The Archaeology Coursebook

Fourth Edition

This fully updated and revised edition of the best-selling title *The Archaeology Coursebook* is a guide for students studying archaeology for the first time. Including new methods and key studies in this fourth edition, it provides pre-university students and teachers, as well as undergraduates and enthusiasts, with the skills and technical concepts necessary to grasp the subject.

The Archaeology Coursebook:

- introduces the most commonly examined archaeological methods, concepts and themes, and provides the necessary skills to understand them
- explains how to interpret the material students may meet in examinations
- supports study with key studies, key sites, key terms, tasks and skills development
- illustrates concepts and commentary with over 400 photos and drawings of excavation sites, methodology and processes, tools and equipment
- provides an overview of human evolution and social development with a particular focus upon European prehistory.

Reflecting changes in archaeological practice and with new key studies, methods, examples, boxes, photographs and diagrams, this is definitely a book no archaeology student should be without.

All three authors have considerable experience in teaching archaeology, examining and field archaeology. **Jim Grant** is Vice Principal at Cirencester College. **Sam Gorin** was formerly a Curriculum Director at Newark and Sherwood College. He has been widely involved in field archaeology in the East Midlands. **Neil Fleming** is Upper-Sixth House Master at Christ's Hospital, Horsham.

The Archaeology Coursebook

Fourth Edition

An introduction to themes, sites, methods and skills

Jim Grant, Sam Gorin and Neil Fleming

LONDON AND NEW YORK

First edition published 2001
Second edition published 2005
Third edition published 2008

This fourth edition published 2015
by Routledge
2 Park Square, Milton Park, Abingdon, Oxon OX14 4RN

and by Routledge
711 Third Avenue, New York, NY 10017

Routledge is an imprint of the Taylor & Francis Group, an informa business

British Library Cataloguing-in-Publication Data
A catalogue record for this book is available from the British Library

Library of Congress Cataloging-in-Publication Data
Grant, Jim, 1958–
The archaeology coursebook: an introduction to themes, sites, methods and skills/Jim Grant, Sam Gorin and Neil Fleming. – Fourth edition.
pages cm
"Simultaneously published in the USA and Canada"—Title page verso.
Includes bibliographical references.
1. Archaeology – Study and teaching (Higher) 2. Archaeology – Methodology. 3. Archaeology – Examinations – Study guides.
I. Gorin, Sam, 1946– II. Fleming, Neil, 1955– III. Title.
CC83.G7 2015
930.1076—dc23
2014031586

ISBN: 978–0-415–52688–3 (pbk)
ISBN: 978–1-315–72783–7 (ebk)

Typeset in Palatino and Bell Gothic
by Florence Production Ltd, Stoodleigh, Devon, UK

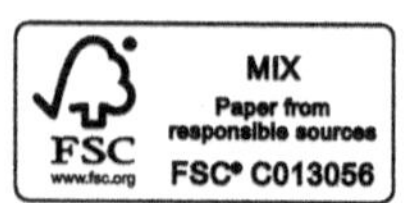

Printed and bound in Great Britain by
TJ International Ltd, Padstow, Cornwall

Brief Contents

Contents

Acknowledgements

Once again we would like to thank all those who contributed to previous editions of this book, much of which is retained here. Thanks are also due to Liz Burton for guidance and to Matthew Gibbons for backing the project.

New key studies have been researched and we acknowledge the support given to us by busy professional fieldworkers and academics. In particular thanks are due to Mike Luke of Albion Archaeology (Bedford), Simon Mortimer (CgMs Consulting) and David Wilson Homes for their time and effort to provide information and illustrations of the excavations at Biddenham Loop, to Tom Dawson and Joanna Hambley (University of St Andrews) for ensuring the key study of Scottish Coastal Archaeology and the Problem of Erosion (SCAPE) gives a clear reflection of their long-term study, to Angela Gannon (RCAHMS) for assisting with the study on St Kilda, to Ian Roberts and Paul Gwilliam (Archaeological Services WYAS) for illustrations of their excavations and finds from Leadenham and to David Mason (Archaeological Services University of Durham) for information on and illustrations of Binchester.

Colleagues (Eileen Appleton, Charlie and Gareth Dean) have generously given us their time to discuss significant points of the modern world of archaeology and 'units' so that hopefully the text is as up-to-date on issues as is possible.

A number of A-level students (Millie Bath, Louisa Manning, Helen Ohlsson, Francesca Roberts, Emily Tabernor and Will Yuill) gave permission in 2011 for their coursework to feature in this new edition. In the past three years our plans for the book have been amended so that their work or extracts from it may be found instead in the companion website. We appreciate their support and hope that their degree experiences were the better for their success in Archaeology A-level!

Thanks and love to Sally for support and patience during this project.

Sam Gorin, June 2014

Most chapters have been completely rewritten and many people have provided new illustrations. I'd particularly like to thank those people in various parts of the world who responded so generously to my emails: Ejvind Hertz for the Alken Enge material, Rengert Elburg and Dietrich Hakelberg for the amazing pictures of the LBK well, Dr Wolfgang Haak for the stunning picture of grave 99 at Eulau, Anne Birgitte Gurlev for the beautiful pictures from Vedbaek, Petr Kvetina and Martin Kuna for access to the Bylany material, Richard Nunn for producing a dramatic ice-core image on request, Dani Nadel for the shot of Ohallo II and Eduard Vasiljević for the shot of the centrepiece from the excellent Krapina Neanderthal Museum. Closer to home I'd like to thank Mary Alexander and Neil Holbroke of Cotswold

Archaeology for giving me access to digs and finds processing, Glen Brearly for the startling Lidar images, Dr Hannah Cobb for the ghostly viking sword X-ray, Jude Plouviez for enabling me to include Ipswich, Caroline Wickham-Jones for the Sand and Orkney images and Nicky Milner, James Barrett and Paul Nicholson for material and information on Star Carr, medieval fishing and petrology respectively and Inge Bødker Enghoff for the fish-bone images. Thanks also to Project Gutenberg for permission to use the *Beowulf* extract.

Even closer to home I'd like to thank my ex-students Dougal McDonald, Beth Nash and Georgia Noyes for images from their coursework projects and Pete Moore, Martha Page and Alice Austin for their illustrations. Becky Osborne produced two great line drawings interpreting Dolni Vestonice and Dorestad, plugging a big hole in those key studies and Zack and Marnie Grant chipped in with additional images. Particular thanks are also due to my fantastic and inspirational co-teacher, Aidan Scott, for his enthusiasm and encouragement as well as several images.

Finally, a huge thank you to Dawn, Zack and Marnie for tolerating disruption to our lives during the writing of the book and the numerous holiday diversions to yet another site.

I'm dedicating this book to my father, William – who passed away aged 94 just as I was completing it. He was a Coal Miner and RAF Navigator and passed on to me his love for maps and the countryside. His bomber squadron was one of many that flew photo reconnaissance missions after the Second World War which left us with an amazing archive of vertical aerial photographs of monuments and field systems before modern development obscured them. A great legacy for archaeology and one I'm always reminded of whenever students use RAF Aerials from the late 1940s.

Jim Grant, January 2015

Illustration Acknowledgements

We are very grateful to those below for supplying illustrations and permission to use them. All other illustrations are the authors'.

Alice Austin (2.16)
Ginny Baddiley, Nottinghamshire SMR (1.3)
Dr James Barrett, University of Cambridge (13.13)
Glenn Brearly, Forest Research (1.34, 1.35)
G. Brovad and Inge Bødker Enghoff (13.16 a and b)
Chris Butler (1.25, 2.20)
Cirencester College (1.15, 1.18, 2.12)
Royston Clarke (3.29, 7.12)
Christina Cliff (7.6)
Dr Hannah Cobb, University of Manchester (3.18)
Sarah Cole (3.37)
Controller of Her Majesty's Stationery Office (1.30)
Tom Dawson, University of St Andrews (1.8)
John Dewar (11.61)
Rengert Elburg, Landesamt für Archäologie Sachsen (2.24, 3.41, 9.27)
Empingham Archive (1.32, 2.34, 12.13)
Alice Gibbs (6.6)
Jamie Gibson (13.9)
Zack Grant (13.4)
Martin Green (2.6)
Anne Birgitte Gurlev, Vedbaekfundene Museum (11.35)
Paul Gwilliam, Archaeological Services WYAS (2.26, 3.9, 3.16)
Dr Wolfgang Haak, University of Adelaide (3.36)
Dietrich Hakelberg, Freiburg University (9.29)
Amanda Hart and Jude Barratt, Corinium Museum (7.37, 10.29, 10.76)
Ole Tage Hartmann, Rudersdal Museums (2.45, 8.14, 13.20)
Ejvind Hertz, Skanderborg Museum (2.38, 3.38, 3.39)
Gwilym Hughes (2.14)
Institute of Archaeology (13.1)

Colin Jarvis (1.10)
Dave Jones (2.13, 2.15, 2.17, 2.43, 3.20, 11.60)
Mick Jones, Lincoln Unit (2.25)
David Knight (2.28, 2.29)
Petr Kvetina and Martin Kuna, Institute of Archaeology ASCR, Prague (0.3, 7.40, 8.48, 8.49, 10.86)
Brona Langton (2.2, 5.17)
Mike Luke, Albion Archaeology (2.1, 2.18, 11.16, 12.14, 12.19, 12.21, 12.22, 12.23, 12.24)
Ben Maggs (5.18)
Dougal McDonald (1.18)
Marine Sonic Ltd (1.37)
Marnie Moo (7.44, 8.58, 10.2, 10.75, 10.89, 13.7)
David Mason, ASUD (1.26)
Pete Moore (3.28, 8.8, 10.23)
Mike Morris (English Heritage and Chester City Council) (2.4, 2.5)
Dani Nadel, Zinman Institute of Archaeology, Haifa University (8.32)
Beth Nash (1.9)
Dr Paul Nicholson, Dept of Archaeology, Cardiff (3.10)
Norfolk Archaeology and Environment Division (2.31)
Georgia Noyes (1.22)
Richard Nunn, National Ice Core Laboratory (4.12)
Becky Osborne (6.25, 9.55)
Martha Page (10.36)
Andy Payne (English Heritage) (1.25)
Jude Plouviez, Suffolk County Council (7.65, 7.66, 7.67, 7.68)
Thomas Reuter, Landesamt für Archäologie Sachsen (5.13, 8.47, 9.28)
Matt Reynolds (2.9)
Clive Ruggles (13.19)
Jim Russell (13.18)
Dan Schofield (3.8 and 3.42)
Aidan Scott (2.36, 4.4, 7.3 and 10.26)
Sarah Scott (3.14, 3.23, 3.32, 3.49, 4.2, 5.16, 5.25 (after Reynolds and Klausmeyer), 6.1, 6.5, 6.5 (after Wenke), 6.9, 6.22, 7.1, 7.28, 7.39, 7.48 (after Drewett), 7.49 (after Drewett), 7.54 (after Binford), 7.55 (after Binford), 7.61, 7.63 (after Stone and Zimansky), 8.10, 8.23, 8.25, 8.29, 8.31, 9.21 (after Svendsen), 9.22 (after Burov), 9.49, 9.52, 10.13, 10.53, 10.66, 10.87, 13.17)
Dr. Bettina Stoll-Tucker (3.36)
Jane Timby (2.33)
Nick Trustram-Eve (1.13, 1.17)
Jonathan Tubb (2.10, 2.11)
University of Cambridge Air Photos (1.31)
Eduard Vasiljević, Krapina Neanderthal Museum (6.8)
Kate Walton (3.48, 5.12, 11.21)
Tracy Wellman, MoLAS (2.44)
Robin Wichard (2.7, 5.2, 11.56)
Caroline Wickham-Jones (1.39, 7.9, 7.10)

Several illustrations are drawings based on other examples. Those not credited in the captions are 5.14 (after Gamble), 6.4 (after Isaacs), 7.46 (after Milner), 7.26 (after Fischer), 7.21 (after Gaffney), 7.23 (after a Hedges and b Renfrew), 8.56 (after Waddell), 10.56 (after Whittle), 10.75 (after Whitelaw), 10.76 (after Whitelaw), 10.88 (Ammerman and Cavalli-Sforza).

A number of photographs are of interpretive displays at the following museums: Andover Museum of the Iron Age (5.24), Burren Centre, Kilfenora (10.9), Devizes (10.36), Hochdorf Keltenmuseum (10.61), Isbister Tomb of the Eagles (11.13), Smithsonian Museum of Natural History, Washington DC (11.32), Sutton Hoo (9.11).

Introduction

The Archaeology Coursebook is about archaeological literacy. Whether you are a student or someone who wants to know more about archaeology, you probably have never studied it previously. This means that there is a whole new technical language and set of concepts to grasp. This text will enable you to get to grips with them. It cannot pretend to cover the whole of a degree programme nor is it a field guide to archaeological methods. A fantastic array of books and websites is already available to fulfil these functions. The aim of this book is to get you started with understanding archaeology.

WHAT IS NEW?

As authors, our collective experience includes professional and amateur archaeology and teaching in both state and private schools and in colleges. We also have extensive experience of successfully preparing students of all ages on A level, IB, Access and HE programmes. In writing this new edition, we have responded to feedback from students, teachers and general readers of *The Archaeology Coursebook* about what they liked and what was less useful. Amongst these changes are:

- Introducing a major new range of detailed and up-to-date key studies. In some instances we have included two or more from the same period to enable comparisons to be made.
- Improving and adding to the range of diagrams and illustrations used to explain ideas.
- Adding a new chapter on human origins.
- Introducing Harvard referencing for key sources for new material and significantly expanding the bibliography.
- Moving chapters on examination success and studying archaeology to the companion website so that it is easier to update and to make use of hyperlinks.

Each chapter has had a major overhaul to reflect continuing changes in archaeology, including excavation and managing the past. The large economics chapter has been divided in two to make it manageable. Most chapters have been totally rewritten. Archaeology is a rapidly evolving discipline. While great discoveries continue to be made in the field, our understanding is also being revolutionised by rapid advances in science. Since the third edition these have included:

- Publication of studies into ancient human fossils from Chad, Croatia, Georgia and Siberia which challenge the way we understand our human family tree.
- The widespread use of Bayesian modelling to refine radiocarbon dates, resulting in much greater precision in understanding events in later prehistory.
- A growing body of genetics data which is radically revising our understanding of

population movements in the past and the origins of present populations.
- The widespread use of biochemical techniques to analyse excavated materials and which are unlocking secrets on topics as wide-ranging as diet, herding and marriage partners in the past.
- Far greater emphasis on scientific analysis reflecting the increasing importance of the lab in generating archaeological knowledge.

For those of you studying archaeology, we hope this book will be of use at every stage of your course, from understanding new terminology to producing assignments. The explanations and the key studies are pitched at a level which covers both A level and the first half of most degree courses. If it equips you to produce good essays and to understand what is being discussed in lectures and seminars, it will have done its job. You will, of course, need other sources too, including specific key studies for your course, and to look at examples of fieldwork reports. Directions are provided on the companion website to point you in the direction of additional resources for topics you may want to investigate further. By your final year of university, you will need far greater depth of material. However, by then you will know everything that is in this book! For those of you approaching archaeology from interest, the book provides a detailed insight into the techniques used by archaeologists to investigate our buried past and a survey of what they have revealed.

HOW THE BOOK IS STRUCTURED

The structure of previous editions followed the A level Archaeology course studied by students in England and Wales. This is due to be revised and we have taken the opportunity to significantly broaden the book beyond that course to make it more accessible to a wider readership. This means that some very specific material on religion and ritual and examination preparation has been moved onto the website. While overall organisation is not chronological, each thematic chapter has been reordered to follow the broad outlines of European prehistory.

Throughout the book we have introduced the most commonly examined archaeological methods, concepts and themes. Whole books have been written on the meanings of particular terms and there may not be consensus on their use. We have largely concentrated on providing you with working definitions and examples rather than debating meaning. The book is organised into three broad sections:

- *Part I: Understanding archaeological resources* is an introduction to how archaeologists work – how they find sites, excavate them and analyse, date and interpret the material they recover. It will help you understand how we get archaeological knowledge.
- *Part II: Studying themes in archaeology* begins with a new chapter on human origins and then covers the broad topics of settlement, economics and material culture, society and religion and ritual. We have concentrated on defining key terms, providing examples and highlighting the sources and methods used to explore these themes. These are relevant to all periods and regions of study. However, our own expertise and the main focus of many of our readers are on Europe, including the British Isles, so most of the examples are drawn from that region.
- *Part III: Issues in world archaeology* covers the protection and management of our archaeological heritage. It addresses the social and political role of archaeology and introduces a number of current debates. It also looks at who does what in archaeology and how archaeological knowledge is presented. While these topics are universal, legislation is specific to different states so we have largely used examples from England or the UK for illustration.

A key feature of this book is that it is designed to be used alongside the companion website. We have retained a couple of suggestions for further reading for each of the technical chapters but all web links have been transferred to the website so that they can be updated. Part of the website mirrors the structure of the book and provides access to a huge range of websites to look for examples and illustrations. Archaeology is such a visual subject and so well served by many excellent sources on the Internet that it is foolish not to use it. The significantly revised website also contains additional activities and material for those studying archaeology and updated information on higher level study.

HOW TO USE THIS TEXT

There are so many different ways in which lecturers can structure courses that it is unlikely you will follow the exact order of our contents sequence in your own study. We have taken this into account by providing a full index and a contents list that includes all the main subheadings. For those of you who want to follow 'the story' chronologically, signposts are provided in Figure 0.1. We have also used a system of cross-referencing throughout the book from one topic to related topics. Content, skills and resources are all linked. Look out for the ▶ signposts which guide you to related material on another page. We have introduced and defined key terms as they have arisen in the text. Where this is not possible, a short working definition is provided with the 🦴 symbol. The glossary contains a working definition of words printed in **bold** in the text and more.

In addition to examples for most of the points, a new range of major key studies is provided to deepen your understanding of the ideas and methods discussed. Where they are relevant to your course (they are about the right length and detail for essays up to the second year at university), you can use them as content to support your written work. **Key studies** are situated within a chapter where they are particularly valuable but all of them will be useful and provide insights and additional detail on topics in other chapters. For example, all of them are relevant for Chapters 3 and 5. We have included the following icons in the study boxes to indicate where a key study from these selected chapters would also be useful in another:

 Reconnaissance (Chapter 1)

 Excavation (Chapter 2)

 Settlement (Chapter 7)

 Economics A (Chapter 8)

 Economics B (Chapter 9)

 Social archaeology (Chapter 10)

A complete list of links for all the chapters is summarised in Figure 0.1. Clusters of broadly contemporary key studies have been selected to enable you to explore links between them or to use them to compare and contrast in essays, for example Ipswich and Dorestad.

CONVENTIONS

A variety of abbreviations are used in archaeology for dating and measurement. We have tried to use the following:

- BP – Before Present (1950) for most of prehistory
- BC – for later prehistory where dating is more precise
- 3rd millennium BC etc. – when discussing broad changes over several hundred years e.g. 3000–2000 BC

Key studies	Period						Chapters												
	Palaeo	Meso	Neo	Bronze	Iron	Medi	1 reconn	2 exc	3 post-ex	4 dating	5 interp	6 origins	7 settle	8 eco A	9 eco B	10 social	11 religion	12 manage	13 present
Scottish Coastal Archaeology and the Problem of Erosion (SCAPE)							■											■	
Surveying an abandoned landscape on St Kilda							■												
Contrasting approaches: Empingham and East Kent Access Road							■	■										■	
The Chester Amphitheatre project								■										■	■
Boxgrove	■							■			■	■		■					
Eulau: human remains and Neolithic relationships			■					■	■							■	■		
The decline of the Maya						■		■		■			■			■			
Lipids, cheese and the European Dairying Project			■						■		■			■					■
Dating the destruction of Minoan Crete				■						■						■			
The Vézère valley and Neanderthal replacement	■							■				■	■	■		■			
Dolni Vestonice and the Moravian Gate	■											■	■	■		■			
Lewis Binford and Nunamiut ethnoarchaeology											■		■	■					
Oronsay, Sand and seasonal movement around the Inner Hebrides		■					■				■		■	■					
Head Smashed In	■	■											■	■		■			■
Minoan settlement hierarchy				■									■			■			
Star Carr revisited: changing interpretations of a classic site		■						■			■		■	■				■	
Pincevent, Mask and site structure	■										■		■	■					
Mashkan Shapir				■			■						■			■			
Tracing the early development of Ipswich						■		■					■		■	■			
Stellmoor and specialised reindeer hunting	■							■			■		■	■					
Tybrind Vig and late Mesolithic foragers in the Baltic		■						■					■	■	■				
Ohalo II and the Palaeolithic origins of food production	■							■			■		■	■					
Tell Abu Hureyra and the transition to farming		■	■					■			■		■	■		■			
Karanovo and early farming villages in the Balkans			■								■		■	■		■			
Vaihingen and pioneer farmers in central Europe			■					■	■		■		■	■		■			
Hallstatt and the organisation of salt mining				■											■	■			
Dorestad and the birth of medieval trade in the North Sea zone						■		■			■		■		■				
Varna, gold and social status in Copper Age Europe				■							■		■		■	■			
Hochdorf and hereditary chiefdoms in the Iron Age					■			■	■							■	■		
Mead halls and power: Gudme, *Beowulf* and Sutton Hoo						■		■			■		■			■			
Vucedol and the birth of inequality at the dawn of the Bronze Age				■									■		■	■			
Knossos and the emergence of Minoan palace civilisation				■									■	■	■	■	■		
Military technology and organisation: the Illerup Hoard					■			■							■	■			
Was there an Anglo-Saxon invasion?						■							■			■			
Newgrange																	■		
The Biddenham Loop: modern developer-led archaeology in action				■	■		■	■	■									■	
Ancient and modern Celts																			■
Archaeology, conservation and the medieval fishing industry						■			■		■				■				■

■ **Figure 0.1** *Table showing which key studies are the most useful to different chapters*

- C12th AD (e.g. twelfth century AD) for broad changes within the historic period.
- mya – million years ago.

Metric measurements are used with m = metres (m^2 = square; m^3 = cubic) and km = kilometres used as abbreviations.

Amongst the geographic terms we have used are:

- Eurasia (Europe and the adjoining regions of Asia)
- Iberia (Spain and Portugal)
- Anatolia (Turkey)
- Near East (the region containing Syria, Israel, Iraq and western Iran)
- Britain (the island comprising England, Wales and mainland Scotland)
- British Isles (all the islands of the archipelago including Britain and Ireland).

GETTING STARTED

Archaeology is the study of our human past from the material people have left behind. These physical remains include the buildings and objects they made, environmental evidence and the bones or bodies of people themselves. This evidence is always incomplete. Archaeology tries to explain human behaviour in the past. In particular it examines the way people in the past adapted to their environments and the way in which human societies changed over time. Explaining our past contributes to our understanding of humanity today.

Archaeology and related subjects

Archaeology is sometimes thought of as the period before history. It is but it is much more than just 'prehistory'. Archaeology covers a period of over six million years. At one extreme, archaeologists excavate the fossils of our earliest ancestors to study human evolution while others excavate the battlefields of the C20th to understand the nature of warfare for ordinary soldiers. History (the period for which there are written records) overlaps with less than 1 per cent of archaeology. It is more useful to see the difference in terms of sources and methods. Historians rely largely on collating and interpreting written documents which are particularly useful for understanding specific events and the lives and views of elites in past societies. Archaeologists use physical evidence to interpret the economy, social structure and technology of the past and to shed light on the lives of ordinary people. In many cases the two disciplines complement each other; for example, when investigating the Roman army or medieval towns.

In Europe many C19th archaeologists worked within an evolutionary framework to classify their finds. As a result, archaeology is often associated with earth sciences. In the USA, by contrast, archaeologists worked with anthropologists to study the native peoples who still lived in North America. As a result, archaeology there is seen as a branch of anthropology. In fact archaeology has close ties with many other disciplines. It is a magpie subject that borrows techniques and insights from both social and natural sciences, from mathematics to linguistics and from computing to history. As a result, archaeology is highly dynamic with new ideas and techniques, constantly providing new ways of studying physical remains from the past. We have highlighted many examples of these in this new edition. What unites these eclectic sources is the way archaeologists use them to help answer questions about people in the past. For example, archaeologists draw on information gathered by palaeoclimatologists from ice cores taken from glaciers in Greenland. They do this not because they are interested in past weather patterns but because information on temperature and rainfall may help explain why some people in Syria and Israel decided to plant crops at the end of the last ice age. The focus is always upon human behaviour.

Some key archaeological concepts

The Glossary (▶ p. 629) contains a detailed list of technical terms used by archaeologists and which we introduce in this text. However, there are a number of fundamental terms which crop up so frequently that you need a working knowledge of them before you start:

Artefacts are things made or modified by humans. They are usually portable and examples include a stone axe, a pot or a wooden spear.

Ecofacts is a term given to all the environmental data or natural items which provide clues into past human behaviour. Examples include pollen, human remains and food waste such as

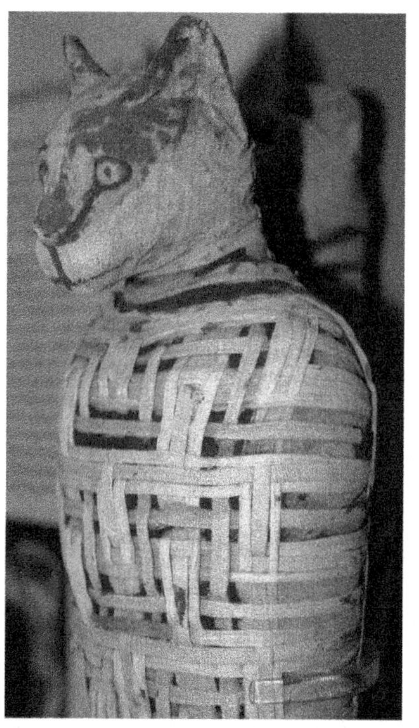

Figure 0.2 *Ecofact or artefact? Inside this Egyptian cat-mummy are the remains of an animal (natural material). However, it has been transformed by human activity including mummification, wrapping and painting into a ritual object.*

Figure 0.3 *Sites contain, and are made up of, features. These dug features are the remains of massive post-holes from a Neolithic longhouse at Bylany (▶ p. 499). Photo Archives of the Institute of Archaeology ASCR, Prague, No. FT-40257. www.bylany.com*

butchered animal bones. A bone processed for meat is an ecofact, a bone carved to make a spear point or needle is an artefact.

Features are marks or materials left in the ground by human activity. Sometimes only the trace remains such as a dark circle of earth where a post once stood, while in other circumstances there might be a complete stone wall. Examples of features include hearths, ditches and buildings. Features are generally non-portable but some larger artefacts such as sunken ships are sometimes also described as features.

Assemblages are clusters of distinctive artefacts and sometimes ecofacts which are repeatedly found together. For example, pottery beakers, flint arrowheads and copper daggers buried with crouched human skeletons in Britain are known as the Beaker assemblage. Sometimes different assemblages are used to distinguish different cultural groups of people.

Archaeological sites are locations where evidence of human activity has been found. Traces might include ecofacts, artefacts or features. Examples range from shipwrecks to burials, campsites to entire landscapes. Where a single artefact such as an arrowhead or coin is found, archaeologists tend not to classify that place as a site but as a find-spot. However, archaeologists have become increasingly interested in the pattern of use of the wider landscape or 'off-site areas'.

The **archaeological record** is the raw data for archaeology. The physical remains of past activities include features, artefacts and ecofacts (including human remains). The archaeological record comprises these remains in the contexts in which they come down to us. It is not static and constantly changes through the impact of natural forces and modern human activity.

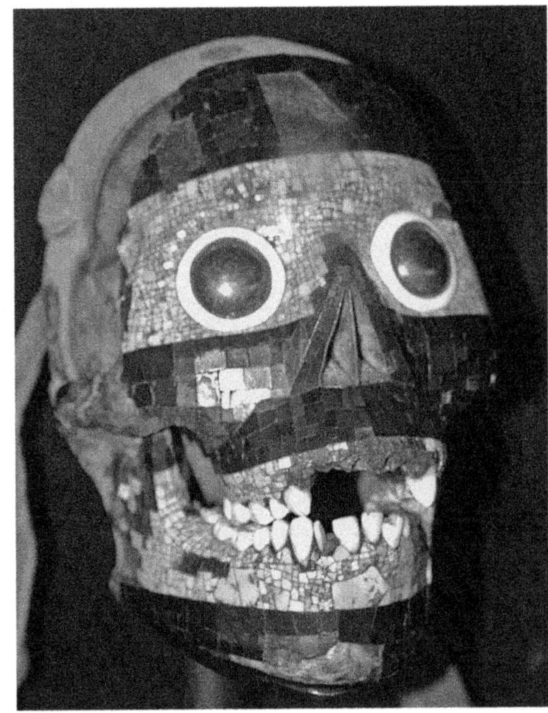

Figure 0.4 *And this one?*

Archaeological sites are unique and non-renewable. Excavation destroys sites so the record then becomes the plans, photographs and reports made by archaeologists and the archive of finds they have preserved.

Archaeological research has been likened to that of detectives using clues to piece together past human behaviour. Another analogy is that it is like putting a jigsaw together but with no picture on the box and many pieces lost or damaged. The challenge is to find techniques to squeeze the maximum information from material remains (artefacts, ecofacts and features) in order to understand human behaviour in the past.

Part I

Understanding Archaeological Resources

Chapter 1

Archaeological Reconnaissance

This chapter introduces the key methods used by archaeologists to locate sites and to reveal and investigate the details of known sites without excavation. We have outlined some strengths and limitations of the most important techniques and identified the way in which different techniques are used for locating and investigating sites in particular circumstances. Reconnaissance is developed in other chapters, including Chapter 7 and the Biddenham Loop key study in Chapter 12.

HOW SITES ARE FOUND

Archaeologists use a wide range of reconnaissance techniques to locate new archaeological sites and to investigate known sites without excavating them. Some archaeologists predict that future advances in non-invasive, and non-destructive, methods will see them become a viable alternative to excavation, not least because of the costs of digging. Reconnaissance techniques are also used to map evidence of human activity across a landscape (▶ p. 229). The particular methods chosen will depend on the question being investigated, the terrain and the scale of the study. The time and resources available are also key factors.

Every year hundreds of new sites are located in the UK and many thousands worldwide. Some result from organised landscape surveys or from the discovery of artefacts by metal detectorists or divers. The 2009 Staffordshire Hoard of Anglo-Saxon metalwork is a significant example of the latter. Some sites are spotted from the air or even from satellites in space. Google Earth has proved a valuable tool in finding sites as diverse as coastal fish traps, Roman villas and hundreds of prehistoric tombs in the Arabian Desert. Some of the most important archaeological discoveries have come about completely by chance. The discoveries of the body of Ötzi the Ice Man by skiers and of the Altamira cave art by children are classic examples. A Neolithic tomb at Crantit in Orkney was found when a digger fell through the roof! Farming and industrial extraction processes such as quarrying, dredging and peat cutting all regularly produce finds of material or features. Some named sites which were documented in the past were located by using written sources. Schliemann's discovery of Troy is the classic example but many battlefields and shipwrecks also fall into this category. Of course some archaeological sites were never 'lost' to begin with. Stonehenge and the Pyramids were well known before the development of archaeology. Then there are buildings from the last 200 or more years which are still in use and the traces of our industrial heritage in both urban and rural landscapes.

Most field archaeology in the UK is developer-led and before any project, large or small, planners demand that an archaeological evaluation (▶ p. 573) is carried out to reveal the impact development proposals might have on the historic environment. Such evaluations have the potential to reveal new sites as well as review earlier evidence. Similarly, research excavations will start with an evaluation of what is already known about a site or landscape from existing records. However, reconnaissance should not be seen simply as the precursor to the real business of digging. In some cases sound survey and evaluation is capable of providing all or most of the evidence needed.

There are many reasons for archaeologists to undertake reconnaissance work including evaluations for developers, major university or government projects, amateur local society investigations and students involved in personal studies or as a piece of extended research for a degree or for a post-graduate thesis.

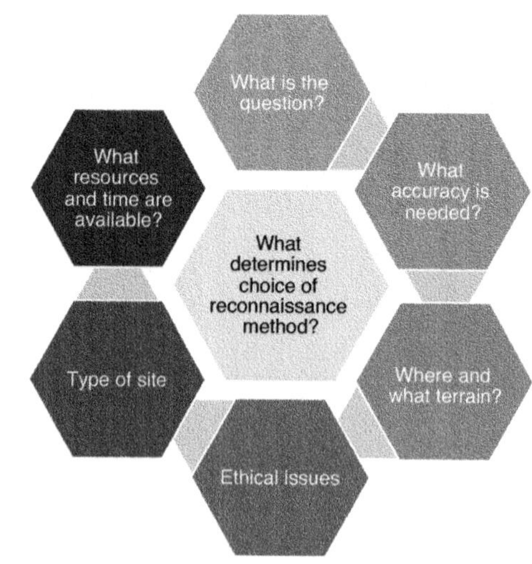

Figure 1.1 *Factors influencing the choice of reconnaissance methods*

Reconnaissance methods

To locate or explore sites during research or ahead of development there are four broad and complementary categories of methods that are commonly used:

- desktop study
- surface survey
- geophysical or geochemical survey
- aerial survey and, increasingly, remote sensing.

Technically speaking an archaeological site can only be discovered once. All subsequent investigations are designed to add information to the initial discovery. Primary methods at the archaeologist's disposal are capable of making that first identification of a new site; for example, aerial photography or fieldwalking. Other methods can be viewed as secondary (in sequence not importance); for example, some geophysical surveys are better suited to developing understanding of details on known sites. However, this distinction is not rigid. 'Primary methods' are also deployed in a secondary context: a site which has been identified from aerial photography may still be investigated later by fieldwalking or vice versa.

A classic case of survey, reconnaissance and targeted excavation can be seen in the pioneering Shapwick Project in Somerset which investigated the development of an estate owned by Glastonbury Abbey. Here a battery of reconnaissance methods including evidence from maps, historical sources and environmental data were combined with limited sampling of deposits through shovel pit testing, geochemical survey and excavation. The results when all sources of evidence were brought together enabled the production of regression maps (▶ p. 8) showing the development of settlement in the area.

DESKTOP STUDY OR 'DESK-BASED ASSESSMENT'

As its name suggests, this is an activity largely conducted indoors using a range of documents and records including those available online. All archaeological research starts here. Some archaeologists, usually concerned with shipwrecks, aircraft crash sites or historical individuals, may gain most of their answers from such sources

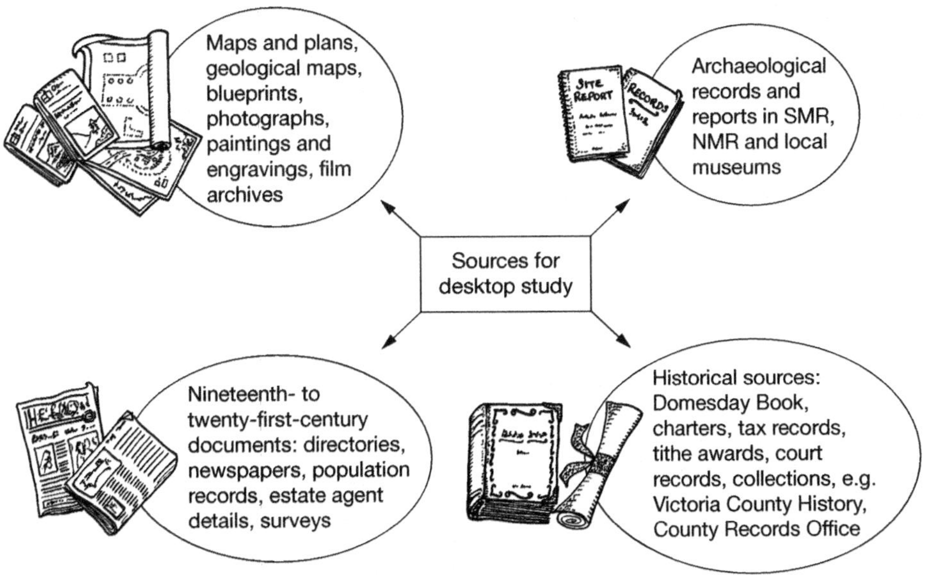

Figure 1.2 *Archive sources commonly used for desktop study*

because there may well be relevant information already capable of answering their question. More commonly archaeologists want to understand what information may be accessible and to interrogate those records as a precursor to fresh investigation. It is quite remarkable how much original research does indeed take place but more often than not it links to earlier finds or discoveries and helps to extend and develop our knowledge and understanding. In some cases desktop work makes fieldwork unnecessary. A recent example was where the Trent and Peak Archaeological Unit was contracted to carry out an evaluation ahead of the new A46 dual carriageway on the Fosse Way in Nottinghamshire. Desktop research enabled them to advise the contractors to avoid two significant Romano-British settlements in favour of a route which only impacted on some minor sites. These were excavated ahead of the road building.

Desktop study involves researching maps and historical or archaeological documents including aerial photographs about the area under investigation. If they are not in private hands, these are most likely to be held in planning departments, county records offices, Historic Environment Records (HERs), local Sites and Monuments Records (SMRs) or the National Monuments Record (NMR) offices. Details of previous archaeological work and records of stray finds for much of Britain are held in local HERs. These records are increasingly digitalised and a national version is being built up at the various NMR offices. Printouts which include lists of earlier research can be made by inputting grid references.

The Portable Antiquities Scheme (PAS) (▶ p. 579) has been in existence since the late 1990s and is moving towards recording 1 million finds. Its website allows archaeologists to search for finds

KEY TERM

Historic Environment Record (HER)

The new name for SMRs. The local authority archive of records and databases covering archaeology and the built environment.

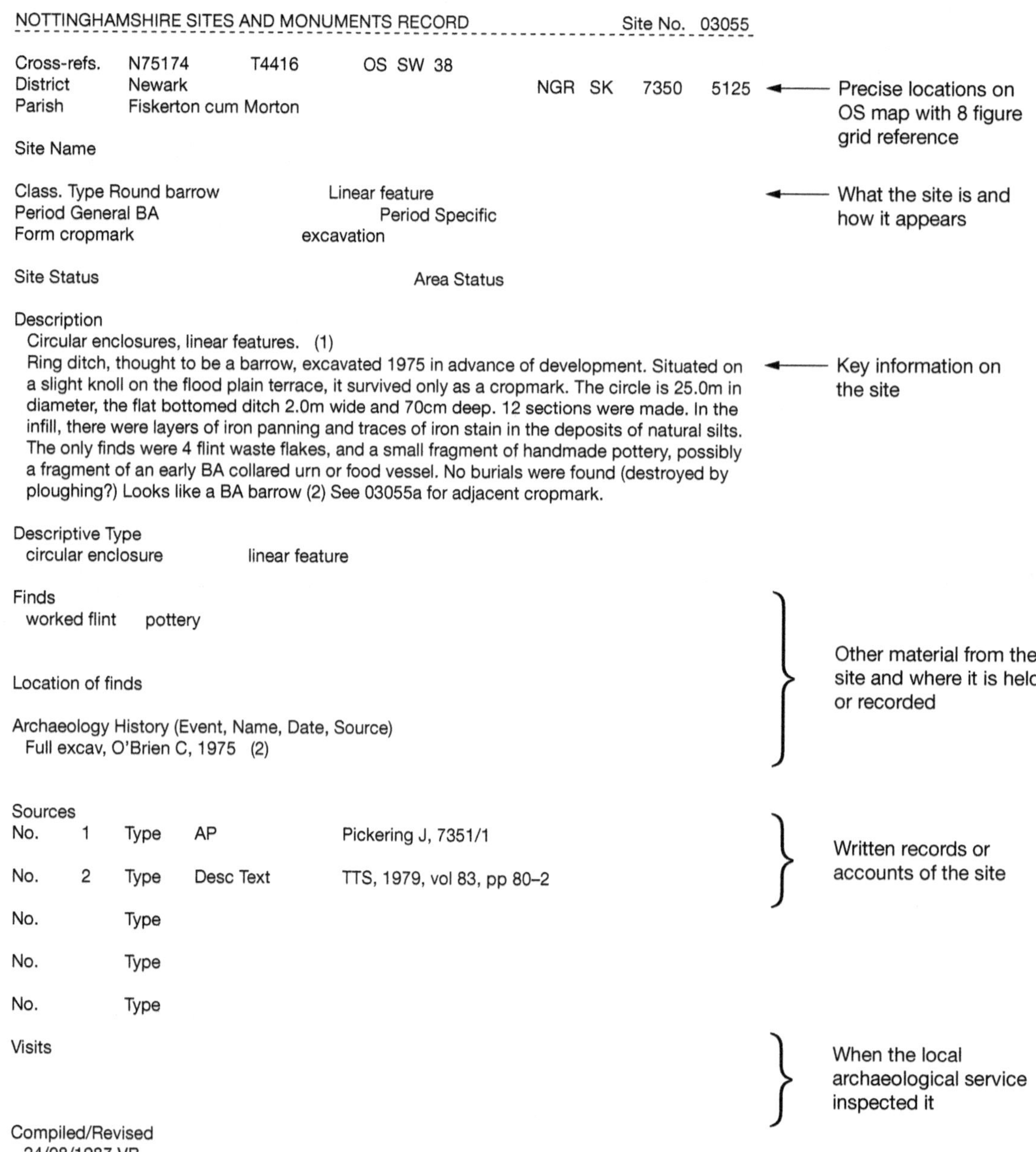

NOTTINGHAMSHIRE SITES AND MONUMENTS RECORD Site No. 03055

Cross-refs. N75174 T4416 OS SW 38
District Newark NGR SK 7350 5125
Parish Fiskerton cum Morton

Site Name

Class. Type Round barrow Linear feature
Period General BA Period Specific
Form cropmark excavation

Site Status Area Status

Description
Circular enclosures, linear features. (1)
Ring ditch, thought to be a barrow, excavated 1975 in advance of development. Situated on a slight knoll on the flood plain terrace, it survived only as a cropmark. The circle is 25.0m in diameter, the flat bottomed ditch 2.0m wide and 70cm deep. 12 sections were made. In the infill, there were layers of iron panning and traces of iron stain in the deposits of natural silts. The only finds were 4 flint waste flakes, and a small fragment of handmade pottery, possibly a fragment of an early BA collared urn or food vessel. No burials were found (destroyed by ploughing?) Looks like a BA barrow (2) See 03055a for adjacent cropmark.

Descriptive Type
circular enclosure linear feature

Finds
worked flint pottery

Location of finds

Archaeology History (Event, Name, Date, Source)
Full excav, O'Brien C, 1975 (2)

Sources
No. 1 Type AP Pickering J, 7351/1
No. 2 Type Desc Text TTS, 1979, vol 83, pp 80–2
No. Type
No. Type
No. Type

Visits

Compiled/Revised
24/08/1987 VB

Figure 1.3 *How to read an SMR/HER printout*

by date and place. The distribution patterns may primarily reflect the distribution of metal detectorists who report their finds but PAS can still have a role to play in providing a picture of past human activity in an area. Other archives may be found at some universities, archaeological societies, cathedrals, museums and libraries, although these vary widely across the country. Increasingly documents, including archaeological site reports, are being digitised and made available online. A major source of information is English Heritage's website PastScape, which gives easy access to over 400,000 records. Other key resources include the Archaeology Data Service at the University of York and the Heritage Gateway, which provide free online digital resources including searchable databases and many reconnaissance and excavation reports.

Historical documents

A diverse assortment of documents may be of value to the archaeologist. These will vary by county, area and period. In much of the country, known documents are archived or recorded in the County Records Office. In many areas, useful sources have also been catalogued in a volume of the Victoria County History (VCH). Based at the University of London, the VCH has been recording and publishing detailed county and parish histories since 1899 and covers most of England. This is often the first resource researchers turn to.

Type of record	Examples and content	Useful for understanding
Legal documents	Records of ownership, charters or court records of disputes often included physical description of property. Wills and inventories which can be linked to particular buildings may provide lists of contents.	Boundaries and occasionally land use Clues to that building's use
Tax records	Tax surveys, tithe awards and the Domesday Book	Landowning units and the economic uses of land
Economic records	Order and sales books and C19th directories e.g. Kelly's Estate agents' bills	Functions of buildings and industrial archaeology Changes in historic buildings
Pictorial records	Paintings, engravings and photographs Aerial photography archives	Identification of sites and tracing changes to standing buildings and landscapes
Written accounts	Descriptions of places in books, diaries, newspapers and travelogues	The function, construction methods and identity of many sites
Antiquarian records	Reports of early antiquarians such as Stukeley on Avebury	Descriptions of monuments as they were before the modern period
Archaeological journals	National journals such as *Archaeologica*, published by the Society of Antiquaries, go back to the C18th. Many regional or specialist period journals go back to the C19th.	Previous excavations and illustrations and descriptions of artefacts

Figure 1.4 *Historical sources for desktop study*

Only a fraction of early records have survived and those that have need translation and interpretation. Amongst the potential range available, the categories shown in Figure 1.4 are important.

Maps

Maps are amongst the most basic tools and sources used by archaeologists. They are used to locate and explore sites and to answer questions about previous use of the landscape. They are of particular value in tracking changes through time (settlement shape and location, boundaries, land units, fields and hedges). They can also be used to relate sites to geology and topography. Medieval archaeologists are often able to produce their own maps for periods before mapping began. They do this by working back from the oldest available map and cross-referencing historical sources and fieldnames. This technique is known as regression. Medieval fieldnames provide a kind of oral map of the landscape as seen by farmers of that time while post-enclosure fields often refer to nearby features such as woods, mills and lime kilns. Those researching archaeological sites need to be able to use scales, at least six-figure grid references and to 'read' contours and hachures (the marks used to indicate earthworks). They may also use other evidence such as photographs and written accounts to interpret maps and plans. A wide variety of maps are used by archaeologists, including the following.

Early maps

Maps from the C16th tend to show the properties of the rich. They are not always to scale but may

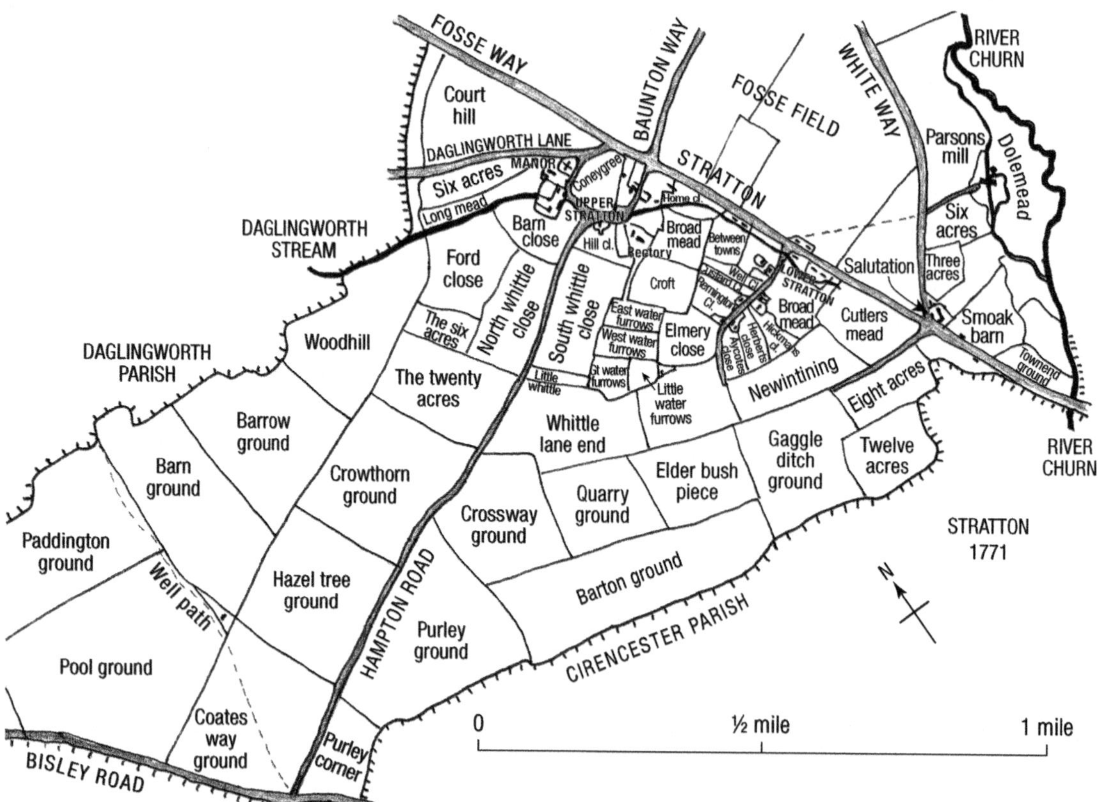

Figure 1.5 *1771 enclosure award map*

provide visual information such as illustrations of specific buildings. John Speed's maps of the early C17th are classics and his town plans are often the first visual records of these sites. From this century too there are route maps such as Ogilvy's Road Book, which is a series of linear strips. Maps were produced to show the proposed routes of turnpikes, canals and railways in order to gain permission from parliament for building to take place.

Changes in rural landownership from the C18th onwards were recorded on enclosure award maps, while taxes owed to the church by landowners were sometimes written on tithe award maps. Sometimes these can be cross-referenced and both can provide information about fieldnames, routes and boundaries, which are vital for landscape archaeology. Other maps show landscaped gardens and battlefields or provide plans of factories and mines. These early maps are often held in county record offices but some may be in private hands or belong to churches.

Ordnance Survey (OS) maps

During the early C19th the OS mapped each county at 1 inch to 1 mile (corresponds to 1:50000 today). From the 1880s OS 6 inch to 1 mile maps (corresponds to 1:10000 today) provided more detail of individual buildings and even hedge species. OS maps established a new standard in accuracy and a comprehensive system of coding and keys for features. A grid system was used which covered the whole country and enabled precise references to be given. By examining a succession of maps for any area,

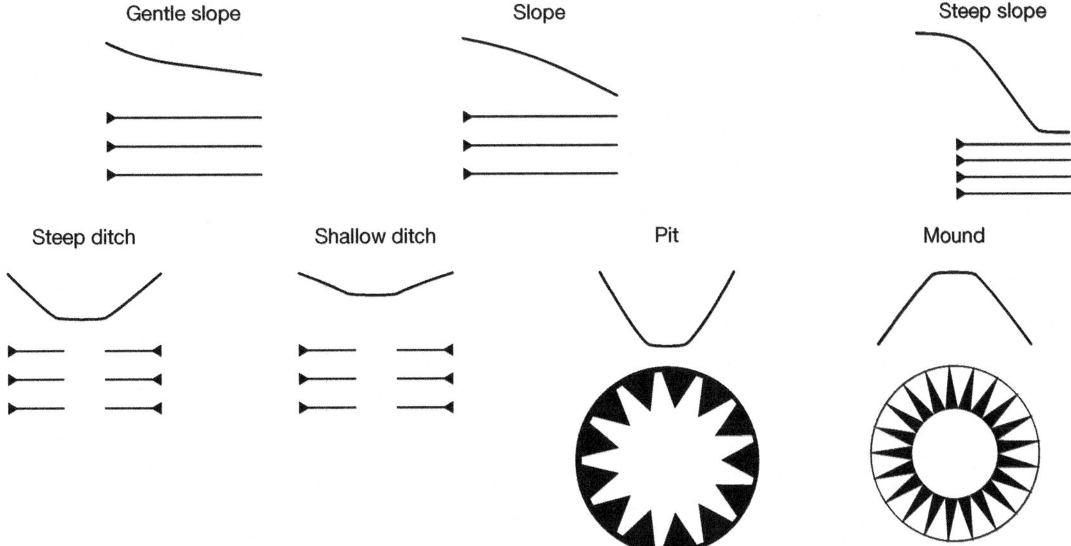

Figure 1.6 *How to read hachures on a map*

Hachures are used on maps and plans to indicate the presence of slopes. Shown wider at the top of a slope and reducing in thickness towards the bottom of the slope they indicate both the steepness and length of the slopes. Short and thick hachures represent a short and steep slope whereas a long and gentle slope is depicted by long and thin hachures. The closer hachures are clustered, the steeper the slope. Some surveyors use elongated triangles or 'T-shapes' while others draw symbols rather like tadpoles where the wider 'head' end can be remembered as being to the top – as in a pond – and the tail wiggles downwards. To read hachures off site plans, learn to look for the thicker ends of the marks which are the tops of slopes so that you can recognise rises and falls in the landscape.

changes in land use and the built environment can be easily seen.

Maps used in archaeological research

The OS 1:25000 series show the location of some archaeological sites but planning maps that use the OS grid system are required for investigations. The 1:10000 (old 6 inch) maps are sometimes the most detailed available for mountainous, remote and some rural areas but 1:2500 (old 25 inch 1 mile) rural or 1:1250 urban planning maps are normally used. For fieldwalking 1:10000 or 1:2500 is used and for excavation the 1:2500 or 1:1250 provides a base. A 1:2500 map allows you to identify individual metre squares with a ten-figure grid reference. These maps are held in county or district planning offices. Copies can be ordered from specialist map shops. Other maps sometimes used include the Geological Survey series, street maps, factory plans, vegetation and climatic maps, land use and classification, soil surveys and specialist archaeological maps. Increasingly archaeologists are using computerised mapping systems based around Geographic Information Systems (**GIS**).

Online versions of maps will increasingly be important. The more powerful of these can incorporate old maps and aerial photographs within national or international grid systems. Google Earth is the best known and its Stonehenge Riverside Project app hints at the potential of this medium but there are many others.

Geographic Information Systems (GIS)

GIS are powerful databases which can store many layers of data against individual map grid references. This can include details of topography,

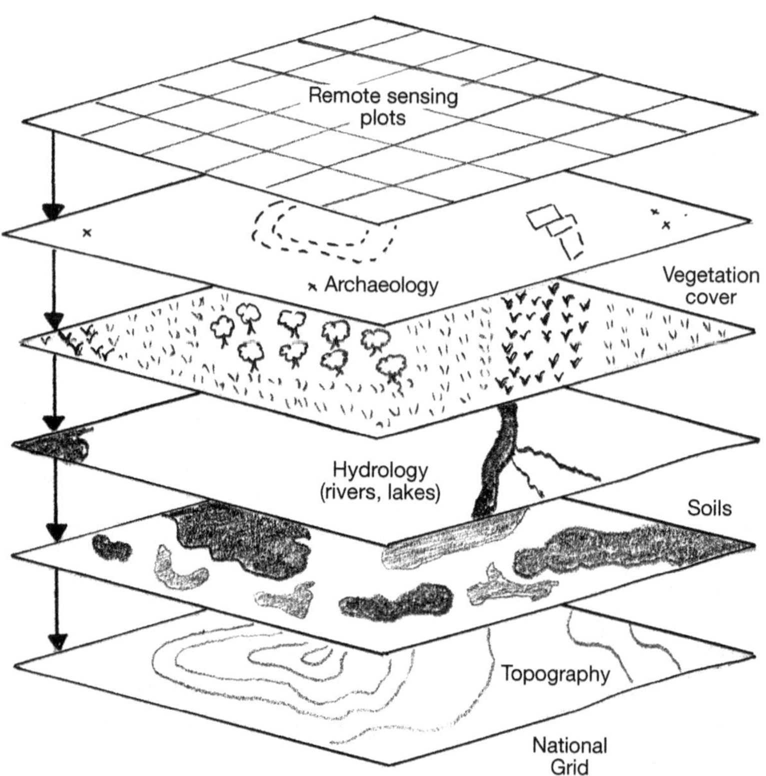

Figure 1.7 *GIS overlays*

geology and vegetation as well as archaeological data. GIS can integrate data from satellites with field recordings. It is revolutionising the recording, presentation and interrogation of archaeological data.

GIS enables direct mapping and recording of data at the excavation site. This allows for immediate access to the data collected for analysis or it can be incorporated with other relevant data sources to help understand the site better. For example, the location of sites can be examined in relation to things like distance to permanent water, changes of slope, extent of view, intervisibility with other sites and contemporary vegetation cover. The southern Hebrides Mesolithic Project (▶ p. 235) used GIS to examine patterns and views from Mesolithic flint scatters and hunting sites on Islay. This 'viewshed approach' enabled them to gain insights into hunting strategies. GIS was used at Castle Hill near Crewkerne in Somerset to establish and map what areas of the landscape were visible from the hilltop and thus to allow discussion on the possible importance of the site in the early medieval period. GIS can produce topographic maps and site plans in three dimensions and perform com-

KEY STUDY

Scottish Coastal Archaeology and the Problem of Erosion (SCAPE)

SCAPE's activities in the area of archaeological reconnaissance highlight how a community approach and professional academic survey can be combined to research and record an aspect of our threatened heritage.

You may be familiar with the Neolithic village of Skara Brae, Orkney (▶ p. 274), and its dramatic exposure following a great storm in 1850. This site is just the most famous of thousands of archaeological sites located close to the sea and subject to its potential destructive effect (▶ p. 569).

Research

To obtain an understanding of the extent of the sea's threat in terms of the number and variety of sites at risk, Historic Scotland began a programme of coastal survey in 1996 and the management of this task passed to SCAPE five years later. SCAPE's aim with the surveys is to search for sites along the foreshore, the coast edge and a strip of land extending back from this some 50m or so. This is a truly monumental task given that the Scottish coastline stretches for approximately 15,000km and as of 2011 only about a third of this has been explored. Within those 5,000km over 12,000 sites have been plotted (an average of 2.4 per kilometre), half of which were previously unrecorded, and about a third of them (3,700) now carry recommendations for further work. SCAPE has a new project which is asking the public to revisit sites with recommendations to check their condition and to help prioritise action at the most threatened. Details of sites are available on an interactive website and an app allows for sites to be recorded in the field using a mobile phone.

SCAPE also manages the Shorewatch Project, which aims to encourage and assist members of local communities to locate, record, monitor and even excavate archaeological sites around Scotland's coasts. Local groups can organise themselves to be on hand to note damage and changes that occur after storms or high tides. Many of these groups have been trained in how to recognise sites and record them using specially designed forms to ensure all relevant information is collected. Detailed planning and surveying often occur as follow-ons from initial recordings.

Figure 1.8 *The SCAPE Project*

Surveying activity in process at Baile Sear next to an exposed hearth. It proved to be the site of an Iron Age wheelhouse. Credit: Ronnie Mckenzie / The SCAPE Trust

Investigations

As in any reconnaissance situation, a small number of key sites are subsequently investigated thoroughly. In the case of Shorewatch local teams work in collaboration with professional archaeologists as at Baile Sear, North Uist. Here an Iron Age settlement was exposed in 2005 and accurate plans were drawn at intervals as the team monitored its gradual erosion over the following months. This was followed up by a full excavation at two of the wheelhouses, locating walls almost 2m high and uncovering many pits within the buildings containing thousands of sherds of pottery, burnt animal bones and some human remains. At a second site at Boddin in Angus, C18th lime kilns were threatened by collapse so a laser scanner was used to provide a digital recording of the monument backed up by photography and desktop historical research.

The fieldwork element of SCAPE's work is complemented by other archaeological survey methods. When the Coastal Zone Assessment Survey of the coast of Angus north of Dundee was undertaken in 2009 the first phase was a full desk-based assessment, using information from the Sites and Monuments Record, Aberdeen and the National Monuments Record (held by the RCAHMS). Old maps, historical texts and excavation reports were also checked, together with aerial photographs. The information was added to a database and plotted onto maps using GIS. The second phase was completed by surveyors walking the entire route.

SCAPE's website provides access to a wealth of information as to how this Trust and the Shorewatch Project pursue their aims to record Scotland's eroding past.

plex statistical analyses. It can even be used to predict site locations based on known patterns (▶ p. 247).

Several other related computer tools which are proving useful to archaeologists are often lumped together with GIS. These include computer cartography, 3D rendering and computer animation. These techniques are especially useful for creating accurate maps and digital terrain models (DTM) which allow the archaeologists to view sites and data in both two and three dimensions.

Oral accounts

People are an important resource for archaeologists. Farmers and others who work on the land or within the built environment could have valuable information for archaeologists who may lack local knowledge. Interviews with people provide clues as to the use and development of recent buildings. Farmers, for example, may be able to identify areas where building rubble has been ploughed up or where dressed stones have been removed. Sometimes estate management records may hold this information for earlier periods. Fishermen or divers can often provide insights about underwater sites (▶ p. 309).

SURFACE SURVEYS

This term can be used to encompass fieldwalking, surveying and even planned aerial photography. We will concentrate on non-destructive visual surveys at ground level. These can range from slow, painstaking searches on foot to quite rapid examinations of a landscape from a vehicle looking for upstanding earthworks. Since most sites lack visible features, the former is more common. Fieldwalking is often concerned with finding traces of unrecorded sites, though it can be used as a follow-up to aerial photography to ascertain the potential chronological period of, say, a cropmark site. Scatters of building rubble or artefacts or slight undulations in the surface can reveal where there may be buried walls or house platforms. Differences in soil or vegetation may also be indicative of past human activity. For studies of the Mesolithic and Neolithic in Britain, scatters of flint and animal bone are often the only traces of human activity visible in the landscape. To study the activities of these mobile populations, careful identification and plotting of these scatters is essential. Surveys can also encompass the study of hedges and woodlands for traces of past economic activities and to help locate settlement areas (▶ p. 243). Surface surveys can cover large areas such as Webster and Sanders' work in the Copan Valley of Mexico or coastal areas in the Scotland's First Settlers project (▶ p. 235).

Waddington's (1999) study of hunter-gatherer exploitation of the landscape in the Milfield basin of Northumberland combined several reconnaissance methods with some limited invasive techniques. He identified five ecozones in the basin from gravel terraces around the River Till to sandstone uplands and studied a transect across them. In arable areas he was able to use fieldwalking but in pasture areas he used shovel pit testing (▶ p. 23). Patterns of finds were used to construct a model of land use. This suggested settlement was largely on the gravel terraces where wetland resources could be exploited. However, task groups (▶ p. 232) travelled to the uplands to hunt deer and gather wood and other resources. His study was also valuable in understanding why finds are more likely in some areas than others. Sediment coring revealed the way in which soil slip and build up affected buried archaeology and the way in which erosion in one particular area of peat was leading to more finds of lithics than in other areas and thus distorting the overall pattern of finds.

Surveying features

Surface investigations of known sites include micro-contour surveys of the topography. These detailed studies involve the precise use of

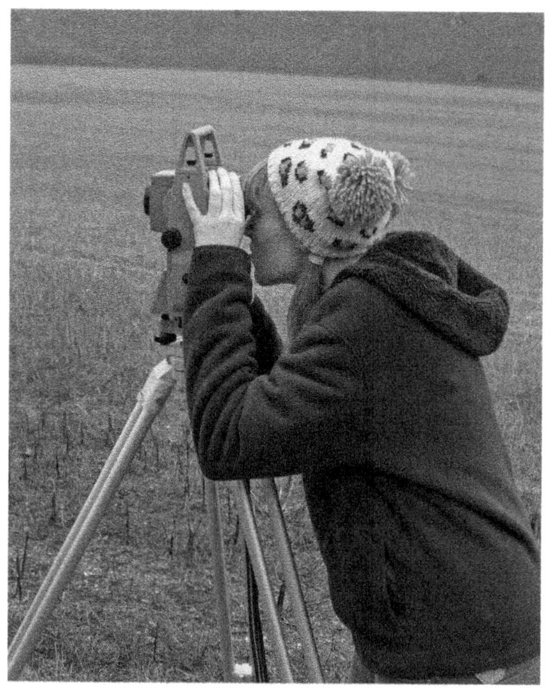

surveying tools to build up a picture of variations in height and levels. Micro-contour surveys often reveal hidden features that could not be detected with the naked eye. In most studies, the areas to be surveyed are measured using surveying equipment or Global Positioning Systems (**GPS**) and are set out with rows or squares of pegs, cane or marker poles. This is to enable accurate sampling and recording. Data from surveys can be loaded into digital terrain modelling (DTM) software to create 3D images of the landscape and features within it. It can also be combined with other data such as that from geophysics. Most professional surveys will use a total station. This combines sighting lens, level, laser measuring and an on-board computer to calculate angles and distances. More sophisticated models include GPS.

Figure 1.9 *Using a total station*

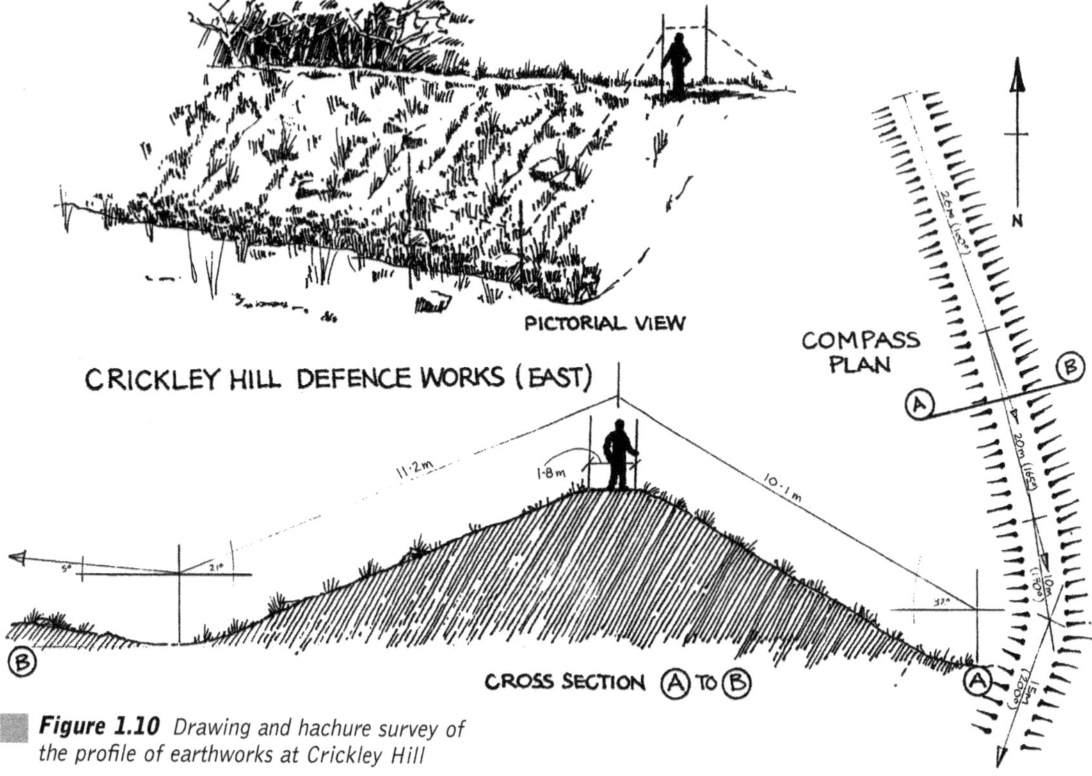

Figure 1.10 *Drawing and hachure survey of the profile of earthworks at Crickley Hill*

Another long-standing method of manual survey is known as plane table survey. This is a much more complex approach and requires a wider range of equipment and understanding. The plane table is levelled and orientated and an alidade (a sighting device) used to observe the key points of a site. A tape is used to measure from alidade to point and both distances and angles recorded as a series of 'rays' from the plane table. The English Heritage pamphlet *With Alidade and Tape* (2002) provides a detailed description of what is needed and how the various pieces of equipment can be used in combination to achieve the best results. An even simpler alternative where precision is not essential or for a rapid survey of a large site is to use pacing and compass directions to measure linear features. Clinometers,

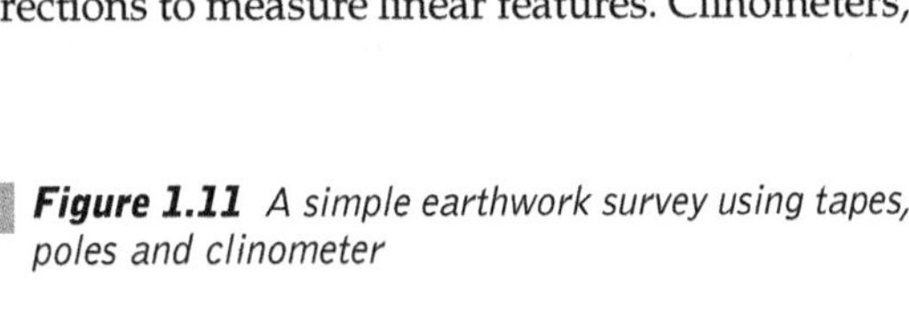

Figure 1.11 *A simple earthwork survey using tapes, poles and clinometer*

KEY STUDY

Surveying an abandoned landscape on St Kilda

This joint survey project between the Royal Commission on the Ancient and Historical Monuments of Scotland (RCAHMS) and the National Trust for Scotland aimed to evaluate the current state of the archaeological remains on the four main islands of the St Kilda archipelago, and to identify, map and record them systematically. These remote islands are 40 miles west of the Outer Hebrides and were continuously inhabited for over 2,000 years until the population was evacuated in 1930.

Much had been written about various aspects of life on St Kilda, but it quickly became apparent that the locations of the archaeological sites were largely unmapped. This seemed all the more amazing given that St Kilda is a Mixed World Heritage Site (▶ p. 577) in recognition of both its natural and its cultural heritage. What was previously known depended on local knowledge and some sketches of features plotted in the 1970s onto copies of the OS maps, plus the results of an RCAHMS survey in the 1980s and the work of a PhD student. To remedy this shortfall in the record, the project team adopted a methodology that combined the use of GPS survey equipment with high-definition ortho-rectified (geometrically corrected to remove distortions) aerial photography.

On the main island, Hirta, archaeologists mapped in detail a landscape with the most recent settlement (evacuated 1930) comprising cottages with strips of land running back from the seashore

continued

to the 'head-dyke' – the boundary that divided agricultural land from rough grazing. On the seaward side of the head-dyke just over one hundred cleits had been recorded, and at least another 1,200 have now been plotted across the rest of the island. Cleits are small multipurpose drystone structures which were originally roofed with stone and turf and are unique to St Kilda. They were used for drying and storing seabirds, eggs, peat and crops. The date range of the cleits is not known, but desk-based research shows some marked on a C17th map as 'pyramids' while late C19th photographs show that others cannot have been built until the early C20th. Field boundaries predating the head-dyke were also observed, though some of these features had been planned in the 1980s RCAHMS survey and through a study by archaeologist Mary Harman. Recording the cleits comprehensively for the first time demonstrated how much more information can be teased out with a fresh pair of eyes.

The most remote of the four main islands is Boreray. Archaeologists and other visitors had previously noted cleits and bothies (small basic dwellings or shelters), plus linear features which had been interpreted as channels to collect water. Reference had also been made to a 'wheel-house'-type structure, suggesting much earlier occupation – perhaps prehistoric. In 2010 fieldworkers spent a week on Boreray. The majority of the archaeological remains lie on a south-west facing grassy slope that plunges steeply into the sea. What had previously been considered as water channels were now better interpreted as field boundaries, and a hitherto unsuspected complex field system was revealed, stretching across the slope and incorporating cultivation terraces, garden plots and lazy beds (a form of spade dug cultivation that looks a bit like ridge and furrow).

Figure 1.12 *Survey work on St Kilda. Note the GPS staff held on the left*

It became clear as work progressed that the cleits and bothies on Boreray consistently overlay the banks and terraces, thus revealing a relative chronology (▶ p. 145), with the field-system earthworks clearly the earliest. The discovery of three settlement mounds added complexity to this sequence, though field observation alone could not establish a direct relationship between the mounds and the field system. Of the mounds, some contained elements of internal structures: these could be interpreted as prehistoric, but equally might date to the 1st millennium AD. Detailed surveys such as the one on Boreray challenged old ideas and revealed entirely new interpretations of the apparently inhospitable landscape; a most unlikely place to settle.

Data and pictures from this survey are available online from the Royal Commission on the Ancient and Historic Monuments of Scotland website which provides another example of a large, free archaeological database.

tape and ranging poles can be used to estimate heights and the lengths and angle of slopes.

Recording standing buildings

One specialised area of archaeological surveying focuses on the built environment and links archaeology to architectural science. Detailed studies of the material and construction techniques of structures are made both to enhance knowledge of the development of buildings and to provide a record against future destruction or decay. Laser scanning is used in some buildings which are covered with lichen to see how they are constructed. Records will range from written description to CAD (computer aided design)-based recording of every brick or stone. Most recording of buildings occurs as part of the planning process (▶ p. 572) or during conservation work. Two examples are the Defence of Britain project, which collected records on surviving defensive monuments of the Second World War, and Sutton Scarsdale Hall, an English Heritage site near Chesterfield in Derbyshire where site evaluation, geophysics and architectural survey were combined to record this large but derelict property. The recording of standing buildings is covered in Chapter 2 (▶ p. 77).

Sampling in archaeological fieldwork

Whatever is deposited is a fragment of past material culture. Dependent upon the material, a variable portion of these deposits will survive. Archaeologists will recover a sample of these. Not every site can be fieldwalked, let alone excavated. Choices have to be made. If these choices are arbitrary (non-probabilistic) they could lead to bias in the **archaeological record** with certain types of evidence being neglected and others over-represented. For example, if archaeologists chose only to study hillforts from the Iron Age or, as often happens, if development only led to excavation in one part of a town, it might create an unrepresentative picture of life in the past.

When archaeologists design reconnaissance or excavation research strategies, they use a rigorous form of probabilistic sampling to reduce bias in recovery. This means that the chance of anything being recovered is known. First, the plan of the total area or site to be surveyed is divided up either into a grid pattern of numbered squares or a series of equidistant parallel lines or transects (▶ p. 21). Both are usually aligned north–south to link into the national survey grid, although sometimes grids in fields are aligned on a particular boundary. With large areas it is common to select a sample of grids and then use transects within them. The scale varies according to the task. An initial surface survey of a whole

Figure 1.13 *Rock art survey using GPS and GIS*

The survey of rock carvings or petroglyphs illustrates many aspects of reconnaissance and recording techniques. In addition to a detailed record of each petroglyph being made by tracing and photographing at this site near Valcamonica in Italy, the position of each petroglyph is identified by GPS. Its height above sea level and orientation are also measured and the information entered into a GIS database. This enables 3D presentations to permit the study of relationships between petroglyphs and topography or between each other.

landscape might start with 100m or km squares and then have transects between 10 and 50m apart depending on terrain and resources. For test pitting on a known site, the initial grid might be 1m square. You need to understand four basic approaches to sampling. Our illustration is for grids but the principles are the same for transects.

A simple *random sample* (A) works like a lottery. The numbered units are selected by computer or number table. This is fair as each unit has an equal chance of being selected, but it can also lead to clustering and thus miss features.

Stratified sampling (B) overcomes clustering bias by first dividing the sample universe into sections. For example, if the site has natural zones such as hills, valley and plain, then numbers are selected randomly for each zone in proportion to its area.

Systematic sampling (C) overcomes clustering by selecting at evenly spaced intervals; for example, every third grid or every 10m. This ensures a more even selection although it could miss things that are regularly distributed. It usually requires a higher number of samples.

Stratified systematic sampling combines the last two methods and could be used to take more samples in particular zones than others.

FIELDWALKING

Fieldwalking, or surface collection, involves the systematic collection from the ploughsoil of artefacts which might be indicative of human settlement. This is based on the reasoning that material on the surface reflects buried remains. Sometimes high-density scatters of particular

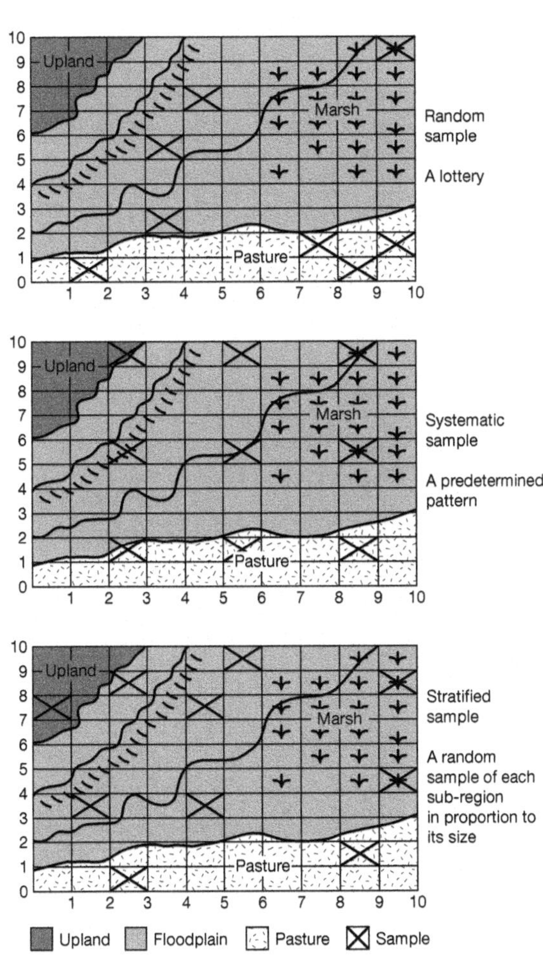

Figure 1.14 *Models of different approaches to sampling*

materials such as building rubble or broken pottery enable specific sites such as buildings or kilns to be identified. More typically, the method helps identify locations of past settlement or activities such as hunting. Ceramics and worked stone are the most commonly gathered materials but metal, bone and burnt stone are often also collected. The method is destructive in that archaeological material is removed, but as it has been disturbed by ploughing, it is not in its original context anyway.

Decisions about sampling have to be made when planning fieldwalking. Not everything will be collected, particularly when building rubble is involved. For instance, will all ceramics be collected or just diagnostic pieces or those over a certain size? Decisions also have to be taken about the width of transects or size of grids.

These are linked via a base point to the national mapping grid. Sometimes the fieldwalk plan will align with the national grid but boundaries and other features in the landscape may make this impractical. In order to link site grid to national grid and to establish the height above sea level of the site, theodolites have traditionally been used. In the UK these enable visual links to be made to Ordnance Survey benchmarks. Benchmarks were established nationwide on existing features such as bridges or on stone or concrete pillars to provide a system for the accurate calculation of levels linking back to the Ordnance Datum at Newlyn (ODN), Cornwall. Most benchmarks are of the 'cut' variety with a horizontal line (for which the height relative to ODN is given in the records) above an incised arrow. The Ordnance Survey's website allows a search by OS kilometre square which provides an instant list with notes and eight-figure grid references to enable location of benchmarks in any area. With the correct equipment the benchmarks are a valid source for levelling but are probably more of historical interest allowing another route to exploring the historic environment's record. They were a vital part of any surveyor's toolkit until the use of Global Positioning Systems (GPS) superseded them. Although about 500,000 still survive, their number is decreasing as a result of development and removal of their original sites. The Ordnance Survey no longer maintains them. The Royal Institute of Chartered Surveyors and the Ordnance Survey have jointly produced a leaflet entitled 'Virtually Level' which offers a clear explanation of the change from benchmarks to GPS.

Timing is important. Ideally ploughed soil should have been broken down by weathering and recent rain will have cleared dust from the surface. Walkers either proceed along a transect

Figure 1.15 *Fieldwalk finds from a Roman site*

Figure 1.16 *Ordnance Survey benchmark*

in a series of stints or search a grid. These are carefully set out with marker flags or poles. Grids are slower to walk and tend to be used when total coverage of a field is required. The material collected is bagged and tagged with the number of the grid or stint for processing and analysis. Once washed and identified by specialists, finds are counted for each grid or stint. They can then be plotted on a distribution map to show patterns and concentrations. There are many ways of displaying this information. Phase maps or a series of clear plastic overlays for each period or type of find are commonly used. Computer displays using GIS have an edge here since several types of data can be linked to any point and comparisons easily made.

Fieldwalking is a well-established method because it has many strengths. It is a relatively cheap way of surveying large areas since volunteer labour can be used to collect and wash

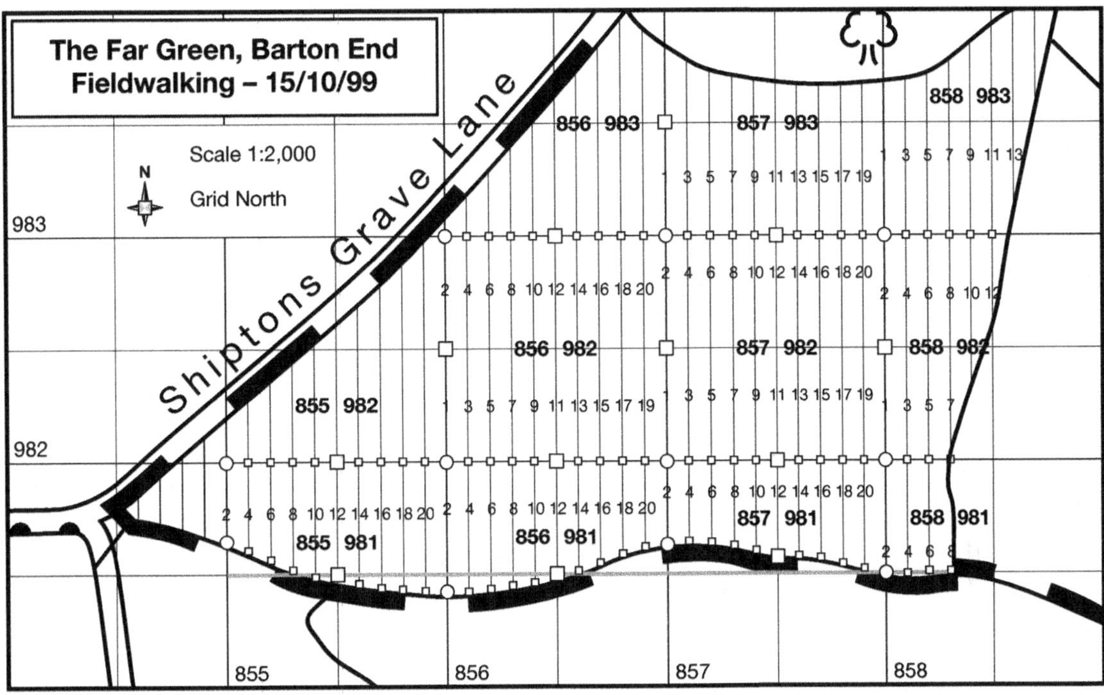

Figure 1.17 A planned fieldwalk which has been linked to the national grid system. Transects are 10m apart with 50m stints.

> **KEY TERM**
>
> **Transects, traverses and stints**
>
> A **transect** is a sampling line which could be across a single site or an entire landscape. It is usually aligned north–south and tied into the national grid. In fieldwalking, transects are usually divided up into manageable chunks or stints of 10 to 50m where one walker will use one collecting bag. 'Traverse' is a term used largely in geophysics and sometimes aerial photography to describe the straight, parallel paths passed over by the surveyor. So a magnetometer survey might use traverses set at 0.5m apart.

finds. It can help establish the function and period of a site without excavation and provide insights into location and exchange. Consideration does need to be given to time and effort. For example, to completely cover even a relatively small field (100m x 100m) an individual would walk 50 x 2m stints each 100m long – the equivalent of 5km – on ploughed soil! Better to find four friends!

Limitations of fieldwalking

Fieldwalking can indicate the spread and foci of evidence. It does, however, have important limitations too. It is only really useful on arable land and then only at certain times in the agricultural cycle. In addition, its results cannot always be taken at face value as, for example, medieval manuring practices may have transferred much domestic refuse to the ploughsoil thus hinting at sites that simply do not exist.

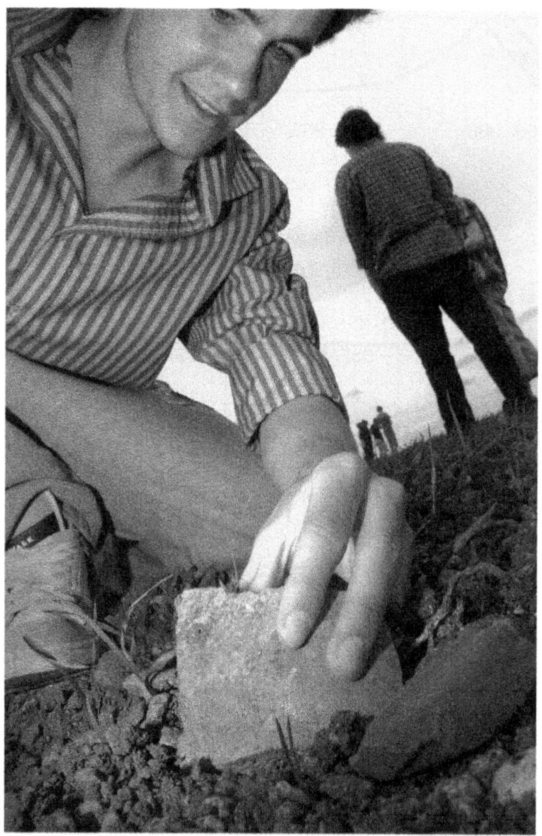

Figure 1.18 *Fieldwalking in progress. The experience and training of fieldwalkers and the conditions on the day all affect what is recovered.*

As with other survey methods, further research is always needed to substantiate preliminary findings. Chris Gerrard's work on the Shapwick Project sheds additional light on the limitations of fieldwalking. Different materials were found to behave differently in the same soil. Repeated walking of the same fields and monitoring ceramics in them showed that some material migrated further than others. Patterns for pottery from different periods were also very different. It was not always a good indication of settlement. A second variable was the differential collection by different fieldwalkers. Analysis of their finds showed that some were good at recognising and collecting one type of material but poor with another. This applied to experienced walkers as well as novices. Their performance varied according to weather and slope. Taken together it means that what is recovered is a sample of what was in the topsoil and the topsoil holds a sample of what lies below. In both cases the sample varies for each type of find. Fieldwalking results therefore need to be cross-checked with other data before conclusions can be drawn.

Alternatives to fieldwalking

There are a number of other prospection methods which provide alternatives to fieldwalking although all are potentially more destructive. **Shovel pit testing** can take place in woods, pasture and gardens where fieldwalking is impossible. This approach to sampling is very common in the USA. Only the top few centimetres are sampled. In each sample a standard volume of soil is sieved through a fine mesh for ecofacts and artefacts. Recent examples of test pitting in the UK are at Kibworth, Leicestershire, where the work was coordinated by Michael Wood for the BBC and in villages around Cambridge by Carenza Lewis.

Coring and **augering** are also used to sample the subsoil. This can provide a snapshot of the stratigraphy and the sample can be examined for artefactual or environmental evidence. An auger is driven or screwed into the ground. It extracts a sample of the subsoil in much the same way as an apple corer. It has been widely used in south-east Europe to detect building horizons. **Probing**, which involves pushing a rod into the ground, is more useful for tracing shallow buried features such as walls on known sites (▶ p. 355). This method proved the simplest and cheapest form of plotting the route of the Fosse Way Roman road and its side ditches across grassland in Leicestershire. Although allowing for a degree of subjectivity on behalf of the person with the probe, traverses across the proposed line of the road were undertaken with the probe inserted at 0.5m intervals and decisions made as to whether

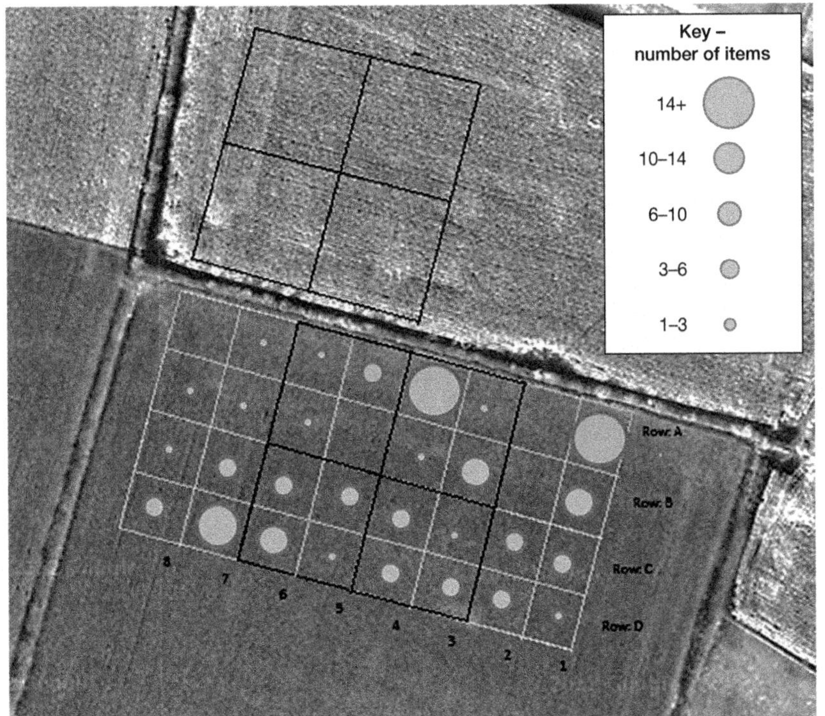

Figure 1.19
The density of Roman pottery plotted in relation to each stint. Amounts of selected materials can also be shown with shapes or dots where the size and colour or shading represent the numbers of finds.

Figure 1.20
Shovel pit testing and dry sieving at Bodie Ghost Town

Figure 1.21 *Probing for stone field boundaries buried under peat at the Ceide Fields (▶ p. 355)*

the probe hit stony ground ('road'), softer fill ('ditch') or standard substrata (between ditch and road or indeterminate readings). The resultant plots showed the road's course (plotted in red), the two ditches (plotted in blue) and other 'responses' (plotted in pencil). Simple but effective and cheap!

Geochemical prospection

These relatively new methods and expensive techniques attempt to locate areas of past human activity by detecting differences in the chemical properties of the soil. All living things produce organic phosphate as waste or through decay. Unlike phosphate in modern fertiliser, this remains in the soil where it was deposited. Where settlement is suspected from other methods such as fieldwalking, samples of soil are taken and levels of phosphate measured in a laboratory. Once plotted, concentrations of organic phosphate may indicate settlements or animal enclosures since this is where most deposition would be expected. Similar principles apply to heavy minerals such as lead and cadmium and to lipids (fats). These techniques may become increasingly important in the future. One possibility is that different chemical combinations could identify 'signatures' (▶ p. 176) for different activities.

GEOPHYSICAL SURVEYS

Perhaps the most noted development in field archaeology over recent times has been the increasing ability to 'see below the ground' using modern technology. With a shift in emphasis amongst archaeologists in favour of preservation in situ rather than excavation, these techniques are now commonplace.

In the UK, the *Time Team* programmes have highlighted the use of 'geofizz' as an almost essential element in an archaeologist's armoury. Given that they usually start with the topsoil intact (and three days to reach a conclusion), some guide as to where to excavate is essential to avoid wasted time and energy and so geophysical methods are quickly combined with other survey methods. Television viewers could be forgiven for thinking that no excavation can operate without a geophysical survey. This is not true. Geophysics is established as a major part of archaeological research and prospecting but the need for it is not universal; for example, where all topsoil has been stripped down to the top of the 'natural' prior to sand and gravel extraction features can be identified by eye in the traditional way (▶ p. 51).

'Geophysics' covers techniques that detect features through their physical differences from the surrounding soil. The most common techniques detect magnetic and electrical anomalies and require considerable skill to interpret. Nearly all these techniques were by-products of military inventions developed to assist bombing or detect hidden locations. Given the heavy investment in research for defence purposes, further new technologies are to be expected.

Resistivity survey

This involves passing an electric current through the ground and noting differences in the ability of the subsoil to conduct electricity. Electricity is conducted through the soil by mineral salts contained in water. The more moisture there is, the better the conductivity of the soil. A buried ditch or grave will generally retain water better than the surrounding soil. A buried wall or road will conduct poorly and therefore resist the current more than the surrounding soil. Electrical current flows close to the surface so it can be measured using shallow probes. Meters are usually mounted on a 'zimmer-like' frame and have a data logger on board to record results. The method works better with some soils than others. Clay retains moisture well so differences in resistance between the soil and buried ditches or pits may be impossible to detect. This also applies to many soils if they become waterlogged in wintertime. Plants, rocks and variations in the depths of soils can also create misleading readings. While relatively easy to use, resistivity meters are not fast and are best suited to detailed exploration of a site or a possible site, located

Figure 1.22 *Resistivity surveying*

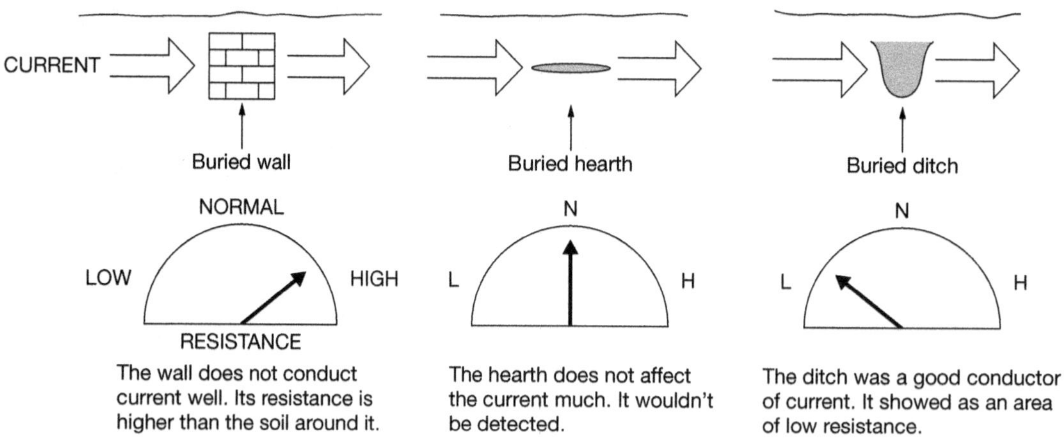

Figure 1.23 *A simplified diagram illustrating the principles of resistivity*

through surface finds or aerial photography, rather than initial prospecting.

Resistivity can also be used to create pseudo-sections of buried linear features. This involves taking a series of readings from a line of probes placed across a buried feature such as a ditch. Increasing the spacing between probes, rather than using narrowly spaced probes, can produce data on the deeper parts of a feature. The depth to which this technology penetrates the soil is limited and readings require considerable interpretation, as the sensitivity of the meters is not great. At Hindwell in Wales, a feature interpreted from the resistivity survey as a 4m wide ditch turned out after excavation to be a series of massive postholes with construction ramps.

Magnetometer surveying

The earth's magnetic field is generally uniform in any one place. However, local magnetic distortions can be caused by past human activity. Topsoil contains haematite (Fe_2O_3), an iron oxide. In some forms its crystals are magnetic. A ditch which has filled up with topsoil will contain more haematite than the surrounding area. Its fill will therefore be slightly different magnetically and this difference may be detected by sensitive, modern magnetometers. A second type of distortion is caused where topsoil has been subject to considerable heat. This erases the magnetic properties of the iron oxides. For haematite, heating to 675°C is required. When the soil cools, the iron oxides become permanently magnetised according to the polarity of the earth's magnetic field at that time. Since this field changes over time, the sites of kilns and hearths appear as magnetic anomalies.

The earliest magnetometers were cumbersome and slow to use. The manufacture of increasingly reliable instruments for archaeology has seen magnetometry become a standard technique. Handheld fluxgate gradiometers, sometimes using twin sensors a metre apart, enable the technique to be used to rapidly scan quite large areas of soil, grass and crops to highlight anomalies. Magnetometers are also used in detailed site investigations where they can detect small features up to 1m down and provide images of some buried features. For very detailed work, traverses are set 0.5m apart with samples every 0.5m. Gaps and sample intervals of 1m are more common.

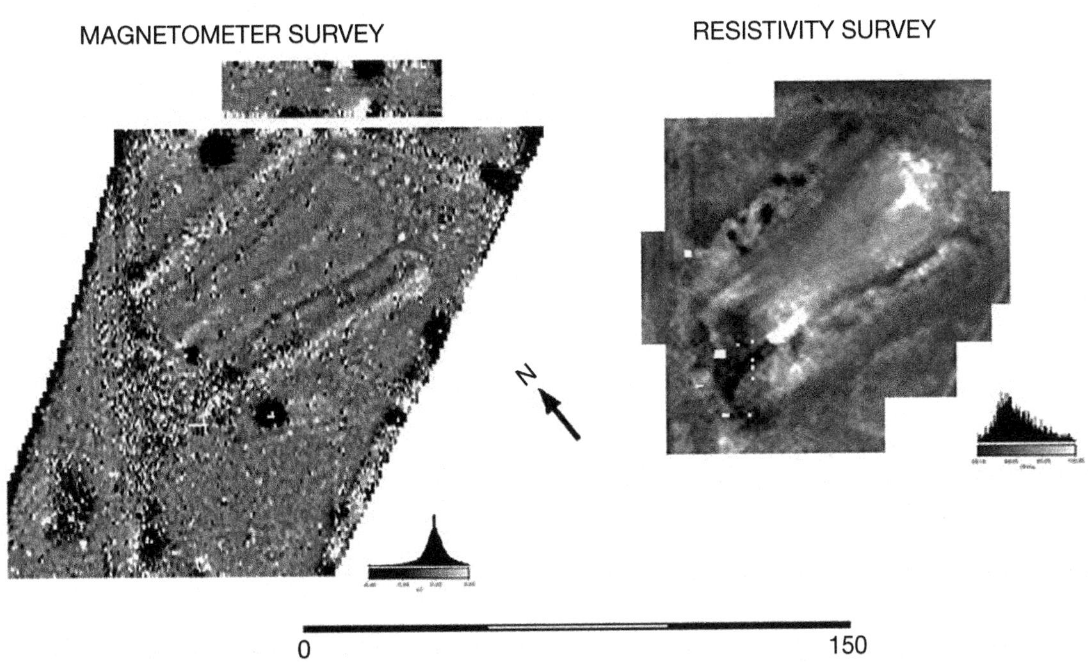

Figure 1.24 *Resistivity and magnetometer plots compared. The essential complementary nature of these techniques can be seen in these plots from English Heritage's survey of White Barrow.*

To be able to detect anomalies, the magnetic background of the soil has to be measured and magnetometers calibrated against it. The measuring of this magnetic susceptibility of the topsoil can also be used as a crude but rapid survey technique in its own right. Magnetic hotspots suggest areas of past settlement or industrial activity, which could be surveyed using other methods.

Sensitive magnetic instruments are easily disturbed by iron, including nails, pipes and wire fences as well as the zips and piercings worn by archaeologists. A further limitation can be background interference from magnetic bedrock or where a long period of occupation has left a magnetic layer over a wide area. Sandy and clay soils often do not provide sufficient contrast. Fluctuations in the earth's magnetic field also have to be taken into account. Data can be quickly downloaded to a laptop in the field but it requires considerable skill and experience to interpret the results.

Magnetometers are also capable of performing on underwater sites.

Caesium vapour (CV) magnetometers

These are many times more sensitive than conventional magnetometers and are more commonly used in Germany and Austria. Typically several machines are used close together on a large wooden handcart. They work by pumping caesium vapour and taking rapid measurements at around 25cm intervals. This alkali is so sensitive to minute variations in magnetism that it can detect and define the edges of buried features formed by traces of magnetite. This iron oxide (Fe_3O_4) is concentrated in the remains of the bacteria which consumed the wooden structures such as posts which once stood there. It has been used at a number of well-documented sites to reveal more of their secrets. Work at Stanton Drew stone circle in Somerset revealed the 'ghosts' of hundreds of postholes in concentric circles. Caesium magnetometers suffer less from the background 'noise' which occurs with handheld devices but at £40,000 per machine and perhaps four machines on a cart, this technique is expensive.

Marine versions of caesium magnetometers are towed behind ships and measure variations in the earth's magnetic field. They can detect ferrous material on or under the seabed.

Other non-invasive methods

Metal detectors are useful for metal objects down to about 15cm. Some archaeologists use them on site to provide information in advance of digging, such as the position of burial deposits. Skill is required to avoid time being wasted exploring buried slag or modern metal debris. Similarly they can sweep areas in advance of detailed geophysics to identify concentrations of metal that might distort readings; for example, on battlefield sites. Danish museums routinely work with local metal detectorists to recover and record metalwork from the ploughsoil around sites and to identify where metal finds are likely to be made prior to excavation (▶ p. 443). This enables the lead archaeologist to check that the diggers did not miss any small finds. Issues around metal detecting are explored in Chapter 12.

Ground penetrating radar (GPR), which was developed for defence and engineering, is increasingly used in urban areas where deposits are often deeply buried and where pipes and cables hamper other geophysics methods. GPR works by transmitting pulses of energy into the ground and

Figure 1.25 *Handcart mounted GPR*

recording the time taken by and strength of the return signal. This can indicate the density and depth of buried deposits. Data based on different energy wavelengths can be plotted as a series of 'time slices' to build up a 3D picture of buried remains. A team at the Bronze Age site of Gordion in Turkey has used GPR as an alternative to excavation and has mapped buried features such as tombs so that they can be protected. More routinely, GPR is useful for detecting buried floors, voids and walls. It has been particularly effective in revealing the internal structures of buildings and exploring burials. It is the only effective geophysics technique in urban centres where it can even penetrate tarmac. Due to its cost and the availability of quicker methods, it has not been used widely outside urban areas in the UK although this is starting to change. The Anglo-Saxon Hall at Lyminge in Kent was discovered using GPR. GPR works poorly on clay soils.

Combining geophysics techniques at Binchester Fort

The Roman fort lies next to the point where Dere Street, the Roman road running north from York to Corbridge, crossed the River Wear in County Durham. Although the site has been known about and in part researched and excavated since the early C19th, it was only when detailed geophysical surveys were undertaken between 2004 and 2011 that a comprehensive understanding of the scale and complexity of the site's features became possible. The original, large timber fort (*c.* AD 75–80) of 7.5 hectares had been abandoned and replaced by a stone fort of 4 hectares in the middle of the C2nd. The underlying features, including ditches from the two forts, shown as marks on aerial photographs taken in the 1940s, were clarified by the geophysics and the *vicus* (civilian settlement) that surrounds the fort was shown to extend to an impressive 12 hectares.

Binchester is a good example of where the three major elements of geophysical survey – resistivity, magetometry and GPR – have been combined to provide the quality and quantity of survey evidence to underpin informed decision making on how best to excavate this 'research' site. A Geoscan resistance meter and a fluxgate gradiometer together provided data to compile a plan of probable features such as roads, ditches and structures. Magnetic data had suggested that the *vicus* was protected in part by a ditch in later Roman times and what appeared to be small, square stone structures were located just outside this ditch. GPR was then focused on these structures and revealed at least two mausolea and part of a third at the edge of the surveyed grid. *Time Team* subsequently based their trench location on this data and were able to recover the physical evidence of the features in their excavation just where the geophysics had predicted. However, a later geophysics survey by ASUD (Archaeological Services University of Durham) provided corrections to their interpretation of the sequence. Binchester is a good example of community engagement (▶ p. 583). The excavation team is led by Durham County Council, Durham and Stanford universities and the local archaeological society. Members of the public can pay to take part.

AERIAL PHOTOGRAPHY

The first aerial photographs (APs) were taken from hot-air balloons. Today, most photographs are taken from light aircraft, although kites, balloons, radio-controlled helicopters or very long poles have been used on occasions. APs can support both archaeological reconnaissance and analysis. Comparatively large areas can be covered in the search for evidence or 'marks'. In some circumstances these lead to initial site discovery while in others they enable more comprehensive investigation of known sites. Aerial photographers devise schedules to ensure that they have the best opportunities for seeing sites and recording them. It involves planning and research to ensure the best possible conditions

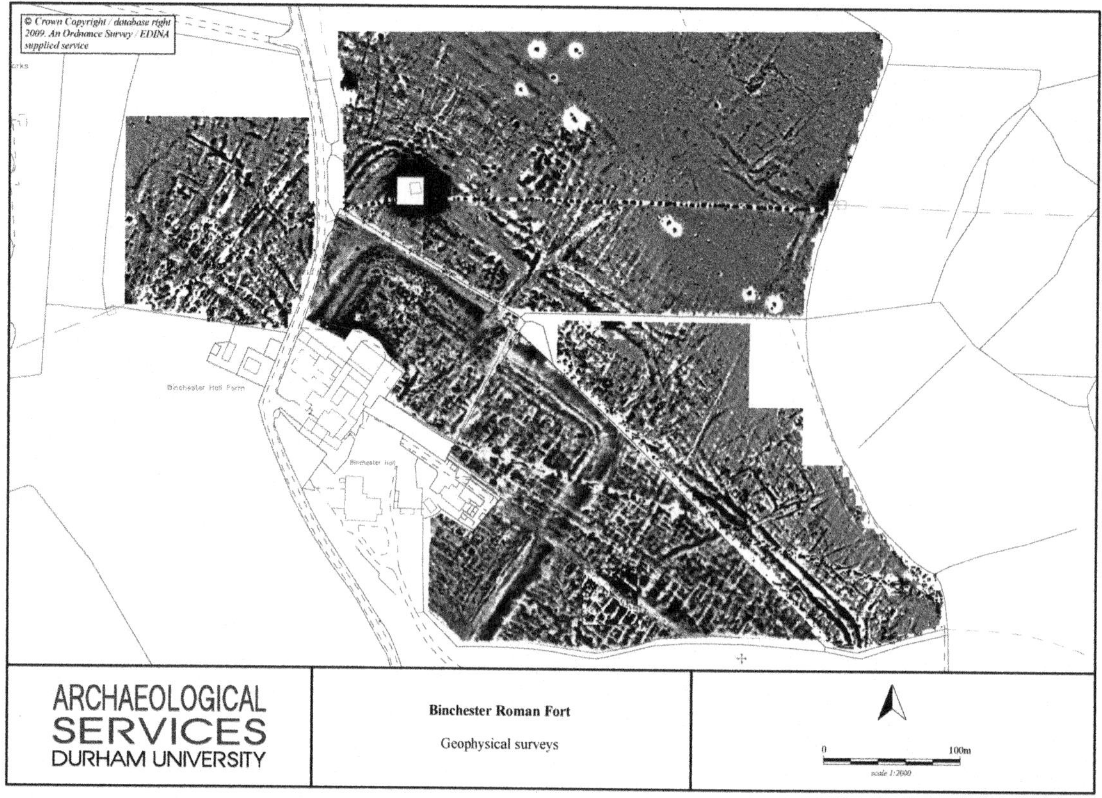

Figure 1.26 *Survey interpretation from Binchester. Excavation sequences blended with the latest geophysics. (ASUD)*

in terms of seasons, weather patterns and agricultural activities. Aerial photographs can aid mapmaking but the main focus here is on reconnaissance and the following paragraphs reflect how different 'marks' can be located and interpreted as archaeological features or sites. It is important to remember that most archaeological sites cannot be detected from the air and that interpretation for all but the most obvious examples requires skill and experience. In particular, interpreters rely on recognising repeated patterns or 'signatures' based on previously investigated sites. Substantial archives of aerial photographs are available publicly and commercially so new research should be based on adding to the current base rather than repeating it at considerable cost. Archives include the impressive Cambridge University collections built up by Professor J. K. St Joseph, the national archive at the NMR, Swindon and regional collections such as the South Yorkshire collection built up by Derek Riley and others.

Aerial photographs used for mapping are taken with the camera pointing straight down at the ground (*verticals*) with the aircraft flying along grid lines. Often these are taken from high altitude and are black and white to maximise contrast. This is the case with the RAF archives dating from the 1940s which are now housed at the NMR. Unless clouds intervene, features can usually be seen clearly and they provide an excellent desktop source for initial study of landscape developments. Usually photographs are taken in an overlapping series so that they can be viewed through a stereoscope to see the landscape in 3D. Their main value is in planning

Figure 1.27 *An aerial photograph of Downton deserted medieval village in Northamptonshire using shadows and highlights to reveal the earthworks. The shadows cast by the trees can be used to establish the position of the sun and thus allow for interpretation of the ups and downs in the landscape. In terms of relative chronology, a later canal cuts through the remains of the village.*

and illustrating sites. Because of the angle of photograph, there is no distortion at the centre of these photographs although some occurs towards the edges. Where some dimensions in the photograph are known, reasonably accurate plans can be drawn of sites, including their contours. This is known as photogrammetric mapping.

Oblique photographs are more widely used in archaeology to reveal sites and features. These are taken from low-flying aircraft with the picture taken at an angle to the ground. Aerial reconnaissance often precedes field survey as it can quickly provide evidence of sites invisible to archaeologists at ground level or add clarity and pattern to those that can be seen; for example, low earthworks which would otherwise require hours of basic field survey and recording.

There are three main types of 'mark' by which archaeological sites show up from the air.

Shadow marks

In low light, either at the start or end of the day, shadows are at their longest and strongest. This means that even quite minor variations in ground level will cast shadows on slopes away from the sun and reflect highlights on up-slopes facing the sun. Careful study of such photographs – once the sun's direction has been established – can reveal sites such as almost ploughed out barrows, the remains of early field systems or hut circles within the interior of an Iron Age hillfort. In an interesting but rather less frequent scenario, shadows are also created where crops have grown to different heights (▶ p. 33) as a result of sub-surface features and some new sites have been detected as a result of this phenomenon. Winter is the best season for shadow photography as the sun is particularly low and vegetation which might mask sites has often died down. Snowfall and flooding can accentuate the appearance of hollows and earthworks and create some of the most dramatic images of **shadow sites**. This technique is most frequently used to illustrate and investigate known sites.

Cropmarks

The ripening and growth rate of crops is related to the amount of moisture their root systems can access. Plants, particularly cereals, with better access to moisture will often grow taller and ripen at a slower rate than those plants around them, thus exhibiting a different tone or colour. Conversely, plants growing over, say, a buried wall are likely to be more stunted and ripen sooner. If there are buried archaeological features under a field, this can result in patterns showing in the crop. It is the contrast between unripe (when most of the crop is in this state) and ripened crops –

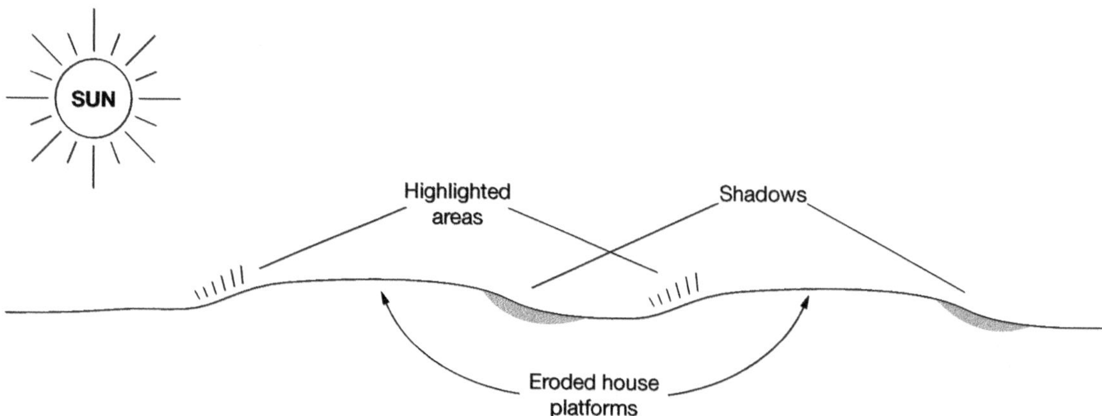

Figure 1.28 *Why earthworks are visible as 'shadow sites'*

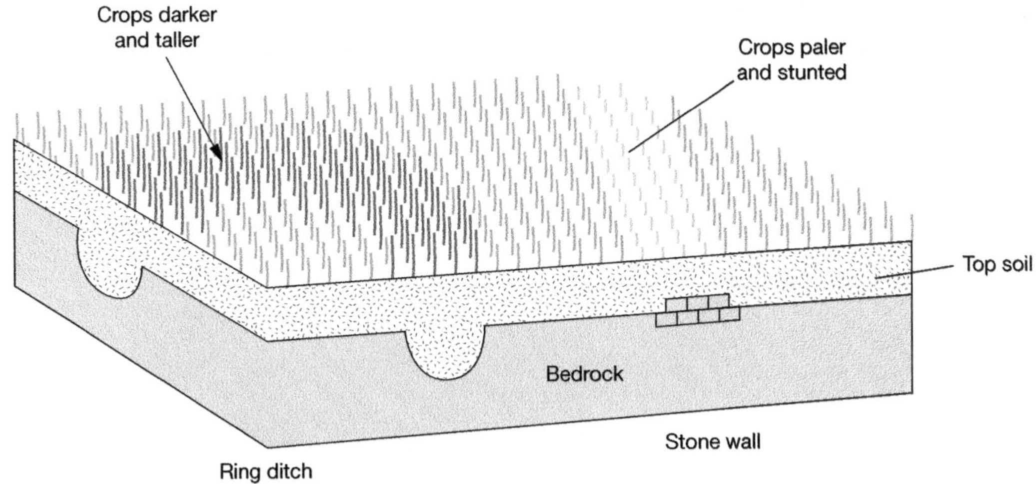

Figure 1.29 *Three-dimensional cross-section of cropmarks*

negative cropmarks – which reveals plans of buildings or routes of Roman roads and the contrast between ripened crop (when most of the crop is in this state) and unripened crop – positive cropmarks – which shows up buried ditches. 'Parch marks' show on grass as negative marks and can often be seen revealing hidden walls under English Heritage's manicured grass at monastic sites.

Cropmarks sometimes only show for a few days a year. Repeatedly flying over areas over time can pick up new and different features. Some only show up in drought conditions when crops with access to moisture have the greatest advantage and colour contrast is exaggerated. The technique works best on fast draining soils such as river gravels but is less good on clay or areas with deep topsoil, where the soil retains moisture well. Major studies have been undertaken along both the Upper Thames and the Trent Valley (sand and gravel zone) based on cropmark evidence of settlements from the Iron Age and Romano-British periods. When the known marks are transferred onto modern maps, the density of earlier evidence shows how intense the settlement patterns were. Cropmarks show up best in cereal crops such as wheat and particularly barley. They do not show up in many other crops – for example, peas and beans – and the effect of differential moisture can be overcome or masked by irrigation or fertiliser. Care has to be taken with interpretation, as geological features such as periglacial cracks and modern field drainage and underground pipelines also create cropmarks. Trial excavation is often the only way to firmly identify many sites. Cropmarks are the most prolific source of new sites, particularly for the late Neolithic to early medieval periods, and are also used to investigate existing sites such as the extent of the harbour at Fishbourne Palace. The lost Roman city of Altinum, near Venice, was extensively photographed in 2009 and sophisticated examination of the cropmarks has revealed remarkable details of the town plan. Italian archaeologists intend to build on their current research using Lidar (▶ p. 37).

Soil marks

On freshly ploughed soils where there is a marked contrast between the colour of the topsoil and subsoil, evidence of ploughed-out monuments can occur as **soil marks**. On chalk, the dark brown of ditch infill will contrast with the chalk

Figure 1.30 *An Iron Age 'banjo' enclosure on Cranborne Chase showing as a dark cropmark. The crops growing over the ditches of the feature are darker because their roots have better access to moisture than the surrounding crops. (Crown Copyright 1955 and 1959/MOD)*

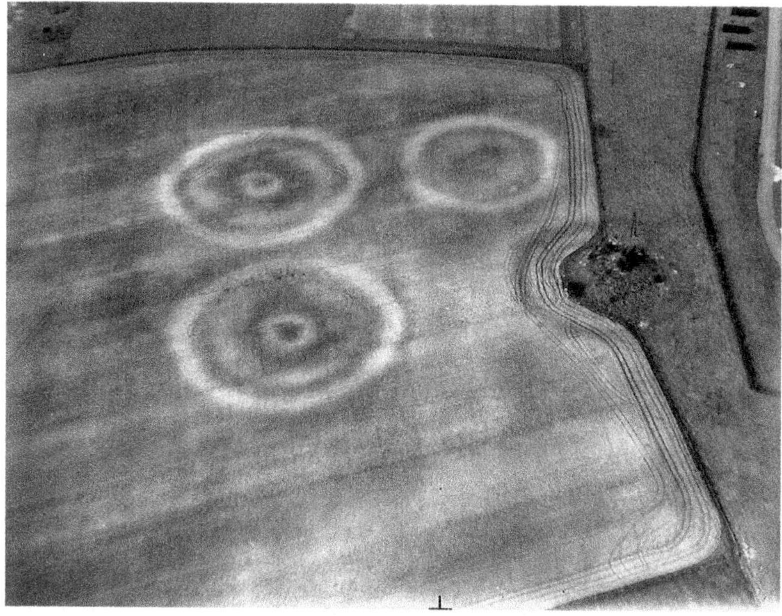

Figure 1.31 *Winterbourne Stoke round barrow cemetery showing as soil marks. The difference in tone between the topsoil and the material used for the barrow provides a clear contrast. The monuments would not be easily detected on the ground. (Crown Copyright 1955 and 1959/MOD)*

KEY STUDY

Contrasting approaches: Empingham and East Kent Access Road

This key study dates back to the early 1970s when plans were drawn up to build a dam across a small river valley and thus create a large reservoir now known as Rutland Water. It highlights the combination of many of the survey methods described in this chapter and the extent to which they contributed to the discovery of the various archaeological sites. Finally a contrast is made with the methodology behind the reconnaissance for sites along the route of the East Kent Access Road on the Isle of Thanet in 2010.

Empingham

The first indication of interest was when a farmer showed an Anglo-Saxon brooch he had ploughed up to a local archaeologist – an early form of the Portable Antiquities Scheme. The fact that such finds are usually associated with burials led to an exploratory excavation (now called 'evaluation') which when extended eventually revealed a small inhumation cemetery of fourteen burials. Conversations over coffee during the dig included issues of how sites can be found and fieldwalking and its potential contribution was raised. The farmer then took the archaeologists onto an adjacent field where they picked up a quantity of Romano-British pottery. An excavation later uncovered a farmstead (aisled barn, well, buildings and farmyard) at this location.

The planned dam and reservoir works constituted a 'threat' in Department of the Environment (now English Heritage) speak and grants were made to enable excavation to progress, though this was limited mainly to the summer season. Part of the area was under pasture (the fields along the River Gwash itself) while arable farming was practised further back up the valley slopes. No shadow or crop marks were visible on the aerial photographs available and mapwork showed only a medieval moated site in the village itself some 500m from the Anglo-Saxon and Romano-British sites. However, the presence of archaeologists working in the area brought in information from other farmers, and trial trenching (▶ p. 56) with a JCB in a field across the river but directly opposite the farmstead revealed a second Romano-British site which was subsequently excavated and shown to be a simple 'villa'.

At this point, as construction work on the dam began, Anglian Water, the consultant engineers and the earth-moving teams all readily accepted the need for a watching brief (▶ p. 575) during the work as an area of almost 1km^2 was scraped off by heavy plant machinery. Careful observation of these exposed surfaces over a period of three years revealed traces of an Iron Age settlement, two more significant Romano-British farmsteads, some Anglo-Saxon huts and a second much larger Anglo-Saxon cemetery with 133 inhumations and a single cremation. All these sites were investigated but the major excavation was of the AS cemetery where immediate salvage work had to take place. The excavators employed the services of a metal detector under controlled circumstances to give initial indications of grave locations. The Department of the Environment's geophysics team used a fluxgate gradiometer to see if magnetic anomalies could show outlying graves and the ditch which formed the cemetery's western boundary.

Modern approaches

In the modern scenario the earliest stages of the Empingham story might well be repeated but plans for such significant engineering works would today require a major archaeological assessment

continued

Figure 1.32 *Excavation of Grave 5 Empingham*

(▶ p. 573) and evaluation. Anglian Water would be required to fund this and react to and support any necessary archaeological research and fieldwork. Whether the survey methods of today's professional archaeological contractors would have fared better cannot be stated but the overall activity and presence would be far greater than the ad hoc situation that prevailed in the 1970s.

The 2010 dig on the East Kent Access Road on the Isle of Thanet studied 48 hectares (about half the area stripped for the works at Empingham) over a nine-month period, moving directly to a substantial investigation – a big dig – rather than spend time on extensive field evaluation. While the features and finds on the Kent excavation far exceeded the Empingham record, it is noteworthy that much of the material evidence was once again revealed during top-stripping overseen by a resident team of archaeologists.

rubble of a bank and the lighter brown of the ploughsoil. At Flag Fen, a Roman road appeared as an orangey stripe against the black peat soil.

REMOTE SENSING

This can be a rather confusing term. Usually it is used to distinguish between the imaging techniques used from planes and satellites and those of ground-based prospection. This may or may not include aerial photography. Sometimes it is used to describe all techniques that do not remove material. When you come across it, be sure to check which sense it is being used in. We are using it in the first sense. The results of all these techniques need to be checked at ground level.

Most methods work by recording radiation in the form of light reflected from the earth's surface. Tiny differences at the surface in terms of vegetation, minerals, water, loose or packed soil, texture or temperature all impact on that reflected light. Only a small range of wavelengths within the electromagnetic light spectrum are visible to the human eye (visible light). Infrared and ultra-violet light are invisible. The development of sensors to 'see' these other wavelengths and computers able to analyse them was originally intended for military use but offers huge potential to archaeology. The earliest development was colour infrared film, which was used to detect hidden installations and tanks during the Second World War. It was subsequently used to detect buried archaeology from slight differences in vegetation.

Airborne and satellite techniques, including thermal imaging and infrared photography, are able to record temperature, dew and frost dispersal variations invisible to light-sensitive film. They all work on the principle that anomalies such as disturbed earth, ditches or buried walls will absorb and retain heat or moisture at different rates to the surrounding ground. These can be identified from differences in colour on screen or printouts. Computers can be programmed to search for particular types of anomaly. Remote sensing can be particularly valuable when exploring large or inaccessible areas.

Cost means that it is not used in most surveys while commercial equipment is really only suitable for large features because each pixel has a side of up to 30m. However, one can anticipate that increases in sensitivity from military purposes will eventually filter through to satellites which prospect for minerals or monitor glaciers and these in turn will benefit archaeology. An example is the discovery of hundreds of buried tombs (including seventeen pyramids) through

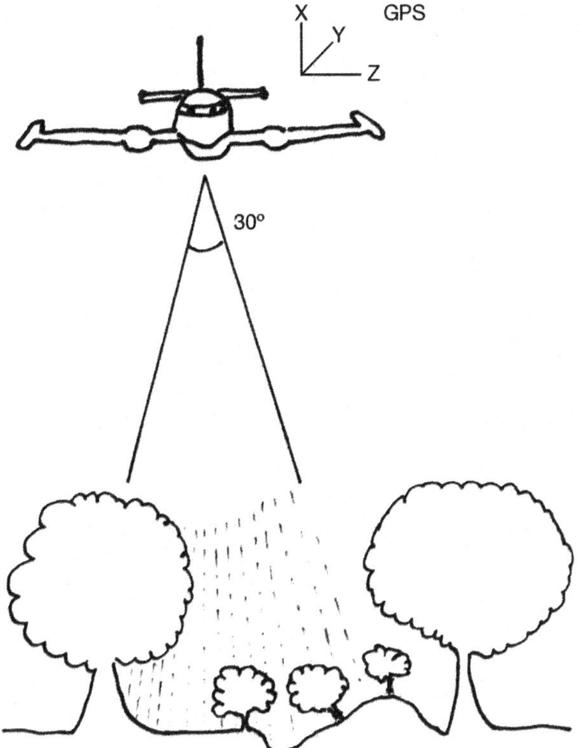

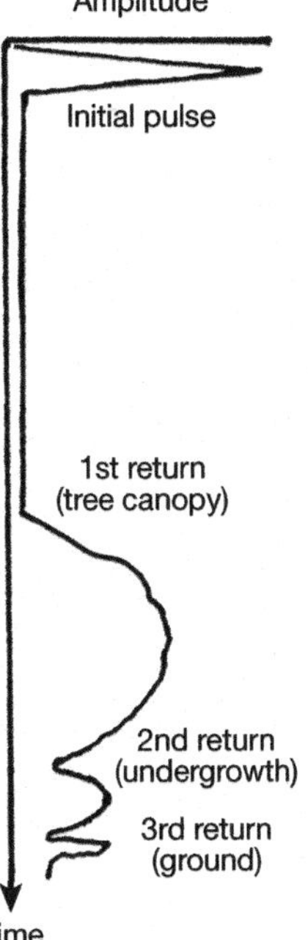

Figure 1.33 *How LiDAR works*

Figure 1.34 *Earthworks at Welshbury before LiDAR survey. Very little is visible through the trees. (Crown Copyright. Courtesy of Forest Research, based on Unit for Landscape Modelling data. www.forestry.gov.uk/fr/lidar)*

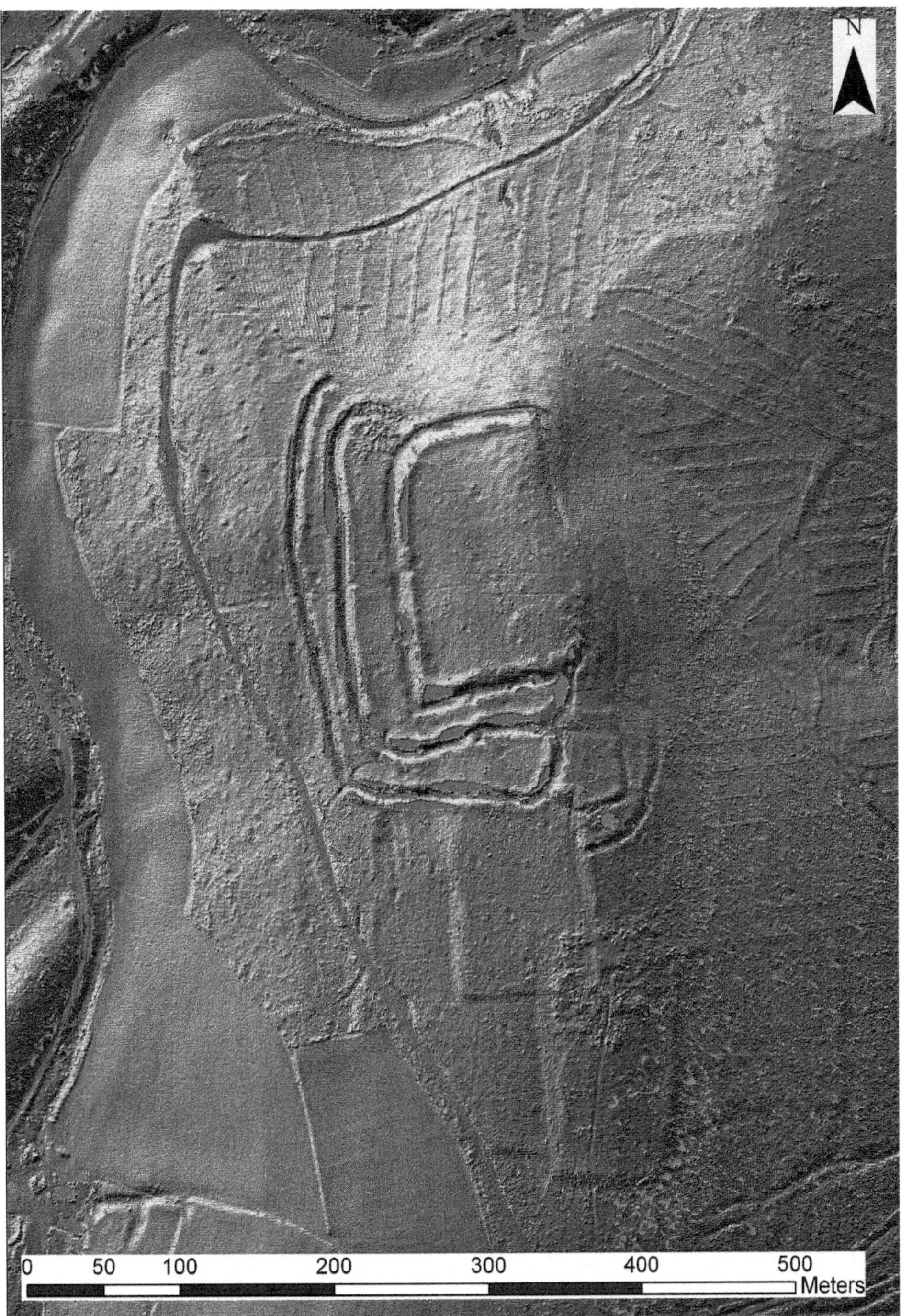

Figure 1.35 *Earthworks at Welshbury after LiDAR survey. The vegetation layer has been digitally removed to reveal the lost landscape. (Crown Copyright. Courtesy of Forest Research, based on Unit for Landscape Modelling data. www.forestry.gov.uk/fr/lidar)*

infrared satellite images by a University of Alabama team at Tanis in Egypt.

Satellite survey

The rediscovery of the lost city of Ubar, a key trading point for camel trains carrying frankincense across the Arabian desert from the Bronze Age to around AD 300, illustrates the potential of remote sensing. Historic records suggested the town lay in a vast area of sand dunes known as the empty quarter. Radar images from NASA's space shuttle failed to locate the city because it was buried too deeply. Thermal and infrared imaging from the Landsat and SPOT satellites was more successful. These can detect minute differences in the earth's surface and present them as colour differences for analysis. Reddish streaks indicated several routes which differed from the surrounding desert by having fewer rocks, more dust and soil enriched with camel dung (Blom et al. 1997). These converged on the village of Shisr. Archaeological investigation revealed artefacts from as far away as Greece and Rome, which testified to its likely importance in long-distance trade. Further examples of the use of remote sensing are explored in Chapter 7.

Lidar

Experimentation with the use of lasers in meteorology led to the development of a number of techniques involving light to provide highly accurate images of objects or surfaces. Lidar (Light Detection and Ranging) uses lasers mounted in a light aircraft to transmit 400 pulses per second of scanning laser beams which are reflected back from the ground surface and recorded on sensors. The time taken for light to bounce back determines the precise distance from the aircraft. This method records differences every 10cm across the survey area and is far more sensitive to tiny variations in terrain than conventional photographs of shadow marks. Beams bounce back from both the top of vegetation and the ground surface. This means it can penetrate forest canopies while the time difference between the readings enables the height of vegetation to be calculated. This has been particularly useful in surveys of Mayan sites in the jungles of Belize. Lidar can be used seamlessly over land and sea to a depth of around 50m. When mapping the seabed it is known as Bathymetric Lidar.

Sonar

Sonar (Sound Navigation and Ranging) was developed to detect submarines and is a form of acoustic sensing. It uses pulses of sound waves to locate objects underwater. For archaeology, side-scan sonar is used to map the topography of the seabed. Usually a 'tow-fish' containing the sonar transmitters is towed behind a survey vessel and emits a fan of acoustic pulses on either side. A sound signal or echo is reflected back and recorded. Raised or protruding features have a strong return and appear as light areas while shadow areas have little or no return. This enables continuous virtual photographs of the seabed to be made relatively quickly. High-resolution sonar can be used to create virtual photographs of submerged objects. The online Museum of Underwater Archaeology provides a wealth of information and case studies on marine surveys.

EXPLORING LOST LANDSCAPES

The value of reconnaissance techniques in revealing new archaeological information is evident in recent studies of the seabed around the UK. Archaeological reconnaissance and records of stray finds have been combined with data from oil-exploration companies. High-resolution bathymetry uses lasers to record and provide images of seabed topography. The use of 3D seismic research records sound waves 'bouncing' back off the seabed from low frequency pulses generated by airguns. This reveals the geological nature of the seabed. Coring and grab sampling provide data on sediments including environmental

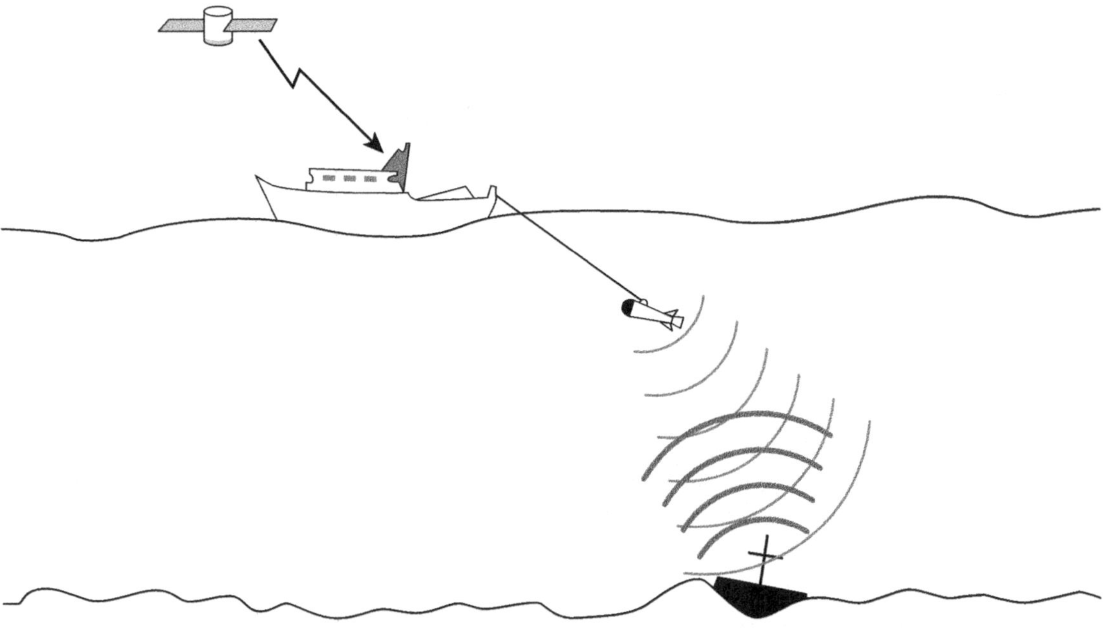

Figure 1.36 *How side-scan sonar works*

Figure 1.37 *Side-scan sonar image of a submerged aircraft. This US Navy PB4Y-2 Bomber was recorded by high-resolution sonar mounted in a tow-fish device. The aircraft is at the bottom of Lake Washington in the USA under 164 feet of water. (Picture courtesy of Marine Sonic Ltd)*

Figure 1.38 *Doggerland*

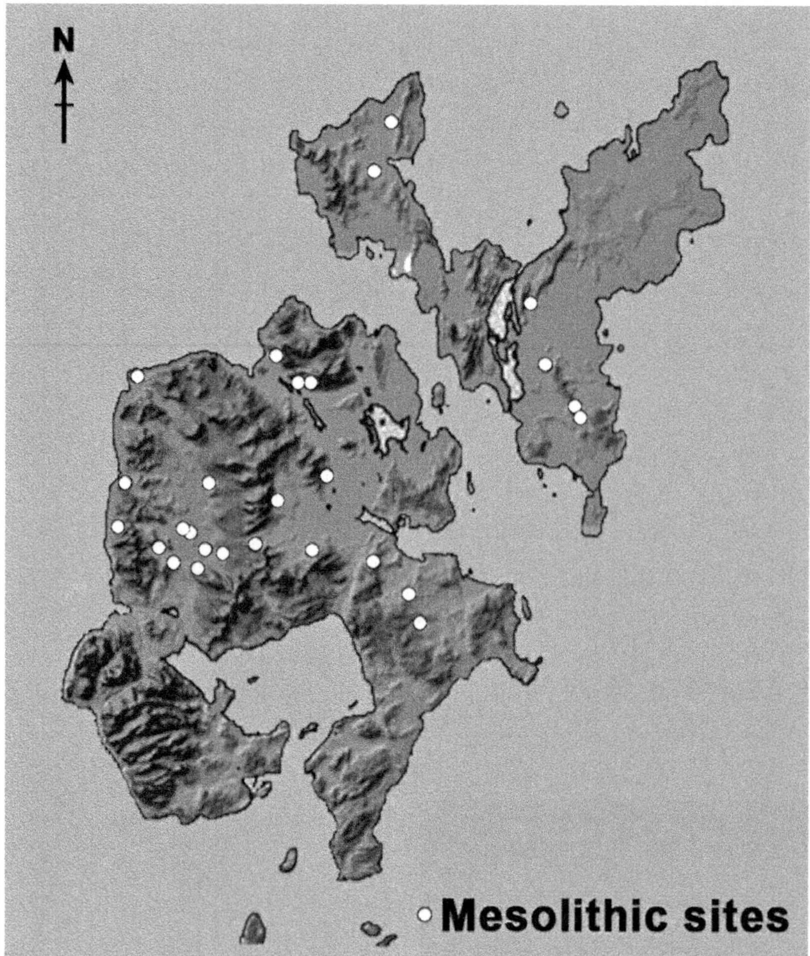

Figure 1.39 The Orkney Islands during the Mesolithic were significantly larger. The Mesolithic sites marked were once on the coast but most were drowned as sea levels rose to their present levels around 4500 BP. (C. Wickham-Jones: Rising Tide Project)

remains. Some of the most spectacular results have come from the area known as Doggerland between the east coast of England and Holland. Before this was finally flooded in 7500 BP, this had been dry land. Researchers at Birmingham University have mapped and produced images of the old land surface and reconstructed vegetation and fauna.

Most people think of this simply as a 'bridge' over which Mesolithic settlers walked to Britain. However, the great plain of Doggerland with its broad river valleys and low ranges of hills (today's Dogger Bank) was inhabited. Some writers have suggested that this area with slowly rising sea levels bringing marine food would have been a more attractive area for forager settlement than thickly forested parts of the mainland. Professor Gaffney, the project leader, has called it the best preserved prehistoric landscape in Europe if not the world. Around the Orkney Islands the Rising Tide Project is documenting another lost Mesolithic world.

Chapter 2

Archaeological Excavation

This chapter explores why and when excavation is undertaken and identifies the advantages and disadvantages of common excavation strategies. We discuss the key concept of stratigraphy and techniques for recording sites and recovering archaeological materials. The final part of the chapter deals with the challenges of excavating different types of sites. Many issues arising from excavation and the legal and planning frameworks surrounding it are dealt with in Chapter 12. Most of the key studies in this book include sections on excavation and a full account of a modern dig is provided by the Biddenham Loop key study in Chapter 12 (▶ p. 587).

To many people, archaeology simply means excavation. Often their interest in archaeology stems from witnessing an excavation or viewing one on television. Excavation is often the public face of archaeology. It is only when people 'dig' deeper into the subject that they are able to recognise the role that excavation plays in the wider nature of the discipline. It has its own methodology – which constantly evolves to reflect new ideas and improving technologies. There can never be one set of rules for excavation, although there is general agreement on key elements of the process. This chapter will try to reflect that current consensus.

APPROACHES TO ARCHAEOLOGICAL EXCAVATION

Archaeology is different from many professions both in its wide public appeal and the involvement in fieldwork of professional workers, academics and amateur 'volunteers'. Archaeology's origins in the UK lie in the work of amateur enthusiasts and in particular the rescue movement of the 1960s and 1970s, although since the 1990s most excavations have been undertaken by units of professional archaeologists (▶ p. 581). This issue and the concept of community archaeology are discussed in Chapter 12. Unlike Medicine or Law there is no one umbrella body either to regulate archaeology or to coordinate excavations. Nevertheless, its practitioners try to adopt and maintain a core of accepted practice and standards which underpin the discipline and ensure the quality of research. At local or regional level attempts are made to establish 'research frameworks' – good examples can be found on the English Heritage website and at the South-West Archaeological Research Framework. Such frameworks seek to coordinate what is already known, what archaeologists would like to know in addition and strategies for making these discoveries, including excavation opportunities.

EXCAVATION: RESCUE OR RESEARCH?

These two terms are commonly used to categorise the rationale behind excavations. The most basic distinction is between a planned campaign to answer particular questions and excavation to recover archaeological evidence before the developers move in.

Research excavations continue the long-standing tradition of archaeologists selecting sites to dig where they believe they will find evidence to advance understanding and answer key questions. The Stonehenge Riverside Project (SRP) provides an example in which several universities, English Heritage and organisations such as the Society of Antiquaries and the Prehistoric Society combined forces to investigate the links between monuments and the landscape around Stonehenge. Such projects are often lengthy. The original funding for the SRP was from 2003 to 2009 but some work is ongoing, and if further funding is secured, more excavation will follow.

Rescue excavations now comprise by far the majority of digs. They are largely undertaken by archaeological 'units' who tender to win fieldwork contracts from developers in what is known as commercial archaeology (▶ p. 573). When archaeological remains are threatened by roads, buildings, quarries or other modern developments, local planning officers will require the archaeological record to be fully considered (▶ p. 574). Surveys are carried out and exploratory work regarding the nature and extent of archaeological deposits (impact assessments or evaluations) informs discussions between archaeologists, planners and contractors (see Chapter 10). To avoid the heavy costs and delays in construction caused by full excavation, a series of 'mitigation strategies' are often adopted. These can involve using building techniques or redesigning building plans in an attempt to minimise damage to archaeology. This is often referred to as **'preservation in situ'**. However, where excavation does go ahead, archaeologists will often set their priorities against research questions as well as time and cost considerations. Unless they miscalculate or uncover unexpected remains, they should have time to carry out their work according to proper archaeological principles. When the time designated for excavation has elapsed and the contractors move in, archaeologists negotiate a 'watching brief'. This means that they can stop building work to record archaeological features which turn up unexpectedly.

Occasionally sites are not discovered until land clearance begins. Rapid recording and rushed excavation in these circumstances is often the best that can be done. This is sometimes called 'salvage archaeology'. Some excavations in intertidal areas still fall into this category (▶ p. 79). The term is used in the USA interchangeably with 'rescue archaeology'.

Similarities and differences

Amongst the key differences between the two approaches is the ability of research archaeologists to select sites and implement the excavation policy most appropriate to them. Rescue archaeology has to reflect the particular issues raised by the on-site non-archaeological development and the designers, engineers and construction teams involved in the project. This can sometimes result in many smaller 'keyhole' excavations into parts of sites rather than the excavation of large parts of them.

However, sometimes the differences can be overstated. The Channel Tunnel rail link from London to Dover resulted in the largest archaeological project to date in the UK. Engineers and archaeologists from eight different groups worked together to ensure that archaeological issues were fully considered. All forms of survey work were carried out; over 2,000 trial trenches and test pits were dug. Fieldwork informed the setting of priorities about where to excavate. Some 55 hectares of the route were identified as requiring detailed archaeological investigation. Planning of the work gave archaeologists time to 'painstakingly' record the archaeological deposits on the sites selected for detailed work. Other areas were subject to watching briefs. In this particular scheme the archaeologists were empowered to

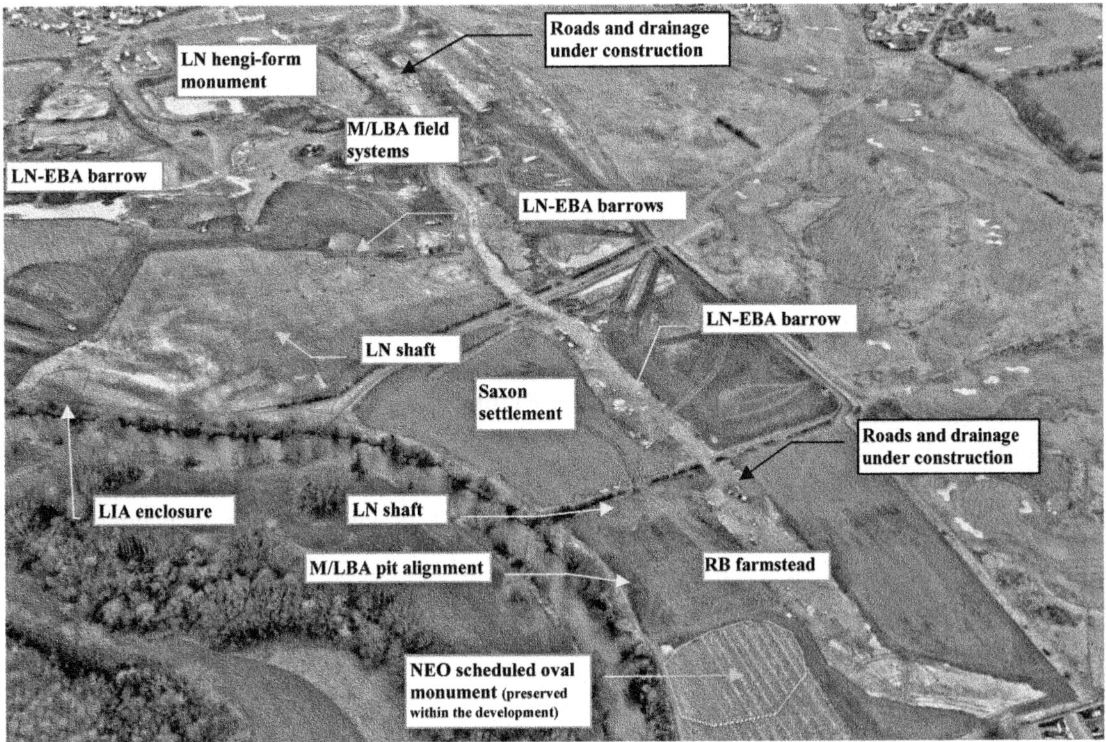

Figure 2.1 *Aerial view of the Biddenham Loop excavation (▶ p. 587) illustrating the size and complexity of major commercial excavations. (Albion Archaeology)*

KEY: NEO = Neolithic, LN = late Neolithic, EBA = early Bronze Age, M/LBA = middle/late Bronze Age, LIA = late Iron Age, RB = Romano-British

stop construction work if 'features of significance' were identified. Over forty sites were excavated with dates ranging from the Palaeolithic to the Second World War. The impact of the new evidence will alter many current perceptions of Kent's archaeology.

To excavate or not?

Any removal of the accumulated evidence of the past is a finite act. Once disturbed, trowelled, shovelled and bucketed away that material cannot be replaced as it was before the excavator removed it. Hence it has frequently been said that 'all excavation is destruction'. Today no one condones excavation as it took place in the C19th: for the pleasure of the excavators and to establish collections of artefacts. In all but extreme circumstances where chance discovery of remains demands a prompt response, there should be controlled planning. This should establish the rationale for excavation and formulate a series of questions which, it is hoped, the excavation might answer.

Often a full and rich record of a site can be gathered if a wide range of reconnaissance methods has been applied and there are sufficient clues about hidden features or structures. In many cases, once the record of such survey activities is carefully housed in an appropriate archive (▶ p. 5), archaeologists leave the physical remains untouched. If, however, a decision is made to excavate, it is viewed as a very serious step. While most scientific experiments can be repeated over and over again in the laboratory, archaeological excavation, although scientific in its approach, does not, by its very nature, allow a second chance. Some excavation procedures, somewhat confusingly referred to as sampling strategies, have been developed to try to ensure that not all the evidence is removed in the primary investigation of a feature or deposit. Nevertheless, destruction is minimised if the archaeologist pays appropriate care and attention to the way the excavation is conducted and particularly to the quality of the records kept. This is sometimes referred to as '**preservation by record**'.

There are other considerations. A balance must be struck between the desire to protect archaeological remains for future generations and the need to develop the discipline and advance our knowledge through excavation. It is also important that archaeology is kept sufficiently in the public eye to receive the support it needs. All these issues are explored further in Chapter 10. If handled appropriately, excavation can move beyond the possible results of survey and get to the real core of archaeology – the hard evidence of their existence left by previous people.

Planning for excavation

The decision to dig will originate either in a research project or because remains are due to be destroyed. In either case the excavation director

Figure 2.2 *No, it isn't a row of onions.*

The reuse of ceramic containers for drainage purposes in the town walls at Cremona in Italy presents an archaeological dilemma. Should all the vessels be recorded in situ and excavated by hand or treated as fill and a sample of complete and diagnostic pieces kept and the rest discarded?

will base plans on what is known from desktop surveys and reconnaissance (▶ p. 3). These plans will aim to answer a series of questions at different levels. An example of a question linked to wider debates might be 'Did towns decay early in the fourth century AD?' A more specific question might be 'Why was this site abandoned?' Below that might be a whole series of questions such as establishing the date of deposits and understanding site formation processes (▶ p. 165). These questions along with constraints of time and money will lead to decisions about where, how and how much to dig.

The first requirement is to produce a clear research design. This is a plan for how the archaeological project will be conducted in order to meet its goals. This may include:

- what is already known from previous local archaeological work;
- justifications for digging the site;
- the use of survey techniques to plan excavation strategies;
- the extent of the excavation required to enable interpretation;
- sampling policy and analysis of samples;
- determining the methods of investigation to be used;
- the recording system to be used;
- ethical considerations such as dealing with human remains;
- identifying the facilities or specialists for post-excavation work;
- how the research will be published and disseminated.

Figure 2.3 *Trench with health and safety features*

At an early stage there will be political and ethical issues arising from relationships with landowners, the local community and the agency funding the work. Once underway, the director will need to maintain professional standards while working under time and economic constraints and adapt the design in the light of events and discoveries on site. One further issue which excavators have to be aware of is the health and safety of their diggers. Precautions range from hard hats and reflective clothing on developer sites to ensuring that deep trenches are properly shored up or have stepped sides. With deep trenches carbon monoxide may be an issue and meters may be needed. In most instances consideration needs to be given to how spoil will be safely extracted and how to prevent materials falling onto the diggers. Safety issues are most evident on underwater sites where air supply, currents, cold and sharks are amongst the potential hazards not faced on land.

KEY STUDY

The Chester Amphitheatre project

A major partnership between English Heritage and Chester City Council was launched in 2004 to sponsor a research programme focused on, but not wholly devoted to, a re-examination of the archaeological evidence for the Roman amphitheatre. The first main phase of the project ran for three years from 2004 to 2006. Central to the aims and principles established for the project was that it should have a strong basis of community links and involvement.

The archaeological mission was to validate and enhance the data recovered from previous excavations, to reappraise the evidence and the quality of its survival, and to establish the occupation/building phases of the site pre-amphitheatre, during the amphitheatre's development and in the subsequent use of the site post-amphitheatre. This would focus on the amphitheatre and also its contemporary Roman context (in particular the adjacent legionary fortress) and possible post-Roman early Christian development. Methods appropriate to this mission included non-destructive research involving ground penetrating radar and photography including photogrammetry and aerial photography and large-scale excavations. It was anticipated that this would lead to a reinterpretation of the site.

Four wider aims for the project were to:

- establish a new research centre with a community focus that would engage and interest the people of Chester;

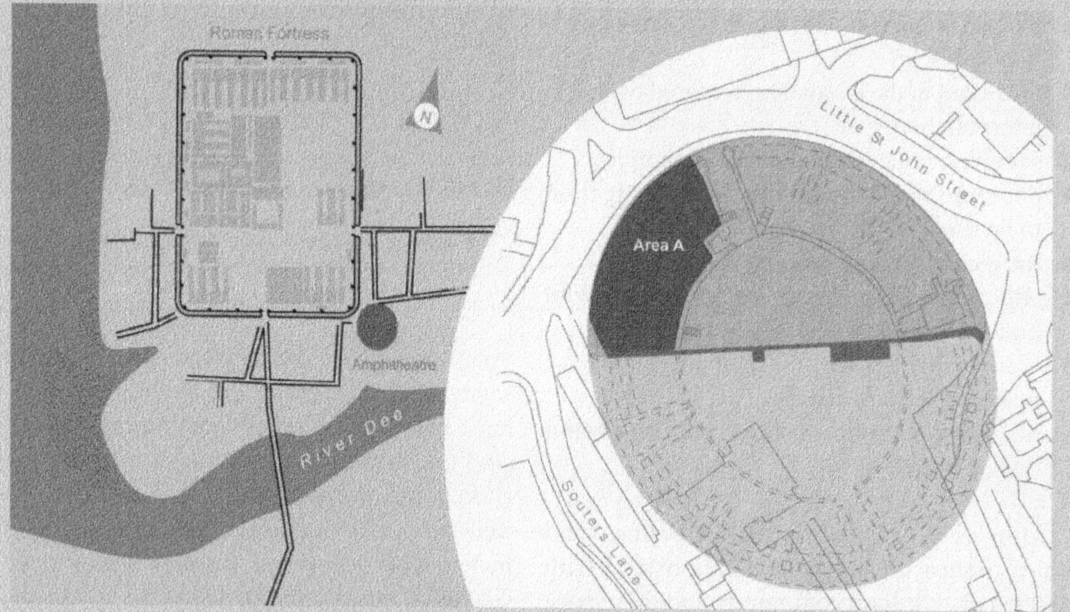

Figure 2.4 *Location of Chester amphitheatre*

Plan of Chester in Roman times showing (1) the relationship of the amphitheatre to the fortress and (2) the location of Area A in the north-west quadrant of the amphitheatre. (English Heritage and Chester City Council)

- encourage visitor interest – an important economic factor;
- have an educational emphasis through display, development of teaching and learning materials and, during the excavations, to enable local people to be trained in basic archaeological field techniques;
- plan for the future of the site.

These four objectives ensured that this was not another 'unit' excavation undertaken behind fences and inaccessible through health and safety legislation. The whole process was conducted in full view of the public (special viewing platforms were erected and guided tours arranged) and the media played their part in recording and broadcasting updates.

Following the three seasons of excavation and related research, the following phases were identified on the main site:

1. Pre-Roman soil levels produced pollen samples which suggested the area may have been the site of an Iron Age farm.

Figure 2.5 *Excavation of Chester Amphitheatre*

Area A from the east. The two lines of the curving external amphitheatre walls are visible with the earlier one on the left and the one from the enlarged site on the right. Note the very public display of excavation in this community project. (English Heritage and Chester City Council)

continued

2. The first amphitheatre, probably built AD 80–100, had a stone outer wall and a stone arena wall with clay dumped in between the two and timber seating erected on this. Upper seats were reached by external stairways. Outside the amphitheatre postholes cut into a cobbled surface provide unique evidence for the presence of booths and stalls – in today's context the souvenir/programme stand and burger van. A possible small shrine was found near the north entrance and may have been dedicated to the goddess Nemesis (Fate).
3. At a date not yet determined, the first amphitheatre was partly demolished and replaced by a much grander construction, the biggest amphitheatre in Roman Britain. New foundations 2m outside the original line and 2.7m deep supported a large stone outer wall with added buttresses, stone entrances and the upper rows of the tiered seating would have been carried on vaulting reminiscent of similar sites elsewhere in the Roman world; for example, Nimes in Provence.
4. At some time possibly in the C10th or the C11th and certainly before the C12th and C13th, the main walls of the amphitheatre were robbed out as building material, first the inner wall and second the massive outer wall of the later rebuild.
5. From the C12th onwards over much of the site medieval cess pits were dug through the Roman levels. These have provided a wealth of finds and particularly environmental evidence such as seeds, fish bones and parasite remains.

EXCAVATION STRATEGIES

Defining the site in question is a key issue. In excavation terms some 'sites' are in fact a series of smaller 'sites'. For example, cropmarks may indicate a series of features (enclosures, pits, tracks) which can be separated out for investigation while a Roman town has a street plan and a variety of public and private buildings each capable of individual excavation. Sites are set within a landscape context which a successful excavation will take note of. So the director needs to decide whether it is the entirety of the site that is the focus of their attention or whether concentration on certain parts offers the best chance to answer their questions. If there are many similar features – for example, storage pits – it is likely that a number will be sampled rather than excavating every one. This means that some deposits are not recorded to the same extent as others.

There is no set manual for archaeological field practices either in relation to where to put the holes in the ground or in how to proceed once the excavation trench is underway. This is not because archaeologists have a laissez-faire attitude to standards and procedures but because of the variety in the nature of sites, evidence and questions asked. Most texts on excavation express their ideas about appropriate 'good practice' and add new methods as they evolve. The archaeological world constantly shares its experiences and a general consensus of current good practice is evident when one looks at images of modern excavations. Practitioners learn from one another and try to keep their methods in line with current thinking, therefore ensuring that their results, when published, stand up to scrutiny and are accepted by their peers. For example, many archaeological units use the Museum of London Archaeological Services' excavation manual which is freely available online.

The nature of the archaeological record in the ground is often complex. Human nature and life circumstances ensure that most sites have a developmental history which the archaeologist needs to unravel. The people who left the evidence went about their daily business without a thought for how their activities might leave

KEY TERM

Features and cuts

Features are traces in the soil of past human activity. A distinction can be made between:

- Constructed features which were deliberately built such as a wall, hearth, fish trap or pond. The term 'cut' is used to describe dug features such as pits, ditches and postholes.
- Cumulative features which develop from repeated actions. Middens, hollow-ways and the shallow gullies known as drip rings which encircled round houses are good examples.

While some features are obvious, many are not. Only the faintest traces of a stakehole may survive as slight variations in the colour or texture of soil and may only be detectable by an experienced excavator. Many features such as ditches or postholes may in fact be elements in one larger feature which is only revealed when excavation recording is complete.

The site below is seen top-stripped before Green's (2000) research dig at Monkton Up Wimborne. The major features or cuts are revealed as discolorations in the chalk but excavation was required to identify them. They proved to be a ring of pits with a central pit 10m wide and 1.5m deep. Hidden in this pit was a burial of a woman and three children and a 7m deep shaft down to a seam of flint.

Figure 2.6 *Features at Neolithic ritual site at Monkton Up Wimborne*

traces for future investigators. They were not simply creating 'features' much of the time, nor did they often build a structure and leave it unaltered. However, their constructional or daily activities will have created a sequence of deposits or **contexts** (the words are often used interchangeably) which build up to create the archaeological record. These deposits are linked to the features and structures of the site. Contained within them are the artefacts of pottery, metalwork, etc. and ecofacts, which provide sources for understanding the chronological, cultural and environmental nature of the site.

Why context is everything: the theory of stratification

In any text about archaeological sites you will come across terms such as 'level', 'layer', 'deposit', 'stratum'. They describe the make-up of the excavated ground in terms of deposits. These were created either by people or by nature. Archaeologists attempt to carefully record these strata – the stratification. By studying their relationship they can identify the sequence of events on the site. The study of the strata is known as **stratigraphy**. It is the key concept in archaeology and enables us to understand the chronology or dating (Chapter 4) of the site and how the site was formed (Chapter 5). The surfaces of strata are sometimes referred to as interfaces.

In an ideal situation, one could assume that deposits at the bottom of any stratigraphical sequence are older than those at the top. The earliest was laid down first and each successive deposit was laid down after the one directly below it. The 'higher' the deposit, the later it is. This is sometimes referred to as 'the law of superposition'. But life and archaeological sites are not usually that simple. As well as establishing which deposits overlie others, archaeologists have to identify intrusive features such as pits and ditches which may cut down into earlier deposits. Occasionally there will also be disturbed deposits where the sequence has been jumbled (▶ p. 169), perhaps by flooding.

Figure 2.7 *Telling a story using the law of superposition*

The female skeleton is lying above the mosaic at Kingscote and covered by building debris. The interpretation is that she was one of a number of 'squatters' who occupied the derelict villa but was killed, possibly trying to escape, when it collapsed.

Each individual element in the stratigraphy is a context. A context might result from a single event such as a fire or roof collapse or a build-up of soil against a wall over several years. The task of the digger is to identify each context and to trace the boundaries or 'interfaces' between contexts. This may only be detectable by minute changes in the colour, texture or composition of

Figure 2.8 *The vertical profile of an excavation is called a* ***section****. In this case the ditch of a Neolithic enclosure is being sectioned.*

the soil and archaeologists can differ in their interpretations of them. Sometimes geological cards with illustrated sediment grain sizes or Munsell soil-colour charts are used to distinguish similar-looking contexts.

Typically contexts will be marked on a label nailed in the side of a trench (▶ p. 73). A description is also noted on a context sheet (▶ p. 69). Once recorded, the stratigraphic relationship between contexts can be determined and a vertical, chronological sequence based on successive 'events' established.

It is within the deposits that the artefactual, environmental and dating evidence is located. Deposits are a time capsule which hold the clues to the immediate context of finds and structures. Plotting the position of each deposit within the site helps determine chronological patterns. Materials in any deposit are likely to be broadly contemporary and can be dated by association with dateable evidence from that deposit. Even if an exact date cannot be given for a find, its context may provide a relative date (▶ p. 145). The key to the interpretation of material remains is the notion of archaeological context – the location of a find within a site and its relationship to other material remains. Archaeologists are able to interpret artefacts, features and ecofacts by examining which kinds of remains are associated with one another, how they are distributed spatially, and how they relate to the larger landscape and environment in which they are found. For example, a pottery vessel found near a hearth in a kitchen may have a very different meaning from one found within a burial pit. In order to preserve as much information as possible about archaeological context, archaeologists typically record the exact 3D location of artefacts

KEY TERM

Context

A context is a deposit of soil which the excavators have been able to distinguish from others above and below it. It is the basic unit for understanding the site and its contents are considered to be contemporary to each other. Contexts might include layers, features, cuts, walls or burials. Context is also used in a general sense when talking about finds and their relationship to deposits. This is based on the principle that objects found together in the same deposit are roughly from the same period and can be dated by association with dateable evidence from that deposit (▶ p. 143).

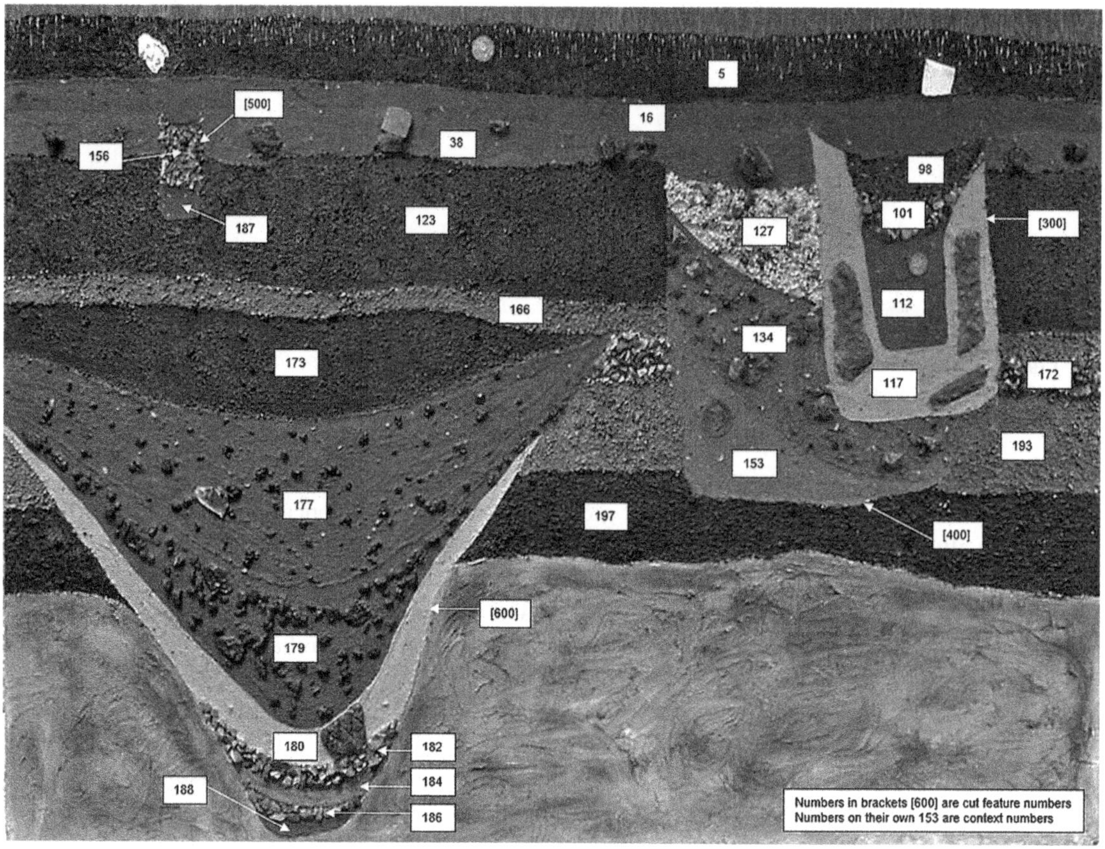

Figure 2.9 *Teaching example of a section*

Figure 2.11 (facing page, foot) *Excavations of the palace complex at Tell es Sa'idiyeh*

The tell was the focus of a long-term British Museum excavation (Tubb 1997) to understand the long-term development of settlement in the region. The great depth and the complexity of the stratigraphy is evident in this excavation by an international team of archaeologists working with Jordanians in the early Bronze Age palace (▶ p. 256) area. They revealed evidence of production on an industrial scale of wine, textiles and pottery as well as extensive storage.

Figure 2.10 *Tell es Sa'idiyeh*

This huge mound is actually the remains of Tell es Sa'idiyeh, site of the biblical city of Zarathan. The tell is made up of 3,000 years of settlement debris including the remains of mudbrick houses. It sits at a crossroads of trade and dominates the fertile land of Canaan east of the River Jordan. Occupied from the 3rd millennium BC to the C7th AD, it began as a village of Neolithic farmers. By 2900 it was a large planned city falling under the influence of several empires, particularly the Egyptians. Despite such changes it provides evidence of long-term Canaanite (▶ p. 405) cultural continuity. The deep stratigraphy at tell sites is invaluable for providing evidence of long-term changes.

and features within a site. They also record the type of matrix (soil) in which an artefact is found and other artefacts that are associated (found together) with it. Archaeologists get upset when artefacts are dug without their context being recorded (provenance) because they will not be able to tell as much about them.

HOW TO DIG?

Debates around excavation methodology centre on the fact that all sites have two key elements: a vertical sequence of deposits containing structures and finds, and the horizontal layout of an occupation area or individual structure. It is difficult for a method to explore both equally well but to record both elements is vital. Unless the archaeologist can establish the correct succession of levels, an excavation will have limited, if any, value. Similarly failure to produce the **plan** (layout) of a building or a cemetery leaves the researcher well short of the required results. Archaeologists have therefore developed a series of methods appropriate to different types of site.

Trenches

The term 'trench' has been applied to any linear excavation and sometimes to any hole cut into the ground by archaeologists, whatever its surface shape. A stricter definition is a rectangular-shaped excavation of variable width and length. Test pits or 'sondages' are essentially square trenches, usually 1m square. Trenches and test pits are used either to evaluate the stratigraphy of a site before a decision is made on whether or not to excavate or as part of an excavation sampling strategy. Test pits can also be used in a trench during its excavation to reveal the depth of deposits still to be investigated. By digging down either to bedrock or the bottom of the archaeological deposits, the vertical profile of part of the site can be examined. This reveals information about depth of deposits and complexity of contexts. It also provides an opportunity for sampling environmental remains. Sometimes mechanical diggers are used to dig part or all of the trench, in which case the trench width may be determined by the dimensions of the digger's bucket.

Viewers of the TV programme *Time Team* will be familiar with the use of trial trenches to investigate possible features identified by reconnaissance methods. This is also done on many sites after 'top-stripping' of topsoil (▶ p. 51). On large sites trenches are used to investigate linear features such as ditches by being placed at 90 degrees to the alignment of the feature. The trenches cut by Alcock through the defences of South Cadbury hillfort in Somerset provide a classic example. By strategically placing a series of 2m wide trenches around the hill he was able to study and report on the developmental sequence of the site's fortifications. This had the added bonus of disturbing only a small proportion of the site in return for a large volume of evidence. Most of the site was left undamaged for future archaeologists. Other linear features such as roads and boundaries can be cross-sectioned in this way. Offa's Dyke, an early medieval feature running from North Wales to South Wales, was the focus of a long-term study by Manchester University and over one hundred trenches were put across it to check and confirm details of its construction.

Test pits

Sometimes test pitting is the main method used. The site is gridded with 1m squares and sampling used to select a number of locations to dig. This produces a series of vertical profiles across the site which gives some idea of the horizontal plan. Cutting lots of test pits or trial trenches into a site is quick, cheap and provides valuable information about stratigraphy. However, they are relatively poor as a means to understand how a site fitted together. Test pits look a bit like shovel pits (▶ p. 23) but their purpose is entirely different.

Figure 2.12 *Test pit with pottery find*

Area excavation

This is the form of excavation most commonly seen in the media or archaeological magazines. 'Area' or 'openstripping' occurs where the extent of the features to be uncovered determines the size of the excavation. This does not mean that the whole of a site is necessarily excavated. While this can be the outcome, factors may limit the total recovery of evidence. Only a sample of the site may be needed to answer the director's questions, financial constraints may limit the amount of digging or perhaps development only threatens part of the site so the rest is left 'in situ'. On some research digs such as those run by universities digging may take place over several seasons. Different areas of the site are opened up and recorded each year. Silchester Roman town and Star Carr (▶ p. 267) are examples of this strategy.

Area excavation has become the key approved method for several reasons:

- Complete structures can be studied.
- Complex relationships between features can be clarified.
- It provides excellent recording possibilities.
- A total understanding of horizontal relationships is possible.

When area excavation became fashionable, there was criticism from those traditionalists who had used trenches. The sides of trenches have the advantage of revealing the vertical sequence of deposits and there was concern that this essential record might be lost. The depth of deposits can vary and this issue is of greatest significance where the stratification is deep and complicated. This problem can be addressed by leaving baulks (undug strips of ground) at strategic points or, increasingly, by carefully recording the horizontal picture of a site context by context and feeding the data into a computer. This process is referred to as 'single context recording'. The data can then be interrogated to produce sections along any chosen line. The problem is that without baulks no check is left in place if the director wishes to refer back, so the recording systems must be of the highest quality. To provide a check, the contexts and their relationships are sometimes photographed.

Box-grid or quadrant systems

These sit in an intermediate position between trenches and area excavation. They offer archaeologists the better aspects of each by giving access to both the horizontal view and the vertical cut simultaneously.

The box-grid system owes its origins to the work of Sir Mortimer Wheeler in the first half of the C20th. He would set out a grid of square

Figure 2.13 *Area excavation at Goldfields Romano-British Farm*

This training dig (▶ p. 582) has adopted an area approach. Once top-stripped the individual features such as the ditch in the foreground are sectioned or excavated. Barrow runways ensure spoil is quickly and safely removed and protect the surface.

Figure 2.14 *A round barrow excavated using the quadrant method*

'boxes' to be excavated with baulks left in between them (▶ p. 60). This resulted in a dig resembling a patchwork quilt. An advantage was the chance to record four sections for every 'box'. Removal of spoil was also easier as baulks provided barrow runs. However, the whole layout of a site was not revealed until the baulks were finally removed. Important relationships between features or structures might not be understood while digging was progressing. The system was complex, costly of time and manpower and of little use on sites with very deep stratigraphy. It is little used in the UK today although it is still popular in other countries.

The 'quadrant system' is a similar approach that is still sometimes employed. It is particularly relevant in the case of sites that are approximately circular in nature, such as round barrows (▶ p. 58). On a micro-scale, this method can be used on features such as hearths or pits. The feature is cut into four quarters by lines intersecting at the middle. Opposing quadrants are excavated first. It is possible after only removing half the remains to see patterns of features in plan (which if they show common elements suggest that they continue under the undug areas) and to totally record the vertical profile of the site in two directions.

KEY STUDY

Boxgrove

The chance discovery in 1993 of a human shin bone in a quarry by Mark Roberts led him to initiate the most famous recent example of box-grid excavation. The ongoing excavations have revealed much about the lifestyle and environment of Homo heidelbergensis, one of the earliest of our ancestors to reach Britain. The bone enabled scientists to suggest that these hominids were large and heavily built like a modern sprinter. Cut-marks on two human teeth found nearby showed that they used their teeth to hold meat while they cut it. The geology revealed that the site had been a beach backed by chalk cliffs. A spring at the foot of the cliffs fed a small freshwater pool that attracted animals. In and around the pool were scatters of animal bones and flint tools including 450 well-made hand-axes and hammer-stones (for removing marrow from bone). Many of the bones had cut-marks from the tools and even fragments of flint in a knife cut.

Excavation methods

Box sections enabled precise cross-referencing of the freshwater sediments laid down by the stream. The base of each section was marked with the site grid to ensure precise planning. Each find was given a coloured flag depending on the material and both compass direction and angle of dip were recorded in order to determine whether water movement had moved them (▶ p. 169). Chalk ensured excellent preservation and enabled scatters of flint and bones to be studied where they had fallen. Some of the silts were so fine grained that individual episodes could be recorded. In one case it was possible to tell from waste flakes how the flint knapper was sitting.

Examination of finds

SEM examination of a rhinoceros bone revealed human butchery marks under the tooth marks of a scavenging carnivore. In other words, the human had got there first. Hunting evidence came in the form

continued

Figure 2.15 *Box sections*

Figure 2.16 *Recreation of horse butchery site*

of a horse scapula with a very neat circular perforation on the outside and a splintered 'exit wound'. This suggested a high-velocity projectile, perhaps a fire-hardened wooden spear such as the ones discovered at Schöningen (▶ p. 200). Experimental archaeology (▶ p. 181) involving a javelin thrower and a deer carcass produced very similar damage to the excavated bones. This suggests that these hominids were hunters rather than scavengers. They used speed and throwing weapons to kill, and stripped the meat from the horses, deer and possibly rhinoceros visiting the pool. The hominids repeatedly exploited their understanding of animal behaviour at the waterhole while evading other predators, whose presence is evident from wolf teeth marks on the shin bone.

Faunal dating (▶ p. 148) showed that the site was in use during a warm interglacial period 500,000 years ago. Lions, elephants and tuna bones suggest a warmer climate than today. As well as bones of large grazing animals, wet sieving enabled the recovery of bird and fish bone and the remains of extinct water voles. These tiny rodents evolve rapidly. For example, their teeth lost their roots over time. Minute differences and the extinction of many species have enabled researchers to construct a detailed picture of vole evolution in Europe for a million years. Voles can be used to date the stratigraphic layer they are found in. Since different species have different habitats, they also help us understand local ecology at the time. The level of development of vole teeth enabled Boxgrove to be compared to examples from other sites dated using absolute methods (▶ p. 150). The 'vole clock' showed that Boxgrove was older than 478,000 BC.

The find of an 'antler hammer' potentially provides a new perspective on human mental capacity and behaviour for this period. It suggests a degree of planning, forethought and 'curation' that was believed to be beyond the capacity of hominids at this stage in evolution. The hammer also provided corroborative faunal dating evidence. The antler came from a giant elk which became extinct *c.* 500,000 years ago.

Figure 2.17 *Living floor (▶ p. 176)*

Recognising features and the planum method

On most sites features can be identified once a surface has been cleared and trowelled. However, if a site lacks clear stratification and generally comprises similar soil rather than stones or building materials, it may be impossible to differentiate contexts by eye. In this case an alternative approach is to repeatedly 'plane' off levels or spits of a standard thickness of 10cm or 5cm across the whole site. Each revealed surface is planned and photographed and its contents recorded as if it were a context. In effect, slices or spits are removed across the site to reveal and record a series of images much the same as an MRI (Magnetic Resonance Imaging) body scan provides cut-through views of the human body for doctors. On some sites hoes can be used as a more efficient way of removing material than trowels at this stage of excavation. One application of this method is the excavation of grave fills where ground conditions have adversely affected the survival of the burial and/or any associated objects. The painstaking excavation of cave deposits at Creswell Crags took this planum method one step further by also dividing the deposits vertically so as to create small cubes of cave earth for precision in recording ecofacts and artefacts.

THE PROCESS OF EXCAVATION

Archaeologists have developed a variety of methods for removing archaeological deposits from the ground in which they have lain to suit the varying circumstances of archaeological sites. Topsoil is removed by top-stripping with a mechanical digger or by using picks, mattocks and shovels. Soil is either mechanically lifted or wheel-barrowed away to start a spoil heap. This has to be far enough away to avoid it spilling over and contaminating deeper layers or burying the diggers. Although mechanical diggers can be used for trial trenches, most excavation is by hand. According to the time available and the nature of the deposits, tools could range from shovels to dentistry instruments for recovering tiny fragments of material. The most familiar toolkit includes a mattock, a short pointing trowel, a brush, a shovel and a bucket. In the USA, long-handled shovels are used which are better for a digger's back than spades, while hand hoes are an alternative to trowels. Eventually, and very neatly, what was an archaeological resource is converted into a hole in the ground. The extracted evidence must be subjected to a rigorous recording process or the excavation will have destroyed the site and its potential. Recording requirements will vary for sites with less obvious collectable material or with particular distributions of evidence.

Layers of deposits in the ground are recognised as contexts, labelled and removed in sequence without mixing them. On many sites such as Roman or medieval where pottery sherds and animal bones are common, their collection is linked to the contexts in which the material is found. They are collected in labelled 'finds trays' so that all the finds from each layer can be put together. They will subsequently be washed, dried and coded to their particular layer for recording. Less common objects like metal, worked bone or stone will usually be classified as 'small finds'. A distinct and more comprehensive recording system will ensure that the precise location of each find is recorded in three dimensions by triangulation and depth measurements. They are collected in finds trays or plastic bags and given unique reference numbers. On a working floor (▶ p. 61) associated with a prehistoric flint-knapper, careful plotting of each flake is necessary to recreate the sequence of the earlier activity. Sometimes their position in a layer is marked by a small flag so that distribution patterns can be recorded (▶ p. 61). These finds will be kept separately and the nature and fragility of each object will determine their post-excavation scientific treatment.

Figure 2.18 *Excavating the fill of a pit which has previously been half sectioned. (Albion Archaeology)*

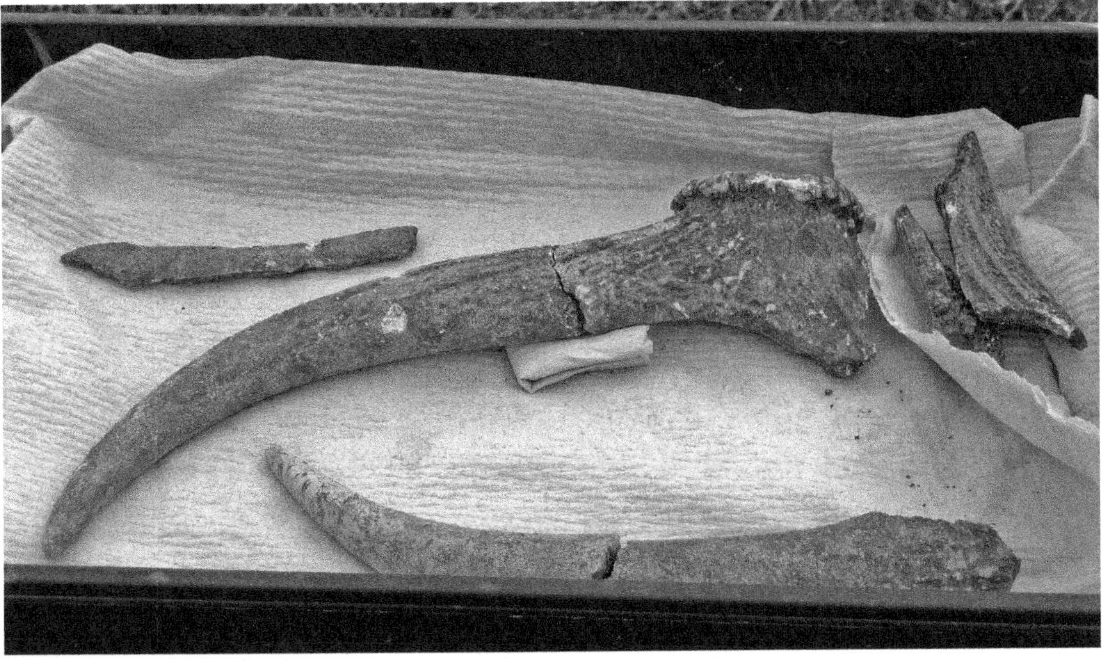

Figure 2.19 *A finds tray containing a Neolithic antler pick*

Occasionally excavators will deviate from the stratigraphic approach where they judge that the nature of finds justifies it. A good example was the excavation of waterlogged ditch deposits at Vindolanda, where letters from c. AD 100 survived on hundreds of fragile, wet, 'leaf-tablets' (postcard-size slivers of wood). Had they been trowelled then they would have been destroyed, so the decision was taken to lift them in blocks and excavate by hand back in the lab. While digging them out risked cutting some tablets, these could be restored and the rest recovered intact. As a result, this site has recovered far more of these valuable artefacts than any other.

RECOVERY OF ENVIRONMENTAL MATERIAL

Not all the material to be retrieved can be recovered by trowelling. The ground contains much smaller and less obvious evidence, in particular faunal (animal) and floral (plant) evidence such as snail shells, small fish or bird bones, insect remains, seeds and pollen grains. Not all of these are visible to the naked eye. Tiny fragments of metal or worked material such as flint or glass present the same problem. This material can be recovered on site by using sieving or flotation or by taking strategically selected soil samples for later analysis.

Sieving

Sieves with a 10mm or 5mm mesh are commonly used for dry sieving soil samples and are particularly effective for recovering artefacts on sites with sandy soils. Dry sieving is not effective with clay soils. On larger sites buckets of soil samples are tipped into a large sieve usually suspended from a frame and riddled over a barrow to ensure that finds not detected in the digging process are retrieved. A series of sieves with increasingly finer mesh improve collection chances and also collect

Figure 2.20 *Dry sieving at Barcombe Roman Villa*

Figure 2.21 *Flotation and wet-sieving equipment*

different-sized material in each sieve. The introduction of water to create 'wet sieving', whether by spray or dipping into a tank, helps to remove the soil particles and means finer mesh sizes down to 0.5mm can be used. Wet material is often easier to identify and locate by colour contrast. Experiments have shown that trowelling and dry sieving recovers a higher proportion of tiny sherds of red pottery but that grey and brown sherds are often missed, especially in wet conditions. Wet sieving is more effective for recovering ecofacts such as seeds, insects or small bones and can give greater control than flotation, although it is much slower.

Flotation

This usually involves putting soil samples from single contexts into a dustbin-like container full of water. Lighter materials such as plant remains, charcoal and even fish scales float to the surface while the soil drops to the bottom of the container. Heavier soils are stirred to break them up and release material. Some flotation bins have graduated screens inside the bin to separate heavier material too. Improvements to this basic methodology include adding oil to hold tiny particles on the surface and bubbling air from below the water with a frothing agent (e.g. detergent) to create a 'froth', which holds and separates lighter organic material (froth flotation). Water containing the 'flot' is drained from the top through a sequence of increasingly finely meshed sieves down to 0.25mm. Flotation is quicker than wet sieving but has a lower recovery rate.

Soil sampling

Some recovery of environmental remains occurs off site. Bags of soil samples are taken from

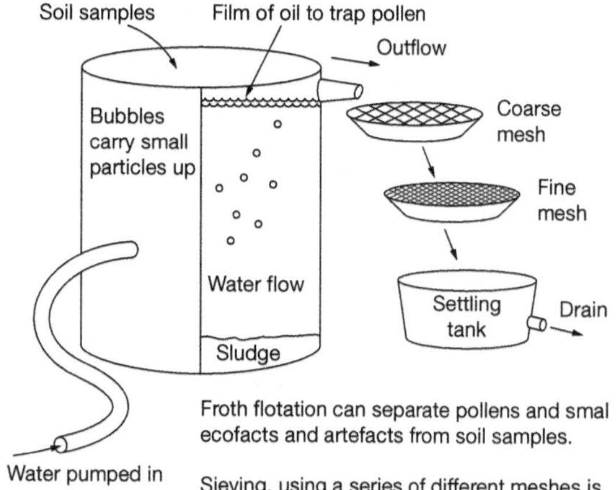

Figure 2.22 *How a flotation bin works*

selected locations such as pits, ditches or other similar diagnostic features or layers. On some sites, including peat sites, sampling tins, known as Kubiena tins, are hammered into freshly dug sections, removed and quickly sealed in plastic to avoid contamination. They are then placed in cold storage before detailed analysis in the laboratory. The pollens and plant remains in them will be used to provide vegetation sequences and help date the site. With recent developments in radiocarbon dating (▶ p. 154), each bone, seed or piece of charcoal is now a potential dating source for a sample. Soil may also be sampled for chemical analysis, particularly for phosphates (▶ p. 105). One aspect of soil sampling which has often been neglected is attempting to recover dietary and other evidence when excavating human remains. Studies have suggested that around 70 per cent of burials have evidence surviving in abdominal soils. This can range from fragments of hair or nails to traces of cholesterol.

Metal detection

Although not strictly a method of recovering environmental material, on some excavations, and directly under the control of the director, it is appropriate to use metal detectors. They can be employed as part of the initial survey as a piece of geophysical equipment but they can also be used to check the spoil heap for finds. This would be applicable if the site had been stripped by machine rather than by hand or if soil removal had been by pick and shovel without subsequent sieving. Any such finds would be classed as unstratified. Metal detectors can also be used to alert diggers to potentially fragile metal objects in areas they are trowelling. At Lerje, Denmark, the site of a Dark Age hall (▶ p. 442) was swept by metal detectors so that the diggers would know in advance to look out for tiny metal finds.

Figure 2.23 *Using a metal detector on site*

On-site conservation

In whatever way the finds are identified and collected, it is vital that the methods used allow their full potential to be exploited in post-excavation analysis and dating procedures. Directors of excavations have to make valid decisions about the processes they adopt in order to balance the needs of the dig to make sufficient progress with the demands of post-excavation studies. This often means taking decisions about what not to collect (e.g. building stone) as well as how to deal with what is recovered. It also means deciding whether lithics or pottery will be examined for residues or whether they can be washed on site or immediately afterwards. Similarly, finds which may be used for dating or DNA analysis (▶ p. 130) have to be protected from contamination. Specialist conservators may be involved from an early stage if there are unusual or fragile finds. This is particularly the case where wet material will be lifted. The key is to keep such material wet, cool and away from sunlight.

Fragile finds will need immediate care if they are not to deteriorate. Plant remains are particularly fragile and are usually placed in a wet, sealed container until they can be examined in the lab. Some finds are wrapped in fine cotton cloth

Figure 2.24 *Excavating a Neolithic well*

This 7,000-year-old well was part of a settlement discovered during the building of a new airport at Leipzig, Germany. The timber structure was several metres in depth and had been sealed in anaerobic conditions below the water table. It was of great archaeological importance as the oldest timber structure in the world and because it appeared to be packed with artefacts and environmental material (▶ p. 384). After precise plotting of the visible timbers in situ, they were block-lifted as a 70 tonne unit and removed for micro-excavation. Every timber and find from the 4m section of well was then carefully excavated and recorded with timbers laser-scanned (▶ p. 386) to provide a precise 3D record including every tool mark on the surface of the wood. ()

or a similar textile while soil or peat samples may also be placed in a refrigerator to prevent decay. Bubble wrap, cling film, corrugated plastic and plaster of Paris are all used in particular cases for 'first aid'. Some metal finds may also require conservation to arrest oxidisation or other forms of chemical change. Where special treatment is necessary to stabilise finds, to prevent either disintegration or decay, then archaeologists try to apply it without making irreversible changes unless absolutely necessary; for example, by using water-soluble adhesive and resins to stabilise fragile materials or soil blocks. Particularly valuable deposits, including rich burials, may be block-lifted for micro-excavation under laboratory conditions (▶ p. 434).

WHAT RECORDS DO ARCHAEOLOGISTS CREATE?

Different directors will approach the task of recording, as they will the excavation itself, from slightly different standpoints. But certain common themes will feature: field notebooks, context sheets, plans, sections, photographs, video, artefact collection systems and, increasingly, the use of on-site digital recording. They also make use of a range of surveying equipment to plot the exact positions of finds and features. Each excavation has a complex reference system. A site grid allows each point to be surveyed and key finds to be linked to the national grid (▶ p. 10). Finds are numbered and linked to contexts. Each context has its own distinct reference number too. Tapes, dumpy levels and theodolites are still in use alongside Electronic Distance Measures (EDMs) but increasingly total stations (▶ p. 14) are used. More recently GPS (Global Positioning System) has proved an even more attractive option for many archaeological surveys. With GPS there is no dependency on permanent landscape features or the need to maintain a line of sight. Surveys may be completed with consistent centimetre accuracy with setting up and surveying time significantly reduced.

Archaeological contexts are recorded in two ways. Sections or profiles provide a vertical view of strata and contexts while plans provide a horizontal (bird's-eye) view.

Context sheets

The 'single context recording system' has, with some slight variations to suit local circumstances, become the established norm for recording purposes. A separate proforma context sheet is used for each identified context, which also has its own unique reference number. The context sheet is designed to ensure that the person making the record addresses all possible questions and compiles a clear description including the maximum level of information in order to facilitate reliable comparison between one context and another. On larger excavations where all the staff are experienced, each site assistant will be autonomous and expected to take responsibility for particular contexts and their recording. Thus the context sheets provide detailed records of layers and other elements of the stratigraphy of the site. They also allow associations between finds to be explored post-excavation. They will be used in post-excavation analysis to reconstruct the phases of use of the site and its features. Other non-standard proformas have been devised for more complex sites to cater for the recording of, for example, masonry structures and skeletons.

Plans

Detailed plans are used to show the location and horizontal spread of features, artefacts and structures. On a site employing the single context recording system, every context, except fills of small pits and postholes, will be drawn separately. A complete set of depth measurements will be taken as an essential element in ensuring that the context's unique profile is fully recorded. Large-scale plans are used to illustrate individual features. For example, an excavation of an Anglo-Saxon cemetery requires an overall plan to show

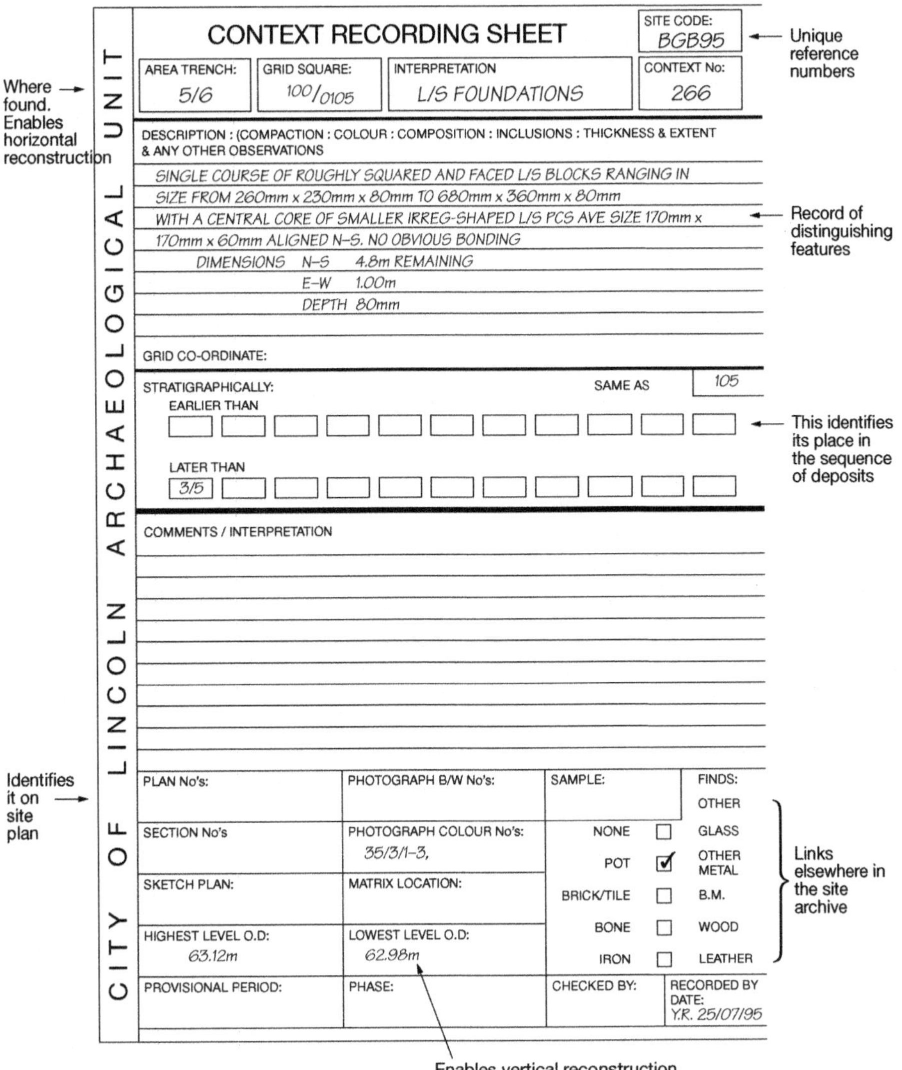
CITY OF LINCOLN ARCHAEOLOGICAL UNIT

CONTEXT RECORDING SHEET

SITE CODE: BGB95

AREA TRENCH: 5/6 | GRID SQUARE: 100/0105 | INTERPRETATION: L/S FOUNDATIONS | CONTEXT No: 266

DESCRIPTION : (COMPACTION : COLOUR : COMPOSITION : INCLUSIONS : THICKNESS & EXTENT & ANY OTHER OBSERVATIONS

SINGLE COURSE OF ROUGHLY SQUARED AND FACED L/S BLOCKS RANGING IN SIZE FROM 260mm x 230mm x 80mm TO 680mm x 360mm x 80mm WITH A CENTRAL CORE OF SMALLER IRREG-SHAPED L/S PCS AVE SIZE 170mm x 170mm x 60mm ALIGNED N-S. NO OBVIOUS BONDING

DIMENSIONS N-S 4.8m REMAINING

E-W 1.00m

DEPTH 80mm

GRID CO-ORDINATE:

STRATIGRAPHICALLY: SAME AS 105

EARLIER THAN

LATER THAN 3/5

COMMENTS / INTERPRETATION

PLAN No's: | PHOTOGRAPH B/W No's: | SAMPLE: | FINDS:

SECTION No's | PHOTOGRAPH COLOUR No's: 35/3/1-3,

SKETCH PLAN: | MATRIX LOCATION:

HIGHEST LEVEL O.D: 63.12m | LOWEST LEVEL O.D: 62.98m

PROVISIONAL PERIOD: | PHASE: | CHECKED BY: | RECORDED BY DATE: Y.R. 25/07/95

NONE ☐ | POT ☑ | BRICK/TILE ☐ | BONE ☐ | IRON ☐

OTHER | GLASS | OTHER METAL | B.M. | WOOD | LEATHER

Figure 2.25 *How to interpret a context sheet*

the relationships between graves and associated features. A detailed plan drawing of each individual grave will be required to show the position of skeletal remains and the location of grave goods. The position of some of the artefacts may be better explained by a close-up drawing featuring, perhaps, the chest area of the burial.

All these drawings relate to the fixed recording grid on the site. Their position is plotted using surveying equipment and their dimensions carefully scaled onto paper. Typically, a planning frame is placed over the feature to assist the production of accurately measured drawings (▶ p. 71). The scale of drawing will vary according to the complexity of the site being recorded. For a large area with few features, scales of 1:20 or more may be used but where there is a mass of detail to record the scale may be 1:5. Considerable effort after the excavation often goes into producing cleaned up versions of these plans for

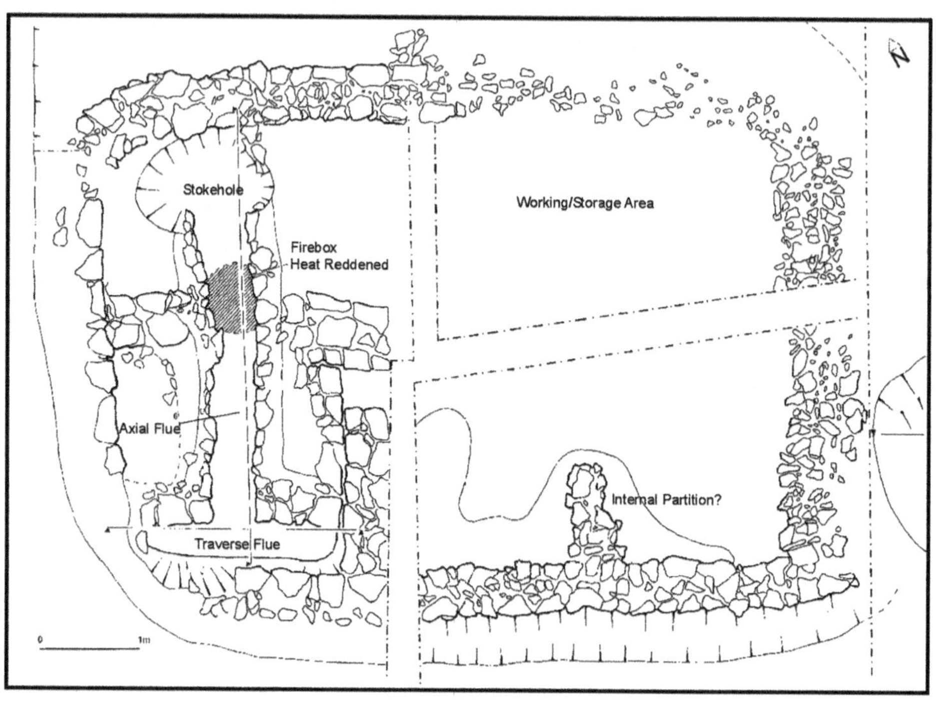
N
Stokehole
Working/Storage Area
Firebox
Heat Reddened
Axial Flue
Internal Partition?
Traverse Flue
0
1m

publication. Often finds and features will be plotted on a series of overlays related to soil and topography. Different plans will be produced to show different aspects of a site such as a contour map of the surface or all the features and structures associated with a single phase. Increasingly, plans are plotted onto tablet computers because of the flexibility they allow in presenting data. GIS is revolutionising this process. Its 3D database enables the production of any section or plan and the testing of complex models.

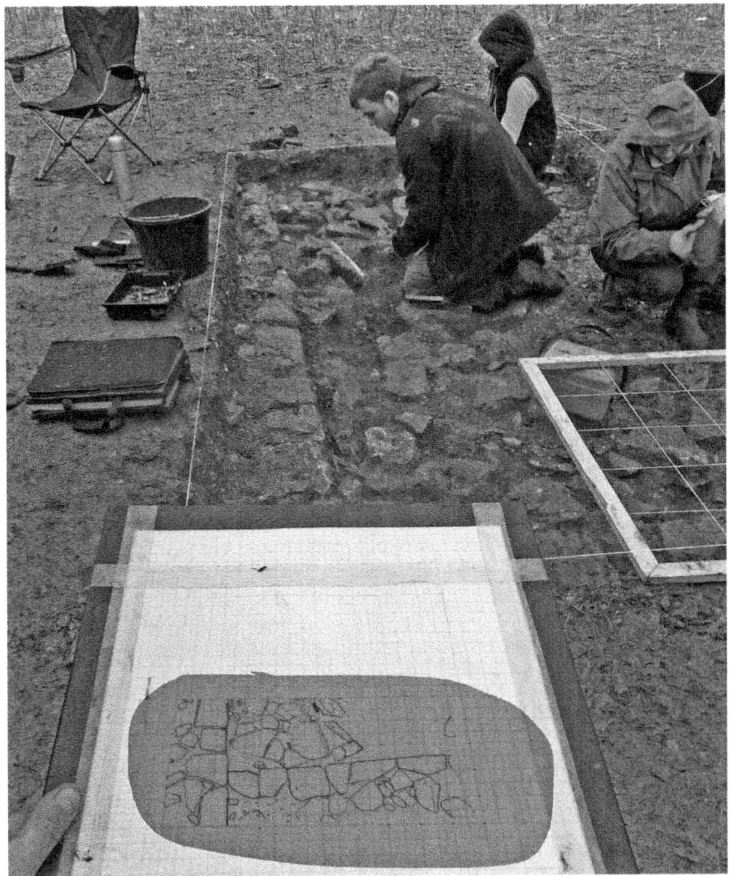

Figure 2.27 *Using gridlines to draw a plan*

In this excavation of a Roman building, the wooden planning frame is 1m square and divided by string into 10cm squares. The gridlines make it easier for the recorder to keep to scale and ensure each piece of stone is included. Each 10cm square on the planning frame is drawn as a 1cm square on the planning sheet to give a 1:10 ratio. Measurements are frequently taken during drawing to ensure the finished record is as accurate as possible.

Figure 2.26 (facing page) *Excavation and plan of a later Romano-British (C4th) corn-drying oven at Leadenham*

The oven consisted of a stoke hole which enabled a fire to be maintained from which heat was channelled via a T-shaped flue to warm a slabbed floor above. Analysis of the carbonised grains found in the structure revealed a high proportion of them to be germinated spelt wheat, suggesting a link to the malting process. (Archaeological Services WYAS)

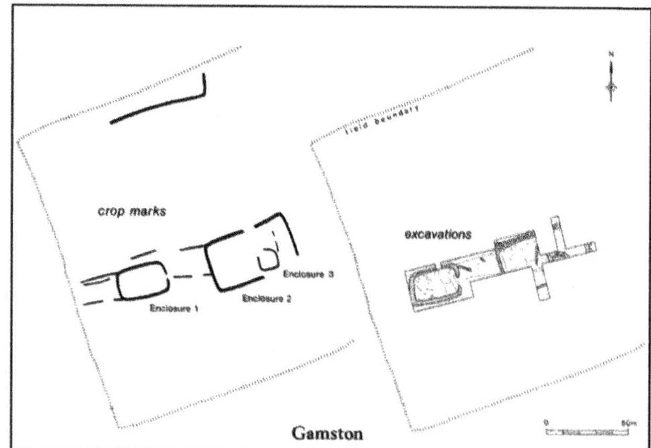

Figure 2.28 (left)
Plot of crop marks and overall excavation plan from Gamston

Figure 2.29 (below)
Phase plans of the Iron Age settlement and field system at Gamston in the Trent Valley. These relied on rigorous attention to stratigraphy and provide a sequence of occupation at the site.

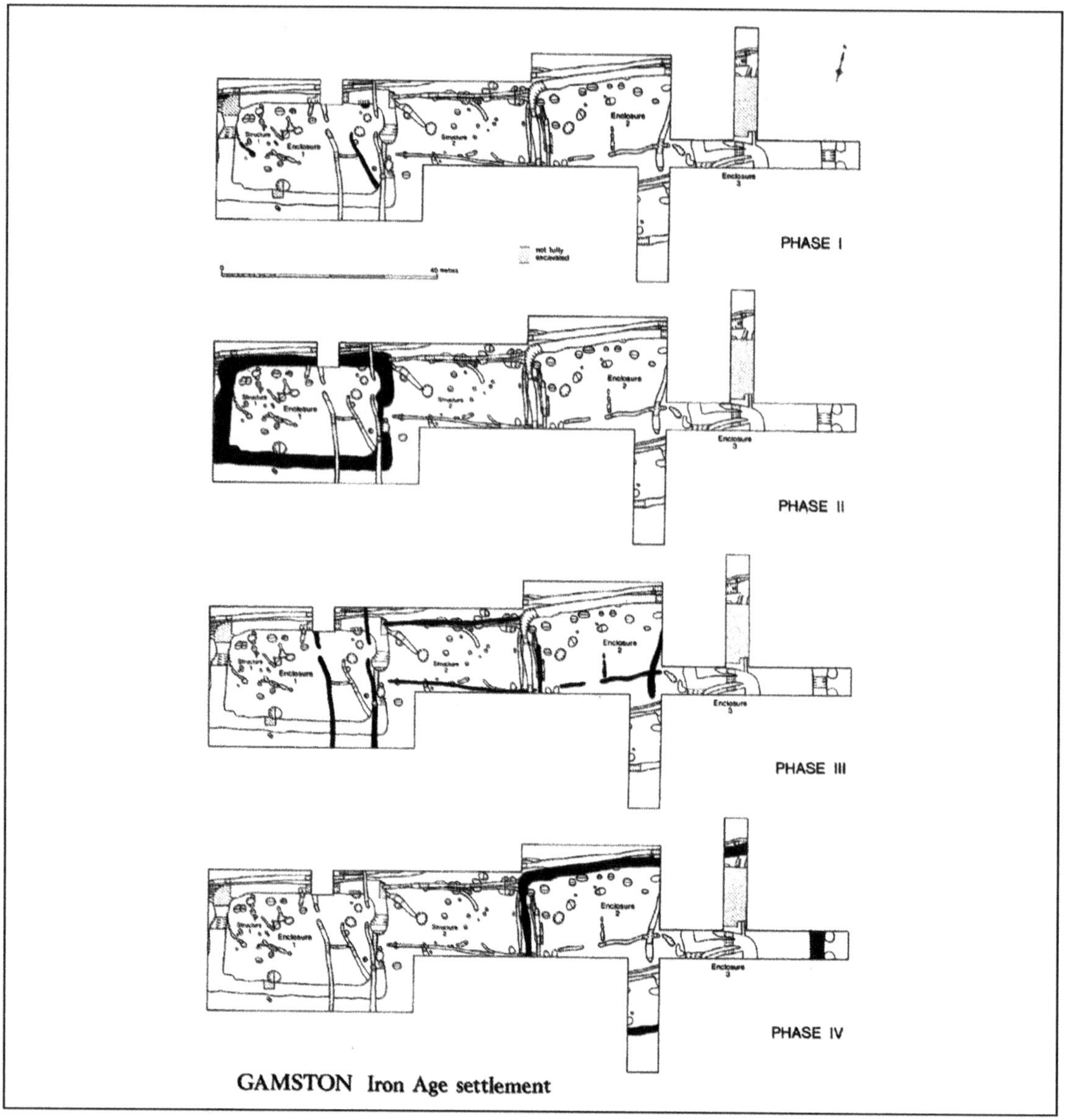

PHASE I

PHASE II

PHASE III

PHASE IV

GAMSTON Iron Age settlement

Section drawings

The sides of excavation trenches, strategically placed baulks or cuts through the fill of features such as ditches, pits or postholes offer vertical slices through the constituent layers of an archaeological site.

Although methods of recording the horizontal spread and depth of each deposit have improved over recent decades, an accurate scaled depiction of the vertical relationship of layers remains the common way of demonstrating the development of a site or feature. For example, the relationship of a 'post pipe' – the evidence for the location of the post itself – within a posthole and to any packing material is best shown in drawn form. As with plans, a key advantage of section drawings is that they can highlight subtle differences in the colour, texture or composition of layers. These are difficult to pick up with photographs. Before drawing it is essential that the face of the section is cleaned up and in some instances sprayed with water to improve contrast. Soil structure and Munsell colour charts are sometimes used to enable specific and standardised descriptions.

Where a section results from a continuous period of excavation, it may be some time before it is ready for recording. Archaeologists note the presence of layers as the dig proceeds by pinning labels with context numbers to the side of the excavation to ensure that when the section is drawn it is still possible to recognise the finer points of the stratification.

Once completed, drawings are usually accompanied by a written interpretation or schematic record such as the Harris matrix. It must be stressed that drawings are always interpretations and the quality of on-site drawings does vary according to the skill of the draughtsperson and the conditions they are working under. For instance, there may be time pressure or risk of decay to organic elements. Back-up photographs can be an additional record.

Figure 2.30 *Recording a section across an excavated ditch*

The tapes against the vertical section help the recorder to produce an accurate profile on gridded paper. The context labels on the face of the section ensure that slight changes in the fill noticed during excavation but which might be very difficult to see or photograph are recorded (▶ p. 590).

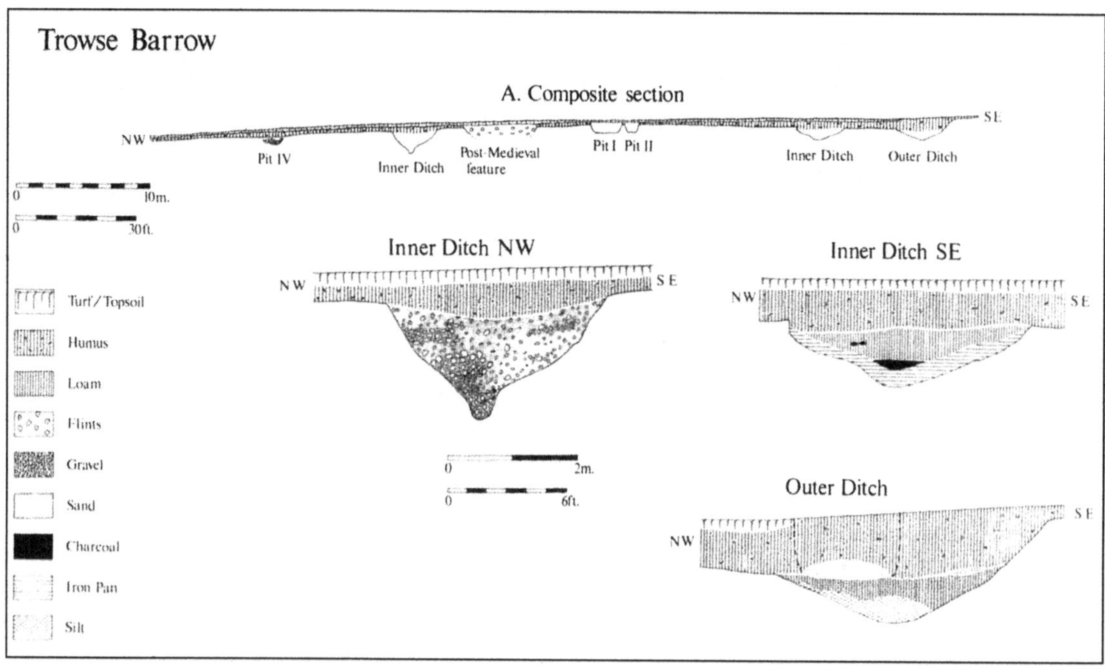

Figure 2.31 *A section drawing of Trowse Round Barrow*

This barrow has two incomplete ditches surrounding it. The main composite cross-section shows the inner ditch twice, the outer ditch once and several other features. The inner and outer ditch sections are enlarged to give greater detail. A key is provided to demonstrate the soil types present. (Reproduced with the permission of the copyright holder, Norfolk Archaeology & Environment Division)

Harris matrix

Stratigraphy is usually recorded in section drawings (▶ p. 73). However, since 1973 the Harris matrix has revolutionised the presentation of the sequences in schematic diagrams. This interpretative system can be applied to standing buildings and rock art as well as to excavated remains. Once sequences and associations of finds are established, different phases of the site can be determined. This relies on recognising significant changes in the assemblages of artefacts or ecofacts or type of structures. For example, the first phase with pottery on a site might be preceded by a final aceramic phase. Other archaeologists will use published data about the stratification to assure themselves of the authenticity of the conclusions reached about phasing on a site.

Photographs

The camera is a key aid to recording, although archaeologists believe that it is less comprehensive in the detail it can show than the drawn record. In reality, photographs usually capture everything but are more difficult to 'read'. Although rulers or ranging rods are usually seen in photographs to give an idea of scale, distances are distorted and film cannot be used to provide precise measurements. The camera clearly offers the chance of accurate views of what features and sections looked like, whereas the draughtsperson can emphasise elements that the camera might obscure; for example, similar coloured soils which have different textures. The two methods complement each other and both are normally used. Some archaeologists continue to use conventional

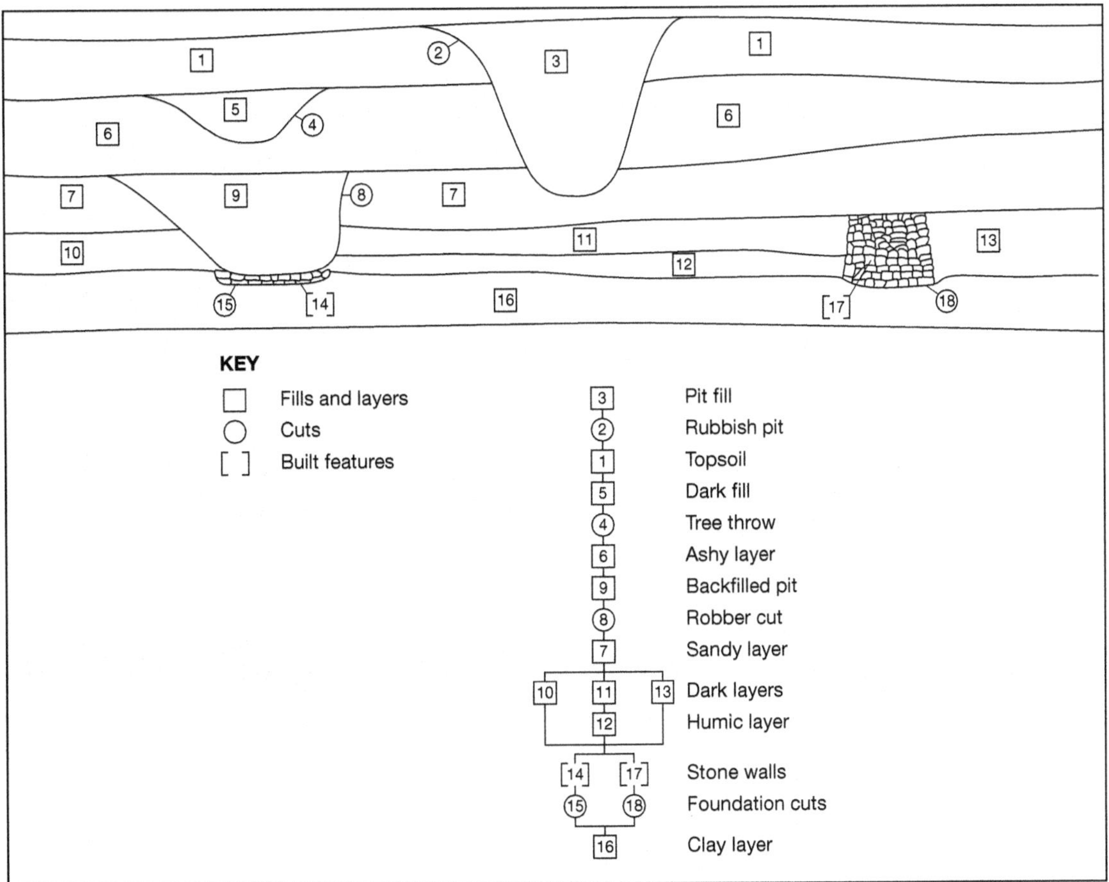

Figure 2.32 *A Harris matrix*

Down to layer 7 in this example, the law of superposition can be applied. Layers 10, 11 and 13 are similar but may not be exactly the same because of the building floor 12. These are shown in parallel. Similarly, the two walls are likely to be contemporary.

black and white film for recording. Digital photography and film are having a major impact, particularly as a support to the site diary. Digital recording also enables the excavation to be viewed online.

The essence of site photography lies in ensuring that the parts to be captured on film are clean, edges of individual structures or bones are well established and careful spraying is used to accentuate coloration changes and contrasts. As in any photography, lighting conditions play a key part in ensuring quality. The use of photographic towers or other means to get a camera above the excavation is common (▶ p. 265). Overlapping vertical photographs with scales can be used as an aid in the creation of plans. This technique (photogrammetry) is particularly popular in underwater archaeology where it is relatively easily to hover above a site and the ability to cover a large area quickly is an advantage.

Increasingly new digital technologies are being employed to record excavations. Bar codes are sometimes used to enable rapid plotting of find points, individual bones or contexts (▶ p. 76).

Ipads are being used for drawing (using touchdraw), making field notes, tagging site photographs and blogging during excavations. The Harvard excavations at Ashkelon in Israel were one of the first to use them.

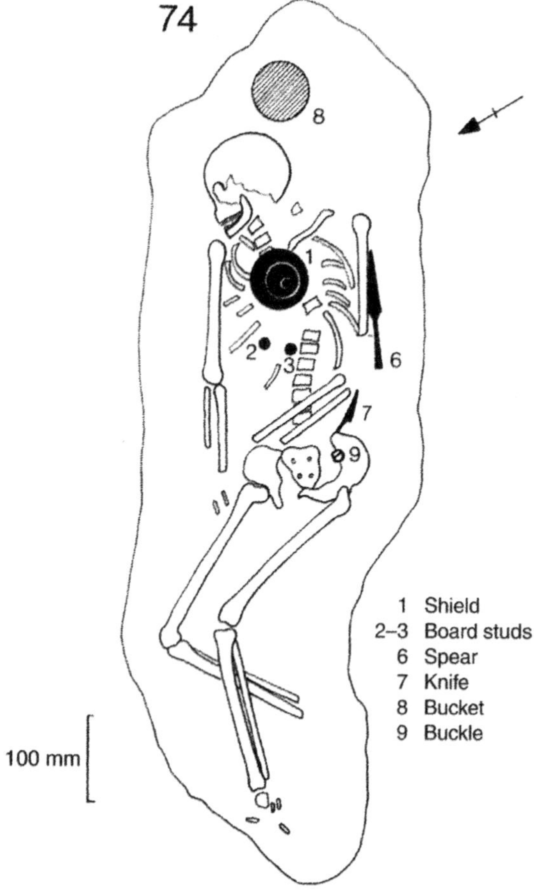

Figure 2.33 Photograph and drawing to allow comparison of the different information provided

The plan of Burial 74 at Empingham shows positions of bones and grave goods. The skeleton of a male aged about 25–30 years was accompanied by a shield boss, two studs, a spearhead, an iron knife, a copper alloy-bound wooden bucket and an iron buckle. Preserved wood remains in the spear socket were identified as willow and poplar and in the bucket as yew.

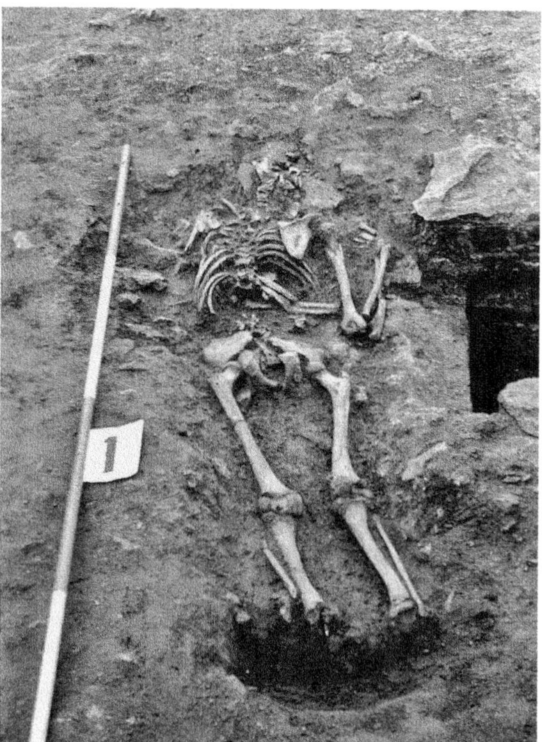

Figure 2.34 Another grave from Empingham. Compare this record with Figure 2.33

Figure 2.35 Using a total station to rapidly plot the position of finds. At Spitalfields so many skeletons were discovered that digital means of recording their position were used including barcodes

Figure 2.36 *Recording using photography*

This trench has been cleaned up ready for photographing. Ranging poles provide a scale and a north-pointer shows orientation. Also in view is a board with the feature or context number to enable identification and location afterwards.

SPECIAL CASES

Most of the points in this chapter apply to all sites but there are some issues that apply to particular types of sites.

Archaeology of standing buildings

In 'traditional' archaeology, interpretation of excavated evidence relies on the basic principle that the deeper the deposit, the earlier it is – the basis of relative dating by stratigraphy. Although standing buildings require a different approach to their study, the basic principles remain the same. One of the objectives of recording is to enable the developmental sequence of the building to be traced. Where a feature has been inserted into an existing one (e.g. a window or door inserted into a standing wall), it follows that the inserted feature is later than that into which it was inserted. Similarly, later walls may be of different construction to the original or may be butt-jointed (simply butted up against earlier walls rather than properly bonded). All these clues help archaeologists to build up a sequence of development in the same way as on an excavation. Recording standing buildings may involve reconnaissance techniques (▶ p. 14), dismantling, excavation or a combination of these approaches. The amount of information which may be recovered from a building will depend on many factors. Cosmetic renovation of a structure may give only a few clues (e.g. glimpses beneath floor boards or behind small areas of plaster), whereas a building undergoing substantial alterations or even demolition will be far more exposed to study. The aim should be to identify the earliest structural remains on the site and then, having plotted them, begin to add in later stages of development. Additions or changes to a building are never random: they will always serve a clear purpose which archaeologists try to detect; for example, the extending of a room or rebuilding of a façade.

The recording of standing buildings should be every bit as rigorous as the recording of an excavation. Alongside drawings and written descriptions a full photographic record should be maintained, indicating scale and the exact point on a master plan from which the view was taken, along with any other relevant information. Sampling should include examples of different mortars and plasters. Substantial timbers may be sampled for **dendrochronology** (▶ p. 150). Details of the fabric and construction of the building, alterations and dating evidence are gathered through drawing and photography. Elevations of buildings are often drawn stone by stone using grids as the completed drawing can often reveal patterns not obvious to the naked eye. Very precise photographic recording to within 10mm can be achieved using photogrammetry. In this technique, also used for aerial photography, two precision cameras are used together to create a 'stereo' recording. When combined with readings from an EDM, specialists can use CAD to produce a 3D record of the building, including very fine decorative or architectural detail. It is considerably faster than traditional recording and is both cost effective and accurate. It is used particularly where historic buildings are being restored.

Wetland archaeology

Waterlogged sites are where the natural water table has maintained a wet or damp environment since the deposition of the evidence. They have been a major factor in adding to our knowledge of past cultures. **Anaerobic conditions** prevent or impede normal bacterial and chemical decay processes and can result in widespread survival of organic material such as wood, leather and textiles which would normally perish. Intertidal sites share many of the same features but with the additional problem of submersion twice every twenty-four hours. The studies of Illerup (▶ p. 483) and Star Carr (▶ p. 267) illustrate some of the particular issues of wetland sites.

Intertidal archaeology presents a specific range of challenges. Organic material exposed between tides such as shipwrecks or structures has often been well preserved but will rapidly decay. It needs to be excavated and recorded quickly but twice a day it is submerged, covering the site with sand or mud. This makes work difficult or dangerous. A salvage approach is usually adopted, with material where possible being removed from immediate danger for study in a laboratory. Unfortunately this action can also destroy the context of the site. Sometimes to buy time a barrier is set up to encircle the site and keep the sea at bay. Protection can range from a cofferdam made from a wall of metal sheeting to a ring of sandbags.

Strategies for excavation, conservation and post-excavation analysis on wetland sites need to factor in the time and cost of dealing with additional evidence as well as the particular challenges associated with waterlogged sites. In particular, there are often large quantities of environmental material, especially plant remains. While the complete removal of all material for close examination is not usually a viable proposition, much emphasis is put on the selection of large numbers of samples of site deposits for laboratory analysis. This has been the case with excavations of London's waterfront, where huge amounts of large timbers could not all be preserved. Those selected for recovery enabled the development of carpentry and construction techniques over a long period to be studied. This

Figure 2.37 *Salvage archaeology at Seahenge*

Until erosion by the sea, the timbers and land surface of this ritual site had been preserved, perhaps with associated deposits. By the time it was discovered in 1999 much damage had been done and English Heritage felt it was not worth rescuing. Under pressure from archaeologists, they relented and began a fairly basic salvaging of the main timbers amid mud, tides and some angry pagans who saw excavation as sacrilege. Little else was recovered and it provides a good contrast with recovery at Boxgrove (▶ p. 59). Each of the fifty-five timbers was at least 30cm across, which meant that the circle was almost closed and focused on a massive upturned oak stump. The timbers were dated by dendrochronology to 2050 BC. In 2007 the conserved timbers were partially reconstructed in a new museum. This site illustrates both differential survival and recovery.

revealed the way older timber buildings were recycled by builders. Once taken out of water, organic material will be stored in tanks of water prior to conservation. The consequence of exceptional preservation is that while the information from 'wet' sites is considered a real bonus in archaeological study, the costs of obtaining it considerably outstrip those of excavating 'dry' sites.

Unlike 'dry' sites where you can walk carefully across the site, pressure on wetland deposits can cause considerable damage. Excavators at Flag Fen (▶ p. 543) erected a series of platforms on scaffolding to allow diggers to lie above the features they were excavating. Such restriction to movement makes digging, cleaning, planning and photography more difficult. Other factors to be overcome are the weight of waterlogged deposits, the need for water management (e.g. pumps) and often cold working conditions. Finds are usually maintained in bags with water or kept in cling film. Once wood is removed from a wet environment, decay sets in rapidly unless proactive measures are taken. Observations at Oakbank showed that excavated wood when freshly broken retained the colour of fresh timber, but once exposed to the air the wood turned black in

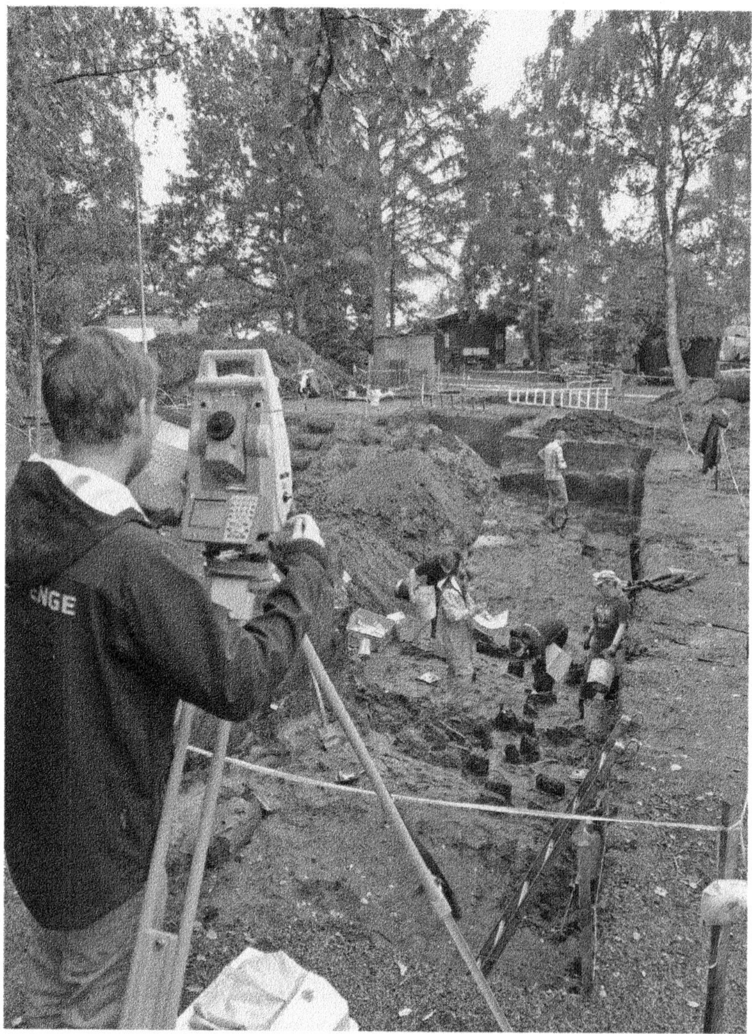

Figure 2.38 *Surveying a 3m trench at Alken Enge (▶ p. 118), Denmark*

Beneath a 2m layer of peat at this 40 hectare wetland site are the remains of a vanquished army. A small team of specialists are carefully excavating the bones of soldiers which were thrown into a lake around AD 0. (Skanderborg Museum/Ejvind Hertz)

about 20 seconds. In the short term, wood is kept wet with biocides added to the water to prevent fungal growth.

Underwater archaeology

Although underwater sites follow the same basic rules as dry sites – the need for survey, careful excavation and recording – being below water presents additional challenges. The excavators usually require watertight diving suits, air tanks and weights and are usually limited to four hours diving a day. In extreme depths, as with the *Titanic*, remotely controlled vehicles may be used. In addition to underwater hazards, cold temperatures may make it difficult to remain stationary for long periods while poor visibility may require excavation using touch rather than sight!

Figure 2.39 *Reconstruction of Oakbank Iron Age Crannog*

Crannogs are artificial islands with a wooden platform supported by piles driven into lakebeds or boulders dumped on the lakebed. They were used for some 5,000 years until the C17th in Scotland and Ireland as farmsteads, halls and defensive refuges. At Oakbank, underwater archaeologists were able to recover organic remains including food, artefacts and structural timbers. Exceptional finds included a butter dish containing butter and a canoe paddle. Like many wet sites, Oakbank has shed light on the extent to which large timbers were felled, shaped and moved in the past.

To inform excavation strategy, a form of sampling is often employed to gain a feel for the site. One example of this is the Tudor warship the *Mary Rose*, whose position and condition was examined and investigated for several years before a sufficient understanding enabled full excavation. Where little or no wooden remains are present and finds are in a dispersed state, plans are drawn and trial trenches excavated to determine the extent of the deposits.

Plastic 2 x 2m or 4 x 4m recording grids are set out and the usual land-based methods of planning and context sheets employed where possible. Synthetic paper (mylar or permatrace) enables pencils to be used underwater. Photography is likely to be limited to close-up shots or carefully rigged photogrammetry rather than general views but digital pictures can easily be combined to produce an overall montage of the site. One advantage of underwater excavation is that the archaeologist can cross the site without treading on a trowelled surface! The diggers remove sediment by 'fanning' with their hands or by using either a water dredge or airlift which sucks water and sediment away to the surface where it is sieved using a fine mesh. Water lances may be used sparingly to shred sediment but can damage the archaeology.

Objects may have suffered corrosion and created concretions that need to be broken apart. Decisions have to be made as to whether to use hammer and chisel below water or to bring the whole mass to the surface. Ordinary finds are placed in open containers, fragile finds in sealed

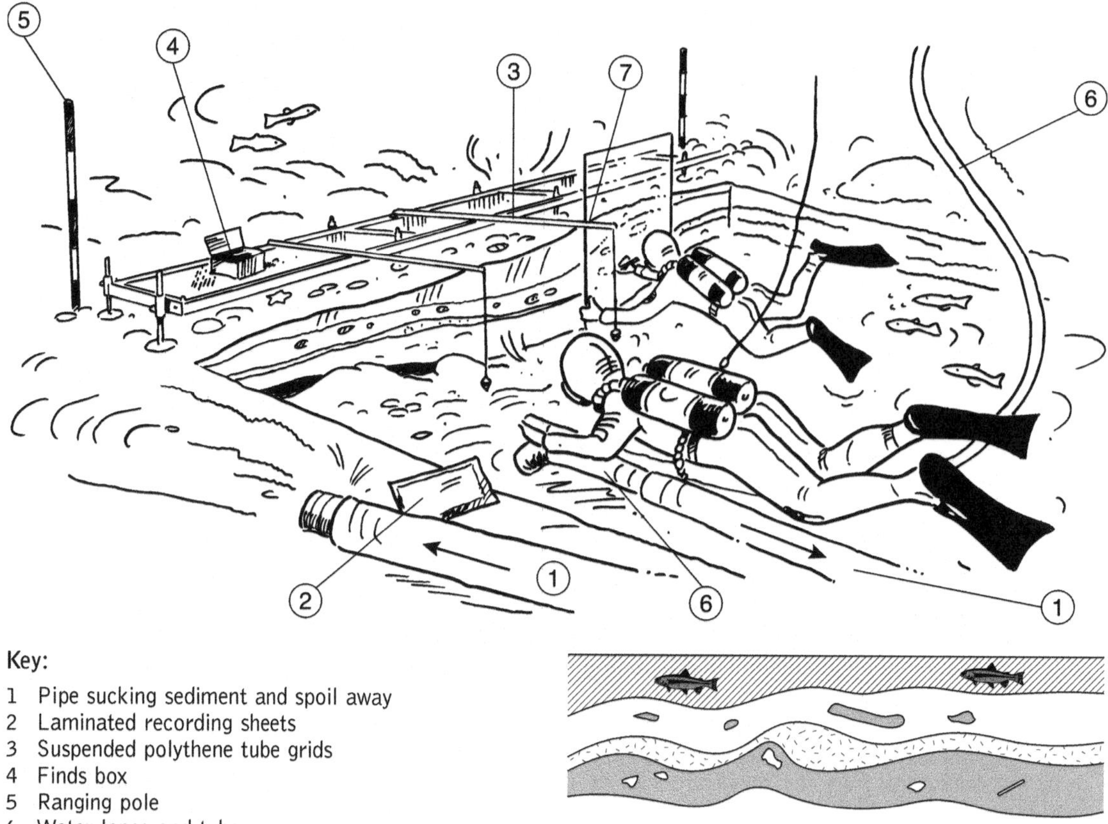

Figure 2.40 *Illustration of some of the equipment used at Tybrind Vig (▶ p. 309) (after Thomasen in Anderson 1985)*

ones and larger objects air-lifted by the use of inflated air bags or balloons. As with waterlogged sites, organic material is susceptible to damage if it is allowed, even briefly, to dry out during excavation. In some cases material has to be stabilised to prevent chemical decay arising from removing it from salt water. Once such material is removed from the water, it must be quickly put into appropriate storage including sometimes refrigeration.

Many underwater sites have now been examined and the range of sites includes Cleopatra's Palace, Alexandria; *La Belle*, a French ship wrecked off Texas and excavated within a cofferdam; the Bronze Age *Uluburun* (▶ p. 403) and the *Titanic*.

Urban archaeology

While it is clear that there is a great variety in the nature of archaeological sites in rural areas, archaeologists working on urban sites face very different challenges. Here open ground is at a premium and so it is usually the clearance of a site for development that provides archaeological opportunities. The area involved is often tightly constrained by other buildings and therefore only parts of buried sites are available for study.

Figure 2.41 *Area excavation of a Roman cemetery, Cirencester. Note the hoarding erected out of respect for the burials.*

These do not necessarily correspond to the areas which archaeologists would choose if they were making the site selection on academic grounds; it is a good example of rescue archaeology being dictated by developer activity. Such excavations are like keyholes into the past because a full view is rarely obtained. Nevertheless there has been an increase in the number of urban excavations with much focus on sampling via evaluations and test pits. Planning permission (▶ p. 572) places an emphasis on avoiding damage to the stratigraphy and checking the depth of deposits. The depth of stratification is usually far greater than on rural sites because of frequent reuse of the same site over time. It is particularly difficult to forecast the range of features that will be encountered and the time it will take to excavate them all properly. Deep excavation also presents additional safety hazards.

Survey methods applicable to rural sites such as aerial photography and many of the geophysical procedures are ineffectual or inappropriate in preparatory work. Indeed, at a large excavation in London at Number 1, Poultry in the 1990s the evaluation consisted of a desktop survey and four shafts between 3m and 5m deep to reach the top of the natural geology. These gave indications of the sequences and structures which might be encountered. The excavation also produced 'wet' archaeology including about 1,500 datable (by dendrochronology) Roman timbers. Normally archaeologists have to complete their work before the building contractors arrive on site but this extensive urban excavation (the on-site budget exceeded £2m) continued for twelve months below the construction of the new building.

Excavating and recording human skeletons

Human remains are quite a regular element of archaeological fieldwork and should always be treated with great respect. However, it is essential that any recovery work should aim to retrieve the

Figure 2.42 *Excavating a skeleton. Note the use of a modelling tool to clean the soil around the ribs.*

maximum possible information and the information which osteologists (bone specialists) can provide will be enhanced by careful recovery of the evidence. Key facts to emerge for each individual from these studies will potentially be age, sex, stature, diet, dentition, injuries and burial position; cultural factors for a group will be evident from funerary practices including alignment of burials and deposition of grave goods which may highlight social attitudes to death and demographic profiles for a community (▶ p. 432).

On the practical front, anyone entrusted with excavating a skeleton should make themselves aware of the details of a human skeleton and the changes from infant to child to juvenile to adult form. They need to be aware of different positions in which the body may have been deposited. Most burials are either extended (usually on their backs but some are face-down) or flexed (sleeping position) or crouched (knees drawn up tightly to the chest). Some grave cuts contain more than one individual, an infant and adult not being unusual. It goes without saying that choice of tools for excavating is paramount. Trowels are too large for such delicate work and a range of smaller spatulas and dentists' equipment often features. Unless a site is really dry, brushes should be avoided as they can apply a coating of soil to freshly revealed bones. If feasible, it is recommended to start the excavation with the skull and work down the length of the body towards the feet. To minimise DNA contamination of the remains, excavators frequently wear gloves and increasingly forensic-style barrier clothing.

Some cultures buried objects with the body and we generally refer to such items as grave goods. While some may be metal, many other materials are found, including stone tools, ceramics and worked bone or antler. Organic remains may well have been deposited at the original ceremony and care needs to be taken in case some evidence survives. Food offerings were one such

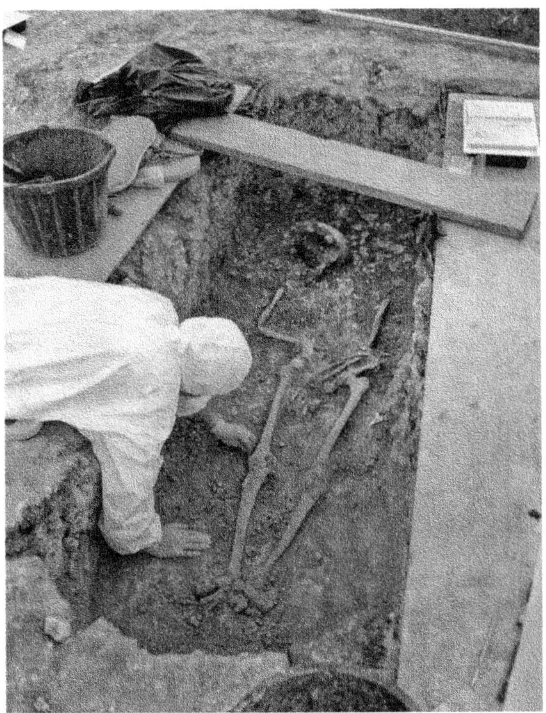

Figure 2.43 *Removing a skeleton. The special clothing worn by the excavator is to minimise DNA contamination.*

practice and therefore the need to recognise the bone from a pork-chop and not confuse it with the burial is another skill the excavator should develop.

As with other archaeological features, recording is essential and a plan should show the grave outline, the position in detail of the burial(s) within it and the location of any grave goods. Both drawings and photographs should be included in the record. Care is needed when lifting a skeleton as often some parts of it or grave goods may not be visible after the first cleaning. If chemical analysis of grave fill is to be undertaken, samples are taken from undisturbed soil around the head and other parts of the body as well as control samples from above and below the grave.

Forensic archaeology

It is quite surprising that forensic ('used in or connected with a court of law') archaeology should only have been seen as a significant contribution by the discipline in the last twenty years. Scientific archaeological excavation has a long history and throughout that time law enforcement agencies have needed high-quality evidence in their enquiries. The material in this chapter and the ones preceding and following it apply equally to archaeologists and forensic investigators. Such agents use search capabilities including geophysics and aerial photography, recovery methodologies largely focused on excavation but also linked to surface depositional activities, identification of evidence and its recording and conservation. Following retrieval of the evidence, their laboratory techniques involve detailed analysis of artefacts and ecofacts just as in a traditional post-excavation context.

One only has to review the detailed examination of bog bodies or Ötzi the 'Ice Man' (▶ p. 104) to recognise that similar processes are also needed for more recent discoveries, often linked to crime. The careful and considerate approach adopted by archaeologists can contribute to a fuller understanding of individual burials or mass graves such as were revealed and investigated in Bosnia.

In Europe an approach called *anthropologie de terrain* examines evidence for changes post-burial in order to understand mortuary practice and to avoid jumping to conclusions based on observations at the point of excavation. For example, compression of the rib cage and clavicle bones can be due to the body being wrapped. Analysis of the position of the upper body of the 18-year-old girl at Vedbaek (▶ p. 531) suggests that she had originally been lying on a cushion of some sort. As it decayed, her bones moved back and down to the position they were found in. Similarly, analysis of the position of ribs in the twin female burial at Vedbaek suggested that they had been tightly wrapped during burial.

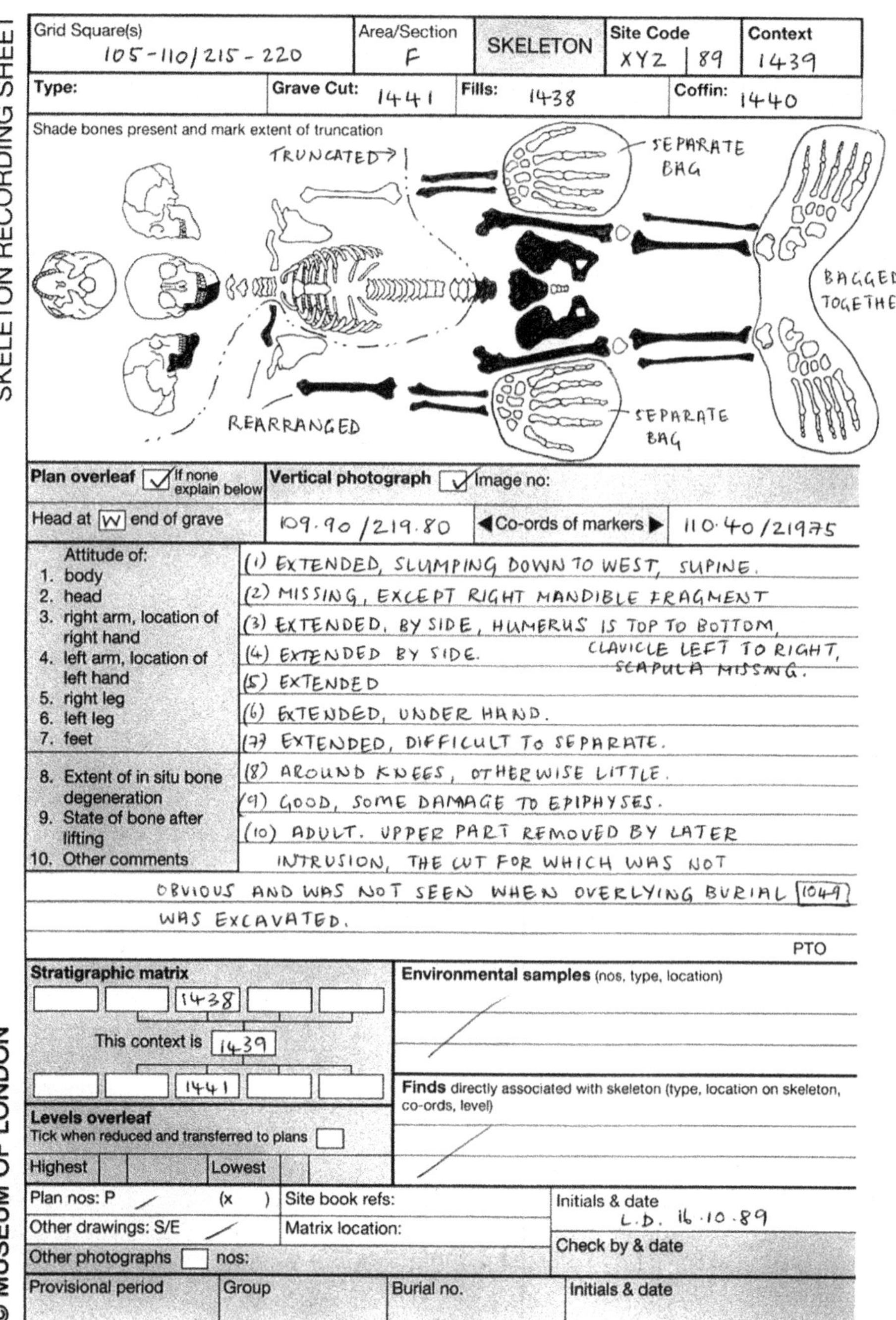

SKELETON RECORDING SHEET

Grid Square(s)	Area/Section	SKELETON	Site Code	Context
105-110/215-220	F		XYZ 89	1439

Type:	Grave Cut: 1441	Fills: 1438	Coffin: 1440

Shade bones present and mark extent of truncation

Plan overleaf ✓ If none explain below	Vertical photograph ✓ Image no:		
Head at W end of grave	109.90/219.80	◀ Co-ords of markers ▶	110.40/219.75

Attitude of: 1. body 2. head 3. right arm, location of right hand 4. left arm, location of left hand 5. right leg 6. left leg 7. feet	(1) EXTENDED, SLUMPING DOWN TO WEST, SUPINE. (2) MISSING, EXCEPT RIGHT MANDIBLE FRAGMENT (3) EXTENDED, BY SIDE, HUMERUS IS TOP TO BOTTOM, CLAVICLE LEFT TO RIGHT, ~~SCAPULA MISSING.~~ (4) EXTENDED BY SIDE. (5) EXTENDED (6) EXTENDED, UNDER HAND. (7) EXTENDED, DIFFICULT TO SEPARATE.
8. Extent of in situ bone degeneration 9. State of bone after lifting 10. Other comments	(8) AROUND KNEES, OTHERWISE LITTLE. (9) GOOD, SOME DAMAGE TO EPIPHYSES. (10) ADULT. UPPER PART REMOVED BY LATER INTRUSION, THE CUT FOR WHICH WAS NOT

OBVIOUS AND WAS NOT SEEN WHEN OVERLYING BURIAL [1049] WAS EXCAVATED.

PTO

Stratigraphic matrix

[1438]

This context is [1439]

[1441]

Levels overleaf Tick when reduced and transferred to plans

Highest | Lowest

Environmental samples (nos, type, location)

Finds directly associated with skeleton (type, location on skeleton, co-ords, level)

Plan nos: P — (x)	Site book refs:	Initials & date L.D. 16.10.89
Other drawings: S/E —	Matrix location:	Check by & date
Other photographs nos:		

Provisional period	Group	Burial no.	Initials & date

© MUSEUM OF LONDON

Figure 2.44 *Skeleton recording sheet*

For dealing with human remains, excavators increasingly use a specialised recording system as this example from the Museum of London demonstrates. Note the stratigraphic (Harris) matrix which records the burial (context 1439) overlying the grave cut (1441) but underneath the grave fill (1438).

Figure 2.45 *Grave 22, a twin female burial from Vedbaek. (Ole Tage Hartmann/Rudersdal Museums)*

AFTER EXCAVATION

Once the digging is completed, attention switches to the laboratories and the processing of finds and site records. This is dealt with in Chapters 3 and 4. The eventual outcome of the excavation used to be a full excavation report with text on the features and structures, catalogues and drawings of finds and specialists' reports. Today the emphasis is on producing a quality 'archive' which can then be adapted as appropriate into reports, more popular publications or to provide research opportunities. Increasingly records are stored digitally, which offers tremendous potential for disseminating data to different audiences in different ways. There is additional discussion of the importance and nature of publications in Chapter 13.

Chapter 3

Post-excavation Analysis and Archaeological Materials

This chapter outlines general approaches to post-excavation work and the range of specialisms involved. The bulk of the chapter outlines the initial analytical techniques used with the most common organic and inorganic materials. Where a method is used with several materials it is dealt with at the first example and only referenced thereafter.

The final section focuses upon lab-based techniques which are usually applicable to a range of materials. These include new techniques adapted from biochemistry which are revolutionising our understanding of the past. Further examples and more detail of their uses can be found throughout Part II of this book.

POST-EX

Reconnaissance and excavation might be the most visible part of archaeology but the most extensive part of the work takes place after digging has finished. Each week of digging creates months

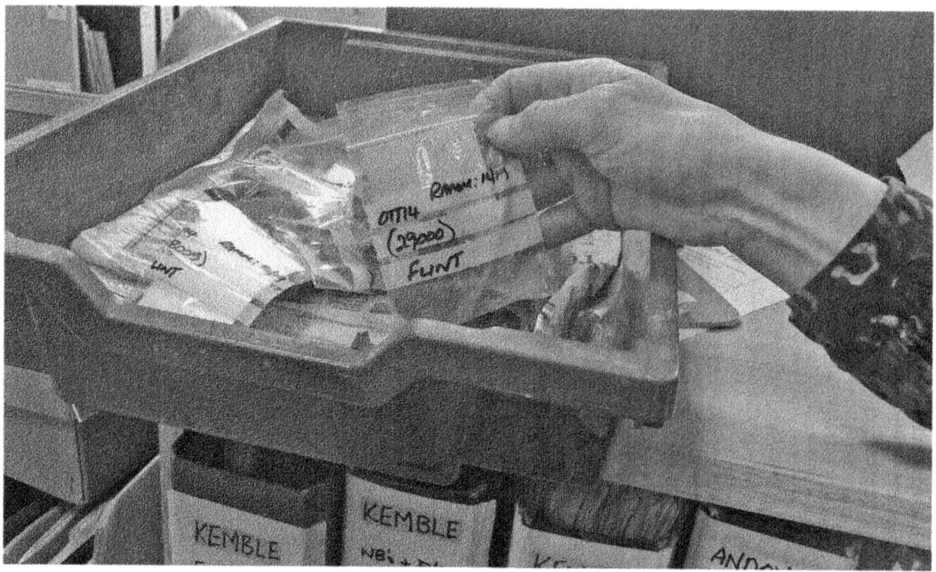

Figure 3.1 *Each find comes in with site and context numbers*

of post-excavation or 'post-ex' processes and interpretation using the materials recovered and the records made by the excavators.

Materials are stored in a temporary archive at the base of the excavation unit, university or museum which carried out the fieldwork. Typically this base will have areas for cleaning and processing finds and rooms for the various specialists who are part of the team. These might have particular expertise in bones, environmental remains or small finds. Only the largest outfits will have a complete range of specialists. Most organisations outsource analysis to freelance experts. This is particularly the case where lab-based processes are involved. Palynologists (pollen), pathologists and geologists are just some of the specialists contracted to analyse material. Radiocarbon dating is also undertaken in more specialist facilities. One room is given over to careful technical drawings of finds and of crucial site documents such as plans, sections and elevations, complemented where appropriate with photographs. Close by are housed the site archives from previous excavations and projects – that is, the collections of context sheets and registers normally stored in a series of ring-binders until needed for publication. Finally there is the suite of computers in the publishing room which produces the finished site reports. Analysis does not stop there. Archived materials and reports are investigated by other researchers as new questions occur to them or as new techniques for analysis are developed. Increasingly, great leaps in our understanding of the past are made in this way.

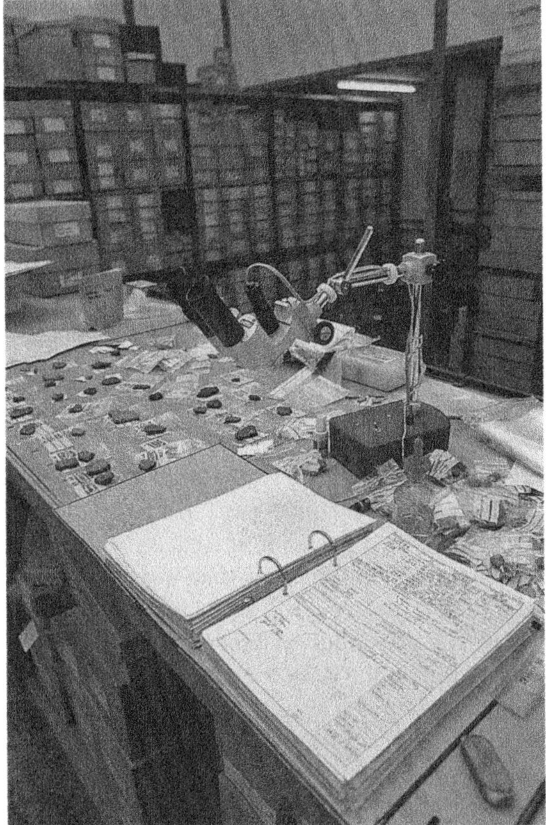

Figure 3.2 *Post-excavation processes normally take longer, cost more and involve more people than excavation. It is the hidden face of archaeology. This desk is set up for the identification and recording of samples.*

INITIAL PROCESSING AND CONSERVATION

On arrival, materials are treated differently according to their properties. Robust artefacts such as flint tools or pottery are cleaned in water unless analysis of residues or wear is to be undertaken. Materials which will be sent to labs for analysis are treated with great care. Ancient textiles are easily contaminated and are often stored in a light-free environment interleaved with acid-free paper or pure cotton cloth. Simply handling pottery will contaminate it with fatty acids from our fingers which may interfere with lipid analysis (▶ p. 136), while handling the edges of lithics will impede use-wear analysis (▶ p. 94). Fragile organic materials such as wood, textiles and bone and some metal artefacts are handled with delicacy and usually require conservation work before analysis can begin. The quantity of material and the availability of specialists can mean that materials have to be temporarily stored in as stable a condition as possible, for example,

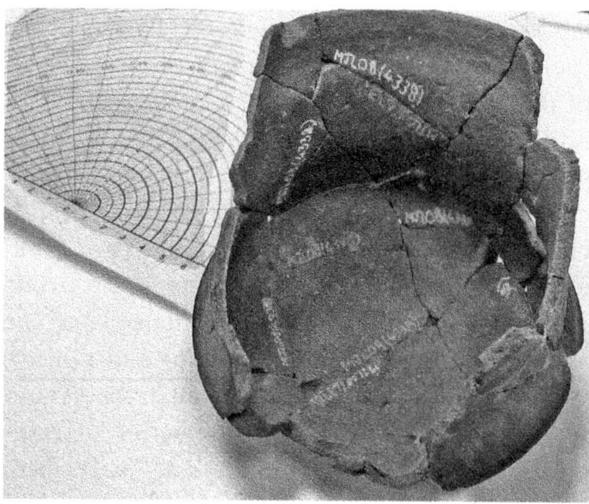

Figure 3.3 *Initial reconstruction of a pot after cleaning. The grid sheet in the background helps with both shape and measuring the radius and circumference. Much reconstruction work is now undertaken by independent specialists.*

keeping waterlogged wood submerged in water or storing soil cores for pollen analysis in a fridge to prevent bacterial decay. Prior to conservation, many materials require cleaning. In the case of waterlogged wood or leather, soft brushes or sponges are used gently with water to avoid damaging surface detail. Dental tools, ultrasonic devices and small vacuum cleaners may also be employed. Washing in moving water, sometimes with mild chemicals, may be required to remove salts from organic materials, while iron may be immersed in a chemical bath containing alkaline sulphite to remove corrosion. The Dornier bomber recovered from the English Channel in 2013 has spent months at RAF Cosford being showered in a lemon juice solution to neutralise alkaline deposits and clean the metal of marine life. Once cleaned, many artefacts have a code written on them in indelible ink which links to the context where they were found.

The main purpose of conservation is to stabilise materials and prevent deterioration. For example, bone may be treated with polyvinyl acetate (PVA) to stop it crumbling, while organic samples may require mild fungicides to halt decay. Dry (dessicated) materials such as leather shoes recovered from salt mines (▶ p. 376) can be brittle so are treated with oils or polymers to restore some flexibility or prevent further deterioration.

Waterlogged materials often present the greatest challenges. Shipwreck timbers, for example, may have the consistency of wet cardboard and consist of 80–90 per cent water. They are unstable and as soon as they are exposed to air, drying out begins, which leads to irreversible shrinkage and cracking. To prevent this they need to be impregnated with a bulking agent to replace the water and then slowly dried. Small wooden objects can be slowly heated to 60°C in a solution of water-soluble wax such as polyethylene glycol (PEG) which gradually replaces the water within the wood. A cheaper method is to use a solution of sucrose. For hardwoods, dehydration with the solvent acetone and impregnation with rosin (pine resin) is sometimes preferred. Vacuum freeze-drying of small artefacts is much faster but requires expensive, specialist equipment. At Vindolanda the huge number of wooden finds led to the development of a simple, cost-effective solution whereby wood is repeatedly sprayed with water and then wrapped in cellophane. Over time the re-spraying becomes less frequent until the artefact has stabilised. In general, conservation is expensive and in some cases can take years. The timbers of the *Mary Rose* were sprayed first with fresh water and then for seventeen years with PEG before they were placed in a purpose-built 'Hot Box' in 2013 to be air-dried for a further five years. The principles for other organic materials are essentially the same but with variation in the bulking or lubricating agents used. Complications arise where artefacts are made from more than one material. For example, PEG can be corrosive for some metals. Leather artefacts present particular challenges. Leather can be made from most animals including mammals and reptiles and created using a wide range of vegetable or mineral tanning processes. Each of these might require a different conservation approach and is

Figure 3.4 *A painstakingly reconstructed Neolithic vessel*

The convention is for plain clay to be infilled in the gaps to recreate the solid shape while making clear which parts are original.

further complicated by artefacts frequently being composites of several different materials.

Some conservation is ongoing. Organic samples may need regular checking for mould and in some cases treatment with fungicides. In the case of textiles, preventing fading or loss of colour from light pollution means storage in darkness. For some organic display items such as leather artefacts, some conservators avoid the use of oils because it can alter their appearance. In these cases environmental controls are essential to maintain optimum levels of temperature, light and humidity and ensure that insects, dust and mould are kept at bay.

Visual examination and recording

The first analytical stage for most materials involves categorisation. Artefacts will be sorted according to physical characteristics or attributes and classified into categories by material and typology. The physical feel of artefacts is often used as well as appearance. Characteristics such as grittiness or greasiness are best determined by touch. Classification of finds is often done by a small finds specialist. Most excavations do not have specialists for every type of material, so some of this work is outsourced to freelance experts. Specialists use their knowledge to categorise finds but they also refer to their set of 'diagnostics' (e.g. a type-series of pottery sherds) or illustrations to aid identification. These are sometimes called parallels or a reference collection. In addition they will use published or online archives from sites of the same period and particularly the same region. Some materials, particularly metals, will require further tests. Microscope examination of marks on some materials can also provide clues to their use. In particularly well-equipped facilities, scanning electron microscopes (SEM) may also be employed. Environmental samples, once removed from soil, are

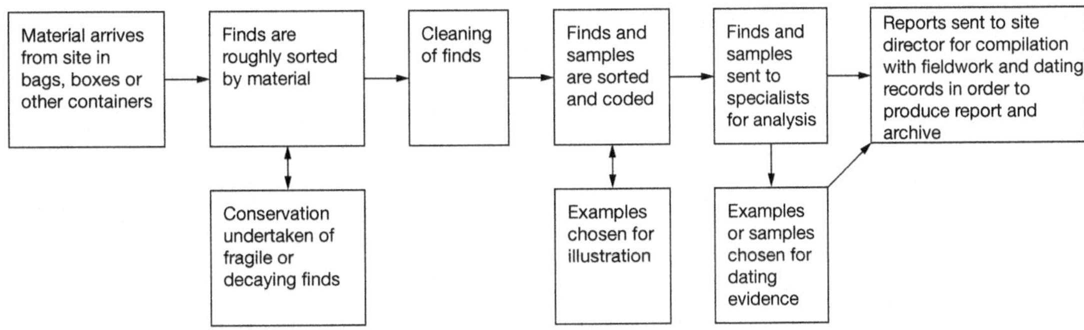

Figure 3.5 *Simplified diagram of the post-excavation process*

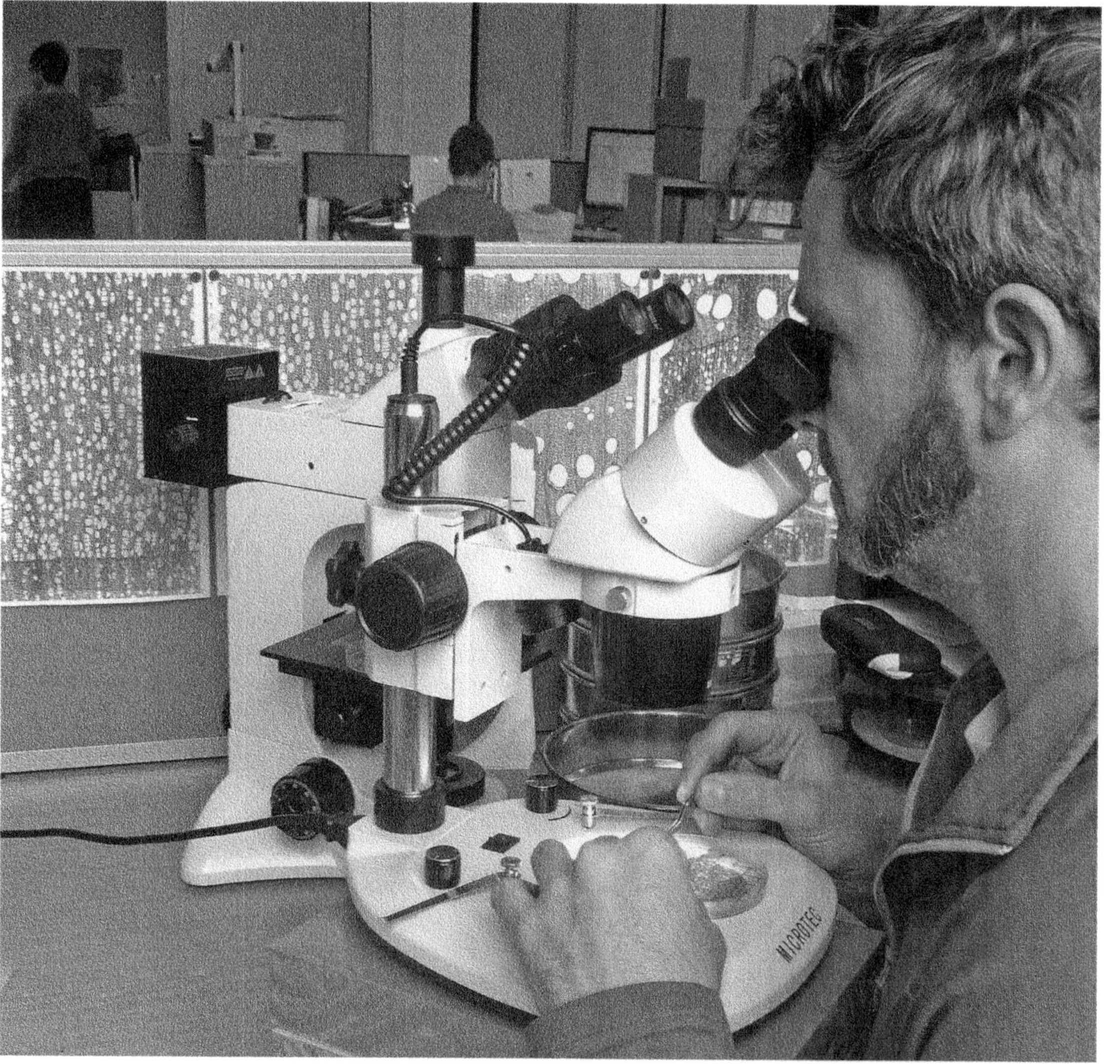

Figure 3.6 *A botanical specialist at Cotswold Archaeology examining soil samples for charcoal. The typical patterns in the grain of the different species of wood are displayed behind the microscope.*

identified by species and then analysed in similar ways, using microscopes for plant and invertebrate remains. Once identified and categorised, material is quantified and recorded through drawing or photography. A descriptive report is then produced by the specialist undertaking the work – often illustrated with drawings, charts or tables.

ANALYSIS OF INORGANIC MATERIALS

Lithics

Lithics or stone tools are virtually indestructible. They have been used for all but the earliest stages of human development and for many sites and periods are the only definite sign of human activity. Lithic artefacts can tell us much about

Figure 3.7 *Lithics*

This hoard of unused Neolithic, polished flint axes from a Danish bog illustrates a high level of knapping skill. The drawn record of these daggers would aim to show size, shape, thickness and the method of manufacture including direction of flaking.

technology, manufacturing and what they were used to process. Artefacts can be sorted by type of stone, colour and **typology**. Most hard stone has been used at some point in the past and lithics also include related materials such as obsidian (volcanic glass) and flint. Specialists will use reference material for relative dating and suggestion of function. Amongst the common classifications of stone tools are core (where a tool has been made by removing material) and flake (where a tool has been made from a fragment struck off a core). A blade is a long flake where the length is more than double the width and thus has a very long cutting edge. Microliths are made by snapping a blade to form tiny, rough, triangular shapes. These were used in the Mesolithic to make barbs for harpoons and in the Neolithic as edges for sickles. Arrowheads are classed as projectile points as we are sometimes not certain that they were not small spear tips, while tools which are flaked on two sides to get a sharp edge (e.g. hand-axes) are called bifaces.

The method of manufacture tells us much about the skills of the maker and the technology involved. The earliest tools (**Oldowan**) from around 2.5 mya (million years ago) (▶ p. 196) were stones from which a few chips had been removed by striking the core with a hammer-stone to give a sharp edge. This technique is called direct percussion and for most of human history this was the only technique. The angle of impact determines how much of the core is flaked off and whether the flake is thick or thin. More control over flaking is gained by using a punch between the core and the hammer-stone. This is indirect percussion. Striking with a soft hammer such as antler can produce thinner flakes than with stone, while tiny flakes can be removed by pressing with antler or wood in what is known

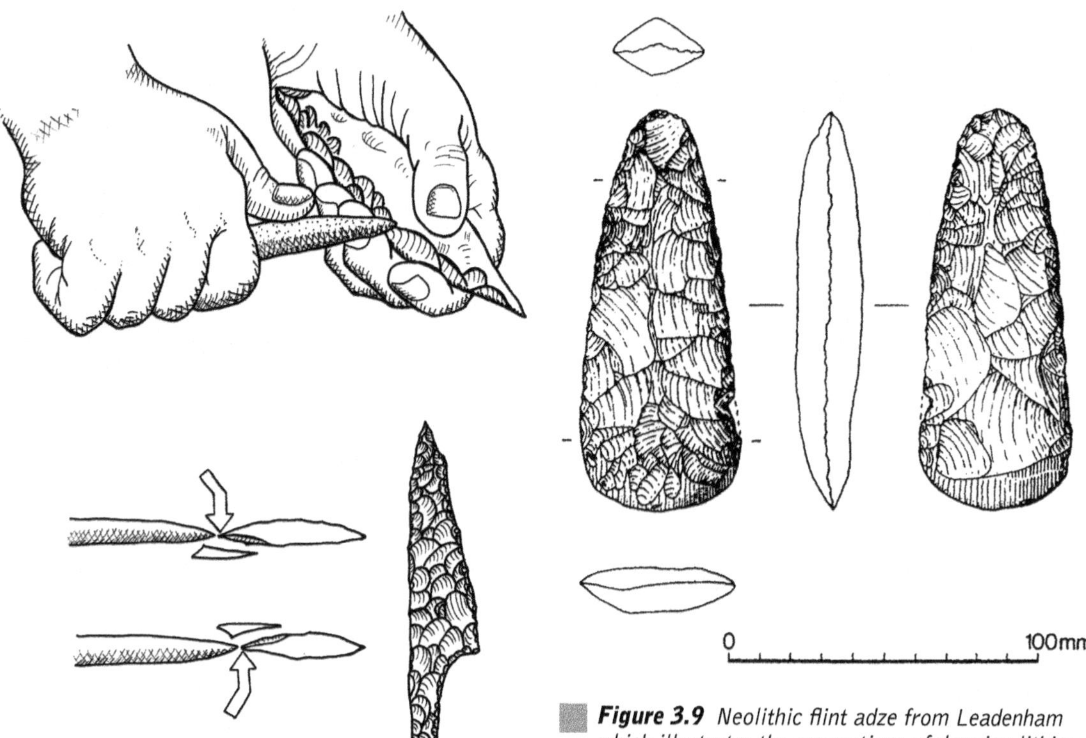

Figure 3.9 *Neolithic flint adze from Leadenham which illustrates the conventions of drawing lithics. (Archaeological Services WYAS)*

Figure 3.8 *Pressure flaking*

Pressing with bone or antler will prise thin flakes away from a part-finished artefact to gain greater definition or sharpness. Recording of markings on the artefact would enable researchers to understand how this technique had been used.

as pressure flaking. A second manufacturing technique is polishing. An artefact might be roughly shaped by chipping and then its surface would be ground using an abrasive such as sand and water. Using this painstaking method, stone jewellery and polished stone axes were manufactured from the Neolithic onwards. With the addition of a drill (▶ p. 182), this method was adapted to make sockets and to bore holes through stone.

Examination of their surface can determine whether lithics were manufactured by flaking, pecking or polishing the original stone. Reference to experimental or ethnographic examples (▶ p. 180) can explain how the techniques were carried out and also suggest how the artefacts were used. Manufacturing debris (debitage) such as flakes or chips is of particular value. It provides evidence of raw materials, the production process and the tools used. Sometimes debitage can be refitted to show the exact sequence of manufacturing (▶ p. 61). The surfaces of stone artefacts will often bear scratches, chips and polishes from their use. For example, half an hour cutting cereals will leave a polish on a flint blade very different from the use-wear from cutting bone. Use-wear studies (microwear analysis) combine microscope examination with information from experimental archaeology to try to identify the signatures (▶ p. 176) of past activities. However, this may only reveal the last activity the tool was used for. The detection and description of wear marks is greatly enhanced by the use of a scanning electron microscope (SEM). This sweeps a band of electrons over the surface of the tool and gives much improved depth of focus and higher magnification. This enhanced image can then be displayed on a screen. Examples include the study of starch grains on stone blades and the analysis of blood residues on some of the equipment carried by Ötzi the Ice Man (▶ p. 104). In some cases DNA analysis can tell us which animal the blood came from.

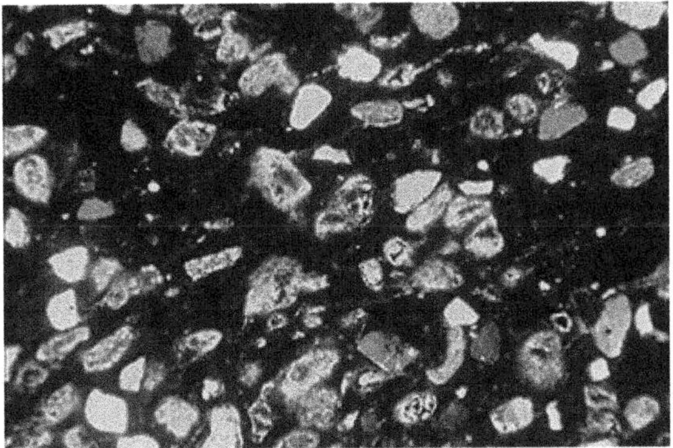

Figure 3.10 *Thin section from an amphora found at Amarna (▶ p. 405) in Egypt*

The clay fabric (Amana Fabric 1) of this vessel contains chalk, limestone and quartz sand inclusions which enabled it to be sourced to the coast of Israel or Lebanon. Tiny quantities of basalt and chert enabled refinement of the location to the Jezreel Valley where identical vessels have been found. (Dr Paul T. Nicholson)

Characterisation

The exact type of raw material and sometimes its precise source is determined through characterisation studies. These are based on identifying the elements and mineral structure within the material. Sometimes the distinctive colour and shape crystals of each mineral can be seen using handheld magnifiers but in other cases specialist equipment is required.

Petrology

This is a geological technique developed for identifying and locating the source of minerals. A small sample of a stone artefact is cut and then glued onto a glass slide and ground and polished till it is about 0.03mm thick. At this point it is transparent and the thin section is examined under a polarising microscope. This highlights colour contrasts between minerals by filtering out particular lightwaves. Its high-resolution image also enables distinctions to be made by degree of transparency, texture shape and the nature of fractures. Thin sections of pottery can also be studied to provide information about manufacturing techniques. By identifying particular combinations of key minerals, the original source of lithics and ceramics (▶ p. 368) can be established with reference to geological maps. The technique can be used for building materials including stone and, in some cases, brick. It has been used extensively in Egypt to identify the quarries (▶ p. 370) used to build the temples at Karnak and the pyramid complex at Giza. Extensive studies which plot the locations of finds of the same material have helped us understand ancient trade patterns (▶ p. 402). For instance, the sources for the early medieval period trade in lava quernstones throughout north-west Europe have been traced back to quarries in the Eifel Mountains of Germany (▶ p. 409). Petrology does not work in all cases. Thin sections of obsidian and flint look remarkably similar regardless of where they originated. Similarly any ceramics which lack distinctive mineral tempers will require other techniques in order to source them. While petrology has been the most widely used means of characterising lithics, other techniques (▶ p. 131) are increasingly used.

Ceramics

Like lithics, materials of fired clay survive well in most environments and are found on most archaeological sites from the Neolithic onwards. Ceramics are often the most numerous surviving artefacts. They provide dating evidence and are used to make inferences about exchange, economy and society. The earliest fired clay artefacts actually come from the Gravettian period of the

Figure 3.11 *Prehistoric pottery making*

These pictures illustrate the process of local pottery manufacture in much of prehistory. Local clay would be mixed with a variety of tempers (a) which might include grit, chaff, shell or the remains of previous vessels. Mineral inclusions will be the key to sourcing the pot for archaeologists. After kneading, the pot shape is formed by coiling (b). This can be detected by examining sherds in cross-section. The vessel is smoothed and decoration is applied – in this instance using cord or shell impressions but twigs, feathers and fingernails were also used (c). These marks are clearly seen through a microscope. Finally the pot would be fired in a bonfire.

Upper Palaeolithic *c.* 30,000 BP in the form of figurines (▶ p. 220), with the earliest pottery developed by Jōmon hunter-gatherers in Japan by 12,000 BP. Bowls and other vessels to process and store food were manufactured by Neolithic farmers in both the Middle East and Far East *c.* 10,000 BP and the technology spread with farming.

Wet clay is a plastic material which means that it can be moulded into a greater variety of shapes than stone, from miniature animals through cups and plates to amphorae. Firing in bonfires and kilns transformed clay into a hard material. Early pots often had rounded bottoms which may have been to help them survive firing. In order to give the clay strength and prevent it from shrinking and cracking or exploding during firing, tempering materials were added at an early stage. These vary hugely between time and place and include shell, sand, grit, plant fibres and grog (crushed pottery fragments). Before firing, the pottery was usually sun-dried to remove moisture. Early firing in a bonfire, pit or kiln produced earthenware at between 900 and 1000°C. This slightly porous, 'biscuit-like' (terracotta) pottery was similar to modern flowerpots. The clay often changed colour depending on the minerals within it. From the earliest periods, ceramics were decorated for symbolic or artistic reasons. The simplest embellishments involved incising or stamping the pottery with bone, fingers or flint or impressing it with cord. Burnishing involves rubbing the pot before firing with a hard material to produce a polished finish. Coloured clays or other additives varied the colour of the final product or produced patterns.

Figure 3.12 *Key concept – 'type site' artefact styles are normally named after the site where they were first recognised (a 'type-site'). This early Minoan (▶ p. 256) Myrtos-style jug is named after the Neolithic settlement at Myrtos on Crete. The fabric and the decoration of red lines on light background are clear and it would not require further typological analysis.*

Glazing probably developed as a form of decoration but also helped make earthenware watertight so that it could hold and store liquids. A material is dusted over or brushed onto the finished pot, sometimes after an initial firing. When fired it fuses with the pot and covers the surface with a glassy coating and new range of colour. The development of more advanced kilns during the 2nd millennium BC enabled the production of stoneware. At temperatures from 1,100 to 1,300°C, the clay and glaze fused to produce a harder, glass-like ceramic. In China *c.* AD 600 a further development involved mixing white kaolin with powdered granite and firing it between 1,200 and 1,400°C to make the fine 'china' called porcelain. Manufacture by hand was slow and each pot looked different. The 'slow wheel' invented in the early Bronze Age before 3000 BC allowed the coiled pot to be spun easily by hand on a wooden turntable during manufacture to finish it. The development of a fast

Figure 3.13 *Sorting pottery according to attributes. The obvious useful attributes are material (fabric, colour, texture), morphology (form, including size, shape, design, etc.), and style (more elusive – including design, decoration, etc.).*

wheel which spun on an axle enabled lumps of pottery to be 'thrown' into desired shapes quickly and without using coils. It was powered by a large, parallel 'kick-wheel' below the bench on the same axle, with a fly-wheel being a later refinement. Wheel-thrown pottery could be mass produced, although the range of shapes is more restricted.

Analysis of ceramics

To categorise sherds, colour is described by reference to the Munsell Soil Colour Charts. There are similar charts for hardness and the grain size of inclusions in the temper. Such analysis may require the use of polarising microscopes. Manufacturing by hand, coil or wheel methods can usually be determined visually, as can form. The key indicators here are sherds from the rim, neck and base of vessels. Experts on regional pottery can usually quickly identify the type and form and often suggest the origin of artefacts from microscopic examination of the temper and inclusions in the fabric. Where possible pots are reassembled by specialists for recording (▶ p. 90).

In many cases, analysis is helped by data from refiring experiments and ethnography (▶ p. 180), which can provide insights into manufacturing techniques. The fabric colour and hardness provide clues to firing temperatures. Clay often contains iron, which forms a red oxide if it is heated in an oxygen-rich environment or a black/grey oxide if it is oxygen-poor. The colour of the molecules of clay indicates which was the case. If the clay is vitrified (where minerals have melted and fused together), it indicates that firing occurred in a kiln at temperatures in excess of 1100°C. Slips and glazes provide additional clues to origins and period.

In quantifying pottery finds there is debate amongst archaeologists over whether the number or weight of sherds is more useful. On most sites it is rare to recover entire pots either intact or in pieces. A large urn may break into several large but heavy pieces while a small pot may shatter into many small, light fragments. Depending on which measure is chosen, the results can be widely different. Good practice is to record both weight and number of sherds for each fabric and form. Weight used in conjunction with average

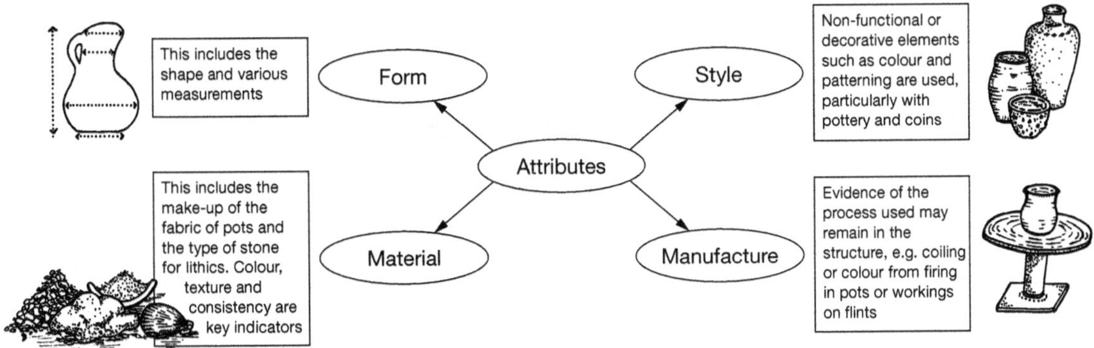

Figure 3.14 *Examples of attributes which could be used to sort material*

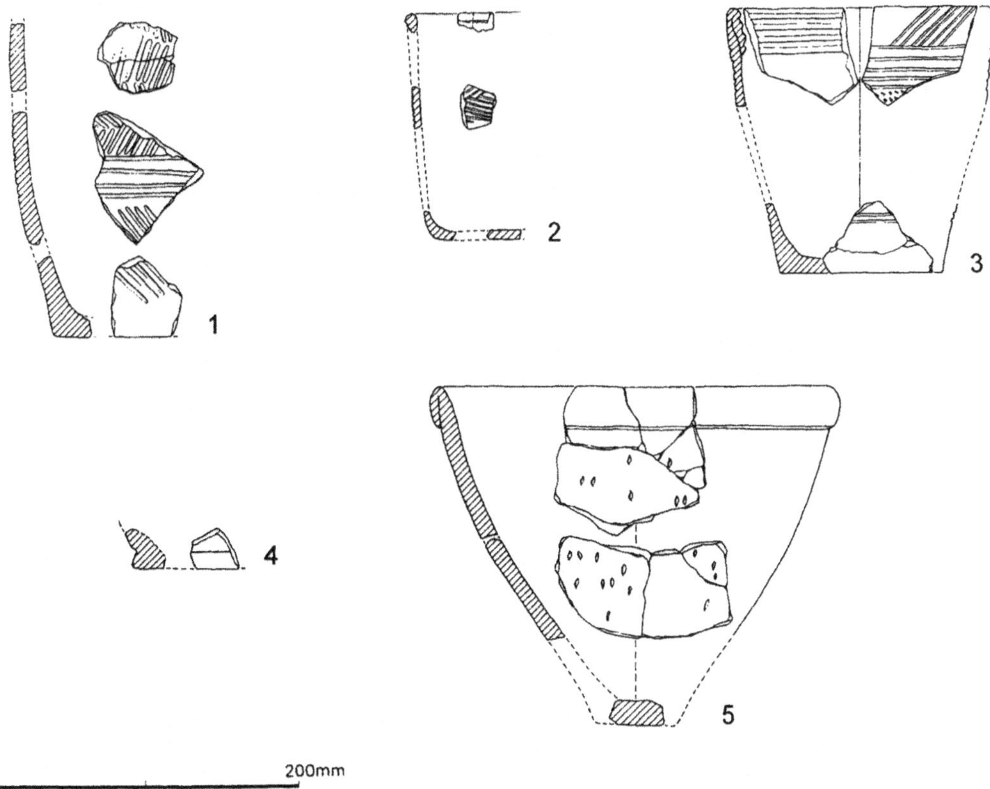

Figure 3.15 *The standard way to record and illustrate ceramics*

The whole vessel is drawn in outline but the left side is a cross-section to show internal and external shape and dimensions. Sometimes the area of decoration is limited to the area of the actual sherds recovered, as in this example of prehistoric pottery from Leadenham. (Archaeological Services WYAS)

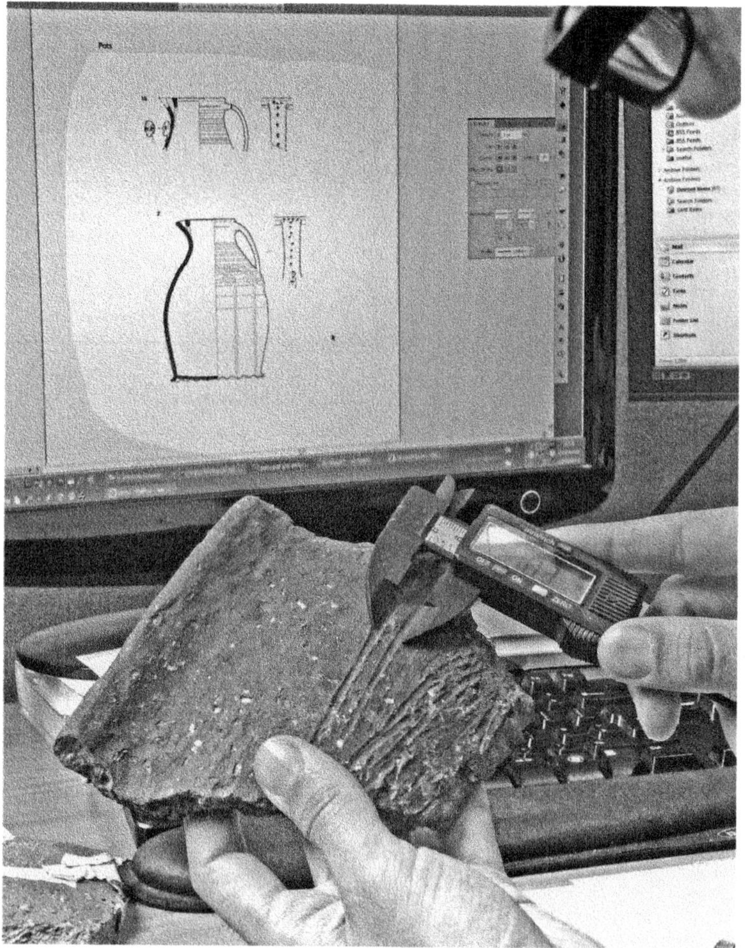

Figure 3.16 *Producing digital records*

Increasingly drawings are produced digitally. In this instance the ceramic vessel has been measured using calipers and a profile gauge and the basic image is then scanned into a PC for refinement (Cotswold Archaeology). In some cases (▶ p. 175) laser scanning is employed to ensure no detail is missed.

sherd weight can be used to reduce variability caused by different sizes of vessels. Various attempts have also been made to work out 'estimated vessel equivalents' (EVE) or 'minimum number of vessels' (MNV). Techniques vary from counting elements which only occur once such as the base to dividing the total angles of rim sherds by 360 degrees.

Clay is almost entirely formed from eroded sedimentary rocks, but a tiny percentage of the material is made up of trace elements. Petrology and other scientific characterisation techniques (▶ p. 131) can be applied to pottery and bricks, although 'fingerprinting' clay sources is much more difficult and less developed than is the case with stone.

Metals

Metal tools are the third type of inorganic artefacts which are commonly found on archaeological sites but are usually much rarer than either

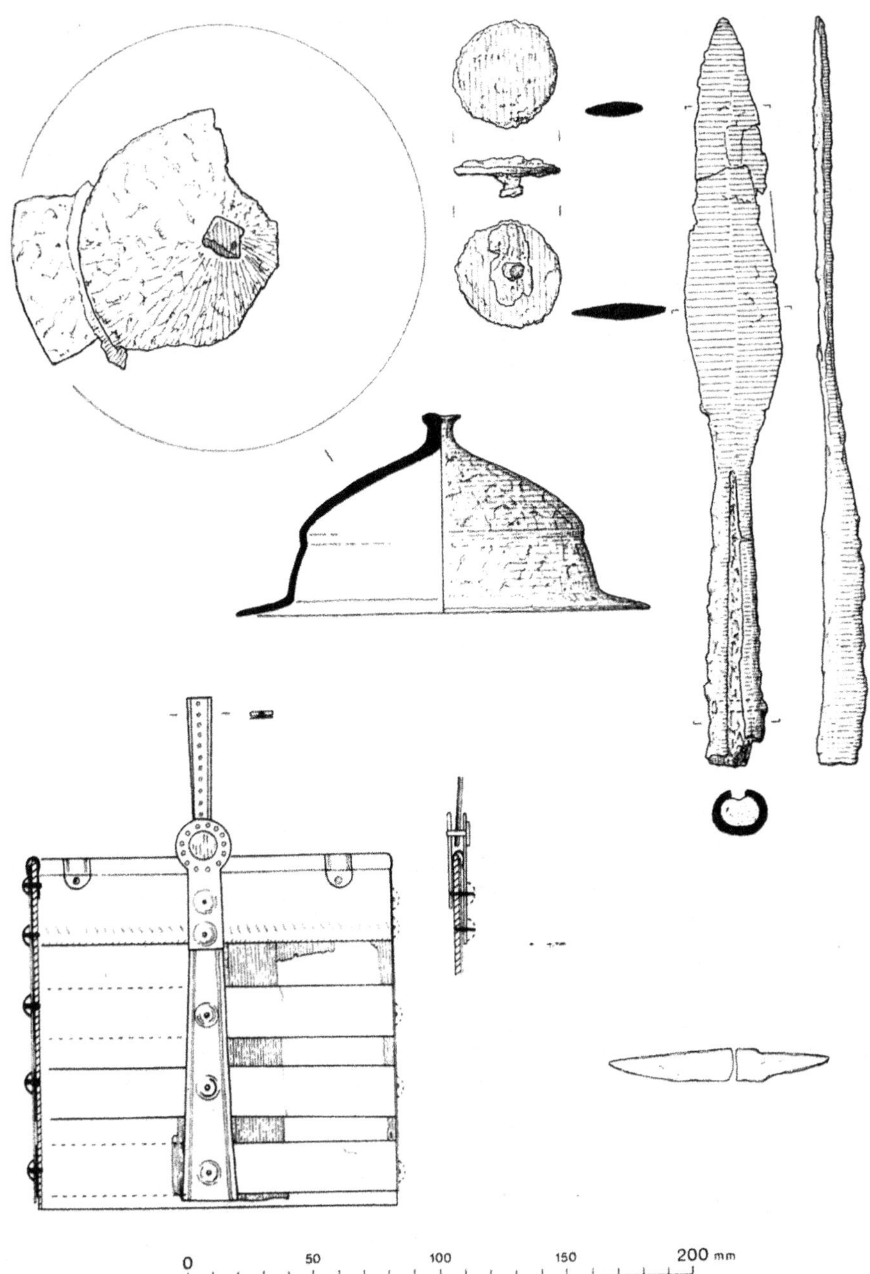

Figure 3.17 *Anglo-Saxon grave goods from Empingham*

This illustrates many of the conventions for drawing inorganic artefacts. The shield boss is shown partly reconstructed as with pottery. The button and spear are shown in several views so that shape is communicated. Compare this with the photographs and grave plans (▶ p. 76). Aside from the bucket this might look like a warrior grave. However, there is some evidence that such grave goods were a mark of ethnic identity in the early medieval period rather than a direct link with what a person did (▶ p. 432).

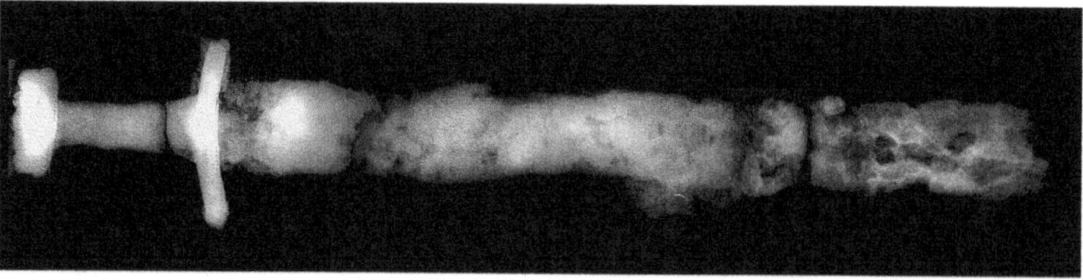

Figure 3.18 *X-ray of the corroded Viking sword from the C10th Port an Eilean Mhòir ship burial. (Ardnamurchan Transitions Project)*

stone or ceramics. This is because metal is scarce and harder to work and also because some metals decay easily. Iron and zinc, for example, corrode in most soils whereas gold and silver survive well. Conservation includes careful treatment to remove corrosion. The development of metallurgy is covered in Chapter 10.

Metallurgical analysis

Some metal artefacts, particularly those which are badly corroded, may be X-rayed. This can enable the object to be identified, to clarify markings on the surface and to identify cracks or seams where several pieces of metal were joined to form complex artefacts. Used in stereo, X-rays can give a 3D view of an object and reveal elements of the construction techniques and process such as pattern welding in swords: the manufacture of iron sword blades often involved hammering folded layers of metal. This process can also be detected by examining a cross-section of the blade with a powerful microscope. **Metallography** includes examination of the size and shape of the grains of minerals in the material for traces of heating, working and alloying. Where they are available, SEMs are preferred. Their magnification at 1000x may be similar to the best optical microscopes but the depth of field they provide enables fine detail to be identified. This is particularly important when exploring the manufacturing techniques used in jewellery making. Once identified, most or all individual metal artefacts would be drawn as part of the site archive. Metalworking waste is often equally important to understanding a site. Slag, crucibles and, if metalworking has occurred, then soil samples (▶ p. 381) may have been taken to analyse residues.

Figure 3.19 *Early medieval pattern welded sword blade. The blade has been formed by welding two twisted rods of metal with the twists running in opposite directions to give a herringbone effect. A steel cutting-edge was then welded on.*

Figure 3.20 Bloom. Finds of material from various stages in the production of metals are crucial to understanding manufacturing technology. In this experiment the cooling metal or bloom is being lifted out of the furnace leaving slag behind.

While most metal artefacts will initially go to a 'small finds specialist', coins are a particularly specialised area of study. For example, Roman coins can be used as an approximate form of dating and have been used to explore topics as diverse as trade, territories and particular events. All excavations will have a contact who is a coin expert to interpret the images and inscriptions on their surfaces. Coins were formed by stamping or hammering a metal disc using two engraved metal dies.

ANALYSIS OF ORGANIC MATERIALS

Site reports usually feature chapters produced by individual experts in plants, various types of animal remains and soils and are largely concerned with detailed visual examination and comparison with reference material. In some cases the surfaces of objects are laser-scanned to create a 3D image which can reveal tool marks, for example axe marks on timber. X-rays are also occasionally used to understand hidden aspects of artefacts such as the stitching of leather shoes or to examine remains that have been block-lifted prior to micro-excavation. With major research projects there has been an increasing trend to use a battery of lab-based analytical methods. These are often delivered by multidisciplinary teams – for instance, in bioarchaeology – based at a few well-equipped universities or commercial companies.

Organic artefacts

Organic artefacts include anything made from something that was once alive like an animal or plant and includes wood, hair, shell and leather. They are far rarer on excavated sites than those made of stone and clay because they decay. Inevitably this has distorted our view of the past because so much material culture is invisible to us. For many periods in the past most artefacts and structures were made of organic material. Sites where organic finds survive in large amounts are unusual and in some cases may not be 'typical' sites (▶ p. 171). They are often waterlogged or underwater, frozen (▶ p. 104), dessicated (dry) or in preserving chemicals as in a salt mine (▶ p. 373). However, they do provide tantalising glimpses of the skills, culture and economics of the periods in the past from which they came (▶ p. 267). Occasionally traces of organic artefacts can be found as impressions on other materials. This is the case with textile impressions in metal corrosion at Illerup (▶ p. 483) and on ceramics at Dolni Vestonici (▶ p. 218). Organic materials may also be mineralised (▶ p. 388) in the same way that bone becomes fossilised. Organic material is broken down by bacteria and replaced by minerals such as calcium from the surrounding soil.

Like other textiles, leather survives only in anaerobic conditions. Leather was one of the most important materials before the industrial revolution and was used for clothing, artefacts, cordage and as part of major structures from boats to

Figure 3.21 *Medieval leather shoe from waterlogged deposits in Dublin*

housing. Survival of artefacts from medieval towns such as Dublin and York enables an understanding of the leather trade, clothing and the exploitation of animals (▶ p. 294). The earliest woven fabrics used thread from plants such as nettle (▶ p. 389) and flax. Grasses and lime bast were also used for some items before wool became widely used in the later Neolithic and Bronze Age.

Ötzi the Ice Man

The amazing discovery of an ice mummy of a Copper Age man from the Alps has been one of the greatest single archaeological discoveries of all time. While his individual story is fascinating, it is his technology which is staggering. Aside from a few tools and weapons, his possessions were largely organic. They include items we may have glimpsed at Mesolithic sites (▶ p. 383) but nowhere has this technology been as fully revealed. His clothes were designed to trap air as those of a modern mountaineer would but he used animal and plant fibres rather than Gore-tex™. His hat was bearskin and bear was also used for the lower part of his boots, deerskin providing the uppers. The boots were stuffed with grass for insulation. He wore a kind of vest, leggings and other clothes made of leather and topped it off with a woven grass cape. In a pouch on his belt were several fungi including one which may have been medicinal and another which was part of the kind of fire-lighting kit which was in use till modern times. He had a rucksack on his back made from a U-shape birch frame and plant fibre netting and carried two birch-bark containers. Besides a copper axe, he had a bow, arrows from a variety of trees and a quiver with a flap to keep the arrows dry.

Figure 3.22 *Textiles. This Bronze Age burial from a Danish bog contained a full set of clothes made from plant and animal fibres.*

Figure 3.23 *Ötzi the Ice Man*

Ongoing post-excavation research has continued to provide surprises. The latest news is that not only was Ötzi shot with an arrow, but he may also have been finished off with blows to the head. The latest forensic techniques have suggested that he may have lost consciousness from blood loss and either hit his head on a rock or someone else hit him with one. Someone also appears to have pulled the arrow shaft from his shoulder. His body has provided an insight into life at the time. His various injuries and ailments and the treatments he received – including acupuncture – suggest a difficult existence. However, sourcing the materials he carried including both plant remains and lithics reveals a society where people did move beyond their village and may have had links over a great distance. Isotope analysis of his teeth and of plant remains on his clothes suggests he came from northern Italy but he was a long way from home when he died. Pollen from the hop-hornbeam tree which he had ingested while eating suggested that he died in early summer. Ötzi himself had dangerous levels of arsenic in his hair from working copper. For the first time we have a definite example of one of the mysterious metalsmiths (▶ p. 391) who were transforming material culture.

Soil

Geoarchaeology is the study of preserved soils and the natural and human processes which created them. It combines organic chemistry with geology to understand the components and structure of soil. Microscopic analysis of the make-up and fabric of soil is called micromorphology.

Soil structure and content can be examined microscopically by creating thin sections in a specialist laboratory. A sample is impregnated with a polyester resin to bond it and then cut into 1cm slices. These are ground flat and bonded to a slide, then lapped (ground down) to a translucent thickness of 30–40μm and then polished with oil. The slide can then be analysed using petrological polarising microscopes and images recorded as photomicrographs. The specialist will record the soil texture in terms of the relative quantities of particles of sand (small), silt and clay (large). Colour is noted as this is indicative of mineral content and how well the soil drains. Orange, browns and yellow soils, for example, are often indicative of high iron contents. The shape of clusters of soil particles (peds) varies from plates to columns to balls with different-shaped and -sized gaps (pores) between them which hold water, air and organisms. These peds and pores make up the soil structure and will vary according to their composition, how they were formed and their history. For example, a surface that has been repeatedly walked over will have a slightly different structure from surrounding soils with identical composition.

Soil can provide clues to the type of vegetation and, by extension, the fauna and agriculture it could support. The early farmers in central Europe, for example, seemed to favour particular soil types (loess – a fine glacial soil deposited by the wind) for their farming settlements. Soil change can also record site formation processes (▶ p. 165), such as the impact of humans on the land. Sediments in valleys in Cyprus were analysed to explain the abandonment of Bronze Age sites. Deforestation or overgrazing had led to erosion of the topsoil on the hillsides which had then been deposited in the valleys. Understanding sedimentary profiles is essential to interpretation of phasing, dating and the way archaeological sites changed over time. Chemical analysis (▶ p. 136) as well as observation is important when 'reading' the story in a soil column sample. Ash, humic fills and enhanced nitrogen levels may be indicative of human enriching of soils (plaggen cultivation) using burning and manure in order to improve yields (▶ p. 356). Conversely, poor mineral levels where leaching has taken place and peats may indicate over-exploitation and the creation of iron pans (▶ p. 242).

At a microscopic level, soil is also analysed for what it holds. Pollen, invertebrates and even microbes can be recovered to provide clues about environment and economy. Soils differ in their ability to preserve materials. Pollen survives well in acidic contexts whereas alkaline environments are better for snail shells. Micromorphology can provide clues to different activities in rooms or areas on sites, the nature of deposits on the floors of caves and whether fields were manured. Analysis of the content of graves can reveal traces of clothing, organic artefacts, disease and the mortuary treatment of the body.

Dry sites sometimes also provide coprolites (preserved faeces). Analysis of these can recover hair, bone, seed and parasites to reveal information about diet and health. Analysis of sewage deposits from the latrines at Bearsden Roman Fort, Scotland (Dery 1997), revealed little trace of cholesterol, suggesting that the legionaries ate little meat. Instead there were large quantities of cereal bran from wheat. Foreign grain insects suggested that much of this had been imported. Beans, lentils, figs and some of the herbs they had used to flavour meals were also imported as they did not grow in Britain. The supply of food from Europe and the Mediterranean to these legionaries testifies to the sophistication of Roman logistics. However, the soldiers also gathered wild fruit and nuts to supplement their rations.

Figure 3.24 *A latrine at Housesteads fort*

Analysis of soil at similar sites has provided valuable evidence about the diets of legionaries.

Faunal remains

Zooarchaeology is the study of the remains of animals from archaeological contexts. Faunal (which includes fish and birds as well as mammals) remains are vital to archaeologists in two

Figure 3.25 *Animal bones after washing*

Figure 3.26 *Processed deer shoulder blade*

This bone has had a circular section cut away with a flint tool to make a ring for personal decoration. Evidence of large-scale production of rings at the Mesolithic site of Ringkloster (▶ p. 316) provides an insight into the range of uses to which animals were put as well as being a source of food. It also indicates a degree of specialisation and probably exchange.

ways: to reconstruct past environments (▶ p. 127) and to identify the contribution which animals made to human diets and economy (▶ p. 294). Most dead animals which are excavated were processed either by humans or by other animals and so remains are usually fragmentary.

The mineral element in bones can survive well in alkaline soils such as sand or gravel. Acid soils usually dissolve all but burnt bone, although in certain conditions bone collagen can sometimes be recovered. Waterlogged, arid and frozen sites provide the best preservation. This means that some sites may have vast amounts of bone, such as West Stow (▶ p. 494), where two tons were recovered, whilst others have very little. This bias applies to different types of bone. Larger bones and teeth enamel survive far longer than small bones. Similarly tiny fish and bird bones do not survive as well as cattle bones. Even where they survive, they are rarely recovered unless sieving or flotation is used or soil samples are taken. As a result, their importance in the past is often underestimated (▶ p. 309).

Identification and enumeration

The first task for bone specialists is to identify the type of bones and then the species of animal from which they came. Mammals have similar numbers and types of bones, so reference collections supplement the expert's knowledge. This also applies to fish and birds. To understand the significance of particular species in an **assemblage**, the number of animals represented has to be determined. However, it is rare for complete skeletons to be recovered, so several different ways of counting the bones of each species are used:

- NISP. The number of identified specimens (bone fragments) present. However, only parts of some animals may have been taken to a site.
- Weight. This is biased to animals with heavier bones.
- MNI. Minimum number of individuals. Working out the smallest number of animals which could produce the assemblage. This can be done by counting bones, or parts of bones, which only occur once; for example, the skull or pelvis or the distal (furthest from the body) end of the right femur. So, for instance, three bovine left femurs must indicate at least three different animals.

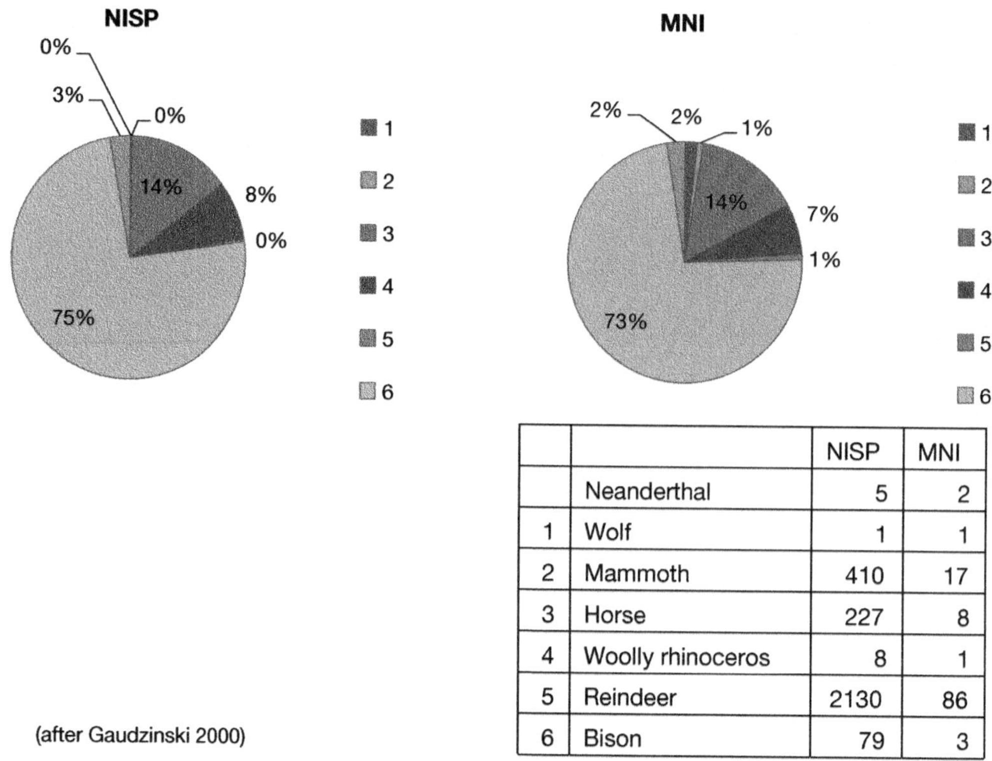

		NISP	MNI
	Neanderthal	5	2
1	Wolf	1	1
2	Mammoth	410	17
3	Horse	227	8
4	Woolly rhinoceros	8	1
5	Reindeer	2130	86
6	Bison	79	3

Figure 3.27 *Counting the faunal assemblage at the Neanderthal site of Salzgitter-Lebenstadt from c. 55,000 BP. The proportions vary slightly depending on the method used; e.g. the single wolf bone does not register on the 'individual specimen' count but does on the 'individuals present'.*

The raw data only shows the relative abundance of a particular species, not how important it was to people and their economy. There is more meat on a cow than on a sheep, so while the MNI for sheep may be greater than for cows, they may contribute much less to the overall diet. Several additional measures have been developed to assess dietary contribution such as meat weight versus bone weight. A further complication arises when we consider the body elements that are present. Some animals may not have been slaughtered on site and bones that are low in meat, such as the spine and feet, may have been discarded off site rather than dragged back to base. This is common in hunting societies and is sometimes called the 'Schlep Effect'.

Careful examination of butchery marks can reveal the process by which animal bone reached the site of deposition, particularly when compared with modern butchers' techniques. Marks might include cuts at the ends of bones where joints were separated, scraping marks on long bones where flesh was removed or on the fronts of skulls which might indicate skinning. Broken and split bones suggest that everything was being processed including the marrow. In a C3rd Romano-British well at Empingham (▶ p. 35), Rutland, a single context provided evidence of the 'butchery waste bones' (skulls, jaws, lower limb bones) of seventeen sheep, indicating that these animals had been slaughtered and roughly butchered on site with the meat-bearing bones

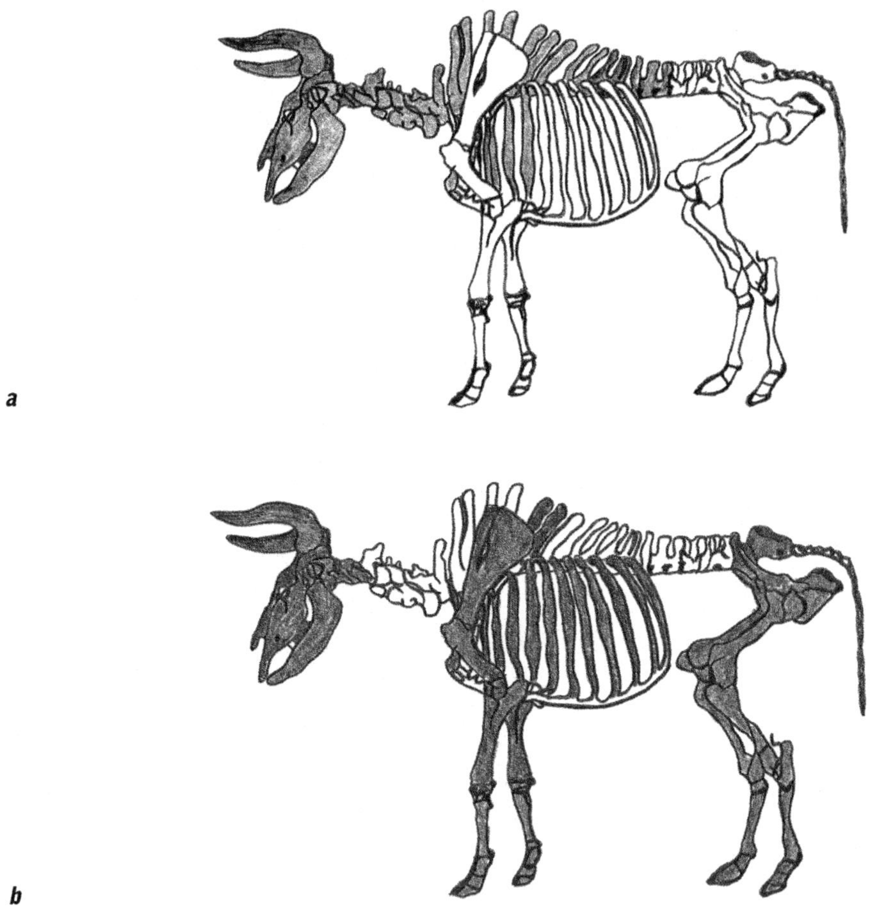

Figure 3.28 *The Schlep Effect: two Auroch from (a) Potsdam Schlaatz and (b) Bedburg Konigshoven. The meat-bearing bones are all missing from (a), suggesting a kill site. With (b) only the spinal column has been discarded, suggesting that this was a home base where meat was consumed (after Rackham 1994).*

being taken away, presumably to market at Great Casterton.

Sexing and ageing specimens

The sex of bones can be identified from anatomical features such as antlers (deer), large canines (pig) and penis bone (dog) in males and pelvic shape and structure in females. The dimensions of bones can also be used as males are larger in many species. The ratio between two or more measurements from one bone is used rather than a single measure (e.g. length) as size may be dependent on the age of the animal. Identification of changes in the skeleton is useful for establishing age, especially patterns of teeth eruption, growth and wear and bone fusion. The ends of long bones are called epiphyses. In a young animal these are joined to the bone by cartilage. As the animal ages, this calcifies until, by a process known as epiphysial fusion, the ends and bones are joined. This allows adults and juveniles to be differentiated. Tooth eruption and antler shedding may also establish the season of death of the animals. However, such analysis is not always

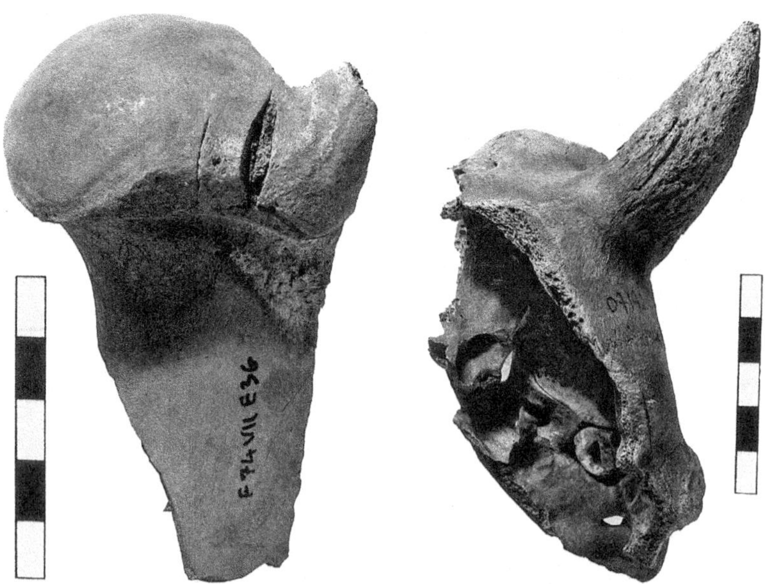

Figure 3.29 *Neolithic animal bone with evidence of human butchery. The cattle bone on the left has cut marks while the sheep skull on the right has been split open with a sharp tool.*

reliable, as bones may not have been deposited at the time the animals were killed. Note that Star Carr was thought to be a winter site from antler evidence, but recent discoveries of stork and crane bones suggest it was used in summer too. Antlers may have been accumulated over a long period and can therefore be unreliable as a guide to season of occupation (▶ p. 267). Other faunal remains used to investigate seasonality include the presence of migratory birds and fish such as geese or salmon.

Establishing the profile of age and sex of the animals represented in a bone assemblage can help reconstruct the system of hunting or agriculture practised (▶ p. 294). For example, the sex ratio and age structure in herds of cattle kept for dairy products are different from a beef herd. The dairying assemblage would be likely to feature many young animals and a few older ones, whereas the meat assemblage would comprise many young adult-sized animals. Kill ratios are indicative of particular strategies. An assemblage where the age and sex of dead animals will be the same as the make-up of a typical herd is called a 'catastrophic profile'. This is due to entire herds being killed through unselective hunting; for example, using stampedes (▶ p. 253). Over-representation of particular animals provides evidence of more selective hunting. Natural predators tend to pick off the old, young and sick and early human hunters were probably similar. This does not endanger the survival of the herd and creates an 'attritional bone profile'. Comparing profiles from related sites can also reveal the relationship between sites. In the Balkans, research from later Neolithic sites has shown some differences in sheep and goat profiles between high pasture sites and those in the valleys which may indicate seasonal patterns of movement (▶ p. 350). Assemblages can also indicate particular activities. Large amounts of bones which have not been fully processed are usually interpreted as evidence of feasting.

Animals provide clues to the environment, although we cannot always be certain that they occupied similar habitats to today's animals.

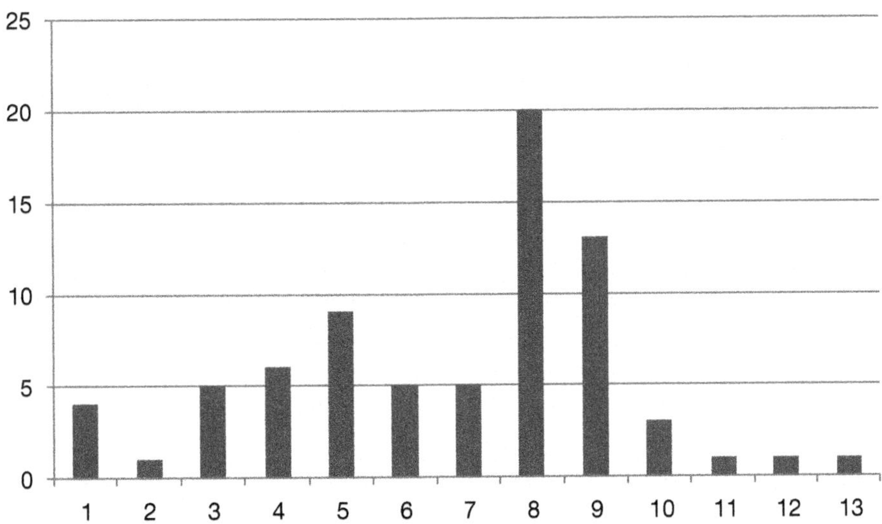

Figure 3.30 *Age profile of reindeer from Salzgitter-Lebenstadt. Numbers of individuals are on the left axis, ages on the bottom.*

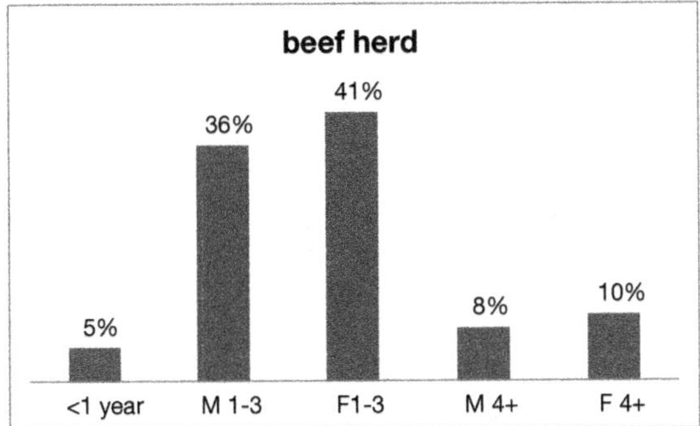

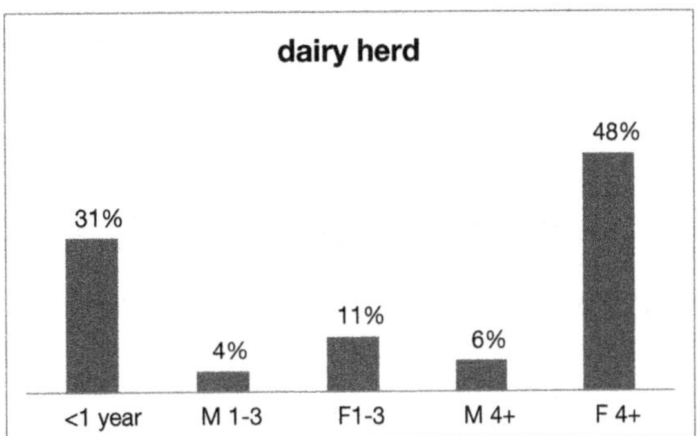

Figure 3.31 *Comparison of the faunal assemblage by age created by two types of herding practice (after Wilkinson and Stevens 2003). The profiles plot age of animals against the percentage of individuals in the assemblage.*

Bones can also provide insights into human behaviour. The spread of species may be related to trade or human migration. DNA research is also shedding light on the origins of modern animal species (▶ p. 317). Analysis of damage to bones provides data on hunting, butchery and craft technology (▶ p. 295). The Origins of Medieval Fishing Project (▶ p. 612) provides a major key study in what can be learned from faunal remains.

Human remains

Human remains can be divided into two major categories: hard and soft tissue. The evidence that these two types provide and the conditions in which they are preserved vary considerably.

Hard tissue

Bone is much more frequently recovered by archaeologists than soft tissue. Osteologists (human bone specialists) carry out similar analysis to that used on faunal remains to age and sex bones and determine the composition of entire assemblages of human remains. They will report on sex, age, stature and physical signs of illness, injury or genetic differences. Biochemical testing, such as isotope analysis (▶ p. 133) is carried out in specialist laboratories and only in some cases. Analysis begins with carefully recording measurements from individual bones. In particular the length and diameter of particular diagnostic bones are calculated to enable comparisons to be made between different groups. Stature is estimated from surviving long (preferably leg) bones and by comparing them with statistics from reference collections.

Sex and age

Like other apes (▶ p. 191), humans are sexually dimorphic with males generally having larger bones and teeth than females. However, there is widespread variation amongst adult humans including gracile (slender) males and robust females, which means that no physical method of sexing human remains is totally reliable. This is particularly the case if skeletons are incomplete. It is almost impossible to sex children. The best diagnostic bones are those making up the pelvis. Amongst several indicators, the pelvic gap (the space in the middle) is a wide oval shape in females (to allow childbirth) and narrower and vaguely heart-shaped in males. The sciatic notch at the bottom of the pelvis is wider in females and narrower in males. Male skulls tend to be more robust with heavier eyebrow ridges and larger mandibles (jaws). In general males are larger with more robust bones and more pronounced muscle attachments. However, this is only a general rule. Larger women who lived hard physical lives in the past would exhibit many of these features. DNA testing is accurate, but expensive.

For children and younger adults, the sequence of tooth eruption and the length and fusion of long bones (epiphysial fusion) usually means that age of death can be identified to within a couple of years. There are also changes in bone structure as we age, although microscopic analysis would be required to assess it. Adults over thirty are more difficult as there is no standard sequence of changes and the eruption of wisdom teeth can be protracted. Using wear on bones and teeth to estimate age for older individuals is also notoriously unreliable. Teeth wear depends on diet while skeletal signs of ageing such as arthritis are also related to activity and environment. Theya Molleson (Molleson et al. 1993) made a comparative study on the collection from Spitalfields Crypt, where the actual ages were known from the coffin plates. In the case of Louisa Courtauld, the archaeological estimate of her age using bone was wrong by over twenty years. However, a newer technique of thin-sectioning teeth, which relies on measuring the amount of translucence in the root, provided a much closer estimate. Most skeletal reports will provide a ten-year range or estimated age of death.

Health and physical trauma

Where a large sample of human bones is recovered, one can *start* to gain some tentative insights into age structure and health of the population. Specialists investigating the marks that injuries and diseases leave on bones in this field of palaeopathology are often trained doctors. Tooth decay and disease and osteoarthritis are the most commonly observed but leprosy, polio, tuberculosis, syphilis and various types of cancer can also affect bones. This also applies to genetic disorders such as cleft palate. Healed fractures are relatively common, along with torn muscle attachments. Early medical treatments such as trepanation (cutting or drilling a hole in the skull) can also sometimes be identified. Except in extreme cases, such as battlefield graves, it is usually impossible to give the precise cause of death. The major killer diseases in the past, particularly of children, such as measles, typhoid and cholera, struck quickly and left no mark on bones. The same is true for heart attacks and soft tissue wounds. Where large numbers of skeletons have been studied, it is

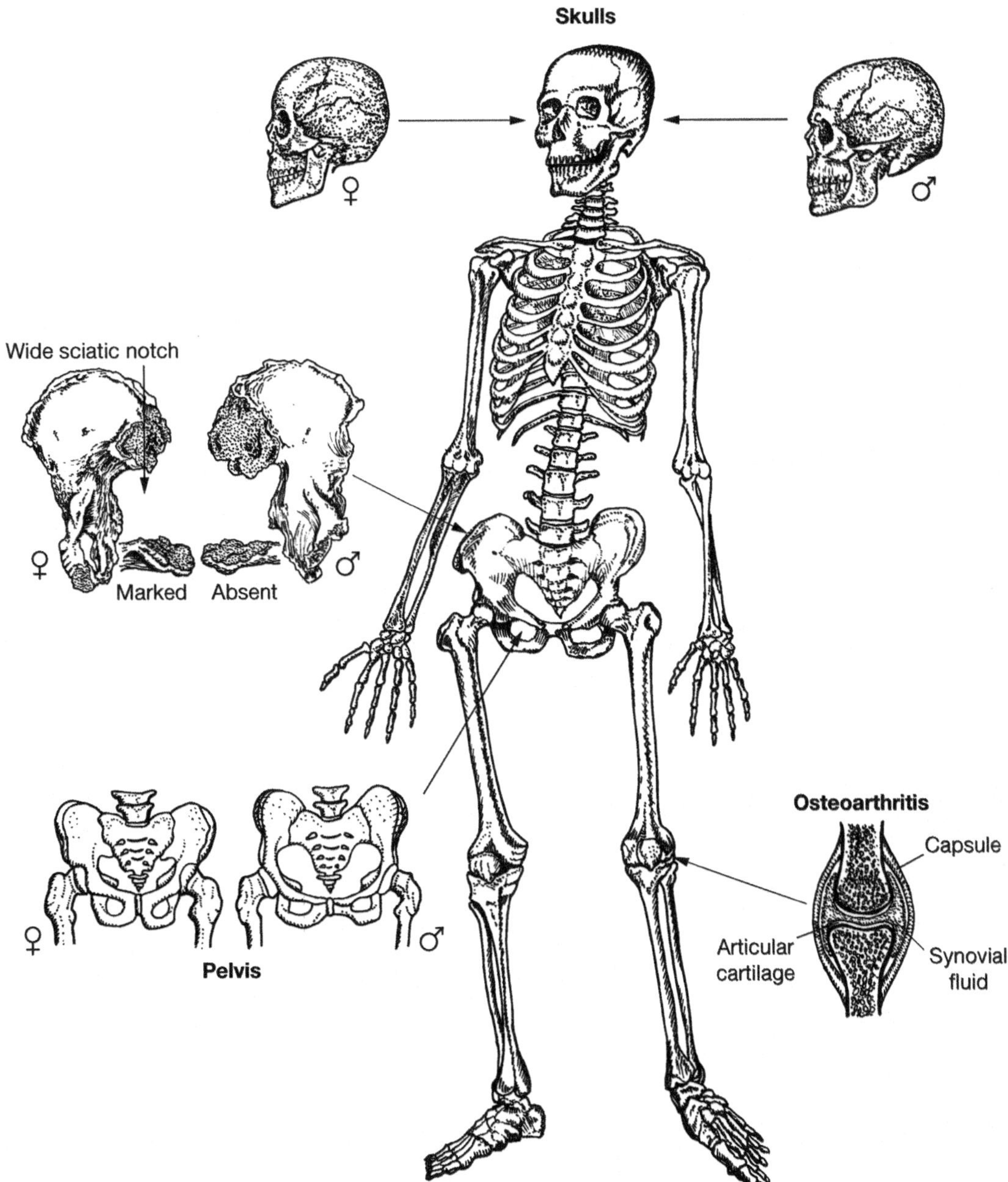

Figure 3.32 *Drawings of human skeleton*

The key parts of the skeleton used by archaeologists to sex and age the body are labelled. The close-up of the pelvis indicates the difference between the narrow arch of males and the wider arch in females. In the blade of the pelvis, below the socket for the hipbone (femur), is the sciatic notch. The rough 'rule of thumb' of the forensic anthropologist Rebecca Storey is, 'You stick your thumb in and if it wiggles it's female and if it doesn't it's male!' The skulls illustrate potential variation between male and female skulls, although there is more of a continuum here.

possible to start to construct tentative demographic profiles of the buried population. This can give insights into life expectancy, infant mortality, sex ratios and age structure, although conclusions are limited by the knowledge that not all of a population are ever buried in the same manner.

DNA can be extracted from both soft and hard tissue, including hair, but for archaeology bones and teeth are the main sources. DNA analysis (▶ p. 130) can be used to reveal information about health, origins, sex and relationships between individuals.

Lifestyle and diet

Evidence of trauma and wear on the bones can provide insights into lifestyle. For example, a shiny ulna or elbow joint is caused by bone rubbing on bone because the cartilage has been worn out by repetitive action. Possible activities which might cause this include rowing if both ulnae are affected or throwing spears if only one is affected. In the latter case the arm bone in question may be thicker than the other one as a result of greater activity; for example the right arms of archers from the *Mary Rose*. Damage to the skeleton through accidents, activities undertaken during life, murder and warfare injuries and even childbirth can all be evidenced by physical traces left on bone. Female skeletons at Tell Abu Hureyra (▶ p. 332) were shown to have traces of arthritis from using grindstones, while the murder of prisoners at the Battle of Towton (▶ p. 479) has recently been investigated through meticulous examination of skeletons from a pit near the battle site.

The main approach to diet relies upon studies of isotopic traces in bone (▶ p. 133). Particular diets such as one dependent on marine foods or one heavy in maize consumption will leave a signature in the bone collagen. Soil from the abdominal area of buried skeletons can be analysed for pollen and seeds which may have been in the stomach (▶ p. 120), while material may also be recovered from the gut of preserved bodies (▶ p. 104). Harris Lines – horizontal lines near the ends of long bones – are caused when growth is reduced during a period of stress and can provide evidence of periods of malnutrition or disease. Amongst farmers this is most likely immediately before the harvest period whereas foragers are often at risk in the late spring when

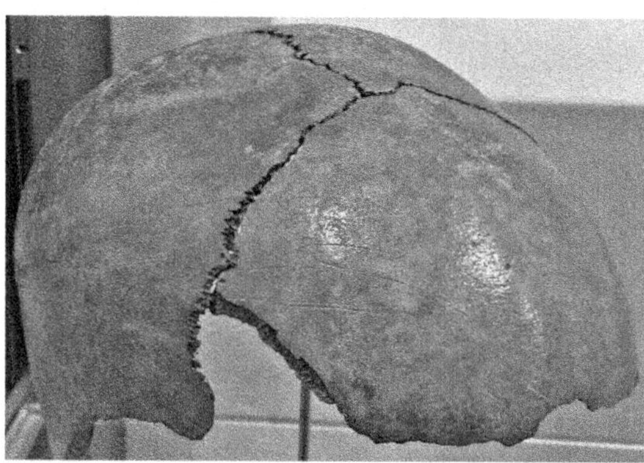

Figure 3.33 *Human cranium with cut-marks possibly from defleshing*

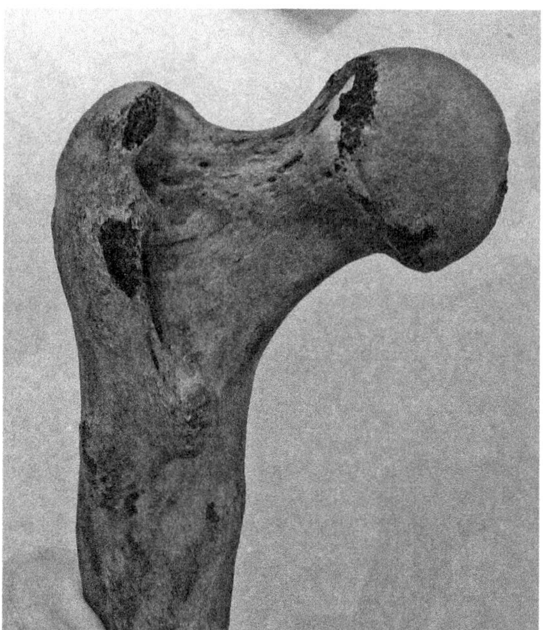

Figure 3.34 *Human hip joint with worn surfaces indicating arthritis and probably pain*

plant foods are in short supply. Similar, horizontal grooves in teeth enamel are known as enamel hypoplasia. Wear and damage to teeth can also be indicative of particular diets, such as from grit impurities left in flour, or from activities such as softening leather. Dental mutilation and cranial deformations (caused by binding the soft skulls of infants) give us insights into cultural practices.

Soft tissue

Like other organic remains, soft tissue is only usually recovered on sites with unusually good preservation. They are not likely to be a representative sample of the wider population but are useful none the less. With well-preserved bodies the same battery of investigations that are carried out in hospitals can be employed including X-ray, CAT scans and endoscopes with mini cameras.

Figure 3.35 *'Ginger'*

Nicknamed from his colour, this naturally mummified Egyptian from *c.* 3400 BC is testimony to the preserving power of arid conditions. The hot sand desiccated the body by absorbing its water content. As a dried out piece of leather, there was no moisture for the flesh-eating bacteria which cause decay. Ginger is surrounded by pre-Dynastic grave goods.

Desiccated bodies such as Egyptian mummies often preserve facial features well, if a little distorted from the drying process, together with internal organs, nails and hair. Accurate sexing of the body can usually be done from the external sexual organs, or from facial hair. There are always exceptions. 'Mummy 1770', which had probably spent some time in the Nile as a result of an unfortunate encounter with a crocodile, could not be sexed at the time of mummification by the priests. He/she was therefore prepared for either eventuality in the afterlife by being given both a false penis made of a roll of bandage and gold nipples. In addition to providing details of clothing and mortuary practices, tissue samples can be rehydrated to give useful evidence about disease; for example, the sand pneumoconiosis suffered by one of 'The Brothers' in Manchester Museum.

Frozen corpses provide similar evidence to dry bodies except that stomach contents are often preserved as well. The general level of distortion and decay is often so low that these bodies can almost seem asleep, not dead. The Peruvian Inca children are especially extraordinary in this respect. In one case the trauma that caused death – a blow to the head – could still be identified in a CAT scan. In another example the red-stained vomit from the symbolic 'achiote' dye that the child had been forced to ingest still marked his face and the front of his clothing. Without Ötzi's preserved skin, we would not have known about his tattoos, which may be the earliest evidence of medicinal acupuncture.

Bodies from anaerobic conditions such as the famous 'bog bodies' of northern Europe, including Lindow Man and Tollund Man, have been used to study diet, internal parasites and trauma. The acid nature of bogs can lead to the almost complete demineralisation of bone while tanning

KEY STUDY

Eulau: human remains and Neolithic relationships

The site

In 2005 a Neolithic burial site was discovered beside the River Saale in Germany. A cluster of four multiple burials was found, at least three of which had once been marked with ring ditches and possibly mounds. The thirteen undisturbed skeletons comprised five adults and eight children and were exceptionally well preserved. Distinctive styles of ceramics and axes plus the position of the bodies identified them as belonging to the Corded Ware Culture. Stratigraphic evidence suggested that all the bodies had been buried in one phase. They were quickly recognised as an unusual and important discovery and were excavated under controlled conditions by local state archaeologists from Saxony-Anhalt. DNA samples and teeth were extracted at the site by excavators wearing face masks and other protection against contamination. Those involved had their DNA tested as a control measure. Most of the finds were then block-lifted and taken back to the State Museum in Halle for micro-excavation. Samples were tested in several laboratories including DNA at Johannes Gutenberg University Mainz and strontium isotopes at Bristol University. The burials were radiocarbon dated to 4600 BP.

Context: Corded Ware Culture (CWC)

Corded ware (▶ p. 456) is a ceramic style found across central Europe north of the Danube from the Rhine to the Volga. The name comes from hemp or flax cord impressions on the pottery. Starting *c.* 2800 BC in the final Neolithic, it was in use in the early Chalcolithic to *c.* 2300 BC. It was contemporary with Bell-Beaker culture and in some regions is known as the Single Grave or Battle Axe Culture. CWC burials are quite common in the river valleys of northern Germany but finds of settlements are rare. Most of our knowledge comes from graves. CWC burials are usually flexed and facing south with male heads to the west and women to the east and the adults at Eulau followed this pattern. Eulau was unusual because of the simultaneous burial and the presence of children. Children were buried facing particular adults and in some cases appeared to have been placed in their arms or had interlinked arms.

Investigations

Radiocarbon dates for all the burials were effectively identical, which supported the phasing interpretation of them all being buried simultaneously. Male burials had stone axes while females had flint tools and animal-teeth jewellery. In grave 98 a boy was also buried in the male position with an axe. In each grave there was a deposit of butchered animal bones, which suggests food offerings were also part of the mortuary process. At least one adult and many of the children in each grave showed clear evidence of violent trauma which had caused their deaths. Wounds included damaged skulls and defensive 'parry' fractures to the left forearms, wrists and fingers. One female had two stone arrowheads lodged in her bones.

DNA evidence established the sex of several of the children and their genetic relationship to the adults. This appeared to have been reflected in burial positions with children facing relatives. In grave 99 both children were boys yet the way they were placed over-rode the normal gender rules in order to emphasise the family relationship. Both boys shared the Y halpogroup R1a with the man but the

Figure 3.36 *Grave 99 at Eulau. The drawing indicates the genetic relationships. (Landesamt für Denkmalpflege und Archäologie Sachsen-Anhalt, Andrea Hoerentrup (State Office for Heritage Management and Archaeology Saxony-Anhalt))*

Key: (1) ♂MtDNA Hg U. Y Hg RIa; (2) ♀MtDNA Hg K; (3) ♂MtDNA Hg K. Y Hg RIa; (4) ♂MtDNA Hg K. Y Hg RIa

MtDNA haplogroup K with the woman. Samples of tooth enamel were analysed to determine ratios of strontium isotopes. Soil samples from in and above the graves and from rodent bones from the site were used to provide controls. Data from enamel samples were compared with the controls and regional geological data. It showed conclusively that while men and children had grown up locally, the women originated at least 50km away.

Grave	Male	Female	Children	DNA
90		25–35	4–5	Too poorly preserved
93	25–40		4–5, 5–6	Too poorly preserved
98		30–38	0.5–1, 4–5, 7–9	2 children were siblings but unrelated to woman. Position may suggest aunt or stepmother
99	40–60	35–50	4–5, 8–9 both male	Woman and boys had same MtDNA. Boys and man had same Y haplogroup R1a. = Nuclear family

Figure 3.37 *Table of relationships from Eulau*

continued

Conclusions

Dr Haak (Haak et al. 2008), who led the research team, believes that genetic links have established burial 99 as a clear (and the earliest) evidence for a nuclear family. The strontium evidence suggested a system of exogamous marriage where people married outside their social groups and patrilocality, whereby women moved to the villages of their husbands. Dr Pike, who led the Bristol team, believes that this would be to forge kinship networks and alliances between villages although it would also prevent inbreeding. The scientific evidence demonstrated that those who buried the dead knew their social relationships. The burial pattern suggests that family relationships were more important in burial position than gender. Aside from two men, all the dead were women and young children. Older children and younger adults were not represented. The two men showed evidence of earlier injuries, which may have meant that they could not take part in all physical activities. The grave goods with the grave 98 male child suggest that there might have been a rite of passage where adult status was gained.

The burials have all the hallmarks of a massacre. Unlike other Neolithic examples (▶ p. 480) most of the adults appear to have survived and returned to bury the victims. Whether they were working elsewhere, were hiding in the forest or on a raid elsewhere is unclear. The motive might have been feud, cattle or people stealing or simply competition for land. The burials were on a loess soil, which is associated with early farming in Europe because it was fertile and easily tilled. It also is the reason why so little settlement evidence survives because these soils have been constantly farmed since then. A regional study of over 300 earlier Neolithic (LBK) burials (▶ p. 346) by an international team led by Professor Bentley of Bristol University has found a strong correlation between burials of men with adzes and strontium isotope ratios, which suggests they were born locally. Conversely, men without adzes tended not to be from the place where they were buried. Taken with other evidence, this suggested that some men were inheriting the most productive land whilst others – herders or even foragers – were excluded. Given the evidence for patrilocality in this early period, it suggests that the loess farmers (those with adzes) had higher status.

Eulau provides an excellent key study of the wealth of information about social organisation that can be gained from modern excavations of human remains.

the skin to perfection. In some soil conditions, in East Anglia for example, where the soil is damp and acid, neither hard nor soft tissue survives well. The only surviving trace of a body may be a stain in the bottom of the grave that provides a silhouette of the original corpse. The 'sand man' in Mound 1 at Sutton Hoo is such a burial.

Excavating an army at Alken Enge

In wetlands around Lake Mossø in Jutland, archaeologists from Skanderborg Museum, supported by the Carlsberg Foundation, are carefully excavating bones from under 2m of peat. The area is already known for Iron Age deposits including the vast hoard of sacrificed weapons at Illerup (▶ p. 483), in the same valley. The wetland meadows cover an area of around 40 hectares and most trenches are turning up bones. The disarticulated remains of 200 people have been discovered so far with estimates of the numbers lying under the wet meadows being far greater. The bones have been well preserved in anaerobic conditions and DNA has survived in many instances. Excavation is extremely careful to avoid contamination and also to avoid damaging the bones so that detailed analysis can be undertaken. The bones have been dated to the start of the C1st AD.

Figure 3.38 *Excavation at Alken Enge. (Skanderborg Museum/Ejvind Hertz)*

Initial examination of the bones is revealing clear patterns. The bones are not found as skeletons. Most common are skulls and leg or jaw bones. Small bones such as toes and fingers are missing. Some joints have animal gnawing marks. This suggests that the corpses rotted down at a different location before the bones were brought to this site and literally thrown into pools in the bog. The bones are from males, mostly young adults and often strongly built. Many of them have unhealed wounds from warfare. This was the remains of an army. However, what is surprising is that few exhibit healed wounds. These were not men who had seen much combat before. Very few weapons have been found so the identity of these men along with information about their diet, health and lifestyles will rely on detailed analysis of the bones. The site provides yet another example of bog or water sacrifice during this period in northern Europe.

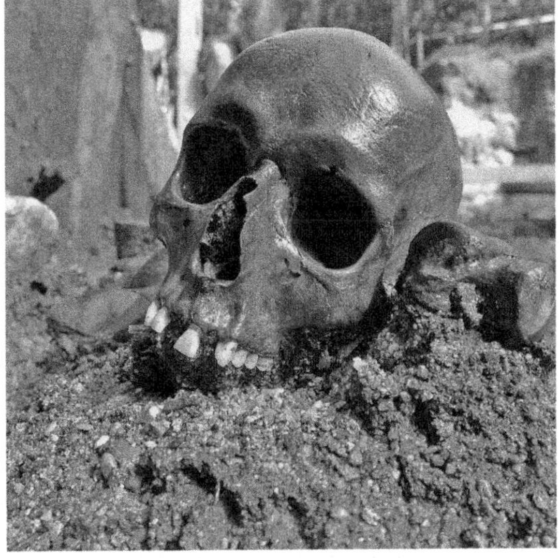

Figure 3.39 *Skull in situ at Alken Enge. (Skanderborg Museum/Ejvind Hertz)*

Plants

Archaeobotany is the study of plant remains from archaeological sites. Palaeobotanists study plant remains to reconstruct past environments (▶ p. 127) while palaeo-ethnobiologists study the relationships between people in the past and plants (▶ p. 321). The terms are sometimes used interchangeably. For the archaeologist, samples of plant remains divide into the macroscopic and the microscopic. Both types usually require specialised methods of conservation and analysis.

Plant macrofossils

Plant macrofossils are specimens that are visible to the naked eye. They include seeds, leaves and twigs. As with other organic materials, they are normally only preserved in unusual circumstances, where the bacteria that cause decomposition are inhibited. Wet, anaerobic conditions in wells, bogs and other waterlogged soils or underwater are the most likely. Examples of survival include bran from the stomach of Lindow Man or moss which had been used as 'toilet paper' from Viking York. The glacier that held Ötzi the Ice Man also preserved plant remains, as does permafrost, with examples including coriander seeds from the 'Ice Maiden's' grave or the stomach contents of Siberian mammoths. Arid environments including deserts and within buildings can also preserve well. A second type of survival is where the plant matter has been transformed to resist decay. Sometimes elements such as manganese and iron in groundwater replace the minerals in the plants. Much more commonly, charring in a hearth or fire carbonises the remains. This was the case in the grain pits at Danebury (▶ p. 184). Finally, indirect survival comes as impressions in mudbrick, pottery or daub, for example corn cobs at Ceren and olives at Pompeii.

The quantity of plant material in natural sediments is usually low but on archaeological sites can be abnormally high, especially where activities such as deposition of food waste and human faeces (**coprolites**) or food processing and storage have taken place. In these case samples are taken for analysis. Samples are usually washed in running water, although chemicals and flotation are needed if they are embedded in sediments. The flot is recovered in a fine mesh and samples identified and sorted under a binocular microscope. Different species are counted in order to draw conclusions about environments or crops. However, care must be taken in presenting data if the sheer quantity of small seeds produced by some species is not to artificially dominate an assemblage at the expense of other species which produce fewer and larger seeds. A comparison between the size of poppy seeds and almonds makes this point. Differential survival may distort the range of plants known from a particular period because some plants (such as tubers) do not preserve well or because they grow in locations lacking suitable conditions for preservation. People may also have introduced plants into the site either deliberately through plant collecting or cultivation or by

Figure 3.40 *Carbonised Neolithic grain*

Figure 3.41 *Preserved ear of einkorn wheat from waterlogged condition in a Neolithic well at Leipzig. (© Landesamt für Archäologie Sachsen, Rengert Elburg)*

accident as in the case of Ötzi the Ice Man, in the form of cereal grains adhering to his grass cape. This means that the archaeologist must study the formation processes (▶ p. 165) very carefully to understand why plant remains might be recovered from a particular deposit.

Each species of plant has a natural habitat. Plants can therefore tell the archaeologist about past climate, the nature of past environments and environmental change. This includes domestication (▶ p. 322) and the introduction of cultivated grain into new regions at the start of the Neolithic. When samples are from farming societies, the presence of weed seeds which were often accidentally gathered with the crops provides clues to the environments which were being farmed and the nature of harvesting. Pulling ears of grain and using sickles, for example, are likely to produce different weed assemblages. The state of preserved crops will give us insights into processing, storage and cooking and may identify the function of specific areas or rooms. High concentrations of chaff in a settlement usually indicates that harvests were brought there for threshing and winnowing. The nature of remains in storage areas or pits will indicate whether whole plants, ears or grains were stored. Plant macrofossils provide information relating to diet, the collection of wild resources, the keeping of livestock, clothing and their use for medicinal and narcotic purposes.

Wood

Wood survives in the same circumstances as other macrofossils but also can be preserved within buildings. Its larger size makes it more likely to survive but also presents problems in conserving it following excavation (▶ p. 90). Wood from wet contexts, though flimsy and insubstantial, retains much of its form and details such as axe marks. Wood from dry contexts also sometimes survives but is frequently warped and distorted.

Shipwrecks (▶ p. 403) such as the *Wasa* or *Mary Rose* are amazing time capsules: a moment frozen in time. Inside these two warships were a huge, bewildering array of wooden artefacts from mundane spoons and bowls to sophisticated navigational aids as well as the ships' timbers themselves. Archaeologists cannot study carpentry practices from the past, which involved complex joinery, without part of a ship or other structure to show how the joint was made (▶ p. 384). Such finds reveal the huge range of uses to which wood was put in the past: from firewood to monuments.

Wooden structures not only tell us about carpentry and construction techniques but also about woodland management. The cellular structure of trees varies so it is possible to identify different species using a microscope. Research frequently reveals that specific tree species were selected for specific tasks. At Corlea a 2km long

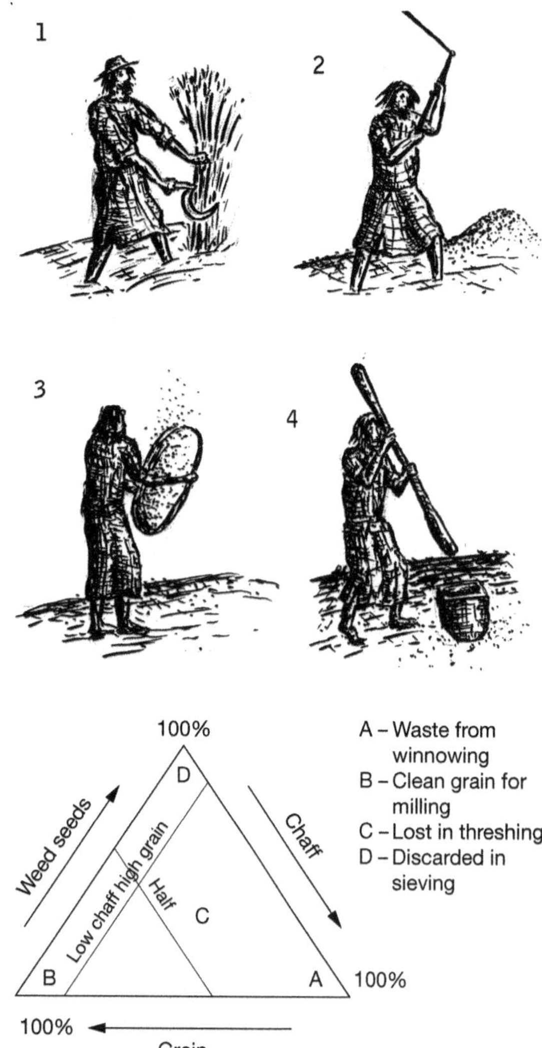

Figure 3.42 *Stages in grain processing and the resulting assemblages*

Through ethnographic study (▶ p. 180) of contemporary societies that rely on simple technology, archaeologists can understand the main stages of grain processing. Each stage produces a signature assemblage of plant macrofossils from the waste or what is left. After reaping (1) ears, bits of stalk and various weeds are taken to the farm. Threshing (2) breaks up the ear and separates the grain from the chaff. Winnowing (3) removes straw and husks – often to be fed to animals. Pounding (4) starts to break up the grains. Singeing to remove waste and sieving to remove smaller weed seeds may occur before storage and finally grinding.

Figure 3.43 *Wood from the Corlea trackway*

trackway was built across a bog using the timber from 370 oak trees. This was laid on alder and elm runners above a platform of brushwood. The planks were split skilfully with wooden wedges and were anchored down with pegs through mortises. Causeways are common in the area and are mentioned in Celtic stories such as the *Wooing of Etain*. However, the scale of Corlea is exceptional and would have required a high degree of social organisation to construct it. There are no ruts from carts or wear on the surface and, unlike the Sweet Track (▶ p. 385), the Corlea trackway sank within a decade. Its purpose can only be guessed at but may relate to ostentatious display. Ancient timbers such as these are vital for constructing dendrochronological sequences. The timbers from Corlea were all felled in 148 BC.

Indirect evidence for the use of wood can also be detected. At Sutton Hoo the imprint of an Anglo-Saxon ship's timbers remained in the sand, while at Garton Slack there was a stain from the vanished spokes of a chariot's wheels. Charcoal is a common find on many archaeological sites. In addition to providing samples for radiocarbon dating (▶ p. 154), it can reveal much about local environments. Microscopic analysis can reveal not only species but also whether firewood came from coppiced trees. Finally, archaeologists can also study living trees (▶ p. 243).

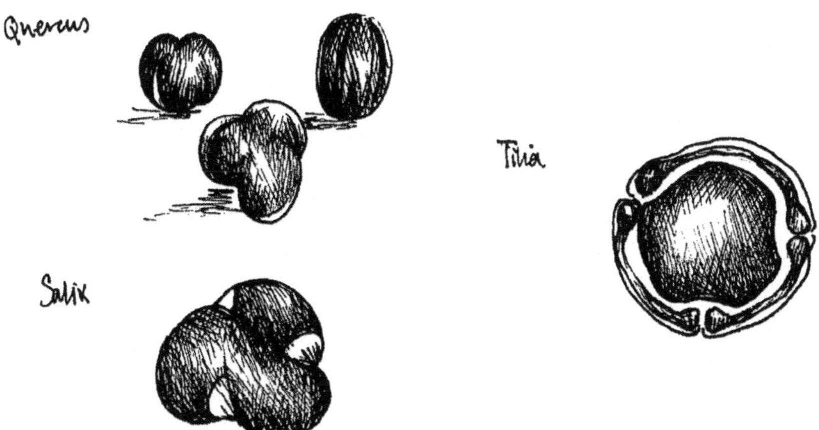

Figure 3.44 *Drawings of examples of magnified pollen grains of oak, lime and willow illustrating the different shapes for each species*

Plant microfossils

Plant microfossils are remains that can usually be studied only using microscopes. Three types that are important to archaeologists are pollens, diatoms and phytoliths.

Pollen The study of pollen is known as **palynology**. The species of individual grains of pollen are readily identifiable by palynologists through their characteristic shapes. They survive well, especially in wet, acid conditions, because they possess a tough outer case. Pollen can be retrieved from most soil samples but is most useful when taken by coring peat or lake sediments or from a column of samples from a ditch or pit.

Species frequency in samples can be counted and the numerical data plotted to show relative quantities. Some species produce more pollen than others, so, depending on wind, animal and human action, a particular assemblage of pollen may represent a very local or a more regional sample. The relative quantities of pollens provide a record of environmental change. Information is represented stratigraphically in pollen diagrams, which show the vegetation sequence for a given site.

In well-researched areas it has been possible to define pollen zones which characterise particular periods according to the relative amounts of each species. These pollen assemblages can be used to assign relative dates to samples from other sites according to where they match the established environmental sequence. This is known as **pollen dating**. The samples can also be dated using radiocarbon dating. The best-known application for this was in reconstructing the sequence for tree colonisation of Denmark following the last Ice Age (▶ p. 238).

Diatoms Diatoms are microscopic single-celled plants usually found in open water or in wet conditions such as bogs and waterlogged soils. They are very sensitive to changes in their local water. Their hard outer shell survives well in alkaline or anaerobic conditions. Changes caused by human action such as deforestation or pollution can be inferred from changes in the species of diatom. They have been invaluable in studies around London in determining where the braided channels of the Thames were in prehistory and whether they were tidal.

Phytoliths Phytoliths are silica from the cells of plants. They survive well enough in both mild acid and alkaline soils across a pH range from 3 to 9 and can be identified to particular groups of

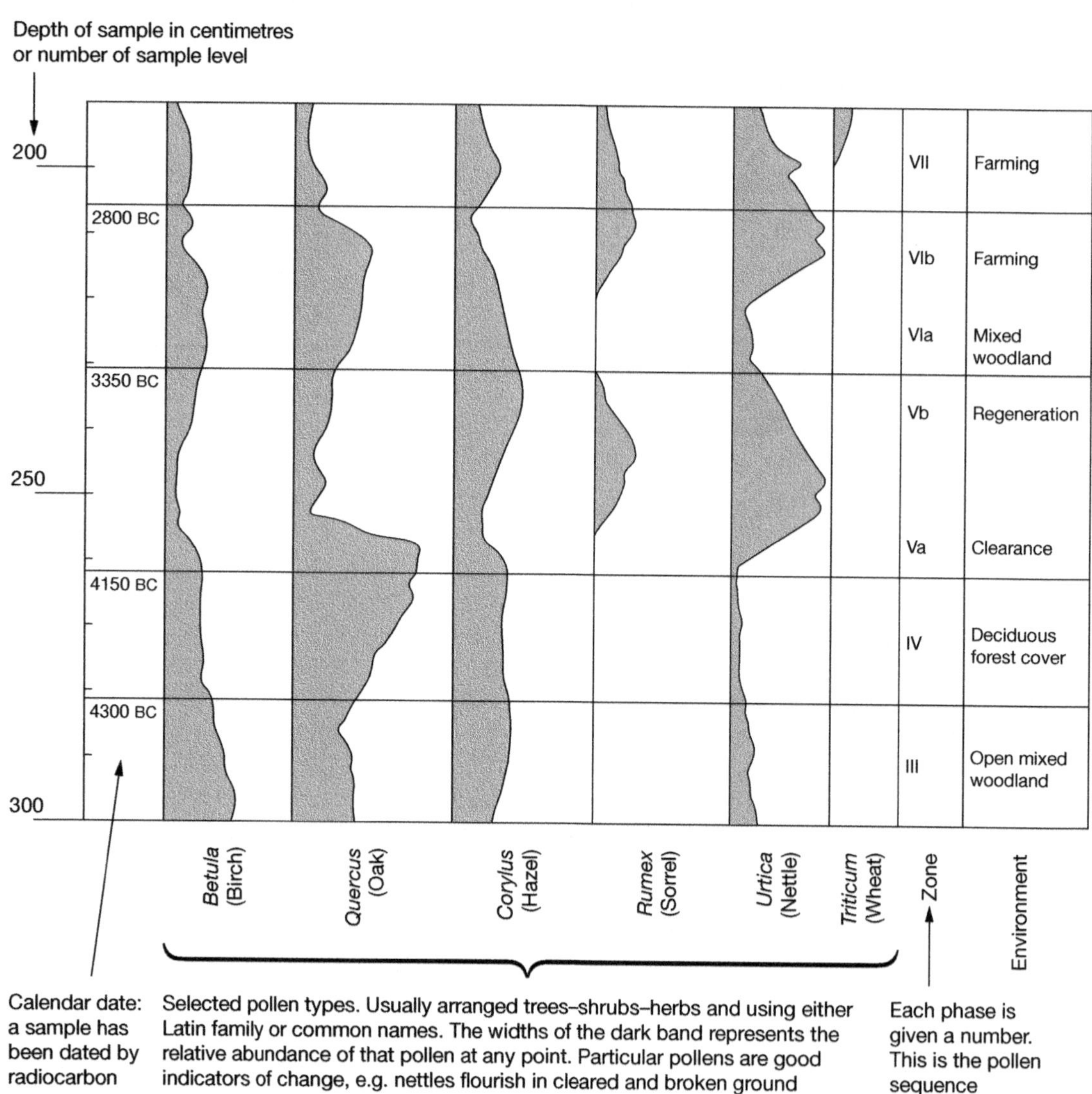

Figure 3.45 *How to read a pollen diagram*

plants and parts of plants. Like pollen, deposits represent the plants or plant-use in the immediate area. Roman waste pits at Silchester contained wheat and barley phytoliths from stems and leaves that enabled researchers to conclude that processing had taken place on site and that reeds and sedges had been used for raw materials. At Amud Cave in Israel, phytoliths from wood and grasses were recovered from Middle Palaeolithic sediments dating back to before 50,000 BP. These have been interpreted as Neanderthal fuel and bedding, with seeds being collected as food. It has been suggested that sickle gloss on flint blades from the early Neolithic in the Near East is indirect evidence of abrasive cereal phytoliths, while in Mesoamerica maize phytoliths have been used to demonstrate the spread of agriculture. In an investigation of late

Mesolithic diets in northern Europe (Saul 2013), food crusts were scraped from potsherds and analysed for both lipids (▶ p. 311) and cellular remains. In addition to meals of fish and meat, phytoliths of garlic mustard suggested that food was being spiced up to improve its taste 6,000 years ago.

Invertebrates

The shells of many tiny living creatures are surprisingly resilient. They provide evidence of the local environment and in some cases human diet and activity, as with the layers of seashells in coastal middens. Two important categories are insects and molluscs.

Beetles

Beetles (or Coleoptera) are one of the most diverse types of invertebrate and they can be found in virtually every environment. The hard shell casing or 'exoskeleton' of a beetle is very resistant and varies sufficiently between species to enable identification under a microscope. In evolutionary terms, beetles have changed very little for tens of thousands of years, so comparison of samples with modern reference collections is relatively straightforward. The large number of types of beetle can make species lists rather unhelpful as there may be up to fifty species present in a collection of one hundred specimens with only one or two in each category. A more profitable approach has been to group species together by their food or habitat preferences into classes such as 'phytophages' (plant eater) or 'obligate aquatics' (living in water). Archaeologists can then discover their local habitat and what taphonomic processes (▶ p. 171) led to their decomposition in a particular deposit.

Beetles along with other indicators have been used to reconstruct past vegetation and climate. The discovery of *Oodes gracilis* in southern Britain during the Palaeolithic has been used to infer the existence of much cooler conditions during glacial periods since this species now has a largely Arctic distribution. On sites, beetles can reveal local ground surface conditions. Buckland (1976) used beetles to analyse the floors of houses at Reykholb, Iceland, in order to infer the use of different rooms. They can also provide information on stored products and the utilisation of plant resources. In Roman granaries at York, grain beetles have been discovered which prove the exploitation of cereals even though there is no physical evidence of the plants themselves.

Figure 3.46 *Beetles from an environmental sample*

Other insects

Insects often inhabit very specific ecological niches which makes them valuable in identifying materials and environments. As with beetles, particular 'pests' tell us about crops, building materials, food storage, animal housing and sanitation. Human and animal parasites reveal health, living conditions and diets while scavenging flies and beetles provide forensic evidence of the stages of decomposition of corpses. Analysis of insects from Viking York (Yorvik) revealed that rotting animal products from butchery and leather working lay in the streets. Evidence from cesspits and houses showed that people suffered from parasites including whipworm, lice and fleas.

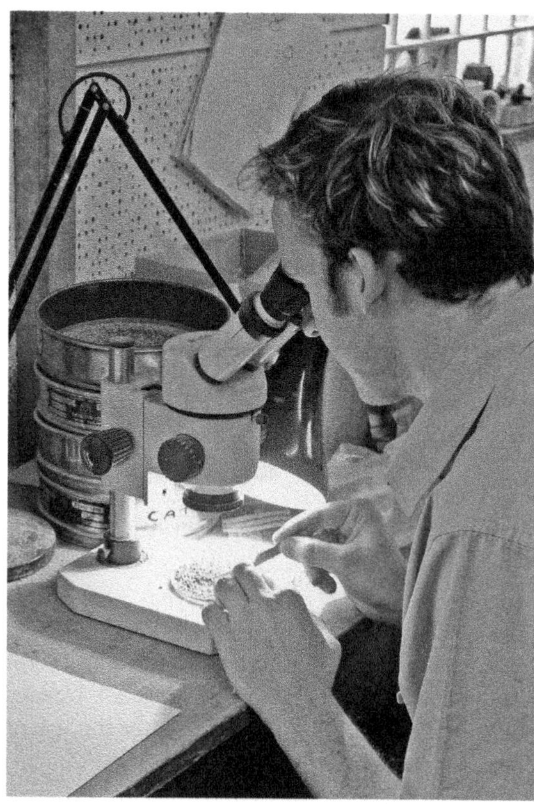

Figure 3.47 *Laboratory examination of snails. A microscope is used to identify the different species to provide insights into local habitats.*

Punctum Pygmaeum

Cecilioides acicula

Vallonia costata

Figure 3.48 *Drawing of magnified snails to illustrate the varied shapes which enable each species to be identified*

Molluscs

Land snail shells are preserved in calcareous, chalky soils because their shells are made of calcium carbonate (chalk). Most snails are so small (around 2mm) that you cannot normally see them. Those larger snails you may have seen, or even eaten, are much bigger and represent only a small proportion of the hundreds of species of snail. Snails are especially useful to archaeologists as different species have particular vegetation habitats. At Skendleby on the Lincolnshire Wolds, excavators found the shell of a *Ceciliodes acicula*, which is an air-breathing land snail. It was located inside the skull of a Neolithic burial and provided evidence to support the theory that Neolithic burials were exposed at ground level for a considerable period of time before the earthen long barrows were erected over them.

Microscopic shells are carefully sieved out of the soil (rather like seeds), identified and counted by the specialist. All snails need shade as they must not dry out, but some species are more tolerant to areas with less shade. This enables classification into three broad groups. Open country species can survive in grassland areas with little shade, unlike the woodland group. A catholic group is frequently found in both habitats, but some have quite specific preferences. Snails do not move far, so although you cannot tell what any past habitat was like from just one or two shells, you can from a whole assemblage. Snails have also been used to inform studies of trade routes. Two species found on the *Uluburun* shipwreck (▶ p. 403) came from the same area around the Dead Sea as resins in the cargo. They were probably brought on board clinging to thorn branches that were used to pack the jars of resin.

HOW DO ARCHAEOLOGISTS RECONSTRUCT ANCIENT LANDSCAPES?

In order to understand past activity in the landscape and the reasons for the distribution of sites across it, we need to understand what that landscape looked like. There are two key elements. The physical topography of hills, rivers and plains and the underlying soil provides the bones, while vegetation and fauna provide the flesh and skin. To do this, archaeology uses survey techniques that borrow from geology, biology and environmental science.

Reconstructing the morphology (shape) of the land is the starting point for research. Today's landscape has been shaped by human and natural activity on top of a geological base. The most significant are usually N-Transforms such as water (sea and river) action, wind erosion, peat deposition and glaciation. For the Palaeolithic and Mesolithic, understanding of geological changes is essential. For example, sea levels and the courses of rivers were often radically different. Many of the remote sensing techniques described in Chapter 1 are useful in understanding these. At Elveden, an early hominid site in Suffolk, geophysical survey was used to map ancient river channels running west–east through a series of narrow gorges. Today the land is utterly different: it is flat and drains north–south. Major investigations such as this will use GIS to produce digital maps and 3D models of past environments.

For most periods, data on soils is essential both to understand the environment it may have supported in the past and to track changes in its composition due to human activity (▶ p. 242). For example, the soils of many upland areas, including Dartmoor, show that they were once wooded. Clearance and agriculture in the Bronze Age contributed to erosion and degradation of the soil, including the formation of 'iron pans' which have prevented their use for crops since then. Studies of eroded layers of soil from the highlands of New Guinea around Kuk Swamp enabled Bayliss-Smith (1996) to identify the start of slash and burn agriculture in the surrounding forests.

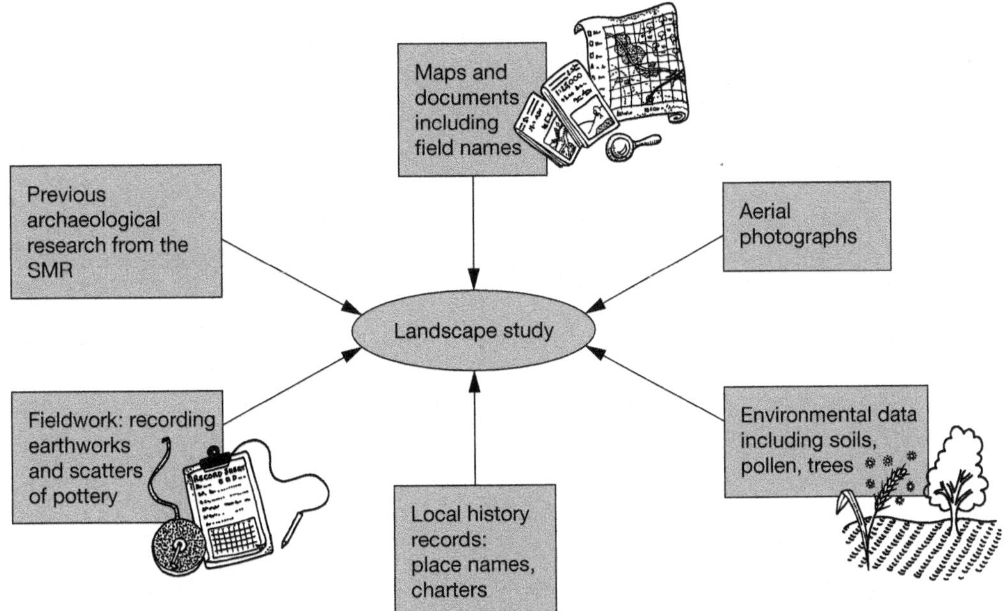

Figure 3.49 *Sources for reconstructing past landscapes*

KEY STUDY

The decline of the Maya

The mystery of the collapse of the Maya civilisation of Mesoamerica in the C9th AD illustrates the way in which the application of a succession of archaeological techniques has led to very different explanations. It also illustrates the value of environmental data in understanding social changes. During the peak of the Classic Maya civilisation between AD 600 and 800, around sixty large cities were supported by rural populations which may have reached 19 million. The rulers of the city states such as Tikal and Copán fought each other, built great monuments and recorded their victories and genealogies in calendars (▶ p. 416) carved on stone stelae. The last of these was carved in AD 904, around which time the cities were abandoned and covered in jungle. Many early attempts to explain their fate focused on a catastrophic war, revolution, pestilence or volcanic eruption but no convincing evidence was found to support them. However, in the 1980s a series of long-term projects explored the countryside around the great centres and radically changed our understanding. Rue (1989) collected pollen samples by coring a peat bog to produce a long, thin column of sediment which encapsulated the environmental history of the Copan Valley. The dominant view was that Mayan society declined rapidly after AD 800, so Rue expected this would be reflected in the pollen evidence with maize being less prominent and tree pollen becoming dominant as the forest cover regenerated. In fact maize continued to be planted until at least AD 1100 and only after that did hardwoods like mahogany, suggestive of fully established rainforest, return on a large scale. Either the standard textbooks about the Maya were wrong or Rue's data was. His results were supported by Freter (1993), who was working on obsidian hydration dating (▶ p. 148) of blades found on Mayan sites of this period. Her dates also suggested a long drawn out

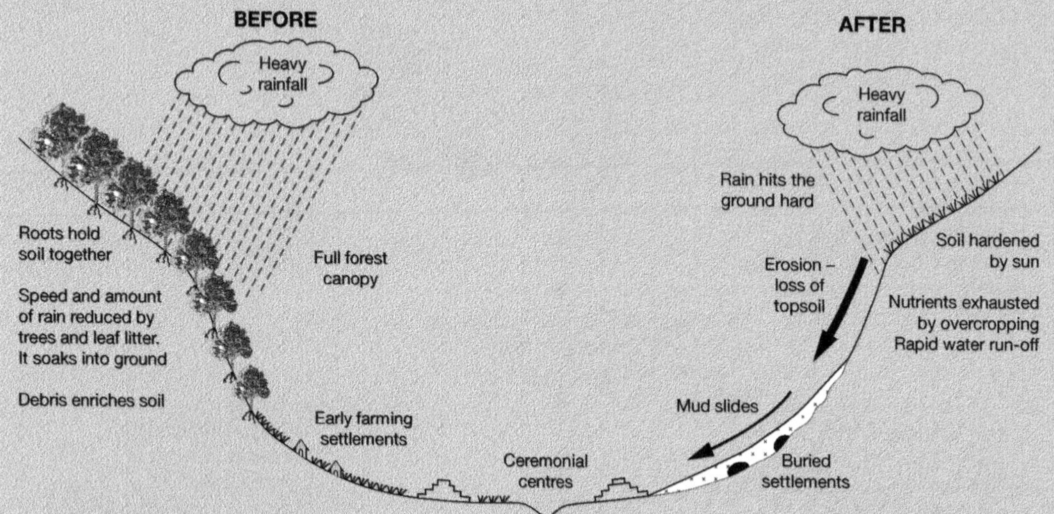

Figure 3.50 *Ecological disaster at Copan*

The extension of farming onto thin hillside soils and removal of tree cover led to environmental damage. Rain washed nutrients from the hill soils. The sediments covering valley settlements were caused by topsoil sliding down from the hills.

decline over several hundred years rather than a cataclysmic demise for the Maya. Other research teams exploring settlement mounds found significant evidence of soil erosion and traces of anemia in the skulls of Maya from all social classes. This provided a new 'model' to explain the end of Mayan civilisation. Webster et al. (1992) used a computer simulation to model the impact of over-farming of the fragile forest soils in order to feed rising populations. Environmental degradation led to famine and the collapse of the ruling elite *c.* AD 800 but population levels remained high until crashing by 90 per cent between AD 1000 and 1200.

Environmental degradation became the new dominant theory until it too was challenged by new evidence. Soil samples taken from lake sediments across the region showed a similar pattern to Copan with tree pollen being replaced by herbs and grasses by AD 800. Forests were being cleared for farming but also to provide fuel for construction. Twenty trees were burnt to turn limestone into just $1m^2$ of lime plaster used for building (Coulter 2009). However, after that date there were increasing signs of drought. Researchers from NASA created a computer model to simulate the impact of forest clearance on temperatures. They discovered (Cook et al. 2012) that while dark rainforest absorbed solar radiation from the atmosphere, light-coloured farmland reflected it back. This in turn reduced evaporation of surface water and led to a drop in rainfall by 5–15 per cent, which would have been enough to cause crop failure. Support for the drought theory came from researchers analysing cave deposits in Yok Balum Cave in Belize. Analysis of oxygen isotopes in the annual growth rings in stalagmites provided a sequence of climatic data which showed a succession of wet and dry periods over 2000 years. Uranium-thorium dating (▶ p. 159) enabled each 'growth ring' to be dated to within seventeen years. Maya expansion was associated with a long period of high rainfall. Conversely, the period after AD 660 was increasingly dry with a major drought from AD 1020 to 1100 (Kennett et al. 2012). The team argued that drought led to falling crop yields, political instability and social collapse. Some archaeologists remain sceptical of a single explanation, particularly given our current interest in climate change. Others suggest that there may have been regional variations in rainfall. While it is the latest dominant explanation, there is still room for more research to explain the sequence of events in Mayan society triggered by environmental disasters.

ARCHAEOMETRY

Scientific advances have a major impact on archaeology with those in dating, DNA and reconnaissance being the best known. However, just as inventions such as sonar and GPS were developed for military rather than archaeological purposes, archaeologists have adopted an impressive range of techniques from other disciplines in order to analyse artefacts and ecofacts. The growth of **archaeometry**, the scientific analysis of archaeological materials, has led to the creation of a whole range of new archaeological specialisms as well as archaeological science degree courses. It has also seen the development of institutions which link archaeological research to wider social issues. For example, the Ancient Biomolecules Centre at Oxford University researches ancient DNA but is funded by Wellcome because the findings will help understand the development of disease and the impact of past climate changes.

Laboratory analysis of finds can determine their composition, structure, date, and in the case of artefacts, their manufacturing history. The type of analysis selected in any particular case will depend on factors including cost, the importance of the individual sample and the questions the archaeologists are asking. For example, **petrology** is relatively cheap, but it is also destructive and limited in the precision of its 'fingerprinting'. **X-ray fluorescence** provides a dearer alternative, which does not cause damage, but it can only analyse the surface of objects. **Atomic absorption spectrometry** is very accurate, but destructive and more expensive. Only selected materials are sent to laboratories and only with clear questions in mind which will help address overall research questions.

DNA analysis

DNA analysis is the best known of the lab-based techniques which have become common over the last few decades. High-profile cases such as the exhumation of members of the Russian royal family who were executed in 1917 and the discovery of the grave of Richard III under a Leicestershire car park have made the news headlines. The applications of the method are changing all the time as is its accuracy and it has become a powerful tool for answering a broad range of questions.

DNA is essentially the coding instructions in the cells of all living organisms which determine what they do. Creatures of the same species, including humans, have the same combination of genes. Genes control our physical traits such as height and hair colour and our rates of development and also metabolic traits such as ability to process particular foods. However, some genes have several forms which are called alleles. For instance, there are several variants of the human gene for eye colour and also for blood type. These differences originated in natural mutations within the gene. These mutations can be due to environmental factors such as solar radiation but also occur spontaneously through errors made when the DNA reproduces itself. Where a set of DNA mutations are inherited they are called haplotypes. Most mutations are not passed on but those that are account for the observable differences between individuals of the same species. Some mutations survive because they provide an evolutionary advantage; for example, the ability to process milk (▶ p. 138). Others survive because they are valued more socially and therefore individuals with those genes are more likely to be successful in mating and thus passing on their genes to their descendants. By analysing sequences in individual strands of DNA and comparing them to others in the same species, geneticists can establish the degree of variation within a population. There is usually greater variation where mutations have been taking place for the longest period. Computers can model the likely rate of mutations in order to provide a family tree of genetic changes within which particular evolutionary traits first appeared (▶ p. 193).

DNA has a number of applications for archaeology beyond the identification of family members (▶ p. 116). Considerable emphasis has also been given to tracing human origins (▶ p. 192), including the relationship between our species and the Neanderthals (▶ p. 203). The identification of haplogroups, people sharing a particular mutation or 'marker', is used to trace the movement of population groups, for instance the spread of farmers across Europe during the Neolithic (▶ p. 499). The technique is not just used on human populations. Most of the world's crops and domestic animals have been traced back to their areas of origin by comparing modern and ancient gene pools for different parts of the world. Often the results confirm other archaeological evidence such as locating the Fertile Crescent (▶ p. 317) as the original source of domesticated cereals. Sometimes results are more surprising and can be contradictory. The first domesticated livestock in Europe were found to have originated in the Near East. However, in the case of pigs, the Near Eastern line of pigs declined rapidly and was replaced with pigs of European origin. Essentially European farmers had begun to domesticate the larger European boar population which may also have had an advantage in being adapted to local environmental conditions.

CHARACTERISATION STUDIES

Scientific analysis of artefacts and building material can reveal their chemical make-up. This is valuable because while stone or metal of the same type is largely composed of the same elements, their exact chemical composition varies. Each stone or metal ore was extracted from a specific location under particular geological conditions. These unique circumstances mean that they contain slightly different combinations and quantities of 'impurities'. Copper, for example, may contain minute amounts of arsenic, silver and lead. These '**trace elements**' occur as a few parts per million and may have negligible effects on the material, but they provide it with a distinctive 'chemical fingerprint'. Where the geological sources of metal, clay or stone have been mapped, archaeologists may be able to identify the actual mine or quarry from which the materials came. In turn this leads to greater understanding of patterns of trade and exchange. Characterisation studies are particularly useful forensic techniques and are used to detect poisons, gunpowder residue and blood; all of which have archaeological applications.

X-ray fluorescence (XRF)

This technique is one of the cheapest and quickest methods of analysing the surface composition of most materials, particularly metals, obsidian and pottery. It can be non-destructive and requires little or no preparation and therefore is suitable for assessing objects prior to conservation. Either the surface or a small powder sample of an object or feature can be analysed. A beam of high-energy radiation (X-rays) excites atoms in the sample and in some cases ionises them (they lose an electron). This releases energy as light or fluorescence which can be measured. The amount and colour of fluorescence relates to the elements present and their relative abundance. Amongst its applications are detecting layers of glaze on ceramics, the composition of

Figure 3.51 *Gold lunulae from Irish bogs*

These incredible gold collar ornaments or lunulae are rarely found outside Ireland and testify to the great skills of early goldsmiths there. The chemical signature could be accurately determined by NAA but that would mean destroying a sample. XRF would probably be sufficient, particularly since the objects are quite thin.

coins and metal jewellery and decorative pigments used in frescoes. It is particularly useful where destructive samples cannot be used either because of the value of the object or where it would be prohibited; for example, with Native American artefacts protected by NAGPRA (▶ p. 603). It has even been used to 'read' completely worn inscriptions on stone by detecting minute particles left from the iron chisels used by the carvers.

The development of handheld devices is adding a new range of capabilities to both survey and initial characterisation of finds. This includes investigating soils in situ on a site to determine potential areas of activity which leave a chemical signature such as hearths, burials or animal pens. Integration with GPS enables the rapid plotting of environmental data on site plans. Handheld XRF can also be used on standing buildings and was recently used on York Minster to analyse mortars and decay in the stonework as part of a conservation project. The technique does have some limitations. For example, it cannot characterise very small components or distinguish isotopes or ions of the same element.

Optical emission spectrometry

Spectrometry covers a range of methods that derive from physics and involve using radiation (e.g. X-rays) to force a small sample of material to produce light (another form of radiation) which can be measured through spectrographic analysis. In the way that sunlight can be split into a rainbow, the light emitted by different elements shows different characteristic patterns when split by a prism into a spectrum. This is projected onto a viewing screen or photographic plate, so that information can be recorded. In a compound of elements, the balance of those elements is shown by the intensity of the lines in the spectrum. This is compared with control spectrums of known composition produced under the same conditions. Trace elements of a few parts per million can be recorded in this way. An alternative approach is to use radiation, such as infra-red, of a known frequency, some of which will be absorbed by the atoms vibrating at the same frequency in the sample. Particular frequencies are characteristic of particular elements. Spectrometry is a very accurate method for quantitative analysis and only requires small samples (less than 10 milligrams) to be taken. This makes it suitable for valuable archaeological material. It has been widely employed for metal analysis but is also used for glass, faience, pottery, obsidian, amber and occasionally flint. It is increasingly being replaced by inductively coupled plasma spectrometry (ICPS).

Atomic absorption spectrometry (AAS)

AAS is a more precise technique than optical emission spectrometry but is a slower process. A minute sample is dissolved in acid and then vaporised. When a beam of light of known wavelength is passed through the gas, the amount that is absorbed indicates the concentration of atoms of a particular element present. A series of beams (and lamp) are required for each element tested for, so researchers need to be clear about what they are testing for. It is most effective when testing for the rarer, heavy-metal trace elements such as magnesium, sodium and nickel. AAS is also widely used to characterise bronze and copper and can even analyse flint. The technique has been used to trace the C7th debasement of coins in the Merovingian Empire. A limitation of this technique is that where metal artefacts were made from several sources, the 'fingerprint' is obscured. In the ancient world, valuable commodities such as bronze were often recycled with new artefacts made from scrap from a variety of sources.

Neutron activation analysis (NAA)

This is the most accurate and reliable **characterisation** technique and can be used on liquids and gases as well as solid material. It is non-destructive since the sample is not burnt, vapourised or chemically altered and can therefore be used on valuable artefacts or ecofacts. Outside archaeology it has been used for moon-rock samples and dinosaur bones for this reason. In archaeology its applications have included analysing coins, pigments, ores, shells and even arsenic poisoning in hair or fingernails.

Samples are bombarded with neutrons in a reactor. This creates unstable isotopes in the sample which give off distinctive patterns of gamma radiation, the spectrum and intensity of which can be measured with great precision. Unlike AAS, it is a multi-element technique, which means that elements can be analysed simultaneously. The technique is so sensitive that at least sixty-five different elements present in a few parts per billion can be detected. Unlike X-rays, neutrons pass through most materials and the middle of a sample can be analysed as well as the surface. This means, for instance, that clays can be sourced from minute variations in trace elements. The technique has been used at Manching in Germany to explore the wide distribution of similar types of ceramics across Iron Age central Europe (Gebhard et al. 2004). The stylistic uniformity of painted and wheel-turned wares suggested a common point of manufacture. However, NAA identification of trace elements within the fabrics revealed many different sources. This established that it was the technology and designs which were exchanged over wide areas rather than the pottery. Visual examination alone could have led to the opposite conclusion. NAA has relatively few limitations besides the cost of the facilities but is not effective with elements which do not form isotopes. Care has also to be taken initially with irradiated samples.

Isotope analysis

Atoms of the same element which have the same number of protons and electrons but different numbers of neutrons are called isotopes. By determining what isotopes are present, and in what proportions, materials can be linked to known sources with the same ratios.

Archaeology borrowed this technique from geology, which had established that similar minerals from different areas had slightly different ratios. This technique was used to analyse metal artefacts from early Bronze Age Crete. These had distinctive Cretan styles but there are no metal ores found on Crete. Ratios for lead isotopes in bronze and silver artefacts enabled

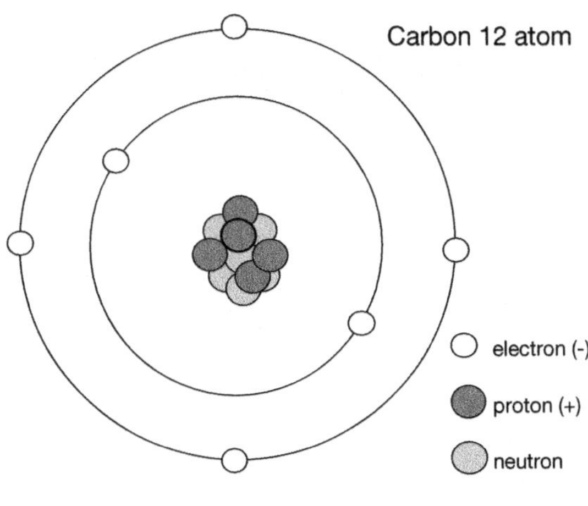

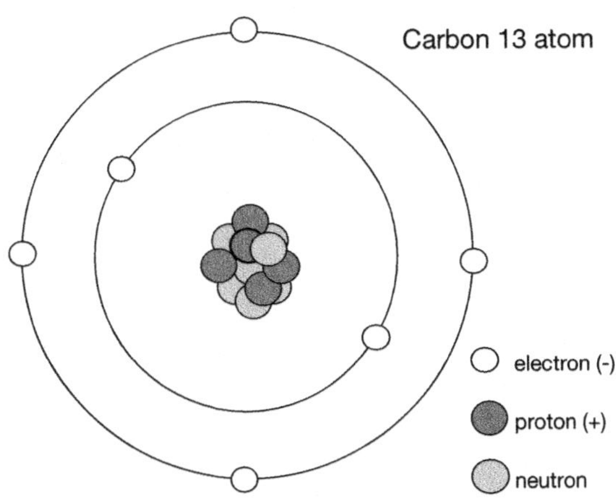

Figure 3.52 *Carbon isotopes. Carbon 13 has one more neutron than Carbon 12. Carbon 14 has two more neutrons than Carbon 12. The atomic weights of the three isotopes vary as a consequence.*

Figure 3.53 *Copper 'oxhide ingots' from Minoan Crete*

Copper was exchanged across the eastern Mediterranean in the early Bronze Age. These distinctive ingots are found at palace sites and also shipwrecks (▶ p. 403). Shape, moulding marks and inscriptions have been studied to identify patterns but lead isotope studies were able to locate the mines to Cyprus.

the material to be traced to sources elsewhere in the region. This showed that raw materials rather than finished objects were being traded. Trade in copper and marble around the Mediterranean has also been traced using isotopic analysis. In the case of marble, petrology had been unable to identify the source quarries but isotope analysis could. In recent years isotope analysis of a wider range of elements has been widely used forensically to trace the geographical origin of everything from poached ivory to the cotton fibres in forged notes.

A second major application of isotopes has been in identifying the sources of minerals in human and animal remains in order to study diet or population movement. Bone, teeth and even hair can be analysed to identify the isotopes present. Particular combinations of isotopes are only found in specific geographic areas. Variations in oxygen isotopes which humans acquire from local rainwater during childhood become locked into teeth enamel. Using oxygen in conjunction with isotopes of heavy elements such as strontium has also proved useful in tracing origins including over short distances (▶ p. 350). Analysis of some Beaker burials has shown that some of them originated in central Europe, possibly the Rhineland. Research is currently underway using this technique to determine the impact of Crusader settlement on populations in the Near East. Sulphur isotopes in collagen are being explored to see if they too can be used to trace migration. Analysis of oxygen isotopes in marine shells on archaeological sites can provide an approximate guide to the season of collection. The technique is also being used to identify seasonal movement of cattle (transhumance ▶ p. 318) and to understand herding practice (▶ p. 352).

YOU ARE WHAT YOU EAT

Developments in organic chemistry in the last few decades have opened up many exciting new areas of potential evidence for archaeologists including the re-examination of archived finds.

Every living thing and every mineral is composed of material drawn from the earth or atmosphere. The atmosphere contains elements such as carbon, oxygen and nitrogen; the earth is the source of elements such as lead and strontium. In many cases these elements occur in several different atomic forms called isotopes. Carbon isotopes include ^{12}C, ^{13}C and ^{14}C. Some of these isotopes such as ^{14}C are unstable, which means that they decay over time – this is the basis of radiocarbon dating. Others are stable and these are the ones used for isotope analysis because they do not change over time and they behave in

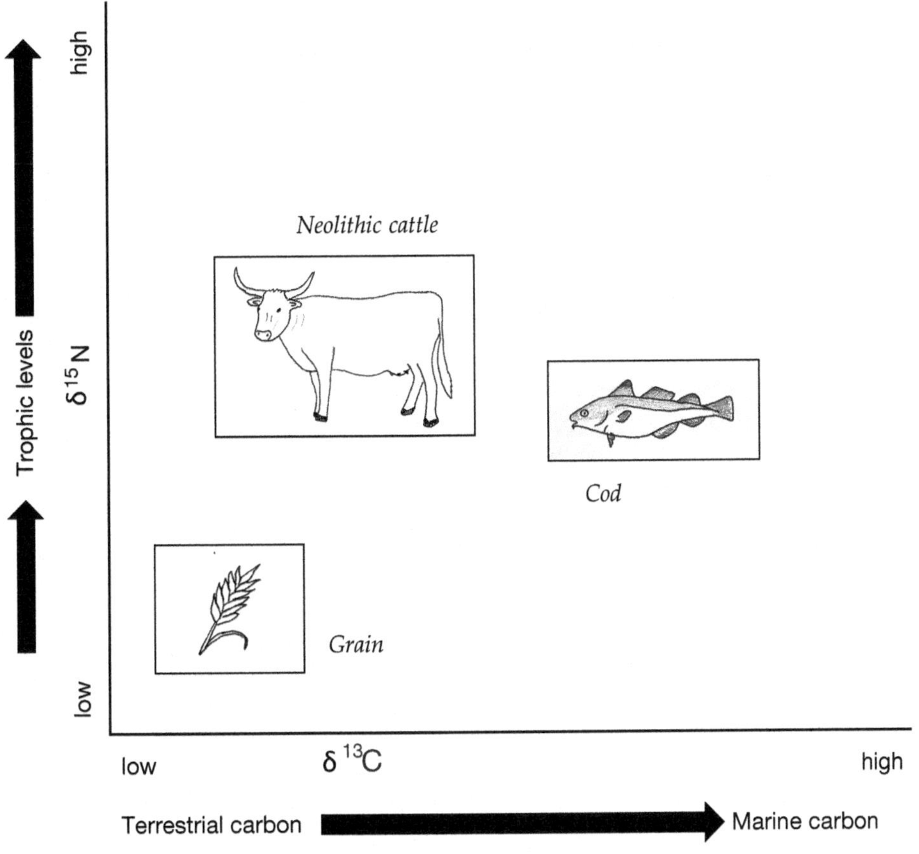

Figure 3.54 *Isotopes and diet*

Plants taking in terrestrial carbon are bottom left while plankton are bottom right. Animals are placed in relation to their main source of carbon left to right. The higher up the food chain they are, the higher up the table. Top predators would be at the top.

similar ways. For instance both ^{12}C and ^{13}C can combine with oxygen atoms to make carbon dioxide. Each has a slightly different atomic weight due to its composition. The isotope ^{12}C has six neutrons and six protons in its nucleus, while heavier ^{13}C has seven neutrons and six protons. Around 99 per cent of atmospheric carbon is ^{12}C with most of the rest being ^{13}C. The normal ratio in which the two isotopes are found is 100:1. In isotope studies the ratio of a heavier and a lighter stable isotope is compared between the sample in question and that in reference material (a standard). These are reported in a form called 'delta notation' (δ). Most living things will have a lower ratio of $^{13}C : ^{12}C$ to the carbon standard and will have a negative δ carbon value. So plant $\delta^{13}C$ measures the stable carbon isotope ratio of that plant. In the case of wheat, the reading might be –27‰.

Carbon isotopes in the food chain

Plants absorb carbon into their cells during photosynthesis. However, they store it in slightly different ways, which means that the ratios of ^{12}C and ^{13}C vary. Those originating from hot and dry parts of the world with long growing seasons store carbon in compounds with four carbon atoms. These are called C4 plants and include maize, sugarcane and millet. They absorb ^{13}C faster than plants which originate from wetter areas or forests and have a slightly higher ratio of ^{13}C to ^{12}C than this second group. The latter originate in more temperate regions and are called C3 plants because they store carbon in compounds with three carbon atoms. They include rice, wheat, barley and potatoes. Plants in the sea store a higher proportion of ^{13}C than terrestrial plants.

When plants are eaten by other creatures, the carbon passes up the food chain but the ratios between the isotopes remains very constant. So a rat eating only maize would have a $\delta^{13}C$ value similar to maize. If it ate a mixed diet of maize and barley, its $\delta^{13}C$ value would be a weighted average of the two. Sulphur isotopes behave in the same way but nitrogen is different. The two stable isotopes of nitrogen (^{14}N and ^{15}N) are also absorbed by plants but in differing ratios. However, as nitrogen passes up the food chain, the lighter isotope is gradually excreted in urine and proportionally more of ^{15}N is stored. Consequently a top predator would have a higher ratio of ^{15}N to ^{14}N than a plant eater. A breastfed baby would have a higher ratio than its mother. Most mammals will have a positive δ nitrogen value. The exact ratio will depend on what they have eaten. However, results can be misleading; for example, when crops have been manured. This can boost ^{15}N so that a diet based on manured plants appears similar to a meat-based one. Analysis of $\delta^{13}C$ and $\delta^{15}N$ in pig bones from medieval York (▶ p. 410) investigated whether the pigs had been kept in the city and fed scraps or pastured outside in fields and woodland. The expectation was of high $\delta^{15}N$ levels due to consuming meat and fish waste but this was not the case. Most pigs had similar levels to local sheep and were raised on a plant-based diet outside the city.

The application of carbon isotope analysis

Carbon from bone collagen, tooth enamel or hair can be analysed using mass spectrometry. Although collagen is replaced over time, analysis of bone collagen does provide a broad guide to the individual's main source of food. This knowledge has been used to trace the spread of maize in Mesoamerica because it increased the $\delta^{13}C$ in human remains. Nitrogen and carbon isotope analysis have been used in tandem to determine whether human populations ate terrestrial or marine food. This method has been used to investigate the Mesolithic–Neolithic transition and suggests that there was a rapid switch from marine to terrestrial diets. In Greenland it has been used to study why early Viking settlers died out during the C14th 'Little Ice Age' while indigenous Inuit (Eskimo) survived (Arneborg et al. 2012). The main initial theory suggested that climatic deterioration prevented their crops from growing and they died out through malnutrition. Relatively few fish bones have been recovered from midden sites so it was thought that they had failed to adapt to climatic change. Collagen from Viking burials also showed that they had initially eaten a C3 rich diet, much of which would have come from imported or locally grown cereals, while the Inuit lived on marine food, particularly seals. However, by the C14th they were eating over 50 per cent marine food, so had adapted to their situation. The work on skeletal remains suggested that younger women were underrepresented in the later period, which may mean that younger people had migrated and that the population eventually declined to a level where it was unsustainable. This may simply reflect the increasingly harsh conditions which made all forms of farming difficult. Faunal evidence suggests that animal stocks fell significantly from the C12th onwards.

ORGANIC RESIDUE ANALYSIS

This is the best known of a number of biochemical processes which are revolutionising our understanding of processes in the past. Residues from cooking occasionally are visible on the surface of pottery. However, during the 1970s biochemists demonstrated that far more residues including sugars and fats had been absorbed into the fabric of unglazed vessels, usually during cooking, where they had survived intact. The most valuable substances to date have been lipids. Lipids are fatty or waxy organic molecules which are found in most foods including meat, milk, honey and olive oil. They will generally decay in sunlight, water or air but sealed in the pores of ceramics they are protected. Pioneering work led by Professor Evershed of the Organic Geochemistry Unit at Bristol University has identified a series of 'biomarkers' (particular molecular structures) which enable different lipids to be isolated and compared with 'fingerprints' known from particular sources.

The process is destructive. Following surface cleaning, a few grams of pottery are ground to a powder and mixed with chemical solvents and reagents to dissolve and extract traces of lipids. These are subjected to lab-based processes such as gas chromatography or mass spectrometry to identify the compounds. For example, stearic acid is commonly found in animal fats and often occurs in ancient pottery. However, gas chromatography can separate out the isotopes to provide greater resolution. Meat fats from cows and sheep (ruminants) have a lower proportion of ^{13}C than fat from pigs, horses and humans. Milk fats have an even lower ratio of ^{13}C. Therefore samples with very low ^{13}C ratios suggest dairying.

Further refinements have isolated leaf vegetables, plant oils and honey (▶ p. 405). The technique has also been applied to other materials. Lipids are present in human faeces and in skeletal material, where the porous surfaces of bones trap organic molecules. Samples from the bandages or remains of mummies have revealed the use of animal fat and beeswax as bases in the application of exotic resins such as frankincense and myrrh during embalming. Substances preserved in shipwrecks such as resins carried on the *Uluburun* (▶ p. 403) or the pitch used to make the *Mary Rose* watertight have been identified. The use of birch resin for glue and manure as fertiliser has also been established using this process. A useful by-product of this research has been the carbon dating of recovered lipids which enables the absolute dating of pottery. Downsides to lipid residue analysis are that individual lipids are not specific to one foodstuff and can potentially be introduced to vessels during all stages of use. In addition, there is not one method of analysis suitable for all types of lipids.

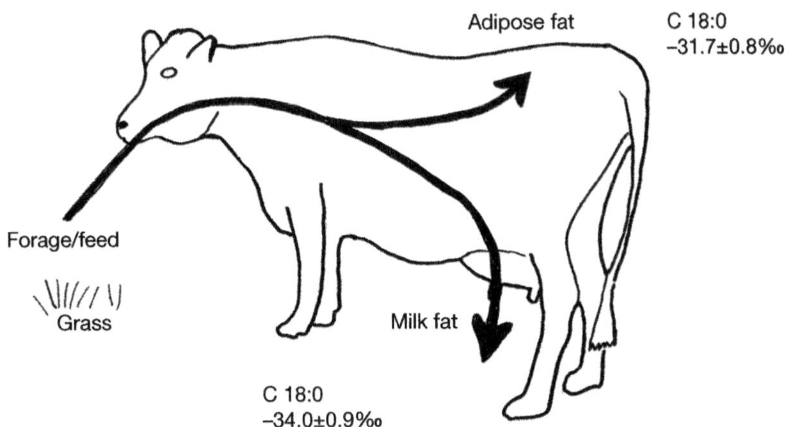

Figure 3.55 *Differing proportions of ^{13}C fatty acids in adipose and milk fat (after Copley et al. 2005). The slight chemical differences enable the sources of lipids preserved in ceramics to be identified.*

KEY STUDY

Lipids, cheese and the European Dairying Project

This example illustrates the revolutionary impact that a range of recent scientific advances are having on our understanding. In this instance, long-standing archives are being re-examined to unlock secrets as well as research being undertaken on new sites. Not only is the approach multidisciplinary, including biochemists, geneticists and zooarchaeologists, but the team is also multinational. Also significant is the subject, which is central to understanding the Neolithic but which also may help address modern health and diet issues. Part of the research is funded by the EU 'Lactase persistence in the Cultural History of Europe' (LeCHE) project.

Lactose tolerance

Even today, most adult humans are naturally lactose intolerant, which means that they cannot digest milk products. When they try to drink milk, the results range from cramps to vomiting and diarrhoea. This is especially true in southern Africa and the Far East, where there is no tradition of consuming dairy foods such as milk, butter or cheese. For this reason archaeologists have tended to see dairying developing much later than the initial domestication of cattle because lactose tolerance would emerge slowly. Sherratt's idea of a Secondary Products Revolution has been particularly influential, seeing dairying as part of a process of intensification and change in the early Bronze Age which included horse riding, rearing sheep for wool and the use of animals for traction. During the 3rd millennium BC there does appear to be a spread of particular new forms of drinking vessels and other containers from the Balkans and eastern Europe and the use of horses certainly followed that path from the area of original domestication on the central Asian Steppe. In several parts of the world, including northern Europe, most people today have the enzyme lactase in their gut which enables them to break down the sugars in milk to digest it. This is called lactase persistence because normally this would disappear when a child was weaned and it is due to a genetic mutation. DNA research has failed to identify this in Mesolithic or early Neolithic skeletons. The LeCHE programme aims to track the emergence and spread of this trait. This mutation was a particularly valuable one since it allowed people to obtain animal protein and fat all year and massively increased the calories provided by a single animal. Those with lactase had a clear evolutionary advantage. Dairying would have also greatly enhanced the value of sheep, goats and cattle.

Identifying the shift to milk consumption

Faunal evidence is ambivalent. Modern dairying herds are made up of adult female cattle. The archaeological signature might be a disproportionate number of remains of calves, young male animals and much older females and this is the case at the Neolithic causewayed enclosure of Hambledon Hill. However, for early breeds of cattle the calves had to be kept present for cows to give milk, perhaps only being slaughtered on weaning around nine months.

Lipid analysis, however, has been able to establish when and where lactose tolerance emerged. Evershed's team analysed nearly 1,000 archived pottery samples across a range of prehistoric sites in southern England, including those from Windmill Hill which had been excavated by Keiller between 1925 and 1939. Milk fats were found in ceramics from every site and from over half of the samples

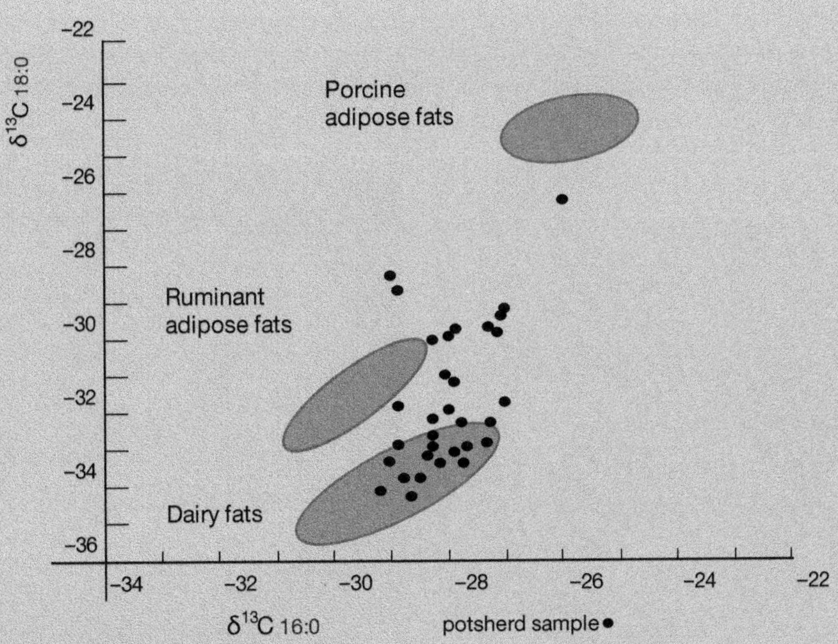

Figure 3.56 *Windmill Hill lipid analysis. Samples of fatty acids recovered from ceramics at the Neolithic causewayed enclosure plotted against (grey) typical ranges for pork, beef and dairy fats (after Dudd et al. 1998).*

overall, including 25 per cent of the Neolithic sherds. This suggests that dairying arrived in Britain with the introduction of the first domesticates by 4000 BC.

This work has been extended into the largest organic residue survey so far with over 2,000 samples analysed from early farming sites in the Near East and the Balkans. Around 15 per cent contained animal fat, mostly dairy. The earliest dated from before 6500 BC with north-west Turkey emerging as the possible area where dairying originated. There is strong evidence that dairying was well established in the Hungarian basin before 5000 BC and from there was spread into central and western Europe by the first Linearbandkeramik (▶ p. 346) farmers. DNA analysis of their bones has revealed that they had the lactase persistence gene. Dairying spread east across Asia but not as far as China, although independently Mongolians had developed the ability to drink mares' milk. At least one independent adaptation seems to have occurred in Africa.

Lactose intolerance may have been initially overcome through the milking of sheep rather than cattle or by consumption of products such as cheese or yoghurt. Fermented cheese is much lower in lactose than milk and therefore could be consumed without side effects. Yoghurt also contains lactase produced by the bacteria which transform it from milk. Evidence for the making of cheese comes in strange ceramic bowls perforated with hundreds of tiny holes. Their role in cheese making had been suspected through their resemblance to modern cheese-strainers but Evershed's team proved it. Examples from central Europe and Anatolia were shown to contain dairy lipids. Many other cooking and storage pots from the same sites did not contain dairy fats but had been used for meats. Some had also been sealed with beeswax,

continued

presumably to make them watertight. The perforated ceramics were sieves used to separate the fatty curds from the runny whey that contained the lactose. Today dairy fats are often seen as unhealthy but in the Neolithic they were an important element of diets. Cheese not only provided a valuable source of protein but was also in a form that could be stored and transported.

Figure 3.57 *Neolithic ceramic strainers, possibly used for cheese making*

IS ARCHAEOLOGY A SCIENCE?

The adoption of scientific techniques and the overlap between archaeology and biology in the study of human origins led some archaeologists to claim that archaeology was now a science. This would have advantages for university departments since science enjoys higher status and better funding than the humanities. However, the use of scientific techniques in itself does not make a subject a science. To be accepted as a science, archaeology would have to demonstrate that it is following the principles of empirical methods with a view to establishing 'laws', or 'middle range theory' as it is often called. Although many research archaeologists have adopted the scientific model of generating a hypothesis and then testing, it is difficult for archaeologists to form law-like generalisations from their findings. While the relationships explored by scientists in laboratory experiments can be tested repeatedly under controlled conditions, archaeologists investigate unique events from the past and deal with material which, once removed from its context, can never be re-excavated. However, many people working in archaeology are scientists and in their lab-work are applying scientific methods, so there is certainly archaeological science.

After analysis

Readers should not conclude from what has been written about the range of different methods available for post-excavation research that all archaeologists eagerly pursue all such lines of enquiry. Anyone conducting fieldwork and its associated post-excavation processes has to be conscious of costs and consideration is given to what is possible, what can be afforded and, most importantly, what is commensurate with the size and importance of the excavation. The potential of archaeological methods and scientific support is immense and increasing, but like the dating methods considered in the next chapter, the exercise of some control is needed in the real rather than the theoretical situation.

Finally all the reports are united with the dating evidence and the fieldwork record as a complete site archive. At this point the archaeological record becomes a collection of written, graphical and electronic data. It still needs to be interpreted (▶ p. 164). In the tradition of scientific reporting, published archaeological reports tend to be descriptive and analytical with a fairly minimal amount of assessment and interpretation. The archive is there for others to draw their conclusions from. For members of the public and many students, reports are often frustrating. What they want are the works of synthesis and interpretation that are largely produced by academic rather than field archaeologists. The examples and discussions in Part II of this book are largely drawn from these interpretative accounts.

The vast majority of finds from excavations remain in museum or other archives and are only seen by specialist researchers. In some cases material is re-analysed many years later (▶ p. 298). For example, new scientific techniques can be deployed on material excavated many decades earlier as with the studies of lipids using archive collections of ceramics.

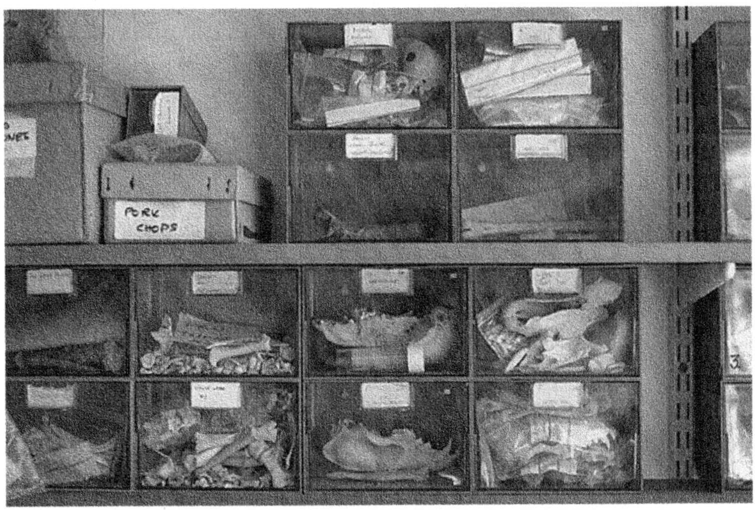

Figure 3.58 *After excavation, finds are stored in archive boxes. This enables future researchers to access them.*

Chapter 4

Understanding Dating in Archaeology

This chapter explains the underlying principles of dating and how the more common techniques work. It also identifies examples where specific techniques are appropriate for particular situations. Archaeologists have used many different techniques to work out the age of artefacts and sites for which they have no historical dates. These dating techniques can be broadly subdivided into two groups:

- **Relative dating** techniques, which identify the order in which sites or artefacts were used in a sequence from earliest to latest. These are based on an understanding of stratigraphy (▶ p. 52). Using the 'Law of superposition', a deposit and anything within it is younger than the deposit below it and older than the deposit above it. You can arrange them in order but you do not know the actual dates. Cross-dating, derived from geology, involves comparing the stratigraphy of different sites or parts of a large site to relatively date layers within the local sequence.
- **Absolute dating** techniques, which try to establish an exact or approximate calendar date for a site, deposit or artefact. The earliest

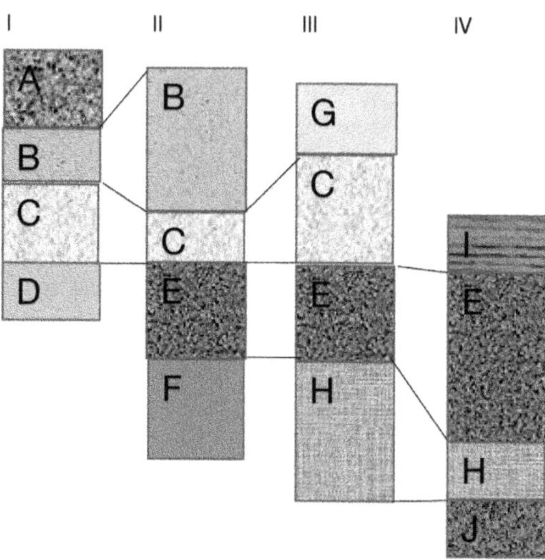

Figure 4.1 *Cross-dating. In this example the sequence in site I can be used to relatively date layers B and C in site II, etc.*

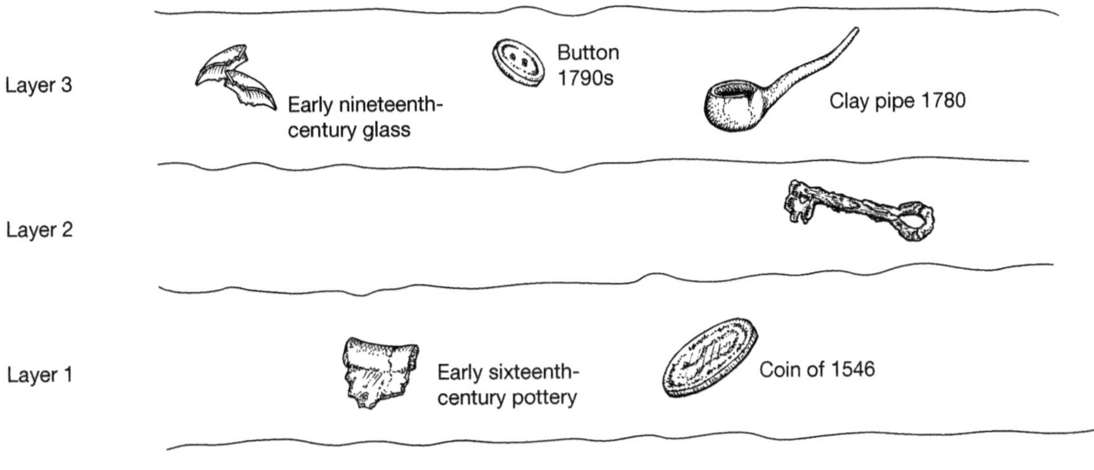

Figure 4.2 *The use of finds to provide earliest and latest dates for a deposit. The key can be dated by association to the deposit.*

way of doing this was to use artefacts with a known date such as coins or ceramics with known date ranges. Where these are unavailable or may be unreliable, a number of lab-based 'chronometric' techniques are used.

In practice archaeologists use both methods. Most remains will not be absolutely dated but will be tied by stratigraphy into a relative sequence that includes dated material or deposit. Direct dating dates a particular artefact whereas indirect dating relates it to something it was found with and is sometimes called the principle of association. This will commonly be something of known age, such as an artefact of a particular style or an artefact marked with a date such as a coin. It only works if neither object has been disturbed and both remain in their primary context (▶ p. 52).

The dating techniques selected depend on the specific task and evidence available as well as practical considerations such as cost. Many of the scientific techniques are expensive and require high levels of technical skill to use and to interpret them. The span of human history studied by archaeologists is so vast and environments so varied that techniques suitable for one place and period may be unsuitable for another.

PERIODS IN ARCHAEOLOGY

In the historic period, archaeologists make use of period names which are broader and often different from those used by historians. The C5th to C7th AD are a case in point. In history books the period following Roman Britain is usually referred to as the Saxon Period or the Dark Ages. The latter term has been used to relate to both the decline in Christianity and urban life and the paucity of written documents from the period. To archaeologists it is certainly not 'Dark' since there is a wealth of artefactual evidence. In those parts of north-western Europe where the Iron Age was not interrupted by Roman occupation, it is either referred to as the later Iron Age because of continuity in technology and society or the 'migration period' because of population evidence. In England, the 'Early Medieval Period' is sometimes used to indicate discontinuity with the Roman period and greater similarity with later centuries. In general, history will name periods after peoples or individual royal families while archaeologists use labels that reflect more gradual changes in material culture and social and economic arrangements.

It is worth noting that periods often start and finish at different dates in different regions. For example, the Neolithic in south-east Europe occurred earlier than that in the north-west and reflects the gradual spread of agriculture out from the Balkan region. By the time Britain was 'in' the Neolithic, the Balkans were 'in' the Copper Age or Chalcolithic (*c.* 5000–3200 BC). Britain's Copper Age did not occur until between 2800 and 1800BC!

For each period there are diagnostic artefacts. A key indicator of the Mesolithic, for example, is the development of microlith-based technology which can be distinguished from the blade-based technology of the Upper Palaeolithic. Within these broad periods of several thousand years, subdivisions are usually named after sites where variations in artefactual evidence were first noted. These subdivisions differ across wide regions. For example, in France and parts of central Europe the term 'Sauveterrian' is used for part of the early Mesolithic. This is named after the type-site of Sauveterre le Lémance, where assemblages containing numbers of geometric microliths were first identified. In northern Europe a broadly similar period is termed 'Maglemosian' after the type-site of Maglemose in Denmark, where flint microliths were found alongside a range of distinctive wood and bone tools.

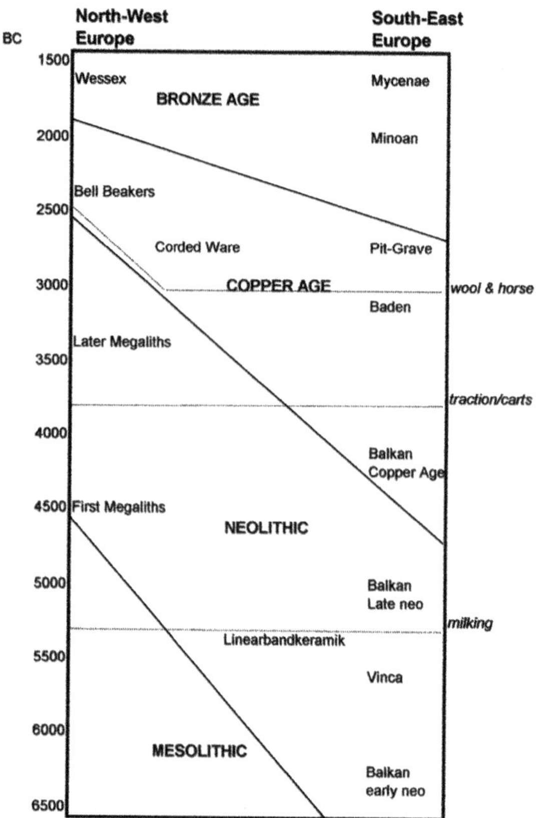

Figure 4.3 *Potentially confusing labels for the past*

This simplified diagram (after Sherratt 1997) illustrates broad patterns between south-east and north-west Europe during a period where the first metal-using civilisations were developing in the Near East but northern Scandinavians were continuing with the same foraging lifestyle that had been developing since the last Ice Age. So was it the Mesolithic, Neolithic or Bronze Age? For example, the Balkan Neolithic at Karanovo (▶ p. 339) had begun by 6500 BC but the Neolithic did not reach Britain until just after 4000 BC. By that time the Balkans (as at Varna (▶ p. 423)) had been in the Chalcolithic for around 1,000 years.

Historical dating

For sites less than 5,000 years old there may be written or artistic evidence which can provide precise dates as long as the original language can be decoded. For example, coins, seals, inscriptions, reliefs, statuary and clay tablets were used by the civilisations of the Mediterranean and Middle East. These may depict or refer to a date, ruler or event which we can link into a known chronological series. In some regions this might be a calendar or list of rulers. Such finds would provide the earliest possible date (TPQ) for that deposit or structure. This has allowed sites such as Egyptian tombs or Mayan temples to be precisely dated. Many early investigations in the

Figure 4.4 *Coin of Flavius Magnus Magnentius*

Magnentius, a Roman general of barbarian origin, was one of the 'usurper' emperors of the C4th AD. He rebelled in AD 350 and controlled much of the western empire before defeat in 351 and suicide in 353. The reverse of the coin shows Victory holding a chi-rho (Christian) symbol. The find of this coin on a Roman site in Gloucestershire provides a TPQ date for the layer in which it was found.

KEY TERM

Terminus post quem (**TPQ**): the earliest possible date for an archaeological deposit.

Terminus ante quem (**TAQ**): the latest possible date for the deposit.

Mediterranean or Near East were undertaken by classical or biblical archaeologists looking for particular historical civilisations. The most famous instance was Schliemann at Troy but others include Evans at Minoan Knossos and Layard at Nineveh. They attempted to tie their discoveries into existing historic and literary chronologies.

RELATIVE DATING

In its simplest form, relative dating involves putting a number of finds into chronological order. On a site with a clear and undisturbed stratigraphy, items from lower levels are older than those in higher levels. Based on his observations in the C19th, Thomsen, the original curator of Denmark's National Museum, argued that stone artefacts were older than metals. His student, Worsaae, went on to prove that deposits which only held stone tools were always below and therefore older than any containing metal artefacts. This led to the creation of a time frame for prehistory known as the '3 Age System', based on the introduction of tools made from stone then bronze then iron. The Stone Age was subsequently divided into old (Palaeolithic), middle (Mesolithic) and new (Neolithic), based on major developments in lithics. While this scheme oversimplifies differences and changes, particularly between regions, it is still the basis of the way we label the past and of typological dating. Where artefacts are used for dating, it is critical that their precise position within the stratigraphy is accurately recorded.

Typological dating and seriation

Initially artefacts were placed into chronological sequences based on stratigraphy. Finer refinements depended on ever more precise classification of those artefacts into types based on their attributes and function. By the late C19th typologies of ceramics, lithics and metal artefacts were being independently developed in many European countries. A refinement of this technique was added by Flinders Petrie in the 1900s. He was an Egyptologist who excavated many tombs including Tanis and Amarna, the finds from which can be seen in the Petrie Museum and the British Museum. He noted that the design and decoration of pottery from the Egyptian tombs he excavated changed gradually over time rather like fashions but his problem was that he could not link each burial site merely by stratigraphy. His solution was to cross-date sites using seriation. Essentially this involves creating clear typological sequences for different sites and then comparing them. There are two main variations of seriation: contextual and frequency (▶ p. 147) seriation. Contextual seriation looks for the presence or absence of particular types or designs in assemblages. So a layer with a new design or shape may be younger than a similar layer which does not contain them. This works best with artefacts from the same cultural tradition and which were commonly used for a relatively short period of time. Think about the sequence of changes in mobile phone or PCs in your lifetime.

By comparing sequences for different sites, Petrie was able to build up a master-sequence of changes in designs and assign them to periods and through association with inscriptions to give them approximate dates. The sequence he pioneered in Egypt was then used to cross-date sequences elsewhere in the Mediterranean where typologies overlapped, such as those for Mycenaean Greece and Minoan Crete (▶ p. 162). He had already noted imported Minoan Kamares Ware (▶ p. 471) in his excavation of Lahun in Egypt and dated it to 2000–1800 BC and he also looked for records of particular types of Egyptian ceramics appearing on Crete. This enabled him to produce a chronology for the Minoan civilisation. This kind of typological dating can work with other types of assemblages and also with buildings and structures. For example, the first deposits which contain domesticated animals or crops are generally assigned to the earliest Neolithic in a region. For more recent periods the exact dates for the introduction of many artefacts from clay pipes to beer bottles are known and can be used to date sites.

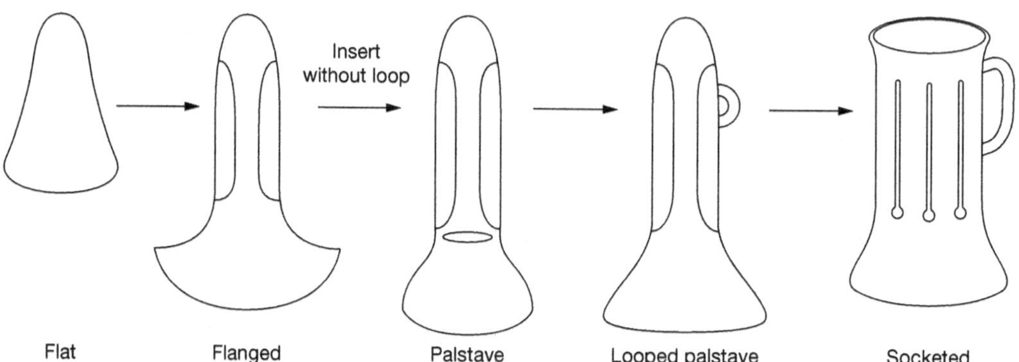

Figure 4.5 *An example of a typological sequence: the development of copper and bronze axes*

Successive groups (or assemblages) of contemporary artefacts, which are commonly found together, have been used to form culture sequences over wide periods. Before the advent of absolute dating techniques, this technique enabled a timetable of the spread of 'cultures' across Europe in later prehistory to be constructed, based on changing combinations of grave goods.

Diffusion and culture history

In the early C20th, typological sequences combined with anthropological interest in distinct human cultures to develop 'culture histories'. Pioneered by Kossina in Germany and then Childe in the UK, they identified particular aspects of material culture with different peoples (racial or ethnic groups) in order to make sense of the past. Given that the earliest civilisations were known to be from Mesopotamia and Egypt, it was assumed that major changes such as farming and metalworking had developed there first. New ideas spread from those regions through diffusion of ideas or by the movement of peoples migrating or invading other areas. A glance through most English texts published before the 1970s will probably reveal references to successive immigrations by the Windmill Hill or Peterborough Folk who brought farming, the Beaker People bringing metalworking (and beakers) and the Celts with iron, woad and torcs. Diffusion fitted with colonial experience of worldwide progress flowing from more 'civilised' to 'backward' peoples. A generation of classically trained archaeologists explained how the people of Bronze Age Wessex built monuments in imitation of and with help from advanced Mediterranean civilisations. Such culture histories were undermined by the rise of absolute dating techniques, particularly radiocarbon, which showed that Stonehenge pre-dated the Mediterranean monuments it was supposed to have been influenced by. However, culture history labels and concepts remain in use.

Frequency seriation is a second typological dating variation which can be used with large assemblages. It works on the same principle that things are initially very rare and gradually become popular before declining over time. This can be seen most clearly by plotting the abundance of particular types or designs in each deposit as bars on a timeline. The pattern revealed

Figure 4.6 *A Funnelneck Beaker Culture ceramic assemblage*

This distinctive type of 4th millennium BC pottery with funnel-neck beakers and a range of stylised containers for liquids is the calling card of the first Neolithic farmers along the Baltic. Debate continues over whether they were incomers or converted foragers (▶ p. 322) but finds of this type provide a relative date for the contexts they are recovered from.

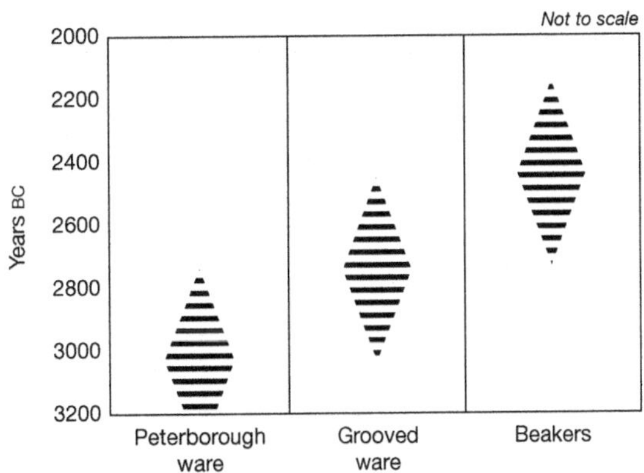

Figure 4.7 *A simplified diagram to show how a model of seriation can be constructed*

The relative proportions of pottery types at a new site would be compared with the seriation chart to give it an approximate date. On our diagram, a site with lots of grooved ware but only one beaker might be relatively dated to soon after 2800 BC.

is known from its shape as a 'battleship curve' because it looks like an aerial view of a battleship. Different sites and regions with overlapping patterns can be compared in order to cross-date and also to identify the direction in which innovations spread. Modern use of frequency seriation employs computers running sophisticated statistical packages to compare very large data sets.

Problems with these techniques

- Although sites and artefacts can be put into order, they can only be used to provide approximate calendar dates where elements of the sequences are tied to historical data.
- The advent of radiocarbon dating showed that archaeologists had underestimated timespans in prehistory. They had mistakenly constructed sequences which fitted their assumptions that all developments happened around the Mediterranean and then spread north and west to 'less civilised' areas. The most famous instance is Stonehenge, which proved to be many centuries older than the societies that were previously thought to have influenced it.
- One type of artefact does not always succeed another. For many years it was thought that pointed hand-axes were earlier than oval ones after they were found in lower levels on some sites. However, at Boxgrove both were found together, suggesting that other influences on choice were important. Seriation assumes that new artefacts are phased in gradually as others are phased out. This does not always happen. Some artefacts, such as medieval knives or axes, change very little over long periods.
- **Curation**, the preservation of valued artefacts, can lead to items being deposited a long time after their manufacture. Basing dates on a few isolated artefacts can lead to errors.

Geoarchaeological, pollen and faunal dating

For the Palaeolithic, some archaeologists, particularly those using environmental data, will refer to climatic periods such as Holocene or particular glaciations such as Devensian. As the climate alters, so too do the types and relative numbers of different plants and animals. Where organic preservation is good, changes can be traced by analysing pollen (▶ p. 123) contained in sediments and animal bones (▶ p. 240). To provide a pollen sequence a core through a deposit such as peat is taken and for each layer the proportions of different types of pollen are identified. Sites within these deposits can then be cross-dated relative to particular phases of climate history in local sequences. Analysis has to take account of many factors including the different amounts of pollen produced by each plant and the different distances the pollen travels. Similarly, sites can be relatively dated using biostratigraphy or faunal dating. This involves studying the fauna in each deposit and comparing it (cross-dating) with other known examples to find a match. This is particularly useful where the sequence of the appearance or extinction of species (e.g. mammoths) is known. Small mammals such as voles generally provide the best indicators as they evolve quickly and particular species are often only found in one layer. The use of distinctive vole teeth to assign a deposit to a period is sometimes referred to as the 'vole clock' (▶ p. 59). Absolute techniques are needed to date these sequences. For the relative dating of major climatic sequences, international studies of deep-sea cores, varves and ice cores (▶ p. 153) are used.

Obsidian hydration

Obsidian is a volcanic glass that can be worked to provide razor-sharp cutting edges. In the Middle East and Mesoamerica it performed a similar function to flint in northern Europe. As soon as a piece of obsidian is broken it begins to absorb water from the atmosphere at a known rate (in much the same way as a stick of rock which goes soft on the outside). This chemically alters a thin layer on the edge of the break where water has penetrated (hydration) into the

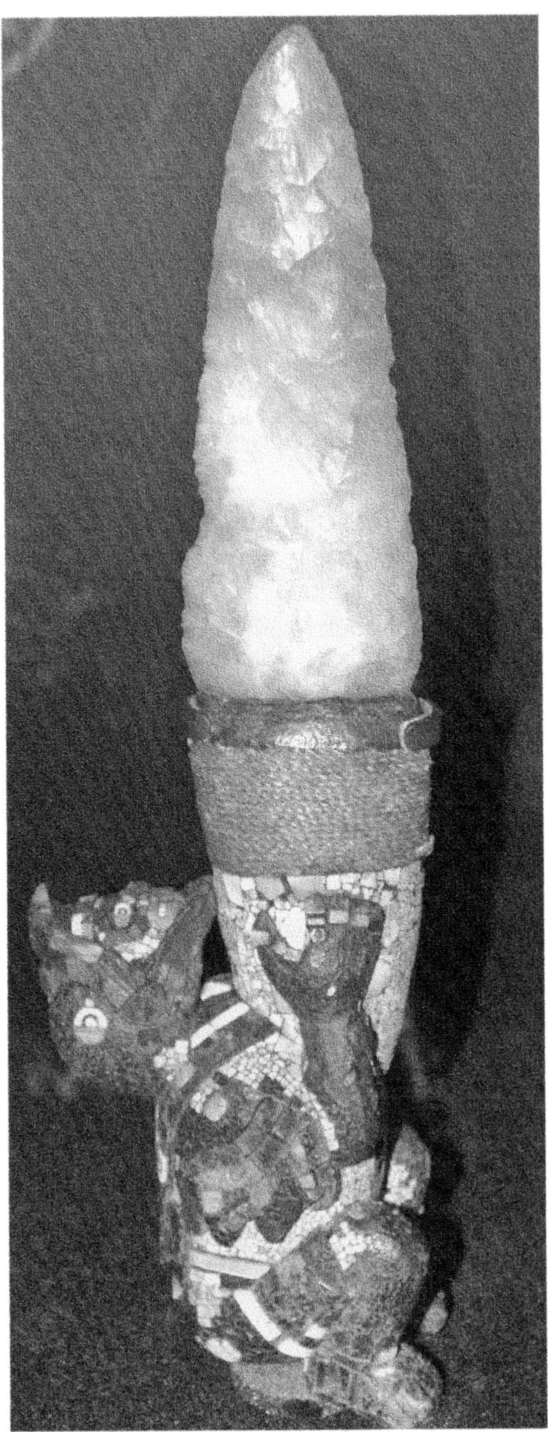

Figure 4.8 *A core of obsidian. Blades were struck from this core during the Neolithic.*

obsidian. The thickness of this layer depends on the length of time since the break and can be measured to provide a date relative to other samples on the same site or to compare sites. In some cases, results can be calibrated to provide absolute dates but that requires considerable additional data since the speed of hydration varies with local temperatures and the chemical make-up of the obsidian. This is one of the cheaper laboratory dating techniques. A limitation is that breaks in obsidian after its use or discard will 'reset' the clock and could suggest much 'younger' dates for a site.

Hydration also occurs in other rocks and the potential of quartz for dating is currently being explored. This works in a similar way with water diffusing into a cut surface to form a measurable layer. Experiments on artefacts with known dates including Olmec pendants in Mexico has led to claims that quartz hydration may be able to date artefacts between 100 and 100,000 years old. However, not all archaeologists currently accept this method.

Chemical dating of bones

Buried bones, antler and teeth absorb fluorine and uranium from water in the ground whilst their nitrogen content declines as collagen in the bones decays. These processes occur at uniform rates so it is possible to establish the relative age of different bones by measuring the proportions of these chemicals. Bones buried at the same time would have similar relative proportions of fluorine and nitrogen. Fluorine dating was used in 1953 to expose the fossil 'Piltdown Man' as a forgery. A medieval human skull and modern orangutan jaw had been stained to look convincingly like an ancient 'missing link'. Fluorine testing revealed very different dates for the various parts and established that all were less than 50,000 years old. The method is limited because fluorine in groundwater varies between sites as does the rate of organic decay in different soils.

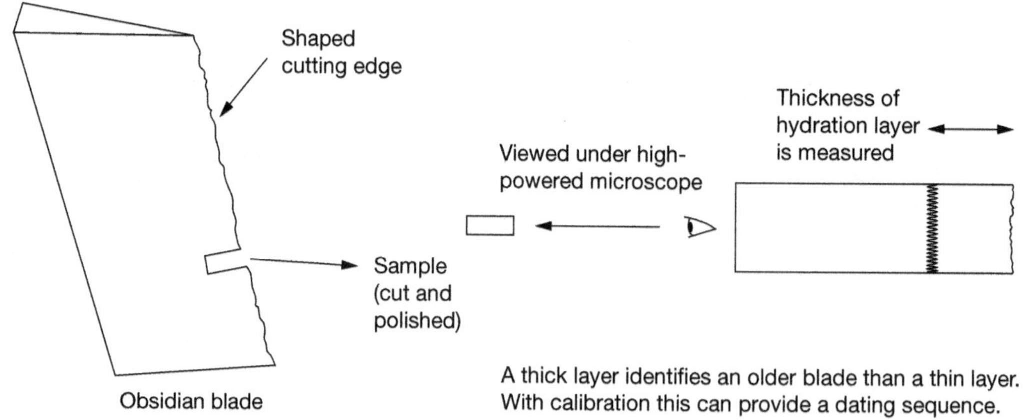

Figure 4.9 *How obsidian hydration works*

ABSOLUTE OR CHRONOMETRIC DATING

Since the mid-C20th a range of new chronometric methods have been introduced. This means that they measure time from a particular event to provide dates in years before the present (BP). With the exception of dendrochronology, most are radiometric, which means that they are based on the regular rates of decay of radioactive isotopes. In these cases the dates are probabilities which are calculated statistically and are provided with an error margin or standard deviation (▶ p. 154).

Dendrochronology (tree ring dating)

This is the most accurate chronometric dating method. Early in the annual growing season trees produce thin-walled 'earlywood' cells. Towards the end of the year thick-walled 'latewood' cells are produced. This cycle produces a visible 'ring' in the wood each year under the bark. The thickness of the rings is directly related to local temperatures and rainfall each season and year of the tree's life. The rings are wider in good weather conditions than in poor ones and therefore provide a record of local climatic variation. Trees in the same area will have similar patterns of rings, which enables wood from different periods to be cross-matched in overlapping sequences. By counting rings and 'wiggle matching' pattern sequences, the outer rings in ancient wood can be tied to the inner rings of younger trees in order to provide precise dates for each ring. Californian bristlecone pines can live for over 5,000 years and have been linked to deadwood to provide sequences of 8,000 years. In Europe, oaks preserved in bogs have been used to create master sequences going back 11,000 years. The precision of the method is such that the felling date of the central stump of Seahenge (▶ p. 79), which had its bark attached, has been pinpointed to between April and June 2050 BC.

Dendrochronology does have some limitations. Sometimes carpenters discard the softer sapwood just under the bark. This is important as in England there may be 15–55 or so 'sapwood' rings on an oak. In such cases researchers can only estimate an 'earliest possible felling date'. Not all areas have sufficiently varied seasons or enough surviving timber to be able to construct sequences. This is particularly the case in tropical areas where there are not clear seasonal patterns to create distinctive rings. To effectively date wood, between thirty and fifty complete rings are needed on a sample. Since this represents quite a thick piece of wood, the technique is better for dating building timbers than artefacts. Its direct

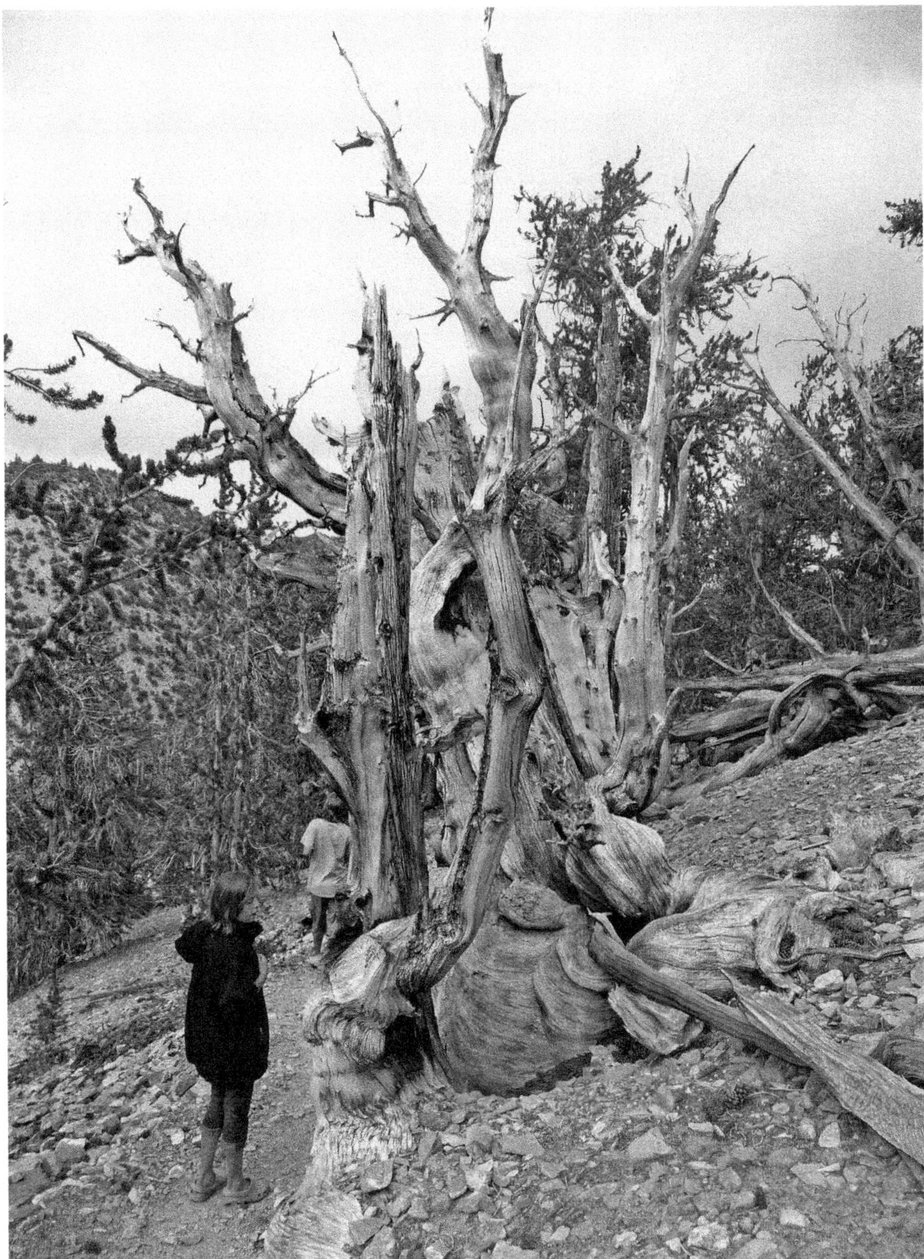

Figure 4.10 *Bristlecone pine from the Methuselah Grove area of the White Mountains, California, where a tree was 5,065 years old when this book was written*

Such trees may live for longer but in the extreme climate at an altitude of 3,000 metres the outer rings are gradually sand- and ice-blasted away by strong winds. The earliest rings are lost this way. The cold, dry location means that deadwood exists from up to 10,000 years ago and a sequence of 8,000 years has been established. Bristlecones are not usually found in association with artefacts so their main value is in calibrating radiometric dates.

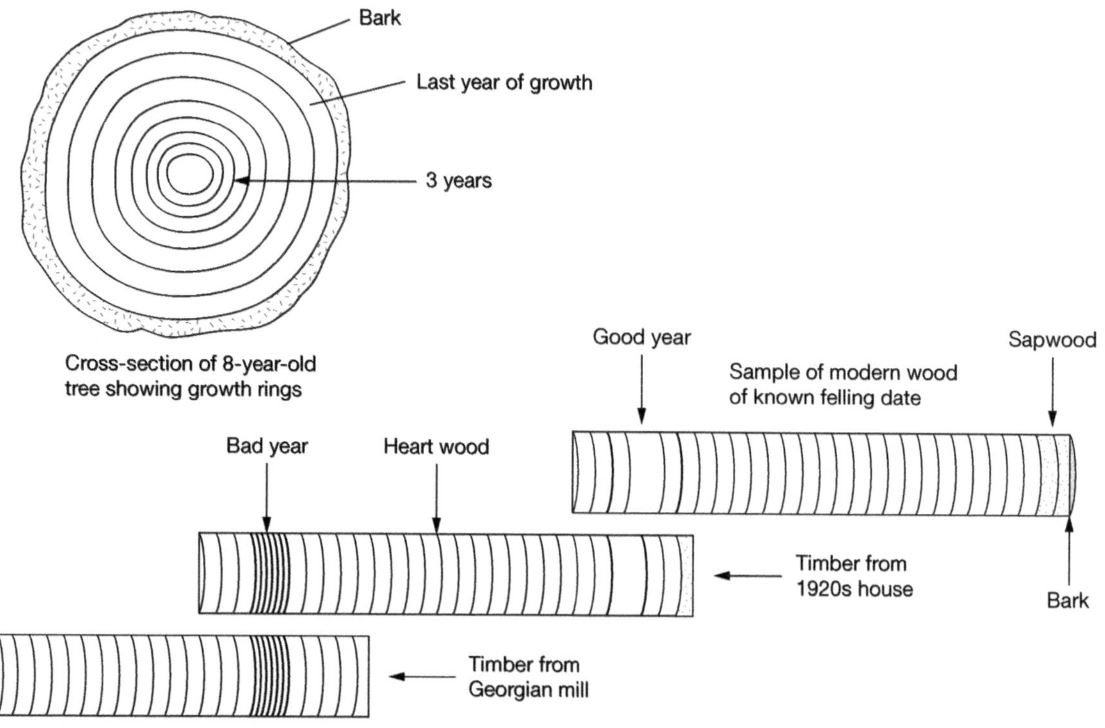

Figure 4.11 *The key principles of dendrochronology*

The principle of tree ring dating: overlaps are matched to take the sequence back from a known date to date old timbers. Samples are taken at 90 degrees to the grain and numbers of rings and their thickness measured by eye or computer.

use is from the Neolithic onwards and it has been widely applied to medieval ships and buildings. Where wood has been recycled, as often happened with structural timbers in the past, this method can overestimate the age of a structure.

Deep-sea cores, ice cores and varves

For the dating of major climatic sequences, international studies of deep-sea cores, **varves** and ice cores are used. These methods involve the examination of annual layers, which reflect climate at the time. The sea is full of tiny organisms such as plankton and corals which are sensitive to contemporary oxygen levels.

Preserved in layers of sediment on the ocean floor, their microfossils contain oxygen absorbed from the sea when they were alive. They are recovered for analysis by deep-sea coring. The balance of two oxygen isotopes – ^{16}O and ^{18}O – varies depending on temperature so their ratios in each layer within a core provide information on how cold the sea was and by extension, the size of the ice caps.

Similar principles apply to ice cores taken from major ice-sheets such as Greenland. Snow deposited on the glaciers in the summer is exposed to more sun and forms a different annual layer from the thicker, winter layer. The thickness of the layers reflects the extent of annual thawing and the length of summer so the pattern over several years varies.

Strata of ice laid down at the poles also reflect the temperature and salinity of the ocean at that

Figure 4.12 *Ice core. Richard Nunn, the assistant curator of the USGS/NSF–managed National Ice Core Laboratory, holds a 16,000-year-old ice core sample from the Greenland Ice Sheet Project.*

time. Ice contains trapped bubbles of air. These too can reveal oxygen ratios as well as concentrations of gases such as methane. The ice also traps atmospheric particles including debris from volcanic eruptions. The climatic data provided helps us understand the big picture of environmental changes and puts human developments into perspective. For example, the climatic period we have lived in since the last Ice Age is called the Holocene. In its early stages, *c.* 11,500 BP, Greenland ice cores record a rapid rise in temperatures starting with a dramatic 15 degree increase in ten years.

Varves are annual layers of sediment on the beds of glacial lakes. During the winter when liitle water flows into the lake, a layer of fine, often dark, particles are deposited. In spring the melt-water from the glaciers washes down large amounts of coarser material while tiny organisms such as algae and diatoms bloom and die and their remains sink to the botttom. This creates a pattern of a thin, dark winter ring and a thick, coarse and lighter summer ring for each year. Cores taken from the lake bottom can be analysed and double rings counted. A sequence of 17,000 years has been established in Scandinavia and 20,000 in the USA. Their main value is for providing a record of climatic conditions. Changing climate will lead to changing deposits which can then be cross-referenced over large areas. Where varves contain pollen they can be tied to geoarchaeological sequences.

Varves provide an alternative source of calibration for techniques such as radiocarbon and archaeomagnetism. Recent research in Japan has used fossilised twigs and leaves from the bed of

Lake Suigetsu to provide an alternative benchmark stretching back 52,000 years. Currently experiments are assessing the potential of ice and ocean cores and of corals to provide calibration beyond the range of dendrochronology.

Radiocarbon dating

There are three carbon isotopes (▶ p. 133) in the atmosphere which exist in very different quantities. A total of 99 per cent of all carbon is ^{12}C, 1 per cent is ^{13}C, and there are minute traces of ^{14}C. The first two are stable but carbon 14 is radioactive, which means it constantly decays over time. It is produced when cosmic radiation in the form of neutrons causes nitrogen atoms in the atmosphere to break down. Carbon isotopes are absorbed in their ratio by plants during photosynthesis and then passed on to the animals that eat the plants. When the animal or plant dies, it stops absorbing carbon and the amount of carbon 14 in its remains diminishes at a predictable rate. The time taken for half of ^{14}C to decay (half-life) is 5,730 years. In 1949 the atomic scientist Willard Libby recognised that by comparing the ratio of $^{12}C{:}^{14}C$ he could measure how much decay had taken place and use a formula to work out the number of years since the creature or plant had died. This principle could be extended for about ten half-lives or about 50,000 years, by which point there is very little ^{14}C left. Most organic materials can be dated in this way including bone, shell, charcoal, antler and peat. It is more precise with wood samples from twigs and nuts than from trees that may have lived for hundreds of years. Recent advances in extracting ancient lipids and other residues from ceramics (▶ p. 138) mean that individual foods or stored products can now be dated (Stott et al. 2003).

Radiocarbon dating appeared to provide the answer to dating on most archaeological sites but as its use became widespread its results were questioned. Many prehistoric dates were much older than had been expected while dates given for Bronze Age sites in Egypt and Mesopotamia where actual calendar dates were known were several hundred years out. Over the next decade a number of problems were identified. Libby had originally estimated the half-life to 5,568, which was too low. In addition, the amount of carbon in the atmosphere has varied over time because of fluctuations in solar activity. As a result, many dates for the last 8,000 years were underestimated. For 5000 BC this was by around 1,000 years! Results for the last 200 years are less reliable because of the amounts of carbon caused by burning fossil fuels since the industrial revolution. More recently scientists have also identified a 'marine reservoir' effect. Carbon in the food chain in the sea is up to 400 years older than that on land, with the result that dates based on bones of populations which ate a lot of marine food may be inaccurate. Results can also be thrown out by contamination in the ground; for example, by burrowing animals or during excavation and handling by archaeologists. Where possible, samples are packed in airtight packaging made from chemically neutral materials. Errors in measuring the miniscule quantities of ^{14}C in samples can also have major effects. It is common when looking at radiocarbon dates for a site to have a number of samples where the dates appear to conflict with the rest so multiple rather than single samples are always preferred. A further complication is that living things take up the carbon isotopes in slightly different ratios. The net result of these discoveries is that complex calculations have to be done with the raw results so that the final date is given as a statistical probability to within 1 standard deviation. This means that there is a 68 per cent chance or one 'level of confidence' (LOC) that the date is right and therefore nearly a one in three chance that it is wrong. For example, a ^{14}C date of 3000±100 BP means that there is a 68 per cent chance that the date is between 3100 and 2900 before the present. There is a greater chance of accuracy if a wider date range is given so at two standard deviations (or 2 LOC) there is a 95 per cent chance that the date is within a statistical error margin or

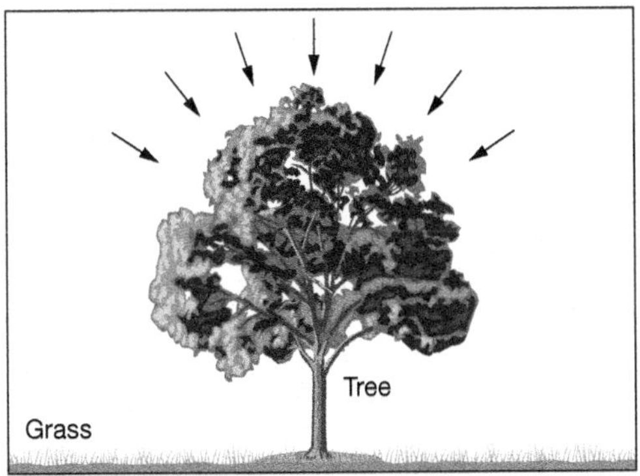

^{14}C is formed by cosmic radiation in the atmosphere and absorbed by plants through photosynthesis.

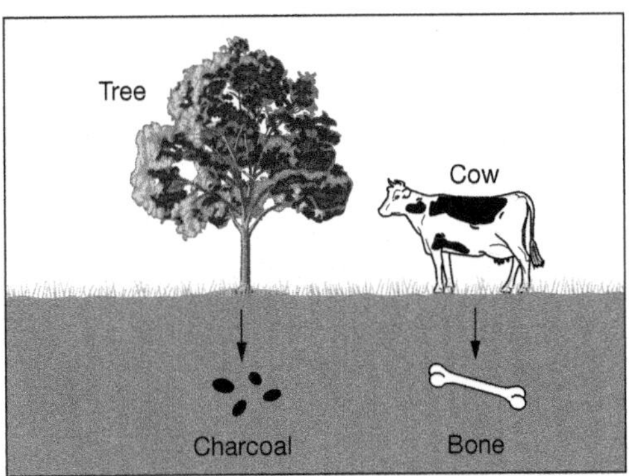

^{14}C is absorbed by animals from plants. It enters the archaeological record in burnt wood (charcoal) or bones.

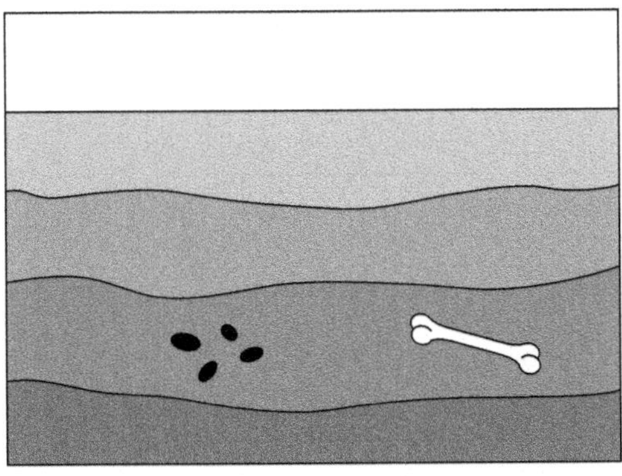

Archaeologists recover charcoal and bone samples to date a layer. Great care is taken to avoid contamination.

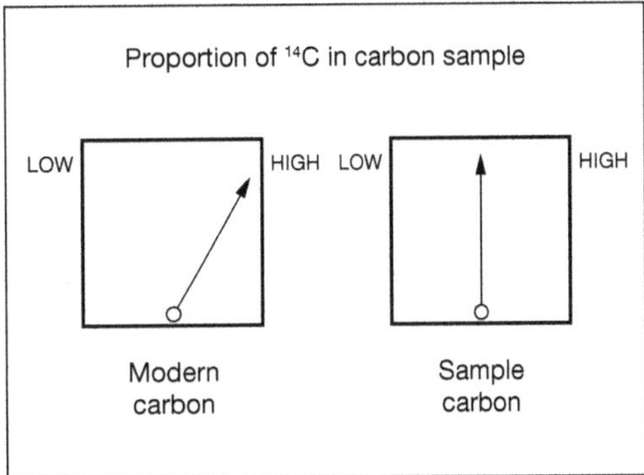

Laboratory analysis gives time since animal or plant died and ^{14}C decay began.

Figure 4.13 *How radiocarbon reaches the archaeological record*

tolerance. In our example 3000±200 BP would give us a 95 per cent chance that the date was between 3200 and 2800 years before the present. In other words, there is a trade-off between probability and precision.

Calibration using dendrochronology

To get round the problem of error margins, radiocarbon dates are calibrated. **Calibration** involves turning measures of time into calendar dates by comparing results from one method with dates from a more precise method. Dendrochronology is the most widely used method for calibration. Essentially, wood of a known age is tested for its ^{14}C date and the two dates compared. Once a large range of comparisons has been made, a chart can be produced which enables scientists to read off a calendar year against a sample date. Calibration curves are modified as new data on ancient wood is published. New ^{14}C results are compared with data in the tree-ring calendar to identify a ring with the same amount of ^{14}C. For some periods there will be more than one possible result since the relationship cannot be plotted as a smooth curve. The fluctuations in the amount of ^{14}C in

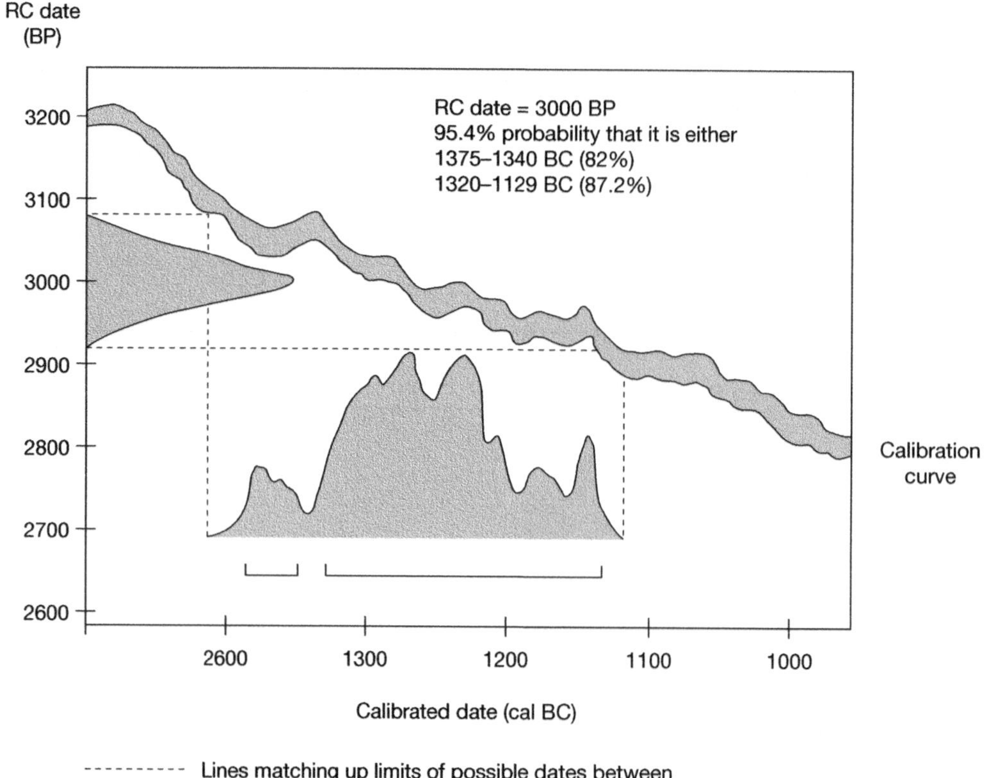

Figure 4.14 *How calibration works*

This diagram is intended simply to illustrate principles. In the example plotted you can see that where the calibration curve is steeper, raw dates are converted to a relatively short range of calibrated dates while where the curve is shallow the range would be much longer.

the atmosphere give several 'wiggles' to the curve. In 2010 scientists at Queen's University Belfast unveiled a new calibration curve called INTCAL09 which uses ice cores, climatic data and dendrochronology to cover the full radiocarbon range back to 50,000 BP.

Radiocarbon dating revolutionised our understanding of prehistory. Earlier chronologies had been founded on typological dating and classicist assumptions that change always spread out from the eastern Mediterranean to the rest of Europe (diffusion). The megalithic tombs of the Atlantic coast were shown to be a thousand years earlier than the pyramids (Renfrew 1973), while the village of Skara Brae (▶ p. 274) proved to be Neolithic rather than Iron Age.

^{14}C dates are expressed in the following ways:

- Lower case letters are often, but not always, used to show that dates are uncalibrated, whereas capitals should mean they have been calibrated. Increasingly 'Cal' is added to a calibrated date to avoid any confusion.
- Calendar dates are expressed as ad or bc (uncalibrated) and BC, AD, Cal BC, Cal AD (calibrated).
- Radiocarbon dates are expressed as BP or Cal BP (calibrated). BP means 'before present'

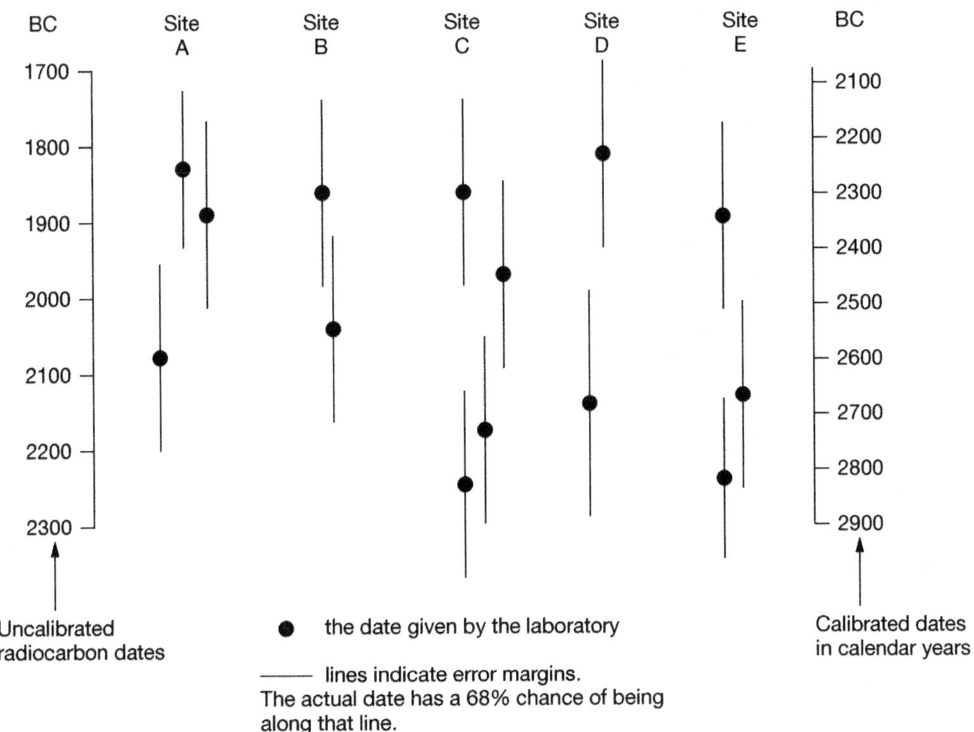

Figure 4.15 *Reading a radiocarbon table*

(1950) and is often preferred for early prehistoric periods for which BC (and AD) is relatively meaningless.

- Standard deviations are used to explain the statistical likelihood of a date actually being within the range or 'margin of error' stated. At one SD there is a two in three probability that the date falls within the given range.

Accelerator mass spectrometry (AMS)

Radiocarbon's practical use is for periods from 200 to about 10,000 years with less reliability to around 50,000 years. Until recently at least 10 grams of charcoal or 200 grams of bone were needed for results. The development of AMS has enabled samples as tiny as one grain of cereal or a fragment of cremated bone to be dated. Potentially this means a greater range of material can be utilised. Instead of calculating the number of decays within a given time, AMS uses energy to accelerate the carbon molecules in such a way that they can be separated by weight and then individually counted. This technique improves accuracy and speed and reduces the error margin but is significantly more expensive. Ultrafiltration is a new technique for slowly purifying bone collagen samples for AMS dating. By removing contaminants that might skew the result, it allows much greater accuracy. It is currently being used to re-date Neanderthal bones across Eurasia (▶ p. 201) with dramatic implications for our understanding of what happened to the Neanderthals.

Thermoluminescence (TL)

Buried deposits are subject to low-level ionising radiation from the surrounding rock and soil.

Where deposits include crystalline minerals such as quartz, calcite or feldspar, they trap some of the electrons from the radiation. This leads to a gradual build-up of electric energy in the crystals at a known rate. The electrical charge is released as light (luminescence) when the crystals are gradually heated to over 450°C. The amount of light is due to the number of trapped electrons which in turn relate to the length of time the minerals have been exposed to radiation since they were last heated. Each reheating resets the clock. The more light, the longer the time since the 'clock setting event'. The glow of light energy released by a given weight of a sample (palaeodose) can be measured in a laboratory to calculate the number of years since the minerals were heated.

$$\frac{\text{Palaeodose (total energy acquired since last heated)}}{\text{Annual dose (average amount gained in a year)}} = \text{Age in years since last heated}$$

This technique can be used for sediments and materials such as glass and burnt flint or stone for periods from the present to over 400,000 years ago. It can be used for ceramics but is usually unnecessary since dated typologies exist for most. It is significantly less accurate than ^{14}C dating and can give false readings due to varying radiation from the soil, heating after burial or, in the case of ceramics, where the initial firing was at low temperature. However, it is useful for older periods and instances where there are no organic remains including dating cave deposits and the Upper Palaeolithic figurines from Dolni Vestonice.

A similar principle underlies **Optically Stimulated Luminescence (OSL)**. Electrons from decaying radioactive elements are trapped in crystals of quartz or feldspar which form part of many sediments. When stimulated with laser-light (not heat), the electrons free themselves, giving off luminescence (light energy) in the process. The amount released can be used to

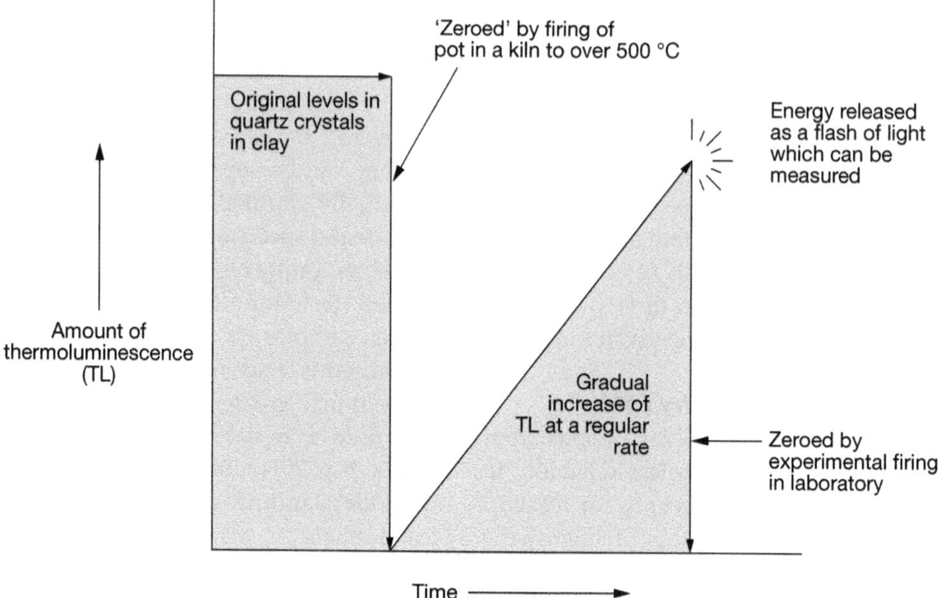

Figure 4.16 *How thermoluminescence works*

date the last 'clock setting event'. Dates from 50 to 1 million years can be calculated with more accuracy than TL. OSL measures the time since sediments were last exposed to sunlight or in the case of ceramics when they were last heated to over 400°C. OSL was used to date silt around the Uffington White Horse to the Bronze Age rather than the Iron Age, to which it had been dated stylistically.

Potassium–argon (K-Ar) dating

K-Ar dating has been used by geologists on volcanic rock samples which are 4.3 billion years old. It has the potential therefore to date the earliest archaeological deposits. When rock melts, gases contained within it are released into the atmosphere. When rock recrystallises to a solid state, it becomes impervious to atmospheric gases. However, one of the more common elements in volcanic rock is potassium and 1 per cent of potassium is the unstable isotope Potassium-40 (^{40}K). Radioactive potassium (^{40}K) in rock crystals decays to produce argon gas (^{40}Ar) and calcium (^{40}Ca) with a half-life of 1.25 billion years. Eleven atoms of ^{40}A are formed from the decay of every one hundred ^{40}K atoms and are trapped in the crystals. Measuring the amounts and ratios of these atoms in a laboratory provides a date at which the crystal was formed. It has been used in volcanic regions to date layers of rock which sandwich human remains. The dates then are indirect and provide TPQ and TAQ for the archaeology. These dates have much larger probability ranges than radiocarbon, often as high as 10 per cent. For instance, at Koobi Fora in East Africa early hominid remains were indirectly dated to 1.89 million years BP ± 10,000 years. The technique can be used for periods from around 200,000 to several million years ago but it is limited to sites with the right geology. If rocks are re-heated – for example, by later volcanic activity – their 'clock' is reset and they cannot be used for dating deposits.

	How it works	Which materials?	Which periods?	Limitations	Examples
Amino acid racemization	The chemical structures of the amino acids found in all living things decay slowly over time at a known rate	Bones, teeth and shell	1000 to 1 million years	Must not be cooked Needs calibrating Varies with climate	Ostrich eggs on Palaeolithic sites in Africa
Archeomagnetism	The earth's magnetic field changes over time. When iron oxide is heated to around 600°C and cools, it records the magnetic field at that time. Variations in the earth's field have been calculated which enables the date of initial heating to be established	Ceramics,lava, hearths and kilns that contain iron oxide	Up to 5,000 years	Local variations in magnetism. Sites must be undisturbed when measured. Needs to be calibrated, e.g. by varves. Can provide inaccurate dates where the same polarity occurred more than once	Clay ovens in south-west USA
Electron spin resonance (ESR)	Electrical charges build up at a known rate in some crystal structures. The time since the process began can be calculated by measuring the charge	Teeth enamel, shells, calcite deposits in caves	50,000 to 1 million years	Works best in dry environments Wide error margins	Palaeolithic sites in Israel and Africa
Fission track dating	Uranium decays regularly through fission (splitting), which releases energy and damages crystalline structures, leaving a 'track'. Tracks accumulate at a known rate and are counted to estimate the time the process of decay has taken	Glass, burned obsidian, heated stones containing uranium. Sites sandwiched between volcanic layers	Mainly 100,000 to several million years although some recent glass has been dated	Difficulty in differentiating tracks from crystal defects Over 10% error margins	Homo habilis bones at Olduvai Gorge from around 2 million years ago
Uranium series	Uranium isotopes U235 and U238 are soluble in water and decay to produce deposits of thorium and protactinium at known rates. By measuring the ratios of the elements the date at which the deposits were laid down can be established	Analysing calcium carbonate deposits where water containing uranium has seeped into caves and been deposited (e.g. as stalactites). Teeth enamel, shells	Early human sites in Europe 50,000 to 500,000 years	Prone to ambiguous results Needs a high uranium content	Dentine on Neanderthal/early human teeth in Israel

Figure 4.17 *Comparison of other major scientific dating methods*

Other absolute dating techniques

Figure 4.17 covers less commonly used methods, some of which are still at an experimental stage. Like radiocarbon dating, most of them rely on data showing known rates of chemical change or decay that can be measured in laboratories. Several of them measure the age of layers rather than the archaeological deposits themselves and are thus limited to particular types of geology. Most methods are used in combination to cross-check dates.

A new dating revolution? The application of Bayesian statistical analysis

Radiocarbon dates are essentially statements of probability. For example, 3500 ± 125 years means that the date has a 68 per cent chance of being somewhere within a 250-year period and a 95 per cent chance of lying within a 500-year period. These broad date ranges have meant that archaeologists have been unable to discuss particular events and discussions of sequences and changes have often been at a very general level. The application of a new statistical technique to radiocarbon dates offers the possibility of much greater precision and is challenging current beliefs about many periods in the past.

The Rev. Thomas Bayes was an C18th amateur mathematician. He developed a statistical model based on accumulating evidence in order to assess the probability of a given hypothesis being correct. This involves using observations and common-sense knowledge to modify probability statements. To take an extreme and simplified example: there might be a 5 per cent chance in any given year of snow falling on 25 December. However, if we knew that it snowed on the 23rd and 24th, the probability of snow falling on the 25th would increase significantly.

If we take our 250-year date range of 3500 ± 125 BP, there are 250 potential outcomes which have equal probability of being the right date. A Bayesian approach would be to update this hypothesis using other information available to us. For example, we may already have secure relative dating information based on stratigraphy or typology of artefacts or features which might lead us to reject parts of the date range. This is known as using 'informative' prior beliefs. Modern excavation techniques and the use of Harris matrices (▶ p. 74) for recording provide fine detail about the chronological order in which each context, ecofact or artefact was deposited. Subject to an understanding of site formation processes (▶ p. 165), we can then be clear about the sequence of dated material and which dates are more likely to be correct. As a result of combining different types of evidence, we might update our hypothesis by stating that it was probable that a smaller part of the range contained the probable actual date. In this case we might narrow the probable date range to fifty years rather than 250. This advance is possible because of recent developments in computer-based simulations and complex mathematical methods of translating archaeological data into formats where it can be analysed statistically. There is some criticism of the approach because it contains elements of subjectivity but it has generally been embraced by dating specialists.

Recovering the history of the Neolithic

The Neolithic in Britain has tended to be seen as a period of gradual changes and of monuments which were in use for millennia. This view is being transformed by an English Heritage programme of applying Bayesian analysis to over 2,000 radiocarbon dates. One of the first monuments to be investigated was the long barrow at Wayland's Smithy. Excavation in the 1960s recovered fourteen skeletons from its chambers and radiocarbon dates suggested it had been used periodically for 1,000 years. Recent forensic examination suggests that three of the people may have been killed by arrows. Two of the skeletons may have been scavenged by dogs or

Figure 4.18 *The façade of Wayland's Smithy*

wolves as they lay in the open before being recovered and buried. This may suggest that the people were killed at the same time in a raid or feud. Detailed observations of stratigraphy and the relative positions of each bone narrowed the range to a few decades from 3590 to 3560 BC. This opens up the possibility that the monument was related to one event or series of events and suggests that the middle of the 4th millennium BC was a time of social tensions. Re-processing of radiocarbon dates from four other long barrows including West Kennet and Hazleton revealed that the final burials in each of them dated to *c.* 3640 BC. In each case the tombs were in use for a few generations rather than hundreds of years.

Causewayed enclosures were also found to have been built over much shorter periods than previously thought and were almost certainly an idea imported from Europe. Hambledon Hill appears to have been built in 3685–3640 BC and used for perhaps 300 years. Windmill Hill may have been built and abandoned within a single lifetime. Alex Bayliss (2009), who leads the EH

Date range	Event	Notes
4100–4000 BC	Neolithic package arrives in the Thames Valley	Domesticated crops and animals, ceramic bowls, leaf arrowheads, flint mines
3900–3700 BC	Neolithic spreads westwards	Slow expansion suggests some immigration
c. 3800 BC	First long barrows built	Initially in the south east and spread westwards
	Polished stone axe exchange	Initially from Cornwall and Wales
	Causewayed enclosures built	Introduced to the Thames Valley
c. 3700 BC	Neolithic package crosses the Severn	It has taken 200 years to get this far
3700–3600 BC	Neolithic spreads to Northern Britain	Rapid change in 50–100 years suggests largely adopted
3600–3500 BC	Long barrows abandoned	Most only used for 30–50 years

Figure 4.19 *A tentative Neolithic sequence for Britain*

KEY STUDY

Dating the destruction of Minoan Crete

Several different explanations have been put forward for the apparent sudden end of the Minoan civilisation (▶ p. 470) on Crete including tsunami, earthquake, insurrection and invasion by the Mycenaeans or combinations of these. Apart from identifying evidence to test each idea, archaeologists have been divided over when the civilisation collapsed and it provides a good key study in the way different methods can conflict with or support each other. An overview chronology is given on p. 475.

Seriation and cross-dating of the latest pottery (Late Minoan 1B) found in the destroyed palaces (▶ p. 256) with Egyptian sequences put the end at *c.* 1450 BC – the time of the 18th Dynasty in Egypt. It was known that the volcanic island of Thera (Santorini) had blown up around this time and this quickly became the favoured explanation: ash clouds, destruction of Minoan ships and a tsunami resulted in the collapse of the Minoan state. The idea gained strength from the discovery of a buried Minoan town (Akrotiri) on the remains of Thera. Akrotiri was even suggested as the site of the mythical Atlantis. However, absolute dating techniques suggested that this explanation was flawed. Dendrochronology is useful in helping pinpoint climatic events which had a disruptive effect on past societies. Major volcanic eruptions throw dust up into the atmosphere and can significantly alter weather patterns and affect tree growth. Sequences in both northern Europe and the USA have very narrow growth rings for several years after 1628 BC, which indicated a very cold, wet period. This could have been the result of a major volcanic eruption. However, this is over 150 years too early to have destroyed the Minoans. Radiocarbon dates ranged from 1663 to 1599 BC, which overlapped the dendrochronology but not the seriation range. In addition there was increasing evidence of occupation of the palaces after their destruction and little sign of a tsunami.

The use of AMS has given us more precision with the date of the eruption. An olive tree buried in pumice on Thera was radiocarbon dated and then 'wiggle matched' to calibrate its death to 1621–1605 BC (Ramsey 2004). Then in 2006 tsunami deposits of mud and ash were located on the north-eastern coast of Crete near the Minoan sites of Malia and Palikastro (Bruins et al. 2009). Large quantities of marine organisms were found in these deposits. Geologists estimate that successive tsunami with waves up to 12m high had hit the island. Bone in these deposits produced calibrated results of 1682–1619 BC at 1 LOC. Analysis of Greenland ice-cores gives a peak of acidity at either 1642 or 1645 BC. Taken together these dates support each other and suggest that the Minoans suffered a catastrophe in the early C17th BC. This date is clearly at odds with the Egyptian dates and the reasons have not yet been resolved. It may be that the tsunami was the beginning of the end rather than the end itself and the civilisation was destabilised and declined slowly rather than collapsed. The Mycenaean explanation has been dealt a blow by recent strontium isotope studies of bones in rich burials dating after the palaces were finally destroyed. Nafplioti (2008) established that these possible rulers were raised on Crete, which tends to support the idea of revolt or civil strife bringing the civilisation to an end.

team, believes that we may now start to be able to identify specific events and changes within the early Neolithic at the level of generations rather than centuries. The use of 'BC' rather than 'BP' in their reports emphasises the revealing of 'history' in 'prehistory'. Their research suggests that monuments that we once saw as contemporary can now be seen as part of an emerging sequence. Neolithic ideas, and probably some people, arrived in the south east in the C41st BC. It took 200 years for Neolithic ideas to be adopted or to colonise the south but *c*. 3700 BC a tipping point was reached and the rest of Britain was rapidly 'converted'. The speed of this final change suggests ideas were adopted by the indigenous population. Monument building appears to be a brief period, perhaps linked to the founding generations.

Although first applied to radiocarbon dates, Bayesian statistics are being used in a range of other dating methods including thermoluminescence, uranium series and obsidian dating to improve the resolution of dates and in other areas of archaeometry where results are expressed in terms of probability.

Chapter 5

Archaeological Interpretation

This chapter explains why the way in which the archaeological record is formed is so important. It examines some ideas which archaeologists use to interpret archaeological remains and identifies strengths and weaknesses. This chapter links the first four 'method' chapters with the 'themes' which follow.

The goal of archaeology is to explain behaviour, but archaeologists do not dig up behaviour. They excavate material remains from the past and then infer human behaviour and the ideas that motivated behaviour from the clues this evidence provides. To make these inferences they use theories or models from the present or compare with similar examples that they have come across.

Figure 5.1 *Excavation of this dark circle of earth can define shape, dimension and content. Establishing what it once was will always require interpretation. This example was a lime kiln.*

As humans, we use theories and models all the time to interpret the world around us. It is impossible to describe something or another person without likening them to something or somebody else. The same is true for archaeology. For example, you need to have seen or read about excavated buildings to interpret a dark circular mark on the earth as the decayed remains of a posthole. This way of thinking about material remains in order to use them to interpret past behaviour is sometimes called 'middle-range' theory to distinguish it from 'big' theories about evolution (▶ p. 191), the origins of farming (▶ p. 324) or the development of states (▶ p. 468).

MIDDLE-RANGE THEORY

So before we can start to answer questions about how people lived or what their houses were like we need to ask, 'How did the data get like this?' Middle-range theory tries to understand how and why those traces of past activities that we excavate got into the ground in the first place and then how they were changed before and after burial and finally by excavation. If we do not understand these processes, then we cannot hope to understand what remains might tell us. Archaeological reconstruction is not like putting a jigsaw puzzle together. We never have all the pieces, some pieces are from different jigsaws and many pieces are in such poor condition that we do not know what they show or where they fit.

***Figure 5.2** Sites contain, and are made up of, features. This stone-built feature from Kingscote Roman Villa was identified as a kiln or corn dryer through reference to other sites, ethnographic example and experiment.*

Debates between archaeologists frequently stem from differences in their inferences about how archaeological data was created and how one should interpret it. University level involves the study of theories about the nature of archaeological knowledge. Until then a basic grasp of aspects of middle-range theory is useful to help you assess the strengths and weaknesses of different interpretations of particular sites. The debate over the Upper Palaeolithic site of Pincevent (▶ p. 278) is a classic example.

HOW DID IT GET LIKE THIS?

In order to be in a position to interpret data and determine its significance, archaeologists have to know which materials went together and can therefore be used to provide evidence of specific past behaviour. For example, a clustering of broken pottery, burnt stones and processed animal bones could represent a cooking area or it could be the result of many people spreading their domestic rubbish on a field as fertiliser. This is where archaeology becomes detective work. To determine which explanation is most likely to be correct, we need to understand the processes by which data reached us. Not all the materials used in human activity enter the archaeological record. Once there, some materials survive, others do not. For example, Neolithic sites from Orkney such as Skara Brae (▶ p. 274) have survived better than any others in the British Isles because the absence of suitable trees meant that they had to be built from local flagstone. Finally, there is better recovery of materials on some sites than others. **Transformation processes** or formation processes are labels for the way evidence from human behaviour in the past has been shaped by human and natural forces into the data recorded in archaeological reports. There are four broad stages:

- behavioural processes
- depositional processes
- post-depositional processes
- recovery processes.

 **KEY TERM**

Transformation processes

All the human and natural forces that shape archaeological evidence from the point of creation to post-excavation analysis.

Formation processes

Behavioural processes include all the things people did prior to an object, butchered animal or structure entering the archaeological record. This includes getting the raw material (acquisition), making or processing it (process), using it (use) and disposing of it (discard). For example, a fox is caught in a trap (acquisition), it is skinned with a flint blade (process), the fur is worn (use), the carcass is thrown onto a midden (discard). Each stage potentially leaves telltale clues.

Depositional processes are the ways in which remains actually find their way into the ground. If humans are responsible, we need to try to understand their logic. Why was an artefact discarded rather than being reused, recycled or repaired? These questions also apply to structures and ecofacts. Most items are discarded as rubbish. However, not all rubbish is discarded in the same way. Smaller items tend to be dropped where they are used (primary refuse). Larger or smellier items tend to be removed a greater distance (secondary refuse). The former can usually tell us something about where and how a process occurred while the latter can often just tell us that it happened. However, small items of primary rubbish are more likely to be subsequently moved through cleaning and trampling. When a site is abandoned, the pattern of discard will depend on whether the people had planned to leave, had to leave suddenly or were wiped out in a natural disaster as at Pompeii. As in our own homes, a few objects are kept for several generations. It accounts for why old artefacts sometimes turn

Stage of formation process	*Example*	*We need to know*	*May enter the archaeological record as*
Acquisition	Collecting flint, feathers and resin, cutting wood	Where and how the materials were gathered Why they were chosen	Flint mine
Process	Shaping the flint, feathers and wood to make an arrow Heating the resin to make glue	What techniques and tools were used	Waste flakes Antler tools
Use/purpose	Used to hunt animals	How it was used, which creatures it was used on	Lost or broken points
Discard	Buried with its owner or in the remains of an animal	Was it thrown away, lost or deliberately abandoned?	Arrowhead in burial or bone debris

Figure 5.3 *Example of the way in which a flint-tipped arrow might enter the archaeological record*

KEY TERM

Curation

Deliberately keeping and preserving an artefact.

up amid much more recent material. Artefacts might be curated for sentimental reasons, heirlooms, rarity, beauty or because they were particularly useful. Curated articles (particularly small, portable objects) are more likely to be taken away when a settlement is abandoned. Curation can distort the record in other ways; for example, in early medieval Europe fine classical pottery often continued in use while metal vessels were recycled. Sometimes articles or even buildings are recycled with a new use. A spear point may be reworked to a scraper, a house can become a barn. What has been curated in your home?

While there have been odd instances of faked evidence such as 'Piltdown Man', it is highly unlikely that archaeological material has been buried to fool later generations. However, there are still codes to be broken. Archaeologists carefully map buried finds to see if there are patterns. Where these exist, they may indicate 'structured' rather than random deposition. This is where material was deliberately deposited in the past rather than simply discarded. Structured deposition has been particularly influential in studies of ritual practices in European prehistory; for example, at Flag Fen (▶ p. 543) and at Hjortspring. Here an assemblage of weapons, personal ornaments and a sea-going ship from AD 300 represents the sacrifice of booty from a successful battle. Careful plotting of the position of artefacts and tracing links between different piles of equipment enabled archaeologists to establish that this was one big sacrifice rather than deposits over a long period. The objects had been 'ritually killed' prior to being deliberately placed in a bog.

Natural forces may also have created particular deposits. These might include erosion, flooding or volcanic activity. By understanding formation and transformation processes, archaeologists learn to differentiate between what was caused by humans and what was caused by nature.

Figure 5.4 *Finds from the Hjortspring hoard*

KEY TERM

Structured deposition

Patterns due to material being deliberately deposited in the past, often during rituals.

How does archaeology get buried?

Leaving aside deliberate burial and sites buried by cataclysmic events such as landslides, a key player is the humble earthworm. Worms process waste vegetation and throw up 'worm casts'. Over many years these raise the soil level to cover discarded material and abandoned structures. Time-lapse photography would show the archaeology literally sinking into the ground. In rural areas other burrowing animals such as moles also move topsoil. Animal droppings and dying vegetation, particularly leaf mould on dry land and peat on wetland, create new soil and can rapidly cover quite large structures. The wind also deposits dust, sand and eroded soils from elsewhere. In urban areas buildings are often raised on the levelled ruins of earlier structures. This is at its most spectacular on tell sites (▶ p. 339). Until recently, rubbish was often burnt or buried in towns and this increased the depth of soil, as did the addition of human remains and coffins in churchyards. As a result, archaeological

Figure 5.5 *A collapsing building*

Once the roof begins to leak, structural integrity is quickly lost. Rot and insects destroy the supporting timbers until the roof collapses. Water now has access to the interior and seeps into the walls where freeze/dry action gradually breaks the masonry or brickwork apart. Plants start to grow in the crevices and extend cracks as they grow. The doors and windows rot and allow more weathering. Slowly the walls collapse until just the lower courses remain, covered in vegetation. Further build-ups of soil from rotting vegetation may bury them entirely.

Figure 5.6 *A vanished experimental Mesolithic hut at Maelmin. The structure of branches and thatch became unstable after several years and was dismantled. Very little evidence remains beyond a slight circular depression.*

deposits in towns are usually much more deeply buried than contemporary remains in the countryside. Archaeologists want to know whether material they excavate is where it was originally discarded (primary context) or whether it has been moved or disturbed after initial burial (secondary context).

Post-depositional processes

Once buried, further modifications take place. The archaeological record is not a safe place for artefacts or ecofacts and it is unusual for artefacts to be found exactly where someone dropped them thousands of years ago. Archaeological materials move and are changed in the soil due to disturbance by both human and natural forces. The rearrangement of soils by tree roots, earthworms and other living things is called bioturbation. Experiments have shown that smaller materials can be moved upwards while larger, heavier materials often move downwards. In extreme cases this can confuse our understanding of their stratigraphic relationships.

The causes of these transformations after burial are usually grouped as:

- natural forces or 'N transforms', including bacteria, acid, water, erosion, gravity, ice, worms, sunlight, roots, freezing and thawing, drying out (desiccation), silting, gnawing, burrowing, and oxidisation
- human or cultural 'C transforms', including grave robbing, looting, bombing, mining, re-use, ploughing, collecting, trampling, building and draining.

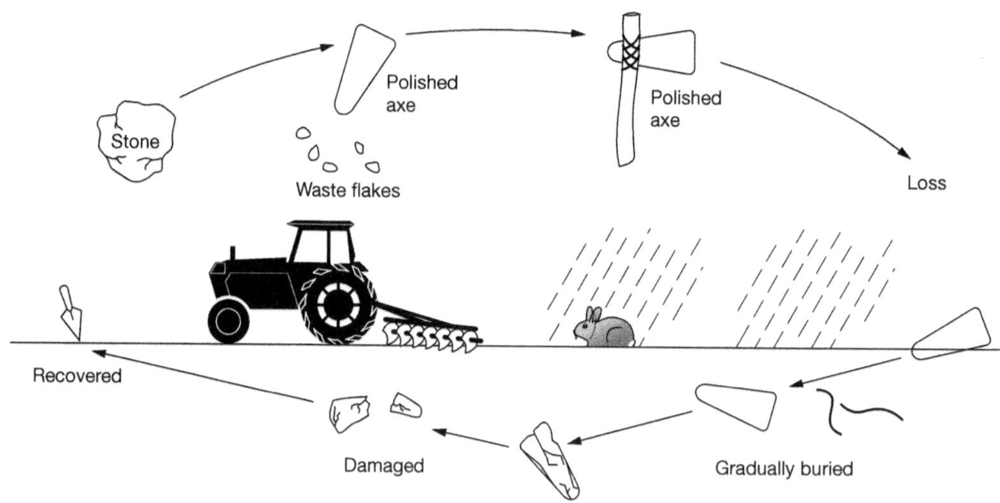

Figure 5.7 *Examples of transformation processes affecting a polished stone axe*

Figure 5.8 *N transforms: the destructive power of the North Sea, eroding, moving and demolishing a Second World War pillbox*

Taphonomy

Taphonomy (the law of burial) is the name commonly given to the study of the effects of such processes on animal and plant remains. These factors can result in changes including movement, destruction, partial decay, colour-loss, texture and shape changes, and alteration of chemical composition. However, this is never even; the extent of change varies between different materials. Inorganic materials are preserved best. Stone, pottery and high-quality bronze, for example, are particularly durable.

Consequently, there is a systematic bias in the archaeological record towards artefacts made from these materials. This can also be seen in museum collections and archaeological research. By contrast, organic materials such as wool, wood and bodies are far less likely to survive. Similarly, large animal bones generally survive better than plants, which is why there has been more focus on big-game hunting rather than gathering when considering prehistoric economies (▶ p. 298). There is also variability between similar types of materials. Gold and silver, for example, do not oxidise and survive far better than copper and iron. The size of buried objects, their depth of burial, climate and the nature of the soil further complicate these basic distinctions. Bones, for example, will decay more slowly than normal in soils with little oxygen such as clay. We can gain an insight into the wealth of material that is usually lost by studying finds from sites with exceptionally good organic preservation. In these cases, remains are often protected from the bacteria which normally consume organic material by climatic conditions or low oxygen levels (anaerobic conditions).

Even in waterlogged environments there can be considerable variability. Organic materials in sediments on a stormy coast are less likely to survive than those at the bottom of a lake. The chemistry of the water is also critical. Horn and animal fibres such as wool survive best in slightly acid conditions whereas bone and plant fibres such as flax survive best in slight alkaline conditions. The bias this can create was clear at Illerup (▶ p. 483). Seawater is also corrosive, particularly of iron.

Special preservation

In arid sites, often in desert regions, remains can dry out (desiccation) before they have a

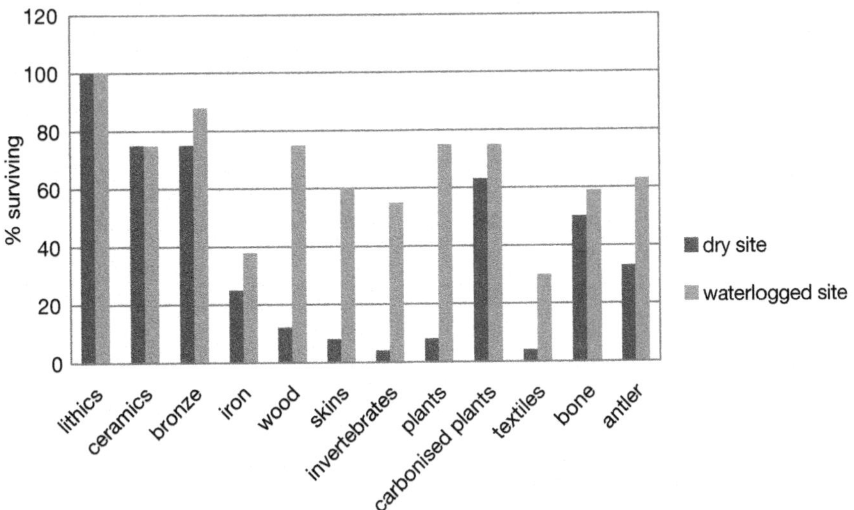

Figure 5.9 *Survival rates of different material*

chance to decay. In the case of bodies, this process creates natural mummies (▶ p. 115). Other classic examples include Mesa Verde in the south-west USA, where wooden and leather items were preserved. Deep caves have their own microclimates which can lead to good organic preservation. The wooden tapers and fragments of cordage from Lascaux (▶ p. 529) are a good example.

Waterlogged sites including peat bogs or submarine sites have been particularly important in European archaeology. Examples include Star Carr (▶ p. 267), bog bodies (e.g. Tollund Man), Tybrind Vig (▶ p. 309) and the wreck of the *Mary Rose*. On most sites, organic finds make up a small proportion of recovered materials. On wet sites they usually provide over 75 per cent of finds. The question for archaeologists is whether wet sites are typical and whether they can assume that other sites originally had the same volumes of organic material.

Frozen sites have produced some incredible finds. Perhaps the best known are the bodies of Ötzi the Ice Man (▶ p. 104) from the Alps and the Pazyryk 'Ice Maiden' from Siberia. Their skin has been so well preserved that tattoos and acupuncture marks can be studied. Such sites may be anaerobic but, more importantly, freezing temperatures inhibit fungal and bacterial action.

Rapidly buried sites can also reveal much that is normally lost. Examples include Pompeii volcanic ash, Copan earthquake and Ozette in the USA, where mudslides also preserved organic material.

Other situations with exceptional preservation include caves and salt (▶ p. 373) or copper mines where chemicals inhibit bacterial decomposition.

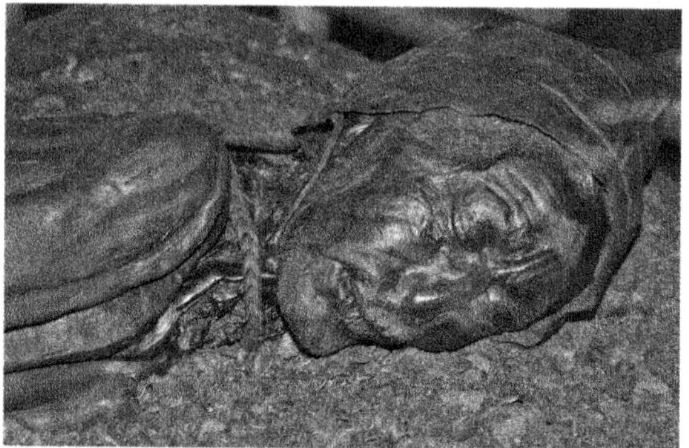

Figure 5.10 *Extreme preservation. A: casts of victims of Pompeii. B: Tollund Man, the best preserved Danish bog body. C: wooden buildings surviving in arid conditions at Bodie ghost town, California.*

Recovery processes

As if these processes were not enough, there is one final hurdle for archaeological remains to cross before they can be used to explain the past. Archaeologists themselves structure the archaeological record in the way they recover data. This results in some materials or sites being better represented than others. Sometimes this may simply be due to chance factors such as discovery or whether archaeologists can get access to particular sites. Decisions about how much of a site to excavate, which samples to take and what period to prioritise all 'structure' what is recorded. Similarly, while pottery and metals finds are usually recorded, animal bone is sometimes not. For example, in the USA during the depression of the 1930s, excavation of Native American settlement and burial sites was carried out as one of a number of welfare for work programmes for the unemployed under the New Deal. With so many inexperienced diggers, ceramic artefacts tended to dominate recovered assemblages while much environmental evidence such as bone or charred wood was discarded. At Star Carr in the 1950s, environmental evidence was valued but the excavators were so overwhelmed by the sheer quantity of wood and bone that recovery policy was to only keep items larger than a fingernail.

The techniques available for recovery are also important. Depending on the mesh size, sieving (▶ p. 64) can dramatically increase the recovery of earth-coloured pottery, coins, lithics and organic remains. However, sieves are not used as widely in Britain as in the USA. Not all excavations will use flotation (▶ p. 65) techniques to recover pollen, metal debris and small bone fragments or have the laboratory support to analyse them. Finally there may be variations in the skills of the diggers and those recording the finds. Once away from the site, the care taken in analysis and storage may continue to transform the record.

MAKING SENSE OF THE DATA

The net result of transformation processes is that archaeologists do not simply piece together recorded data as if they were pieces of a jigsaw to produce a picture of the past. Archaeological evidence cannot speak for itself and needs interpretation. Whatever was deposited was a fraction of the material used by people in the past. Only some elements of this will survive and only a sample of them will be recovered. By understanding transformation processes, archaeologists gain insights into what shaped the various samples. This enables them to understand which of the patterns in their data actually result from human behaviour in order to begin interpreting them. For example, human skeletons are often found with the head turned to one side. At face value this might seem a significant part of a belief system and mortuary ritual. However, forensic science has revealed that the slumping of corpses' heads is due to natural processes of decay. Some aspects of past behaviour are easier to reconstruct than others. The way stone tools were made, animals were hunted and butchered and buildings were laid out is much more straightforward to see than how societies organised themselves, what they believed and the nature of gender roles. However, even with a topic like diet, we can never be sure that a rubbish pit or midden is truly representative of what people ate. Have a look in your own dustbins to see if this is valid for you too. In 1954 Hawkes produced a model which has come to be known as 'Hawkes' ladder of inference'. In it he identified a hierarchy of aspects of past societies according to how easy they were to infer. Technical processes were seen as the easiest and thus at the bottom followed by economics with political institutions and religious beliefs at the top.

Partly because of all these factors and the limitations of our analytical techniques, archaeological reports often contain minimal amounts of interpretation. Their writers follow a scientific tradition of reporting their findings and analysis of data but leaving interpretation to others. An unfortunate by-product of this strong emphasis on scientific approaches has been that sometimes archaeologists have not always addressed, or clearly communicated on, the more difficult topics. This has sometimes enabled pseudo-archaeological explanations to fill the void with

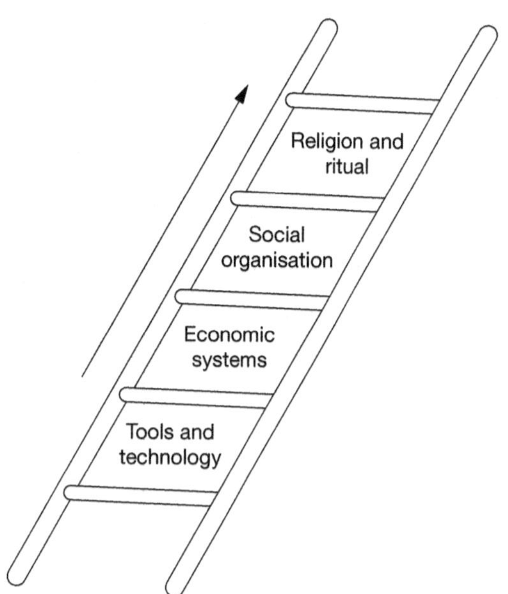

Figure 5.11 *Hawkes' ladder of inference*

misleading explanations based on sweeping generalisations, faith or evidence taken out of context. Recurring themes include the existence of lost advanced civilisations such as Atlantis and the role of space aliens in prehistory. A classic and best-selling example was the way the author Von Däniken interpreted the Wakah Kan relief carving from Palenque as evidence of alien astronauts.

In Mayan beliefs the 'world tree' or Wakah Kan linked the underworld, the realm of the living and the sky. The king dressed in the image of the Wakah Kan to emphasise the special relationship between the ruler and the spirit world. He provided a conduit for supernatural powers. Religious belief serves to sustain the authority of the king. In the relief, King Pacal is shown falling into the jaws of the earth monster. Underneath is an altar with a bowl of blood sacrifices burning and thus opening up a portal into another world. The smoking axe in Pacal's forehead is a mark of his divinity and he wears a jade net skirt which reveals that at his moment of death he had become the 'Maize God'. Above

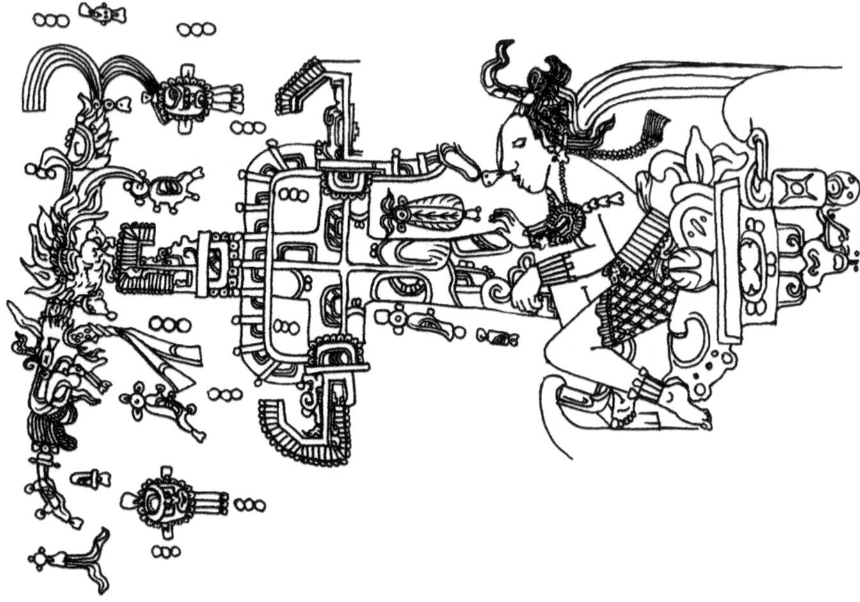

Figure 5.12 *Drawing of the Wakah Kan or 'Raised up sky' from Palenque*

him the cross branch of the tree represents the doubleheaded 'vision serpent' of life and death. This sceptre of power is depicted on altars being handed on from one ruler to the next rather like a relay baton. Perhaps influenced by the contemporary moon-landings, Von Däniken (1969) simply interpreted the image as portraying the front of an alien craft. This alleged recording of extra-terrestrial visits was then cited as 'evidence' to support alien involvement in building Mayan cities and other ancient sites such as the Nazca lines or the pyramids.

KEY TERM

Assemblage

Where a certain group of artefacts and/or ecofacts from the same period are repeatedly found together.

Analysing spatial and temporal patterns

Having identified archaeological material and taken account of various transformation processes, archaeologists try to identify what human behaviour lies behind them. Initially this involves pattern recognition in both space and time: plotting vertical and horizontal relationships between finds, structures and sites. Materials found grouped together from the same context (▶ p. 54) are called an assemblage. So a cluster of animal remains in one place is called a 'bone' or 'faunal assemblage'. Where the focus is purely upon technology, the term 'industry' is often used to group similar tools and methods of manufacture; for example, the Neanderthal Mousterian Industry (▶ p. 201).

Where a certain group of artefacts, features and symbols are repeatedly found together, they are called a cultural assemblage to indicate that they were created by a specific people during a particular time; for example, the Beaker burial assemblage (▶ p. 456). Groups of related assemblages and features (▶ p. xxxiii) are referred to as 'Archaeological Cultures' and are used to distinguish different peoples in the past. The Linearbandkeramik (LBK) farmers of 6th millennium BC Europe are a classic example (▶ p. 346). Today archaeologists do not assume that groups with the same archaeological culture necessarily recognised themselves as one ethnic group or even spoke the same language.

Repeated patterns of artefacts and ecofacts are also taken to be evidence for behaviour. For example, a scatter of flint tools amidst the bones of an animal might indicate a butchery or kill site involving humans in scavenging or hunting. Archaeologists carry mental templates around in their head for many common, recurring patterns which they come across in their work. For example, fires or hearths usually colour the earth

Figure 5.13 *Linearbandkeramik pot (laser scan)*

Along with massive timber longhouses (▶ p. 347) and woodworking adzes, the distinctive ceramics decorated with linear bands make up key elements of the LBK cultural assemblage. Such finds immediately enable archaeologists to identify the approximate period and the likely type of settlement. (© Landesamt für Archäologie Sachsen, Thomas Reuter)

KEY TERM

Signature

A recurring pattern of artefacts, ecofacts and features which are associated with particular activities.

reddish-orange while smelting or metalworking leaves slag and other waste products. Archaeologists will 'read' these **signatures** when they come across similar finds or features on new sites.

Site or palimpsest?

Sometimes what appear to be patterns can be misleading. Where a location has been subject to repeated activity over very long periods of time, there can be a build-up of archaeological material from many diverse episodes of activity. On excavation this mass of material can appear to represent a significant area of human activity. This particularly applies to Palaeolithic sites such as the shore of a waterhole which may have been repeatedly used by both humans and animals over hundreds of years. Discarded bones from predators and humans and occasional stone tools dropped by their users are trampled into the mud, moved around by water action and finally buried.

Olduvai Gorge (▶ p. 197) in East Africa features dense concentrations of stone tools and animal bones. Some archaeologists interpreted these as 'living floors' or base camps where activities took place in a single period of occupation. Other archaeologists suggest that such sites are in fact **palimpsests,** that is, accumulations of material from different times caused by natural forces as well as human activity. The term is also sometimes used for multiperiod sites where so many features intercut each other that it is difficult to identify distinct phases.

The Homo heidelbergensis (▶ p. 200) site of Bilzingsleben, Germany, illustrates some of the problems of unpicking site formation processes to understand human behaviour between 412 and 320,000 BP. Preservation was good since water levels slowly inundated the site, which was situated on the shore of an ancient lake. A range of deposits including thousands of stone tools, animal bones (including elephants and rhinos) and some human remains were buried under lake sediments. Mania (1991), the excavator, interpreted patterns including a series of large rings of faunal remains and tools as being the

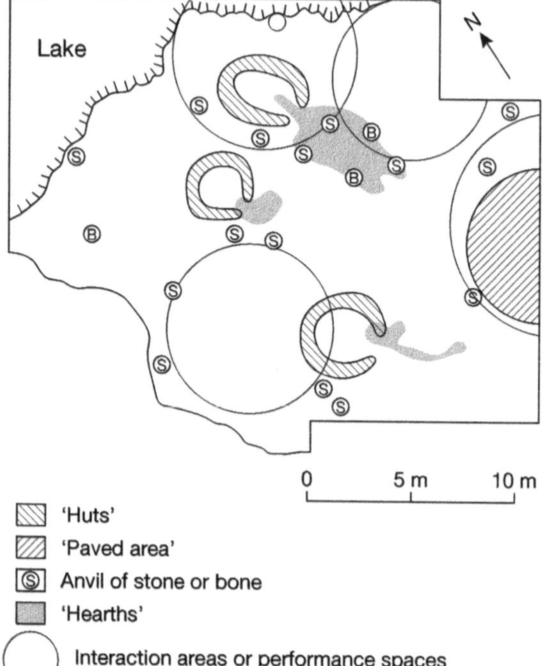

Figure 5.14 *Bilzingsleben*

KEY TERM

Palimpsest

Accumulated, unrelated archaeological material deposited on multiple occasions in the same place over a long period of time.

remains of a camp site with four distinct activity areas for processing wood, stone and antler. Gamble (1999) used a statistical model to challenge this view, arguing that the apparent patterns were the result of successive visits to a 'locale' and that the circular patterns were not the outline of huts but palimpsests of materials which built up around trees. Gamble's gathering places are marked with circles on the plan. These two radically different interpretations offer very different verdicts on the sophistication of heidelbergensis society. Support for Gamble's view has come from a study of the large numbers of red deer antlers accumulated on the site. Vollbrecht (2000) examined hundreds of antlers and only found five where wear marks could not be explained by fluvial (water) action. Terra Amata, France, is another contemporary site which appears to have been structured with hearths and possibly huts but here, too, many archaeologists remain sceptical.

Use of analogies

The next stage of archaeological interpretation tends to vary according to the ideas about knowledge held by the archaeologist. In most cases they will use analogies or analogs to formulate theories about what the data can provide evidence of. This involves using something with which we are already familiar to interpret a new thing or phenomenon. It is based on the idea that if two things are similar in one way then they may be similar in others. When we describe an artefact as a hand-axe or an enclosure as a hillfort, we are using analogies. Analogies range from interpretations of how something was made or worn to what the social systems or patterns of religious

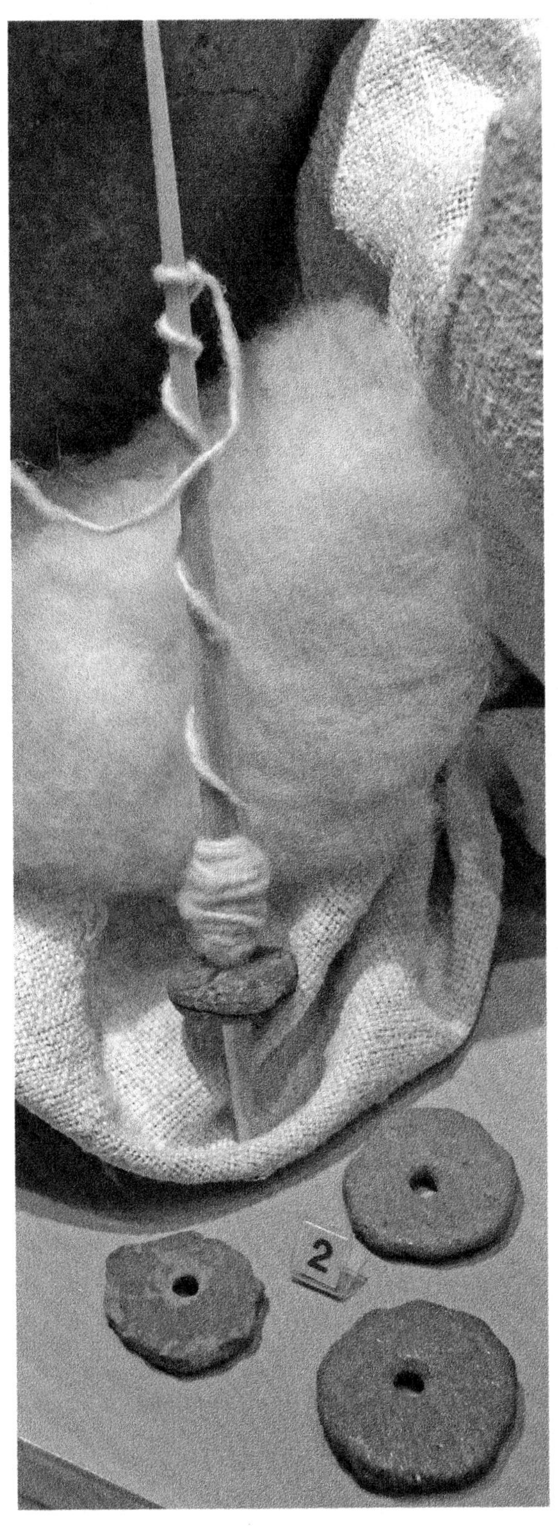

Figure 5.15 *Spindles*

These composite artefacts for twisting wool into thread are made of both organic and inorganic materials. Only the clay or stone 'whorl' is likely to survive. Interpretation is needed to reconstruct it.

belief in the past might have been. Analogies cannot prove anything about the past but through identifying similarities they can tell us much about what was possible. They can widen our horizons, generate new lines of enquiry and provide theories to be tested against further evidence to see how robust they are. They can lead to widely differing interpretation because when we think we are discovering patterns in archaeological data, what we are really doing is organising data so that it reflects the structures already in our minds. For example, a female skeleton in a prehistoric burial with a flint arrowhead by her neck might be automatically interpreted as a victim if you have already assumed that only men fired arrows. Archaeologists with other assumptions might see her as a hunter or warrior. Many female burials in museums were originally sexed in the C19th or earlier C20th solely on the basis of grave goods. At that time a mirror, earrings or hair accessories in western societies were automatically assumed to be female so it made sense. With changing fashions in our societies and greater use of ethnographic analogies we may be less certain (▶ p. 449). Where two things are compared because of similarities they are sometimes termed formal analogies; for example, the mortuary practice of the Merina of Madagascar has been used to provide insights into Neolithic beliefs (▶ p. 532). Comparisons based on historic or cultural connections are termed relational analogies.

Sources of archaeological analogies

There are four main sources of analogy: models from other disciplines, history, ethnography and actualistic studies, which includes experimentation.

Analogies imported from other disciplines

Archaeology is a magpie discipline. As well as borrowing a battery of techniques from science, a wide range of models have been imported, especially from social sciences. Many examples are explored later in this book, particularly the impact of geographical models on interpretation of settlement patterns (▶ p. 245).

Historical accounts

Classical accounts of the world such as the descriptions of Ancient Egypt by Herodotus or Roman accounts of Britain have been particularly influential in understanding social and religious practices such as 'barbarian' sacrifices (▶ p. 483). Literary and artistic sources such as the poetry of early medieval Europe have been used to provide models of social organisation such as the nature of Anglo-Saxon kingship (▶ p. 442). Travelogues written by the first western people to visit areas largely unaffected by European culture provide insights, albeit from an outside perspective, into dwellings, technology and warfare. For example, reports from fur traders and explorers provide insights into the economy of Native Americans at sites such as Head Smashed In (▶ p. 253). These accounts are often called ethno-histories. Where there is continuity in population, environment and some cultural forms, the direct historical approach (DHA) uses relational analogies based upon studies of, or oral accounts from, current peoples.

At San Jose Mogote, Marcus and Flannery (1994) combined several key interpretative methods in their exploration of Zapotec beliefs. The Zapotec civilisation flourished in the Oaxaca Valley of southern Mexico between 200 BC and AD 700. There was evidence of great continuity in local populations from Zapotec times until the Spanish conquest in the C16th, which enabled the archaeologists to use a direct historical approach. Spanish priests had documented local 'pagan' customs that were used to form a hypothesis for testing by excavation. The archaeologists predicted that anything with breath would be sacred and that ancestors would be worshipped. The burning of copal incense and sacrifices of blood, jade, living things and exotic goods would be

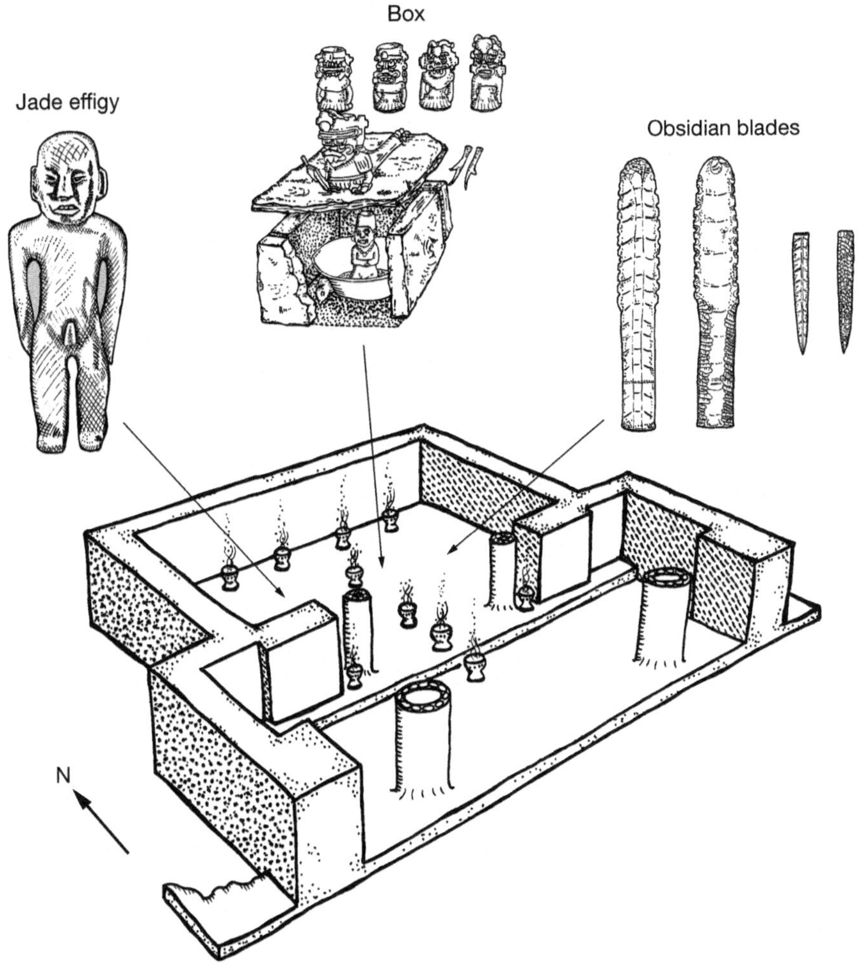

Figure 5.16 *The partial reconstruction of a Zapotec temple showing the position of key finds and the layout of the structure*

made to petition elemental forces such as earthquake and lightning. They expected to find evidence of priests who lived in two-roomed houses with sacrifices made in the inner room and who used drugs to reach ecstatic states.

Excavations at San Jose Mogote revealed symbolism in the architecture and repeated patterns of structured deposition. There were a series of two-roomed buildings with the same east–west axis superimposed upon them. The inner rooms had been kept scrupulously clean, although there were traces of repeated burning in them. Tiny pieces of debris in the corners were frequently from obsidian blades or stingray stings, used for bloodletting until historic times. Buried in the floor were tiny statues, jade beads and the bones of quail, a bird believed to be pure. The Spanish had not recorded this aspect of religion. Underfloor offerings also included effigies of the lightning clouds, hail and wind. Research amongst local people revealed that they called the statuettes 'little people of the clouds'. Ancestors were also known as cloud people. Through a mixture of historical records, analyses of excavated architecture and artefacts, and ethnography, Marcus and Flannery were able to reach conclusions about Zapotec reverence for ancestors and natural forces and the types of ritual practice involved in worship.

Ethnography or anthropology

Ethnography is the study of people in the world today while anthropology compares human cultures to identify general principles. Ethnographic analogies draw on the wide range of current and historically recorded cultures to interpret archaeological evidence. General models drawing on broad comparisons across many cultures such as Service's band–tribe–chiefdom model of social evolution (▶ p. 419) have been used to categorise and interpret past societies. Our society does not include all the rich variety of human activity and culture that has existed. To rely on it as the sole source of analogies would be limiting and lead to Eurocentric and anachronistic interpretations. Specific analogies have been used to explore particular archaeological phenomena. Sometimes these are simply insights into tool use or provide alternative models for past structures. Romanian peasant farmers have traditionally stored grain off the ground in six-poster granaries. This kind of structure has provided a formal analogy to interpret four- and six-post settings on Iron Age sites such as Danebury (▶ p. 184).

Amongst the most well-known ethnographic studies are those of the Hadza of Tanzania and !Kung of the Kalahari Desert who were used in the 1960s to provide social and economic models for pre-agricultural humans as 'man the hunter'. In particular the 1957 film of a !Kung giraffe hunt, *The Hunters*, was uncritically used to interpret early hominid sites. Archaeologists also have to resist the temptation to select the single examples that make most sense to them. Most ethnographic studies come from the C19th and C20th, when most of the world was already influenced in some way by European civilisations. There is often also a huge gulf in time and place between ancient peoples and the modern groups who are the source of analogies. While taking us beyond Western models, ethnography can also limit our imagination. It is highly likely that ideas, social organisations and ways of doing things existed in the past but are not present in any current societies. The greater share of variation in human societies has already been lost. Settlement archaeology (▶ p. 229) and studies of past religious beliefs (▶ p. 505) have been particularly influenced by ethnographic analogies.

Figure 5.17 *Romanian six-poster*

Ethnoarchaeology

Ethnoarchaeology involves studying how contemporary communities use material culture from an archaeological perspective. By correlating modern activities with physical remains we may start to understand what behaviour is reflected in which data. Examining the distribution of remains within modern hunting camps may help identify the functions of particular areas. Binford's (1978) study of Nunamiut caribou hunters in Alaska (▶ p. 229) is a classic in this respect. By following the hunting parties he was able to record their activities and have the sites and assemblages explained to him. He used the understanding gained there to provide insights

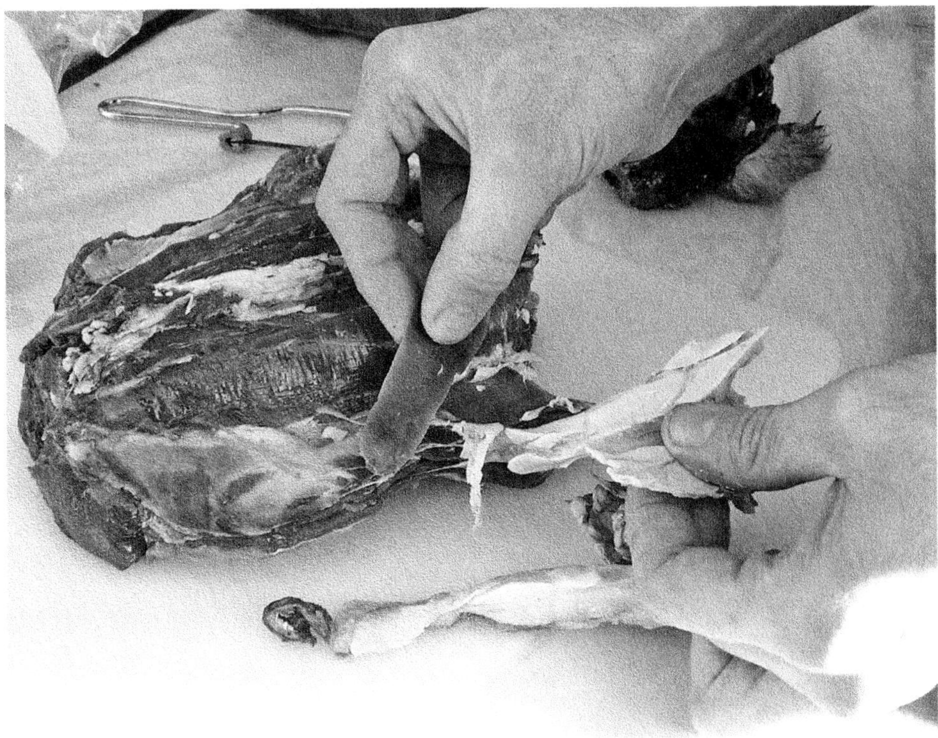

Figure 5.18 *Experimentation with flint blades to process a deer*

into Upper Palaeolithic reindeer hunters (▶ p. 298), who lived in a similar climate. Studying people who manufacture stone tools and the debris they leave can help us identify the signatures left by different processes. Ethnoarchaeology may also help reveal 'invisible' influences such as gender or ethnicity.

Experimental archaeology

Experimental archaeology involves forming a hypothesis about a process, artefact or ecofact and testing it using similar materials to those found on archaeological sites. Replica artefacts can be used to test the potential functions of real examples. Replicating lithics and using them to test their efficacy on a variety of tasks has a long tradition in archaeology. For example, flint axes can be tested to see how effectively they can chop down trees and then the wear patterns compared with Neolithic examples. Experimental studies of lithics have demonstrated that the wear and distinctive polishes on the surface of tools varies depending on the material being processed (e.g. bone or meat) and the type of action being carried out (e.g. cutting or scraping). Identifying each 'microwear' signature (▶ p. 176) enables the functions of tools from the past to be interpreted with greater accuracy than traditional typologies and ethnographic analogies. A second approach is to understand the technology itself by replicating processes. Knapping experiments are the best example of this. The distribution of experimental debitage (waste material) can be compared with archaeological examples to understand the knapping sequence and whether the knapper was standing, seated and left- or right-handed. During the Neolithic, stone artefacts were polished and drilled in order to take a haft.

Figure 5.19 *Neolithic drilled stone artefacts*

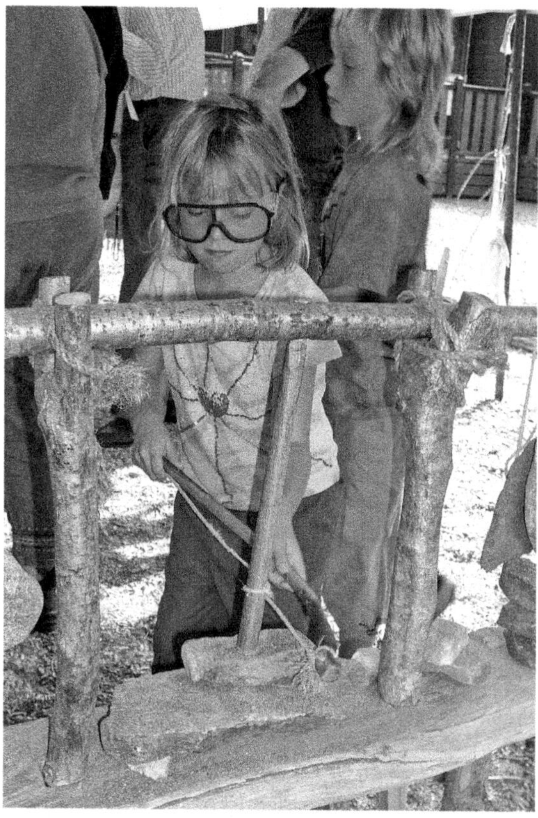

Replication can tell us something of the effort that went into this and perhaps, by extension, the value. Such artefacts were often made from exotic rocks, which suggests they may have been prestige items. We can also learn of the processes required to manufacture them.

Reconstructions use data as the basis for models that can be tested. For example, experimental archaeologists used post settings and other features to inform experimental structures to test hypotheses about the design and materials used to make the walls and roofs and then about the use and function of the buildings. It is important to remember that while everyone refers to these buildings as 'reconstructions' they are not really reconstructions. We cannot be

Figure 5.20 *Replication as education*

Reconstructions of tools such as bow drills enable researchers to test their effectiveness on a range of materials and to identify signatures for their use. Replica tools are also widely used at archaeological attractions to enable the public to connect with the past by appreciating the skills of past people.

entirely sure what an Iron Age roof was like, so modern versions should properly be called constructs or models (Reynolds 1989). Similarly we cannot know if the house was decorated or whether people slept on the ground or on platforms that lay across the roof beams. Experiment can only show what might have been and then test it to failure.

Iron Age experiments at Butser

A common feature on many Iron Age sites are four- and six-post structures. Ethnographic analogy (▶ p. 180) suggested that the four- and six-posters might have been raised granaries. To test this idea several full-scale models of different structures were built at Butser Ancient Farm. This innovative open-air laboratory had already been one of the first places to experiment with 'constructs' based on excavation floor-plans. Apart from the postholes, another clue was provided by traces of wattle and daub panels which might have been the walls of these structures. The Butser model made sense as it kept grain out of reach of rats and allowed air to circulate to prevent damp.

Experimental roundhouses were also constructed. The walls, beams and roof itself drew on knowledge of Iron Age carpentry and engineering. These constructs enabled the exploration of ideas about the roof pitch, light, efficiency of fires and whether a smoke hole is needed. Reynolds (1989) demonstrated that a smoke hole would have turned the house into a furnace. Instead smoke filtered through the thatch where

Figure 5.21 *View of Butser Ancient Farm*

Figure 5.22 Reconstruction of four-poster, raised granaries at Danebury

it may have also contributed to waterproofing and reduced vermin. Butser also answered questions about how long a roundhouse might last and the amount of woodland needed to build and maintain it.

Iron Age settlements also feature large numbers of beehive-shaped pits. Those at Danebury hillfort were 1m wide and up to 2m deep with a grain capacity of over 2 tonnes each. Initially it was thought that the pits had been sealed and covered with a basketwork lid so that their contents would last over the winter. How they did this without rotting was unclear. To investigate, archaeo-botanist Hillson conducted a micro-excavation in his lab of a sample of carbonised grain from a pit. As he removed and counted the seeds layer by layer, he discovered that there were more germinated seeds at the bottom, next to the chalk. Reynolds (1979) tested Hillson's findings at Butser by digging a replica 1.5m pit and filling it with grain. Instruments were inserted to measure humidity, temperature and gas exchange. The pit was sealed with an airtight layer of clay. The results were impressive. The grain around the edges, especially where it was in contact with the chalk, began to germinate and produced shoots. This gradually used up the available oxygen and produced carbon dioxide, creating an anaerobic environment, and germination ceased. While the seal remained intact, the grain lay dormant and survived the winter in good condition. When the pit was opened, most of the grain could be used except for that around the edges, which was full of mould and fungi. If the pit was to be used

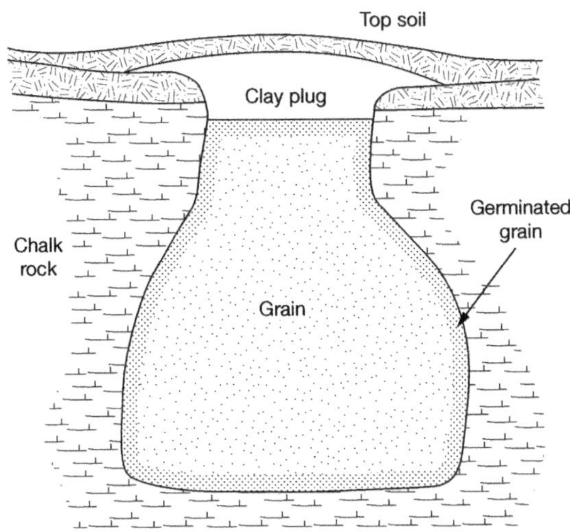

Figure 5.23 *Section of 'Beehive' grain storage pit*

again, this waste had to be disposed of. Reynolds suggested that it was burnt in the pit, which accounted for the carbonised grain at the bottom. It is likely that the grain was taken out in one go, perhaps for sowing or trading, rather than the pit being used as a larder for food. Ladders and baskets or buckets would be needed to empty a pit of this depth. Excavation on contemporary sites suggested that pits were usually backfilled to preserve their narrow entrances from collapse and not present a hazard. It was easier to re-dig them than start a new pit.

Experimental archaeology is, of course, weighted towards technological understanding. There may be social or religious reasons for particular designs and materials being used which reconstructions cannot directly address. Where

Figure 5.24 *Replica Viking ships from Roskilde, Denmark*

the remains of such an experimental village are examined, there might be an overlap with ethno-archaeology. However, the people in the experiment would clearly be very different from those in archaeological examples.

Recreated boats have broadened our understanding of seafaring in the past. Well-preserved Viking vessels have enabled the construction of replicas. The Viking museum at Roskilde has built replicas of several different types which are enormously valuable in helping us understand the skills and potential of past seafarers. The building process provided insights into the skills required of specialised shipwrights and the materials they would have needed. The ships themselves help us understand seamanship, speed, range, loads, handling and function. Taken together they help address the question of why the Vikings were so successful as traders and raiders in the early medieval period (▶ p. 408). Other recreations are primarily educational, for presenting ideas (▶ p. 624), or to test assumptions. The Kon Tiki raft, which sailed across the Atlantic to test the possibility that the Ancient Egyptians could have reached Mexico, falls into this category. However, its successful voyage does not prove that Mexican civilisation or its pyramids derive from Egypt.

Taphonomic studies

The final category involves observing transformation processes in order to understand their impact on archaeological material and interpret patterns on real sites. Experiments in Africa have explored the effect of scavengers on the distribution of bones from a carcass or the effects of streams on artefact movement. The bones or artefacts can then be subjected to microwear analysis to identify signatures for particular kinds of processes such as flash flooding or trampling. One example was a square metre which was created to simulate a portion of the Palaeolithic site of Klithi in northern Greece. The simulated site was positioned along the path leading to the site so that it was regularly walked on by diggers going to and from the site. It was also 'trampled' by the regular passing of goat herds along the valley. After a period of time the simulated site was excavated and the position of the artefacts

Figure 5.25 *Accidental experimentation at West Stow*

recorded. Comparisons were then made between the original position and condition of the artefacts and where they had moved to both spatially and within the stratigraphy. This provided information about taphonomic changes within the rock shelter. With all experiments, replication is a key element in determining their validity. Where several researchers get similar results from similar experiments, those results are more widely accepted. The production of lithics falls into this category as do the experiments at West Stow (▶ p. 494) into sunken-floored buildings. When one of the houses at West Stow was burnt by arsonists, the archaeologists were naturally disappointed. However, it did provide them with evidence about what would survive from burnt buildings from the past and the signature they would leave in the ground.

WHY DO ARCHAEOLOGISTS OFFER DIFFERENT INTERPRETATIONS OF THE PAST?

Since archaeologists disagree about how or whether past behaviour can be reconstructed and because the archaeological record is so flawed, it is hardly surprising that their accounts can differ. Evidence is often contradictory with different conclusions being drawn depending on the materials being examined. For example, archaeologists studying the transition to agriculture around the Baltic (▶ p. 501) might see a dramatic change if they focused upon the form of ceramics or ritual practices. If they focused upon ceramic fabrics, site locations, palynology, human diet or lithics, they might see continuity. Their own specialisms, the questions asked and even their political and social assumptions and views on the relative importance of ecology or human choice will influence them. This is not because they are being biased but because they have to make choices based on what they find most persuasive.

Data is constantly being reinterpreted as archaeologists make new discoveries, ask different questions, use new techniques or find new sources of analogs. They also borrow models and methods from other disciplines and then there are academic fashions as there are in all subjects. For example, in the 1960s processual archaeologists adopted scientific methods including mathematical modelling to explain and generalise about past behaviour. They tried to use empirical evidence and quantification as if they were analysing a natural system such as a food chain or weather patterns. So the collapse of the Maya civilisation by AD 900 (▶ p. 128) was explained in terms of problems in the system (ecological disaster, overpopulation or disease) rather than individual events or changes in social organisation or belief. The late 1960s and 1970s also saw settlement archaeology borrow models from geography such as site catchment analysis and central place theory. In the 1980s and 1990s there was a reaction to the limitations of scientific approaches with what is called post-processualism. This drew heavily on cultural and gender studies and emphasised issues such as interpretation, meaning and human agency. It was particularly influential in focusing attention on belief systems and how prehistoric people understood the landscape (▶ p. 229). Conversely, since the 1990s many of the most exciting advances in archaeology have come via developments in biochemistry (▶ p. 133). This has provided powerful new tools for interpreting trade networks, diets and population movements amongst other things. The continued debate amongst archaeologists is a sign of the subject's vitality. Examples of these debates are explored in the next five chapters and particularly in the key studies.

Part II

Studying Themes in Archaeology

Chapter 6

Human Origins

This chapter provides a broad introduction to the sequence of human evolution and the main causes of changes. There is particular focus upon the debates around the point at which our ancestors started to behave in a way we would consider 'human' and around the circumstances in which our own species, Homo sapiens (wise man), developed, and in particular, our relationship to other species such as the Neanderthals. The Dolni Vestonice key study introduces themes which are explored further over the next five chapters.

Human origins has its own distinct range of specialists, terminology and evidence which can be confusing at first. Palaeo-anthropologists are scientists from different disciplines who study fossil humans. Physical anthropologists study human and primate evolution and are increasingly called biological anthropologists because of the use of genetic evidence and other links with biology. Primatologists observe modern great apes and provide insights into the potential capabilities and behaviours of ancestral apes. Traditionally, human ancestors have been classified according to the Linnaean system used in biology since 1758. On the basis of observable morphological (physical) similarities and differences, Linnaeus classified animals into class: order: family: genus and species. According to this model we are mammals: primates: hominids: homo and Homo sapiens. The big picture that our ancestors evolved from the great apes (including gorillas and chimpanzees) is well known but the precise timing, sequence and reasons are still subject to debate. Our understanding of human origins is one of the most rapidly changing areas of our past. Each month brings new discoveries and the application of new technologies. Some assumptions that were widely held when the first edition of this book was published look increasingly shaky. Amongst the key developments at the centre of debates are bipedalism (walking on two feet), tool making, cooperative behaviour, meat eating, hunting, speech and culture.

A CHANGING FAMILY TREE

Until recently, differentiation between species was based on identifying morphological differences from the shape of bones and teeth. For example, compared with chimpanzees, Homo sapiens have feet, knees, spine and pelvis adapted for upright walking. We have rounder skulls, larger brain cavities, flatter faces but pronounced chins and noses and much smaller teeth. In order to identify the point where the two species went their different evolutionary ways, scientists trace back tiny physical changes in fossils to the point at which they were virtually identical; this is generally thought to be around 5 mya. The very limited survival of evidence from such distant periods means that information has to be squeezed from very fragmentary remains. This may be a mandible (jaw), part of a skull, teeth or a femur. For example, only about 40 per cent of the famous fossil 'Lucy' (▶ p. 195) was recovered. Progress relies on sharp-eyed discovery in the field followed by reassembly of thousands of bone and stone fragments. From these scientists make inferences about locomotion, diet and behaviour. Inevitably there may be more than one way to 'reconstruct' the missing parts. Every new discovery is precious and adds something to our understanding, often challenging existing knowledge. There is also no way of directly dating fossils from these periods. Instead, geological methods such as potassium argon (▶ p. 159) are used to date the rock layers where finds occur.

Genetic analysis has had a tremendous impact on evolutionary studies. DNA analysis has shown that we share at least 98.7 per cent of our

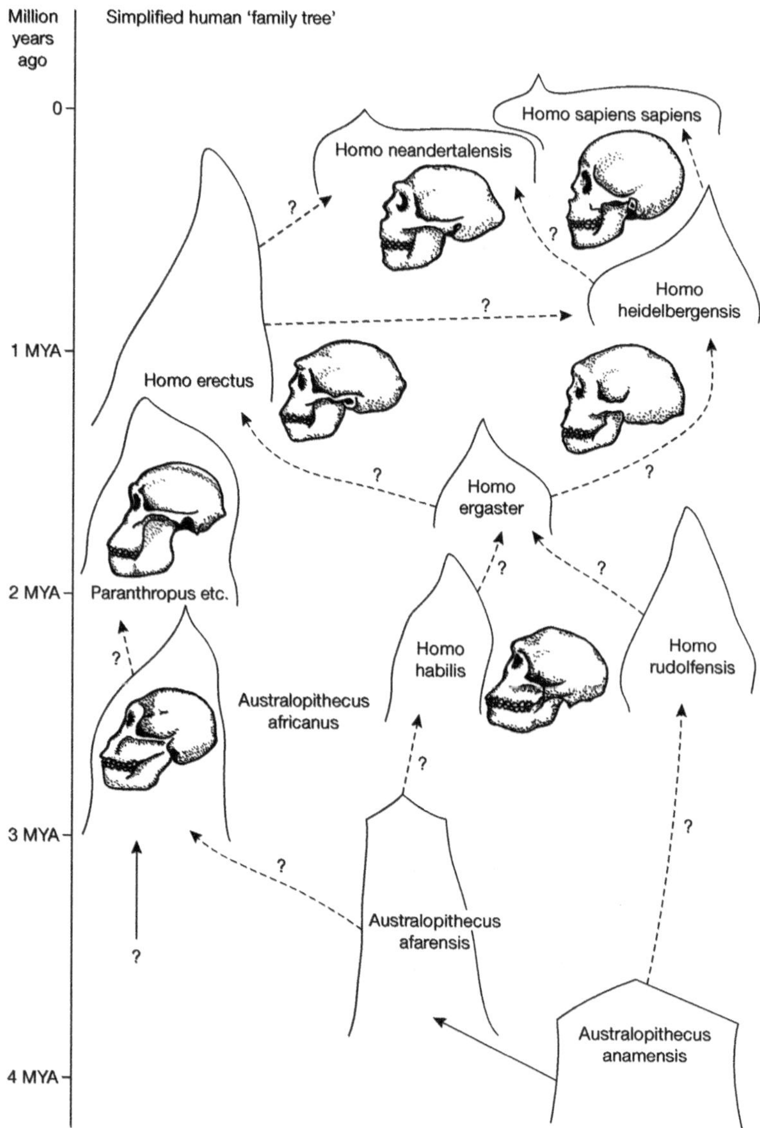

Figure 6.1 *Human family tree*

genes with chimpanzees and around 98.4 per cent with gorillas. These differences arose over time through successive mutations. Mutations occur at an approximately known rate, which enables modelling of the time required for modern differences to emerge. This has given greater precision to estimates of the point where ancestral lines separated. In the case of humans and chimpanzees, it is pushing it back to 6–7 mya. Genetics has also clarified the relationships between different species, sometimes in a way which has overturned the old morphological distinctions. For example, a chimpanzee might look closer to a gorilla than a human but genetically it is closer to us. Increasingly, models of our origins look less like a family tree and more like a bush with multiple branches.

In addition, a host of new fossil discoveries since the 1990s have also contributed to a revolution in ideas about human origins. However, this new information often only leads to tentative conclusions. Two similar but different fragments from two skulls may represent different species or may reflect variability across one species. A skull discovered in Chad in 2001 provides a good example of this. Sahelanthropus tchadensis lived 6–7 mya and had the small brain (350cc) and face of an ape but small teeth and the opening for the spinal column underneath its skull. This suggests that it stood upright on two legs like a human rather than on all fours like an ape. Whether it is related to chimpanzees or the earliest of the human line is much debated. It does suggest bipedal walking developed several million years earlier than previously thought.

As a result of these discoveries, the classification of our ancestors is currently in flux with the following precise, but still confusing, model becoming increasingly accepted: **Hominids** are members of a family of primates sometimes referred to as the 'Great Apes'. A subgroup or tribe of this group are called **hominins** and include humans and chimpanzees. Humans and their extinct bipedal ancestors are termed **hominans** with the term **human** applying to both our species and extinct members of the genus Homo. Humanoids are earthlings encountered by aliens.

HOW DID HUMANS EVOLVE?

The order of mammals called primates originated 65 mya as squirrel-like creatures adapted to a life hunting insects and fruit in the trees of tropical forests. Adaptations included opposable thumbs for gripping branches, an upright stance, fewer teeth and an increasing reliance on eyesight rather than sense of smell. Over millions of years further specialised adaptations took place. One group, the Hominids, developed rotating shoulder joints that enabled them to hang while feeding and gradually lost their tails. Hominids also spent increasing time on the ground. Their brains grew larger and their infants remained dependent for longer. Other primates such as lemurs, monkeys and gibbons remained in the trees. The reason for the change is probably related to a cooling of the earth's climate around 15 mya which led to sparser forests and increased grassland or savannah. Many types of ape died out but the great apes (Hominids) survived by switching between trees and foraging for food on the ground. Further diverging adaptations separated the human lineage from first the gorillas around 9 mya and finally the chimpanzee and bonobo. However, no intermediate fossils have yet been found from between 13 and 7 mya.

Gorillas survived as plant-eating quadrupeds by becoming large and powerful enough to deter most predators. Chimpanzees continued to live both on the ground and in trees and became more omnivorous. However, it is important to realise that they have also evolved. Modern chimpanzees get 5 per cent of their diet from meat and do hunt monkeys. The human lineage increasingly moved towards bipedalism. This may have been for easier movement between trees, for standing to pick fruit from trees or to transport food to a more dependent mate or infant. A further benefit may be that upright walking enabled better cooling and exposed less of the body to the sun, thus reducing water loss. Bipedalism required significant skeletal and muscular changes and much of the work of scientists researching our ancestry focuses on identifying and sequencing developments in the structure of feet, joints and pelvis. In many other respects, these ancestors remained similar to chimpanzees with small brains and ape-like skulls.

Ardipithecus Ramidas ('Ardi'), a species first found in Ethiopia in 1994 and only fully published in 2009, may be the earliest of these ancestors (so far) clearly different from chimpanzees. Dating to between 5.5 and 4.4 mya, its teeth suggest that it was omnivorous and it shows very early signs of bipedalism. Since it lived in wooded environments, it suggests that initial moves towards upright walking occurred before moves into savannah environments. Similarly, Orrorin tugenensis, found in Kenya in 2000 and dated to 6 mya, was the size of a chimpanzee with ape-like arms and teeth suggesting a plant-based diet. While it was clearly a good climber, its leg bones suggest it walked upright. Its teeth enamel was relatively thick like our own, whereas that of 'Ardi' was thin like an ape's. It seems unlikely that both are our direct ancestor but it is not clear which one is most likely.

The Australopithecines

More well known are the Australopithecines (southern Apes). First identified in the 1920s in South Africa by Raymond Dart, these were the first true bipeds and had a mix of human-like legs, pelvis and opposable thumbs and ape-like skulls. While they could walk, they were probably not good runners and some have curved hands similar to those of chimpanzees and which are used for 'knuckle walking'. Footprints preserved in ash at Laetoli in Kenya and dated to 3.6 mya showed that Australopithecines had short stride lengths but had a modern, efficient, heel-strike mode of walking. Australopithecus afarensis lived between 3.9 and 3 mya in the grasslands of east Africa and had a brain size of 390–545cc. This is slightly higher than chimpanzees. Marked sexual diamorphism (males being significantly larger

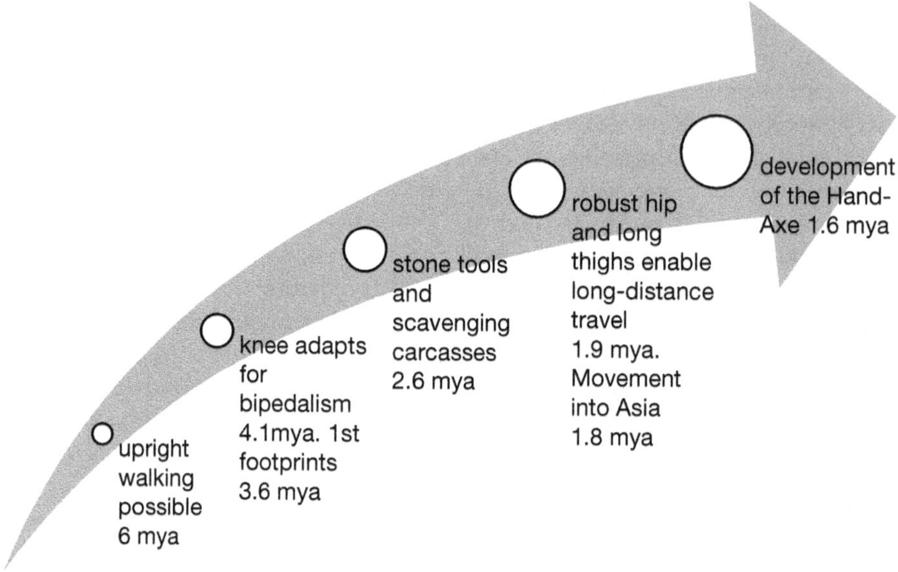

Figure 6.2 *Key stages in the Lower Palaeolithic*

than females) suggests that they may have lived in 'harem' groups like gorillas. They remained ape-like in being proportionally stronger than modern humans and some scientists believe they continued to sleep in trees for safety. 'Lucy' was the name given to an afaransis specimen discovered by Johansen in 1974 which demonstrated clear evidence of bipedalism. Several bones including pelvis, femur and ankle had been adapted for balance, upright stance and efficient walking. However, in most other respects she remained like an upright chimpanzee. In fact the early hominins differed little from other apes except that they successfully adapted to seasonal grassland areas as rainforests shrank. Upright walking enabled them to spot predators and food sources over tall grass and to hold tools and infants as they moved.

Figure 6.3 *Cast of Laetoli footprints*

Over the next 2 million years many different species developed from the early Australopithecines, although the exact sequence is unclear. Several different types existed at the same time in southern and eastern Africa down to around 1.1 mya and from one of them the Homo lineage developed. Australopithecines are usually divided into at least eight gracile (slender) types such as Australopithecus africanus (3–2 mya), who might have been a human ancestor, and more robust types such as Australopithecus boisei – previously known as Zinjanthropus – (2.1–1.1 mya), who was not. The teeth of africanus suggest a diet of fruit and leaves; however, carbon isotope analysis has revealed levels of carbon 13 which must have come from eating either grasses or herbivores or both. Africanus may have begun foraging for food on the grasslands including scavenging for meat. The robust group were heavily built with very large molars and massive facial muscles for chewing coarse plant foods such as bark and sedges. This group – which led to an evolutionary dead-end – are increasingly relabelled the Paranthropus genus to differentiate them from our lineage. Current consensus is that the Homo genus was another development from one of the early gracile Australopithecines.

Homo habilis

Homo habilis (handyman) lived from 2.4 to 1.4 mya and differed from the early Australopithecines in having a larger brain (500–800cc) and an anatomy clearly adapted to walking rather than climbing. Its legs and feet were modern if rather short. It was also the first fossil associated with stone tools and meat eating. Stone tools have been seen as one of the markers of more intelligent hominans. Chimpanzees use rocks and sticks as tools but they do not make tools. The 'Oldowan' tools first found in Olduvai Gorge around 1.75 mya are crudely but deliberately sharpened. While they required little to manufacture, lithics at Koobi Fora had been brought from outcrops 3km away, which suggests planning. The transition from using a rock or a stick as a tool to deliberately creating a new tool by using one material to shape another suggests increased intelligence. Tools were mainly used for cutting and pounding food and are frequently associated with animal carcasses. For example, faunal remains at Koobi Fora KBS dated to 1.8 mya include gazelles, pigs and hippos. Tools may have developed as a response to the need to seek roots underground or to scavenge effectively. Analysis of wear marks on lithics, cut-marks on bone and experimentation are key areas of research into tools. It is only with the advent of stone tools that researchers can be sure that butchery evidence on animal bones is due to hominan activity. However, archaeologists need to be sure that collections of lithics and bones at such ancient sites were deposited there by hominins rather than being palimpsests (▶ p. 176) caused by water action and other taphonomic factors.

Current revisions

Until recently it was thought that only the Homo genus was capable of making tools. However, the 1996 discovery of crude stone tools in Ethiopia associated with animal bones bearing cut-marks and fossil remains of the gracile Australopithecus garhi has challenged this. The layer in which they were found was dated to 2.5 mya, making it possible that Australopithecines developed tool making before Homo habilis. Some archaeologists now argue that Homo habilis should be reclassified as an Australopithecine or an 'early transitional human'. This highlights the problem that so few remains have been discovered that timelines for different species are only approximate. Each new fossil can overturn established models and sequences. A further example was the discovery of a new group of fossils called Australopithecus sediba at Malapa in South Africa in 2009. Dating from 2 mya, sediba had a very modern hand capable of precise tool making as well as climbing. Its pelvis was a human–ape mix but its foot was still ape-like. Phytoliths (▶ p. 123) on its teeth came from grasses, sedges and leaves, suggesting a largely vegetarian diet. Its brain (440cc) was smaller than those of Lucy and Homo habilis but had a more modern shape. Some archaeologists think sediba is now more likely to be our earliest ancestor. At least two species of Australopithecines co-existed with Homo habilis and considerable variation has been documented between habilis fossils. One large-brained example has been relabelled Homo rudolfensis. The overall evolutionary sequence currently combines species from southern and east Africa but neither region has a complete sequence.

WHAT IS THE EARLIEST EVIDENCE FOR COMPLEX SOCIAL BEHAVIOUR?

Humans are usually differentiated from other species by complex social behaviour, control of technology and creation of culture. In particular the ability to communicate large amounts of knowledge including abstract concepts is absent in other modern species. Another key difference is food sharing. Apart from meat, chimpanzees do not share food. Humans may have developed reciprocal food sharing within social groups in order to minimise risk when supplies were scarce. Meat eating is generally thought to have been a key element in the evolution of a more intelligent species. Meat is a more concentrated source of protein than plants and may have been necessary for larger brains to develop. Our brains are 2 per

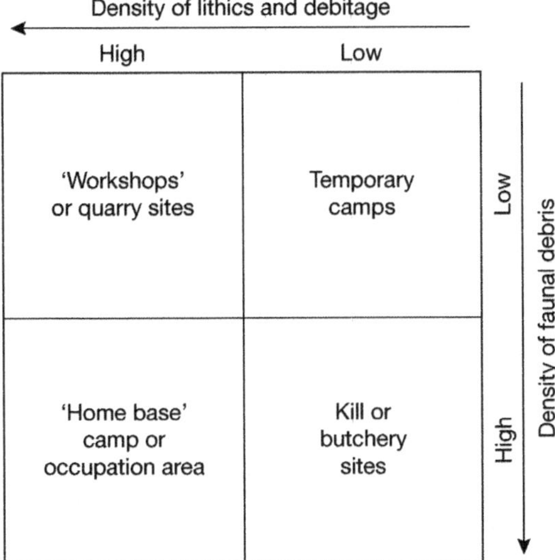

Figure 6.4 *The home-base model*

cent of our weight but take 20 per cent of our blood and oxygen.

Home bases or palimpsests

The coincidence of hundreds of lithics and broken animal bones, evidence of meat eating and larger brain size suggested to Leakey and Isaacs (Bindford 1989) that Homo habilis hunted and behaved socially more like modern humans. Habilis had a brain up to 35 per cent larger than earlier Australopithecines and therefore may have been capable of rudimentary speech. Isaacs (1978) originally interpreted different assemblages of animal bones and lithics as indicators of different types of human activity. He argued that sites at Olduvai Gorge and Koobi Fora were actually 'living floors' or 'home bases' and reflected hominans sharing food and working cooperatively. In this he was influenced by the ethnographic work of Washburn and also Lee and De Vore (1968), which provided a social model of nomadic, human foragers very distinct from those of other hominids and baboons. Isaacs' model was rejected by Binford (1983) because of insecure evidence.

Binford drew on taphonomic (▶ p. 186) studies of bone distributions from predator kills and experimental work on site formation processes affecting tools and bones in the region (Schick and Toth 1993). He suggests the sites might be palimpsests. Microscopic analysis of the bones suggests that humans scavenged the bones after other predators had processed them. Binford also argued that such 'sites' were unsafe for vulnerable early humans. He interpreted the assemblages (▶ p. 175) as palimpsests of animal kills and human

Figure 6.5 *Binford vs Isaacs: competing interpretations of bone and lithic assemblages at Olduvai Bed 1*

scavenging activities. As a consequence he argued it did not support the idea of Homo habilis living in bands and sharing food.

Binford highlighted the danger of archaeologists projecting modern behaviour onto past species. His work led to a more rigorous approach and greater openness to the use of alternative approaches or analogies to fill in the considerable gaps in our knowledge. This has included primate and other zoological studies and experimentation to understand potential economic strategies and site formation processes (▶ p. 165). Bunn and Krall (1986) carried out detailed studies of animal kill sites to identify the proportion of particular bones which were processed by particular animals. These were compared with archaeological evidence from Koobi Fora, Olduvai bed 1. The results suggested less carnivore processing at the hominid sites, which led Bunn to propose 'power scavenging', where hominids drove other scavengers away from kill sites. An alternative view of 'passive scavenging' emerged from Blumenschine et al.'s (1987) study of dry season scavenging opportunities on the Serengeti. He analysed fresh kills and measured the amount of nutrients which could be extracted from carcasses after they had been processed by lions and leopards and by major scavengers such as hyenas and jackals. He demonstrated that tiny Homo habilis could harvest significant calories by using simple tools to rapidly extract bone marrow from processed carcasses. Finding this specialised niche in the food chain may have enabled this species to survive. Today, most archaeologists accept that habilis might have scavenged kill sites but they were not advanced enough to establish and protect base sites.

OUT OF AFRICA I

Homo erectus ('upright man') stood around 1.8m in height and with an 800–1200cc brain was considerably more modern in appearance and capabilities than Homo habilis, although retaining an ape-like face. Their longer legs and modern hips were suitable for travelling long distances or running rather than tree climbing. Emerging around 1.8 mya and surviving until at least 300,000 BP, they were a very successful species for over a million years, during which they colonised much of the world. All were more robust than modern people, although there was considerable variation over such a long time. Asian fossils such as 'Peking Man' were shorter and sturdier than those in Africa such as 'Turkana Boy'. Their role in our lineage has become more complicated with the discovery of Homo ergaster, who coexisted in East Africa with several early Homo types and late Australopithecines between 1.8 and 1.3 mya. Scientists are divided over whether Homo erectus developed from Homo ergaster or if they were parallel species. Increasingly, African fossils are referred to as Homo ergaster with Homo erectus used for the Asian variant.

Both erectus and ergaster used a sophisticated, standardised set of tools chipped on two sides which archaeologists call **Acheulean**, including

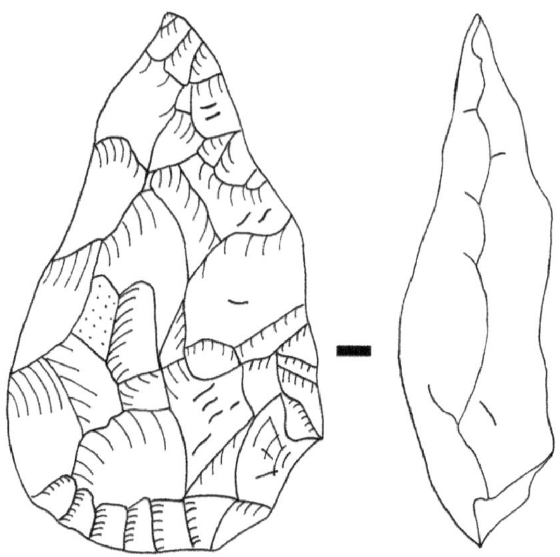

Figure 6.6 *Acheulean hand-axe from Um-Qatafa (after Benito)*

the classic hand-axe. These required planning to make. They may also have been the first to definitely use fire and develop a form of language. It is possible that they progressed from scavenging to hunting, particularly of small animals, but there is no evidence of weapons. However, they had fully rotating shoulder joints like ours, which meant they were capable of throwing rocks or other missiles. Analysis of animal bones by Walker and Shipman (1997) found examples of Homo erectus processing bone before other scavengers, which suggests they may have moved up the pecking order. Their large brains meant that, just like modern humans, babies continued developing outside the womb because the birth canal was too narrow for females to give birth to babies with fully developed brains. Since infants would be helpless, this meant that a parent had to look after them and probably would rely on others to bring food. Their large brain also needed more calories to supply it. Pair-bonding, parental roles and food sharing between adults may have developed in order to ensure the survival of offspring, dependent infants and nursing mothers. Extended childhood may have also led to greater communication of knowledge and skill development. Survival appears to have been precarious. Estimates for their breeding population around 1.2 mya are only 20,000. This would make them a more endangered species than gorillas are today!

Homo erectus and contemporary species

Currently, the dominant view sees Homo erectus leaving Africa at around 1 mya with migrations as far apart as China and Europe. This is marked culturally by the spread of the ubiquitous biface or hand-axe (though not east of India). Erectus and ergaster developed into a number of different variants in different parts of the world including Homo heidelbergensis in Europe, 'Java Man' in Asia and Homo rhodesiensis in Africa. Part of the reason for divergence may be because this species survived for so long. Some Javan dates may be as late as 30,000 BP, which would have meant 10,000 years of coexistence with Homo sapiens. The term 'archaic humans' is sometimes used as a general term for the descendants of Homo erectus.

Movement from Africa may have been forced by climate change or because our erectus were intelligent enough to adapt to new environments. Low sea levels enabled them to spread as far as Java using land bridges. Finds from more distant Indonesian islands means they must have made sea crossings either deliberately on rafts or possibly swept across with vegetation in tropical storms. Stone tools on Flores have been fission-track dated (▶ p. 159) to over 800,000 BP. Acheulean tools are known from Europe but no erectus bones have been found. However, several skeletons were found at the bottom of a natural shaft at Atapuerca in Spain dating from 800,000 and may suggest the first evidence of ritual. Scientists are divided over whether this was heidelbergensis or an intermediate species called Homo antecessor.

For many years archaeologists have debated whether or not Homo erectus and its immediate descendants thought or behaved like modern humans and whether they used fire and made clothing and shelters. Evidence increasingly supports the idea that they were very capable. Tools found at Pakenham, Suffolk, in 2005 were dated to 700,000 BP while those from Happisburgh, Norfolk, in 2010 were from 950,000 BP. This demonstrated that hominins were surviving in temperatures 3°C colder than today in northern Europe. At Gesher Benot Ya'aqov, Israel, excellent organic preservation has preserved clusters of burnt seed, wood and flint debitage from 790,000 BP. These have been interpreted as hearths. Cooking transforms food, enabling the body to absorb more nutrients, and reduces the energy spent digesting it. At Wonderwerk Cave, South Africa, wood ash 30m from the entrance provides more conclusive evidence from 300,000 BP.

Recently two apparently new species have been discovered which complicate the picture further.

Fossils discovered in 2002 in Dmansi, Georgia, were dated to 1.8 mya. Homo georgicus was smaller than erectus, being about 1.5m in height with a 600–800cc brain. Their face and brain case was similar to habilis but their lower legs were very modern. This suggested they were intermediate between habilis and erectus but their date is well before Homo erectus is thought to first have left Africa. The specimens were also interesting in terms of sexual diamorphism and considerable variation between remains of the same sex (Lordkipanidze et al. 2013). This has increased the view amongst some scientists that some remains labelled as separate species simply reflect variation in one species. In 2003 the even smaller fossils of a tiny 1m Hominin were discovered on Flores and dated to as recently as 38,000–18,000 BP. Their 400cc brains were just larger than those of chimpanzees and their feet were similar to those of Australopithecines. However, they used fire, made relatively modern stone tools and hunted a variety of unusual species including dwarf elephants and giant rats. Scientists named them Homo floresienses, although much of the press predictably called them hobbits. Scientists are divided over whether they are an offshoot of Homo erectus or a dwarf variety of another species. Dwarfism amongst larger mammals has been observed in other islands in the past.

Figure 6.7 *The old view of Neanderthals as primitive. Statues outside Krapina Cave.*

How early did hunting begin?

Dates for the origin of hunting vary widely from 2.5 mya to perhaps 400,000 years ago. Smashed animal bones including many with tool cut-marks have been found as far back as 1.8 mya but were probably from scavenged carcasses. It is also possible that small animals, fish and birds were hunted but no evidence has survived. The best case for big-game hunting comes *c.* 400,000 BP with yew spear tips from Lehringen, Germany, (found within an elephant rib-cage) and Clacton and seven complete javelins from Schöningen, Germany, found alongside butchered horses. There is also indirect evidence of tools with animal remains at Torralba, Spain, Bilzingsleben (▶ p. 176) and Boxgrove (▶ p. 61). At the latter, lesions caused by a fire-hardened wooden spear were found in the scapula of a horse and also a skeleton of a rhinoceros was found, showing carnivore tooth marks overlying knife cuts from a flint knife – probable evidence of successful hunting of large and dangerous prey. It implies that these hominins could scare off other predators, secure a carcass and dissect it in a leisurely fashion. This is likely to have been the work of Homo heidelbergensis, who lived in Europe from around 600,000 to 250,000 mya. A calcified skeleton of heidelbergensis was recently discovered at Altamura in Italy and dated to 400,000 BP. Taller and more muscular than modern humans, their brain was only 50cc smaller than our own. Despite these discoveries some archaeologists believe that really secure evidence for hunting does not emerge until the Neanderthals or Homo sapiens during the Ice Age. This view sees humans having to develop hunting in an environment where there was little plant food for much of the year.

Ice Age adaptation: the Neanderthals

From *c.* 250,000 BP as Europe and Western Asia underwent a series of Ice Ages, a new species, Homo neanderthalensis, adapted to this environment with shorter limbs, squat, muscular bodies and thicker facial features. These were all ideal for preserving heat. Brain sizes have been estimated to be as high as 1500cc, which makes them comparable with the 1350cc average for Homo sapiens. They developed a new technology called **Mousterian** with a range of scrapers and small hand-axes produced by using the Levallois technique. This involved preparing a stone core to form a standard 'blank' and then striking flakes away with soft hammers to create the desired shapes. This is a more controlled technology than Acheulean and required more skill and planning. One of the reasons there is more evidence about the Neanderthals than earlier species is because they used cave sites where remains were more likely to survive. They also buried their dead. An example from Shanidar in Iran, where flowers appeared to have been buried too, suggests they may have had rituals and beliefs. Archaeologists are divided about whether they could speak and use projectile weapons for hunting. They certainly used unselective hunting in instances such as La Cotte de St Brelade, Jersey (▶ p. 304), and Mauron, France, where herds were driven over cliffs. The overdeveloped right side of Neanderthal skeletons and the large size of their spear points suggests that they primarily used thrusting weapons to ambush large animals. They did so in extreme conditions. Faunal remains from the open-air site of Salzgitter-Lebenstedt (▶ p. 108), Germany, from *c.* 55,000 BP (Gaudzinski 2000) showed that they had adapted to hunting herds of reindeer in arctic conditions during their autumn migration. Large numbers of reindeer, horse and mammoth had been butchered. The reindeer were largely animals in their prime, suggesting selective hunting. In addition to lithics, the Neanderthals also used a range of points carved from mammoth bones. The evidence from this site bears some similarities with the nearby, but much later, site of Stellmoor (▶ p. 298). Unsurprisingly, they had a high meat, high protein diet. Bones of Neanderthals from Vindija Cave, Croatia, have similar stable isotope profiles to those of wolves. The discovery of a Neanderthal hyoid bone in the Kebera Cave, Israel, dating to 60,000 BP suggests that they might have had a similar larynx (voice box) to modern humans. They also had the Fox P2 gene, which is associated with speech. At Divje Babe, Slovenia, a bone drilled with two holes was dated to 43,000 BP and may be evidence of a Neanderthal flute. Other DNA findings include genes for pale skin and red hair.

Analysis of Neanderthal bones

The largest single find of Neanderthals came from Krapina Cave, Croatia. From 1899 to 1906 Gorjanović-Kramberger systematically excavated deposits dated from 130 to 50,000 BP including hundreds of Neanderthal bones and teeth from up to eighty individuals. He also pioneered the use of X-rays to examine fossil bones and fluorine dating (▶ p. 149). The detailed records created by this early palaeontologist have enabled extensive secondary research over recent decades which, allied to new technologies, continues to reveal secrets about the Neanderthals, particularly about population and behaviour. Modern surveys have brought the number of specimens up to 884, including 281 teeth and fourteen pelvises, which represent Neanderthals ranging from infants to around forty years old. They had hunted large herbivores such as rhinoceros, auroch and elk using tools flaked from local flint and stone. SEM analysis of the angle of scratches on their incisor teeth from holding and cutting meat with a blade have enabled researchers to show that some were left handed and others right handed. CAT scans and computer tomography have given us a much better understanding of how they may have looked. The contrast between the modern view of the Neanderthals as almost human and the more ape-like view as recently as the 1970s shows just

Figure 6.8 *The modern view of Neanderthals as similar to modern humans. Diorama at Krapina Cave Museum. (Tomislav Veić, archives of MKN)*

how much impact modern analysis has made. Many of the bones from the cave have been broken. The predominant view is that this is evidence of cannibalism. However, Cook and Ward (2008), whilst reviewing the conservation of the bones using high-resolution microscopes, noticed very regular cuts on some of the bones. One skull, Krapina 3, had a series of parallel grooves which were not associated with butchery. Cook argues that this may have been mortuary practice with the dead laid face down and defleshed and dismembered as part of a ritual. Similar butchery was observed at Moula Guercey, France. Defleur et al. (1999) found the remains of six individuals dated to 220–100,000 BP which had been processed in the same ways as animal bones in the same cave. Meat and marrow had been extracted, brain cases broken open and in one case, the tongue removed. However, badly injured Neanderthals appeared to have been cared for by others at Shanidar and La Chapelle aux Saints. Neanderthal skeletons show frequent signs of injuries due to accidents and stress due to poor nutrition. They appear to have lived in small family groups and may have been nomadic within limited ranges. Their population density is likely to have been low, perhaps reflecting the difficulty in existing in such a hostile environment.

Anatomically modern humans

At some point *c.* 40,000 BP Neanderthals were joined in Europe by Homo sapiens, sometimes called Cro-Magnons after a rock shelter in France where remains were dated to 32,000 BP. After a period of possible coexistence, Neanderthals gradually disappeared, with the last pockets in the Crimea, the Balkans and the Iberian Peninsula *c.* 30–24,000 BP. Archaeologists are divided over whether Homo sapiens out-competed them for food or exterminated them, or whether they interbred. DNA results initially led most scientists towards a replacement theory but not all are convinced. Social cooperation, problem solving and the interchange of ideas may have been what helped Homo sapiens survive in worsening conditions, unlike Neanderthals who, for all their physical advantages, were less well equipped to adapt quickly.

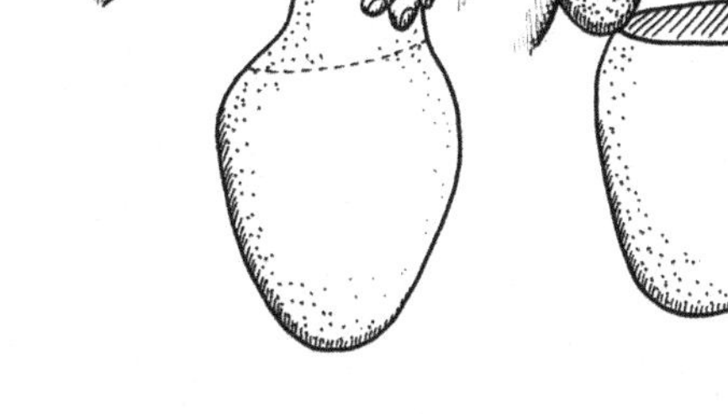

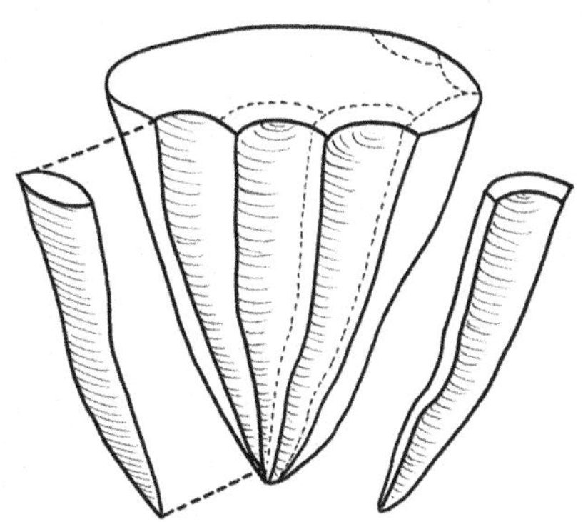

Figure 6.9 *Blade technology*

This was a key to the success of modern humans during the last Ice Age. Prepared pyramidal cores were struck repeatedly around the edge of the flat platform to produce long, thin blades. With a backing these could be used as knives but they could also be incorporated in composite tools or broken to produce points for projectile weapons. They were very efficient because they maximised the cutting edge produced from a given piece of flint.

KEY STUDY

The Vézère valley and Neanderthal replacement

The Vézère valley has for the last century been seen as the crucible of the clash between Neanderthals and anatomically modern humans (AMH). Rock shelters and cave sites were known to fossil hunters from the early C19th and in the 1860s serious exploration by antiquarians and geologists made a series of important discoveries. These included the painted cave of Font de Gaume, Neanderthal tools and remains at Le Moustier, modern-looking skulls from the Cro Magnon rock shelter and beads, tools and AMH remains from La Madeleine. These provided the type-sites for the Mousterian and Magdalenian periods while Cro-Magnons became the name by which the first AMH in Europe were widely known. Subsequently over 150 habitation sites and twenty-five painted caves were discovered including the Neanderthal rock shelter of La Ferrassie, the Aurignacian complex of shelters at Castel Merle and, in 1940, Lascaux. This valley and neighbouring rivers became known as the location where long established Neanderthal groups were first joined by and then replaced by AMH bands. In 1979 it became a World Heritage Site (▶ p. 577).

continued

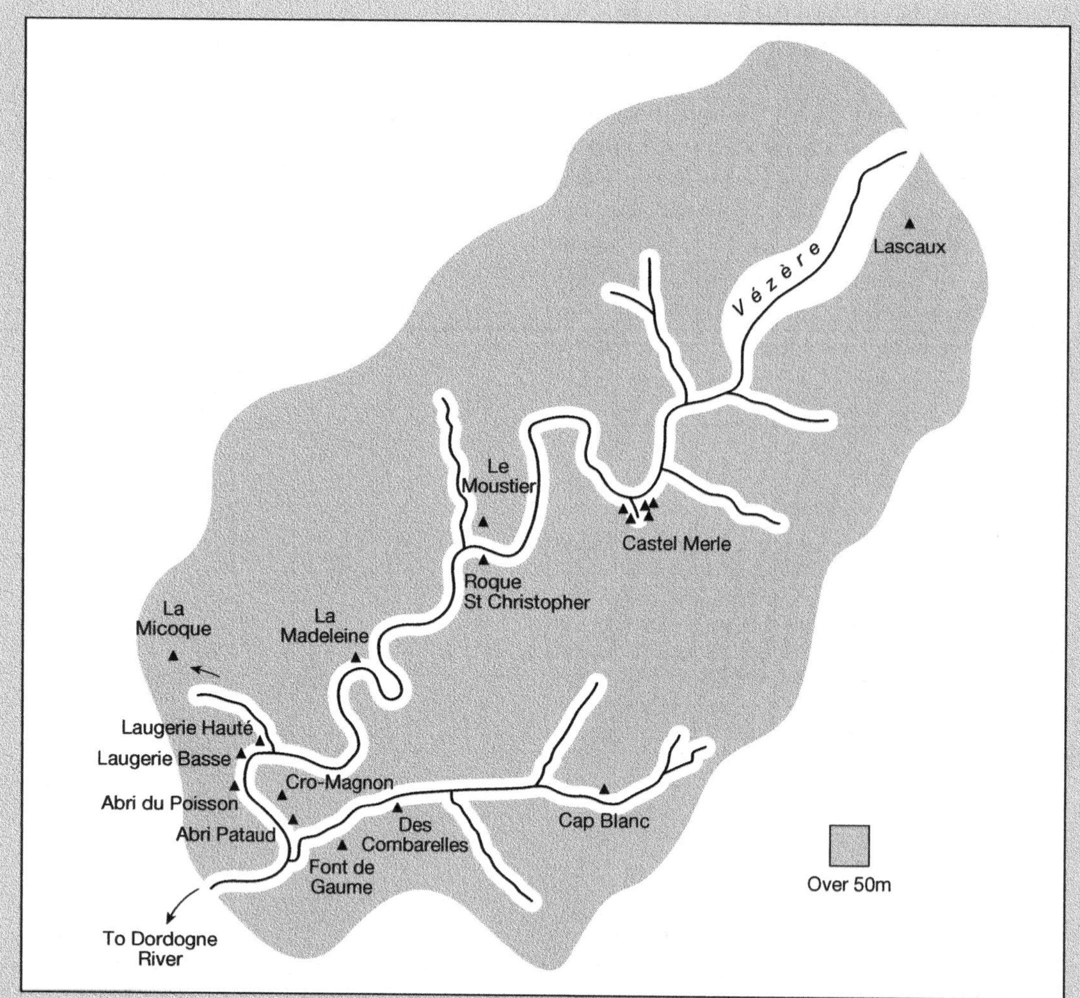

Figure 6.10 *Map of the Vézère valley*

Neanderthals in the Dordogne

The Vézère of south-west France is a tributary of the neighbouring Dordogne and is one of a series of east–west running rivers that originally drained the glaciers of the Massif Central into the Atlantic. The fast running river cut through the limestone uplands to create a deep valley featuring overhanging cliffs and deep cave systems. The valleys attracted so much prehistoric activity because they were well stocked with game and fish, on migration routes for herd animals while rock shelters (or abris) provided ideal habitation sites. Early explorers of these sites focused on creating typologies of artefacts. The deep stratigraphy in many abris enabled sequences to be recorded in detail while faunal dating (▶ p. 148) provided a secondary cross-referencing to establish periods. The earliest sites in the Vézère valley feature Acheulean hand-axes and other tools from *c.* 150,000 BP. However, most date from the last Ice Age with sites with Mousterian flake tools from 80 to 35,000 BP overlapping with sites with Aurignacian technology from *c.* 40,000 BP. A process of re-evaluating dates using the latest techniques is currently revising our understanding of this crucial period in human development and many dates of known rock shelters are likely to change. Regardless, the number and range of sites in the Vézère valley means that it remains the single most important area for understanding these Ice Age changes.

Neanderthal finds in the region

Figure 6.11 *The massive Roche St Christophe rock shelter on the Vézère*

Neanderthal remains were first discovered in Germany but the first complete skeleton was recovered from La Chapelle aux Saintes, dating from *c.* 60,000 BP. This specimen was mistakenly reconstructed in 1911 in such a way that it appeared hunched, brutish and very different from modern humans. This fitted with assumptions at the time that Neanderthals and AMHs were not related. Further discoveries along the Vézère provided details of Mousterian technology, diet, burial practices and important clues about social organisation. At Combe Grenal, a few kilometres upstream on the Dordogne, Bordes excavated 13m of Neanderthal deposits and meticulously recorded sixty-five stratigraphic layers. These provided evidence of 75,000 years of Neanderthal adaptation to a changing climate. The earliest layers (65–56) before 125,000 BP include the butchered remains of reindeer and the Acheulean tools, such as hand-axes, common to both Homo heidelbergensis and early Neanderthals. This was followed by a

continued

period of warm, wet climatic conditions (layers 55–38), during which pollen records the spread of trees such as elm, alder and hazel. The fauna changed too with red and roe deer, horse, auroch and pig being the main food animals. From *c.* 75,000 BP (layers 38–35) the climate became much colder. Reindeer returned as nearly all the trees vanished to be replaced by steppe-like grassland. Mousterian technology dominated the tool assemblages. The final layers suggest a bitterly cold climate with a few mild periods during which pine, hazel and alder spread and deer and horses occurred in the faunal record. At *c.* 50,000 BP the occupation sequence ended. The sequence at Combe Grenal demonstrates how detailed faunal and pollen records in conjunction with lithic typology could be used to cross-date other sites. It also demonstrates the tenacity of the Neanderthals in surviving in bitterly cold conditions. The eight well-preserved burials from La Ferrassie (70–50,000 BP) include foetuses, children and adults and provide the basis of our understanding of what Neanderthals looked like. The upper levels at La Ferrassie include AMH artefacts from the Aurignacian and Gravettian periods. This documents the replacement of Neanderthals in the valley during the Middle to Upper Palaeolithic transition.

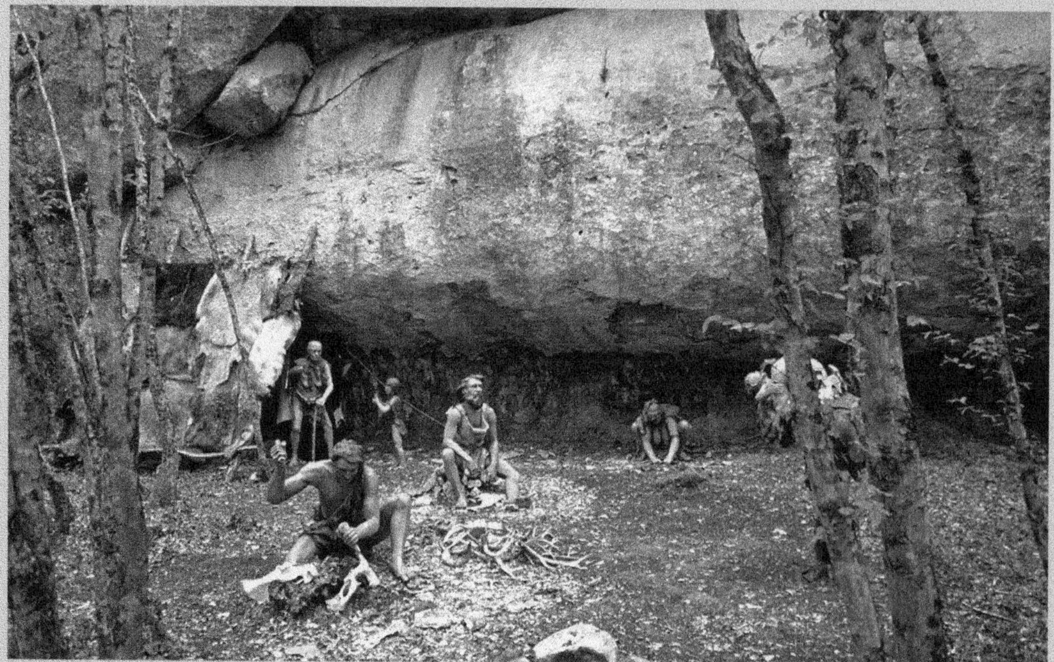

Figure 6.12 *Replica of a rock shelter*

Anatomically modern humans along the Vézère

The discovery of AMH remains in the Cro-Magnon shelter in 1868 was the first find of early Homo sapiens in Europe. These were identified as primitive modern humans but more advanced than the Neanderthals. Prior to discoveries in southern Africa and the Rift Valley, it was widely believed that modern humans first appeared in Europe. Further up the Vézère valley is a complex of ten shelters

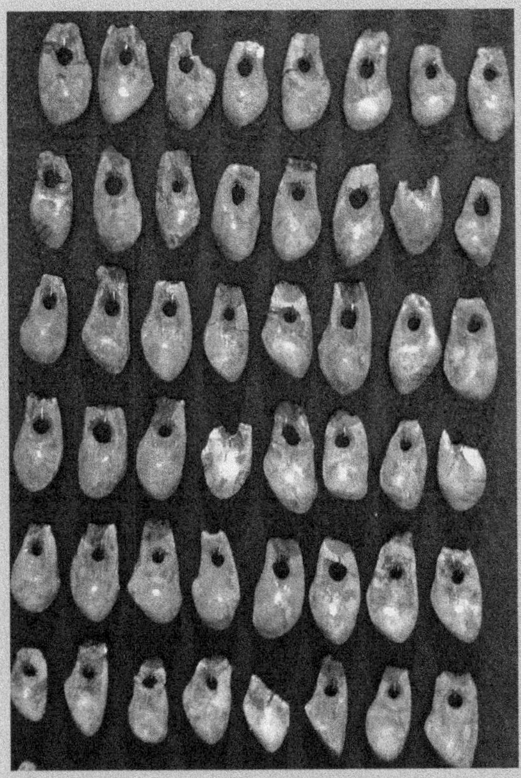

Figure 6.13 Basket-shaped beads

(abris) at Castel Merle, where excavation continues today. Assemblages are all AMH and include examples from Aurignacian, Gravettian and Magdalenian cultures with dates ranging from 37,000 to 10,000 BP. Although the location is within 200m of the river and has springs nearby, it is in a north-facing side valley which is cooler than most other sites. It is also unusual because of the size and density of occupation and the evidence of symbolic activities (White et al. 2012).

Bead making at Castel Merle

At the Aurignacian site of Abri Castanet (37–35,000 BP) a series of raised rings ('anneaux') appear to have been gouged into the soft rock along the lip of the roof of the rock shelter and possibly along the floor. These were possibly used to fasten skins to create an awning for the rock shelter and keep the elements out. Beads were recovered at Abri Blanchard by a local farmer – Marcel Castanet – in 1909 in an early example of using wet-sieving (▶ p. 64) to recover small finds. Since then, thousands of beads have been found in various stages of manufacture in contemporary layers in other abris in the complex. Materials include shells which have been sourced using strontium isotope analysis (▶ p. 133) to the Mediterranean and Atlantic Coasts over 100km away, soapstone from the Pyrenees and ivory which may have come from as far as Germany. Many materials were carved into tiny 'basket-shaped' beads less than 1cm in length. This has led some archaeologists to infer a degree of specialisation perhaps involving women and children in their manufacture. Each bead required considerable effort to make. A rod of stone or ivory was initially carved and polished before being snapped into smaller pieces for gouging the hole and for final polishing. Experiments suggest that each bead took up to three hours to make. Teeth from foxes, deer and even humans, none of which were significant food animals, were also drilled to use as personal ornamentation. Bergerac flint used for tools came from over 40km away but lithic manufacture does not appear to have taken place in these shelters. The local geography has preserved remains far better than open sites. The collapsed roofs of the shelters effectively sealed in occupation floors. This enabled archaeologists to explore the spatial distribution of material which would otherwise have been redistributed through natural and human action (▶ p. 169). White's (2012) excavation at Abri Castanet involved excavating around 100m^2 in 75cm^2 blocks and recovering particles of cultural material as small as 1mm in size. Over 150,000 artefacts have been recovered (White et al. 2012). Distribution plots reveal the way the site was organised while magnetic susceptibility surveys have located the fire places around which activities took place. Most of the bead manufacture was

continued

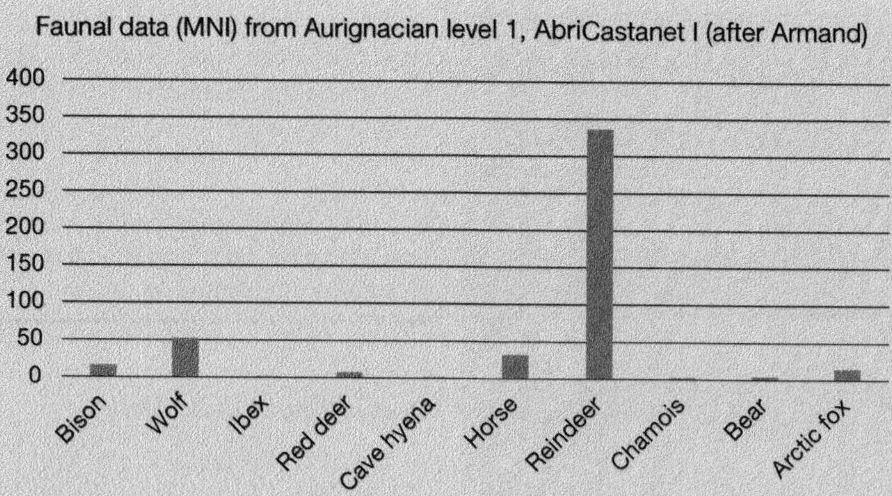

Figure 6.14 *The reindeer economy*

concentrated in a 3m square near the front of the shelter, while the production area of antler spear points was deduced from burnt flakes around one of the fire places. Other areas appear to have been used for sharpening stone tools or creating art (White et al. 2012). This includes engravings of animals and a vulva on the shelter surfaces or plaques of stone. Traces of images of auroch and bison created using red ochre and manganese are the earliest known examples of painting.

The AMH economy on the Vézère

Like the earlier Neanderthals, the AMH economy at Castel Merle revolved around hunted reindeer, although they occasionally diversified including the killing and skinning of hibernating cave bears. However, these sites suggest very different societies. Space is organised and the AMH groups are four to five times larger, suggesting a more efficient division of labour. Bead production provides evidence of long distance exchange networks and the use of symbolism to create group or individual identities. The early evidence of art hints at ritual as a reason for seasonal aggregation instead of communal hunting. White (2012) argues that most reindeer were killed individually rather than en masse. He sums up the importance of the sites by pointing out that under one huge block of fallen roof from *c.* 36,000 BP at Abri Castanet he has more human material than in all of the rest of the world up to that date. The rapid technological development of modern humans is well documented along the Vézère. At Laugerie Haute finds of harpoons suggest seasonal salmon fishing, while the nearby Abri de Poisson includes a 25,000-year-old carving of a salmon. During the Magdalenian period, just after the peak of the last Ice Age, the extent of creativity is revealed by the cave art at Lascaux and the burials at La Madeleine. The latter included a three-year-old (10,000 BP) with 1,500 shell beads sewn to its clothes and its headpiece. Elsewhere stone lamps, bone needles, antler harpoons and flint blades testify to understanding of materials and design. Portable art includes horses engraved on antler and bone and a number of beautifully carved, zoomorphic spear throwers.

How and why Neanderthals were replaced

Better tools?

The circumstances of Neanderthal replacement along the Vézère have been subject to repeated reinterpretation including insights drawn from other Neanderthal sites. For many years it was thought that the technological superiority of AMH meant that they were more successful hunters and killed or simply out-competed the Neanderthals. The fact that the Dordogne was settled slightly later than Spain and south-eastern France was thought to be evidence that it was a Neanderthal stronghold and was initially avoided by incoming AMH bands. However, the earliest Aurignacian tools were not significantly better than the Neanderthal's Mousterian toolkit for hunting and butchery, while faunal studies suggest very similar diets. Recent studies have shown that clusters of both Neanderthal and AMH sites may represent similar hunting ranges to those of modern foragers. They also show that Neanderthals selected animals in their prime to kill which testifies to their prowess as hunters. At the deeply stratified cave site of Grotte XVI on the Ceou, close to the Vézère, eleven occupation layers have been identified. Some 50,000 artefacts have been recovered from around the fire places and many more fragments of animal bones. To ensure accurate recording, a metal grid has been fixed along the cave ceiling with weighted cords hanging to the floor. Each digger excavates a single metre square and records their finds in three dimensions. Rigaud et al. (1995) used TL (▶ p. 157) to date hearth sediments to between 65,000 and 12,000 BP. At *c.* 40,000 BP the tools become similar to AMH artefacts yet the bones remain Neanderthal. It is only *c.* 30,000 that AMHs settle in the cave. Comparison of the Neanderthal and AMH assemblages reveals great similarities (Grayson and Delpech 2003). The same eight or nine species of herbivore were hunted. The only variation was the balance of red deer and reindeer depending on the climate. Bones of pike and trout were found around the well-preserved fire places in both Neanderthal and AMH levels (Wong 2000), while analysis of the degree of processing and

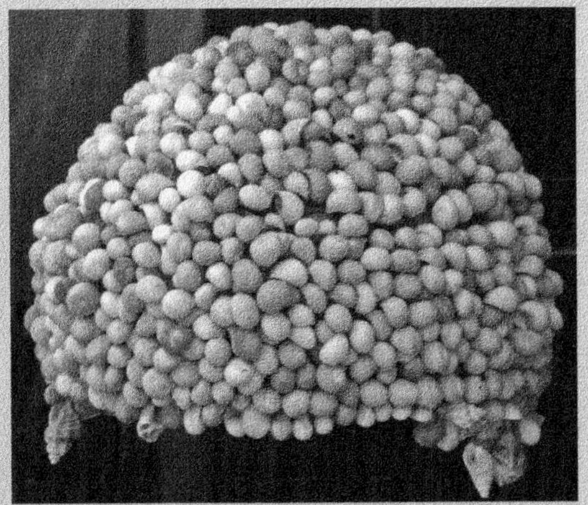

Figure 6.15 *Recreation of Magdalenian bead work*

continued

fragmentation of animal bones suggests similar levels of intensity. Grayson and Delpech (2003) conclude that AMH superiority is overstated until the Magdalenian period.

Smarter adaptation?

Neanderthal Châtelperronian culture after 35,000 BP appears to have produced lithics copied from Homo sapiens. However, there is less evidence that they copied their sewing kits. Australian research suggests that Neanderthals were well adapted to cold with skin and fur clothing but the peak of the last Ice Age may have proved too much for them without the tailored, layered clothing worn by their rivals. The main technological gulf appears to have been the development of nets and better projectile weapons by AMHs as the Ice Age reached its peak. The decline of tree cover made Neanderthal ambush-hunting difficult while climatic change or over-hunting may have reduced the numbers of large herd animals. The evidence from the Vézère shows how AMH successfully diversified to hunt fish, birds and small mammals such as rabbits using nets, atlatls (spear throwers) and harpoons. Nevertheless, there is evidence elsewhere of some Neanderthal diversification, although it may have been too late. Faunal remains from Gorham's Cave, Gibraltar, showed that the last Neanderthals did include birds, lizards and tortoise in their diet. At Shanidar (Iran) and Payre, France, traces of starch grains from plants on Neanderthal teeth and lithics suggest that they did not just eat meat. Payre also has evidence of fish and birds being eaten.

Social factors?

An increasingly popular view is that while the two species were more similar in abilities than previously thought, Neanderthals were less socially adapted in terms of communication and the ability to work with others. Tiny, isolated clans of Neanderthals did not appear to mix or communicate with strangers. Evidence for this comes from the size and distribution of sites. Mellars and French's (2011) study of south-west France found that Neanderthal numbers were small and stayed small while AMH numbers and sites rapidly expanded to reach around ten times the population levels of Neanderthals. The potential for innovation and adaptation offered by the aggregation sites and exchange networks also gave the AMH an advantage. This is supported by Pearce et al. (2013), who discovered that Neanderthal eyes were larger and probably more specially adapted to northern climates than Homo sapiens'. Processing extra optical information would have occupied a significant amount of the Neanderthal brain. The structure of Homo sapiens brains is very different, with more processing power available for innovation and managing complex social relationships with wide networks of people.

Division of labour may also have been a crucial AMH advantage. Net hunting for small game was much less hazardous than ambush hunting with spears and may have reduced deaths and injuries, particularly amongst AMH females. This may have given them a reproductive edge. In contrast, Neanderthal females were very muscular. The number of genetic mutations in a population is related to the size of the population. The low genetic diversity in Neanderthal populations after 70,000 BP has led to estimates of females in Europe as low as 1500–3500 and probably indicates inbreeding. Today we would consider them an endangered species at those levels. Neanderthals rarely lived beyond thirty and half of all remains are children, suggesting high infant mortality rates. As the Ice Age peaked, Neanderthal numbers, which were never great, may have dwindled below the levels needed to maintain breeding populations. They had successfully adapted to a series of periods of extreme cold but perhaps the last glacial maximum was just too cold. In Spain temperatures in areas which had usually been

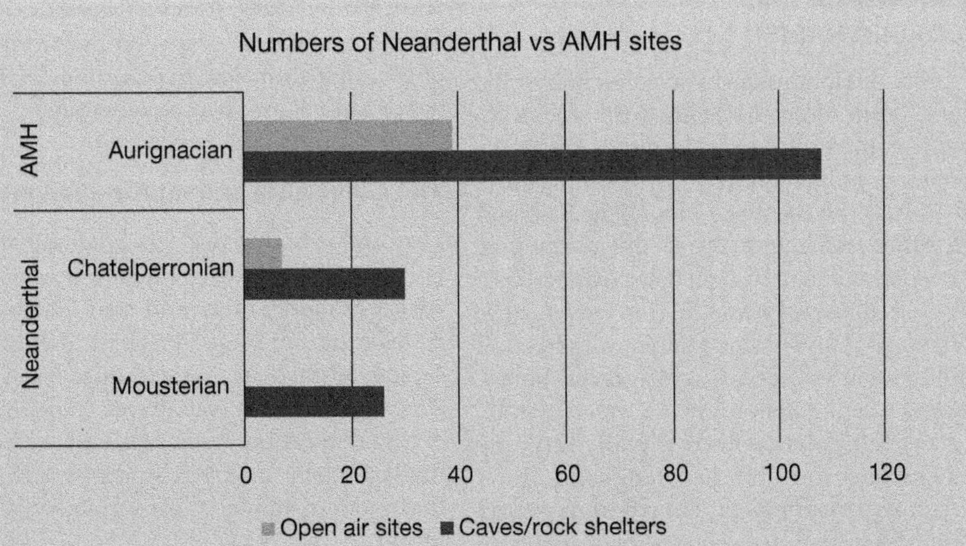

Figure 6.16 *Density of Neanderthal and AMH sites in south-west France (after Mellars and French 2011)*

refuges for Neanderthals plunged below previous levels. Perhaps they reached their limits in terms of adaptation. Some 40 per cent of Neanderthal bones exhibit signs of hypoplasia, which suggests that they lacked nutrients, while their higher metabolic rates mean that they needed more calories than AMH to sustain them. Alternatively they may have been displaced. Mellars and French (2011) used a statistical analysis of sites across the Dordogne region to determine that AMH populations were ten times the levels of Neanderthal populations and their settlements considerably larger. Perhaps the AMH took over the best hunting sites, gathered the fuel and occupied the warmest shelters. Alternatively there may have been interbreeding, with the Neanderthals genetically swamped (▶ p. 213). Two alternative hypotheses based on modern examples of epidemics are that cannibalism led to an illness similar to mad cow disease or that a virus contracted from AMHs proved fatal.

Did they ever meet?

A new series of dates in Russia suggests that the two species may never actually have met. Pinhasi et al. (2010) combined ultrafiltration to purify bone collagen samples for AMS dating (▶ p. 157) with Bayesian modelling (▶ p. 160) to date a Neanderthal baby from Mezmaiskaya Cave in the Caucasus to 39,000 BP rather than the previous date of 30,000 BP. Neanderthals here died out well before the arrival of AMHs. Similar techniques have significantly revised dates for Spanish Neanderthal sites (Wood 2013). Instead of Spain being a last refuge *c.* 30,000 BP Neanderthals may have vanished as early as 45,000 BP. The Oxford team (Pinhasi 2011) believe all existing Neanderthal dates before 39,000 BP to be unreliable and are currently redating using the new technique. If correct, this points to a very brief period of contact with AMH and strengthens the argument that our ancestors were responsible for their demise. Refinement of dates along the Vézère suggests there was still an overlap of up to 2,000 years, *c.* 40,000 BP, but this is a significantly smaller window than previously thought.

OUT OF AFRICA II VS MULTIREGIONALISM

The origin of Homo sapiens remains one of the greatest debates in archaeology, with archaeologists often bitterly divided. The oldest anatomically modern human (AMH) fossils dating from up to 130,000 BP have been found in East and South Africa and from 90,000 BP in Israel, where they overlap and may even predate Neanderthals. DNA projections put AMH origins back further to 150,000 BP. AMHs differ anatomically from all previous hominid species with gracile bones, flatter faces, high foreheads and a rounder skull. The mental differences were equally striking. Homo sapiens probably had language, ritual and art from an early stage. The oldest recovered art from Blombos Cave, South Africa, dates to 70,000 BP and Venus figurines (▶ p. 528) date to 30,000 BP. They developed an extensive range of stone tools and their pace of technological change seemed to increase after 40,000 BP, suggesting greater communication. Their expansion across the world was equally impressive, reaching Australia by 55,000 BP and America *c.* 13,000 BP. Their population levels soon outstripped those of all other primates. Explanations of how this happened fall into two broad groups.

The candelabra and multiregion models

The candelabra model was predominant in the mid-C20th and involved human ancestors leaving Africa around 2 mya and then independently developing into the different-looking Homo sapiens found in Africa, Europe, Asia and Australasia. It was initially discredited because of its association with racist ideas but more fundamentally by DNA studies which showed that modern humans are virtually genetically identical – which would not be possible if they had been isolated for so long.

Multiregionalism, championed by Wolpoff, suggests modern humans evolved from regional Homo erectus populations but that they also shared exchanged genes with humans in other parts of the world through migration. Some of the

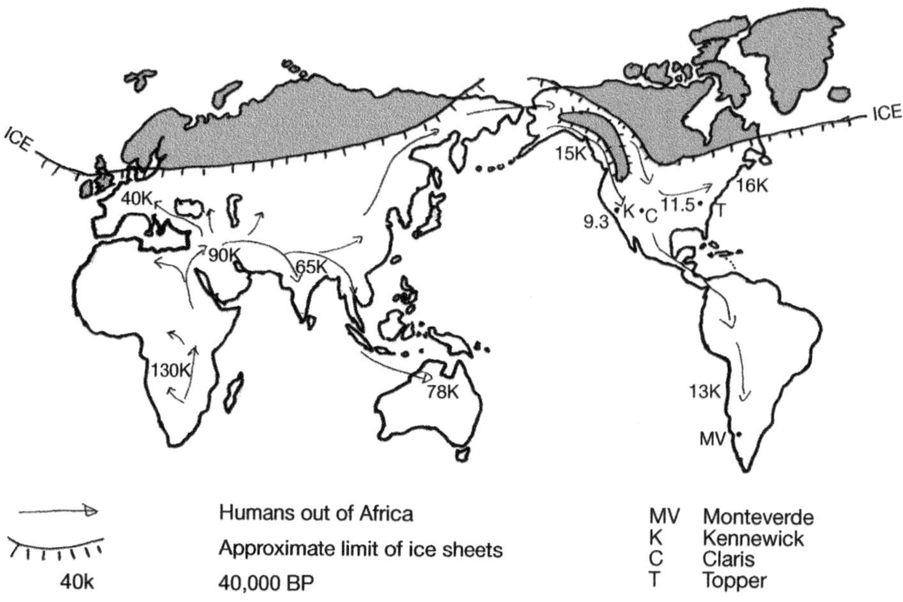

Figure 6.17 *The spread of modern humans out of Africa*

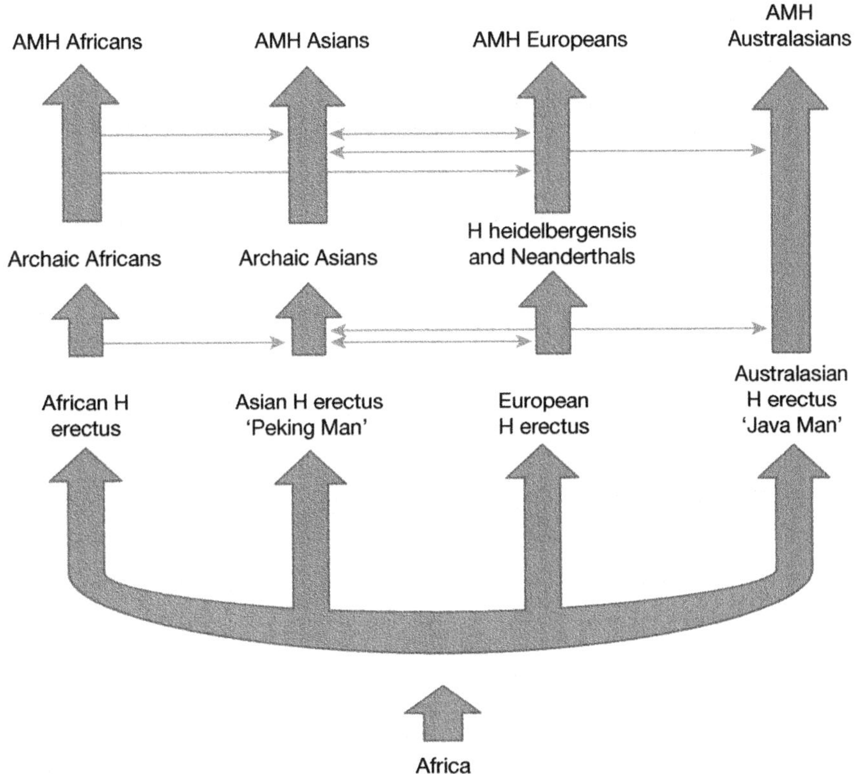

Figure 6.18 *Candelabra and multiregion models. Key genetic flows of the multiregion model are superimposed on the basic candelabra.*

minor differences in skeletal appearances between people from different parts of the world seem to reflect differences in earlier species. Homo sapiens therefore developed in parallel in Africa, Asia and possibly Europe. Thus it is claimed that modern Chinese populations share with ancestors who existed over 500,000 years ago certain physical traits such as shovel-shaped incisors.

Replacement and assimilation models

These theories suggest that all modern humans originated from a single small population in Africa. After evolving in Africa, the 'Noah's Ark theory', championed by Stringer and others, sees a complete and comparatively rapid replacement of all earlier species throughout the world by fully modern people. As a result, there is no significant genetic differences between modern peoples. Assimilation theories broadly align with this interpretation but allow for some interbreeding with other species during this process.

In addition to the study of fossils, stone tools and various types of site, genetic studies of ancient DNA have had a massive impact on this debate. Pioneering work by Cann et al. (1987) into mitochondrial DNA (mDNA) found that the greatest genetic variation amongst modern humans is in Africa. In other words, they have had more time to accumulate the mutations that signal differences between populations, which suggests that Homo sapiens have been evolving there the longest. Studies in mDNA also predict that all modern people share their mDNA with one woman, the so-called African 'Eve' who lived *c.* 200,000 years ago. By 2000, with initial studies

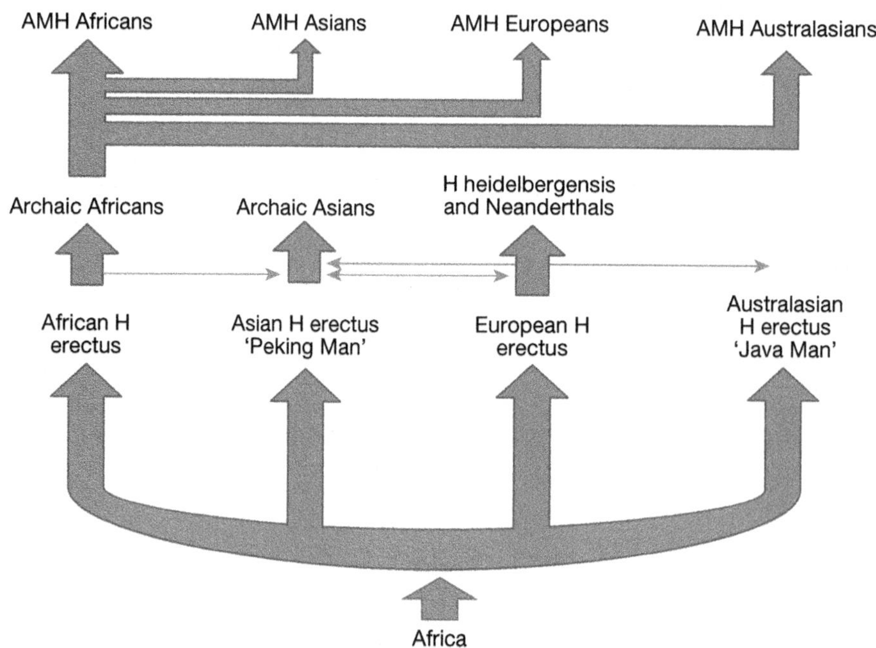

Figure 6.19 *The replacement or Out of Africa II model*

of Neanderthal DNA suggesting no link between them and modern people, it looked as though the replacement model would triumph.

New discoveries and methods

However, as with other aspects of evolution, new discoveries constantly lead to reappraisals. Modern human remains from Lake Mungo in Australia have been dated to 40,000 BP with some scientists claiming that their DNA indicates a date closer to 60,000 BP. However, DNA modelling elsewhere suggests that the first Homo sapiens only reached India by 65,000 BP and so could not have arrived in Australia before 55,000 BP. The 1998 discovery at the Lagar Velho rock shelter of a Neanderthal child with Homo sapiens traits from 24,500 BP reignited the debate about interbreeding. The 3- to 4-year-old had a modern jaw and teeth but the limbs were Neanderthal. The burial was more typical of Homo sapiens with ochre, rabbit and deer bones in the grave. The child wore a necklace of pierced shells. Conclusive evidence came with the mapping of the full Neanderthal genome in 2008 from samples taken from the Vindija cave in Croatia and dated to 44,000 BP: 1–4 per cent of Neanderthal genes were shared with modern Eurasian populations but none with Africans. This provided support for at least the assimilation model.

A further twist came with the discovery of skeletal remains at Denisova, Siberia, in 2010. Dated to 80,000 BP by thermoluminescence (▶ p. 157) of the rock shelter floor, the bones were more similar to Neanderthal than Homo sapiens. However, mapping of their genome in 2012 revealed that 6 per cent of their genes are shared by modern people from Papua New Guinea and smaller amounts by other islanders from Australasia (Racimo et al. 2014). This suggests some interbreeding with Homo sapiens before the colonisation of Oceania. The complete mapping of the DNA from a female Neanderthal toe bone from the same cave and dated to 50,000 BP revealed more evidence of interbreeding and

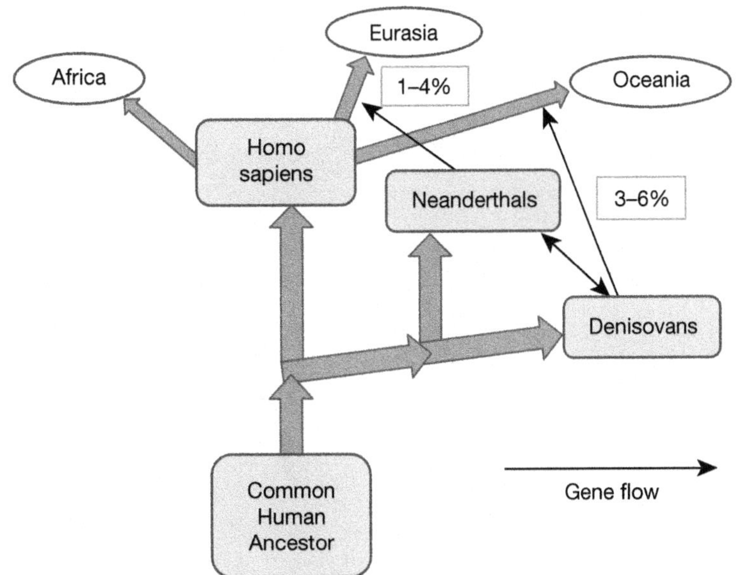

Figure 6.20 *The complex relationships between later human species (after Racimo et al. 2014)*

inbreeding. The woman's parents were both close relatives but she also shared DNA mutations with the Denisovans which are absent in AMH DNA. The research (Racimo et al. 2014) suggests that these two species split from the AMH lineage *c.* 400,000 BP and then Denisovans divided from Neanderthals *c.* 300,000 BP.

As well as the differences in interpretation of and weight given to various categories of evidence (DNA or anatomy), some underlying political ideas are involved. These relate to the way people would like to look at our modern population. Multiregionalism has been portrayed as racist (for emphasising differences between modern humans) or nationalistic by its critics. Out of Africa II has been called overly religious (Genesis and Eve) or politically correct. Part of the problem in arriving at a conclusion is that no DNA research is accepted universally. The fossil evidence base remains small and every year new discoveries are hailed by either side as proof of one theory or the other. It also seems that the modern human evolutionary sequence and links with and between earlier humans appear to be more blurred than once was thought. Small populations of related species appear to have interbred on several occasions, which currently is interpreted as support by both multiregional and assimilation camps.

Evolution of our species continues. Skeletal remains from the Upper Palaeolithic were around 25 per cent more robust than the skeletons of modern people. Average tooth size has continued to decline, especially among those populations which were the first to start farming.

WAS THERE A 'CREATIVE EXPLOSION' AND WHEN DID IT HAPPEN?

At some point after 50,000 BP (some archaeologists put it as late as 30–15,000 BP) there was a rapid blossoming in human culture. This involved a much greater variety of tools, including those carved from bone and antler, the development of art, music, symbolic behavior (▶ p. 505) and structured open-air settlements. This coincides with rapid expansion by Homo sapiens into harsh climates and uninhabited parts of the world including Europe. It has been ascribed to the way that Homo sapiens had to adapt in that

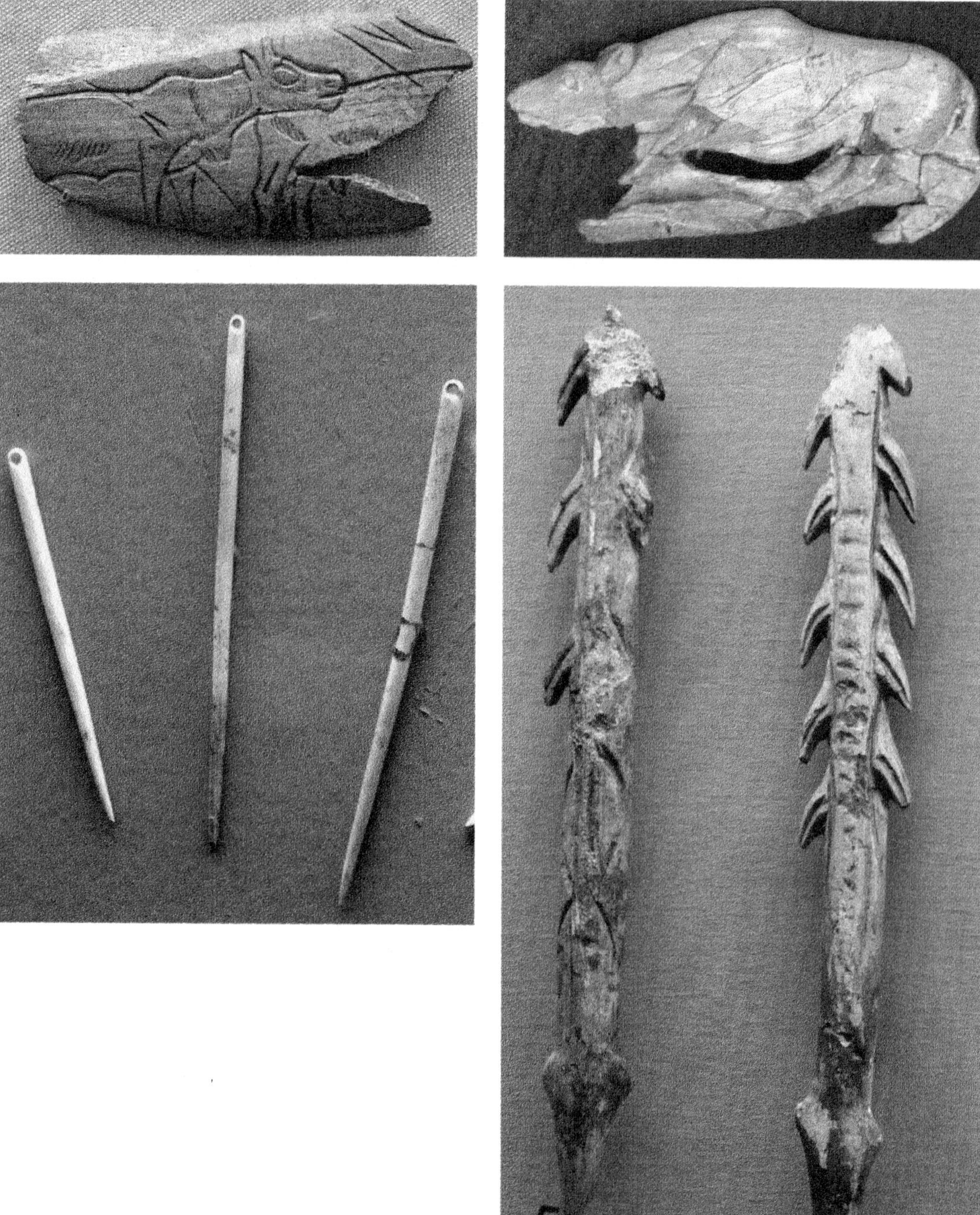

Figure 6.21 *Upper Palaeolithic innovations, figurative art, needles and harpoons*

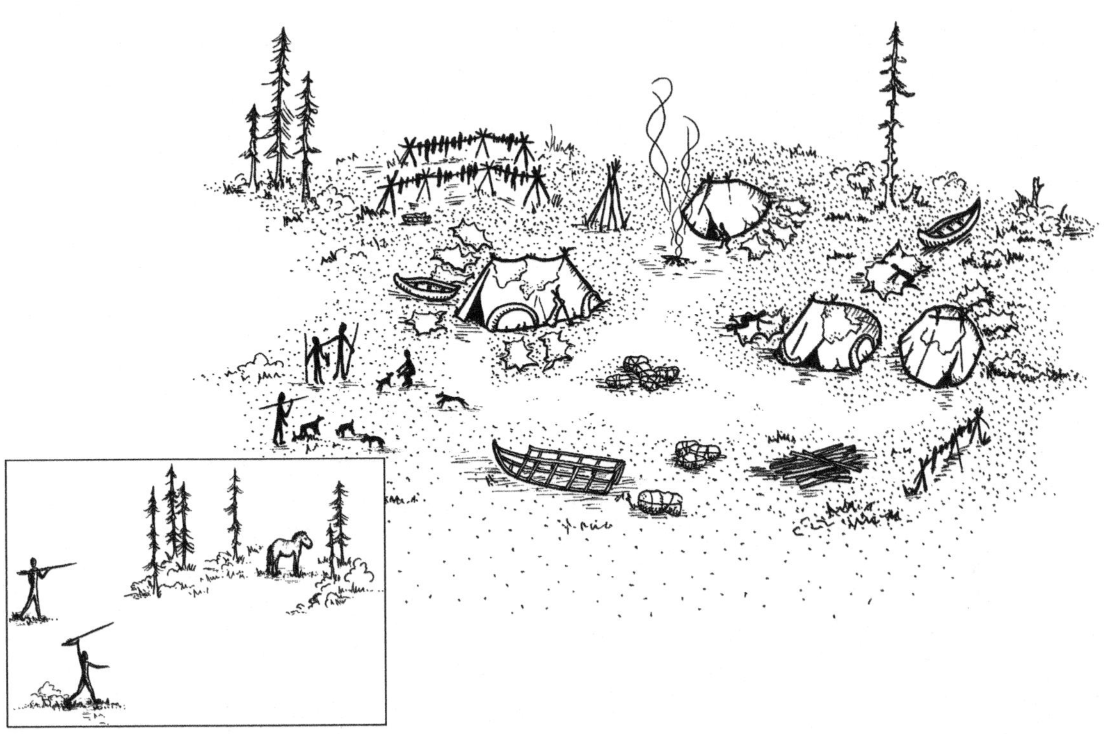

Figure 6.22 *Creative hunters*

By the end of the Ice Age tents, dried food, atlatls, domesticated dogs and possibly sleds and canoes enabled adaptation through better technology.

Ice Age world. Modern humans adapted to terrible climatic conditions socially and technologically rather than physically. Larger aggregations may have led to greater efficiency through a division of labour and cooperation. The development of tents, layered clothing and storage techniques such as drying fish or meat was also significant. More efficient projectile weapons such as stone-tipped darts launched from an atlatl enabled large prey to be killed at a distance. The Upper Palaeolithic is also associated with a rapid growth in population. Caspari and Lee's (2004) investigations into comparative ages of death of humans revealed that at this time up to five times as many people were surviving into old age than previously. This may have given Homo sapiens an edge in terms of accumulated knowledge or the 'Grandmother Revolution' which may have freed up younger adults from childcare to specialise, including manufacturing and exchange. These unprecedented and obvious changes in the archaeological record have led some archaeologists to argue that this is the point where we became modern people and to differentiate between anatomically modern humans (AMH) arising in Africa after 200,000 BP and behaviourally modern humans who developed in Ice-Age Eurasia.

A great leap forward?

While symbolic artefacts such as beads and occasional abstract carvings from earlier, African cave sites indicate a long genesis of symbolic behaviour, nothing approaches the Eurasian 'creative explosion'. Jared Diamond (1998) dubbed it 'The great leap forward'. It includes elaborate burials, a diverse wealth of technology moving well beyond stone tools, symbolic and figurative art, permanent dwellings, large social groups and evidence of exchange. The speed of change outstrips anything earlier and leads to regional diversity of technology and evidence of tremendous inventiveness including spear throwers, sewn clothing, barbed fish-hooks, textiles, fat-lamps and eventually bows. One explanation has been that there was a biological event *c.* 50,000 BP, possibly a neurological change in the brain which improved communication and creative thinking. However, no physical evidence for this has survived. An alternative view is that there were often primitive precursors for many of these developments but what happened in the Upper Palaeolithic is that ideas were quickly shared, improved on and led to further development. This points to a social or behavioural cause of change. Mega-sites where different groups came together, such as Dolni Vestonice, may provide the answer.

Gradual change

Not everyone agrees that there was a sudden change. Bednarik (1992) highlights evidence for the use of symbolism by earlier humans (▶ p. 212). He argues for the possibility that organic materials were a medium for expression and cites rare survivals such as the Schöningen spears (▶ p. 200) as evidence of woodworking. There is also increasing evidence of personal ornamentation, art and possibly ritual from before 50,000 BP. At the cave site of Grotte des Pigeons in Morocco, beads made from Nassarius shells have been found with traces of red ochre and microscopic wear patterns which suggest they were hung from cords. The shells had been transported 40km from the coast and were used *c.* 80,000 BP. Very similar shell beads were found in Blombos Cave, South Africa, dating to *c.* 75,000 BP. Vanhaeren et al. (2013) were able to identify slight changes in the way beads were strung over time which may indicate changing fashions. Nassarius beads from the Skhul Cave in Israel have been securely dated to *c.* 100,000 BP, which suggests that symbolic behaviour originated much earlier, possibly soon after modern humans first appeared. Red ochre may have been used for decoration from 164,000 BP and a possible carved figure from Israel dates from 250,000 BP. Vanhaeren et al. (2006) have pointed out that the range of early beads is much narrower than those from Upper Palaeolithic Europe and they may have had a more restricted range of functions. They argue that their use may have been in gift exchanges between groups to establish reciprocity networks. Perforated shells have been discovered at Ucagizli in south-eastern Turkey dating from 60,000 years ago and these may be markers of modern peoples en route to western Europe.

KEY STUDY

Dolni Vestonice and the Moravian Gate

Dolni Vestonice is the best known of a cluster of sites in central Europe dating from the Gravettian period of *c.* 30–20,000 BP. These were large open-air sites and are particularly concentrated around 'gates' in the central European mountains through which migratory animals could pass from the Danube valley to the south onto the North European Plain. As with most Palaeolithic cultures, the Gravettian period is usually identified by its lithic assemblage. However, these sites are also remarkable in their development of new materials, their art and their unprecedented size (over 100m in diameter) and permanence. Dolni Vestonice was

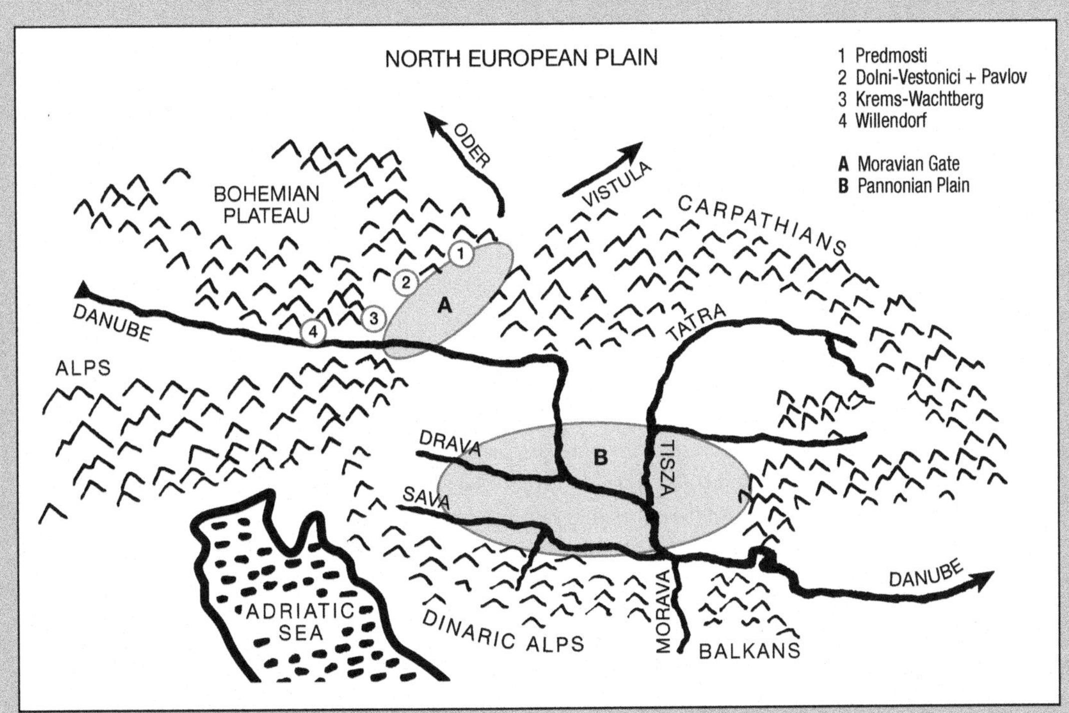

Figure 6.23 Location of Moravian Gate sites

occupied repeatedly from *c.* 30,000 to 25,000 BP. It lies in the 'Moravian Gate': a narrow corridor of flat land between the Carpathian Mountains and the Bohemian Massif. A string of clustered, open-air sites are located with fairly regular spacing along this corridor and on slopes close to rivers. They include Predmosti to the north and Willendorf and Krems to the south. These patterns and types of locations are similar to that of Kostenki (▶ p. 224) in the Don Valley but the Moravian sites are significantly larger and more complex.

Dolni Vestonice lies on slopes south of the River Dyje close to the modern town of Brno and was systematically excavated between 1924 and 1938 by Karel Absolon. Further finds emerged after the Second World War when a brickworks and then terracing for vineyards cut into the thick layers of loess which covered the sites. Since then a series of rescue (in advance of a dam being built in the 1980s) and research excavations have taken place, revealing a constellation of local sites including Pavlov, about 700m to the south-east. Pavlov I was excavated over several decades from 1952 on a large scale by Bohuslav Klíma. Today research continues as part of the Moravian Gate Project which involves several European institutes and universities including Cambridge. Archaeologists named each successive excavation DV I, DV II etc. but this can be misleading. Several of the excavations or trenches are in fact different elements in the same large, contemporary Gravettian settlement. Palaeobotanical research including the analysis of charcoal fragments, molluscs and faunal remains suggests that the environment was open grassland but with marsh areas and pockets of woodland featuring cold-adapted trees such as spruce and larch.

continued

The excavations

Dolni Vestonice I was sited by a stream close to a marsh and protected by a boundary made from mammoth tusks and bones. Four clustered rings of heavy stones and bones had provided weights to hold down skins which had been draped over wooden frames to make large tents. Ash from a large external hearth showed that animal bone had been the main fuel used. Vast numbers of animal bones littered the site, including the remains of hundreds of mammoths. Many showed signs of butchery and processing by the many stone tools left around the hearths. Other animals included horses, reindeer, hare, wolf and fox. Some 80m upstream of the tents a shelter had been dug into the hillside and side-walls built up with rocks and clay. Inside was a dome-shaped kiln and scattered over the floor were fragments of hundreds of figurines. These were made from a fired mixture of river clay and powdered bone and were mainly in the form of animal heads or human figures and are the earliest known ceramics. Most appeared to have been deliberately broken. The most famous is a Venus figurine similar to that from Willendorf (▶ p. 453). Other figurines were discovered around the hearth at the main site along with some made of ivory. At Dolni Vestonice II futher dwellings were found close to a marshy ravine containing large numbers of mammoth bones and remains from manufacturing lithics. At DV III analysis of one of the hearths revealed the remains of ground plant tissue. Several burials were found at this site including a triple burial of three young adults and one of a child wearing a fox-tooth necklace and covered by a mammoth shoulder blade.

Figure 6.24 *Recreation of a mammoth bone house*

Pavlov was very similar. At least ten structures were excavated at Pavlov I along with hearths, another kiln and hundreds of broken clay figurines. Grindstones were found amongst the lithic debris, although they appeared to have been used to process coloured minerals rather than grains. Relatively few remains of mammoths were found, although a male burial was found also covered by a mammoth shoulder blade. In 2007 the digging of a new canal revealed a single living unit (of Pavlov VI) in an otherwise undisturbed area, comprising a hearth and several pits containing the remains of two mammoths and other animals. The largest pit was over 1m wide and the dark, humic fill contained stones which had been heated. It was interpreted as a roasting pit while smaller pits were thought to be boiling pits. Around the hearth were fragments of ceramics, some of which were marked with impressions from fingerprints and textiles. Other decorative items included drilled stones and shells decorated with ochre and small tools which were used to carve mammoth ivory.

Faunal remains

The faunal assemblage of over 40,000 bones at Pavlov I was dominated not by mammoths but by reindeer and large numbers of small animals including birds, Arctic foxes and hares. The most common birds were grouse and ptarmigan, which were used for food, but the presence of so many fur-bearing animals, particularly carnivores such as wolves and wolverine, suggest that pelts were also important. Cut-marks on bones revealed skinning processes as well as butchery. Animal bones were also processed to make tools – possibly including wind instruments – and ornaments. Drilled teeth were commonly worn as necklaces or sewn into clothing.

In 2009 another accidental discovery occurred when a road close to the village of Milovice collapsed into an old cellar, in the walls of which were mammoth bones. Huts and mammoth butchery sites were already known from a side valley close by but this new site (Milovice IV) lay lower down and contained rich environmental data. Wet sieving and flotation retrieved pollen, charcoal and the bones of small vertebrates. Many of these were typical of aquatic habitats. Many of the 20,000 animal bones recovered were highly fragmented and records made by Binford (▶ p. 229) in Alaska were used to interpret the patterns. In addition to skinning and butchery, marrow and grease (for fuel, food or processing hides) had been extracted and many bones subsequently used as fuel.

The settlements

The huts varied in size, with the largest being around 16m x 6m and containing five hearths. While the lower walls of huts were constructed from large mammoth bones and tusks, the upper parts were made from wood, with hide the most likely covering. Repeatedly used postholes suggested that the site was used for a long time or on many occasions. Huts could hold between eight and fifteen people, so if occupation was contemporary, the population of Dolni Vestonice could have been as high as one hundred. This number included children, several of whom left their fingerprints on clay artefacts. These were easily the largest and most permanent settlements to that date. Activity appears to have revolved around the external hearths. These were the focus for the production and use of thousands of artefacts and processed bones. Most of the flint, ochre, fossils and stone used were local but some stones (radiolarite) and shells had travelled a considerable distance. Lithics were most commonly blades, scrapers, burins and Gravettian backed or shouldered points. Bone and ivory were used for needles, shovels, hoes, picks, spear-tips and possible whistles and weaving battens. Both bone and ivory were

continued

carved to make jewellery and ornaments with drilled teeth (including a fossil shark tooth), ivory, stone and shells used for necklaces. Many had traces of red or black ochre. One carved mammoth bone appears to be a female portrait and another has been interpreted as a map. Both would be firsts. In addition to figurines there were many other lumps of fired clay. Over forty have revealed woven textile, cord or knot impressions and even a fragment of mesh or net. Experimentation showed how a range of cordage may have been produced by processing crushed nettles and then spinning and weaving. Other plants had been used to make baskets. Outside the huts and often surrounding the hearths were ash-filled pits. Distribution patterns of materials suggest that activities including manufacture and butchery may have been separated into zones.

Economy

These 'mega-sites' appear both complex and long-lasting. Some archaeologists see them as the first permanent open-air settlements. Others believe that they built up their artefact density through repeated short occupations. Analysis of growth stages on reindeer and carnivore teeth supports year-round occupation. The long-lasting structures, kilns and burials may also support permanence. Most of the sites are situated at around 200–240m with a good view across the plain and above the swampy areas where mammoths and other herds would congregate. In most cases all animal bones were present at the site, which means the inhabitants had brought them there. Some archaeologists believe that while most animals were hunted, mammoths were scavenged. However, the sheer number of bones supports the interpretation of the excavators that these were specialist mammoth hunters. Klima (Svoboda and Klima 2005) believes that hunters worked in groups, possibly using whistles to communicate. Natural features such as blind valleys, swamps and cliffs could have been used to trap or kill the animals and this is supported by butchered remains from these areas. Other animals hunted in this way included horses and reindeer. Small animals such as hares and birds were probably trapped using nets. Other animals appear to have been hunted primarily for fur including the full range of carnivores. Nets or harpoons would have been needed to harvest fish from the nearby river. While there is no evidence of domestic dogs from this site, there are skulls at the contemporary site of Predmosti which may show the first signs of domestication. Bringing huge mammoths back to the camp must have been a considerable feat of organisation and the people made use of every part of the animal including for food, lamps, tools, buildings and fuel. Skins may also have been used for shoes. Trinkaus (2005a) found that from *c.* 26,000 BP little toes became progressively weaker than in previous populations. This is because they were no longer flexing for traction with the likely cause being the use of protective and supportive footwear.

Society

The view that Dolni Vestonice was dominated by male hunters has been challenged by Olga Soffer. Many previous interpretations had assumed that women were mainly concerned with child rearing while men hunted. Soffer et al. (2009) argued that the age and sex profile of dead mammoths was similar to those that died around modern waterholes in Africa. They argue that sites were located near places (such as swamps) where dead mammoths could be harvested for resources rather than hunted. Drawing on a range of recent ethnographic data and some of the more unusual discoveries from the site, they argue that women may have made the most significant contribution to food through gathering plants and net-hunting of small animals. These make up nearly 50 per cent of the faunal assemblages. This sort of hunting, driving hares and grouse into nets, is safe and could have involved women with young children. Other archaeologists argue that despite the climate, plants may also have been important, particularly roots and berries, which could have been pounded using the grindstones. Palaeobotanical research in the region has shown that many plants which are used by modern peoples in the Arctic for food and medicine were available. Subsequent research has recovered charred roots and berries from Gravettian hearths. If plants, eggs and even insects are added to the small game, then women may have contributed most of the food consumed at the time. Soffer has used this economic argument to interpret the 'Venus' figurines as representing female power. The figurines have generated considerable debate with interpretations including male pornography, female ritual artefacts and celebrations of fertility. Today the latter two ideas predominate. The accuracy of some of the depictions of very overweight women suggest that the artists had seen obese women. It may be that having large fat deposits was seen as a social ideal or demonstration of wealth as it has been in some modern cultures, or that it made the survival of babies more likely.

Ritual

Besides their economic function, these mega-sites may have had ritual functions. Experiments with the many broken ceramic figurines have shown that their method of manufacture led them to explode during

Figure 6.25 *Dolni Vestonice triple burial (after Libor Balak)*

continued

firing. Their sheer number suggests that this was deliberate. Other symbolic activities may have involved the use of paint or dyes. Manufacturing ochre powder is one of the possible uses of the grindstones and ochre was used to colour artefacts and in burials to cover parts of the body. Burials are often associated with animal tooth and ivory beads, while mammoth shoulders often covered the corpse. Whether this was symbolic or to prevent scavengers accessing the body is unclear. One burial was of a woman in her forties holding the body of a fox. She was old enough to be a grandmother and represents a trend in the Upper Palaeolithic of people living longer. Caspari (Caspari and Lee 2004) argues that older people would have had considerable status because of their knowledge. Others have argued that in the 'grandparent revolution', rather than being a burden, older people were able to look after children, thus freeing up younger adults for more productive roles. The elaborate nature of her burial may support the idea that she had higher status or was a shaman.

The triple burial has provoked the most debate. The slender, central female is partially overlapped by the two robust males. One is face down while the other lies on his side with his hands touching the pelvis of the female. Their heads were covered with red ochre as was the pubic area of the female. The hip area of the female was deformed either from birth or illness, which may have crippled her, and one of the males may have been speared in the side before or after death. Aside from this, the young people

Period	Date range BP	Culture	Species	Distinctive material culture	Key sites
Upper Palaeolithic	17–11,000	Magdalenian	Homo sapiens	bows & arrows, fish hooks, tents	Lascaux
	22–18,000	Solutrean		leaf-shaped and shouldered points	Laugerie-Haute
	29–22,000	Gravettian		ceramic art, harpoons, mammoth bone houses, Venus figurines	Dolni Vestonice
	45–29,000	Aurignacian		blades, bone & antler points, needles, figurative art	Kostenki, Chauvet
	40–34,000	Chatelperronian	Homo neanderthalensis	elements of both Mousterian and Aurignacian	Grotte du Renne, La Ferrassie
Middle Palaeolithic	c. 90–40,000	Mousterian		flake tools, spear points, awls	La Chapelle aux Saintes, Krapina, St. Cesaire
Lower Palaeolithic	900,000–c. 90,000	Acheulean	Homo erectus, Homo heidelbergensis, Homo neanderthalensis	core-tools, hand-axes, crude flake tools, scrapers, wooden spears	Bilzingsleben, Torralba, Boxgrove, Happisburgh

Figure 6.26 *Periods in the European Palaeolithic*

appear to have been healthy at the time of death and interpretations have focused upon the relationships between the two and possible social taboos. One theory is that it represents a 'married' couple and another man with whom the woman had had sex. This may have transgressed social laws which reinforced marriage either to prevent disorder or because of the need to provide for children. The face-down burial may represent shame or disapproval. An alternative view is that the woman is not a woman but a gracile male and this represents a same-sex relationship which may also have broken taboos. Damage to its hips means that the sex of the central skeleton is ambiguous. Most burials are similar to others in Ice Age Europe in terms of position of the body, burial goods and the use of ochre. This supports the idea of similar sets of beliefs at that time.

Evolution

Dolni Vestonice is also at the heart of a debate about when we became modern. Although Homo sapiens are known from 160 to 120,000 BP in southern Africa, there is an unprecedented explosion of culture in Ice Age Europe and western Asia between 40,000 and 20,000 BP. Innovation flourished and ideas spread widely. This points to a social or behavioural cause of change. Aggregation sites like Dolni Vestonice may have facilitated these changes.

Chapter 7

Sites and People in the Landscape

Settlement Archaeology

This chapter begins by considering the relationship between people and the environment and then considers the techniques archaeologists use to interpret the function and status of sites and structures. It builds on Chapters 1 and 2 and should be read in conjunction with Chapter 5, which introduces underpinning ideas about interpreting sites and their formation.

WHAT DOES THE ARCHAEOLOGY OF SETTLEMENT COVER?

Settlement is a central topic in both thematic and chronological studies of the past. However, the term has several meanings. Today, when we talk of settlements we mean cities, towns and villages. However, for most of human history none of these existed. When humans were mobile hunter-gatherers rather than **sedentary** farmers, they created a range of temporary camps for processing raw materials and food. Sometimes caves or rock shelters were repeatedly occupied and their rich archaeological deposits have survived. Other sites simply consist of scatters of debitage (▶ p. 94) from a single episode of stone tool making or bones from the butchery of an animal. The duration of use of a site might range from a few hours for a hunting site to thousands of years for a town. Rather confusingly, a settlement is just one type of site but the archaeology of settlement includes all sites and some which you may feel are not sites at all. Settlement archaeology, therefore, includes the study of both permanent and temporary sites (including their structures and features) and the interaction of humans with their landscape. Settlement archaeology seeks to identify and explain the spatial distribution of past human activities. This might mean understanding the location of sites within a landscape or the arrangement of structures within a settlement. At a micro-level it includes studying activities within a room or living floor. The key questions asked usually revolve around identification of functions or the reasons for patterns in their distribution. The meticulous plotting in three dimensions of artefacts, ecofacts and features is the key evidence base in studying the distribution of ancient activities. The specific forms of sites studied vary according to the period: kill site, barrow, motte, mill, etc.

For most of their existence humans lived by hunting and gathering within a natural environment. The common image of 'hunter-gatherers', or 'foragers' as they are increasingly known, is of a small group wandering around the landscape in a nomadic fashion seeking food or following animals. They are usually portrayed living in

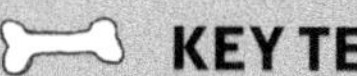

KEY TERM

Sedentary

Living in one place.

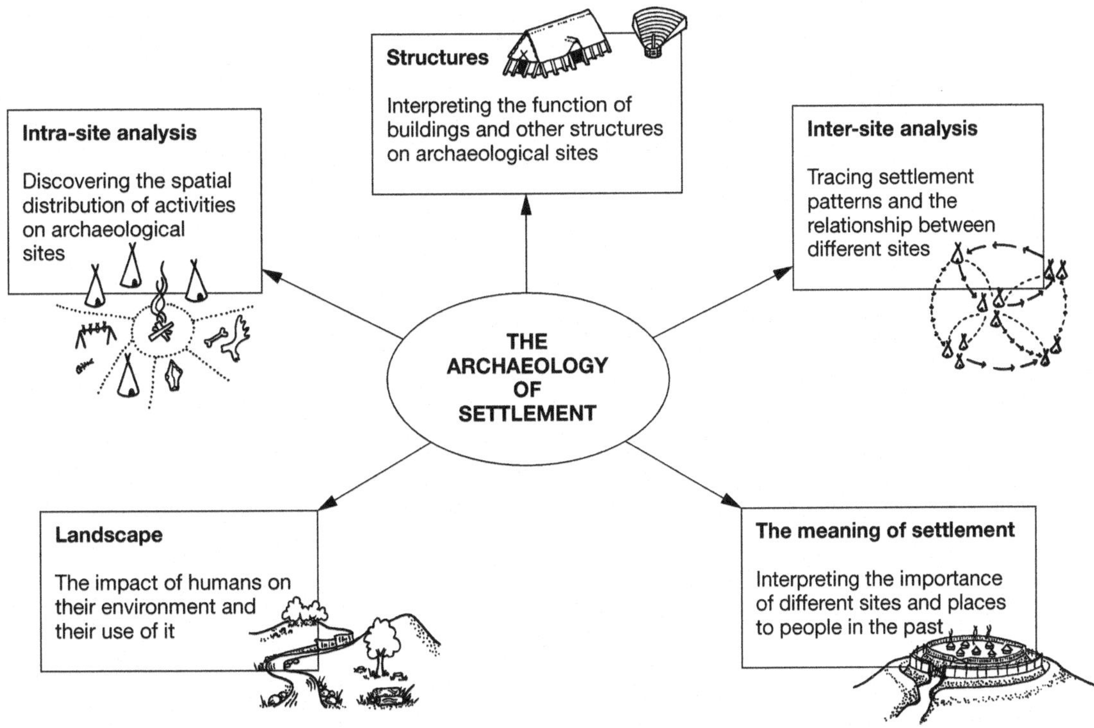

Figure 7.1 *The archaeology of settlement*

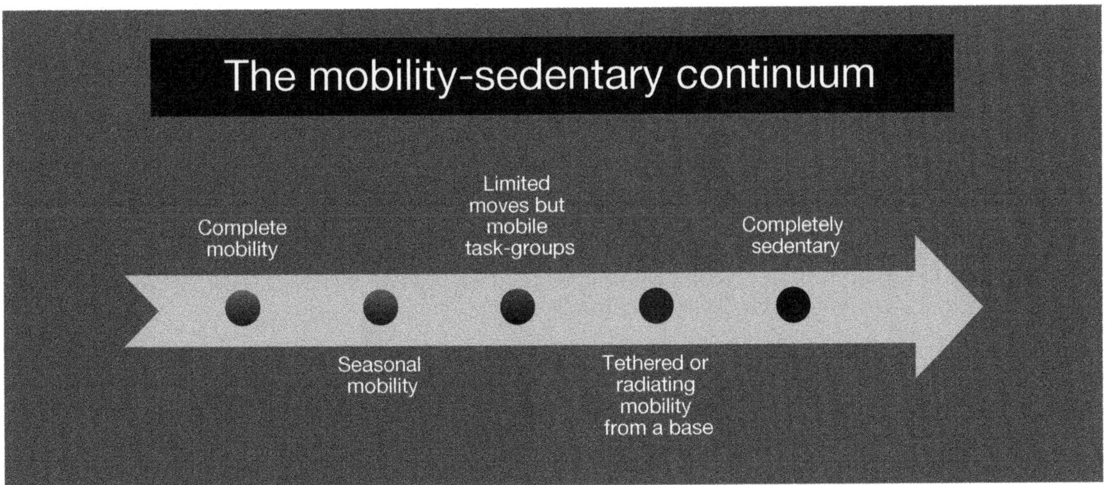

Figure 7.2 *The mobility–sedentary continuum*

Figure 7.3 *Semi-sedentism in the Mesolithic*

Mobility is a strategy to reduce risk. However, during the later Mesolithic, rich coastal environments and technological innovation enabled Ertebølle foragers around the Baltic to become almost sedentary. Generally the group remained in their favoured location but task groups might go out on seasonal foraging trips for short periods. These might be to islands to exploit seals or sea birds or inland lakes for migratory waterfowl. Signs of greater permanence include cemeteries and built structures (▶ p. 281).

harmony with nature and have little in the way of possessions or settlement. This image, based largely on colonial ethnographies from Africa and America, is increasingly inappropriate for later prehistory, especially for temperate or Arctic regions. Another problem is that hunting and (mainly) gathering lifestyles range from the earliest hominid ancestors in Africa around 2 mya to the sophisticated Ertebølle culture (▶ p. 309) of the 4th millennium BC. A considerable amount changed during that time. Research increasingly demonstrates that the old view that people only 'settled down' with the advent of farming is no longer tenable. Evidence from archaeology and anthropology suggests a more complex reality. Many cultures have existed whose settlement pattern lies somewhere between the two poles of mobile and sedentary. A wealth of terms such as 'semi-sedentary' and 'radiating or tethered mobility' have been used to describe these patterns.

PEOPLE AND THE LANDSCAPE

However, for much of the past people probably identified with an area of the landscape through which they may have moved on a seasonal basis, rather than necessarily living in one fixed place. Neither 'site' nor 'settlement' adequately describe repeated activity in approximately the same area or 'locale' (▶ p. 177), nor the range of activities which took place across the landscape. Some writers call this the 'taskscape'. For many past societies, these 'off-site areas' that we sometimes detect as flint-scatters, woods or field systems were as important as the 'sites' which archaeologists have tended to 'excavate'. The work of Binford (▶ p. 229) in particular demonstrates that individual sites can provide a rather biased picture of activity in the past and that there is a need to consider the whole 'settlement system'.

The term 'cultural ecology' is used to describe the relationship between people and landscape. Humans are part of the ecosystem like other living organisms and climate, environment and natural food sources impose limits on human populations and how they live. However, unlike that of other mammals, human movement around and use of the landscape cannot be explained solely in terms of biology and the physical environment. Humans adapt to their environment through the use of cultural technology. They can extend the range of resources and territory they exploit beyond their natural biological limits by, for example, harvesting sea fish through the development of boats, traps and nets during the Mesolithic (▶ p. 382) or using irrigation to farm arid areas. To understand the dynamics of human adaptation, archaeologists need to understand both the environment of the area studied and the technology available to the people living there. Humans can also modify their environment and their own fertility. Population levels and settlement density are not just determined by the carrying capacity of the land, as the modern world demonstrates. Human impact on the landscape from forest clearance to division into fields and territories is also a vital part of settlement study. Finally, humans also have a mental and emotional relationship with the landscape which includes concepts such as ownership, territory and beliefs. Bradley (2000b) argues that natural places were significant in past belief systems (▶ p. 522) and a relationship between ancestors, spirits and places is common in many cultures.

Seasonal patterns of movement

People in the past often exploited different parts of the landscape at different times of the year. Ecofacts have been used on many transitory sites

KEY STUDY

Lewis Binford and Nunamiut ethnoarchaeology

Binford's (1978) classic ethnoarchaeological research amongst the Nunamiut examined their hunting activities and the dynamics of their settlement pattern through seasonal movement from an archaeological perspective. The Nunamiut ('inland-people') live around Anaktuvuk Pass in Alaska and like the Inuit (Eskimo), to whom they are related, they mainly ate meat. Apart from the plant contents of caribou stomachs, Binford estimated that they only ate a cup and a half of plant food each year. Mostly they subsisted on dried reindeer meat supplemented by some traded fish and seal meat and fat. Traditionally in spring and autumn the Nunamiut trapped

continued

migrating caribou in corrals, although by the time of Binford's study they were hunting using guns. As with the Blackfoot buffalo hunters (▶ p. 253), all parts of the animals were used. Caribou provided their clothes, tents and cordage. Carcasses that could not be processed immediately were stored in caches on the frozen ground under piles of rocks to keep them from scavengers.

Binford's studies revealed the huge range of territory covered and the factors that influenced the location and timing of campsites. Specialist camps were established for hunting, carcass processing and sexual liaisons while non-residential sites included caches of meat and deadfall traps. Binford was able to argue convincingly that since humans do not confine their behaviour to identifiable sites, we should study sites as part of a wider context. Drawing an analogy with the parts of a car engine, he showed that in order to understand the activities of a mobile society we need to fit all the parts of the system together to see the whole picture, from hunting stands to skinning sites. Observation enabled him to understand Nunamiut activities and then record the discarded material associated with it. He put particular emphasis upon documenting the spatial relationship between lithic and bone evidence.

Foragers and collectors

The most influential idea Binford developed from this study was his distinction between foragers and collectors and his models of their differing settlement patterns. While careful not to draw direct parallels

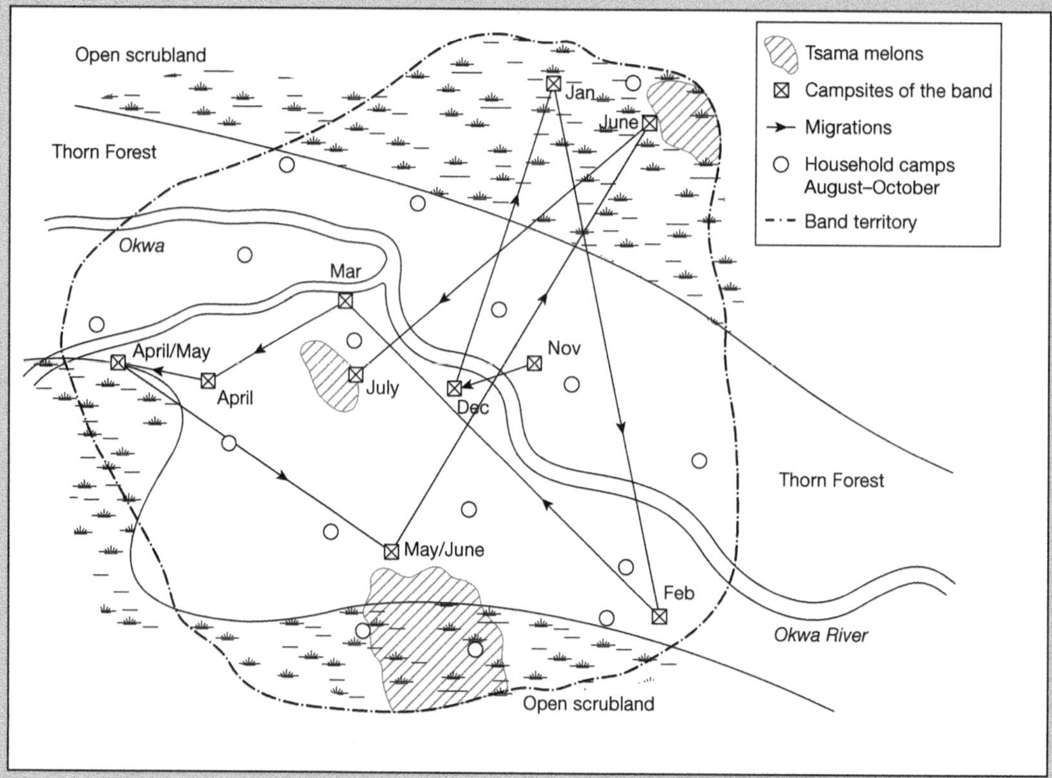

Figure 7.4 *Foragers: seasonal migrations of the Efe pygmies in the Congo (after Bailey 1991)*

between Nunamiut and Palaeolithic hunters, Binford (1978) felt that they provided more appropriate analogs for interpreting sites such as Pincevent (▶ p. 278) than models archaeologists derived from tropical Africa. He drew on the comparative ethnographic studies of Murdock and Morrow (1970), which showed that residential mobility was greatest at the equator and in the Arctic and also that the further from the equator, the greater foragers' reliance on meat and on storage.

He described forager settlement patterns as being daisy-like. They would set out each day from the home base into the bush and encounter resources at various 'locations' scattered across the landscape. These included kill sites, bushes with berries or sources of water. Foragers take what they need back to home bases, where processing and manufacturing takes place. This strategy does not involve storage because the finding of resources is highly predictable and there is limited seasonal variation. If resources

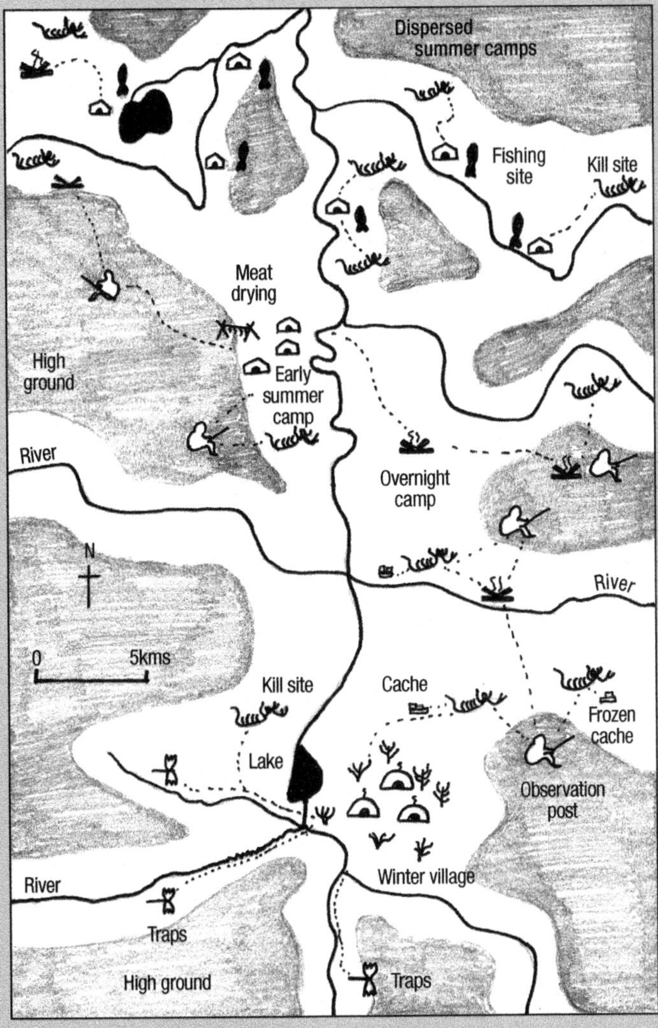

Figure 7.5 *Binford's model of logistical collectors (after Binford 1978)*

continued

run low, the group splits up or moves to a new area. 'Mapping the group onto resources' (Binford 1980) or 'residential mobility' is a key characteristic of foragers in Australia and southern Africa. However, groups varied hugely in how often they moved camp, the numbers living together and therefore the amount of evidence left behind.

In contrast, the Nunamiut were 'logistically organised collectors'. Logistics is the planned management of resources. The Nunamiut operate in a landscape with great seasonal variation, where risk of not finding food is greater and where resources are too far apart to move a group close to them all. They solve this problem by storing food in caches for some of the year and transporting food and other resources from a variety of procurement sites back to the main residential base. This can involve the establishment of temporary field camps by specialist task-groups rather than the whole band. It also involves planning the locations they will use rather than hoping to encounter resources. Sites will vary according to their purpose in the type of material discarded and therefore their 'signature'. Some, such as 'stations' where observers watch for caribou, might leave fleeting traces while a butchery site would have large amounts of low-meat bones.

Binford was not saying that Palaeolithic hunters were all logistical collectors. However, he was suggesting that on the continuum between forager and collector, their strategies and settlement patterns were likely to be closer to the 'logistical mobility' of collectors as they adapted to their harsh environment.

to identify periods of occupation. The season of periodic activities around the Palaeolithic site of Torralba was identified from the bones of migratory birds while seasonal occupation of midden sites has been distinguished from growth lines in shells. These methods are not without controversy. The antlers found at Star Carr (▶ p. 267) have been used to argue for the site's use in almost every season. Seasonal mobility is not limited to hunter-gatherers. Herders (pastoralists) often follow a yearly cycle, spreading out onto higher grazing areas in the late spring and returning to more sheltered areas for the winter (▶ p. 318). Contrasting examples of seasonal movement are explored in several key studies including Head Smashed In (▶ p. 253), Pincevent (▶ p. 278) and Vaihingen (▶ p. 350).

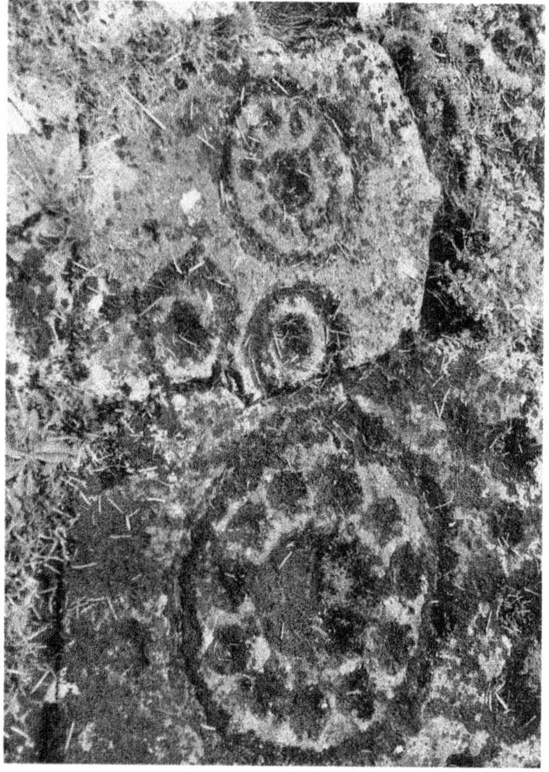

Figure 7.6 *Ormaig rock art panel, Kilmartin*

Like many other petroglyphs in the area it is located on poor agricultural soil near an entry point into the Kilmartin Valley. It may indicate territory, a route through the landscape, seasonal pastures or a significant 'off-site' location.

KEY STUDY

Oronsay, Sand and seasonal movement around the Inner Hebrides

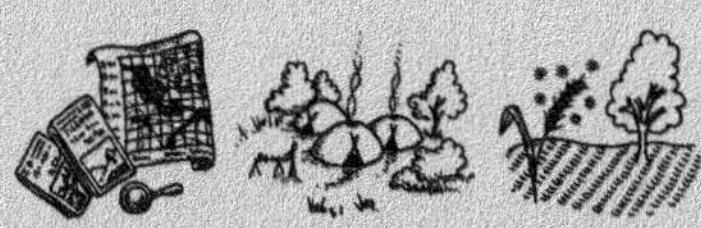

Oronsay is a small island in the Inner Hebrides connected by a causeway to the larger island of Colonsay. From the 1870s antiquarians excavated the shell middens which stand on raised beaches on the island, recovering Mesolithic stone tools, shell beads and barbed antler and bone points. There were also 'bevel-ended' (think blunt chisel) bone and antler tools which have been interpreted as limpet hammers. Since red deer were not present on the islands, an early interpretation of the site was a summer camp where people crossed from the mainland to harvest shellfish as part of a wide-ranging inland–coast pattern of mobility.

Mellar's (1987) excavations in the 1970s using dry sieving subsequently recovered well-preserved faunal material and some human teeth and bones from the shell layers (mainly limpets) which were sandwiched between deposits of wind-blown sand. There were numerous hearths within the middens and a circular ring of stake holes about 3m in diameter. Amongst the local faunal remains processed were seabirds, crabs, otters and particularly seals. Many were pups killed in the autumn. As previously, remains of red deer and pig were found which had been brought to the island. Better recovery methods also produced a large fish-bone assemblage, most of which were saithe (cod family). Fish processing had been a significant activity at the middens. Mellars believed that seaweed might have been used for food but it leaves little trace, and few other plant foods apart from hazelnuts were recovered. Environmental samples containing pollen and snails showed that the island still had areas of mixed woodland in the Mesolithic. The team dated the middens to 6200–5200 BP.

Saithe provided a vital clue to the pattern of human activity on the island. Saithe (also known as pollack or coley and a major component of fishfingers) spawn off the Hebrides in February to April and the young fish are found inshore for the next two years. Saithe grow quickly, reaching 45cm (and over 5kg) in three years and over 1m as an adult. Traditionally, harvests of saithe have been smoked or dried and some stone settings in Cnoc Coig midden on Oronsay have been identified as possible drying or smoking places. The rapid growth of saithe makes it possible to establish their age at death by measuring their otolith or ear-bone and sectioning it to count annual growth rings. Lengths of otoliths from four middens were compared with modern samples of known ages. The results were surprising as each midden produced fish bones from a different season. This suggested that the people may have lived permanently on the island, moving around it over the year. There must also have been trading or hunting expeditions elsewhere to bring pig and deer across since these were butchered at the middens. Later research involving stable isotope analysis of human bone from Cnoc Coig midden appeared to support this view as it suggested that these people had largely consumed marine protein (Richards and Mellars 1998). Interestingly, isotope analysis of a lone human bone from Caisteal Nan Gillean II midden was different and suggested a mixed diet of terrestrial mammals and seals.

Alternative explanations

Mellar's interpretation was challenged by Mithen (2006), who argued that it was unlikely that foragers would restrict themselves to such a small island unless there were particular ritual reasons. The marine foods would have been unreliable at certain times of year. The limited range of tools found on Oronsay

continued

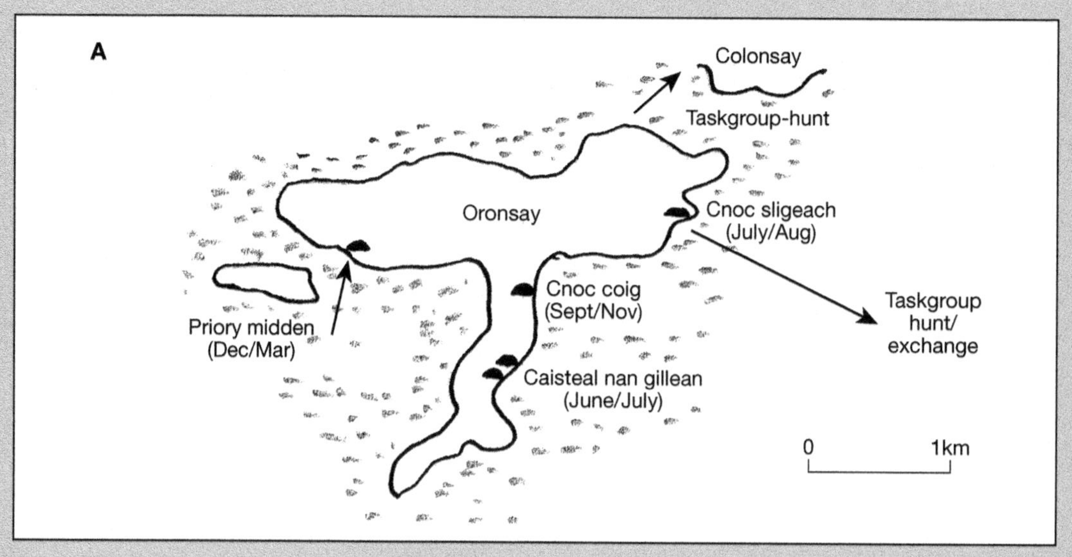

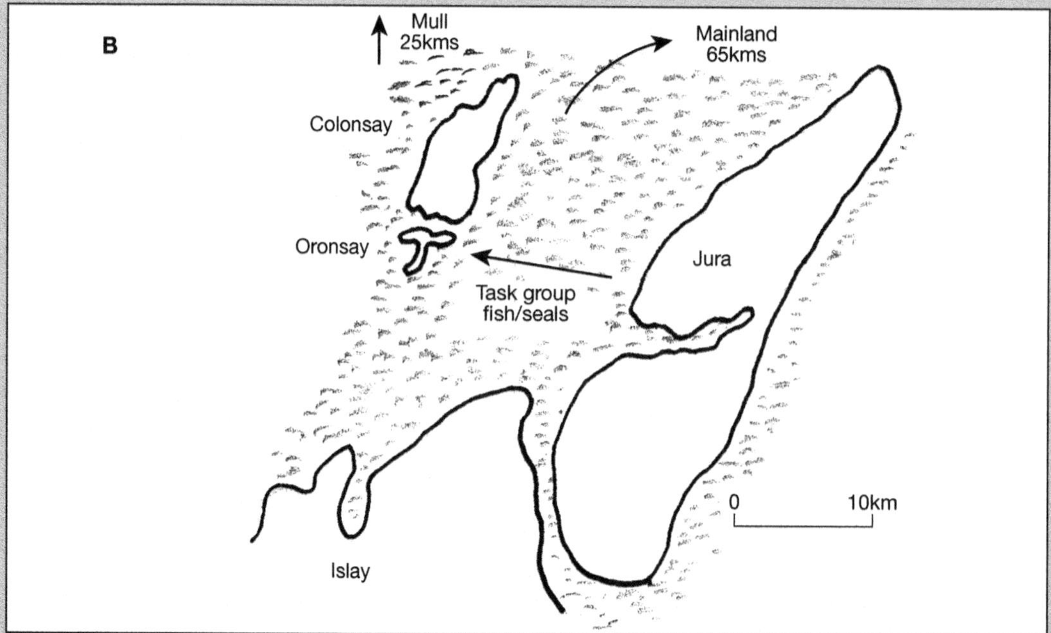

Figure 7.7 *Alternative explanations of seasonal movement at Oronsay*

and the existence of more diverse habitats on the larger islands led him to suggest that the middens were the result of short-term specialised expeditions for sealing or fishing by people from those larger islands. The red deer bones may provide a clue. They were often not major meat-bearing bones, which suggested that they had been brought partly for tool making. Remains have been drawn from two separate populations of deer. One group were small animals, which may be the result of a population being isolated on an island. The other group included large individuals and may have come from the mainland.

Mithen suspected that the absence of contemporary sites on nearby Colonsay and Islay was simply because non-midden sites had not been discovered yet. The Southern Hebrides Mesolithic Project looked for evidence across the islands in the area, including successfully locating and excavating over thirty new flint scatters. GIS analysis of the position of sites on Islay examined the views from these sites (a 'viewshed' approach) and found that they were commonly located above valleys, ideal for spotting and ambushing animals. They also discovered a pit on Colonsay dating to 9000 BP which contained hundreds of thousands of charred hazelnut shells and lesser celandine tubers and provided evidence of large-scale processing, possibly for storage. However, none of the dates for the new sites overlap those on Oronsay.

Sand

Further north, the seascape around the inner sound between Skye and the mainland has been intensively surveyed as part of the Scotland's First Settlers project. This included surface survey to document middens, rock shelters and microlith scatters, test pitting and at Sand, the excavation of a rock shelter midden. The site is in a sheltered position on a tidal inlet and was dated to 7600–6260 BC.

Much of the faunal material recovered from the midden was highly fragmented and deposits had been transformed (▶ p. 165) both by movement down-slope and disturbance by later periods of

Figure 7.8 *Sand rock shelter*

Figure 7.9 *The midden at Sand being sectioned (Caroline Wickham-Jones/Scotland's First Settlers project)*

continued

occupation. Flotation was used to recover remains using sieves with tiny 1mm and 0.3mm meshes (Hardy and Wickham-Jones 2002). Mammal bones were rarer than expected and often highly fragmented. A narrow range of animals was hunted including pig and deer, however, the assemblage of bird and fish bones was enormous with over 16,000 specimens identified. Fish were largely inshore species such as saithe and were generally under 50cm in length. The presence of smaller fish such as wrasse suggested that nets or traps had been used since these produce a by-catch of smaller species. The most common

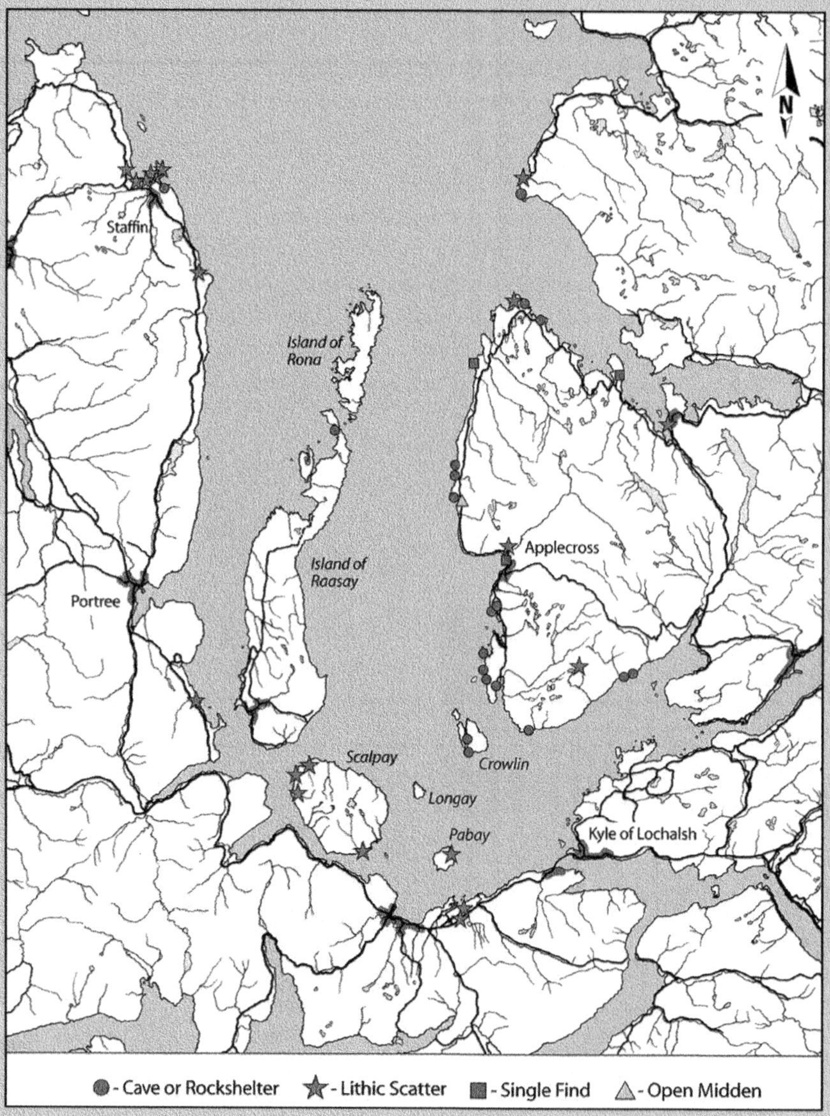

Figure 7.10 *Mesolithic sites around the Inner Sound. Sand is the triangle just north of Applecross. (Caroline Wickham-Jones/Scotland's First Settlers project)*

birds were guillemots and razorbills, which spend most of their lives far out at sea. They only come ashore to breed in late spring and to moult in late summer. In both periods they are relatively helpless and it is likely that the foragers occupied Sand to harvest birds during one of them. Other food remains included charred hazelnuts, vast quantities of limpets and crabshells. Burnt stone may have been used as 'potboilers' in cooking (Wickham-Jones 2000). The excavators believe that intertidal resources such as crustaceans were probably an important source of food and may have been gathered by children.

Evidence from tools and waste suggests the manufacturing of shell ornaments, lithics and hide processing. Petrological examination (▶ p. 95) identified a number of disparate sources of stone. Quartz was probably sourced locally but baked mudstone and chalcedonic silica is largely found at Staffin Bay on Skye across the sound. The nearest sources of bloodstone are 60km away on the island of Rùm. There is strong evidence at Sand for seasonal occupation to exploit particular resources and that some people at least were using boats to cross the sea.

Collectors in the Trentino

Clark's (2000) study of Mesolithic hunters in the Trentino Mountains of northern Italy illustrates a complex pattern of human use of the landscape and some aspects of Binford's settlement system model. Clark was able to detect diachronic or gradual change over a long period in assemblages of animal bones (▶ p. 108) and lithic tools from well-preserved deposits in valley rock shelters.

Figure 7.11 *Chamois*

During the early Mesolithic, bone and lithic data from the rock shelters suggests that bands of hunters operated over wide areas, exploiting resources on a seasonal basis. Partial ibex and chamois bone assemblages at the rock shelter sites suggest selected joints of meat were being brought down by the hunters from the high altitude pastures where they lived. Fieldwork in these mountain areas revealed scattered assemblages of lithics and bones indicative of hunting and field butchery. Through comparative analysis of the assemblages at high altitude sites, Clark traced changes in use of the landscape and hunting patterns. In the early Mesolithic, small tasks groups operating from open-air hunting camps had gone up into the mountains to hunt ibex, chamois and red deer herds. To minimise the risk of wasted trips, they developed arrow technology to maximise their chances of killing animals at well-chosen ambush sites such as Colbricon. To facilitate this they had to acquire flint from quarry sites and bring it with them into the mountains.

By the late Mesolithic, pollen evidence showed trees colonising the high pastures, pushing herd animals and ibex beyond the reach of the hunters. High-level hunting became less reliable. The intercept sites were abandoned and bone assemblages from the valley rock shelters increasingly

Figure 7.12 *A Mesolithic hearth at the Grotto D'Ernesto rock shelter*

The positioning of artefacts and ecofacts around the hearth provides clues about the size of the group and the activities they were involved in. Charcoal and bone collagen provided radiocarbon dates around 8500 BP. Most of the bones were from young male animals, which suggests very selective hunting. Upper leg bones were rarely found here but were found in larger shelters, which suggests that this site was not a 'home base'.

comprised whole carcasses of animals from the lower woods and river valleys. Lithics also changed in order to kill forest animals. This suggested a switch to broad spectrum foraging within a much more restricted territory. Riverine resources increasingly supplemented forest animals killed through encounter hunting strategies. To reduce risk and to adapt to a changed environment, new strategies, tools and landscape exploitation patterns had been adopted.

The impact of climate change since the Ice Age in northern Europe

Climate has significantly impacted upon human evolution (▶ p. 191) and by extension, settlement. In northern Europe during our current interglacial period, the Holocene, the relationship between climate, landscape and humans has been particularly complex and dramatic.

During the last Ice Age, glaciers covered Scandinavia while much of Europe to the south was tundra. This was a relatively open landscape with some clumps of dwarf birch and junipers. Large cold-adapted fauna predominated including mammoths and herd animals such as horses and reindeer. Then *c.* 11,500 BP Greenland ice cores record a rapid rise in temperatures, starting with a dramatic 10 degree increase in ten years. The glaciers retreated and land was colonised by successive waves of plants moving up from the south. Over the next 2000 years,

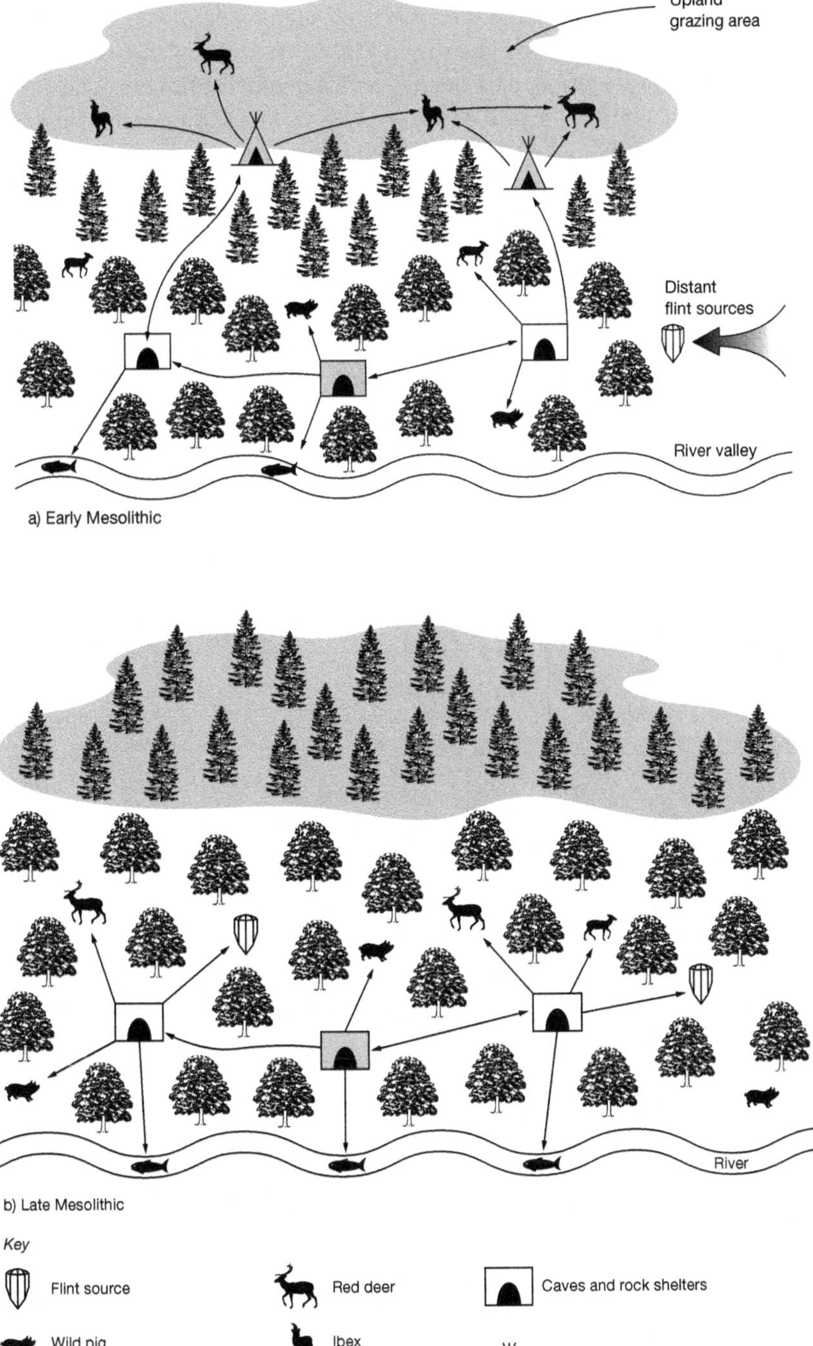

Figure 7.13 *Changing patterns of settlement in the Trentino*

tundra species were joined and then replaced by pine and birch woodland. Fauna changed too with mammoth and horse largely disappearing and the vast herds of reindeer that had been hunted in the Upper Palaeolithic (▶ p. 208) retreated to the Arctic Circle as the trees advanced. Beaver, elk and red deer were amongst the species that thrived in these new conditions. Further temperature rises brought broadleaved trees such as ash, oak, elm, lime and hazel. By 7000 BP the open landscape had been replaced with a dense, continuous wildwood except for the edges of lakes, mountains and coasts. Red deer adapted to this environment along with woodland fauna such as auroch (wild cattle), roe deer and pig. Melting glaciers and rising sea levels

Climatic period	Approx dates BP	Temperature	Sea level	Dominant vegetation	Main prey species	Period	Cultures and sites in this book
Sub-Atlantic	2500+	V slow rise		grasses, cereals, pine and beechwood spread	domestic animals	Iron Age	Danebury
Sub-Boreal	5000–2500	Slow rise. Cool & dry. Warmer than now	slow rise	mixed oak incl. ash. Increasing grass	red deer, roe deer, pig, domestic animals	Bronze to Iron Age	Corded Ware, Eulau, Hochdorf, Flag Fen
Atlantic	8000–5000	Rising. Warmer and moister than now	rising	wildwood: mixed oak, elm, lime		Final Mesolithic, Neolithic	Ertebølle, LBK, Tybrind Vig, Vaihingen
Boreal	9000–8000	Rising. Similar to now	rapid rise	mixed woodland pine, birch, hazel and oak	red deer, roe deer, elk, pig, auroch	Mesolithic	Doggerland, Oronsay
Pre-Boreal	11,500–9000	Sudden rise	rapid rise	taiga: birch and pine forest		LUP, earliest Mesolithic	Maglemosian, Star Carr
Younger Dryas	12,800–11,500	Abrupt freeze	slow rise	tundra			
Allerød Oscillation	13,700–12,800	Rapid warming	rapid rise	park tundra & birch woods			Ahrensburgian, Stellmoor 2
Older Dryas	14,000–13,700	Rapid freeze	slow rise	tundra			
Bølling oscillation	14,600–14,000	Rapid warming	rapid rise	park tundra	bison, reindeer, elk, red deer		Magdalenian, Hamburgian, Stellmoor 1, Pincevent
Oldest Dryas	18,000–15,000	Freezing	V slow rise			Late Upper Palaeolithic (LUP)	
Devensian Glaciation	pre 18,000	V slow warming from glacial	rising	tundra	mammoth, reindeer, horse, bison	Upper Palaeolithic	Gravettian, Dolni Vestonice

Figure 7.14 *Climatic sequence since the last Ice Age*

continued to alter the landscape in a way that must have been noticeable to (Mesolithic) foragers at that time. For example, the slow flooding of the North Sea basin would have meant the continued abandonment of coastal locations (▶ p. 40). The Baltic changed from a freshwater lake to a sea and by 8100 BP Britain was an island. Post-glacial processes continue with some land rising once the weight of the ice had gone (isostatic uplift) and other areas sinking (▶ p. 42).

These environmental changes had a profound impact upon human populations. In the wildwood, hunters had to adapt to new prey and their movement was constrained by a sea of trees. Settlements clustered on the coast and inland lakes. These were often areas favoured by grazing animals and where berry and nut-bearing plants could get access to light. Layers of charcoal in some soil sediments from the Mesolithic have been interpreted as deliberate burning to open up areas for hunting or to encourage useful plants but overall human impact on the wildwood was very limited. While many foragers were still mobile, it is likely that the distances covered were significantly less than their reindeer-hunting ancestors. Evidence of this is visible in the earliest monuments in the landscape. Across Atlantic Europe from Portugal to Scotland huge middens, such as that at Ertebølle (▶ p. 309), Denmark, were formed by the discarding of tons of oysters and other shells over many years to stand several metres high in places. They represent repeated seasonal occupation by Mesolithic people to exploit marine and lacrustine (lake) resources. Although shells form the bulk of the finds, fish and animal bones, hazelnuts, tools and human burials are often present. Hearths and traces of dwellings are frequently found in middens.

Figure 7.15 *One of the Culleenamore middens (▶ p. 522) on Ireland's west coast*

Human impact on the landscape

Later changes in the landscape owe more to human activity than to nature. Deforestation to create grazing and farmland is usually traced by patterns in pollen cores (▶ p. 124) and invertebrate samples. The earliest Neolithic farming in northern Europe is often hard to detect since plots were small and clearing dense forest was a considerable undertaking. Initially the signature is a decline in tree pollen and rise in grasses and disturbed ground indicators such as nettle, dock and ribwort plantain. This is sometimes accompanied with increased finds of charcoal resulting from burning to clear forests or dispose of fallen trees. The next phase usually includes the first cereal pollens. Sometimes this is followed by woodland regeneration, which may indicate that plots were abandoned after a few years in what is called slash and burn or swidden agriculture. Hazel pollen is a good indicator of this since it grows quickly in forest clearings or abandoned plots. By the Bronze Age, human impact was considerable with removal of much natural vegetation (and habitats) and changes in the soil where farming had become permanent. By the arrival of the Romans and certainly by the time of the Norman Conquest, most of the wildwood had been cleared. Only around 15 per cent of England was recorded as woodland in the Domesday Book of 1086. Farmers also inscribed the landscape with boundaries. Where stakes or perhaps hedging was used, these are difficult to detect but earthworks or stone boundaries are sometimes still visible today (▶ p. 31).

Bog formation

One very significant change for archaeology which combined human agency and climate was the spread of blanket bogs over much of the west of the British Isles. During the later Mesolithic and Neolithic, temperatures averaged around 2°C warmer than today. The spread of farming and forest clearance on thin, upland soils led to soil erosion and made it easier for rainfall to leach nutrients out of the soil. In the wetter and colder conditions after 3000 BC, these soils gradually became more acidic and the leached minerals often formed a hard 'iron pan' which restricted the roots of cereals and prevented drainage. Under these conditions dead vegetation cannot rot and forms a layer of waterlogged peat suitable only for plants such as mosses and heathers. During the later Bronze Age, between 1600 and 900 BC, rainfall increased and conditions were worsened by other climatic events such as the eruption of Hekla III in Iceland *c.* 1100 BC. This period saw huts and field systems on higher and marginal land such as Dartmoor and much of western Ireland (▶ p. 356) abandoned. Many of these early settlements are now buried several metres under blanket bogs. During this time of disruption, the bogs themselves become the focus for much ritual activity (▶ p. 543).

During the medieval period, several centuries of warmer weather saw another expansion of farming until the 'little Ice Age' from *c.* 1300. This period is associated with crop failures, famine and of course the Black Death. This was just one of several causes of the deserted medieval villages (DMVs) which can still be seen in the landscape. Over the last 500 years human impact on the landscape has accelerated, dramatically changing its appearance. All these changes impact on the archaeological record and are also topics of study, particularly by industrial archaeologists. They include quarries and mines, enclosures and emparkment, canals and railways, drainage and river and coastal management, forestry and of course ever more settlement.

As human populations grew and agriculture expanded, they caused many examples of devastating impacts on natural environments well before the modern era. The fate of Copan and Mashkan Shapir (▶ p. 286) provide examples of environmental damage leading to catastrophes. These processes are complex, however, and occasionally have an upside. The Burren, a limestone plateau in County Clare in the west of Ireland, had been wooded with pine, birch and hazel prior to the

Figure 7.16 *Limestone pavement on the Burren*

arrival of farmers. Clearance and the breaking up of soil led to rapid erosion of the soil so that some ancient field systems can be seen surrounding bare rock. Local people adapted by using the uplands for winter grazing of cattle in a reverse of usual transhumance (▶ p. 318) patterns. This led to a successful local pastoral economy and the creation of a unique natural environment.

Researching changes in the landscape

Settled agriculture brought the division of the landscape into fields which can often be traced through surviving boundaries. For more recent periods, a wider range of evidence becomes available. Historical sources and the analysis of woods, hedges and buildings can all contribute to our understanding of past landscapes. The types of plants growing on specific soils can also provide evidence of past microclimates. For example, bluebells and oxlips indicate where ancient woodland grew. Research often reveals patterns of earlier land use 'fossilised' within today's pattern of fields and woods. Fieldnames provide clues to land use; for example, *assart* refers to land cleared from woodland, while *wick* and *chester* refer to settlements. Studying landscapes in historic times will start with desktop research. A classic example is Rackham's (1986) study of Hayley Wood. He drew on estate documents from the C14th onwards and fieldwork to show how this ash and hazel woodland was managed to produce renewable crops. His work demonstrates the range of evidence available to the woodland archaeologist including monuments, banks and the trees themselves. Timbers were felled and replanted on a thirty-year cycle and coppiced on a seven-year rotation. Coppiced and pollarded

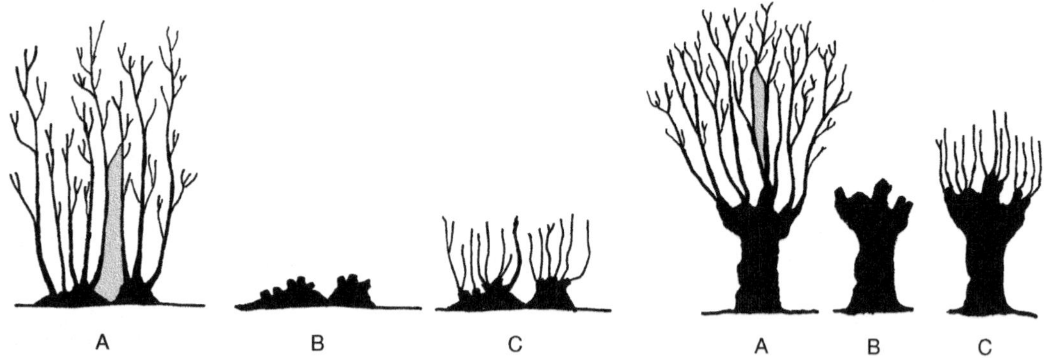

Figure 7.17 *Coppices and pollards (after Rackham 1990). A, B and C show before and after harvest and then after one year of new growth.*

trees still remain from managed woodland. These are two of the easiest examples of woodland management to spot. Coppiced trees are repeatedly cut back to a stool. This encourages the growth of lots of long straight shoots suitable for fences, arrows and kindling. Where animals are present which might eat the shoots, pollards are used instead. The tree is repeatedly cut back to about a few metres in height (a bolling). Even when management has ceased and the tree has reached normal height, the distorted trunk or broad stool is a give-away. Indirect evidence of coppicing can be inferred from the vast quantities of wooden stakes required to build fish traps in the Mesolithic.

Some boundaries may date back to at least Roman times and the hedges that mark some of them may be almost as old. The idea that there is

Figure 7.18 *Coppiced woodland*

a direct relationship between the number of species in a hedge and its age is well established. Hooper's hedgerow hypothesis held that the number of species in a 30m stretch equalled the age of the hedge in centuries. It assumed diversity increases over time as new seeds take root. However, this model only really works for the last 1000 years in particular conditions. Through examination of the species in Cotswold hedges, Reece (1998) found that periods in which hedge management lapsed led to domination by a few species and the elimination of slow-growing species. This means that the Hooper method may underestimate the age of the oldest hedges. Reece found that combinations of certain key species such as wayfaring tree and guelder rose were better indicators of older hedges. He noted that since hedges were used to separate arable land from pasture and border trackways, they would normally be planted within a doughnut-shaped zone around settlements. In the Cotswolds, settlements between the C5th decline of Roman towns and villas and the C11th emergence of known villages are hard to detect. The absence of dateable ceramics from the archaeological record means that fieldwalking has contributed little and there has been no major excavation of a village. Through comprehensive mapping of richer (older) hedges, Reece hoped to test the possibility that hedgerows may be indicative of past settlement locations.

SPATIAL DISTRIBUTION: THE PATTERN OF SITES WITHIN THE LANDSCAPE

The study of the way sites are distributed across a landscape and the relationship between different sites is generally known as intersite analysis. Patterns are studied because it is believed that there is a correlation between the distribution and nature of sites and the type of society and economy that used them. In the 1970s, archaeologists investigating how humans exploited their environment and located their settlements borrowed several analytical techniques from geography. These included site catchment analysis and central place theory. They shared a scientific or mathematical approach to evidence and sought to identify repeated patterns which amounted to 'laws' of human behaviour or developing predictive models. They all assume that people seek to exploit resources, including land, as efficiently as possible. These approaches moved archaeologists beyond a focus on single sites to try to understand them in the context of their territory or surrounding settlements.

Site catchment analysis

Site catchment analysis was adapted from geographical catchment analysis by Higgs and Vita-Finzi during research in the Middle East and Greece. They were trying to understand how foragers used the environment around their sites in order to reconstruct their economy. They hoped that this would shed light on the transition to agriculture. Site catchment assumes that settlements were not located randomly across the landscape but were sited to maximise efficiency and minimise effort in gathering resources. In other words, the point where it ceases to be worth expending energy to obtain resources is the limit of a site's catchment. This is the basis of what is known as a 'time-distance' model, where people make their decisions based on economic benefits and costs. It may also be the edge of its territory. Ethnographic studies of site exploitation territories were used to determine average distances which people might travel for subsistence resources. For instance, foragers such as the !Kung bushmen of the Kalahari rarely walk more than 10km (about two hours' walk) from their base with a range of 20–30km to other sites with whom they trade and areas they occasionally visit; for example, for building materials, clay or summer pasture. Studies of peasant farmers suggest that their normal limit is just 5km. Site catchment analysis begins by drawing a circle around the site at the appropriate distance as was the case with Higg and Finzi's (1970) pioneering studies of

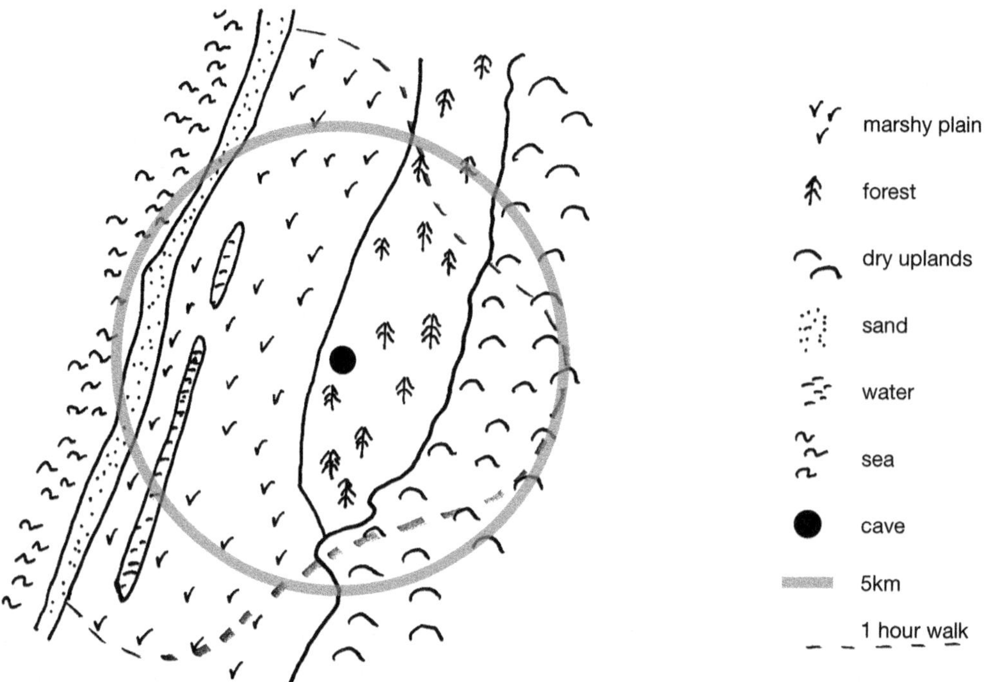

Figure 7.19 *Site catchment at Mount Carmel*

early farmers in coastal Palestine around Mount Carmel.

A problem with drawing a circle around a site is that natural terrain may have influenced the 'shape' of the catchment. If a site is on the edge of a mountain range and a plain, its catchment is likely to extend farther across the plain than into the mountains. At Mount Carmel, a plain, mountains and the sea were potentially within the catchment but systematic walking from the cave for two hours established a more realistic 'shape' for the catchment. However, this is time consuming and can be distorted by the pace of an individual surveyor and the weather during the survey. A more precise approach has been to borrow path-distance models from geography. These involve dividing the area map into a series of grids and then calculating the 'time and energy cost' of moving through each square. A grid square with a marsh, steep slope or wood will 'cost' more to cross than one on a grassy plain.

Through surveying the catchment around a site, archaeologists try to identify resources which the site's inhabitants might have exploited. This helps them understand its location, function and the subsistence strategy of its inhabitants. This is not easy. It depends on accurate reconstruction of ancient landscapes, which is difficult since traces of much of the flora and fauna may not have survived. However, once constructed, the model of resource exploitation provided by the survey can be compared with archaeological evidence such as food remains, pollen and artefacts and human skeletal remains (▶ p. 111). The Mount Carmel study showed that these foragers had a wide range of soils, plants and animals available within their catchments, which may explain why they were not the first to develop agriculture.

Site catchment can also be used to understand settlements in the historic period. Aston's (1985) study of Ashington in Somerset pioneered this technique to illuminate the way that medieval

Indicators of intended long-term camps	Indicators of intended short-term camps	Neutral indicators
Mudbrick houses Storage structures Thorn fences Food processing areas Cooking areas Manufacturing/processing (e.g. hides) areas Animal enclosures Formal refuse dumps	Overall smaller area per head Smaller range of structures Less durable structures (grass, woven branches, thatch)	Windbreaks Hearths Huts Informal storage areas (e.g. wood piles) Roasting pits Ash dumps around hearths

Figure 7.20 *Indicators of intended long-term occupation (after Kent 1989)*

farmsteads organised their exploitation of the local environment. This included identifying the pasture, arable fields and woodland within the catchment. Resources needed on a daily basis were produced in or close to the settlement with less frequently needed resources located further out (▶ p. 496). Aston showed how the landscape could be used as a text to read off past activities and relationships. Another approach is to identify catchment ecozones by analysing weed seeds in plant assemblages.

Criticisms of site catchment analysis (SCA)

SCA sets sites in context and does help us understand the relationship between place, resources and technology. However, like other geographical techniques it does focus narrowly on economic or ecological explanations, which has led to criticisms that it is deterministic. It assumes that people in the past were aware of and could access the resources we can identify today. It also assumes that their behaviour was economically 'normal'. That is, they always sought to maximise returns for the least effort. It may well be that spiritual, cultural or political considerations were as important factors in decisions about site placement as economics. Kent's (1989) ethnoarchaeological study of modern sites in the Kalahari tested the importance of economic motives in determining difference in size, complexity and period of occupation between different settlements. She compared the camps of different groups of farmers and foragers to see whether ethnicity or a major source of subsistence was critical, and was able to talk to the people themselves about their behaviour. The data she gathered could largely be explained by social factors. For example, the layout and range of features was determined by how long people expected to remain at the site. Kent's work reminds us never to overlook human choice even when investigating environmental issues.

GIS and satellite-based spatial surveys

Since the 1990s the development of GIS (▶ p. 10) and remote sensing has given intersite approaches a new lease of life and research has grown at the whole landscape level including major studies in the Middle East and on the seabed (▶ p. 41). GIS enables a vast amount of data to be stored digitally and then combined in different ways in order to plot or test relationships between sites. Data variables might include soil, vegetation, height above sea level, prominent landscape features and water sources along with sites, aerial photographs, individual artefacts and ecofacts. GIS enables large-scale analysis in a way that could only have been dreamed of back in the 1970s. Dates, sites and finds can be presented visually in sequence to show the way the landscape filled up and the emergence of larger sites.

Contemporary sites can be plotted against other data. Clusters or patterns in site distribution can be analysed to determine their relationship and their association with natural resources. Multivariate statistical analysis can rapidly determine the significance of such results and identify new patterns. Correlations between different types of data can be swiftly identified and plotted on maps. Questions can be asked about site catchment, territories, the association of sites with particular soils and landscapes, intervisibility between sites and even how the landscape might have appeared to people as they travelled through it. GIS can also be used in a predictive way to suggest where there may be undiscovered sites or suggest the relationship between sites. In the USA, the Department of Transportation uses GIS to model likely archaeological hot spots as part of impact assessments for new infrastructure projects. On the Croatian island of Hvar, an international GIS project explored the relationship between soils, terrain and different settlements in a number of periods. A path-cost model was used to establish site catchments for each of the major Bronze and Iron Age hillforts. Gaffney and Stanic (1996) compared data on land quality and water sources to establish whether hillforts had been sited to maximise control of the best land. There was a strong correlation with the catchments but the actual locations of the hillforts were often on poor sites. The explanation is that these were selected as defensive positions on high ground but still close to farmland. In the Roman period, however, villas are invariably sited on good land with the best climate for agriculture. Analysis of the Stari Grad Plain, an area with no climatic variation, demonstrated clearly that land quality was the most important determinant of settlement location.

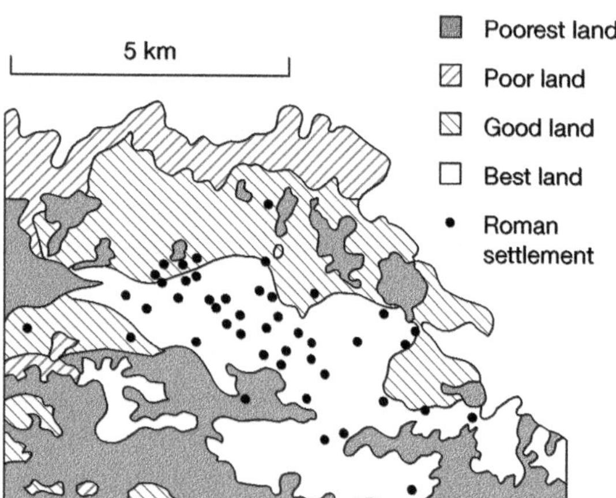

Figure 7.21 Distribution of Roman settlements in relation to land quality on the Stari Grad Plain, Hvar (after Gaffney)

A second technological advance has been the use of satellites to survey vast areas. This data can then be combined with terrestrial GIS data sets for analysis of features. The Finnish SYGIS project (Lönnqvist 2013) used such techniques to study forager and mobile pastoralist cultures over the 1 million hectare area of the Jebel Bishri Mountains of central Syria. Remote sensing data was largely used instead of traditional foot- and vehicle-based surveying. Digital maps of the area and information on vegetation were obtained from the visible light and infrared surveys carried out by Landsat-7 for NASA. Additional highly detailed, 3D images of the land surface were provided from the thermal imaging surveys carried out by the USA-Japanese ASTER programme. Finally, high-resolution images from the commercial Quickbird satellite enabled identification and plotting of features such as rock shelters, hunting blinds and corrals (animal pens). GIS analysis showed that the corrals were all within 1km of a seasonal water source and was also able to estimate the grazing potential of the pasture within the catchment. A number of random checks were made to verify findings on the ground but the bulk of the information was supplied remotely.

Geometric models

Central place theory (CPT) draws on the models of the geographer Christaller to explain the distribution and relationships between settle-

Figure 7.22 *Features of a central place at Roman Salamis*

A major commercial centre for 2,000 years, most of the remains at Salamis are from the Roman period. This view illustrates some of the extensive public buildings. The re-erected columns would have supported a stoa or covered walkway. It surrounds the gymnasium square (palaestra). Adjoining it are hot and cold public bath houses and a forty-four-seat latrine. Nearby is an amphitheatre and theatre. Much of the construction is faced with marble. This indicates the wealth and importance of this centre.

ments in a region. It is based on the idea that as the landscape fills up settlements will be spaced evenly across it. Where settlements are more or less of equal size, this reflects a fairly equal society. Where there is considerable variation in size, it reflects a hierarchical society. Larger places perform central functions and provide a wider range of goods on behalf of a cluster of smaller satellite settlements. Geographers have used the model to understand markets, political territories and transport networks. Central places also emerge at regular intervals across the landscape. The most efficient pattern of spacing forms a hexagonal lattice so territories for each central place are modelled by drawing hexagons around them. Applications to archaeology have included Neolithic ritual centres, Roman settlements and medieval market towns. In some regions such towns were sited 4–6 miles from their neighbours and served a hinterland of dependent hamlets and farmsteads. Time-cost studies and ethnographic research suggests that peasant farmers tend to use markets which they can walk to and from in a day. However, even in geographic studies of modern settlement on the plains of the American Midwest, there is often a poor match between the theoretical model and actual places on the ground. Partly this is because no region is completely uniform but there are also cultural and historic factors which the model cannot take into account.

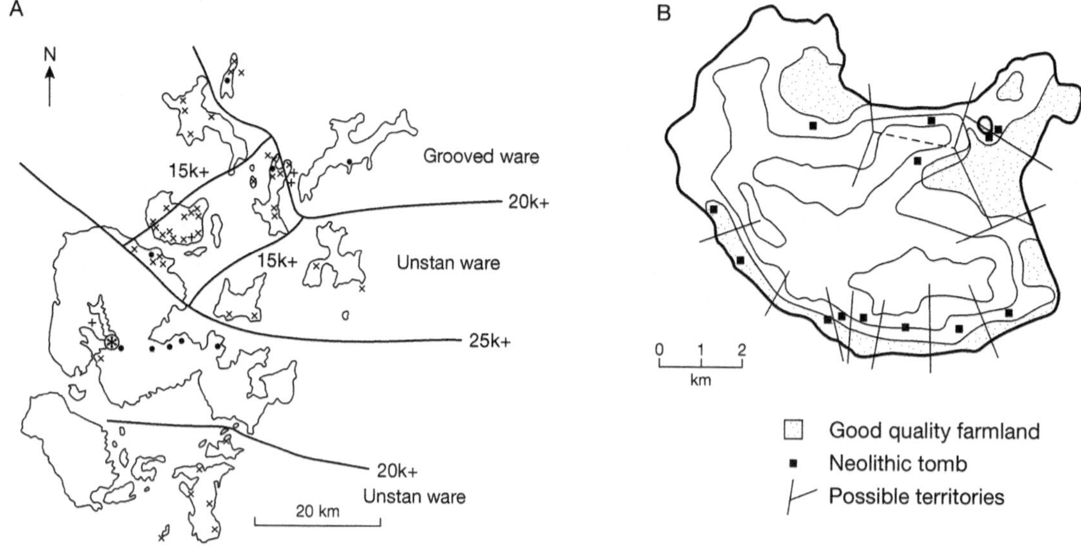

Figure 7.23 *Territories in Prehistoric Orkney (after Renfrew 1973)*

Figure 7.24 *The C12th tower at Clonmacnoise Monastery*

A less purely theoretical variation on CPT uses **Thiessen polygons**. These also derive from geography and are used to define territories between real settlements which tend to have an irregular distribution pattern. Polygons are created by identifying the midpoints between settlements of equal status, and then joining the midpoints up to form irregular-shaped zones of influence and exploitation. Applications have ranged from estimating the territory associated with Iron Age brochs to the territories of Mayan cities. Renfrew (1973) used this model to interpret the distribution of burial monuments on Orkney and Rousay as the territories of groups of pioneer farmers. He reasoned that each tomb might represent a family group who owned a strip of land going back from the sea to the rocky hills. Each unit would have some arable and some grazing land and access to the sea. The tombs marked their claim and also linked the remains of their ancestors to the fertility of their land. He found that the territories he had identified were similar to the holdings of modern crofts.

Criticisms of these methods

As with SCA, these theoretical models tend to neglect social and cultural influences on settlement and the effect of topography. CPT fits all known sites into one of the categories in a hierarchy of sites, which may not be realistic. A single pattern of settlement may be the physical expression of many different social systems. Belief, defence, social relations and political considerations can be significant. For example, the distribution of Roman towns could reflect administrative areas for tax and law and order as well as the influence of markets. Some small sites may also have considerable social or ritual importance, which means they were of greater importance in their region.

Clonmacnoise, Ireland, illustrates the complexity of site location and the emergence of a central place. Clonmacnoise began as a tiny wooden monastery established by the missionary St Ciarán in AD 545. However, this apparently remote location was well chosen for commercial as well as spiritual reasons. Underwater archaeologists have discovered traces of an adjacent, ancient bridge which indicates that it was sited at a crossing point over the Shannon. This enabled the monastery to gain income from travellers and

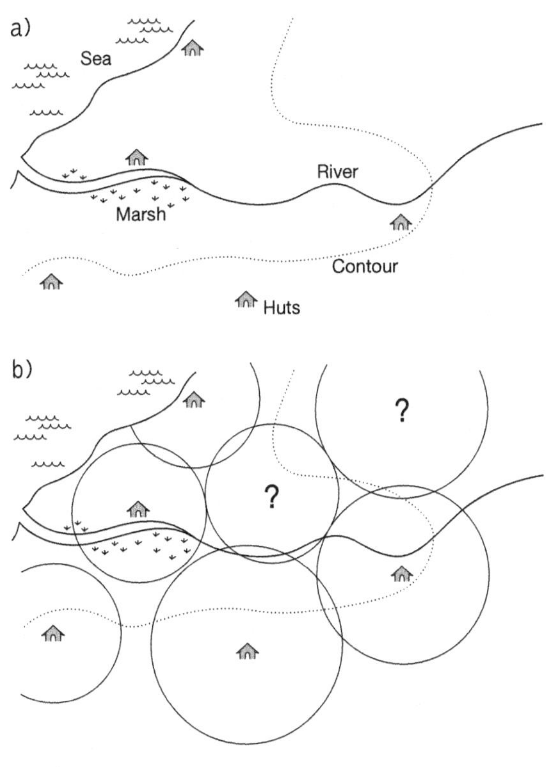

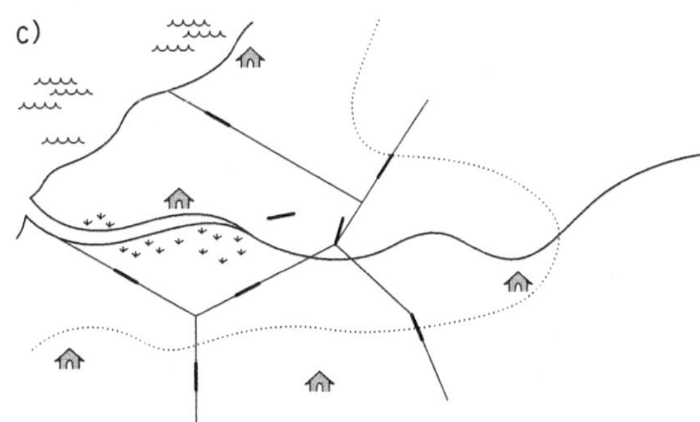

Figure 7.25 *Territorial models from geography. The effects of modelling with CPT (b) and Theissen polygons (c) on a prehistoric landscape (a).*

pilgrims. The monastery was rebuilt in stone and became one of the richest in Ireland and a centre for learning and craft production. Some of the finest medieval metalworking and manuscripts were produced there and it became the burial site of kings. It also attracted unwanted attention and was frequently raided, starting with the Vikings. A Norman castle alongside it hints at the strategic value of such a location.

One also has to be confident that all the plotted sites are contemporary and that no significant ones have been omitted. If not, the analysis is of archaeological discoveries rather than of decisions made in the past. Models can also be criticised for focusing too much on establishing patterns rather than understanding settlements. However, the key point is that these are models. Despite their limitations when compared with real archaeological data on the ground, these models can be used to generate hypotheses to test ideas about territory or catchment. CPT could also be used to suggest where there might be undiscovered sites. These can then be tested against archaeological data rather than fitting data to a model.

EXPLAINING THE LOCATION OF ARCHAEOLOGICAL SITES

In trying to understand past decision making about the location and establishment of settlements, most archaeologists have focused on resources (as with SCA) or landscape features. The latter include defensive features such as the Whinsill of Northumbria on which Hadrian's Wall was built and the natural harbour at Hengistbury Head in Dorset which became an Iron Age port. Sometimes correlations with natural resources such as soils can be clearly seen, as at Hvar (▶ p. 248), or between pioneer European farmers (▶ p. 346) and loess deposits. However, this can also lead to assumptions which can limit our understanding. For example, many older texts argue that Anglo-Saxons settled on lighter soils because they lacked heavy ploughs. At that time there had been relatively little excavation of modern rural settlements but with the massive expansion of urban development since the 1980s in areas such as the Thames Valley many new rural sites have been uncovered, particularly in river valleys. The association of Anglo-Saxons with light soils therefore reflected the fact that most excavation had been of abandoned sites on lighter soils. Conversely, sometimes the wealth of archaeological evidence in a region can be used to predict where more settlements might be found. The building of the Oresund Bridge between Denmark and Sweden in the 1990s provides such a model. Danish archaeologists had observed a pattern in the positioning of fish traps at entrances to lagoons or where streams entered the sea. They reasoned that settlements would cluster around such suitable locations. The results of underwater surveys which had mapped the topography of submerged landscapes on the sea-bottom were used to predict where sites might be found. When divers investigated these locations, their success rate was over 75 per cent and included well-preserved settlement remains.

Studies of prehistoric ritual sites have drawn on ethnographic models rather than economics and resources to explain the siting of monuments. The position of individual stones, cairns or stone circles has been interpreted in terms of ancestral places or divisions between the living and the dead. The referencing of later monuments on earlier ones is clear in many ritual landscapes (▶ p. 522), while some archaeologists have argued that natural features such as mountains and rivers have also influenced choice of site. People in the past would have had an awareness of particular places before sites developed there. The location of Stonehenge on the site of a much earlier Mesolithic timber monument provides an interesting example. Cirencester provides another where Roman sensitivities to local people or perhaps towards their ancestral spirits may have led to the building of Corinium in a less than ideal location in a river bottom 1km away from where it would have been expected. The town

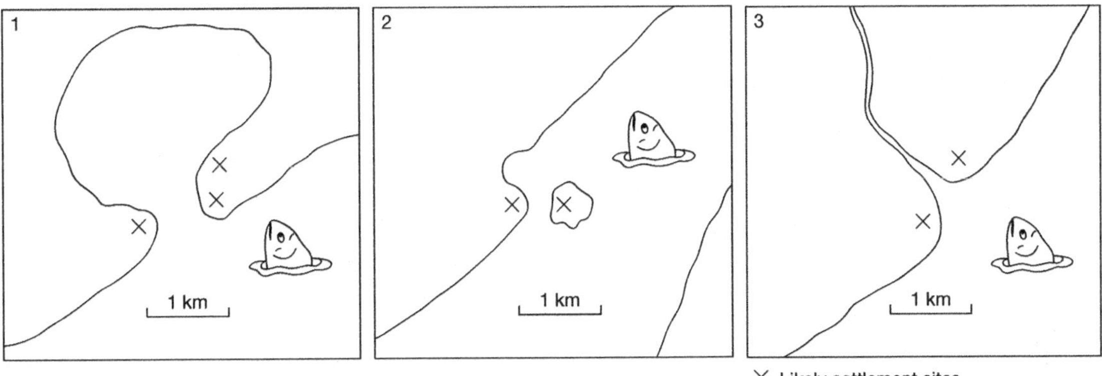

Figure 7.26 *Finding Mesolithic sites on the seabed – Oresund Bridge project*

began as a fort at the river crossing and a crossroads on the Fosse Way. However, Ermin Street, which connects Silchester to Gloucester, appears to deviate from its path at Corinium and takes a more difficult route as a result. Recent research has found a major Iron Age burial complex where the crossroads would have been expected. The suggestion is that Roman road builders deliberately diverted to avoid the complex for political or religious reasons. During the medieval period, builders appear to have taken the opposite approach with many examples of churches being built inside or over earlier prehistoric monuments. This may have been either to show their power or to take on the importance attached to the place. Knowlton Henge in Dorset provides a classic example.

Political and social factors are also evident in site location, particularly during the historic period. The Shapwick Project (Aston and Gerrard 2013) revealed that many of the villages which appeared to have always nestled in the landscape were in fact the product of a reorganisation of that landscape by estate owners. Nucleated villages were easier to control and to tax than scattered farms. Similarly, the deserted settlement of Badbea in Sutherland is relatively recent. It was founded in the late C18th by destitute highlanders who had been cleared from their farms by landowners to make way for sheep. The location on extremely poor soil on a clifftop was the only one available to them. Modern field patterns strongly reflect the enclosure movement of the early C19th, which was pursued for similar reasons.

KEY STUDY

Head Smashed In

The UNESCO world heritage site of Head Smashed In in the Canadian Rocky Mountains was in use for nearly 6,000 years since before 3700 BC by the ancestors of the North Peigan tribe, part of the Blackfoot Confederacy. It is a place where ethnographic, historical and archaeological data combine to provide an unrivalled picture of a society and economy based around communal hunting. It also illustrates human use of a landscape and the importance of 'off-site' areas to understanding past activity. The name of the site is a translation of the Blackfoot *estipah-skikikini-kots*, which refers to the fate of a young man who chose to watch the buffalo jump from underneath the cliff.

continued

The site

Figure 7.27 *Buffalo*

The site comprises several linked areas over a wide area of around 600 hectares. The jump site itself is a 300m stretch of cliff over which buffalo were stampeded to fall around 10m down to the kill site. When excavated, this proved to be an 11m deep stratified midden of rock and bone which produced a long typological sequence of lithics. These include blades, choppers and thousands of points and arrowheads. The most recent layers around AD 1850 contain metal points indicating that the site was in use when European traders first arrived on the plains. The site probably went out of use when escaped horses spread north from Spanish colonies and a new method of hunting developed. North-west of the jump site is the drainage basin of Olsen Creek. This is a grassy area of 40km^2 surrounded by the Porcupine Hills with two exits leading directly to the cliff. Buffalo would be herded into this basin along stream valleys. Within the basin are numerous lines of hundreds of cairns, each approximately 1m in diameter. The cairns led towards the exits which in turn led straight to the cliffs. These are drive lanes along which buffalo would be stampeded. South-east of the cliffs is a flat area with many hearths, pits, tipi circles of stones (▶ p. 279) and huge amounts of smashed and processed bones. Artefacts include bone awls and beads, some pottery and lithic scrapers, butchery tools and drills. There are also huge quantities of fire-cracked rock.

Interpretations

To interpret these finds archaeologists made use of historical accounts including that of Peter Fidler, an English surveyor working for the Hudson Bay Company. He was taken through the area in 1792 by a Peigan band and witnessed the use of a jump site. There are also Blackfoot ethnographic records which provide detail of social organisation for the most recent use of the site. Blackfoot society was based around the family and then the band. These were relatively fluid groups or 'lodges' of 80–200 people living in tipis. They followed a nomadic lifestyle and settlement pattern well adapted to the climate and food sources of the plains. During the winter, the Blackfoot bands were widely dispersed in sheltered valleys where there was fuel, water and some food. In the summer bands would come together for tribal ceremonies and communal hunting. This is sometimes called a fission-fusion model of social organisation. The movements or 'seasonal round' of the tribe were structured around the migration of the buffalo. In the autumn they would gather at traditional buffalo 'jump sites'. The organisers of the hunts derived status, wealth and influence over the tribes. They included ritual specialists who would encourage the buffalo to come.

How it worked

Young men would lure the buffalo into the gathering areas by imitating the sounds of lost calves. Other hunters would move in upwind of the herd and scare them into the drive lanes. The cairns may have hidden other hunters or supported branches which would move in the wind and further alarm the animals. Once the herd was stampeding, the animals at the front could not stop and the entire herd would plunge over the cliffs. At the bottom, hunters would finish off wounded animals and begin the butchery process. In the processing area, meat, horns and hide would be stripped from the bones, which were smashed open to extract marrow. Pits were lined with buffalo hide, filled with water and brought to boiling point using hot rocks from the hearths. This would render the grease from broken bones. Tons of fire-cracked stones littered the processing area. This vast processing operation provided for most of the tribe's needs. Bone was worked into tools and ornaments. Skins provided clothing, containers and clothes. Meat was consumed in a feast but the great majority was stored. Thin strips of meat were dried on racks by the sun or a fire, pounded with rocks and then mixed with an equal amount of fat and marrow. Sometimes flavoured with powdered berries, this 'pemmican' would be stored in envelope-like pouches made from raw buffalo hide (called parfleches) for months or even years. During the processing work, families would live in their tipis. The rings of stones mark where the edges of the tipi were anchored to the ground. Once the work was completed they would disperse, dragging their tipis and carrying pemmican to get them through the winter.

Today an exhibition centre explains the site and its archaeology but also explores Blackfoot history and life. Blackfoot guides conduct tours of the site and lead workshops. The centre is seen by them as important in preserving and perpetuating their culture (▶ p. 603).

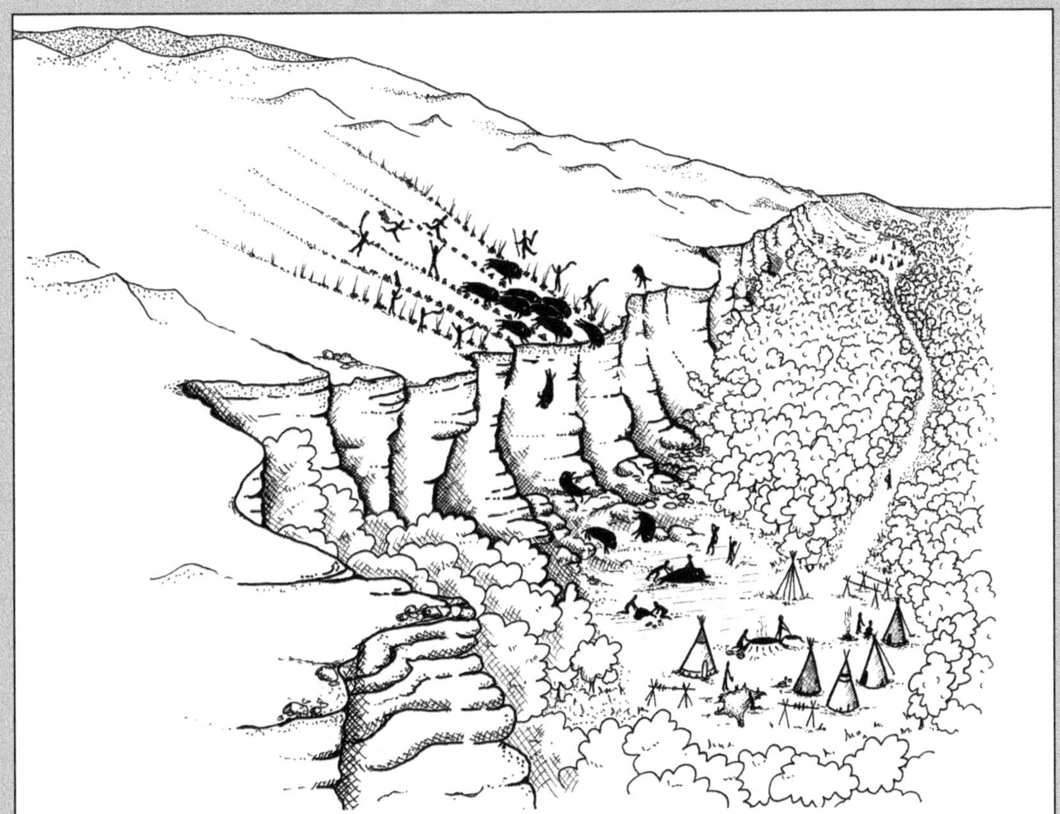

Figure 7.28 *Reconstruction of main features at Head Smashed In*

SETTLEMENT HIERARCHIES

From the Mesolithic onwards, archaeologists are able to identify different levels of sites. Amongst hunter-gatherers this may largely be a matter of function and duration (▶ p. 228) but amongst sedentary farmers and later societies it becomes a question of size and status too. A site hierarchy might rank in order of size: farmstead–hamlet–village–small (local) town–large (regional) town–city. However, as with CPT, one has to be careful not to assume that the larger settlements were always the more important. In Wiltshire at the time of the Domesday Book of 1086, Wilton was a royal burh (fortified town) and the shire administrative centre but nearby Sarum was a significant royal residence and the seat of the local bishop, who was building a cathedral there. Cricklade was also a burh, with a larger area than Wilton, while Malmesbury was both a burh and the site of a bishopric and one of the most significant religious complexes in England. Which was the highest status settlement?

A key sign of increasing importance is complexity in terms of functions and buildings. In particular the inclusion of public buildings is usually taken as the sign that a settlement provides services for others around it. These might include temples, markets, courts or arenas. Others might include evidence of a garrison, significant storage, the residence of high-ranking or wealthy people and manufacturing areas. High-quality architecture, prestige goods, significant defences and a dominant position in the landscape might also be used to infer status.

KEY STUDY

Minoan settlement hierarchy

Europe's first civilisation developed in early Bronze Age Crete *c.* 2000 BC and it provides an excellent example of how archaeologists attempt to rank settlements. It was centred on large 'palace-complexes', of which Knossos is the most famous. These palaces surrounded by houses are comparable in scale with all but the largest Bronze Age towns of the Middle East, yet are very different. No Minoan town has anything like a complete defensive wall. As a result, the internal settlement pattern is not dictated by those walls in the way that it was in cities such as Mashkan Shapir (▶ p. 286). Apart from the palace complexes, there is no zoning of different activities or industries and little evidence of street plans being imposed. Workshops such as forges occur in the palaces or are scattered in residential areas while some residential houses doubled as workshops for pottery or woodworking. Mesopotamian and Egyptian cities are dominated by colossal religious and political architecture such as ziggurats and statues or reliefs of deities or rulers (▶ p. 476). While Minoan palaces were prominent, and may have been inserted into existing settlements, they were never overwhelming and their leaders remain unknown to us. There are no major Minoan temples either. There are some small shrines in the palaces but religious emphasis seems to have been towards remote sites such as caves and mountains.

Palace complexes

The palaces were complex groups of multistorey buildings. Knossos is the largest, more than twice the size of the next two at Malia and Phaistos. Some, such as Phaistos, appear to have been built to a plan while others, such as Knossos, were built into an existing settlement. The public areas include a

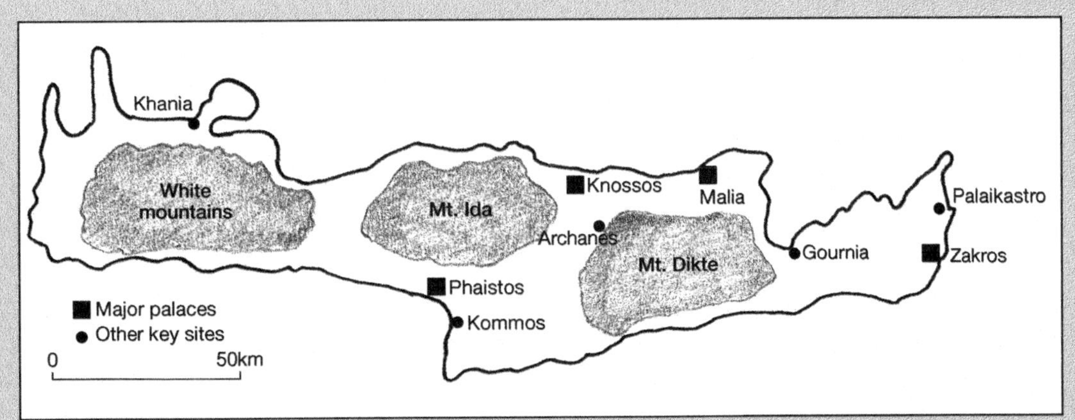

Figure 7.29 *Map of Minoan Crete*

Figure 7.30 *Central arena at Phaistos*

The larger Minoan towns were characterised by extensive public spaces including 'theatres' or arenas. It is unclear what kind of performances took place in this arena but it is clearly linked to the high-status buildings to the left and extensive storage areas to the right.

continued

Figure 7.31 *Entrance to palace complex from central courtyard at Phaistos. The columns, facings of gypsum and construction from ashlar (sawn stone) blocks indicate a prestigious building.*

large, rectangular central courtyard (usually north–south) and often huge stepped areas that may have been for ceremonies. All had public halls, living areas, workshops and significant areas of storage, which suggests that they were central places. The west wings of the palaces were high-status areas with frescoes, gardens, bathing or ritual pools and innovative light-wells which brought sunlight and fresh air down through the building. Some featured the earliest plumbing in Europe. A range of material was used, including sawn (ashlar) blocks of limestone for lower courses, marble for some floors and timber for columns and much of the structure. Some walls in public areas were faced with gypsum. We have a good understanding of Minoan building from depictions in art including seals and also models. The upper stories were built from timber and mudbrick with windows and possibly chimneys. Ordinary Minoan houses appear to be larger than those in the Near East.

Exotic artefacts including fine pottery (▶ p. 471), jewellery (▶ p. 391) and imported Syrian seals and Egyptian scarabs were also found in these areas. There were also extensive magazines or storerooms. Some held huge ceramic jars called pithoi, others had lined vats in the floor. Elsewhere at Knossos there were huge silos thought to be granaries. This huge storage capacity identifies the palaces as redistributive centres. Their fertile hinterlands provided a surplus including grain, wool, honey, olive oil and wine

Figure 7.32 *Ceramic model of a Minoan house from a workshop in the small town of Archanes. In addition to windows and chimneys, we know they were often two-storey and used wood as well as stone and mudbrick in their construction.*

Figure 7.33 *Storage magazine at Knossos with pithoi and lined vats. There was room for hundreds of these giant pithoi.*

(▶ p. 473). Palace accountants used Europe's first written language – Linear A – to record stores and transactions. Palace workshops produced fine pottery, metal and stone artefacts often using imported materials such as ivory and copper. Cult rooms housing ritual artefacts and figurines provide evidence of other specialists. Palaces were generally unfortified and clustered around the central buildings were more ordinary dwellings. Populations in these 'proto towns' were quite high. Estimates for Knossos reach 20,000.

Rural settlements

In the countryside around each palace were villas: smaller two-storey buildings with many of the features of palaces but without large public areas. These rich houses also had storage areas. Perhaps a local elite controlled agriculture from villas and supplied the palaces with their craftsmen, architects, masons and administrators. Finds of identical seal (▶ p. 417) impressions have allowed some reconstruction of exchange networks between particular villas and palaces. In a classic redistributive model (▶ p. 427), the palaces appear to have converted regional surpluses into ritual, exotic imports and possibly performances. The nature of the social organisation which ran the palaces is explored in Chapter 10.

The mountains of Crete prevented an even distribution of large towns across the landscape but there still seem to be patterns. Branigan (2001) identified one large town per 200–250km^2. Allowing

continued

for some discoveries in the future, he suggested the ratio between large and small towns might be something like 1:5. Both had 'palace' complexes but the scale, range of public buildings, storage capacity and evidence for administration was far greater at the large regional sites than at the smaller provincial sites. There were also some small towns which seemed to have a specific economic function, such as a port (▶ p. 472) or market. Below these urban centres were villages, hamlets and individual farms. Some of these would have a 'villa' or mini-palace at their heart. Driessen (2001) argues that the towns were central places and of higher status than other sites in their region. However, a problem for all these models is that we still know little about rural settlement in Minoan Crete. Archaeologists have focused on the palaces and it is only recently that the suburbs, villages and wider language have been studied in depth.

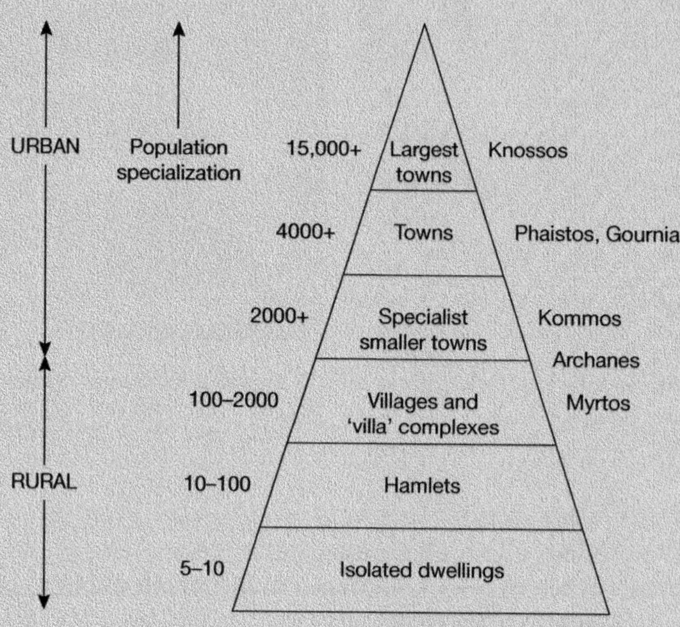

Figure 7.34 *Hierarchy of settlement in Minoan Crete (after Branigan 2001)*

THE SOCIAL LANDSCAPE: TERRITORY AND BOUNDARIES

Both of these categories describe the ways in which people divide up and give social meaning to the landscape. Territories are usually considered to be the area of land controlled by a state. However, the definition is often widened to mean an area controlled by some form of political authority which might include land held by a tribe, settlement or religious or elite leader. For forager or pastoralist societies it is sometimes used to mean hunting range or the pastures used on an annual cycle of transhumance. Boundaries include the edges of territories but might also be used to describe the limits of individual fields or settlements or the thresholds of houses or tombs. Some boundaries include physical barriers while others may have symbols or are merely 'known'.

Figure 7.35 *City walls, Famagusta*

Some city walls were meant to control trade but these massive examples from Famagusta in Cyprus clearly had a particular threat in mind. The 3km long low, outer wall shields the main ramparts from artillery. Attackers then have to traverse a 46m wide moat (which could be flooded) with vertical sides to reach the curtain wall. Projecting bastions provide a field of fire within the moat. The main ramparts are 8m thick and 15m high. Built by the Venetians, its 8,000 defenders withstood a siege by a Turkish army of 200,000 for ten months in 1570–1 before starvation led to surrender.

Territorial markers

For early periods there may have been markers of territory which have not survived. These might have included totems or the appearance of peoples themselves. From the Neolithic or early Bronze Age, rock carvings or petroglyphs have survived in many parts of Britain with hard stone including Cumbria, Argyle and Yorkshire. There are extensive views from the carvings but they cannot be seen from a distance. There are several interpretations of their function including that of territorial markers. Waddington (1998) argues that they 'inscribed grazing areas'. In other words, they identified secure upland pasture for particular groups which was used in summer as part of annual transhumance cycles. Bradley (1997) believes that intervisibility between the sites is more significant and that they may denote pathways through the landscape.

Social territories can include many sites and are not obviously shaped by geography. The British Empire of the C19th was not limited by proximity to the British Isles, for example. For state societies, written records often exist which help to identify centres and their territories. The stone stelae of the Maya (▶ p. 416) and Roman inscriptions have both been used in this way. As the second largest Roman town in Britain, Corinium had massive and extensive city walls and a range of public buildings including temples, a basilica and an amphitheatre. Its high status is also suggested by the lavish mosaics and frescos in opulent townhouses. Proof of its

Figure 7.36 *Petroglyphs in a rock shelter overlooking the Milfield Basin*

political importance comes from this massive carving which stood in the forum or market place and included carvings of several deities. On a nearby inscription stone, a General (Septimius) dedicated the column to Britannica Prima. This indicates that Corinium was the capital of the south-western province.

Figure 7.37 *Part of the Jupiter Column from Cirencester*

For some states the extent of political control is indicated by physical boundaries. Hadrian's Wall and the Great Wall of China are well known from the ancient world but during the C20th fortified borders became the norm for nation states. The ruins of France's Maginot Line and the 'Iron Curtain' dividing East and West Europe provide classic examples. Less certainty surrounds the purpose of early medieval earthworks such as Offa's Dyke or Wansdyke. Artefacts of administration also provide clues to territories and the influence of central authorities. These include clay seals (▶ p. 417), emblems, standard

Figure 7.38 *The Devil's Dyke. Probably a boundary of the Anglo-Saxon kingdom of East Anglia.*

weights and measures and coinage. However, influence and territory are not identical. Well-recognised currencies were used in the past outside their area of issue just as the US dollar is today. The evidence may be contradictory in other ways. For example, zones of pottery styles and coin distribution do not always match up.

Human remains

Bioarchaeologists use skeletal material to find out about lifestyle but it can also help us understand settlements and society. Recent studies by Shulting (2007) in south-west Britain are shedding new light on territories and economies during the Mesolithic. Dating of remains from Aveline's Hole (AH) in Somerset suggest that the cave had been used for burials over a long period. Strontium isotope analysis of eight molars and some faunal remains showed that all had grown up close to the Mendips while carbon and nitrogen isotope analysis showed that they had a terrestrial diet. Faunal remains suggested red deer and pig were their main prey animals. This implied a relatively small annual range of movement since nearby marine resources were not exploited. Aveline's Hole is sited in an area where food would have been scarce, suggesting it was a significant location for other reasons, perhaps spiritual. It is what is sometimes termed a 'persistent place'. Similar tests were undertaken on Mesolithic samples from the Caldey Island (CI) and Gower areas of South Wales. The Caldey group had a largely marine diet while coastal samples from Worm's Head (WH) suggested a more mixed intake. Inland samples were comparable to those from Aveline's Hole. These results point to groups continually using small territories over long periods of time rather than seasonal movement between coast and uplands. Perhaps inland and coastal groups adapted in different ways, with

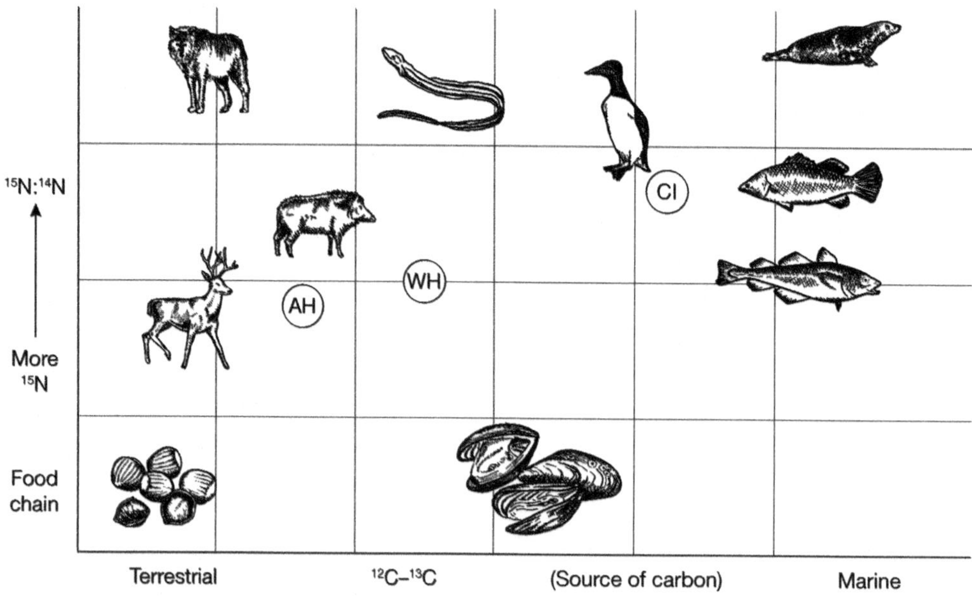

Figure 7.39 *Tracing diet and territory through isotope analysis*

Carbon on the horizontal axis varies depending on whether food sources are more terrestrial or marine. The vertical axis shows the enrichment of Nitrogen 15 moving up the food chain (or trophic levels). The approximate position of each human group is shown.

different tool kits and knowledge. Their separateness may help to explain the evidence for violence in some late Mesolithic societies (▶ p. 480) if territories were seen as exclusive. It may also help to explain differential adaptation to changes in the Neolithic. The dietary evidence from Shulting's study suggests each territory was approximately 25km in diameter.

IDENTIFYING THE FUNCTION(S) OF ARCHAEOLOGICAL SITES

Archaeological sites are usually categorised by function. Really this means determining the primary function since most sites have several. For example, Knossos Palace (▶ p. 256) may also have a domestic, economic and political function as well as being a status symbol. Archaeologists therefore try to identify what activities were carried out and whether there are any significant patterns in the evidence that might indicate that those particular spaces (areas, buildings or rooms) had specific functions. For example, was food preparation separated from storage? Taken together these enable the functions of the site to be described and assessed to determine their relative importance.

Evidence of human activities varies widely according to period, degree of preservation and the resources available. In historic periods there may be written accounts, artistic depictions, plans and for the last few centuries maps, photographs, film and even living people! However, evidence for most sites will come from excavation or reconnaissance survey. Archaeologists will then try to recognise and explain patterns in the data. This relies on the comprehensiveness and accuracy of excavation recording (▶ p. 68) for its validity. This presents particular problems for early prehistory. While there are cave sites and rock shelters with deep deposits of cultural material that have been sheltered from erosion, these sites are not typical. Most Palaeolithic sites have been subject to the ravages of a full range of transformation processes (▶ p. 165) and any interpretation has to take these into account. In particular the better survival of lithics and the bones of larger mammals has led to most sites being labelled in terms of hunting or manufacturing when they may have had other equally important functions for which evidence has not survived.

How are different types of activity identified on archaeological sites?

Studies of the use of space on archaeological sites are known as **intra-site analysis**. Most commonly this is an attempt to define activity areas; in other words, what went on in each zone. From this archaeologists will then use analogs (▶ p. 178) to make inferences about social relationships on topics such as gender, control and specialists and also on belief systems. Ethnographic research has repeatedly shown that ideas and belief 'structure' behaviour and therefore the patterns left behind from that behaviour. The assumption is therefore that there is a relationship between assemblages and the activities that produced them (▶ p. 175).

Features

Boundaries such as internal and external walls, fence alignments or ditches usually separate different activities, animals and people whether in a building, farm or town. Clear demarcation with boundaries makes detecting patterns of finds or space and comparing finds and features in different areas easier than on open sites. Where boundaries are identified, their shape, size and

Figure 7.40 *The distinctive pattern of postholes and ditches from LBK (Neolithic) longhouses (Archives of the Institute of Archaeology ASCR, Prague, No. FT-40257. www.bylany.com)*

orientation alone can provide indications to their use, although analogies (▶ p. 178) will be needed to interpret them. Certain shapes and patterns (e.g. 'four-posters' or 'church shapes') may occur frequently. This enables interpretation of features on new sites through reference to identified examples from known ones. Shapes of buildings and patterns can also be detected from detailed aerial photographs or by remote sensing. Archaeologists also use their experience and data from excavation reports to identify connected groups of features. For example, a particular group of holes might be suggested as the postholes of a house from their size, depth, fill, date and because the archaeologist recognises their pattern. Other evidence will be examined to see if the interpretation can be corroborated.

The distribution of activities can be most clearly seen where buildings remain. Distinctive features such as ovens, drains and traces of fixings provide important clues. Decorative features, the size of the room and the nature of doors and windows provide hints to both function and status.

Artefact distribution

Association of artefacts and other finds with particular areas is the key to understanding what took place where. Detailed 3D plotting of the distribution of finds across entire excavations enables patterns of activity to be identified. Examples include clusters of hide or bone working flints or the association of particular artefacts with particular features, such as loom weights in pit-houses (▶ p. 479). Through experience and reference to other site reports archaeologists learn to recognise the signatures of different activities from surviving evidence. However, one has to be careful not to assign function on the basis of a few finds. Computer applications (including GIS) make sophisticated cluster and density analysis possible and the establishment of ratios of finds to area or volume of earth excavated. The latter analysis can suggest which areas were most used for particular activities and may counter the bias created by large finds or raw numbers of finds. Similar analysis has been used on pits to suggest that they were not used solely for refuse disposal. Areas with few finds present more of a challenge. The apparent deliberate clearing or 'purification' of an area can be a signature of ritual activity. For example, the ditch at Avebury or the temples of San Jose Mogote (▶ p. 179). However, absence of finds alone is not proof of ritual purification!

Other clues

Analysis of soils or other environmental evidence has been used successfully on some sites to determine activity. Phosphate or heavy mineral analysis can indicate where animals have been penned and there is some suggestion that different animals may have different chemical 'signatures'. Other environmental data including the remains of invertebrates with specific habitats can also provide clues (▶ p. 125). The immediate context of a site can also provide clues to its general function and the activities that may have occurred there. A site surrounded by arable fields is likely to have had areas for processing and storing crops while evidence of watercourses may help to identify the remains of a building as a mill. This is least easy to do in towns where a picture of overall patterns can only be built up over a long time through a series of 'keyhole' excavations. It is also still relatively rare for an entire site to be excavated.

There are, of course, limits to the conclusions that can be drawn about any site. Archaeologists are usually investigating at the end of lengthy post-depositional processes and need to understand the impact of these on the evidence. For example, is it a site or a palimpsest (▶ p. 176)? Partial survival, partial recovery, accuracy of find identification and the quality of sampling will also influence what is there to be studied. For example, not all excavations will have recovered environmental evidence.

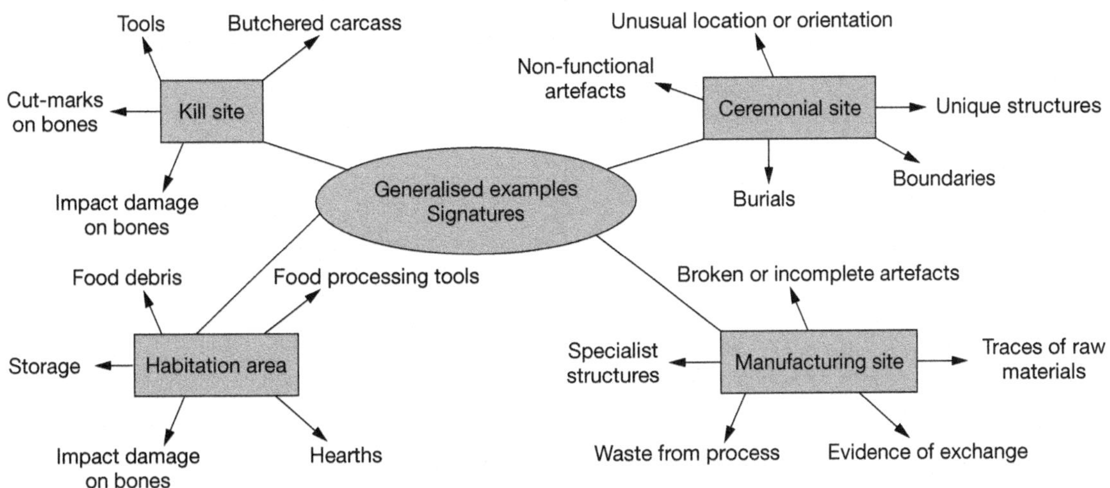

Figure 7.41 *The evidence from four different types of activities which could be used to develop a signature for each*

KEY STUDY

Star Carr revisited: changing interpretations of a classic site

Star Carr is Britain's best-known Mesolithic site. It also provides excellent examples of the ways in which interpretations of sites change over time. Lithics and then organic remains had first been discovered during land drainage in 1947 by an amateur archaeologist. Clark's excavation in 1949–51 was groundbreaking in attempting to combine environmental data with material culture and the use of ethnographies in order to understand past economic activity. It also demonstrated the huge value of waterlogged sites. The site had exceptional anaerobic preservation under a layer of peat. Clark radiocarbon dated the site to *c.* 7600 BC but AMS dates calibrated against European oak sequences now gives an earlier range of 8700–8350 BC. The most recent excavations have pushed the date back to *c.* 9000 BC. This was immediately after the retreat of the ice sheets, making Star Carr part of the earliest Mesolithic. Pollen analysis set the site in an area of open birch-wood and reed swamp at the western end of what was then Lake Pickering. The lake was surrounded by the North York Moors, which were sparsely covered with new woods of pine and birch. The coast, where some of the flint came from, was about 12km away and there, rising waters were slowly drowning the North Sea basin (▶ p. 41).

Economy

The occupation area featured a brushwood 'living platform', scatters of thousands of pieces of flint debitage and butchery and antler working debris. Stone tools included microlithic arrowheads for hunting, burins for working bone, scrapers for hide, antler tine wedges for splitting wood and adzes for carpentry

continued

Figure 7.42 The environment of Star Carr: birch-wood and reed swamp beside a lake

alongside a range of organic artefacts. These included a canoe paddle, rolls of birch bark, elk-antler 'mattocks' and, most famously, twenty-one 'antler headdresses'. The antlers had been skilfully thinned and trimmed to make them light enough to be worn. Holes drilled in them showed where leather thongs or cordage would have been used to attach them to the wearer. Their use has variously been interpreted as hunting, teaching and play but most writers believe they had a ritual function, perhaps as part of more extensive costume. Imported finds included amber from the coast.

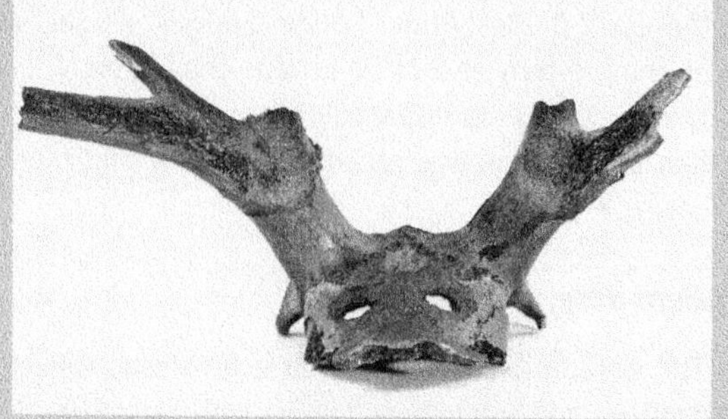

Figure 7.43 Antler 'headdress' from Star Carr

Perhaps more significant were 191 barbed antler harpoons or spearheads: 95 per cent of all such artefacts surviving from the Mesolithic in Britain. Experimentation and examination of tools and antler debitage revealed how an awl was used to carve two parallel grooves into the antler beams and then a long splinter levered out. It could then be crafted with flint into needles or points. This 'groove and splinter' technique dates back to the Upper Palaeolithic and was first recognised at

Stellmoor (▶ p. 298). Star Carr brilliantly demonstrates the impact of differential survival on the archaeological record and our inferences about technology by showing that the Mesolithic was really a 'wood age'. Compared with tools, finds of personal ornaments were rare, with a few drilled shale beads and an amber pendant.

Faunal remains included larger herbivores such as elk, boar, auroch and red deer. There were also bones of beaver, roe deer, hare, hedgehog and water birds but no fish. The technology for fishing existed and there is evidence of fishing at other contemporary sites. Did the people at Star Carr choose not to fish or have remains of these meals not survived? Similar points can be made about plants. Berries, tubers and seeds were all available and could have provided both food and, in the case of reeds, cordage. Little evidence of their exploitation was recovered beyond hazelnuts and water lilies.

The remains of two dogs, however, may indicate some of the earliest domesticates in Britain. Carbon isotope analysis of the dog bones showed one had isotope ratios associated with marine food. This was taken to support the idea that Star Carr was a temporary site, with people moving seasonally across the landscape.

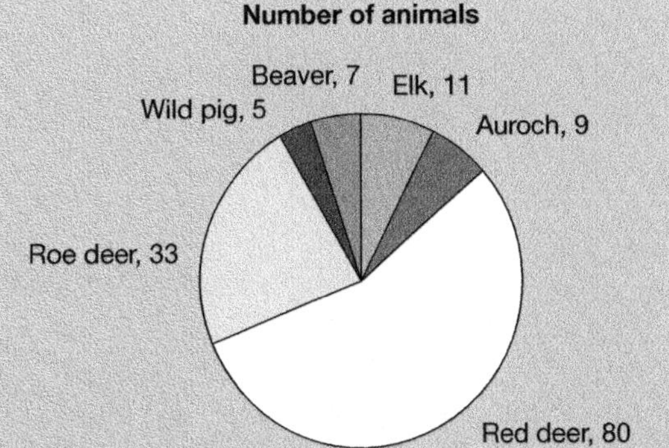

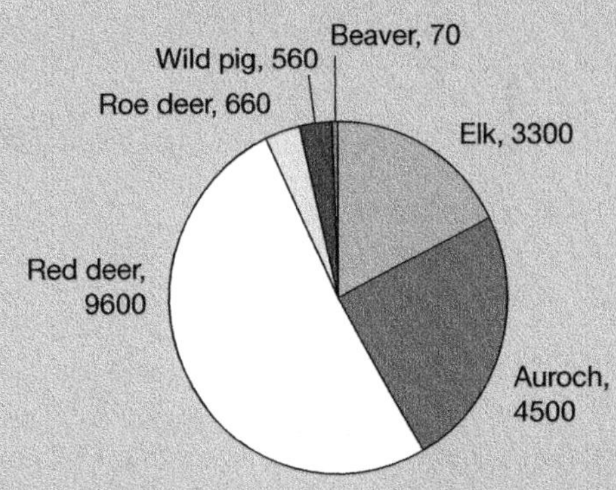

Figure 7.44 *Pie charts showing numbers of individual animals processed at Star Carr and their contribution as food in terms of meat poundage*

Nature of settlement

Clark initially inferred from the growth stages of antlers and other faunal remains that Star Carr was a seasonal hunting and butchery site occupied in the winter or spring over a period of about six years. Ethnographic studies including Thomson's 1939 study of the Wik Monkam of northern Queensland provided his models for a regular seasonal 'round' of movement. Clark suggested that hunting groups would disperse and fan out over the hills or to the coast in the summer months and autumn. His model of patterned mobility with winter aggregation in a valley and summer movement dispersal onto high ground was very influential in later Mesolithic studies such as at Morton and Oronsay (▶ p. 233). He estimated the group size from the flint scatters and faunal remains to have been a band of about twenty-five people in several family groups. They would have slept on the brushwood platform, probably with some sort of skin or bark shelters (▶ p. 283). Comparison of the artefacts with others known at the time led him to identify Star Carr as being from the early Mesolithic, Maglemosian Culture (first identified in 1900 by the Danish archaeologist Sarauw at Maglemose). This enabled inferences to be made about other technologies including dug-out canoes and bows (▶ p. 384).

continued

Figure 7.45 *Red deer*

The wider context

Since the 1970s considerable archaeological work has gone on in the surrounding landscape. Pollen and charcoal samples from across the North York Moors (as in other upland areas such as the Cheviots) suggest periodic burning of woodland. Ethnographic research from North America and Australia has demonstrated that foragers use fire in hunting or to create open areas in which to forage. Pollen and sediment studies from peat cores taken from Lake Flixton reveal that reed swamps around the site had also been repeatedly burnt. This too may have been to provide a hunting area or perhaps improve access to the lake. Either way it may be the earliest landscape management found in Britain. Equally surprising have been the number of other Mesolithic sites discovered in the area. Clark thought that he had excavated all of Star Carr but by the late 1980s it was apparent that there were many small sites dotted around the lake and that there were further remains close to his original dig site. This pattern is very similar to the Maglemosian site of Klosterlund on Bolling Lake (▶ p. 626) in Denmark.

Re-excavation

Test excavations in the 1990s revealed that the site was rapidly degrading and becoming more acidic, possibly in relation to land drainage. Bones were found to have lost their mineral element, leaving only a collagen jelly. A major joint-university research project with significant public funding involving Cambridge, UCL, Manchester and York has been ongoing since 2003 to understand the local context of Star Carr and to recover more information from the site itself before the organic material is lost. Its national importance was recognised when it was scheduled in December 2011.

Excavations close to Clark's dig have shown that the extent of lithic scatters and antler working areas was far more extensive than previously thought. It appears that Clark only excavated the most waterlogged area and he found an activity area rather than where people lived. One new feature is a 6m trackway running out through the reed beds to the edge of the open water which may have provided access for canoes. Aspen logs had been split along the grain using antler tines as wedges. Along with many wood chippings this is Europe's earliest evidence for carpentry. As well as axe and adze marks, beaver teeth-marks have been found on some of the wood archive material. The quantity of wood processed may suggest coppicing was going on. A second timber 'decking' platform has been discovered at the water's edge while in a dry area are the remains of Britain's earliest house. It comprised a ring of posts surrounding a hollow area 3.5m in diameter filled with a soft flooring of reeds, moss and grasses and containing a hearth. Amongst the organic tools recovered is the oldest example of a digging stick – made of willow and used for digging up roots and other plant foods. Research teams have also contour-mapped the ancient lake area and used augers to gain environmental details. Test pits every 15m were used close to the original trenches to see how far the site extended and whether there were other sites

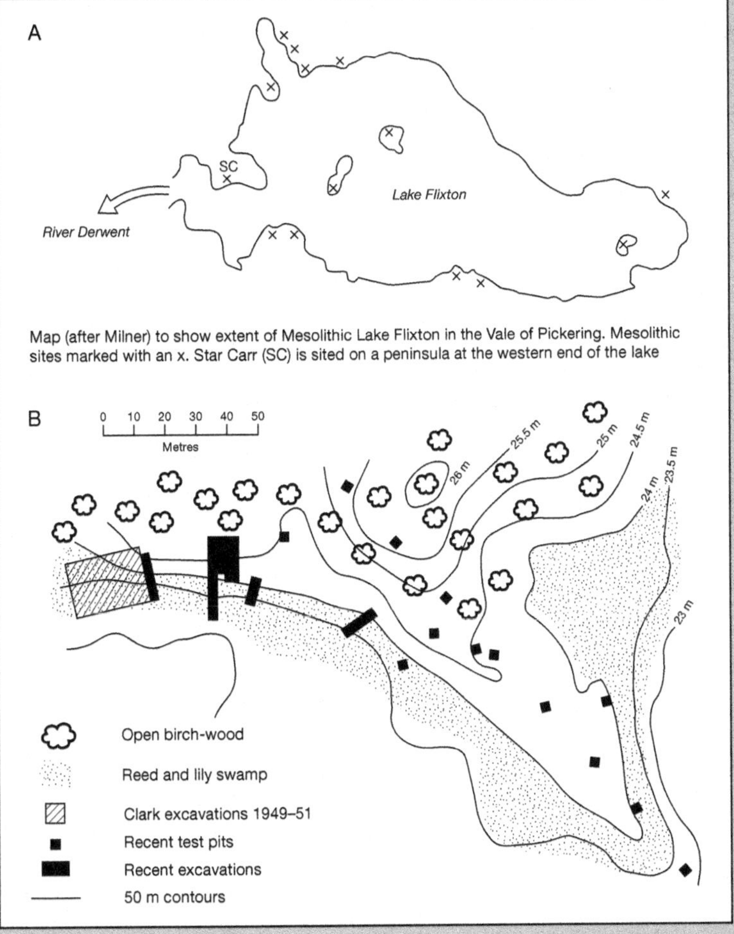

Figure 7.46 *Map of Lake Flixton in the Vale of Pickering, showing positions of Mesolithic sites*

continued

close by. Star Carr itself is now known to cover most of a small peninsula at the point where the lake is drained by a stream. Whether this was chosen for economic or social/ritual reasons is unclear. Distributions of finds suggest different activities were taking place in different areas, with wood often found on the lake margin, bone and antler at the swamp edge and flint on drier ground. Painstaking excavation is recovering evidence of single tool-making events. Meanwhile, other surveys are looking at other Mesolithic activity – mostly flint scatters – across the Vale of Pickering. A possibility is that Star Carr was an **aggregation** site for particular activities for groups widely dispersed across the landscape for much of the year.

Re-examination of the site has been hampered by a limited archive and few notebooks but some gaps have been plugged through interviews with Clark's colleagues. In order to manage the overwhelming number of finds, Clark imposed a 'fingernail rule' for recovery. This meant that micro-debitage and tiny bones were not collected and almost certainly biased overall findings. Bones of fish-eating birds were recovered but not fish bones. In the current excavations everything is sieved or processed by flotation. Particularly promising deposits have been block lifted for lab-based microanalysis while some of Clark's trenches have been re-excavated to recover what was missed.

Reinterpretations

Star Carr has been interpreted in many ways as archaeologists have used different analogies to interpret remains. Periodic new discoveries have also transformed the debate. Deer skulls with antlers still attached initially led Clark to see it as a seasonal site from winter to spring, although he later revised this in the light of other evidence. Examination of plant remains led others towards summer occupation, as did the idea that the antlers had been gathered elsewhere and brought to this manufacturing site. The discovery of the second platform, a much larger site area and the house may tilt interpretations towards it being a more permanent base camp. Similarly the prime function of the site has been identified as a hunting stand, a butchery site (many meat-bearing bones were missing from the assemblage), a specialist antler manufacture site (with deer hunted for their antlers) and a ritual location. Much of the debate focuses on the significance of the red deer bones. They dominate the assemblage but did they accumulate over a short period of time (which would suggest specialisation) or gradually over a hundred years? Despite being so well known, Star Carr's main function remains unclear. The newest dates suggest much longer, albeit perhaps intermittent, occupation for several hundred years. It may therefore be a palimpsest where use varied over time.

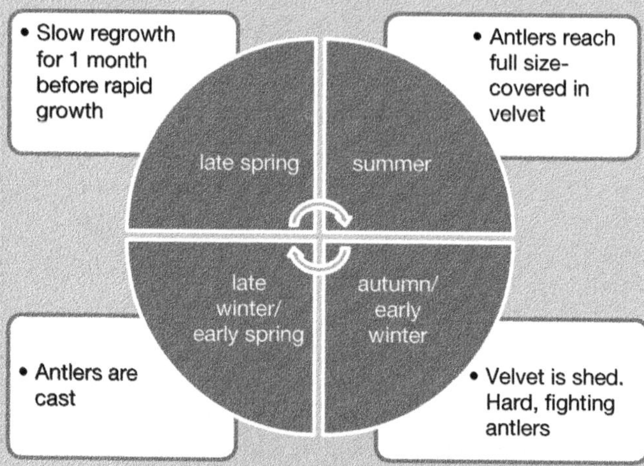

Figure 7.47 *Antler annual cycles. These patterns have often been used to estimate the season of occupation of Mesolithic sites.*

INTERPRETING THE USE OF SPACE ON ARCHAEOLOGICAL SITES

In exploring the reasons why sites within the same area differ in their internal layout, archaeologists draw heavily upon ethnography and ethnoarchaeology. This is important in providing insights but also in countering the modern values and assumptions of the archaeologists themselves. This is particularly important when considering space in relation to gender, status or age groups. Binford's work with the Nunamiut (▶ p. 229) showed that it was wrong to expect the same group of people to produce homogeneous sites. Sites differed due to their role in the overall settlement system. Even hunting camps differ widely. The site of a successful hunt will generate many additional activities compared to an unsuccessful one. Ethnoarchaeology has helped identify some of the problems that can occur if the distribution of artefacts and features on a site is interpreted as a direct record of economic decisions and activities. Site maintenance and the practice of disposing of rubbish may create misleading patterns in the archaeological record. Different materials are treated differently, some being thrown aside while others are recycled or deliberately taken to dumps. Some activities are deliberately sited to be near heat and light while tasks that require a lot of space are rarely in areas where people socialise.

In Clarke's (1972) study of Glastonbury Lake Village, he used artefactual evidence in relation to spaces marked by boundaries to identify a series of zones which went beyond economic activity. Distinct compounds for carpentry, leather and iron working were identified and interpreted, using ethnographic examples from Africa, as male working areas, while zones for spinning and baking were interpreted as female areas. Clarke also identified some differences in the value of artefacts in different huts, which he saw as evidence of a ranked society (▶ p. 419) with differences in status. Drewett's (1982) excavation of part of Black Patch Bronze Age farmstead drew on Nigerian ethnographies featuring similar settlement layouts combined with detailed analysis of plots of different categories of finds to suggest the site's functions and social organisation. The largest hut, which had its own

Figure 7.48 *Settlement at Black Patch showing subdivisions and land use based on surviving features and assemblages (after Drewett 1982)*

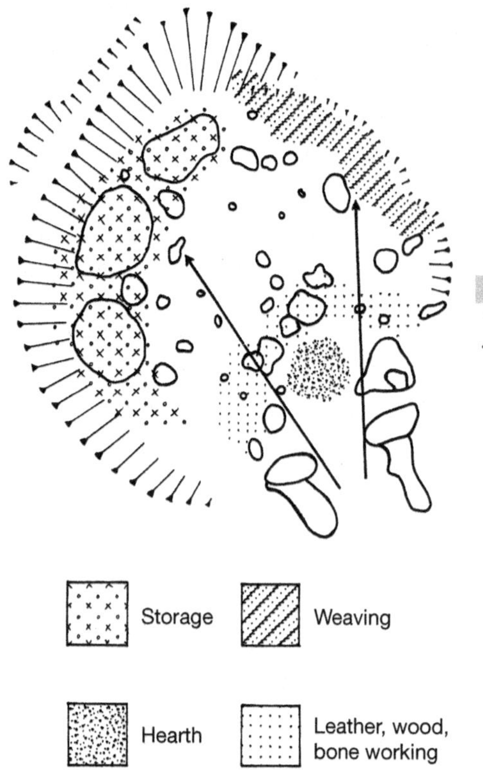

Figure 7.49 *Main hut at Black Patch (after Drewett 1982) with activity areas based on clusters of loom weights, flint debitage and metal finds*

compound and pond and contained finer pottery and evidence of a loom, was the home of the headman. The smaller huts were for food preparation, storage and accommodation for the rest of the headman's extended family. Detailed study of finds within the huts was related to likely sources of light to identify areas for weaving, leather working and storage.

Room interpretation at Skara Brae

Surviving buildings enable greater exploration of the social use of space than on excavated sites. This involves analysis of what the use of space meant and how social relations were structured by the architecture. For example, the household is the fundamental organisational unit for most known societies and buildings 'enclose' separate households and families. However, exceptions are known where more extended social groups live under one roof. Skara Brae, a cluster of cell-like Neolithic houses on Orkney, may fit this pattern. The site was buried under sand for 5,000 years, which partly accounts for the amazing state of preservation. The other factor is the use of local flagstone for building. Even furniture has survived. At least ten houses from three phases of development have been identified, although others may have been lost to sea erosion. The final phase features eight near-identical houses linked by passageways, sharing a drainage system and sunk into a pre-existing midden, possibly to provide insulation. The dry-stone walls are up to 3m thick while the roof would have been made from whalebone or timber washed up on the beach. The floor-sizes of the houses are all around 40sqm and all but one house have a central hearth, box-beds, 'dresser' and storage areas. The exception, house 8, lacks furniture and may have been a ritual area or workshop. From the initial excavation onwards, archaeologists have speculated about the impact of the layout of the houses upon both movement and people. To the left of the thresholds, flagstone boxes hindered access and forced those entering to turn right. Many cultures have rules about the 'right way' to move round a building including examples from Bali and the Amazon basin (Darvill and Thomas 2000). These rules may relate to ritual or to social norms, particularly around gender. Drawing on C19th Hebridean blackhouses for an analogy, the excavator Childe (1931) interpreted the larger bed on the right as male and the smaller one as female. Beads, pottery and possible paint pots were recovered from the left side of some buildings, which reinforced this idea and suggested that there was a male/public side and a female/private side. However, this view makes some big assumptions including that only women wore beads.

House 7 is unusual in that it could be barred from the outside and two female skeletons were

Figure 7.50 *House at Skara Brae*

found beneath the floor. A variety of analogies such as jail, initiation, birthing or menstruation rooms have been suggested but without supporting evidence these are just speculation. Others have noted the similarity in structure between the houses and contemporary ancestral tombs nearby (▶ p. 533). Finds from the village include pottery, bone and stone tools, loom weights, personal ornamentation and small, carved artistic objects. Ecofacts suggest that they practised mixed farming (▶ p. 338) but supplemented their diet with marine food. The architecture and finds suggest a tight-knit, egalitarian and related community of farmers. The real division is between the band inside and those outside.

In contrast, physical space between clusters of buildings may represent social distance, while a building that physically dominates others may be the home of a social leader. The broch at Gurness provides an example where social relations may be literally 'set in stone'.

Access analysis at Gurness

Brochs are double-walled, drystone tower houses surrounded by clusters of other buildings. Recent studies of this Iron Age broch on Orkney by Historic Scotland have challenged the idea that it was simply a defensive site. The great tower of the broch dominated the nucleated settlement of small houses which were ranged either side of a single entrance passage which leads into the broch itself. Foster (1989) analysed access to space around the site and demonstrated how movement was controlled by the architecture, with those in the tower having considerably more right of

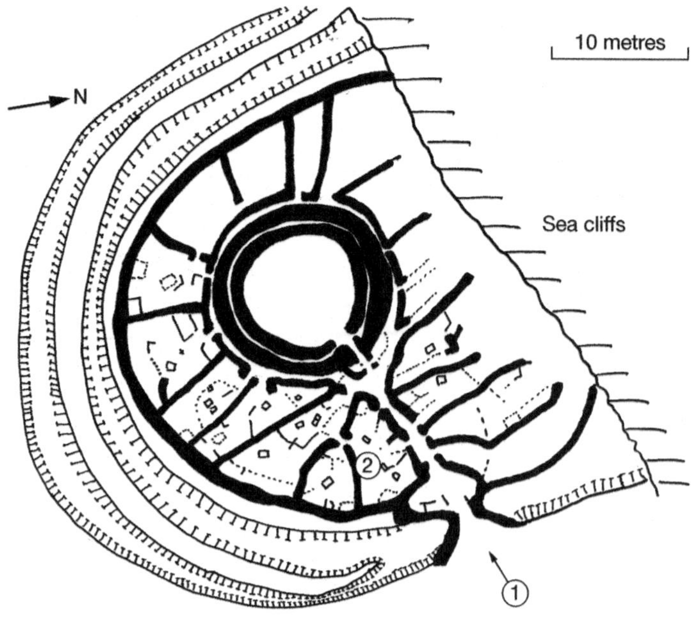

Figure 7.51 *Simplified plan of Gurness to show how the tower dominated the other buildings and the access route. The places where the photographs in Figures 7.52 and 7.53 were taken from are indicated by 1 and 2 respectively.*

access. Movement around the site also constantly drew attention to the tower and could be observed from it. The access map for this site was significantly more complex and hierarchical than one produced for nearby Skara Brae. Interestingly, the layout of the individual houses at Gurness are similar to the cellular dwellings at Skara Brae.

Gurness provided a home to a chieftain and protection for his followers. The physical height of the tower and the hierarchical use of space made his dominance of the people and the area visible. In helping to build it and living under its shadow, the local people accepted his authority.

This 'access analysis' has also been applied to investigations of gender relations. Gilchrist (1995) suggests that the layout of domestic areas of medieval castles reflects and reinforces contemporary views on the differences between men and women. On a larger scale, the differing size and elaboration of buildings may suggest a stratified society, while controlling elites might be inferred from settlements structured along gridlines or with fixed orientations. Elsewhere, the buildings of an elite are expected to be larger and richer in finds and decoration than humbler versions. Key features such as unusually large storage facilities and exotic finds are also indicators of status (▶ p. 431).

In the analysis of space, boundaries are of particular importance and archaeologists are careful not to see ditches and entrances as simply functional. In prehistory there is clear evidence on many sites that boundaries were influenced by belief systems. The predominant orientation of Bronze and Iron Age roundhouses and enclosures towards the south-east may be such a case. Experiment has shown that a southerly orientation would maximise light. The choice of south-east or west may reflect beliefs linked to the rising or setting sun. Hillfort entrances also appear to have been selected for reasons other than defence. In addition, special deposits, including human remains, were frequently placed at boundaries and thresholds.

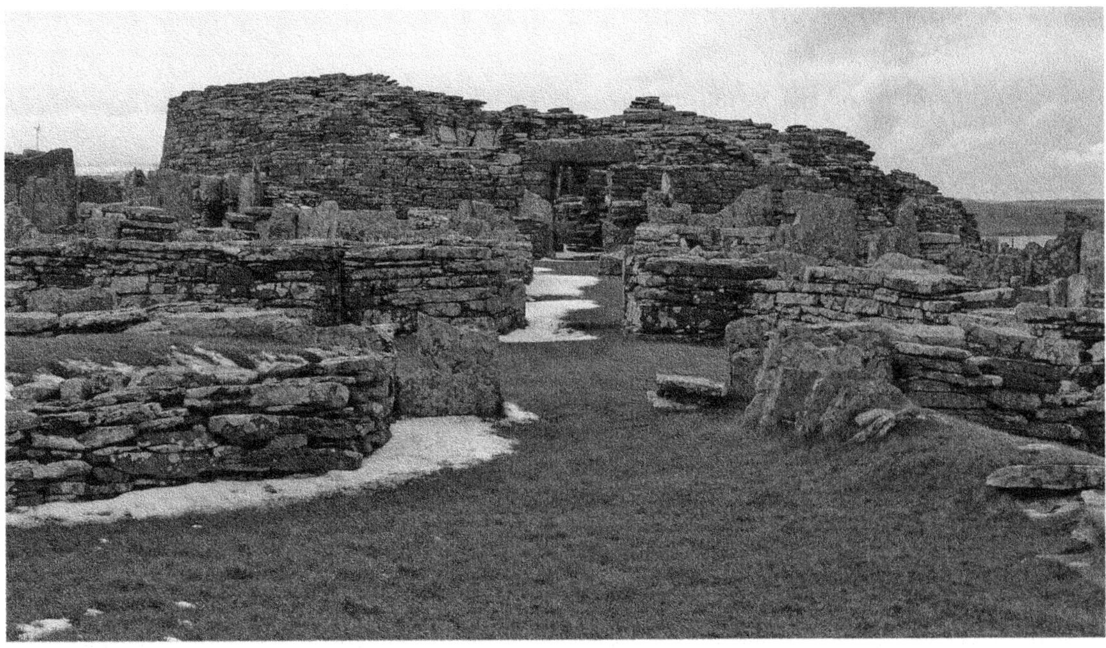

Figure 7.52 *The broch at Gurness, looking down the entrance corridor to the central tower*

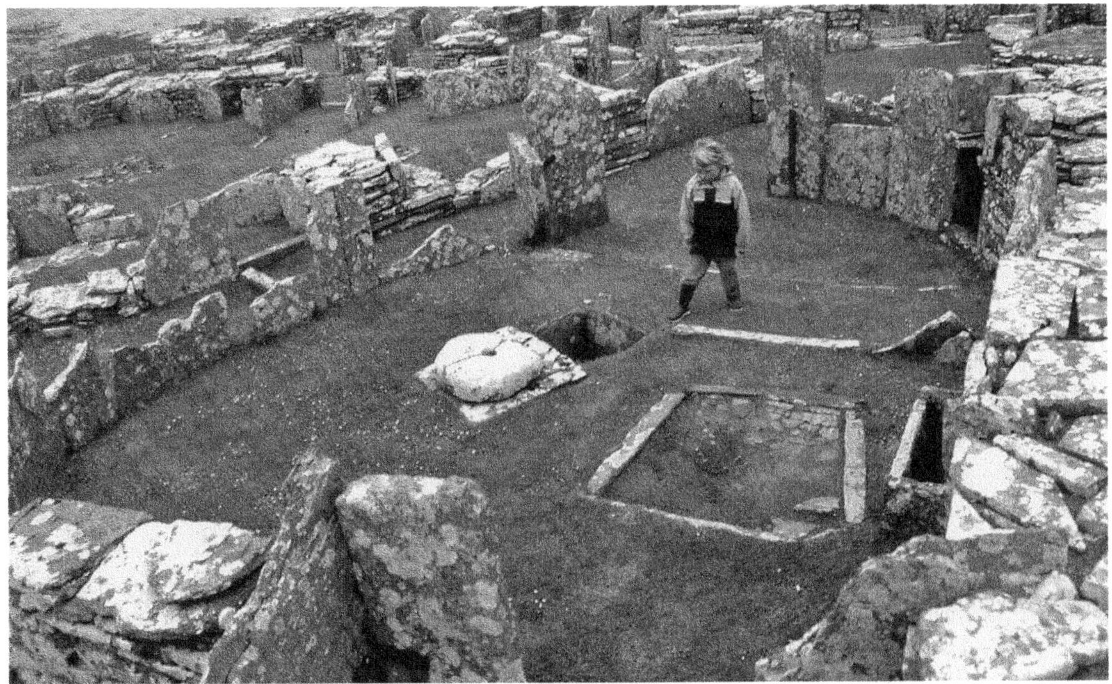

Figure 7.53 *An example of a smaller cellular house at Gurness*

KEY STUDY

Pincevent, Mask and site structure

Probably the most famous archaeological debate about site structure concerns the late Ice Age site of Pincevent. The site was on the bank of the Seine, south of modern Paris, and radiocarbon dated between 13 and 12,000 BP. The landscape at the time would have been tundra and cold grassland which was grazed by large herbivores. Preservation was exceptionally good and Leroi-Gourhan, the excavator, pioneered an approach he called *décapage* to expose entire horizontal levels of the site to reveal and enable study of the 'living floor'. In addition to planning, he undertook a complete vertical photographic survey of the site. He reasoned that finds on the living floor would represent a particular event or relatively brief period of activity. By observing clusters of finds and their relationship, he hoped to infer what activity had taken place. Pincevent was a particularly suitable site for this approach as the nearby river periodically flooded the area and deposited a fine layer of silt. As at Boxgrove (▶ p. 61), silt layers separated each successive occupation of the site surface, allowing the spatial pattern of finds and features to be studied.

The finds

Initial excavation of one section of the site revealed three major arcs of stone and debris from butchery and lithic manufacture associated with a number of hearths. Many of the longer pieces of bone and lithics were in line with the overall arc, which suggested that they had been pushed or swept up against a barrier. Binford (1983) interpreted these arcs as waste material which had built up around the outsides of three linked skin tents. Larger flint nodules were interpreted as being used to hold down the tent sides against the wind. The bones of mammoth, horse and hares were recovered but the most significant prey species was reindeer. Faunal remains initially suggested to Leroi-Gourhan that Pincevent was occupied in winter and that it was a base camp for reindeer hunters.

Rival interpretations

Binford (1983) used insights from his observations of behaviour and the use of space around a hearth by modern Nunamiut caribou hunters at the Mask site in Alaska to challenge Leroi-Gourhan's interpretation. At Mask the hunters had sat around the hearth on the windward side to avoid the smoke. Where they had sat, Binford identified an irregular doughnut-shaped distribution of material. He divided this into drop and toss zones according to the way the hunters disposed of rubbish. Larger debris was tossed behind the hunters or across the fire while small pieces were dropped around where they sat. Over time this created two concentric arcs of material. Binford noted that different numbers of hunters created different distribution patterns. He also noted that hearths tended to be spread by people searching for food in the ashes and that when the wind changed direction, the hunters would turn around and start another hearth. Binford contrasted this behaviour with observations of hearths and debris inside structures where hearths and resulting ash are usually surrounded by stones to prevent the spread of fire and to provide working surfaces. People also tend not to throw rubbish over their shoulders when they are in a tent. Instead it is sometimes dumped outside or moved to a separate refuse area. He argued that lithic patterns from two Pincevent hearths showed close correlation with the 'drop and

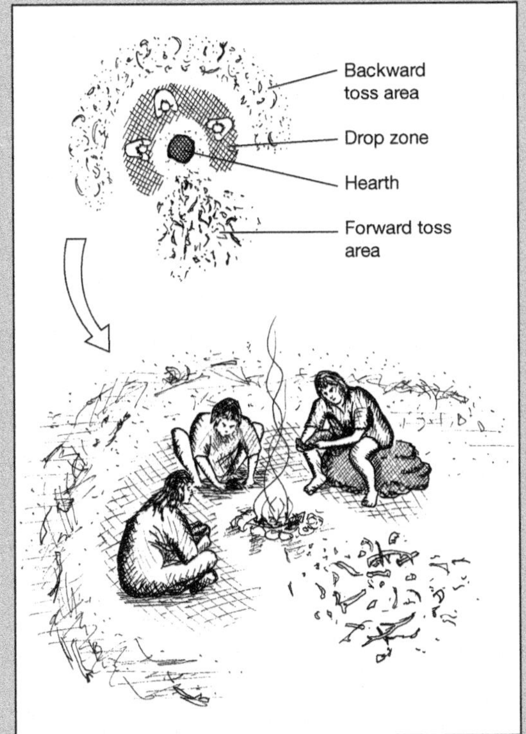

Figure 7.54 *Drawing of the Mask site*

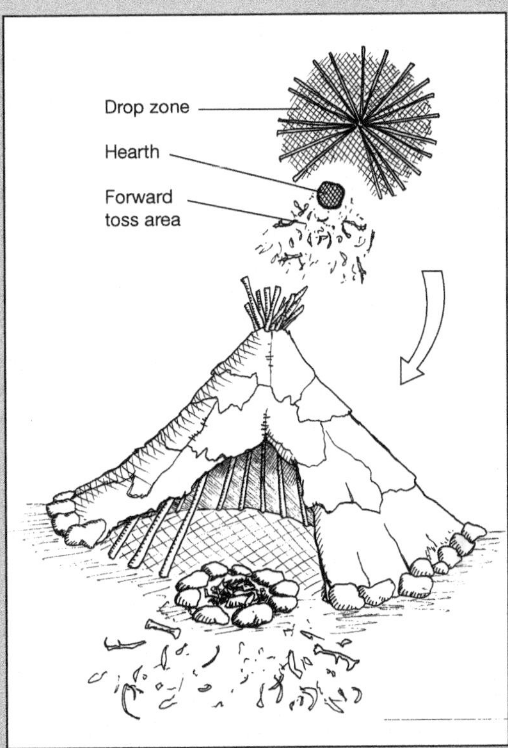

Figure 7.55 *Drawing and alternative interpretations of Pincevent*

toss' pattern from Mask. He suggested that these were open hearths and that larger stones had been used to hold down hides for processing and only the third arc was a possible tent. He observed that people tidied up long-term base camps and therefore the toss and drop patterns would not normally survive. Rather than being a base camp, he saw Pincevent as a more specialised hunting and processing site which was occupied on relatively brief visits.

Since 1966 an area of almost 5000m^2 has been excavated, revealing many stone-lined hearths and areas associated with butchery, lithic manufacture, habitation and refuse. On each living floor research has been undertaken to refit lithics and fragmented animal bone. This has revealed evidence of food sharing between hearths of bones from the same reindeer (Enloe 1992). This implies generalised reciprocity (▶ p. 399) within the band. A number of different approaches to identifying clusters of material have been employed using the detailed original records. Point-pattern analysis involves plotting finds on a grid and then adding X and Y axes in order to carry out significance tests (e.g. chi-square) to see whether patterns are random or clusters deriving from an activity. GIS is used to store and plot this data as contour density plans which enable patterns to be seen more easily. Frequencies of particular finds are counted for each area to identify and then test the significance of clusters. Both approaches have been widely applied to other Upper Palaeolithic sites including Hengistbury Head in Dorset (Barton 1992) and Verberie (Keeler 2007). Areas relatively free from debris but surrounded

continued

by discarded bones have been identified as butchery areas with meat being piled up on the reindeer hides. Use-wear analysis on flint blades from this area showed that they had last been used to cut meat (Enloe 1997). Bone and antler working occurred around the hearths.

Recent research

The seasonality of the site has been revised as a result of subsequent research. The absence of foetal reindeer or very young animals suggests occupation was not in winter or spring. Both male and female reindeer were killed. They tend to be found together during the autumn migration. Both males and females have new antlers from early summer and that was the case here. Finally, analysis of tooth growth on young animals also points to a later summer–autumn season for the site (Enloe and David 1997). The location close to a river suggests that the herds could have been ambushed while fording it as at Stellmoor (▶ p. 298). Just upstream the river narrows, while two tributaries join the main river nearby. Interestingly, one of the jewels of the British Museum is a mammoth ivory carving of swimming reindeer from the Montastruc rock shelter by the Aveyron River in southern France. It has been dated to 13,000 BP. Also at Montastruc was part of a reindeer antler atlatl or spear thrower, which may suggest how the animals were hunted. Analysis of the kill profile of reindeer reveals hunting to have been highly selective, with animals in their prime preferred and males over-represented in relation to their proportion in natural herds (Enloe 1997).

Research on contemporary sites in the same region has also provided a little more potential evidence for tent rings, although this is not conclusive. However, tent rings have been found on reindeer hunting sites close to the glaciers in the southern mountains of Norway from *c.* 7900 BP (Bang-Andersen 2003) and the Saami reindeer hunters of the Arctic lived in a tipi-like tent called a lavvo. It is possible that more flimsy dome-shaped 'benders' (▶ p. 283) of wood from bushes or large antlers covered in ten to twenty skins were used for sleeping. Comparison of the hearths has not revealed any evidence of social differences. This appears to have been an egalitarian 'band' society (▶ p. 421) with several households (or hearth-groups) living and working together. It may also suggest kinship ties between the groups (Enloe 2006). Pincevent itself is generally not now seen as a complete residential base site but as part of a settlement system (▶ p. 229). The lack of reindeer vertebrae suggests that kills and initial butchery took place elsewhere. This contrasts with the smaller site of Verberie in the same region which did have vertebrae and also other debris scattered in patterns which Binford (1978) had identified as a signature of butchery. This is an area of bone and occasional lithic debris surrounding an empty space. Binford had observed Nunamiut hunters processing caribou on their own skins and creating this 'doughnut' pattern. This suggests that Verberie was primarily a butchery site. There is no direct evidence for storage at Pincevent, although the frequent absence of rib bones accords with Binford's (1978) observation that these were the most commonly dried for storage among the Nunamiut. The processing of large amounts of bone at one time including marrow extraction has also been cited as a possible indicator of storage (Enloe 2003).

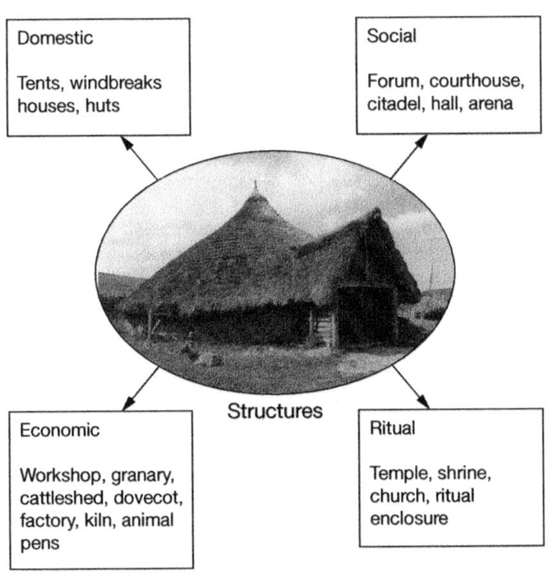

Figure 7.56 *Structures in archaeology*

UNDERSTANDING STRUCTURES

Structures are past features built by humans. So buildings, fences, fish-traps and a windbreak around a hearth are all structures while caves, kill sites and rock shelters are not. Tents, benders and boats are all mobile structures. Many of the points made in relation to sites and features also apply to structures, but the main focus of the study of structures is understanding how they were built from the traces recovered by excavation. Key questions revolve around why particular designs were selected and the technology and materials used to construct them. While ground plans can be estimated from hearths, postholes or foundation trenches, archaeologists have to make imaginative leaps to reconstruct the walls and roofs (▶ p. 183).

The first buildings

The earliest man-made structures in Europe are Upper Palaeolithic huts made from the bones of large herbivores, particularly mammoth. Examples include Mezin in Ukraine and Dolni Vestonice (▶ p. 218). Detailed stratigraphic study (Soffer et al. 1997) at Mezhirich, Ukraine, suggests these were occupied seasonally rather than all year in what would have been an extremely hostile climate. The evidence for this was a series of thin deposits sometimes with sterile layers of sand between them. Analysis of Dwelling 4 provided evidence of food processing, cooking and manufacture of tools and clothing. Limited debris inside the hut and finds from external middens suggested periodic cleaning. The site was structured. At least two dwellings were in use at the same time and each had storage pits and a midden associated with it. These sites represent seasonal hunting camps. Bands would return to the favourable locations and reuse the bone structures, probably by draping a skin roof over the framework. Soffer et al. (1997) suggest that these were winter sites both from the suggestion of stored resources and the amount of activity taking place indoors.

Sources of analogies

Early archaeological interpretations sometimes reflected modern perceptions of people in the past as less intelligent. An example was the way in which Anglo-Saxons were often depicted as living in pits. In some cultures, such as the Anasazi of the south-west USA, sunken buildings made sense because their thermal properties made life bearable in the desert heat. In damp climates this would be less so. However, over the last few decades a greater understanding of building techniques and organic materials has been gained from sites with exceptional preservation (▶ p. 171). In particular, insights into construction techniques, tools and the type of wood used have greatly improved our understanding of prehistoric carpentry skills (▶ p. 384). These insights, combined with the development of experimental archaeology, have been particularly important in investigating structures from prehistoric and medieval times. The development of experimental structures such as those at Butser

(▶ p. 183) have used this information to test hypotheses about the design and materials used to make the walls and roofs and then about the use and function of the buildings. As a result, we can be reasonably sure about the pitch of a roof or whether there was a smoke hole but we cannot know if the house was decorated or whether people slept on the ground or on platforms that lay across the roof beams. Experiment can only show what might have been and then test it to failure. Experimental archaeology is, of course, weighted towards technological understanding. There may be social or religious reasons for particular designs and materials being used which reconstructions cannot directly address.

At the Anglo-Saxon site of West Stow, Suffolk (▶ p. 494), building materials had not survived in the sandy local soil but postholes, pits and beam slots from over seventy structures were preserved (West 1985). Most were identified as 'Grubenhäuser' – after the German term for sunken-featured buildings (SFBs). SFBs were thought to have been introduced by migrants from northern Europe and comprised a rectangular plank-built structure built around a pit. There was a large post at each end which would have supported the

Figure 7.57 *Wattle and daub. Used for walls during prehistory and the early medieval period.*

Figure 7.58 *Experimental Iron Age roundhouse from Archaeolink*

Figure 7.59 *Recreation of a Mesolithic 'bender'-style tent*

ridge of the roof. The excavators faced the familar problem of interpreting the above-ground structure of the buildings. Previously SFBs had been interpreted as pit dwellings, which in part reflected the view amongst classically influenced archaeologists that their inhabitants really were barbaric. With increasing knowledge of Anglo-Saxon carpentry and construction technique the excavators at West Stow used experimental archaeology to test alternative models.

The excavators had recorded the distribution of artefacts in relation to traces of burnt timbers. The patterns suggested that there were originally plank floors over the pits. The building of two experimental versions, one floored and the other open, enabled this to be confirmed through a

Figure 7.60 *Faience (glass-like) models of Minoan houses. These miniatures along with models and illustrations have provided much information about the construction of Minoan houses.*

study of the differential build-up of soil in the pit during use. It is now thought likely that Grubenhäuser had suspended floors like the deck of a ship with the rubbish entering the pit after the building's abandonment. There is also a debate about the internal decoration and use of buildings and whether the roof was thatch or wood shingles. Inside these huts fires were lit on top of clay beds to protect the timbers. The pits in many of the SFBs contained loom weights, which led to them being seen as workshops or weaving sheds. Surviving metal tools showed that the villagers worked wood while combs and pins in various stages of manufacture provided evidence of bone and antler working.

Ethnographic models have been most heavily used for Palaeolithic (▶ p. 300) and Mesolithic (▶ p. 167) structures. For example, at Mount Sandal (Ireland) and Morton (Scotland) excavation revealed small rings of stakeholes and several hearths. These have been interpreted as the traces of skin-covered 'benders' or tents. Depictions of houses on objects or as models have also been useful for reconstructing the upper stories of buildings (▶ p. 259).

THE DEVELOPMENT OF COMPLEX SETTLEMENTS

Understanding the development of an individual settlement starts with an understanding of stratigraphy and, in particular, phasing. For historical periods this is augmented by documentary sources including maps, charters and legal records such as by-laws and deeds. Understanding the reasons for development on specific sites will combine an understanding of the site itself within its wider context. General ideas about the development of larger and more complex urban settlements will tend to focus on that wider local context but will also include broader ideas about the emergence of more complex societies.

Labels such as 'town' and 'city' are often used interchangeably when discussing larger settlements. However, most archaeologists discussing the emergence of civilisation or of states (▶ p. 468) will tend to see cities as distinct. Towns or at least very large villages existed from at least 7000 BC. Some, such as Jericho, had walls, others had temples, granaries and long-distance trade networks to acquire key raw materials such as obsidian or luxuries such as lapis lazuli or cowrie

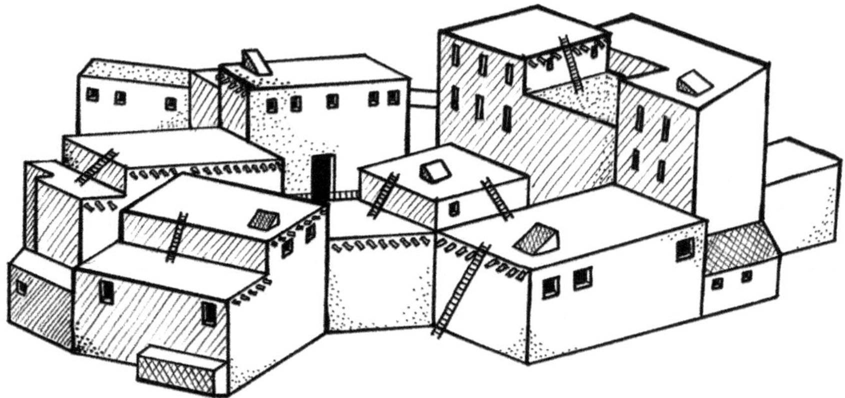

Figure 7.61 *Çatal Höyük*

This cluster of interlinked dwellings became one of the earliest towns. It was occupied from the early 7th to 6th millennia BC and the eighteen layers of mudbrick dwellings housing several thousand people eventually became a tell (▶ p. 55). Unusually, access to the houses appears to have been through the roof; there are no streets. Similarities in house size and contents have been interpreted as being the result of a fairly egalitarian society (▶ p. 421).

shells. In Mesopotamia they are sometimes surrounded by irrigation canals which were used to increase the productivity of the land. Some, such as Çatal Höyük in Anatolia or Ubiad in Mesopotamia, had several thousand inhabitants but they were not yet cities. The threshold between these 'proto-cities' and the first real cities is usually defined by scale and complexity. The first cities (in Mesopotamia) had large, densely settled populations (over 5,000) who were not directly involved in agriculture, a complex division of labour and monumental public buildings which served the wider region. They are associated with specialisation, the development of writing, social hierarchy, armies and codified laws. In return for services, trade and craft production, they controlled the surplus of their hinterlands.

The gradual development of settlements such as Uruk in Mesopotamia, which originated as a large village but by the early 4th millennium BC had become a city, is reasonably clear. It began as one of a cluster of densely packed villages full of mudbrick houses with little social differentiation. Over several hundred years it first acquired a temple then other public buildings and gradually grew in size to dominate its surroundings. Successive phases of public buildings grew both in size and elaboration, in particular the temple complex with several shrines and a ziggurat: a massive stepped platform which raised a shrine into the sky. The temple complexes in these early Sumerian cities were associated with workshops, storage, cylinder seals and clay tablets (inscribed pictographs which eventually mutated into the earliest written script, cuneiform (▶ p. 415)). By 3000 BC the population was numbered in tens of thousands and the city needed a much larger hinterland to provide food and raw materials such as stone, timber and metals.

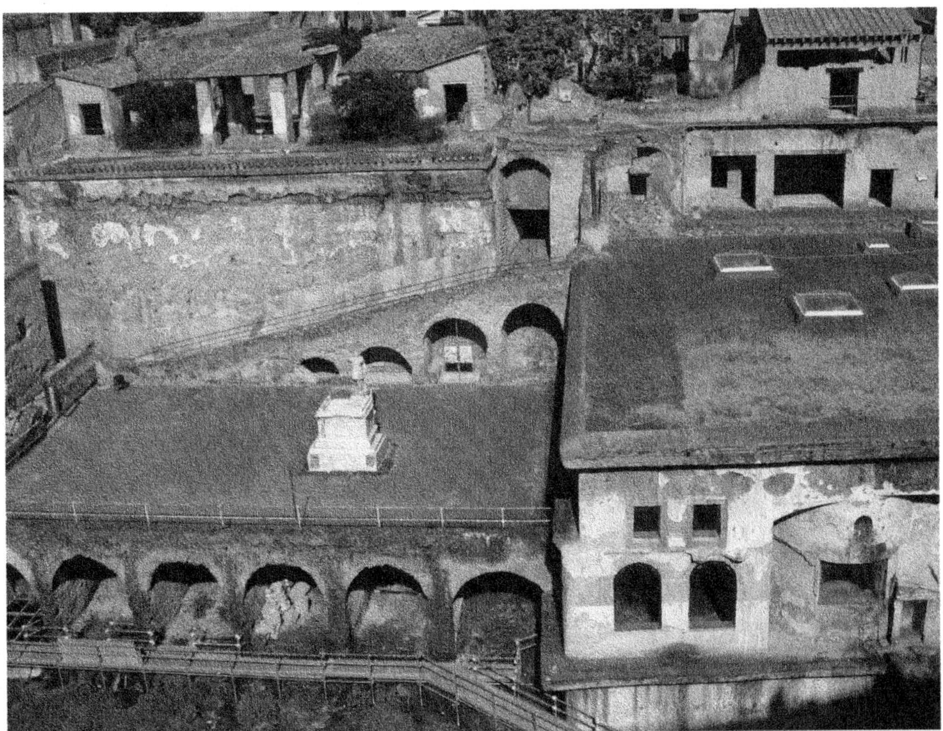

Figure 7.62 *The Roman town of Herculaneum, preserved under volcanic ash*

KEY STUDY

Mashkan Shapir

Unlike other Mesopotamian cities which have been identified from extensive settlement mounds or tells, Mashkan Shapir, 140km downriver from Baghdad, was discovered by satellite photography. From space the traces of long filled-in waterways were visible in the Iraqi desert. At the point where they converged, archaeologists found the remains of buildings up to 2m in height and scatters of Bronze Age artefacts in the sand. Aerial photography was not allowed, so the ground plan of the site was mapped using a camera mounted on a kite. The name of the city, which means 'encampment of the overseer', was revealed when clay cylinders covered in cuneiform writing were deciphered. These texts commemorate the building of the city wall and suggest that the city was founded *c.* 2000 BC by the King of Larsa (one of the larger Mesopotamian city-states), who had ordered the construction of a trade canal between the Tigris and Euphrates rivers. Holding a strategic position and controlling trade in wood, metal and stone coming down the Tigris, Mashkan Shapir grew rapidly. With a population of around 15,000 it became the second largest city in the kingdom but was suddenly abandoned *c.* 1720 BC apparently after a war with Babylon.

The site

Because it was abandoned rather than built over, archaeologists were able to investigate the spatial organisation of the city. By mapping the location of remains and artefacts on the surface and then checking with limited excavation, a picture began to emerge of life in the city. There were several entrances to the city for both roads and canals. Inside the fortified mudbrick walls was a large area of some 70 hectares. It was divided by canals into zones dedicated to manufacture, administration and living areas. Canals were important for water, fish (many fish-hooks were found) and transport. Mesopotamian texts record the city as having 240 boats. Two harbours joined to canals were probably commercial areas while an empty area with some storehouses near a gate was possibly a market and another was probably a garden.

The southern zone, cut off by a wall and canal, seems to have been a religious sanctuary dedicated to Nergal, the god of death. Within the mudbrick platform which would have supported a pyramid-like ziggurat were clay effigies of people and animals. Enclosed between a wall and a canal at the south-west end of the central area was a large cemetery. Here the dead were buried in ceramic jars along with weapons and jewellery. Usually the dead were buried in domestic areas so this may have been a special burial site for particular social groups.

A smaller walled-off area directly over a canal to the west is thought to be the administrative area. It included many regularly built buildings, a possible palace and unusual artefacts including clay pieces with seal marks which are thought to mark out storage areas. Many miniature chariots with effigies of Nergal or the scythe, which was his symbol, were also found here. The excavators believe that these were used for oath-taking. The other zones appear to have been mixed residential areas with concentrations of buildings along the canals. Different-sized houses were grouped together, which suggests rich and poor were not segregated. Symbols of authority such as seals and high status metal artefacts were widely dispersed, as were manufacturing sites including kilns and slag from pottery making and copper smelting respectively. Fragments of grey-black rock were also discovered which seem to have been by-products from the manufacture of synthetic 'volcanic' rock to be used for grindstones and building material.

Interpretations

Elizabeth Stone and Paul Zimansky have argued that the layout of Mashkan Shapir represents a very different kind of urban society from those recorded from excavation of palace sites. Absolute rulers tend to exercise control and centralise authority by keeping religious, political and administrative buildings close to them, sometimes within their palace complex. However, early Mesopotamian texts describe citizens exercising power through assemblies rather than being controlled by their rulers. At Mashkan Shapir, power seems to have been dispersed with both rich and poor living in the same neighbourhoods. Commerce, production, administration and religion all appear to have been separate. The lack of concentration may suggest a more heterarchical society.

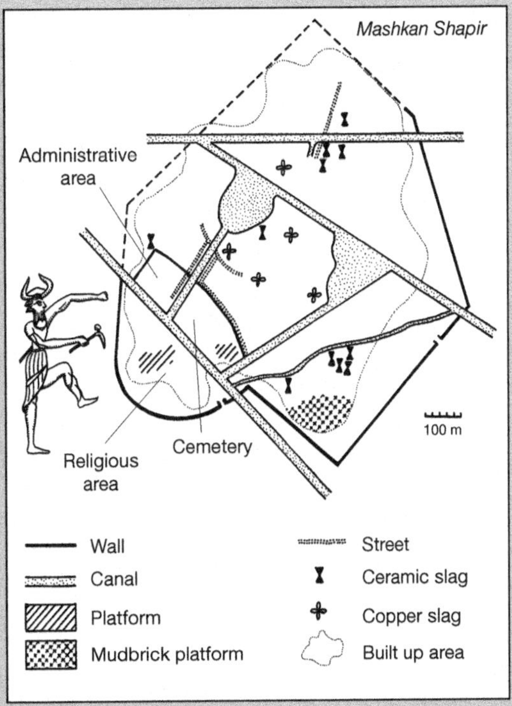

Figure 7.63 *Plan of Mashkan Shapir (and image of Nergal)*

Other research at Mashkan Shapir has concentrated on parallel evidence for decline. The area is now desert but in the Bronze Age irrigation had brought agriculture to the area. The canals were raised above the levels of the fields so water fed into them by gravity. However, in a classic example of negative feedback, the water evaporated and left mineral salts behind. Ultimately the soil became toxic to plants due to salinisation and crop yields fell. Across the region agricultural production may have collapsed for this reason.

Unfortunately war intervened before exploration of the site could be completed. Excavation halted with the first Gulf War in 1990, and since the second (Iraq War), Mashkan Shapir has been comprehensively looted. The site is pock-marked with hundreds of holes where artefacts have been dug up.

The reasons for the emergence of urban centres and cities in general is addressed in Chapter 10 since they are linked with the emergence of states. Where significant amounts of excavation have taken place, it is often possible to piece together the particular reasons for the growth of individual towns. This often reveals the interplay between a range of factors which explain why one small settlement grew rather than another. In Britain, York, Southampton and Ipswich have particularly rich and detailed archaeological archives.

KEY STUDY

Tracing the early development of Ipswich

Ipswich rivals Southampton as the oldest English (rather than Roman) town. Unlike Roman towns, which were founded by a central authority to provide defence or governance in a region, Anglo-Saxon towns grew more organically with commerce initially often more important than politics or ritual. Like most early towns, the original settlement of Ipswich is buried underneath modern houses and businesses so glimpses of it are only gained during redevelopment. However, in addition to regular 'keyhole' excavations, there have been two major phases of urban renewal which have enabled archaeologists to learn a great deal about medieval Ipswich, although only just over 2 per cent of the original town has been excavated (Scull 2009). During the redevelopment of the commercial districts in the 1960s and 1970s, much of the original town centre and manufacturing areas were revealed, while recent conversion of the old port into a university, housing and businesses has enabled study of the original port. Unlike towns which were transformed by industrialisation or war, the layout of the middle of Ipswich preserves elements of one of the earliest medieval street patterns in Europe. This has made it easier to understand locations and enable cross-referencing with historical documents. The earliest of these is a reference in the Anglo-Saxon Chronicle to a Viking raid on Ipswich in AD 919. Before then its development is only known from archaeology.

Context

Ipswich is sited 12 miles up the River Orwell at a point where tidal salt water is joined by the River Gipping. The original name of the town was Gipeswic, with 'wic' possibly indicating a port or deriving from the Scandinavian 'vig' for bay. It was the lowest point where the river could be forded and became a bridging point on a Roman road from Colchester. Medieval Brook Street is thought to be on the line of this road as it climbed above the marshes heading north. Stray finds indicate that there had been prehistoric and Roman settlements in the area and a substantial C2nd AD Roman villa was built 3 miles to the north. The line of Carr Street, which forms the main east–west thoroughfare through the town, was originally a 'corduroy' timber road which may predate the town. The first Anglo-Saxon settlements were a mile west up the Gipping, where Boss Hall and Hadleigh Road cemeteries have been excavated, dating from the C6th AD or earlier. Scull (2009) argues that these largely represent kin-based groups of farmers while Fairclough (2010) claims that they were Germanic warriors, possibly mercenaries. He cites the weapons and Anglian jewellery in the graves and the discovery of Grubenhäuser (▶ p. 495) over the Gipping at Handford. It seems that continental artefacts and possibly people were coming into the area up the rivers but no evidence of a port has been found. It may be that for occasional landings of small trading vessels none was needed.

Early trading growth

In the early C7th AD things changed with the growth of a small town covering about 6 hectares on the north bank of the Orwell by the crossing point. Domestic refuse includes local hand-made pottery and fine, imported Merovingian black-ware and glass. Some of the inhabitants were likely to have still been farmers at this point as field boundaries abut the town but elsewhere there is evidence of greater social

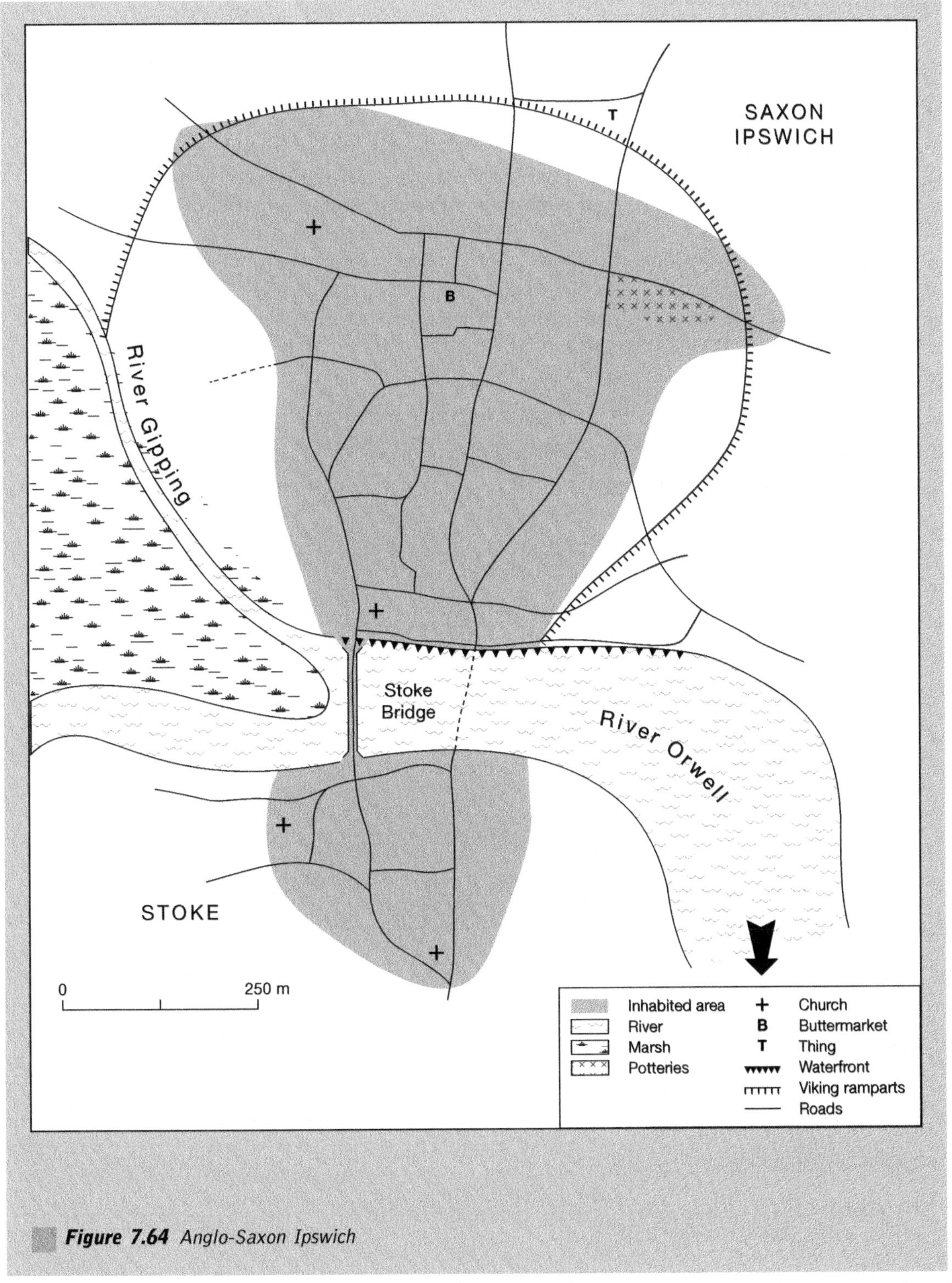

Figure 7.64 *Anglo-Saxon Ipswich*

continued

differentiation. The major C7th cemetery excavated in 1987 during the building of a shopping complex at the Buttermarket included several rich burials. Some had strong continental associations including a log coffin and Merovingian artefacts (Scull 2009). Wade (2001) argues that Ipswich, along with contemporary Hamwic (Southampton) and Lundenwic (London), was an emporium – a trading site contemporary with those emerging on the continent at Dorestad (▶ p. 408) and Hedeby. Emporia may initially have been seasonally active and were not originally manufacturing centres but developed into them. Each emporium is associated with a kingdom. The proximity between Ipswich and the East Anglian royal burials at nearby Sutton Hoo is unlikely to have been a coincidence. All over Europe, rulers were establishing control over trade and one element of that was to concentrate commerce in towns. It may also have reflected growing volumes of trade, not just for luxuries but agricultural produce and key raw materials such as lava quernstones, which were imported from Frisia and the Rhineland (▶ p. 410) and then traded up English rivers.

Figure 7.65 *The Buttermarket excavation with a Middle Saxon street and adjacent posthole structure (copyright Suffolk County Council)*

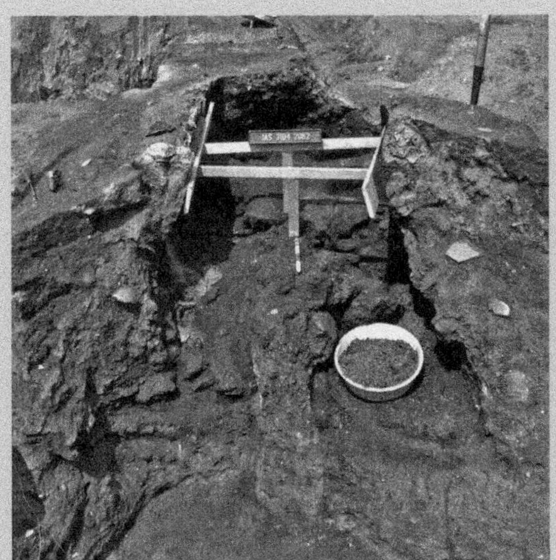

Figure 7.66 *Kiln from the Buttermarket site under excavation (copyright Suffolk County Council)*

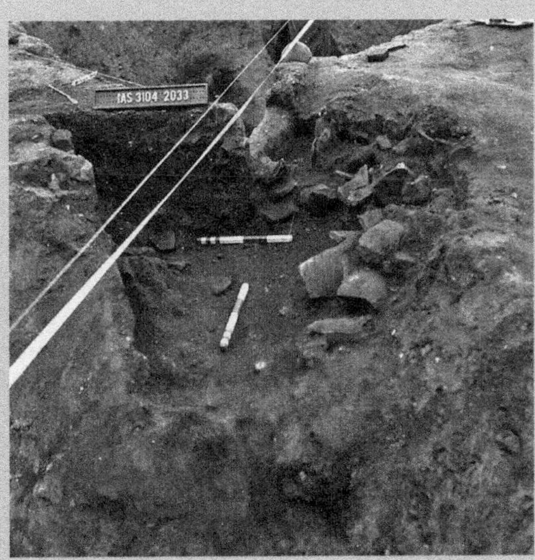

Figure 7.67 *Kiln from the Buttermarket site with chamber excavated (copyright Suffolk County Council)*

The developed town

The town grew rapidly to around 50 hectares in the C8th AD both north of the early settlement and at Stoke, on the south side of the ford. In the C7th, Frisian potters had established England's first large-scale pottery industry along a 160m stretch of Carr Street in the north-east of the town where their kilns and workshops equipped with slow-wheels (▶ p. 412) produced well-fired, quality vessels including the first English pitchers (Blinkhorn 1997). 'Ipswich Ware' came in several different fabrics but the finest, a smooth, grey tableware, is found on higher status sites across England, as far west as Gloucestershire and from the Thames to Yorkshire. It had the widest distribution of any Anglo-Saxon pottery type. Workshops for antler and bone working and metallurgy have also been discovered along with domestic textile production. Different parts of the town appear to have been the focus for particular production including leatherworking near the river, where large quantities of cobblers' waste have been recovered from waterlogged areas (Alsford 1998). Excavation behind the modern dock following the demolition of Cranfield Mill in 2006 also found preserved Anglo-Saxon boardwalks, jetties similar to those at Dorestad (▶ p. 408) and timber revetments, which provided quaysides in water deep enough for ships to reach. Over successive generations further revetments were moved out into the river as land was reclaimed and silting prevented ships from mooring.

Continental links

Imports included Frankish pottery, Norwegian honestones and wine. Wine barrels were frequently used to line wells. One excavated from Lower Brook Street was dated by dendrochronology to after AD 871 and the sequence matched to that of Mainz on the Rhine. Coins from the emporiums of Domburg and

continued

Dorestad (▶ p. 408) emphasise the importance of trade across the North Sea. Exports are likely to have included agricultural produce, wool and possibly fish. The pottery industry continued, now using the fast wheel and producing fine Thetford Ware which was distributed across East Anglia. The wealth of the town is evident from its size, the establishment of significant churches such as St Peter's, and East Anglia's first mint. Silver sceattas (pennies) of King Ælfwald, *c.* AD 713 to 749, are thought to have been produced in Gipeswic and it is likely that it was under his control that a grid street-pattern was laid out, part of which overlay the earlier Buttermarket cemetery. Royal patronage is also hinted at in a dedication found to St Mildred close to the church named after her. St Mildred, who died in AD 700, was linked to the Wuffingas.

Following the conquest of East Anglia by a Viking army, Ipswich was under Danish rule from 869 to 917. During this period earthen ramparts and a ditch were constructed around the town, their position preserved today in the road called Tower Ramparts. Ipswich continued to thrive following the defeat of the Danes by Edward the Elder. Its wealth was evident from Viking raids, the defences, the minting of royal coins from 970, eleven churches and the large number of taxpayers before 1066 recorded in the Domesday Book. During the later medieval period, renewed development saw large religious foundations and merchants' houses built over much of the old area of the town, which testified to its continued importance as a commercial centre and port.

Figure 7.68 *A late Saxon cellared building with a Thetford Ware storage jar from School Street, Ipswich (copyright Suffolk County Council)*

Chapter 8

Economics A: Foraging to Farming

The exploitation of plants and animals

Economics is concerned with how people manage the cultural and natural resources available to them. At its most basic it involves wresting energy from nature to survive. Subsistence is the range of strategies people use to get the food they need:

- **Foraging** is the collecting of wild food. It encompasses hunting or scavenging for meat and gathering plants.
- **Horticulture** is the cultivation of small plots or gardens using digging sticks or hoes. In the tropics these are often created by cutting or burning down jungle (slash and burn) and growing crops for a few years until the soil is exhausted, then moving on to another plot. In some cases it may simply involve weeding and watering particular plants to encourage them. Horticulture is small-scale and cannot support large populations.
- **Pastoralism** is the breeding and herding of domesticated animals.
- **Arable agriculture** involves the use of ploughs to break up the soil and circulate nutrients. Animal traction is used to pull ploughs and large fields of crops are grown.
- **Mixed farming** includes both arable agriculture and animal husbandry.
- **Storage** is a strategy to stockpile resources until they are needed. This encompasses ensuring year-round supplies of food and hoarding produce in order to trade.

Most modern societies have been concerned with far more than just subsistence. A broader definition of economics might include all the ways in which people acquire materials, manufacture products, exchange goods and consume resources. These aspects are covered in the next chapter.

The focus of this chapter is on the nature of subsistence and the exploitation of plants and animals and how we recognise this in the archaeological record. It is organised chronologically with case studies to exemplify each stage of adaptation to changing climatic conditions and then the spread of agriculture. This chapter should be read in conjunction with Chapter 3 for analytical methods and Chapter 5 particularly for the use of ethnographic and experimental analogies. There are also strong links with the archaeology of society. Many writers consider that the type of economic system used largely determines the nature of society. Indeed, archaeologists define many societies according to how they

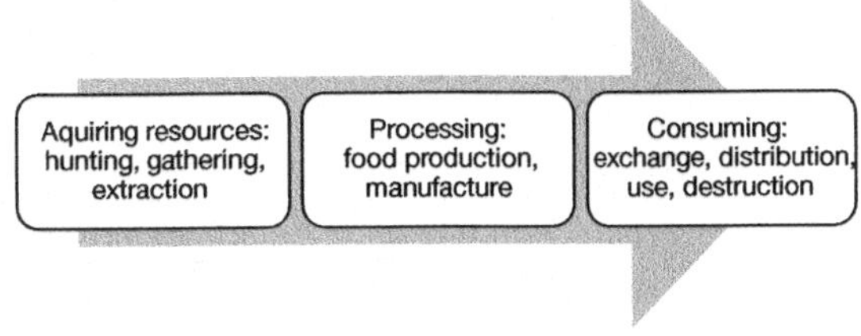

Figure 8.1 *The three stages of economic activity*

acquired their food. For example, foraging economies seem to support fairly egalitarian, small-scale societies (▶ p. 421). Their rituals and rules focus on the group and their relationship with their environment. Agricultural societies which produce a food surplus seem to develop marked social hierarchies and laws and rituals which promote the interests of an elite. A key element in this is productivity. Foraging cannot support high densities of human populations and rarely produces large-scale surpluses. Agriculture can increase the carrying capacity of the land to support large populations and provide surpluses.

SUBSISTENCE: HOW DID PEOPLE IN THE PAST FEED THEMSELVES?

Faced with different environmental challenges, humans have always adapted to minimise the risk of starvation. Archaeologists try to identify the strategies they adopted and the reasons for those choices. 'Hunter-gatherer' is a label used to cover a wide range of societies across over 90 per cent of human history. However, hunting only developed following a very long period of scavenging and gathering. The origins of hunting are discussed in Chapter 6.

THE EXPLOITATION OF ANIMALS

The direct contribution of animals to human economy takes four main forms:

- a source of food products such as meat, blubber, fat or marrow
- a source of secondary food products such as blood, milk, cheese and butter
- a source of raw materials for artefacts, light and fuel including antler, bone, skins, grease, dung, hair and wool
- a source of traction, haulage and transport.

Primary products require the killing and butchery of animals and include meat and bone. Secondary products include food, energy and materials from living animals including dung and wool.

Identifying the nature of exploitation: interpreting bone assemblages

The interpretation of the contribution of animals to the economy of a site depends upon recovering a sufficiently representative bone sample of the animal population and the identification of its age and sex structure (▶ p. 106). Bone assemblages also provide insights into preferred food sources, although the archaeological record has a

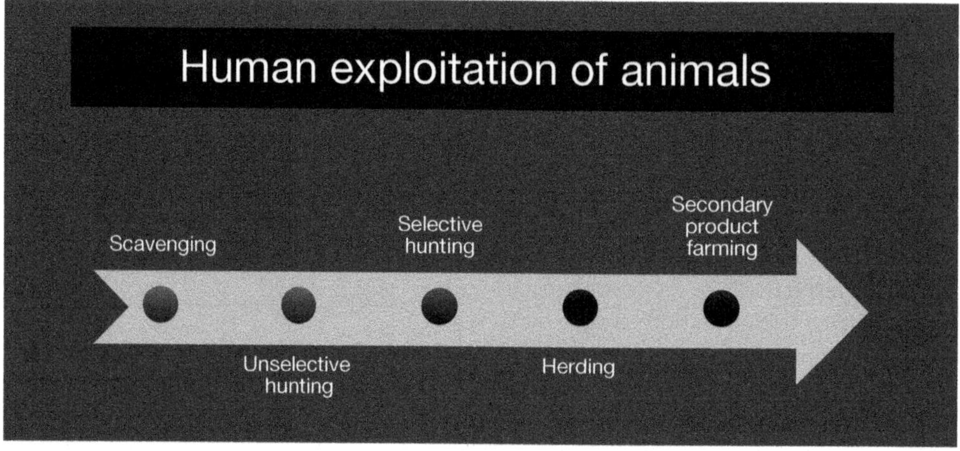

Figure 8.2 *The range of human exploitation of animals*

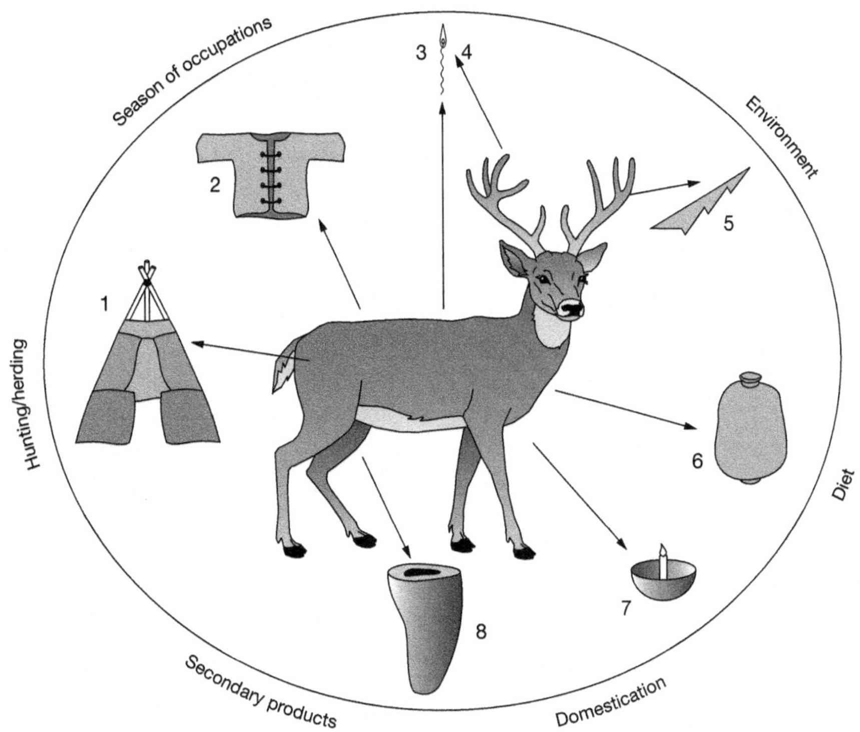

Human exploitation of animals and areas which archaeologists can explore using surviving evidence

Key to primary use of animal

1. skin for tent
2. skin for clothes
3. sinew for thread
4. bone for needle
5. antler for harpoon
6. intestine for water container
7. fat for fuel or lamps
8. meat

Figure 8.3 *Human primary exploitation of animals and some related topics*

preservation bias towards larger bones and large mammals (▶ p. 171). Inferences about the importance of fish and birds can be made from the remains of fish traps, specialist fowling tools or even art, as in Egyptian tomb paintings. Assessing the use of invertebrates, with the exception of molluscs, is much harder. Modern excavation techniques have also added to our knowledge. Animal fats have been recovered from Upper Palaeolithic cave sites while phosphate analysis has been used to identify stalls and paddocks. Tools, once they have been interpreted, are used to make inferences about hunting and processing animals. Use wear marks (▶ p. 94) and traces of blood on tools can also be examined. Experimental archaeology (▶ p. 181) can show the capability of hunting tools and provide insights into the ways in which they might have been used. It can also indicate how the animal was processed through comparison with modern butchery practice and experimental observation of scavenged carcasses. Cut-marks near the joints may indicate butchery for meat while smashing the mid-section of long bones suggests marrow extraction. Experimental studies have demonstrated that many past societies smashed bones to extract marrow fat or boiled bones to get grease. Fat has far more calories than other parts of an

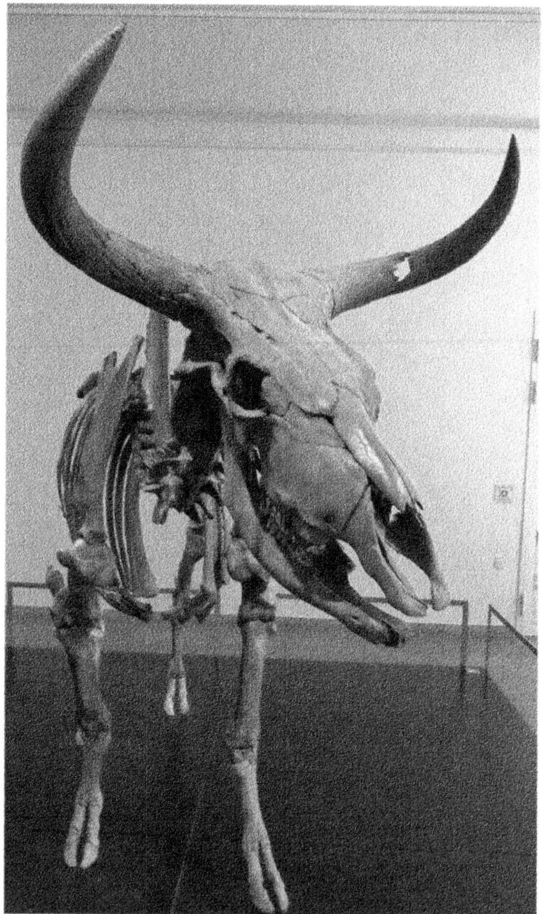

Figure 8.4 The Vig auroch

Standing 2m at the shoulder and weighing around 1000kg, the auroch was a formidable quarry for early Mesolithic hunters in European forests. The skeleton from Vig showed signs of an earlier brush with hunters as well as damage and the remains of three arrowheads from the fatal encounter. The wounded animal swam into a lake where it drowned and which ensured the survival of the skeleton.

Figure 8.5 Healed impact injury on rib of Vig auroch

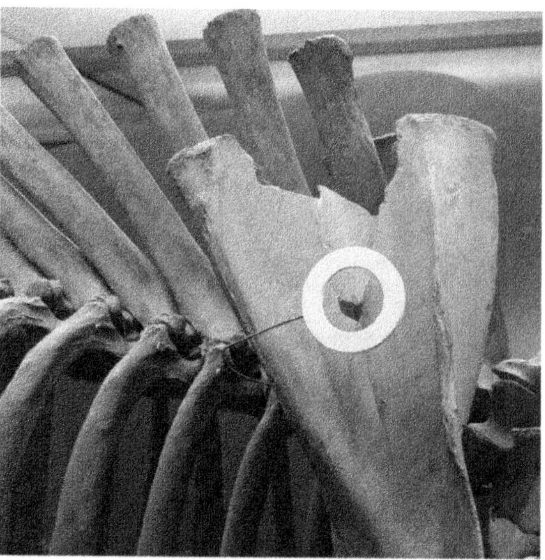

Figure 8.6 Unhealed impact injury on shoulder blade of Vig auroch

animal and was attractive in cold climates or at times of food shortage. This was particularly pronounced amongst the Greenland Vikings. Fat can also be used for fuel, softening skins and waterproofing. Bone assemblages at 'Head Smashed In' (▶ p. 253) suggest that fat was extracted from buffalo, probably for pemmican making. Similarly, angled cut-marks on animal skulls may indicate skinning (▶ p. 312). Assemblages comprising particular meat-bearing bones possibly indicate storage. Their absence from kill sites suggests that consumption occurred at a home base. However, butchery in the past has some differences from modern practice.

TRACING DEVELOPMENTS IN HUMAN EXPLOITATION OF ANIMALS

Scavenging

For most of their existence, humans have been scavengers rather than hunters. This topic is addressed in Chapter 6. For Middle Palaeolithic sites such as Boxgrove (▶ p. 61), the evidence is more ambivalent and archaeologists are often divided over whether hunting or scavenging was going on. The site of Lynford, Norfolk, illustrates the problem. At Lynford gravel quarry in 2002, a Neanderthal flint hand-axe was identified in conjunction with a mammoth tusk by knapping expert John Lord. An excavation was funded by a tax on aggregates. Gravel was stripped away to reveal a dark, peaty layer full of artefacts and bones (Boismier et al. 2012). These included large herbivores such as reindeer, mammoth, horse and bison and predators and scavengers including bear, wolf, hyena and Arctic fox. Herbivore remains were disarticulated, weathered and gnawed. Horse and reindeer bones had been broken to extract marrow. Organic preservation was excellent so soil samples were sieved to 1mm to recover plant remains and microfauna. These indicated that it had been a marshy, treeless environment where grass and reeds were grazed by groups of large herbivores. The climate was colder than today and similar to that of Sweden. The site was dated by optically stimulated luminescence (▶ p. 158) to *c*. 60,000 BP. The remains had been preserved in an oxbow lake by layers of sediment. Several hundred flint artefacts were found including around fifty hand-axes. Debitage (▶ p. 94) showed that these had been brought to the site as blanks and finished off there before being discarded.

The initial interpretation was that it was a mammoth hunting site. Neanderthal hunters either drove animals into the swamp or knew it as a reliable place for animals to become trapped. Either way they turned up prepared for butchery. However, detailed lab-work on the bones and careful analysis of the stratigraphy has called this interpretation into question. Shreeve (2006) noted

Figure 8.7 *What a mammoth trap might have looked like. If only . . .*

that the bones were damaged through weathering and trampling and tools seem to have largely been used to extract marrow from horse, reindeer and woolly rhinoceros. Many of the mammoths showed signs of illness. She interpreted the site as a 'natural freezer' where carcasses from dead animals were preserved for carnivores, including Neanderthals, to scavenge. Smith (2012) also noted that there were no cut-marks on the mammoths and only one possible case of impact marks on a horse. He also suggested that water action may have contributed to the positions of bones and artefacts in the assemblage. While he thinks the Neanderthals exploited many of the animals, he does not accept them hunting the mammoths.

Selective hunting and specialisation in the Upper Palaeolithic

Modern human hunts are more persistent than the charges of predators and rely on cultural knowledge and communication rather than instinct. Hunters often work together, exchange information and share food in base camps. Knowledge is needed – for example, of how to create balanced, aerodynamic spears and where to penetrate large animals to kill them. This requires communication and the debate about modern hunting is closely linked to debates about when human social attributes developed. The evidence for selective hunting includes specialisation. The Upper Palaeolithic has generally been seen as a time of specialised hunting of large animals such as mammoths, horses and reindeer (▶ p. 208). Sites such as Roc de Combe, France, where 99 per cent of remains are reindeer, suggested that some human groups were almost entirely dependent on one species. The final part of the Ice Age, the Magdalenian Period, is sometimes called the 'Age of the Reindeer'. Recently this view has been criticised since it could rely on differential preservation and recovery. Most of our knowledge comes from cave sites, which are easier to find and often have well preserved stratigraphy (▶ p. 52). However, open sites such as Le Flageolet I often have a broader range of prey species including red deer and aurochs. There is also some evidence in the sex-ratios amongst reindeer bones from cave sites that suggests these were used for seasonal hunting and may not therefore reflect the all-year economy. Migrating reindeer move too fast for humans to follow them for long and their populations tended to crash periodically. Focusing on a single species would therefore be a high-risk strategy. Plants and small animal remains survive very poorly from this period and are also generally absent from cave paintings. However, the existence of fishing technology and possibly textiles, impressions of which were found on clay models at Dolni Vestonice (▶ p. 218), suggests that a broader spectrum of food sources was exploited than previously thought. There is currently a major debate over both the extent of specialisation during this period and whether it marked a significant change in strategy. Most kill profiles are attritional (▶ p. 110), while specialised artefacts indicate sophisticated hunting technology.

KEY STUDY

Stellmoor and specialised reindeer hunting

Discovery and excavation

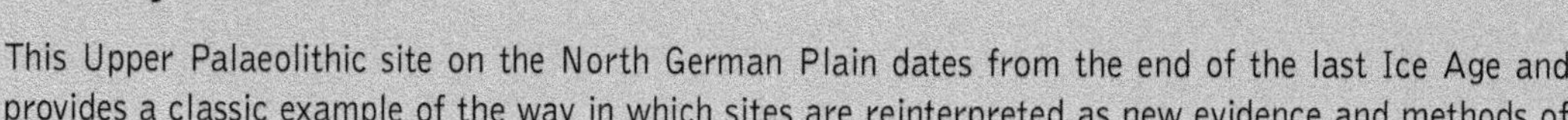
This Upper Palaeolithic site on the North German Plain dates from the end of the last Ice Age and provides a classic example of the way in which sites are reinterpreted as new evidence and methods of

analysis emerge. In 1930, Alfred Rust, an amateur archaeologist, began exploring the Ahrensburg 'tunnel' valley north-east of Hamburg. This 'U-shaped' valley had been formed by glaciation and the bottom was covered in thick layers of peat where a lake had existed after the glacier melted. Rust's first discoveries were made at Meiendorf on the north side of the valley. Here, on the sandy terraces above the marsh, he discovered large numbers of lithic artefacts from what became known as the Hamburgian Culture. The following year he extended his excavation to a large area of boggy meadow on the edge of the marsh, where he recovered more artefacts including antler points along with faunal remains, particularly reindeer. During 1932–4, he switched his attention to another wet meadow on the south side of the valley which was overlooked by Stellmoor Hill. This part of the valley narrowed from around 400m to a bottleneck only 150m in width. Rust used coring to explore the site and then pumps to drain the waterlogged sediments during excavation. This site had further Hamburgian deposits but these were overlain by a 5m layer packed with material from the later Ahrensburgian period. These deposits were the product of many episodes of hunting over a long period. They included wooden tools, lithics and carved bone. A further Hamburgian site at Poggenwisch was excavated later. Typologically, Hamburgian assemblages were distinguished by 'shouldered points' similar to Magdalenian examples from France while Ahrensburgian assemblages contained 'tanged points'. Huge quantities of faunal remains were found, again dominated by reindeer. There were also the remains of what appeared to be a pine post. Close by, Rust recorded several rings of stones which he interpreted as 'tipi rings' used to anchor skin tents.

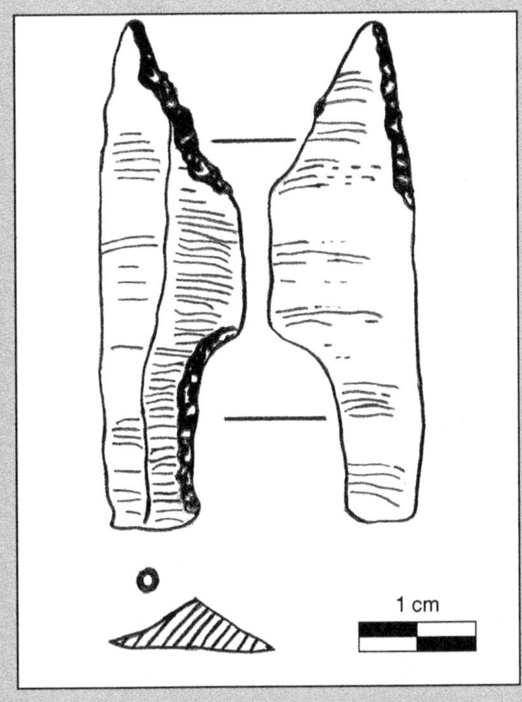

Figure 8.8 *Hamburgian shouldered point*

Artefacts and ecofacts

At Meiendorf, Rust found flint points which may have been fired from atlatls and evidence of the 'groove and splinter' technique of producing needles or points from antler. At Stellmoor he found 105 long pine arrowshafts. Thousands of tanged points (arrowheads) were also recovered including two with their tangs still embedded in shafts. These are the first clear evidence of the use of bows in the world. Other pieces of pointed wood may have been the remains of a bow. Other tools included axes, harpoons and a possible mattock. A number of decorated artefacts of amber, wood and the ribs of horse or elk were also found. Most of the hundreds of animal bones Rust recovered were reindeer. This included twelve complete skeletons from the Ahrensburg layer, some of which appeared to have been weighted down by stones placed in the thorax (chest cavity). Rust reported that these were all adult females,

continued

Figure 8.9 *Possible dwellings used at Stellmoor. Tent shapes from northern Eurasia: conical (tipi), dome, ridge (after Faegre 1979).*

although his zoologist, Kollau, reported them as being of all ages and including males (Bratlund 1996). At least 1,300 antlers were recovered, mostly from male animals. Other species included elk, horse, wolf, marten, hare, beaver, swan, ptarmigan and water birds. In the case of at least one fox, cut-marks associated with skinning were discovered.

Interpretation

Rust proved that Palaeolithic people had adapted to a tundra environment. He drew on ethnographic examples from Canada and Eurasia and used the antler and water bird evidence to interpret Stellmoor as the summer camp of specialist reindeer hunters. They had travelled north during the brief Arctic summer to ambush migrating herds at an ideal point in the valley in what is known as an intercept strategy (▶ p. 237). The pine post may have been from a fence used to direct animals towards the ambush or to provide cover for hunters – a technique used by Native Americans. From the predominance of male antlers he believed they were selectively killing mainly male animals. The finds from the Ahrensburg Valley seemed to confirm the impression from cave sites and cave paintings in France that the Late Palaeolithic was a 'Reindeer Age' where people depended upon one species for all their needs. Rust interpreted the complete animals weighted down in the lake with stones as offerings. Unfortunately many of the artefacts and faunal remains and some site records were lost in the destruction of Hamburg during the Second World War.

Modern dating and environmental evidence

Radiocarbon dates have been allied to environmental data to enable a partial reconstruction of the landscape and conditions at the end of the last Ice Age. The climatic sequence has been based on studies of ^{18}O frequencies in varves (▶ p. 152) and ice cores combined with palynology. Some of the data appears contradictory, which has led to radically different interpretations of the site. Geological research has established that there was a shallow, ribbon-like lake running along the valley floor. Palynological research suggests that by the time the first Hamburgian hunters arrived *c.* 12,500 BP the area had been clear of glaciers for over 1,000 years and had developed into open tundra grassland with occasional scrub consisting of dwarf shrubs of birch, willow and juniper. Populations of reindeer and mammoth were well established. The area seems to have been abandoned during the cold snap of the Older Dryas *c.* 12,000 BP but trees quickly resumed their spread with poplar, birch and pine present during the cold, dry climate of the Younger Dryas down to 10,000 BP. It was during this last phase that the Ahrensburg hunters re-occupied the valley. Pollen cannot distinguish between dwarf and normal trees of a given species but the existence of woodland species such as beaver and bison suggest that in sheltered areas away from the tundra there were probably stands of trees.

Economy and season

The detailed re-examination of the surviving faunal remains by a series of osteologists has challenged many of Rust's original findings. Most of the reindeer were killed in the autumn rather than the summer, although there was also evidence of some low-level reindeer hunting during all other seasons, particularly spring (Bratlund 1996). Examination of the bones rather than the antlers has shown that animals were killed in the same proportions that they exist in normal herds (Weinstock 2000). Other faunal remains also point to all-year occupation of the area with swans, geese and horses killed in the summer (Bratlund 1996). Stable isotope research (▶ p. 133) using teeth and antler samples is being used to try to establish the nature of reindeer migrations. In living animals, bone is constantly replaced and so acquires minerals throughout the animal's lifespan and is not useful as a guide to migration. Antler is grown each summer and provides clues to summer pastures, while tooth enamel develops in a predictable seasonal sequence before birth and in the first two years of the reindeer's life. Some teeth reflect the mother's diet in the spring, others reflect the first summer and winter and so on. Tooth enamel survives well and provides the best prospect of tracing the migration routes. Initial research (Price et al. 2008) comparing reindeer and red deer from the region clearly shows a difference, with the red deer being local and the reindeer migratory. Researchers are divided over which direction the herds were moving in at the autumn kill site at Stellmoor. Bokelmann (1991) argues that they spent the summer in modern Holland and travelled north to spend the winter on dryer pastures close to the Swedish glaciers. Others argue the reverse with reindeer wintering in German forests and travelling north to summer pastures

continued

in Scandinavia or out onto the North Sea Plain. The discovery in Denmark of reindeer remains from both summer and winter adds to the confusion. In southern Jutland at Jels and Slotseng there is another concentration of hunting sites from both Hamburgian and Ahrensburgian cultures within the Nørre valley. Nevertheless, Rust's notion of the hunters migrating long distances following the reindeer herds has largely been discounted. Studies have shown that reindeer average 7km/hour when they are moving slowly and can sustain 10 km/hour for long periods. Humans would not be able to keep up.

No evidence of plant foods was recovered by Rust because techniques for recovering environmental data had yet to be developed. Recent excavations of contemporary sites in France and Spain have shown that acorns, pine-nuts, sloes and rowan berries were being collected, while eggs were on the menu at Pincevent. Further east (Kubiak-Martens 1996) on Polish sites, sedge bulbs, bogbean and thistle seeds were consumed. At Mirkowice burnt bones of fish (especially pike) were also discovered in a hearth, which hints at another resource available close to Stellmoor.

The nature of hunting

Lesions (impact damage) on bones can be analysed to determine the angle and velocity of the projectiles. Rust identified some as having traces of flint in them while subsequent researchers have used experimentation to identify lesions caused by bone points as well as additional flint point damage. Bratlund (1996) found that reindeer from Hamburgian layers had been shot in the side or from behind in the body. In the Ahrensburg layers, animals had been hit from all directions, with one distinctive group shot in the head and neck from behind and above. She interpreted these as hits on swimming reindeer. The hunters predominantly used head shots or shots towards vital organs in order to maximise damage and blood loss. Most animals had been hit several times and lesions were all unhealed, which suggests they were all fresh and there were several hunters. Large numbers of arrows (which had missed) were also found in the Ahrensburg deposits but not in the Hamburgian layers. The backs of many skulls were smashed, which could indicate the clubbing of fallen animals or the removal of brains. Bratlund ascribes the difference between the assemblages to a switch from spears to bows and arrows and a shift in the type of hunting.

Bratlund's (1996) detailed examination of butchery marks on reindeer bones suggests that most animals were skinned, starting with cuts around the feet and up the legs. The head and the sinews in the back were then removed before filletting the meat-bearing bones. The vertebrae, pelvis, scapula and humerus, which are of lowest nutritional content, were the most frequently discarded, sometimes without being fully processed. This was more pronounced in the Ahrensburgian deposits where there was also little sign of systematic removal of marrow from the bones. Two new interpretations have challenged the idea that complete skeletons were sacrifices. One is that they were simply discarded, perhaps because they were not needed for food. The second (Bokelmann 1991) is that they were stored underwater away from foxes and wolves until they were needed. There are ethnographic examples of this from the Inuit and Lapp peoples and it accords with Rust's reports of large stones weighting the carcasses down. The massive difference (9:1) in the ratio of male to female antlers is now thought to be the product of collecting shed male antlers and stockpiling them as they are a better resource. The huge quantities of bone dumped in a nearby lake margin suggest the hunters were processing more meat than they could consume. Ethnographic analogy suggests storage practices could have included caching, drying or making pemmican.

Technology

There is no direct evidence for bows in the Hamburgian layers and most writers conclude that the faunal evidence and points suggest the use of atlatls (spear throwers). By the Ahrensburgian phase, bows were being used. Wood was now more easily available either locally or within the wider region and bows are also more suited to hunting in woodland and at distance than the atlatl. This may explain why people were able to adapt to the area during such a harsh climatic period. The possible campsite at Stellmoor has not been re-examined. At other sites on the North European Plain, depressions or shallow pits, stone slabs, hearths and possible rings of stones (▶ p. 279) have been recorded, which suggest that some form of tents, probably of reindeer skin, were being used.

New interpretations

The ambush site appears to have been carefully chosen just beyond a bend at a narrow point in the valley. The hill of Stellmoor would have provided an ideal lookout point for animals moving in the area. Large herds of reindeer would be driven past the hunters and possibly diverted into the lake shallows where they were shot while swimming. Groups of archers brought the animals down and finished them off with clubs. Most other excavated sites from this period are in similar 'bottleneck' locations on rivers or lakes (▶ p. 204). However, while hunters aggregated in the valleys for the migration hunts, they did not constantly follow the herds. They stayed in the areas for much of the year in smaller groups, hunting other prey by stalking and possibly trapping and gathering, perhaps retreating south in the winter.

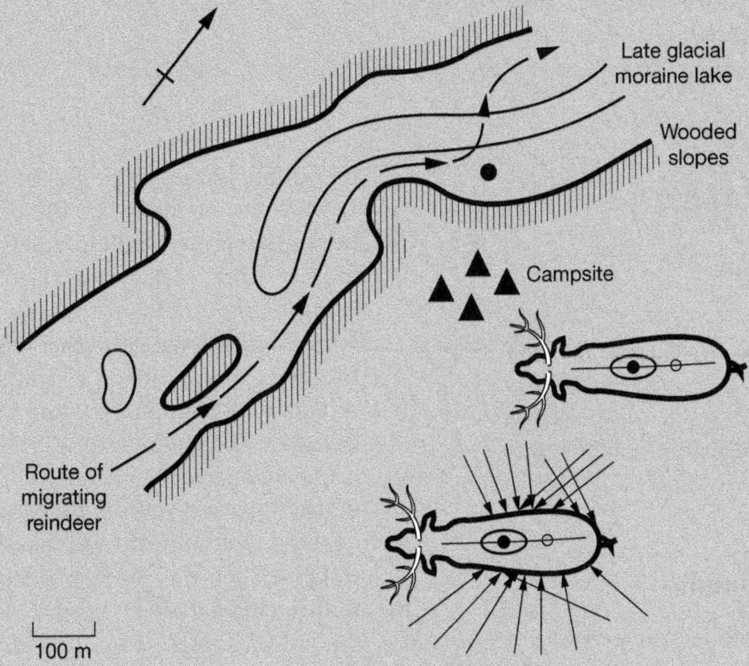

Figure 8.10 *Location of Stellmoor kill site in the tunnel valley*

continued

The stockpiling of antler and possibly meat and the focus on harvesting sinew and skins supports the idea of continued local habitation and suggests that the reindeer drives were about gathering resources to last through the long winter. Research on the finds and other new sites in the region will no doubt lead to further refinements of interpretation.

Figure 8.11 *Magdalenian spear thrower contemporary with Stellmoor, carved from mammoth ivory*

During this period humans domesticated the dog from Eurasian wolves as a hunting companion. The earliest faunal remains of dogs suggest a date of 11,000 BC in the Near East. However, DNA points to 13,000 BC in East Asia as being more likely. Humans adapted to challenging environments using their conceptual abilities and technology. Their material culture transformed their position in the food chain to dominant predator. Knecht's (1994) study of the evolution of projectile points during the Upper Palaeolithic helps explain how they did this. She demonstrated how people used an understanding of design and the physical properties of raw materials to produce increasingly efficient and flexible spears which were easy to repair. Her experiments with a goat carcass confirm the accuracy and penetrative power of spears thrown by hand or by spear thrower or atlatl. Technology enables humans to hunt large, dangerous prey effectively and from a safer distance than previously possible. Spear throwers (atlatls), nets, harpoons and bows were all developed during this period. As with much innovative technology, tools could also be art as expertly carved spear throwers illustrate.

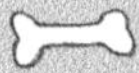 **KEY TERM**

Intensification

An economic strategy to increase productivity from the same resource base; for example, the development of more effective projectile weapons for hunting or the use of two-piece moulds to speed up the manufacture of bronze axes.

Unselective hunting

Any hunting method where any, or all, animals are killed is essentially unselective. The Neanderthals are known to have driven animals over cliffs as at La Cotte de St Brelade, Jersey, and the use of 'buffalo jumps' (▶ p. 253) by modern humans is well documented. The use of walls to funnel herd animals into a killing area is known from the 'desert kites' of Upper Palaeolithic Syria and using fences is known from the C18th in North America. Trapping is another unselective form of hunting. Stone-lined pit traps for migrating reindeer in Scandinavia date from at least the Iron Age (Bang-Andersen 2003) and may have originated earlier in prehistory. The development of fish traps and weirs in the Mesolithic (▶ p. 383) enabled communities to passively hunt fish trapped each day by ebb tides. Their productivity enabled these foragers to become sedentary. Faunal evidence from the Mesolithic site of Ringkloster (▶ p. 316) provides indirect evidence of trapping land mammals. Deadfall traps may have been the method used, but in its simplest form – a rock held up by a stick – it is archaeologically invisible. European fur traders adopted the snares and deadfall traps of Native Americans from the C17th but these techniques were clearly much older. Images of snares are depicted on C11th Mimbres ceramics from New Mexico. The development of boats and nets capable of deep-sea fishing in the Middle Ages (▶ p. 612) intensified the harvesting of fish to feed Europe's growing towns.

UNDERSTANDING FORAGING STRATEGIES

Humans have been hunter-gatherers for most of their existence. Today this part of our history is rarely studied and almost never below university level. In the 1960s attempts were made to explore prehistoric hunting through ethnography. One surprising finding was that even in hostile environments hunter-gatherers spent much less time working than did farmers. Although some have questioned the romantic view of hunter-gatherers as the original affluent society (they were time-rich whereas we are rich in consumer goods), sites with good organic preservation have revealed that they often had rich diets and rich cultures. A second finding was that in most societies the bulk of the food came from gathering. Where a diverse range of food resources was exploited, many archaeologists now use the term 'foragers' to describe the economic strategy. Foragers are not usually nomadic but often move around an area during an annual cycle (▶ p. 229). This is rarely random. It is a strategy to exploit different environments in turn and minimise seasonal shortages. However, not all foragers need this mobility.

Optimal foraging strategy

To try to understand the decisions made by foragers, archaeologists have drawn on evolutionary biology, economics and psychology. A popular concept has been 'Optimal Foraging Theory' (OFT), drawn from predator studies in zoology. It sees behaviour as being shaped by natural selection with decision making based on maximising returns (usually in calories) for the least effort and risk. There are several models of OFT (e.g. diet-breadth and patch-choice) but essentially they work by predicting the likelihood of encountering and killing potential prey in given environments and then estimating the time and effort required to butcher them and transport meat back to base. Foraging for different foods can then be ranked in terms of efficiency in obtaining calories. Since the 1960s both contemporary foragers and the archaeological record have been studied to understand and test predictive models. Joachim's (1976) pioneering study used mathematical models to predict Mesolithic settlement, diet and population densities on the basis of the available resources in the forests of southern Germany. He saw these foragers as economically rational, making a cost-benefit analysis in determining what to hunt and where. He found that the available faunal evidence did fit this pattern, with single species often dominating assemblages at particular sites. He also correctly predicted the importance of locations along the Danube and its tributaries for autumn to spring settlements with summer sites clustering around the Federsee (lake) for fishing and fowling. OFT has been criticised for over-focusing upon large game, whereas ethnographic studies away from polar regions suggest plants and small game are more important. This has led to an over-emphasis on male hunters against female gatherers. While the discrepancy between predicted and actual food remains can illuminate cultural choices, OFT can also promote a one-dimensional view of foragers by minimising social and individual choices in human behaviour. The tendency to only see the Mesolithic in ecological terms was lampooned by Bradley (1984) as 'farmers have social relationships with one another, while hunter-gatherers have ecological relationships with hazelnuts'. There are many instances in prehistory where potential

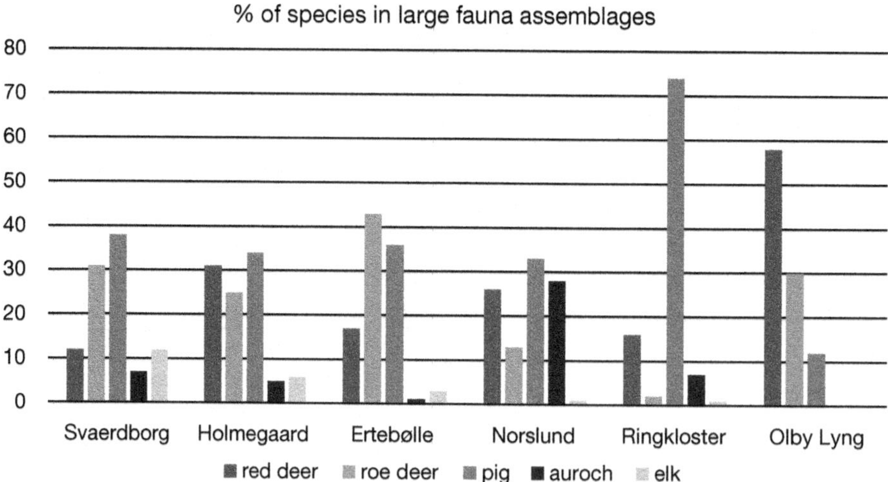

Figure 8.12 *Comparison of faunal assemblages from six Danish Mesolithic sites. Different patterns may reflect specialisation, local conditions or seasons.*

resources have been deliberately neglected or selected for cultural reasons, including possible taboos on eating fish in Neolithic and Iron Age Britain.

Mithen and 'Thoughtful foragers'

Mithen (1990) challenged the deterministic nature of OFT and argued that foragers actively solved problems rather than simply trying to maximise calorific returns. He linked this creative decision making to the way the human mind evolved. He drew on a wide range of ethnographies to show that hunter-gatherers process a vast quantity of data before and during foraging. This includes vegetation changes, weather, tracks and faeces, sounds, terrain and information from other people. Choices are also influenced by taboos, divination, social events and myths. He tested OFT by using computer simulations of different forager strategies, group size and skill levels of hunters and employed the psychological concepts of optimiser (maximiser) and sufficer to create different objectives. Essentially an optimiser seeks the best from a situation while a sufficer just wants sufficient to meet their needs. He then used environmental data to reconstruct large animal population densities for Mesolithic Denmark and southern Germany and used a string of probability calculations such as 'the likelihood of seeing a given animal' or 'the likelihood of killing it with an arrow' to simulate a series of hunting expeditions. He then compared his predicted faunal assemblages for pig, red deer and roe deer for each objective with actual archaeological data from the two regions. The results were striking. In neither region were people hunting the first thing they came across, which suggests that they were not on the edge of starvation. The German hunters fitted a 'sufficer' pattern where they avoided coming home empty-handed, while the Danish hunters appeared to be more choosy – only wanting the best. This tends to fit with other evidence about the richness of the choices available around the Baltic in the Mesolithic (▶ p. 309) and may suggest that hunting large mammals was less vital for sustenance. Already having rich and diverse staple resources, the Baltic foragers may have hunted for prestige, status, feasts, antlers and tusks, seasonal risk-buffering or to supplement seafood diets. Interestingly the two areas also adopted farming in radically different ways (▶ p. 353).

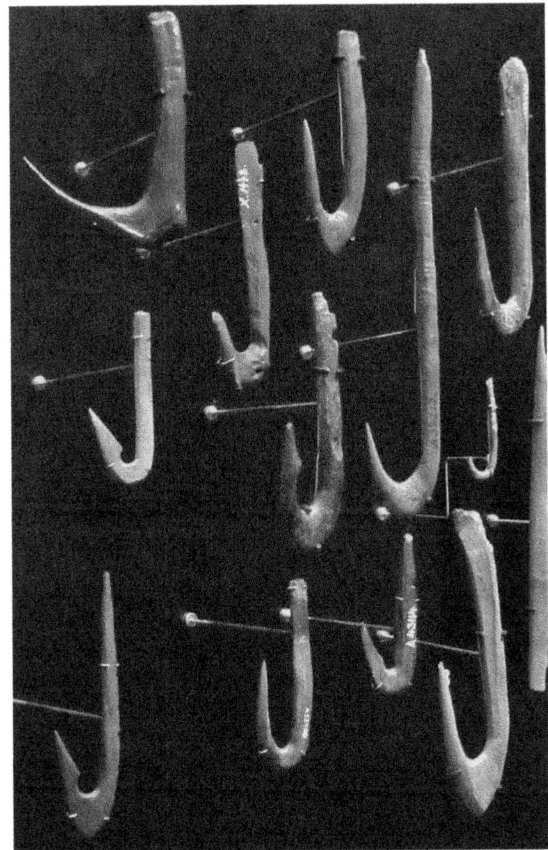

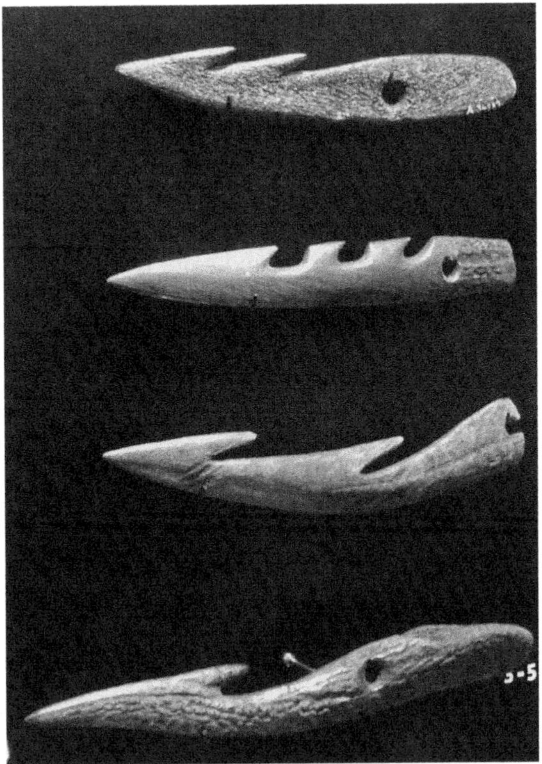

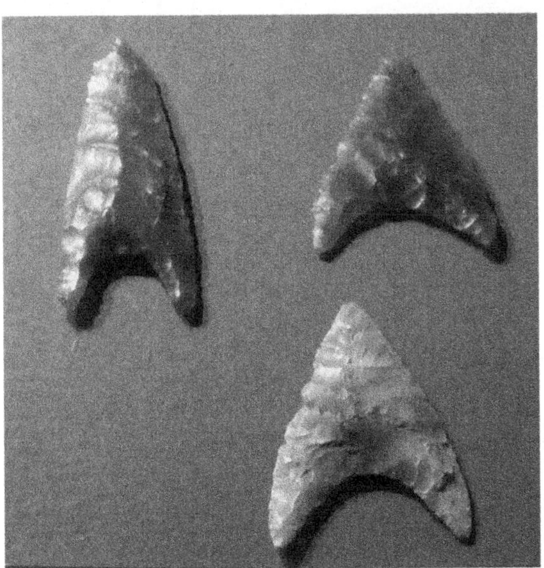

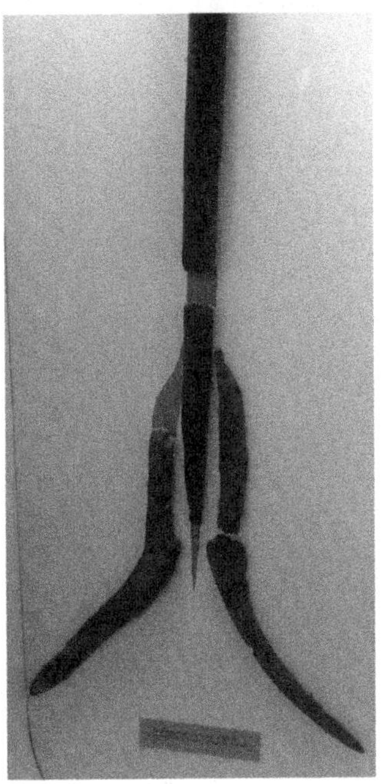

Figure 8.13 *Mesolithic foraging technology including leister (fish spear) and harpoons*

Broad spectrum foraging

If the Palaeolithic was based on 'big game hunting', the Mesolithic saw diversification into a broad range of animals, plants and marine foods. Hazelnuts and shellfish are the most visible in the archaeological record but where there is good organic preservation, birds, marine mammals, fish, seeds, berries and plant roots have all been recorded. Flannery (1969) argued that the extinction of large Ice Age mammals forced foragers to broaden their resource base, which in turn laid the ground work for farming. He called this change the Broad Spectrum Revolution. This increased range of foods is associated with greater sedentism, especially on coasts, rivers and lakes (▶ p. 228) and with a series of technological advances. Mesolithic arrows developed in response to smaller, fast-moving prey in thickly wooded environments. Bows, canoes, fish traps, baskets, pottery, grinding and digging tools are all examples of the way humans adapted to living in new eco-systems. The best-known examples are the Ertebølle Culture of Denmark and Scania (southern Sweden) but similar cultures existed at many other points around the Baltic and North Sea coasts from Finland to Holland. Continuity in flint technology and skeletal shape suggests stable populations, while site density and the absence of much disease from human bones suggest that they were well nourished. Isotopic evidence from human bone and a range of specialised equipment suggests an intensification particularly focusing on marine foods.

Fishing equipment included hooks, nets, harpoons and weirs. Remains of whales and sharks in coastal middens may indicate offshore

Figure 8.14 *Recreation of fish trap and midden area at Vedbaek (Ole Tage Hartmann/Rudersdal Museums)*

fishing, although they could simply represent strandings. The faunal assemblages on some sites suggest some specialisation, possibly on a seasonal basis. Examples include fur-bearing mammals and breeding seabirds. Seals in particular may also have been hunted for their fat at lagoon sites such as Skateholm and on islands such as Gotland. Large numbers were killed and several sites have produced rough, shallow bowls which have been interpreted as blubber lamps. Exotic artefacts from inland areas may have been traded for seal oil. Analysis of faunal assemblages indicates selective hunting of deer, pig and aurochs, possibly even herd management of smaller species. Key sites such as Ertebølle, Vedbaek and Skateholm had hearths, pits, cemeteries (▶ p. 531), various structures and their own distinctive pottery. Mobility is a strategy to reduce risk. However, such rich coastal environments and technological innovation allowed Ertebølle foragers to become sedentary. This has been called tethered or radiating mobility, where a band has a main base but task groups go on seasonal foraging trips for short periods. This might be to outer islands to exploit seabirds and seals in the spring or inland lakes for migratory waterfowl in the winter. The increase in investment in a site through burials and the building of traps and other structures might eventually lead to a mobility pattern paralleling that of early farmers. Their rich culture is further evidence of the success of their subsistence strategy.

KEY STUDY

Tybrind Vig and late Mesolithic foragers in the Baltic

Discovery and description

Tybrind Vig is a shallow, sandy bay on the west coast of the Danish island of Fyn. Some 6,000 years ago the bay was a lagoon and a hunter-gatherer settlement stood by the inland mouth of the lagoon. This part of Denmark has been gradually sinking since the last Ice Age due to post-glacial rebound or isostatic adjustment. Essentially, much of northern Scandinavia had been pushed down by the huge weight of glaciers. As the ice melted these areas have risen but others have been tilted downwards. Much the same is happening in Britain with Scotland rising and southern England sinking. The effect on Tybrind Vig was that sea levels rose over several hundred years and drowned the settlement. This was a relatively gentle process and parts of the settlement originally at the water's edge and protected by a reed bed were preserved under organic mud called gyttja. This anaerobic sediment preserved an unprecedented range of organic artefacts including wooden tools, textiles and wooden structures. The mud itself has been stabilised by eelgrass, a tough flowering plant that grows underwater and which anchors itself by its spreading rhizomes (mass of roots).

Since the late 1950s amateur divers had recovered Mesolithic artefacts which had eroded out from the protective gyttja and were scattered on the seabed. In 1978 ten summers of systematic excavation began, led by Professor Søren Anderson of Aarhus University. Although the area of roughly 50m x 10m was only in 3m of water and just 300m from the shore, it was a challenging undertaking for the team of mostly archaeology students and volunteer divers. It became the largest submarine excavation of a settlement at that time and post-excavation research continues today. Divers still recover large numbers of finds from the area, most spectacularly in 2007, when a double adult burial was recovered.

continued

Underwater excavation (▶ p. 80) is slow and expensive because it requires a great deal of specialist equipment including boats, pumps and air compressors. Some university research funds and private and commercial donations supplemented volunteers from amateur diving groups. Controlling the progress of the excavation was a challenge to the director, while safety issues were also more pressing than usual. The team innovated in order to contend with water movement, unstable sections and the recovery and first aid for vast numbers of fragile finds. Unusually for a Stone Age site, at least 60 per cent of finds were organic. To support the divers a raft was constructed and permanently moored above the site. Fire hoses were attached to the pumps that sucked sediment away from the excavation and large nails and ranging poles were used to mark out grids. A special 10m section rail was designed to sit horizontally above the seabed. It provided a datum point and guide for grids and incorporated plumb lines for sections. Divers worked on individual 1m grids, plotting artefacts in 3D using acrylic sheets and wax crayons. Larger sheets were literally used to trace sections. Tiny finds which would otherwise have been lost such as fish bones and charcoal were recovered from a 6mm x 6mm mesh in the vacuum pump, one grid at a time. In the most recent excavations, human bones were put straight into plastic bags underwater to prevent DNA contamination. Sediment samples were also taken from around bones to see whether DNA had survived there.

The site

The lagoon had been fed by a series of freshwater streams as well as the sea. This created a brackish environment surrounded by reed-bed swamps and rich in wildlife. Evidence of contemporary Mesolithic activity was found all around the lagoon. The main excavation was of a section of shore, reed bed and open water which included the refuse dump for the site. The settlement area itself had been destroyed by waves during erosion, although evidence from contemporary sites enables us to understand what it would have been like. Radiocarbon dates suggest that activity took place over long periods with dates ranging from 5500 to 4000 BC. This places Tybrind Vig in the Ertebølle Culture from the late Mesolithic.

Stretching into the lagoon were hundreds of pointed hazel sticks up to 4m in length. Some tips were embedded upright in the gyttja. These were the fence-like remains of a major fish weir or trap. Many other examples of these have subsequently been found, notably at Oresund bridge (▶ p. 253), where complete wattle fence panels survived along with metres of posts. These structures provide convincing evidence of woodland management. Coppicing (▶ p. 244) was needed to produce so many long, straight hazel rods. The traps indicate a predictable harvest of fish where basket traps or fish spears would be used to catch fish at low tides. Two types of portable, throated, wicker traps have also been identified which could have been used in the weir or in other locations such as streams. Fish can swim into these but not get out. Other fishing tools at the site included hooks made from red deer ribs (one with line attached), a wooden float and three-pronged fishing spears called leisters. The central prong would pierce the fish while the others would grip it to prevent escape. Knotted lime-bast fibres provide evidence of cordage (string) and also nets. Large numbers of fine wooden points were recovered which some archaeologists believe may have been fish-rakes used to harvest shoals of herring from a boat. Remains of three canoes had survived, the most intact being over 9m long. They were carved from the trunks of lime trees, chosen because lime is light and does not absorb water easily. Each had an oval charred area at the stern and one had a 30kg rock for ballast. The interpretation was that the charring was from a fire used to attract fish, particularly eels, when night fishing using leisters. Paddles were also recovered. These were made from ash with heart-shaped blades which were beautifully decorated with abstract motifs similar to those found on amber, antler and bone at other Ertebølle sites. Evidence of the importance of wood was everywhere, ranging from waste chips from tool making to an elm bow and hazel arrows.

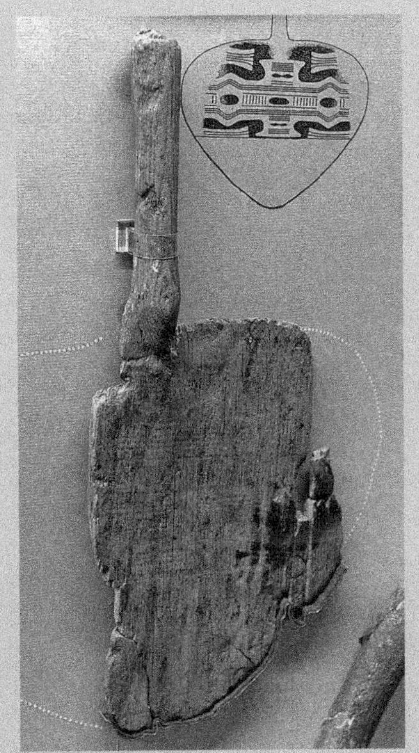

Figure 8.15 *Decorated canoe paddle from Tybrind Vig*

Ecofacts and artefacts

The water's edge served as a dump area. Waste came from the manufacture of bone, antler and stone tools and faunal remains from the animals that had been hunted. Large numbers of bones of fur-bearing animals, particularly pine martens, were recovered. Some had symmetrical fractures on their skulls which may have been caused by traps. Virtually all the cut-marks on their bones are associated with skinning. Other faunal remains included deer, pigs, seal, water birds and shellfish. Every habitat from the deep forest to the reed beds was exploited for resources. In common with most Ertebølle sites this represents broad spectrum (▶ p. 308) foraging; a strategy that minimises risk as well as providing variety. Besides the faunal remains, twenty-three species of edible plant have been identified including acorns and hazelnuts, raspberry, strawberry, crab apple, hawthorn, dock, nettle, fat hen and bulrush.

Figure 8.16 *Remains of Ertebølle culture fish trap*

There was also pottery. Although usually associated with the Neolithic, the Ertebølle had their own distinctive pointy-bottomed pots (pointed either to stand in a fire or to strengthen against cracking). Residue on Ertebølle pots comprised mixtures of blood, plant and fish. Carbon on the bottoms suggests that soups were heated on open fires. Clay had also been moulded to form rough, oval bowls which were probably lamps which burnt seal fat. Although the occupation surface did not survive, some human remains have. Individual human bones and several human burials have been

continued

Habitat	Species	Caught	Most likely method
Brackish water (mix of fresh and salt)	Flatfish (brill, flounder), small species (goby, stickleback, blenny), pipefish, young cod	Lagoon	Static traps and nets, spear
Salt water	Herring, mackerel, wrasse, spurdog, dab, larger cod	Sea	Hook and line, net, rakes (herring)
Fresh water	Stickleback	Streams	Weirs, traps, nets
All conditions	Eel, salmon	Everywhere	All methods

Figure 8.17 *Fish from Tybrind Vig and their environments*

Most of these fish could have been caught in the traps. However, the range of fishing gear and the different habitats of each species caught suggest a variety of fishing methods and locations. Not all the fish may have been for food. Some, such as stickleback and herring, can produce fish oil for lamps or to exchange.

Figure 8.18 *Fox and pine marten skull with cut marks from skinning*

Faunal remains	Spring	Summer	Autumn	Winter
Non-migratory fish				
Migratory fish, e.g. mackerel, eel and salmon				
Fish seasonally in-shore, e.g. wrasse, dab, dogfish				
Plants (Kubiak-Martens 1999)				
Migratory birds (Andersen 1987a)				
Juvenile red deer teeth (Carter 2001)				

Figure 8.19 *Seasonality at Tybrind Vig. There are strong indicators here of both winter and summer occupation. In addition there are remains from animals that were available all year round.*

discovered including the double burial of a teenage girl and newborn baby. Initial carbon isotope results support the idea of marine food being an important component of their diet.

Seasonality

Floral and faunal remains provide important clues to seasonality. There is strong evidence for occupation from summer to winter. There are less clear-cut indicators for spring, although non-migratory species could have been hunted and it tends to be a time of year when sedentary communities rely in part on stored food. Ethnographic evidence from foragers and herders in Eurasia and North America suggests that we might expect them to dry some fish and meat from periods of surplus.

Context

Most of the finds from Tybrind Vig are similar to those from other Ertebølle sites. However, the range of foods and evidence for a wide range of fishing strategies is unprecedented. The Ertebølle culture are named after a classic midden site from Jutland. Although they were called *kökkenmödding* (kitchen middens) because of the millions of oysters and cockles that made up the bulk of the remains, excavation since the C19th revealed evidence of hunting, tools, domestic activity, hearths and burials within the middens. Over 400 such middens existed around Denmark with many more along the Atlantic coast of Europe. As with other Mesolithic groups, the Ertebølle were first identified across southern Scandinavia by their lithic and antler tools. The survival of bones of large mammals such as red deer, pig and aurochs led archaeologists to interpret them as mobile hunters, pursuing game in the forests and coming to the coasts in particular seasons to hunt seals and seabirds and harvest shellfish. Excavations of wet and submarine sites since the 1970s have transformed that view. Instead of being a culture defined by lithics, their culture was based on wood. Wood not only provided most of their tools but also shelter, transport, fishing traps and cordage. Their choice of wood for different tasks shows a great understanding of the properties of different trees while the sheer volume of particular types of timber suggests that they may have been coppicing the forest to obtain it. Was tree management (arboriculture) the first farming in Europe?

Structural evidence from settlements has rarely survived but there is enough to establish their existence. At the submerged site of Ronaes Skae, a complete external clay hearth was found including

continued

Figure 8.20 *Students standing on the remains of the Ertebølle midden*

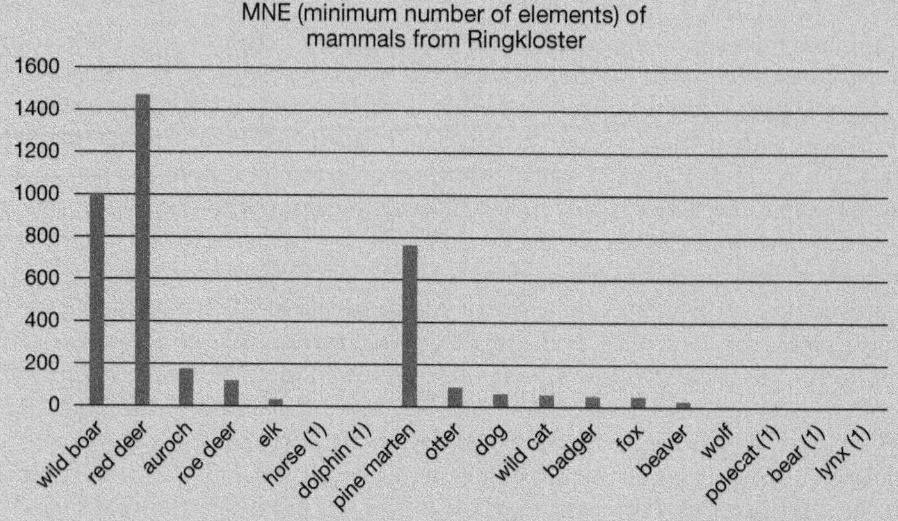

Figure 8.21 *Mammal assemblage from Ringkloster suggesting the specialised exploitation of fur-bearing animals. For MNE each type of bone from a specimen is counted once to avoid distortion due to fragmentation. It provides a more accurate representation of relative proportions of species.*

charred driftwood still arranged in a spoke-pattern and tinder fungus for fire-lighting. At the underwater site of Møllegabet II, the remains of a bark and brushwood platform survived in a hut-pit measuring 5m x 3m and 20cm deep with stakes along the wall line and two posts along its axis. Interpretations have ranged from wood, bark or skin tent structures to log cabins. Also at Møllegabet II, a burial in a lime-wood canoe and a child's bow were found. Cemetery sites such as Vedbaek and Skateholm show some signs of social differentiation while the proportion of individuals who had met violent deaths or recovered from serious wounds suggests competition and perhaps warfare.

The Ertebølle culture calls into question the view of Mesolithic people as mobile hunters. Extensive fish weirs represent a considerable investment of time in both equipment and place.

Figure 8.22 *T-shaped antler axes from Ringkloster. The distribution of these axes may indicate exchange.*

Figure 8.23 *Recreation of Tybrind Vig*

continued

It represents what economists call a delayed-return strategy. Instead of a hand-to-mouth existence, going out to get food when needed, they would plan ahead and then harvest the return. This extensive exploitation of marine resources provides an example of economic intensification (▶ p. 360). There are hints from the faunal assemblages at some sites of the beginnings of herd management (not yet herding) of red deer and of specialisation in hunting, fowling, trapping for fur or sealing. At Ringkloster, huge amounts of antler and the bodies of fur-bearing animals were simply dumped in the lake. This faunal assemblage could simply reflect the local environment but the volume of remains suggests that some hunting was done to provide exchange products including fur, bone rings and T-shaped axes. The existence of exotic finds on Ertebølle sites, including polished stone axes and occasional finds of domestic cattle bones or cereals from the farming communities in northern Germany suggest extended exchange networks. It may also suggest that waterways rather than tracks through the dense forests were the main avenues of travel and communication. The densest concentrations of settlement are on the coast, particularly around lagoons or stream mouths where there was richest variety of habitat and food sources. There is some evidence of contact and movement between some inland sites such as Ringkloster and the larger and more permanent shore settlements. Whittle's (1996) concept of tethered or radiating mobility, where task groups go out from a fixed base for particular purposes, may fit the evidence better than that of mobile foragers.

The cemeteries, canoes, huts, ceramics and the prime locations all suggest a more sedentary population. The numbers of sites and long runs of radiocarbon dates suggest long periods of occupation and relatively high populations. The sophistication of this culture with its impressive technology, abstract art and increasing evidence in burials of social hierarchies has led to the Ertebølle being termed 'complex hunter-gatherers'.

HERDING AND THE DOMESTICATION OF ANIMALS

What is domestication?

Domestication describes the process whereby humans take control of animals through restricting movement and through selective breeding. They gradually change the composition of herds and the nature of the animals themselves. It is a symbiotic relationship since humans exploit the animals for resources but also protect them and ensure that they can access food and water. In regions where domesticates originated, herding may have been the end point of a long period of parasitic herd management or selective hunting during which humans acquired knowledge of animal behaviour. An analogy may be the Sami of Lapland, who only switched from hunting to herding of reindeer in the C17th under pressure (to pay tax) from the developing states of Norway and Sweden.

The timing, nature, location and exact reasons for the transition from hunting to loose herd management to domestication have long been debated. Partly this is because evidence is ambivalent. Morphological (shape) changes in animals, such as reduced horns, smaller stature and less robust bones than their wild ancestors, have been used as indicators of selective breeding. Essentially herders kill the most aggressive animals and breed the docile ones. However, climate can produce similar changes. Most animals have reduced in size since the end of the Ice Age. In situations of strict control – for example, modern dog breeding – changes can occur rapidly but 10,000 years ago there was no understanding of genetics so changes were slow. By the time morphological changes are detectable, herding could have been well established. Consequently, where archaeologists have dated domestication solely from changes in the size of animals or certain features such as horns, they may have underestimated the date at which herding began. Art, artefacts, specialist buildings and burials of humans with animals provide potential alternative evidence but each could apply to wild animals or occur after initial domestication. Where large bone assemblages survive, archaeologists have tried to reconstruct animal populations. Domestic flocks and herds do differ from wild groups since more female animals survive to adulthood in order to maintain breeding numbers whilst excess young males are harvested for meat. Especially in northern climates where animals may need to be fed over the winter, many surplus animals will be killed towards the end of their first year. As a result, faunal assemblages from herding sites tend to be dominated by younger animals and young adult males with fewer, older females.

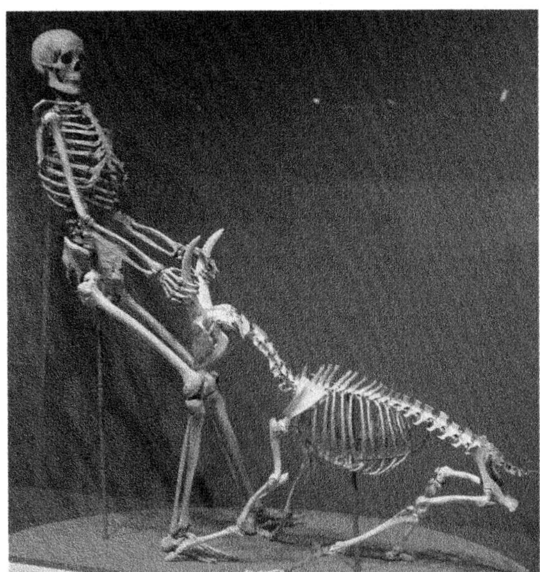

Figure 8.24 *Domesticating goats. The wild ancestors of goats would have been challenging to tame. Smithsonian Museum of Natural History, Washington DC*

Where did domestication take place?

The existence of early farming sites identified the Near East as the likely source of many common domesticates and genetic research into animal DNA has corroborated it. Essentially DNA of wild and modern animals along with excavated remains are compared to establish the closest genetic matches. The number of mutations enables an estimation of time since the two groups separated. Refinements of dating technology and DNA are revealing surprising results. New ^{14}C dates for sheep (from the Asiatic Mouflon) and goat domestication (from the Bezoar goat) around the Zagros Mountains of Iran and Iraq have been pushed back to at least 8000 BC. MtDNA sequences suggest there may have been two independent goat domestications in the same region. Unlike modern sheep, the first domesticated sheep were strong, agile animals and brown haired rather than woolly. DNA research on pigs suggests simultaneous domestication in the Near East and China from wild boar. One study from Hallan Chemi in Turkey detected a significant change in pig bones *c.* 9000 BC with a high number of suckling pigs being killed. If this represents domestication, then it predates cereal farming in the area. Most accounts still see a date of 7000 BC as more likely. The situation in Europe is more complex, with domestication of wild European boars taking place after domesticated pigs were introduced from Anatolia. Larger, and perhaps hardier, European pigs appear to have totally replaced the imported strain fairly quickly.

Cattle in Eurasia (Bos Taurus) and North Africa are descended from the aurochs (▶ p. 109) which existed across a huge region, unlike sheep and goats which had more restricted ranges. In South Asia the zebu was domesticated instead. Aurochs were huge, strong, dangerous animals, which makes them unlikely domesticates and, unsurprisingly, were domesticated later than sheep or pigs. MtDNA research by Bollongino et al. (2012) estimated that as few as eighty female auroch provided the ancestors of all European

Figure 8.25 *Wild and domestic cattle and sheep*

cattle. One possibility is that they were originally captured as status symbols or for ritual purposes. Çatal Höyük, Turkey (▶ p. 284), is one of a number of locations where cattle horns are found in what appear to be ritual sites but it is unclear whether the animals there were domestic or wild. Morphological changes put domestication at *c.* 6000 BC but DNA research has pushed it back closer to 8000. Some recent DNA research (Beja-Pereira et al. 2006) suggests that domesticated cattle may also have reached Spain from North Africa.

Pastoralists

Domestication required adaptation by human populations. Animal husbandry may have replaced hunting but was more labour intensive. Flocks needed moving between pastures, protecting from wolves and feeding through the winter. Initially this may have led to specialist roles such as shepherds and herders within families or communities but at some point communities arose which relied largely or almost entirely upon their herds for food and resources. These were pastoralists, a term which covers a wide range of strategies. At one extreme are modern livestock farmers with sedentary flocks and herds which are fed in barns on relatively small farms. They control all aspects of an animal's life, dictating where it feeds (by creating fields), dictating its mate (by creating single-sex herds) and so on. At the other extreme are nomadic pastoralists who move their herds and their families between seasonally available pastures over vast distances. The best-known examples are in central Asia and Mongolia, such as the Kazakh and Mongol peoples, but the Tungus reindeer herders of Siberia and Bedouin of North Africa are also nomadic pastoralists. Much of this region was unsuitable for early arable agriculture and a dominant idea is that pastoralists were originally poorer farmers who were forced onto marginal land. These semi-arid areas cannot support large herds for long or regular periods and so mobility is the only strategy. Horses, camels and yaks were herded in this way as well as sheep and goats and, to a much lesser extent, cattle. Sheep and cattle herding had spread around the Caspian Sea to Turkmenistan by 6000 BC and faunal remains document the spread onto the Western and Kazakh Steppe after 4000 BC. This was the region where the Botai culture had just domesticated the horse (▶ p. 458), the use of which can be traced spreading in the opposite direction during the 3rd millennium BC (▶ p. 459).

Transhumance

In between the extremes of sedentary and nomadic pastoralism is transhumance. Transhumance pastoralists take their animals up onto high mountain pastures in late spring and return to the valleys in autumn. This practice continues today across much of Europe including the Alps and Carpathian Mountains. The earliest signs in the Alps were changes in faunal assemblages during the 3rd millennium BC at lakeside settlements such as Lagozza in Italy. An increase in the bones of mature young adults suggests produc-

Figure 8.26 *A transhumant flock on the annual journey to the mountain pastures*

tion for meat alongside existing dairy herds. Beef animals can be raised further afield than those that require regular milking. This suggests a wider area was being exploited and given the limited space in the valleys, alpine pastures are the most likely. 'Layer-cake' deposits in some upland rock shelters in the late Neolithic have been interpreted as seasonal sheep and goat droppings and charcoal sandwiched between white silt from the rocks themselves. Signs that the upland meadows were being exploited include an increase in finds generally, evidence of copper working in the mountains and most famously the discovery of Ötzi the Ice Man. Palynological research to the north of the Vinschgau valley from which he is thought to come have revealed an increase in meadow plants, which are indicative of pasture, from *c.* 4000 BC. However, these can also occur as a result of increased rainfall due to climate change. Deforestation, soil erosion and the remains of herders' shelters are other potential clues. A current project by the University of Innsbruck is searching for evidence of temporary settlements and shelters on modern transhumance routes in the Vinschgau area in order to test the transhumance model (Oeggl 2008). Isotope analysis on faunal remains at the LBK settlement of Vaihingen (▶ p. 350) suggests that distant pasturing had developed as early as the 5th millennium BC.

Elsewhere evidence of transhumance includes shelters built by herders and possibly rock art (▶ p. 232). In Scotland, the word 'shieling' means both a summer pasture and a shelter and both are indicative of transhumance farming of cattle up to the early C19th. Ruins of stone-built shielings often occur in small groups, close to water in upland areas and occasionally with small areas of cultivation (rigs) alongside. Corn-drying kilns and occasional whisky stills suggest additional economic activities alongside pastoralism at some of these sites. Few have been excavated and

Figure 8.27 *Shepherds' huts in the Cretan mountains*

dating material is scarce so we currently know little about the development of this way of farming. In the Balkans, where sheep transhumance remains important, a project comparing faunal remains from valley and high altitude sites has tried to identify its origins (Arnold and Greenfield 2006). In a transhumance economy, the faunal remains from the two areas should be complementary. The sheltered sites should have remains of animals culled in the winter and also very young animals that died at birth or in their first months. Upland sites would be expected to have bones of juvenile animals and particularly animals killed during the summer. Three methods were used for ageing: the pattern of tooth eruption, tooth wear and cementation analysis. Cementum is the surface layer of the tooth root which grows in annual cycles. A stained cross-section of the tooth root examined under a microscope reveals rings in much the same way as dendrochronology. The study revealed no change in patterns of pig bones but in the early Bronze Age remains of sheep and goats began to conform to the transhumance model, with cattle

Sheep and goats

	0–2 months	2–6 months	6–12 months
lowlands			
highlands			

Cattle

	0–1 month	1–8 months	8–18 months
lowlands			
highlands			

Figure 8.28 *Faunal remains indicative of transhumance (after Arnold and Greenfield 2006)*

doing the same in the late Bronze Age. This accords with pollen and settlement evidence which shows the first colonisation of the upland areas in the Chalcolithic. It would take time for clear patterns to emerge and suggests that social and economic pressures during that period (▶ p. 461) led to strategies to exploit what had been marginal land. References to shepherds and their way of life in pre-classical Greek literature attest to the economic importance of transhumance by late Bronze Age.

THE EXPLOITATION OF PLANTS

For foraging peoples, research has focused on identifying which plants they used from plant remains and specialised artefacts such as digging sticks and grinding stones. Site catchment analysis has been used in conjunction with environmental data to suggest possible resources. Glimpses of the range of non-food uses of plants have been obtained from sites with exceptional preservation. Nets, boats and clothes (▶ p. 383) have been recovered from later prehistory and probably represent only a fraction of plant uses. With the development of pottery, twisted cord was used for decoration, suggesting that the use of rope was well known. In the historic period, the economic importance of agricultural produce means that there is considerable historical documentation of various sorts, including the earliest writing (▶ p. 415), and artistic sources that provide information on techniques, organisation and productivity.

In most parts of the world foraging was followed by agriculture, which provided the economic basis for life up to the Industrial Revolution. Sedentary farmers are usually associated with societies from the last 10,000 years. In some regions they were preceded by mobile horticulturalists whose pattern of farming was very different from that of arable (crop) agriculturalists of historic times. Most farmers have practised animal husbandry, the rearing of animals for food, alongside arable (crop) farming.

The Neolithic revolution

The shift to food production has rightly been seen as the most significant single change in human history. For over 90 per cent of our existence as a species we were foragers and it is only in the last 10,000 years that the huge changes in terms of population, technology and society which make up the modern world have occurred. These would have been impossible without agriculture since foraging cannot support very large or dense sedentary populations. Urban civilisations (▶ p. 284) developed because they could be fed with cultivated wheat, barley, millet, rice, maize or potato. The Neolithic (or New Stone Age) was identified from the introduction of pottery, new stone tools such as querns, sickles and polished axes, settled village life, domesticated plants and animals and crafts such as spinning and weaving. Relatively speaking this was a rapid change in human evolution and before the advent of accurate dating methods the discovery or adoption of a range of domesticates appeared to have happened simultaneously. The phrase 'Neolithic Revolution' was coined in the 1920s by Gordon Childe, who was influenced by Marxist ideas about society evolving through a series of revolutions. He saw it as a Stone Age version of the Industrial Revolution. Working backwards from his own excavations at Skara Brae on Orkney, Childe traced the spread of Neolithic artefacts through the Danubian (▶ p. 346) culture of central Europe from the Near East. Here in the area already referred to as the 'fertile crescent', he argued that agriculture had begun. It was also the area where the earliest civilisations then developed. However, subsequent discoveries have shown that domestication occurred independently in other areas of the world, particularly South and Central America and East Asia. Nevertheless, the Near East has the earliest dates for the shift to farming and is the focus for the rest of this section.

Figure 8.29 *The 'Neolithic package'*

The classic assemblage associated with the introduction of agriculture included domesticated plants and animals, a new range of tools including grindstones, polished stone axes, and pottery. The 'package' for southern Scandinavia is shown here. There are slight regional variations but the essence is similar. For southern England substitute Windmill Hill Ware, polished axes and long barrows.

What is plant domestication?

As with animals, plant domestication involves a series of changes, some of which can be identified archaeologically. Essentially the process begins with a desirable wild plant being encouraged through weeding, watering or helping plant its seeds. The latter point is key. Once humans understood that cereals grew from the seeds they had been harvesting, they were able to deliberately replant in suitable habitats. This must have been a long period of experimentation with many 'blind alleys' involving unsuitable plants, soils or locations. By replanting seeds from preferred plants, genetic changes start to multiply. This might involve selecting plants with the largest seeds, those which ripened most quickly or those where the seed heads did not shatter as easily during harvesting or could be stored the longest. All these slight differences arise from naturally occurring genetic mutation in plants but human intervention ultimately made some mutations particularly successful. Sometimes two plants would hybridise to form a new variant. While foragers would not have understood the science behind this, they would have recognised a better plant and encouraged the spread of the most useful hybrids. This process will have been the same for all potential crops once similar discoveries about planting tubers (roots) or cuttings had been made. Agriculture appears to have begun with small seeded cereals which are relatively inefficient to gather and process. It may be that experimentation with cultivation was a stop–start process, only worth bothering with during periods where wild food became scarcer.

Domestication implies an increase in dependence on a narrow range of plants which were exploited intensively. This involved modifying the land through clearance, weeding and perhaps irrigation. The range of early domesticates native to the Fertile Crescent included the cereals einkorn and emmer wheat, barley and rye and legumes such as pea, broad bean, lentil, bitter vetch and chickpea. Flax also grew in the area and was useful as a source of both linseeds and fibre for cordage and later textiles. Later, fruit and tree-crops such as plums, grapes, figs, olives and almonds would be added. Settled agriculture is known in the Fertile Crescent from *c.* 10,000 BP,

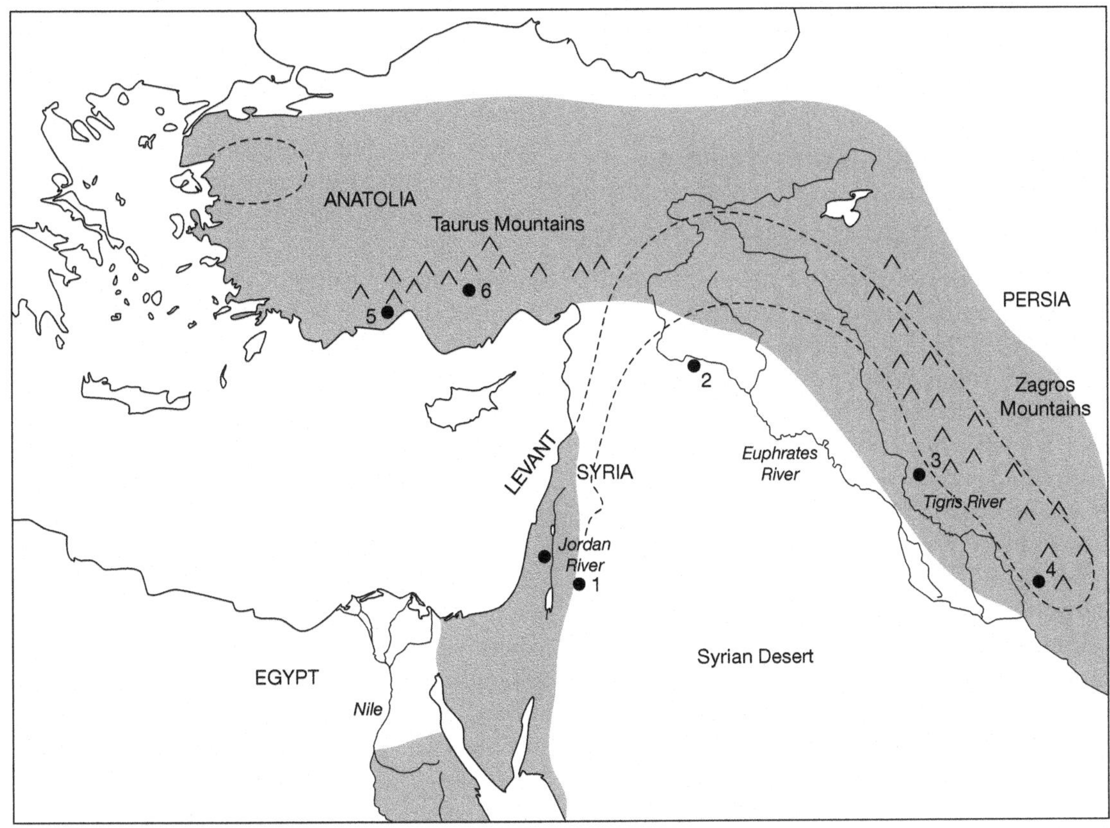

Natural habitat of wild sheep and goats

● Key early farming sites. 1 Jericho. 2 Tell Abu Hureyra. 3 Jarmo. 4 Ali Kosh. 5 Hacilar

● 6 Slightly later site of Çatal Höyük

Natural distribution of wild grains including Emmer and Einkorn wheat and barley. Note the crescent shape this makes

Figure 8.30 *Map of the Fertile Crescent. The two 'wings' of the crescent provide very different environments: in the north and east the 'hilly flanks' of the Taurus and Zagros Mountains and in the west the 'Levantine corridor' of the Jordan valley and desert oases. Woodlands, grassland and semi-arid zones are in close proximity, providing access to a broad spectrum of resources. These included sheep, goats and cattle and a range of cereals.*

from where it spread south to Mesopotamia and the Nile valley, east to the Indus valley and north into Anatolia. Up to eleven other 'hearths' independently domesticated different packages of crops and animals. In China millet, rice and soya were domesticated *c.* 9500 BP, probably followed by pigs. Thailand was also a 'hearth' for rice around the same time and probably chickens, while New Guinea appears to have domesticated the root crop taro. Potatoes and beans were grown in South America from 8000 BP with corn (maize), squash and peppers in Mexico shortly afterwards.

EXPLAINING THE CHANGE TO FOOD PRODUCTION

Until the 1960s agriculture was assumed to be superior to foraging and the change seemed a natural step in human evolution where our ancestors left the other animals behind and began to control nature. Once people understood that planting seeds could produce crops on demand, they would settle down and start farming. However, ethnographic research with hunter-gatherers (Lee and DeVore 1968) showed that foraging was in many ways easier than farming. Despite foragers all over the world having great knowledge of local plants and animals, it is only in a limited number of regions that people began farming. In much of the world, foraging remained the major strategy until recently, including some, such as Australian Aborigines, who encourage particular plants to grow through 'firestick farming'. Recent oesteological research has shown early farmers were less healthy and possibly less robust than earlier forager populations. They also suffered more from disease and periodic bouts of malnutrition (Cohen 1991). If agriculture was a choice rather than inevitable progress, then the reasons for that choice needed explaining. The most common view is that it was an enforced choice. Theories emphasise one of a number of factors which pressurised people into abandoning a successful way of life. Some explanations reflect academic fashions but new discoveries and advances in the many branches of science involved constantly provide evidence to support one theory rather than others. Currently there is no consensus about why farming began.

Early theories of domestication

Childe did not believe that progress was inevitable without a shock that forced people to innovate. The Oasis theory he developed from Pumpelly's work offered an early environmental explanation. At the end of the last Ice Age the climate became very dry, leading to the spread of deserts (desiccation). Human and animal populations were forced into restricted ranges close to water such as the Euphrates Valley. Through close association people gained the knowledge which enabled domestication. This version paralleled the biblical Garden of Eden but was undermined by the advent of radiocarbon dating which showed that other sites in the region domesticated first. Climatic data in the 1950s also suggested a trend to wetter rather than dryer conditions. An alternative location was provided by Braidwood's Hilly Flanks hypothesis. He argued that a more likely location for agriculture was on the lower slopes of the Zagros Mountains of Iraq above the dry floodplains of the River Tigris. This was where wild relatives of early domesticated plants and animals still lived. His pioneering environmental research from the 1940s at the early Neolithic village of Jarmo revealed evidence of many early domesticates and processing artefacts. He argued that domestication occurred across the Fertile Crescent in this kind of habitat as foragers became sedentary due to the wealth of plant and animal resources. However, he was unable to offer an explanation of why agriculture replaced foraging beyond the time being right. A key problem is that farming requires a very different mindset from foraging. Foragers acquire most of their food each day except in the most extreme environments where storage strategies become essential (▶ p. 363). They have an immediate return on investment of effort. Agriculture is a delayed-return system where considerable effort is invested for an eventual reward – assuming the harvest is good. Archaeologists needed to explain why people would give up an easy life.

Demographic theories of domestication

In the late 1960s many archaeologists turned to population growth as the key factor. In Sauer's Hearths Theory, foragers settled in areas with good resources and began to experiment. They developed some aspects of farming and storage to make up for lean periods of wild resources. Ultimately, populations rose and farming became essential. Binford's Edge Zone hypothesis suggested that as sedentary forager populations within the Fertile Crescent grew, they expanded into more marginal areas where they were forced to begin cultivation to ensure enough food. These demographic models assumed sedentism occurred before farming. Cohen, in *Prehistoric Food Crisis* (1979), addressed the issue of timing by arguing that successful hunters had eliminated large herbivores at the end of the last Ice Age whilst raising their own population levels so they had to focus on plant foods in order to survive. However, there is no evidence for very high population densities in the key areas. A variation was provided with Flannery's 'Positive Feedback Model'. He also argued that the decline in large herbivores led to a shift to broad spectrum foraging including small seeded grasses. These provided a low return in calories for the effort of collecting them but could be gathered by women and children in large quantities during annual harvests. As a result, foragers became sedentary. These wild foods responded to humans spreading their seeds and perhaps clearing away other plants by growing in dense stands. An increase in available nutrition enabled forager populations to rise and to expand into new areas. Eventually human populations grew to exceed the natural carrying capacity of the land. There could be no going back to foraging and so more intensive cultivation of cereals developed. This theory of one change leading to a 'feedback' response works best with corn/maize in Mesoamerica, which mutated in spectacular fashion from the small-seeded grass teosinte to the large ears of early maize. Nothing quite fits with this theory in the Near East and it cannot explain the different timing of agriculture in different regions nor why some regions with potential domesticates did not cultivate them. Ethnographic research has also shown how foragers maintain stable population size through mechanisms such as extended breast feeding. A question remains over whether rising populations led to agriculture or whether it was the other way round. A different way of looking at the problem was provided by the co-evolution ideas of Rindos. He argued that humans adapted to plants and animals as much as they adapted domesticated crops and herds. Humans modified other species to suit themselves and increase productivity but then had to change their own behaviour to ensure their supplies of food – for instance, by tending crops and looking after herds. However, this does not explain why some foragers did not make the change.

Social theories of domestication

The 1960s had seen archaeology borrow models from ecology and geography but the 1970s saw more emphasis on people making choices as social actors. A different range of ethnographic accounts provided new concepts and ideas. Prominent examples were the Bigmen of Papua New Guinea, who gained fame through competing at pig-feasts (Moka), and the Kwakiutl of the Pacific coast of North America, with their potlatches (▶ p. 399). Hayden (2009) argued that prospective leaders from the Mesolithic onwards may have gained prestige and shown their power through feasting (▶ p. 427). In order to do this they needed to assemble large surpluses of food and other resources. They achieved this with new technologies such as the use of static fish traps (▶ p. 315) and by developing storage (▶ p. 363). Food production was another element in a

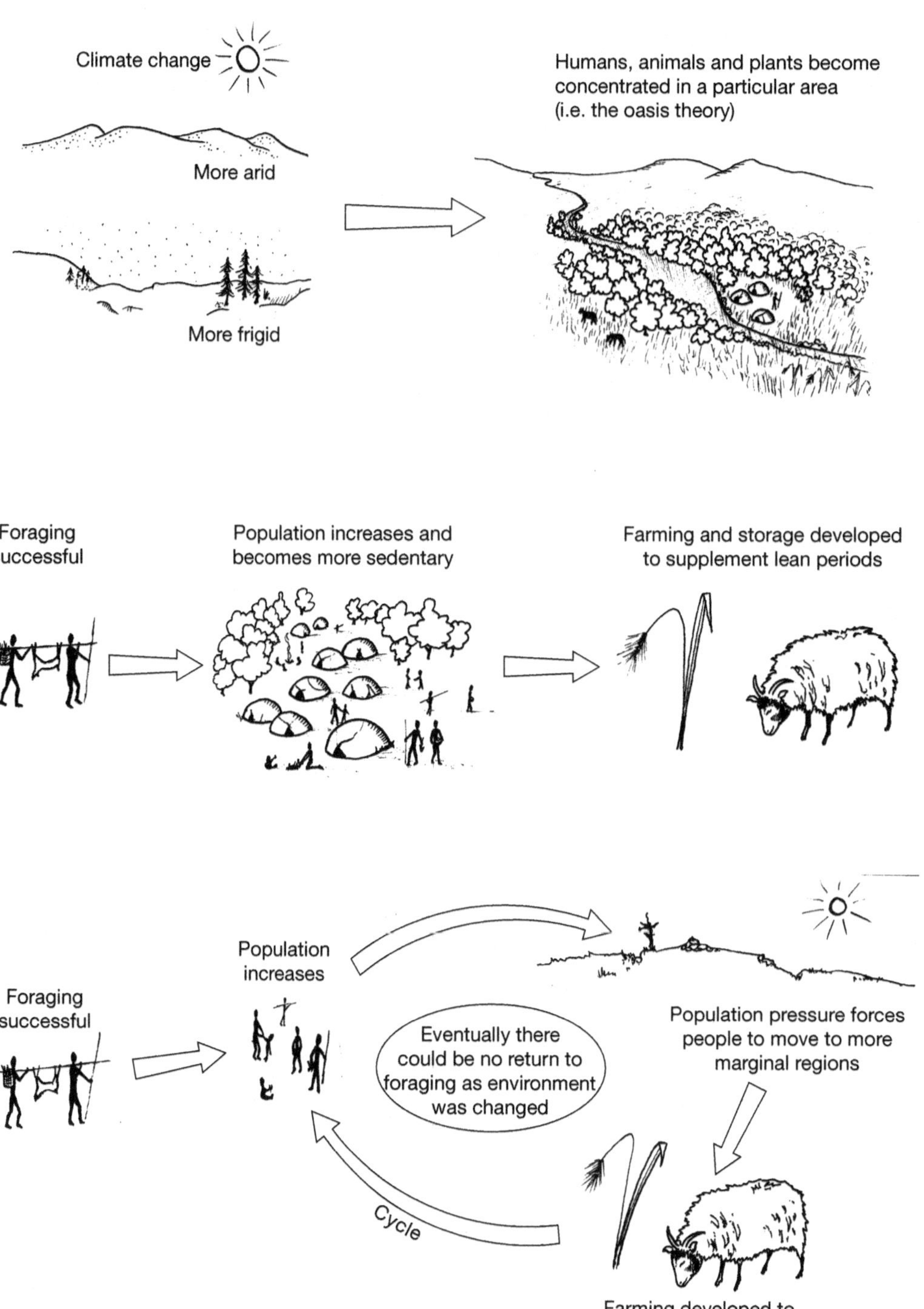

Figure 8.31 *Explanations for the adoption of farming*

competition to accumulate resources. Bender made a similar case for surplus produce being used to exchange with other groups for high-status goods. These **social theories** rely on large-scale storage but that does not appear to have happened in the earliest phase of farming. Both Hayden and McGovern have more recently suggested that alcohol may have been another reason to adopt farming. There are chemical traces in early pottery from China and Iran which are associated with wine and beer respectively and wild cereals do not appear to have been a major component of local forager diets before cultivation began.

Climate change and extended domestication theories

Today the environmental sequence from the end of the Ice Age is much better known and this has led to climate change returning as a factor, with Bar-Yosef providing the best-known accounts. During the late Upper Palaeolithic, there is increasing evidence from 20,000 BP that foragers in the Near East supplemented hunting with a wide variety of plant foods including small seeded grasses. They developed some new technologies, including grindstones, to process them. However, these grasses were probably not central to their diet. By the end of the Ice Age *c.* 14,000 BP, Kebaran foragers had spread across the western wing of the Fertile Crescent using a microlith-based technology to hunt gazelles and other animals but also gathered a wide range of wild plants. Bar-Yosef (1998) argued that near the coast, foragers became semi-sedentary due to the increasing range of available resources as temperatures rose. This group are called the Natufians, after the type-site of Wady-en-Natuf, and had a distinctive material culture including picks, sickles, and pestles and mortars.

The rapid period of cold, dry weather from 13,000 BP reduced food availability. In the desert steppe area foragers developed more mobility but in the Levantine corridor the Natufians coped with a decline in some wild foods with greater emphasis upon cereal processing. When warm, wetter weather returned, they expanded their territories and populations still further across the Levantine corridor. These were sedentary foragers living in cave sites such as Mount Carmel or small villages of pit-huts with rough stone walls. Excavated examples include Ain Mallaha and Mureybet. Stratigraphic deposits suggest long periods of occupation. Willcox (2012) argues from significant records of harvested wild emmer wheat at several sites that there was a period of pre-domestic cultivation between 13,000 and 10,000 BP. The seeds of wild cereals were sown to extend the stands available for harvesting. The Younger Dryas *c.* 11,000 BP provided a more severe challenge. Several centuries of cold, dry weather disrupted plant and animal populations and many settlements were abandoned. In the central part of the region (Sinai and the Negev), the Harifian culture returned to a very mobile, foraging lifestyle. The Natufian response was different and provides the earliest evidence of land clearance and planting as domesticates began to replace wild cereals. Rapid global warming and wetter conditions after 10,000 BP at the end of the Younger Dryas suited this strategy and these groups quickly became successful. This period is often called the Pre-pottery Neolithic A (PPNA) because ceramics, which many associate with the Neolithic, were absent. Farmers spread onto the fertile alluvial soils of the Jordan valley and western Syria and their populations rose rapidly. By 8000 BP farming villages of the later PPNB could have as many as 500 people living in them and were rearing domesticated animals.

However, even this change may be too fast. Modern excavations, such as Tell Abu Hureyra (▶ p. 332), with good recovery of environmental remains have revealed that the process of domestication took place over a much longer period than previously thought. The explosion of DNA research into the origins of plants and animals is also pointing to an extended sequence over 10,000 years with domestication events in a number of separate geographic locations. The full 'Neolithic package' did not come together in one place for two to three thousand years. While there is still much debate about origins, there is consensus around the varying nature of domestication events in different parts of the world and the complexity of the process of adaptation. Instead of a single cause, the adoption of agriculture appears to have involved social, demographic and environmental factors. These are best understood in relation to sequences in specific regions.

KEY STUDY

Ohalo II and the Palaeolithic origins of food production

During drought conditions in the 1980s, falling water levels at Lake Galilee, Israel, revealed traces of an ancient settlement. The remains of brush huts, an oven and grinding stones suggested it might be Neolithic but it was radiocarbon dated to 23,000 BP. The site appeared to have been burnt down and soon afterwards was submerged by Lake Galilee as waters rose at the end of the Ice Age. Like Tybrind Vig (▶ p. 309), gentle flooding and a protective layer of silt provided exceptional preservation of organic materials including the largest collection of Upper Palaeolithic plant remains. Normally the site lies 3–4m below the surface but modern extraction for irrigation reduced water levels and during a drought

Figure 8.32 *Ohalo II Hut 1 under excavation (photo courtesy of Dani Nadel, Zinman Institute of Archaeology, Haifa University, Israel)*

the site re-emerged. It was excavated by a team from Haifa University led by Dr Dani Nadel from 1989 to 1991 and suspended when water levels rose again, before completion in 1998–2001. The main features were the remains of six oval brushwood huts made from oak and willow with slightly sunken floors. They varied in size between 5m^2 and 13m^2 and had been constructed by piling up tree branches followed by grasses to form the walls. External hearths were located in between huts rather than right next to them. All the huts had been burnt down. Elsewhere on the site there was a grave and a midden. Scattered across the site were vast quantities of plant and animal remains along with a wide range of lithics.

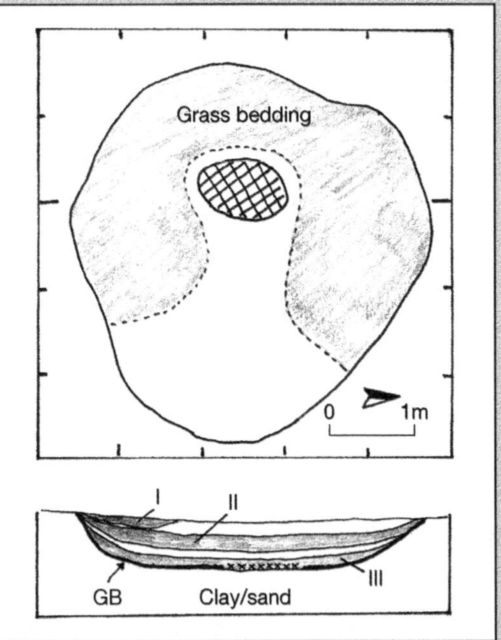

Figure 8.33 *Plan and section of Hut 1 (after Nadel et al. 2012)*

The finds

Detailed environmental analysis including flotation was undertaken across the site, resulting in the recovery of hundreds of thousands of plant specimens, most of which had been preserved by charring. Millions of fish bones were the most numerous faunal remains, particularly carp and tilapia. Bird bones were largely from waterfowl, while mammals were dominated by gazelle. Other prey included fallow deer, pig, auroch and tortoise. Analysis of soils from the huts has revealed a wide range of invertebrates. Over one hundred species of plants have been identified with the seeds of small-grained grasses, wild barley and emmer wheat being the most numerous. There were also remains of millet, sunflowers and legumes. Nuts and fruit were also gathered in large amounts and included almonds, pistachio, acorn, olive, fig, grape and wild raspberry. Anvil stones were found in a number of huts and flint debitage from the production of small blades and flakes was littered across the site. Since the date for Ohalo is earlier than Kebaran Culture sites in the region, its lithics are described as a proto-Kebaran industry. Some stone pebbles appeared to have been used as weights while a large flat stone had been used for grinding. Analysis of starch remains (Nadel et al. 2012) showed that barley had been processed in this way. Long points had been made from polished bone, mainly gazelle leg-bones, and some appeared to have been decorated with parallel lines. Several wooden artefacts have also been recovered but their function is unclear. Other artefacts include shell beads from the Mediterranean (60km to the west) and traces of plant fibres.

Intrasite analysis

Much of the carbonised grain came from around the inner walls of the huts, which suggested it had been stored. The doorways of huts appeared to have been the site of flint knapping, while grinding seeds occurred inside, which has led some archaeologists to speculate that there may have been a gendered

continued

division of labour between manufacturing and food production. In Hut 1 grass bedding appeared to have been laid around a central hearth. The external hearths do not appear attached to particular huts and may suggest communal rather than family use. Debris in the ash suggests different activities may have taken place around particular hearths. The stratigraphy of the site suggested lengthy or repeated occupation. Plant and faunal remains suggested that it was occupied at least in the spring and autumn with the excavators convinced that it was inhabited all year. The burning in the site may have been accidental or to destroy insects which infested the huts and middens.

Significance

Most of the interest has been in the vast amounts of cereals and small-grained grasses. The latter are harder to harvest than cereals and produce little nutrition for the work involved in processing them. Weiss et al. (2004) argue that this scattergun approach shows that broad spectrum foraging involved plants as well as animals and began much earlier than Flannery (▶ p. 308) originally thought. Processing evidence suggests that the idea of transforming seeds by grinding to a flour which could then be made into porridge or flat bread was already known. However, these were foraged foods rather than cultivated crops and prove that cereal processing began many millennia before farming. The evidence from Ohalo II strongly supports the idea of domestication developing over a very long period. The site is also notable for the earliest wooden huts yet discovered and the evidence for large-scale exploitation of fish.

IDENTIFYING THE SHIFT TO FOOD PRODUCTION

Modern domesticated plants and animals look quite different from their wild counterparts and agricultural systems with fields, boundaries, irrigation and specialised buildings are easy to detect archaeologically. As with herding, the earliest horticulture is much harder to identify. Archaeobotanical studies have focused on identifying the morphological changes in plants that suggest they were being selectively encouraged by human activity. Wild cereal grains are small with tough husks for protection and are joined to the plant by brittle rachis. They often have spikes to enable seeds to cling to animals' fur and therefore spread themselves further. The ears of these cereals shatter easily in order to disperse the seeds. This is not ideal for harvesting since cutting the stalks will shake the seeds, scattering them everywhere. To farm efficiently, plants had to be selected that would not shatter easily.

Identifying morphological changes

A key signature of domestic grain is the tough rachis. This mutation prevented seed heads from shattering when disturbed and enabled ears of grain to be harvested whole by plucking or sickle. It can be identified microscopically from the scar on the plant. Initially thought to have been a rapid change, it is now thought this trait which is due to a single gene took 3,000 years from *c.* 9000 BP to become dominant. The slow pace of this change may have been due to constant replenishment of stocks from wild seeds (Willcox 2012). The ideal grains therefore were large, with easily removed husks and fewer spikes. Each of these changes can be tracked microscopically from charred grains and chaff (waste material). The earliest examples with these morphological changes come from emmer wheat samples from Tell Abu Hureyra and Tell Assad *c.* 8500 BP (Ozkan et al. 2002). New hybridised cereals can also be identified and may represent human intervention, although these do occur naturally.

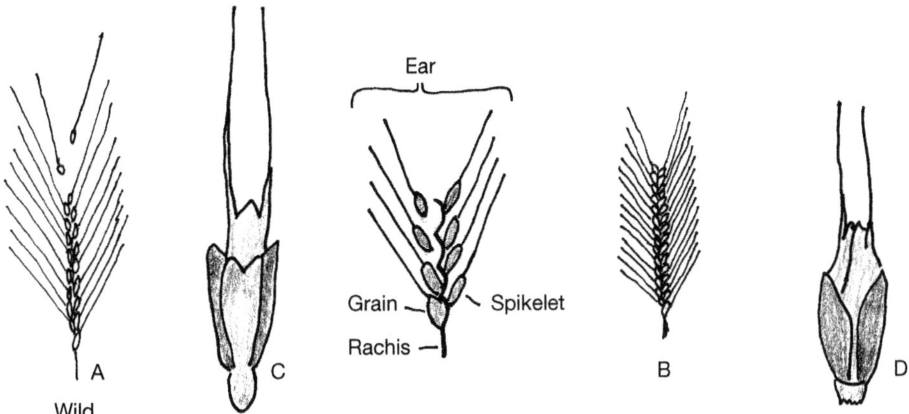

Figure 8.34 *A key signature of domestic grain is the tough rachis which attaches the grain to the stalk (D). This leaves a rough scar at the nodal point compared to the smooth scar of the brittle, wild variety (C). The wild ear (A) has long, barbed awns (spikes) while the domestic ear (B) has plumper seeds and shorter unbarbed awns.*

Palynological studies are useful in providing a general outline of vegetation patterns such as indicating forest clearance. However, because cereals are native to the Near East rather than new species, their presence is not unusual, and changes in the prevalence of particular mutations of each plant are not easily recognised in the pollen record.

Contradictory evidence

What is also becoming increasingly clear is that there was a pre-domestication phase of cultivation using entirely wild plants which cannot be detected morphologically. Wilcox (2012) argues that charred cereal grains from Jerf el Ahmar in Syria *c.* 11,300 BP provide the clearest evidence of this. The assemblage was dominated by wild barley, rye and einkorn. In the case of rye, the surrounding environment was not its normal habitat, which suggested that seeds had been imported. Similar suggestions have been made at Tell Abu Hureyra. The scale of processing of these grains is hinted at by the large amounts of chaff found on site and which was used as a binding agent in building. Large numbers of saddle querns were found including three set into the floor of one room. Remains of domestic house mice and their droppings suggest that grain was being stored. Large numbers of large flint blades were found to have plant silica gloss from harvesting. These are best suited to dense stands of grain rather than isolated plants. At least fifteen different weeds associated with disturbed ground had also been harvested. These provide indirect evidence of planting. Taken together it seems that the foragers of Jerf el Ahmar focused upon a narrow range of wild plant foods which they were encouraging through planting. Seed heads are slightly larger than average, which may suggest favoured location, the beginnings of selection or tending.

It used to be thought that technological changes marked the onset of farming but we now know that foragers had already developed harvesting and grinding tools. Microscopic Natufian sickles have revealed glosses on the blades which could have come from cereals. However, non-shattering cereals had not yet developed, so a possibility is that sickles were originally used to harvest plants such as reeds for thatch or bedding. Instead, swinging a basket through a stand of wild grain may have been the initial method of harvesting seeds. Baskets are multifunctional and do not survive well, so this practice is archaeologically invisible. Similarly, while sedentism and houses are associated with the Neolithic, we now know that successful foragers often abandoned mobility and the Natufian culture provides examples of pre-agricultural houses. Field systems were a relatively late development. The earliest farming appears to have involved small plots. Many of these indicators are of more use in tracking the spread of agriculture than pinpointing its initial development. DNA research is currently revolutionising the tracing of plant origins. The genetic make-up of modern crops can be compared with wild species and with well-preserved archaeological remains. Although there are limitations including contamination of ancient DNA and sequencing estimates of the rates of mutations, DNA offers the possibility of identifying the original locations of domesticates and the approximate date of their introduction.

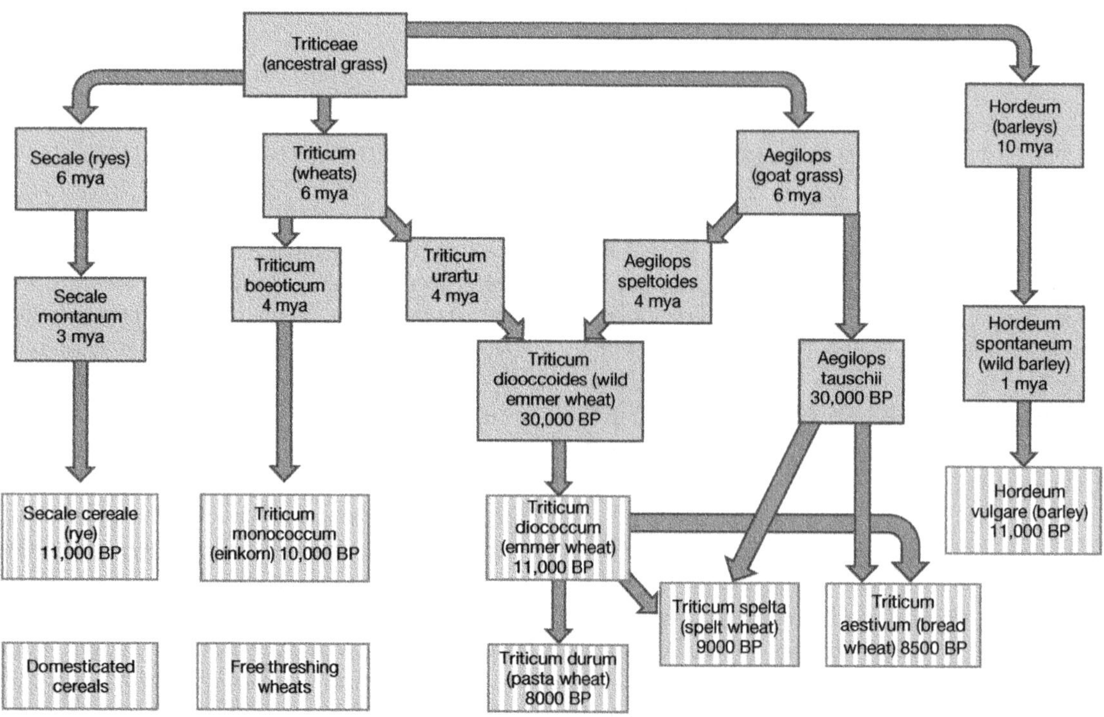

Figure 8.35 *The wheat family tree*

KEY STUDY

Tell Abu Hureyra and the transition to farming

From 1968 to 1974 the Syrian government was building a huge dam to provide hydroelectricity and irrigation water from the River Euphrates. The middle Euphrates valley was known to contain sites from the Mesolithic onwards which would be flooded under the new Lake Assad once the dam came into use. As a result, a series of international projects with UNESCO support were launched to investigate and record archaeological remains before they were lost. One of these sites was a hill beside a dry tributary of the Euphrates which was littered with flint. This suggested it might be a very early settlement. When investigated by the archaeologist Andrew Moore, the 8m mound proved to be a **tell** (▶ p. 55) – an artificial hill made up of successive layers of mudbrick houses. Radiocarbon results suggested occupation had lasted from 11,500 to 7000 BP, which straddled the period before and after the start of farming (more recent dates suggest it may have been occupied before 12,000 BP). A salvage excavation was launched to recover as much as possible.

Excavation

Seven large trenches up to 8m deep were dug into the tell to expose its stratigraphy. All the soil was dry sieved to recover artefacts and faunal remains while flotation was used to recover smaller faunal remains and artefacts and carbonised plant remains. The results documented the story of the shift from a foraging settlement to an agricultural village. Only a relatively small area of the tell was excavated but it has provided over forty years' worth of research materials. The Syrian government was so keen to get the many sites in the region excavated that they allowed large numbers of finds to go abroad where they continue to be studied today.

The forager phase

Abu Hureyra I was a Natufian forager camp comprising a series of circular pit houses built with timber and reeds. The inhabitants had mainly hunted gazelles but also gathered around 150 different plant

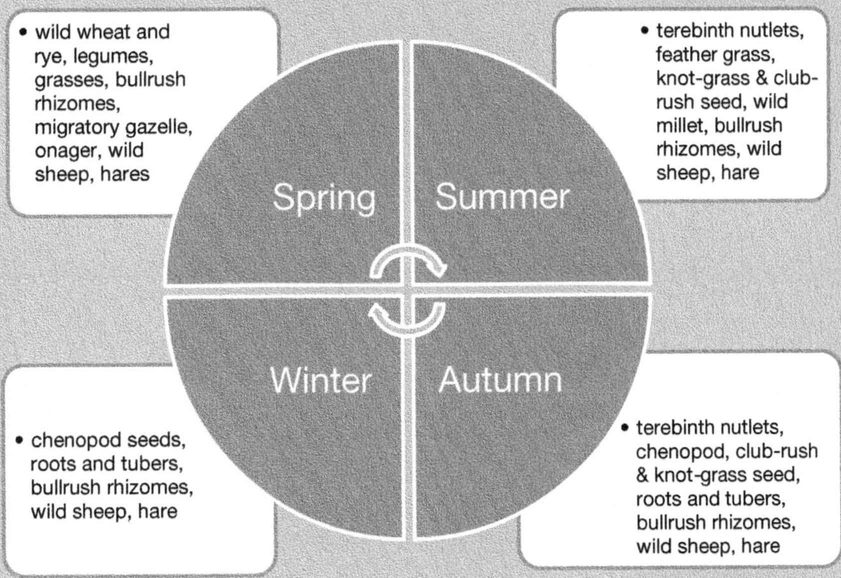

Figure 8.36 *Becoming sedentary at Tell Abu Hureyra. Evidence from plant and animal remains suggested four-seasonal occupation.*

continued

species including wild einkorn and emmer wheat. The different harvesting times for these resources suggested that the settlement was occupied all year. Some huts contained pits for storage. It is thought that 'desert kites' – made from converging stone walls – were used to trap migrating gazelle so that they could be killed with spears. At *c.* 11,000 BP the range of plants declined rapidly and the people began cultivating wild rye (Hillman et al. 2001) and possibly lentils. These cultivated cereals had slightly fatter seeds than their wild counterparts, which is an early sign of selection for domestication. The experiment appears to have been unsuccessful and the site was abandoned and the dwellings filled up with soil and rubbish. It may be the people had to return to a mobile foraging lifestyle due to the climatic changes of the Younger Dryas. There is evidence of later temporary forager camps on the site but with people living in more flimsy huts rather than pit houses.

The farming phase

Abu Hureyra II was a Neolithic reoccupation of the site coinciding with the return of warm, wetter weather after 9500 BP. The new village was occupied from *c.* 9400 to 7000 BP with people living in multiroomed, rectangular, mudbrick houses. Some had been rebuilt as many as eleven times. It was a significantly larger settlement with populations as high as 5,000 compared with the 200–300 in phase I. Domestic crops were present from the start and the variety increased during the levels of the settlement until there were eight main plant foods comprising emmer and einkorn wheat, barley, rye, oats, lentils, beans and chickpeas. Wild foods were also gathered in the early Neolithic phase. The early farmers continued to hunt for meat but *c.* 8300 BP gazelle and other wild prey were largely replaced with domesticated sheep and goats. These two species are often lumped together and referred to as 'ovicaprids' since it is difficult to distinguish between their bones at this early stage of domestication.

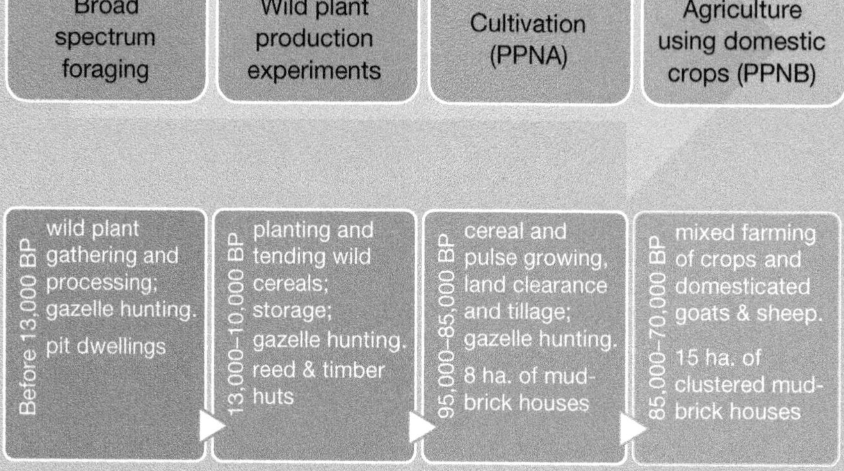

Figure 8.37 *Tell Abu Hureyra and food production. The deep stratigraphy provided evidence of all transitional stages to farming (after Harris et al. 1996).*

Later morphological changes such as horns changing from curved to curly make the distinction much easier. Gazelle could never have been domesticated because they lacked the behavioural traits which made sheep and goats more manageable. Artefacts included many lithic artefacts for processing seeds. One large basalt saddle quern had been brought from 60 miles away. Other items included stone axes, bone needles and arrowheads. Weaving of either animal or plant textiles and pottery manufacture is evident during the 7th millennium BC, with the village finally abandoned *c.* 7000 BP. Soil appears to have deteriorated due to overgrazing and a drier, warmer climate and perhaps yields fell to an unsustainable level.

The impact on people

The transition to agriculture also left traces in the bones of the human inhabitants. A total of 162 skeletons were recovered from burials underneath their houses. As with most early farming settlements, there is little sign in burials or houses of social inequalities. Most appeared to have lived into their

Figure 8.38 *Neolithic saddle querns and pestles and mortars*

The processing of grains to produce flour led to the development of grinding tools, which are one of the first indicators of settled agriculture. Grain rubbers or quern stones were quarried from very hard stone and became an early trade item.

continued

fifties and most had thickened arm and leg bones from heavy labour. Many, particularly the young, had degenerative changes in their necks, possibly from carrying heavy loads such as building material or water on their heads. Male skeletons had lesions and strain injuries to their arms as might be associated with spear throwing. This fits with faunal evidence for hunting gazelles. The effort involved to process flour was considerable and women in particular had arthritic knees and big toe joints and worn vertebrae. This damage had been caused by rocking backwards and forwards whilst kneeling with the big toe curled under as a lever and repeatedly pushing and pulling the quern stone for long periods. This suggests a division of labour with women processing food and men hunting and perhaps cultivating. In the early Neolithic levels, both sexes had tooth damage caused by hard kernels of the larger domestic grains and grit which got into the flour. Many teeth were worn down or had been lost. This was less noticeable in later populations as the development of pottery allowed grains to be soaked to make a kind of porridge which required less chewing (Molleson et al. 1993). However, sticky porridge is also a possible culprit in the appearance of dental caries at the same time. Some people, particularly women, had grooved marks on their teeth which ethnographic research suggests came from making baskets or weaving. Phosphate and other chemical analysis of soils showed that the narrow spaces between the houses were used as refuse areas, yet the people did not show any signs of epidemic diseases (Moore et al. 2000). These were yet to develop.

Tell Abu Hureyra in context

Hillman et al. (2001) argues that the evidence from Abu Hureyra shows that foragers were driven to start cultivation by a crisis. The characteristically skinny wild cereals disappeared during the Younger Dryas period with those that needed the most water going first. In order to replace them, foragers brought wild seed from further away and planted it in damp areas close to the tell. They would have cleared the scrub from these planting sites and tended the crops but there is no evidence of irrigation. Moore et al. (2000) argue that foragers already had a good understanding of plants which enabled them to shift to cultivation. They also argue that communication helped. Finds of Anatolian obsidian and Mediterranean shell beads attest to long distance exchange contacts. Knowledge and domesticates could have spread in the same way. Emmer was first domesticated in the Jordan Valley, while chickpeas were domesticated in Anatolia. Both domesticated varieties turned up at Tell Abu Hureyra.

IDENTIFYING THE SPREAD OF AGRICULTURE

Identifying the arrival of agriculture in new areas is relatively straightforward. Where domesticated animals were not native, farming can be dated by the arrival of their bones in the archaeological record. The same applies to cereal grains. However, care has to be taken that a few exotic food or sacrificial imports are not mistaken for farming. Broader environmental data such as palynology has traditionally been used to identify forest clearance through the decline in tree pollen and the rise of open-ground weeds. However, it may underestimate the earliest dates because pioneer agriculture was very small-scale and considerable clearance would be needed to substantially impact upon regional pollen records. At a site level it can provide more precision along with microfauna and soil analysis (▶ p. 105). Human remains contain some clues, in partic-

Clockwise from top left: a) flint crescent sickles; b) reconstruction of a bone sickle with flint bladelets glued into a groove; c) long flint blades; d) Neolithic carbonised grain and pot; e) ceramic drinking vessel with impressed grain decoration and goats

Figure 8.39 *Neolithic technology*

ular worn teeth due to grit from grindstones in porridge or bread. Settlements and artefacts provide the other key indicators, particularly where there is a clear break in local traditions. Polished stone axes, pottery, stonegrinding, harvesting and digging tools along with permanent houses have been the most widely documented. Taken together with the main domesticates, they make up what is often referred to as the 'Neolithic package' to which ancestral tombs (▶ p. 532) are usually added for Atlantic Europe.

Understanding the spread of agriculture across Europe

Understanding why farming spread is another matter. In the case of Europe, the spread was not steady and included several standstills and rapid advances. The form it took also mutated so that the first agriculture in Britain looks quite different from the earliest farming in Greece or Bulgaria. It provides a fascinating study of the interplay between social, environmental, technological and probably religious factors in shaping varied agricultural strategies across Europe. Most works on the origins of agriculture before the 1970s assumed small hunter-gatherer populations either embraced agriculture or were overwhelmed by farming colonists. However, recent work on successful foragers (▶ p. 309) provides an opposing view. For up to a thousand years the Mesolithic peoples of north-west Europe did not adopt farming in what is termed the 'Neolithic standstill'. There were farmers to the south with whom they were in contact (▶ p. 353) so the ideas and crops were available, but they chose not to adopt them. Why should people give up economic strategies that produced a wide variety of foodstuffs and other resources and may have provided surpluses? Farming is hard work and would have produced a monotonous diet. Eventually agriculture did spread and this raises another question, why then? Theories include environmental change, the prestige attached to cattle and grain and even religious conversion. What is clear is that the transition to farming was not a simple process and that a variety of economic strategies were selected by people according to social requirements as well as ecological pressures. Increasingly, archaeological studies have examined the social significance of different models of food acquisition including gender relations and social structure.

The first European farmers

The earliest farming sites in Europe are in Greece and Bulgaria and both domesticates and most of the technology clearly came from across the Bosphorus in Anatolia. Mudbrick houses in Greece, ceramics and tells (▶ p. 55) also show clear links to the Near East. Unlike the Near East, where cereal production preceded herding, the whole 'package' arrived in Europe at the same time. It is unclear whether the spread of agriculture into this area was due to migration of farmers or adoption by foragers but most archaeologists have emphasised the former. Emerging DNA studies suggest it may be more complicated. Farming, with an emphasis upon sheep and goats, quickly spread across the eastern half of the Balkan Peninsula, where there were suitable soils and a broadly similar climate to where domesticates had originated. There is debate amongst archaeologists about the scale of crop growing, with most interpreting the arable remains as the produce of small plots (horticulture) cultivated with hoes and digging sticks. Weed assemblages suggest that harvesting involved ear-plucking as well as sickles and that some winter as well as summer crops were grown. It was very labour intensive and very uniform. Virtually identical crop assemblages have been found at sites across the region (Kreuz et al. 2005).

The spread of farming into central Europe

From the Balkans, farming spread both west along the Mediterranean coast and north towards the Danube basin. The earliest Neolithic in the northern Balkans and Carpathian basin from *c.* 6200 BC to *c.* 5500 BC is known as the Starčevo-Körös-Criş complex because of similarities in their ceramic styles. The three names reflect research in Serbia, Hungary and Romania respectively. Although the same domesticates were adopted in these areas, settlements are not as large or long-lasting as those further south and a gradual economic change is observable. Faunal remains indicate greater utilisation of wild food, including fish in Hungary and gradual emphasis

KEY STUDY

Karanovo and early farming villages in the Balkans

Discovery and description

The large tell of Karanovo in the Maritsa Valley of central Bulgaria was one of the earliest villages in Europe. Excavations led by G. I. Georgiev took place from the 1930s with the main published report from 1961. The 12m of occupation layers started *c.* 6000 BC and continued for 4,000 years from the Neolithic to the Bronze Age. The houses of the inhabitants were made of wooden frames plastered with mud. Once each generation a house would need renewing, so it would be demolished and its successor built alongside or on the same spot. Each demolition resulted in another 15cm of mud debris being added to the tell. Much of the early exploration of tell sites in this region was focused on establishing artefact-based chronologies (culture-histories), in particular by the use of sondages. These were particularly useful for understanding stratigraphy but less so for spatial relationships. The material culture finds from the site were hugely valuable but recovery of environmental data was in its infancy at the time with little dry or wet sieving. Subsequent excavation both at Karanovo and other tell sites has focused on open-area excavation of building horizons, which leads to a better understanding of settlement. Recent environmental research is beginning to fill in gaps in our understanding of the economy.

Figure 8.40 *The tell at Karanovo*

continued

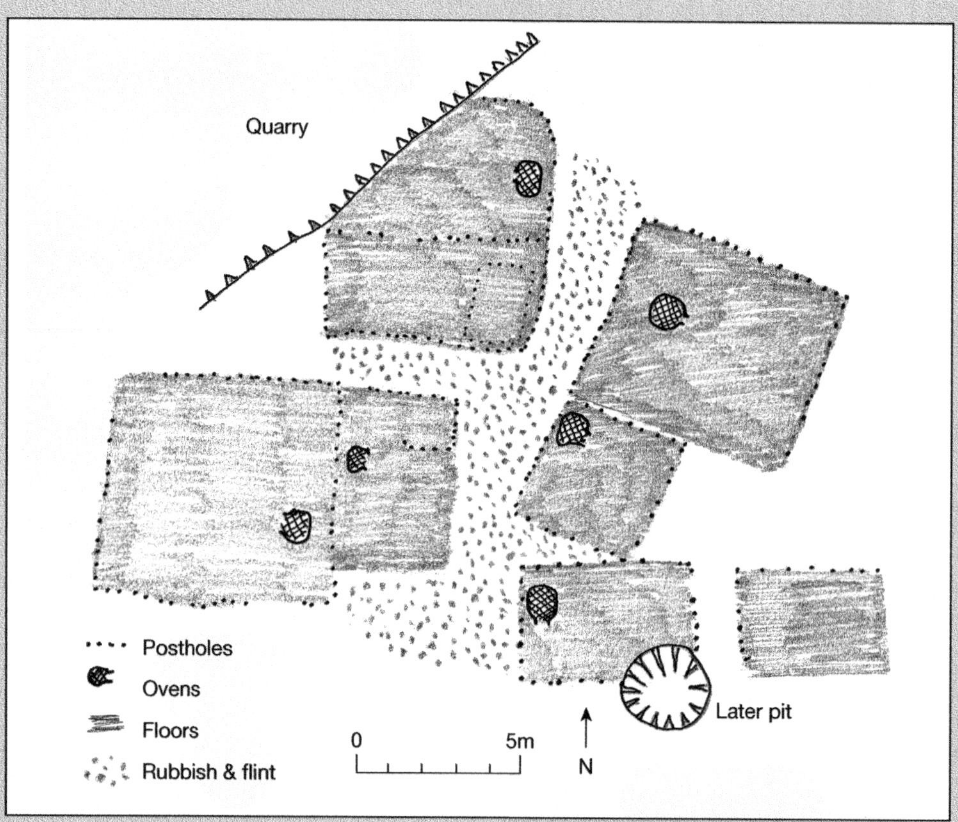

Figure 8.41 *Plan of horizon 4 at Karanovo (after Hiller and Nikolov 1997)*

Stratigraphy from seven main phases of occupation provided a ceramic sequence which supplied a chronology for cross-dating for the region. Karanovo culture became the name for the earliest Neolithic in Macedonia, Bulgaria and southern Romania while to the west it was named after Starčevo in Serbia. From the onset, there was considerable diversity in ceramics manufacture. In addition to a variety of vessels, figurines of buildings, people and animals were produced. The lowest levels (Karanovo I) represent the earliest Neolithic in the region and were characterised by first white and then red painted ceramics. In the third level (Karanovo III) dark, burnished pottery and carinated (fluted or a sharp angle between body and neck) styles appeared. The late Neolithic of Karanovo IV and V features graphite painted ware and artefact styles known across the Balkans as the Vinča culture. A tiny burnt seal from 4800 BC was found in this level. Divided into quarters, it features a number of abstract, linear symbols and has variously been interpreted as constellations or Europe's earliest writing. In Karanovo VI, *c.* 4500 BC, we reach the Chalcolithic with a tiny copper awl in a bone handle followed by beads and pins of beaten copper. This period is called Gumelniţa culture and is associated with female figurines and the rich cemetery at Varna (▶ p. 423). Houses are larger and more rectilinear than previously with plastered and painted interiors. Karanovo VII is the top layer and represents the Bronze Age, after which the great mound was abandoned.

Neolithic houses

The earliest phase had around sixty houses well spaced out within an area of about 250m x 150m although only around half would have been in use at one time. This implies 100–200 people lived in the village. The square, single-roomed houses were virtually identical. All were roughly 6m x 6m with a hearth or stone and clay-plaster oven along one wall, clay platforms either side of the door and storage vessels sunk in the rammed earth floor. One large unfired clay vessel could hold 100 litres. Inside the houses were grindstones, stone tools and waste from crop processing. Outside were activity areas and pits filled with debris. Later buildings were rectangular, larger and two- or three-roomed but frequently reflected the orientation and/or floor plan of the previous building. Although later levels had streets and fences, and the houses were even more closely packed, the connection between different generations of houses continued. The interior organisation of space continued too. Later buildings were often plastered and in some cases painted. A common problem with tell sites is that floors were often destroyed through overbuilding or digging of rubbish pits in later levels. A better understanding of houses came from a chance discovery during the building of a hospital in nearby Stara Zagora in 1968 with the discovery of two of the earliest and best-preserved Neolithic houses in Europe. The two were joined and were single-roomed. The larger measures approximately 8m x 6m with the smaller adjoining house being 5m x 3m. Wattle walls were built by weaving branches through a row of posts and then plastering on clay and straw. The earth floor was covered in clay and possibly planks. The roof was made from reeds or straw on a wooden framework. Clay models (▶ p. 344) suggest that it would have been pitched. However, the walls alone could not have held it up so there must also have been some supporting timbers. The houses were deliberately burnt, which effectively 'fired' the floor and lower walls and preserved

Figure 8.42 *Stara Zagora houses. Dome oven in centre background.*

continued

hundreds of artefacts. A domed clay oven with arched entrance stood against the north wall. Around it were a clay platform, grindstones, and serving and storage vessels which contained charred seeds of cereals. Both houses had pots sunk into the floor for storage. Figurines were deliberately buried near the entrances and others found inside. Other finds included ceramics, querns, bone spoons, antler picks, a goat horn, a necklace of imported beads and a flint sickle. Carbonised wheat, barley and lentils indicates their staple diets. Dating from the 6th millennium BC, the houses are preserved in situ in a museum.

At Slatina Tell a larger, two-roomed building had large, central support timbers which suggests a pitched roof. It also contained the remains of wooden furniture (possibly a bed) and a partition screen. Over 200kg of carbonised cereals and beans were found in storage vessels sunk in the floor. Space appeared to have been demarcated for different activities including stone tool production and domestic textile production (spindle whorls) from wool or flax. Other insights into dwellings are provided by numerous clay models of houses and ovens which add details of windows, roofs and internal features. Analysis of carbonised plant remains from rubbish pits suggests that all stages of crop processing took place in the villages including winnowing, roasting or parching, pounding and grinding.

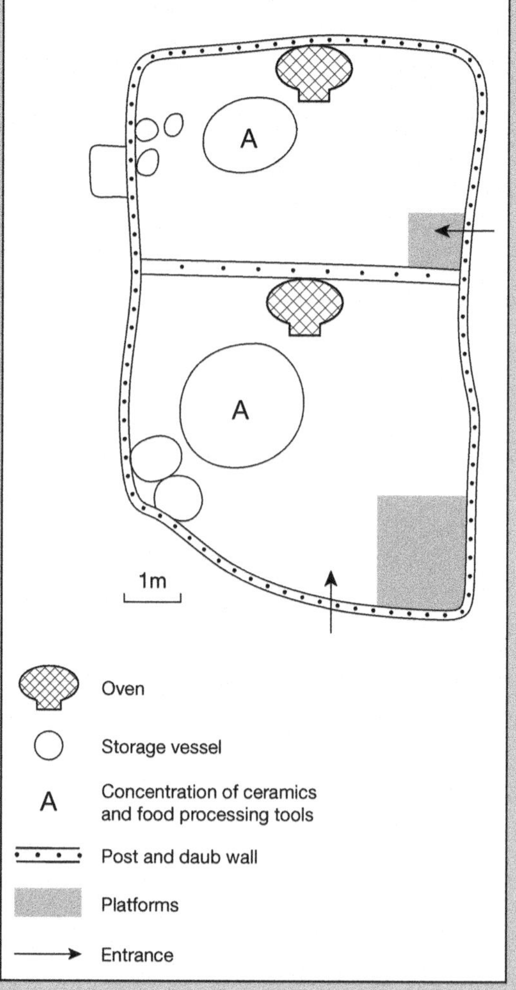

Figure 8.43 *Double house at Stara Zagora*

Key finds

Burials from the earliest levels are rare but some inhumations, particularly of children, have been found under floors or in the rubbish pits in the village. Grave goods are even rarer but consist of stone and bone tools and ornaments. More common are anthropomorphic and zoomorphic stone and clay figurines. At Ovcharovo Tell, over one hundred were excavated. Some are abstract but a significant number, particularly from the late Neolithic and Chalcolithic layers, were of women. Male figurines are rare, although a number of possible phallus-like artefacts exist. Besides anthropomorphic figurines, there are frequently ceramic miniatures of chairs and tables, ovens, pottery and altars. Exotic finds from tells include stone tools from distant sources and obsidian and spondylus shell from the Mediterranean. Whether these came via long-distance trade or a series of short-distance gift exchanges is unclear.

Economy

Figure 8.44 *Decorated pottery from the Balkan Neolithic*

The site of Karanovo lies just south of forested hills in a place where alluvial soils were ideal for cultivation. To the south, plains with heavier soils provided rich grazing land. Several other tells such as Chevdar have similar locations, suggesting that a mix of environments and resources was preferred. Caprines (sheep-goats) dominate faunal assemblages but there were also pigs, dogs and cattle, while wild food still supplemented agricultural produce. At Starčevo on the Danube these included red deer, birds and fish, particularly catfish and pike. Environmental research suggests that seasonal grazing patterns or transhumance (▶ p. 318) would have been likely, with animals moved on to hill pasture in the summer when the plains dried out and then back down in the late autumn when the snows came. It is also the case that cattle, sheep and pigs prefer different grazing habitats and Karanovo was ideal for all three. Carbonised remains of emmer and einkorn wheat, lentils, vetch (pea family) and barley were the main cultivated crops recovered at Karanovo. Other wild plant food included acorns, pistachios, cherries and plums. More recent research in the region suggests that flax was also grown. The plough had not been invented so cultivation was of small 'garden-agriculture' plots using digging sticks or mattocks. These plots were close to the tells.

Who were the farmers?

For most of the last century, archaeologists assumed that both farming and farmers arrived in Europe from the Near East, bringing the 'Neolithic package' with them. Farming certainly did. Although some tools to process wild foods existed in the Mesolithic, the forms of most of the grinders and sickles are not of local origin. DNA studies of domesticates prove that they originated from Anatolia and the 'Fertile Crescent'. There are also some similarities in buildings, burials and female domestic symbolism as at Çatal Höyük in Turkey. However, they are not identical. Little is known about the last forager communities of the Balkans, although some continuity of both artefacts and settlement has been recognised at Lepanski Vir on the Danube. The combination of crops is not exactly the same as in Anatolia and there is some evidence that some local legumes were domesticated. DNA studies are inconclusive but do not support the view that there was total population replacement. This suggests a mix of incoming ideas and people and a transformation of existing cultures. There certainly was local adaptation as not everywhere has tells and the relative emphasis on herding and cultivation also varies.

The impact on people

Agriculture must have had a profound impact on the lifestyles of the local people. The activities of clearing, digging, planting, weeding, harvesting and crop processing were far more labour intensive than

continued

foraging. Herd animals provided meat but also brought responsibilities. In particular sheep and cattle would have required protection and moving between pastures. The slaughter and consumption of different animals may also have had an impact. Pigs were small and bred quickly so were probably consumed at household level. Cattle, however, required a significant investment of time to rear and were too large for a household to eat. It is likely that their killing was a prelude to a larger social event such as a feast which would have linked several households or possibly a whole community. The effort of maintaining cultivated plots and rich pastures constituted considerable investment in one place. A clear sign of this phenomenon were the tells themselves. Built on the homes and burials of ancestors, they are the largest man-made monuments in Europe and after a few generations must have appeared to have always existed. This anchoring of people to a place only became common in Europe from this point.

Permanent houses would have had an impact both on society and on the way people understood the world. Houses define households and impose order and everyday rituals on their inhabitants. The common size and plan suggests fairly uniform family structures and physically separates the private and public

Figure 8.45 *Ceramic model houses from the Balkans. Note the ovens.*

sphere in a way that campsites do not. The tendency in later tells for houses to adhere to particular orientations (at Ovcharovo they all run north–south) suggests the direction of movement may have been significant. Ian Hodder, who directed the excavation of the major Neolithic settlement of Çatal Höyük (▶ p. 284) in Turkey, has argued that the concept of the home or household was a powerful symbol in 'domesticating' Europe and enabling people to live in a new way in larger groups with a more ordered lifestyle. He sees the symbolic elaboration of the house though decoration, burials and the focus on the hearth as evidence of an ideology in which farming and village life were linked with new social relationships, processes and rituals.

House burning

Most tells have a burnt house horizon of ash and fired clay, which has been interpreted as the result of domestic accidents, arson or raiding. However, Ruth Tringham (2013), who excavated Podgoritsa Tell, found that individual buildings were very thoroughly burnt and there was often an unburnt strip around them. Most of the buildings were old and had collapsed in on themselves. There were rarely burnt human remains in them. Experimental burning of reconstructions has not been able to replicate the destruction since it is difficult to fully burn wattle and daub buildings. This suggests that it was not a raid, village fire or accident. Native American ethnographies suggested burning could have been about purification on the death of a key member of a household. Derelict buildings could have been pulled down, recycled or built over. Instead they were deliberately burnt at a high temperature in what would have been a dramatic, sensuous and emotional event. The rubble and ash was often left exposed and weathering for a long time before finally being deposited in pits. Fire was likely to have been symbolic,

Figure 8.46 *Domestic Neolithic figurines in a reconstructed 'cult scene'*

continued

given its ability to transform dough, clay and later metals. This voluntary killing of a house (domithanasia) may have been a communal event to help people adjust to a change, for example, the death of the head of a household. The mound of debris may have become a monument to that person.

Farming societies

Most archaeologists see these stable early farming societies as essentially egalitarian. There is little sign of ranking in either houses or burial assemblages. Gender is more controversial. Female anthromorphic figurines and the absence of weapons or rich male graves led Maria Gimbutas (▶ p. 458), who had excavated Sitagroi Tell, to develop a model of 'old Europe' as both matriarchal and peaceful. She believed that some figurines represented goddesses. She went on to characterise the Neolithic as the 'civilisation of the goddess' and contrasted it with the male-dominated and warlike societies of the Bronze Age (▶ p. 456). Other archaeologists have disagreed with her interpretation, usually on the grounds that she may have imposed a modern understanding on the evidence but also because of increasing evidence of violence elsewhere in the Neolithic. Some suggest that the figurines represent ancestors, while Douglass Bailey (2000), who excavated Podgoritsa Tell, argues that whether they are votives, idols or toys the key thing about them is that they are miniature objects. In handling or playing with them people entered another world and came to understand themselves and their social group. He notes that styles vary between communities, which could mean they had differing ideas about what 'their' people should look like.

on pigs and particularly cattle rather than sheep and goats. Possible reasons include the role of indigenous foragers in adopting aspects of the 'Neolithic package'. However, environment was also a key factor. Signs of stress on sheep bones (Bartosiewicz 2005) suggests that the wet river valleys were unsuited to Mediterranean breeds. Cattle were better suited to the Danube Basin. It was also the limit for several Mediterranean crops. Chick peas, for example, were grown in Bulgaria but not as far north as Hungary. Similarly, barley and naked wheat (an easily processed strain) did not spread further despite better yields. One theory is that these crops were less able to recover from central European rainstorms. During this transitional period the spread of farming appears to pause for several hundred years – perhaps while farmers adapted to central European conditions – before the next phase of expansion.

The Linearbandkeramik (LBK)

From *c.* 5500 BC to 4900 BC agriculture expanded rapidly eastwards into the Ukraine, northwards into Poland and westwards as far as northern France in an archaeologically distinctive phase. The debate over how this happened is covered in Chapter 10 (▶ p. 499). Previously called the Danubian culture because of the early sites found along the river which is the gateway to central Europe, it is usually known as the LBK, an abbreviation of the German name for its pottery. From its origins in Hungary to later settlements close to the North Sea, there is a little regional variation but overwhelmingly one pattern of culture and economy is evident. Aside from pottery incised with linear bands, the clearest distinguishing features are the unique, massive, timber longhouses. Typically 20m in length, though some have been found 45m long and 8–10m wide, these were the largest buildings in the world at that time. Their floors have been

Figure 8.47 LBK pottery from a well at Leipzig (▶ p. 386) (copyright Landesamt für Archäologie Sachsen, Thomas Reuter)

Figure 8.48 LBK longhouse from Bylany, Czech Republic (Photo Archives of the Institute of Archaeology ASCR, Prague, No. FT-40257. www.bylany.com)

Figure 8.49 *Oven from Bylany (Photo Archives of the Institute of Archaeology ASCR, Prague, No. FT-40257. www.bylany.com)*

destroyed by later ploughing but enough evidence remains to establish that they probably formed three modules. These comprised a sleeping area, a central living-working space where charcoal is concentrated and a cattle byre and storage area, possibly with loft-space used as a grain store. 'Borrow pits' running along the side provided daub and later were filled with rubbish. Houses were usually orientated the same way (SSE) and when abandoned after thirty to fifty years were left as mounds while replacements were built alongside. These have been interpreted as becoming monuments to the ancestors that lived there and a possible origin of barrows (Whittle 1998; Bradley 1998). Other features include pits, ovens, kilns, wells and enclosures. Some later sites have cemeteries and others enclosures, a few of which are thought to be defensive. The waterlogged elements of wells provide an insight into LBK carpentry, being built from planks into a square box-shape using halved joints. The heavy, woodworking adze is their most distinctive tool and appears also to have been pressed into use as a weapon (▶ p. 116) as well as being used for grave goods.

LBK farming

Settlements tend to cluster in groups of ten to twenty longhouses, usually along river valleys and particularly on loess soils which were fertile and easy to till. Palynological research suggests that areas of forest were cleared (using polished stone and flint axes) to create small plots which were repeatedly cropped and possibly pasture. Shade-loving weeds in crop assemblages suggest that these were literally clearings in the forest. The LBK only used five of the original Neolithic crop package, which implies a very different economy

Figure 8.50 *Early European crops: a) wild emmer, b) emmer, c) flax, d) millet, e) oats*

from that of the Balkans. Emmer and particularly einkorn wheat, lentils, peas and flax may have been selected for their ability to cope with the cooler and wetter climates of central Europe. Einkorn has a relatively low yield but is tough and remains standing after heavy rain (Kreuz et al. 2005). Farmers had also to rely on summer crops due to a shorter growing season and harsher winters and therefore storage became increasingly important. While some wild foods such as deer, fish, nuts and berries were exploited, 80–95 per cent of assemblages are domesticates. Cattle in particular but also pigs, sheep and goats were important. However, the limited areas of pasture have presented a puzzle. Forest grazing has been suggested – which would leave little archaeological trace – but recent research (▶ p. 318) has identified transhumance to upland pastures as part of their strategy. The first pigs were of Anatolian origin but the LBK quickly replaced them with larger, hardier boars from the surrounding forests. During the later LBK phase, ceramic sieves have been interpreted as an element in cheese making and recent lipid analysis of pottery (▶ p. 138) suggests that dairying was a key source of food.

LBK houses appear to have been the centre of their world, with most activities including knapping, food processing and manufacturing taking place around them. There is, however, also evidence of contact well beyond their forest clearings. In burials as far west as Elsloo in Holland, spondylus shell jewellery from the Mediterranean has been found. Obsidian from Hungary has been found at sites along the Danube, while stone axes also travelled significant distances. At Bylany in the Czech Republic, flint came from 320 km away. While LBK settlements were self-sufficient, exchange networks were clearly important to them. Other forms of contact were less welcome. Many later burials show signs of violent deaths, which may suggest increasing conflict over resources with local foragers or other LBK farmers (▶ p. 480).

KEY STUDY

Vaihingen and pioneer farmers in central Europe

The Neolithic Linearbandkeramik (LBK) settlement at Vaihingen lies on fertile clay and loess soils close to the River Enz north-west of Stuttgart in southern Germany. It was discovered during work in advance of industrial development in 1994. Trial trenching revealed the well-preserved remains of longhouses while aerial photography established that the site extended over several hectares. Work was halted while the Baden-Württemberg state archaeological team led by Dr Rüdiger Krause undertook a rescue excavation. Initial finds suggested that it was a very early but long-lasting LBK settlement with good preservation of plants and bone. As a result, an extended research excavation continued until 2003 to recover as much information as possible.

The enclosed settlement covered 6 hectares and contained over one hundred longhouses with around forty in use at one time. It was surrounded by a flat-bottomed ditch over 1m deep and 2m wide plus several smaller ditches and a line of post settings. This was possibly part of a palisade but multiple entrances suggested that it was not defensive. Stratigraphy revealed that the ditch had been built after the village had existed for some time. It was open for a relatively brief period before being used for around eighty burials. Other skeletons, buried in the same crouched style, were found in nearby pits. Some burials had grave goods, mainly pottery, but others appeared to have been simply dumped in the ditch. Disarticulated human remains were found at points across the site. As with most LBK settlements, later ploughing had destroyed most of the floors of the longhouses but their size and positions were clear from 'borrow pits' outside their walls and postholes from their main structural timbers. The largest were 32m in length. Most were orientated NNW–SSE. Besides distinctive LBK pottery, artefacts included stone and bone tools and a large amount of worked deer antler. Many artefacts came from the southern half of the site which, combined with the apparently regular spacing of longhouses, suggests an element of planning had gone on. The settlement was dated to approximately 5400–4900 BC, during the earliest Neolithic in the region.

Arable farming

Preservation of plants was excellent and a detailed soil-sampling and wet-sieving exercise was undertaken across the entire site to try to map activity areas. Some 3,700 samples of approximately 5 litres each were analysed. This revealed little variation in distribution. Repeated, dense finds of chaff and charred spikelets of emmer and einkorn wheat suggested that each household was independently processing its own food. The distribution of other crops such as peas, lentils and flax (for oil or fibres) and remains of wild foods such as hazelnut shells and strawberry seeds reinforces this impression. Opium poppy appears also to have been grown for oil and possibly as a drug but was only found in one area of the site. Analysis of crop-weeds by Bogaard et al. (2013) in relation to their preferred soil types revealed marked differences in the weed assemblages between different zones of the village. This implied that some family groups were farming plots close to the settlement while others used more distant land including plots in the forest. The consistency in these patterns suggests that the land was exploited over a long period with plots 'owned' by the different groups. The 'in-field' soil was more productive and therefore may indicate that those farming it were better off and perhaps of higher status.

Social organisation

Through detailed analysis of the way lithics and ceramics had been made and decorated, five distinct variations were identified. The excavators interpreted these as five different kinship traditions. Each variant appeared to be clustered in one or more zones of the site, implying that people lived in family groups. Houses within each zone had repeatedly been replaced, which again suggests that kin groups 'owned' particular spaces. When this information was combined with the crop-weed data, Bogaard (2013) found that kin group A had the highest proportion of good land close to the settlement while kin groups C and

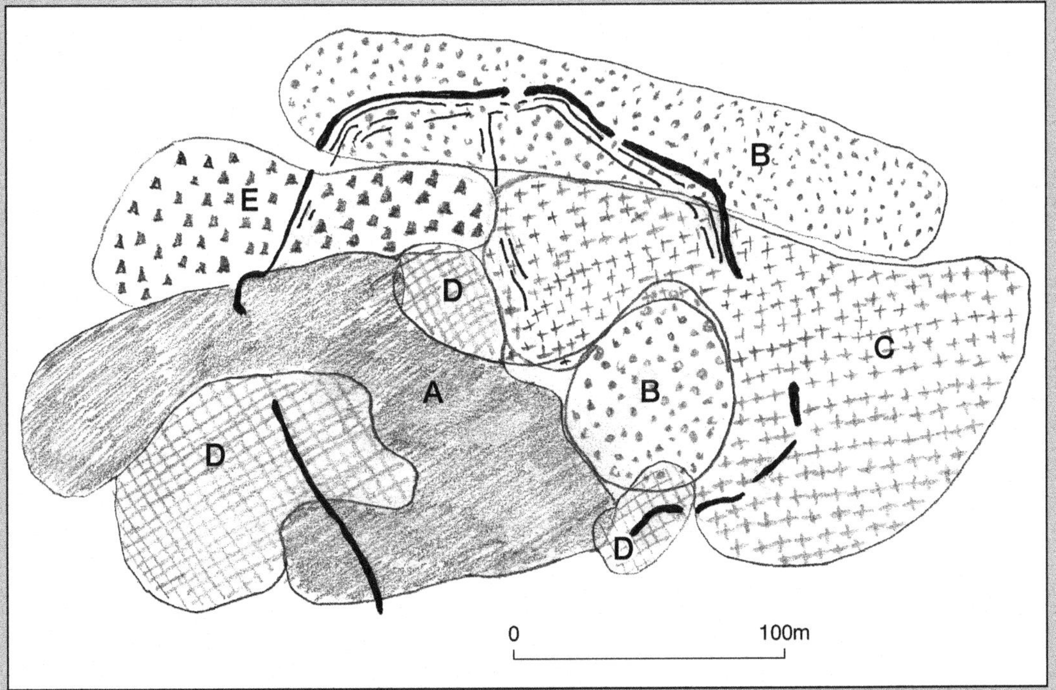

Figure 8.51 *Clan groups at Vaihingen (after Bentley 2012). Dark lines indicate settlement ditches*

continued

E were travelling further to use forest clearings. Not only does this strongly suggest kin-based land tenure but it also provides a motive for some families to break from the community in a search for better land.

Burials were mainly flexed and in mixed age and gender groups. These too are suggestive of different kin groups. Like other LBK burials (▶ p. 480), many show signs of trauma. The scattered bones are generally more robust than those which were buried. This has led to speculation that they were ethnically different: hunters rather than LBK farmers. Both human and animal bones from the site have been subjected to strontium isotope ($^{87}Sr/^{86}Sr$) analysis of tooth enamel to determine where they were raised. There is considerable geological diversity in the region and local strontium ratios have been mapped using modern pigs' teeth. Analysis of excavated human teeth supported the idea that those buried in the ditch were more likely to be incomers or outsiders. Those males buried with goods, particularly adzes, almost always grew up in the vicinity of the settlement (Bentley et al. 2003). Again this could indicate a different cultural group or perhaps a division between pastoralist and arable farmers. As with other Neolithic sites in the region (▶ p. 116), females tended to have been raised away from the site, which suggests the practice of patrilocality whereby women move to live in their husband's village.

Pastoral farming

Bentley (2004) also found that LBK pigs had, as expected, been reared in the vicinity of Vaihingen, probably in the surrounding woodland. Some sheep and cattle, however, had isotope ratios which

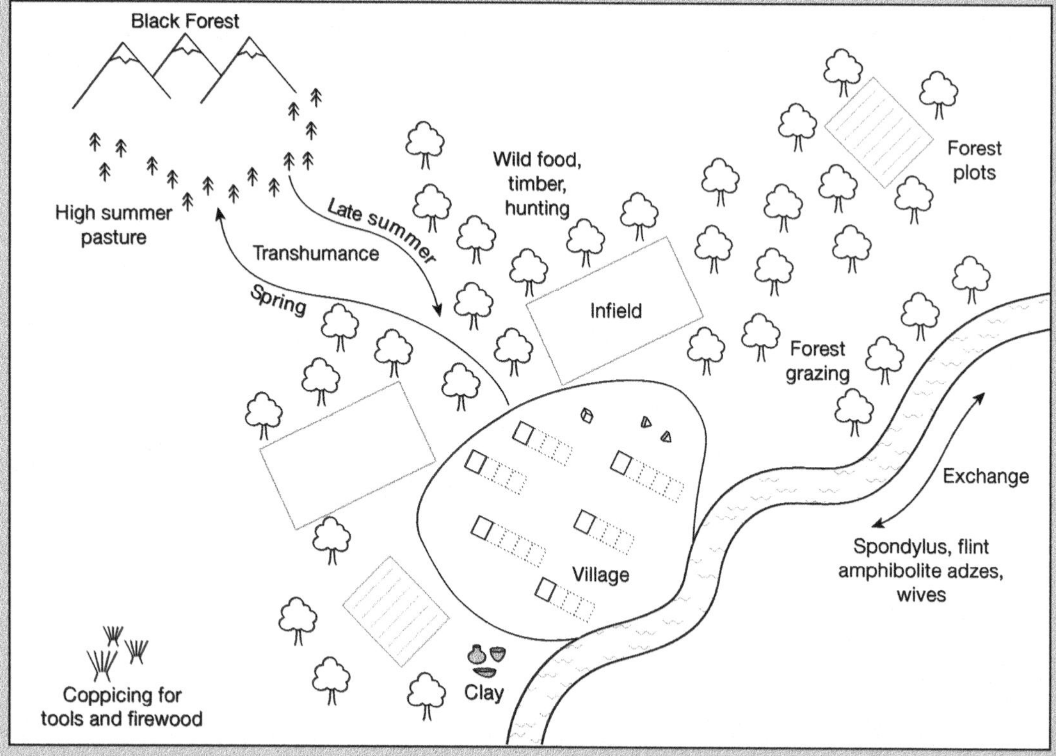

Figure 8.52 *Land use at Vaihingen*

indicated they had been raised in the Black Forest uplands. This may indicate a **transhumance** economy involving at least some of the villagers and perhaps different kin groups using different upland pastures. A surprisingly high proportion (15 per cent) of the thousands of faunal remains were from wild animals (Bogaard et al. 2013). Cattle declined from two-thirds to one-third of the assemblage over the life of the settlement, with pig gradually becoming predominant. The age and sex of the cattle does not suggest dairy herds and bones show no signs of deformity caused by ploughing. This means animals were reared for meat. Taken together, the evidence from Vaihingen points to the emergence of both livestock and land as key sources of wealth and social differentiation between individuals and families.

This densely settled site differs from the more typical dispersed pattern of LBK settlements previously excavated in the Rhineland area such as Langweiler. Here there were a similar number of longhouses but they were clustered into at least eight different farmsteads strung out along river terraces in the edge of the forest. It is more similar to other large, nucleated LBK settlements such as Elsloo in Holland or Bylany in the Czech Republic. Bylany also contained over one hundred longhouses along with kilns, ovens and wells and was in use for around 500 years.

Early farming in the British Isles

After 4900 BC the LBK culture disintegrated into many regional variations and agriculture spread from the loess areas up to the North Sea and Baltic coasts. Bogucki (2000) explains the 'mosaic' of different settlements and economies as local foragers selectively adopting elements of food production. There is particularly strong evidence for this at Swifterbant sites in marshlands around the Rhine estuary. Zvelebil (1998) presents a similar case for the Ertebølle (▶ p. 309) of the Baltic coast. A wider range of domesticated crops were used including spelt and bread wheat and barley. Southern Britain appears to fall into this pattern later. Prior to 4000 BC there is little confirmed evidence of domesticated crops or animals despite their existence for over 1,000 years across the Channel. From *c.* 4000 BC most of the early finds of cereals and pig and cattle bones come from ceremonial sites such as causewayed enclosures (e.g. Hambledon Hill) and long barrows, suggesting that economics may not have been the sole or even main reason for importing them. This transition is currently the subject of a major redating programme (▶ p. 161).

In Britain but not Ireland there was a lag of hundreds of years between the appearance of the first sign of arable crops and evidence of widespread farming. Relatively few farming sites have been excavated before the middle Bronze Age, which has led many writers to suggest that the population was mobile rather than sedentary and that wild resources were still important. Houses or indicators of field systems are also rare. Darvill's survey of known domestic buildings (Darvill and Thomas 2000) was only able to identify just over one hundred. They varied hugely from small rectangular houses as at Fengate through massive longhouses as at Balbridie to the stone cells at Knap of Howar in the Orkney Islands. Several of the houses have also been interpreted as being of ritual rather than domestic significance (▶ p. 274). Elsewhere, clusters of pits and small postholes suggest more mobile settlement patterns. On the coast there is often continuity at midden sites (▶ p. 241) from the Mesolithic and many sites where wild food such as deer or hazelnuts were still exploited.

Incomers or indigenous adoption?

The low visibility of arable farming has led many archaeologists to suggest that a form of pastoralism was the main form adopted. The cattle bones at Hambledon Hill and Windmill Hill have

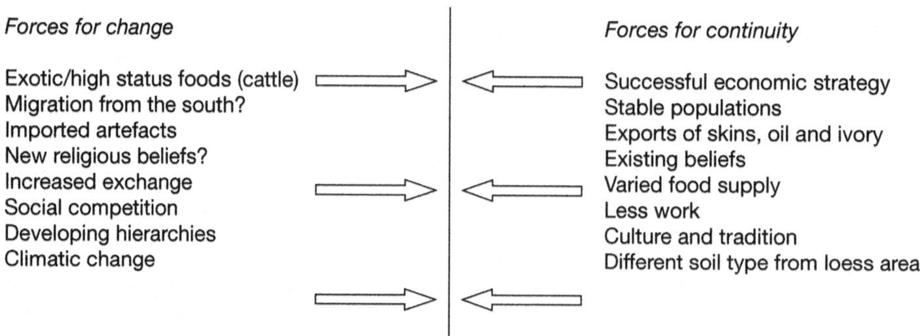

Figure 8.53 *A force-field diagram to illustrate the different pressures and motives which influenced the 'Neolithic standstill' in the Baltic. A shift in the strength of some of these eventually led to a very rapid conversion.*

Figure 8.54 *A Neolithic bow ard*

The ard, or scratch plough, was used to cut a shallow furrow for sowing on light soils. It may have been used to create furrows at right angles as appear under South Street long barrow at Avebury.

suggested herd structures associated with dairying (▶ p. 111). Support has come from carbon isotope analysis of human bones, which suggests a dependence upon animal protein and traces of dairy fats on the earliest ceramics on many sites (Evershed et al. 2003). Many of the carbonised grain deposits found are 'clean' – having been fully processed elsewhere, and may represent special deposits. Pollen evidence is ambivalent. There is evidence of the opening of clearings in the forests but there is also evidence of a major decline in elm trees at this time, which may have been caused by disease. Far more is known about the monuments of this period and there is consensus amongst archaeologists that these were central to the Neolithic. A common view is that they created a focus and sense of identity for scattered communities (Whittle 1996). Archaeologists are divided over whether these were sedentary mixed farmers or mobile pastoralists who practised small-scale horticulture. The debate over who the farmers were continues (▶ p. 499). Until the 1970s, the colonisation argument supported by the alien domesticates and continental-

Figure 8.55 *Iron Age roundhouse from the Peat Moors centre*

Although the first farmers in central Europe lived in massive rectangular longhouses, the preference in Britain when arable farming became common during the Bronze Age was usually for roundhouses. These are the commonest large structure on sites up to the Roman period. Their universality suggests that similar-sized groups of extended families (▶ p. 420) were the basic building block of society and probably of production and consumption too.

style ceramic bowls held sway. DNA evidence (▶ p. 502) does not support wholesale colonisation. Most now believe indigenous people adopted elements of the 'package' but are divided over how and to what extent. The latest dating research (▶ p. 161) is starting to clarify this. In Ireland the picture is different again with more visible evidence of houses and fields from an early date and pollen records documenting clearance and cereals (Bradley 2007). It appears that in Ireland farming may have swiftly replaced foraging in many areas but with a narrower 'package' of domestic crops than in Britain.

Europe's earliest field system

The Ceide Fields (pronounced K-Ja) on the coast of Mayo in Ireland provide evidence for some of the earliest farming in the British Isles and perhaps also its environmental impact. They were revealed by peat-cutters who discovered drystone walls underneath the peat. Excavation uncovered a landscape of rectangular, enclosed fields, houses and tombs all buried beneath blanket bog. It is the oldest field system in Europe and dates from the early 4th millennium BC. While some features have been excavated, the site is too large (around 20km^2) to open up. It is too wet for resistivity so researchers have used 2m probes to trace the buried walls (▶ p. 24). When the pole hits a wall, a cane is placed in the hole and the walls can be traced from the canes. Fields form coaxial patterns with the main axis running north down the slope towards the sea and other walls coming off at right angles. This suggests that the walls were planned and were roughly

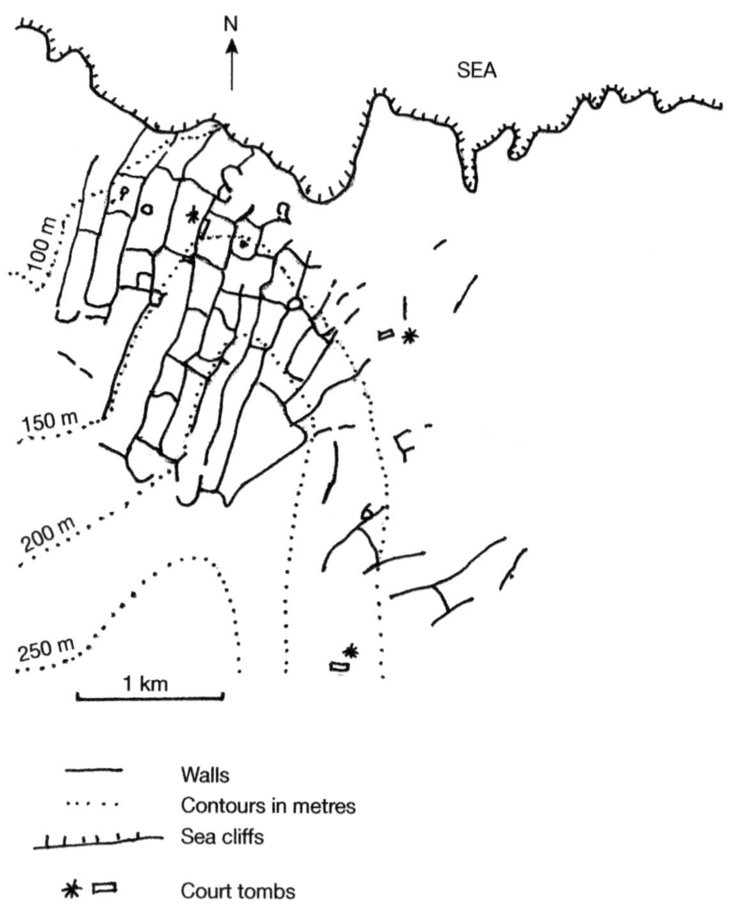

Figure 8.56 *Map of the Ceide Fields*

contemporary rather than gradually built up over time. The extensive field pattern demonstrates considerable social organisation and must have involved a sizeable community clearing woodland and building and maintaining walls. Bone and environmental evidence suggests the fields were mainly pasture for cattle rearing. With a warm climate in the 4th millennium BC, grass for grazing would have grown for eleven months a year. Archaeologists' interpretations of the main function of the fields include protecting herds from wolves or rustlers, controlling grazing patterns, separating animals to ensure selective breeding and keeping cattle and crops apart. There is some evidence for arable farming. Ard marks have been found along with the stone point of an ard and pollen analysis has revealed that wheat was grown. Buried mineral soils from this site and others nearby were compared with earlier Mesolithic soils. Organic phosphate was higher in all cases than the Mesolithic soils and highest in those fields with ard marks. The same fields showed a high level of bile acid from cattle dung when subjected to lipid analysis. This suggests that farmers were manuring the soil to enrich it.

Integrated within the field systems are domestic enclosures and the postholes and hearths remaining from small circular huts. These occur roughly once for every strip of land. Relatively few artefacts have been recovered but pottery and lithics, including arrowheads and quernstones, have been found. There are also stone-built court and portal tombs spaced out evenly across the landscape every 1–2km. This suggests that family groups lived amongst the field systems and may also have been buried there. The lack of differentiation suggests a relatively egalitarian society. Although the dominant model of the Neolithic in Britain is that people were seasonally mobile, Ceide is very different. People here were firmly anchored to a relatively small area. Cooney (Cooney and Grogran 1999) argues that people would have had a much stronger sense of place and a community identity. Furthermore he argues that there is evidence elsewhere in Ireland, the Northern Isles and the Atlantic seaboard of Britain for long-lasting sedentary settlements. Certainly other field systems with similar relationships between tombs and round or rectangular houses are known elsewhere along the Mayo coast. It is likely that many more are hidden under the bogs that cloak much of the region. A growing number of durable, oak-built houses have also been discovered in Ireland including one at Ballyglass, close to the Ceide Fields. In other words, the Neolithic took many forms and we need to be careful not to extend a model from one area to everywhere else. By 3000 BC the fields were abandoned as blanket bog (▶ p. 242) developed.

Investigating early agriculture

Once arable agriculture was established in Britain, its traces are relatively easy to detect archaeologically, particularly through changes in pollen sequences. Field and irrigation systems, storage pits and specialist equipment from ploughs to sickles become common from the late Bronze Age. Interest then shifts to the productivity and use of agricultural products. Experimental archaeology has been valuable. Butser Ancient Farm has demonstrated the kinds of yield possible with ancient crops and explored their response to a range of growing conditions. Detailed analysis of plant assemblages to examine weed types and ratios of weeds to grain and grain to chaff enables archaeologists to identify whether crops were grown and processed on site and suggest where the fields were (▶ p. 121).

A SECONDARY PRODUCTS REVOLUTION?

Early agriculture was at a subsistence level, providing meat and harvest crops for the farming communities. Essentially they substituted domesticates for wild food. There is little evidence of significant surpluses or social change during the Neolithic. However, from 3500 BC civilisations (▶ p. 468) emerged across the Near East based on the control of massive agricultural surpluses. In south-eastern Europe in the 3rd millennium BC societies became unequal, with warrior-elites (▶ p. 457) controlling land, animals and people to provide weapons, prestige goods and feasting. These social transformations were enabled by a series of technological changes that intensified agricultural production. Sherratt (1981) saw these changes as relatively contemporary and connected them together as the 'secondary products revolution' (SPR) to differentiate their impact from the original 'Neolithic revolution'. Primitive ploughs and draught animals extended the area which could be farmed to include heavier soils while the use of manure increased crop yields. Donkeys and wheeled carts enabled excess produce to be moved to a central place (▶ p. 400) or market. Milk massively increased the calories that could be provided by cattle and provided an all-year source of protein and fat. The development of a breed of woolly sheep (which also provided milk) similarly increased the value of herds and provided a new, versatile textile to supplement flax and other plant fibres. Halstead (1981a) estimates that a society subsisting on sheep meat would need flocks two and a half times as large as one combining milk and mutton to provide the same calories. This would require several

Figure 8.57 *Animal traction. Yoked oxen pulling a plough. Similar technology spread across Europe in the Bronze Age.*

thousand extra animals for a typical village. Horses appear to have been used for riding rather than as draught animals but may also have supplied milk and blood as secondary products. Wool and grain provided commodities which could be traded or taxed and controlled. Farming land became valuable but cattle and sheep also provided mobile sources of wealth. It is unsurprising that herd animals became both symbolically important (▶ p. 423) and the focus of early accounting systems (▶ p. 416). The expansion of agriculture, particularly herding, as the result of these changes led to the construction of field systems and the development of transhumance pastoralism in unsettled, upland areas.

Identifying the SPR in the archaeological record

The 'secondary products revolution' remains a widely used concept because it describes a significant transformation of economy and society but there is less acceptance today of the short time frame and direction of change (from Mesopotamia) in Sherratt's original account. He based the dating of the SPR on changes in faunal assemblages, art and specialised artefacts. These indicators all provided evidence of the new practices but none of them could identify when they began. The predominance of older females in assemblages can indicate dairying, wear from traction can lead to stress or arthritis in animal bones and skeletal changes occur where bullocks (castrated bulls) were used. However, these are not always easy to identify. Sheep are often sexed according to their horn cores, but these do not always survive. Spindle whorls and loom weights provide evidence of textile processing from the late Neolithic onwards but can be used for flax and hemp as well as wool.

Recent research (▶ p. 138) has shown Sherratt was right to suspect perforated ceramic bowls of being milk sieves but that dairying may be even older than he thought. New approaches to the ageing of animal teeth combined with biochemical analysis of pottery have provided possible evidence that Near Eastern farmers were milking sheep by the early 8th millennium BC. Helmer and Vigne (2007) go further and suggest that milking may have been the original reason for domesticating animals. They argue that heating the milk to drink or make porridge may have made it easier to digest. Milk certainly appears to be part of the initial Neolithic package in western Europe and may also have been an early element elsewhere. Environmental data can provide indirect evidence of increased herding. The abandonment of many tell sites in the Balkans *c.* 4000 BC is associated with deposits of eroded hillside soils (Dennell 1978). This may indicate that forest clearance and perhaps over-grazing had begun in the 5th millennium BC. New species such as horses or donkeys and new breeds such as the larger fleecy sheep are easier to identify. Horses were first domesticated on the Eurasian Steppe, although when and where is disputed. Outram et al. (2009) established from bit wear on horses' teeth and from horse milk fats in pottery that the Botai of Kazakhstan had domesticated horses as early as 5500 BC. DNA research published by Warmuth et al. (2012) pointed to multiple sites of domestication across the Steppes, probably caused by herders replenishing their stock by capturing wild horses. By the 5th millennium BC horses were being herded by the Sredny Stog culture of the Ukraine and *c.* 3500 BC horse bones and harness fittings appeared in eastern Europe. Their association with high-status sites and burials suggests that they were initially a symbol of prestige, to be ridden rather than used as draught animals. Donkeys, by contrast, appear to have been used primarily for carrying or pulling loads. They were domesticated from the wild African ass during the 5th millennium BC and widely used in Near Eastern civilisations but do not appear to have arrived in Europe until later in the Bronze Age, *c.* 2000 BC.

Figure 8.58 *Symbol of a new world: a Bronze Age rock carving of a ploughman from the World Heritage site of Tanum in Sweden*

The first wooden ploughs, or ards, were effectively long hoes drawn by people or animals and were used to scratch shallow furrows in order to plant seeds. They probably originated in Mesopotamia and are depicted in pictograms (▶ p. 415) from the Uruk period *c.* 4000 BC. This technology spread quickly with characteristic scratch marks being recorded in several places in Europe in the 4th millennium BC. The oldest surviving ard dates to 2300 BC and was made from a single piece of oak. It was preserved in a bog at Lavagnone, Italy. Wheeled carts are also thought to have originated in the Uruk period, although there is some evidence of simultaneous invention in the Ukraine. A possible abstract depiction of a cart is also shown on the Bronocice Pot from Poland from 3635 to 3370 BC. The oldest surviving wheel was preserved in the Ljubljana marshes of Slovenia and dated to 3000 BC. Like other early wheels it was solid and made from ash planks with an oak axle that rotated with the wheel.

Secondary products did not arrive as a unified package in Europe. Dairying may have been present from the Neolithic and herding of all kinds probably expanded in the Chalcolithic. Ploughing and the use of carts followed in the 4th millennium BC as did the horse. Donkeys, vines and arboriculture (tree crops) arrived much later during the Bronze Age after the main economic and associated social changes had already begun.

Figure 8.59 *Cart image on the Bronocice Pot*

Secondary products did, however, transform Europe and establish a common pattern of mixed farming and agricultural surpluses from the Balkans to the British Isles.

Ceramic technology was used to create wine and olive oil as part of the secondary products revolution. Their wide distribution suggests intensive processing of agricultural produce occurred in the countryside with finished products being taken to the palace sites.

Figure 8.60 *Wine press from the Minoan villa at Archanes*

AGRICULTURAL INTENSIFICATION

Intensification of agriculture involves increasing control over the productive capacity of the land. It is often associated with population pressure or social demands to create surpluses (▶ p. 461). The earliest traces of intensification can be detected from the soil and pollen evidence for forest clearance and pioneer farming. For example, around Avebury cycles of forest clearance and later regeneration in association with fluctuations in the intensity of agricultural exploitation have been traced.

Irrigation

More dramatic evidence comes from areas of the world where artificial ways of supplying rainfall to crops were needed to raise yields. Starting in Mesopotamia, canals, ditches and dams were built to store water and divert it to dry areas. This enabled the expansion of arable areas and raised yields while reducing risk. Some ancient canals survive as earthworks as at Monte Alban in Mexico or crop or soil marks but others are not immediately visible. The 3rd millennium BC network of canals suppling water to the fields and the port of Mashkan Shapir (▶ p. 286) is buried under sand but was detected by satellite imaging (▶ p. 37). In the Oaxaca valley of Mexico, a field survey at Arroyo Lencho Diego located 20m of sediment which had accumulated behind a vanished dam. The inhabitants had used the dam to irrigate the whole of the valley in an area of otherwise unpredictable water availability. Tomb paintings supplement the archaeological evidence for irrigation schemes in Ancient Egypt. Early agriculture here involved planting as soon as the Nile floodwaters receded. By building a series of banks or dams the Egyptians learned how to hold some of the floodwater in a basin and release it more slowly or to extend the area watered. Illustrations depict the technology for lifting water from canals to fields including the shaduf and later the Archimedes' Screw, an early bronze version of which may have watered the famous 'Hanging Gardens of Babylon'. More visible are the terrace irrigations of the Far East. Banks and ditches guide water from the tops of hills or mountains along a series of steps or terraces. The most spectacular example are the 2,000-year-old rice terraces of the Cordilleras in the Philippines which were the first landscape listed by UNESCO. Terracing was also used in the Andes to grow potatoes rather than rice. An alternative approach was taken in Mexico, where the Aztecs developed an intensive system of agriculture based on floating gardens or 'chinampas'. Rafts were covered in weeds and mud and anchored in rows. Over time more mud was added and the root systems of trees bound the rafts together as fertile islands. They could be cropped two to three times a year. The Aztec capital Tenochtitlan received most of its food from chinampas. Irrigation was also the basis of water meadow systems built across southern England from the early medieval period. These spread water and silt across floodplains to create lush grazing to fatten animals for market.

Figure 8.61 *Terraces at Machu Picchu*

These Inca farming systems effectively distributed moisture to crops on each level while retaining heat within the walled terraces.

Drainage and colonising marginal land

In other instances there was too much water for successful cultivation and land had to be reclaimed before farming could begin. At Kuk Swamp in New Guinea a huge network of drainage ditches was first revealed by aerial photography, showing as dark lines several kilometres long in modern tea plantations. Excavation revealed that early farmers had built them to drain the swamp in order to intensively cultivate the fertile soil and grow taro (a starchy root) and other crops (Bayliss-Smith 1996). In many areas, drainage schemes from the past continue in use. Some of England's most productive farmland was low-lying marshy fen until C17th Dutch engineers built drainage canals and windmills to lift water from field ditches into them. The complex pattern of dykes (banks), ditches and sluices survives along with straightened rivers. More commonly, farming from the Iron Age onwards often involved ploughing to build a well-drained ridge of earth which could be planted. The corduroy pattern of medieval ridge and furrow is often visible today in pasture and in aerial photographs. In addition to draining bogs, agricultural production was also raised by extending onto more marginal land. Evidence for this can be seen in many upland areas which were put under cultivation during periods of warmer climates or during times of shortage or warfare. Often these were not sustainable due to climate deterioration or soil degradation. The intensification of production including the exploitation of stock animals resulted in the construction of elaborate field systems and land divisions such as the Bronze Age Dartmoor 'reaves'. These and

Figure 8.62 *Sail-wing windmill from Crete*

Windmill technology arrived in Europe by way of Persia in the C12th. Unlike their Islamic predecessors, European mills had a horizontal axis. This may have been because that was used in existing watermills. Mills such as this were used to pump irrigation water and grind corn.

contemporary settlements such as Shaugh Moor provide evidence of more extensive farming. Medieval attempts to intensify production by extending the area of arable land can be identified through place names and earthworks such as strip lynchets where hillsides were ploughed.

Soil fertility

Altering the chemistry of the soil itself is another way of raising productivity. Manuring is known from the Bronze Age in Holland where dark, humic layers can be detected in otherwise sandy soil areas. The source of manure can be determined by examining insect remains. Flies and their eggs from farmyards will differ from those which lay eggs in cowpats in fields. At Gurness, Orkney (▶ p. 275) and Dun Vulan in the Hebrides during the Iron Age, seaweed, dung, domestic midden deposits and ash were amongst the materials used to enhance naturally thin soils with phosphates and other nutrients to create rich plaggen soils. Medieval manuring to increase yields is generally recognised from the halo of pottery scattered in the fields around settlements (▶ p. 19). The production of lime for increasing the pH content of soils as well as providing mortar for building is evidenced by the remains of kilns in rural areas across much of Britain.

Agricultural specialisation

Specialisation can raise productivity, particularly if it is large-scale, and can also be efficient by matching crops and animals to environments. Intensive stock rearing can be identified from enclosures and specialist sites. The Iron Age site of Mingies Ditch near Oxford provides such an example. The wet floodplain was unsuited to cereals so was used to rear horses. The specialised nature of the settlement meant that other sites had to supply the subsistence needs of those living there. Tree crops provide another variation. These require long-term investment to nurture them while they grow and are unproductive but then can provide significant returns once they enter production. Olives in the Mediterranean region (▶ p. 473) are the best known but orchards, coppiced woodland (▶ p. 244) and vineyards provide other examples.

STORAGE

Storage is an economic strategy. It may be used to overcome fluctuations in food supply or to hoard a surplus to use in exchange. Storage can be linked to social power (▶ p. 256), perhaps used by an elite to control the distribution of resources to gain prestige or power. The concept of storage can be used to include energy, information, and even the dead. Archaeologists study both the methods of storage and the social and economic reasons for it.

Direct evidence of storage comes from the containers or other features used to hold produce.

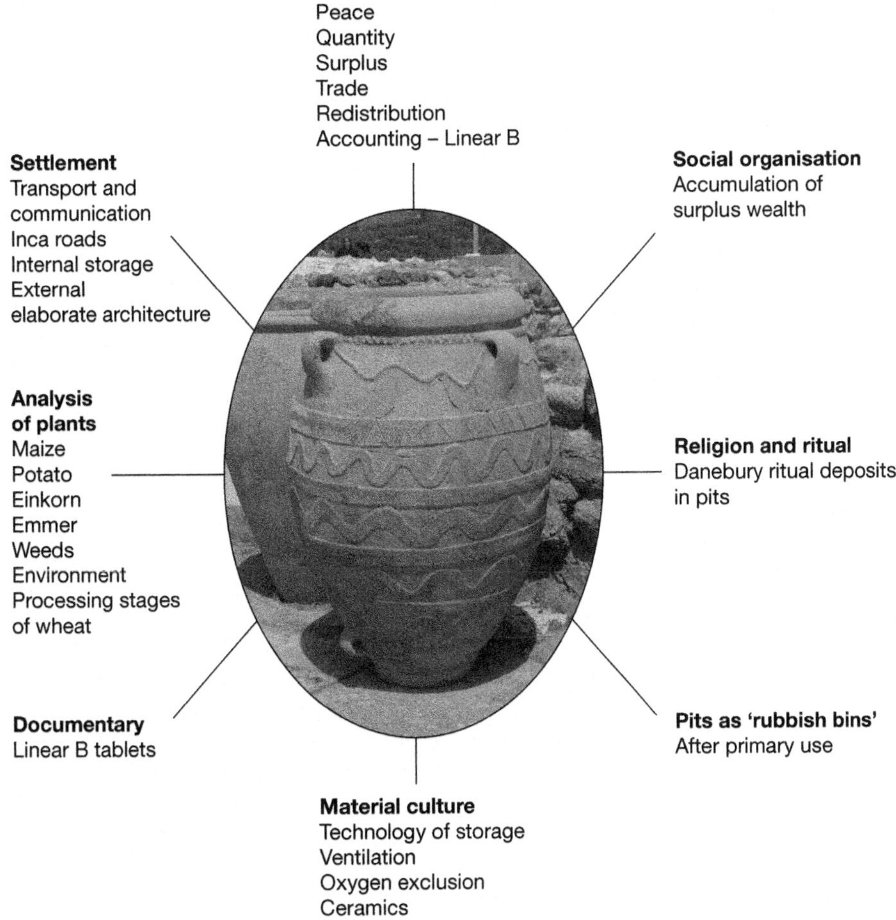

Figure 8.63 *The archaeology of storage*

Figure 8.64 *Roman granary from Corbridge*

Built to standard plans, military granaries were raised to reduce damp and allow dogs to hunt rats underneath. They testify to the economic organisation of the Roman army, who did not just rely on local food sources. Grain surpluses were transported to bases and stored to ensure a constant supply for the troops. This is also a good example of redistribution (▶ p. 400).

Many ancient civilisations developed central storage facilities (▶ p. 259) to hold food and other agricultural produce. At the Inca site of Huanuco Pampa, circular, ventilated warehouses which were once used for freeze-dried potatoes still survive. The same is true of many medieval tithe barns. Sometimes they contain traces of their former contents or illustrations on their walls. Dumps of raw inorganic materials such as coal or stone will also leave at least small traces of minerals in the topsoil. Similarly, features such as pits or silos of arable farming communities are frequently recognised and contain pollen or carbonised grain which indicate their uses. On a smaller scale, storage vessels including pottery and glass can be examined in the same way for external decoration or residues of former contents (▶ p. 136). There may also be written or artistic

Figure 8.65 *Iron Age four-poster grain store from Hochdorf*

sources that illustrate storage, including tax records and tomb paintings. Other traces of storage need greater interpretation. Drying racks and off-ground structures will only be represented in the archaeological record by postholes.

Different forms of storage

Landscape features may represent very different types of storage. Millponds, for example, may be stores of power, fish and water. Herds of animals are a form of storage in themselves. Dense clusters of posts or ditches may represent corrals or stockyards for storing food on the hoof. Phosphate analysis may confirm their function. It is important to recognise this because there is a tendency to associate storage with sedentary societies, yet ethnography has shown many examples of storage practised by mobile pastoralists.

Other forms of storage leave only indirect evidence. Salt production is often traced through the distinctive 'briquetage' containers used to transport it. On some sites inferences can be drawn from the nature of the food remains. The restricted range of bone types at La Cotte de St Brelade suggested the 'caching' of meat. At Stellmoor (▶ p. 298) the sheer quantity of meat

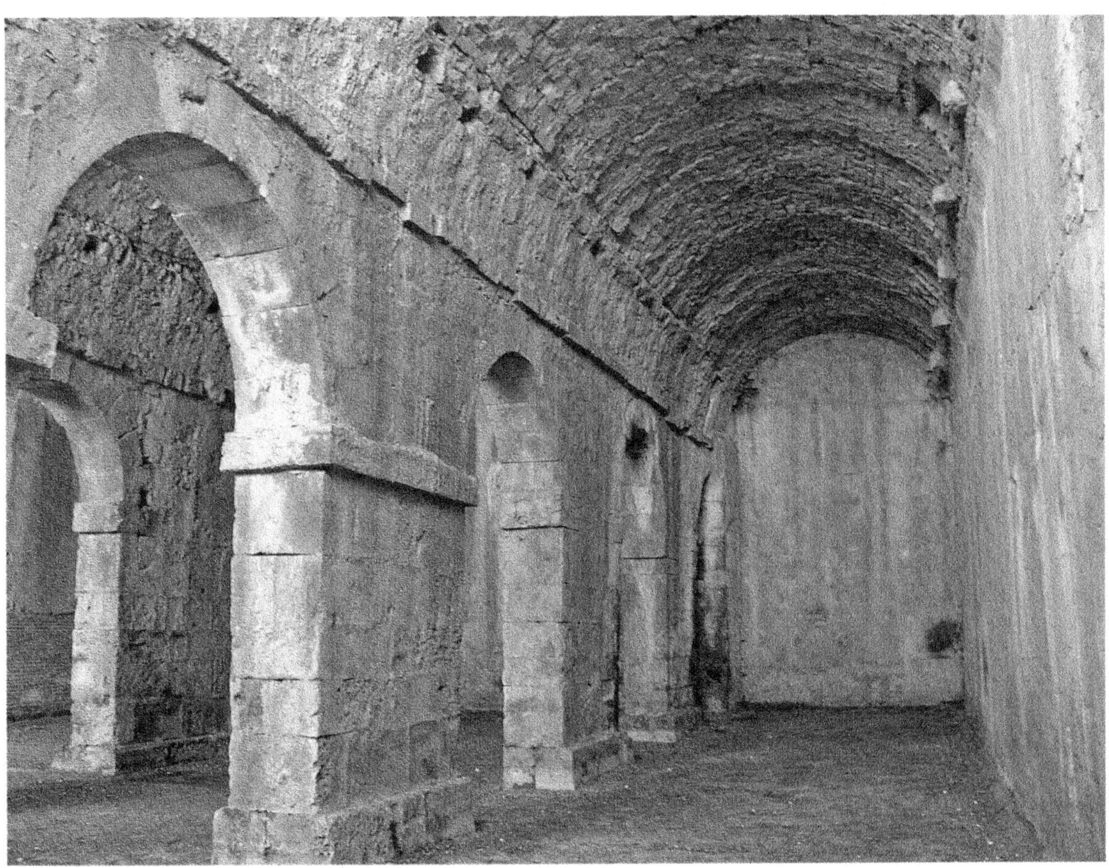

Figure 8.66 *Storage of water*

One of three massive Roman cisterns at Aptera, Crete. The function of the vaulted underground cisterns was to feed the baths on the site, to provide drinking water for the people and to enable the hilltop city to withstand a siege. It is an impressive example of public works (▶ p. 285).

Figure 8.67 *Minoan harvester vase. The farming year with its cycle of activities and festivals dominated the lives of most Europeans until the C19th AD.*

was suggestive of pemmican making (▶ p. 253). Insects associated with particular foodstuffs also provide clues; for example, grain beetles from Roman York.

Finally, there are forms of storage which leave no trace. Binford's study of the Nunamiut recorded them wind-drying caribou meat on willow bushes while woodpiles are one of the commonest types of store on any site but both are archaeologically invisible. Organic containers such as baskets and skins only survive in exceptional circumstances. The same is true of some agricultural produce, particularly tubers. Symbolic or abstract forms of storage are visible in the archaeological record from later prehistory. Instead of raw materials themselves being stored, they are exchanged for something which is widely accepted as symbolising a value in those materials. Coins are a particularly sophisticated method of symbolically storing value. They can be converted into goods at a later date. They have the advantage of being easily transported and concealed. Jewellery, cattle, carpets and cowrie shells have been used in a similar way. The concept of social storage should also be considered under this heading, although it is much more difficult to recognise archaeologically. This is where one person stores value in others. In simple terms, if I give you a gift of a cow, at some point in the future you will give me something of at least equal value (▶ p. 399). In practice, social storage is often highly complex and can encompass marriages, feasting and military alliances. Social storage blurs economics with social and political affairs. However, for most of human history these areas have probably been inextricably linked.

THE IMPACT OF AGRICULTURE

Farming transformed the world. Within a few millennia surpluses enabled some people to become non-farming specialists and ultimately the first urban societies. It also led to increasingly unequal societies as elites gained control over surpluses, land or people. The explosion of the human population is directly attributable to agriculture. The impact on health is less clear. Cohen (1979) argued that nutrition declined except amongst elites and that infectious disease spread in sedentary agricultural populations. Evidence for this comes through studying human bones for signs of deficiency, stress and infection as well as average size and age at death. Most studies confirm that early farmers were less robust than their foraging predecessors and had much narrower diets. The environmental effects of farming are well known, including erosion (▶ p. 128), destruction of habitats and salination (▶ p. 286). The archaeological evidence for these largely comes from site abandonment and soil studies (▶ p. 105).

Chapter 9

Economics B

Extraction, Manufacture, Material Culture and Exchange

This chapter deals with the acquisition of materials, production of goods and artefacts and exchange. Many of the methods used in studying materials were covered in Chapter 3, with interpretative techniques in Chapter 5. This chapter builds on them, providing context and key studies. It also relates to the economic functions of settlements (Chapter 7) and the relationship between economy and society (Chapter 10). Key concepts covered include:

- **Extraction**: the technologies used to acquire resources, particularly through mining. The acquisition of organic resources from plants and animals was largely covered in Chapter 8.
- **Production**: how artefacts are manufactured including the technology, tools and organisation of those doing the making.
- **Material culture**: the artefacts (and structures) that people made and what they signified. 'Biographical approaches' research the raw materials used, how they were obtained and worked and how the finished products were used. A second approach involves 'reading' the symbolic meanings embedded in artefacts and structures. This is based on the idea that the beliefs and values of a culture are expressed to some extent in the material things it produces. People's actions are 'structured' by the beliefs, ideas and knowledge of their culture. These actions in turn shape the things they create.
- **Technology**: the tools used in particular tasks and the underlying skills and knowledge required to accomplish them.
- **Exchange**: the social and economic aspects of human behaviour governing the way materials are distributed. It ranges from the exchange of gifts to complex international trade systems. Consumption is the final aspect of exchange and is covered in Chapter 10.

ACQUISITION OF STONE AND MINERALS

Underground mining is unknown before the Neolithic. Previously, stone and minerals for artefacts were gathered from surface deposits, outcrops and water courses. This applies to material such as flint, chert, obsidian, gold and building stone. Most such early sites are archaeologically invisible except where artefacts can be matched by their chemical fingerprint (▶ p. 131) to a source or there is extensive debris from repeated visits. In many cases, as with semi-precious stones such as cornelian and chalcedony, attractive colours, shapes and reflective qualities led to selection for beads and other trinkets. The rich Chalcolithic grave goods at Varna (▶ p. 423) and Duran Kuluk on the Black Sea were dominated by personal adornments created from polished, hammered and drilled materials gathered in this way. Early salt extraction also leaves little or no trace. Salt springs would have been identified from the effect on surrounding vegetation and the crystals left from evaporation collected in bags or baskets. It is not until the use of distinctive coarse pottery (briquetage) that this process becomes visible.

Grimes Graves and flint mining

Aside from identifying the sources of materials, ancient extraction sites such as mines and quarries provide insights into technology and scale of production. At the Neolithic flint mines at Grimes Graves, 350 vertical shafts were dug 10m down through chalk and flint to seams of dark, floor-stone flint. This was prized for its colour, purity and ease of working. Recent dating evidence suggests the whole site was in use for hundreds of years with one to two shafts dug each year, so a relatively small number of people were involved at any one time. From the bottom of the shafts, galleries radiate out following the flint seams. Antler picks, shoulder blade shovels and stone axes were used to dig the mine and extract the flint. Some were left behind by the miners and the marks made by these tools can be seen on the walls. This helps us understand the processes of extraction. Pillars were left in the galleries to prevent roof collapses and baskets and ladders probably used to get in and out with the flint. Smoke stains from burning animal fat on the roofs of galleries show that miners used lamps or textiles soaked in fat to provide light. However, this was not just an extraction site. There was no need to dig this deep to get flint for tools. There are hearths and evidence of feasting in some chambers. There are special deposits of unusual artefacts and animal bones and also some human remains. It is highly likely that ritual was also important.

Europe's largest flint mine at Krzemionki, Poland, was used for over 2,000 years from 3900 BC and includes 700 shafts spread over several kilometres. The site includes settlements and

Figure 9.1 *Grimes Graves flint mining*

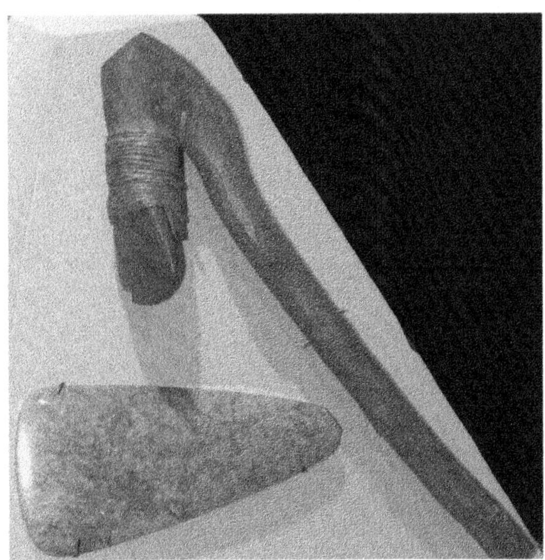

Figure 9.2 *The stages of manufacture of stone axes*

flint knapping areas where distinctive banded, spotted or chocolate flint artefacts were produced. The technology was the same as Grimes Graves with shafts up to 9m in depth and drifts fanning out from the shaft bottoms. Here, too, mining was unnecessary to extract flint, as it occurs on the surface in some clays and limestone soils. However, quality, colour and perhaps the dangerous, underground world from which it came made mined flint more desirable.

Langdale stone axes

The distribution patterns of polished stone axes during the Neolithic in northern Europe also suggest that materials with unusual colours and which were extracted from dangerous sites on mountains were particularly sought after. Suitably hard stone exists in many hills and mountainous areas but quarry sites were often particularly remote. Amongst the most spectacular is the Langdale 'axe factory' in the heart of the Lake District which produced around a quarter of all known axes in England (▶ p. 370). Langdale greenstone comes from a band of volcanic tuff found on the highest mountains in the area. From *c.* 3800 BC rocks were being selected from debris at the top of the mountain around 700m rather than the scree slopes near the valley bottom. Rocks were roughed into a rectangular blank with a hard hammer of stone. Evidence of producing these rough-outs at the site occurs in the form of debitage and broken rejects. Blanks were then taken from the mountains and distributed across Britain and Ireland. Somewhere on their journey softer hammers and pressure flaking techniques were used to refine the shape and smooth the surface. Finally a laborious process of grinding and polishing with leather, sand and water produced wedge-shaped axe heads up to 28cm × 7cm in size. A very fine abrasive would be used to give it the final polish and make it a thing of beauty. They are perfectly functional and hafted examples have been found. However, many were deposited without being used including several in the Thames and one at Grimes Graves. Bradley and Edmonds (2005) argue that remote, dangerous (perhaps sacred) quarry locations gave these axes particular significance and made them prestige items.

Figure 9.3 *Langdale Pike is on the far left. Most of the peaks are associated with Neolithic axe-factories.*

Figure 9.4 *Langdale greenstone polished axe*

Quarrying

Petrology (▶ p. 95) analysis of ceramics can suggest location sites for ancient clay extraction but, as with surface extraction, traces of early activity are often destroyed by subsequent quarrying and mining. At very local levels, borrow pits for clay to provide daub can sometimes be found in settlements in the same way that quarry ditches are found alongside long barrows or LBK longhouses but rarely anything large-scale. From the Roman period onwards, quarries became more substantial and are more likely to survive as landscape features or later field names such as 'querns', 'clay pits' or 'lime kilns'.

Occasionally prehistoric quarries do survive. At Aswan, an incomplete 41m long red granite obelisk was discovered from the 2nd millennium BC along with clues about the technology. Workers holding balls of diorite found at the site, a stone even harder than granite, laboriously pounded a metre-wide trench around the outline. This process left characteristic rounded marks on the trench side and base. At an estimated weight of 1,168 tonnes, it would take several hundred workers over a year to quarry the obelisk. Recent discovery of a buried canal linking the quarry to

Figure 9.5 *Roman stone quarry on Brac, Croatia*

the Nile reveals how the monster stone would have been floated to its intended destination had it not cracked. With softer rocks, holes would be created using bow-drills (▶ p. 182) and sand then filled with wood which was then soaked to expand and crack the rock free. This can be seen from drill marks and organic residue on the bedrock in other Egyptian quarries.

On Crete, the Minoan civilisation used similar methods to quarry a range of softer rocks. At the coastal quarry of Mochlos, sandstone for building the town of Gournia was removed by using bronze picks to gouge out trenches around blocks. By starting close to the water and working up the cliffs, the quarrymen were able to slide blocks on chippings from earlier extractions down to the sea, from where blocks could be put on rafts (Waelkens and Herz 1992). Stone blocks were dressed using chisels or in the case of some soft rocks such as gypsum, large bronze saws. Ten of these have been found at Zakros. An abrasive such as sand was probably used as well. While these saws could have been used for timber, there are stone blocks that do have saw-marks. Other stone such as serpentine and soapstone was also quarried but to make vessels and ornaments rather than building materials.

The first copper mines

Unlike lithics, the extraction of metals involves at least two steps. The mined ore requires processing to separate metal from waste (slag). Some of the earliest evidence for metals extraction comes from the Balkans from *c*. 5000 BC. The technology used was similar to that in flint mines. At Rudna Glava in the mountains of Serbia, old mine workings were exposed by a modern open cast iron mine. Excavations in the 1970s recorded over twenty vertical shafts following veins of copper down through the limestone rock to a depth of 25m. Horizontal galleries connected the shafts or

Figure 9.6 *The unfinished obelisk, Aswan*

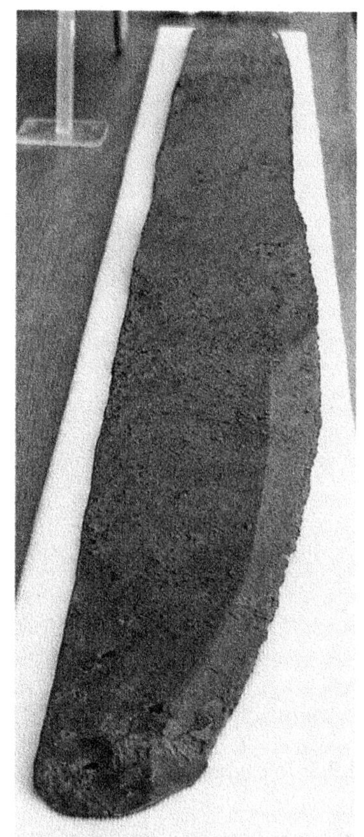

Figure 9.7 *Bronze saw from Zakros Minoan palace*

followed seams of copper into the mountain for around 15m. In some of these, stone had been piled up to support the roof. Finds included hundreds of mauls: large, smooth rocks with a groove around their middle where they had been tied and signs of damage where they had been used. Antler and bone picks were common, as were ceramics. Several complete vessels had been deliberately preserved in cracks in the rock (Craddock 1995).

The twelve mines at Aibunar in the mountains of central Bulgaria were contemporary with Rudna Glava. Trenches up to 80m long and 10m wide were used rather than vertical shafts, although these went to similar depths. Similar tools were used with the addition of a copper axe and an adze, both with shaftholes. Pottery was linked to phases IV and V of Karanovo (▶ p. 339), which was just to the south, and metal from Aibunar has been found at Karanovo. Additional organic artefacts included wooden wedges and shovels and the remains of leather bags. Charcoal mixed in with shattered rock enabled the mining process to be reconstructed. Fires were lit against the rock face (fire-setting) and then water was thrown on it. This shattered the limestone and enabled it to be broken up with mauls and picks or by hammering wedges into cracks. Nuggets containing ore would be identified by colour – green for malachite and blue for azurite – and removed to the surface in bags or baskets. Here the rock was pounded with other mauls to

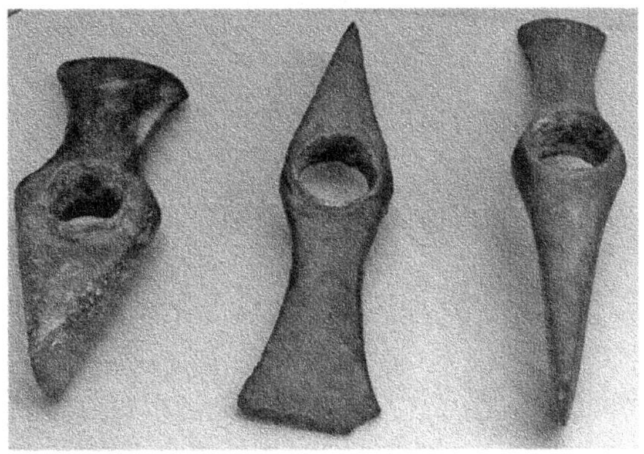

Figure 9.8 *Adzes and axe from Aibunar*

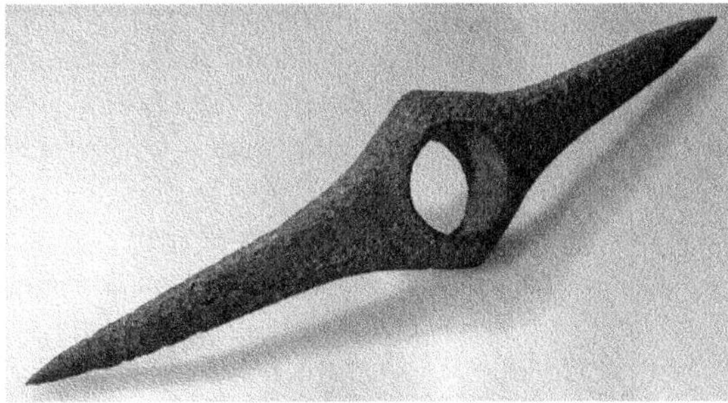

Figure 9.9 *Copper alloy pick from Stara Zagora*

separate ore from waste. At neither site was there evidence of smelting. The ores were taken to other locations for processing. Both sites were abandoned when the accessible ores were exhausted. The development of mining and copper artefacts in burials across the region led to this period being called the Chalcolithic or Copper Age. Similar mines have been found in areas with native copper deposits including Mount Gabriel and Ross Island in Ireland and Great Orme in North Wales which date from *c*. 2000 BC. Great Orme began with surface trenches and technology similar to those at Aibunar, but as those seams were exhausted after 1500 BC, shafts and galleries were dug to over 30m in depth. The different phases appear to be marked by a shift from largely bone tools to copper or bronze in the later period. The volume of rock removed suggests that Great Orme was a particularly large-scale operation (Lewis 1996).

KEY STUDY

Hallstatt and the organisation of salt mining

Hallstatt in the Dachstein Mountains of Austria is best known for the cemetery 400m up the Salzbergtal (salt mountain valley) which gave its name to the early European Iron Age. Hallstatt is also known for the world's oldest working salt mines. 'Hall' is the Celtic word for salt and indicates the importance of this site and the connection between salt and wealth in prehistory.

Mining records from the C16th AD onwards document the discovery of strange finds including the preserved bodies of miners. These were assumed to be recent victims of accidents and reburied locally. By the C19th greater curiosity about the past led amateur archaeologists to dig areas where finds were reported. In 1846 workers digging a gravel pit uncovered a grave. Johann Ramsauer, the director of the salt mine, recognised the burial as prehistoric and began excavating the surrounding area. By his death in 1874 almost 1,000 graves had been excavated. The cemetery may have originally held over 2,000 burials but many were destroyed by mining and in the early days of excavation cremations were not recognised by the diggers. Unusually for this period, Ramsauer dug methodically, used measurements and meticulously recorded his finds in line drawings and water colours. While environmental information including human bone was lost and many artefacts given away to visitors, a valuable archive was created for others to study. Ramsauer's records of metalwork provided the basis for a typological study by Paul

continued

Reinecke, who defined four chronological phases which became the basis of central European dating of the late Bronze Age (Hallstatt A and B) and early Iron Age (Hallstatt C and D). The artistic style decorating the Iron Age weapons, jewels and ceramics combined the curvilinear designs of late Bronze Age central Europe with figurative art including both stylised human figures and the natural world in a new 'Celtic' form. It was influenced by both Etruscan and Greek traditions. New metallurgical trends included repoussé work on sheet bronze and the use of brooches to supplement decorated bronze pins as clothes fasteners. Recent surveys suggest there may be more burials yet to be discovered. Investigations of old mine workings began with Ramsauer but the most spectacular finds have come in recent decades from excavations led by Barth and Reschreiter of the Vienna Natural History Museum. Their work includes taking 3D laser scans and photo mosaic records of the mines and linking them into a GIS database to enable digital recreations of the workings. Much of this recent archaeological work has been sponsored by the main mining company Salinen Austria AG. In 1997 UNESCO declared Hallstatt a World Heritage Site.

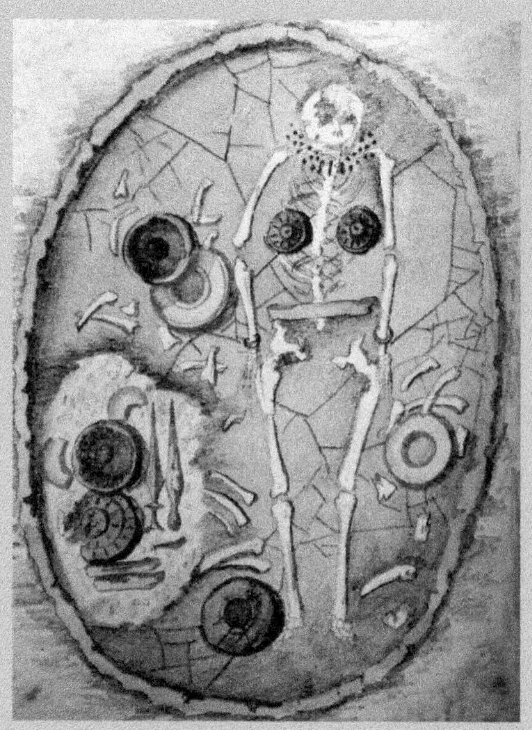

Figure 9.10 *Watercolour from Hallstatt*

The burials

The cemetery is in a hanging valley directly in front of the salt mining area. Surviving graves are largely from the Iron Age of Hallstatt C and D. Cremation and inhumation burials were found in approximately even proportions and in all phases. Bodies were aligned east–west and buried without coffins. There is no evidence that grave markers were used. Cremation burials were richer and included those identified as 'warrior burials' from the grave goods. This may seem counter-intuitive but cremation pyres were expensive in terms of labour and provided spectacular funerals. The early Hallstatt culture graves (800–650 BC) are marked by an increase in inhumations, and new artefacts including long bronze and iron swords and winged axes. Later assemblages (650–475 BC) include ornate daggers, a wide range of jewellery and imports from the Mediterranean area. This may reflect a change in display of wealth from the funeral pyre to graveside deposition. The distribution of grave goods implies an increasingly ranked society. Around 5 per cent were rich, most had daggers and some personal ornaments but 25 per cent had no goods. There was a clear gender divide with female graves mainly containing personal ornaments including headdresses and males having weapons and vessels. Examination of surviving bone suggests that many of those buried may have been miners. Males have very developed shoulder muscles

Figure 9.11 *Rich Hallstatt cremation burial*

which can be caused by swinging picks while females have muscular arms caused by carrying heavy weights. Even children show signs of strenuous labour (Kern et al. 2009). Bronze Age burials have not yet been located.

The salt mines

The earliest evidence of salt extraction comes from Neolithic antler picks similar to those used from Stonehenge to Aibunar (▶ p. 372) and dating from 5000 BC. However, no mines have been found so it is likely that salt exposed by evaporation around saline springs was exploited. The middle Bronze Age *c.* 1400 BC saw the first significant workings when copper mining techniques were adopted including driving a shaft down (through 30m of rock) and then following seams to create galleries. Three parallel shafts over 100m deep are known with galleries radiating out from them. In the Christian von Tuschwerk gallery, salt had been removed to create a space 8m high and up to 40m long. The large-scale nature of these operations was made clear by the discovery of a 1.2m wide wooden staircase in one gallery which has been dendrochronologically dated to 1344–43 BC (Kern et al. 2009). It was made by fitting wedge-shaped steps into slots cut in trunks of spruce and fir trees. Debris from mining was simply thrown down the shafts, where it provides a treasure trove for archaeology. Salt is a very effective preservative because it removes the moisture which microbes need to survive and therefore prevents decay taking place. The result is that rope, textiles, wooden tools and human faeces are all preserved.

Mining

Salt was mined using bronze picks which have left grooves all over the gallery walls. Rock debris on the floors suggests that the ceilings of galleries were mined by miners standing on piles of debris to access the next layer of salt. All the voids they created were later filled by rock falls. Chips of salt were shovelled into trugs or buckets. These were emptied into carry-sacks and taken to the shafts. Here salt was poured into sacks and hauled up on ropes. Those working the ropes wore hand leathers to protect them and several 'pitches' of rope were used. From the surface, carry-sacks were used to take the salt off the mountain. Ladders and staircases enabled movement within the mine and to the surface. Tools and sacks are of standardised designs, which implies an organised mining operation. These mines went out of use *c.* 1250 BC, when they were filled with mud and surface debris probably from a landslide. After a gap of 400 years, Iron Age mines opened and lasted till 350 BC, when they too were destroyed by landslips. These mines were very different, with angled shafts and much longer galleries. Some of these later mines were 200m deep with huge galleries up to 20m high and 150m long. Miners continued to use bronze picks and also mallets and chisels to excavate large blocks of salt including distinctive heart-shaped tablets. In contrast to the Bronze Age, waste chips of salt were left where they fell and it was only the blocks which were carried to the surface. The telltale wear on discarded shoes shows that miners spent much of their lives going up and down ladders.

continued

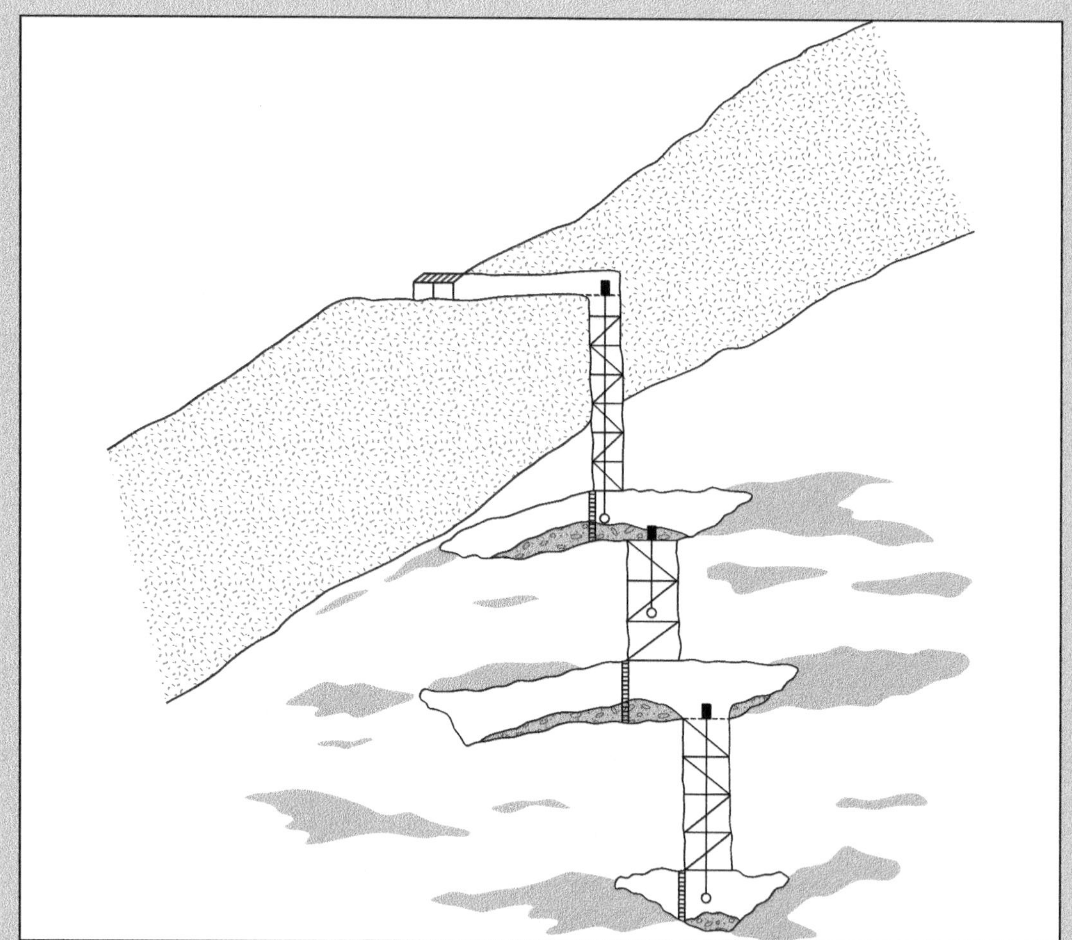

Figure 9.12 *Bronze Age mining at the Christian von Tuschwerk mine, Hallstatt (after Kern et al. 2009)*

Artefacts and ecofacts from the mines

Wooden artefacts include thousands of 1m fir and spruce tapers used to provide light. Some had teeth marks on the end but most would have been held by hand, possibly by children. Fir stumps were hollowed out to use as buckets and trugs (troughs) and the tree itself provided timbers (Grabner et al. 2009) for pit-props, ladders and scaffolding. Wood also supplied pick handles and shovels while bast (fibres under the bark) provided cordage. Some of this was twisted into heavy-duty cable up to 4cm thick and capable of hauling 100kg of salt. Grass also provided fibre for string but most textiles came from animals rather than plants. A selection of woven woollen cloths were found which provide valuable insights into the development of looms and weaving. Most are rags, possibly used in bags or slings. Several cloths were dyed using minerals and plants to produce blues, yellows and reds. Animal skins provided bindings, hand leathers, fur hats and bladders to hold drinking water. Carry-sacks were made by cutting cow

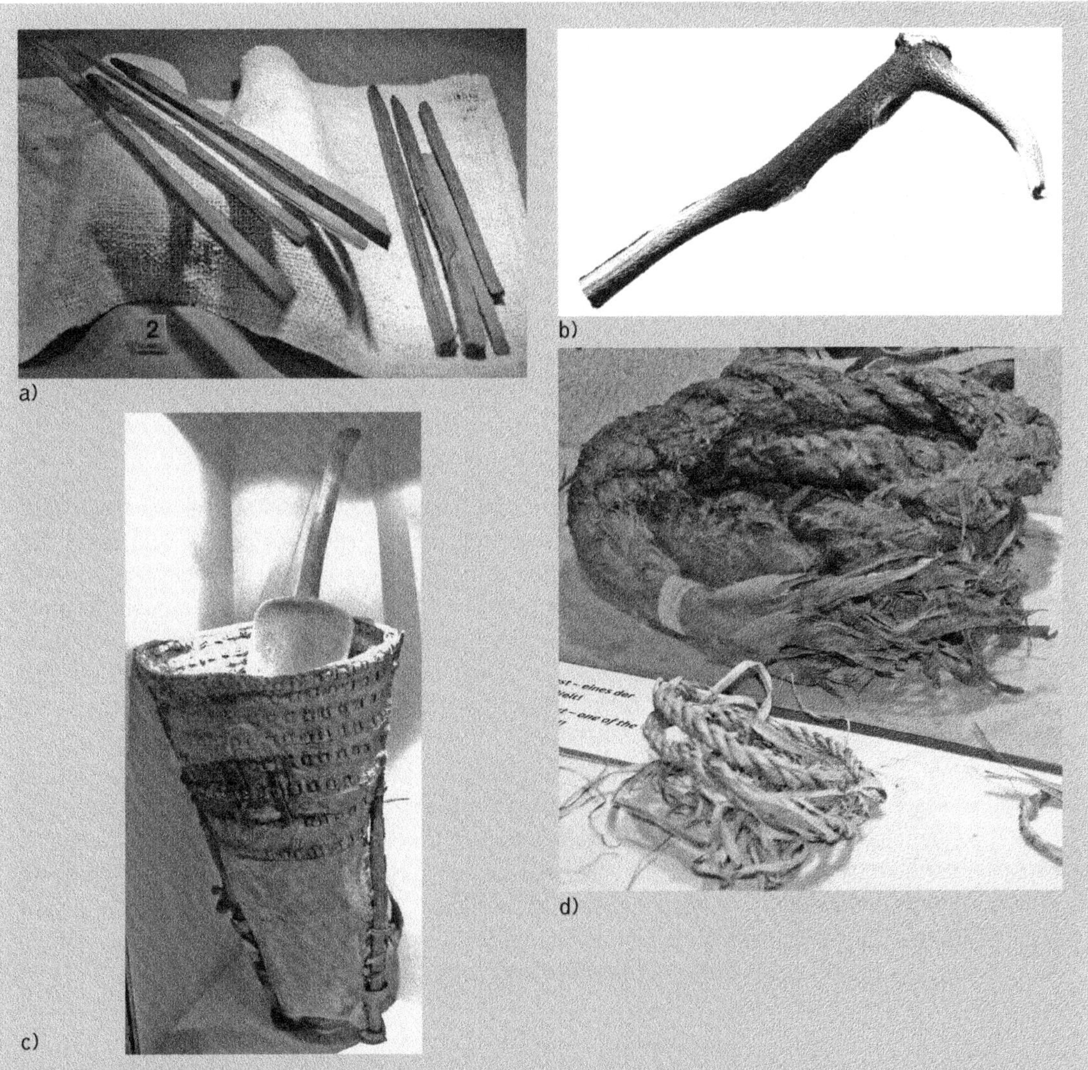

Figure 9.13 *Preserved artefacts from Hallstatt: a) pine tapers; b) antler pick; c) leather rucksack and wooden shovel; d) rope*

hides and sewing them up to make a cylindrical pack 80cm tall by 35cm in diameter. They were designed to be carried on the right shoulder and could be emptied of up to 30kg of salt with one arm movement (Kern et al. 2009). Food scraps included some animal bone and wooden boxes that held cheese but the most useful information on diet has come from the large amount of human faeces perfectly preserved in the mines. The lack of animal fibre suggests that miners ate stews of barley, millet and beans – probably from wooden bowls. They were also afflicted by parasites including intestinal worms and lice, which would have spread easily in the insanitary conditions in the mine. Background pollen in the faeces suggests mining took place all year.

continued

Surface features

Finds of domestic pottery hint that the settlement of the miners may have been close to the mine but is probably buried under several metres of mud from landslides. However, there are remains of some remarkable log-built buildings which are close to the mine and littered with thousands of animal bones. Some 60 per cent of bones were pigs aged 1–2 years with the rest being cattle, sheep and goats (Kern et al. 2009). Low-meat parts of the skeletons such as skulls and vertebrae were often missing, which suggests they were butchered elsewhere. In the case of pigs, the articulated, meat-bearing elements appear to have been carried up the mountain using the jaw bone as a 'handle'. Environmental evidence and experimentation has shown that the buildings were salting troughs where up to 200 pigs could be cured at a time to produce ham. Initial curing would take about ten days followed by a longer period of smoking in dry conditions – possibly the mine itself. The cured hams could then be transported onwards.

Mining in context

Both the Bronze and Iron Age mines were sophisticated industrial and social operations which each lasted for over 200 years. Evidence points to a segmented workforce below ground with particular individuals specialising in mining, carpentry, carrying or hauling. It is likely that whole families were engaged in these processes. Above ground others prepared food, logged trees and brought in other supplies, particularly food (Kowarik et al. 2009). Bronze Age house foundations with bones of domestic animals have been found on high pastures in the surrounding mountains and these may have supplied the mine with meat and dairy products. Others were engaged in trade and at the apex of the social pyramid in the Iron Age were those buried with exotic, high-status objects in the cemetery. Salt was important not just as a preservative but also for improving the taste of food, dyeing cloth and tanning leather. It was an expensive commodity and trade in 'white gold' brought great wealth to those who controlled the mines and distribution. Hallstatt was part of a system linked to the Danube trade and beyond to northern Italy. The trade involved chiefs who controlled rivers from hillforts such as Heuneberg (▶ p. 437) and were buried in great tumuli such as Hochdorf (▶ p. 434). From *c.* 600 BC Hallstatt had a rival in the Dürrnberg mines at Hallein close to Salzburg but both centres prospered as the demand for salt grew. Its social impact is discussed in the next chapter.

PROCESSING METALS

Most early metal artefacts were relatively simple and often imitated stone ones. The earliest metallurgy involved hammering nuggets of pure copper or gold into simple shapes or drilling them to make beads. However, hammered copper became brittle and would easily break. The eventual solution to this problem was to anneal the copper by heating to 200–300°C then rapidly cooling in water to make it more plastic. It was then hammered on an anvil to drive out the impurities. By 5,000 BC a variety of flat, sheet and rolled copper artefacts were being made. They were valuable because of their rarity, the mystery of their production and their shininess. Two common forms of copper, malachite and azurite, are bright green and blue respectively. Ores may have originally been crushed for body paint or to decorate pottery or houses. Copper was largely used for personal adornment including bracelets, earrings, brooches and thin coverings for other artefacts. Gold was rarer but used in much the same way, as can be seen in the contemporary Varna (▶ p. 423) cemetery. Early seams of pure

Figure 9.14 *Bun of copper and flat axe. The axe was cast in a single piece mould.*

Mining	• digging, fire-setting, collecting • mines, picks and mauls, fire-cracked rock, charcoal, stray artefacts
Smelting	• sorting, crushing, heating in a kiln or furnace to >1085 °C, use of flux or roasting to remove impurities • crushing stones, powdered ore, slag, crucibles, hearths or kilns, charcoal ash, tuyères
Smithing	• casting, forging, annealing, soldering, finishing, decorating • anvil, slag, tools (punches, hammers, smoothers), finished artefacts, moulds, hearths

Figure 9.15 *The copper mining process*

Figure 9.16 *Early ceramic tuyères from Anatolia*

copper were quickly exhausted and new techniques were required in order to process the more common sulphide ores.

For most ores of copper, iron, lead and tin a second stage of extraction or **metallurgy** was required. This is smelting. A reducing agent is heated with the ore to remove impurities. For example, charcoal (mainly carbon) heated with copper oxide ore in a kiln to 1,100°C will produce relatively pure copper plus CO_2 gas. The liquid copper will gather at the bottom of the crucible and is poured out, leaving other waste material as slag. Some ores such as copper sulphide require roasting before smelting in an oxygen-rich environment. This produces copper oxide but also gives off poisonous SO_2, sulphur dioxide gas. During the 4th millennium BC, the time of Ötzi (▶ p. 104), coppersmiths in the Alps were smelting sulphide ores in enclosed charcoal furnaces.

The earliest metal to be smelted was lead, which is rarely found naturally and has to be separated from its ore, galena. Cast (and therefore smelted) lead beads were found at Çatal Höyük in Anatolia and dated by association to 6500 BC. The process was probably discovered at an earlier date and almost certainly in conjunction with ceramic manufacture, since lead can easily be smelted at the temperatures reached in early kilns. Tin may also have been smelted first in Anatolia since cassiterite (tin oxide ore) and galena are both found in the Taurus Mountains to the south. Cassiterite also melts at a relatively low temperature.

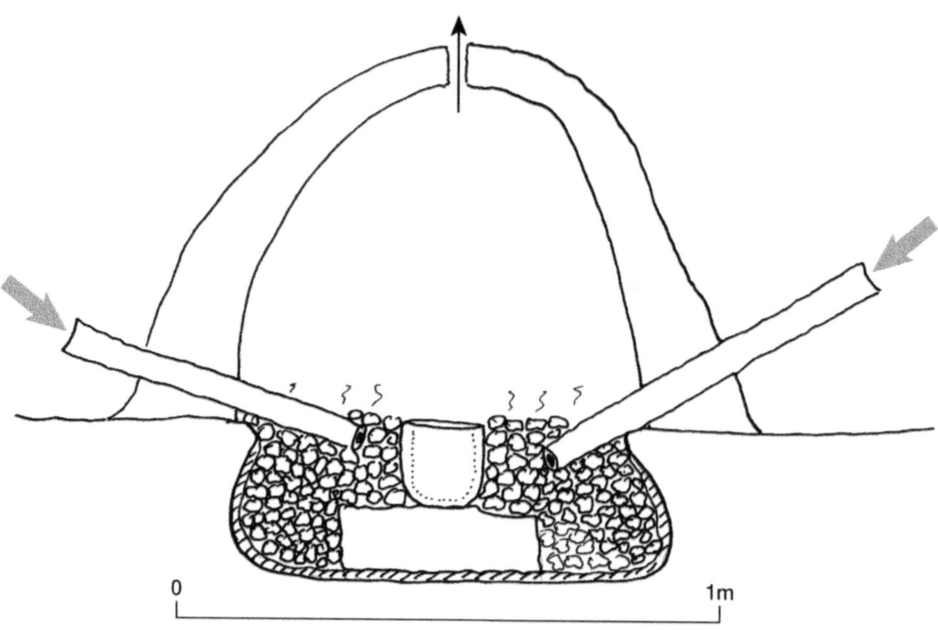

Figure 9.17 *Early smelting technology*

Air is forced into the kiln through tuyères, probably using bellows, in order to raise temperatures. Metal is smelted in the crucible seated in the charcoal at the bottom of the kiln.

Little evidence from early copper smelting had been found in the Balkans until the publication of results from Pločnik in Serbia in 2008. This site had been known since 1927 but new finds and dating took the date of copper smelting back to 5500 BC. The village had been burnt down with collapsed buildings preserving inorganic materials in situ. Large cast-copper chisels and axes were found along with processing waste and a metalworking building. An unusual furnace was built outside one building with a series of tuyères (ceramic pipes) to remove fumes and bring in air. These were probably once attached to leather bellows. Several pots contained traces of copper, which suggested they had been used as crucibles.

Copper and Cyprus

In the Bronze Age, copper smelting becomes much more visible. Processing sulphide ores involves large amounts of charcoal which in turn requires considerable numbers of trees to be felled. The environmental impact is most clearly visible in Cyprus, a major source of copper, where large-scale deforestation took place. However, the richness of Cypriot copper seams means that much archaeological evidence has been destroyed by more recent mining. Most Mediterranean archaeology has focused on palaces and urban areas. These have revealed much about the final processes of artefact production and trade, but little of the smelting process. To investigate this, archaeologists have undertaken extensive field surveys to identify 'off-site' activity areas. One such example is the early smelting workshop of Phorades (1600 BC), which was built into a stream bed close to the source of ores. It was identified by fieldwalkers from slag and furnace lining eroding out of a stream bank. Some 3.5 tonnes of slag and other debris was excavated but little copper, almost certainly because its value meant that every drop was removed (Knapp et al. 2002). Pieces of furnace debris enabled the design of the smelting furnace to be recreated while well-preserved tuyères (ceramic pipes) revealed how high temperatures were reached.

The furnaces at Phorades were cylindrical and about 44cm in diameter. Scorching on the tuyères suggests they were inserted into the mouth of the furnace from above. Their role was to force air into the chamber to raise temperatures above 1,200°C in order to smelt the copper. Elsewhere ceramic bellows have been found but none were present at Phorades. This may be because they were organic or because workers simply blew down the tuyères, a method depicted in some Egyptian wall paintings. Despite the large slag heap, Phorades was a small-scale operation. Only around 300kg of copper was produced, which would have been enough for only ten oxhide ingots (▶ p. 134). Other small workshops such as Almyras were scattered across Cyprus but also only covered the first parts of the production process. There may have been some large-scale production but no such sites have been found yet. Final production took place in specialised workshops in the urban centres on the coast such as Enkomi, which grew rich on the trade in ingots and finished artefacts. Lead isotopic analysis of seventy-eight ingots discovered across the Mediterranean found that they could be linked with the Apliki mine in northern Cyprus, which confirms the island's key role in the development of trade (▶ p. 403).

Iron

Pure iron from meteorites was used in much the same way as any other exotic material – for beads – from at least the 5th millennium BC. Individual finds of cast iron artefacts are known from the 3rd millennium BC but were probably made from meteoric iron. Iron ore is a common mineral but iron cannot be cold-worked and does not melt below 1,538°C, which early furnaces could not reach. As a result, iron ore mining did not really begin until after 1500 BC, with smelted artefacts providing indirect evidence. These appeared first across the Near East, particularly as weapons and, as with most novel materials, particularly in high-status burials. It took several hundred years to start to replace bronze and become the most common metal used. Iron smelting is usually attributed to the Hittites of Anatolia because many early finds came from that culture but more artefacts have since been found across the region, particularly in Egypt, and there is some evidence for early smelting in India. As with copper, early iron working has proved hard to pin down. Iron extraction from ore is a multistage process involving distinctive furnaces and producing a range of different slag. Ore is first crushed and then roasted in the open to oxidise it. Ore is then reduced in a special furnace known as a bloomery, where it is mixed with charcoal and air at around 1,250°C to force it to produce 'bloom' and give off carbon monoxide. Bloom is a tangled, spongy mix of metallic iron and slag. The basic forging technique involved repeatedly reheating bloom and then hammering it on an anvil to force out impurities and produce wrought iron. The same technique could be used to shape the iron into artefacts from nails to swords. Evidence of this process can be found in the tiny fishscale-like flakes of iron oxide called hammerscale which were produced during forging.

The earliest definite smelting site discovered is at Tell Hammeh in Jordan. Around a tonne of slag along with ash, tuyères, ceramics and up to 5 mudbrick furnace stuctures have been excavated (Veldhuijzen 2007). The site was radio-carbon dated from olive-wood charcoal used in the smelting process to *c.* 920 BC. Analysis of the slag showed that temperatures above 1,200°C were reached, which means that bellows were probably used. The site appeared to have been chosen close to local sources of clay, haematite ore, water and olive trees. There were no signs of houses and distinct stratigraphic layers suggested several episodes of smelting. The excavators

Figure 9.18 Crucible containing liquid bronze

Figure 9.19 Forging iron on an anvil (with hammerscale)

estimate that it was a small-scale, seasonal operation producing no more than 200kg of iron a year which would just require a few donkey-loads of ore to provide (Veldhuijzen 2007). The process of iron smelting spread much more quickly than that of copper, reaching Greece by 1100 BC and Britain by 700 BC.

PRODUCTION: HOW ARTEFACTS WERE MADE

Manufacturing using plants

The growth of bushcraft as an activity and a subject for television programmes has encouraged interest in the aboriginal peoples of Europe. Poor survival of organic materials from the Upper Palaeolithic and Mesolithic has meant that much of our understanding of past skills draws heavily on ethnographic examples of other people in the modern world who exploit wild resources for food and technology. However, across northern Europe there are sites, usually waterlogged, which provide insights into what was more a 'wood age' than a 'stone age'. Star Carr (▶ p. 267) and Tybrind Vig (▶ p. 309) are examples. As with plant food, plant technology is under-represented in archaeological assemblages, although it almost certainly predominated. Plant fibres made from nettles or bast were used as binding, thread and to make mats. The survival of large numbers of fish-hooks tells us that plant fibres were used to make fishing line. Plants were used for fabrics, impressions having been found on ceramic material as far back as Dolni Vestonice (▶ p. 218) during the last Ice Age. Wood was crucial to Mesolithic technology and there is growing evidence of the use of large quantities of coppiced (▶ p. 244) wood which might suggest that wood-

Figure 9.20 Bushcraft Mesolithic style: Mesolithic fire lighting kit: flint, pyrites and tinder fungus

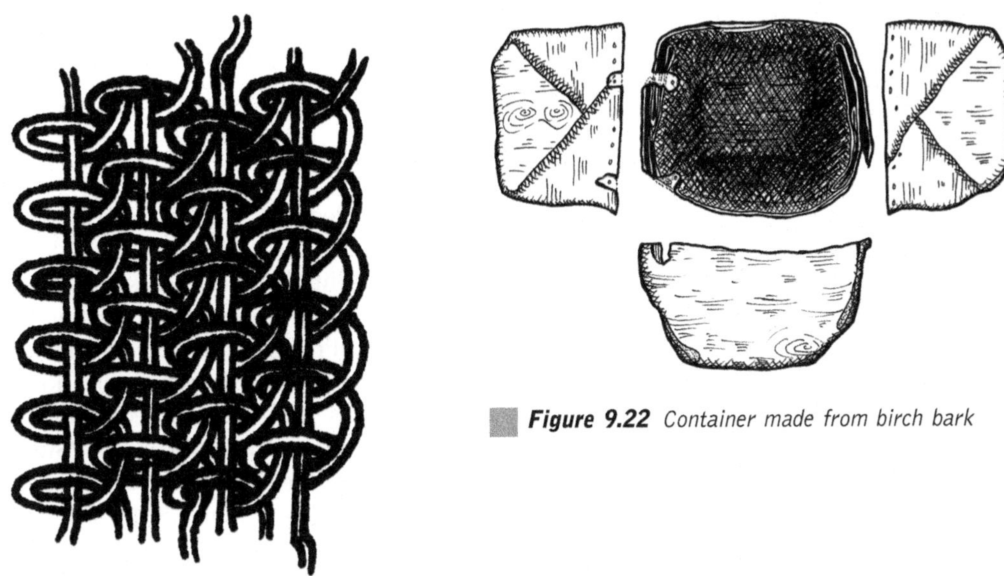

Figure 9.22 *Container made from birch bark*

Figure 9.21 *Net made from lime bast fibres*

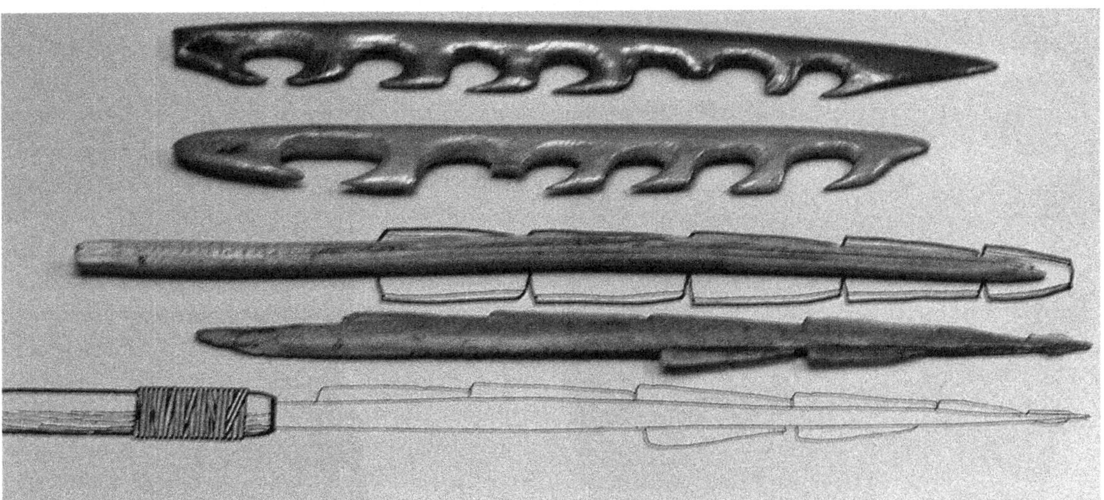

Figure 9.23 *Antler harpoons*

land management preceded farming in northern Europe. A fish-trap at Nekselo, Denmark, for example, was constructed using around 7,000 3–4m long rods of hazel and many longer, straight poles. Wood was carefully selected for different properties. Lime was favoured for canoes, possibly because it does not crack as easily as other woods with repeated wetting and drying, while paddles were ash. Lime bast was used for nets while hazel, and to a lesser extent willow and cherry, were used for fish traps. Willow was used for wicker baskets while birch bark provided

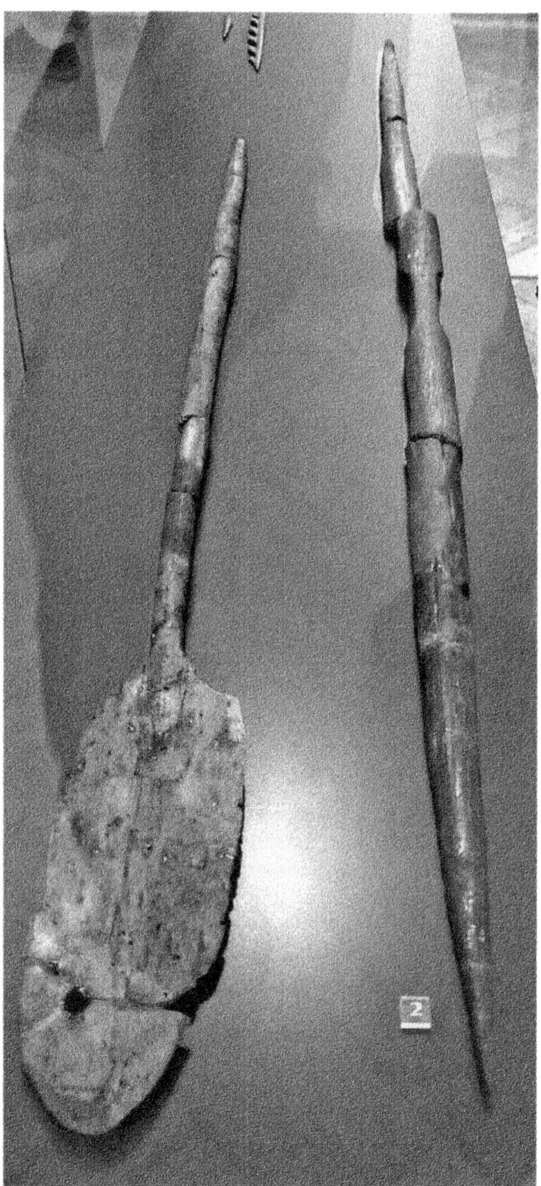

Figure 9.24 *Mesolithic elm bow and ash paddle*

alternative containers. Elm was the favoured wood for Mesolithic bows. Points were secured using pine and birch resin. In addition to knowing their trees, Mesolithic people knew their fungi. Examples of tinder fungus, which is used in fire lighting and to carry embers, have been found at Vedbaek and other Danish sites, while the Neolithic 'ice man' (▶ p. 104) was carrying several types of fungi.

Carpentry

Our knowledge of ancient woodworking largely comes from exceptional wet sites. A key example is the Neolithic 'Sweet Track' which connected knolls of high ground in the Somerset Levels wetlands. Prehistoric people faced the problem of ensuring effective communication between settlements and they solved it by constructing sophisticated trackways. The 'Sweet Track', named after the farmer who discovered it whilst clearing a drain, was an 1,800m artificial wooden walkway through the swamp. Anaerobic conditions had preserved the structure, which has been dated by dendrochronology to *c.* 4000 BC. Its construction reveals considerable woodworking skill and woodland management. The planks of the walkway were created by driving wedges into a tree trunk to split it. Other components were made from coppiced wood from oak, hazel and alder. Coppiced wood can be identified both by sheer quantities of uniform-sized rods and from the way shoots curve at the base from the plant as they move out from the tree and rise towards the light. Coppicing implies both sustainable management strategies and forward planning. The line of the track had been staked out with wooden posts. Construction involved creating a series of X-shapes using posts that rested on a submerged wooden rail. The planks were laid on the X-shapes to create a walkway above the water level. Items found alongside the track, such as jadeite axes from Europe, suggest far-reaching exchange contacts. Precise dating of the timbers revealed that the Sweet Track was built fairly quickly and only lasted some eleven years before going out of use, probably due to rising water levels (Coles and Coles 1976).

The recent discovery of a series of wells on LBK (▶ p. 67) settlements near Leipzig in Germany illustrates the sophistication of Neo-

Figure 9.25 *A replica of the Sweet Track*

lithic carpentry. Three wells were so well preserved that they were block-lifted for micro-excavation under lab conditions. In one case where the lower 4m were intact, this meant a 70 tonne block was raised. Photogrammetry and precise surveying was carried out prior to moving and, once cleaned, the timbers were all laser-scanned to reveal every tool mark and provide 3D reconstructions of the wells (Tegel et al. 2012). The contents of the wells were wet sieved and dendrochronology samples taken. The wells had been constructed from oak felled with stone axes between 5206 and 5098 BC and split in the same way as the Sweet Track. Stone adzes had shaped and smoothed the planks. For the base of the wells a square frame using mortice and tenon joints had been constructed and locked in place with peg-wedges. The rest of the well had been built up using log-cabin style halved joints (Tegel et al. 2012). Interestingly, few experimental models of prehistoric houses have used halved joints, although they are still used in Scandinavian

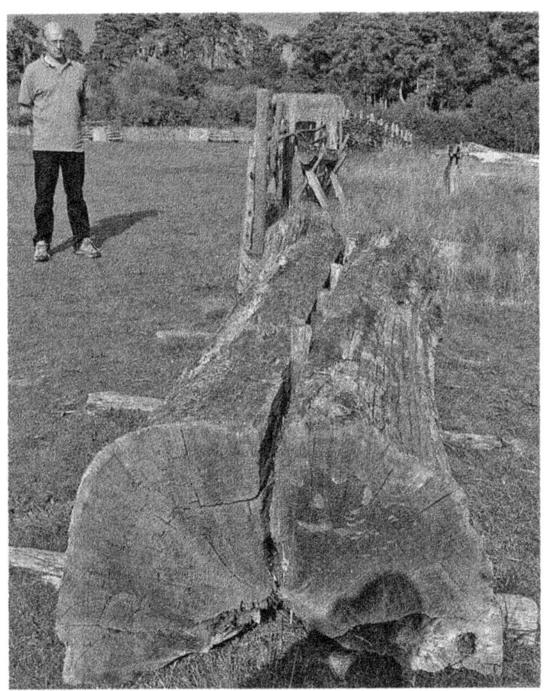

Figure 9.26 *Splitting wood with wedges*

Figure 9.27 LBK well and contents being excavated, Leipzig (copyright Landesamt für Archäologie Sachsen, Rengert Elburg)

buildings. The use of mortise and tenon joints in prehistory is better known, not least from the (unneccesary) use of them at Stonehenge.

Mortice and tenon joints were used in ancient ships including the model Khufu ship from a pit at the Great Pyramid, Giza, dated to 2500 BC. Since shipwrecks are one of the most likely situations for wood to survive in, it is unsurprising that they are a key source of interpreting structures on land. Many early boats were plants sewn together using bast from lime and other trees. The Iron Age Hjortspring boat in Denmark

Figure 9.28 Laser scan of LBK well timbers from Leipzig showing adze marks (copyright Landesamt für Archäologie Sachsen, Thomas Reuter)

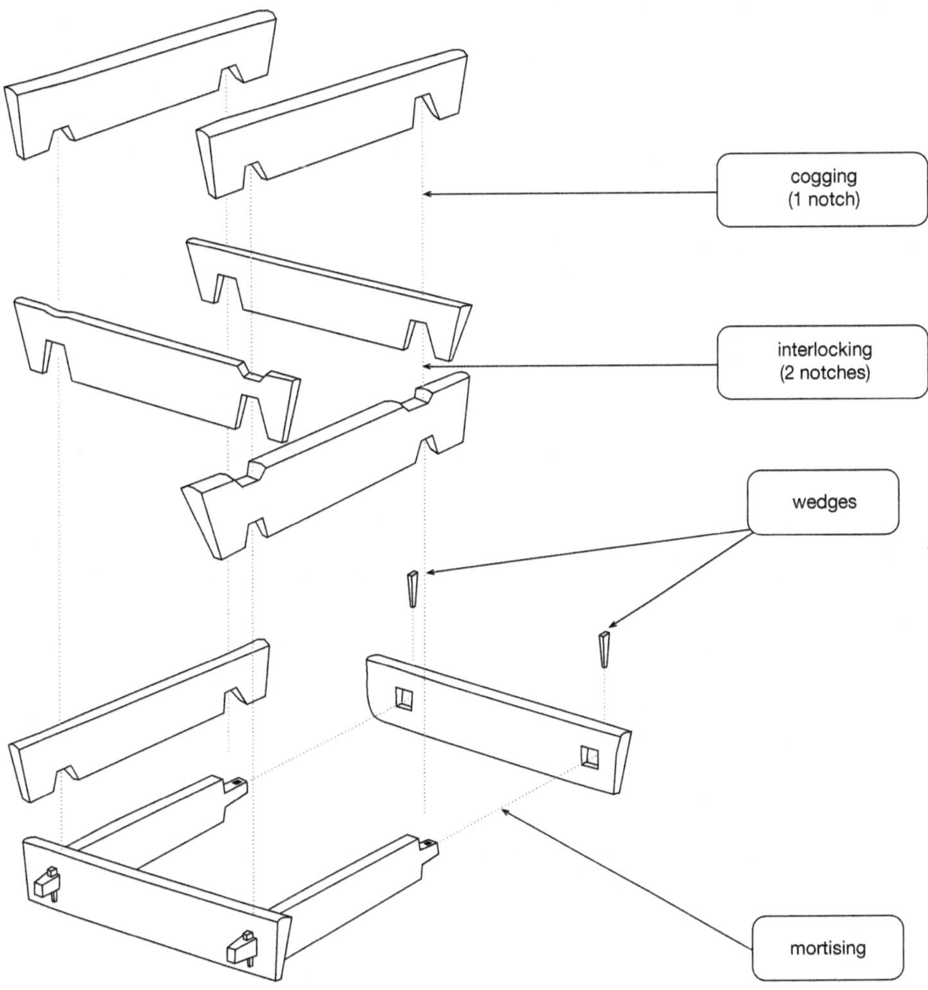

Figure 9.29 *LBK well construction diagram showing carpentry joints used (copyright Landesamt für Archäologie Sachsen, Dietrich Hakelberg, University of Freiburg/Br)*

and the Bronze Age Dover Boat are examples. All these early boats display the same understanding of the properties of different woods that we can see from the Mesolithic. The use of wooden pegs or 'tree nails' is evidenced from the *Uluburun* (▶ p. 403), while a variety of plant materials including moss and tree resin were used to caulk joints. Other developments in shipbuilding are covered later in this chapter (▶ p. 404). Many smaller artefacts from bows to spoons were carved from wood using flint or later metal tools. Most people would have made whatever they needed themselves since the technology was ubiquitous. However, carpentry was one of the earliest manufacturing processes to be mechanised with the invention of the lathe. Turned bowls have survived and in 1997 a waste disc from the bottom of a turned bowl was recovered from Loch Tay at Oakbank Crannog (▶ p. 81). Dating from the Iron Age, the disc has a hole in the middle where it was fixed to a lathe and gouge marks from the blade which carved the bowl. Once the bowl was finished, the disc was removed from the bowl and discarded. Manufacture had clearly taken place at the settlement – as other woodworking debris confirmed. The lathe sped up production from a day to less than an hour and provided a more regular product. Pole lathes are a common sight at re-enactments. Prehistoric lathes may have been similar but none have survived.

Textiles

Textiles include woven or knitted cloth, fibres that that have been made into yarn and related fabrics such as felt. Textile production was one of the most important forms of manufacture in all periods but has also been one of the least visible or understood archaeologically. Even fifty years ago it was common to see people depicted in textbooks wearing wrapped skins – Flintstone-style. We now know that if that ever did happen with our species, it was in our very distant past. Evidence from Upper Palaeolithic sites of skin processing and bone and antler needles shows that for 40,000 years people have worn manufactured and tailored clothes. Textiles provided more than clothing. Containers, sails, nets and carpets are just a few of their many uses. Their expressive potential was developed from an early stage, first with sewn decoration with shell, bone and stone and later with dyes. Fine fabrics such as silk quickly became a status symbol and certainly from the Bronze Age a major aspect of trade. Ethnographic and historic data suggests that textiles production was a major aspect of most families' lives and that it was organised on gender lines.

Preserved textiles

Textiles are made from organic material so unsurprisingly most of the physical evidence recovered through excavation are tools used in textile production such as loom weights and clothes-fittings such as brooches. Situations of exceptional organic preservation have started to fill in many of the gaps. Scythian and Viking burials in permafrost regions have provided textiles as have burial assemblages in desiccated conditions such as the tomb of Tutankhamun, although in both cases these may not represent everyday fabrics. Accidental burials such as Ötzi the Ice Man (▶ p. 104), who provided us with a complete set of clothes, and scraps preserved in salt at Hallstatt (▶ p. 373) provide more typical insights. The bog-burials of Bronze and Iron Age Denmark present a partial picture depending on the acidity of the bog. Animal fibres survive best in acid conditions such as those at Huldremose, while plants survive best in alkaline bogs such as Hjortspring (▶ p. 167). The Huldremose burial was of a woman wearing a complete woollen plaid dress and scarf under two woollen cloaks and a leather cape. Her undergarments are likely to have been linen, which has not survived. Votive deposits from Thorsberg bog include a woollen tunic and trews which give us an insight into what male clothes looked like. Indirect preservation of textiles comes in the form of pseudomorphs and negative imprints. Pseudomorphs occur when salts from metal artefacts leach out into surrounding textiles and chemically protect them from bacteria rather like fossilisation. Textiles from Hochdorf (▶ p. 434) were preserved in this way. Impressions of textiles and cordage are also found on ceramics including deliberate pattern-making on corded ware pottery and the accidental traces on ceramics at Dolni Vestonice (▶ p. 218). Other evidence of early textiles comes from art, such as Venus figurines (▶ p. 528), the Gundestrup Cauldron (▶ p. 397) and Minoan frescoes (▶ p. 627). Some of the earliest written documents from the Sumerian city of Ur record textile trade on cuneiform (▶ p. 415) tablets. Other indirect evidence includes beads – which were fastened with thread (although this could be leather) – and fastenings such as pins, buttons and buckles. Plant fibre also survives in a carbonised state, such as the twine from Ohalo II (▶ p. 328).

Textiles from plants

The earliest fibres used were from plants. Stringy plants such as nettles, hemp and flax were widely used along with bast from under the bark of lime and willow trees. Flax was the earliest textile crop but may have been grown for linseed rather than linen. When it is grown for textile production, it is harvested before the seeds fully develop, which makes it hard to detect archaeologically. Plant fibres are stiff and best suited to weaving into baskets or nets or twisting to make cord, although cotton, a much softer fabric, was being used in India in the Bronze Age. Several fabrics were brought together during the 4th millennium BC Bronze Age amongst the pastoralist farmers of the Majkop Culture north of the Caucasus. At a kurgan (mound) burial at Novosvobodnaya, traces of linen, cotton and a new textile, wool, were detected. Wool was superior to flax in its flexibility, warmth and ease of dyeing.

Textiles from animals

Sheep were domesticated for meat and possibly milk rather than wool. The fleece of a sheep contains three different fibres – long, coarse outer hair, brittle kemp and a soft undercoat. Through selective breeding the undercoat (wool) became dominant. Evidence is indicated by a shift in the balance of herds to include large numbers of castrated male sheep which produce the best wool. Their horn cores are distinct from those of rams and ewes. Wool was probably initially used to make felt. When wool fibres are rubbed in water they become matted. Under pressure the fibres bond to become a fabric. Felt is known from at least the Bronze Age in Siberia, where it was used to provide outer clothing, hats, rugs and tents (yurts).

Textile production

Textile production involves several stages. Flax for example has to have seeds removed (rippling) and is then soaked in water to rot the pectin that binds the fibres together (retting). The dried stalks are broken open and the fibres cleaned and combed. Wool processing begins with plucking or shearing followed by sorting, washing and combing. Evidence for these processes may come if special flax pits were dug for retting (although rivers were used if available) and particularly from wood or antler carding combs. In both cases yarn was produced by twisting the short fibres together to give them strength and length. This became easier with the use of spindles: long rods of wood weighted with a whorl of clay or stone. Spindle whorls (▶ p. 177) tend to be the main evidence of this process and were found from the late Neolithic in the Near East. Yarn could be used for sewing or knitting. It could be plaited and used as cord (the same process was repeated to make thicker cables) or knotted together to make bags or nets or it could be woven to produce carpets or cloth.

Figure 9.30 *Upright loom – reconstruction of an Anglo-Saxon loom. This design was in use from the late Neolithic.*

Early weaving involved cards or discs until the invention of the loom during the Bronze Age. A horizontal, ground loom is depicted on a cylinder seal from Susa in Mesopotamia from the 4th millennium BC (Wild 2003) but since they would have been constructed entirely of wood none have survived. The real calling card of weaving is the loom weight made from clay or stone. These were used with upright looms to weight the vertical (warp) threads while the weaver passed the weft thread between the threads horizontally. From the late Bronze Age, loom weights and spindle whorls (▶ p. 167) appear on virtually every settlement site across Eurasia, testifying to the household level of textile production. The final stages of production are also largely invisible including washing, bleaching and dyeing. Occasionally the sources of dyes can be evidenced by remains such as piles of murex sea shells (purple) at Kommos (▶ p. 472) but more commonly these are identified through chromatography and spectrometry. Experimentation is important in providing comparative material for both weaves and dyes. A wide range of materials was used for dyeing including the plants woad (blue), madder (red), safflower (yellow) and insect kermes (red). After cutting and sewing into garments, further adornment was added including embroidery and fastenings. The archaeology of textiles has shown us that people in the past were not simply dressed in browns and greys but from at least the Bronze Age would have worn clothes with colours and patterns that would have told others something about the wearer.

Figure 9.31 *Late Neolithic loom weights displaying wear from threads*

ORGANISATION OF PRODUCTION

The basic level of production is at the level of the individual, group or household. At this small scale, people just produced what they needed. This included flaking the tools needed to butcher an animal, grinding cereals to make flour or spinning wool into yarn to make clothes from. The evidence for self-sufficient domestic production is that similar tools, for instance spindle whorls, would be found in all houses in a settlement. This is not to say that some people would not have become more skilled and perhaps exchanged an impressive hand-axe or set of arrows for something else but it would only be the case for some products. There is some evidence for this kind of part-time expertise in the Upper Palaeolithic of the Vézère Valley (▶ p. 203), with increasingly well-crafted and standardised lithics and the manufacture of beads.

Economic specialists

During the Bronze Age, two broad types of economic specialists become visible in industries where high levels of technical knowledge were required and particularly for those producing high-status artefacts. Attached specialists live in close proximity to a high-status person. They may be employed by them or kept as slaves or may be part of their extended family. Examples include craft workers in the Minoan palace workshops such as at Knossos (▶ p. 256). The Roman army also provides a range of examples of attached specialists within an organisation. Independent specialists produce goods to market for their own profit. They are not controlled by anyone else

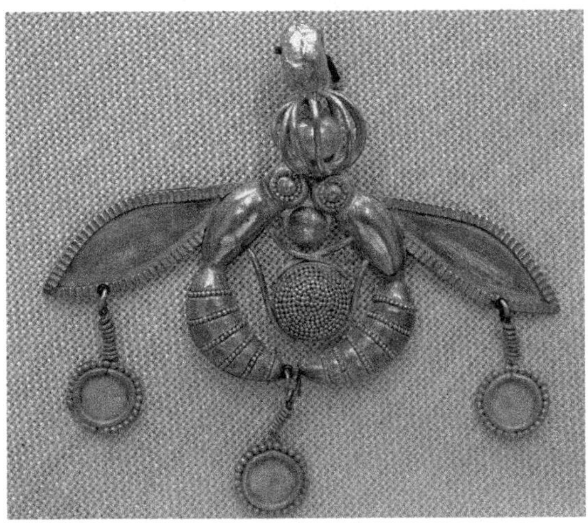

Figure 9.32 *Malia bee pendant*

This exquisite gold pendant from a burial at Malia is evidence of professional metalworking. A new technique – granulation – had been developed by Cretan goldsmiths in order to produce realistic images such as these bees on a comb of honey. It is evidence of sufficient food surplus to support craftsmen since it would take years of training to develop the skill required here. It also suggests an elite who wanted such artefacts. Palace workshops suggest that the goldsmiths were attached craftsmen (▶ p. 470), with raw materials provided by their masters.

Figure 9.33 *Antler comb manufacturing*

but may well depend on elite individuals for protection, business and raw materials. In some cases these specialists might be itinerant, moving to where there is work or manufacturing to order. The Amesbury Archer might fall into this category as perhaps did the Transylvanian metalsmiths who produced the Gundestrup Cauldron (▶ p. 397).

From the Iron Age it is possible to recognise specialism even in rural settlements, with certain areas or buildings being associated with different activities. Full-time specialisation and larger-scale production is evident in the developing trade centres (emporia) or wics of the early medieval period. C8th Ipswich (▶ p. 288) had distinct areas with concentrations of pottery production and iron, leather and bone working. When identifying specialist areas and individual manufacturing, debris can be important, as can the very names of locations where craft workers concentrated, which may have survived, albeit in altered form, over time. Both of these sources are illustrated in Viking York (Jorvik), where the name of the most famous excavation site – 'Coppergate' – comes from the Old Norse for 'Street of the Barrel-Makers'. The rectangular, oak-built houses of the craft workers were built on long, narrow plots with workshops on the street front and living quarters to the rear. Debris and tools enable the craft specialisms of the inhabitants to be identified. There is much waste material from leather working and trial pieces for carving in bone while other independent specialists made jewellery, metal goods or antler combs.

Metalworking specialists: from sorcerers to smiths

Unlike lithics manufacture, casting and forging metal artefacts required highly specialist tools, skills and knowledge. These specialists are called smiths and the first practitioners may have been viewed as magicians, turning rock into shiny, exotic objects. In some cultures an association remains between metalworking and other transformations including elements of divination (▶ p. 526) and shamanism.

Once smiths learnt how to use bellows to reach the high temperatures needed to smelt ores in crucibles, the potential metals could be realised. This development almost certainly came through advances in kiln technology for pottery production. Smelting also enabled the production of alloys, which were blends of two or more minerals. Arsenic, which is often found with copper, was probably the first deliberate addition. Arsenical copper is harder than pure copper and therefore could be used to make weapons. The spread of arsenical copper artefacts by 3000 BC is evidence that alloying was deliberate and this is confirmed by the invention of bronze, which alloyed 5–15 per cent tin with 85–95 per cent copper. Bronze had a lower melt point than copper and therefore could be cast more easily. Bronze is harder than copper and was used for a wider range of artefacts including swords, armour, buckets and tableware. However, it remained relatively rare due to the scarcity and location of the raw materials and the skill used to work it. The skill was in blending the metals in the right proportion in the crucible so that the finished alloy was not too soft or too brittle. Crucibles were usually small, open-topped ceramic containers and typically grey-black from being heated in a reducing furnace. The high temperatures often vitrified the clay, giving a glossy surface, while particles of the metals being cast can bond to the crucible and be detected under a microscope. Moulds enabled new shapes to be produced; casting enabled their mass-production. One-piece (flat) moulds were initially made of stone, where the required shape was laboriously carved into the rock. Stone moulds

Figure 9.34 *Stone and wood two-piece moulds. The lost-wax process is illustrated top left.*

could be used repeatedly to produce awls or flat axes. For metals with low melting points such as lead, hard wood (often charred) moulds could also be used. Clay was commonly used but survives less well because moulds were poorly fired, leaving them friable (crumbly). Two-piece moulds were introduced in the 3rd millennium BC and can be indirectly evidenced by more complicated 3D castings, particularly shafthole axes. Clay would be pressed around an artefact or a carving of one to create the mould shape. For complex castings such as fibulae brooches where fine decoration was required, the lost-wax technique was developed. Here an artefact would be carved from beeswax and encased in clay. When metal was poured in, the wax would melt and the metal filled the void in the required shape. From the Iron Age, metal with a higher melt-point than the metal being cast was used to make reusable moulds.

A goldsmith from Upton Lovell?

This early Bronze Age barrow excavated by antiquarians in 1802 is possibly one of the earliest examples of a specialist in Britain. Whether he was a shaman, goldsmith or both is unclear. Across his chest and by his feet were rows of drilled bone points. He also had several boars' tusks and bone buttons or toggles. These have been interpreted as decoration or fastenings on his clothes. These were unusual in themselves, but the stone artefacts were even more fascinating. On the chest of the extended skeleton was a large highly polished flat round stone and a high-quality stone battle axe. At his feet was an array of different stone artefacts.

The exotic battle axe suggested the man may have taken part in ceremonies where his bone-tasselled clothes would have been very distinctive. The polished stone was also unique. Some shamanic cultures use polished, reflective surfaces as an aid to divination (like a crystal ball). The other stone tools were more of a puzzle. An A-level student who happened to be an amateur goldsmith noted the similarity of the burial assemblage to his own tools. He suggested how each of the smooth stones might be used to produce the hammered gold trinkets visible in

Figure 9.35 *Artefacts from Upton Lovell*

To the left are three stone axes in front of three hollow flints with a fine, stone axehead at the back. To the right are whetstones in front of smoothing stones and hammers.

Figure 9.36 *The Upton Lovell burial as a Shaman*

This interpretation at the excellent Devizes Museum where the artefacts are displayed explains the possible use of the bone artefacts, the battle axe and polished stone. The significance of the latter two is enhanced because they were placed on his chest.

several of the other cabinets. The flint nodules could be tiny crucibles. The only thing missing is the gold. Historically goldworkers have often not owned gold. It has been supplied either by their patron or, in the case of independent specialists, by the person commissioning an artefact. It is possible that the man was both goldsmith and shaman. In many cultures, metalworkers' ability to magically transform material has classed them with other 'liminal' roles such as midwives, musicians and diviners. Xrf (▶ p. 131) analysis of the tools in 2004 did find traces of gold.

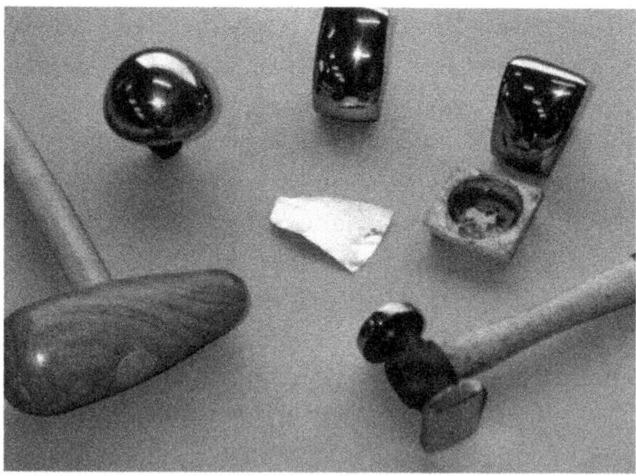

Figure 9.37 *Modern gold worker's toolkit*

As with the grave goods, an array of hammers and tiny anvils is used to produce sheets, cones and circular artefacts from gold similar to those at Varna.

Ironsmiths

Between 1200 and 800 BC ironsmiths developed new forging technologies to manufacture artefacts. Forged iron itself is hard but brittle. Objects were less likely to break if they were annealed by slowly heating to soften them. Brittleness could be reduced further by repeated heating to force out impurities and slow cooling (tempering), which resulted in a stronger, more resilient metal. This finally enabled iron to replace bronze. A further refinement was to roast the finished product on charcoal to add carbon and then quench it suddenly by plunging it into water. This produced a layer of steel which was harder but less brittle. Stone tools were finally superseded by iron. Within a few hundred years everyday tools such as saws, chisels and nails as well as most weapons were made from iron.

An early smithing site

The smithy at Beth-Shemesh in Israel illustrates artisan workshop-level production. Broadly contemporary (900 BC) with the smelting site at Tell Hammeh (▶ p. 381) and using similar tuyères, its location tells us something about the different parts of the manufacturing process. Hammeh, where iron was produced, was a rural site away from settlement, whereas the smithy was in an industrial area of a city close to the customers. The floor of the workshop was covered in slag and other debris so the excavators took the opportunity to recover every piece of waste and plot it on 25cm × 25cm squares to understand the different aspects of processing in the smithy. A handheld magnet in a plastic bag was dragged over soil samples from each square to recover tiny magnetic flakes of hammerscale (▶ p. 382). High concentrations in conjunction with ash enabled the hearth location to be identified, while low concentrations mark where the smith and possibly the anvil stood. Hammerscale from working bloom is lighter coloured and thicker than the fine, dark flakes produced when working finished articles. Most of the hammerscale was of the latter type, enabling the excavators to identify it as a place of 'secondary-smithing' where artefacts were forged or repaired rather than iron being produced. It was the second half of the process begun at Tell Hammeh (Veldhuijzen and Rehren 2007).

Craftsmen as artists

Art is a term applied to images and objects which show appreciation of aesthetic qualities. It may include decoration on functional objects or decoration that forms part of a system of iconography. While it is clear that people in the past appreciated the beauty of particular objects, their conceptions of art are likely to be very different from modern ideas such as 'art for art's sake'. In other words, their art may be functional or infused with morals, lessons or religious values. The meaning of art is culturally embedded and may prove difficult to access. In archaeology it is usually studied as part of the archaeology of religion (▶ p. 520). The alternative approach is to concentrate on the technology of execution rather than on interpretation. While there is debate about the meaning of Palaeolithic cave paintings (▶ p. 529), we can be more certain about the techniques. The skills of draughtsmanship, paints used and the techniques of painting become the focus for research. Research has discovered the use of ferrous and manganese oxide for paint, chewed twigs and fingers as brushes and stone lamps with animal grease or pine torches for light. Experiments have established that paint was blown through leather stencils to create handprints.

There are some major gaps in our understanding of artistic expression in the past including houses, textiles and perhaps the human body.

Figure 9.38 *Close up of the spout of a Basse-Yutz flagon*

In each case there is a small but growing amount of evidence to suggest that these were important 'canvases' for artists in the past. A broader conception of art than painting is evident in the past with artefacts the most numerous and most likely to survive in the archaeological record. The high level of craftsmanship in the form of brooches, shield bosses and fine ceramics is certainly artistic. The Sutton Hoo burial contains several examples from all over the Anglo-Saxon world, in particular a tiny pyramidal jewel that had been originally attached to a sword hilt. Each face is a plate of gold with tiny 'cells' built up on it with gold wire in the technique known as cloisonné. Each cell is fitted with an individually cut prism

Figure 9.39 *Beads and identity*

Beads are frequently found in burials (▶ p. 209). These examples are from a Beaker burial from Wiltshire and a Mesolithic burial from Vedbaek. In both cases the beads are fashioned from unusual – perhaps wild – materials including boars' teeth and amber. The beads themselves are therefore expressing an aspect of the deceased's identity.

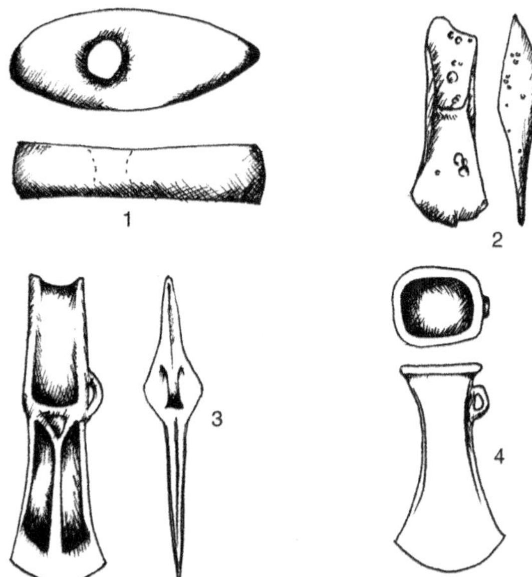

Figure 9.40 *Diachronic change: the development of axes. Lithic axes evolved to polished stone axes such as (1). The first metal axes were flat copper. Later developments included a stop-ridge (2), flanges (3) and sockets and loops (4).*

Figure 9.41 *Jewellery from Sutton Hoo illustrating cloisonné technique*

of garnet and some are provided with chequered metal foil underneath to enhance the glitter of the stones. The precision and exquisite craftsmanship of the worker at such a small scale is breathtaking. That so much time and effort was lavished on what is really a tiny detail of the king's burial goods is also a testament to his status.

The Gundestrup Cauldron

The Gundestrup Cauldron is a magnificent, silver Iron Age feasting bowl found in a bog in Jutland and measuring 70cm in diameter. It provides evidence of highly skilled silversmiths and also the dangers of associating material culture and art too closely with particular ethnic groups. For many years the images on the cauldron were viewed as the peak of Celtic art. The many scenes had been created using repoussé, where rough shapes had been beaten to raise a design on the reverse side of the flat, silver plates. To achieve this the metal was placed face down on pitch (resin), sand or wax to prevent damage. Chasing on the front side using punches created a series of shallow grooves or dents which enabled fine detail to be added. Embossing is the general name given to these techniques. Scenes appeared to show Celtic warriors and scenes from Celtic and Greek mythology. The plates were then welded together to make the cauldron. Analysis of punch-marks with an SEM (Larsen 2005) suggested that several toolkits had been used to create the designs. This implied that there were several craftsmen involved. Taylor (1997) compared manufacturing techniques, other artefacts and imagery to identify Transylvania as the likely location for the workshop and to suggest the ethnic origins of the craftsmen. They were independent craft specialists or at least independent of final owners of the cauldron. Further work by Taylor (1997) on the iconography of some of the scenes identified influences from India and Persia. The cauldron cannot solely be called Celtic in design or manufacture. It provides further evidence of the extent of exchange networks within Europe and contacts, at least in terms of ideas over a much greater area.

Figure 9.42 *The Gundestrup Cauldron*

Figure 9.43 *Replica panel from the Gundestrup Cauldron*

WHAT IS MATERIAL CULTURE?

This term is used in a general sense to mean the artefacts and structures produced by a given people with emphasis sometimes given to things that are unique to them. A significant part of the development in archaeology as a discipline has been concerned with cataloguing these differences and changes and that remains the case in some countries such as France. Examples of this are the slight differences in lithic styles and assemblages as well as location which identify the Hamburgian, Ahrensburgian and Bromme cultures at the end of the last Ice Age (▶ p. 298). Similar designation is often made using pottery (e.g. LBK) and to a lesser extent metalwork. Archaeologists also explore the way that material things symbolised values and in turn structured the way in which people thought about and interpreted their world. For instance, certain artefacts (e.g. beakers) may have been used to express social identity, particularly through burial assemblages.

Beads and symbolic behaviour

Beads are currently at the centre of a debate about when modern human behaviour began. This is because beads are an example of a symbolic medium through which humans express their individual identity and communicate with others. Unlike clothing, tattoos and hairstyles, beads made from stone or shells are much more likely to survive in the archaeological record. Beads are found in the ethnographic record for virtually every culture. Their functions include use as social markers denoting ethnic or tribal group, ranking and marital status. They are used for self-expression and in courtship and can also be gifts or media for exchange. Particular beads may also be used to ward off evil or have ritual connotations. What these uses have in common is their symbolic nature. They communicate with others who have the ability to interpret or 'read' them. This shared understanding also implies language. Beads have long been associated with developments amongst modern humans in Europe. The burials at Sungir, Russia, from 28,000 BP with around 13,000 ivory beads are the best-known example. Finds at Castel Merle (▶ p. 208), France, are considered as part of a technology of ornamentation developed in response to increasing populations and the need to communicate with strangers.

To 'read' artefacts as texts, archaeologists look for repeated patterns in the way they were made, their form and the contexts in which they are found. Ethnographic studies suggest that both the production and the form of pottery are often determined by cultural rather than purely material considerations. A pot can be functional in terms of its ability to hold its contents and withstand heat but other aspects are more to do with its social use than its functionality, particularly decoration and colour. Beliefs and values determine the 'right way' for things to look even when that way is not the most functional. In Middle Saxon Southampton imported pitchers became popular. They were more functional for pouring liquids than existing pots, yet local potters did not copy them. Instead they continued to turn out traditional vessels. Another instance where symbolism may have outweighed practicality was the use of flint as temper in some prehistoric pottery. There are usually alternative tempers available and flint would be painful to work in. A classic example of comparing form and context would be the way in which Gimbutas (▶ p. 458) interpreted the clay figurines found around hearths in early Neolithic houses as expressing a matriarchal society.

Why does material culture change?

Gradual change over a very long period is called diachronic change and is usually ascribed to people making a succession of tiny changes to their technology to make it more effective. An example is the gradual improvement in the efficiency of stone tools from Oldowan pebble tools through Acheulean and Mousterian types to the 'creative explosion' of the Upper Palaeolithic and blade technology. It may also be related to adaptation to environmental changes; for example, the development of microlith technology to arm small projectiles for forest hunting during the Mesolithic. More sudden changes in material culture may derive from internal factors such as new discoveries. An example is the flourishing of metal artefacts and changes in some burial assemblages following the development of copper smithing in the Balkans. Alternatively, external factors may be responsible. These could include invasion, trade, the spread of ideas or emulation. The latter can be seen in the late phases of the Ertebølle culture (▶ p. 309), where the design of some artefacts was influenced by those of the farmers to their south. Often the cause of the change is unclear and the subject of debate. For example, were the first Cretan palaces the invention of a Daedalus-like genius architect or were they the development of existing indigenous structures or copies of public buildings in Egypt or Syria (▶ p. 256)?

TRADE AND EXCHANGE

Early archaeological studies largely interpret the movement of artefacts and materials as trade or the movement of peoples. Movement was traced by plotting the distribution patterns of particular durable artefacts and then using stylistic or characterisation studies (▶ p. 95) to determine their origin. However, not all exchange is trade nor does it necessarily involve goods. Ethnographic studies have led to recognition that the aims of exchange are often social rather than maximising economic gain. Often the relationship is of more value than what is exchanged, as with modern Christmas cards. The exchange may involve social obligations which help bind society together. Exchange in its widest sense includes any transaction between people. This can include exchange of information, services and people. For instance, the spread of bell-beakers throughout Europe and North Africa in the 3rd millennium BC was due to exchange. Archaeologists have been divided over whether the mechanism for this exchange was movement of people or the spread of ideas, drinking culture or religion. Three main categories of exchange have been adopted by archaeology from ethnography. These are reciprocity, redistribution and market exchange.

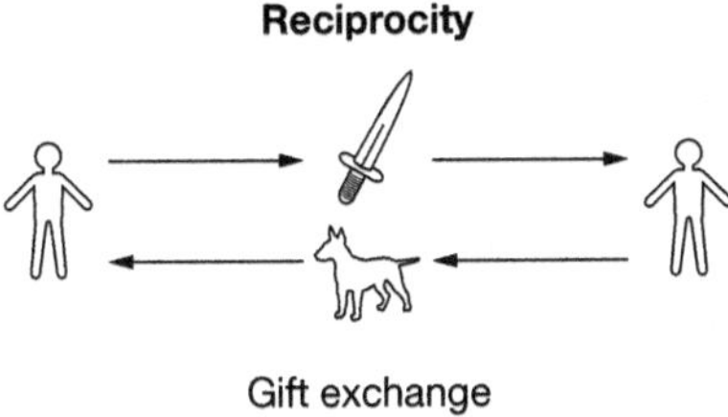

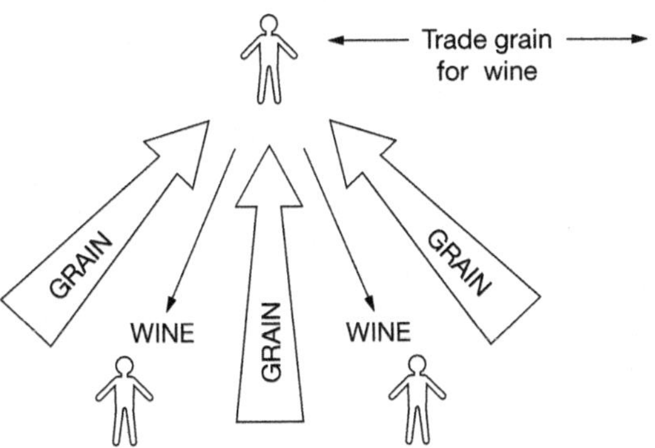

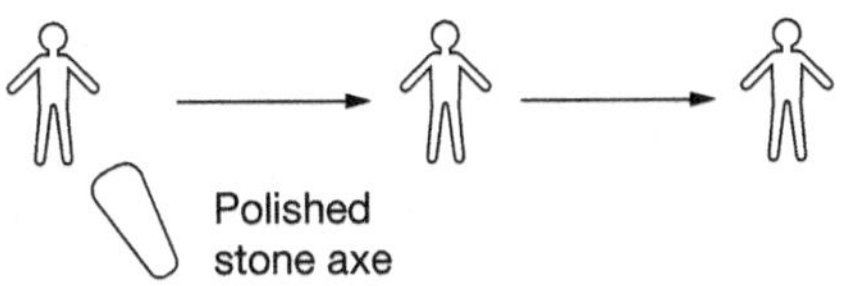

Figure 9.44 *Some types of exchange identified by archaeologists*

Reciprocity

This involves transactions where a gift from one person creates an obligation to return something at a later date. In the UK we do this when we buy a round of drinks. In many societies reciprocity is the basis for social stability. In some cultures marriage involves payment of bridewealth from the husband's family to the bride's family. This is to compensate for their loss of a fertile worker. Payments may be in goods and may take place over time. Such exchange reinforces the relationship between the two families. Feasting and the sharing of food with others are often a powerful example of reciprocity. It creates an obligation to return the favour at a later point. This may have been the case with hunters sharing meat around the hearths at Pincevent (▶ p. 278). Reciprocity could also be seen in an exchange of food for social prestige. A popular example for archaeologists has been the Big Man Mokas (pig feasts) of highland New Guinea. Here status is acquired by throwing huge feasts at which party-goers are given generous gifts of meat or livestock. A related concept is social storage. Here a gift or favour is given which stores up future gifts or assistance for times when they will be needed. Extreme examples of this are provided by ethnographic accounts of the Potlatch and Kula Ring (Orme 1981). Reciprocity can involve an equal exchange (balanced reciprocity) but can also be positive or negative if one partner does better. Ethnography once again warns against imposing our values on the evidence. In an example which is incomprehensible in terms of modern economic logic, Islanders on Yap in the Caroline Islands gained prestige by spending their savings on huge stone discs, which they then buried under their homes. One of the earliest examples of reciprocity is suggested by the movement of beads over vast distances in the Upper Palaeolithic (▶ p. 208).

Historical sources such as Homer and Egyptian tomb paintings have provided insights into prestige goods exchange. High-status individuals established and cemented relationships through reciprocal exchanges. This continues at a symbolic level amongst leaders of state today. These exchanges used to involve marriage partners and exotic goods or creatures. Archaeologically this sort of exchange may be recognised where special artefacts such as gems, amber, jade and ivory move long distances. In these cases archaeologists have talked of 'prestige goods chains'. A classic example is Renfrew and Shennan's (1982) explanation of the movement of amber from the Baltic to Mycenae during the Bronze Age and some of the fine metalwork that travelled in the opposite direction from central Europe. Amber was valued as both a beautiful and a magical material. It is warm and light unlike a stone, and when rubbed, can attract light objects. 'Electricity' is derived from the Greek word for amber. Almost all the amber recovered in Mycenae has come from burials and grave goods and special votive deposits have often been

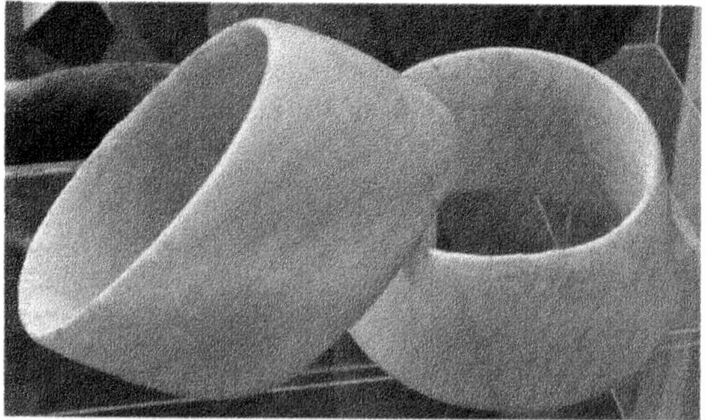

Figure 9.45 *Spondylus bracelets from the Chalcolithic. These were one of the most visible prestige items exchanged from the Neolithic onwards.*

the source of such prestige material for archaeologists. The rich graves at Varna (▶ p. 423) contained bracelets of spondylus, a Mediterranean shellfish. One interpretation is that these were exchanged for gold from sources close to Varna. However, the LBK (▶ p. 346) farmers who were also buried with spondylus did not have access to gold and their side of the exchange is a mystery. It may be that, as with other prestige goods movements before the historic period, considerable exchange of perishable luxuries such as furs, slaves, silk and feathers went on which is archaeologically invisible. Materials which have travelled far from their source and which are relatively rare in the context where they are found are referred to as 'exotics'. This term also often implies a high 'value' for the material in the eyes of the people using it and consequently its possession may suggest high status.

Redistribution

This model involves a central authority collecting together resources and then redistributing them. Our welfare state is a giant version of this, while harvest festivals symbolise it. In the past, redistribution tended to be operated by individual rulers to whom it gave both prestige and legitimacy. Ethnographic studies have tended to emphasise this as a feature of chiefdoms, particularly in areas of economic diversity. Redistribution shares out particular resources to areas that lack them; for example, fish to farmers and crops to fishers. Literary accounts such as Celtic histories suggest that rulers used redistribution to reward their followers with weapons, cattle and exotic goods in order to secure their loyalty. As with reciprocity, the social aspects of the exchange may be important and feasting may be the vehicle for the exchange. This is highlighted in the Anglo-Saxon poem *Beowulf* and documented by finds from sites such as Lerje (▶ p. 442) in Denmark.

Archaeological evidence for redistribution includes sites with massive central stores as at Knossos (▶ p. 259). Patterns of distribution where valuable goods have been widely redistributed are also potential evidence of redistribution to local leaders from a central chief. The distribution of Bronze Age swords in Wessex may be such a case. The clearest evidence of redistribution comes from those sites where records have been recovered, as at Vindolanda. The Roman army itself is a model of redistribution whereby a service was provided from taxes gathered centrally. At Vindolanda and other forts around Hadrian's Wall, food and materials were stock-piled to provide for the needs of the army. Evidence ranges from massive granaries (▶ p. 364) to strong rooms which held the pay. Further east the fort on the Tyne at Arbeia imported and warehoused grain and other resources. Lead seals (▶ p. 417) were used to control these exchanges. The Vindolanda letters document some of the problems in the supply chain and provide insights into the range of materials the central authority needed to supply to maintain its far-flung garrisons.

Market exchange

In its simplest sense 'a market' suggests a recognised place where bargaining takes place. The easiest to identify are those where defined areas or buildings exist. The public space of the agora in Greek towns is an example. Another clue is the development of mechanisms to regulate

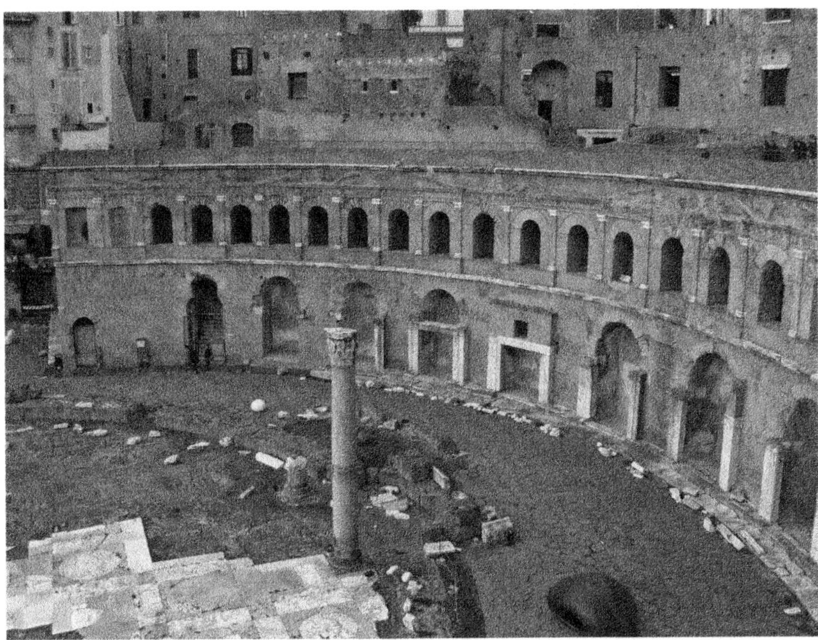

Figure 9.46 *Trajan's market – a Roman shopping mall*

amounts or to make exchange flexible such as weights and coinage. Of course, not all market exchange happens in a fixed place and not all currencies are archaeologically visible. Itinerant traders can be documented from at least the Bronze Age and at times organic goods such as blankets and carpets have been used as standards against which value can be measured. Concentrations of artefacts from many areas would be expected at a port or market. The Iron Age settlement at Hengistbury Head, with its modified harbour and apparently defensive wall, may be such an example. Finds included imported pottery, glass and figs, with evidence of metals and perhaps hides and corn being exported. However, in some cases the pattern of finds could equally represent a religious or high-status site. The many interpretations of Neolithic causewayed enclosures typify this sort of ambivalent evidence. While reciprocity and redistribution are fundamentally rooted in social ties between people, market exchange is more rooted in concepts such as value, price and profit. Although markets today are almost entirely about buying and selling, they too have had social functions in the past. Ethnographic studies have noted their role in information exchange, tax collection and as places for social gatherings. Historic and artistic sources are again useful.

Figure 9.47 *Amphorae stamps*

IDENTIFYING PATTERNS OF EXCHANGE

The origins of materials used in exchange are tracked using characterisation studies (▶ p. 95). For example, Roman documentary sources tell us very little about trade, but amphorae are very common finds on excavations and in shipwrecks. The fabrics of the millions of Roman amphorae that were traded all over the empire have responded particularly well to petrology, with the result that we now know where most types were manufactured. As a result, it is possible to study the sources and distributions of important agricultural products such as Italian wine, Spanish fish sauce or North African olive oil. Seals or marks on the ceramics themselves may indicate their place of manufacture. For example, many Roman amphorae have potters' stamps and some even have handwritten inscriptions, written in black ink, giving details of their contents and origin. Archaeologists plot finds of materials with the same origin on maps to show the distribution pattern. This is the first step to understanding the scale and nature of exchange. Find spots are typically shown as dots, with large dots representing multiple finds. While this technique can often suggest trade routes (e.g. along rivers), it can also be biased towards places where much development (and therefore archaeology) has taken place, such as river valleys. An attempt to overcome this is the use of trend surface analysis, which turns the dots on a map into contours to smooth out the distortion caused by chance finds. This has been used to map the distribution of Neolithic stone axes from their source.

Fall-off analysis can be used to plot the decline in finds the further one gets from the place of manufacture. A sharp fall suggests very local exchange, a smooth decline suggests 'down the line' trade, while a pattern with several blips in the curve indicates secondary trading or exchange centres. Obsidian provided an essential cutting edge for hunting, harvesting and manufacturing tools. Its exchange in the Neolithic from Anatolia as far south as modern Iran provides a classic example. When finds were plotted against distance, they formed an exponential fall-off pattern. This suggested that people close to the obsidian outcrops mined their own flakes but that it reached those further afield by being exchanged from settlement to settlement in what is termed 'down the line exchange'. A very different pattern is evident in the Oaxaca valley of Mexico, where clustering of finds of obsidian and other exchanged materials occurred at San José Mogote. This may represent a redistribution point from which a leader or 'middleman' operated. This illustrates a limitation of this approach since chiefly redistribution and market trading are very different yet remarkably similar in the resulting spatial distribution of artefacts. Sometimes only one side of an exchange can be found, as at Gudme (▶ p. 442). There are also cases where there was no exchange. Instead, people moved, taking artefacts with them. More commonly, people collected local materials themselves. This is thought to be the case with the movement of obsidian from Melos, which has been found in nearby settlements on the Greek mainland. Identifying instances of trade in perishable goods is more difficult. The well-preserved Pazyryk 'Ice Maiden' from the Altai Mountains helped provide clues. Pazyryk tribes were known to have trade links with China. When silk in her clothes was analysed, it was expected to have been made of yarn from cultivated Chinese silkworms. To the experts' surprise it turned out to be characteristic of wild Indian silk. This indicated that the Pazyryk traded to the south as well as in China.

Shipwrecks

Well-preserved shipwrecks are like time capsules from the past. They provide insights not only into ship construction and woodworking but also into exchange and social relations. Two wrecks near to Turkey and excavated by teams led by George Bass provide a glimpse of developing trade patterns in the ancient world. In each case the ship is named after where it was found.

Uluburun, Turkey, c. 1400 BC

The oldest sea-going ship in the world was 50m long with a short mast and square sail. It was a slow, heavy vessel similar to those depicted on Egyptian reliefs, with at least 15 tons of goods on board. These were painstakingly excavated and raised by lifting balloons and nets. Cargo included a 'sumptuary' range of exotic goods from across the eastern Mediterranean. The wreck was dated from Egyptian rings and seals. Also from Egypt were scarabs, gold artefacts and elephant tusks along with seals (▶ p. 417) from Mycenae and Mesopotamia, 6,000 Canaanite and Mycenaean swords and Baltic amber. Hundreds of copper oxhide ingots (▶ p. 134) were sourced by lead isotope analysis to Cyprus while tin ingots probably came from Turkey or even Afghanistan.

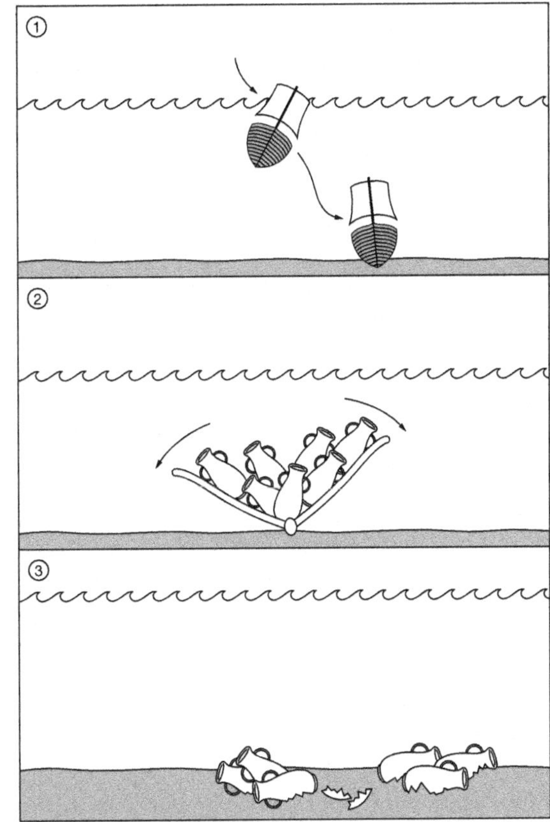

Figure 9.48 *The decay of the Kyrenia wreck*

Figure 9.49 *The Uluburun ship*

Amongst organic finds were African ebony logs, pistachios, almonds, figs, olives, spices and grain. Most of the 130 amphorae contained terebinth resin used to make perfume. Fine pottery came from Canaan, Cyprus, Mycenae and Syria and there were murex shells (used to make purple dye) and thousands of glass beads. A wooded, wax-covered writing table and balance weights suggested someone on board kept records. The personal effects suggested a Greek or Canaanite crew. Bass interpreted this as a royal cargo. Contemporary inscriptions and tablets document gifts sent as tribute, dowries or to seal alliances between rulers. En route the ship had put in to many ports and bought, and probably sold, different goods. This wreck demonstrates how long-distance trade could have developed on the back of reciprocal exchanges.

Kyrenia, Cyprus, c. 300 BC

This wreck was a small merchant vessel with a cargo of 400 amphorae from the island of Rhodes, identifiable by their seal stamps, and millstones. There were very few personal possessions, only a few bone eyelets from a sandal and some fig seeds. Underneath the hull a collection of concretions were recovered. When opened and used to produce resin casts, they proved to be iron javelins, some of them bent from impact on the hull. Since there are no natural hazards in the area, this evidence led the excavators to believe that pirates may have sunk the *Kyrenia*. The vessel had settled down onto the ocean bed, and gradually became covered in silt. As its mast and rigging rotted away, the lower part of the hull was forced outwards by the weight of the cargo and broke apart. Protected by the silt, which choked off oxygen and killed the marine worms that infested it, the remains of the hull were preserved. The ship was built in the traditional way of the classical Greeks, which is 'hull first'. Planks are carved by eye to fit along a keel, with timber selected for its natural curvature as appropriate to different parts of the vessel. The sculpted planks were held together along their edges by thousands of mortise and tenon joints which gave a very strong hull braced only with frames at a later stage. The pine frames were clenched together with treenails, fastened with copper nails. This process wasted 70–80 per cent of the wood used and required a high standard of craftsmanship from the shipwright. It would only be possible in a society which valued craftsmanship, where raw materials were abundant and where time was no problem. The man who built the *Kyrenia* was probably a slave and his time was his master's. Over its life, the 90-year-old vessel had been much repaired and partly sheathed in lead to remain watertight. She was engaged in what has been called 'tramping': sailing (usually within sight of land) between

Figure 9.50 *Cargo of the Kyrenia wreck*

Figure 9.51 *Construction of the Kyrenia*

ports on a long circuit of the region, taking on and selling cargoes as she went.

This partial reconstruction shows the amphorae densely packed in the bottom of the vessel. It is not clear if it had a deck over the hold but the pottery was packed in thorn branches (dunnage) to protect it. The millstones are also visible. There may have been textiles on top but no trace of them survives.

The freeze-dried hull of the ship reveals structural elements and construction techniques. The degree of carpentry skills which went into building the vessel is clear.

NETWORKS OF EXCHANGE

The ultimate goal of distribution studies is to recreate the system which connected producers, middlemen and consumers and to understand both their social interactions and the way goods were transported between them. A variety of sources have been used to build up a picture of trade in the eastern Mediterranean in the Bronze Age. On a clay tablet found at Tell el Amarna in Egypt, the King of Alashiya apologises to the pharaoh for sending a smaller shipment of copper than expected. The mountain of Alashiya was recorded across the Middle East as the major source of copper. Characterisation of the minerals in the tablets has located the clay source to south-west Cyprus. Similarly ingots of copper found across the region have also been sourced by lead isotope (▶ p. 133) analysis to Cypriot mines. Ten tonnes of copper ingots were also found on the *Uluburun* (▶ p. 403) in what represents the first find of a bulk metal cargo. Shipwrecks in general have been useful in understanding the mechanisms of trade as well as the cargoes. Artistic sources can provide considerable detail. The tomb of the Egyptian official Rekhmir from Thebes has pictures of Cretans bearing goods while the frescoes from the Minoan town of Akrotiri on Thera depict the kind of vessels in which they sailed.

The Canaanite Amphorae Project

Amphorae – large pottery storage vessels – have been found on Bronze Age sites across the Middle East and eastern Mediterranean. Through typology and petrological study of clay fabrics, several styles of vessel have been linked to particular areas of origin. In this particular case it was the area of present-day Israel, Lebanon and

Figure 9.52 *Canaanite amphora*

Palestine known in biblical times as Canaan. They have a particularly wide distribution, appearing in the cargo of the *Uluburun* off modern Turkey and in great quantities on Egyptian sites up the River Nile. To understand what was being carried in the amphorae and provide insights into trade, this project involves data collection and residue analysis from across the region. An early focus has been on sherds recovered from the Egyptian cities of Amarna (capital of the Pharaoh Akhenaten) and Memphis (capital of New Kingdom Egypt).

Researchers began by establishing a detailed typology of the amphorae based on visual attributes using material from the Amarna project and collections held in museums. Binocular microscopes were used to classify fabric types. These were checked using petrology and NAA (▶ p. 132) and compared with reference material on pottery and geology from across the region. Amongst inclusions in the Fabric 1 clays (▶ p. 95) were minerals which only occur together in Israel's Jezreel Valley. Identical pottery was found in Bronze Age settlements in this area.

The archaeologists now knew where the amphorae had originated but not what they held. A few had inscriptions including references to honey and oil but most did not. Organic residue analysis was unsuccessful with the honey or for pinpointing the vegetable oil. This was probably from olives which were produced on a large scale in Canaan and one particular amphora type was linked to this trade. A considerable quantity of resin was also found in broken amphorae or extracted from the fabric with solvents. It was also found on textiles and local bowls which are known to have been used for incense burning. The nature of this incense has long been debated. The Egyptian word *sntr* has been translated as incense and generally thought to mean frankincense, a gum resin from trees grown further south

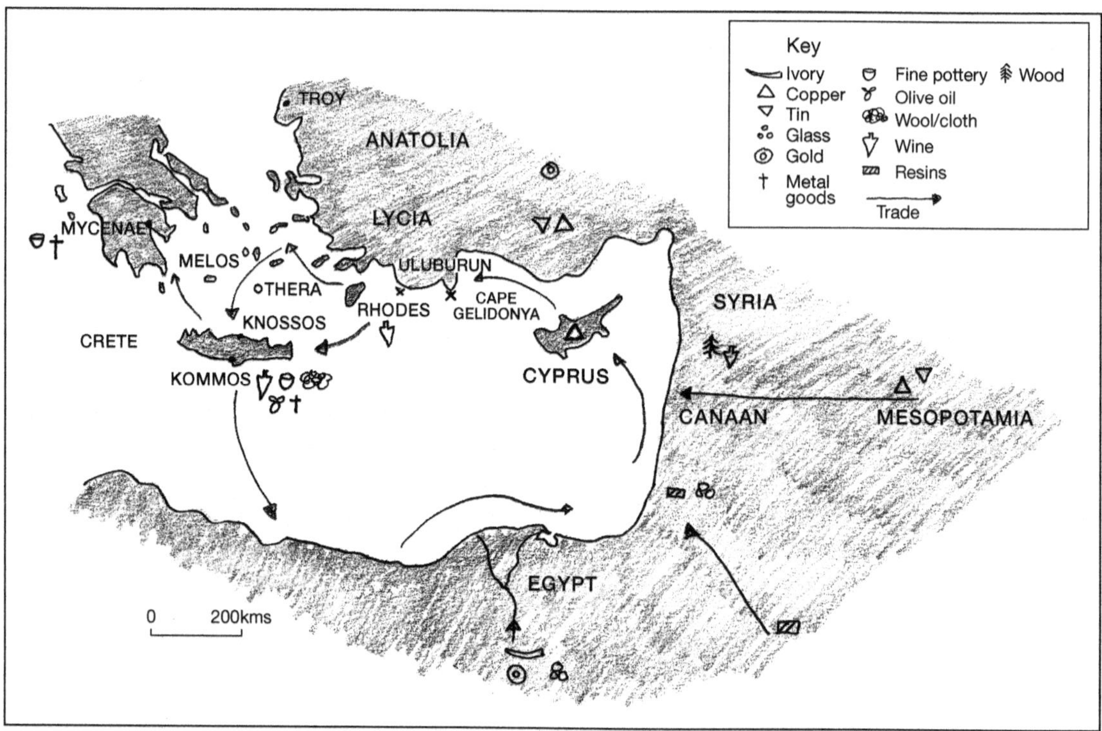

Figure 9.53 *Bronze Age trade in the eastern Mediterranean*

in Africa. However, this resin came from pistacia trees, probably terebinth. A similar resin was found on the *Uluburun* (▶ p. 403). Traces of beer were found in a few vessels. As a result of this research, there is now a detailed reference collection of vessel and fabric types which will enable identification of ceramics and their origin using hand lenses or microscopes. There is also a reference collection of biomarkers which will help researchers identify products more easily in the future. Finally, they have been able to identify part of the Bronze Age trade network across the region.

Iron Age trade to Britain

A number of models from modern economic and development studies have been used to try to understand past exchange systems. A particularly influential model has been World Systems Theory, which divides trade zones up into a rich core and a poorer periphery which it exploits for raw materials. Cunliffe (1994) used this model to explain the relationship between different groups in Iron Age Britain. In the south-east the core tribes monopolised trade with the advancing Roman Empire to secure the kind of feasting luxuries that appear in the late C1st BC Welwyn Garden City burial (▶ p. 545). Diplomatic ties were established, mercenaries may have fought in return for gold during the Gallic Wars and cross-channel trade became orientated towards the Thames estuary. The evidence for this comes in distribution patterns of imported luxuries including fine tableware, Italian metalwork and wine vessels. The predominant distribution of earlier Dressel 1A amphorae had been up the south-coast rivers from ports such as Hengistbury Head, while the later Dressel 1B amphorae are found in the south-east. Most of the trade flowing back to Roman Gaul is invisible but the Roman author Strabo lists slaves, dogs, minerals and agricultural produce. Some of this may have been produced in the core zone but definitely not minerals such as tin, silver and gold, which are only found in the west. In the periphery zone from Dorset to Yorkshire there are far fewer imported luxuries and less use of coinage. The suggestion is that this area produced goods or traded or raided them from the tribes on the Atlantic coast. The discovery of slave chains at a number of sites hints at least at some raiding to feed the markets developing at oppida (high-status settlements) such as Verulamium or Camulodunum.

Identifying trade routes

A series of recent studies have begun exploiting new technologies to study the medieval 'silk roads' which carried trade from China to the Mediterranean. These developed out of regional trading networks from the Bronze Age onwards and used pack animals, particularly camels, to transport precious metals and stones, spices and fine textiles over long distances. In some areas such as Persia and China there were actual road systems but much of central Asia was simply vast tracts of grassland or desert. The Karakum Routes Survey used geographic and satellite data in conjunction with historic records in a GIS database (▶ p. 10) to predict likely corridors of movement using cost-distance (▶ p. 248) models. This highlighted areas for surface surveys to search for surface scatters or pottery or structural evidence of caravanserais (roadside inns where the camel caravans would rest on their journeys). The related research of the Ancient Merv Project is examining the development and trade links of this great oasis-city in Turkmenistan (Wordsworth 2013). So far a number of large structures have been identified on the probable route from Merv through the desert to the River Oxus as well as smaller campsites. Further investigations will examine whether the large structures were part of an imperial road designed to protect and control the lucrative trade. The nature of this research is best appreciated from online resources such as Archatlas.

Where they exist, the remains of permanent tracks and roads such as the Roman and Inca road systems can indicate increasing traffic on routes. Intense use of these features can sometimes be inferred from wear such as rutting and evidence of frequent repairing. The same may be true of wooden walkways through wetlands such as the Sweet Track (▶ p. 385) or the recently discovered Plumstead trackway dating from *c*. 4000 BC. Wheeled transport can also be indicative of increased movement of materials. The development of vehicles can be traced through artistic depiction, from models such as the 4th millennium carts in burials at Uruk and through the first finds of wheels (▶ p. 360). Similarly, evidence for the use of animals for riding and draught purposes can sometimes be determined by bit-wear marks on teeth or artefacts associated with harnesses (▶ p. 359). Artistic sources and shipwrecks (▶ p. 403) provide evidence of the evolution of river and seaborne transport.

KEY STUDY

Dorestad and the birth of medieval trade in the North Sea zone

According to the economic historian Pirenne (1927/1969), the end of the Roman Empire and the disruption of Mediterranean trade routes by Moslem expansion in the C7th AD led to the collapse of Western trade. A period of local self-sufficiency ensued until the emergence of towns around religious and royal centres from the late C10th. This fitted notions of the early medieval period as a backward 'Dark Age'. There are relatively few historical sources for trade in this period but that does not mean there was no trade. The accounts of missionaries such as Anskar or travellers such as Othere contain many references to sea travel and ports. Archaeological evidence increasingly supports the view that this was in fact a golden age of the north during which commercial trade and towns were reborn.

Between the late C7th and late C9th AD Dorestad emerged as the hub of trade in north-west Europe. The town was located in the Rhine Delta at a fork in the river which had previously been the site of one of a series of Roman forts (Levefanum) marking the northern border of the empire. Using 3D Lidar mapping and geological survey data on ancient river channels showed that the site originated on a high natural levee (Kosian et al. 2013) safe from seasonal flooding and at the heart of a network of channels which enabled ships to avoid hazardous areas of the Dutch coast. The Kromme Rijn (Crooked Rhine) gave access to the North Sea and the River Lek to the River Schelde estuary of present-day Belgium. The Rhine itself provided access to much of western Germany. Dorestad began as a Frisian trading post but grew in importance to become a possible Frisian capital prior to its conquest by the Franks around AD 700. Under the Franks, Dorestad was protected but also became a source of wealth for the Carolingian emperors, who levied customs duties and river tolls. Its trade network connecting the Christian Frankish Empire with pagan Scandinavia and Anglo-Saxon England survived until its destruction by Vikings in the 840s.

Excavation

A riverside port was first identified in the 1920s but major salvage excavation occurred in advance of large-scale housing developments from 1967 to 1978. With a small excavation team, director Wim van Es of the Dutch Archaeological Service controversially chose to try to understand the whole town rather than focus on a few parts of it. As a result, an area of over 30 hectares was machine stripped and

Figure 9.54 *Layout of the settlement at Dorestad*

Ships would dock against the long wooden jetties in the foreground. Further back are the warehouses and farmsteads associated with each part of the waterfront. A wooden road runs along the wharf.

followed up with targeted excavation to identify the various components. This was advantageous in revealing the layout of the town but less good in terms of stratigraphic understanding and recovery of artefacts. More recent excavations in surrounding settlements and the old vegetable market of the current town have provided much more detail to complement van Es' pioneering work.

The undefended port stretched for 3km on the banks of the River Kromme Rijn. At the water's edge, lines of timber piles at right angles to the shore marked wooden jetties which would have been 6–8m wide. These were constantly extended as the slow-moving river silted up and meandered, some being 200m long. On the shore was a roadway backed by up to three rows of closely packed buildings. These buildings, also at 90 degrees to the river, were grouped in rectangular 'parcels' of land about 20m wide and each linked to a pair of jetties. The excavators interpreted this as representing different businesses, each with their own wharf, storage and workshops (Van Es and Verwers 2010). This systematic pattern also suggests organisation and perhaps control. Behind the trade settlement or vicus were at least sixty fenced compounds each with boat-shaped longhouses, byres and wells. These were interpreted as farms which fed and supplied the town. Estimates of population size range from 2,000–3,000 people.

Artefacts

Traded materials found at Dorestad included large quantities of Mayen lava quernstones from the Eifel Mountains of Germany. Querns were an essential item for farming communities and those living around the North Sea coasts lacked sources of hard stone. Lava was relatively easy to quarry and work, had

continued

a good grinding surface and was light enough to transport long distances (Pohl 2010). Lava debris in the workshops tells us that querns arrived as blanks to be finished and drilled at Dorestad. The Rhine also brought pottery from Mayen, fine cream-coloured Badorf tableware from kilns around Cologne and both glass and wine from the Rhineland. The wells in Dorestad were lined with wine barrels made from Rhineland oak or silver fir from Bavaria (Jansma and De Natris 2009). In Dorestad itself, manufacturing waste and tools tell us that wood, antler, leather and bone were worked along with weaving and the manufacture of iron goods from hooks and nails to Frankish swords. Ships were built and glass-workers used recycled Roman artefacts to produce beads and drinking vessels. Wheel-thrown cooking pots were produced in large numbers and precious metals were imported in order for the Dorestad mint to strike coins including silver derniers (pennies) with distinctive ship motifs. The distribution of these coins in conjunction with Dorestad pots and Rhineland imports (especially quernstones) provides evidence of the wider reach of Frisian merchants across the northern world, linking Mainz, Ipswich (▶ p. 288), York and Ribe in Denmark. Much of the returning trade is invisible apart from Baltic amber. Partly this is because some commodities simply passed through while others left no physical trace. From the historical sources we know these included furs, textiles, dogs and particularly slaves. Bede described Frisian slavers buying prisoners in London, while in France St Eligius reportedly bought slaves from Frisians in order to free them. Fish (▶ p. 612), grain, iron, wood and wool are other likely bulk cargoes. A clue to the latter has come from increasing finds through metal detecting of Dorestad silver sceattas in areas such as the Cotswolds and Yorkshire which were associated with sheep rearing. The sceattas themselves (the word is Anglo-Saxon for wealth) were at one time thought to be elite tokens of value rather than indicators of a money economy. However, the distribution and numbers recovered of these and Anglo-Saxon imitations suggests that they were used as a currency.

Figure 9.55 *Coin from Dorestad*

Figure 9.56 *Mayen quernstone*

How was trade organised?

Evidence of a high volume of trade of everyday artefacts, food and bulk goods and of the wide distribution of sceattas suggests that this was commercial trading rather than prestige goods exchange or simply

	Commodities	Prestige goods
Germany	lava quernstones, timber, grain*	wine, glass, fine pottery, fine metalwork
Scandinavia	stockfish, soapstone, whetstones, iron, timber,* furs, wax,* antler	amber, ivory
England	wool, woollen cloth,* grain,* hides,* food,* salt, linen*	slaves,* honey,* dogs*
Frisia	fish, cloth*	
Dorestad	finished quernstones	fine ceramics, fine metal goods, coins
Other origins		precious metals, gemstones, fine metalwork, coins, glass, spices, silk,* dyes,* ivory

***known from historical sources**

Figure 9.57 *Dark Age trade goods*

providing an elite with Frankish luxuries in return for raw materials. Elites may have protected and taxed the emporia as they developed but they do not appear to have initiated the trade networks. A new source of analog has also been used to explain the way in which the system developed and functioned. Borrowing from network science, Sindbæk (2007a) argued that a range of different types of trading expeditions tended to cross paths at particular locations. These 'nodal points' or 'traffic junctions' developed as unfortified settlements because of trading rather than being established to control or attract trade. These were not necessarily the central places of religious or political authority, although the latter eventually followed. These 'network towns' or emporia grew organically and can be identified both by their 'black earth', indicating long periods of occupation, and by large numbers of long-distance trade artefacts. They were often located geographically at points where journeys had to be broken or goods transhipped. Sindbæk (2007a) compared different towns in Scandinavia and found that only five (Ribe, Kaupang, Birka, Aros and Hedeby) had significant evidence of long-distance trade items. Additionally they featured yellow Badorf cooking pots from the Rhineland which appear to be associated with traders rather than trade. Almost all sites have the waste from manufacturing iron goods, textiles and bone combs but only the network towns cast bronze or made glass beads. Both industries depended on imported raw materials. Sindbæk (2007a) argues that in a hazardous world where no authority yet protected commerce, traders would tend to use predictable locations where they knew they could meet other traders to buy and sell relatively safely and perhaps had contacts. Each node would be connected by a web of local trade to other settlements as exemplified in Blinkhorn's (2012) work on Ipswich. Historical sources suggest that the traders who developed these networks were largely Frisian, the same peoples who had traded across the North Sea under the Romans. There is also evidence from York, Mainz, Ipswich and Hedeby of Frisian merchants living in those emporia.

continued

What was the relationship between an emporium and its hinterland?

Blinkhorn (1999) investigated the relationship between Ipswich (▶ p. 288) and other sites within East Anglia. Across the region, finds of Ipswich ware demonstrated close links between rural settlements and manufacturing in the emporia. Finds of Mayen quernstones and Frisian coins on many sites showed that many rural sites were getting access to the wider trade network through Ipswich. Blinkhorn (1999) argues that changing settlement and enclosure patterns suggest a reorganisation of land ownership and field systems during this period. This included cultivation of heavier but more productive soils and agricultural intensification through specialisation in order to provide 'cash crops'. These included grain, cattle for meat and hides, furs, salt or beeswax. For example, plant remains from North Raunds suggest a focus upon wheat, while a high proportion of the Ipswich ware sherds found there contain traces of honey. Similar relationships between other 'Wic' sites such as Hamwic (Southampton) and Eoforwic (York) have been identified by other researchers. The interdependence between settlements and the increasing importance of a market economy in England reflected larger-scale specialisation along the Rhine. This included viticulture (wine production), quarrying and pottery production.

Until recently it was thought that early medieval trade was begun by political elites who established 'gateway communities' such as Ipswich to obtain luxuries (Hodges 1982). While there does seem to be one emporium for each of the emerging English kingdoms (e.g. Hamwic for Wessex), the volume of

Figure 9.58 *Ipswich ware*

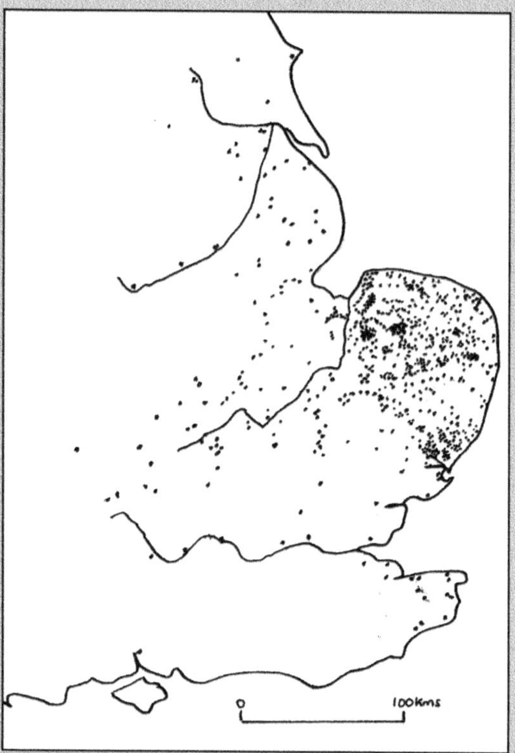

Figure 9.59 *Distribution of Ipswich ware (after Blinkhorn 1999)*

trade which is being revealed through recent finds and excavations suggests much wider involvement and not just for prestige goods (Loveluck and Tys 2006). The church also appears to have played a leading role. O'Connor (1991) argues that evidence of increased production and imported goods on monastic estates suggests they were supplying the emporia and almost certainly hosting their own seasonal fairs or markets. From literary sources we also know that East Anglian monks had close links with the Rhineland. Many of the find sites for Ipswich ware outside East Anglia are monasteries and abbeys such as Beverley in Northumbria or Brixworth in Mercia. There also seems to be a lower level of trade between coastal and inland areas based on the raw materials each had access to such as fish and salt or wool and iron (Loveluck and Tys 2006).

The expansion of trade

Evidence of the Frisians' increasing reach is provided by Skyre's (2013) examination of imported goods from the C9th AD Norse port of Kaupang. Some finds could have been the result of raiding but the

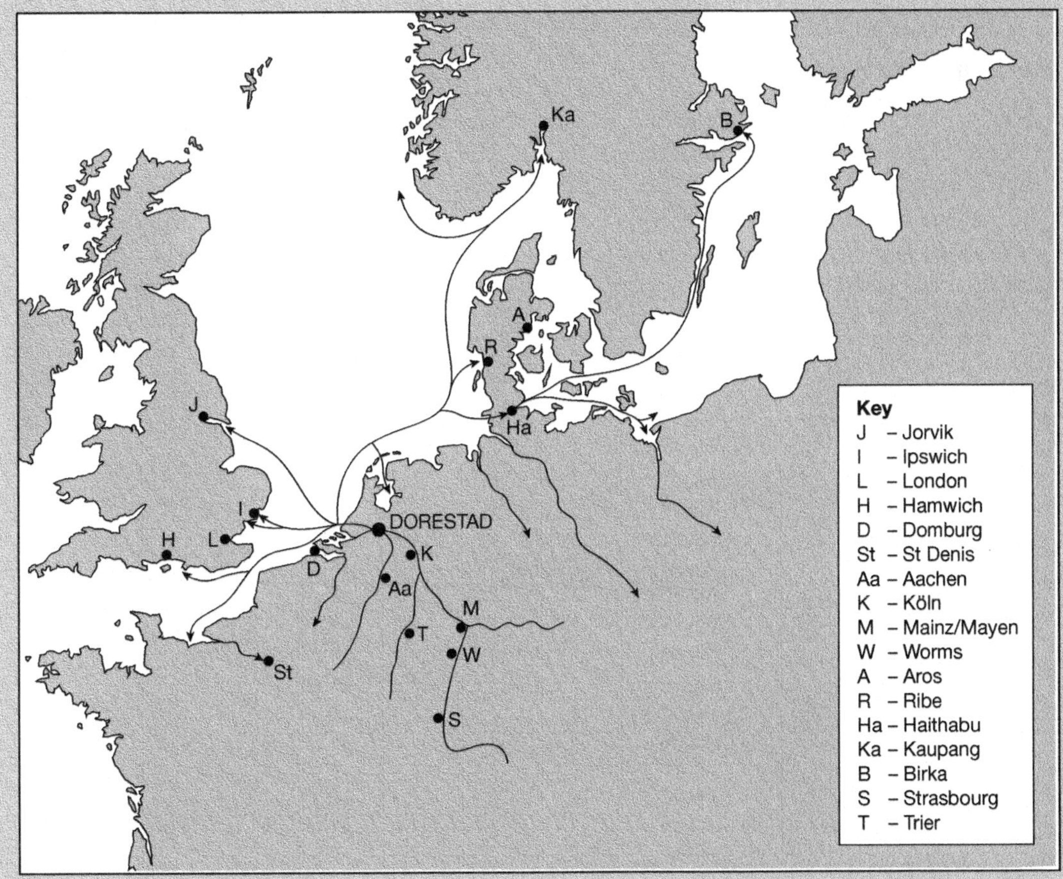

Figure 9.60 *The North Sea emporia and trade network*

continued

range strongly suggests trade. It included Frankish metalwork, glass and coins along with Islamic glass beads. Raw materials included lead, copper and glass waste. Most of the pottery was Frankish or Frisian cooking pots (especially Badorf ware) but they appeared to be related to particular houses and were more likely to be personal possessions rather than trade goods. Finds from house A301 provided some strong clues. There was more pottery than in most other buildings and most of it was Frisian. A set of everyday, worn, bronze Frankish women's dress fittings, some weights, four pieces of hack-silver (used as a basic currency), Islamic beads, amber and Rhenish glassware were found there. Unlike the other houses this building did not contain a workshop. Skyre interpreted this as the house of a Frisian trader and his family. Large numbers of iron fragments were found in the floor deposits. From later periods we know that Vikings traded furs, slaves, iron, amber, soapstone and whetstones. There is no evidence that the last two were being traded at this date but the other commodities are documented. While iron is a common mineral, Norwegian ore is particularly high quality and became prized for making swords. The Frisian nature of the network is evidenced by the decline in many of the emporia such as Ribe after the sack of Dorestad by the Vikings. Their dominance was replaced by that of the Vikings from the late C10th, who extended the network to the Arctic, Ireland and the rivers of Russia.

Dark Age cargo vessels

The boats used for this commerce had to have shallow draughts to navigate rivers and for beaching at Scandinavian ports where there were no wharves, but be strong enough to cope with the North Sea. The most likely candidate is the knarr, a shorter, wider and deeper cargo-version of the longship. Like the longship it was clinker-built (with overlapping planks), which made it light and flexible. The Scandinavian tradition of using trenails (wooden rivets) or tree-bast fibres to hold planks together was often used due to the cost of iron. Modern reconstructions have used several hundred kilograms of

Figure 9.61 *Dark Age cargo vessel*

The knarr on the right can clearly be differentiated from the warship by its deeper and broader hull, built for carrying bulk rather than for speed.

nails. The knarr had a small crew and relied on a square woollen sail for power, only using oars to manoeuvre from port. No Frisian knarr has yet been found, although images are known including those on coins. However, an example was recovered from Roskilde Fjord (▶ p. 185) in Denmark and remains of others are known from Norway. A replica of that wreck, the *Ottar*, has been used to demonstrate speed, range, seaworthiness and how the steering and rigging would handle (▶ p. 414). Over time, wear and damage to this vessel will help us understand the problems and repairs of the historic vessels. Knarr were tough, stable ships and could carry up to 24 tonnes in their two holds. They were used by the Vikings to reach Iceland and possibly Greenland. Smaller versions called byrthing or keels were used for inshore and river trade as they had a shallower draught and were more portable.

EXCHANGE AND THE FIRST WRITING SYSTEMS

Writing is a technology which primarily developed as a means of recording and administering trade. Although there is potential evidence from the 5th millennium BC in the Balkans, it has proved impossible to decipher, so the first real writing system is considered to be Cuneiform, which emerged in Sumer (Mesopotamia) after 4000 BC.

Merchants needed to ensure their goods arrived at distant destinations. During the late Neolithic they made tokens shaped like each of their goods such as cattle or jars of oil. These were enclosed in a hollow ball of clay which was sealed using their unique cylinder seal. The recipient could be sure who had sent the shipment from the seal. The tokens inside would tell them how many of each item should have arrived. Writing developed from the tokens and the symbols on the seals. By the Chalcolithic Uruk period, the volume and complexity of exchange in Sumer led to the development of a set of pictographs (ideas expressed as images, e.g. modern toilet signs) to standardise information and assist memory. Cuneiform was inscribed on clay tablets using a wedge-shaped (Latin – cuneus) stylus and gradually developed into an ideographic or logographic system, using abstract symbols to signify a word (e.g. the way '4' symbolises 'four'). Early Egyptian hieroglyphics were also ideographs but from about 2000 BC other characters were added which represented the phonetic sounds of an alphabet. The Mayan writing system used glyphs as both ideographs and to represent phonetic sounds. It developed in parallel to Eurasian writing systems.

Modern European alphabets from the Romans onwards are based on the Greek alphabet. That in turn can be linked back via the Phoenicians to the Semitic language of the Egyptian alphabet. Greek included vowel sounds and from 1500 BC used a linear writing style – Linear B.

From the point writing developed, the rulers of early states recognised its potential to proclaim their laws, deeds and ancestry. Their monumental inscriptions are often the best-known examples of early writing.

Decoding writing systems

Egyptian tablets and inscriptions potentially offered a vast amount of information to scholars. The problem was that nobody could read them. The breakthrough came in 1799 when Napoleonic soldiers found a stone with inscriptions built into a wall in Rosetta in Egypt. The Rosetta Stone dates from 196 BC, when the Greek dynasty of the Ptolemies were the ruling pharaohs. It was written by priests to praise the pharaoh using three different scripts: Egyptian hieroglyphs (the script of the priesthood), Egyptian demotic (the linear script used by ordinary people) and Greek. Since all three said the same thing it was possible

Figure 9.62 *The sedge (plant) and bee represented the Nile Delta and Upper Egypt respectively. Shown above the two original mounds of land these hieroglyphics announced the Pharaoh as ruler of both kingdoms of Egypt.*

Figure 9.64 *Minoan Linear A tablet*

Figure 9.63 *'Jaguar' in Mayan glyphs*

Figure 9.65 *This merchant's cylinder seal from Crete has been rolled on wax to display the inscription. Cylinder seals themselves provide strong evidence of trading systems.*

for the French scholar Champollion to work out how hieroglyphics worked and decode what they said. Unfortunately, we cannot be sure of Egyptian vowels, which is why there are alternative spellings for many words and names, for instance Imen/Amen/Amun.

When explorers discovered the ruins of Mayan cities in the jungle in the mid-C19th, they realised that the glyphs which covered the monuments were the remnants of a lost language. Until recently little progress was made with the translation. It was assumed from the little that could be read that the Maya were a society of peace-loving astronomers with an obsession with mathematics and a complex calendar. Recent breakthroughs have allowed most glyphs to be translated. Unfortunately, few Mayan texts survive because Spanish priests burnt them. However, the carvings survive and the stories of gods, wars and rulers such as Pacal at Palenque (▶ p. 128) and the kings of Copan can be read. The glyphs provide us with information about real, named people. This is impossible for periods without writing.

Not all ancient languages have been deciphered. The clay tablet in Figure 9.64 is in Linear A, the writing used by the Minoans. However, there is sufficient similarity between it and the later Linear B (the writing of the Mycenaean Greeks) to establish that it was used by palace accountants to record agricultural produce entering and leaving the storerooms. The tablets were made of soft clay and could be reused. Normally they would not survive because they decay over time but in this instance it provides an example of preservation by fire. When the Palace of Zakros (▶ p. 429) burnt down, hundreds of tablets were fired and thus preserved as ceramics.

Chapter 10

People and Society in the Past

Since this is the penultimate thematic chapter of this book, there is danger of repetition. Where possible, we have cross-referenced issues here to earlier chapters. However, we have also included a larger number of key studies, both to illustrate aspects of social archaeology and to pull together themes from across the book.

WHAT IS SOCIAL ARCHAEOLOGY?

Social archaeology can usefully be divided into three main subsections:

- Social organisation ranges from the basic social units of family, **kin** and **bands** to nation states and empires. It is related to political organisation, which comprises the way social groups take decisions and the distribution of power within societies.

social organisation	social action and change	social divisions
• band • tribe • chiefdom • state • household • family • kin • politics	• social evolution • population growth • migration • competition • conflict • warfare	• age • gender • ethnicity • status • rank • stratification • class • elites

Figure 10.1 *What is social archaeology?*

- Social differentiation is the way in which people in social groups are viewed and treated differently according to features that society sees as significant. Examples include age or gender, status or class.
- Social action and change includes warfare, immigration and how and why societies transformed themselves.

Understanding social archaeology

Hawkes (▶ p. 174) identified past social systems as problematic for archaeologists. Despite this, most archaeologists have written with confidence on the societies they have studied, drawing on many different models (particularly from ethnography) to help interpret their sources. For recent societies there is written and even oral evidence to draw on but for pre-literate societies, archaeologists have relied heavily on burial evidence. The advantages of the association between grave goods in particular and different individuals are obvious but burial assemblages can be misleading. They are, after all, a symbolic collection placed with the deceased by the living and not necessarily what the person would normally have had around them. It is important to cross-reference burial evidence with other physical sources. These include artistic depictions, artefacts, buildings and settlement patterns. To these traditional sources should be added the scientific analysis of human remains which is revolutionising our understanding of relationships between people in the past in ways unimaginable just a few decades ago. Since the strengths and weaknesses of each type of evidence are similar for each topic, we have tackled them more fully for status and avoided repetition on the other topics. It is therefore advisable to read this chapter in order.

FORMS OF SOCIAL AND POLITICAL ORGANISATION

Social evolution

Archaeology developed in the early C20th when evolutionary ideas were being applied in the social sciences and when much of the world was directly ruled by colonial powers. It is understandable then that evolutionary models of social development were applied to the past. As societies became increasingly 'advanced' and 'civilised', they were expected to develop along similar paths. Early archaeological research sought to trace this development and identify reasons for particular regions being more advanced than others. Western models of social development have been challenged in recent decades, but what are now termed neo-evolutionary models of social development are still commonplace. In particular the degree of social complexity within a society is often stressed. In the simplest societies there is little differentiation of roles as everyone forages, makes tools and shares food. In the most complex societies there are a vast range of specialists from soldiers to priestesses to fresco painters and a growing proportion of the population live in urban centres and neither forage nor farm.

The best known of the socio-evolutionary models which seek to define different types of society and to chart and explain linear progress from simple to complex society are those of Service and Fried. There are similarities between them but not complete overlap. Service's (1971) model of Band to State differentiates in terms of

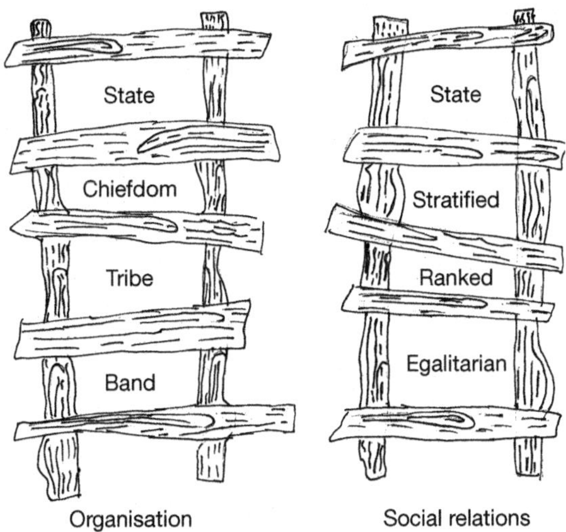

Figure 10.2 *The social evolutionary ladders of Service and Fried*

the type and scale of social and political organisation and is the more widely used. However, defining the divide between each level is difficult. Fried's (1978) model focuses on the changing relationships between people in a society with increasing inequality and formal roles. While the terms make sense, it has proved particularly difficult to differentiate between ranked and stratified societies and it has been less useful in archaeology. Nevertheless, there seems general agreement that complex societies tend to be larger scale, more stratified and with more permanent institutions. However, some prehistorians use 'social complexity' to describe changes in Palaeolithic or Mesolithic society; for example, the apparent emergence of flint-working specialists and the 'grandmother revolution' of the last Ice Age (▶ p. 224).

All the terms used to classify social organisation over-simplify and conceal considerable variations. However, we need to use such concepts as our starting point when comparing and contrasting social groups and discussing them. We also know that not all societies developed along the same paths and that there have been many 'dead ends' where there was no progression to the next level and even where 'progress' was reversed. It is also worth noting that bands, tribes and chiefdoms all still exist today in many parts of the world including within modern states.

Families

Households or families are the basic building blocks of all human societies. From the point when humans began sitting round campsites or living in tents or rock shelters, evidence about the form of residential groups accumulated. While pair bonding (▶ p. 199) of parents was probably important, the precise forms and degree of permanence of early families is unclear. The appearance of permanent houses at Neolithic sites such as Karanovo (▶ p. 339) marks a fundamental social change (at least in the archaeological record) because walls define the living arrangements, possessions and activities of one group while excluding others. The importance of houses, often on sites which were used for several generations, and their households has been emphasized in numerous studies. They literally set relationships in stone or at least wattle and daub. Households live together, eat together and in most historic societies, work together. Households became the basic social unit for production of food and other artefacts, consumption (replacing meals round an open hearth) and socialisation. They also became the focus for rituals in many societies including burials under floors and the use of cult objects (▶ p. 520). Any internal divisions in houses also tell us something about differences within this basic group. In the Balkan Neolithic, there is persuasive evidence that houses were ritually burnt (Tringham 2013), perhaps upon the death of the head of the household, before being replaced. This suggests a symbolic importance beyond a simple place of work and shelter. Similarly, longhouses (▶ p. 499) may have been the inspiration behind long barrows (▶ p. 161). Households are not the same as families. LBK (▶ p. 346) and medieval longhouses included animals as well as people while residences of richer people such as villas, palaces or castles often contained several families as well as servants, officials or slaves.

Families are couples and their offspring. This is not to say that any particular model such as the nuclear family always existed in the past, although the evidence from Eulau (▶ p. 116) may support it. At some point in the past in most societies particular relationships were socially recognised as exclusive through marriage. The triple burial from Dolni Vestonice (▶ p. 218) has been suggested as evidence of a taboo or social rule against either adultery or homosexuality. Ethnographic studies of the range of forms of marriage or families in historical societies suggest that all societies would have had rules governing relationships. In some, families are two-generational nuclear families headed by a wife and husband but many also lived as extended families involving several generations of people linked by marriage.

The archaeological clues are in the size of houses and their relationship to others. Multiple small, evenly spaced houses with similar features are likely to be indicative of nuclear families while larger compounds or buildings with major subdivisions might indicate extended families. Such an arrangement was identified by the excavator of the Bronze Age site of Black Patch (▶ p. 273), with several linked compounds and huts representing the homes of a family head and other relatives. Some cultures have had marriages of one man and several wives (polygyny) and occasionally one woman and several husbands (polyandry). Many have had rules governing marriage partners and where new families can settle. Endogamous marriage involves finding a partner within the social group, while exogamous marriage requires a partner from outside. Matrilocal marriage involves the new family joining the household or settlement of the bride's family, while patrilocal marriage requires them to settle with the husband's. Until recently, stylistic studies of artefacts and analysis of morphological traits on skeletal remains provided the only clues to these patterns. DNA and stable isotope analysis (▶ p. 133) are providing startling new insights including evidence of exogamy and patrilocality at LBK sites such as Vaihingen (▶ p. 350).

Kinship

Whether they lived together or not, **kinship** is important in most societies, although the significance attached to blood or marriage ties varies widely. People from the Neolithic onwards were particularly aware of lines of descent or lineages which created bonds between people beyond their immediate households. This is suggested both by burials under houses or by monuments (such as long barrows) built to venerate collective ancestors. In some historic cases whole communities are known to have believed that they were descended from a common ancestor, mythological figure or creature such as an eagle or bear. An example was medieval Scotland, where groups of lineages claimed descent from a common ancestor in what is known as a **clan** system. Different societies stress the importance of the male line of descent (patrilineal), female (matrilineal) or both (bi-lineal). Kinship provided a network of assistance in economic activity, finding marriage partners, exchange, assistance and other matters. It also provided a basic political structure for dealing with disputes, outsiders and negotiations with the older, more experienced members of the group likely to take the lead. Although the relevance of kinship in modern Western society has declined, there are still exceptions, most notoriously the Mafia. Kinship affiliations are researched through skeletal remains and the clustering of particular forms of artefacts as at Vaihingen (▶ p. 350). A number of other bonds recorded by anthropologists include age-based groups and 'moieties'. Moieties are formed by dividing people into one of two groups at birth or through induction. They may have distinctive emblems or totems (▶ p. 510), can be important for rituals including organisation of feasts and burials and often require marriage partners to be from the opposite moiety (exogamy). The existence of such groups means that individuals may have several different affiliations.

Bands and tribes

Bands are self-sufficient groups of a few families numbering up to fifty or one hundred individuals. They are usually linked through kinship or marriage and may consider themselves to be a clan. They were most commonly found in mobile forager societies who lived in temporary camps. While some members had particularly valuable expertise, there were no full-time specialists. To some early anthropologists bands appeared to be egalitarian societies, although recent ethnographic research has shown that some inequalities exist in

Band	<100	Broadly egalitarian	Temporary camps	Boxgrove, Trentino, Pincevent, Ohalo II, Ringkloster, Oronsay, Stellmoor, Star Carr
Tribe	100s–2–3000	Segmentary. Transegalitarian	Permanent camps. Villages	Karanovo, Tell Abu Hureyra, Vaihingen, Eulau, Varna? Tybrind Vig?
Chiefdom	up to 20,000	Ranked. Kinship	Elite centres, forts, ritual complexes	Hallstatt, Hochdorf, Vucedal? Danebury, Stonehenge? Gudme
State	over 20,000	Class-based elite/stratified	Urban	Knossos, Ipswich, Dorestad, Nineveh, Copan

Figure 10.3 *Social organisation. Service's model matched against studies from this text.*

many modern bands. The term is most frequently used in archaeology for the Upper Palaeolithic and Mesolithic. Bands were probably fluid, with families or individuals moving between groups at times. They may also have only lived together during particular seasons. Leaders are likely to have emerged because of experience or personal qualities but may have been temporary. With mobile populations it is difficult for leaders to become permanent since it is easy for their prospective subjects to move away. Stellmoor (▶ p. 298) is likely to represent a band-level society. The early farming site of Skara Brae (▶ p. 274) may represent another.

Tribes are larger than bands, with numbers ranging from a few hundred to a few thousand. Tribes are associated with horticulturalists, pastoralists and some forager societies. Amongst mobile tribes people may live in one of a number of bands for part of the year but the tribe itself has its own identity too. A cycle of fission into bands and fusion into a tribe can be seen at Head Smashed In (▶ p. 253).

Hedges (2000) suggested that different animal remains found in Neolithic tombs on Orkney represented totems (▶ p. 510), each linked to a tribal group. Renfrew (1984) suggested a similar pattern with his study of the distribution of tombs and ceramic styles (▶ p. 251). Farming tribes will often live in permanent villages. However, a tribe is not simply a collection of bands. Kinship and marriage networks provide bonds which link the tribe together but there are also ceremonies and communal activities which reinforce tribal identity. Tribes often have activity leaders who are recognised as having skill and authority in particular areas such as hunting or ritual. Potentially most adults may achieve leadership in some areas and therefore none may stand out overall. Of the models of political organisation and leadership that have been borrowed from anthropology for tribes, the most influential has been the **Bigmen** of New Guinea. These are individuals who rise to prominence through their personal charisma and skill in key areas of economic and social life such as organising feasts or warfare. Their position as Bigmen allows them to conduct trade and alliances on behalf of their tribe. Their position is cemented by their ability to provide generously for their followers. They accumulate wealth, usually pigs or another food source, and redistribute it at major feasts. The position is not hereditary and they can be replaced by others who are better placed to dispense generously. Some tribes may have leaders called chiefs but these individuals also rely on their personalities and powers of persuasion to influence the group. Most societies from the Neolithic into at least the Bronze Age were probably tribal although their nature is debated.

Transegalitarian societies

Ethnographic studies (Weissner 1982) have identified a range of ways in which modern foragers minimise risk. Some of these strategies can be identified from the Upper Palaeolithic including food sharing, mobility and more efficient weapons as at Stellmoor (▶ p. 298) and environment manipulation and broad spectrum foraging in the Mesolithic (▶ p. 308). There are hints in the exchange of prestige items such as beads that social networks may also have played a part in enabling groups to call on help in times of need. The development of alliances for this purpose as well as to acquire other resources or marriage partners is well known. It is also one of the means by which individuals could gain social status, particularly when exchanges included events such as feasting. Hayden and Dietler (2010) argue that in complex hunter-gatherers such as the Ertebølle (▶ p. 309), competition developed between individuals to acquire surpluses for prestige goods exchange or conspicuous displays of consumption such as feasts. Other methods might include gift-giving or organising exchange networks or ancestor cults. This aggrandising behaviour changed egalitarian bands into what Hayden and Dietler (2010) term

KEY STUDY

Varna, gold and social status in Copper Age Europe

Discovery and description

The Varna necropolis was discovered by chance during construction work in 1972 when a tractor driver noticed green and yellow objects in a cable trench he was digging. The flint and copper artefacts were recognised as dating to the Chalcolithic (Copper Age) of the 5th millennium BC but the gold was unprecedented in such an early site. Led by Varna Museum archaeologist Ivan Ivanov, 294 graves were excavated revealing the richest collection of grave goods in European prehistory. The total number of graves was probably well over 300 as some had already been destroyed but 211 undisturbed graves with similar orientations were recorded. Most of the graves contained a few artefacts, particularly ceramics, but a small number were packed with exotic and valuable artefacts. Amongst them were 3,000 gold artefacts weighing over 6kg in total. These were the earliest examples of gold metalworking in the world.

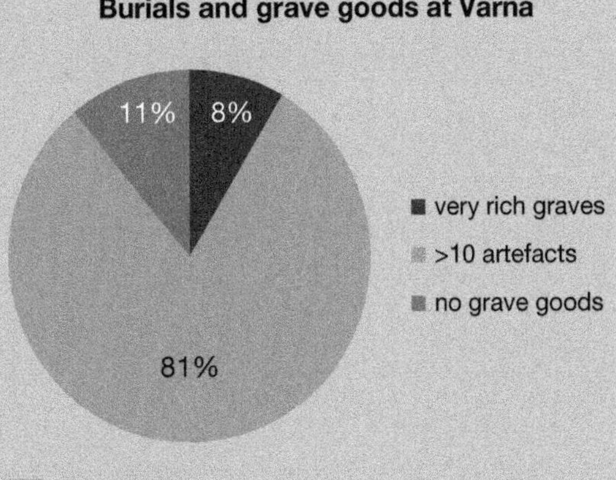

Figure 10.4 *Distribution of burial goods at Varna*

Grave goods

Besides pottery, many graves held tools, with an emphasis on over-sized flint blades or copper woodworking tools. Many were unused. Most of the remaining artefacts were jewellery. Hundreds of local dentalium (tusk-shells) and white spondylus shells from the Mediterranean had been worked into bracelets and beads. The distance these shells had travelled probably added to their value as personal ornaments. Other beads were made from drilled and polished semi-precious stones such as red carnelian and agate, marble and malachite. Gold had been hammered into sheets and then rolled, pierced and cut to make over twenty different shapes. These included loops, discs, beads and zoomorphic representations of horns and cattle. Many had small holes to enable them to be sewn onto clothes (appliqués – rather like large rhinestones) or attached to hair. Gold was also occasionally wrapped round other artefacts such as a stone axe and there is at least one pot with traces of gold paint. However, some more ancient burial goods persisted including deer teeth and red ochre. Based on the style of artefacts, the cemetery was dated to the Gumelniţa Culture of 4900–4400 BC. Recent AMS radiocarbon dates of samples of human and animal bones have narrowed this to 4600–4450, with some suggestion that the wealthier graves are amongst the earliest. A 40- to 50-year-old man buried in Grave 43 had the richest assemblage including nearly 1,000 gold artefacts weighing a total of 1.5kg. Body ornamentation included gold ear or lip plugs, rings, arm-rings and a gold penis sheath. He wore 890 gold beads. Gold appliqués and flat plates at his waist and discs over his knees were sewn onto his clothes. Sheet gold was also wrapped

continued

Figure 10.5 *Grave 43 at Varna. Note the hair and facial ornaments, penis sheath and the way objects have been enhanced by wrapping with gold foil.*

around his axe handle, bow and spondylus bracelet. In addition he had copper tools, stone axes, ceramics, bone points and several flint blades and points. One flint blade was 39cm long.

Burial patterns

While the cemetery held burials of men, women and children, the records are not clear enough for patterns of either grave goods or body position to be fully analysed. A large number of graves had a few exotic goods of gold or shell but the richest grave goods came from either male burials or cenotaphs (empty graves). Three cenotaphs contained clay face-masks with gold earrings and lip and nose rings.

The forty-three cenotaphs are particularly puzzling. Possible explanations have included memorials for relatives lost in battle or at sea or a collective ritual deposit. The latter view has gained some support from the location of the cemetery itself, which is not close to a settlement (a break with earlier burial practice), and where all areas of the cemetery were used simultaneously. The most recent dating evidence also suggests three to four burials a year, which is unusually high for a cemetery of this date. Higham (2007) suggests that several social groups were using it and that the cemetery was an important focal point for a wide network.

The role of prestige artefacts

The prestige goods in burial assemblages at Varna provide evidence of a significant social change in south-eastern Europe, possibly including the emergence of a ranked society. The recent dating evidence suggests this change may have been concentrated in a relatively short period of perhaps fifty years when the richest burials were deposited. This brief period of spectacular burials (and possibly funerals) may have been part of the way in which an elite established their position. The precise social model is not clear, with some archaeologists describing it as a chiefdom, others as a 'Bigman' or transegalitarian society. The artefacts at Varna had been acquired to be worn, given away or displayed in some way. However, some artefacts such as sceptres (a rod wrapped in gold) have been interpreted as formal symbols of office or power, which would suggest that it had moved beyond competitive display to become a permanently hierarchical society.

Figure 10.6 *Dentalium shells from Chalcolithic necklaces*

The high value assigned to the artefacts comes from both their exotic nature and the time and skill required to produce them. Early metal artefacts of copper (▶ p. 373) and gold had all these features as well as the magic of metallurgy. Chapman (1981) analysed the depositional context and properties of exotic artefacts and argues that early farming communities prized colourful and reflective objects. This could represent sun or moon symbolism or the development of their own aesthetic which valued objects that shone including polished bone tools, obsidian and painted ceramics. This is why they spent so much effort on manufacturing and accumulating them. While burnished pottery was associated with the home, polished stone tools and shells were found outside. All these shiny objects were buried with the dead. Copper extended the range of colours available and was perhaps first used to create greenish paint while graphite-painted pottery created a silver effect. Gold, the colour of the sun, fitted into this pattern and its rarity and brilliance made it the most valuable of all. All this would have made funerary rituals spectacular events in which differing social positions were reinforced.

Varna in context

Evidence from other contemporary sites can help us understand the context in which the Varna elite emerged. As farming spread northwards from the plains of Thrace and across the Danube into present-day Romania and Hungary, a number of changes occurred. Some large tells remain but increasingly, as at Polyanitsa and Ovocarovo, they are laid out systematically with common orientation of houses, settlement boundaries and external cemeteries. However, there is still little differentiation in either houses or grave goods compared with Varna. There are also increasing numbers of scattered small 'flat' sites of a few pit-houses or less permanent huts. The faunal assemblages change too as the environmental limits of the original 'Neolithic package' were reached. Cattle adapted better than sheep to wetter and cooler climates and a pastoral economy developed. Herds of cattle are a mobile source of wealth and

continued

may have made it possible for some kin groups and individuals to accumulate more than others. Cattle also became more productive through the development of dairying. Cheese moulds have been found from this period and it also coincides with the emergence of lactose tolerance in European populations which enabled them to drink milk. The cattle appliqué and jewellery at Varna may reflect their prestige and value. Copper provides another potential source of wealth. Not everyone would have had the skills or access to materials to produce metal tools. Finally there is exchange. Extensive networks took spondylus shells and obsidian from the Aegean to Germany while Balkan copper reached the Volga and the Caucasus. Precious stones and salt may also have been traded. Those who controlled these exchanges could acquire prestige, wealth and perhaps power. The societies they dominated increasingly included people with new skills who smelted and moulded metal, and produced fine wares, figurines, textiles and new foodstuffs. While they may have been part-time roles, they suggest the start of social complexity.

Figure 10.7 *Cenotaph burial*

This was a society that buried its most valuable products and Varna is not the only source of treasure from this culture. Other cemeteries confirm the pattern of more exotic goods in male graves and cenotaphs. Burial position (crouched or extended) and orientation of burials varied between cemeteries, suggesting group traditions were more important than gender or age distinctions. Considerable quantities of gold objects have also been excavated at Hotnitsa and Durankuluk in Bulgaria. At the latter site on an island in a lake close to the Black Sea, over 1,200 graves have been excavated alongside a tell dating from the late Neolithic to Chalcolithic. The settlement appeared to be planned and successive buildings stood on the same spot. By *c.* 4600 BC some buildings were becoming larger and more substantial. Some had stone walls, others planks plastered with clay. Most had two or three rooms. Like Varna, there was a huge variation in the goods in individual graves. The abandonment of these cemeteries and collapse of the culture that used them has in the past been attributed to the invasion of horse-riding nomads from the Steppes (▶ p. 458). However, it could equally be because the exchange network collapsed or the Balkan copper mines were exhausted.

transegalitarian societies. This is where individuals gain status and rise to prominence but their position is not sustained. Their status is not necessarily inherited by their children and does not lead to permanent classes or inequality. Transegalitarian models and the political importance of feasting have been widely applied in later periods (▶ p. 442).

Segmentary and ranked societies

Both bands and tribes, particularly those living in villages, are sometimes referred to as **segmentary societies**. This is where society is made up of lots of similar-sized groups with little difference in wealth, status or power between individuals or groups. Segments are organised horizontally rather than vertically. Such societies are broadly

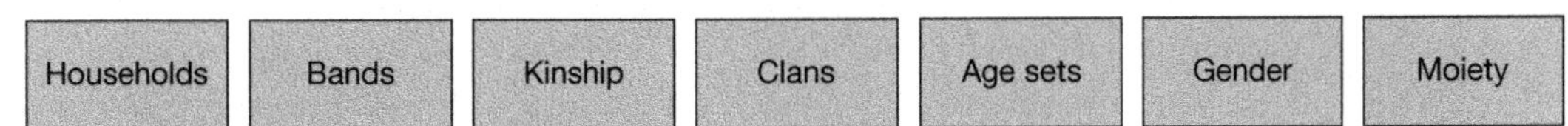

Figure 10.8 *Segmentary social divisions*

egalitarian with similar houses or base camps, similar artefact assemblages and little variation in burials. Most exchange within such groups takes the form of reciprocity, although there may be some trade in exotic items. Although they may have come together for particular communal activities such as ritual (▶ p. 511) or hunting (▶ p. 298), they were generally small autonomous groups who regulated their own affairs.

In contrast, larger tribes and less complex chiefdoms are sometimes referred to as **ranked societies**. This means that a hierarchy is beginning to develop where people or groups are graded in terms of prestige but not really in terms of access to resources or power. Over time particular individuals or lineages may have more social status but this does not become hereditary. The beginnings of ranking are usually from the late Neolithic onwards, particularly where there are rich burials as at Varna (▶ p. 423). However, the burial of many exotic artefacts (which were not then available to the children of the deceased) in what was probably a dramatic event suggests that rank was often ephemeral. Greater variety in houses, large monuments, defended settlements and evidence of extensive exchange networks also provide clues to a more ranked society.

Chiefdoms

Chiefdoms are more formally organised and ranked than tribes. Within ethnographic literature there is a huge range of different forms of chiefdom with numbers of followers ranging from around 1,000 to 10,000, so we can assume the same is true of the past. Within a chiefdom, some decision making and power is centralised in the permanent office of chief which is held by an individual. Some chiefs are elected but most are hereditary, although the role may alternate between a group of families rather than remain in just one. As a result, chiefs and their relatives are often viewed as an elite, different from the rest of the social group, perhaps as a nobility. A key element in chiefdoms is redistribution. Resources are gathered into a central place and directly or indirectly returned through feasts, gifts or services ranging from ritual to protection. Chiefs also usually have an important ritual role as well as law giving, warfare and organising labour. Their permanent position and high status may result in other differences including more marriage partners and more or different possessions. Social hierarchies in chiefdoms can be very elaborate and at least one of their settlements is likely to be a ceremonial centre. Chiefdoms all feature ranking, where people have different social statuses. Status can be ascribed at birth, perhaps being born a noble or commoner, or achieved, perhaps through successful trade, farming or raiding. Where different noble groups compete for prestige, chiefdoms can be unstable. Where power is distributed amongst a number of similar groups in a society it is known as a heterarchy. The most complex chiefdoms may be stratified. That means that the hierarchy is more fixed, with each stratum having different levels of prestige and often access to resources and power. People will then tend to be born into a stratum or class; for instance, nobles and commoners. The later Bronze Age is generally held to be the period where chiefdoms became common but archaeologists frequently disagree over whether societies are tribal or chiefdom in nature. This is because settlement, burial and artefact evidence can be contradictory.

Figure 10.9 *Cahercommaun*

This early medieval fortified settlement had a triple ring of defences and was perched on the side of a very steep ravine. It looks defensive, a view that was strengthened by the discovery of underground passages (souterrains) under each of six houses, one of which came out on the cliff. One interpretation is that it is the base of the representative of the King of Cashel and its function is to collect tribute. Alternatively it is the high-status, fortified farmstead of a local clan chief who depended on cattle-raising supplemented by raiding. Around forty people would have lived in it. It fits the model of a ranked society where kinship remains important. Thousands of such ring-forts once existed in Ireland.

States

States are political systems where permanent institutions develop independent of individual leaders. All modern societies are nation states. States first emerged in the Bronze Age in Mesopotamia as a network of walled cities, each with its leaders controlling an army and bureaucracy and enforcing laws. States claim sovereignty over a territory, regulating trade with particular weights and measures and often currencies used within its borders whilst maintaining roads. In some states kinship remains important, particularly in those kingships which are also states, but this need not be the case. State societies are pyramid-shaped hierarchies with ethnicity, wealth and class providing some of the common divisions. States are associated with large urban populations supplied by agricultural surpluses collected from the countryside. They are socially complex, which means that there is a high degree of differentiation between people but also a high degree of interdependence. Skills are increasingly concentrated in specialists who provide goods or services but equally depend on others for food, protection or materials. Key archaeological indicators of early states include large

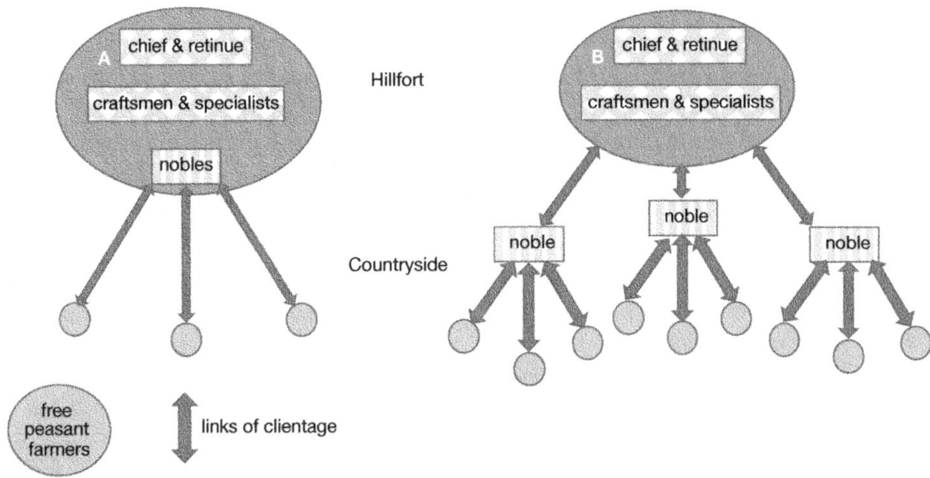

Figure 10.10 *Cunliffe's models of Iron Age chiefdoms*

The two models vary only in terms of whether all the elite lived within the hillfort or not. The chief provides protection, gifts and feasts to the elite in return for loyalty. The clientage links to the peasantry involved cattle being 'loaned out' in return for tithes (taxes) of agricultural produce.

Figure 10.11 *View of Zakros palace from the north*

urban settlements with public buildings such as temples, palaces and central stores used to control food surpluses. The Minoan (▶ p. 429) Palace of Zakros, for example, shows clear signs of planning and evidence of specialisation including areas of craft production and rooms containing the seals, tablets and calendars associated with a palace bureaucracy.

Looking from the town area, the central courtyard is top left. To the right is a colonnaded ceremonial hall and behind that archive rooms, 'lustral basins' for ritual purification, treasury and shrines. Bottom right are the storage magazines while top right are the craft workshops with more to the south of the courtyard. Immediately left of the courtyard are the 'royal' apartments backing onto a hall with a cistern and other water-related rooms. Off to the left are more courtyards and some industrial buildings on the road to the port. The walls of ashlar cut into blocks with two-man saws indicate the scale and size of the buildings. Attached workshops included stone cutting, perfume making and ivory carving. The palace was destroyed by fire but the boxes of clay archives (▶ p. 416) on shelves survived as a result.

Within states there is also likely to be a clear hierarchy of settlement types (▶ p. 256) from city to hamlets and farms. Evidence of the power of the rulers may be determined from reliefs and monuments (▶ p. 554) documenting their deeds and their ability to mobilise labour to complete major building projects such as canals and monuments. Close links between the elite and religion were a feature of most early states including the portrayal of rulers as gods or descended from them, as with Egyptian pharaohs. Their lavish tombs, such as the pyramids, testify to the degree to which states were unequal as well as complex. Some writers add **empires** as a fifth evolutionary stage where one state becomes dominant over several others. Rome was a particularly complex and highly centralised state. Its patrician (noble) elite controlled a vast empire in which raw materials, particularly agricultural surpluses, were transported through an elaborate transport infrastructure. Its army (▶ p. 479) illustrates formal hierarchy and epitomised organisation that was bureaucratic rather than along personal lines.

Developed states are perhaps the easiest to identify archaeologically. However, at the margins there is ambivalence, where some of the key aspects of social complexity are present but others not. Minoan Crete (▶ p. 470) is a good example of this and is sometimes referred to as a proto-state, suggesting that it is in the later stages of transition into a true state. Early states often continued features of chiefdom but the ruler now had power to make and enforce laws and led a standing army. This can also be seen in the evidence of post-Roman societies such as the kingdoms of Anglo-Saxon England (▶ p. 445). **Kings** (▶ p. 476) can differ from chiefs simply in terms of scale. Kings will usually preside over several social groups, each with their own sub-king or chief. The term was used for C19th Africa as well as for the classical and medieval worlds so variation is considerable. Today we would consider some of these kings to have led chiefdoms and others states. The position is hereditary with some, although not all, being seen as divine. They are likely to have a larger than usual household and may have permanent social and economic organisations based close to them; for example, a permanent guard. Their need to display their position through exotic goods and provide gifts to supporters may mean that their household included attached specialists.

THE ARCHAEOLOGY OF RANK, STATUS AND STRATIFICATION

These terms are often used interchangeably but do have slightly different meanings. Status is associated with social prestige and describes the social standing of one person relative to another. Status can be derived from physical aspects such as age, gender or appearance or from possessions, achievements or individual talents. Rank implies a position in a society which carries distinct rights and responsibilities or where particular abilities are valued. Both status and rank may be inherited or acquired during life by an individual. **Ascribed status** is where an individual inherits social position, usually at birth; for example, being born into royalty. This is common in non-egalitarian societies. **Achieved status** is where the individual earns or obtains position due to their actions; for example, a great warrior or successful farmer. Rich burials of children are often interpreted as evidence of ascribed status. Evidence of societies based on ascribed status is usually easier to find partly for this reason. In societies where status is more fleeting, evidence may not enter the archaeological record. In Bigman societies (▶ p. 422), fame is achieved by giving away resources. A successful Bigman might be buried with very little. Not all marks of status are easily preserved. Clothing, tattoos and tribal scars may have been very significant in life but are usually invisible to archaeologists.

While there may be a social hierarchy in a ranked society, it may be fluid and families do not necessarily monopolise the top levels over long periods nor is there great inequality in wealth or power. With a stratified society this is different. Those people at the top of the hierarchy may have greater access to resources, status or power and the gulf between those at the top and bottom of the social scale can be massive. Where there is unequal access to both wealth and power in

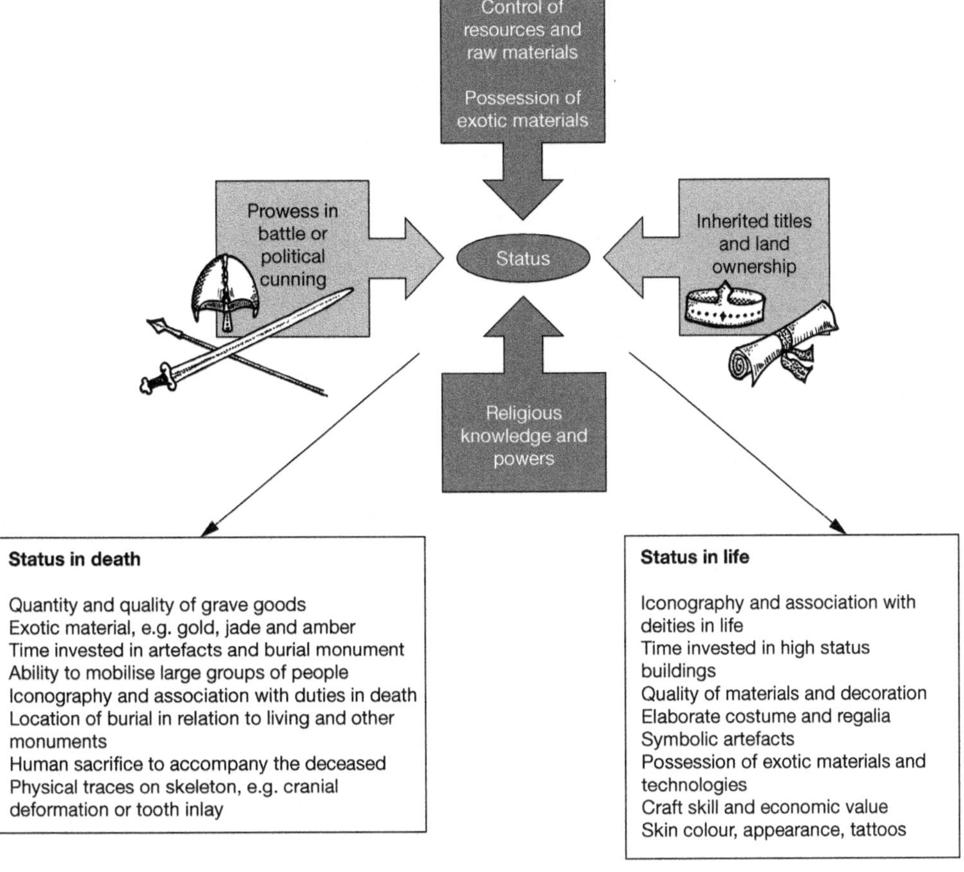

Figure 10.12 *Status and the archaeological evidence for it*

stratified societies, they are often referred to as class societies. Bogucki (2011) defines **wealth** as the accumulation of possessions which could be translated into status or passed down through families and lead to structured differences between those with wealth and those without. Agricultural surpluses represent income and can be used to gain fleeting status through feasting, but it is only by translating them into wealth that this may become permanent. The form wealth takes will depend upon what a society values but it might include land, herds, draught animals, key raw materials such as metal or prestige artefacts.

IDENTIFYING STATUS, RANK AND STRATIFICATION

For some periods artistic depictions (▶ p. 476) provide insights but in general archaeologists rely on material culture to provide answers. In their analysis they try to isolate particular variables that will allow differentiation between sectors of a society and between individuals. The origins of status differences lie in ways in which humans mark themselves out both individually and as members of groups. In most societies there is usually a correlation between status differences and artefacts or houses. However, this is not universal and identifying differences is usually easier than understanding meanings or the reasons for them.

Burial evidence

Personal status is usually suggested on the basis of grave goods and mortuary monuments. Rich burials such as those at Sutton Hoo (▶ p. 442) are usually interpreted as being those of high-status individuals. Sometimes there is additional evidence to confirm this. In the Royal Cemetery at Ur, mortuary practice involved the sacrifice of attendants with royalty. The grave of Pu-abi included a 40-year-old woman who is identified as a queen on a seal-stone buried with her. She was accompanied by exotic objects, including a lyre with a golden bull's head decoration, gold and silver vessels, a magnificent headdress of golden leaves and rosettes and twenty-three of her courtiers. These 'victims' seem to have gone to their deaths willingly as there was no sign of coercion. Human sacrifice to accompany the dead may help establish the power and status of an individual. Equally there are many instances where such behaviour is more significant for the whole community in terms of the fertility of the earth or the continuity of cyclical events.

Human skeletons can provide some general clues to status, particularly in stratified societies where advantage was inherited. In extreme examples such as the Maya, deliberate deformities to the skull and teeth were signs of high status. More typically those of higher rank are taller and healthier. This is primarily about better access to food rather than medical care.

Differences in the investment of labour in particular graves and the ranges of artefacts tell us that burials were not just about religious beliefs and that both the goods and the rituals reflect the status of the deceased in life and the relations they had with others. These marked differences are most visible in the archaeological record from the end of the Neolithic onwards. In cases such as the Chalcolithic cemetery at Varna (▶ p. 423), the lavish deposition of exotic and shiny artefacts may have enabled the family of the deceased to exchange wealth for status on behalf of the deceased or their own lineage. There are glimpses of this from earlier periods such as the Palaeolithic burials at Sungir. These imply that there was a long period where inequalities between people emerged and were celebrated in death but without giving rise to stratified societies.

Measuring wealth

However, we need to take care that we do not impose our values and assume that certain materials held the same value and prestige in past societies as in our own. In some cases symbolic associations may be an equally important factor in the choice of raw material, such as jade in Mesoamerica. Even the gold at Varna (see cover) may not be what it seems. Some of the richest graves there are empty 'cenotaphs'. It may be that the gold represents offerings from the living rather than the belongings of the deceased. Another complication occurs with vessels such as beakers. Their contents may have been more valuable than the pottery. Other organic materials such as textiles, food or wood may have been placed in what to us appear to have been 'poor' graves, but these rarely survive.

O'Shea (1981) compared C18th and C19th ethnographic descriptions of the Omaha by European explorers with burial evidence to test the visibility of status and social grouping in mortuary data. Where social divisions were vertical or ranked, evidence could usually be seen in the grave goods. Horizontal social divisions based on clan, moiety and age tended to be archaeologically invisible. This could lead to misleading conclusions being drawn about the relative importance of individuals. Rank which was archaeologically visible was concentrated in particular age and sex groups in the population. Horizontal divisions were more equally distributed. However, historic accounts revealed that some horizontal identities had been celebrated during funerary rituals whereas a person's ranking had not. This may indicate that the horizontal divisions were more significant in life. It also tells us that we cannot hope to read all status from burials.

Status is only likely to be represented *in* death where the person held that status *at* death. In cases where status or rank did not stay with the

Ethnographically observed				
	In life	**In mortuary practice**	**Archaeological evidence**	**Examples**
Horizontal				
Family				Mourning for 4 days. Care for the corpse
Clan				Face painted. Clan animal skin
Gender				Particular artefacts
Adult/child				Particular artefacts
Patrilineal residence				Today isotope analysis could identify this
Secret society				Special mortuary rituals. Symbol placed on grave
Vertical				
Chief				Public mourning. Horse sacrifice on grave
Ranked male				Particular artefacts
Ranked female				Particular artefacts
Ranked child				Buried in village rather than sky burial where died (▶p. 514).
Wealth				Personal ornaments

Figure 10.13 *Comparison of ethnographically and archaeologically observed status (after O'Shea 1981)*

individual for their whole life, it may not be visible. Similarly, where beliefs dictate that people should appear equal in death (as in Christianity), indicators of status may be absent. In general, ascribed status is easier to detect than achieved status. The position of burials, their orientation and any funerary monument associated with them can also be used to examine status. Various models and formulae have been developed correlating graves, population and frequency of rare materials. Perhaps the best known is Shennan's (1975) systematic approach to evaluating the social significance of grave goods from over 300 rectangular pit graves at the early Bronze Age Únětice culture (▶ p. 466) site at Branč, Slovakia. Instead of assuming modern values applied – for example, that gold was of most value in the past – she used other measures to determine value. The key one was energy expenditure. Artefacts that required more skill, effort and resources from long distances were likely to have been most prized. At Branč some individuals had more valuable assemblages than others. Gender differences were evident in the way bodies had been laid out. Males predominantly lay on their right sides and females on their left. Her interpretation was that wealth and status was inherited (ascribed). This suggested that ranking was a feature of central European society by the late 2nd millennium BC.

KEY STUDY

Hochdorf and hereditary chiefdoms in the Iron Age

The Hochdorf burial mound was discovered by an amateur archaeologist who identified stones from a monument in ploughsoil and in 1977 a ring of boulders. By then ploughing had reduced the mound to 1m in height. Dr Jörg Biel, chief archaeologist of Baden-Württemberg, Germany, then used a range of modern excavation techniques to rescue the undisturbed burial chamber from destruction by further ploughing.

Figure 10.14 *The Hochdorf mound recreated to its original size*

The burial itself was below ground level and had been protected from looters in a double-walled chamber of oak timbers with the wall cavity filled with 50 tons of stone. The contents of the square chamber had been preserved (albeit crushed) when the roof collapsed and filled it with rocks. Inside on a grass pillow, badger fur and cloths woven from hemp and animal hair lay the skeleton of a 1.8m (6 foot) man aged about 45. He lay on an ornate, 2.75m long wheeled, bronze couch. The back of this was decorated with repoussé scenes depicting warriors and horse-drawn wagons. Its eight legs were bronze female figurines, highly decorated with jewellery and coral inlay, standing on castors. Apart from a decorated, conical birch-bark hat, no clothes survived but the man wore over 500g of gold jewellery including a decorated torc, fibulae brooches and belt plate. His shoes and the hilt and scabbard of an iron dagger were decorated with gold foil. Accompanying him were a large axe, an iron knife, a quiver of iron hunting arrows, a comb and a razor. A nail trimmer and fishhooks were in a cloth bag on his chest. His hat is identical to one worn by a life-size stone statue from the nearby burial mound of Hirchlanden.

Excavation

Organic preservation was excellent, so to avoid losing fragments of artefacts during excavation, the archaeologists used a vacuum cleaner prior to sieving finds from collapsed couch and skeleton. Key areas were block-lifted to be safely micro-excavated in batches in a laboratory environment.

Figure 10.15 *The reconstructed Hochdorf burial chamber*

continued

Soil blocks were kept damp and cold in polystyrene containers and freezer bags. X-rays of the blocks showed the position of metals and scanning electron microscopes enabled identification of artefacts. Needles and fine spatulas were then used to gently separate the finds. As in a regular excavation, photographs and plans were used to provide a record since the organic material began to degrade in contact with the air. Binding materials such as acrylic stabilised the soil around fragile remains.

Block-lifting was particularly beneficial for textiles and fur. Often traces of textile are lost when metal artefacts are cleaned but here they were separated. On excavation textiles looked grey and brown but gas chromatography combined with experimentation on the effect of different soils on wool and silk enabled dyes to be identified. Comparisons were also made with textiles and skins preserved in the Hallstatt salt mines. Dyes had provided vivid colours including indigo from woad and crimson from the insect kermes vermillo that lives on Mediterranean oaks. The deceased had been wrapped in a red and blue checked cloth. Twenty-eight different textiles were identified including wool, hemp, linen and cloth made from badger and horsehair.

The grave goods

Opposite the burial, against the east wall and laden with nine bronze plates and other banqueting equipment, was a wooden wagon sheathed in iron. It had four wheels, a yoke and bronze harnesses to attach two horses. On the south wall hung nine great drinking horns of eastern European style, decorated with gold bands. The largest (1.23m and holding over 5 litres) was iron, the remainder made from auroch horns. Opposite them was a huge bronze cauldron and a golden ladle. The cauldron was decorated with cast bronze lions and had been made in Greece or Italy. A 'ring mark' of beeswax and grain showed it had been full with 500 litres of liquid. Analysis of pollen preserved in the honey residue suggests the drink was mead flavoured with sixty different late summer plants. The huge amount of honey used suggested that it was a strong drink and that at least fifteen hives had been required. Textile fragments survived on the floor and in corrosion on metal objects, which suggested carpets, wall hangings and that the wagon and many of the objects had been covered in cloth. The style of the artefacts allowed the burial to be dated to the mid-C6th BC. Also under the mound were traces of workshops where most of the artefacts had been specifically made for the funeral. This proved that the chamber and the mound had not been built at the same time, which suggests a lengthy mortuary process. Although animal hairs had been found on the couch, no human hair was found. This may mean the body had been temporarily preserved in salt or honey prior to inhumation. Plants had also started to grow on the floor of the burial pit before it was enclosed. The mound had originally been 6m high and 60m in diameter and was encircled with large stones and oak posts (Biel 2006).

The settlement

In 1989 during the building of a new museum devoted to the burial, the remains of Iron Age houses were found. Further investigation included the use of augers to locate man-made layers while open-area excavation revealed a mass of postholes, storage pits, beam sills (where horizontal wooden beams had supported walls) and house pits. The 1.5 hectare, fenced settlement dated from the C6th BC, just after the Hochdorf burial. Remains of wattle and daub helped provide evidence of building structures while analogs drawn from surviving timber superstructures in wet sites north of the Alps provided models for the recreation of examples of the buildings at the new museum. These include substantial houses of up to 140 m^2, covered storage pits, raised granaries and up to forty rectangular sunken weaving huts. The settlement is planned and the largest house was thought to be the residence of the chief.

Economy

Charred plant remains in house pits and silos provided evidence of processing cultivated barley, spelt wheat, millet, peas, lentils, broad beans and sweet peas. Flax (for linen) and poppies were grown along with a range of other vegetables and herbs including celery, beet, dill and parsley. Several U-shaped, 1m deep trenches contained thousands of grains of charred barley. Dr Stika, an archaeobotanist from the University of Hohenheim, used experiments to reveal the close resemblance between these grains and malt barley. He concluded that they were the by-product of large-scale beer brewing. The earliest beer was brewed in Mesopotamia *c.* 3500 BC but evidence of how ancient beer was brewed is rare. At Hochdorf barley was soaked in the trenches until it sprouted and then dried using fires at the ends of the trench. This malting process turns starch to sugar. The mash of water and fermented barley itself was probably heated using hot stones with fermentation (to turn it to alcohol) caused by natural yeast or that from fruit or honey. Experimentation suggested the beer was dark, cloudy, sour and smoky. Other botanical evidence pointed to wild carrots, mugwort and even henbane being used for flavouring. The Roman emperor Julian described Celtic beer as smelling like a goat. Hops were not used for another millennium.

Archaeozoologists examined over 30,000 bones. Sheep had been kept primarily for wool and oxen as draught animals. Goats and pigs were reared for meat and butchery marks suggested dogs, domestic fowl and hares were also eaten. A wide range of wild birds had also been hunted but deer and boar were rare. This suggests a fairly open countryside. Finds of wheel-turned pottery, loom weights and small metal artefacts such as pins and brooches were common. More exotic finds included some bronze precision weights, fragments of Greek pottery and quantities of briquetage – the thick-walled ceramic vessels used to heat brine and transport salt.

Context

In the Hochdorf region, the early Iron Age is called the Hallstatt culture (▶ p. 373) after the typological sequence established from the cemetery there. However, some late Hallstatt burials such as Hochdorf are of a different scale from those at Hallstatt. Up to one hundred very rich graves have been documented in the western part of the Hallstatt zone including the 'princess' of Vix in France. Most were covered by tumuli and included feasting equipment and in several cases wagons. This suggests a similar elite culture existed over a wide area. High-ranked burials were often associated with high-status sites. At least sixteen strongly defended hillforts have been identified, such as the massive Heuneburg 120km to the south overlooking the upper Danube. In addition to their size and fortifications, hillforts contained imported exotic goods and workshops for iron, bronze and other materials. In Germany these are called *Fürstensitz* (princely seats). The combined evidence suggests the emergence of strong, territorial elites. Most archaeologists believe that elites grew rich by controlling long-distance river trade whereby salt and northern goods such as furs, iron ore, amber and slaves were exchanged for Mediterranean exotic goods including wine, fine wares, fabrics and coral. Salt was so valuable because it allowed meat from animals slaughtered each winter to be preserved. The most likely source was the Hallein mines near Salzburg. The Heuneburg has been firmly linked to a trade system including the Greek colony at Massilia

continued

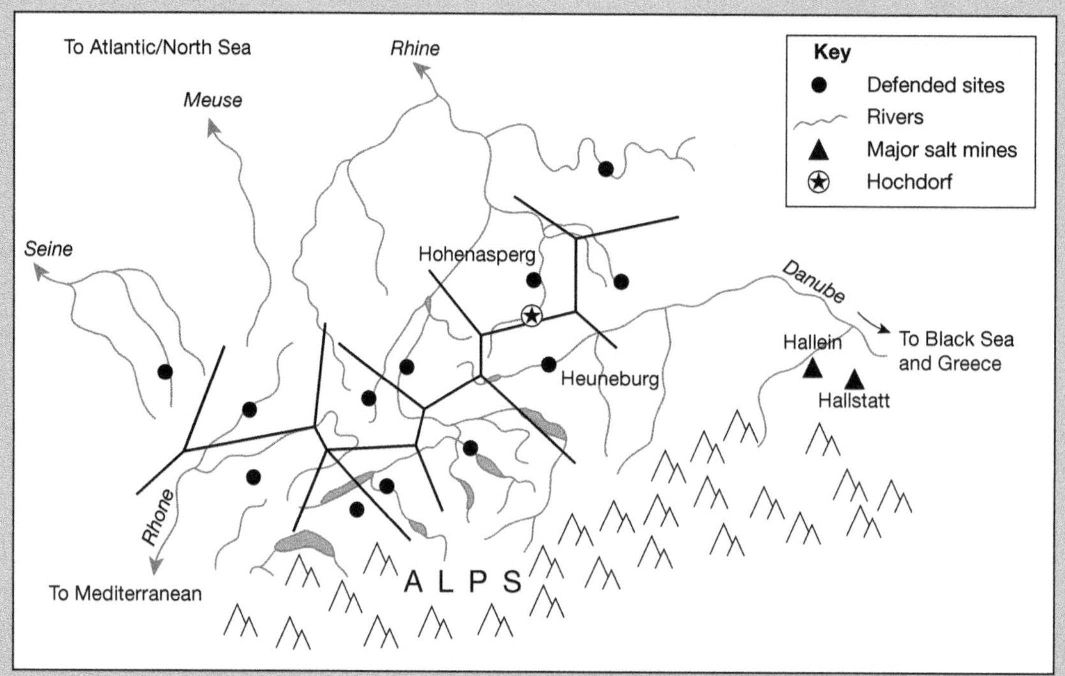

Figure 10.16 *Thiessen polygons suggesting possible territories of chiefdoms linked to Hallstatt exchange networks (after Harke 1979)*

(Marseille) near the Rhone delta by local wine amphorae and Greek black-figure pottery. Its fortifications also have a Mediterranean influence including mudbrick walls on stone foundations and rectangular bastions. Some have argued that the hillforts were redistributive centres or even proto-towns. Certainly the emphasis on weapons and feasting equipment supports the idea of powerful warlords able to bind their followers with protection, banquets and gifts. Archaeologists are divided over whether feasting was influenced by the Greek 'symposium' or Etruscan or Eastern sources as suggested by the drinking horns. There is also no agreement about whether high-status imports are gifts from traders who wanted to exploit Celtic resources or prestige artefacts acquired by Celtic (▶ p. 467) princes for redistribution or for conspicuous consumption or display to increase their own power and prestige.

Interpretation

The monumental mound, exotic and high-status grave goods and a cauldron of mead commemorate a powerful chieftain or 'prince' who died *c.* 550 BC. Some artefacts including the gold torc and hat may be insignia of rank, although items deliberately selected (and manufactured) to go into the grave are not necessarily those that would have defined him in life; for example, those artefacts which portray him as a hunter. He was much more than that. Small secondary burials were covered by his tumulus or are clustered around it; close by were twenty-four additional tumuli; three or four different levels of burials are present in the area with simple cremations being the most common; 10km away the massive fortress of the Hohenasberg dominates the upper Neckar valley and may have been his seat of power – it too is surrounded by more rich burial mounds. Skeletal evidence suggests that the elite were taller than average; perhaps suggesting a richer diet. Most writers believe that kinship was a key element in relationships between them. Current DNA studies on skeletal remains from these rich burials are exploring family relationships to establish whether it was a hereditary elite. Hochdorf fits a consistent pattern of a complex, hierarchical society with an elite controlling territory and trade.

Artefactual evidence

Besides from graves, personal adornments are recovered from settlements, where they can provide a more general indication of social differentiation. A broad distribution of particular artefacts might indicate a more egalitarian society, while concentrations of valuable finds may suggest locations used by important individuals as at Lerje (▶ p. 442). Evidence of long-distance trade in exotic or prestige goods or of the craft workshops of attached specialists can also be important. Their skill and effort is not easily duplicated so their products are rare and therefore valuable (▶ p. 395). Objects may also gain prestige from their own histories. A relatively ordinary sword associated with a great hero becomes an object of value. Tolkien was well aware of the biographical value of objects when he wrote *The Lord of the Rings*. This aspect is difficult for archaeologists to recover.

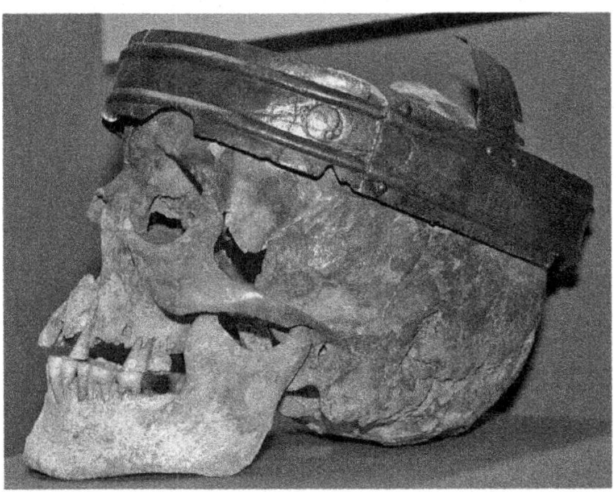

Figure 10.17 *Skull and crown from Deal Iron Age cemetery*

This discovery of a young man wearing a crown has been interpreted as evidence of royal families. It is unlikely a man would have achieved kingship by around twenty so it is more likely that the role was inherited. However, the crown bears an uncanny resemblance to the headgear of later Romano-British priests. This raises the possibility that the young man might be a priest or druid.

The palette of Narmer

This cosmetic artefact illustrates both status and rank in relation to a named individual. It was excavated at Hierakonpolis in Egypt and dates from just before the First Dynasty (*c.* 3000 BC), when the rules and icons of kingship were being established. It is a classic example of the manipulation of iconography to support an individual's status. It is also one of the first examples of hieroglyphics (▶ p. 416). The king's name is written at the top, surrounded by a frame which is reminiscent of the architecture of the royal palace. The catfish (Nar) and chisel (mer) spell out the Horus name (▶ p. 559) of the king: 'Narmer'. The king stands, left hand clasping the topknot of a kneeling captive, with a mace in his right hand. The hieroglyphs tell us that the prisoner's name is 'Wash'. The design immediately above him shows a falcon on papyrus plants pulling back the head of a figure who looks like 'Wash' and the location is the Nile delta. The main figure wears the white crown of Upper Egypt and holds a flywhisk, early symbols of kingship. Below are defeated enemies and a sign representing a fortified town. We are clearly being told that the king has won a victory over an enemy in the northern delta.

Figure 10.18 *The palette of Narmer*

On the reverse of the palette the king, carrying the mace and flail, and this time wearing the red crown of Lower Egypt, is explicitly labelled and accompanied by standard bearers called 'The Followers of Horus'. They march within a panel representing the gate of the royal palace towards two rows of bound and decapitated prisoners. The dead prisoners are now powerless and returned to order, compared with the figures on the other side who have spread-eagled limbs. This may be symbolic of the Egyptian concept of order. In the central panel are two mythological beasts with their long necks entwined to symbolise harmony and perhaps the unification of the two lands of Egypt. This is echoed by the two crowns, which would later be incorporated into the 'Double Crown', indicating that the pharaoh was 'The Lord of the Two Lands'. At the bottom right, a raging bull represents the king's anger, trampling a man and a walled city. Those who defied Narmer can have been in no doubt as to what lay in store for them.

Settlement evidence

Segmentary societies are associated with lots of small, scattered, similar settlements. A mix of small and very large settlements suggests a more unequal society, with large settlements expected to be the residence of powerful individuals. The palaces at Knossos and the hillfort at Danebury have both been interpreted in this way. High-status individuals might be expected to have different houses from other people. Houses may simply be bigger because the inhabitants have more to store or they may have larger household units. They may also occupy a prominent position. Higher-status buildings might be more physically imposing and may have inscriptions or artwork that marks them out. They may also dominate the buildings around them through positioning or size. Landowners in the C18th chose to build in prominent positions in the landscape to emphasise control over land. Rich merchants in earlier periods clustered in central positions in towns. Their houses are often larger, more elaborate and built from better quality materials – part of a general display of wealth and status, which might also include dress and visible forms of consumption. Higher-status people are also more likely to enclose their property in a more visible way than are others. The layout of a site may reveal individual status through the control of access and space and therefore the way people relate to each other. This can clearly be traced in medieval castles and monasteries. Gurness (▶ p. 275) encapsulates many such features including both protecting and controlling a client population and using height and central position to reinforce status.

Figure 10.19 *Reconstruction of the Palace of Knossos*

Conspicuous consumption

Consumption involves the ways in which materials such as food or drinks are consumed in particular social situations using particular artefacts. A way to gain and demonstrate prestige or status is through visible displays of generosity or sacrifice. Feasting, extravagance and the destruction of valuable goods (▶ p. 397) signal the ability of an individual to reward their allies and challenge those with whom they are in competition (▶ p. 477). We know from classical and medieval literature of the crucial importance of feasting as a way of binding leaders and followers together (▶ p. 442). Large and elaborate items of feasting equipment such as drinking sets, flesh hooks and cauldrons suggest feasts and elites capable of supplying such hospitality. Sherratt (1997) interpreted bell-beakers (▶ p. 493) as signifying a new drinking culture, perhaps in imitation of the metal drinking and feasting vessels of classical Greece. Rewarding followers through redistribution seems to have been a key element in the emergence of chiefdoms from the late Bronze Age. Food and drink were dispensed (with the order of serving reflecting rank) along with gifts of weapons, animals and exotic artefacts in return for loyalty. This may explain why fine goods, harness equipment and swords are often found across many sites rather than concentrated in places where one might expect rulers to have lived. The association of elite warriors and feasting is evident in the archaeological record from the Iron Age until well into the Middle Ages. Hayden (2009) argues that the scale and purpose of some feasting behaviour changes with the transition from transegalitarian to more permanently stratified societies such as chiefdoms and early states. Feasting also became a pretext for collecting tribute from the population. Hayden (2009) interprets the massive 65,000m^3 of feasting debris at East Chisenbury midden near Stonehenge as an example. Faunal evidence from such events suggests a high level of waste and a strong association with ritual (▶ p. 521). Ritual consumption involving deposition of valuable materials in water (▶ p. 520) or resources used in the construction of monuments (▶ p. 559) would also confer status upon those coordinating activities. The events at West Kennet (▶ p. 541) may have fitted this pattern.

Figure 10.20 *The Battersea cauldron provides evidence of elite metalworking, feasting and ritual*

KEY STUDY

Mead halls and power: Gudme, *Beowulf* and Sutton Hoo

The late Iron Age or migration period in Scandinavia corresponds to the early medieval or Anglo-Saxon period in England. The two regions share literature, history and a range of distinctive artefacts and site features. Classical historians labelled the C4th to C6th as the Dark Ages to contrast with the supposed 'light' of the earlier Roman and later medieval periods but archaeology has revealed it as the golden age of northern Europe.

Discovery

In 1833 a ploughman on the Broholm Estate near Gudme in Denmark unearthed six gold rings. Further investigation led to the recovery of more gold artefacts including arm and finger rings, brooches and medallions called bracteates. The hoard dated from the C6th AD, weighed 4.5kg and became known as the Broholm Treasure. Further hoards have since been recovered by labourers, treasure hunters and most recently metal detectorists. These are often on the sites of farms and include coins and scrap gold, bronze and silver from Roman tableware and statues. From a 1km strip on the nearby coast at Lundeborg, archaeologists have recovered slag and other waste from metal workshops and other Roman imports including glass and fine pottery. In addition to manufacturing, ships were also built at Lundeborg. It was Scandinavia's first port, although it was probably used seasonally with boats pulled up on the beach rather than sheltered in a harbour. It was part of an exchange network that reached to the Mediterranean. Precious materials were imported, particularly from the Roman world, to be buried or recycled into beautiful Scandinavian jewellery, much of which was then deposited around Gudme. The gold may have been booty, payment for mercenaries or profit from trade but it appears to have been offered to local deities. Gudme, the local township, means 'home of god'. Iconography on the bracteates suggests that the god was Odin. However, archaeologists believed that there was also likely to be a seat of political power associated with such a powerful and wealthy location. Eventually, in

1994, they found it. Top-stripping during the building of a sports hall at Gudme revealed the outlines of large post and plank-built buildings. Excavation identified one as a massive C3rd AD hall 47m long and 10m wide – the largest structure in northern Europe at that time (Hedeager 2002).

Figure 10.21 *Gold bracteate from Gudme featuring Odin healing Baldur*

A high-status building

Further investigation exposed the remains of five more halls in a sequence extending to the C6th. Plotting with metal detectors prior to careful digging enabled archaeologists to recover many tiny items of gold and silver jewellery. Excavation of C1st–C2nd cemeteries in the area also produced Roman imports, which implies that Gudme was important for over 500 years. Waste products and discarded tools from metallurgy, woodcarving and jewellery making surrounded the hall, suggesting that attached specialists had their workshops there. Hedeager (2002) argues that Norse mythology associated the work of skilled craftsmen with royal power and they produced gifts for the warriors who lived nearby or in the surrounding farmsteads. Although Gudme-Lundeborg was not a town, it was a central place (▶ p. 248) and established a pattern linking trade and political power which we can see in the later emporia (▶ p. 408).

The huge open space inside the building, feasting evidence from faunal remains and pottery and the concentration of precious objects suggest that this was a mead hall of the kind known from literature. It would have been the residence of a lord or king who rewarded his warriors with gifts and feasts. The best known is Heorot, the legendary hall of King Hrothgar from the early English poem *Beowulf*. This is set during the C6th, almost certainly in Denmark. The poem (recorded in the C11th) recounts Beowulf's battles with a series of monsters but contains valuable physical descriptions of a mead hall and its functions. These can help interpret finds and features.

> The greatest of halls; Heorot he named it
> Whose word held sway among chieftains.
> His promise unbroken, he gave arm-rings
> And treasure at feasts. The hall towered up
> High gabled and horn-crested, long between antlers

> Heorot groaned . . . and rattled.
> 'Twas a wonder that the wine-hall withstood
> The battling foes and did not fall to earth,
> Excellent earth-hall it was fastened firmly

continued

By fetters of iron, forged by the smith.
Mead-benches splintered and gold fittings scattered
Where the grim ones struggled.

(Adapted from Project Gutenberg 2005 version of *Beowulf*)

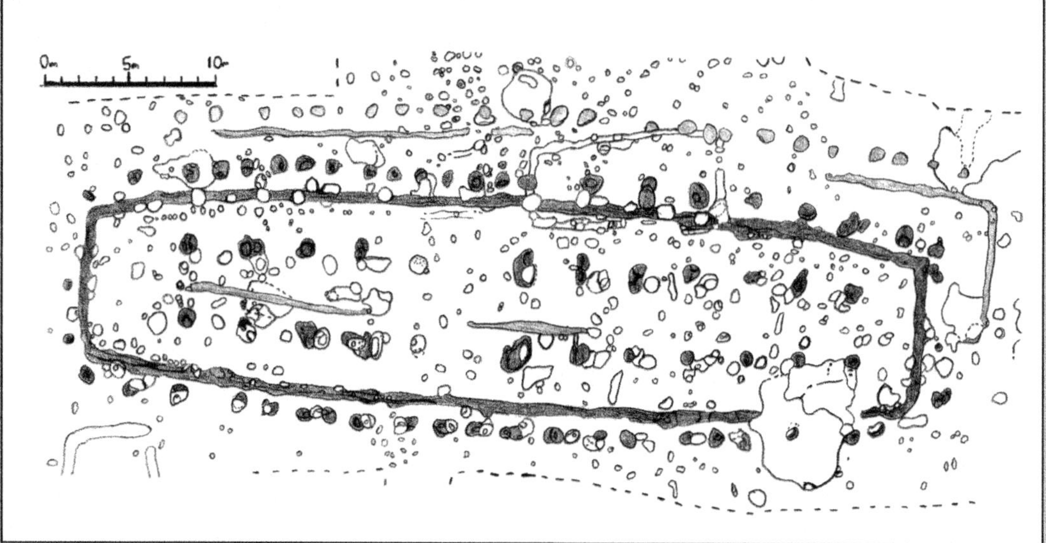

Figure 10.22 *Plan of mead halls at Lerje*

Figure 10.23 *Model of mead hall at Lerje*

Mead halls in context

Mead halls are known from across north-western Europe from Borg in Lofoten in northern Norway to Lyminge in Kent. All are longhouses, sometimes over 60m in length and with a large central space around one or more hearths. In several cases these halls are close to rich burial mounds as at Lerje in Denmark. Pollington (2003) identifies mead halls as places where people would swear oaths, marry, feast, dispense justice and make alliances. They were centres of power and crucial for establishing social status and identity.

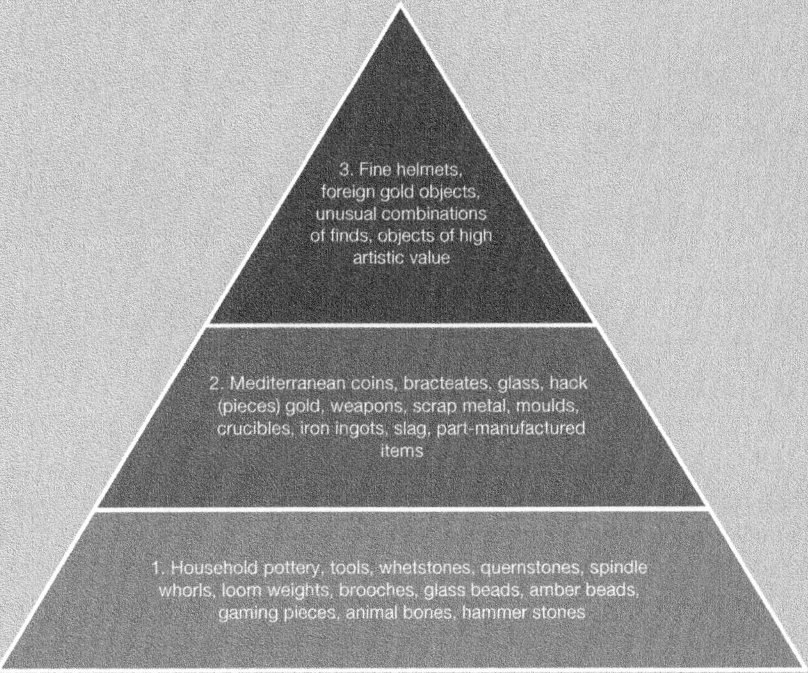

Figure 10.24 *Identifying places of power (after Fabech and Ringtved 1999). 1. Ordinary settlements. 2. Local power centres. 3. Regional power centres.*

The English connection

Beowulf is not the only English connection with Gudme. At early Anglo-Saxon sites the same motifs as on metalwork at Gudme are often found on cremation urns; for example, at Spong Hill cemetery in Norfolk. At Lakenheath, Suffolk, a similar bracteate was discovered, inscribed with runes and dating to AD 450–500. The most dramatic link is the royal burial at Sutton Hoo in Suffolk. This early C7th ship burial beneath a mound shows strong parallels with royal burials at Vendel, near another hall at Uppsala in Sweden. Sutton Hoo is widely believed to be the grave of Rædwald, king of East Anglia and Bretwalda, (over-king) of the Anglo-Saxons. His family, the Wuffingas, are thought to have come from Sweden and the ship, helmet, shield and armour all fit that tradition. The paraphernalia of status can clearly be seen in the carefully laid assemblage of rare, symbolic and everyday artefacts in the

continued

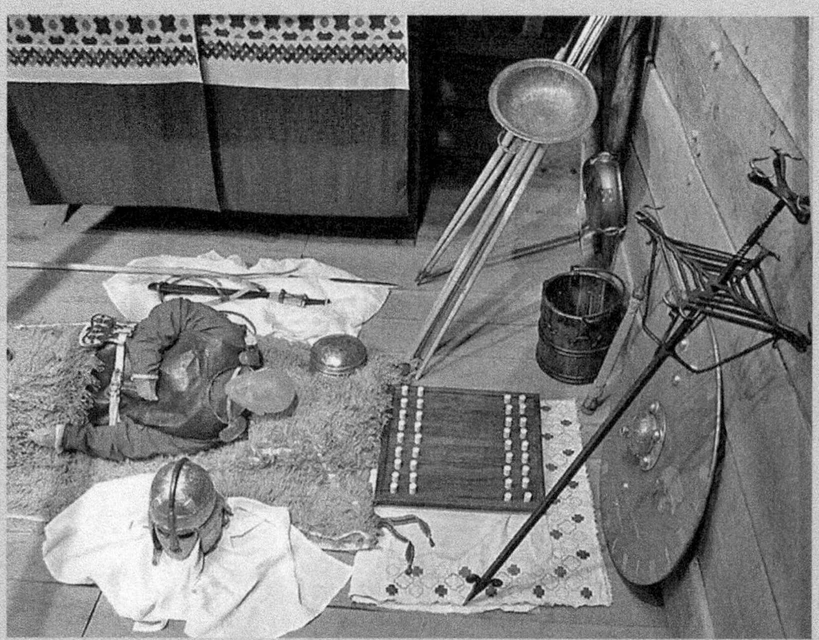

Figure 10.25 *Recreation of the burial assemblage inside the Sutton Hoo ship*

Sutton Hoo burial. The grave goods are some of the finest produced by contemporary European craftsmen including millefiori (coloured glass) and cloisonné metalwork using enamel and garnet inlays and gold. Artefacts and artistic styles draw on British and Mediterranean traditions as well as Scandinavian. Exotic materials included coral from the Red Sea, ivory from the Arctic and silver tableware from Byzantium. The prestige goods testify to Rædwald's wealth, the Roman-style helmet and standard and the weapons projected his power. Drinking horns, tableware, lyre, bucket and cauldrons confirm the centrality of feasting. Rædwald was the kind of king who was depicted in *Beowulf* and his funeral fitted the tradition described in the poem. He would also have held court in a hall similar to that at Gudme, probably at nearby Rendlesham. Herschend (2000) noted that ship burials are spatially organised in the same way as halls. He argues that the ship, packed with feasting equipment and gifts, was a symbolic hall for the afterworld.

Further C7th royal burials from the Northumbrian site of Redcar on Teeside and the East Saxon site of Prittlewell in Essex also link status symbols, international networks and craftsmanship. Taken together they provide an insight into the nature and exercise of power during this pivotal period in the emergence of states in northern Europe. Rulers who may have begun as leaders of warbands were using trade and taxes to augment wealth gained from raiding. Rædwald, for example, is likely to have benefited from the emergence nearby of the emporium of Ipswich (▶ p. 288). These new kings adopted the trappings and symbols of the Roman military but their relationship with their main supporters remained personal. Gift giving was part of a reciprocal (▶ p. 399) exchange and was returned through loyalty and service (Pollington 2003). The Anglo-Saxon poem 'The Wanderer' makes clear how vital it was for men to have a lord for protection while in *Beowulf*, the king, Hrothgar, is referred to as 'ring-giver' or 'giver of gold' and he provides gifts, drink, food and entertainment for his followers. A generous (and victorious) lord bound men to him and he in return gained from their swords, labour and taxes. The kinds of rings he would have given were the arm and neck rings found at Gudme.

Figure 10.26 *Continental motifs on Anglo-Saxon pottery. On the left one stamp comprises runes spelling the name of the Norse god Tew.*

Invisible indicators

Personal ornamentation (▶ p. 218) was probably the first way in which people expressed individuality, group identity and status. Besides jewellery this may have included body paint, tattoos, hairstyles and clothing. These rarely leave traces except in circumstances of exceptional preservation such as Hochdorf (▶ p. 434) or in images such as hairstyles of figurines from Dolni Vestonice (▶ p. 218). Clothing was probably at least as significant for most of our history as it is today. Researchers at the Max Planck Institute, Germany, established that the human body louse mutated from the head louse between 42,000 and 72,000 years ago. While head lice lay eggs in hair, body lice only lay them in clothes. This suggests that humans have been wearing clothes for between 50,000 and 100,000 years.

DNA may hint at other socially determined indicators of status. Northern Europeans have greater variety in hair and eye colour than other human populations. Uniquely these traits include the genes for blond hair and blue eyes. It would have taken around 800,000 years for these traits to become common naturally but our species has only existed for a fraction of that time with Europe only settled after 45,000 BP. The answer lies somewhere in the small, isolated populations of the last Ice Age. An environmental theory is that the lighter skin tone associated with these mutations was more efficient in absorbing vitamin D in northern climates. Recent analysis of Neanderthal DNA also identified a gene for fair skin and reddish hair which may support either the environmental argument or a case for some interbreeding with modern humans (▶ p. 211). A third explanation may be that sexual selection was the main driver. Frost (2006) argues that during the Ice Age people were more reliant on food from male hunting than from foraging. Men died hunting large prey in freezing conditions which led to an imbalance between males and females. In a situation with competition for mates, women with particular traits which were seen as socially more desirable gained a slight evolutionary advantage. They were slightly more likely to pass on the genes for blue eyes and blonde hair than those without them. Consequently more blonde children were born, which created greater variety in eye and hair colour in Europe.

THE ARCHAEOLOGY OF GENDER

Archaeologists usually distinguish between sex, which is biologically determined, and gender, which is identity assigned to different sexes by society. In the early stages of hominid development, males were up to twice the size of females but this distinction had largely disappeared by the time modern humans emerged. Nevertheless, there are some differences between the roles of men and women in all human societies. This stems from the fact that women give birth and that there are obvious anatomical differences between male and female. Gender explains these differences and specifies what is to be done about them. There is tremendous variation from one society to another. Paradoxically, gender differences were far more extreme in late C19th and early C20th western European societies than they were among historically known food-foraging peoples.

Assumptions about 'natural' roles and their significance profoundly influenced the development of archaeology up to the 1970s. In particular, males were portrayed as the active sex in human evolution. For example, hunting was seen as the key humanising activity in evolution (▶ p. 200). Since then the importance of scavenging and gathering and the likely role of women in early horticulture has been recognised from ethnographic studies. Even among the !Kung bushmen, often seen as archetypal hunters, women actually contributed more protein to the daily intake of the group than did the men. Hunting was very hit and miss, while gathering of wild plant foods made up 60–80 per cent of the !Kung diet. Nevertheless, the tendency to assume a gendered division between childcare, gathering and domestic roles, on the one hand, and hunting, warfare and public roles, on the other, continues to shape interpretations. It is also the case that activities considered male such as tool manufacture, hunting and warfare tend to dominate archaeological accounts. Engendered archaeology began in the 1970s by trying to reveal the role of women in the past. Increasingly, studies consider the construction of sexuality and gender (e.g. Taylor 1997), including homosexual and transgender identities (▶ p. 225). Archaeological studies of gender have relied heavily on burial evidence including human remains and grave goods. Settlement and architectural analysis and artistic sources, where they survive, have supplemented this.

Human remains

Differential evidence of disease can be used to identify gendered patterns of activity or consumption. Canadian Inuit hunter-gatherers from the 1890s show osteoarthritis in the right hand and jaw of women, combined with tooth loss. These women spent considerable time preparing skins and sewing. They made the thread by rolling sinews against their cheeks. Areas most pressured by this activity reveal damage. The men hunted with harpoons, which sometimes caused disease of the right shoulder and elbow, while kayak paddling also resulted in distinctive wear of the bones. Other studies of damage and wear have identified gender-specific activities as diverse as basket-making, fighting and grinding corn. These patterns are echoed in the skeletons from Tell Abu Hureyra (▶ p. 332). The quantity and quality of food consumed may relate to status including gender. Chemical analysis of prehistoric Native American skeletons shows that women have a higher strontium:calcium ratio than men in the same community. This may indicate that they ate a smaller share of the available meat.

However, strontium levels also alter when a woman is pregnant or breastfeeding. Differential care and nutrition of female and male children might also show up in X-ray analysis of bones (▶ p. 114). Recent advances in DNA and isotope analysis are increasingly revealing other patterns of gendered behaviour as at Vaihingen (▶ p. 350).

Graves and grave goods

The association of male and female burials with different ranges of grave goods and burial positions (▶ p. 453) has been noted in many cultures. During the Bronze Age, arrowheads, axes and other weapons are predominantly found in male burials, which suggests that hunting and warfare were male-dominated or that this was how males were distinguished in mortuary rites. During the same period, women were regularly buried with a variety of ornaments and jewellery such as pins, necklaces and bracelets. While this may indicate different roles in life, there are two potential problems with this analysis. Until recently, sexing of burials often relied on the grave goods. Jewellery without weapons was expected in female graves so these finds were used to define female burials. Today there is less confidence in this interpretation. A rich Iron Age burial from Birdlip illustrates this problem. The burial from a barrow contained a mirror, jewellery including amber and shale objects, and some bronze bowls. It was initially interpreted as a rich woman's grave. Some even speculated that it was Boudicca. However, recent examination of the skull has revealed masculine traits. The assemblage is also notable in that the artefacts have all been broken and one of the vessels was placed over the face of the skeleton. The mirror may also not be what it seems. Scrying (divining) mirrors are used by some shamans for divination (▶ p. 526). Could this be the burial of a male shaman rather than a princess? Meanwhile DNA analysis at West Heslerton (▶ p. 494) showed that some females were buried with weapons (perhaps ethnic markers) and some men with jewellery. Many museums are currently reviewing their labelling of burials as male or female. Differential survival can be an issue when trying to infer gender differences. In the Mesolithic period, men, and especially older men, appeared to receive special treatment, being buried with ochre, antlers or stone artefacts. However, if women had grave goods of organic materials, perhaps offerings of plant foods and medicinal herbs and tools or ornaments of wood rather than joints of meat, these would not have survived.

A second issue is the way in which such burial evidence has been interpreted differently for men and women. From the Bronze Age onwards, rich male graves are often interpreted in terms of what *he* earned or won, whereas when a woman is found with elaborate grave goods they are often attributed to her husband or father. For example, if women over a certain age have certain grave goods and younger ones do not, it may be argued that these represent goods transferred at

Figure 10.27 *The Birdlip mirror*

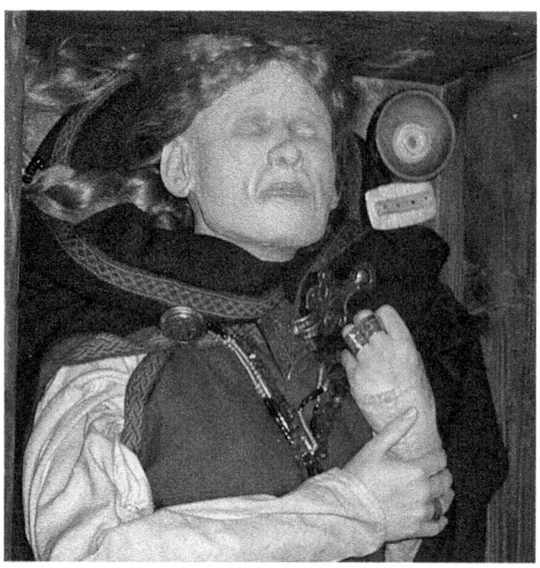

Figure 10.28 *'Mrs Getty'*

The woman aged 25–30 in this C6th burial from the Lechlade cemetery (▶ p. 494) got her nickname from her exceptional grave goods which included 500 beads. Unlike most, she had a wooden coffin concealed under stone packing. Inside, her possessions came from far beyond the Anglo-Saxon world. Along with Baltic amber and metal bowls from the Rhineland were cowries from the Red Sea, garnets from India, Spanish glass and an ivory purse mouth. Her bronze brooches and silver spiral rings were also rare. Despite the humble spindle whorl in her coffin, she was a woman of high status. Forensic reconstruction of her face along with detailed excavation records has enabled the Corinium Museum to present her as she looked at her funeral.

marriage. The possibility that women have achieved their own wealth is rarely considered. Nevertheless by the Iron Age there are a number of clear examples of high-status female burials including Wetwang Slack, which features a 'chariot' burial surrounded by rich grave goods, and the Vix Burial at Saone, which includes a gold torc, huge Greek bronze krater (wine-mixing vessel) and decorated metal bowls. The female graves at Khok Phanom Di, Thailand, may indicate that craft specialisation played a role in achieving higher social ranking.

Settlement evidence

Evidence that there were areas of sites where activities took place have been used to infer gendered activities. Clarke (1972) at Glastonbury (▶ p. 273) and Flannery and Marcus at Guila Naquitz both used differential distribution of artefacts to identify male and female activity areas. However, even if they are correct about the activities, they still rely on inferences about who was carrying them out. Another approach has been to look for repeated patterns of association. At Tell Abu Hureyra (▶ p. 332), women were most often buried under the floor of houses and in early Neolithic houses there appears to be a symbolic link between the hearth, food processing and female figurines, as at Karanovo (▶ p. 339). This has been used as evidence that the domestic world was female-dominated (▶ p. 458). Studies of architecture have been used to explore the way in which societies structured gender in the past, particularly differential access to space. Gilchrist's (1995) study of the relationship between ideas of chivalry, gender roles and the different zones of medieval castles is a good example.

Artistic sources

Depictions of males and females in scenes on pottery, reliefs, wall paintings (▶ p. 524) and metal artefacts have been quarried for information about gender roles. Some appear fairly straightforward and provide evidence for a division of labour. C6th BC pottery from Sopron, Hungary, depicts women engaged in weaving and spinning; one is dancing or praying while another figure, which may also be female, is playing a lyre. Men in comparison are riding horses, herding animals and leading horse-drawn wagons. Other material is more ambivalent. A depiction of a person gathering wild honey from a tree at Bicorp, in Spain, from 7000–4000 BC has been interpreted as both male and female by different commentators. The majority have assumed it is a woman due to the size of the buttocks and the

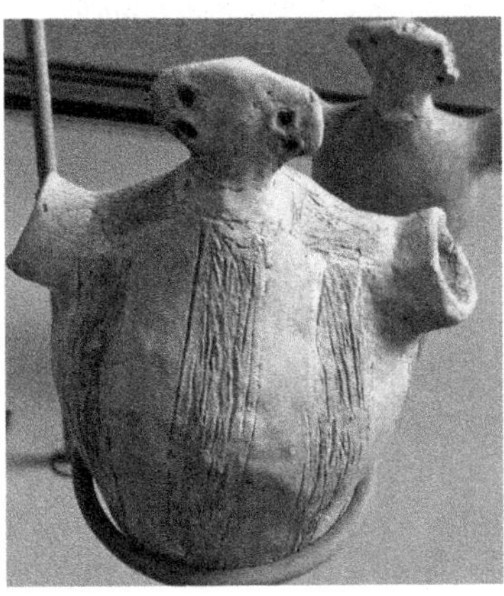

Figure 10.29 *Female figurines from Neolithic hearths, Bulgaria*

flowing hair. At Knossos (▶ p. 470), frescoes produced by painting with plant and shellfish dyes onto wet plaster show women and men involved in different activities. They are easily distinguished as the Minoans painted women as white-skinned while men are painted brown. Women are depicted more commonly than men and additionally many figurines of bare-breasted women with full-length skirts have been found. Taken at face value it seems that elite women may have had more status and the right to participate in a wider range of activities than women in many other societies. Some writers have gone further. These images and an absence of fortifications, male statues, temples to gods or boastful inscriptions might be evidence of a matriarchal (headed by women) society.

'Venus figurines', the Upper Palaeolithic carvings of female figures which have been found across Europe, exemplify the difficulties in interpreting values from the past. They are fairly uniform in character and style over thousands of years and a vast area. Most appear to be associated with hearths and home bases. They are made from a range of materials including baked clay (Dolni Vestonice), mammoth ivory (Lespugue)

Figure 10.30 *Minoan fresco of a procession of young men towards a priestess*

and limestone (Willendorf). They have been variously interpreted as evidence of veneration of a mother goddess deity by the first modern humans in Europe, primitive pornography, fertility symbols or high-status women. Trinkhaus (2005b) observed that they often accurately portray obese women, which implies that artists had seen such women. This is puzzling because Palaeolithic lifestyle skeletal remains suggest that people were lean and muscular. He argues that they could have temporarily put on excess fat during sedentary periods when there was an abundance of food.

The nature of Neolithic societies provokes similar debate with the 8th to 6th millennium BC site of Çatal Höyük at its heart. Amazingly well-preserved female figurines in houses and grain stores, and wall paintings appeared to depict males and females differently. Mellaart (1967), a classically influenced excavator, interpreted one ceramic figurine of an obese and naked woman on a leopard throne as a mother goddess figure. Gimbutas (1991) developed this idea into her thesis of a lost matriarchal world of peaceful farmers, which particularly influenced interpretations of the first farming settlements in Europe (▶ p. 339). However, subsequent excavation by Hodder (2004) contradicts her interpretation. Detailed examination of human remains suggested little difference between men and women in terms of diet or lifestyle. Burials of men and women were identical and skulls of both were plastered and kept with the living. The only clear differences were in paintings associating men with wild animals, especially bulls, while figurines and art associated women with plants. This suggests that while there may have been different roles there did not appear to be structured inequality or evidence for matriarchy.

AGE

Similar evidence and indicators are also used to study age differentiation. The relationship between children and adults in burial practice is often a focus; for example, whether they are buried in a similar fashion and with similar assemblages. One of the most common forms of status is being a full member of a community. Uniform practices, as seen in early medieval cemeteries or as at Tiszapolgar, might suggest

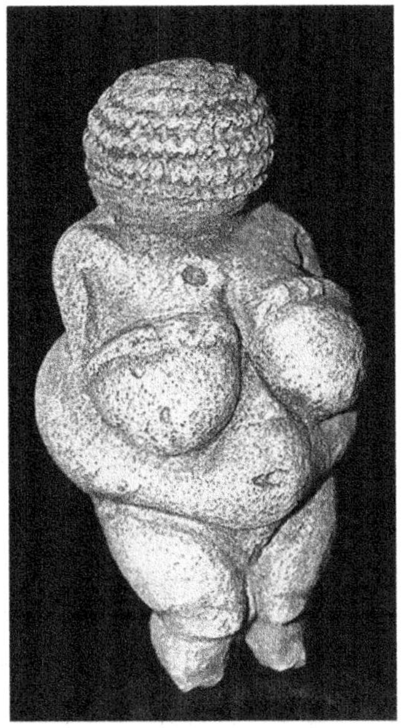

Figure 10.31 *'Venus' figurine from Willendorf, Austria*

Strongly sexed	Polished stone tools, flint tools	
Weakly sexed	Fire-lighting kits, bone tools	Ceramics
V. weakly sexed		Spondylus, personal ornaments, ochre
No difference	Grinding stones, dentalium, river and Atlantic shells	

Figure 10.32 *LBK grave goods associated with male and female burials (after Bickle and Whittle 2013)*

	Male	Female
Increase	Atlantic shells, fire-lighting kits, bone tools, flint tools, pottery, polished stone tools	Atlantic shells, ochre, pottery, polished stone, flint tools
No change	Dentalium beads, river shells, stone ornaments	Dentalium beads, river shells, stone ornaments, grinding stones, bone tools
Decrease	Spondylus, shell ornaments, ochre, grinding stones	Spondylus, shell ornaments

Figure 10.33 *Changes in LBK grave goods in relation to age (after Bickle and Whittle 2013)*

that children were considered to be members of the social group in the same way as adults. The 'swan wing' burial at Vedbaek (▶ p. 531) is interesting in this respect. Where rites differ – for example, burials of children under houses in some early Neolithic cultures – it may indicate that they were not yet full members of the society. A major survey of LBK burial practice across central Europe (Bickle and Whittle 2013) found some clear patterns related to gender and age. Aside from status, there is less focus upon older people, with the grandmother revolution (▶ p. 224) of the Upper Palaeolithic an exception.

SOCIAL CHANGE

Social changes range from the enclosing of small families in Neolithic houses to the emergence of empires in the late Bronze Age. Reasons for change broadly fall into two groups: external factors including immigration, diffusion, conquest and environmental change; internal factors including evolution, competition and innovation.

The beginnings of ranking and social divisions in Europe

One of the great debates in European prehistory focuses on the nature of social changes in the Chalcolithic after 5000 BC – the period between the late Neolithic and early Bronze Age. Neolithic societies are generally viewed as more or less egalitarian (Renfrew 1987), with some archaeologists arguing that in 'Old Europe' (Gimbutas 1991) there was also gender equality or even matriarchy and that it was peaceful (▶ p. 458). By the early Bronze Age there are many indicators of a growing inequality and conflict including prestige goods, individual burial monuments and clear evidence of weapons. Most archaeologists see this as evidence of the rise of a warrior elite with some adding warfare and partriarchy. This period is also when linguists believe that Indo-European languages (the forerunners of most modern European languages) arrived in Europe from Asia. Key questions include the extent of the changes, the reasons for them and the related reasons for language changes. Traditionally answers were largely sought through construction of detailed typological sequences

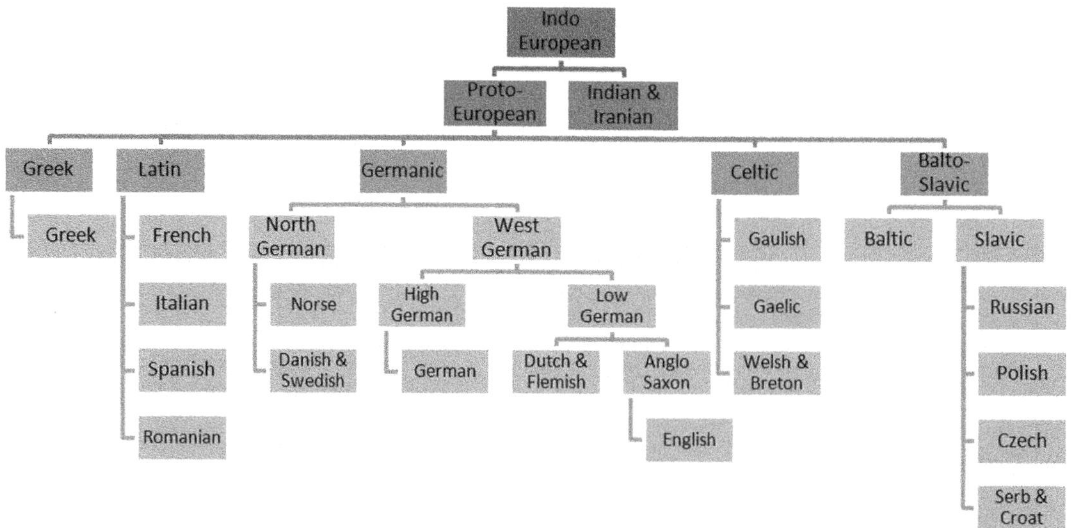

Figure 10.34 *The European family tree of languages. Many share words with Proto-Indo-European roots. These include relationships (mother, sister), numbers and agricultural terms (plough, mead, horse and milk).*

(▶ p. 175) of cultural assemblages (ceramics and then metals). Linguists added comparative studies of language, identifying shared words and using them to plot the family tree of European languages (▶ p. 454). Genetics is now making a contribution.

Changes by the 3rd millennium BC

While there was still marked regional diversity across Europe by 2500 BC, a number of broad common changes from the Neolithic are evident. A greater emphasis upon pastoralism can be seen from the importance of cattle reflected in symbolism and burials. Widespread evidence of secondary products (▶ p. 357) includes spindle whorls, loom weights (▶ p. 389), cheese strainers and models of carts. Early forms of agricultural settlement such as the Balkan tell sites (▶ p. 339) and LBK villages were abandoned. Settlement was more dispersed and new areas settled including upland areas. Environmental evidence suggests widespread land clearance well away from the loess soils, the use of mountain pastures for grazing and an intensification of mining including flint. However, while copper and gold artefacts are the focus of much archaeological attention, most tools continued to be made from stone until the Iron Age. While permanent villages are known in some areas, such as the Alpine foreland home of Ötzi (▶ p. 104), and fortified sites in others, over much of the continent settlement evidence is thin. This may suggest a degree of mobility, perhaps associated with pastoralism. People are more visible in the burial record, although there was considerable variation in practice. Before 4000 BC, aside from particularly rich examples such as Varna (▶ p. 423), there

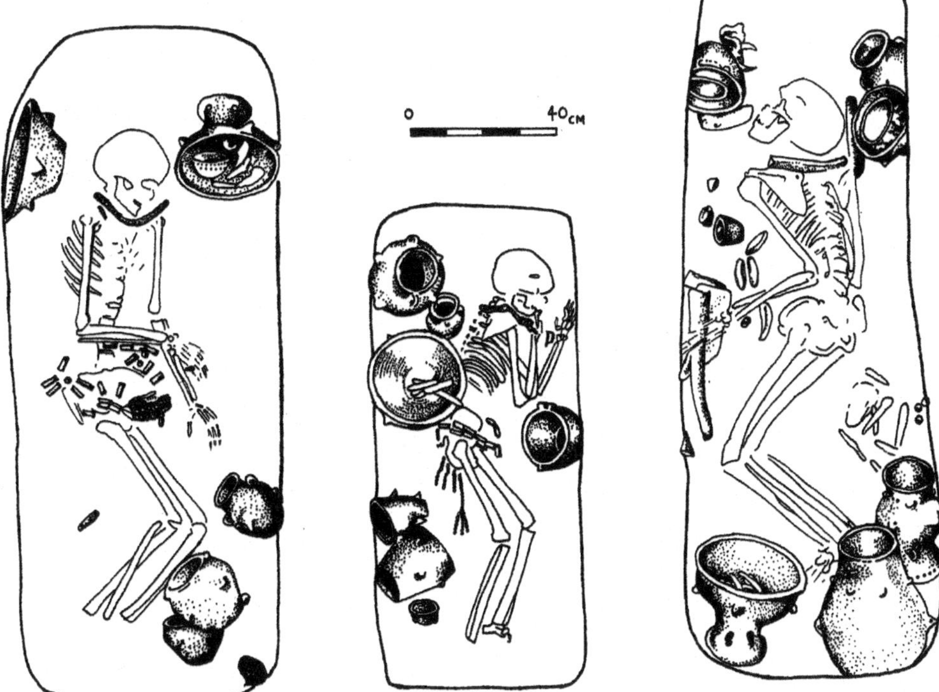

Figure 10.35 *Burials at Tiszapolgar (after Orschiedt 1998)*

seems to be relatively little evidence of status differences in burial assemblages. There were also slight variations in grave goods and body position between men and women as can be seen from the Chalcolithic cemetery at Tiszapolgar, Hungary.

Tiszapolgar

This large cemetery which was largely excavated in the 1950s revealed repeated burial patterns over a long period from *c.* 4500 to 3600 BC. Most of the 157 graves followed the same alignment and were not cut by later burials, which suggests that there may once have been markers which may have been socially significant. Males were buried on their right sides, females on their left. Gendered grave goods hints at different roles and statuses for men and women. Males are associated with weapons and tools and also with animal bones including wild boar and dogs. They are also associated with exotic imports such as copper, obsidian and spondylus. These goods may symbolise hunting, agriculture, exchange and possibly fighting. Small tools, pebbles and greater amounts of pottery are found in female graves, which may symbolise domesticity or perhaps ceramic production (Milisauskas 2002). Personal ornamentation is also gendered. Derevenski's (1997) statistical significance testing showed that women usually had a girdle of beads over the pelvis and a ring on their left hand. Men tended to have an arm-ring on their right and beads over their torsos. In both cases, beads could have been sewn into clothing. Burials of children were gendered too, with similar assemblages to adults. For example, the longest flint blade was found with a child lying on its right side. Age seemed to be significant including an association between younger adult women and girdles which may relate to fertility or marriage. Derevenski (1997) also noted that gendered grave goods changed during the lifetime of the cemetery, perhaps indicating that the social construction of gender was changing.

Corded Ware Culture and beakers

Differences became more marked with the trend towards single burials marked by monuments in the late 4th millennium BC. In the Pannonian (Hungarian) Basin some graves were covered by a tumulus (mound of stone or earth) as at Kétegyháza or marked with stelae (stone slabs) as at Mezõcsát. Within these burials there was

FEMALE
crouched skeleton on left side
pebbles
jug and other ceramics
finger ring (left)

Adult female only
flower-pot vase
mussel shells
limestone beads
bone awl
girdle of beads over pelvis

MALE
skeleton on right side
copper awl and pins
obsidian
stone tools incl. flint blades
domesticated animal bones incl. dog
wild boar and auroch bones
spondylus
arm ring (right)

Adult male only
weapons
shafthole axe
copper dagger

Figure 10.36 *Gendered grave goods at Tiszapolgar (after Milisauskas 1978 and Derevenski 1997)*

Figure 10.37 *Single grave axes*

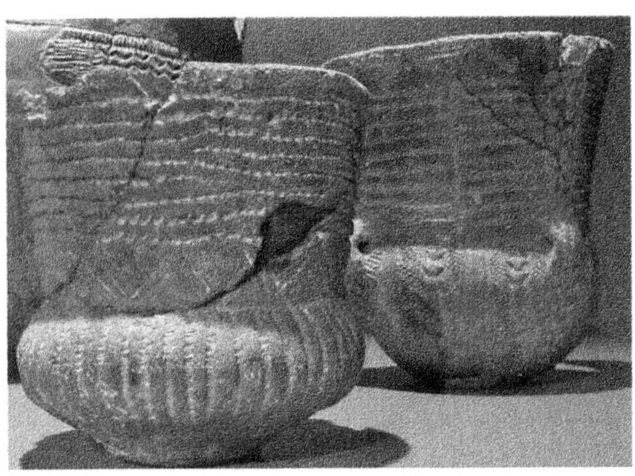

Figure 10.38 *Beakers. These examples include cord-impressions.*

a bias towards adult males associated with horses, cattle, weapons and drinking vessels, while females were particularly associated with ceramics and beads. Variations of this mortuary practice spread across Europe and a series of major cultural groups are named after artefacts recovered from tumuli or other flat cemeteries. The Corded Ware Culture (▶ p. 116) from *c.* 2900 BC was the most widespread across central Europe and Russia with variations in Scandinavia (Battle Axe Culture) and north-west Europe (Single Grave Culture). Common diagnostic artefacts were ceramics decorated with cord (probably hemp), especially beakers, and stone battle axes. Generally men lay on their right side and females on their left, although this was reversed in some regions. The bell-beaker burial assemblage, which spread from 2800 BC along the Atlantic seaboard from Denmark to Morocco, contained many similar aspects. The British variation substituted archery equipment for battle axes (▶ p. 460), with a range of round barrows and cairns as well as flat cemeteries. These burials contain the earliest evidence of new technologies such as copper daggers, metal ornamentation and horse riding gear as well as exotic materials such as amber beads. Associated ritual changes included a decline in female figurines in the Balkans while in the West the late Neolithic from 3500 BC saw the construction of great timber and stone ceremonial monuments (▶ p. 522).

EXPLAINING THE EMERGENCE OF ELITES

Sherratt (1997) describes Corded Ware Culture as reformatting Europe. The question is what new social form had arisen. Individual monuments suggest that lineages were important and burial evidence suggests increasing inequality. However, while some individuals acquired wealth and perhaps some power, there is no persuasive evidence yet of permanent elites. Burying that wealth means it was ephemeral and not passed on to descendants. There is no strong evidence either for the kind of palaces or high-status residences that would emerge in the Mediterranean Bronze Age.

The reasons why greater inequality emerged are much debated. Before the widespread use of radiocarbon dating, the diffusion of ideas and metallurgy from the new urban centres in the Near East was the dominant explanation. Certainly some forms of drinking vessel and some technologies including viticulture (wine production) do have Near Eastern origins, yet copper smelting probably developed simultaneously or earlier in Europe. Additional internal reasons for changes include the adaption to new environments, climate change and the spread of pastoralism, which helped transform productivity

Figure 10.39 *Drinking vessels made from metal and ceramics. Sets of special drinking vessels including jugs, ladles and cups are associated with Corded Ware Culture and related cultures.*

and helped raise population levels. It was a Europe where both prestige goods and ideas, including language and probably beliefs, spread across vast areas. Across Europe a wider range of materials were being produced and the opportunities to turn surpluses into wealth and status were increasing.

A second external influence was from the Pontic Steppe, which stretches north of the Black and Caspian Seas. The Sredny Stog culture of the late 5th/early 4th millennium BC Ukraine had horses and copper alloying before Europe and late 4th/early 3rd millennium BC Yamna (pit-grave) Culture had kurgans (burial mounds), wheeled vehicles and cord-impressed pottery with solar motifs. This was also the region where linguists have searched for the origins of proto-European languages for over two centuries. The theories of Gimbutas and Sherratt are the best-known explanations for the 3rd millennium BC changes and illustrate these different influences.

Gimbutas and the Kurgan hypothesis

Marija Gimbutas (1991) used archaeological and linguistic evidence to argue that there were

Figure 10.40 *Horses from the steppes. The first horses into Europe would have been pony-sized animals looking similar to Przewalski's wild horses.*

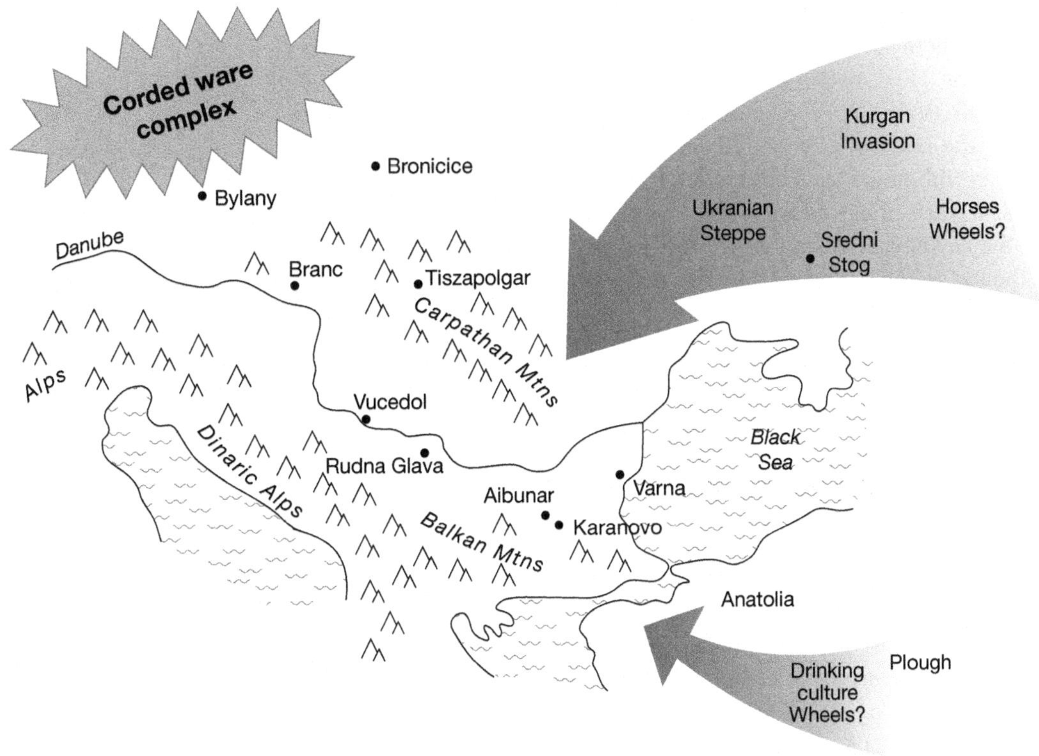

Figure 10.41 *The end of 'Old Europe'. European society was transformed partly through influences from the Steppes, the Near East and the spread of Corded Ware Culture.*

repeated invasions of the Danube basin by Proto-Indo-European (PIE)-speaking nomads from the Steppes. These horse and chariot-riding warriors sought booty and grazing land and conquered the peaceful horticulturalists of south-eastern Europe. She saw their language as the source of pastoral words in European languages in contrast to agricultural terms which derived from Neolithic farmers. She called them the 'Kurgan Culture' after the distinctive Kurgan tumuli which mark their progress into Europe. She identified the 4th millennium BC Baden and Vucedol (▶ p. 462) cultures as being 'kurganised' and the Corded Ware Culture as representing an invading group. From the 1970s she added a feminist perspective, claiming that Kurgan people brought a patriarchal society, new (male) sky-gods of the type associated with pastoral societies and endemic warfare. She noted that contemporary, new Near Eastern religions such as Judaism were also patriarchal and rooted in pastoralism. The peaceful, matriarchal and earth goddess-worshipping culture of 'Old Europe' was replaced with the cult of the warrior male.

Sherratt and the secondary products revolution

Andrew Sherratt (1997) also acknowledged influences from the Steppes, but argued that animal traction, horse riding and developments in metallurgy probably came through trade and exchange rather than invasion. Simultaneously he argued for influences from the urban Near

East via Anatolia including the cult of warriors drinking together, wine and textile production and dairying. He used dated typologies of artefact design and assemblages to underpin his theory. He saw the corded ware as fusing these two traditions with new ideals linking leaders, hospitality and a self-image as warriors. Livestock became the key new source of wealth but exchange was the key to the spread of this new way of life.

Influences from the Steppes

Undeniably horses came from the Steppes (▶ p. 458), although their early use in battle rather than as transport has largely been rejected because the riding equipment to control them is lacking. Clay models and the earliest finds of wheeled vehicles provide evidence of carts for transport (▶ p. 360). However, evidence for warfare pre-dates Kurgan influences, which brings the peaceful nature of 'Old Europe' into doubt (▶ p. 459). Similarly, Bentley's (2012) identification of patrilocality amongst LBK farmers (▶ p. 350) undermines claims of universal Neolithic matriarchy. Linguists have demonstrated that the pastoral–arable division of words is unfounded (Krell 1998) as steppe peoples had both sets of words. Gimbutas has been criticised (Anthony 2007) for lumping many different cultures across long periods together under the Kurgan banner, some of whom did not even have burial mounds. The dates of her waves of invasions have also been challenged. Some changes in fact, particularly in metalworking and agriculture, spread eastwards around the Black Sea from Europe, thus demonstrating the movement of ideas rather than people. Sherratt's model has principally been criticised for its timing, since secondary products are now known to have arrived over a much longer period, including through internal developments (▶ p. 318) rather than as a new package. In his 'Anatolian Hypothesis', Renfrew (1987) argued that Proto-Indo-Europeans (PIE) arrived much earlier with the first farmers in the Balkans. This fits with the demonstrable spread of farming across the continent, much or all of which would have involved the movement of people (▶ p. 499). However, many words in PIE refer to technologies which did not exist when farmers entered Europe *c.* 7000 BC.

Figure 10.42 *Shafthole battle axes*

Since the end of the Soviet Union in 1991 much more research has been carried out into steppe cultures. Anthony (2007) demonstrated that horses were first used for food and then ridden to herd other animals. They enabled the Sredny Stog (who had flat cemeteries not kurgans) and other 5th millennium BC cultures to extend the territories they exploited from the river valleys onto the open steppes, thus increasing their productivity. By 4200 BC they were riding on long-range raids to steal livestock since horses enabled surprise and a quick escape. The later Yamna Culture (who did have kurgans) similarly used carts to enable migrations with herds by *c.* 3000 BC. Anthony agrees that there was migration from the Steppes in several very gradual stages but argues that this was largely peaceful rather than being military. He also sees the Western Steppe as the home of Proto-Indo-Europeans.

Recent developments in genetics may potentially resolve migration issues, although some of the earliest results have been contradictory. Recent analysis of a Corded Ware burial in Germany (Lee 2012) revealed female haplogroup U5, which was unknown amongst earlier Neolithic populations and therefore may indicate migrants. Similarly the distribution of the male haplogroup R1a, which is associated with Indo-European languages, is common right across the Steppes to Siberia. The Corded Ware males at Eulau (▶ p. 116) had this haplogroup. However, there are some continuities in both lithics and ceramics between the Corded Ware Culture and earlier cultures such as the Funnelneckbeaker (TRB) of northern Europe, which suggests a degree of continuity amongst at least part of the population. It is likely that the new cultures have mixed roots. The Baden Culture shows clear signs of continuity with earlier Chalcolithic cultures whilst having Steppe-influenced burials in some cemeteries including burials with cattle. This suggests some movement of people but not necessarily conflict. Wetter climates and the spread of milk consumption in this period may have encouraged a shift to pastoralism while the new technologies themselves would have been disruptive.

Bogucki and the emergence of wealth

Bogucki (2011) argues that by 4000 BC across central Europe the population lived in clusters of households or small hamlets. Earlier farmers such as the LBK (▶ p. 346) had successfully adapted agriculture to this environment but had been 'risk averse' and not deviated from that formula. As a result, society was **transegalitarian**, where individuals were unable to accumulate sufficient wealth to transform society. However, from *c.* 4000 BC there are signs of farmers taking risks. This includes cultivating different soils and

Figure 10.43 *Scandinavian fishtailed daggers*

This hoard of 'fishtail' daggers from a Danish bog illustrates a peak in knapping skill. Possibly weapons and certainly prestige items, the design seems unnecessarily difficult for a flint weapon and is probably based on early copper or bronze weapons. It is a good example of a form suited to one technology crossing over into another.

landscape and different balances of crops and livestock. Emmer and spelt wheat became increasingly common while einkorn, which produced lower yields, became less so. Barley and increasingly millet were also grown.

Their motivation was to acquire wealth. Bogucki (2011) reworks Sherratt's secondary products model to explain why this happened at this point. First, communication increased as evidenced by developments in water craft such as the Dover Boat. At a local level, wheeled carts allowed crops, timber, materials and carcasses to be transported over shorter distances. Increased communication offered opportunities for exchange of goods and the spread of ideas. This can be evidenced in the way designs travelled even if materials did not, as with Scandinavian fishtail daggers, which were flint copies of central European status symbols. Metals provided for the first time truly durable goods that could be accumulated and inherited. Animal traction enabled heavier soils to be exploited and households able to sustain and train a pair of oxen were able to break through a productivity threshold. Agricultural intensification would have enabled higher populations and surpluses and stimulated exchange. Cattle themselves became a key form of wealth which could reproduce itself. Metallurgy and animal husbandry also created new roles and took people into new locations. All these changes created differences and offered opportunities for individuals to amass wealth and perhaps power. Those households able to amass a surplus could become wealthy. Those unable to became relatively poorer. Bogucki (2011) calls oxen the 'killer app for secondary products'.

KEY STUDY

Vučedol and the birth of inequality at the dawn of the Bronze Age

Site

The type-site of Vučedol perches on a bluff above the west bank of the Danube just downstream from Vukovar (▶ p. 477) in Croatia. Deep stratigraphy from continuous occupation includes cultural layers from the Neolithic Starčevo culture of *c.* 5000 BC to the Bronze Age after 2000 BC. Although the lower levels are reasonably well preserved, the rich loess soil continues to be ploughed so later surfaces are degraded. The site has suffered from river erosion and has significant damage from being used as an artillery base in 1991 during the Yugoslav Civil War. Less than 10 per cent of the site has been excavated, with much more underneath a vineyard.

The distinctive Vučedol culture layers represent the late Chalcolithic from *c.* 3000 to 2600 BC. The Chalcolithic site was large, covering at least 3 hectares. Within probable enclosure were the remains of houses, storage pits, graves and working areas. The highest point – Gradec – was enclosed by double ditches and possibly a palisade and contained a large rectangular structure measuring 16m x 10m (Durham 1988) associated with residue from copperworking. It has been variously interpreted as a chief's hall and a metalworking centre.

Well over 1,000 people (Forenbaher 1994) lived in the densely packed, one-room, rectangular houses. These were partially sunken with burnt clay floors and wattle and daub walls. Wear marks show where doors had been and other features include circular hearths and sunken pots – probably for storing water. As at Karanovo (▶ p. 339), ceramic models of houses, ovens and furniture provide insights into how these buildings looked and were used. Hooks for suspending cooking pots were found close to hearths in several buildings (Durham 1988). Outside the houses were external ovens and large numbers of pits which contained traces of carbonised wheat and settlement debris. Some pits had been used for burials.

Artefacts

Recovered artefacts were largely stone or ceramic but with some bone and metal objects. Lithics included weights for fishing nets, querns and polished shaft-hole axes and hammers. As on many central European sites, spondylus bracelets (▶ p. 400) testified to an exchange network reaching to the Aegean. Decorated ceramics were produced including many forms which were ornamental or symbolic rather than practical. These included models of furniture, wagons and items of clothing along with figurines. These depictions provide insights into the wooden and plant materials which have not survived, including leather footwear, carts and embroidered wool and leather clothing. The best known piece is a three-legged container known as the Dove of Vučedol (possibly a partridge). Thought to be a cult object (▶ p. 520) because of the double axes motifs on its neck, it has been adopted in modern Croatia as a symbol both of the nation and of peace. Vessels ranged from large amphorae, cooking pots and tureens to bowls, spoons and cups.

Figure 10.44 *Ceramics from Vučedol. This includes sets of fine drinking vessels.*

continued

The range of tableware, including much of high quality, suggests that eating and drinking was about much more than satisfying hunger. Some perforated vessels have been identified as censers (for incense) and others as sieves used in cheese production (▶ p. 140). Decoration included incrustation, where a paste of powdered white snail shells and resin was baked onto the surface of black pottery or into a shape cut out from the clay. An iron oxide wash was used to create a red surface (Durham 1988). In addition to lines and geometric patterns, sun and star shapes are common motifs. The quality of artistry and the skill of the potters suggest that specialists were producing ceramics. Several of the larger vessels depict constellations, particularly Orion. One is decorated with frames which appear to show the changing appearance (including his summer absence) of Orion over the year and may be Europe's first calendar. Loom weights testify to the importance of textile manufacture, although it is unclear whether this was largely wool or whether plant fibres remained important.

Metallurgy was also advanced and specialised with a number of new artefact forms. Five furnaces have been excavated so far along with two-piece clay moulds and manufacturing debris. The copper itself was usually alloyed with arsenic to give it strength. The whole process from smelting to finishing pieces occurred on this site and the large quantities of finished artefacts suggests mass production of some forms. The most distinctive are small, socketed 'battle axes' but there were also pins and daggers. There are some items of gold jewellery but these are relatively rare. The assemblage contrasts strongly with that from the earlier Chalcolithic site of Varna (▶ p. 423).

Vučedol was first investigated in 1897, with a major excavation by the German archaeologist R. R. Schmidt in 1938. As the earliest and largest of the sites contained a particular range of Chalcolithic artefacts, it gave its name to the Vučedol Culture, although this does not mean it was the earliest. Vučedol Culture artefacts, burials and settlement types are found along the Danube valley as far north as Prague and into northern Italy. Several similar sites have been found with elevated locations and possible palisades and concentrations of copper artefacts, particularly battle axes.

Figure 10.45 *Hoard of battle axes from Vučedol*

Economy

The existence of such a large settlement suggests that its inhabitants, particularly the groups of specialists, benefited from agricultural surpluses. The local chenozem (black-earth) soils are particularly fertile and easily tilled, while the Danube floodplain provides excellent grazing for cattle. Most faunal remains were domesticates with cattle and pigs predominating. However, wild food was still important, particularly deer. Deer also provided skins and antler for tools, especially hooks and harpoons, while there was at least one burial of a stag (Trbojević Vukičević 2006). Water bird and fish bones emphasise the importance of the Danube as a food source as well as the source of water and a communication artery. Up to 40 per cent of domesticates were cattle, especially mature females, which is indicative of dairying (Trbojević Vukičević, 2006). The remains of only one horse have been recovered, which suggests that it was still an exotic animal at this time. Carbonised wheat has been recovered from the houses and pits but otherwise recovered information on plant foods is scant. The location, population and assemblages suggest a wide site catchment including a range of environments, some, especially grazing, at a distance from Vučedol. Archaeologists differ over why the site was so economically successful. Stock breeding, control over local farmers or dominating the manufacture and luxury trade in copper and other artefacts are all possibilities. Little archaeological research has been carried out beyond the site itself and further surveys including the recovery of environmental data would help resolve many questions about the economy.

Society

There is persuasive evidence from Vučedol of both greater specialisation and a more ranked society than previously. The special compound at Gradac suggests a form of social segregation. The differential burial deposits and the distribution of copper artefacts (one house had fifty copper artefacts) provide additional indicators. Only a small proportion of the population appears to have been buried, mostly being placed in old storage pits in a similar manner to 'sacrificed' domestic animals. Remains may also have been included in middens close to the houses. Burials often contain more than one individual and usually contained grave goods, especially ceramics and food remains. One particularly rich assemblage accompanied a man and woman who had been buried simultaneously. The multiple burials have led to suggestions that some may have been sacrifices but there is no evidence to corroborate this at present. There has been much speculation on the nature of early Bronze Age beliefs, with particular emphasis on the sun and sky gods because of the shift in symbolism in the material culture. Female figurines were still made but they are less abstract and more often clothed than in the Neolithic.

Its size, resources and strategic position on the Danube may well have given Vučedol regional influence and power (Forenbaher 1994). Schmidt (1938) had gone further, drawing on the palisade and new battle axes to suggest that it was the centre of a warrior chiefdom. His illustration of the site with added longships has the look of a Dark Age fortress. While there is insufficient evidence to confirm such an elite, there are early signs of the social differences which would emerge in the Bronze Age. Archaeologists are divided over whether the Vučedol culture owed more to the Chalcolithic, the Baden Culture of central Europe, groups from the Steppes or other local cultures. Today a major new museum is being built into the north side of the site with the aim of making it one of the major Neolithic attractions in Europe and which tells the story of the significant social changes associated with Vučedol.

THE EMERGENCE OF CHIEFDOMS IN BRONZE AGE EUROPE

During the Bronze Age, much of the continent remained a mosaic of farmsteads and hamlets engaged in mixed farming and domestic manufacturing (▶ p. 390) supplemented with wild resources. Most people lived in small round or rectangular houses with little social differentiation. However, the burial record of the 2nd millennium BC implies the rise of chiefdoms, trade and endemic warfare. Nevertheless, unlike the Mediterranean zone, Europe did not develop cities or palace civilisations. European societies borrowed artefact styles, ritual and elements of warfare but not social or economic models. The key questions for this period are about the nature of social organisation and why emergent chiefdoms did not develop into states or more rigidly stratified societies in the same way as Greece or Mesopotamia (▶ p. 286).

Evidence for elites

Evidence for a more hierarchical society, or at least inequalities in wealth, largely comes from the burial record. Bronze artefacts first appear in numbers in the cemeteries of the Únětice Culture of central Europe from 2300 to 1500 BC. Most people were inhumed in a uniform way with north–south orientation and a variety of ceramics, tools and personal ornamentation. However, a small number of barrows were constructed over richer individual burials. These contain the finest metalworkings such as torcs, riveted daggers, halberds and spiral bracelets. Aside from buried hoards of bronze ingots, this new material seems to have been almost entirely to produce ostentatious artefacts to display wealth. The Únětice culture (▶ p. 433) appears to have had long-distance exchange links which brought exotic materials and prestige items. Finds of Baltic amber in Únětice graves and Egyptian influence on the iconography of the Nebra sky disk (▶ p. 452) hint at some of these connections. Elements of its

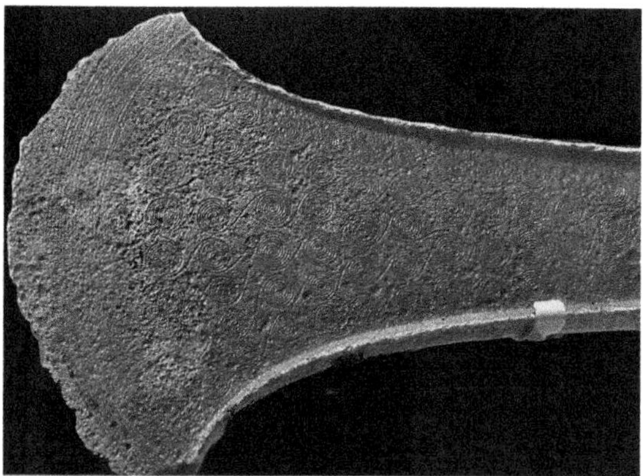

Figure 10.46 *Bronze, patterned axe typifying the kind of high-status metalwork created and exchanged during the Bronze Age*

burial practice and grave goods echo across much of Europe including to the Wessex Culture of southern Britain and rich burials such as that at Bush Barrow. The importance of creating an impressive presentation is emphasised by jewellery and artefacts such as tweezers, razors and cosmetic palettes. As with the preceding period, there is also an emphasis on vessels for drinking and eating. Succeeding phases in central Europe such as the Tumulus Culture and Hallstatt are marked by an intensification of exchange and rich burials.

Sources of wealth

The sources of wealth were similar to the preceding period but with some new developments, particularly in trade. Prestige goods and rare materials such as jet and gold provide evidence of very long exchange networks. Some argue that the amber found in the Mycenaean shaft graves is evidence of prestige goods chains reaching from the Mediterranean to the Baltic. Cornish tin may have been another such commodity. Within regions such as the British Isles valuable raw materials were transported over great distances including copper and gold from the west of Ireland (▶ p. 373). Sea-going boats made the increasing volume of this trade possible. Control over the production and exchange of prestige

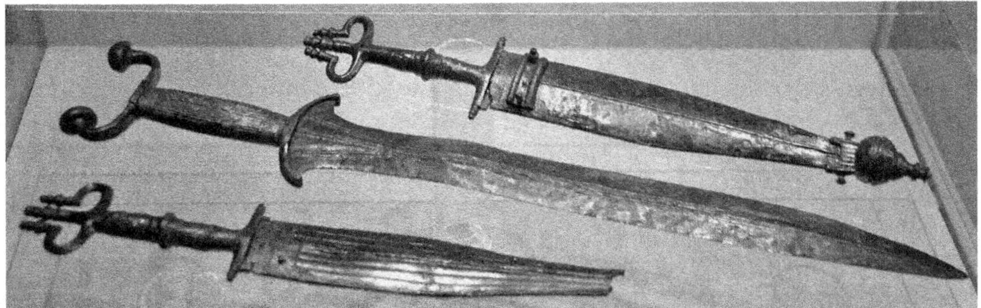

Figure 10.47 *Hallstatt daggers*

goods and valuable materials offered ways to acquire new levels of status. This can clearly be seen in relation to salt from the rich graves at Hallstatt (▶ p. 373).

Less visible but still important was agriculture. There was continued expansion onto previously marginal land (e.g. Dartmoor) as populations slowly rose and pastoralism spread. Cattle remained a major source of (mobile) wealth. Some of the earliest European myths such as the Ulster Cycle probably have their roots in this period and cattle as wealth and the object of raids are central to the stories. Studies in Denmark have found correlations between prestige goods and the most fertile agricultural land. It is also a period where enclosed field systems were established in many areas ranging from grids of tiny rectangular plots to extended 'ranch boundaries'. Land was also improved whether by stone clearance or the creation of banks or lynchets on sloping fields to prevent erosion. This investment and the emphasis on ownership suggests that the productivity of farms was a key source of wealth. Populations anchored to one place were also easier to control or tax.

Mobilisation

An indication of growing political power is the ability to mobilise and organise people. In the Near East this involved great fortifications and tombs for the rulers such as the pyramids but these were largely absent from Europe. The development of large ceremonial and defensive sites from the Bronze Age has been seen by many archaeologists as evidence of the emergence of chiefdoms in the British Isles. Grogan's (1999) regional level study of Irish hilltop enclosures showed that these very visible, although not always defensive, sites were established at regular intervals across the landscape. Finds suggest they were high status. In Britain the phase of megalithic monument building at sites such as Stonehenge did involve mobilisation. Parker-Pearson (2012) argues that it involved an attempt to unify Britain. However, the cluster of burials around the site may suggest a broad elite rather than a few very powerful individuals. Ritual itself may have been significant in Europe as it was in the Near East. Early Bronze Age religion saw an emphasis on the sun and stars (▶ p. 452). New monuments for large-scale ceremonies required people to lead and organise them, which offered new opportunities to acquire power.

Using prestige goods to build social networks

The later Bronze Age saw an increasing emphasis on deposition of objects in wet places (▶ p. 453), sometimes involving displays of conspicuous destruction which only some could afford. This suggests that powerful individuals amassed surpluses to acquire prestige goods on behalf of their communities. At the end of the European gift chain was Ancient Greece. Homer's epics were rooted in this period and feature heroes who 'spent' the agricultural wealth of their communities on gifts of fine weapons and feasts for their followers. Arguably similar warbands developed into chiefdoms elsewhere in Europe. Agricultural surpluses were translated into conspicuous consumption: feasting, votive offerings (▶ p. 520), funerals and, of course, weapons. Finely crafted swords are a feature of graves and votive deposits (▶ p. 512).

Kristiansen and Larsson (2005) argue that there was an increasing tendency towards an elite served by warriors drawn from farming households by the hospitality and gifts they could bestow. Below them in the hierarchy were farmers and below them slaves. They noted that in Scandinavia there was a trend towards fewer but larger chiefly dwellings and smaller ordinary homes. They suggested that these smaller family units relied on a chief for protection rather than an extended kin group as they had previously. In a continuation of patterns seen in the 3rd millennium, Artusson (2009) argues that power structures were based on social networks rather than permanent institutions. Fine metalwork, tableware and textiles, alcohol and prime animals all became part of what Sherratt (1997) called an 'elaborate game of one-upmanship'. Power and status revolved around the ability of key individuals to reward followers, win battles or win over the gods. Rival small and medium-sized chiefdoms constantly struggled for dominance, while competing lineages within chiefdoms made them inherently unstable. Rivals created elaborate networks of alliances to obtain prestige goods and materials. This prevented any one group from becoming permanently dominant.

EXPLAINING THE EMERGENCE OF SOCIAL COMPLEXITY

The term 'Urban Revolution' was coined by Childe (1936) as a development from his earlier 'Neolithic Revolution'. He used it to capture the dramatic scale of developments involved in the emergence of the first states, or civilisations, which were based around large towns or cities. Powerful elites controlled large populations and used agricultural surpluses to fund monumental architecture, armies, a bureaucracy and a wide range of craft specialists. It was the emergence of the latter group that Childe saw as the key to the development of states with a move from domestic to specialist production and the emergence of classes. The state emerged to coordinate the work of specialists. However, specialisation is also found in chiefdoms so in itself it cannot alone explain the emergence of states. We now know that change was more gradual than Childe anticipated and the reasons for it are also complex.

The first urban settlements

Urban settlements such as Jericho and Çatal Höyük (▶ p. 284) emerged *c.* 7000 BC but lacked many of the features of later cities so are sometimes called proto-cities. The first real city-states arose in the Sumerian civilisation of the 4th millennium BC Mesopotamia. Population levels had risen in the region with the development of irrigation systems which massively boosted crop yields. This in turn enabled growing social differentiation. Along with new specialist bronze workers, brewers and potters were priests. Temples became the focal points of towns and played a key role in the economy and politics. Clearly there were also those who organised the building of canals and public buildings, supervised redistribution of food surpluses and led raids into surrounding areas to acquire slaves. By 3000 BC Mesopotamian city-states such as Ur, Uruk (▶ p. 285) and Tell Brak were enormously different from Çatal Höyük. Most were walled with substantial defences, indicating a growth in warfare beyond raiding and perhaps the need for rulers to control their population. Small, hereditary elites now ruled, generally with unlimited power and frequently controlling religion, law and commerce as well as armies and the first government bureaucracies. Religious monuments, such as the Ziggurat of Ur, were often gigantic. So too were the palaces, statues and reliefs of the rulers whose deeds were preserved for posterity by their scribes. Similar states rapidly emerged throughout the Middle East and in Egypt, China and India.

Hydraulic theories

The Mesopotamian epic poem *Gilgamesh* credits the king-god of that name with founding Uruk and building its walls. However, although most scholars date his reign to the mid-3rd millennium BC, the city is much older. Some archaeologists have also advanced mono-causal explanations for the emergence of more complex societies. One is the development of manager-specialists who wield power in order to integrate society. However, this does not explain why they were able to do so at this time. One possibility is that they had a benevolent, managerial function organising public works or the redistribution of agricultural surpluses. In his famous 'Hydraulic Theory' (1957), Wittfogel argued that states developed to mobilise populations to build the irrigation systems and distribute water. This made sense because irrigation massively raised the productivity of the river valleys of the Euphrates and Nile. However, while most early states had irrigation schemes, they were not always centrally organised. Some predated the state while others developed after the emergence of the state as in Mexico and China. Other suggested prime managerial functions were conflict resolution including providing laws for dense populations and organising defence against aggressors. While some aspects of these ideas such as a food surplus and a hierarchy are necessary conditions for cities to emerge, no one explanation seems to be sufficient. Most writers prefer multicausal explanations and tend to focus on the key role of the temples where ritual, political and economic power appeared to come together. The presence of temples and monuments in all early cities encouraged an interpretation that a priesthood or theocracy gained power by accumulating surpluses on behalf of the gods. Rituals then reinforced the beliefs or ideology which led people to serve the state.

Population theories

Unprecedented populations are a key feature of socially complex states but the causal relationship is unclear. There clearly is a relationship between food production and both population density and the number of priests, soldiers and craftspeople who could be supported. Did population lead to social complexity because there were more people or did increasing specialism increase productivity, which enabled populations to rise? Some of the most exciting work on the emergence of urban societies is at the Mesopotamian site of Tell Brak in northern Iraq. Tell Brak from *c.* 4000 BC vies with Uruk (▶ p. 285) and Eridu as the first city and has some of the earliest clay tablets and cylinder seals (▶ p. 417) from 3500 BC. Here satellite and surface surveys have revealed developments beyond the tell itself. Distinct clusters of domestic refuse around the tell led Ur (2007) to the conclusion that different social groups came together around a specialised centre at the site and coalesced into an urban area. This is very different from the city being the creation of a centralised elite as had previously been thought. Rapid population growth followed the building of protective walls. While complexity itself has often been viewed as the key to these new cities, specialists in metalworking or religion do not usually farm and required lengthy periods to acquire their skills so they would need to be supported by a barter economy or through redistribution. This required a significant agricultural surplus to happen.

Conflict theories

Conflict models take two forms. Stress versions seek to explain why conflict emerged which in turn required a state to develop in order to resolve it.

Carneiro (1970) compared prehistoric Amazonia with the valleys of Peru. Both had agriculture and warfare but only Peru developed a state. The key difference was that populations in Peru outstripped available land. Warfare and armies evolved to conquer rivals and make them hand over food as tribute or taxes. New classes included a military elite and a slave group of prisoners. Renfrew and Cherry's Peer Polity Interaction model (1986) argues that warfare was just one of a number of ways in which small proto-states competed including exchange and feasting. State organisation developed to provide the leaders with the resources to compete. Alternatively chiefs used their warbands to coerce people into a state for 'protection'. An extension of this is that the best-organised states were then able to conquer others and increase their power and wealth through tribute and enslavement as with Uruk and the Aztecs.

Consensus versions seek to explain how a ruling elite was able to take control and establish a state to protect its own class interests against the majority. Unprecedented inequality is a feature of early states and can particularly be seen in the lavish tombs and in some cases palaces of the rulers. This may have occurred gradually. Perhaps with increasing differentiation some specialisms became more valuable than others, leading to stratification. Alternatively, some people monopolised trade in the products crafted by specialists and the flow of rare materials which supported their work. Through wealth they acquired influence and were able to control their own attached specialists (▶ p. 390). Or, warrior kings developed either from or to protect the priesthood. In many early states the ruler was also a religious leader. The ruler was able to supplement kinship ties with the devotion of subjects to the state gods.

Rather than search for prime movers, most archaeologists acknowledge that there were multiple reasons and regional variations. Agriculture does not always create a food surplus even where it is possible to do so and there is not one trajectory whereby competition between chiefdoms always led to stratified bureaucracies. Many paths proved to be 'dead ends' in terms of social evolution.

KEY STUDY

Knossos and the emergence of Minoan palace civilisation

The Minoan palace civilisation was arguably Europe's first state. However, both its nature and the reasons for its emergence are unclear. Apart from the myth of the Minotaur and labyrinth (probably Knossos palace), the Minoans were unknown until archaeologists discovered them. Most excavation has focused upon the palaces and a great deal is known about ritual, manufacture and trade. Conversely, relatively little is known about either earlier settlements including those underlying the palaces themselves, or rural settlements. This makes it difficult to understand either sequences or the contexts in which palaces operated. Research in the last two decades, particularly focusing on households and settlement of the final Neolithic and early Bronze Age, combined with regional surveys is starting to address these gaps.

Palace economies

The palaces (▶ p. 256) had several functions we associate with states. The extensive storage for agricultural produce including wine, grain and oil suggests control over the rural economy and a redistributive role. These resources were recorded on clay tablets in Linear A (▶ p. 416) by palace accountants while ownership was marked using seals. Attached specialists in palace workshops produced luxury artefacts using exotic and imported raw materials including copper from Cyprus and ivory from Syria. They were especially skilled in stone (using imported stone and rock crystal) and seal carving and goldworking. Cretan potters made some of the best ceramics in the early Bronze Age. Eggshell-thin Kamares Ware and fine Marine Style vessels with their entire surface covered in sea creatures have been found across the eastern Mediterranean and as far up the Nile as Aswan. Agricultural exports included grain, olive oil, scented oil, honey, wine and probably textiles and timber.

Figure 10.48 *Kamares Ware cup*

Cretan palaces became part of the first major maritime exchange network including both commodities and luxury goods. Shipwrecks such as the *Uluburun* (▶ p. 403) and the use of Minoan weights across the eastern Mediterranean evidence this trade as does the port of Kommos on Crete's south coast. Kommos was protected by an offshore reef while six large sheds probably housed sea-going vessels during the winter. Stone anchors found here have been sourced to Syria and copper ingots to Cyprus. Pottery which once held wine, oil and incense came from all over the eastern Mediterranean. It includes Canaanite amphorae (▶ p. 405). The site had considerable storage capacity and was probably involved in importing and exporting on behalf of the nearby palace of Phaistos (▶ p. 257).

Figure 10.49 *Late Minoan marine-style stirrup jar*

The nature of the Minoan elite

Unlike the Near Eastern civilisations, wealth was not translated into great temples, armies or monuments to the rulers. Instead there is artistic and artefactual evidence for public rituals and possibly sports including boxing and gymnastics. While art depicts religious scenes, much of it appears to have been 'for art's sake' with imagery from nature or daily life. Luxurious rooms, exotic goods, a planned layout and some of the frescoes suggest a ruling elite, perhaps an aristocracy. The degree of specialism suggests a bureaucratic form of organisation. However, the nature of the elite which ran the palaces is puzzling. Although weapons have been found, there are relatively slight defences and no celebration of warrior kings in the manner of the later Mycenaeans. There are none of the statues or monuments to the rulers which were built in the contemporary civilisations with whom they traded. Ritual evidence, images and

continued

Figure 10.50 *Minoan 'ship-sheds' at Kommos*

the repeated symbolism of bulls and the double-headed axe or labrys suggests a priesthood, possibly dominated by priestesses. Minoan religion appears to have been polytheistic with goddesses linked to the natural world, especially plants. Rituals focused on natural places such as springs, caves and mountain peaks and appear to have involved votive offerings and sacrifices. Perhaps the population was controlled through ideology or perhaps the elite were genuinely benign – distributing resources in times of hardship.

Figure 10.51 *Ivory imports to Crete. Both raw ivory and exotic artefacts such as this ivory crocodile were imported via Egypt.*

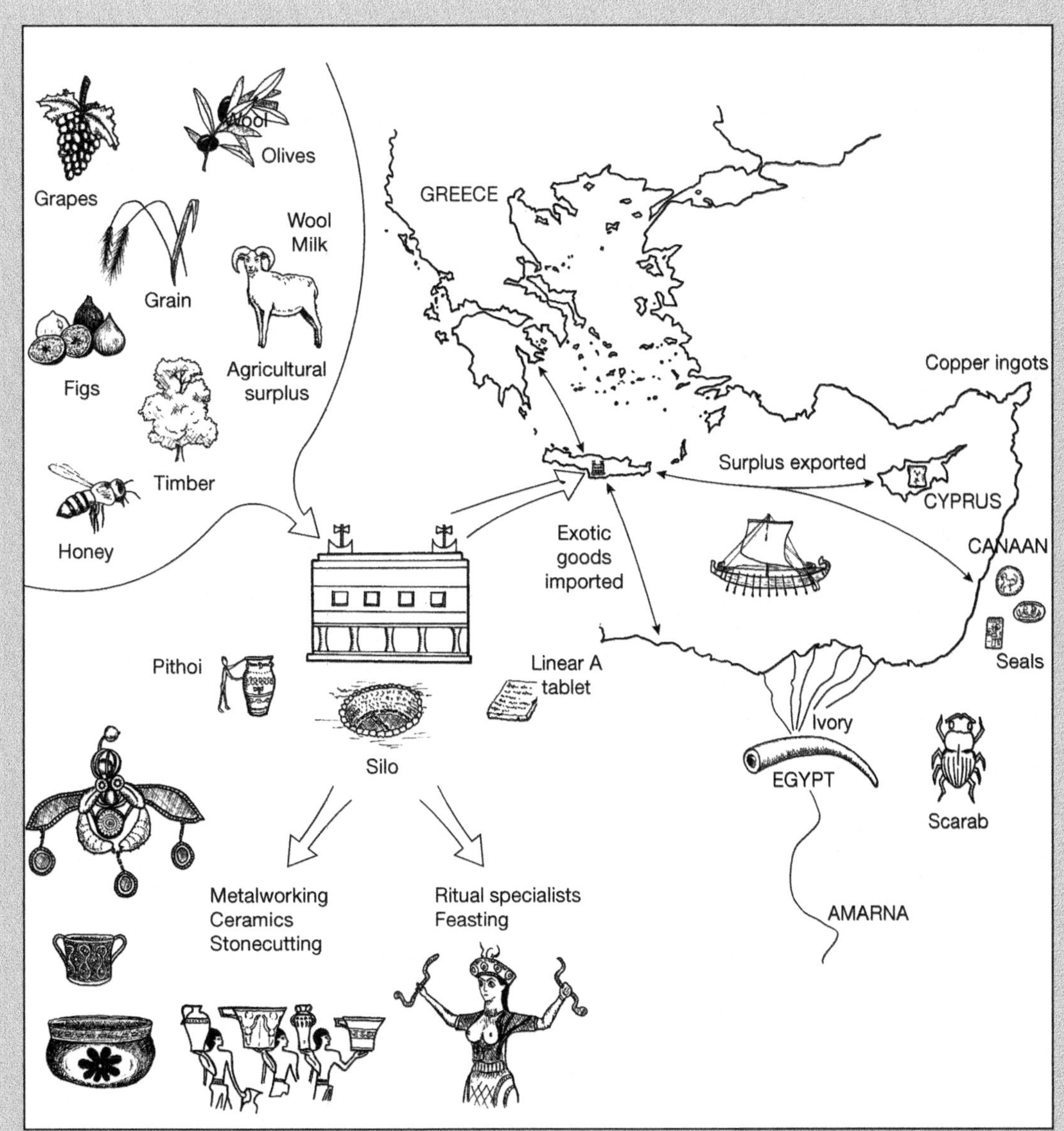

Figure 10.52 *Minoan palace economies and Mediterranean trade*

This diagram illustrates the relationship based around the palace in the centre which centralised agricultural surpluses from rural areas and used this to trade for luxury items and provide redistribution through ritual, entertainment and manufacturing. The map also identifies key sites mentioned elsewhere in this chapter.

Rival explanations

Within 1,000 years Crete developed from broadly egalitarian and self-sufficient farming communities to the elaborate architecture and luxuries of the palaces. Some archaeologists (Cherry 1983) think there

continued

was a more revolutionary change *c.* 2000 BC. The dominant explanation since Evans' excavation of Knossos was based on an influx of immigrants or ideas bringing civilisation from Syria or Egypt in the early Bronze Age. While there was trade with both regions and visible influences in technology and design, the Minoan palaces differed significantly from the empires of the Near East including the absence of massive defences, temples and tombs. There are also innovative features in the palaces such as light wells. Nowicki's (2002) variant on the external argument is based on the emergence of over one hundred new settlements *c.* 3000 BC. These were often in harbour or defensive locations and are similar to settlements in the Dodecanese islands and Anatolia. Recent DNA research (Hughey et al. 2013) which compared Minoan burials with modern populations found little evidence of gene inflow from Egypt. The Minoans were closer to populations in the Aegean. There are particularly strong links between Minoan DNA and the modern population of the Lasithi Plateau in Crete.

Renfrew (1972) presented a counter view based largely on indigenous development. He argued that chiefdoms evolved in the late Neolithic because of redistribution. He linked this to the introduction of vines and olives, which he believed led to greater agricultural specialisation. Palaces developed as a central place to store and redistribute surpluses from different areas. Van Andel and Runnels (1988) developed this model to include craft specialisation and trade goods. Renfrew's view has been criticised because there is no hard evidence of an altruistic elite or detailed information about tree crops. Farmers are more likely to have diversified rather than specialised in new crops. A variation on the redistributive model (Halstead 1981b) suggested that farmers invested their surplus centrally in a form of social storage (▶ p. 400) so that they could call on support from others when crops failed. Certainly arboriculture (tree crops) is likely to have had an impact. This can significantly raise productivity as well as introducing new tradable commodities such as oil and wine but takes many years to mature and deliver a payback on initial efforts. It is likely to have changed attitudes to land ownership and may have amplified wealth differences between families. Equally, the development of prestige goods exchange networks may have enabled some households to outstrip others in terms of wealth – perhaps making their settlements the focus of storage and competitive display (Tomkins amd Schoep 2010).

The Minoan sequence

Arthur Evans, the excavator of Knossos, established a relative chronology for Minoan Crete based on ceramic styles (e.g. Early Minoan EM I, II, III) which he cross-dated (▶ p. 146) against Egyptian imports. His terms remain in use today, although there is no agreement about calendar dates and phases.

Conclusions

Emerging evidence supports the idea of many palace elements being rooted in earlier Cretan phases. Elements of the layout of the courtyard indicate that Knossos may date from the final Neolithic, suggesting that such locations were already important. Knossos was already used for ritual or feasting. Conspicuous and competitive consumption from the same period points to the development of a ranked society. Luxury imports arrived from abroad as early as the EM II period (Colburn 2008). These were mainly items of personal adornment and they were placed, showing wear from being worn, in rich burials. Some artefacts were symbols of power in the cultures from which they came. Colburn (2008) argues that these were used by competing elites to consolidate their status. EM II is also the period where pithoi were first used. However, large-scale central stores and large pithoi with a capacity of over 150 litres only appeared after 1900 BC.

The Minoans tapped into a developing international trade in luxuries across south-west Asia which included spices, incense and precious stones such as lapis lazuli from Afghanistan. Elite households, specialisation and prestige goods exchange all developed before the palaces but the palaces saw the volume and complexity of trade reach new levels. Following Minoan Crete, palace economies developed at many points around the Mediterranean. However, the tipping point where a hetrarchy of competing families shifted to a hierarchical society run from a few palaces remains subject to debate.

Neolithic c. 7000–3300 BC	Agriculture developed by 6000 BC through immigrants from the islands to the north. Some exchange with these islands, particularly for obsidian. Cave sites are a focus for ritual.
Final Neolithic c. 3300–3000 BC	Settlement begins to expand into the uplands. Some coastal sites appear to be based on trade rather than farming. Introduction of tree crops and animal traction via islands to the north. Competition for status is evident through more visible burials. Household production of ceramics but there is an increase in quality. Many new settlements around 3000 BC.
Early Minoan I & II (Bronze Age) 3000–2300 BC	Major advances in ceramics including painted and burnished wares and innovative shapes. The potter's wheel was in use by 2300 BC. Increasing evidence of trade at harbour sites of Poros and Mochlos with metal and stone imported and Cretan pottery exported. Larger (tholos) tombs with some rich burials. A limited number of sites have concentrations of prestige goods. Increasing evidence of specialised workshops for metalworking. New techniques of stone and seal carving and faience making imported from Near East. Growth of some very large agricultural centres including Knossos and Malia. Some have public spaces where later courtyards would be built.
Pre-palatial EM III/Middle Minoan I 2300–1900 BC	Intensification of most of the trends in EM II with specialist smelting sites, advances in metallurgy (granulation) and the development of a Minoan script. The adoption of the sail and appearance of Egyptian imports (particularly in tombs) expand the prestige network. Pithoi are developed to expand storage.
Proto-palatial (old palace) MM II 1900–1650	Monumental buildings at Knossos, Malia and Phaistos which increasingly dominate their regions as storage, trade and craft production are centralised in the palaces. Palaces become a focus for ritual. Kamares ware is widely exported. A major port develops at Kommos. Palaces are destroyed around 1700 BC possibly by earthquakes.
Neo-palatial MMIII 1650–1450	Rebuilding of some palaces and emergence of others such as Agia Triada. Continued developments in crafts culminating in Marine ware. Evidence of a shift in exchange from Egypt and towards Mycenae. Evidence of more extreme forms of religion.
Post-palatial Late Minoan	Knossos and most palaces destroyed and Crete comes under Mycenaean control.

Figure 10.53 *The Minoan sequence*

POWER AND SOCIAL CONTROL

Power is the ability to make others do what you want. It can be through the use or threat of force, personal charisma or authorised through politics or religion. It can be inferred, but not proved, from evidence of mobilisation. It may also be inferred from great wealth, fortified structures or evidence of military organisation. In some cases such as Egypt or the Maya the ideological control exerted by the pharaohs or Maya shaman-kings is illustrated in art on artefacts and temple walls which link their positions to the gods (▶ p. 521). Typically the more powerful figures are also larger and wear more elaborate costumes. Their subjects, or those they have defeated, are smaller and sometimes depicted naked and bowed or lying face down. Certain artefacts are interpreted as symbols of power which legitimised the power of a ruler. These include crowns (▶ p. 439), sceptres (▶ p. 425) and maces (▶ p. 440). Slave chains and dungeons provide striking illustrations of the power of one person over another. Writing systems which document laws or tax and tribute (▶ p. 415) are testimony to the institutionalisation of power relationships between rulers and ruled.

Figure 10.54 *Smiting scene from Medinet Habu*

In a strikingly similar scene to the palette of Narmer (▶ p. 440), Pharaoh Rameses II is shown about to dash out his prisoners' brains with a mace. The iconography for depicting a powerful ruler had become standardised over 3,000 years.

Exploitative relationships between different societies are sometimes interpreted using social science models particularly from World Systems Theory. For example, Rome was a 'core' area in relation to Iron Age Britain, which was a 'periphery' area. Rome was technologically and militarily more advanced and its large urban populations constantly required raw materials and exotic items from a much wider region than its empire. Much of this was acquired through trade networks and some from raiding. The periphery (Britain) was a source of raw minerals, slaves, textiles and grain, for which local rulers received fine manufactured goods such as tableware and exotic foodstuffs, particularly wine. This exchange relationship is one-sided with the core benefiting most. Often an intermediate semi-periphery zone develops which benefits as middlemen in exchanges and is also influenced by the core. This has been used to explain the rise of warrior chiefdoms, raiding and feasting in central Europe and also what Cunliffe (1995) termed the 'bow wave effect' in southern Britain prior to the Roman invasion. Here, local chiefs imported Roman luxuries and perhaps became romanised while exploiting their neighbours inland. The Welwyn burial (▶ p. 545) is a possible example. A danger with such models is that they can lead to assumptions about innovation only going in one direction and that the periphery is somehow backward. These assumptions were prevalent amongst early C20th archaeologists who assumed that change always flowed from the Mediterranean, as in early theories about the origin of Stonehenge. As Figure 10.55 illustrates, there were other sources of influence in the 3rd millennium BC besides the Mediterranean, including Corded Ware Culture and burial practices and the Atlantic Bell-Beaker Culture.

Social conflict

Social conflict involves a struggle between individuals or groups for power or status. Warfare, armed conflict between social groups, is

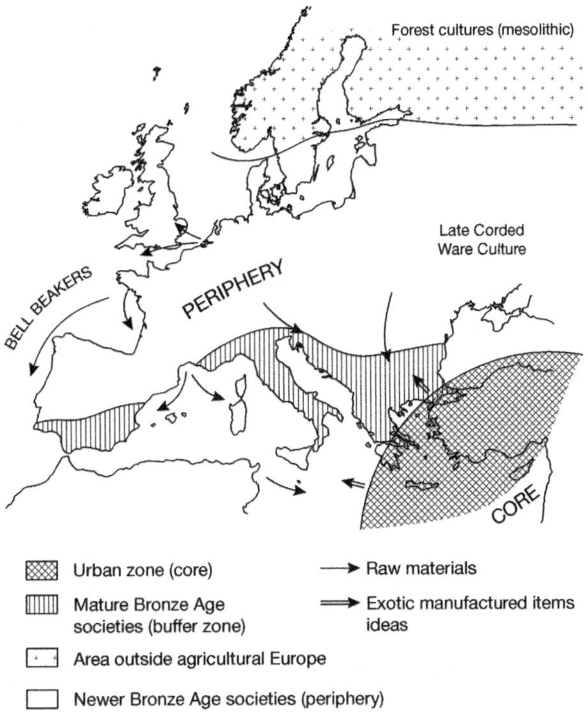

Figure 10.55 *Core and periphery*

Figure 10.56 *Water tower from Vukovar. The house on the left remains riddled with bullet holes from the Serb-Croat conflict of the 1990s. The shell-blasted tower stands as a monument to the defence of the town.*

an example but not all social conflict is violent. Probably its most common form is competition in either display or conspicuous consumption (▶ p. 443). This could include evidence of feasting, personal ornamentation, lavish funerals, elaborate buildings and monuments. Modern society is no different in this respect. Tilley (1996) suggested that developments in the design of Swedish passage graves might have been the product of local competitive emulation. Other writers have come to similar conclusions about the henges of Wessex.

WARFARE

Archaeology is concerned with identifying evidence of warfare and particularly its nature. This includes identifying the participants, motives, weapons, tactics and outcomes. The form of warfare has varied enormously. Warfare in Iron Age Britain, for example, might look more like a cattle raid than pitched battle between rival armies, at least until the Romans arrived. Archaeologists study warfare using weapons, human remains, fortifications, spatial distributions of finds and features on battlefields, stratigraphic evidence of burning or abandonment and from art (▶ p. 440). Skeletons may display unhealed traumas including cuts and depressions caused by crushing. They may also have projectiles embedded in bone. Mutilation, mass graves or signs that bodies were left unburied and scavenged are also potential indicators. Examples include the 'war grave' at Maiden Castle with its famous iron

Figure 10.57 *Memorial to the dead from the Battle of the Somme at Thiepval*

ballista bolt embedded in a defender's spine, or the mass grave at Towton from AD 1461. Here, forensic archaeologists subjected the skeletal remains to the same tests as a murder enquiry in order to identify how each injury was caused. The exact location and sequence of the battle is also being revealed by fieldwalking and plotting metal detecting finds. Towton shows how archaeology can add to and test written sources, many of which are vague or unreliable. Similar research has been carried out at the site of the Battle of the Little Bighorn (AD 1876) and Culloden (AD 1746). Some major battlefields, such as those of the First World War, are well known and precisely recorded on maps and monuments. Other sites are disputed or lost, which hampers the ability of military archaeologists to understand them. Brunaburgh (AD 937), where King Athelstan won the crucial battle which led to the formation of England, has been claimed for locations from Cheshire to Northumberland.

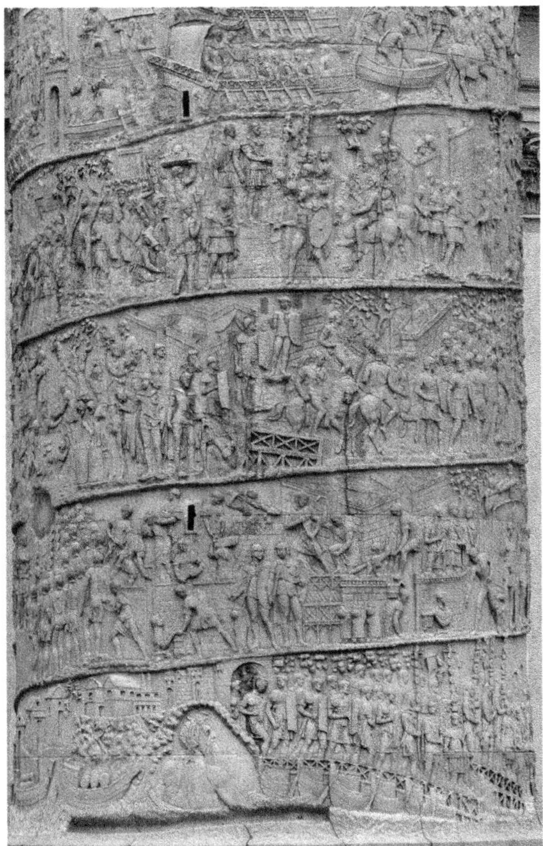

Figure 10.58 *Detail from Trajan's Column*

The use of monuments to glorify the role of individuals is known from throughout the classical world. The glorification of the campaigns of the Emperor Trajan against the Dacians on Trajan's Column in Rome (AD 113) shows in tremendous detail the equipment and organisation involved in the campaign. It provides key insights into Roman tactics, clothing and the role of new specialists such as engineers.

Understanding warfare in prehistory

The absence of unmistakeable weapons before the Bronze Age has sometimes led to claims that warfare was absent. Rousseau, the C18th philosopher, was particularly influential with his depiction of 'natural man' who lived in a 'state of nature' and only developed jealousy, greed and evil with the development of property. He based his view on contemporary peoples who were then coming into contact with Europeans and whom he felt were uncorrupted by civilisation. Others developed the idea of the noble savage and it continues to influence views of both small-scale societies and prehistory. Gimbutas (▶ p. 458) used the absence of weapons to underpin her theory that Balkan Neolithic society was peaceful. Biological and zoological evidence has been claimed to support both peace and war but recent comparative ethnographic studies and archaeological discoveries have tended to suggest that violent conflict began much earlier than the Bronze Age.

Keeley's (1996) historic and ethnographic survey established that warfare occurred in over 90 per cent of known societies with the main exceptions being very isolated groups, particularly nomads. Battles between armies are rare. Most warfare is raiding for goods, people, animals or simply to destroy rivals. This form of warfare was more common (yearly in most

Figure 10.59 *Bronze Age halberds*

There is a debate over the functionality of the halberd due to the way it was riveted to a shaft but trials by O'Flaherty (2007) suggest that it was one of the first specifically designed weapons rather than simply an adaptation of an existing tool. It may have retained a ceremonial role after the development of swords.

Native American societies) and around twenty times more deadly than modern warfare (Keeley 1996). Torture, execution, mutilation and massacre are all well documented in societies prior to contact with European society. Prehistoric warfare was particularly deadly because it was mainly fought face to face with brutally efficient tools, particularly clubs and axes. This was well illustrated by the excavation of a mass grave in a ditch at Crow Creek village in Nebraska where a population of at least 489 were massacred in AD 1325. Their attackers broke through fortifications to slaughter the men, women and children in the village using clubs and arrows, scalping and mutilating them (Willey and Emerson 1993). Gnaw marks on the bones suggests they were initially left unburied while their village was burnt. Young women were under-represented amongst the dead, which suggests that they were taken by the victors. The fortifications and healed injuries on bones (including grown-over arrowheads) implies that warfare was common. Some bones showed signs of previous malnutrition, which has led some archaeologists to suggest climate change and population pressure as a reason for genocide, while others see it as conflict over land. Evidence from Danish Ertebølle culture sites shows that violence was also common amongst late Mesolithic foragers. Skeletons from cemeteries including Vedbaek often have trauma injuries from blunt objects or embedded arrows. Since most arrow wounds and some fatal cuts do not leave skeletal evidence, the proportion of violent deaths was undoubtedly higher.

Neolithic warfare

Persuasive evidence of similar massacres has been found during excavation of LBK (▶ p. 346) settlements in central Europe from the 6th millennium BC. At Talheim thirty-four villagers were killed with stone adze blows to the left side of their skulls or shot in the back with arrows and thrown into a pit. The absence of parry-fractures

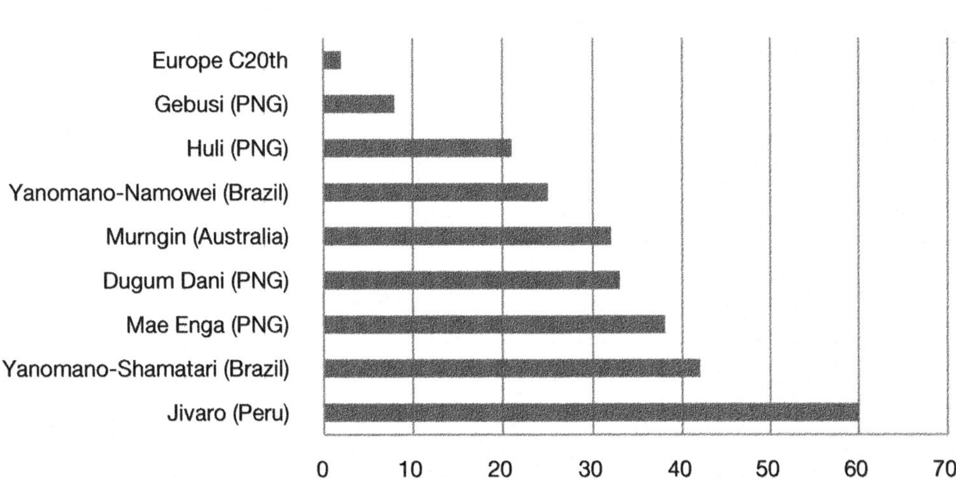

Figure 10.60 *Comparison of impact of warfare between C20th modern and small-scale societies (after Keeley 1996)*

(damage caused to the forearms when trying to ward off a blow) may mean that some were executed after capture. Isotopic analysis (Bentley et al. 2008) showed that the dead belonged to three distinct groups. One group were entirely children with no young adult females, perhaps suggesting that their mothers had been taken captive. Similar patterns were found at the contemporary site of Schletz-Asparn, where skeletal remains of sixty-seven people were recovered from a partially excavated boundary ditch. All were killed at the same time and trauma evidence indicates that adzes and clubs caused their injuries. Evidence of animal gnawing implied that they had initially been left unburied and the settlement was abandoned, suggesting genocide. The total number of dead may have been 300 but again, younger adult females are under-represented. Both Vaihingen (▶ p. 350) and the later site of Eulau (▶ p. 116) display similar features. Golitko and Keeley's (2007) review of published LBK sites found that most had enclosure ditches, many with V-shaped profiles around 2m wide and 1.5m deep. These may be defences but other archaeologists have interpreted them as stock enclosures or ritual boundaries (Whittle 1996). Golitko and Keeley (2007) note that most enclosures and most evidence of violence occurred on the frontiers as the farmers expanded their territory or later in the western part of the LBK culture where there was particularly dense settlement. Here over 30 per cent of skeletons show signs of violence. Ethnography suggests a wide range of potential motives for early conflicts, including land, raiding for cattle, women or slaves, prestige and revenge. Advances in biochemistry, such as stable isotope and DNA analysis, are starting to offer answers about who was involved and why, in ways which were unimaginable a decade ago.

Herxheim: ritual cannibalism or massacre

Not all apparent massacre sites are what they seem. At the LBK enclosure at Herxheim, skeletal remains of over 450 people were recovered. Estimates of the total number may reach 1,500. They had been dismembered and placed in pits or the perimeter ditch over a fifty-year period. Good preservation enabled detailed skeletal analysis which revealed how they had been processed (Boulestin et al. 2009). Shallow cutmarks and scrapes along the bones were the traces of defleshing. Techniques were similar to animal butchery. The skin of the head was slit from nose to neck to reveal the skull which was then cut off and broken open with the tongue removed. The rest of the body was disarticulated, defleshed and many of the long bones smashed open. Tooth marks on the bones were from either dogs or humans. The selection of particular bones suggests cannibalism. Skulls appear to have been modified and may have been trophies or artefacts. However, the reason for death is unclear in almost all cases. Pottery and lithics found in the pits came from a wide area, often up to several hundred kilometres away. The short period each pit was used suggests that these were not normal deaths from one settlement. Golitko and Keeley (2007) argue for warfare while Orschiedt and Haidle (2007) describe the site as a regional necropolis where the dead from many communities were brought for mortuary rituals. Boulestin et al. (2009) argue for ritual cannibalism since the sheer numbers and the repetitive patterns suggest that this was not simply a reaction to hunger. Funerary cannibalism related to normal deaths is unlikely due to the short time frame of site use. They conclude that the dead were either captured in a series of raids or brought to the site for sacrifice, perhaps voluntarily.

The development of weapons

The 'golden age of clubbing' using domestic axes and adzes continued into the Chalcolithic during which, Boyadzhiev (2011) argues, specialised weapons were developed. His analysis of Bulgarian artefacts suggests that drilled stone maceheads were developed specifically because their whole surface could be used to deliver crushing blows. These were followed by stone and then copper shafthole axes. All were hafted via small drilled, and later moulded, holes. This implies relatively small and short handles as in the gold sheathed example from Varna (▶ p. 423). These axe-heads were much lighter than Neolithic stone axes (▶ p. 457) and had shorter cutting edges, which eventually developed beak-like points. They were unsuitable for heavy agricultural work or carpentry but were much easier to wield in one hand during close combat. Boyadzhiev (2011) argues that light, pointed axes were developed to pierce early leather helmets which offered some protection against maces. He points out that the contexts where battle axes are found are usually male graves, particularly rich ones. By contrast, heavier woodworking axes and adzes are also found in settlements. Some children were buried with miniature shafthole axes, which suggests that they had a symbolic importance, perhaps associating maleness with warriors. Metal battle axes continued to develop and become more elaborate in their decoration into the Bronze Age. They were joined in the later 3rd millennium BC by daggers, metal spear tips and by slashing swords once smiths had found ways of overcoming the brittleness of long blades. Swords have no domestic or agricultural use and were clearly for use in combat. Analysis of blades has shown that many have damage associated

Figure 10.61 *Bronze Age Greek-style armour*

KEY STUDY

Military technology and organisation: the Illerup Hoard

In the film *Gladiator*, the Roman General Maximus defeated Germanic tribesmen in a battle of AD 180. The nature and equipment of the Roman army is well known, but what of the 'barbarians'? Often the impression we get is of a mass of recklessly brave but disorganised amateur warriors. The army hoard from Illerup, Denmark, challenges that view.

Excavation

Land drainage of a bog on the site of a prehistoric lake in the 1950s was stopped because of the numbers of swords and spears being churned up. A detailed survey and re-excavation of 40 per cent of the site in the 1970s revealed a 200m by 400m area packed with finds. These finds extended well out into the lake – too far to have been thrown. Rope and textile impressions in the rust on the weapons suggested that bundles of weapons had been taken out by boat and deposited. Many different groups of weapons could be linked where pieces of one artefact occurred in two or more heaps. These deposits were contemporary with one another. Excavating these remains, which were structured like a giant game of pick-up-sticks, was a tremendous challenge. Everything had to be kept wet while detailed recording was

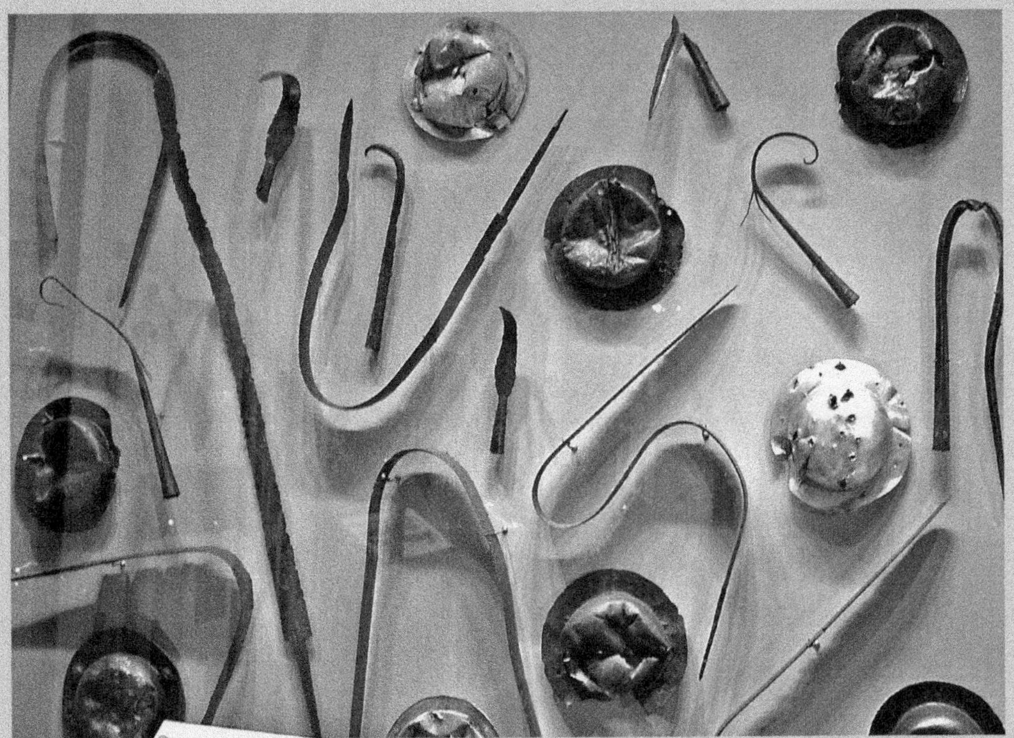

Figure 10.62 *The Illerup Hoard – some of the sacrificed war booty*

continued

made prior to removal. For complex 'heaps' a box was dug in around the finds and a wooden base pushed underneath. This enabled micro-excavation in a lab and X-raying of the soil matrix to locate tiny finds.

Artefacts

Over 15,000 items of metal, wood and bone have been recovered and dated to *c.* AD 200. In Scandinavia (not invaded by the Romans) this was the later Iron Age. These and contemporary finds demonstrate considerable contacts with the Roman world. Glass, bronze and silver reached Scandinavia with amber, fur, textiles, slaves and mercenaries probably travelling in the opposite direction. Amongst the weapons were hundreds of spears, all smashed but uniformly made from split and planed ash heartwood. A concave shaft-plane for repairs was also found. A total of 748 iron lances and 661 barbed spearheads were recovered. The design of these throwing and thrusting weapons tended to change every thirty years or so. This enabled separate deposits to be relatively dated. No warrior seems to have been using old 'inherited' weapons and the forging technology used to produce them was complex. Two of the spear-blades were stamped 'Wagnijo', a name that has been found on blades elsewhere in the Baltic. Was this the name of a war-leader or a manufacturer? Although the Romans banned the export of high-quality weapons, they frequently recruited 'barbarians' to their armies. Was this evidence of someone who had served the Romans and brought the knowledge of their smiths back with him? Over 150 of the swords were two-edged Roman-style weapons designed for both cutting and thrusting. Several were inlaid with images of Mars or Victoria and some had Roman makers' stamps. One of them bore the words 'Nithijo ordered made' in the earliest Norse writing yet found. While most sword blades had locally made hilts including some of ivory, there were some with ornate Roman hilts including one made of gold and silver. For each sword there were three to four sets of throwing weapons.

Survival of over 400 wooden shields enabled a TPQ of AD 207 to be established. Shields were manufactured from thin boards of alder or oak with metal rims and boss. They may also have had an organic backing but this has not survived. Many had been painted red and often had silver or gold inlay. Although leather has not survived, the position of metal fittings enabled the reconstruction of over 300 military belts. These were worn outside tunics and fastened with large iron buckles. Rust impressions of cloth match the weave on contemporary woollen trousers and tunics found at other sites. Hanging from mountings on the belt would have been the essentials of campaign life. These included a knife, fire-starting kit, repairing tools and a leather purse. This contained the most personal possessions. Contents included beads, coins, razors, tweezers, lucky charms and combs. Danish combs tend to be made from deer antler, but most of those found were elk or reindeer and of a design more common in Norway.

Figure 10.63 *Spearhead stamped with the name Wagnijo*

Military organisation

The sophistication of the weapons and the degree of standardisation suggests that some war leaders had their own arsenals with specialist weapon smiths and professional soldiers. The scale of the battle suggests that it was not opportunistic raiding but part of a power struggle during which a largely Norwegian army was defeated. At this time in Scandinavia dynasties of regional kings were emerging and vying for supremacy. These conflicts were made possible by the development of sea-going vessels in the Baltic and can be seen as precursors to later raids on Britain by what were in later centuries called the Vikings.

Figure 10.64 A warrior's possessions

Figure 10.65 Military organisation at Illerup

continued

A common conception of Dark Age armies is that they were undisciplined raiders. However, the Roman view of these barbarians was somewhat different. Tacitus described clear lines of authority amongst the Germans and the control of weapons by powerful leaders. Analysis of the artefacts also seems to support a hierarchical, specialist organisation. Amongst these finds there were clear signs of a specialist, military hierarchy. There were sixty highly decorated baldrics or sword belts, sixteen of which appeared to be Roman. Fittings were either bronze or silver. There were also twelve sets of military equipment for horses. Only six shields have gold or silver bosses and ornamentation, around forty were bronze while the majority were iron. There were similar proportional differences in the quality of weaponry. It seems that there were a handful of leaders, a second rank of about forty well-equipped soldiers and 300–400 warriors with fairly standard kit, spears and other weapons. The Roman Orosius recorded a ritual in Germany where booty was stripped from the bodies of a defeated army and sacrificed by ritual destruction before being deposited in a lake. This may be what happened at Illerup. The sacrificed war booty probably represents the defeat of a semi-professional Norse army of 500–1,000 warriors.

Further down the Illerup Valley in the Alken Enge (▶ p. 118) wetlands the remains of an army from around AD 0 are being recovered. While post-ex work is ongoing, the current hypothesis is that the bones were brought to the lake after disarticulation and possibly decomposition. The Roman writer Tacitus reported the bodies of slain armies being left unburied. It is conceivable that these bones were collected from such a battlefield and brought to this place of sacrifice. Perhaps the remains of the soldiers from Illerup will one day be recovered in a similar location.

with metal-on-metal contact. The earliest metal armour (e.g. greaves to protect the legs) was developed to counter swords in the 2nd millennium BC but leather armour and wooden or leather shields were in use earlier in the Bronze Age.

State-level warfare

From the Bronze Age onwards a wider range of sources provides evidence of new aspects of warfare such as battles between organised armies, sieges and military specialists from cavalry to archers. Finds of slingshots and cemeteries of possible casualties of warfare at Tell Hamoukar and Tell Brak (▶ p. 468) from the 4th millennium BC suggest that siege warfare began soon after the founding of the first cities. The widespread enclosing of cities with walls supports this view. In literate societies, warfare is one of the first things to be documented. It seems likely that in societies with oral traditions it forms a major part of their history too. From Homer we know something of the wars of Bronze Age Greece, while medieval recording of Irish and Icelandic sagas may provide insights into Iron Age warfare in north-western Europe. Tomb paintings and inscriptions in most of the classical civilisations of Eurasia and Mesoamerica provide graphic depiction of the nature of battles.

The palace reliefs of Nimrud and Nineveh from the Assyrian Empire between the C9th and C7th BC provide excellent examples. The use of sculpture to glorify kings in war had been common practice in the region for over 2,000 years and therefore is interesting both as early propaganda and as evidence of the nature of early Iron Age warfare. Imagery is highly stylised and intended to impress and intimidate. Kings are depicted larger than other people and sometimes as high priests linked to the gods. Other high-ranking people have squared-off beards and net

Figure 10.66 *Assyrian cavalry trampling their vanquished foes at the Battle of Til Tuba, c. 653 BC*

skirts. Eunuchs, who provided many of their officials, have no beards. The strength of rulers was emphasised through scenes of them hunting lions. Ashurnasirpal (reigned 883–859 BC) boasted in inscriptions of having killed 450.

The fate of those who resisted him was depicted in scenes of flaying, impaling and beheading. The cartoon strip-style reliefs of military campaigns were also subject to conventions. The sculptures all show well-equipped Assyrians trampling their foes under their chariots, beheading their leaders and bringing booty back to Assyria. No Assyrians were shown dead. While clearly propaganda, they provide unwitting evidence – evidence that was not deliberately distorted – about clothing, technology and tactics. We see chariots, siege towers and inflatable skins being used to cross a river. We can distinguish the lightly armed Aramaic forces who fought alongside the Assyrians from other types of military units. The range of weapons including bows, spears and slings is evident, as is the way they were used. Soldiers are shown holding tall wooden or reed shields as cover while others fire slingshots and arrows from behind them. The origin of the phrase 'taking a head count' is suggested in depictions of the aftermath of victory.

Fortifications

Fortifications provide insights into the changing nature of defensive warfare as well as displays of power and physical means of domination and control. From simple ditches and palisades, massive and complex fortifications developed to counter cavalry, archers and sieges. Playing card-shaped marching camps such as Chew Green in the Cheviots plot the advance of Roman legions and their discipline in taking precautions in hostile territory. Permanent stone fortifications such as Hadrian's Wall provide evidence of more static warfare and the holding of territory. Increasingly sophisticated designs enabled relatively small numbers of defenders to hold out against overwhelming odds. Norman castles developed from early earth and wood motte and bailey castles which provided

Figure 10.67 *Nazi Atlantic Wall fortifications – note shell damage from D-Day*

temporary protection to stone keeps such as Orford and were impregnable to all but the best-equipped attackers. Further adaptations included fighting platforms, arrow slits and barbicans. The response to the development of gunpowder weapons was lower and often angled walls, themselves screened by earth berms (banks) to prevent direct hits by cannonballs on masonry. The surviving shell holes and trenches of First World War battlefields testify to the power of mechanised weapons, specifically machine guns and artillery.

Of course, not everything that looks military may indicate warfare. Both weapons and fortifications can be symbolic. Fortifications can also mislead us about the nature of warfare. 'Hillforts' with their massive circuits of ramparts suggest sieges. There is evidence of attack at a few but these are exceptions. A similar bias would occur if we looked at the major physical evidence of warfare between France and Germany in 1940. The Maginot Line, bypassed by the Germans, is still visible, while traces of the aircraft and mobile tank and infantry formations which bypassed it are harder to discern. Equally, evidence of weapons and fortifications does not mean conflict took place. For example, Blue Streak nuclear rockets were never fired from their silos at RAF Spadeadam in Northumberland.

Finding evidence of resistance to social control in the archaeological record is difficult. It can be inferred from the establishment of fortifications to 'hold down' a population including Roman forts and motte and bailey castles. It is also implicit in the reliefs of the Assyrian kings or the smiting scenes of Egyptian pharaohs. Both were intended

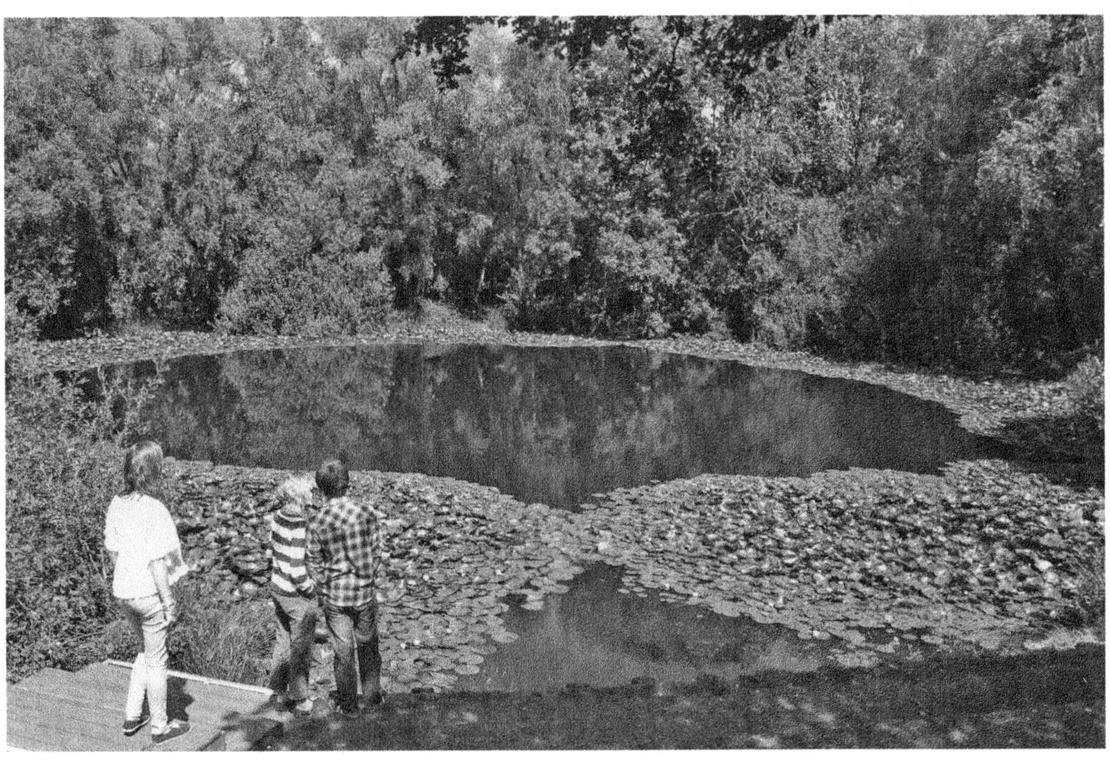

Figure 10.68 *Not a pond but Spanbroekmolen (Lone Tree) crater, France, caused by tonnes of explosives fired in a mine 76m below at the battle of Messines in 1917*

Figure 10.69 *Blue Streak test-firing platforms, RAF Spadeadam*

Figure 10.70 *Oradour sur Glane*

to remind populations of the perils of rebellion. One of the most poignant reminders of resistance is the small French town of Oradour sur Glane, where the population was massacred and the town devastated by Nazi troops in 1944 as a reprisal for French Resistance operations.

POPULATION

Demographic information about past populations is largely obtained from human remains. Where there are large collections from cemeteries they can reveal information about health (▶ p. 112) and population size as well as common illnesses and injuries. DNA offers the opportunity to explore relationships between people and to determine how homogenous any population was. It has also been critical in tracing the evolution of humans. Artistic sources and preserved bodies can fill in details of appearance.

Estimating population size

Where burials exist, attempts can be made to estimate infant mortality and adult life-expectancy. From this attempts can be made to map the age and sex population pyramids and to estimate birth and death rates. Projections about the average size of the population can then be attempted. These methods have been used to estimate world populations by modelling growth rates from the original modern human population over the last 120,000 years. Estimates for human populations before agriculture vary between 1 and 10 million worldwide with most accounts opting for a stable population averaging 3–5 million. By the late Iron Age, estimates exceed 200 million with the Roman Empire holding up to a quarter of the total. For periods where burial evidence is sparse, including much of prehistory, estimates can be based on the carrying capacity of the land. This method was originally used to work out likely population levels of animal species within a given environment. It relies on accurate reconstruction of past ecosystems and transferring ethnographic patterns of population. Archaeologists model different strategies such as foraging or horticulture to work out what maximum density of human population could have been sustained.

For urban areas researchers usually multiply the area of settlement by an average figure for density. This is simple but subject to a wide variety of errors. Ethnographic averages for the amount of space each person needs have been used to produce standard estimates such as ten square metres per person. This is then multiplied up by overall area to project the numbers of inhabitants. However, cultures vary hugely in their use of space and typical household size, both of which impact on density in any particular case. In addition there are many urban areas where the full size of the town is not known. A second method is to multiply an estimate of the number of houses with an average household size. This excludes unoccupied space but can still be distorted by alternative uses of buildings (e.g. workshops) and family size. In some urban centres, particularly those in walled medieval towns where building space was limited, much housing was very crowded with subdivisions being common. This produces a much higher occupation density than average. Excavation bias is also a factor. Archaeology has tended to focus on high-status buildings at the centre of ancient towns which are atypical. More balanced excavation and an understanding of specific local and cultural factors is likely to be the key to successful estimation.

Minoan Crete exemplifies the challenge facing archaeologists in estimating population size. Most attention has been given to palaces rather than surrounding town houses or rural settlements. Whitelaw noted that similar-sized houses were a feature of the smaller towns such as Gournia. He inferred from this regularity that nuclear family units of five or six people were the residential norm. In the central areas of the larger towns such as Knossos, large dwellings clustered around the palaces. Even with the addition of servants, these would not be as densely settled as Gournia or the outlying districts of Knossos. He also found that there were fairly consistent ratios between the amount of space devoted to public buildings (the palace complexes), streets and open areas and residential areas. Using this data he created average densities appropriate for this civilisation of up to 225 people/hectare and estimated the population of Knossos to be 14–18,000. Branigan used a similar model to project a population for the whole island of Crete. His figure of around 80,000 in rural areas and 58,000–78,000 in urban areas gives a figure not far below the 175,000 counted by the Venetians in the first attempt at a

Figure 10.71 *Gournia, a small Minoan town*

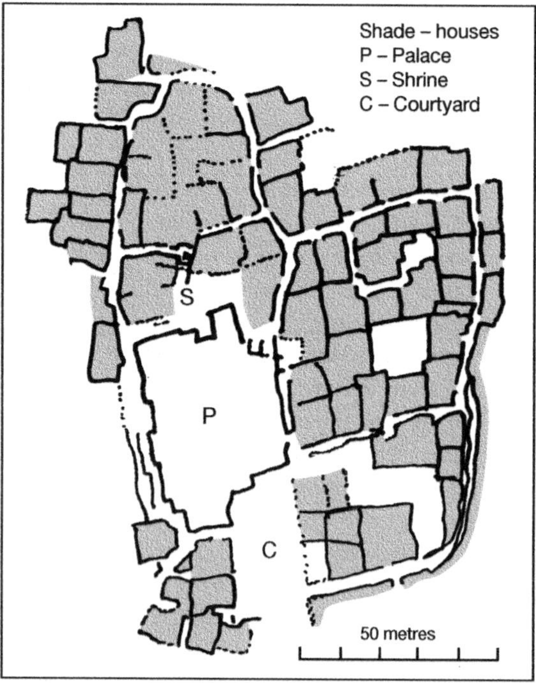

Figure 10.72 *Plan of Gournia*

census in AD 1534. Branigan and other researchers all project that 40–60 per cent of the population lived in urban areas.

An alternative approach is to project backwards from historic periods. However, the earliest recorded figures are guesstimates based on the impressions of travellers or soldiers and may be exaggerated for impact back home. Early historical estimates of population are notoriously unreliable because they are usually based on tax assessments which focused on particular (taxable) elements rather than numbers of people; for example, the Domesday Survey. In addition many surveys have only partially survived. Another approach is to use age and sex information from tombstones. More recently, computer modelling using DNA variations and estimates of the rate of mutations has been used to back-project past population size.

ETHNICITY

Ethnicity and race have the same relationship as sex and gender. One of each pair is in our DNA, the other is in our heads. Racially we are all Homo sapiens but ethnicity consists of cultural norms and values that differentiate one social group from another. Physical differences are sometimes, but not always, used to distinguish different ethnic groups. From the early C20th, culture history (▶ p. 147) approaches to archaeology dominated interpretations. Groups (assemblages) of recurring traits including artefact design and

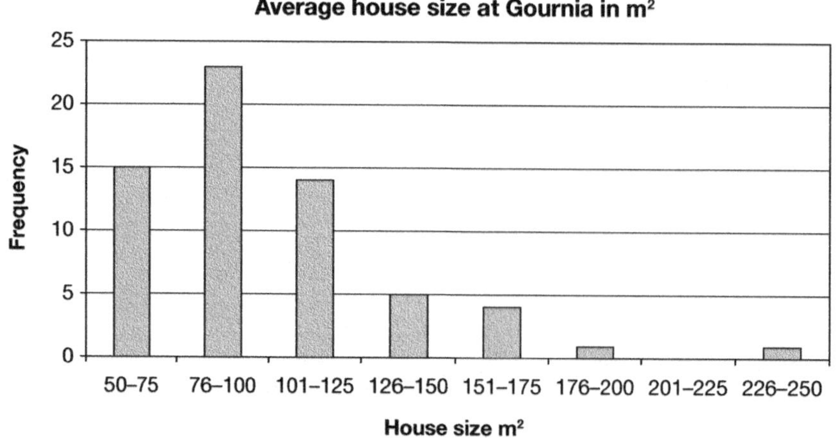

Figure 10.73 *Minoan houses by area*

Figure 10.74 *Tombstone of Sextus Valerius Genialis from Cirencester*

This cavalryman and citizen of Corinium from AD 60 is shown defeating a 'dying Gaul'. However, he was not from Rome but from Thrace. The Roman army was cosmopolitan. Soldiers posted to and often settling in Britain were as likely to have come from the Middle East or north of the Rhine as from Rome itself. Bulgarians and Romanians (Dacians) were living and settling in Britain 2,000 years ago.

manufacture, mortuary practice and house styles were associated with and used to distinguish different cultures. Effectively, pots were people. Culture-history (▶ p. 147) models of social change relied on diffusionist explanations and undervalued the achievements of indigenous people as in the case of Iron Age brochs (▶ p. 275). Absolute dating undermined such approaches while advances in genetics undermined the idea that pure ethnic groups existed in the past. Where expressions of ethnic allegiances relied on body decoration or the use of organic material such as textiles, evidence may not always survive.

MIGRATION AND THE ORIGINS OF POPULATIONS

Even where we know invasions took place, the archaeological record is not always helpful. For example, there is little evidence for the Norman Conquest in sequences of medieval ceramics or house styles, perhaps because this was an elite rather than mass migration. Some evidence is

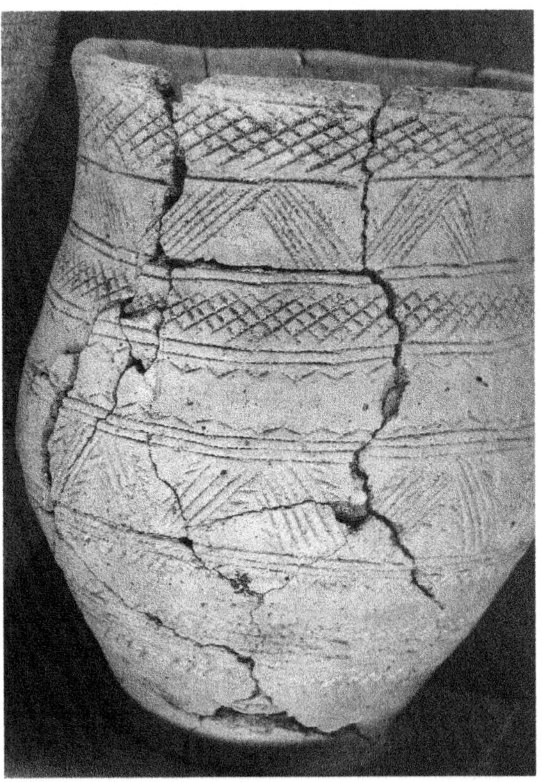

Figure 10.75 *A beaker. Does this represent the movement of a people or ideas?*

ambivalent. Belgic coins found in south-east England from the late Iron Age have been used to support Caesar's description of immigration into the area from Gaul. However, there are other ways in which the coins could reach Britain. Language (▶ p. 454) has also been a major focus of research, although there are several mechanisms by which languages change, including trade and elite migration as well as population replacement. Advances in biochemistry, especially stable isotope analysis (▶ p. 133), are revolutionising archaeological studies of migration. DNA studies tracing different haplogroups (▶ p. 502) are being used to create new family trees for different population groups with estimates of the dates when they separated or moved apart.

KEY STUDY

Was there an Anglo-Saxon invasion? The evidence from three Anglo-Saxon settlements

Historical sources such as Gildas and Bede describe the slaughter or displacement of Romano-British populations in the C5th and C6th AD. Linguistic evidence supports this view. Old English, the language of the Anglo-Saxons, was a Germanic language closely related to Saxon and Frisian. The name 'English' is derived from the Angles, a people from Schleswig-Holstein, and the majority of place-names in the eastern half of Britain are English rather than Roman or Celtic. Most early excavations from this period were of burials and produced artefacts and artistic styles, especially ceramics (▶ p. 447), associated with the continent. Areas where Saxon pottery or metalwork was absent were identified as places still held by Britons.

Large-scale migration was possible by the C5th. Sea-going ships had plied the North Sea during the Roman period and the forerunners of Viking longboats were in use in the Baltic (▶ p. 408). In the likely areas for migrants to have sailed from there was also some evidence of social stress. The Saxon settlement of Feddersen Wierde on the North Sea coast had existed for 400 years before rising sea levels led to its abandonment in the C5th AD. While its inhabitants lived with their cattle in substantial longhouses, their agricultural practices and their artefacts were very similar to those that appeared in East Anglian sites. The inland site of Flögeln in Saxony was also abandoned in the C6th. Pollen evidence in the surrounding region suggests a decline in cultivation. This could be due to emigration or perhaps was the result of plague or famine. However, excavation of Anglo-Saxon settlements in England provides a more complex picture and many archaeologists now reject the idea of mass immigration.

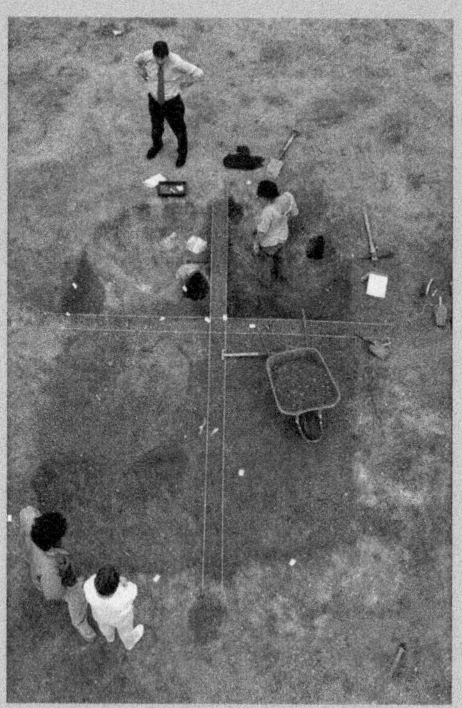

Figure 10.76 *Grubenhaus under excavation at Lechlade*

Figure 10.77 *Reconstructed Grubenhaus at West Stow*

One of the first Anglo-Saxon settlements to be fully investigated was excavated at West Stow, Suffolk. Traces of seven small, rectangular, plank-built 'halls', the largest measuring approximately 10m x 4m, and sixty-nine 'Grubenhäuser' or SFBs (▶ p. 186) were discovered. All were of European style. The settlement appeared to comprise seven farms, each with a number of out-buildings. A detailed pottery typology enabled a sequence from north German pottery styles around AD 450 through to Ipswich Ware (▶ p. 447) by the C7th. This showed that not all the farms were contemporary, with only three or four existing at one time. Flotation and the recovery of 180,000 animal bones enabled a reconstruction of the economy. Fields around the village produced cereal crops including spelt wheat, which is associated with Romano-British rather than German farming. Further out, the River Lark provided fish, waterfowl, reeds for thatch and wet meadows for grazing. Higher, dry meadows were used to pasture sheep. Pigs were kept in woodland, which provided timber, firewood and foraged foods. The settlement appeared to be largely self-sufficient, although there were a few luxury items including glass beads and Red Sea cowrie shells. Contemporary settlements on the site of the nearby Romano-British town of Icklingham may have provided a market for textiles and other agricultural produce. So while cultural indicators suggest change, the economy suggests continuity. Although the inhabitants of the hamlet of West Stow may have arrived as part of Anglo-Saxon migrations, it is also possible that they were descended from a Germanic mercenary group brought over to defend the Roman estate at Icklingham. They may also have been Romano-British people who adopted continental styles.

Part of the problem with attempts to study ethnicity through material culture is the material itself. In some areas such as Oxfordshire it can be difficult to differentiate Saxon from Iron Age pottery, unless it is decorated. Where it can be identified, it sometimes turns up well before historical sources say the Saxons arrived. This may illustrate the point that ethnically distinctive material may be used

continued

Figure 10.78 *West Stow Anglo-Saxon village*

by other groups. Exchange, trade, small-scale migration or adoption and copying by indigenous people would also spread material. Finds of specific types of jewellery have been mapped to distinguish ethnic variations (Welch 1992). Cruciform brooches and symbolic keys or 'girdle hangers' are associated with female Anglian (East Anglia and Lincolnshire) burials while square-headed brooches are more frequently found at female Saxon burials (Kent, Wessex and the south Midlands). Both types of brooch, which were modelled on a Roman design, are also found in burials in Jutland and northern Germany.

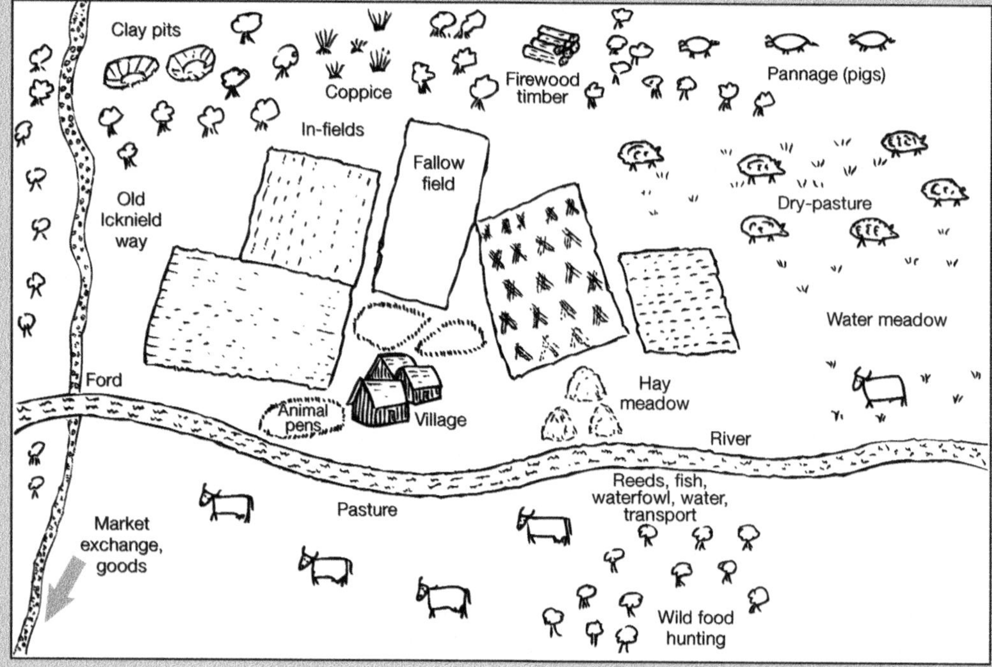

Figure 10.79 *Land use at West Stow*

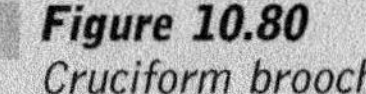

Figure 10.80
Cruciform brooch

Figure 10.81
Square-headed brooch

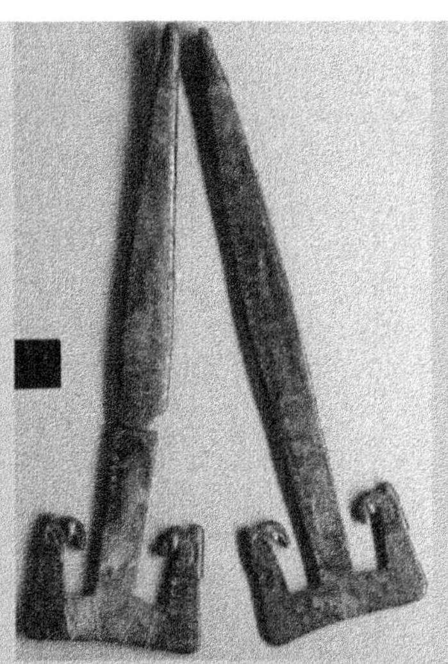

Figure 10.82
Symbolic keys – possibly indicating marital status

According to the Anglo-Saxon Chronicle, modern Gloucestershire was British until the victory of the Saxons at the battle of Dyrham in 577. However, excavations in 1985 at Lechlade provided much earlier dates for burials, with grave goods which were considered to be Saxon ethnic markers. The cemetery contained several hundred inhumations and cremations dating from the late C5th to the early C8th. Graves before AD 600 were pagan and aligned NE–SW while later Christian burials were aligned NW–SE. The long-lasting cemetery and the absence of signs of trauma on all but one skeleton do not suggest a violent period, yet the artefacts do suggest that some of those buried there were incomers. Many women had distinctive Saxon saucer brooches at their shoulders, although a few also had Romano-British brooches. Many early graves contained weapons, particularly spears and shields, but four were distinctive Anglo-Saxon one-sided swords called seaxes. In one case a child was buried with an adult spear. Weapons may have been more symbolic than a sign of warfare. Here warrior burials were not the most significant. The richest burial, a female dubbed 'Mrs Getty', was one of the wealthiest known from the C6th (▶ p. 450). Grave 11, another high-status grave, was of a 5- to 6-year-old child buried with jewellery and metal feasting containers. A local chiropodist examined the feet of the skeletons and identified two main variants (Jackson 2007): narrow feet similar to Iron Age people from the locality and broader feet that may represent Saxon immigrants.

In 1997 an Anglo-Saxon village was discovered adjacent to the cemetery. Like West Stow it contained Grubenhäuser and was long-lived. Its economy was also based on mixed farming of cereals, beans and flax along with cattle and sheep (Bateman et al. 2003). There was evidence too of metalworking, weaving and leather working. However, while this is similar to West Stow, it is also very similar to the picture we get from Iron Age settlements in the vicinity 1,000 years earlier. Indeed this site had been used repeatedly for farms and houses since the Bronze Age.

At West Heslerton, Yorkshire, in the early C5th some distinctive Anglo-Saxon Grubenhäuser were built in what had been a typical Romano-British settlement. Around AD 450 this site was abandoned

continued

and a new, larger settlement replaced it a short distance away. This too combined Romano-British and Anglo-Saxon elements but was otherwise different. It included post- and plank-built buildings and a long hall. The whole site was laid out in an ordered way with distinct zones for agricultural processing, housing and industrial activity. This included bone- and metalworking and the manufacture of pottery and textiles. Imported pottery, metalwork and lava quernstones suggest some of this may have been for trade. The longevity of the site and the excavation of over 200 buildings mean that changes in construction techniques can be traced over time. A massive assemblage of around a million animal bones offers the possibility of understanding the economy and diet. Most cattle which had been butchered on the site were young adults. Mature specimens were rare, which suggested that they were being produced for market. Curiously, some of the new 'Anglo-Saxon' pottery styles were produced using Romano-British fabrics. The evidence of buildings and pottery suggested much continuity of population but the degree of planning and Scandinavian origin of the larger buildings suggested that the site had new, foreign leaders. It also had European connections, particularly with the Rhineland (▶ p. 408), from where it obtained querns, glass and ceramics.

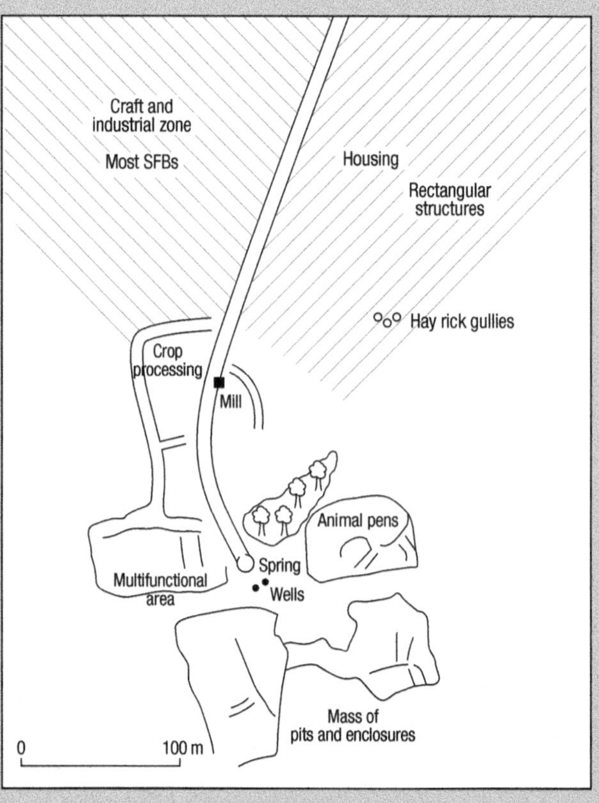

Figure 10.83 *Plan of zones at West Heslerton (after Powlesland 2000)*

Interpretations

Artefacts from burials appears to favour a mixed population. Amongst over 300 burials were many with weapons. Some of these seem to be female graves while others are individuals who do not have 'warrior' builds. This might suggest that weapons had a symbolic value rather than identifying male warriors. This may support Härke's (1990) 'warband model', where an elite of male immigrants took control of but did not replace the indigenous population rather like the Norman Invasion in 1066. Härke estimated that between 12 and 25 per cent of the population were Anglo-Saxons and these then intermarried with the more numerous British to become 'the English'. The dominant culture remained 'Anglo-Saxon'. His study of Anglo-Saxon cemeteries showed that many included Romano-Britons, thus indicating co-existence. Male burials with swords were on average 2.5–5cm taller than those without. This was not due to different diets and suggested two distinct ethnic groups. By the C7th this distinction had disappeared, probably through intermarriage. DNA analysis of several cemeteries revealed two models of Anglo-Saxon immigration. In some, complete kin groups were represented, which suggests entire communities settled here, while in others, males with weapons existed alongside females whose skeletons which showed continuity with the Romano-British period.

Oxygen and strontium isotope analysis of tooth enamel at West Heslerton also identified two distinct population groups. Most had similar profiles to prehistoric burials from the area but some were Scandinavian (Montgomery et al. 2005). This suggests that many of the Anglo-Saxons buried there were first generation immigrants. However, they included men and women and people of low social status. This does not support the elite warband model of immigration. As DNA studies become more refined, the balance in the debate has tilted away from the immigration model towards continuity. Oppenheimer's (2007) genetic study of Britain (▶ p. 503) suggested that Anglo-Saxon immigrants only contributed around 5 per cent to the national gene pool. More controversially, he argues that English was already the language of eastern Britain before the Anglo-Saxons arrived.

Where did the farmers go? The LBK and the DNA of modern Europeans

The spread of farming across Europe transformed the continent but the mechanism by which farming moved has provoked considerable debate. The original view was that it was a folk migration rather like white settlers occupying the plains of North America in the C19th. Less deliberate models include demic diffusion, where one population expands and advances a few kilometres across a frontier each generation, or leap-frog colonisation, where small numbers of pioneers move across that frontier but are surrounded by and perhaps blend with indigenous people. Pioneer English settlements in North America in the C17th fit these two models.

Figure 10.84 *Excavated LBK longhouses at Bylany (Photo Archives of the Institute of Archaeology ASCR, Prague, No. FT-40257. www.bylany.com)*

Figure 10.85 *A Linearbandkeramik settlement*

Alternatives include elite migration, where a conquering group take over and impose their culture on another group as with Norman England, and cultural diffusion, where ideas rather than people spread through exchange. In these two instances there might be little impact on the genetic make-up of the population.

Demic diffusion

The settlements and artefacts of the first farmers in the Balkans (▶ p. 339) were similar to those in Anatolia, suggesting that they were immigrants. The spread across central Europe via the Linearbandkeramik Culture (LBK) from 5500 BC to 4500 BC (▶ p. 346) involved similar domesticates but a novel culture. Most archaeologists believed that LBK farmers were also immigrant settlers who displaced the indigenous foragers. This made sense because farming was assumed to be superior to foraging (▶ p. 305). The apparently uniform nature of LBK culture and the dating of ethnic markers led Ammerman and Cavalli-Sforza (1984) to attribute the gradual pattern of expansion to demic diffusion. Agriculture enabled LBK populations to grow but this growth then created a shortage of land which was suitable for their type of farming (▶ p. 348). This push factor led to part of the population clearing parts of the forest to the west in what became short-range migration. As this process was repeated with successive generations, a series of 'waves of advance' occurred. As LBK populations expanded, the thinly distributed foraging population was gradually squeezed out.

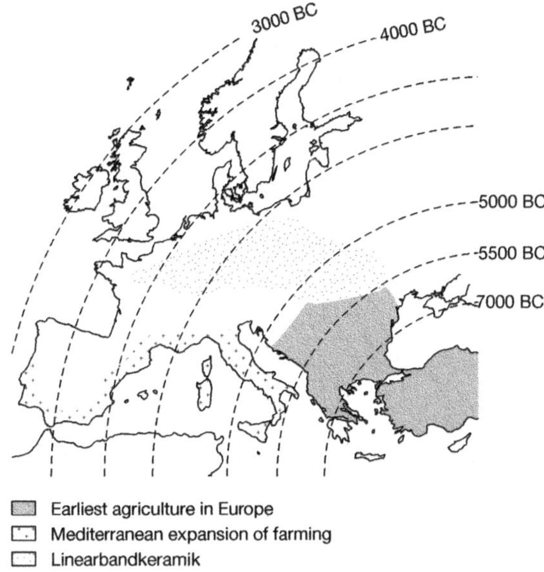

Figure 10.86 *The wave of advance theory*

Computer modelling using settlement dates shows that the spread of LBK advance averaged 1km per year. The conclusion from this model was that there was a genetic replacement of the European population by farmers. Evidence of blood groups across the continent seemed to support this conclusion. However, DNA analysis both supports and contradicts it.

Cultural diffusion

An alternative explanation was that cultural diffusion had occurred. That means the idea of farming and particular languages moved rather than the people. Analysis of LBK skeletal remains by Burger et al. (2005) showed that they had the mitochondrial DNA type N1a, which is common in Near East populations. However, it is very rare in later central Europe. This suggests an incoming group but one which did not make much genetic impact. Insufficient DNA evidence is available on earlier foragers but it seemed that either LBK farmers took forager wives or that the foragers adopted LBK farming lifestyles. Further research by Brotherton et al. (2013) discovered maternal DNA, suggesting an eastern European origin for the LBK but also suggesting that these genetic types vanished *c.* 4500 BC when LBK culture also disappeared. A pan-European study (Gibbons 2000) of the Y chromosome discovered that 80 per cent of European men could trace genetic ancestry back to foragers, which supported the idea of population continuity. However, later studies (Burger 2009) found that most of the forager DNA types were also relatively rare in modern populations. New research into the male Y chromosome (Balaresque et al. 2010) found much stronger links which suggested that 80 per cent of European men are partially descended from incoming Neolithic farmers. The current state of research suggests that there may have been a wave of advance but one that involved people who originated in eastern Europe as well as the Near East and that in the west LBK farmers interbred with indigenous foragers. Overall the genetic contribution of the farmers to the European gene pools is below 25 per cent.

Neolithic standstill

North and west of the LBK settlement zone something very different appears to have happened. LBK settlements did not reach the Baltic or Atlantic seaboard. Dating evidence suggests that there was a lull of up to a thousand years before farming spread to these areas. When this change came, the form it took was very different from that of the LBK and much less clear. Some attempts have been made to explain this focus on the limitations of the type of farming practised by the LBK. Most LBK settlements are on fertile bands of loess. Perhaps they were reluctant to risk farming on heavier clay soils, which may also have been more thickly forested. Also, since the number of frost-free days decline as you move north, arable farming was limited by the length of growing seasons. However, while loess does 'run out' in the coastal areas of north-western Europe, that region has successfully grown cereal crops since the Bronze Age. Other approaches have focused on the relatively dense forager populations of that region. The Ertebølle Culture were thriving without farming (▶ p. 309) and did not need to change. Perhaps they were hostile to incoming farmers (Isern and Fort 2010). There is evidence of violence and some LBK sites were fortified (▶ p. 350). Increasingly archaeologists studying the eventual transition to farming around the Baltic and Atlantic seaboard have rejected the idea that agriculture developed solely as a result of immigration by farmers (▶ p. 353). Instead they believe that the successful foragers of this region chose to adopt aspects of the 'Neolithic package'. The key evidence is that in this region there is continuity in some aspects of material culture and ritual practice, little evidence of houses and fields and the appearance of a variety of new ritual monuments including long barrows. The full transition to an economy based on sedentary

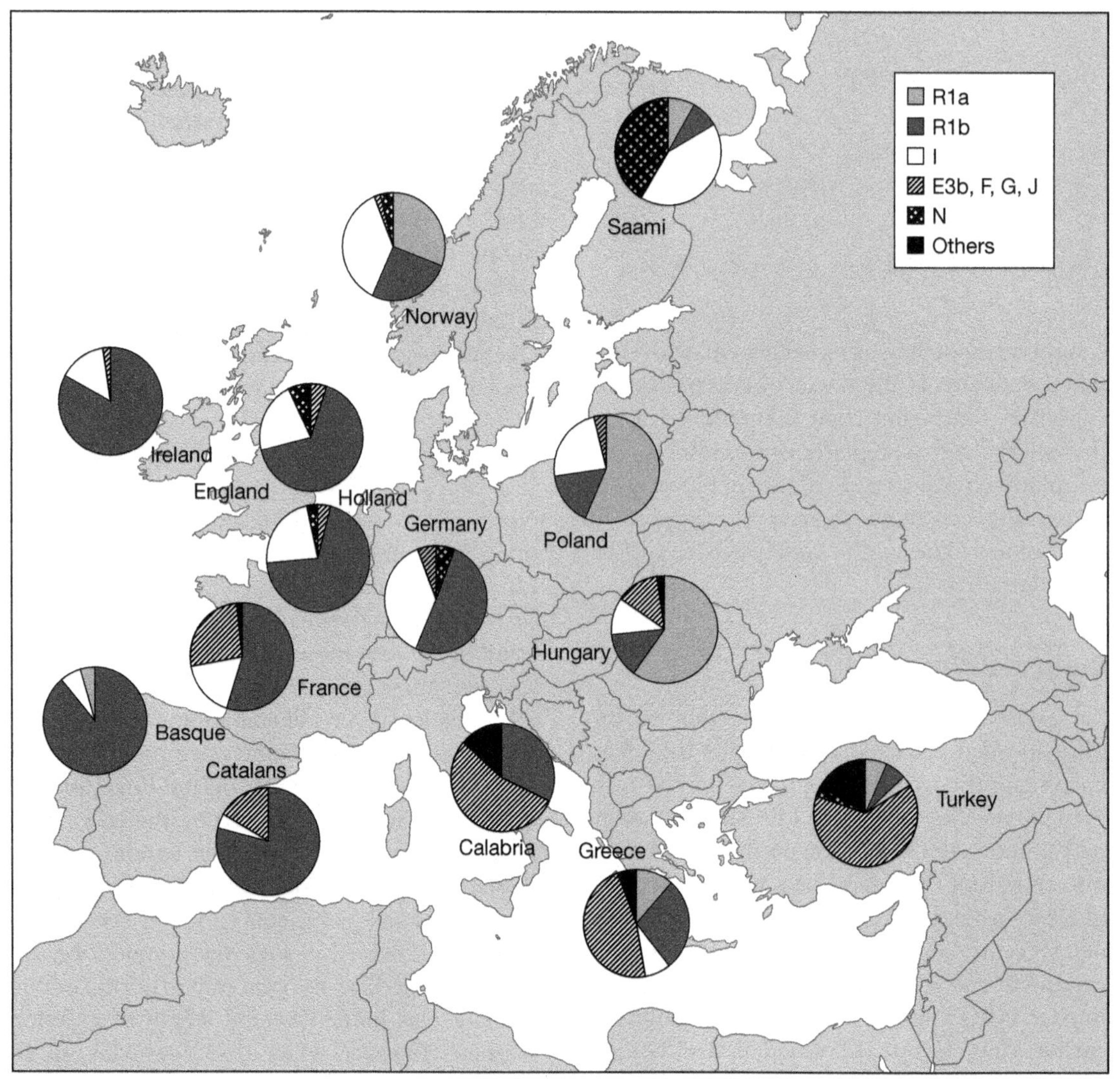

Figure 10.87 *The major European Y chromosome haplogroups*

farming appears to have then taken around another thousand years. This does not rule out some population movement but suggests that there was not a replacement of population everywhere either. The picture is further confused by research into the gene which enables the processing of milk (▶ p. 138). Swedish populations around 4000 BC lacked this gene (Linderholm 2010), which suggests some migration must have come with agriculture. In western Europe mtDNA haplogroup H appears to have spread between 4000 and 2000 BC and is found in 40 per cent of modern Europeans. However, Brotherton et al. (2010) suggest that this may represent movement associated with the Bell-Beaker Culture, possibly from Iberia (Spain). The current re-dating programme of Neolithic sites (▶ p. 160) is likely to shift the balance of explanation again.

The genetic origins of the British

The picture on the Atlantic seaboard appears to be of much stronger continuity than in central Europe. Sykes argued in *The Seven Daughters of Eve* (2001) that 80–90 per cent of Europeans are descended from one of seven 'clan mothers' who lived in the Upper Palaeolithic, particularly 'Helena' (haplogroup H). In part the differences between his findings and others is that he is looking at a much longer time frame. He locates the differences during the peak of the Ice Age when human populations were isolated in three main 'refuges' and some slight genetic variations developed between them. These groups then repopulated Europe after the Ice Age.

One of these refuges was in Iberia and associated with the R1b haplogroup. The Balkan refuge is associated with haplogroup I and the Caucasus region with R1a. His large-scale analysis of the Y chromosome in the British Isles (2006) suggests that the male population has been largely unchanged since the Neolithic when there was an influx of haplogroup R1b. This may represent elite (Beaker) migration and what is known as the 'Genghis Khan' effect, where some men are significantly more successful in passing on their genes. Female DNA suggests continuity from at least the Mesolithic. His research contradicts ideas of major population replacement by 'Celts' or Anglo-Saxons. Oppenheimer (2007) reached similar conclusions. He found that the R1b Iberian connection was strongest in Ireland and the west of Britain, where it provided over 90 per cent of DNA. However, he attributes this to the original colonisation during the Mesolithic before Britain became an island rather than a later Beaker influx in the late Neolithic. Even in eastern England this original population still contributes around 60 per cent of DNA. However, eastern Britain was also colonised via Doggerland (▶ p. 41) by people originating from the Balkan refuge (haplogroup I) and as a result the population are genetically more similar to the Germans and Dutch. Like Sykes, Oppenheimer rejects later population movements as having much impact except for Scandinavian DNA over a very long period. An exception is in Orkney and Shetland, where 40 per cent of the genetic heritage (haplogroup R1a) came from the Vikings. The markers of Near Eastern immigration from the Neolithic are haplogroups E3b, F, G and J, none of which had a major impact in Britain. Every advance in genetics is providing new evidence and as it becomes increasingly accurate and detailed, more evidence is available for examination. There will be more twists to this story.

Chapter 11

The Archaeology of Religion and Ritual

Section A of this chapter outlines the key concepts and terms from sociology and anthropology that archaeologists use to help define and explain past beliefs and rituals. It also discusses the techniques and sources archaeologists use to interpret evidence of religious belief and ritual practices. Section B looks at continuity and change in religion and ritual over time, using the later prehistory of north-west Europe for most examples. Section C focuses upon Ancient Egypt to examine the particular phenomenon of state religion.

SECTION A: CONCEPTS AND EVIDENCE

Where written sources exist, as for Ancient Greece or medieval Europe, archaeologists have tended to use texts as the means to interpret and understand past belief systems. For cultures where there are no written sources, some archaeologists have held the view that uncovering the nature of past religious belief from material remains is beyond their ability. How can you understand thoughts and beliefs from bones, sherds and postholes? This is most clearly expressed in Hawkes' 'ladder of inference' (▶ p. 174). The reluctance of many archaeologists to discuss religion left a gap that was filled by a range of non-archaeological explanations. These fed on the explosion in public interest in ancient monuments and prehistoric religions from the 1960s onwards. Often these involved projecting current concerns and values onto evidence from the past. The most famous was Von Däniken's depiction of God as an astronaut (▶ p. 174). Similar

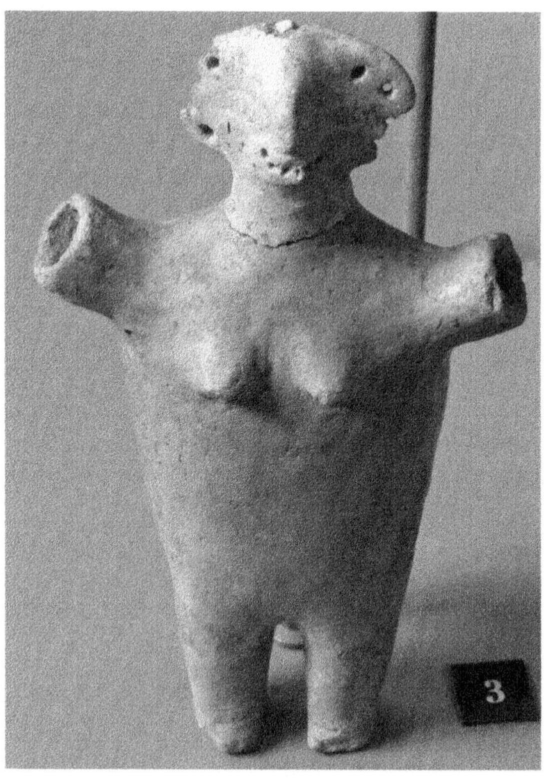

Figure 11.1 *Possible Neolithic goddess figurine from Bulgaria*

views attributed ancient monuments to aliens, the inhabitants of Atlantis or wandering Ancient Egyptians. For example, the Nazca lines in Peru became alien landing strips. More recently a New Age version of prehistory, drawing on the work of the archaeologist Marija Gimbutas (▶ p. 458), has linked together evidence from sites from disparate periods as evidence of a universal cult of a mother goddess.

Partly in response, archaeologists have borrowed a battery of analytical techniques and concepts from other disciplines to explore religion and ritual. It is now a core element of study for most periods. A particularly influential idea from anthropology has been the realisation that in many cultures there is no neat separation of religion and ritual from secular activity. Beliefs and the way they shape understanding of the world influence the way people behave on a daily basis. This in turn leaves traces in their material culture including their art, the orientation of their houses and their use of the landscape. Archaeological discoveries have in turn led to criticism of historical sources for what they omit and because they are often ambivalent. Archaeology, as a complementary source of evidence, may have much to offer the study of religion in the classical period after all.

WHAT IS RELIGION?

Giddens (1989) provides a useful, broad definition of religion as: 'a set of symbols, invoking feelings of reverence or awe linked to rituals or ceremonials practised by a community of believers'. These symbols may be of gods and goddesses, ancestral or nature spirits, or impersonal powers. Rituals can consist of prayers, songs, dances, processions, feasting, drug taking, offerings and sacrifices. People often use ritual to influence supernatural powers and beings to their advantage and to deal with problems that cannot be solved through the application of technology. However, there are also religions without objects of worship. In Confucianism and Taoism, for example, the individual attempts to attain a higher level through correctly following specified principles.

Modern world religions are the most familiar but are atypical of the range of known religions from the past. Christianity, Judaism and Islam, for example, are all **monotheistic** (one god) world religions which provide codes of conduct for life, have permanent religious institutions and offer life after death to believers. There have been religions that have differed on each of these points. At the other end of the scale from **states** (▶ p. 428) which have promoted world religions, are hunter-gatherer societies. They consider themselves as part of, rather than in control of, nature. Their religion may be a constant part of their daily life rather than something for specific occasions. There is far more religious variety in just those small-scale societies which survive today than in all the world religions. They therefore may provide better insights into the wealth of lost belief systems, particularly since Homo sapiens has spent most of the last 100,000 years foraging in bands (▶ p. 421) rather than living in towns and eating farm produce. While an understanding of recent world religions is a useful start point, ethnographies provide a much better insight into the diversity of human beliefs and rituals.

WHAT IS THE FUNCTION OF RELIGION?

Archaeologists are interested in how religion affected the people practising it rather than whether a particular religion accomplished what its believers hoped. All religions cater to basic human social and psychological needs. Some of these, such as the need to explain what happens when people die, may be universal if we are correct in our interpretation of the archaeological evidence for burial and associated activities from the last 40,000 years. The following four key functions can often be identified.

Explaining the unknown

Explanations provide meaning and reduce anxiety. Religions provide a worldview: a set of ideas and way of looking at the world or universe that explains the position of humankind in relation to the physical and supernatural worlds that we inhabit. The layout of the temple at Karnak does this by representing the myth of creation. A belief in a divine force can also provide hope and comfort in difficult times. The death of a family member may be easier to cope with if they are believed to exist beyond death. Ritual at a time of crisis may give people the confidence to cope with problems – for example, praying before a battle – these are often referred to as 'rites of intensification' (▶ p. 512).

Establishing rules and models of behaviour

Most religions put divine power behind definitions of what is right and wrong, good or evil, allowed or taboo. They may tell believers the 'right' way to live. Religion can be manipulated as ideology to enforce obedience to a ruler (e.g. medieval kings) or even to justify rebellion. Ancient Egyptian kings claimed to be the earthly embodiment of the sky god Horus. Horus, the falcon-man son of Isis, was a protector god who destroyed evil. When a king died he became the god Osiris and the new king became Horus. As Horus he could mediate between men and gods. All pharaohs had a 'Horus name' as part of their title, in order to identify them with the deity; indeed, Horus has been identified as one of the very earliest 'kingly symbols' adopted in Egypt at Hierakonpolis from the so-called Dynasty Zero.

The maintenance of social order

This was seen as the primary function of religion by the sociologist Durkheim. His study of **totemism** (▶ p. 510) amongst Australian aboriginal societies suggested that what was being worshipped represented society and its values. By holding collective ceremonies, people reinforce their sense of togetherness and social cohesion. 'Mobilising' a population for a great religious purpose such as monument construction can create or reinforce a sense of social identity.

Transmitting memory

This is particularly important in non-literate societies, by the learning of oral traditions and through repetitive rituals. The classic example of this is the telling of creation myths. Myths are explanatory narratives that rationalise religious beliefs and practices and provide explanations for why certain things are so. Myths invariably

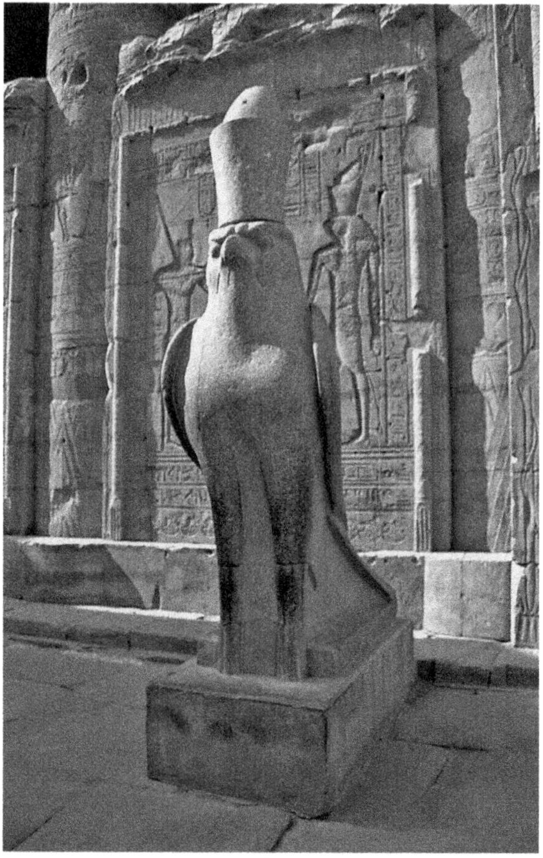

Figure 11.2 *Pharaoh as Horus at Edfu*

Figure 11.3 *Vietnam memorial*

This stunning group of bronze statues are part of a massive complex of funerary monuments in the heart of Washington DC. State memorials to the fallen promote and legitimise values and help create identity as well as providing a focus for remembrance rituals.

are full of accounts of the doings of various supernatural beings and hence serve to reinforce belief in them. The building of religious monuments can literally set collective memories in stone.

WHAT KINDS OF RELIGION HAVE THERE BEEN?

Most known religions include a belief in supernatural beings and forces through whom appeals for aid may be directed. For convenience we may divide these into three categories: deities, ancestral spirits and nature spirits. While some societies have only believed in one of these categories, it has been common for belief in several or all of them to co-exist; for example, belief in evil spirits in medieval Europe.

Major deities

Gods and goddesses are great and remote beings who are usually seen as controlling the universe. **Monotheistic** religions such as Islam or Christianity have one god. In **polytheistic** religions a panoply of deities are recognised. Often each has charge of a particular part of the universe. Hinduism, the oldest major world religion, is around 6,000 years old and is polytheistic. Its original contemporaries included the gods of Ancient Greece: Zeus was the lord of the sky, Poseidon was the ruler of the sea and Hades was

Figure 11.4 *Relief from Temple of Kom Ombo*

Sacred crocodiles basked on the Nile at this point which became the location for this temple which is partly dedicated to Sobek. Sobek, a crocodile god, represented the Nile and fertility. Hundreds of mummified crocodiles have been found nearby.

the lord of the underworld and ruler of the dead. In addition to these three brothers, there were many other deities of both sexes. Each embodied characteristic is seen as typical of male and female roles; each was concerned with specific aspects of life and the workings of the world, or indeed universe. A **pantheon** or collection of gods and goddesses, such as that of the Greeks, was also common in early state societies such as Egypt, Sumer or the Maya. Specific deities are identified from repeated images on buildings or artefacts ranging from mosaics to statues. Evidence of the worship of 'sky gods', including the sun, from the late Neolithic and early Bronze Age (▶ p. 542) is also suggestive of major deities even though we will never know what they were called.

Gods and goddesses

Belief in gods, goddesses or both, and the way that they treated each other, may have paralleled gender relationships between men and women in everyday life. In societies where women have less power than men, the nature of 'god' is frequently defined in masculine terms. This is commonest where the economy is based upon herding animals or on intensive agriculture, which would have been largely male activities. In such societies men may often have been seen as rather distant authority figures by their children. Goddesses, however, appear more often in societies where women make the major contribution to the economy and enjoy some measure of equality with men. Such societies often depend on horticulture or specialised craft production, much of which is done by women. Evidence from Çatal Höyük (Turkey) and Karanovo (▶ p. 339) led some to suggest that pioneer agricultural societies may have venerated female roles. Gimbutas (1991) took this a stage further and argued that both Neolithic 'Old Europe' (▶ p. 458) and a number of later societies including Minoan Crete (▶ p. 470) worshipped a great mother goddess. This monotheistic cult was associated with fertility and a peaceful, matriarchal society. In contrast, she claimed that later world religions developed to legitimise the emergence of patriarchal, warlike societies during the Bronze Age. The masculine god that replaced various goddess cults amongst the Hebrews during the late 2nd millennium BC may have helped establish gender relationships in which women have traditionally been expected to submit to the rule of men. This in turn shaped Jewish, Christian and Islamic society. While many aspects of Gimbutas' views have been shown to be flawed (▶ p. 460), they were complemented by the increasing availability of authoritative ethnographies of groups

Figure 11.5 *Minoan snake goddess or Potnia. This idol found in a hidden cist at Knossos (▶ p. 256) with other cult objects may represent a female fertility deity or a mother goddess.*

such as the San which suggested that the roles of men in spiritual and profane matters had been previously over-emphasised by mostly male archaeologists.

Ancestral spirits

Belief in ancestral spirits originates in the widespread idea that human beings are made up of two parts: the body and a vital spirit or soul. For example, the Maya Indians maintained that each person had a 'spirit-companion' which resided in the blood and could leave the body and move around during sleep. The 'spirit-companion' was envisaged as an animal. One inscription tells us that 'the watery jaguar is the "way" of the Lord (King) of Seibal'. Given such a concept, it is only a small step to believe that the spirit could be freed by death from the body and have a continued existence. It has something in common with recent accounts of 'out of body experiences'.

Where people believe in ancestral spirits, they are frequently seen as retaining an active interest and even membership in society. For example, the 'ghost ancestors' of the Wape of Papua New Guinea might either provide or withhold meat from their living descendants. Like living persons, ancestral spirits may be well or badly disposed towards the living, but they are often capricious and unpredictable, hence the need to appease them with offerings. Whatever their involvement in particular past societies, belief in ancestral spirits provided a strong sense of continuity. These beliefs seem to have been particularly strong amongst early farming communities. Ancestors may have linked past, present and future generations and ownership of particular land.

Animism

Perhaps the most common set of beliefs centre on the idea that the living share the physical and spiritual world with many other spirits. Australian first peoples frequently named particular places after spirits taken from their mythological view of prehistory called 'The Dreaming'. Animals, plants and people all have their own individual spirits, as may springs, mountains, or other natural features. People who believe in animism tend to see themselves as being part of nature rather than superior to it. This includes most hunter-gatherers and many horticultural societies. Many Native Americans subscribed to this view of the world and would pray to the spirits of their 'brothers and sisters' the animals for success in the hunt. They asked animals to give up their lives for the good of people and apologised to them when they were actually caught. Even where there is a belief that gods and goddesses created the world, it is spirits to whom one turns for the ordinary needs of daily life and whom the ordinary hunter may meet while out roaming the woods. Roman statues of the River Tyne or the watery goddess at Bath or the 'nymphs' at Lullingstone (▶ p. 552) exemplify the idea of 'spirit of place'.

Liminality

Liminality is an important concept linked to the idea of the existence of separate worlds such as those of the living and the spirits. Boundaries and spaces which are literally between two worlds can be liminal. It may be between land and water as at Flag Fen or between the living and the dead. Liminal areas can be dangerous and therefore are likely to be marked by ritual. Most well-known ritual sites have well-defined boundaries. People, creatures and even time can be liminal – for example, Halloween/Samhain or the time between the death of a pharaoh in Egypt and the installation of his successor.

Totems

Totemism is a label sometimes attached to particular animistic forms of religion. Here animals or plants with special powers may be worshipped or there may be complex rules about their treatment. Totems are often associated with clans and lineages (▶ p. 421) as their sacred or spirit animals and may have an emblematic significance as heraldic devices especially on 'totem-poles' erected in the Amerindian culture area of the Northwest Coast by the Haida and Tlingit. Totemism has been used as an explanation for repeated finds in prehistoric tombs. Hedges (2000) noted that the Isbister tomb on Orkney contained the remains of at least eight massive sea eagles, while nearby Cuween held the remains of twenty-four dogs and Knowe of Yarso contained deer bones. Local tribal groups may have identified with particular animals. However, these may have been food or in some cases scavengers which entered the tombs independently or as part of the excarnation process (▶ p. 514). Isbister contained the jumbled remains of 342 people including rows of skulls on a shelf. Joints of lamb had been left in the tomb while outside was a pile of deliberately smashed pots and other remains of feasting.

Animatism

Some societies believe in a supernatural power that exists independently of deities and spirits. The people of Melanesia, for example, believe that 'mana' exists as a force inherent in all objects. In itself it is not physical but it can be revealed through its physical effects. When a warrior experiences success in battle, this will not be as a result of his own strength but directly attributable to the 'mana' carried with him in the form of an

Figure 11.6 *Sea eagle talons from the Neolithic stalled cairn at Isbister*

Figure 11.7 *Sioux ghost shirt*

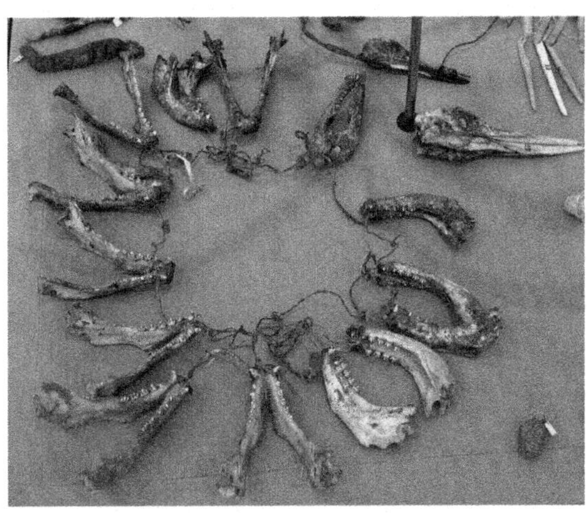

Figure 11.8 *Inuit amulet, Greenland*

amulet that hangs around his neck. In much the same way, in farming societies an individual may know a great deal about the right way to treat plants, about soil conditions and the correct time for sowing and harvesting, but still be dependent on 'mana' for the success of his crop. He may build a simple altar for this power at the end of the field, as often seen in the rice fields of Bali. If the crop is good, it is a sign that the farmer has in some way acquired the necessary 'mana'. The possession of objects containing such power may provide the owner with confidence; for example, in going into battle. Confidence might then lead to fearlessness and victory. This would then 'prove' the power of the 'mana'. The Sioux followers of the Ghost Dance cult provide a less successful example. They believed their magical shirts would stop bullets in their final conflict with the US army in the late C19th. It is probable that some grave goods from the past were seen as having special powers while others may have been buried to avoid the bad luck associated with taking particular items from the dead.

Belief in magic has some similarities with animatism. Magic can involve spirits or particular individuals influencing events resulting in bad luck or unwanted natural phenomena such as storms or disease. Practitioners invoke magic through spells, potions, incantations and manipulation of magical and personal items. The wearing of charms, amulets or talismans to bring good fortune and ward off evil combines elements of magic and animatism. It can also involve divination, astrology and curses such as those found on the walls of Pompeii. In many societies magic or witchcraft exists as a fully functioning and accepted alternative to the explanations of Western science. The best known is the ethnographic study of Evans-Pritchard (1937) into the magic beliefs of the Azande people of north-west Africa. Magic has survived in a watered down way in societies which have been Christian for many centuries.

RITUAL ACTIVITY

Much of the value of religion comes from religious activities. These range from daily rituals to great cyclical events such as Easter or the Egyptian festival of Opet. Participation in ceremonies enables people to relate to higher forces; it is religion in action. Ritual involves repeated performance of religious activities, usually at a particular place. It can reinforce the social bonds of a group and reduce tensions. Participants can feel a wave of reassurance, security and even ecstasy and a sense of closeness. Although the rituals and practices vary considerably, even those rites that seem to us the most bizarrely exotic can be shown to serve the same basic social and psychological function. Anthropologists have classified several different types of ritual, a major division being between **'rites of passage'** and **'rites of intensification'**.

The concept of rites of passage was introduced by the anthropologist Van Gennep in 1909. They are ceremonies which mark transitions in a person's life; for example, birth, becoming an adult, getting married and dying. Documented rites included separate initiation rituals for girls and boys where they were taken from their families to a liminal place and instructed so that they could return as men or women as full members of the group. Rituals vary widely but might involve dancing, mutilation or challenges. While there might be physical signs on a person or changes in dress to indicate that they had undergone a rite of passage, these are difficult to detect archaeologically with the exception of funerary rituals.

Rites of intensification are undertaken when a crisis threatens the group or society. These might include drought, disease, war, the death of a significant person or a key point in the annual yearly cycle, particularly the end of a year. Collective rituals bring society together in a show of solidarity but also might be hoped to influence events. Examples range from rain dances to Remembrance Day. Evidence of sacrifice or festivals may indicate rites of intensification. Most world religions have a cycle of ritual events. Christmas, for example, replaced Iron Age midwinter feasts which may be linked to the winter solstice and the turning of the year. The Iron Age in northern Europe is also noted for the quantities of valuable artefacts, and occasionally people, sacrificed in watery places (▶ p. 118). 'Ritually killed' objects which are destroyed before being deposited 'out of this world' may be indicators of intensification rites for better harvests or victory in battle.

Figure 11.9 *Elaborate shield boss from a huge sacrifice of military equipment in a Danish bog (▶ p. 483)*

Funerary rituals

Funerals blur this neat distinction. The death of an individual can also be a crisis for an entire group, particularly if the group is small. The survivors must readjust, take up new roles and work out how to behave towards one another. They also need to reconcile themselves to the loss of someone to whom they were emotionally tied. This can take extreme forms. One of the funerary rites of the Melanesians was ritual cannibalism. This was felt to be a supreme act of reverence, love and devotion. Funerals offer the opportunity for outpourings of emotions without disrupting society. They can also emphasise that the values of the group outlive the individual. Burials are just one part of the funerary process but they are the most archaeologically visible. This does not mean they were the most important part. For example, the resources required and the participation involved in the event of burning a body on a funeral pyre may outstrip both the value of grave goods and the significance attached to depositing the ashes afterwards. This can be seen at Hallstatt (▶ p. 373).

However, ritual can also be a routine part of everyday life. In many religions, entry into

Figure 11.10 *Washing facilities at a mosque in Cyprus*

Figure 11.11 *Late Minoan 'bathtub style' sarcophagus. These ceramic vessels, large enough to hold a crouched body (or two), were used to bury wealthy Minoans. They include a plughole.*

religious sites is marked by ritual. This may mark a transition from the 'profane' everyday world to a 'sacred' enclosure or building. Ritual washing with its connotations of purity is a good example of this. This kind of categorisation into pure/impure and sacred/profane can sometimes be discerned through archaeology; for instance, where special deposits are placed at thresholds or entrances.

Mortuary rituals and the treatment of the dead

The treatment of the dead can overlap with funerals. The corpse may be prepared in advance for a funeral and the remains may need further ritual treatment afterwards. Much has been learnt from studying the treatment of the corpse, particularly its final disposal. This can take many forms.

Inhumation (burial) is a deliberate setting of the dead outside the world of the living – usually in a hole dug in the ground. Where this occurs it indicates cultural attitudes to the dead. Christian cemeteries are placed apart from the living while some prehistoric burials, as at Franchthi Cave, were kept close to the living. The orientation and position of the body – flexed, extended or crouched – may be significant. For example, foetal positions may indicate some belief in rebirth. Burials may be single or in a cemetery and may have a mound erected over one or more of the graves.

Figure 11.12 *Bronze Age cremation including a ring*

Cremation is more complex. Funeral pyres can leave several kilos of charred bones. The fire may destroy the body and release the spirit but these remains may have to be dealt with in a secondary ceremony. At the Roman fort of Birdoswald on Hadrian's Wall, a geophysics survey along the main road into the fort revealed a number of 'bustum burials', where funeral pyres had been buried after firing. Unlike modern crematoria, funeral pyres could not usually reach sufficient temperatures to reduce bodies to ash. The larger chunks of bone along with charred grave goods were often collected and placed in vessels for burial. Sufficient bone may survive to allow identification and even DNA testing.

Excarnation is a process which involves exposing the body for scavengers and the decay process to clean the flesh from the bones. For example, Parsees expose bodies on structures known as 'Towers of Silence' while some American First Peoples used a scaffold known as a 'sky burial'. The ritual may also happen in a sacred open place as in the Tibetan mountains where the corpse may be disarticulated before exposure to make the task of the vultures easier. The philosophy behind this ritual is that removal of flesh cleanses the body of its animal component and frees the soul to journey to the ancestors or the afterworld. The symbolism of birds carrying remains into the sky may also have been significant. Cleaned bones may be used in other rites or stored in an ossuary. Weathering or cut-marks on bones which were subsequently buried may indicate excarnation. It appears to have been a common mortuary rite in later prehistory. Examples include exposure in the open at the causwayed enclosure (▶ p. 536) of Hambledon Hill.

Figure 11.13 *Recreation of excarnation at the 'Tomb of the Sea Eagles', Isbister (▶p. 510)*

Figure 11.14 *An ossuary at Hallstatt*

Mummification is often an elaborate process, which can involve removing some parts of the body. It may be believed that the body can be used by the person's spirit in another world or the future. Mummification is best known from ancient Egypt but occurred in many other cultures. Salt (▶ p. 373), peat and air-drying have all been used to preserve bodies or particular parts. A dramatic use of mummification was practised by the Anga of Papua New Guinea who removed the organs and then smoked the dead over a fire for weeks. This dried the bodies and reduced bacterial and insect damage. The mummified remains were placed in caves or on ledges overlooking the settlements. Males were armed so that their spirits could protect their descendants while female mummies held digging sticks to care for the garden-plots. The ancestors' spirits remained part of the community. The use of certain types of coffin or funeral vaults that may slow down natural decay processes may reflect similar beliefs. Composite mummies made up from several individuals have been found at the Bronze Age village of Cladh Hallan in the Western Isles of Scotland and they were preserved initially by burial in peat and then removed and used over a considerable period.

Sometimes the dead are hard to find. This may be because they are totally consumed. The Yanomamö grind the cremated remains of their dead to a powder that they then drink. The dead thus remain in the living. There are also ethnographic examples of bones of ancestors being worn by their descendants. For much of prehistory most of the dead are invisible (▶ p. 544). Inhumations are the exception rather than the norm.

Funerary monuments and grave goods

Both of these categories may tell us more about the mourners and society than they do about their religious beliefs (▶ p. 507). Elaborately decorated tombs such as those in the Valley of the Kings or the reliefs carved on Maya tombs do provide detailed information about both beliefs and

Figure 11.15 *Graceland*

The grave of Elvis in the garden of remembrance at Graceland is one of the most visited funerary monuments in the modern world. Like many other pilgrimage sites, it is the focus for a variety of offerings.

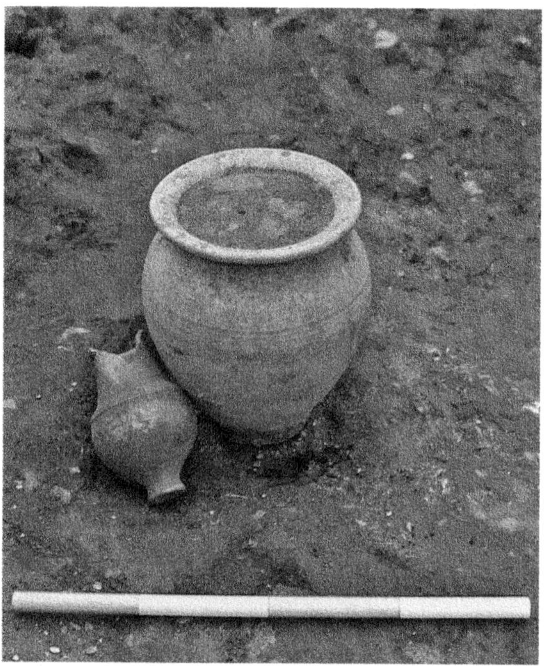

Figure 11.16 *Bustum burial*

In this rare type of Roman burial, funerary goods were placed in a pyre along with the corpse and the burial was not disturbed after firing. Usually a pit beneath the pyre became the grave. In this example from Biddenham (▶ p. 592), the organic fill of the grave as well as the artefacts will be analysed to understand what else (e.g. food and drink) was placed on the pyre. (Albion Archaeology)

rituals but for most periods archaeologists rely on studying the patterns and nature of deposits in order to make inferences (▶ p. 173). Gravestones provide many insights for a variety of cultures, not least about the setting aside of respected areas for the dead. Goods buried with the body or which were consumed in a funeral pyre can suggest an afterlife but this is not always the case. Goods may be placed in the grave by mourners as tokens of affection or because they belonged to the deceased and are considered unlucky or taboo. Tools used to prepare the dead, such as razors or tweezers, may fall into this category. There may also be important offerings of food or organic materials that have not survived. The absence of grave goods does not mean that there was no belief in an afterlife. It may suggest a belief in an afterlife where people are equal and provided for or it may reflect an idealised picture of society that masks differences in wealth. Equally, the repeated deposit of particular artefacts may represent social status or ethnic markers (▶ p. 492) rather than evidence of specific beliefs.

HOW DO ARCHAEOLOGISTS DETECT EVIDENCE OF PAST RITUALS?

A standing joke amongst archaeologists is that anything that cannot immediately be explained must be ritual. While there has been some over-enthusiasm in what is still a relatively new area of archaeological interpretation, most studies are based on far more than an odd-shaped building or one figurine. Egyptologists have the advantage of the Book of the Dead to draw on but for other cultures different approaches are required. Analogies drawn from ethnography have been particularly useful, not so much for direct parallels but to demonstrate a range of possible options and influences and to prevent simplistic interpretation. It may appear common sense that a burial with many goods was that of a wealthy person, yet ethnography has provided examples where this is not the case. Anthropology has taught us that all human societies can be studied both from a holistic perspective, centred on universal values, and from a particularist viewpoint which stresses the differences between them. Rituals often occur at particular times, are repetitive and have repetitive structures. As a result, studies often try to identify and interpret these repeated patterns. These might include symbols that recur in similar places or on specific types of artefact. Non-random patterns of deposition of particular artefacts or animal remains and the distribution of deposits and monuments across the landscape also provide clues. The analytical power of computers, particularly linked to GIS (▶ p. 10), is increasingly enlisted in searching for such patterns. Similar approaches have been used to understand the ritual treatment of boundaries in the past.

Architectural clues

The best known set of indicators of ritual are those of Renfrew and Bahn (2004). In many cases

Figure 11.17 *Temple complex of Srirangam at Triuchirappalli*

This is the largest temple complex in India and a major centre for Hindu worship of the god Vishnu. The huge gopurums (pyramidal entrance towers) are masterpieces of early modern Dravidian architecture. Their height dominates the town and ensures visibility at distance in the same way as European cathedrals.

their four key points – focus of attention, boundary zones, symbols or images of the deity, and participation and offerings – can be ticked off. Focus of attention is essentially any iconographic, sculptural or architectural feature that draws the attention of the onlooker/worshipper such that they concentrate on it and are drawn into the holy nature of the place where it resides. Cult statues such as those at Abu Simbel and the Pylon gateways at Karnak are good examples.

Tombs and temples are the most obvious sites of ritual and also monuments such as shrines and ghats (steps down to a holy river). However, there are exceptions. Such indicators work best for formal religions and for communal rather than individual ritual acts, many of which leave no traces. They also rely on there being a distinct area set aside even if it is just a small area in a dwelling; for example, the altar or 'lararium' mounted on the wall of a Roman house. However, there are societies today where there is no clear demarcation between ritual and the everyday. The layout and structure of houses as far apart as Bali and the Amazon jungle are determined by religious beliefs (▶ p. 544). Their orientation, where domestic activities occur and the direction in which particular people can move around them are all subject to religious rules. Evidence from later European prehistory suggests that people then did not make a clear distinction between domestic and ritual places (▶ p. 339).

Symbolism and indicators of ritual at the Clava Cairns

This group of monuments near Inverness illustrates many of the different features of ritual sites including devices to focus attention, symbolism and evidence for specialists. This distinctive, regional complex comprising ring cairns, passage graves and standing stones had originally been

Figure 11.18 *Clava Cairns. View of the south-west passage grave looking down the main alignment towards the north-east cairn from the direction of the midwinter sunset. The entrance stones, the rays and stones linked to them and much of the chamber were built using pink and reddish stones while much of the kerb and the back of the chamber were white. Note the erosion of the platform due to visitors.*

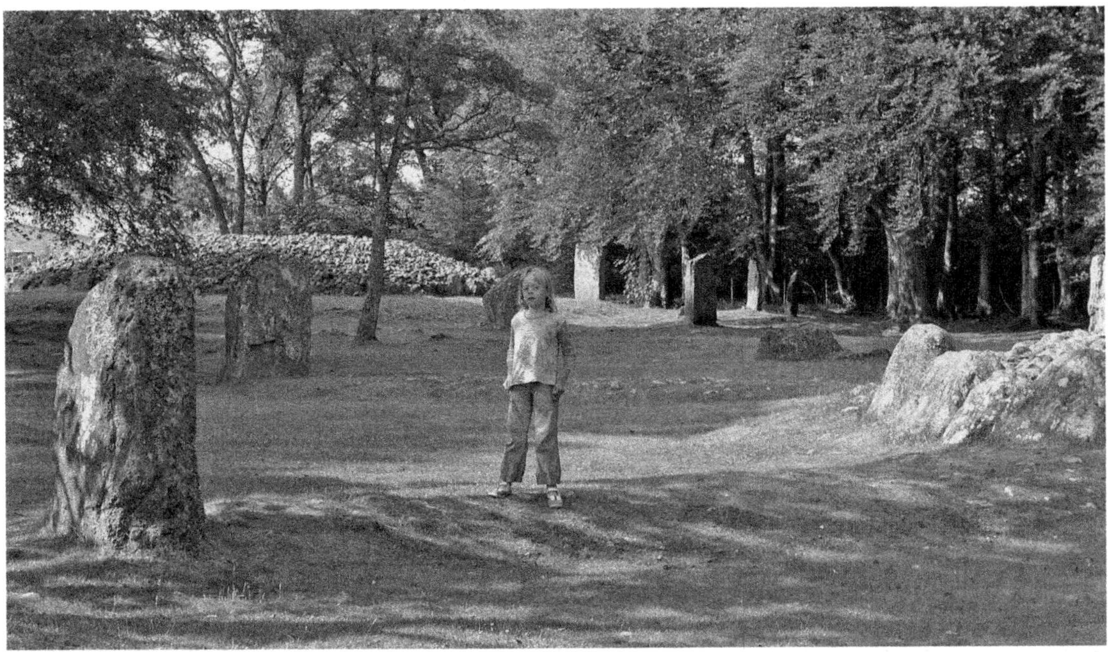

Figure 11.19 *View of a relationship between the features of the monuments. Two standing stones on the left are linked by 'rays' to the central ring cairn. The child is standing on the first ray. This integral relationship could only be established by excavation. Note how small the kerbstones are on the back of the south-west cairn in the distance in comparison with the front ones.*

thought to be Neolithic. Bradley's (2000a) re-excavation revealed that building had begun in the early Bronze Age *c.* 2000 BC. The complex was remodelled in the late Bronze Age and funerary deposits were also made in the Iron Age.

The passage graves are aligned on the mid-winter sunset. When viewed from the passage of the north-eastern cairn, the dying sun disappears over the south-western cairn, thus linking the event to the ancestors. The rays of the setting sun fall on reddish sandstone boulders while the rising sun would have sparkled on white quartz. This symbolism has been found in other monuments. On Arran, red boulders were chosen to face the setting sun with white granite facing the rising sun. The colours red (blood, flesh, ochre and amber) and white (bone, semen and flint) are often associated in grave deposits.

A number of conventions were adhered to in building the monument. The kerbstones of the cairns were carefully graded in height from the south-west. From an engineering point of view this makes no sense but it may have symbolised the passage of the sun. Rock carvings were included both inside and outside the cairns with the same 'cup and ring' designs as others in Britain and Ireland. However, these monuments seem to represent a change in ritual practice. Excavation revealed low platforms covered in seashells and flat stones surrounding the cairns. 'Rays' or ridges of stones led out through the platform to standing monoliths. Excavation showed that these were all integral to the cairns rather than later add-ons. The architecture creates a number of distinct boundaries. The tombs themselves with their narrow passages would only be accessible to one or two individuals during a ceremony. The ring of megaliths provided a permeable barrier between those inside on the platform and onlookers outside. These monuments seem to have been a transitional stage between passage graves, where the views of mortuary rituals would have been very restricted, to stone circles, where ritual may have been much more public and perhaps on a larger scale.

Votive offerings

Unusual concentrations of particular objects or the remains of animals or even people have sometimes helped identify otherwise ordinary features such as wells or springs as being the focus of rituals. Ceramic models of body parts are frequently found at cave and peak sanctuaries in Minoan Crete and later at Roman temples. They were left with offerings by pilgrims who were suffering in some way and hoped the deities would heal them.

Objects cannot be seen as ritual simply because they are exotic. However, the form and location of particular artefacts have been used to suggest ritual objects for most periods. In some cases the material is important. Amber is associated with burials from the Mesolithic onwards. Its colour of blood and fire with slight magnetic properties perhaps marked it out. Pottery vessels with particular designs such as beakers or grooved ware are often seen as ritual artefacts. In some cases these have been repaired but not sufficiently to make them useable. Figurines and statues and non-functional artefacts such as copper axes are more ambiguous unless their context can link them with other indicators. Evidence of sacrifice – which literally means 'to make sacred' – might include deposits of valuable items, animals or even humans ritually murdered to invoke favours from deities. The bodies from Clonycavan and Oldcroghan in the Republic of Ireland, Lindow Man in England, Tollund (▶ p. 172) and Grauballe in Denmark suggest a common cult of human sacrifice in watery places across Iron Age northern Europe. **Propitiation** is the term used to describe making offerings or sacrifices to a spirit or deity. It involves giving something in advance to please the spirits or gods, usually to guarantee success such as when setting out on a new venture or to ward off ill fortune of a personal or wider nature. It may require an offering or sacrifice perhaps in a 'liminal place' (▶ p. 509). The widespread burials of human and animal remains in grain pits, as at Danebury, and bog bodies (▶ p. 104) deposited in rivers or lakes (▶ p. 118) have been interpreted as such offerings. Egyptian temple foundation deposits serve a similar function as do Roman votive altars.

Ritual symbolism

Art and symbolism have also provided indications of ritual. Some, such as the Yaxchilan Lintels, are undoubtedly ritual, others, such as Palaeolithic cave art and Neolithic rock carvings, have been hotly debated. Other approaches to ritual symbolism have focused on repeated patterns including pairings such as left/right, male/female, in/out. This technique has been drawn from media and critical theory. At Durrington Walls, all the ritual structures are made of wood,

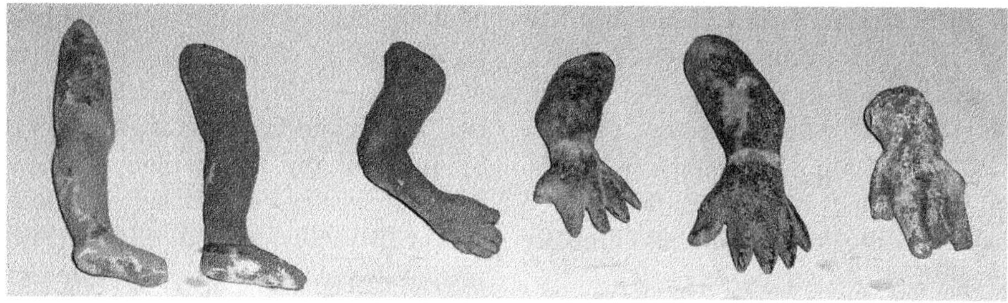

Figure 11.20 *Votives from Minoan cave sanctuaries*

Figure 11.21 *Ritual scene from the Yaxchilan Lintels*

This huge stone slab was originally placed above the entrance to a Mayan temple. It illustrates bloodletting or 'autosacrifice', an extreme form of participation in ritual. Blood, analogous with water, was vital for the fertility of crops and maintaining good relations with the gods. It repaid sacrifices made by the gods at the time of mankind's creation. Here Lady Xoc is perforating her tongue and Shield Jaguar is bleeding his penis. Blood is collected on paper to be burnt as an offering, smoke rising to the gods. They are rewarded by the appearance of an ancestor in the form of an armed warrior dressed as the 'vision serpent'.

which is seen as a symbol of life, while at Stonehenge, closely linked to Durrington by rituals and processional ways, they are made of stone, symbolising death. The standing stones of the Beckhampton and West Kennet avenues at Avebury are regarded as alternately fat and thin, which some have interpreted as representing female and male.

Feasting

The sharing of food is a powerful social unifier and is likely to feature in many rituals, but it can also be secular. The cauldron and dining kits from Hochdorf (▶ p. 434) were probably from social rather than religious feasting. However, in other situations, the remains of feasts can help identify ritual functions. Large amounts of waste and deliberate destruction may also provide clues. For instance, at the large enclosure at Durrington Walls large numbers of pigs were slaughtered in rituals connecting the site with Stonehenge. Evidence of other apparently waste material has also been used to suggest the embedding of ritual in the everyday. In particular Mesolithic middens from Scotland and Denmark (▶ p. 241) with their deposits of artefacts and human remains may not have been simply rubbish heaps.

Landscape, ritual and belief

A combination of the development of landscape archaeology and a growing awareness from ethnography of the ritual significance of landscape has led archaeologists to look beyond burials and individual monuments. Studies from Australia, for example, reveal that to the Aborigines the whole landscape had a mythical dimension and they in turn inscribed it with meaning, including the use of rock carvings. Analogies based on ethnologies have been used to explore ritual use of the landscape in the Neolithic in relation to petroglyphs (rock art) and cursus monuments.

The value of this approach is illustrated by examining the entire landscape in western Ireland rather than studying individual monuments in isolation. The sequence and distribution of monuments to the east of Sligo illustrates the way in which monument builders used natural features and also related different groups of monuments to each other in order to create a ritual landscape. The earliest monuments in the area are shell middens on the coast such as at Culleenamore (▶ p. 523). At *c.* 5000 BC Neolithic dolmens and passage graves were built nearby at Carrowmore. Within the cemetery there appears to be a focus on tomb 51, 'Listoghil' (▶ p. 627), which has

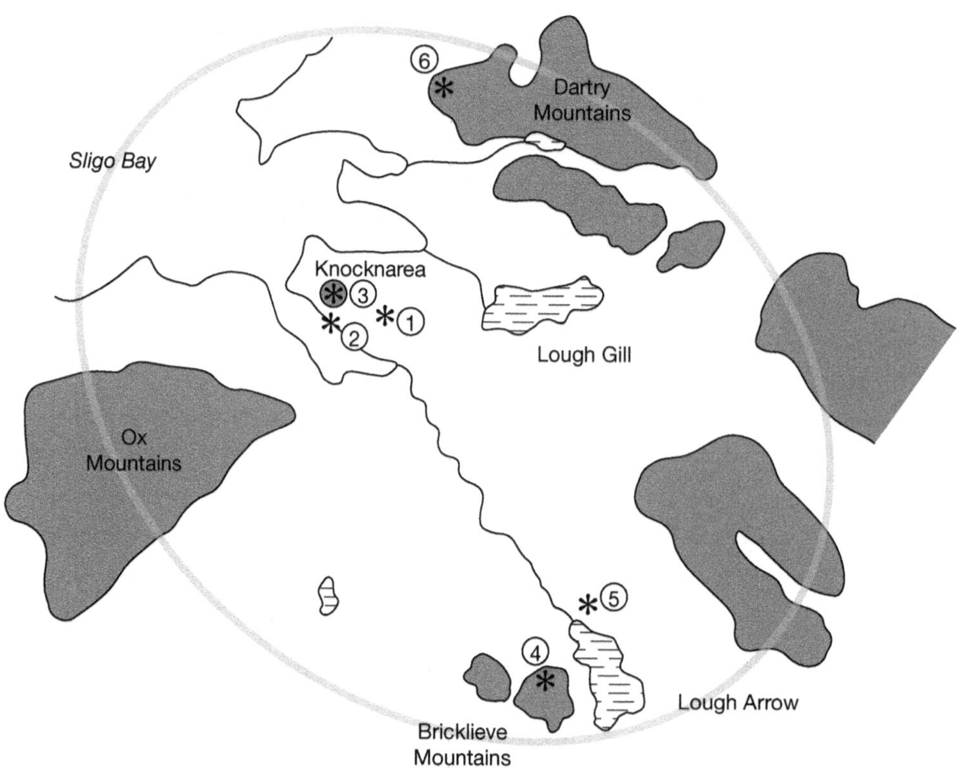

Figure 11.22 *Map of Carrowmore and related monuments*

Figure 11.23 *A ring dolmen from Carrowmore (1 on the map)*

Figure 11.24
Carrowkeel passage graves looking west (4 towards 6 on the map)

Figure 11.25
A ring dolmen at Carrowmore looking towards Knocknarea. Maeve's Cairn is visible as a tiny bump (1 towards 3 on the map)

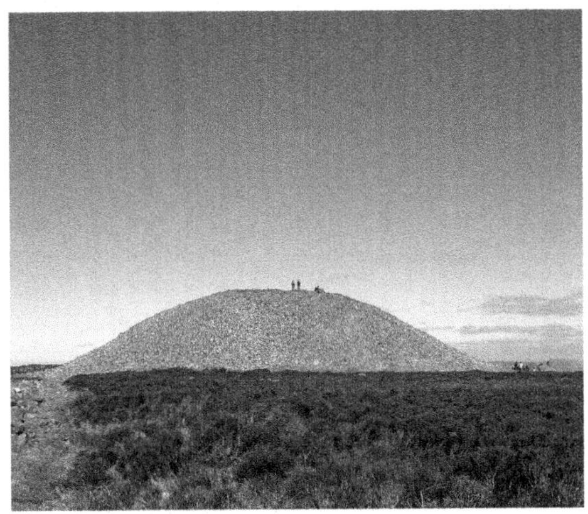

Figure 11.26
Maeve's Cairn on top of Knocknarea (3 on the map)

petroglyphs on some of its stones. There were at least one hundred tombs before quarrying depleted their number.

Other monuments were added in the surrounding countryside. From the Ox Mountains to the south to the distinctive shape of Ben Bulben to the north, all the high ground surrounding the low-lying farmland east of Carrowmore is marked with passage graves. These are orientated on the earlier cemetery. An enormous passage grave (Maeve's Cairn) was also built on the prominent summit of Knocknarea which overlooks Carrowmore from the west. Its position means that many of the passage graves on other hills also appear to be focused on it. In the distribution and orientation of monuments, we can therefore see connections which suggest common belief systems and understandings linked to ancestors and the seasons. If the dates are correct, megalithic tomb building may have spread out from Carrowmore to other parts of the British Isles.

RELIGIOUS SPECIALISTS

In all societies there are certain individuals especially skilled at contacting and influencing supernatural beings and manipulating supernatural forces. They assist or lead other members of society in their ritual activities. Their qualification for this role may be certain distinctive personality traits or they may have undergone special training. A body of myths may help explain how and why they are different from those who lack such powers.

Figure 11.27 *Scene from the Agia Triada sarcophagus (c. 1370 BC)*

This painting on plaster covering a limestone sarcophagus includes many aspects of Minoan funerary ritual. On the reverse a bull is strapped down for sacrifice by priestesses. Here a priestess pours liquid into a krater on an altar. This may be sacrificial blood or water or wine for lustration (bathing) of the altar or for purification rites. Another woman brings further liquid while a man plays a lyre. Birds wait for the gods, perhaps called by the lyre. To the right one of several men carries offerings of animals to a male priest.

Priests and priestesses

Priests and priestesses are found mostly in complex societies that can afford to support full-time specialists of all kinds. He or she will be ceremonially initiated into a religious organisation and given a rank or office similar to those held before by others. They interpret their wishes or commands for other people but may also appeal to deities on behalf of believers. This may be for a fee or for payment in kind. Priests and priestesses may be recognised archaeologically through objects placed in burials, through special equipment and clothing, through literary and epigraphic evidence and through artistic evidence of persons involved in ritual activity. Their presence can also be inferred from the structure of monuments themselves. In most cases monuments physically divide people into those who are in and those who are out, those at the head of a procession and the followers.

Shamans

There have been societies without full-time ritual specialists for much longer than those in which one finds priests and priestesses. However, there have always been individuals who claim to be able to contact the spirit world on behalf of others in society and often have a role as healers. Increasingly, these individuals are called shamans. The earliest image and recording of the term is an engraving in the book *North and East Tartary* in 1692 by Dutch statesman and explorer Nicolas Witsen. His depiction has become a model for interpreting shamanism across northern Eurasia. However, definitions of shamanism vary. Some writers reserve the term for Siberian culture but it is widely applied, particularly to herding, hunter-gatherer and mobile horticulturalist societies from Africa to South America. Increasingly individuals who were previously called witch doctors (Africa), medicine women (North America) or clever men (Australia) are now called shamans.

The common thread is a belief in an 'en-souled world' where shamans, by entering a trance-like state, can see and interact with spirit beings (Lewis-Williams and Dowson 1988). How they do this varies. Some experience this transformation in isolation and may involve bodily deprivation, even self-torture, to try to induce shamanistic

Figure 11.28 *Tungus Shaman, Siberia, from Witsen's 'Noord en Oost Tartarye', 1692. The drumming and dancing were keys to the way the shaman would enter a trance and the spirit world.*

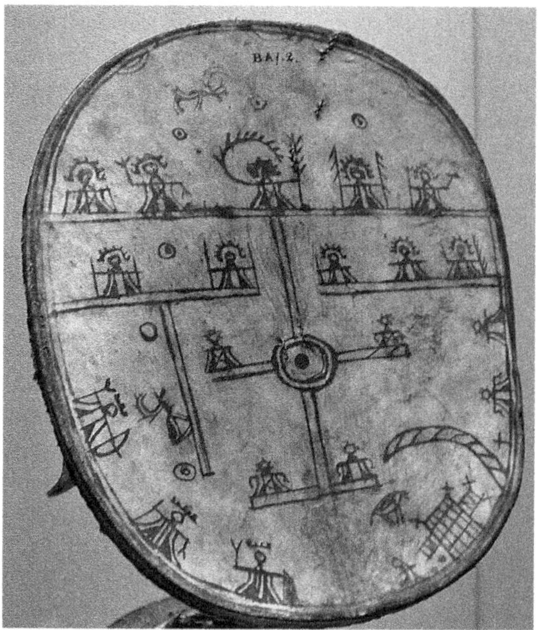

Figure 11.29 *Inuit shaman's drum*

visions. More commonly trances are induced by repetitive dancing, drumming, chanting and the use of psychotropic drugs. Depending on location, hallucinogens have included fly agaric mushrooms, peyote cactus and ayahuasca – a brew made from a vine and used by Amazonian shamans.

A shaman in action may put on a show to involve other members of the group. The musical element may involve performance of mythical stories and traditional songs. Sometimes this is accompanied by conjuring tricks, including the use of elaborate masks or ventriloquism. Extensive collections of shamanic masks were collected by American anthropologists from tribes such as the Kwakiutl on the north-west coast of the USA. Feathers also are a frequent feature on costumes or shamanic paraphernalia along with other musical instruments including rattles and gongs. The shaman may have a 'spirit-helper' in the form of an animal which may be represented by a carved figure that they use in performance.

Through contact with a spirit or visits to the land of the dead, shamans acquire special gifts, such as healing, visions or divination and the ability to deal with supernatural beings and powers. Faith healers and some evangelists in our own society share some of these characteristics. Shamans will battle or bargain with malevolent spirits to free a person from illness or change a bad situation, as in faith healing or exorcism. Shamans often have expert knowledge of medicinal plants native to their area, and herbal treatments are often prescribed. In many places shamans learn directly from the plants, harnessing their effects and healing properties, after obtaining permission from the in-dwelling or patron spirits. The shaman may also help to maintain social control through the ability to detect and punish evildoers. This can backfire on the shaman. If they are believed to work evil as well as good, or are unsuccessful, shamans may be driven out of their group or even killed.

Shamans may be detected through iconography such as images depicting transformations such as the man turning into a grouse at Lascaux. More commonly, burials are the main source of evidence as at Upton Lovell (▶ p. 393). Siberian examples have been found buried face down, tied up and covered with rocks.

SECTION B: RELIGIOUS CHANGE

Comparative studies over long periods often reveal changes in the evidence for religion. This can be useful as the contrasts often suggest much about both the nature of beliefs and society. The overlap between paganism and Christianity revealed in the changing grave goods and orientation of bodies from Anglo-Saxon cemeteries such as Lechlade (▶ p. 494) are well known. Many Christian churches were deliberately built on earlier pagan sites, most spectacularly at Knowlton, Dorset and La Hougue Bie on Jersey. The continuing power and importance of earlier beliefs can also be seen in the reuse of some religious sites. The nature of the religious changes of the Reformation can be seen in the study of structural and decorative changes in churches. This is most evident when medieval wall-paintings are revealed under Puritan whitewash as at Baunton.

This section provides a brief overview from the Upper Palaeolithic to the Roman period to introduce the range of evidence and current interpretations. It also illustrates change and the way in which social and economic evolution impacted on religion. Examples are largely from the British Isles but reference is also made to Europe. You need to be aware that in many respects, particularly monument types, there are regional differences that may be significant; and also that we only know about the mortuary practices for a tiny fraction of the population. They may not be typical. Excarnation or cremation before disposal in natural places (possibly rivers) may have always been the norm from at least the Neolithic onwards.

UPPER PALAEOLITHIC EUROPE 40,000–10,000 BP

The earliest accepted evidence of religious beliefs comes from modern human burials *c.* 100,000 BP. Inhumations in Skhul Cave, Israel, were sprinkled with red ochre and surrounded with stone tools, shells and animal bones, showing both clear signs of ritual and a perhaps a concern for the deceased after their death. A child burial from the same period in Border Cave, South Africa, may reflect similar practices. While the 'grave goods' may have been attached to clothes the deceased had worn, the use of red ochre is different. It represents symbolic behaviour with people expressing ideas about the deceased through ritual and offerings. Other tantalising glimpses of the early expression of ideas are represented by the wearing of beads (▶ p. 218), shell palettes used for mixing ochre paint from Blombos Cave, South Africa and abstract patterns carved on stone. The Neanderthals also buried some of their dead (▶ p. 201) and some archaeologists argue that this reflects beliefs as well as the disposal of human remains. Evidence from Krapina Cave (▶ p. 201), Croatia, where patterns of cut-marks on human bones have been found, may suggest ritual rather than cannibalism or both.

The survival of burials from the Upper Palaeolithic (from *c.* 40,000 BP) is extremely rare but two key elements are repeated. One is the use of the pigment red ochre which appears to have been sprinkled or painted on buried bodies. Its use on living bodies is also suspected at many sites associated with both modern people and even Neanderthals. The second is personal ornaments or grave goods. Most commonly this involves shell, stone and ivory beads, bracelets and pendants. These elements are found in the Paviland Cave (Wales) burial of a young man and most spectacularly in the group of burials at the riverside site of Sungir near Moscow. Both are dated to between 30,000 and 20,000 BP. This period also saw developments which provide insights into the origins of art and its role in religion in particular.

Art

The first of these was portable art. One of the oldest known statues, the 'Lion Man' of Stadel im Hohlenstein, dates from 32,000 BP. This mythical, anthropomorphic figure may represent beliefs in animal spirits or that human qualities were seen in animals. The mobile art tradition includes representing women as so-called 'Venus figurines' including the examples from Willendorf, Dolni Vestonice and Kostienki and they have been interpreted as possible evidence of a mother goddess religion. The detail and complexity of these statues, which mainly date between 28,000 and 20,000 BP, is echoed across Europe and indicates common elements in cultural and religious ideas.

The middle of the Upper Palaeolithic is perhaps best known for cave or parietal art on the

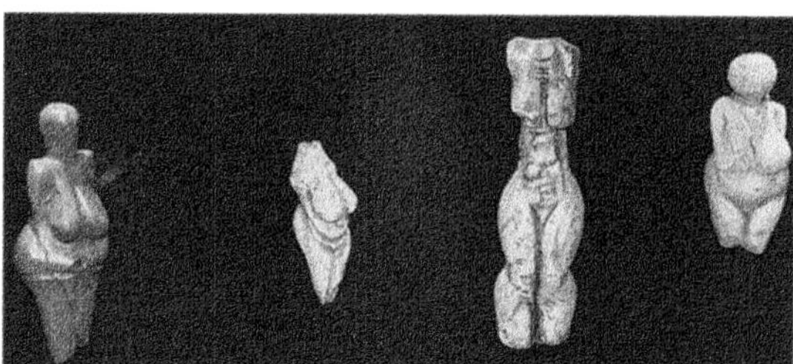

Figure 11.30 *A selection of Venus figurines. These may or may not represent mother goddesses.*

walls and ceilings of caves and rock shelters. Like the statues these also hint at complex ideas and rituals. Examples from France include the 3D sculptures at L'Abri du Cap Blanc with its beautiful frieze of horses; the magnificent bison in clay from Le Tuc d'Audoubert; the horse at Peche Merle carved from a sheet of stalactite with another horse painted in black and white on its surface. This is quite splendid, especially when viewed in context by the flickering light of a pine torch when shadows and imagination enter the viewer's consciousness along with the image itself. Cave art at first sight seems very appealing and accessible and a common misconception is that it consists of 'hunting scenes' which we can interpret through our imagination and appreciate in our modern way as 'art for art's sake'. In fact there are very few if any 'scenes', instead the significance seems often to be in the performance as much as the actual images. In most cases we

Figure 11.31 *Peche Merle – the world of the cave. It is easy to understand how deep caves with vivid colours and twisted stalactites seen in flickering light must have seemed like liminal places before decoration with cave art.*

cannot be sure which images on a particular wall were painted at the same time, never mind whether they 'go together' in any meaningful way. Images of animals predominate but not usually in proportion to their importance as a food source. Reindeer were often the most common prey species but not the most frequently painted. Images of human beings tend to vary hugely. They can be schematic at one end of the scale, as at Lascaux, or intensely realistic, as at La Marche. In addition to the main images there are also many geometric designs or 'signs', which some have interpreted literally as spears, nets, traps and houses.

Cave art has been through a number of different interpretations since the discovery of Lascaux in 1940 including 'art for art's sake', 'male/female symbols' and the idea of 'caves as cathedrals'. Analogies drawn from the Pacific coast of North America suggested the possibilities of totemism or 'sympathetic magic' designed to bring prey to the hunters. The inaccessibility of the galleries also raised the possibility that they were educational, to teach hunting and tracking skills, perhaps as a rite of passage. Until recently no one had attempted to integrate the large number of abstract motifs into the overall schema. Then Lewis-Williams and Dowson (1988) opened up a new approach combining neuropsychology with ethnography. Many of the symbols were shown to be 'entoptic' or geometric shapes that are 'hard-wired' into our central nervous system as humans. They are images that come from within our brains rather than from what we have seen. We project them over the top of images from everyday life when in an altered state of consciousness such as a trance. These geometric shapes are shared by all modern peoples and therefore by the people of the Upper Palaeolithic.

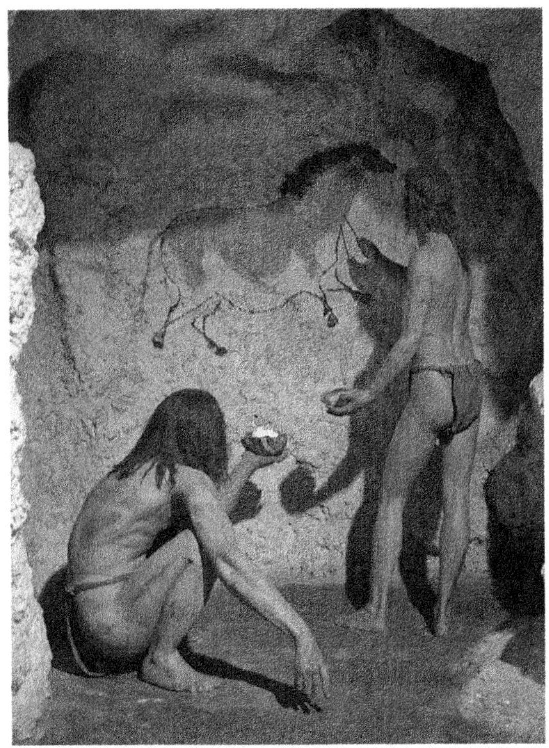

Figure 11.32 *Reconstruction of cave painting. Evidence from Lascaux and other caves of pine tapers, wood brushes, stone 'saucers' with fat and traces of red ochre and manganese oxide enables an understanding of how the work was executed.*

Similar analysis has been carried out on Neolithic rock art. This also drew on the work in South Africa of the C19th linguist Wilhelm Bleeck, who studied Bushmen art and mythology. His records of these people provided the key to understanding Bushmen rock paintings. San shamans often describe themselves as feeling weightless and changing shape during 'trance dances' which they use to reach the spirit world. They record their visions and spirit travels as rock art. Palaeolithic images include a shaman transforming into his animal spirit companions. The human figure is still quite rare despite enigmatic images at Les Trois Frères, Cougnac and Lascaux which suggest that we are dealing with shamans turning into creatures that are half man and half animal – therianthropes. Trancing may have involved the shaman dancing and imitating the movements and sounds of a bird as part of his performance, perhaps

Figure 11.33 *Palaeolithic cave art images which may be of shamans transforming*

dressed in a bird costume and carrying magical artefacts such as the staff. Wider research into links between shamanism and rock art across much of Africa and Eurasia suggests that cave art may be shamanistic in origin. It may also mean that we can even understand elements of ancient religion as far back as the last Ice Age.

MESOLITHIC EUROPE *C.* 10,000–6,500 BP

Animistic beliefs and shamanism appear to have continued into the Mesolithic. The antler 'head dresses' from Bedburg and Star Carr (▶ p. 267) have been interpreted as props for ritual dancing. Human–fish hybrids are also a feature of statues created at Lepenski Vir on the Danube. Amber carvings of animals are frequently of bears, associated with shamans by many northern Eurasian peoples. On a carved elk bone, which may have been part of a staff, an image reminiscent of San rock art appears to show an anthropomorphic figure entering an elk – another creature associated with shamanism.

While cave sites, such as Aveline's Hole in Somerset, were still used for burials, there is more diversity of mortuary practice in the Mesolithic. Disarticulated remains (Oronsay ▶ p. 233) and inhumations (Hoëdic and Téviec, France) have been recovered from inside and beneath shell middens. Cremations, inhumations and secondary burials are all known from the increasing number of known cemetery sites. The numbers of both cemeteries and burials provide archaeologists with greater opportunities than in the Palaeolithic for identifying repeated patterns in order to infer beliefs and practices. The deliberate burial with grave goods suggests a reverence for the dead, most eloquently expressed in the interment of a child on a swan's wing at the Ertebølle Culture cemetery at Vedbaek. Other Ertebølle cemeteries such as Skateholm emphasise natural materials including amber, red ochre, animal bone and antlers. Some of these are associated with burials as far back as the Upper Palaeolithic, which may suggest some continuity of belief.

Similar finds and strings of beads are known from Téviec and Hoëdic, where some bodies were buried in stone cists and at large cemeteries in the eastern Baltic. The largest of these is Oleni Island on Lake Onega in Russian Karelia, with 177 burials surviving from a much greater original number. In addition to tools and jewellery of slate, quartz and flint, there were many

Figure 11.34 *Possible shaman's staff*

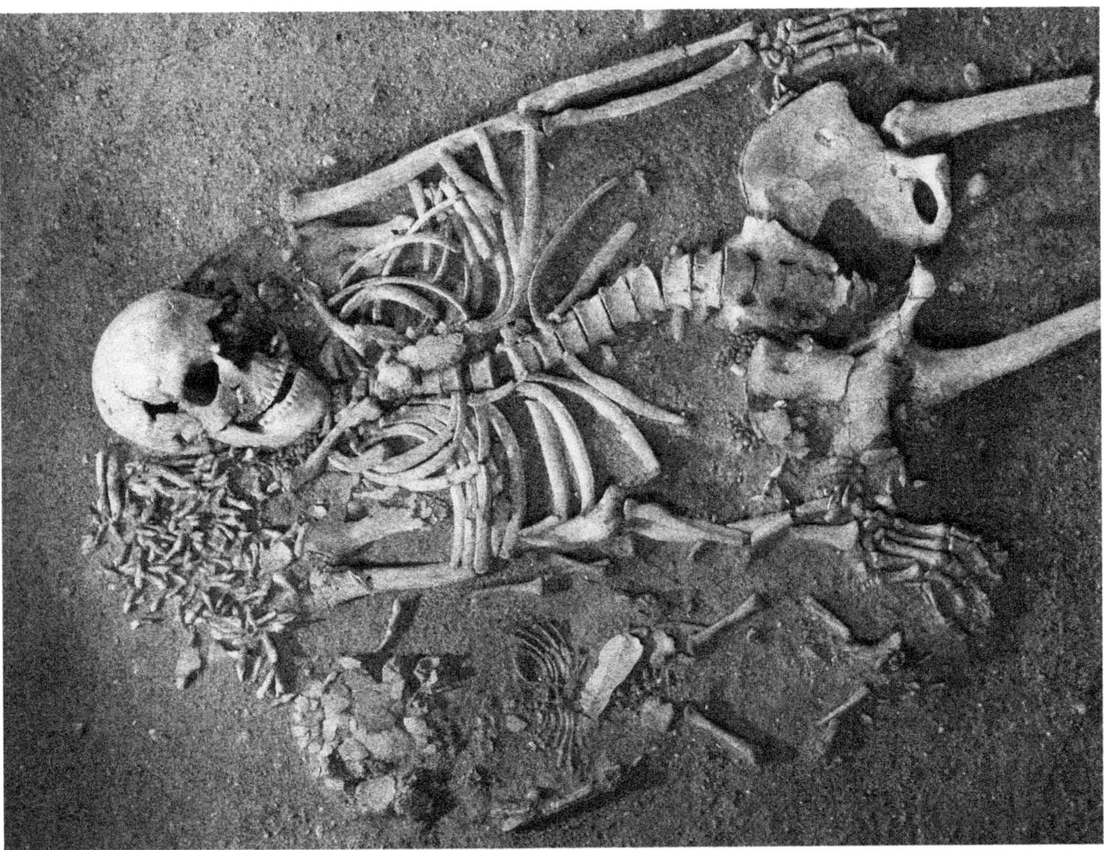

Figure 11.35 *Vedbaek 'swan wing burial'*

Grave 8, the most famous of the burials from this Ertebølle Culture cemetery, contains a young woman, who may have died in childbirth, and a premature baby. The symbolism of the baby on the swan wing has been much debated with suggestions including purity and the ability of a water bird to transcend water, land and air. Certainly both bodies were cared for in death (the disorderly state of the mother's ribs suggests that she may have been resting on an organic 'pillow'), which suggests a belief that the spirit remained with the body. The child's flint blade may symbolise some form of ascribed status while the woman, in common with several others, had a shell girdle. Her headdress (or hair ornaments) comprised teeth from a variety of wild animals including red deer, boar, elk and bear. (Anne Birgitte Gurlev/Vedbaek Museum)

carved artefacts from the bones of beaver, wolf, bear and elk. These included several carved snakes with anthropomorphic faces and also carvings of elk heads. On several sites dogs were buried in a similar way to humans. Taken together the evidence points to beliefs in a spirit world. Perhaps people saw themselves as part of nature rather than in control of it. Mannermaa et al. (2008) noted that adult birds of prey were disproportionally placed in the graves at Oleni Island rather than the more common water birds. This suggested deliberate selection of great grey owls, ospreys and sea eagles for particular burials. They may have represented clan totems or perhaps the identification of people with the power and spirits of these hunters.

A different approach to interpreting these burials was taken by Nilsson Stutz (2003). She applied the French archaeological approach of 'anthropologie de terrain' to Mesolithic burials.

Essentially this involves very detailed taphonological recording and investigation of the site formation processes affecting the bodies. The way a skeleton decomposes and moves within the ground will differ if it is articulated or disarticulated, wrapped or unwrapped, placed in a box or in the soil. If each community had an idea about the right way to treat the dead, then there should be observable differences from these rituals in the archaeological record. Nilsson Stutz (2010) was able to identify mortuary practice at Zvejnieki (northern Latvia) which involved wrapping the dead and differed from Ertebølle sites. At the latter, she found evidence of secondary burials and at Skateholm of some corpses being buried in a sitting position.

Cemeteries mark places in the landscape which were repeatedly visited over many years and may have been seen as sacred places for the dead. Middens also mark the landscape and are effectively the first monuments but they were used by the living as well as being places where they buried their dead, as at Ertebølle (▶ p. 314). There are also Mesolithic pits underneath some later barrows.

THE EARLY TO MIDDLE NEOLITHIC *C.* 4500–*C.* 3000 BC IN THE BRITISH ISLES

The Neolithic brought changes in religion which vary by region, although an increased emphasis on ancestral remains is central. In Britain the Neolithic is seen as at least partly the result of indigenous Mesolithic people adopting new ideas. People's lives in the early Neolithic may have been similar to those in the later Mesolithic: herding rather than hunting but still seasonally mobile. Key elements in the new beliefs were widespread evidence of excarnation, the deposition of manufactured artefacts such as pottery and domesticated animal bones and the creation of monuments. These include ritual enclosures, particularly on hilltops (e.g. 'causewayed camps'), and tombs such as long barrows or long cairns.

Neolithic tombs

A range of hypotheses have been put forward about the nature of the religion of the builders of the passage graves, cairns and long barrows of western Europe. Although these monuments are similar in some ways, there are significant differences in their contents. In long barrows there was a gradual change from individual articulated burials to collections of disarticulated bones as at Hazleton or re-sorted bones as at West Kennet. However, this pattern is not universal, which suggests some regional variety in beliefs. The shape of the tombs may celebrate domestication in its widest sense: houses and control over the fertility of animals. Some writers see the swollen mound of these monuments as evidence for worship of an earth or fertility goddess. The shape of passage graves with their narrow entrances suggests a womb from which the soul is reborn. For farmers, fertility is a crucial issue and reseeding Mother Earth with the bones of ancestors may have been a symbolic gesture to ensure good crops or plentiful livestock. Other archaeologists have noted the similarity between some of these monuments and the longhouses of the first farmers of central Europe. Perhaps inscribing the landscape with permanent markers associated with their dead was to establish land rights.

Not all tombs had entrances. Amongst many that did, the disarticulated bones from different individuals were deliberately mixed and sometimes re-sorted. Perhaps this was to downplay individual differences and mask inequalities amongst the living. The dead became part of a shared group of ancestors rather than belonging to a particular family. The restricted entrance passages and evidence of the transformation of skeletons through sorting hint at the possibility of ritual specialists. Acoustic experiments (Watson 1997) suggest that the design of burial chambers may have enabled specialists, possibly shamans, to create atmospheres and illusions through the use of sound. Similar effects have been noted at

Figure 11.36 *The inside of a Neolithic tomb with disarticulated human remains*

later stone circles. The mortuary rituals in tombs may be linked to activities at other Neolithic sites. At some causewayed enclosures such as Hambledon Hill, human bones appear to have been subject to excarnation. Perhaps the spirits of the dead could not be released until flesh had been removed from bones. Some bones exposed at such sites may have later been transferred to tombs. Around barrows there is often waste from feasting and some human bones. Ethnographic evidence from the Merina of Madagascar (Parker-Pearson 1999) has been used to suggest that the remains of the dead may have been removed from time to time to be involved in rituals. While they are radically different societies, there are interesting parallels. The Merina use communal, chambered tombs to emphasise community and kinship. Skeletons are wrapped in the tomb but are periodically taken out and re-wrapped. These rituals involve both the living and the ancestors.

Soul beliefs

Graslund (1994), in a comparative study of Scandinavian tombs from the Neolithic to Viking periods, concluded that settled societies share a belief in some sort of afterlife and in souls or spirits. He identified two models. The breath soul leaves the body with its last sigh and goes to join the ancestors. The free or dream soul is active when the body sleeps. After death it remains with the body until the flesh is gone. Graslund argued that the treatment of bodies after death reflected different soul beliefs. Where excarnation or disarticulation had occurred before placing in a tomb, it suggested a breath soul. The tomb served as an ossuary. However, where decomposition occurred inside the tomb, it was a grave. The evidence for this is the presence of small bones that would have been lost during excarnation, skeletons in sitting positions and beads that may have come from clothing. There are also fatty deposits in the soil in some tombs. With dream soul beliefs, before the dead could join the ancestors in the tomb, the corpse would have to be cared for as if it were alive. This might also account for the presence of food remains and grave goods. In both cases the dead go through a rite of passage involving defleshing in order to become an ancestor.

KEY STUDY

Newgrange

This massive Neolithic passage grave was constructed *c.* 3200 BC on a ridge overlooking a large bend in the River Boyne, Ireland. It is part of a mortuary complex of tombs which includes the equally massive monuments of Knowth and Dowth. Clusters of small passage graves are aligned on the major monuments. Newgrange measures some 105m in diameter and was once encircled by standing stones. Twelve of around thirty-five of these stones still survive. In common with other monuments in the complex, it has suffered through being used as a stone quarry for road and wall building over the centuries. Around the base of the mound are ninety-seven kerbstones, many of which are decorated. Some of these face into the monument and may have been intended to only be visible to the spirits. The south side of the monument appears to have been faced with quartz which petrology showed had come from the Wicklow Mountains, a long boat journey to the south, while the granite pebbles came from the Mountains of Mourne to the north. The entrance has a light box above it and a sinuous, gently rising 19m passage leading to a cruciform central chamber. This is corbelled to create a domed roof 6m high in the centre. The chamber contained relatively few artefacts, although some items may have been taken over the millennia. Stone basins held disarticulated burials and cremations and some animal bones. On the walls is some of the most important carved rock art in Europe. These include tri-spirals, which are often mistakenly thought to be Celtic in design, zig-zags, herringbone, concentric circles and axe shapes. The chamber was possibly designed to provide particular acoustic effects. At dawn on the winter solstice, and two days either side of it, a shaft of light shines through the light box to penetrate the central chamber. This effect and the womb-like design of the monument have led many to link Newgrange to a belief in rebirth.

Links to other monuments

Newgrange was built in an area where settlement already existed. A mixture of landscapes in the local area meant that both pastoral and arable farming was practised. The sheer scale of the monuments suggests that building them was in some way competitive with a sequence of complexes stretching west across Ireland including Loughcrew, Carrowkeel and Carrowmore. At one time it was thought Newgrange influenced these others but recent dates suggest Carrowmore may have been the earliest. Certainly there were links between them with Carrowkeel-style pottery found at all the sites. There are also polished mace heads of a design common in Orkney. The logistical effort of mobilising and feeding a labour force to complete the project has been seen as signifying an increasingly ranked society. Certainly the design itself structures people into those who would have witnessed the chamber art and the solstice and those who would only see the kerb art. The earliest art in the chamber is incised and largely made up of lines. It is similar to that at Maes Howe on Orkney. Later, often curved, designs were created by 'pecking' and have similarities with megalithic art along the Atlantic seaboard from Temple Wood in Scotland (▶ p. 540) to Iberia.

Newgrange's entrance has the light box above the entrance to the passage and a massive blocking stone with distinctive spiral petroglyphs. The composition of the reconstructed façade, with granite 'peppering' of the white quartz, is clearly visible.

As with many major prehistoric monuments, considerable changes took place during its use. In the 3rd millennium BC the tomb may have been blocked. Certainly the façade had collapsed or been demolished.

Figure 11.37 *Newgrange entrance and lightbox*

The circle of monoliths was built to create a more open type of monument, perhaps more concerned with wider rituals than burials. This is a pattern also seen at the Clava Cairns near Inverness (▶ p. 518). During the Beaker period a cluster of round-houses was built next to the monument and an oval ring of pits and timber post settings was dug. There may also have been a henge, roughly the same size as Newgrange. Grooved ware and animal remains suggest that feasting took place there.

Figure 11.38 *Newgrange curved passage which reduces light entering the chamber on the solstice to a thin shaft*

Newgrange illustrates some of the modern presentational problems faced by Stonehenge (▶ p. 578). During excavation in the 1960s, the decision was taken to reconstruct the monument to enable visitors to appreciate its original features. Antiquarian accounts, experiments and engineering principles were used to determine the final shape of the mound. The result has been much criticised. The controversial vertical façade would probably fall down without the concrete holding it in place while the peppering of the sparkling quartz with granite pebbles is said to make it look like a cheesecake.

A major interpretation centre was built a short distance away with buses used to transport tourists to the tomb and control numbers. Its massive popularity means visits often have to be booked ahead

continued

Figure 11.39 *Newgrange. The controversial quartz and granite façade.*

and a lottery system is used to select those to witness the solstice. While many have criticised the 'reconstruction' of Newgrange, it serves as a tourist 'honeypot' which reduces pressure on the other major tombs and other monuments in the World Heritage Site of the Boyne Valley. The equally large passage tomb at Knowth is currently being excavated, while that at Dowth has not been developed.

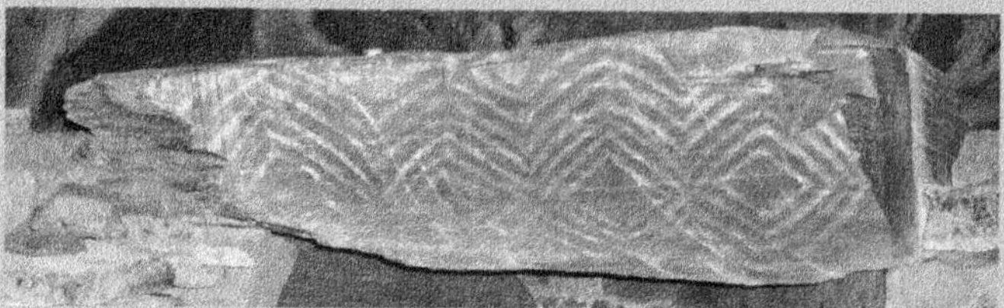

Figure 11.40 *Lozenge petroglyphs from Four Knocks*

Four Knocks passage grave is 16km south of Newgrange and part of the same tradition. Excavated in the 1950s and given a modern domed roof, it contains a variety of Neolithic petroglyphs including zig-zag and lozenge motifs. Statistical analysis has established a significant correlation between these images and entoptic images produced during trancing. This may suggest that shamanism remained important into the Bronze Age.

Figure 11.41 *Zig-zag petroglyphs from Four Knocks*

Other Neolithic monuments

The tombs that hold the remains of the dead are often massive while remains of the settlements of the living are more fleeting. Neolithic people may have been mobile herders so this may not be surprising. Tilley (1996) suggests that monuments were sited in particular places in relation to important places in the natural landscape. Mountains, spurs and crossing points on pathways may have already been important. Causewayed enclosures, which encircle an area with one or more series of intermittent ditches, were originally thought to have been placed on hilltop sites along route ways. However, the development of aerial photography revealed many examples from flatlands as well. Most of these enclosures were not defensive and the ditches contained the remains of animal butchery, pottery and lithics from a wide range of sources and human remains. They have been interpreted as seasonal markets, festival sites, stock enclosures and mortuary enclosures. However, it is perfectly possible that all these elements were present if those using the site did not separate beliefs off from the rest of their lives.

Some Neolithic monuments also appear to have been sited at places which already had ancestral significance. Evidence from the relatively small number of Neolithic houses that have been found suggests that some may not have been domestic at all. Many have odd, non-functional features and strange deposits or unusual artefacts and have been described as cult houses. The massive timber house at Balbridie appeared to have a screen just inside the door which would have made the inside dark and restricted access. Another at Balfarg probably had no roof. It held finds of a beaker which contained possible traces of narcotic substances. The early houses of Orkney reflect the designs of tombs as at Skara Brae (▶ p. 274) and Barnhouse. Even apparently purely economic sites such as flint mines may have had some ritual functions. It seems that in the Neolithic there was no distinction between ritual and practical. Actions were informed by beliefs.

KEY TERM

Structured deposition

Non-random patterns of finds which suggest that artefacts and remains were deliberately placed in particular locations or result from particular, repeated activities.

THE LATER NEOLITHIC AND EARLY BRONZE AGE *C.* 3000–1800 BC IN THE BRITISH ISLES

The veneration of ancestors, communal rituals and belief in spirits continued into the 3rd millennium BC but very gradually a number of changes occurred. The new elements included an increasing diversity of funerary and ritual monuments. Amongst the latter were large-scale constructions such as cursus monuments, stone or timber circles and rows and henges. These are associated with particular landscape features such as rivers, earlier ancestral remains and solar alignments. Particular classes of artefacts are associated with these monuments such as grooved ware with henges and they were frequently deposition sites for valuable objects such as polished stone axes. Rock art, which is found in most areas with hard stone, is also likely to have had a ritual significance.

Large Neolithic enclosures

Amongst the significant developments here are the scale and type of monument and the symbolism of the alignment and positioning of monuments. Many of the larger monuments would have required considerable organisation and millions of man-hours to build. Engineering skills were needed to transport and erect huge timbers and megaliths. Megalith essentially means 'big stone' and is applied both to standing stones and to monuments constructed of large boulders. Increasingly 'megalithic' is used to describe other aspects of society such as art during the time when megaliths were erected – essentially the Neolithic and early to middle Bronze Age.

Large, open monuments may represent a move to large-scale rituals. Certainly there is evidence of extensive feasting at many, such as the slaughter of pigs and cattle at West Kennet timber enclosure. The planning of the architecture and use of space in the monuments suggests the

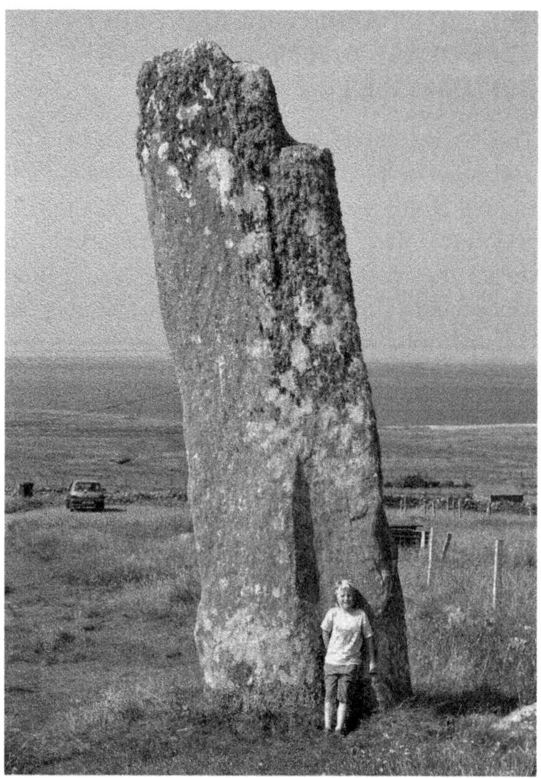

Figure 11.42 *Clach An Truishal, Lewis. This megalith stands 6m tall.*

existence of ritual leaders, while the events that took place in them would have required organisation and coordination.

Linear alignments lend themselves to processions (someone always leads) while barriers, boundaries, elaborate entrances and series of concentric structures on some sites divide people into in/out. The circularity of monuments could symbolise many things; for example, the horizons of their world, as they could see it, the community or the sun. Some writers have suggested that monuments reflected the landscape. Henges often occur in river basins where long views are cut off.

The positioning of later monuments seems to be affected by both the landscape and earlier monuments. Loveday's (1998) work on Dorchester-on-Thames suggested that the cursus might have been aligned on a natural feature: a twin-peaked hill known as Mother Dunche's Buttocks. Other monuments including cursuses are then aligned on it even after it went out of use. Its proximity to the Thames is surely also significant. Rivers, including their springs, do seem to be a focus for ritual activity from at least this period. Henges in particular are often associated with rivers. There are also many examples where monuments are aligned on earlier funerary monuments. The Dorset Cursus was aligned on several long barrows, the Giant's Ring at Ballynahatty on a small passage grave. The new monuments are linked to earlier ancestral beliefs, perhaps to provide legitimacy. Many monuments are also aligned on solar or possibly lunar phenomena. The most famous is the reorientation of Stonehenge towards the midsummer or midwinter solstice. Equally significant are the 'light boxes' on passage graves in Ireland and Orkney. These allow light to penetrate into burial chambers on the winter solstice. This linked ancestors to an annual cycle of death and rebirth.

Neolithic ritual landscapes

Where large numbers of monuments cluster together, archaeologists have used the term 'ritual landscape' (▶ p. 522). The idea that a whole block of land might have been dedicated to gods or spirits was first applied to Cranborne Chase, where the 11km long cursus monument was the focus for burials over several thousand years. Analysis of fieldwalking finds revealed that higher than usual proportions of exotic artefacts and human remains were found close to the cursus with little sign of everyday activity (Green 2000). Whether areas were set aside for gods or spirits, the monuments affected the way people moved around the landscape and saw the world. They probably reinforced ideas about life, death and society. Some of the monuments may have been at points where people met during seasonal movements. The massive henge at Durrington Walls may have been a place where herders

Figure 11.43 *The Ring of Brodgar*

This elemental monument is part of an astonishing concentration of ritual sites on an isthmus where a freshwater and a sea loch almost meet. This World Heritage Site also includes Maes Howe chambered cairn and the huge Stones of Stenness. Like Avebury, a circle of megaliths was erected inside a massive henge, in this case with two causewayed entrances. Brodgar is the third largest stone circle in the British Isles and twenty-seven of the original sixty megaliths remain. It dates to the late 3rd millennium BC and was probably associated with large-scale ritual performances. An alternative view is that the process of construction was the most important aspect, perhaps a way for local leaders to gain status through competition with monument builders elsewhere. As with many stone circles, dancing giants feature in the folklore of the site.

crossed the Upper Avon and spread out into summer grazing lands in the spring. The site may have been important for seasonal rituals or festivals. Many monuments were remodelled several times, perhaps reflecting changing beliefs. At Stanton Drew magnetometer surveys have revealed that the stone circles replaced earlier timber monuments. Recent work suggests that henges might be the final form enclosing ritual sites.

The study of sacred geography involves examining the relation between monuments and landscape and the ways in which the building of monuments affects the way in which people may have moved around or viewed the landscape. Amongst the range of techniques are studies of intervisibility which examine whether monuments were sited in view of each other. This has been assisted by the use of GIS and has been particularly applied to rock art and barrows.

Figure 11.44 *Cist grave at Temple Wood*

This cist grave is the focus for the main stone circle in the Kilmartin ritual complex. It is encircled by a tiny ring of stones only 3m in diameter. A larger ring of megaliths (12m in diameter) – some with petroglyphs – may align on the winter solstice. The cist held cremation burials and had no lid, being originally covered in a cairn of stones. The monument itself dates back to the 4th millennium BC and was originally constructed in timber. The cist was added during the 3rd millennium BC after the large stone circle was built. This filling up of an existing monument may represent particular lineages in the early Bronze Age staking a claim to a shared ancestral past. The monument was still the focus of burials 1,000 years later, demonstrating the continued importance of ritual places even when their original belief system was forgotten.

Attempting to 'read' the way monuments structure experience of the landscape borrows from the sociological approach known as phenomenology and has been pioneered in case studies in Britain by Tilley (1994). This approach has led to a reappraisal of linear monuments. These clearly structure movement in a particular order and direction but may themselves be permanent inscriptions of earlier movements or processions. Barnett's (1998) study of the stone rows on Dartmoor noted how many lead from the valleys onto the moors, perhaps marking a route for spirits or the dead. Similar suggestions have been made for Avebury and Stonehenge, with pathways linking ritual areas for the living and those of the ancestors.

Clues to Neolithic ritual

There is increasing evidence that dramatic events played an important part in ritual. Some monuments appear to have been built in stages over many years so that participation in the project may have been more important than the final product; for example, the Cleaven Dyke. Others were deliberately destroyed by what must have

Figure 11.45 *Petroglyphs from Achnabreck, Kilmartin*

been spectacular fires. Often timber structures were repeatedly built and destroyed as at Dunragit and West Kennet. At the latter site, Whittle's (1998) excavations revealed two massive but short-lived, egg-shaped enclosures. The large number of meat bones which had been discarded without being fully processed provided strong evidence of feasting, as did large amounts of grooved ware. The enclosures were located very close to other monuments and the source of the Kennet. The concept of liminality was used to explain the special attention given to boundaries. In particular, deliberate deposits of grooved ware, bone and artefacts had been made around the entrances. This practice has been noted at other timber enclosures throughout Britain.

Petroglyphs (▶ p. 232) such as that at Achnabreck provide another possible insight into ritual. This slab, with its examples of classic 'cup and ring' marks, and 'stars and spirals', overlooks one of the approaches to the Kilmartin Valley, a significant ritual complex. Other examples have been found throughout north-western Europe on monuments such as Newgrange (▶ p. 535). Analysis of the abstract images suggests that they comprise similar entoptic patterns (▶ p. 529) to those recorded in research into hallucinogens and trancing. If this is the case, then attaining altered states of consciousness through dancing, sound, drugs or fasting may have been a feature of rituals. In addition to some monuments being designed to alter sound, there is increasing evidence that colour was also important in the selection of stone and perhaps related to performances.

Possibly the distinctive pottery (grooved ware and beakers) found in ritual deposits from this period may have held more than just refreshments. Beakers (▶ p. 493) are best known from their place in a new tradition of single burials in graves and cists. As part of a fairly standard assemblage of grave goods (decorated beaker, arrowheads, dagger, wrist guard, etc.), they may represent a more individualised view of an afterlife as well as a more ranked society.

THE MIDDLE BRONZE AGE 1800–1200 BC IN BRITAIN

Once again, there is great continuity from the late Neolithic. This is most obvious in the elaboration of earlier monuments such as the final phases of remodelling of Stonehenge, Avebury and the way new monuments continue to be linked to much earlier ones. Individual burials occur throughout prehistory but there seems to be a shift of emphasis in the Bronze Age. This is most marked in the building of thousands of round barrows or cairns that were often constructed over a primary burial or cremation with satellite burials around it (and often later secondary burials). The development of a range of regional burial traditions could reflect changes in beliefs and society. The old way of life of semi-sedentary herding amongst roughly equal social groups was being replaced by a more unequal society based on control of the land. The new barrows and cairns cluster round earlier monuments and in the case of some small circular monuments, such as Cairnpapple, fill them. This surely represents high-status individuals linking their families to 'the ancestors' and their rights and power. Some burials, particularly in Wessex, included rich and exotic grave goods. The 'Amesbury Archer' and the Bush Barrow burial are the best known. The size of the burial mounds may also indicate the importance of individuals but could also be to provide platforms for funeral pyres. It is likely that the funerary rituals would have been more important at the time than the artefacts which archaeologists recover. Later in this period there was an increasing variety of burial traditions including single and multiple burials, flat cemeteries and particularly cremations.

It was not just monuments which were aligned on the solar features. Orientation also became important in determining the entrances of houses and enclosures. This tradition continued into the Iron Age. Elsewhere in northern Europe a number of bronze artefacts also attest to the importance of the sun. The Trundholm sun chariot is a bronze model of the sun being pulled by a wheeled horse. It is gilded on one side, which may represent the east-west journey of the sun, while the other side may represent the invisible return journey. It was found in a bog in Denmark and

Figure 11.46 *Trundholm sun chariot found in a bog in Denmark and dated to 1600 BC. The sun is being pulled by a wheeled horse.*

dated to *c*. 1600 BC. The Nebra sky disc is from the same period in Germany and features gold images of the sun, moon and stars on a bronze base. It is thought to be a lunar calendar because it may indicate sunrise and sunset at the solstices.

THE LATE BRONZE AGE AND IRON AGE 1200–55 BC

Some archaeologists have approached this period from later Roman accounts while others have traced developments in the archaeological record. These tend to lead to very different emphases. Roman accounts stress a priesthood – the Druids – while archaeology tends to highlight the continued embedding of ritual in the everyday and the importance of deposition in wet places. Society was now based on settled villages involved in mixed farming. Perhaps the domestication of religion reflects a less mobile society. The monument-building tradition was abandoned and is evident in the way later Bronze Age field systems cut across earlier monuments whose faint traces had been respected for over a thousand years. Instead of monuments, natural places seem to have become significant as locations for ritual. In addition to water and pits, deposits occur on hilltops, which may well have been wooded. This is particularly the case with torcs. The Romans mentioned Druids lurking in oak groves! Symbolism was drawn from the natural world. Birds, particularly ducks, feature on some high-status artefacts and bird bones are often found with human remains.

From *c*. 1400 BC the climate became cooler with disastrous consequences for upland settlements (▶ p. 242). Shortly afterwards many of the Mediterranean civilisations associated with the long-distance prestige goods trade collapsed. Whether the two were connected or not there was

Figure 11.47 *Shears from Flag Fen*

This perfect pair of clippers from Flag Fen shows us that Bronze Age shepherds already had technology which would be in use until the C19th. They were not lost or casually discarded. These valuable items complete with their wooden case were deposited from a wooden causeway as ritual offerings. Hundreds of other valuable finds from jewellery through swords to millstones belonged to these structured deposits.

a major change in ritual away from large seasonal gatherings at monuments linked to solar phenomena and towards more extreme votive deposits including that of people. Throughout north-western Europe large quantities of metalwork including the very finest were deposited in rivers and lakes. Examples include the Battersea and Witham shields and the Mold gold cape. Water sacrifices may be acts of propitiation (▶ p. 520), perhaps in appeals to a water or underground deity. It may also be the case that water was always important, but that it becomes archaeologically visible at this point. From Ireland to Denmark there is also evidence of ritual killing and burial in shallow lakes from finds of 'bog bodies'. Such sacrifices may have been connected with fertility but also with rites of intensification.

Iron Age burials

The impressive burials seen in museums such as the 'chariot burials' of Yorkshire and rich burials from Kent are exceptions. Most of the dead disappear. Excarnation seems to have been common with some cremation and possibly water burial. Brück's (1995) study of human remains on sites from this period revealed structured deposition with bones occurring in many locations not necessarily thought of as ritual, including huts and pits. Relatives may well have kept relics of their dead ancestors. Human bones along with animal remains were also used as deliberate deposits at entrances, boundaries and in grain pits. Ninety-eight of the pits at Danebury contained some human remains. Studies of middens and rubbish pits have also shown that their fills were non-random. Rules structured their creation. Some domestic sites also had very patterned orientation. Hill's (1996a) comparative study of Iron Age sites revealed a tendency for houses to face south-east. This may have been to do with light, although in Britain south would be the best direction to maximise daylight entering a hut. Light cannot have been a factor with

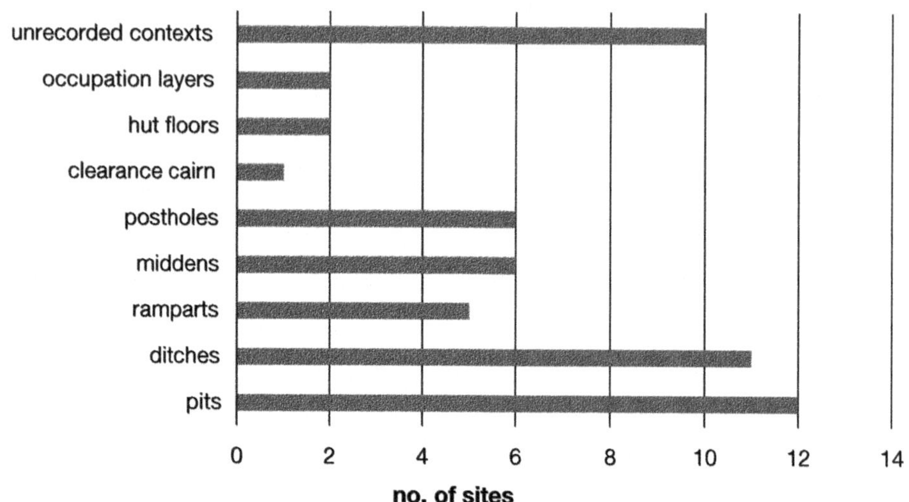

Figure 11.48 *Contexts where human remains have been found on late Bronze Age sites (after Brück 1995). Relatively few people appear to have been buried so it is unclear how most of the dead were disposed of during this period, although there is some evidence for excarnation and deposition in rivers. Brück's survey of excavated sites found that human remains were frequently deposited, or used, on settlement sites. This suggests that ancestral remains provided a kind of symbolic resource.*

Figure 11.49 *Welwyn burial. The cremation was buried with amphorae of wine, fine tableware, games and a variety of luxury items.*

enclosures. These tend to face south-west even when local topography and defensive considerations might suggest other directions. It may be that there was a 'right' direction from which to enter or perform activities. Ritual was a part of everyday life.

Specialists remain elusive. The Mill Hill (Deal) burials (▶ p. 439) include a young man wearing what has been interpreted as a Druid's crown because of its similarity to Roman priests' crowns. The Birdlip burial (▶ p. 449) was classified as a woman's grave but some researchers have reinterpreted the grave goods as shamanistic.

From the very end of the Iron Age a handful of possible temples have been identified. This may reflect a southern elite adopting continental customs along with imported goods in advance of the Roman invasion. Similarly, rich burials such as Welwyn document the influence of Rome in terms of burial goods if not religion. The Romans also provide us with names of local deities such as Sulis at Bath and of the festivals which marked the Iron Age calendar including Samhain, the forerunner of Halloween. Some wooden carvings from bogs and Roman reliefs may also represent Iron Age deities.

ROMAN RELIGION AND RITUAL TO *C.* AD 476

From the Roman period, much of our understanding of religion, particularly of deities and public rituals, comes from classical texts. Archaeology has been particularly useful in helping us understand less recorded aspects such as ritual embedded in everyday life.

Roman syncretism

Religion in the Roman world is a story of classical pantheons, mystery rituals and wonderful syncretisms of local and Roman deities. Early Roman religion was animistic with worship of ancestors and spirits who inhabited or influenced particular everyday places, events and things. Local protective spirits were known as *genius loci.* From the outset, Romans borrowed beliefs and practices from cultures around them, starting with the deities of the Etruscans and Greeks. The image of many gods or goddesses that they worshipped had generally evolved along lines established by Classical Greek artists in the C7th–C3rd BC. For example Zeus became Jupiter. They usually dealt with new ideas through a process of 'syncretism' or equating native gods and their attributes with the nearest equivalent from their pantheon, as in the famous example of Sulis Minerva. The Celtic goddess Sulis inhabited the hot spring at Bath and was equated by the Romans with Minerva, in this case operating in her guise as a goddess of healing rather than

 **KEY TERM**

Syncretism

Combining beliefs and ideas from several sources in a new religion.

Figure 11.50 *Altar from Cirencester dedicated to the genius loci of Corinium. In one hand he holds a cornucopia, with a patera (an offering or sacrificial bowl) in the other.*

wisdom. Clearly, Sulis Minerva was thought to provide curative powers through her hot water spring. Roman votives and 'defixiones' (curse tablets) were thrown into a liminal place that had been special to prehistoric Britons for hundreds of years already. This had the additional advantage of accommodating conquered peoples to Roman rule.

Syncretism did not mean the Romans simply copied older religions. Roman deities had less developed personalities and mythologies than those of the Greeks. Their powers and relationships to each other were more important. The major deities including Jupiter, Mars and Minerva had their own priesthoods, temples and festivals.

Relationships with the gods

This concept of 'you scratch my back and I'll scratch yours' underlies much of Roman belief. This can be seen in thousands of votive altars, plaques and miniature objects found nailed to temple doors or thrown into wells, rivers and springs all over the empire. Offerings could enable you to hedge your bets when embarking on a new business venture, going on a journey or facing potentially life-changing events. Animal entrails were burnt, chickens sacrificed and the flight of birds consulted. This was a reciprocal bargain between mortal and supernatural beings and the gods were expected to perform their side of the deal by using their power (*numen*) to influence events. 'Numen' was also embedded in particular places. This was later enshrined in temples and symbolised by statues of the '*genius loci*' (spirit of the place) such as the British goddess Brigantia and her nymphs in north-east England (e.g. Arbeia) or Sabrina Fluvius, the spirit of the River Severn. The 'numen' was everywhere in the Roman world from poems such as Horace's *Fountain of Bandusia*, 'more glittering than glass', to the end of a bar in Pompeii where one glanced across the top of a wine cup to see the household deities of the owner and the place, the Lares and Penates. Rather like our custom of leaving a mince pie and glass of sherry for Father Christmas, food and drink offerings would be left at this 'altar'.

Temples

Temples were houses of the gods so the Romans built them to look like a house, albeit on a grand scale and in prominent places. Temple layouts followed a defined plan which can be seen throughout the empire from the Temple of Apollo at Didyma (Turkey) to the Maison Carrée at Nimes (France). In the centre was a chamber (cella) in which the cult statue of the deity was visible and where offerings to the god were dedicated. The cella was often surrounded by a colonnade on at least one side and often on all sides. The Romans also liked to put their temples on a high podium so that they dominated the townscape, access being by a flight of steps at the front of the podium, as in the Temple of Apollo in Pompeii. The altar, where the sacrifices to the deity took place, was at the foot of the steps and it was here that people gathered to observe the rituals, rather than in the cella from which they were excluded. Both temple and altar were set within a defined enclosure or temenos whose boundary might be marked by a wall, a ditch, or a simple fence or hedge. This enclosed area, which might contain shrines and sacred groves,

Figure 11.51 *Temple of Mercury at Uley*

Mercury, messenger of the gods, was the patron of travellers (and also thieves!). His popularity in Corinium and at the nearby cult temple at Uley is evidenced by statues, votives and lead 'curse' tablets. Mercury is often shown with sheep or goats (fertility) or a cockerel (herald of the day). The bones of these animals were found in considerable numbers at Uley. The complex with the standard temple design (right) also included shops and hostels for pilgrims which can be seen to the left of the aerial view.

was also sacred to the deity. It often included ancillary buildings for priests and pilgrims. By comparison, later Jewish synagogues and Christian churches shared similar characteristics; both had to be able to hold large numbers of people in a segregated congregation.

Each town had one temple that was, in modern terms, its cathedral; Rome had the temple of Capitoline Jupiter, which he shared with Juno and Minerva. These temples were often lavishly decorated and were built in the most expensive materials available as they reflected the wealth of the town itself and its prestige in relation to other towns in the vicinity. Some of the more famous temples were centres of pilgrimage, or were oracular shrines, such as the earlier Shrine of Apollo at Delphi in Greece. Temple buildings could be built of many different materials – timber, mudbrick, tile, stone, marble – the choice depended upon the local building tradition and the amount of money available to the congregation. The site of a temple was determined by the exact focus of veneration, which in the countryside might be a spring, a grove, the top of a hill, or a crossroads. Once these sacred spots are forgotten, they are difficult to find again, although careful analysis of archaeological finds from surveys or the study of aerial photographs can yield new sites. Inscriptions often tell us who paid for the temples, and these inform us that donors ranged from town councils or wealthy individuals to the guilds, effectively craft-based friendly societies that dedicated temples for the use of their own members. These were clearly designed to meet their own specific needs: temples of Isis or Serapis for Egyptian grain shippers; a temple to Vulcan for blacksmiths. The temple of Serapis copied its façade from those of ancient Egypt with large

Figure 11.52 *Relief of Mithras from Pisa*

Figure 11.53 *Two of three genii cucullati from near Hadrian's Wall. Wearing their distinctive hooded cloaks, these Romano-Celtic gods symbolised healing and fertility.*

sloping pylons and lotus columns, while the Persian god Mithras had to have a building that resembled a cave as this was the focal part of the religious myth.

The priests (flamen) of the various cults were all overseen by the high priest or 'Pontifex Maximus', who in imperial times was the emperor. Their responsibility for organising religion came from law codes found inscribed on metal and stone in local towns. Other specialists included 'augurs' and 'haruspices'. These diviners interpreted the meanings in natural phenomena and the livers of sacrificed animals. They were consulted before important decisions were made. Perhaps the most well known of Roman ritual specialists were the Vestal Virgins, who tended the continually burning flame on the altar of the Temple of Vesta in Rome.

Religion in everyday life

Worship was not confined to temples; individuals looked to their household gods, the Lares and Penates. Higher-status people had their own shrine built into their houses, while for ordinary people worship centred around a simple lararium or set of statues. Pompeii has provided good examples. At the House of the Vettii two brothers had a very fine lararium on the wall, where a magical snake protected the household from evil forces outside. Phallic symbols performed much the same role outside many houses, including the town brothel with its massively endowed depiction of the god Priapus. More noble and richer families often put great faith in the cult of their ancestors and kept masks of them in the house to be carried in festival processions. There was also 'pietas', the sense of love, respect and duty towards both gods and their families, expressed through ordinary people's lives. Contact with the gods was effected in their temples or sacred places, but literary sources, such as letters, make it clear that contact with the gods could take place anywhere, and at any time. Also, those who wished for some help, or had a wish come true, might want to thank the deity responsible. The most obvious example of this are inscriptions: altars set up to record thanks for protection during a journey, or which have been set up as the result of a vision or dream. Successful business deals might be commemorated with an appropriate offering to Mercury, such as a cockerel, a bird identified as the familiar of this particular deity. Letters could also be written to the gods requesting favours, asking for them to help with a particular problem, or requesting them to pursue thieves who had stolen property. These were given to the gods as an offering so that only the god might read them. The votive tablets, letters to the deity scratched into small sheets of lead or pewter, from Bath and Uley show that these letters were written not by priests but by people of middle rank in society who were appealing to the gods to help them.

Roman mortuary practice

Mortuary practice is equally varied with both cremation on pyres and inhumations being

Figure 11.54 *The temple of Vesta in Rome*

common, as seen in the cemeteries of Londinium. There are also pipe burials, mausolea and cremations in jars of ceramic or glass. Thousands of gravestones with their elaborate decoration and Latin inscriptions tell us equally about belief and the lives of the deceased. The spirits of the dead, the *'dis manibus'*, also figure largely in standard grave inscriptions. Families often visited the grave to feast beside the tomb. At Caerleon one cremation could be served drinks through a spout which led down to the urn. Only neo-natal burials were allowed inside the 'pomerium' or town boundary. Cemeteries therefore were kept apart from settlement areas. In Rome burial could be in underground niches or 'loculi' but above ground tombstones were also very common. This was especially so in Britain due to the influence of the army (▶ p. 493).

By the C2nd AD inhumation became the norm across the whole empire. This may be associated with increasing worship of the sun god 'Sol Invictus'. At the same time cemeteries were laid out east–west and in neat rows. Inhumations were usually in the extended position but it is also quite common for the head to be cut off and placed elsewhere in the grave, often between the knees. Grave goods include lamps, jewellery and shoes, usually surviving as sets of studded nails. One of the most spectacular graves is the 'Lady of Spitalfields'. Her unique collection of lead coffin, grave goods and high-quality apparel is displayed in the Museum of London. One

Figure 11.55 *Fresco from the Villa of the Mysteries, Pompeii*

A chamber in this villa at Pompeii is thought to have been the site of female initiation ceremonies. In a series of frescoes, a woman (wearing a scarf) is prepared for rites involving satyrs and the god Dionysus. She emerges to scenes of transformation and later appears as a bride. An alternative interpretation is that she has been initiated into the cult of Dionysus, who was popular amongst Roman women.

distinctive Roman religious organisation was the 'burial club' where people saved money to pay for their burial and tombstones. Such clubs were often affiliated to trade guilds with their own club room for meetings and dining – several of these have been identified at Ostia, the port of Rome. Unlike modern tombstones which tend to be conservative and modest, their Roman counterparts often list in detail the good qualities and achievements of the deceased.

Roman state religion

A strong thread of state ritual is apparent from Claudius' Temple in Colchester to the Pantheon in Rome where the state is personified and the gods that support it are extolled. Imperial expansion following the wars of the C3rd BC added more exotic cults from the East such as Isis. Initial Roman attitudes to new religions were generous, providing that they did not suggest a political challenge to the state. One that did, Judaism, led to ruthless repression.

Despite bad press for their treatment of Christians, the Romans were generally tolerant of other cults. However, during the C1st AD, Tacitus described how a difficult new sect of Jews known as Christians were persecuted – they were burnt as torches by Nero to illuminate the parks of Rome at night. Despite this, Christianity grew in importance and physical evidence of its presence grew more frequent in mosaics, wall paintings,

Figure 11.56 *C4th AD Christian mosaic from a villa at Hinton St Mary, Dorset. It contains what may be the earliest image of Christ in Britain and the Chi-Rho symbol.*

ritual structures, the use of the Chi-Rho monogram and secret word squares which spelt out the words *pater noster* (our Father). Finally in AD 313 Christianity was legalised by Constantine. In 391 Theodosius I declared it to be the sole state religion and many other temples were destroyed.

Religious change at Lullingstone Villa

The Romano-British villa at Lullingstone in Kent encapsulates changes in religion over the period of the Roman occupation from the adoption of native deities to the import of Christianity. Originally built around AD 75 to include a circular temple, it was rebuilt about AD 190 with a cult room created below the villa. This had a pit containing ritual water at its centre and a niche in the wall decorated with a painting of three water nymphs. It must be presumed that the room was dedicated to the worship of these water-goddesses. Elsewhere in the villa, precisely where is not known, the owner had portrait busts of his ancestors carved from Greek marble. The cult room became disused and was blocked off in another refurbishment at the end of the C3rd AD.

In this third phase, mosaics depict mythological scenes including Jupiter in the form of a bull kidnapping Europa. A less well executed panel shows Bellerophon killing a chimera (a Greek mythological creature combining lion, goat and snake). On the edge of the mosaic are swastikas, which represented good luck. The faces

Figure 11.57 *Christian wall-plaster painting from Lullingstone*

of the four seasons were seen at the corners of the mosaic and scenes from Virgil's *Aeneid*. Elsewhere in the villa a mausoleum was built with the burials of a young man and a woman. Between AD 360 and 370 the owner, by now a Christian, converted part of the villa to Christian use. By chance this took place in a room immediately above the earlier cult room. The new facility is perhaps best described as a house-chapel, although no artefacts were found to support its use for worship. However, six human figures are clearly depicted in a wall painting with their arms outstretched in the pose adopted for prayer by early Christians before the change to clasped hands. This 'Orans posture' is similar to prayer stances in other eastern religions. It may also represent the soul. The figures wore blue and saffron robes edged with pearls. Next to them a large Chi-Rho monogram encircled by a wreath was painted as part of the wall decoration. The villa was destroyed by fire in AD 420 and never rebuilt.

SECTION C: ANCIENT EGYPTIAN STATE RELIGION

Although Christianity became a state religion towards the end of the Roman period, Britain never experienced the kind of major state religion that developed in the Near East during the Bronze Age. The rise of complex states (▶ p. 468) was closely associated with changes in the nature of religion and the focus of ritual. In particular, the close identification of gods and rulers provided an ideology to legitimise massive disparities in wealth and power within society (▶ p. 471). The best understood is Ancient Egypt. Knowledge of Egyptian religion is heavily based on surviving papyrus scrolls. Some describe myths, others rituals. Versions of the Book of the Dead survive from 1600 BC because they were placed in tombs to provide the dead with details of the next world and instructions and spells to help them get there. In addition there are much earlier hieroglyphic inscriptions and wall paintings in tombs, coffins and on monuments. Stone-built monuments containing burials of the elite have survived much better than the mudbrick houses and simple burials of the mass of the people.

Egyptian beliefs and deities

The Egyptian creation myth starts with the god Amun coming into being in a watery chaos. He lifted himself out of the water and masturbated himself to produce the two constituent elements of all life: wet and dry. From this act comes the first land in the form of the 'primeval mound' and then the sky and later the first inhabitants of that Egyptian 'Eden': Isis and Osiris. Egyptian temples symbolised the mound with the hypostyle hall, with its forest of columns whose capitals were carved in the shape of plants such as papyrus, representing the 'Swamp of Creation'. Possibly the most important religion concept in ancient Egypt is the idea of 'balance' or order which has its roots in the natural world. The annual cycle of the Nile which provided the fertile black silt that gave the land its name – Kemet or 'the black land' – also gave a sense of regularity which it was the pharaoh's duty to maintain by appropriate behaviour, propitiation and offering. The goddess that personified this concept was Ma'at, usually represented as a seated woman holding an ankh and with a feather on her head. The ankh, symbol of life, shows the crucial gift upon which all Egyptians depended, that is the golden grain that sprang from the black silt. Only Ma'at could keep at bay the forces of chaos that daily threatened to challenge the rhythm of life by allowing the forces of evil, in the form of Seth, to encroach on the long green strip of land either side of the valley. Amun's creation was kept alive and in order by Ma'at. Ma'at also appears weighing the hearts of the deceased against her feather to determine their fate. The importance of this one goddess is summed up in the throne name of one of Egypt's greatest pharaohs –

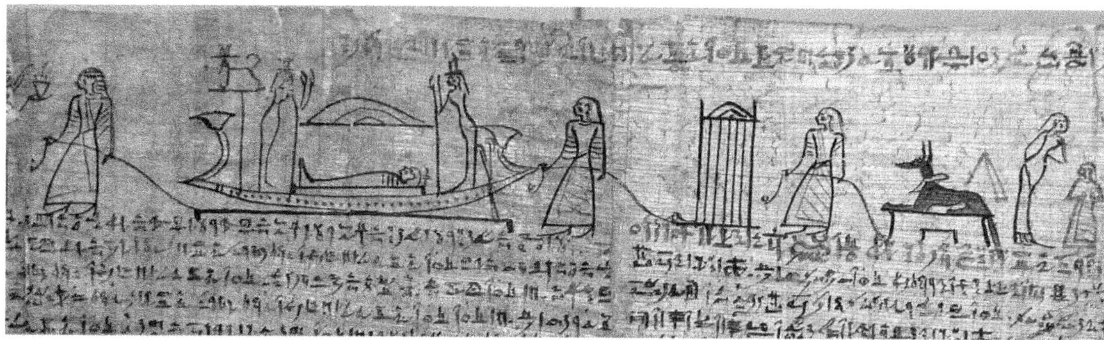

Figure 11.58 *Sequence from the Egyptian Book of the Dead*

Rameses II. It appears on temple columns and walls all over Egypt in very deep relief as User – Ma'at – Re – Setep – en – Re, which means 'strong in truth chosen of Re'.

Deities and rulers

Early Egyptian deities were zoomorphic, reflecting animistic beliefs and the use of animals to represent particular manifestations of gods. Worship of particular deities was often very localised. Gradually a few of the hundreds of deities became more prominent. Increasingly these were depicted in human form but with animal heads. During the early dynastic period of the early 3rd millennium BC the most prominent included Re, the sun-god, who was the creator of the earth and the sky, and the husband and wife Osiris and Isis. Confusingly, deities have quite fluid identities and often had multiple forms and names. At times some were blended together to form single deities with different aspects, a practice known as syncretism. For example, Amun, the main deity of the New Kingdom who represented the hidden power of god, was combined with the visible light of Re as Amun-Re.

Egyptian temples

Temples, such as that of Rameses III at Medinet Habu, were sanctuaries which safeguarded 'the holy' behind huge mudbrick temenos walls and massive pylon gates. Inside through more pylons is the hypostyle hall. Beyond that is the funerary chamber of the pharaoh and eventually the shrine

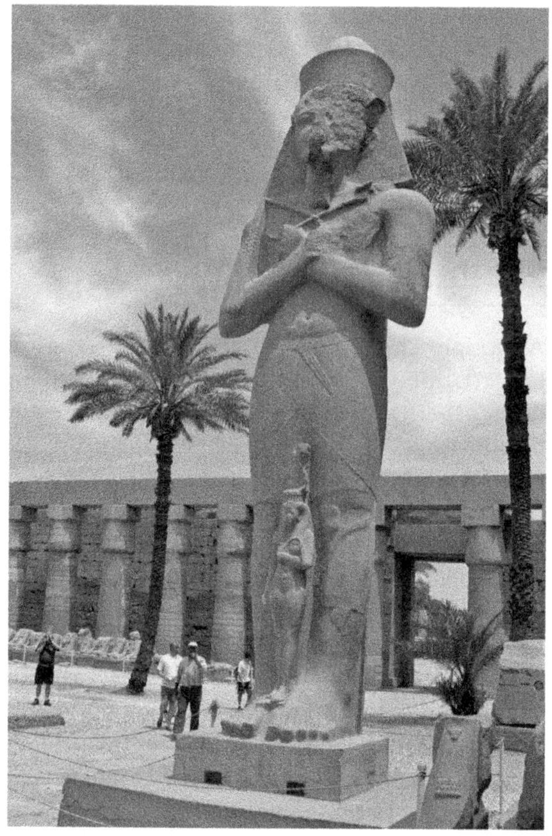

Figure 11.59 *Statue of Rameses II at Karnak*

Figure 11.60 *Aerial view of the Mortuary Temple of Rameses III at Medinet Habu. From left to right can be seen the pylons leading to the open first court.*

of Amun. The interior would have been furnished with doors inlaid with precious metal and jewels. On the walls, massive inscribed reliefs celebrate the victory of Rameses III over the Sea People. Ritual ideas and practices are reflected in the symbolism of wall paintings and the physical structure of the temple building itself. The mound is also symbolised in the inner sanctum of the temples. The shrine contained cult statues and was dark with a raised floor and low ceiling and decorated with reeds. It was the centre of the universe, cut off from the world of mortals by a succession of chambers, each progressively lighter. On the lower half of walls plants are shown emerging from the fertile silt while ceilings depict the stars.

The scale of these temples was unprecedented. The Temple of Karnak at Luxor is the largest in the world. Its 100 hectare area could hold more than a dozen medieval cathedrals. There are actually three main temples inside for the gods Amun, Mut and Montu and several smaller ones. The layout of Karnak was designed as a microcosm of the world at the time of its creation by the god Amun. His temple is at the heart of the complex. Its high walls and huge gates or 'pylons' excluded ordinary people. For the Egyptians the statue of Amun was a house for the god, a place where he could take up residence to interact with mortals. Through his divine presence it became 'alive' in a very real sense. Only priests could enter the temple and they, like all other things dedicated to Amun, had to be pure and clean. They shaved off all their body hair, bathed daily in the Sacred Lake in the heart of the temple and dressed in spotless robes.

At morning, noon and dusk a series of rituals were carried out. Priests would burn incense and sing to the gods before breaking the seals and entering the shrine. After prostrating themselves, they anointed the effigies with oil, perfume and incense and offered food and drink. The priests dressed the statue, applied eye make-up and entertained it as they would the pharaoh himself. In return the god would shower gifts upon humanity and maintain the natural order. One relief shows a group of females playing musical instruments while others clap. They are led by a woman who is identified by the hieroglyphs as 'the Hand of God'. Many scholars believe that the statue of Amun was shown in a state of sexual excitement grasping his erect penis and that the

Figure 11.61 *Hypostyle hall at Luxor*

reliefs are picturing a ritual re-enactment of the original moment of creation induced by the rhythmic music and hand clapping. The question here is whether the ritual was essentially a metaphorical act that happened in people's minds or whether it had some sort of physical reality enacted by the chief priest of the temple or by the pharaoh himself once a year.

Rituals depicted in hieroglyphics include the journey of Amun's sacred boat from Karnak to Luxor with attendants singing and dancing. The desire for the maintenance of order is also featured symbolically in the temple reliefs. Battle scenes show foreigners as disorderly mobs until they have been conquered and brought within the civilising influence of Egypt. Then they are shown in neat lines. In the nearby Luxor Temple this contrast is very clear: the Egyptian infantry and chariots at the Battle of Kadesh are immaculately organised in geometric squads while the opposing Hittites are in total disarray. The south wall of the enormous hypostyle hall records the signing of a peace treaty between Rameses II and the king of the Hittites. It is the earliest record of diplomacy. Successive pharaohs added to the temple over time to ensure their names were linked to Amun.

These rectilinear cult centres were the divine power plants that gave pharaohs the moral, spiritual and economic support to maintain their own position and the whole fabric of Egyptian society that was inextricably linked to the fortune of the royal house. Above all, they were theatres for the crucial rituals which brought humankind into contact with the gods through ritual activity. Temples were off-limits to ordinary people, although people might come to the temple gates for advice or oracles.

The pyramids too may have represented the sacred mound of the creation story from which Re emerged or on which he landed, depending on the version. Their steps represent a kind of stairway to heaven and their shape a solar symbol representing the pattern made by the sun's rays when they fell on the sacred mound. Their sides faced the cardinal points. Orientation is crucial

Figure 11.62 *Entrance to the Temple of Luxor*

too in the Temple of Rameses at Abu Simbel. Instead of being a free-standing structure this was built into the side of a mountain. Rather like Newgrange (▶ p. 534), it was engineered so that the sun's rays would flood through the temple and light up the sculpture in the shrine. At Abu Simbel this occurred in February and October.

Religious festivals

On festival occasions priests would take images out of the temple for processions. Festivals reflected the agricultural cycle, mythology and cosmology. The months in the Egyptian calendar were named after the cycle of festivals with times fixed by the priesthood. Festivals were times of mass participation with pilgrimages, feasting, fortune telling, elaborate decorations and revelry. Several focused on the Nile itself and the flooding which was vital to the fertility of the land. Osiris was worshipped at such key times since the November floods represented his renewal of life and the fall in water levels in the summer represented dying. At these times floating shrines were launched and offerings made to the river. Other festivals reinforced the link between rulers, gods and fertility in the same way as the temples. The Opet festival, for example, which was held around the time of year when the Nile flooded the fields, celebrated the link between the pharoah and the god Amun. People joined a procession from Karnak temple to Luxor. Inside Karnak priests dressed and bathed the statue of Amun, before enclosing him inside a shrine, which was then placed on top of a ceremonial barque. The procession included drums and dancing, before reaching Luxor. Here a ceremony took place, where the divine insemination was recreated. Temple priests distributed beer and bread during the festival as a sign of the god's generosity.

The Heb-Sed Festival was celebrated thirty years after a king's rule and thereafter every three years. This ritual represented regeneration and was meant to assure a long reign. It usually began on New Year's Day with an imposing procession. Many of the ceremonies were performed in front of everyday people and commoners. Special courtyards were built with a throne at one end and seating for an audience at the other. Sculptors reproduced shrines of local deities to show the extent of the king's power over all of Egypt. Rituals included the king giving offerings to Sechat-Hor, who had fed Horus with holy milk – the drink of immortality – and the king receiving the crowns of Upper and Lower Egypt (▶ p. 440) whilst sitting on their respective thrones.

Figure 11.63 *Canopic jars*

Mortuary ritual

Amongst the range of religious specialists were the Sem priests who carried out mortuary rituals. Both the Tomb of Seti I (KV17) and Tutankhamun depict the opening of the mouth ceremony. This involved the purification of the deceased with water, balls of natron (a salt-based drying agent) and incense. A priest who was identified with the god Horus then opened the mouth of a cult statue with his fingers – possibly a re-enactment of the clearing of a baby's mouth at birth. A bull is then butchered and the heart is presented to the deceased. The mouth of the deceased is opened with special artefacts and food and drink are offered. This ceremony reanimated the deceased and was supposed to enable him to see, smell and hear.

The most well-known aspect of Egyptian religion is mummification. However, this mortuary ritual emerged gradually. It probably developed because bodies buried in sandy, desert soils in such a hot climate rapidly became desiccated and were preserved like leather. The practice of embalming began with the royal family and then gradually spread to other, rich members of society. Some animals (▶ p. xxxii) which may have represented deities were also mummified. It was a complex, specialist process involving the removal of all internal organs except for the heart and the application of the soda ash drying agent natron. The washed and dried body was then varnished, wrapped in cloth for protection and placed in a sarcophagus. The internal

Figure 11.64 *Sarcophagus and mummy*

organs were embalmed and placed in canopic jars. The tops of these jars each took the form of one of the four sons of Horus, each of whom was protected by a deity of one of the cardinal points.

Embalming developed around the time that the early mastaba tombs were being built and may have been a response to the problems of preserving bodies in them. Mummification was important because the body would be reunited with the deceased in the afterlife. Death was viewed as a gateway to another world. Grave goods were placed by the dead for their use following resurrection in the realm of Osiris. Ordinary people had simpler burials in graves, often with headrests for the body and a few personal grave goods.

Elite tombs

Tombs were dug deep to help the deceased to reach as close to the underworld on their journey as they could while the second purpose was to contain the grave goods they would need when they were reborn. Wall paintings often depict scenes of the pharaoh adoring the gods and making offerings. Ceiling paintings tend to be to do with the heavens, as the tomb is a microcosm of the world/underworld; for example, vultures representing the goddess Nekhbet, a protective female deity. The main corridor often featured scenes from various Books of the Dead, which provided a detailed guide for the pharaoh as to how to complete the different tasks and to pass different trials en route to the afterlife. Tutankhamun's tomb is particularly significant for archaeology because it is the only relatively unrobbed tomb of a pharoah that we have. In the burial chamber are a variety of paintings, each showing us the different beliefs about death. On one wall are the twelve sons of Ra, depicted as baboons, each representing an hour of the night. Above, the Khepri, in the form of a beetle, is being ferried across the waters of Nun to bear the sun disc across the sky once more. On another wall, Tutankhamun and his Ka (spirit) are being welcomed to the afterlife by Osiris; his Ka is holding an ankh, suggesting his god-like status. Another painting depicts the 'opening of the mouth' ceremony.

Another significant artefact to consider is the sarcophagus itself. It is covered in gold leaf which holds religious significance as the Egyptians believed gold to be the skin of the gods and thus believed that in death the pharaoh had become a god in his own right. Amongst many statues, one of particular interest is a depiction of Tutankhamun on a boat, spearing an unseen hippo. This is startlingly similar to a relief at the temple of Horus at Edfu, in which Horus is spearing Set (who takes the form of a hippo). This statue highlights the importance the Egyptians placed on banishing Seth (Chaos) and bringing Ma'at (Order). Tombs fequently linked the pharoah and the sun, including the pharoah travelling on a solar barque (boat), models of which have also been found. This belief may have influenced Bronze Age belief in Europe where the sun is depicted in similar ways (▶ p. 542). Other paintings depicted the many festivals which linked the ruler, gods, fertility and values such as justice.

Funerary monuments

Ancient Egypt is perhaps best known for the massive monumental tombs known as the pyramids. These developed from more simple mastaba tombs. Mastaba tombs were the first stage of the development of increasingly elaborate funerary monuments for the pharaohs culminating in the great necropolises of the Old Kingdom. Tomb Uj at Abydos is a well-preserved example. It takes the form of a rectangular building (the Mastaba – 'bench' in Arabic) divided into rooms with thin symbolic doorways for the king's Ka to pass though. There were many storerooms for food containing beer, bread and wine jars with square labels with pictures on them which are considered by the excavation director Gunter Dreyer to be the earliest hieroglyph symbols. The main temple on the site dates

Figure 11.65 *Step pyramid of Pharaoh Djoser at Saqqara*

from the New Kingdom during the reign of Seti I, the father of Rameses II, who was largely responsible for the hypostyle hall. The temple is also famous for the 'king list' which holds the cartouches of most pharaohs. Abydos was a place of pilgrimage before 4000 BC since it was thought to be the place where Osiris died and was buried, after 'seeding the womb of Isis' as depicted at the Temple of Hathor in Dendera. Many early kings wanted to be buried there to be near to Osiris. There was a festival to Osiris every year and people gave offerings of pottery, and when the contents had been offered, the pots were then discarded, forming a huge pile of broken ceramics known as Umm El Quaab. Further evidence comes from the walls of tombs in Luxor showing individuals such as Nespaquashuty and his wife making their way to the festival at Abydos.

The first in the line of monumental stone tombs was the Step Pyramid at Saqqara, built *c.* 2700 BC. The high priest Imhotep is usually credited with the design. Originally it would have been faced with gleaming white limestone. It is the most visible element in a major ceremonial complex which appears to have been used for festivals as well as funerary rites.

Pyramids

During the 3rd millennium BC, monumental tombs rapidly developed into the pyramids. Around one hundred were built, the largest being the Great Pyramid at Giza from shortly before 2500 BC. It stands 146m high and with a base of 230 square metres. The Great Pyramid was constructed with limestone blocks built up layer by layer and sheathed in white limestone.

The precision of the engineering is superb. Tiny passages lead into the interior before opening out into hidden galleries and chambers which included the tomb of the pharaoh. It was built as part of a major complex of tombs. These include small pyramids for Khufu's wives and the mastaba tombs of nobles. A large pit contains a boat which may have been intended for the pharaoh to use to join Re or it may have been a barge used in the funerary rites. The Sphinx is also close by, acting as the ultimate protective deity for the whole pyramid necropolis. The Great Pyramid originally had a smooth outer casing of Tura limestone. One theory as to the pyramidal shape is that it is a burst of sunshine, indeed it used to have a cap stone or pyramidion made of gold or a mixture of silver and gold called electrum.

An intriguing theory from the 1990s put forward by Adrian Gilbert and Robert Bauval has suggested a new interpretation of the symbolic meaning of the pyramid complex which makes sense of all three monuments as part of a preconceived plan. Their theory drew first on Egyptian mythology and known connections with the stars. Each pharaoh believed they were Horus during life and Osiris at death and the constellation of Orion represented him in the heavens while his consort Isis was seen in the star Sirius, the brightest star in the sky. The constellation of Orion disappears each year for seventy days under the horizon, which was seen to coincide with the pharaoh's funeral and his rebirth into the afterlife with the stellar 'rebirth' of Orion. In the Great Pyramid there are four ritual shafts which have often been referred to as 'ventilation shafts' but this explanation makes little sense and moreover the southern shaft of the 'King's Chamber' points directly to Orion's belt and those southern shafts from the Queen's chamber point to Sirius. The northern shafts point to the Polar Stars, called 'the indestructibles'. Bauval and Gilbert realised that all the pyramids fitted into a pattern which resembled that of Orion's belt, with the last pharaoh Menkaure's pyramid slightly askew from the diagonal just as in the constellation of Orion. Not all Egyptologists believe this scenario

Figure 11.66 *The Great Pyramid of Khufu. The Pyramid of Khafre appears larger as it is better preserved and stands on higher ground.*

but, if true, it would provide yet another of the ways in which rulers stressed their permanence and right to rule.

It is easy to forget the changes that took place in both ritual structures and the nature of religion during the three thousand years up to the arrival of the Romans in Egypt. The cults of particular deities were identified with by different pharaohs and their popularity changed with new rulers. Styles of ritual, styles of mummification, styles of ritual burial and accompanying grave goods all changed radically over this period to say nothing of tomb location and decoration. King Djoser would have been quite at home next to the Giza pyramids but baffled by the rock cut tombs in the Valley of the Kings, by which time Djoser's own 'Step Pyramid' at Sakkara was already thirteen hundred years old! The Valley of the Kings appears to have been selected because of its location on the west bank of the Nile – where the sun sank into the desert – symbolic of death and the pyramidal peak above it which is a sacred shape. Close by was another necropolis in the Valley of the Queens. Pharaohs of the New Kingdom were buried in the valley from the C16th to C11th BC.

Part III

Issues in World Archaeology

Chapter 12

Managing Archaeological Heritage

This chapter covers several linked topics. The first half covers the key threats to our archaeological heritage and considers the nature and effectiveness of current protection for archaeological remains. This is largely from an English or UK perspective as appropriate but with examples drawn from elsewhere to illustrate other dimensions. The second half outlines the roles of the key agencies involved in archaeology and managing heritage and the key debates about the preservation and ownership of archaeological remains. It should be read in conjunction with Chapters 2 and 13.

THREATS TO ARCHAEOLOGICAL REMAINS

Natural processes (Chapter 5) account for the decay of most archaeological remains once in the soil but the overwhelming threat to surviving monuments, from field systems to buildings, comes from human activity. More has been lost in the last few decades than in the rest of human history. As a result, most excavation since 1960 has been of sites just prior to destruction by development. The rapid growth of towns and transport networks since 1945 combined with declining pasture land and more intensive forms of agriculture are largely responsible. Even seemingly minor changes can have significant impacts. For example, in the aftermath of 'mad cow disease' many farmers in the upper Severn valley ploughed up old pasture to grow maize. Ploughing is much more destructive of archaeology.

The rapid pace of development continues today and debates about the destruction of archaeological remains are rarely out of the media for long. The battle to save Thornborough Henge and the ongoing debate about Stonehenge and its landscape provide examples. Government plans to relax some planning restrictions on house building to cope with the UK's rising population and new infrastructure projects such as wind turbines, roads, high-speed rail links and airports will all have a significant impact. In particular the emphasis on using brown-field sites where possible for urban development is particularly destructive of industrial archaeology. Building and construction make heavy demands on raw materials and sand, gravel and stone quarries operate to fill these needs, creating in turn their own threat to archaeological deposits. Government spending cuts since the late 1990s also threaten many historic public buildings, which are expensive to maintain, including Victorian churches, baths and schools.

Some high-profile sites are simply threatened by increasing public interest in our past. Hadrian's Wall and Avebury are two high-profile sites that have suffered badly from erosion caused by walkers. As World Heritage Sites (▶ p. 577), detailed management plans have been drawn up to try to resolve the conflict between access and preservation.

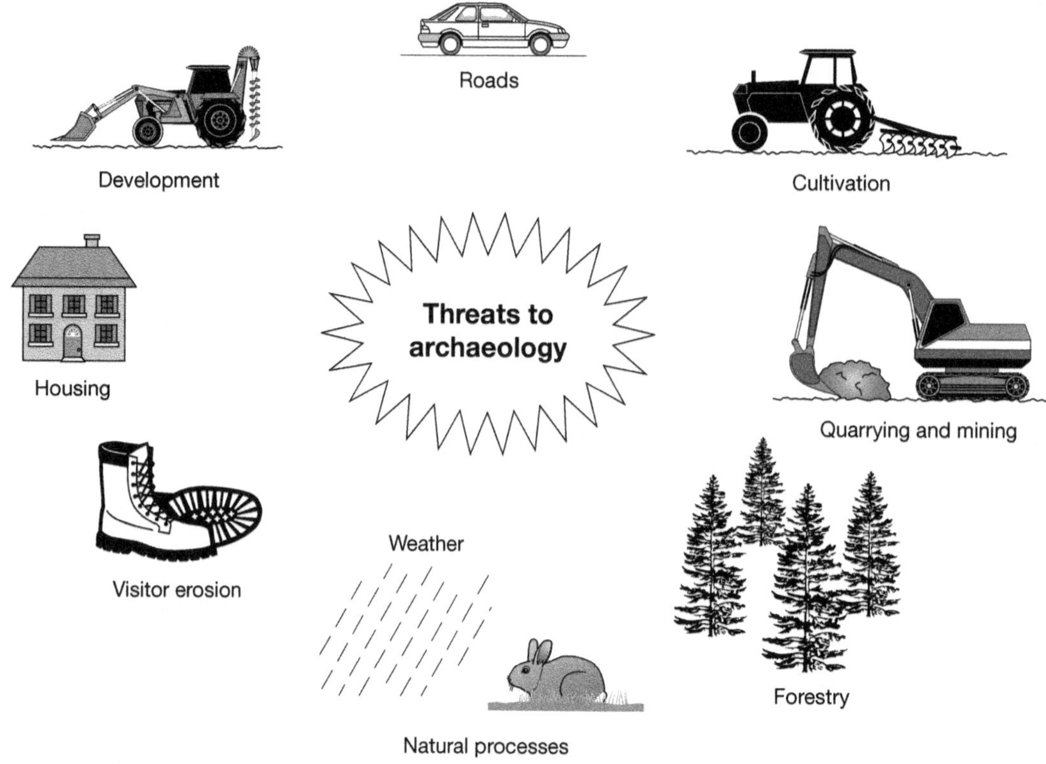

Figure 12.1 *Sources of threats to archaeological remains*

Naturally public attention focuses on threats to famous monuments and exciting discoveries. However, a massive amount of our visible archaeological heritage continues to disappear with little protest. A glance at aerial photographs from the 1940s will reveal how many hedges, water meadows and medieval field systems have vanished. To landscape archaeologists they provide key evidence about land ownership, settlement and use of the environment. Medieval field systems also provided a protective blanket over earlier sites that would otherwise have been eroded. The Doggerland project (▶ p. 41) illustrates the ongoing threat to undersea archaeology from fishing and mineral extraction as well as erosion.

The Monuments at Risk Survey of England (MARS), 1998

Bournemouth University and English Heritage combined to survey the condition of a 5 per cent random sample of England's 937,484 recorded archaeological sites. The study provided a census of the nature, distribution and state of England's archaeological resources. The study started by examining archive records, such as RAF aerial photographs, of the state of monuments in 1940 and then surveying to measure damage since then. Their key measures were loss of horizontal area and loss of height.

The study discovered (Darvill and Fulton 1998) that the south-east had lost the highest proportion of monuments with best survival in the West Midlands. Standing buildings and field systems are most at risk while sites protected

Figure 12.2 *Natural destruction of mining buildings by vegetation in West Virginia*

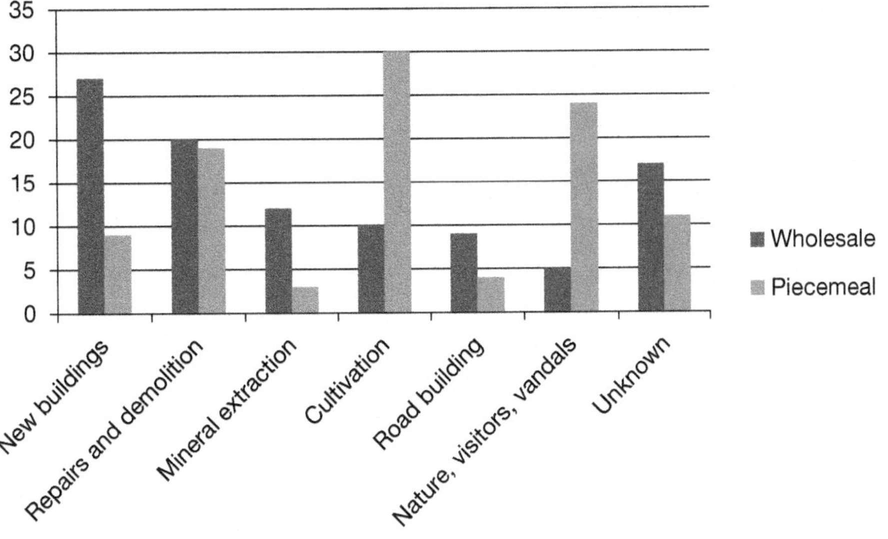

Figure 12.3 *Key causes of destruction of archaeological monuments from the MARS report*

by legislation are at least risk. In total, 95 per cent of monuments had suffered some damage. Since 1945, some 23,500 monuments have been completely destroyed, an average of one site a day. Over 2 per cent of known sites have been lost since the 1998 survey. MARS drew on existing records plus its own surveys but inevitably will have missed many buried sites. Therefore the numbers of all sites destroyed and at risk will be higher. Figure 12.3 summarises the key causes of destruction.

Since 2008 English Heritage has maintained a broad risk register which includes some historic churches, wreck sites and parks alongside listed buildings and monuments. Regional and thematic lists of monuments at risk are published on their website. In 2013 there were 3265 scheduled monuments deemed to be at risk (English Heritage 2013), primarily from agriculture (43 per cent) and the growth of bushes and trees (27 per cent).

Global threats to archaeology

The pace of development across the world means thousands of archaeological sites are lost each year. Few countries have the resources to even record what is lost. For many, archaeology comes an understandable second to feeding and housing their people. In extreme cases, monuments are sometimes deliberately destroyed for political or religious reasons, as has happened recently in Syria and Mali, where shrines and an ancient library have been attacked by Islamists in Timbuktu.

A growing global problem is the looting of archaeological sites to feed the demand of Western collectors for artefacts and artwork. Britain has its problems with 'nighthawks' (▶ p. 585) but looting in much of the world is on an industrial scale. At ancient temples in Mesoamerica and Cambodia, power saws have been used to remove statues and reliefs which are then trucked across borders for export. In Iraq museums were looted following the Second Gulf War and many ancient sites have been devastated by robbing excavations. Civil disorder and war across other countries in the Middle East and North Africa have seen this practice spread. Following the Egyptian revolution of 2011, archaeologists returning to El Hibeh discovered

Figure 12.4 *Altar Q at the Mayan city of Copan*

On this panel the baton of power is passing between a whole dynasty of sixteen kings from the founder Yax K'uk Mo to the last king Yax Pasajh. Despite World Heritage Site status Copan, like many similar monuments, is regularly threatened by gangs of well-organised (and sometimes armed) looters who remove stone reliefs and statues. Much of this material is bought by wealthy 'art collectors' in the West.

Figure 12.5 *Climatic damage to the Sphinx*

that the tombs had been looted and dismembered mummies and broken artefacts were scattered across the site.

Western media often blames corrupt local officials or armies for colluding or even controlling the trade. However, UNESCO has highlighted the one-way traffic in artefacts from poorer countries to the art auction houses in the West and Japan which dispose of stolen antiquities. A search on eBay will quickly give you an insight into the catastrophic scale of looting on world heritage. Ecofacts too are at risk. A growing trade in mammoth ivory is currently being portrayed as an ethical alternative to poached elephant ivory. Michelle Obama has given credibility to this view. However, mammoths are a finite resource and also have a scientific value. On a less industrial scale, sites throughout the world are routinely looted for coins, pottery and other portable artefacts by local people. They supplement their low incomes by selling to tourists and dealers. Some tourists join commercial metal detecting tours to help themselves to artefacts.

Nor is the problem limited to human agency. Climate change appears to be having a growing impact. Examples include erosion due to both rising sea level and the drying out of wetlands, while the thawing of areas of permafrost threatens prehistoric burial sites across central Asia and Thule settlements in Greenland. The Defence of Britain project tried to record our fast-disappearing legacy of wartime structures. While most sites are destroyed by development, the sea is also playing a part. Erosion of East Anglian cliffs (▶ p. 170) is rapidly demolishing coastal defences with pillboxes and bunkers regularly succumbing to the waves, while on Orkney, Skara Brae (▶ p. 274) is threatened.

In parts of North Africa desertification is increasing the sand erosion of monuments and buildings. Human responses to climate change such as building new drains, flood defences and energy-efficient measures also threaten archaeological remains. The Sphinx and many other ancient Egyptian monuments are threatened because irrigation schemes to allow all-year farming are contributing to rising water tables in Egypt. Water and the mineral salts it carries weaken the soft sandstone foundations and walls, causing them to crumble. Upstanding earthworks can be devastated by burrowing animals such as rabbits. English Heritage recently had a research project looking at ways to prevent badgers, whose numbers are increasing with our warmer climate, from destroying round barrows through tunnelling.

Are all archaeological sites valuable?

Archaeological sites are finite and non-renewable so that every time one is destroyed, degraded or excavated it cannot be replaced. However, to argue that everything should be preserved is unrealistic. There are competing claims on land for houses, industry and communications; the question is really about balance and how we should determine priorities. For example, is a rare type of site such as a Mesolithic hunting camp more precious than a more common Roman villa or Iron Age roundhouse? Should quality of preservation, range of materials or the possibility that the site might answer particular questions be the key? Alternatively should economic and social priorities trump heritage except in the most extreme situations? All these positions have been argued, and as in all issues of conservation versus change, there is no right answer. It is always a moral and political judgement. However, what is deemed important varies over time. In the past medieval sites were destroyed in order to reach the more valued classical ruins, while in the 1960s

Figure 12.6 *The Nazi grandstand at the Zeppelinfeld, Nuremburg*

Georgian and Victorian areas of towns were bulldozed to build flats and roads. Archaeologists are not always against developments but they are aware that what we deem most worthy of preservation may change over time. Rich burials attracted C19th antiquarians whereas modern archaeologists might be equally interested in a Bronze Age midden or a medieval longhouse. In the USA, changing political views have been reflected in decisions about heritage. A survey for the National Park Service (Kauffman 2004) revealed that barely 1 per cent of places on the National Register of Historic Places were related to African American or Latino ethnic groups. This research reflected an interest in finding and preserving sites in order to ensure and present a more inclusive heritage. Examples include the C18th African burial ground in New York and the house of James Dexter in Philadelphia. Construction work here around the National Constitution Center Site exposed a series of C18th streets, backyards, wells and privies, which included houses known to have been lived in by African American families. Research showed one of these to have been the home of the ex-slave and campaigner James Dexter and it was selected for detailed excavation.

The Nazi past was not only a source of shame to German prehistorians but also presents a dilemma today over what to do about surviving Nazi monuments. The enormous Party complex at Nuremburg is a key example. While the Party Records Office is now a museum which uses Nazi artefacts to warn against extremism, the parade grounds where Hitler reviewed his supporters is slowly crumbling.

THE PROTECTION OF ARCHAEOLOGICAL REMAINS

Protection in law

Legal protection for archaeological remains in Britain has never been comprehensive and is also fragmented between different types of remains and the various parts of the United Kingdom. What follows here applies to England, although similar measures exist in other parts of the UK, particularly Wales. Some protection has been in place since the Ancient Monuments Protection Act (1882), which listed preservation orders for sixty-nine monuments, and the Town and Country Planning Act (1947), which introduced the listing of buildings. However, the cornerstone of legal protection for archaeology for over thirty-five years has been the Ancient Monuments and Archaeological Areas Act 1979 (AMAA). This required owners of scheduled ancient monuments to seek the consent of the Secretary of State responsible for Heritage before they could make changes to sites. Fines and other penalties could be imposed for damaging scheduled (listed) monuments. It subsequently gave English Heritage the task of recording, assessing and monitoring monuments. English Heritage could also recommend other endangered sites and the land around them for scheduling to the Secretary of State if they were deemed to be of national importance. Under the Monument Protection Programme the number of scheduled sites has risen to 20,000. This is still less than 2 per cent of all the known sites in the country.

AMAA gave legal protection to some visible monuments after years of destruction. It also established the use of mapping as a tool to protect sites. Developers were 'warned off' sites where their plans might be slowed down or halted. Increasingly, landowners have signed management or 'stewardship' agreements to protect sites in return for funding. However, AMAA had serious limitations. Sites which were discovered during development were not protected. Nor were those in areas where permission for gravel extraction had already been given. Landscapes and most marine sites were not covered, while ploughing could continue on sites where it was already taking place as long as the depth of ploughing was not increased. An example is the Roman town of Verulamium. One of the most visible failings of the Act was the way it only protected the upstanding (earthwork) element of monuments. The mounds of many long barrows survive as islands in ploughed fields while their ditches, pits and postholes are still being destroyed. Enforcement was variable. Landowners could plead ignorance as a defence for damaging sites. The cost of protection fell on local or national government, for whom it was never a top priority.

Heritage Protection Reform

Since 2008 a suite of new legislation has been presented to completely overhaul protection for all aspects of heritage including a Heritage Protection Bill, a Marine Bill and a new Planning Act. All proposed legislation embodies a philosophy in which sites and buildings are termed 'assets'. Heritage assets are defined as places which hold meaning for society over and above their current use. The use of the word 'asset' is interesting as it implies a value which could be weighed against the value of a development and reflects wider attempts to ascribe a monetary value to landscapes and heritage. Another key word is 'sustainability', with considerable emphasis on the sustainable ongoing use of 'assets' including adapting buildings to new uses. Briefing documents stress the value of heritage but also the need for development. At the time of publication, this legislation remains draft and AMAA remains in force. However, these themes are developed further in the National Planning Policy Framework (▶ p. 577).

Indirect protective legislation for sites

Laws to protect particular environments or to regulate planning have also benefited archaeology including providing some protection for unscheduled sites and archaeological landscapes. The designation of some areas as national parks, 'Areas of Outstanding Natural Beauty' or Sites of Special Scientific Interest (SSSI) was primarily to conserve landscapes or habitats but also helped to protect archaeological remains. Similarly, measures to encourage landowners to manage their land for the benefit of nature or tourism through tax breaks or stewardship schemes have also brought some measure of protection. The Civil Amenities Act (1967) allowed for areas of architectural or historic interest to be designated as conservation areas. With around 10,000 designations made, much urban archaeology has been indirectly protected. This Act was replaced in 1990 by the Planning (Listed Buildings and Conservation Areas) (England) Regulations which in turn were amended in 2009 and 2013. These allow English Heritage to compile lists of buildings of special architectural or historic interest for the Secretary of State to approve. Registration has been used to protect other types of site, notably the Battlefields Register. However, while listing constrains developers, it cannot guarantee secure protection and does not provide funding for archaeological work. The Marine and Coastal Access Act 2009 was originally part of the new suite of Heritage and Environmental protection. It allows for the creation of Marine Conservation Zones where activity – including development and fishing – is restricted to conserve fish-stocks. It will indirectly provide protection for some submarine heritage.

Protection through the planning process

In the UK decisions about development have traditionally been taken at a local level by the planning committees of councils. However, the government issues guidance to help councils make decisions and increasingly this guidance is treated as if it were the law.

PPG16

The Town and Country Planning Act 1971 allowed local authorities to take archaeology into account when considering planning applications and required them to produce structure plans for future development. Further legislation in

1990 created conservation areas. This did not guarantee that archaeology would be preserved or even recorded. During the 1980s there were many high-profile campaigns to save historic sites from demolition, most notably, in 1989, the Elizabethan Rose Theatre. Despite considerable efforts by some government agencies, many volunteer groups, excavation units and the charity Rescue, some archaeology was lost without recording. In some cities such as Winchester, local planners did not use powers available to them when development threatened buried remains. This, along with the need to get funding from developers, was the key factor behind the introduction of the government policy and planning guide for local authorities called Planning and Policy Guide Note 16 (PPG16).

PPG16 was shaped by English Heritage's desire to protect archaeological remains and to secure a more coordinated approach to excavation and, importantly, funding from developers. It advised planners to consider archaeology at an early stage of the development process and was underpinned by the philosophy that the past is a finite resource which requires management and conservation. Preservation 'in situ' therefore is preferable to excavation. Where excavation is deemed necessary, then archaeology is 'preserved by record'. In order to consider archaeology when planning applications are lodged, most local authorities documented and mapped known archaeological sites in their Sites and Monuments Records (SMRs). Under PPG16 local authority archaeologists advised planners and drew up briefs for any work required. Developers were responsible for funding any archaeological work deemed necessary on the 'polluter pays' basis. They would then put a contract for archaeological work out to tender and contracting units (▶ p. 581) would bid for it. A later guidance note, PPG15 (1994), covered buildings of historic interest. Although PPG16 was not law, planners needed to have good reasons for not following its advice.

The language of PPG16

PPG16 has generated a new range of terminology which needs to be understood in order to follow archaeologists' discussions:

- **Desk-based assessment**: the initial stage of assessing the risk to archaeology involves checks with the SMR and other archives. It may also involve a very brief look at the site.
- **Field evaluation**: where desk-based assessment suggests a potential risk, there would be a survey of the site, which usually includes trial trenching to establish the depth, nature and condition of remains. The sample size is usually 2 per cent. Following assessment, the planning authority, advised by local authority (LA) archaeologists, decides whether remains are of sufficient national importance to warrant preservation or whether a **mitigation strategy** will suffice. Mitigation can range from complete project redesign to engineering solutions which protect archaeological deposits underneath new buildings. Planners then draw up a brief for the developer's archaeological contractor. This includes any post-excavation requirements.
- **Preservation in situ**: excavation is destructive so PPG16 advises that archaeological remains should be left where they are (in situ) if possible. This can mean resting buildings on piles driven through deposits. This method is controversial. In Norway, piling, which damages and interferes with the drainage and stratigraphy of sites, is viewed as destruction rather than preservation. An alternative is to lay a 'raft' of concrete over remains and then build on that. Some archaeologists have questioned the extent of preservation of this nature. Development can alter the water table and chemical composition of the soil. It is difficult to see how the long-term effects can be monitored, and even if they can, what could be done to 'rescue' a site 'preserved' under a housing estate.

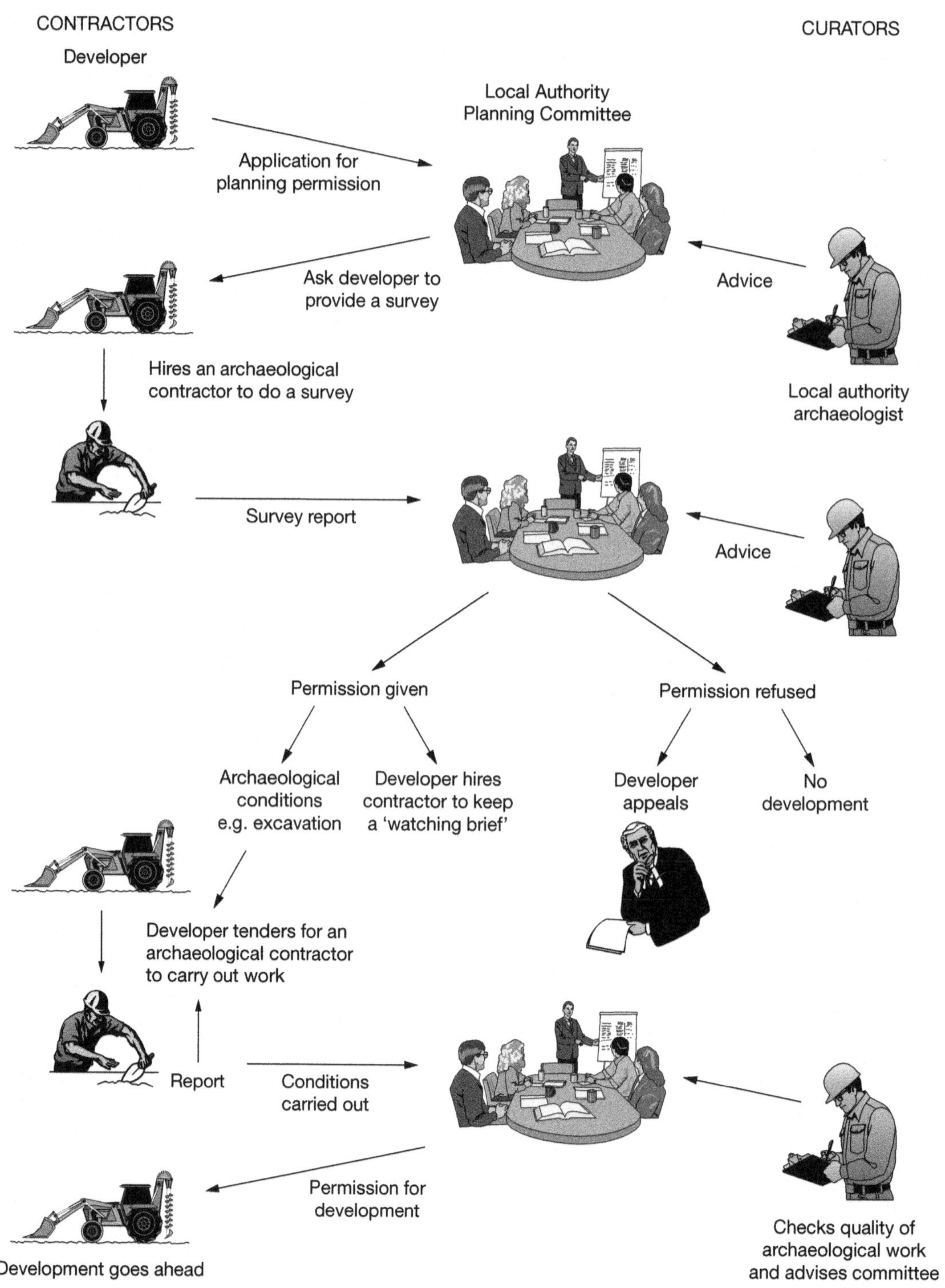

Figure 12.7 *Simplified diagram to show how archaeology is involved in the planning process*

Figure 12.8 *PPG16 in action*

Deposits from the area around the Forum in Cirencester lie around 1m under the surface. Rather than excavate a large area of Roman Britain's second city, planners preferred a mitigation strategy. Test pits and a minor excavation down to the top of the Roman road in the foreground established the depth of deposits. In the picture these are being covered in a concrete raft before houses are built on top. Depending on your viewpoint, this is a wasted opportunity to engage the local community with its heritage or precious remains preserved in situ for a future generation.

Mitigation strategies can range from full excavation to a **watching brief** with the objective being '**preservation by record**'. A watching brief is literally that. An archaeologist will watch as the machines go in to see if any archaeological remains are unearthed and to report on them.

The impact of PPG16

PPG16 did provide much-needed funding for rescue excavation. Although developers have to meet archaeological costs, it has not prevented development. Very few planning applications are refused on archaeological grounds and 'preservation by record' is the outcome of most positive assessments. There are at least three times as many excavations annually as there were before 1990 and around 90 per cent of all archaeological work comes through the planning process. By 2011 developers were spending £125m annually on archaeology (IFA 2011). One unforeseen benefit is the greater range of sites and periods covered than by previous excavation, which tended to

Figure 12.9 *Modern developer-led archaeology*

This was the result of a contract tendered by the developers as part of planning permission for a Waitrose. The small team of professionals from Cotswold Archaeology, dressed in safety gear, worked to tight deadlines through the winter.

have a bias towards visible monuments. For example, more early medieval and Mesolithic sites, which would not have been easily detected from the air or surface survey, have been discovered. Partly this is because development is occurring in areas which had not been intensively explored. These include brown-field sites in towns, the Thames Valley and the locations of major infrastructure projects such as Heathrow Terminal 5 and the Channel Tunnel Rail Link.

PPG16 has also had some negative impacts. Commercially inexperienced archaeological units tended to bid too low for contracts during the early 1990s. This meant that wage levels were low. It tied archaeology to the cycle of the construction industry, which affected the regularity of work for diggers. As a result, there is a high turnover of field archaeologists. Similarly, the costs of post-excavation work, including the use of specialists and storage of remains, was often underestimated. As a result, this work has suffered and many museum archives are now 'full'. Some local authorities (LA) used PPG16 as a way of reducing spending on archaeology and many have their own archaeology units. LA archaeologists now spend most of their time on planning matters. Contracts with developers for archaeological work frequently require professional staff and have strict health and safety controls. This largely curtails opportunities for amateurs to take part or even to visit excavations. PPG16 did not place value on either community involvement or public benefit.

There have been arguments about the quality of contract archaeology but that is a charge that has been levelled at archaeology of any type or period. If there are shortfalls, then the planners do have the power to address it. Perhaps a more relevant criticism is the limitations of the system. Financial pressure from developers on contractors may limit the use of the most expensive dating and analytical techniques. Some archaeologists argue that 5 per cent trenching would provide a more indicative sample of archaeological remains than the recommended (and cheaper) 2 per cent. Perhaps the most persistent criticism has been the fragmentation of archaeological knowledge. Completed excavation reports belong to the developers. They do not have to publish them. As a result, it can take a while for reports to get in to the public domain and the amount of detail can vary. Work in a given geographical area is often undertaken by a range of units, which means that it is difficult to obtain an overall picture of local archaeology. In an attempt to address the problem of 'grey literature', as unpublished reports are known, the Archaeological Data Service (ADS) (▶ p. 7) has made over 18,000 available online.

Planning Policy Statement (PPS) 5 (2010)

PPS5 (Planning for the Historic Environment) briefly replaced both PPG15 and PPG16 in a streamlining of guidance which grouped archaeology with other heritage assets including parks, buildings and landscapes. It was a much simpler and concise document than its predecessors, which made it more accessible for developers and the general public. It continued the emphasis for heritage to be considered in the planning process and added a requirement that initial decisions should be based on evidence held in the Historic Environment Record (HER). These are currently local government archives and databases covering particular counties that provide comprehensive information on local monuments, buildings, landscapes and finds. In many cases information is now digitalised and linked to GIS. PPS5 also addressed the 'grey literature issue'. Developers had to use archaeologists working to professional standards and were required to publish reports and make archives accessible to the public. PPS5 reflected the philosophical changes behind the draft Reform Bill (▶ p. 572) and articulated the importance of heritage in community identity and the economic benefits of heritage tourism. It stated that once lost, assets cannot be replaced. In this it draws on current notions of best practice and 'significance' in cultural resource management internationally such as Australia's Burra Charter (1999).

The National Planning Policy Framework NPPF (2012)

Hot on the heels of PPS5 and subsuming it is an overhaul of the planning process in order to reduce bureaucracy, delay and confusion and to locate planning decisions at the 'right' level. This means that decisions about nationally important infrastructure projects will be taken at national level rather than by local planning committees. Many environmental groups opposed NPPF when it was first proposed because they feared it would favour large-scale development and remove the right of local people to influence major projects. Unlike PPG16 and PPS5 there is no presumption in favour of preserving designated heritage assets. Instead 'great weight' is to be given to conserving designated heritage assets such as monuments and national parks but they will still be balanced against other needs. Councils will have to produce local plans which must assess the significance of local heritage assets and have strategies to conserve them and encourage enjoyment of them. There is also a new presumption in favour of 'sustainable development'.

It is too early to assess what effect that will have on archaeology. Some archaeologists are worried that the 'significance' of a heritage asset is too open to debate and that there are not clear criteria for establishing it. What will it mean for sites deemed to be of 'low significance'? Others have pointed out that the 'significance' of a site (or indeed its existence) sometimes does not emerge until investigations begin. Neither PPS5 nor NPPF offer solutions to problems of archive space or halt the decline in the numbers of units and skilled staff.

International protection

Increasingly decisions taken at the UN or EU are likely to impact on archaeology in Britain. The United Nations Educational, Scientific and Cultural Organization (UNESCO) has drawn up a World Heritage (WH) list of over 850 sites of outstanding international value. It defines these as 'irreplaceable sources of life and inspiration' and includes the Great Barrier Reef as well as the Pyramids and the City of Venice. They are deemed to belong to all the peoples of the world, not just the nations where they are situated.

Most governments including the UK have signed up to the World Heritage Convention (1972) to protect these sites. In itself this provides some protection since it would be embarrassing for a government if a WH site was damaged. The UK currently has twenty-four WH sites including

Neolithic Orkney, industrial Blaenavon and the City of Bath. From 2009 these sites were treated as 'listed' in the planning system. The WH scheme also enables funds and expertise to be channelled to conservation and restoration projects on endangered sites in poorer countries. However, designation does not guarantee preservation and only covers a fraction of sites worldwide. It does guarantee increased tourism, which presents both an opportunity to raise funds and an additional problem to be managed. UNESCO itself is currently in crisis. A total of 22 per cent of its budget comes from the USA, which is withholding the funds following a dispute with the UN over Palestine in 2011.

The Valetta Convention (1992)

This European Charter for the Protection and Management of the Archaeological Heritage came into force in March 2001. It is based on the principle that heritage throughout Europe is threatened by development and needs to be protected. It requires governments to safeguard monuments and regulate archaeology to ensure the proper conservation of excavated sites and the recording and safe-keeping of finds. It also covers the use of metal detectors, the trade in artefacts and the need to raise public awareness of and access to archaeological heritage. Although much of it is similar to existing UK measures (particularly the emphasis on preservation 'in situ'), Article 3, which called for all work to be authorised and carried out by suitably qualified people, caused considerable debate. This was because of fears that it could be used to limit the involvement of amateurs in archaeology.

The management of Stonehenge

Britain's most famous World Heritage Site illustrates a whole series of problems in balancing access against protection. It also highlights the limited strength of WHS designation in securing improvements even in a state as rich as the UK and a site that gets 1 million visitors annually.

A landmark for centuries, its visibility on Salisbury Plain ensured it attracted a road junction. Until 2013 it existed on an island of land next to the busy A303, cut off from its landscape by traffic and surrounded by tourist facilities which made few concessions to the nature of the site. Stonehenge is owned by the government and managed by English Heritage, while much of the surrounding landscape has been purchased by the National Trust. For twenty-five years various governments had accepted that Stonehenge was a national disgrace and in breach of World Heritage conventions and floated a series of ideas to redevelop the site. Disputes about the location of a visitor centre, archaeological opposition to tunnelling (because it would mean excavating archaeological deposits and because proposed entrances were near other monuments) and spiralling costs prevented action. Finally in 2014 a reduced scheme was completed. A stretch of the A344 was grassed over to allow people to

Figure 12.10 *The view of Stonehenge from the cursus round barrows prior to closure of the old car park*

walk across the northern half of the landscape, although the land immediately to the south remains barred by the A303. Solving this problem remains a government 'priority' but no solutions are likely soon. The dreadful 1960s car park and visitor centre have been finally replaced by a new £27m centre just north of the Winterborne Stoke barrow cemetery and just west of the cursus. The centre includes displays of over one hundred artefacts, a burial and a virtual solstice presentation with 'recreated' houses outside. It is out of sight of the stones, although it has a 'low-key visitor transit system' (land rovers pulling carriages) to bring visitors close to the stones.

The protection of artefacts

Legal protection of artefacts focuses on those few examples of high monetary value. The old laws on treasure trove in England and Wales were replaced by the Treasure Act (1996). It defines as treasure objects and coins which are over 300 years old and either over 10 per cent precious metal or at least ten in number. In 2003 'treasure' was extended to cover all prehistoric metal finds. Items substantially composed of precious metal and less than 300 years old are treasure if it can be shown that they were deposited with the intention of recovering them. Finds of treasure have to be reported to a coroner within fourteen days and become the property of the Crown. Rewards are generally paid to the finder or landowner. Apart from general legislation on theft and trespass, the law neglects other materials (e.g. pottery) which may be of greater archaeological value. This means that assemblages that include treasure can be broken up.

To improve the recording of artefacts which fell outside the scope of the Treasure Act, the Portable Antiquities Scheme was introduced in 1997. The government and the Heritage Lottery Fund financed pilot schemes to encourage the recording of all archaeological objects found by members of the public at any site. The scheme extends to all of England and Wales. 'Finds Liaison Officers' provide advice on finds and run 'finds roadshows'. They provide a link between the public, metal detector users and archaeologists and museums. The scheme has been very successful with over 920,000 objects reported by 2014 including an increasing amount of 'treasure'. A considerable number of new sites have been located as a result of this work. Accurate recording enables details to be added to an online database. The jewel in the crown of this scheme was the Staffordshire Hoard discovered in a field by a metal detectorist in 2009. Over 3,500 artefacts including 5kg of gold were recovered. Nearly all the artefacts were military and and it was thought that this hoard was the booty from a major 'Dark Age' battle in the C8th AD. Despite its success, the Portable Antiquities Scheme is currently at risk due to austerity cuts across the public sector.

There is considerable support amongst archaeologists for the United Nations sponsored UNIDROIT Convention on Stolen or Illegally Exported Cultural Objects. This requires the return of stolen or illegally excavated artefacts to their owners and provides a way of checking the provenance of imported objects. It also sets out a minimum standard for the art trade. It would not affect existing collections. The UK has not yet signed up to this convention but may do so in the near future. In the meantime the Portable Antiquities Scheme has reached voluntary agreements with some organisations, notably eBay, to ban the illegal sale of treasure through their service.

WHO ARE THE ARCHAEOLOGISTS?

Within archaeology in the UK there is increasing debate about who should engage in practical archaeology. Archaeology's roots lie with the work of enthusiastic amateurs but since the advent of PPG16 it has become increasingly professionalised. Excavation began with the antiquarians from the C17th onwards. Archaeology provided a hobby for landed enthusiasts right up to the 1950s. Some of these early diggers were little more than grave robbers. However, in the C20th a new breed of more informed and influential practitioners, such as Sir Mortimer Wheeler, pioneered modern excavation techniques.

Learned and excavation societies

By 1900 most parts of the country had societies devoted to gathering archaeological information and communicating it to their members and to the wider public. Most undertook excavations and began journals, many of which continue to this day. Some established museums where their collections could be displayed. This too was largely an upper-class activity, undertaken by those who could afford the time to take part in research excavations. The societies did, however, include more of the public by the 1950s. One of their strengths was their focus on particular localities so that expertise in identifying artefacts, especially lithics and ceramics, was developed. Some of these groups such as the Prehistoric Society continue to be leaders in funding and publishing research archaeology. A modern example is the Vindolanda Trust, which is an independent charity that excavates and researches Roman military remains close to Hadrian's Wall and provides education and enables public involvement. In some parts of the country local societies remain very active and still conduct research excavations. In others their function has shrunk to organising public lectures.

The rescue era

The massive urban expansion and road building programmes of the 1960s and 1970s saw a rapid rise in rescue archaeology. The term was coined in the 1960s when so much development was occurring that the earlier pattern of amateur and university summer excavations could not cope with the volume of archaeological sites being threatened and destroyed. Rescue, a charitable trust, dramatised the threat to Britain's archaeology by using as its logo an image of Stonehenge being scooped up in a giant earth-moving machine's bucket. While that icon itself was never really endangered, it drew attention to the scale and pace of development and the way in which valuable evidence was being lost unless it could be excavated and recorded. Excavation teams were needed all year round.

Numerous local rescue committees sprang up to address the destruction of archaeological sites in their area. Teams of volunteers sought to record what they could before machines or ploughs destroyed the remains. The Iron Age Museum in Andover contains a gallery paying tribute to the contribution of their local volunteers. Typically, excavations involved a small number of professionals working alongside volunteers. The Empingham (▶ p. 35) excavation of an Anglo-Saxon cemetery ahead of flooding to create Rutland Water was a good example of this. Some teams were centrally based within government agencies including universities and local authorities while others were formed locally to combat specific threats. The M5 Rescue Committee is a good example of a group founded with a clear but essentially time-constrained focus. Most of today's archaeological units can trace their origins back to 1960–80s rescue groups. In Oxfordshire five local excavation committees had undertaken rescue work ahead of gravel extraction in the Thames Valley and the building of the M40. In 1973, to improve coordination and access to funding, they united as the Oxfordshire Excavation Committee. That organisation eventually developed into Oxford Archaeology, now one of the largest non-government units in Europe.

Rescue archaeology coincided with a rapid expansion of adult and higher education provision including the development of new archaeological departments in universities. These two developments provided many opportunities for the public to get involved in archaeology and to follow that interest academically. However, excavation was poorly resourced. Rescue teams would identify potential threats to archaeological

Figure 12.11 *How it used to be: an amateur rescue team at Empingham* *(▶ p. 35)*

sites from planned developments such as road building, gravel extraction or pipelines and then try to raise funds. Sometimes they were able to bid for public funding but they often relied on charitable efforts. Sometimes where some funding was available, diggers could be paid. Pay was low, often similar to unemployment benefit levels, and it was difficult to find full-time paid work. Nevertheless, a pool of skilled excavators emerged on 'the circuit' moving between rescue work and major research projects such as Cadbury Castle and Danebury.

In the 1980s some funding did come through government job creation schemes at a time of high unemployment but pay for diggers remained low. The step change was PPG16 and the funding by developers. This meant that some archaeologists could be employed to operate all year round whereas previously almost all excavation was undertaken in the summer months.

Archaeologists since the era of PPG16

PPG16 broadly divided archaeologists into two groups: curators and contractors.

Curators were local authority archaeologists who advised planners on the archaeological sensitivity of proposed development sites. Following a desktop survey drawing on information held by their SMR, they drew up the brief for any archaeological work needed and checked that it was done to required standards. Most of the finds from development work were usually deposited with the local authority museum service.

Contractors were archaeologists who actually carried out the exploratory work or excavations. Developers would put out a contract for the work required by the planners to competitive tender. They sometimes also hired archaeological consultants to contest the local authority decision. Most contracts were taken up by independent trusts such as York Archaeological Trust or small commercial 'units' – often ex-council archaeologists. Others developed from university units such as Archaeology South-East (UCL) or museums such as MoLA (Museum of London). Council units still carry out some work in a few counties such as Suffolk and Surrey but this is becoming increasingly rare. As in any sphere of business there have been mergers and takeovers with the result that, while some smaller units survive, a few large contracting units now dominate developer-led work in what is known as commercial archaeology. These include Oxford Archaeology, AOC and Wessex. These units can offer developers wide-reaching professional expertise and increasingly operate well beyond their original home base including in Europe and other parts of the world. Another development was the emergence of commercial companies such as Environmental Dimension Partnership (EDP), which offers a full range of environmental, consultative and fieldwork services to developers including archaeology.

Archaeology today

Most excavations now fall into the following four categories:

- Assessments and rescue excavations in advance of developments. These are largely carried out by professional archaeologists in the contracting units. Over 90 per cent of excavation falls into this category.
- Seasonal research excavations run by universities. These are largely open to their own students, although some take paying volunteers on training excavations.
- Occasional research excavation by specialists from government heritage agencies.

Figure 12.12 *A professional unit excavation. Note the much smaller number of diggers and the health and safety clothing worn by the team excavating a Bronze Age pit alignment at Biddenham. (Albion Archaeology)*

- Research and rescue excavations by local societies, independent archaeological trusts or amateur enthusiasts.

The development of the concept of community archaeology blurs some of these categories since academics or units may bid for grants to lead amateur groups (▶ p. 584).

Community archaeology

A counter to this trend has been a growth in interest in community archaeology. This recognises the potential of local people to volunteer on a regular basis and gain the requisite skills to work as independent groups or alongside contracted fieldworkers. First pioneered in Leicestershire in the late 1970s, a current example of good practice is Dig Greater Manchester. This project, sponsored by the University of Salford and the Association of Greater Manchester Authorities, is intended to create an opportunity for the local communities in the Greater Manchester region to get involved in a variety of ways in their own history and heritage. The chance will be given to thousands of Greater Manchester residents to get 'hands-on' experience of an archaeological excavation in a safe and healthy environment. The 2012 programme included sites in Bury, Oldham, Salford and Stockport as well as a residential excavation

Figure 12.13 *A community archaeology project. Investigation of a Roman building in Gloucestershire involving students and volunteers from the local village.*

of a multiperiod site in the Trent Valley at Mons Pool, Collingham, Nottinghamshire. The Chester Amphitheatre Project (▶ p. 48) provides another example.

Public engagement is a key theme in Heritage Reforms and new planning guidance, although it is not entirely clear what this will mean. Visions of community archaeology vary hugely. At one extreme the Southport Group of the IFA (2011) advocates professionals paid to communicate with the public and conduct tours of digs, while at the other extreme communities identify projects and carry out research, including excavation, themselves. For example, the CBA host a Community Archaeology Forum and organise bursaries to train community archaeologists. The Museum of London, UCL and EH jointly run the Thames Discovery Programme which trains volunteers to record archaeology on the intertidal zone of the river. In 2014 Crown Estate and Lottery Funding enabled them to roll out a nationwide CITiZAN (Coastal and Intertidal Zone Archaeological Network) community project to monitor and record coastal sites. Faulkner (2000) argues that community archaeology should go further. He notes that research still is largely carried out by amateurs and suggests ways in which this could be extended, leaving development work to the commercial sector. An example might be the Altogether Archaeology project which isorganised by Durham County Council. It used Lottery funding to pay an archaeological team to train and supervise around 400 volunteer diggers to excavate the medieval monastic site of Muggleswick Grange. More broadly, what were once called amateur projects are increasingly called public or community archaeology.

Amateur archaeology

Amateur archaeology is still thriving in pockets throughout the UK, although it is not as widespread as it once was. Amateurs have the advantage of being able to look at local sites and ask questions without the pressure to complete work quickly. The excavators are also often able to become experts in the particular periods they investigate for their area. The Council for Independent Archaeology offers some support for amateurs and has pioneered the development of affordable geophysics equipment. The CIA journal *Current Archaeology* often covers amateur projects and provides a critique of 'official archaeology'. Undoubtedly amateurs have been squeezed out of practical field archaeology in many areas, although many museums rely on them for finds and cataloguing work.

The decline in amateur involvement in fieldwork is related to changes in planning guidance. Developers are expected to hire qualified workers and commercial standards of health and safety must be applied. The units of professional archaeologists which developed in response to PPG16 also had to compete for business to survive. This left little time for the traditional professional role of supervising and training volunteers. Opportunities for amateur involvement in digging began to decline as a result. At the same time archaeology became more specialised. The application of scientific techniques for prospecting, recording and analysing was in most cases beyond the resources of rescue committees and enthusiastic amateurs. Interest groups have different views on the future. The Institute for Archaeologists (IFA) lobbies for the full application of the Valetta Convention partly because the requirement for all archaeological work to be carried out by accredited experts would improve the status of its members. Some amateur groups are concerned that accreditation would mean the same thing as being professional and would restrict all amateur archaeology. Amongst commercial diggers there is a desire for public involvement but concern that the use of volunteers could further depress wages (IFA 2013). Much hinges on whether archaeological work is restricted to professionals or those with professional skills and how these are determined.

Metal detectorists

The gradual exclusion of amateurs from field archaeology has coincided with an increase in metal detecting. Some professionals remain hostile to all detectorists because of damage that has been done to sites or looting by organised gangs of 'nighthawks'. However, most detectorists are not intentionally destructive or members of criminal gangs but simply people interested in the physical past. The Portable Antiquities Scheme has provided funding for liaison and recording work and increasingly county archaeologists work with detectorists. The success of the scheme testifies to the desire of many metal detectorists to contribute to archaeological understanding and it is slowly eroding professional distrust.

CULTURAL RESOURCE MANAGEMENT

This term originates with the US National Park Service but is used to describe the role of what are sometimes called curatorial services or Heritage Management in the UK. It encompasses those employed directly or indirectly by government and whose role involves protecting, administering and managing archaeological sites, landscapes and collections on behalf of the public. The best-known examples are local HERs and museum services and national agencies such as CADW and English Heritage. Most of those working for such agencies will not be directly involved in either excavation or post-excavation research; their primary function is to manage what has already been recorded. Increasingly their archaeological remit is linked

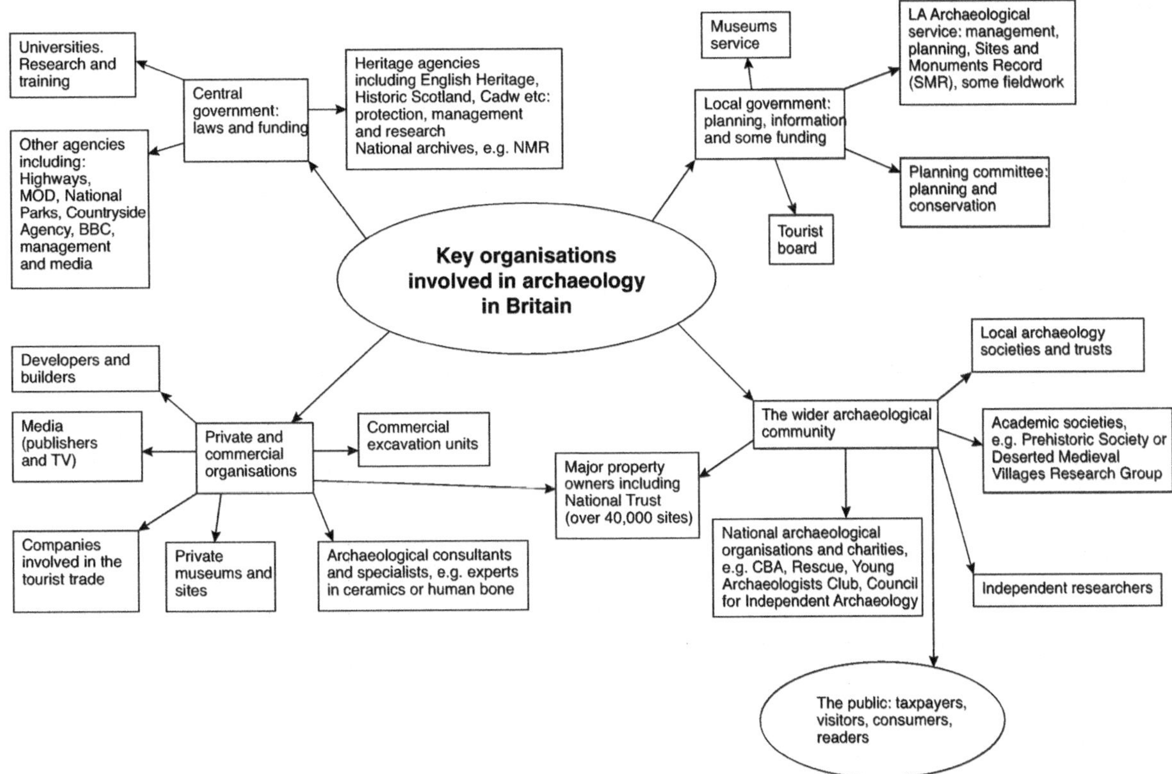

Figure 12.14 *Key organisations involved in British archaeology. The popular view of archaeologists is that they spend their time digging. While many do, there are at least an equal number who do not. For those of you who are considering archaeology-related careers, this chart may prove helpful in identifying opportunities.*

with management of other aspects of culture or the environment.

Specialists and scientists

There is a long tradition in archaeology of specialising in one aspect such as ceramics, animal bones or environmental evidence. The structure of archaeological reports reflects this with different specialists each writing a chapter on their findings. Some universities and larger units have some in-house specialists, although this is getting rarer in the commercial sector. Following the decline in local authority archaeology, fewer specialists are attached to councils or local museums. Usually freelance specialists work with excavated material sent from digs all over the country. Equally, aerial photography, geophysics and other reconnaissance specialisms are also outsourced. For lab-based scientific analysis, university departments and a small number of national or commercial companies are used. In some fields such as radiocarbon dating there is an international market. It can be cheaper to fly samples around the world to labs than to test locally. Many of those working in these areas are not archaeologists but scientists from other disciplines. However, they are increasingly at the forefront of archaeological research. For example the Europe-wide study into the spread of dairying is largely carried out by biochemists.

Campaign and lobby groups

A range of independent organisations, charities and learned bodies such as the Council for British Archaeology (CBA) and Rescue provide information and campaign on behalf of archaeology. This includes lobbying politicians, using the media and providing advice for developers and farmers. There is also the Institute for Archaeologists which promotes (but cannot enforce) high standards amongst those engaging in excavations. It acts as a professional body for a core part of the sector.

IS RESEARCH ARCHAEOLOGY STILL JUSTIFIABLE?

All excavation is destruction and buried remains from the past are a finite resource. That being true then should archaeologists only dig when remains will otherwise be destroyed by either development or natural forces? This philosophy became popular in the 1980s as ideas of conservation influenced archaeology. Research excavation was criticised on technical grounds because no excavation recovers and records everything and therefore potentially valuable information is lost. At some point in the future, techniques (including as yet undiscovered non-invasive technologies) may enable better recovery and recording. A related moral position is that we have a duty to preserve our heritage for future generations. These ideas came to dominate official archaeological thinking in the UK and were embedded in the preference for preservation 'in situ' (▶ p. 573) within the planning system. While well meaning, this ideology also made PPG16 more palatable to developers, who did not have to fund lengthy excavations when remains could be preserved under concrete rafts (▶ p. 575).

Since most excavation is rescue work and that has been increasingly the preserve of commercial units, it has become more difficult for aspiring archaeologists to gain experience and skills in digging. Many (but not all) universities have continued to mount research excavations both to answer research questions and to provide some training for the next generation of archaeologists. Clearly, archaeology would be unsustainable as a profession if some research work did not take place. For many years that gap has been filled by the training excavation. These are usually long-term research projects where volunteers pay to be trained in archaeological techniques. The Vindolanda excavations on Hadrian's Wall are probably the best-known example.

Currently there are signs that the pendulum is swinging back towards more public involvement in archaeological research both in recent legislation and in funding. There is a subtle shift in tone from the public being passive consumers to notions of active engagement with heritage. Similarly there is a shift from archaeological remains being a resource to be preserved untouched for future generations to a recognition that the current population have a legitimate interest in the past and that archaeological remains are an asset which can be used.

Development archaeology and research

A frequent criticism of developer-led archaeology is in relation to research. Unlike the other three categories, sites are not selected primarily to ask a question and in some cases the results are not always fully published or easily available. In addition, the fragmentation of records makes it difficult for researchers to piece together information from large numbers of 'keyhole' excavations in particular areas. Nevertheless many of the leading commercial units are involved in research, often in conjunction with universities and English Heritage. Oxford Archaeology, for example, has a sizeable post-excavation department and is committed to 'Open Archaeology' – making its research findings publicly available online. In addition many developer-financed excavations can be and are linked to wider research agendas. A groundbreaking attempt to synthesise the results of both research and developer-led work was Bradley's (2007) survey of findings from rescue excavations. In it he highlights the ways in which new discoveries from commercial archaeology led him to revise his perspective on later prehistory in the British Isles.

A number of massive infrastructure projects such as Heathrow Terminal 5, Crossrail and the proposed HS2 railway has meant that units often have to work together to undertake projects. While these projects are good news for units, they involve archaeologists frequently having to work at a distance from their homes and can create a shortage of diggers elsewhere. By 2014 a recruitment crisis due to years of low pay and demand from major projects was leading to a rise in recruitment of diggers from abroad. Major research projects also involve organisations combining to bid for funds and to ensure sufficient expertise. Several universities combined to undertake the Stonehenge Riverside Project, while the current Star Carr Project involves the universities of York and Manchester, the York Archaeological Trust and the local Vale of Pickering Research Trust.

KEY STUDY

The Biddenham Loop: modern developer-led archaeology in action

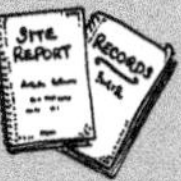

In the past twenty years a great deal of new housing has been required for the expanding town of Bedford and much of it has been built on land in a loop of the River Great Ouse known locally as the Biddenham Loop. The geology of the valley can best be described as river gravels and sand. Aerial photography can be particularly successful on such sites, especially on the gravel terraces, as major studies of the Thames and Trent valleys have shown. Under PPG16 any development has to be preceded by an archaeological evaluation and, where appropriate, fieldwork including excavation. Earlier non-intrusive work and excavation (1990s) was undertaken on 19 hectares of a much larger development by Bovis Homes but more recently (2007–12) another 62 hectares was released for development by David Wilson Homes. They supported an extended evaluation followed by providing the funding for large-scale phased stripping of all this new site and excavation of a wide range of features to investigate and record the archaeological landscape.

continued

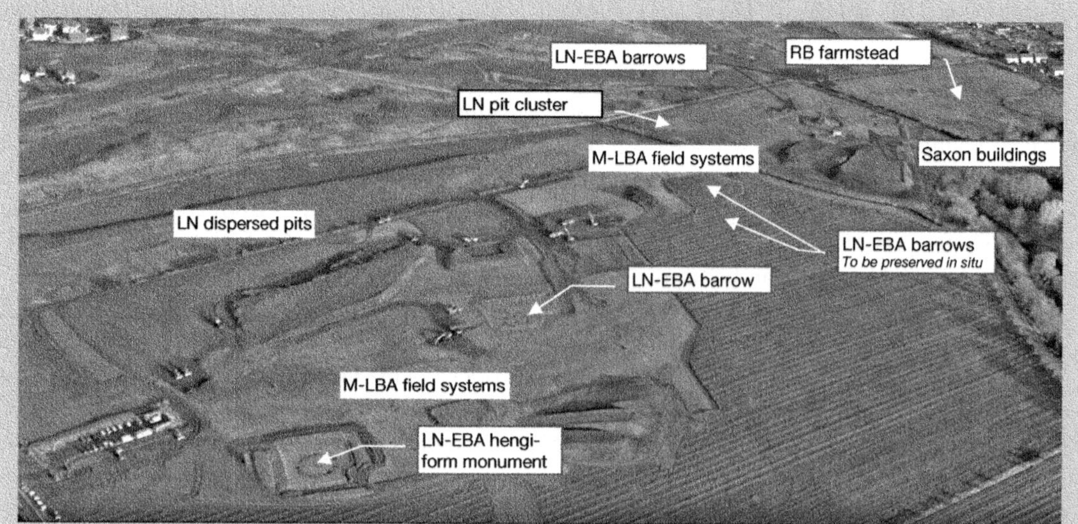

Figure 12.15 *Biddenham Loop main discoveries (Albion Archaeology)*

The four main elements of this work – survey/evaluation, excavation, post-excavation analysis and dating – provide an excellent key study into what can be achieved by a modern archaeological unit working closely with sympathetic developers.

Context

Up to 90 per cent of British archaeological fieldwork now takes place on development sites where strict health and safety regulations often prevent access except for those involved in the work. It is therefore a more hidden yet vital element of archaeologists' work and this description of the Biddenham Loop project should be read as an example of the kind of practices currently followed.

David Wilson Homes (the 'developer') appointed CgMs Consultants to act on their behalf and prepare an archaeological management plan for their Biddenham Loop site. This was approved by the planning department of Bedfordshire County Council, who had made it a condition of the planning approval that appropriate archaeological investigations should take place. CgMs then prepared tender documents related to the archaeological potential of the site and invited bids for the work via a process known as competitive tendering. Albion Archaeology (a professional archaeological organisation based in Bedford) made the successful bid and then commenced to work in liaison with the developer, the consultants, the planning officers and on-site contractors to develop an appropriate strategy for the archaeological investigations.

This strategy involved a Written Scheme of Investigation providing research objectives and looking at logistical issues such as the phased release of areas for topsoil stripping and archaeological investigation before their release back to the contractor for their own work schedule. The archaeologists had a 12-week window for their first phase and then subsequent areas were cleared, excavated and released in an agreed sequence.

Neolithic	At least 3 hengiform monuments (depending on interpretations of crop marks), one of which was radiocarbon dated to the start of the early Neolithic.
Early Bronze Age	11 of 18 ring-ditches/barrows were investigated. The highest status burial was referred to as the 'Biddenham Archer', a crouched male burial located in 2012 and buried with a beaker, two flint arrowheads, a stone wrist-guard, a copper dagger and a wild boar tusk. Also from this period: flat graves, shafts and evidence for settlement from pit clusters and flint concentrations in the ploughsoil
Middle Bronze Age	Field systems and ditches from an agricultural landscape considered as one of the most significant discoveries at Biddenham Loop. Large numbers of burials – 35 human and 4 cattle
Late Bronze Age	3 pit alignments
Middle Iron Age	Pits and several roundhouses from 5 settlements. Pits were used for grain storage then infilled with domestic debris including pottery. One included a spearhead tip, another an inhumation and a third held an animal burial.
Romano-British	4 farmsteads, ditches and 2 trackways. A bustum burial with a jar and C4th Nene Valley beaker. A ritual complex. A cemetery with 33 inhumations was recorded nearby on the Bedford Bypass project. Some imported pottery was recovered but most of the pottery assemblage is characterised by domestic and utilitarian types and forms of locally made coarse wares.
Early Saxon	A settlement with 16 sunken-featured buildings with an additional 8 dispersed on the west side of the Biddenham Loop. Finds included Saxon pottery, bone combs, spindle whorls and iron pins

Figure 12.16 *Finds and periods from the Biddenham Loop (Albion Archaeology)*

What emerged from the investigations was a clear indication that this area of river valley had had fairly continuous human occupation from the Mesolithic to the early Saxon period with evidence from material culture and key features. It is not the purpose here to go into great depth regarding particular features but the list above will indicate to the reader the variety of sites examined and how they can demonstrate continuity of use. As in most archaeological landscape studies, it is the evidence of ongoing activity that is really significant rather than a headline-grabbing discovery such as a chariot burial. The evidence can be analysed to see how generations of people in the past interacted with their own contemporary landscape, reacting to and respecting earlier elements and sometimes reworking and remodelling them to suit the conventions or rituals of their own time.

Archaeological reconnaissance

HER provided lists of an extensive range of ritual monuments and trackways from aerial photography sources. Fieldwalking prior to Bovis Homes' involvement had identified flint scatters, while one oval barrow was listed as a scheduled ancient monument. In other words, there was a corpus of known information before more intensive and focused research began – the presence of archaeological remains and deposits was not a surprise.

Bovis Homes' non-intrusive evaluation in the 1990s had involved fieldwalking and a magnetometer survey by Geophysical Surveys of Bradford, now known as GSB Prospection. In 1994, when this survey

continued

took place, a 50 per cent sample of the area was covered – quite extensive for its day – but now (2014) it would be expected that a 100 per cent survey would be undertaken.

Cropmark aerial photos were sourced from the Cambridge University Collections and those held by Bedfordshire County Council rather than a new aerial survey being commissioned. The nature of aerial photography is such that an existing longer-term collection is always likely to be of more value than photography arranged after development is agreed by planning departments.

Mesolithic flints were identified from fieldwalking using transects at 4m intervals across areas of observed flint concentrations. Field system ditches were 'identified and assigned to the Romano-British period' from surveys but were later dated to the middle Bronze Age by excavation. This is testament to the fact that while a non-intrusive survey dates by typology, excavation can confirm or reject such dates from cultural evidence.

Excavation

Throughout the five years of the excavations (the greatest proportion of the work was undertaken in the first year October 2007–October 2008 and the rest intermittently over the remaining four years) reviews were held and a careful watch kept on the plan and its costings and implementation. Such projects are by nature an iterative process whereby discoveries can influence subsequent decisions and the original Written Scheme of Investigation is often amended or updated by mutual agreement of the parties involved. A good example at Biddenham was the increased focus on the middle Bronze Age field system, once it was recognised as such, owing to the fact that such evidence had not been located in

Figure 12.17 *Recording the lower fills from one of the large pits at Biddenham (Albion Archaeology)*

Bedfordshire previously. The original sampling strategy designed when the features were being interpreted as Romano-British was revised and machines were used to empty most of their lengths. However, it emerged that these ditches had been of greater significance to their creators at points where they turned corners or exhibited bends (at these locations there was a greater deposition of animal and even human remains) and so such vital areas were reserved for excavation by hand.

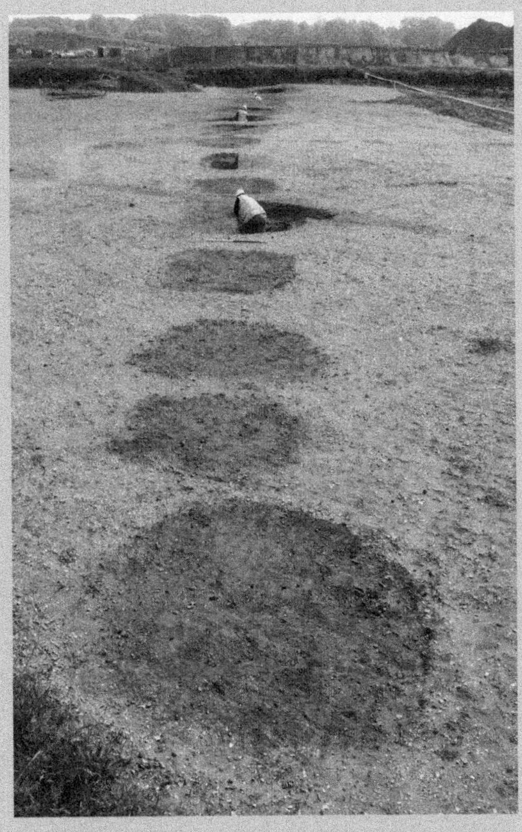

Figure 12.18 *Pit alignment (▶p. 582) under investigation at Biddenham (Albion Archaeology)*

In general terms, all earth cut features were exposed after stripping and their extent was visible against the sand and gravel natural. Thus linear and circular features, pits, graves and sunken-featured buildings could be identified and planned using GPS. Hand excavation or machine excavation was adopted as per the Written Scheme of Investigation but with possible amendment – see above. Larger features were sectioned/sampled to reveal profiles and to recover dating evidence. Smaller features were frequently excavated by removing half of their fill and completing site recording data. Some features had more fill removed depending on the archaeologists' judgement as to their potential to provide extra evidence. Key attention was paid to intersecting features to establish their relative chronology; for example, defining MBA field system ditches as earlier than the pit alignment and the latter as earlier than IA storage pits. Plans, sections and context sheets were drawn and completed in line with the requirements of the recording manual.

Sometimes interpretation of features and a site is seen as an activity which takes place post-excavation when all the plans, sections, context sheets and data from finds can be drawn together in the peace and quiet of the office. The consultants and archaeologists who managed the Biddenham Loop excavations were keen to acknowledge that interpretation is equally a key element of the day-to-day process of excavation. Questions about past usage of a site cannot necessarily wait until after the excavation but the debate about them should inform the process. The landscape archaeology on this site demanded questions be asked about its evolution – Could ditch fillings indicate the presence and/or location of a bank? What was the sequence of opening and filling of a ditch? Had it been cleaned or recut? Some significant answers were obtained – Bronze Age ditches which aligned on Neolithic hengiform monuments stopped short by a distance which would have allowed an earlier bank still to be visible and therefore respected. Romano-British ditches also observed the surviving prehistoric landscape. Large pits were at first interpreted as water pits due to parallels elsewhere but are now interpreted as being dug in association with ritual activity. A few artefacts need ^{14}C dating to confirm this.

continued

Figure 12.19 *Bustum burial (▶p. 516) being recorded at Biddenham (Albion Archaeology)*

Finds were processed and soil samples evaluated off site but during the excavations. This concurrent activity allowed for rapid feedback of information into the excavation strategy. Archaeologists set their discoveries against the current state of local and regional knowledge to target areas which were less well understood or of greater potential significance. Thus the interpretation and site narrative was built largely on site during the excavations.

Post-excavation

Although it has been established that interpretation starts during the process of excavation and is key to directing research objectives, there is no doubt that much activity follows the completion of on-site activity.

The first formal report after the completion of fieldwork is an Assessment and Updated Project Design. As the name suggests, this assesses the significance and condition of the data recovered (artefacts and ecofacts), determines if further work is justifiable in the light of current research objectives and details the proposed methodology for analysis and publication.

Metalwork was sent for X-ray; specialists were used for dating; pollen samples sent to laboratories. This process, whereby a wide range of people are called upon to provide their specialist knowledge and equipment, ensured that a formal analysis could be made of the totality of the evidence and the information capable of being extracted from it.

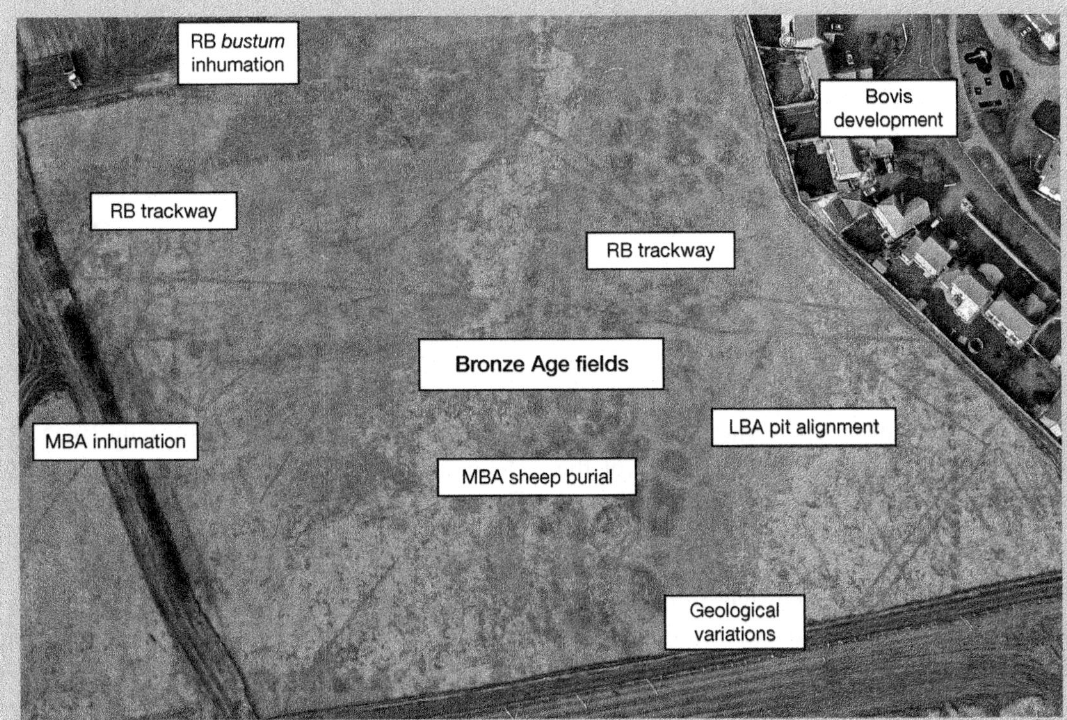

Figure 12.20 *Interpretation of Bronze Age landscape at Biddenham (Albion Archaeology)*

Interim reports were issued during the dig to keep stakeholders and the general public updated on progress. These documents had plenty of illustrations and revealed the interpretations of the site and its features. Amongst those highlighted as of particular interest were hengiform monuments, structured deposits in shafts and pits, the rare MBA landscape and the repeated use of early boundaries over time. The more formal report is scheduled to be published as a monograph in the East Anglian Archaeology series.

Dating

A range of methods were employed to build the chronological picture of the site:

- Typology of artefacts and features: flints (Mesolithic, Neolithic, Bronze Age); pottery (Peterborough Ware/Beaker). Parallels with other sites such as round barrows while the MIA ritual complex was compared with others in France.
- Stratigraphy. This was often shallow but some significant relationships were observed and recorded where features intersected. Later features often 'respected' earlier monuments which were still revered as sacred sites, except the ditch through Biddenham Archer mound.
- ^{14}C: 94 samples were dated by this method and when allied to stratigraphic sequences the date ranges returned by the laboratory could be narrowed using Bayesian modelling (▶ p. 160) to give more closely dated information.

Chapter 13

Archaeology and the Present

Whose Past Is It Anyway?

This chapter centres upon the relevance of archaeology in today's world and some of the political and ethical debates about ownership and presentation of the past. The first half focuses upon the ways in which different groups have sought to use evidence and images from the past. The second half focuses on the various ways in which archaeological knowledge is communicated.

WHICH PAST?

Archaeological knowledge and the images of the past created by archaeologists are not value free. As with history and literature, the selection of what is significant and how it should be interpreted partly derives from the political and social values and structures in present-day society. Archaeology and history have both been used either consciously or unconsciously to justify particular values and social structures. This has profound implications for the choices made by archaeologists including what and where to dig, what to do with the material recovered and how to communicate their findings.

THE POLITICAL USE OF ARCHAEOLOGY

Many governments and rulers have sought to justify their regimes and their territorial ambitions by claiming precedent and symbols from the past. Mussolini, the fascist dictator of Italy (1922–45), claimed to be following in the footsteps of the Romans with his plans for an Italian empire in Africa and for turning the Mediterranean into an Italian lake. Israel, Bosnia and the Indian city of Ayodhya are just three of many places where archaeology has recently been involved in violent political conflicts. In each case the ability to control what is known about the past is used as a tool to legitimise political, social or economic power. The newly independent Republic of Macedonia became embroiled from 1991 in a long-running dispute with neighbouring Greece over its name and particularly its flag – the Vergina Star. This sixteen-pointed golden symbol was found on Iron Age artefacts from the time of Alexander the Great, whose empire included both countries. Both states claimed the same heritage so Greece forced the new republic to change both its name and its flag. From the 1980s Saddam Hussein in Iraq drew parallels between his regime and the Assyrian Empire (▶ p. 487), which dominated the region in the 1st millennium BC. His regime drew prestige from association with that once mighty empire which originated in the area where Saddam's tribe lived.

These and many other attempts to impose a particular version of archaeology and history illustrate the political slogan in George Orwell's book *1984*, 'He who controls the past controls the future. He who controls the present controls

Figure 13.1 *Saddam and his use of archaeological heritage*

the past' (Orwell, 2000). One particularly complex and symbolic example was the 2013 conflict in Taksim Square, Istanbul, between the Islamist government who wanted to redevelop the square and neighbouring Gezi Park and a diverse group of opponents. Gezi Park had been created by the demolition of an Ottoman Empire barracks while Taksim contains both the monument to the Turkish Republic and the Atatürk Cultural Centre, named after the founder of modern, secular Turkey. It was also the site where thirty-four workers were killed by the military during protests in 1977. The government's redevelopment plans include a recreation of the Ottoman barracks as a shopping mall and a new mosque. The destruction of a secular, republican space and monuments symbolises the political conflict in Turkey between the secular Atatürk tradition and Islamists. A third dimension is that Gezi Park was also built over an Armenian cemetery. This contained a memorial to the Armenian victims of genocide by the Ottoman government during the First World War.

Israel, Islam and archaeology

In Israel, the dramatic, desert fortress of Masada was reputedly the site of a last stand by Jewish Zealot rebels against the Romans in AD 73. Excavations in the 1960s revealed the best-preserved Roman siege works in the world but failed to find evidence of collective suicide by the defenders. Nevertheless the site became an important symbol of Israel's refusal to give in to aggression and was used for military swearing-in ceremonies. Not all accept the official, heroic presentation and some Israeli archaeologists have suggested that the Zealots were an extremist group who provide poor role models for modern Israel. In Jerusalem, excavation is even more emotionally highly charged. Excavations in the Silwan area of the city, which has been under Israeli control since the Six-Day War of 1967, are trying to uncover the 'City of David', the original Jewish City. However, some of the work is funded by organisations which promote Jewish settlement in what is currently a largely Palestinian neighbourhood. Opponents allege that excavation and the tours which bring over 350,000 visitors a year are really designed to legitimise the take-over of the area for Jewish settlement. More generally, some Palestinians argue that excavation is simply another means of bulldozing their settlements. In Afghanistan, by contrast, it is archaeological remains which are destroyed for political purposes. In 2001 the Taleban blew up the monumental C6th AD statues of the Buddha at Bamiwan as well as destroying other statues and ancient artwork across the country. Religious leaders had declared them to be idols and therefore against Islam. UNESCO is debating whether to try to reconstruct them as an example of World Heritage (▶ p. 577). In Mali in 2013, Islamists destroyed Islamic tombs such as the medieval mausoleum of Sidi Mahmoud Ben Amar in the World Heritage Site of Timbuktu. The tombs belonged to Sufi (Islamic) saints but the Islamic Fundamentalist group Ansar Dine which is linked to al-Qaeda still regarded the shrines as idolatrous (idol worship), which is forbidden in Islam. Similar destruction of early Christian heritage was being carried out by Islamists in Syria in 2014.

Nazi archaeology

The best-known example of the manipulation of archaeology for propaganda purposes was by the Nazis during the 1930s and 1940s. German prehistorians had pioneered the use of material culture to identify particular ethnic groups of peoples (Volk) since before the First World War. In the 1920s Gustav Kossina took this a stage further to identify territories and homelands for each Volk in what became called 'early history'. Finds of Germanic material culture meant that a site was once German territory. This argument was deployed to oppose the loss of German territory after the First World War. The Nazi Party adapted these ideas in order to draw up racial maps of Europe and identify 'superior' races. The Nazis ensured that German prehistory was well funded at universities for the first time and a new institute – the Ahnenerbe (it means inheritance from our ancestors) – was established to research the history of the Aryan race from which they believed the Nordic peoples (including the Germans) were descended (Arnold 1990). Expeditions travelled as far as Iceland, Tibet and North Africa searching for clues. Within Germany, Ahnenerbe financed new museums, excavations and films to bring archaeology to a wider public. They also pioneered community archaeology (▶ p. 583), bringing archaeologists, soldiers and party members together on excavations to unite Germans in digging and to learn about their heritage and held open days for school children. Major excavations included the Iron Age hillfort of Alt-Christburg or Stary Dzierzgoń near modern Gdansk (Poland), to prove that the area had been German before Slavs settled there (Szczepanski 2009). Key indicators of Germanic occupation were artefacts decorated with particular symbols such as the swastika. The Nazis adopted the swastika, which had become a popular 'good luck' symbol following Schliemann's excavation of Troy in the late C19th. It was believed to be related to the Indo-Europeans (▶ p. 454) who had brought European (including German) languages from Asia. As Nazi armies advanced across eastern Europe, SS archaeological teams excavated artefacts with swastikas or the sun or wheel cross (which they believed to be a Nordic symbol)

Figure 13.2 *Anglo-Saxon pottery with swastika motifs*

to justify their conquests as retaking land which had always been German. One example is the Iron Age fortress of Biskupin in Poland, which the SS excavated from 1940 to 1942. Some of the same evidence was later used by Slavic archaeologists to prove that the area had not been German.

The political use of heritage in the UK

It is not just dictatorships or extremist political parties which have used archaeology for political ends. In Britain, current political priorities and values shape the nature of public archaeology. Promotion of 'community engagement' and of 'diversity' are two of the key issues which organisations currently need to address if they want to bid for public or lottery funds. While it seems only right that public archaeology should try to involve the public when spending public money, there is always a danger that priorities or interpretations may be too closely tailored to fit the current views of whichever politicians hold the purse-strings. Definitions of heritage, identity and therefore what should be excavated, preserved and presented are never value-free. For example, in Wales, the selection of sites for preservation and particularly for promotion has generated debate about which version of the past should predominate: the past of English conquest and castle building or the tradition of Welsh independence and resistance.

KEY STUDY

Ancient and modern Celts

In an uncanny parallel with the work of Kossina and 1930s Germany, a Celtic identity is being created both for the European Union and for separatist movements in Atlantic Europe. Does modern Celticism have a basis in archaeological reality?

Who were the Celts?

The name 'Celt' derives from 'Keltoi', which was a name the Ancient Greeks gave to the Iron Age peoples of Europe. The C6th BC geographer Hecataeus of Miletus used the term for peoples in southern France. The historian Herodotus used the term for people of modern Bulgaria and Romania but also beyond the pillars of Hercules (Spain). In the C3rd BC, Keltoi were held responsible for the attack on Delphi in Greece in 279 BC and as the 'Galatai' for invading Anatolia. The Romans used these terms interchangeably as Celts, Galli and Galatae and applied them to the Iron Age 'barbarians' they encountered north of the Alps. Concerned to conclude his conquest of Gaul, Caesar neatly divided the 'barbarians' into Gauls west of the Rhine and Germans to the East. There is no evidence to suggest that the loose confederations of tribes who fought the Romans had ever defined themselves in that way let alone as Celts. While Caesar recorded an influx of Belgae (from Belgium) into southern Britain, the terms 'Celts' and 'Gaul' were not applied by the Romans to the inhabitants of the British Isles.

The main thing the diverse range of European peoples labelled Celts by the Greeks and Romans had in common was that they were not Greek or Roman. We are also left with various, often contradictory, descriptions of Celts and Gauls amongst which warlike nature, chariots, torcs, moustaches and red hair have been used to create the stereotype which informs the Asterix books. Since the C18th AD these descriptions have been blended with linguistic and archaeological evidence to create new identities.

continued

The invention of Celtic identities

In 1705 the Breton cleric Pezron linked the Breton and Welsh languages to a common Celtic origin. In Wales, Lhuyd extended this link to Cornish and Irish and Scots Gaelic (Hobsbawn and Ranger 1983). These claims led to an enthusiasm for things Celtic as part of the Romantic Movement in the arts. These included an interest in early medieval poetry and the identification of monuments associated with Druids as in the work of the antiquarian Stukeley, who linked them to the 'temples' of Stonehenge and Avebury. These influences came together in the Welsh bardic movement and particularly the druidic rituals of the Gorsedd, which were invented by Iolo Morganwg. Over the next 200 years Celtic languages and literature were revived and linked to particular styles of visual art. This remains in popular culture in Celtic crosses and interlace tattoos, in particular the interlaced decorative style associated with metal finds from La Tène. The excavation of artefacts with similar motifs from Austria to Ireland was used to suggest common cultural links across a wide region. Extensions of this were the idea of a common 'proto-Celtic' language and tracing the migration of Celtic peoples from a central heartland north of the Alps, which included Hallstatt (▶ p. 373) and Hochdorf (▶ p. 434). Archaeologists tried to use differences in skull shapes to identify those of Celtic racial origin. Short broad skulls were Celtic while long narrow ones were Nordic.

Enthusiasm for vanishing languages, imitations of Iron Age artefacts, harps, poetry and Druids also became bound up with nationalism. The French revolutionary government after 1789 emphasised France's Gaulish heritage to contrast with the way the aristocracy had claimed legitimacy from Charlemagne and Frankish invaders. Napoleon III financed excavations at Alésia, where a Gaulish army had resisted Caesar in the last great battle of the Roman invasion. A statue of the Gaulish leader Vercingetorix was erected on the site as an element in unifying France around a Celtic tradition. President Mitterand chose a nearby Iron Age fort at Bibracte to make a similar appeal for national unity in 1985 (Dietler 1994). The European Museum of Celtic Civilisation is at Bibracte. The European Union itself through its Education and Culture Directorate funds exhibitions, education and restoration programmes which promote a view of European history leading from Celtic beginnings to future political integration (Graves-Brown 1996).

For Irish nationalists, Celtic heritage became a key element in creating a distinctive Irish identity, most romantically expressed in 'The Celtic Twilight' by the poet Yeats. Aspects of Celtic culture have been mobilised in other countries and regions which once spoke Celtic languages including Wales, Galicia and Brittany. Occasionally these newly constructed ethnic identities have been used by extremists to promote racist views which are usually anti-English (Scotland) or anti-French (Brittany).

Celtic identity and archaeology

For many years, archaeologists have accepted the Celtic label when studying the European Iron Age. There are degree courses in Celtic studies and departments of Celtic archaeology. The idea of Celtic migration fitted with the dominant models of change in prehistory, and across Europe sites were catalogued with reference to key Celtic type-sites such as Hallstatt. However, growing awareness of the way a Celtic tradition has been constructed (Hobsbawm and Ranger 1983) and a reaction against the idea of pure ethnic identities in the present as well as the past has led many to question the validity of the label. James (1999) argued that there was no united Celtic culture in the past and that links between ancient and modern Celts were tenuous. Collis (2003) distinguished between an invented idea of a pan-European Celtic race or culture and the cluster of languages which are labelled Celtic. Both archaeologists were attacked as English Imperialists for their views (Megaw and Megaw 1998) as the debate became highly charged. Further work, however, brought more support to their arguments.

Taylor's work on the Gundestrup Cauldron (▶ p. 397), often cited as the best example of Celtic art, revealed that it was in fact Thracian. Hill (1996b) showed that Iron Age societies in Britain varied enormously and that while there were occasional finds of 'La Tène'-style metalwork, little else linked them to central Europe. He argued that the use of analogies from medieval Ireland or classical works had imposed a Celtic framework on the Iron Age which got in the way of interpreting the evidence on its own terms. This led to evidence being overlooked when it did not conform to the Celtic model. His research showed Wessex to be a relatively egalitarian society of farmers for most of the Iron Age. Other parts of Britain were different again. Research into the genetic origins of the populations of the British Isles does suggest a major element of common ancestry for Ireland and western Britain and links to Galicia (▶ p. 503). However, migration from Spain had taken place by the Neolithic. There was little genetic ancestry which could be ascribed to incoming Celts from central Europe in the Iron Age. This has led to a refocus on Atlantic links in Iron Age studies. Much of this supports linguistic origins for Celtic languages in Spain (Cunliffe and Koch 2012). The realisation of the importance of long-distance communication and exchange by sea is just one aspect of the period that had been overlooked because of assumptions about diffusion (▶ p. 147) from central Europe.

Archaeological evidence in the British Isles provides little support for a common European Celtic culture. While there are a few rich burials which display continental influences, these can be explained by an elite borrowing specific ideas to enhance their prestige. In the same way, the Etruscans borrowed from the Ancient Greeks but this did not make them Greek (James 2000). Other aspects of Iron Age religion, particularly deposition in water (▶ p. 434), are older and their frequency suggests stronger links to the non-Celtic, Baltic region. 'La Tène'-style material culture can also be explained through the exchange of materials and ideas. This is a more persuasive explanation because there is no wholesale adoption of a 'Celtic package'. While it is likely that many of the Iron Age inhabitants of the British Isles spoke one of several Celtic languages, there is no evidence of a common ethnic identity or social organisation (▶ p. 419). It is likely that there was far more diversity of culture and ethnicity than the Celtic model allows.

Modern Celtic identity, like many other European identities, has been constructed since the C18th from selected evidence from different periods and different places. Since all ethnicities are constructed, there is nothing inherently wrong with this. However, it is misleading and potentially dangerous to impose this concoction on the Iron Age and then to use it to justify exclusive, nationalist politics today.

Figure 13.3 *Celtic art? Should the Great Torc from Snettisham, one of the finest examples of prehistoric goldworking, be classified as Celtic and bracketed with central European art work dating back to Hallstatt (▶ p. 373) and the migration of Celtic peoples in the Iron Age? Or is it the product of an Iron Age tradition in the British Isles which may have borrowed some motifs from Europe?*

NATIONAL DISPUTES OVER THE OWNERSHIP OF CULTURAL ARTEFACTS

Throughout the history of states, artefacts from one country have found their way as gifts, stolen booty and purchases to other countries. The first person to break the tradition of the victorious army taking what it wanted appears to have been the Duke of Wellington, who returned art treasures to Italy that had been plundered by Napoleon. However, this did not catch on. Museums, especially – but certainly not exclusively – in the Western world filled up with artefacts from beyond their national borders. From the late C19th this included materials from excavations carried out by archaeologists from western European countries and the USA. Some of these were in independent states with the consent of the government of the day but many others were in colonies where the local people had no say in what was removed. From the late C20th many of the modern states in areas from which artefacts were removed have requested that they be returned (restitution) irrespective of whether they were simply taken or purchased or taken with permission. An instance of a restitution request to right a colonial wrong is the dispute between the British Museum (BM) and Nigeria about the Benin Bronzes: brass plaques taken from the palace of the king of Benin in 1897 after its conquest by Britain. Some modern governments have declared that legal permissions given in the past to remove artefacts are now invalid because governments in the past were corrupt, illegitimate or foreign. There are many such claims regarding the Ottoman (Turkish) Empire, in which many excavations took place in the mid-C19th from the Balkans to Mesopotamia. Most of these artefacts come from cultures that no longer exist and which bore little resemblance to the modern states that occupy the territory from which they came. Nevertheless, there is an escalating trend towards countries demanding the restoration of artefacts from museums where they are currently housed.

Figure 13.4 *The Pergamon Altar*

Restitution issues

Sometimes claims are backed by threats to withdraw excavation rights (as Turkey did to Germany in 2011) or not to allow other materials to be loaned to the museum in question (as Turkey did to the British Museum (BM)). In the USA a large number of metal and ceramic artefacts have been returned to claimant countries. For example, Yale University returned hundreds of artefacts to Peru that had been excavated from Machu Picchu from 1911 to 1915. Sometimes materials have been returned even where the provenance of the items was not clear. Those supporting restitution argue that even where the artefacts were legally purchased, it was often unclear exactly where they came from and therefore they could have been stolen. They also argue that if museums house artefacts which were once stolen, then how can they morally oppose the modern illegal trade in antiquities (▶ p. 569)? However, restitution of artefacts shows no sign of discouraging the expanding commercial trade in looted artefacts. Those resisting the return of materials deny that current states are really the heirs to past cultures in the same region; for example, Turkey and Troy or Modern and Ancient Egypt. Questions about the quality of conservation and whether materials will remain safe and accessible have also been raised. While this cannot be argued today in the case of Italy or Greece, the looting of museums in Cairo in 2013 has undermined the Egyptian case for the return of the bust of Nefertiti from Berlin or the Rosetta Stone from London. Similarly, the BM sold around thirty Benin Bronzes to Nigeria in 1951 but many have since been lost from the Lagos Museum. The BM now regrets this decision and further sales of artefacts would not be legal. In a test case in 2005 (The Feldmann case) the high court ruled that any 'moral obligation' to the original owners of material that had been acquired, even via looting, did not override laws such as the British Museum Act (1963), which prohibits it from giving up artefacts from its collections, many of which were donated 'to the nation' rather than to the BM.

Figure 13.5 *An ancient Egyptian obelisk in Istanbul. Erected during the Ottoman Empire, it stands on top of a Byzantine plinth in modern Turkey. To which nation does it belong?*

Perhaps the most bizarre dispute concerns art and artefacts taken by the Red Army from Germany in 1945. In 2013 the leaders of Russia and Germany were to speak at the opening of an exhibition at the St Petersburg Hermitage

Museum which was ironically called 'Bronze Age Europe without Borders'. It included the Eberswalde Hoard, the largest assemblage of gold found in Germany, and artefacts from Troy. Speeches by the two leaders were cancelled when it emerged that Angela Merkel, the German Chancellor, was about to call for the restitution of looted artefacts, many of which the Russians had previously denied that they had. The Russian position was that the Nazis had looted many artefacts from Russia in the Second World War and that the artefacts were also compensation for the great losses suffered by the Red Army. The origins of the Trojan artefacts were not discussed.

Claims for the restoration of artefacts are sometimes an element in nation building and at other times simply an expression of nationalism. A new way of looking at this has been to consider whether some materials should be considered world cultural heritage – for all people – rather than for a particular nation. This is an argument which the BM has deployed as part of its defence against calls for restitution or what David Cameron, the British Prime Minister, termed 'returnism'.

The Elgin Marbles

Perhaps the most famous dispute between nations over archaeology is that of the Elgin Marbles. Many of the marble, classical friezes from the ruined Parthenon Temple in Athens were removed by Lord Elgin, the British ambassador in 1812, apparently with the permission of the Ottoman (Turkish) sultan who ruled Greece at that time. Others went to Paris and Copenhagen. Elgin sold his below the market price to the British parliament, who presented them to the British Museum. Meanwhile, Greece gained its independence from the Ottoman Empire and deliberately promoted a classical Greek heritage to promote a sense of identity in the new state (Hamilakis and Alouri 1996). From the 1980s the Greek government campaigned for the return of the marbles, claiming that they had been removed illegally, that they are a key element in Greek national identity and that they should be seen in context on a restored Parthenon. Over the years the full range of arguments has been deployed by both sides. Initially the BM was able to argue that the marbles were better preserved in London – as they had been for 200 years – than they would be

Figure 13.6 *The Elgin Marbles: should they stay or should they go?*

in heavily polluted Athens, and much less at risk of damage. Indeed the Parthenon itself had been lucky to survive plans by the C19th Greek monarchy to turn the Acropolis into a Royal Palace (Hamilakis and Alouri 1996). However, the building of a state-of-the-art museum to house the marbles eventually undermined this position. Both sides have identified damage done to the artefacts in the past, in Greece through fighting and looting and in London during a botched cleaning operation in the 1930s.

The BM would in fact find it legally difficult to return the marbles even if it wanted to but increasingly it has advanced arguments related to the function of 'Universal museums' in a world where humans share a global cultural heritage. Encyclopedic museums such as the BM or the Louvre in Paris or Smithsonian in Washington offer large numbers of people the opportunity to compare materials across many cultures and therefore promote tolerance and a common sense of humanity. Like Greece, the UK can also argue that its culture owes something to Ancient Greece just as it does to the people of Ice Age Europe and Palaeolithic Africa. Furthermore, with globalisation and the increasing migration of people around the world, many cities, particularly London, are global cities. London has large numbers of people of Greek, not to mention Turkish or Nigerian origins who might equally claim a connection to particular artefacts. Interestingly, the city with the third largest Greek ethnic population is now Chicago. The C19th nation state with its ethnically pure population is increasingly a thing of the past, if it ever existed at all. However, 'returnists' argue that the concept of world culture is just another idea to justify Western colonialism. One 'half-way house' option which several museums are pioneering is the loaning of artefacts to claimant states for exhibitions. For example, the Cylinder of the Persian King Cyrus II (559–530 BC), which is claimed to be the earliest law granting human rights, was loaned to Iran by the BM in 2010. The debate between the claims of modern nation states and museums devoted to research and a kind of world cultural heritage remains finely balanced.

REPATRIATION TO INDIGENOUS PEOPLES

The disputes between museums and indigenous peoples is somewhat different. In most cases artefacts and sometimes human remains from these tribal or chiefdom levels were removed without their consent and frequently from excavations of burial sites. Materials taken belonged to, or were linked to, the same culture and belief systems of people living today. This contrasts with many of the disputes between states. For example, most of the artefacts that Iran wants returned from the Louvre in Paris belong to Elamite or Persian civilisations which were radically different from modern Islamic culture. In contrast, there is a widespread view amongst academics and museums that at least some of the material taken from indigenous peoples is a basic part of their identity. The best-known example of conflict between indigenous peoples and archaeologists has been in the USA. By the 1990s the civil rights movement for Native Americans had won a series of legal and political victories. One of these addressed what Native Americans considered to be the 'vulture culture' of archaeologists who had desecrated burial sites to recover artefacts for analysis and display in collections. They viewed archaeology as grave robbing by an occupying power. The 1990 Native American Graves Protection and Repatriation Act (NAGPRA) protected graves and cultural objects from further exploitation and required agencies with government funding to identify material from Native American cultures and to offer its repatriation to the tribes involved. Even where there is no cultural link, Native American groups can still request repatriation. Since 1990, over one hundred collections have returned ritual artefacts or human remains. The US example has been followed in several other Western countries. In

1992 a Ghost Dance Shirt was returned from Glasgow Museum to the Lakota tribe, while in 2005 bones and grave goods were returned to the Algonquins by the Canadian Museum of Civilisation for reburial despite there being a lack of clarity about whether the remains were all Algonquin. In 2007 the UN passed a Declaration on the Rights of Indigenous Peoples which called for their human rights and cultural identity to be safeguarded. Since then disputes have spread to many other countries. In Japan in 2013 the Auni people began lawsuits against several Japanese universities which hold over 1,000 skulls and skeletons excavated from grave sites over the last 150 years. While they cannot prove individual links, the Ainu argue that the ancestral bones belong to the whole community.

In 2004 the Human Tissue Act (▶ p. 608) made it legal for the BM and other museums to return human remains. Since then the BM has returned some materials within its policy limits of 100 years to direct descendants and 300 years to communities with a direct connection. This keeps this issue separate from disputes with states. The test for the BM is whether wider public interest in retaining remains is outweighed by the cultural and religious importance to the claimants. Examples include two ash bundles in animal skin which represent the remains of seventeen people which were returned to the Tasmanian Aboriginal people in 2007. The rationale was that the grief caused by not completing the traditional mortuary rituals outweighed the benefit of retaining the remains in the museum. Similarly, in 2011 the Natural History Museum returned the remains of 178 people to the Torres Strait Islanders. However, in 2012 the BM decided not to return some Torres Island skulls because there

Figure 13.7 *The Museum of the American Indian*

This stunning museum close to the Capitol in Washington is representative of a shift in public policy in the late C20th USA. The museum presents the Native American story from their perspective and combines archaeology, historical artefacts and oral history. This particular display stresses the Native American role in managing the environment, another topical political concern. The state-of-the-art displays include video and motion sensor-activated displays as well as dioramas and more traditional displays. In the café you can eat Native American food.

was insufficient evidence supporting the claim that mortuary practice had been disrupted. The reaction from archaeologists has been mixed. There is clearly great sympathy with indigenous peoples and the wrongs that were done to them by archaeology in the past. However, returning remains makes the scientific study of human remains very difficult and creates particular obstacles for prehistoric excavations in the countries involved.

Science v. repatriation: the case of Kennewick Man

The most infamous conflict between archaeologists and indigenous peoples concerns the discovery of a skeleton at Kennewick, Washington State, USA in 1996. The remains were dated to *c.* 9300 BP and were some of the oldest and most complete found in North America. They were scientifically significant because of anatomical differences between the Kennewick skeleton and modern Native Americans. Early suggestions were that he appeared to have originated in Europe or, more likely, Japan or Polynesia. This was explosive because the claim to land ownership by Native Americans has rested on their identification with cultural remains and burials found there. In addition the oral histories of many tribes say that they have lived on their traditional lands since the start of time. Some Native Americans feared that if they were simply seen as one of a number of immigrant groups, then their claims to land rights would be undermined. The Umatilla, Yakama, Nez Perce and Colville tribes who inhabit the Columbia Valley demanded that the remains should be repatriated to them for burial under NAGPRA. Attempts to perform rituals near the bones led to claims that their DNA was deliberately being contaminated. The US army then dumped rubble over the find-site but were unable to prevent the dispute spreading. It quickly went to court and reached the US Senate, where debate continues. Scientists formed the organisation Friends of America's Past to lobby for the right to carry out research and finally in 2004 a federal court allowed them to do this. However, challenges continued including a halting of DNA research because it destroys bone and would therefore be desecration.

The issue of whether Native Americans have the right to block scientific research is part of a wider intellectual debate about the position of science in modern societies. Relativism (whereby no one set of knowledge is seen as superior) can lead to science being viewed as having no greater importance than mysticism or particular religious beliefs (Gross 1997). This thinking was enshrined in the Vermillion Accord on Human Remains (1989) and the Code of Ethics (1990) of the World Archaeological Congress. The latter recognises that 'the concerns of various ethnic groups, as well as those of science are legitimate and to be respected'. Ironically this has coincided with a significant increase in the range of scientific technologies available to study human remains and the potential benefits of such study. Critics argue that NAGPRA has become profoundly anti-scientific and has resulted in important scientific collections being buried. This has implications for studies into health and genetics as well as for archaeology. Supporters of NAGPRA argue that Western archaeology and science has indeed been a means of colonial domination and that repatriation and reburial are essential for aboriginal groups to re-take control over their identities (Fforde et al. 2004). However, although the debate is now polarised, opinions do cover a wider spectrum. There are Native Americans who welcome some research and there are also major differences about appropriate disposal rites since burial was never a universal custom. Thomas (2001) argues that problems could have been averted over Kennewick Man had scientists established better relations with local Native Americans from the outset. He cites instances where archaeologists have successfully involved native communities in the excavation, analysis and aftercare of remains in what is sometimes called indigenous archaeology.

Archaeologists with indigenous peoples

For many years many indigenous people saw archaeologists at best as thieves, plundering their burials. However, increasingly the value of archaeology in asserting other rights has become apparent. Australian aboriginal groups have used archaeological evidence to prove that their ancestors inhabited particular regions and to demonstrate their right to the land or to compensation for its use by others. Increasingly, native peoples in many parts of the world have also turned to archaeology for help. Examples from the USA include the Oneida of New York and the Tunica of Louisiana, both of whom were able to verify cultural continuity to the periods before white settlers arrived. In the most famous instance, historical records suggested that the Pequot Indian tribe of Connecticut died out following a war with European settlers in the C17th. However, archaeologists working with descendants of the Pequots were able to establish cultural continuity between the original tribe and survivors of the war whose descendants lived on reservations in the area until recent times. The Pequots were able to use archaeological data to gain recognition as a sovereign nation from the US government in 1987 and the return of some of their land. They now have their own Mashantucket Pequot Museum & Research Center with its own archaeological section which researches places of significance to the tribe including battlefield excavations from the Pequot War.

An excellent example of collaborative approaches has been work in the Tongass National Forest of Alaska coordinated by local archaeologist Terry Fifield. Palaeontologists had discovered human remains and obsidian artefacts in On Your Knees Cave on Prince of Wales Island in 1996. Although NAGPRA meant that work had to halt, local tribal leaders from the Tlingit peoples were consulted and consented to excavation and analysis as long as they were involved (Fifield 1996). Renewed excavation involving Tlingit interns revealed further bones which proved to be the remains of the earliest Alaskan, dating to 10,300 BP, but whose DNA differed from that of the Tlingit. Isotopic analysis (▶ p. 134) showed the young man to have had a similar diet to a seal and he clearly had travelled by boat. This is a key piece of evidence in support of coastal migration into North America. Following analysis, the bones were given a festival and burial by the Tlingit, who believe that the discovery supports their own oral history. This collaboration led to the Coffman Cove Community Archaeology Project involving the National Forest Service and the Native American Sealaska Heritage Institute excavating a Tlingit settlement with 4,000 years of deposits. The local Tlingit value the work because it provides employment and because of their interest in their past.

Pagans, human remains and museums in the UK

Most books on Stonehenge feature a picture of the Druids, a C19th order who invented their own ceremonies at the monument based on their interpretation of Iron Age beliefs. Since the 1960s many other groups have also sought to use ancient monuments for rituals and festivals. Pagans have claimed the sites as sacred according to their beliefs and want the right to worship there. For others their demands to hold festivals at the sites symbolise a struggle against an oppressive state. Either way, these demands have led to conflict with those responsible for managing the monuments and archaeologists concerned about damage to remains. In the case of the West Kennet Long Barrow, this includes sarsen stone being damaged by candles. In the case of Stonehenge, disputes over access have led to public order offences and occasionally violence. More recently the authorities have realised that those wanting to celebrate at the sites do not usually want to see them damaged. This has led to more inclusive management plans and a greater emphasis on educating about unintended damage to the monuments. Many New Age websites provide excellent visual records of sites.

Figure 13.8 *A pagan summer solstice at Avebury. This circular gathering at dawn includes both Druids and followers of Wicca.*

Sensitivities about displaying human remains

Not all museums have taken this line. A number have embraced repatriation and/or taking steps to avoid real or imagined public upset or offence. Some have removed exhibits from display, ended public handling of skeletal remains or plan to bury some of their collections. The National Museum in Dublin placed its bog bodies in spiral walk-in chambers so that people could choose whether to see them or not, while the Manchester Museum covered several mummies with sheets in 2008 to prevent public viewing. This decision was reversed following complaints from the public. Critics have suggested that curators are being manipulated by minority pressure groups or have lost their sense of purpose. It can also be seen as elitist and patronising for experts to deny the public the opportunity to see skeletons or bog bodies because they are deemed too sensitive or viewed as sensation seekers. Jenkins (2010) accuses such museums of penalising their visitors who want to learn about past rituals and of making research more difficult. Surveys consistently show that people want to see the remains held by museums and support their use for research. English Heritage (2009) found 91 per cent of people in favour, particularly with older specimens. Where people were most critical, it was of museums which did not provide sufficient contextual information for them to understand burials.

The case of 'Charlie'

Following the growing success of indigenous peoples in repatriating burials, some pagans have attempted to claim the same rights despite having no cultural links to the human remains. In 2008 the Council for British Druids demanded on the grounds of respect for the ancestors that 'Charlie', the skeleton of a four-year-old Neolithic child, should be removed from display at the Keiller Museum in Avebury and buried. The museum took the request seriously and launched

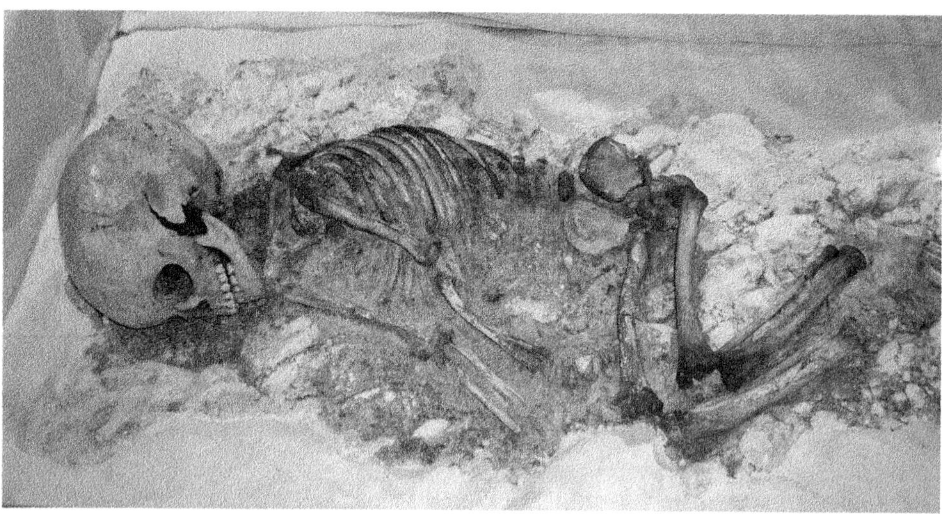

Figure 13.9 *'Charlie'*

a consultation. Partly this was out of concern not to be seen as discriminating against a religious group and partly from the growing sensitivity amongst the museum community about displaying human remains. However, the survey revealed that most people wished the remains to be kept on display and the request was refused. The debate about human remains in the UK was complicated by a major scandal which erupted in 1999 at Alder Hey Children's Hospital, Liverpool, where remains of dead children had been kept without their families' knowledge or consent. This led to the Human Tissue Act 2004, which included a clause to permit the transfer of human remains from museums. This in turn enabled a pagan group 'Honouring the Ancient Dead' to call for reburial of all prehistoric skeletal remains including bog bodies.

The government adopted a balanced view in 2008 when the Ministry of Justice issued new guidance on the treatment of human remains which allowed for alternatives to reburial of remains including retention indefinitely. The guidelines also made clear that while exhumations should be screened to protect the public from being offended or upset by accident, this did not mean that members of the public could not see the excavation. Equally, while a heightened sensitivity about ancestral remains permeates all official guidance on the excavation and display of human remains, it has not gone as far as NAGPRA. Roberts (2009a), in the CBA guide to human remains, argues that preservation and curation can be respectful and that the process of study and revealing the past life of people is an alternative way of honouring the dead. Similarly while the BM's policy (2006) is to ensure remains less than 500 years old are stored with artefacts from the same culture, it intends to retain its collection. The BM mounts a robust defence of its human remains collections because it fosters an understanding of diverse cultures and also provides a resource for scientific research into disease, forensics and evolution.

THE VALUE OF ARCHAEOLOGY

Public interest

The most frequently cited value of archaeology is the level of public interest. Queues to see the Staffordshire Hoard, visitor numbers at archaeological attractions from the BM to Jorvik to Stonehenge and viewer numbers for TV archaeology, particularly *Time Team*, clearly support this. Some would go wider and point to films, books and digital games as evidence of the fascination for archaeology either linked to history or independent of this. This is both surprising and unsurprising. Aside from the small numbers taking an A-level or a degree in archaeology, the subject is excluded from mainstream education beyond the primary years. Perhaps fondly remembered lessons on 'Saxons' or 'Romans' are not erased by the pressures of studying the subject for GCSE? However, in most countries and cultures people have an interest in where they came from both as individuals and as nations. The UK is just unusual in how little emphasis the State gives to this. Public interest is not new and cannot just be ascribed to popular television. The authors recall queuing at the BM as part of the 1.6 million people who saw the 'Treasures of Tutankhamun' exhibition in 1972, while the popular Jorvik Viking Centre first opened back in 1984. Close to 1 million people a year visit Stonehenge alone. The value of this interest seems intangible but it is there. A survey for English Heritage in 2000 found that 76 per cent of the UK population felt that the opportunity to visit heritage sites enriched their lives. This research underlies the concept of community heritage assets in recent legislation (▶ p. 577).

Public involvement

Modern archaeology owes a huge debt to archaeological volunteers. During the 1960s and 1970s most of the salvage work to document sites and recover finds was undertaken by enthusiastic amateurs (▶ p. 580). Since then in many areas commercial pressures and an element of elitism have gradually excluded volunteers from most archaeological work. The All-Party Parliamentary Archaeology Group (APPAG) report (2003) warned that this disenfranchisement might reduce popular support for archaeology at a time when public finance is tough. This is not to say that the public are completely excluded. There are great examples of community archaeology projects, some excavations do an excellent job in communicating their discoveries locally and many local museums rely on volunteers to be able to function. English Heritage too combines the protection of archaeological remains with a duty to advance public understanding. There are some signs that the pendulum may swing back to greater direct public involvement. Recent legislation (▶ p. 577) elevates the public enjoyment of heritage in considerations about archaeological work while public engagement is usually a condition for public or lottery funding. The Southport Group (▶ p. 584) of the IFA shows that this concern is shared by some professionals. The growth in metal detecting can be to some extent seen as the displacement of people who in the past might have got involved in field archaeology. The Portable Antiquities Scheme (▶ p. 579) marks an attempt to bring detectorists back into the mainstream of archaeology.

Tourism

Clearly not all tourism is linked to archaeology but historic landscapes, museums and heritage sites do attract huge numbers of visitors from abroad as well as from the UK. The economic benefits are massive. The UK is the eighth most popular world tourist destination overall with over 29 million visitors a year but its historic buildings are ranked fourth behind only Italy, Egypt and France (UNWTO 2013). Tourism is the fourth largest employment sector with some 2.6 million jobs and over 200,000 businesses (VisitBritain 2012) and is the third highest export earner behind chemicals and finance. Estimates of value vary but Deloitte (2010) estimated that foreign tourism alone contributed £52 billion directly and another £63 million indirectly, over 8 per cent of GDP. They also identify heritage as one of the key areas for future growth. Living within a country it can be difficult sometimes to appreciate these values. To get a sense of context it is useful to look at heritage tourism in other countries. In Egypt tourism, largely heritage

Figure 13.10 *Heritage tourism at Caerleon Roman Fort*

related, was the leading industry but in summer 2013 visitor numbers crashed 80 per cent due to political trouble leading to widespread unemployment. Croatia, by contrast, is encouraging heritage tourism, in particular by investing in two new archaeological museums focused on Neanderthals and the Neolithic as a way of diversifying from beach-tourism and becoming a year-round destination. In the UK archaeological work has a key role in the development of heritage tourism both through new discoveries such as the Staffordshire Hoard and new research such as the Stonehenge Riverside Project which has informed the new visitor centre at Stonehenge.

Advancing understanding

The best way to approach this might be to ask what we would not understand without archaeology. Our knowledge of the past would be limited to the historic period, a maximum of 3,000 years but less in many areas. Beyond that we would be left with myths. Evolution, Ice Age art, the start of agriculture and cities, Egyptian tombs, everything about the Minoans, Star Carr, the colonisation of Australia and America, indeed virtually everything touched on in this book, would be unknown. Even in the historic period there is much about the lives of ordinary people that would remain a mystery without excavations such as Wharram Percy and the *Mary Rose*. Whole chapters of our history such as the Anglo-Saxon and Viking period would be based largely on some very terse statements in the Anglo-Saxon Chronicles, some wonderful poetry and the not entirely accurate lives of saints. Like history, archaeology provides us with a framework and a context for understanding both our past and our present. It addresses fundamental questions which all human societies have needed answers for, such as where did we come from? Unlike most of history there are many, many new discoveries still to be made which will refine or change our view of the past. Examples include the discovery and analysis of Ötzi the Ice Man (▶ p. 104), the application of lipid analysis to existing collections of pottery (▶ p. 138) and the use of satellites to locate hidden sites (▶ p. 248).

Applied understanding

Understanding is good, but can archaeology also help with practical problems? Clearly much of it does not have an immediate application but you never know what challenge or question is around the corner. In the 1960s and 1970s, aside from small numbers of 'green' enthusiasts, there was little serious concern about climate change or waste. That has changed and some archaeological studies have proved to be valuable in addressing the challenges of sustainability. As Diamond (2005) puts it, 'we have the opportunity to learn from the mistakes of past peoples'. Landscape surveys in the Copan Valley led to a much greater understanding of environmental and economic collapse in relation to over-farming of tropical forests and soil erosion. Investigation of the Mesopotamian city of Mashkan Shapir (▶ p. 286) similarly led to a better understanding of salinisation, which can poison irrigation systems and destroy crop yields. Barker's (2008) study of past desertification in Jordan sheds light on the interaction between farming communities and the environment in arid areas. This holds lessons for the third of the world's population living in desert regions today. The Medieval Origins of Commercial Sea Fishing Project (▶ p. 612) enabled an understanding of both 'natural population levels' of fish stocks and the impact of mismanagement. In the USA the pioneering Tucson Garbage Project (Rathje and Murphy 1991) applied archaeological methodology to understanding waste and landfill sites. This much imitated project revealed paper to be the main villain in terms of both volume of waste (40 per cent) and poisonous chemicals from the ink, rather than the expected plastic bags, nappies and fast food packaging. Dustbin analysis revealed many aspects of consumption and discard patterns from incorrect use of contraceptive pills to the preference of lower income families for small name-brand foods rather than value lines. Amongst the many unexpected finds from landfill excavations and temperature probes was that very little garbage actually rots and much food survives for years. Rathje demonstrated that studying discarded material can sometimes tell you more (and more honestly) than asking people about their habits. It also provided a wealth of ideas which have informed modern recycling, packaging and waste management. Finally, the daddy of all global warming was the end of the cold, dry period of the Younger Dryas *c.* 11,500 BP. In little more than a decade average temperatures rose by 10°C with a dramatic impact on vegetation and human foragers (▶ p. 327).

There have also been instances where innovation in the past has been lost and then rediscovered through archaeology. The region around the ruined C10th AD city of Tiwanaku in the high plains of the Bolivian Andes was renowned for thin soils and crop yields which barely fed local farming families. Archaeological investigation (Janusek et al. 2004) of ancient earthworks and other features revealed that there were once extensive field systems and irrigation canals. In an experiment, a section of canal was re-dug and one of the raised beds planted, resulting in a massive rise in potato yields and crops which survived frosts. Ancient Tiwanakuan farmers were several times as productive as their modern counterparts. Once the archaeologists had shown the locals the secrets of the ancient farming methods, they were able to ensure a more plentiful food supply.

Other fields where archaeology has made a telling contribution include providing a long-term understanding of human disease and nutrition which has lessons for public health, diet and understanding the origins of infectious disease. Watchers of the CSI series will also be familiar with the use of archaeologists in forensics. Forensic methodology is firmly rooted in an understanding of stratigraphy. Some osteoarchaeologists are involved in documenting atrocities such as the Rwandan genocide or massacres in Bosnia in order to convict those responsible in war-crimes trials. Parker-Pearson (2011) argues that British archaeologists are among the world's best and make another significant contribution by sharing expertise with other countries.

KEY STUDY

Archaeology, conservation and the medieval fishing industry

Today stocks of fish everywhere are widely seen as under threat but the long-term effects of intensive fishing are poorly understood. To help address this issue researchers across northern Europe collaborated on the 'Medieval Origins of Commercial Sea Fishing Project', which in turn was part of a global census of marine life. The project was part-funded by two educational charities: the Leverhulme Foundation set up by the entrepreneur who founded the chemical company Lever Brothers (now Unilever) and the Fishmongers' Company, who have regulated the London Fishmarket since the C13th. By researching past ecosystems and the impacts of human activity they hope to inform policymaking on sustainable fishing and conservation.

Since the Roman period, documents, particularly customs, tax and legal records, have tended to predominate over archaeological evidence as the basis for research into economics. In the case of fishing, archaeology has been hampered by poor survival of fish bones. From written sources it is known that Viking vessels carried dried cod (stockfish) which were caught from the coastal waters off Arctic Norway and that the C14th Hanseatic League had a monopoly on trading in stockfish in the Baltic. However, historians assumed that large-scale, deep-water fishing was rare until the exploitation of Icelandic and Newfoundland Fisheries from the C15th onwards. The research project focused on archive material from sites with good organic preservation across the region to examine the rise of the world's first commercial fisheries. These included urban areas with deep stratified waste deposits such as York and Southampton in England and Baltic towns such as Ribe and Gdansk. The dates of deposits ranged from AD 800 to 1900.

Figure 13.11 *Woodcut from 1555 showing the abundance of herring in the Baltic*

Methods

The project combined the zooarchaeological investigation of bone assemblages with marine ecology and newer biochemical techniques. Before fast boats and refrigeration, drying was the best way to preserve fish and meat. Smoking and salting were the other two common methods. Dried cod can be identified archaeologically by distinctive butchery marks left on fish bones and the pattern of bone survival. Faunal evidence from Iron Age middens in the Lofoten Islands off Norway suggests that fishermen had perfected a way of preserving cod for several years as 'stockfish' by gutting and beheading them then drying them on racks. These dessicated carcasses became hard and lost 80 per cent of their weight so they were lighter to transport and would not rot. Cranial (head) bones from the landing sites were used to provide signatures for each fishery using biochemical analysis (Orton and Barrett 2012). Stable isotope ratios (13C and 15N) in fish vary according to the temperature and salinity of the waters they are from. These indicators enabled researchers to determine whether fish found in midden deposits in each town were caught locally or imported. In the latter case they could identify the fishing grounds and therefore trading patterns. The average sizes of fish, which were randomly caught, provided insights into fish population structures. The team modelled past fish population levels in order to measure the impact of fishing against other factors.

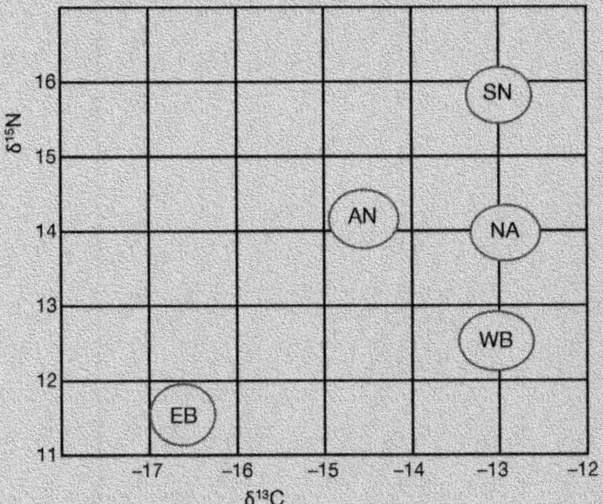

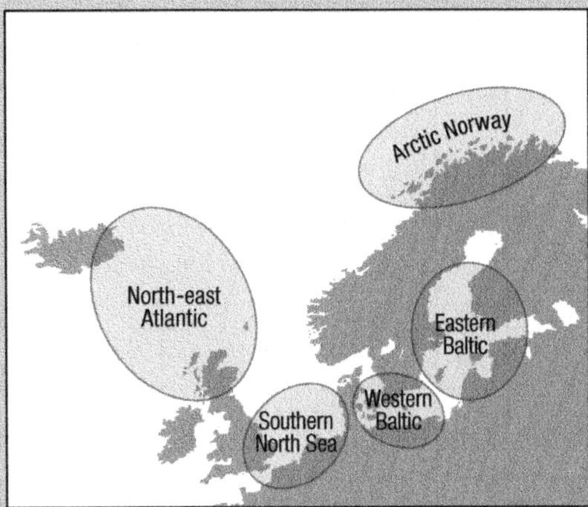

Figure 13.12 *Isotopic signatures (▶p. 135) for different fishing grounds. The initials of each fishing ground are shown on the graph (after Barrett 2012).*

Findings

The team, led by James Barrett of Cambridge University, was surprised to discover a significant 'fish-event horizon' between AD 950 and 1050. In the early Middle Ages most fish recovered from archaeological sites were freshwater species such as pike, trout and bream and migratory fish such as salmon and sturgeon. However, by the late C11th herring and fish from the cod family predominated. A change at this point is surprising because climatic data suggests it was a warm period, which would have meant lower stocks of sea fish and more productive farming on land. Nevertheless, other research across northern Europe revealed the same pattern (Orton and Barrett 2012).

continued

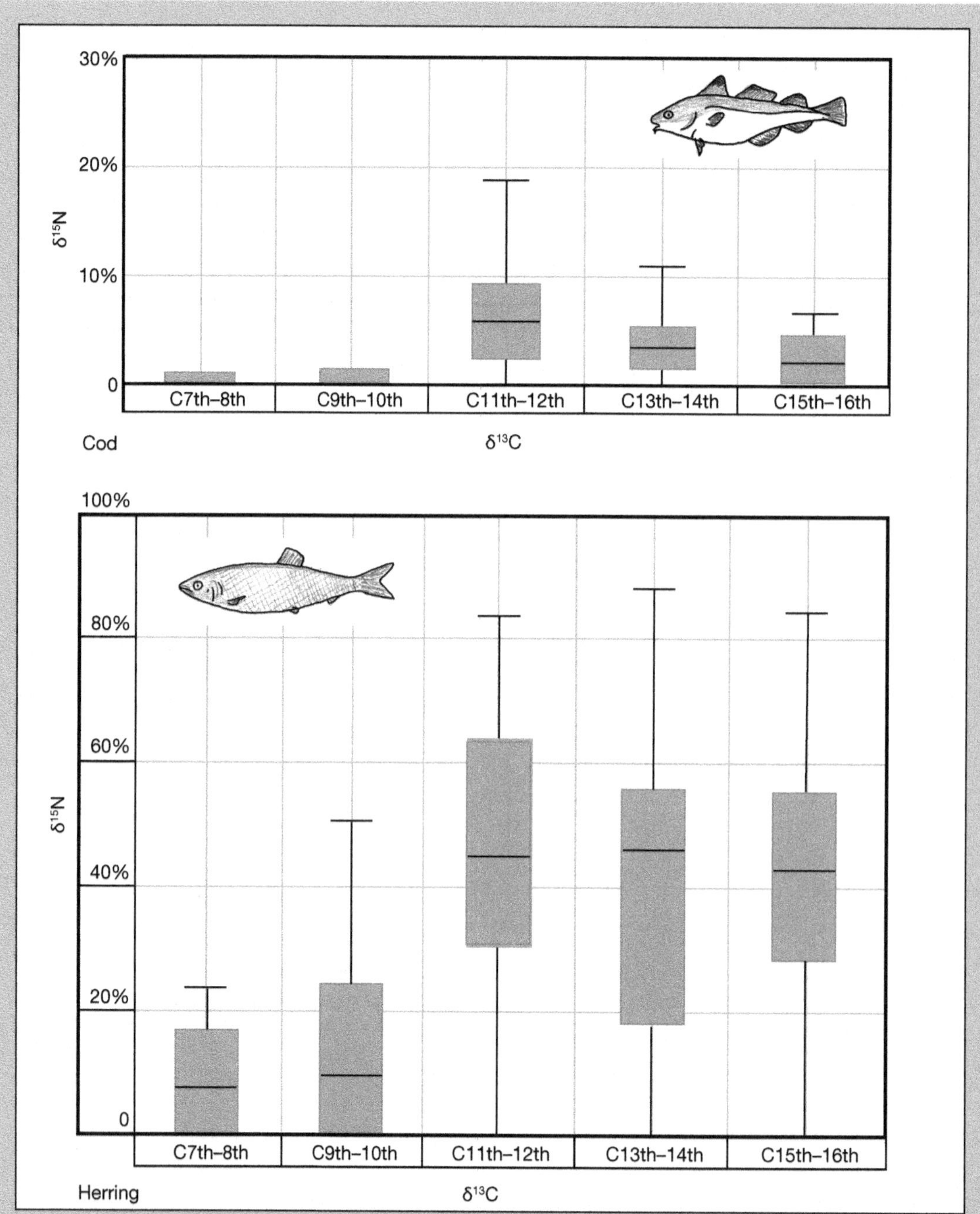

Figure 13.13 *Changes in the proportion of cod and herring consumed in towns (after Barrett). The boxplots show the percentage of each species consumed as part of the fish assemblage across all the towns surveyed. Each box shows the 1st to 3rd quartile range with the median dividing the box. The rapid exhaustion of cod supplies is very clear (after Barrett 2012).*

The faunal remains tell us that most sea fish at this time were caught locally – from the southern part of the North Sea or the Baltic – but this quickly changed. By the C13th fish from the Arctic coasts of Norway and to the north of Scotland were dominating markets from Poland to Belgium. Lofoten stockfish were traded across Europe and the technique was carried by Vikings to Orkney, Shetland and Iceland. Huge quantities of processed bone and the absence of significant human populations at these landing sites suggests that fishing was for export. The isotopic evidence shows where they were also traded. The fish being caught were huge. Most cod specimens from York were more than 1m in length and many other species were larger. From the C12th increasing amounts of fish were also being landed at ports such as Great Yarmouth as English fishermen joined in. It became a year-round industry; northern waters were fished for cod in the spring and summer and the vast shoals of North Sea herring were exploited from summer to autumn. Salted herring packed in barrels became the most important trade commodity in northern Europe in the late Middle Ages and other trading networks grew up around its distribution.

Causes of deep-sea fishing

The Catholic Church prohibited meat consumption for at least 130 days a year so people either ate local fish or preserved sea fish. The team's hypothesis was that over-fishing due to a combination of population rise and religious requirements led to a collapse in stocks of freshwater fish. This crisis was resolved by the exploitation of offshore fisheries made possible by the development of seine and drift nets and square-rigged ships. Certainly declining freshwater fish lengths in York suggested that freshwater stocks were exhausted but a range of other factors may have impacted on demand and supply. Fish was initially a prestige food which was frequently eaten at feasts. There was also rising demand from the growth of towns which needed to import food. This led to the creation of markets and commercial fishing to supply them. Historic records suggested that rivers were over-fished through the use of barrier nets and fishing weirs. In addition the spread of watermills and dams and the creation of fishponds for rich landowners blocked rivers while wetlands were drained. Sediment cores from across Europe and historic

Figure 13.14 *Woodcut from 1555 of fishing in the Norwegian Sea*

continued

records also testify to waterways silting up due to soil erosion caused by more intensive farming. These changes particularly impacted on migratory fish such as salmon and eels, with sturgeon badly affected. It fell from 70 per cent to 10 per cent of assemblages (by weight) across the Baltic between the C8th and C13th. The average size of these huge fish, which once reached half a ton, also fell (Roberts 2009b). The first laws to protect river fish stocks date from the C13th.

Consequences of deep-sea fishing

The solution to the crisis in fish supply was to import the stockfish being offered by Viking traders. Barrett's (2008) research on Orkney and Shetland identified relatively few deep-sea fish on sites prior to the arrival of the Vikings around AD 800. Almost immediately cod, ling and haddock began to appear in assemblages and in rapidly rising numbers. Stable isotope evidence from human bones shows an increasingly marine-based diet. Within a few generations these settlements had joined the Viking trade selling fish to Europe. Historical records from Bergen of the massive volume of stockfish exported to England suggest that the archetypal Viking was as likely to be a fishmonger as a raider. Trade networks based on animal products in return for grain and gold rode on the back of the fish market. Commerce in goods such as walrus ivory can also be detected in the archaeological record. However, a message for today is also encapsulated in these records.

From the C11th huge numbers of the much smaller herring along with increasing numbers of flat fish are found in urban deposits, testifying to diversification by fishermen. Numbers of cod bones in towns decline from the C12th and increasingly those that are recovered have isotopic signatures from Icelandic waters. At Quoygrew on Orkney, where the faunal record had documented a rapid and intensive growth in cod fishing, there was a sudden change. Around AD 1400 average sizes rapidly diminished and cod were replaced with small inshore fish. The industry had collapsed due to over-fishing. By the end of the Middle Ages, the average size of Icelandic fish in urban deposits began to fall, suggesting that over-fishing was starting to occur there too (Roberts 2007). In successive fisheries demand had risen beyond what exhausted cod stocks could supply. This explains the eagerness of

a)

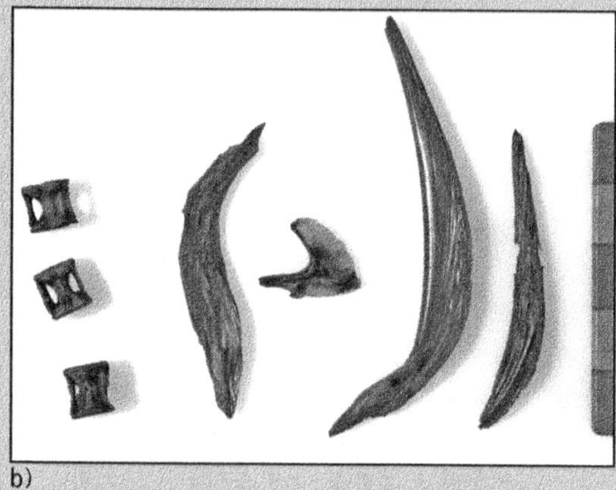

b)

Figure 13.15 *Analysing fishbones (G. Brovad). a) Fishbones caught on a sieve from the Ertebølle (▶ p. 314) site of Maglemosegård. Most of the bones are cod and flatfish. b) Diagnostic bones after analysis: spurdog/plaice/flounder/flounder/dab.*

European fishermen to exploit the waters off Newfoundland following Cabot's reports that swarms of cod could be caught with a basket on a rope in 1497. Research so far has demonstrated that intensive fishing began much earlier than first thought and was driven by a combination of rapidly rising demand and the availability of a new supply. Fish was the key commodity behind the development of northern trade networks. However, while sea-fish populations were initially massive, they were very quickly affected by over-exploitation.

COMMUNICATING ARCHAEOLOGICAL KNOWLEDGE

Before 1990, most archaeological knowledge was communicated via lectures, museum galleries and the printed word. While these are familiar media, it is expensive to produce reports and books and there is often a considerable time-lag before new ideas and discoveries are widely disseminated. Increasing diversity of communication also reflects the growing and changing audiences for archaeology and the way in which their requirements vary. Consider how your requirements of a site or museum might differ from those of a researcher or of a class of eight-year-olds. As a result, what is a perfectly adequate mode of communication for one person may be inaccessible or too shallow for another. The contrast between a specialist pottery report and an episode of *Time Team* illustrates this point well.

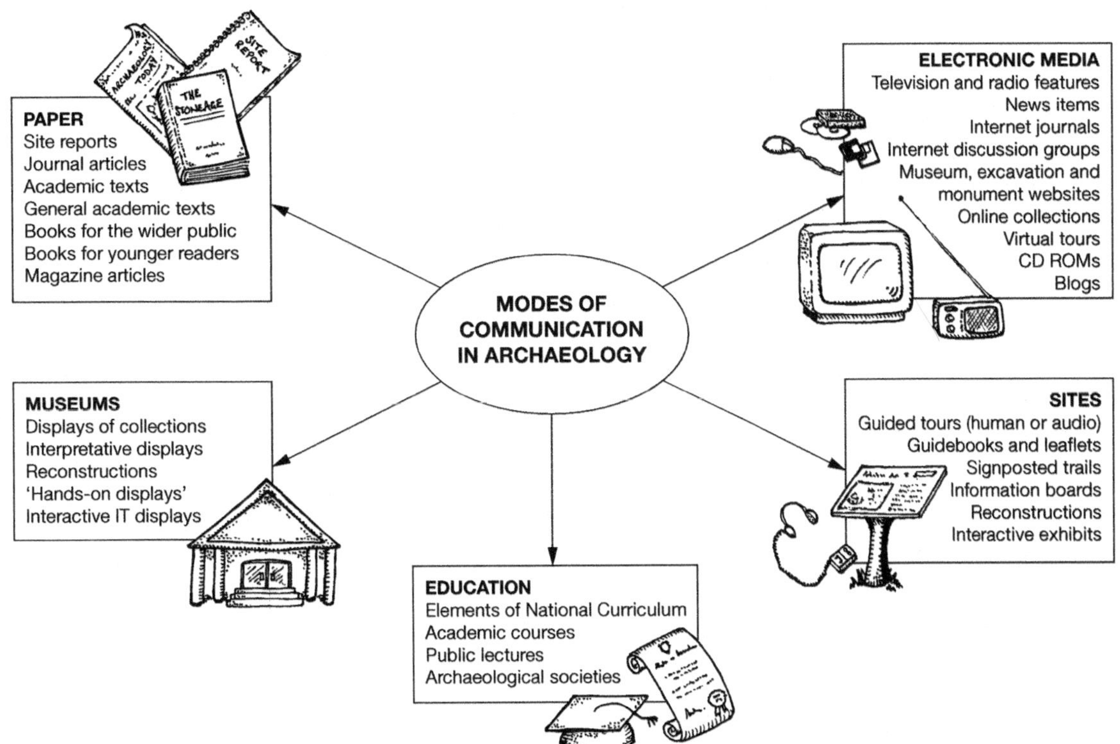

Figure 13.16 *The communication of archaeological information*

Reports

Archaeological reports follow a scientific format either in a book or an academic journal. A series of experts present evidence as accurately and precisely as they can. There is often only limited interpretation and rarely speculation. Often only a few hundred are printed. However, reports are essential reading to specialists in the same field who rely on them to provide data for them to compare findings and detect patterns. Cheaper printing costs and drawing software have increased the range of visual communication in these monographs. Once a site has been excavated, the report becomes the archaeological record. For this reason archaeologists are expected to publish their work, otherwise the site they excavated is lost. There have been a number of scandals where eminent archaeologists excavated sites and then neglected to do the dull follow-up work of report writing. Today there is a new problem. Many reports are produced for commercial clients and are difficult for researchers to access. The Archaeological Data Service is attempting to rectify the situation by making them available online. Digitalisation also offers the opportunity of using interactive reports which are not limited to two-dimensional A4 formats and may enable people to interrogate data at very different levels. Experimentation in this regard can be seen in the online journal *Internet Archaeology*.

Books and journals

The growth in public interest in archaeology has seen a proliferation of types of archaeological publications. Forty years ago there were academic texts – generally expensive and aimed at other academics and students rather than the public – or very simple texts for primary school children. There is now a wide range of popular archaeological books, often linked to television programmes, particular places or periods or mythology. There are also magazines, notably *Current Archaeology* (and now *Current World Archaeology*). This initially targeted professionals and academics but now has a very wide audience. It provides excellent, detailed summaries of the latest major discoveries, ideas and debates to a largely amateur audience. Finally there is a market for novels which draw heavily upon archaeological research. Jean Auel's Ice Age novels (1980) are a well-researched, best-selling set of stories involving Neanderthals and Cro-Magnons. Cornwell's *Stonehenge* (1999) brought the Bronze Age to life and there is even a series of children's novels set in the Mesolithic (Paver 2005).

Television

Archaeology broadcasting in the UK began as part of the BBC mission to impart knowledge through the use of often charismatic experts. Pioneered by Mortimer Wheeler, programmes such as *Buried Treasure* (1954) moved swiftly from talking heads to location and travelogue-based formats (Henson 2005). There was an emphasis upon classical sites but world archaeology also featured, such as the ruins of Great Zimbabwe, which were advertised in relation to the popular novel *King Solomon's Mines*. The impressive Chronicle series was the next development, running from the 1960s to the 1980s, when the BBC axed it for being too 'highbrow'. This brought high-profile excavations into people's living rooms including the BBC-sponsored investigation of Silbury Hill (1968). In the 1970s, archaeology can claim to have pioneered the 'Big Brother' approach to reality television in what began as an experiment with fifteen young volunteers trying to live like Iron Age farmers for a year in *Living in the Past* (1978). In the 1980s, programming swung firmly towards entertainment rather than public education and despite the popularity of films such as *Raiders of the Lost Ark* (1981) and occasional science programmes such as *Horizon*, archaeology had a low profile on TV. Programmes when they occurred tended to mark a return to ancient mysteries and lost (usually classical) civilisations.

Time Team

That changed from 1992 with *Time Team*. Its format drew on the established model used in house and garden makeover shows of a time-limited challenge for a group of personalities. A team of archaeologists raced against the clock to answer a question with three days of fieldwork. Many professionals were scathing about what they saw as the trivialising of their work but they were not the intended audience. *Time Team*'s function was to provide entertainment to a general audience whilst educating them in some aspects of archaeological methods and interpretations. Public understanding of 'geophys' is largely because of *Time Team*. Technical language and ideas were brilliantly communicated simply through computer-generated images while the routine or time-consuming aspects of excavation and post-excavation work were edited out in favour of action involving celebrity diggers. Viewers were involved via the device of using ordinary people to pose the question at the start and camerawork which took viewers right into the trenches. The focus too was different, with farms, factories, villages and huts featuring as well as villas and palaces. *Time Team* became a phenomenon and ran for twenty seasons.

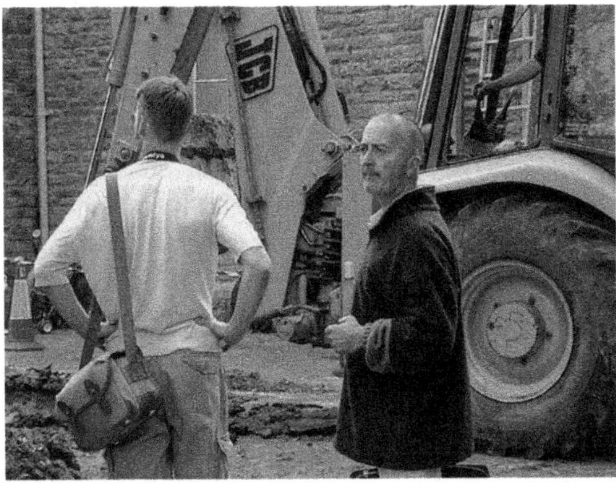

Figure 13.17 *Tony Robinson of the Time Team. His programmes have been outstandingly successful in raising public awareness of and interest in archaeology.*

Its entertainment value is attested to by its high ratings. It caused a huge upsurge in public interest including a major growth in the Young Archaeologists Club. In addition, its website and publications provide opportunities for people to develop their understanding and explore links to educational sites. It opened the door to other series such as *Secrets of the Dead*, *Two Men in a Trench* and *Meet the Ancestors*.

Archaeology on the web

Archaeology is a discipline that lends itself to rapid dissemination via the Internet. Digital photography, GIS systems and film enable the visual aspects of sites, artefacts and lab results to be exploited. Virtual tours enable people to explore sites remotely and study relationships between features. Increasingly such sites include interactive maps or images with 'visitors' able to decide the depth and level they want to investigate to. Similarly, hyperlinks embedded in text offer the chance to satisfy more than one audience at the same time. Not only do digital images readily offer high-quality colour photographs where their use was previously rationed, but they can also go beyond the limitations of two-dimensional illustration on A3 paper. Maps and plans can be presented at a larger scale and 3D modelling is possible.

Online publishing enables the gap between digging and the production of site reports to be bridged including the use of interim reports. Many excavations now offer daily diaries or webcams on their websites. The numbers visiting many of these websites far exceed the numbers of site reports sold. Moreover, the audience is now global rather than largely national. As with other disciplines, the web provides a means of discussing ideas and seeking help from fellow archaeologists through discussion groups such as the CBA's lists for archaeologists and teachers. Many US universities generously give extensive public access to research papers and in some cases teaching materials, although UK universities are far more protective. In a gradual democratisation of knowledge, many academic papers are also available online. Blogs, both academic and enthusiast and of varying quality, abound on all manner of archaeological topics and there has been a growth of sophisticated 'public broadcasts' such as the Smithsonian Human Origins site. Old terrestrial broadcasts are increasingly available both on YouTube and archive sites such as that for the BBC Chronicle series. There are, of course, drawbacks including the sheer volume of material available, which means that you have to be selective and it is often difficult to immediately see what might be relevant. A wide selection of relevant links are on our companion website.

Museums

Museums, like libraries, have found the growth of digital technology a challenge. They are no longer the main way in which the public can learn about our distant past. In order to make galleries 'relevant', particularly to younger visitors, there has been a move away from traditional artefact displays towards the use of computers, interactive screens and recreations. High-tech displays are expensive to buy and are often space-hungry, which leads to hard decisions about what to leave out. Sometimes these new displays are superb as at the Jorvik Viking Museum but others have quickly dated or have led to criticism of 'mission drift'. Museums were once proud of their enlightenment role in spreading knowledge but are they now prioritising entertainment over promoting understanding? Bristol City Museum is an example of a museum which has removed much of its archaeology collection from the galleries to make room for an interactive learning zone and an Egyptian display. Devizes Museum by contrast has maintained a focus on Neolithic and Bronze Age finds and models of the monuments associated with them. These trends are less evident in Europe, where museums tend to augment traditional approaches with new technologies as at the Hochdorf (▶ p. 434) Museum or the national prehistoric museum of Eyzies de Tayac (France). Traditional museums were largely generalist, often featuring geology, finds from the Palaeolithic onwards and clothing and photographs from the last 200 years. Increasingly there is a trend towards specialism. A good example is Andover Museum, which retains some of these other displays but devotes most space to finds and interpretations from Danebury Hillfort. Andover is also interesting both for its gallery celebrating the work of volunteers during the rescue era and for the way it has attempted to provide different commentaries for different groups including low height interpretations for children.

Most museums try to contextualise artefacts, particularly through chronological presentation and association with finds from the same period. The British Museum is a good example of this approach. Another approach to contextualisation is presented at the Kilmartin Museum, where local artists have attempted to evoke aspects of the landscape which may have been important to people in the late Neolithic. Sound and handling material is used to enhance the experience. In contrast, the National Museum of Scotland adopts a thematic approach in order to emphasise similarities between people over time but where all sense of context is lost. The Neanderthal Museum in Krapina (▶ p. 202) makes a great deal out of a relatively small number of actual finds by majoring on context. It sets its startling collection of Neanderthal remains and artefacts into a physical journey as visitors walk through human evolution. Issues of cultural sensitivity have affected museums in different ways. Aside from issues over the repatriation and the removal of human remains has been the degree to which exhibits should be censored. For example, in several countries collections of artefacts with sexual imagery are often kept from public view. In 1999 the British Museum faced a dilemma over whether to display a rare Roman vase that depicted homosexual sex. Similarly, a collection of erotic art from Pompeii was kept until 2000 in

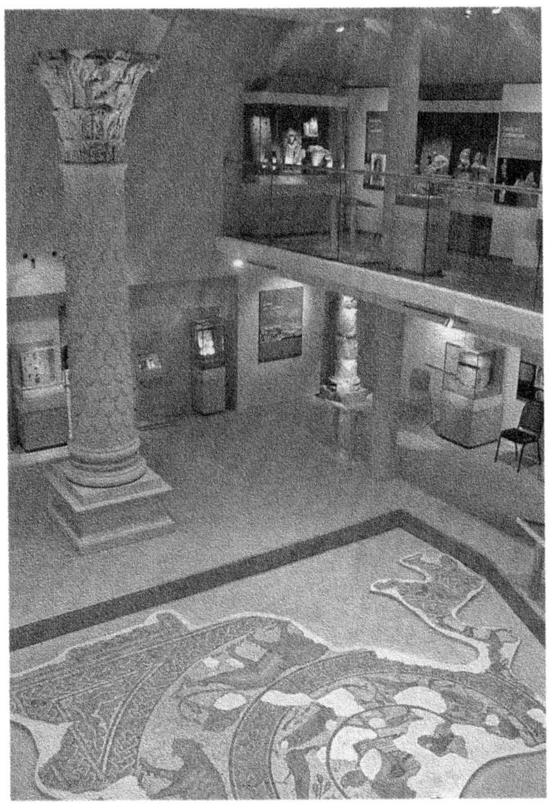

Figure 13.18 *The Corinium Museum. In the foreground is one of the mosaics for which the town was famous and in the background a range of different types of display.*

the 'secret cabinet' at the Naples Archaeological Museum.

The Corinium Museum in Cirencester provides an example of museum makeover. It had a complete makeover courtesy of the National Lottery and exhibits many state-of-the-art features. Families and primary school children are the target audience and little previous knowledge is assumed. Heavy use is made of recreations to explain burials, buildings and technology including hands-on replica clothing and artefacts. Interactive displays allow exhibits and the museum's catalogue to be interrogated at several levels. A particularly innovative feature uses video, sound and lighting in conjunction with tombstones to 'bring the people to life'. Open space has been created in which the town's Jupiter Column has been re-erected to give a sense of scale.

Figure 13.19 *Inside Vedbaek Museum. Displays are arranged to simulate movement through the forest.*

Figure 13.20 *Diorama at Vedbaek. Artefacts and replicas are displayed in context. (Ole Tage Hartmann/Rudersdal Museums)*

Figure 13.21 *Touch panel at Vedbaek. This example features remains and products made by Mesolithic people from wild boars.*

Developments in IT and communications technology have offered archaeologists the opportunities to transform the way they communicate. As a result, the range of methods and modes of communicating archaeological information is rapidly expanding and there is considerable diversity in the way they are used. Rather than cover all periods, the Corinium has chosen to major in Roman Corinium with a minor in Anglo-Saxon Lechlade (▶ p. 494). This kind of specialisation is a growing feature of British museums.

Specialism is particularly evident at the Vedbaek Finds Museum, Denmark. The finds come from the rich seam of Mesolithic material from around what was once the Maglemose Fjord. The catalyst for the museum was the discovery of a cemetery when constructing a new school. The museum includes several of the graves (▶ p. 87), including the famous 'Swan-wing burial' (▶ p. 531). The galleries were designed in the 1970s to engage all the senses in order to communicate an understanding of the Mesolithic. Galleries are organised and decorated so that visitors feel that they are moving between the trees with an occasional glimpse of the sea. Artefacts are displayed alongside replicas which visitors are encouraged to touch and which enable a physical appreciation of cordage, leisters and bows. Collections of materials such as furs are available to enable an appreciation of the different properties of materials. There is even a smell-tube to enable visitors to experience the aroma of the midden. While ideal for kindergarten or primary classes, the museum works effectively on several levels with the amount of detail also appropriate for academic visitors.

Open air museums

A particular range of issues surround open air museums. These tend to combine relocated or experimental buildings, artefacts and 'recreations' often involving actors. The earliest examples were Scandinavian including Den Gamle By (the old town) in Aarhus (Denmark), which opened in 1909 and brought together Danish buildings from the C16th onwards. In the UK St Fagan's National History Museum combines the open air collection of buildings from the C12th onwards with demonstrations of traditional crafts and culture.

A variation pioneered in southern Germany was to try to recreate ancient buildings from archaeological evidence. Neolithic houses on piles were built at the Pfahlbauten on Lake Constance to interpret finds from Federsee in an accessible way. The Scottish Crannog Centre on Lake Tay provides a similar experience. Further along the research spectrum are experimental centres which initially seek to answer archaeological questions but also have an educational role. The earliest was the Lerje Archaeological Research Centre in Denmark, which used contemporary tools such as stone axes to reconstruct Neolithic houses. Other structures from Palaeolithic tents to Iron Age longhouses were also built using excavation plans and evidence of carpentry and other skills. Academic experiments related to both the buildings and ancient technology take place but the site has also become a major tourist and educational destination. In the UK both Butser Ancient Farm (▶ p. 183) and West Stow (▶ p. 494) began as experimental centres and developed into educational ones.

At West Stow constructs were built on the site of excavated features to try to understand their nature (▶ p. 494). Valuable information was gained about the nature of Anglo-Saxon houses but the potential of the site for communicating understanding was also realised. Today the recreated settlement addresses these issues and the problem of communicating to multiple audiences in a number of ways. Visitors can enter and examine all the houses and reach their own judgements against the plans in guidebooks and the visitor centre. Artefacts are displayed in the visitor centre with pictures and reconstructions alongside to show how they were used, while activity areas allow visitors to see how artefacts might have been made. Occasionally this is supported by demonstrations by experts in fields

Figure 13.22 *Open air museum at Etara, Bulgaria. Buildings and artefacts from the Bulgarian revival of the C18th have been collected and reassembled here including this working watermill from 1780.*

Figure 13.23 *The Romans were small people*

such as green woodworking, metalworking or firing pottery. Video presentations show how Anglo-Saxons lived and publications are available at a variety of levels, ranging from infant school to professional.

At the opposite end of the spectrum are what might be termed archaeological theme parks. These are conceived primarily as tourist attractions but with serious educational aspects to them. Archeon in Holland recreates structures and experiences from the Dutch Mesolithic to the Roman period. It adds role-playing actors and the chance for children to dress up in costumes and to try out activities from sword fighting to bread making and moving megaliths. At Archaeolink Prehistory Park small children could dig in a sandpit for artefacts while adults could view excavated remains, reconstructions, workshops, books and New Age presentations. Older children could dress up as Romans and throw javelins. Sadly, Archaeolink was probably too remote to become the tourist attraction Aberdeenshire Council had wanted and it has now closed.

Figure 13.24 *Construct of Iron Age hall at Hochdorf*

Some reconstruction sites have been criticised for misleading the public by presenting things for which there is not yet evidence and sometimes for mixing together aspects of different periods. The founder of Butser, Peter Reynolds, always made clear to visitors that his Iron Age buildings were constructs – experimental models – rather than actual reconstructions (▶ p. 183). Not all sites make this clear and there is a dilemma. Is it better to show how something was used, even if it may be inaccurate, or to provide the evidence and ask people (who are not specialists) to try to make up their own minds?

Presenting archaeological sites

Many of the same issues that face museums and recreations apply to archaeological sites. Indeed the divisions between these different categories are often blurred. For example, at Vindolanda Roman Fort there are ongoing excavations which involve the public, guided tours, a museum, recreations and related activities and groundbreaking research. Alternatively, for many small sites such as isolated long barrows there is clearly much less that can be done. Since there are so many, most ancient sites are only acknowledged on maps. At sites that attract large numbers of visitors interpretation panels are increasingly common, as at Stonehenge or Uffington Hillfort. Sometimes these are supplemented by trail leaflets to guide visitors through what might otherwise appear as series of lumps and bumps. Battlefield sites in the USA such as Fredericksburg (1862) pioneered the way in which guide-sheets and panels, supported by a finds gallery, can enable the public to understand the historic landscape, although guided tours are also available.

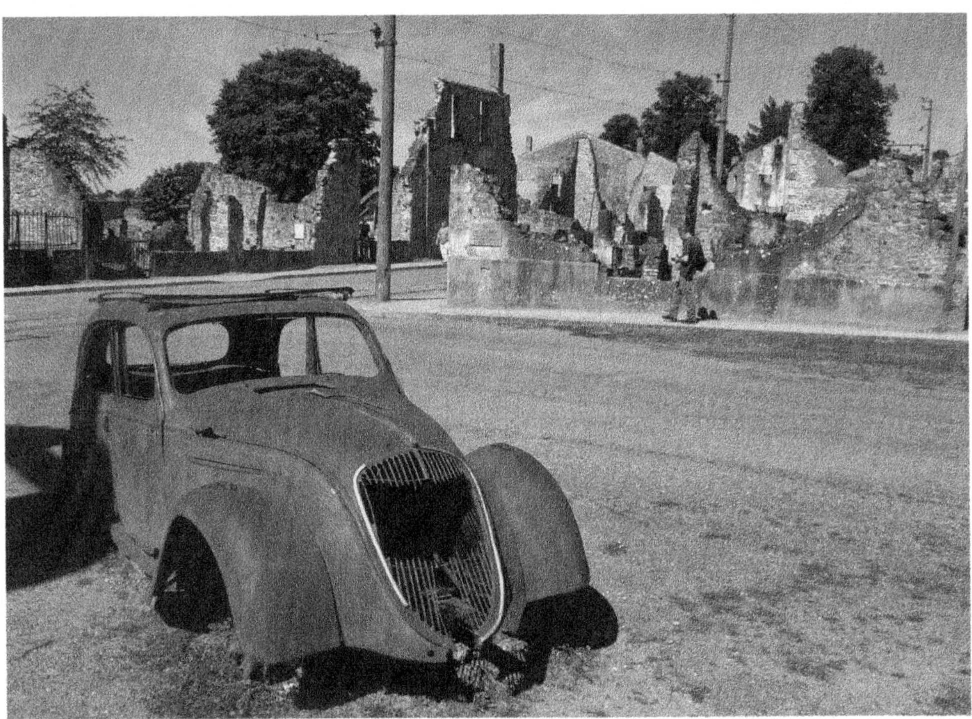

Figure 13.25 *Open air museum at Oradour sur Glane. This museum serves a dual purpose as a memorial to the victims (▶ p. 490) and as a public teaching vehicle about the dangers of political extremism. Audio guides are available in many languages.*

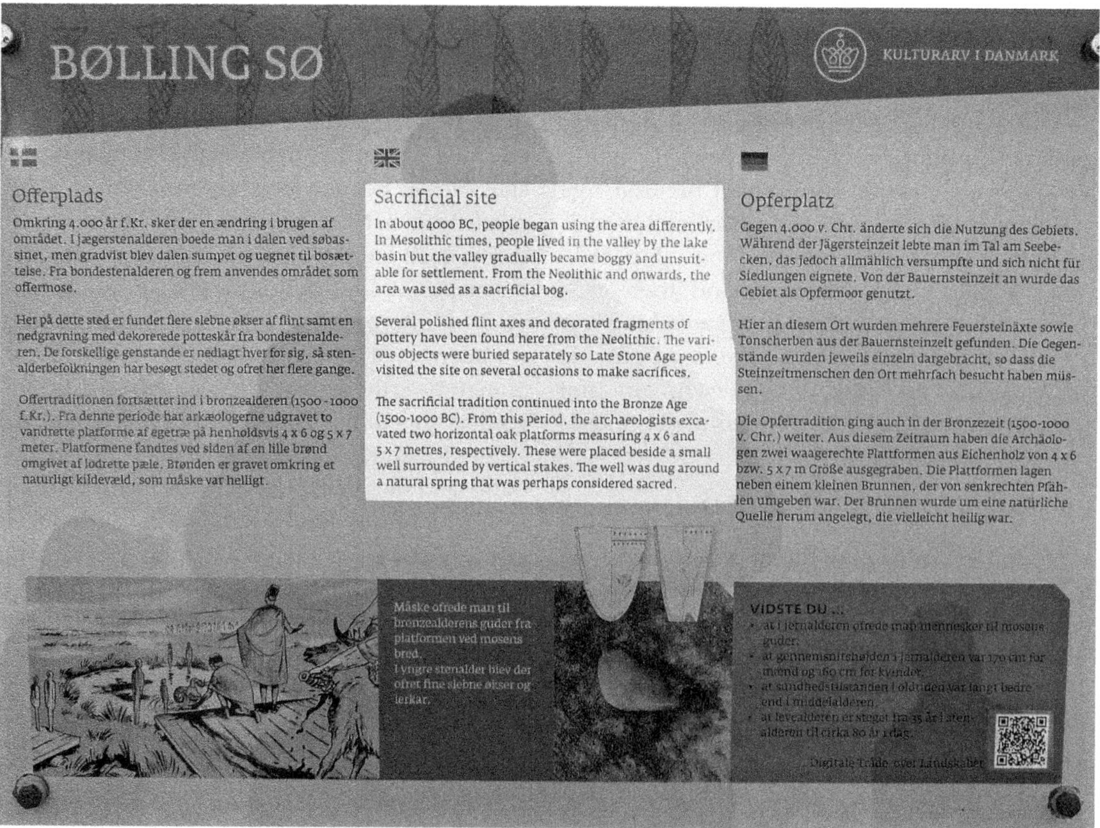

Figure 13.26 *Interpretation panel with QR code at the Bølling Lake, Denmark*

The new interpretation centre at Culloden (1746) has adopted a similar approach. The latest approach is the use of QR codes which enable visitors with smartphones to receive commentary while panning across the site.

Controversial presentations

Controversy about presentation at real sites tends to revolve around the visual impact of visitor amenities and interpretation panels and whether reconstruction should take place. One of the first examples of the latter was Evan's reconstruction – including painting frescoes of some of the rooms – at Knossos. More recently the rebuilding of the façade at Newgrange has also led to debate (▶ p. 534). While large numbers of white quartz stones and grey cobbles were recovered, the technology to cement them into a vertical wall did not exist in the Neolithic. The modern entrance is also new. So while the rebuilding is striking and highly visible, it is not authentic. Archaeologists are divided over whether the quartz formed part of the monument or was always spread in front as an 'apron' in a similar way to materials at the Clava Cairns (▶ p. 518). At neighbouring Knowth, a quartz apron has been laid out to enable visitors to understand this alternative. An even more extreme example is the presentation of 'Listoghil', the central tomb at the Carrowmore Cemetery. After complete excavation, instead of restoring it as a cairn, it was decided to leave the table-like tomb exposed so that visitors could see it. The new design is influenced by modern concerns for health and safety and disability access. Mesh

Figure 13.27 *Reconstructed building at Knossos. One of the earliest, and still controversial, reconstructions by Arthur Evans at the Minoan Palace.*

Figure 13.28 *The reconstructed tomb 'Listoghil' at Carrowmore*

boxes hold the stones of the cairn back to protect visitors. It has been widely criticised on aesthetic, religious and archaeological grounds but it is accessible to everybody. At some sites the sheer volume of visitors threatens the archaeology. At Lascaux the atmosphere which had preserved delicate Palaeolithic cave paintings was threatened by carbon dioxide (from breath) and bacteria which thrived on the light from illuminations and cameras. The response was to close the cave but to construct a copy (Lascaux II) nearby for visitors whilst producing an interactive website to enable virtual exploration of the real thing. At one time a similar reconstruction was mooted for Stonehenge.

An extensive list of suggested websites to follow up many of the issues and sites in this book are on the companion website.

Glossary of Terms and Abbreviations

This list does not pretend to be precise in an academic sense. It is intended to give you a simple definition of words that may be new to you so that you can comprehend the sources you come into contact with. For greater sophistication you should use an archaeological dictionary. Every subject has a lexicon of acronyms and abbreviations. Archaeology (arx) is no different. The glossary contains those which you are most likely to come across and with which you should familiarise yourself.

Absolute dating: Giving the age of something according to a calendar or historic scale, e.g. BC, AD, BP. Also called chronometric dating.

Accelerator mass spectrometry (AMS): An advanced radiocarbon dating method which can work for tiny samples

Acheulean: Lithic industry from about 1.6 mya until 125,000 years ago. It involved flaking from both sides of a core with the hand-axe being the classic form. Associated with Homo erectus.

Achieved status: Position or prestige in society earned through one's own efforts or qualities

AD: Abbreviation of Anno Domini – traditional dating of the last 2,000 years since the birth of Christ

Aerial survey: Locating and defining archaeological sites from the air. Photographing cropmarks and parchmarks during drought conditions usually produces the best results.

Aggregation: Upper Palaeolithic sites where several groups have come together to cooperate in particular activities, for social reasons or to enable specialisation; for example, Dolni Vestonice.

Anaerobic conditions: Where there is insufficient oxygen for the bacteria which normally break down organic materials to thrive; for example, waterlogged sites

Analogy: Interpreting something with reference to something else; for example, 'it is similar to X'

Animism: Belief in spirits

Anthropology: The study of humans. It has many subdivisions including Archaeology and Ethnography.

Antiquarian: C18th or C19th collector of artefacts who may have excavated and recorded sites

Arable: Growing crops

Archaeological record: What survives in the ground before excavation or the records produced by archaeologists after the whole excavation and analysis process

Archaeology: The study of physical remains to help understand the behaviour of people in the past

Archaeometry: The application of scientific analysis to archaeological materials

Artefacts: Can refer to anything made or modified by humans. Tends to be used most frequently for tools.

Ascribed status: Position or prestige in society gained through inheritance

Assemblage: Artefacts from a particular period which typically appear together. Also used to describe a collection of materials, for example animal bones, from a particular site.

Atomic absorption spectrometry (AAS): Measuring light energy emitted by different elements. Different combinations provide different spectra.

Attribute: A quality of an artefact which allows it to be grouped with others, for example colour, texture

Attritional bone profile: A table plotting the age and sex of animal bones which suggests that younger and old members of herds were killed. It suggests scavenging or selective hunting by humans or other predators.

Augering: Using a drill to take a core through deposits in the ground

Band: A hunting and gathering-based society with groups of under one hundred people

Baulk: A narrow strip of earth left between two excavated areas in order to see the stratigraphy

Bayesian statistical analysis: This involves other observations and common-sense knowledge being used to modify probability statements

BC: Abbreviation for Before Christ. Calendar years counted backwards from 0. Sometimes BCE (Before Common Era) is substituted.

Bigman: A non-hereditary position of status in some small-scale societies gained through the ability to amass and distribute resources – often through feasts

BP: Before present (actually 1950). Absolute dating used for periods in the past where historical dates (BC and AD) are irrelevant; for example, the Palaeolithic.

Cache: A store of food or artefacts

Caesium magnetometer: Cart-mounted magnetometers that use Caesium vapour to detect magnetic anomalies. More sensitive than conventional flux-gate machines, they record straight line transects rather than using grids.

Calibration: Using one method to correct inaccuracies in another; for example, using calendar dates from tree ring sequences to calibrate raw radiocarbon dates

Canopic jars: Egyptian vessels in which organs from mummified bodies were stored

Catastrophic profile: A table plotting the age and sex of animal bones which shows the natural distribution of animals in a herd. It suggests that they all died simultaneously in a natural disaster or unselective slaughter.

Central place theory: A geographic model developed by Christaller, which predicts that central places would develop at regular spaces in an ideal landscape

Characterisation: Identifying the origins of materials from their physical characteristics

Chiefdom: A ranked society with the inherited or elected role of chief at the top. Likely to have some specialisation in crafts and types of building.

Clan: A system of social organisation based on blood and marriage ties

Conservation: Specialist work to stabilise an artefact or prevent its decay

Context: The layer of soil in which artefacts or ecofacts may be found

Coppicing: Repeatedly cutting trees back to a stump in order to encourage them to grow long, straight poles which can then be harvested

Coprolites: Preserved faeces

Core: A prepared piece of stone from which tools can be made

Coring: Driving a hollow tube into the ground to get a stratigraphic sample of the subsoil

Cropmarks: Variations in the tone or colour of crops caused by underlying archaeological features

Curation: Deliberately preserving artefacts; for example, jewellery or weapons. This can result in artefacts from an early period being discovered 'out of sequence' on a later site.

Cursus: Linear monuments, sometimes several kilometres long, constructed in the Neolithic period

Debitage: Waste from the manufacture of stone tools

Demic diffusion: Where one population expands faster than another and ultimately disperses till it occupies most of the available land

Dendrochronology: Tree ring dating

Depositional processes: The various means by which archaeological material becomes buried

Desktop study: An office-based search of historical and existing archaeological records about a site

DHA: Direct historical approach. Using oral evidence and studies of a modern population to form hypotheses about an earlier culture in the same region.

Diachronic change: Gradual change over a period of time

Disarticulated: Bones that are mixed up, no longer in the right skeletal order

Distribution patterns: Plots of archaeological finds either on a site or across a region which are analysed to determine the behaviour that caused them

DNA: Deoxyribonucleic acid. The material that makes up genes and determines the nature of living things.

Doggerland: The ancient landscape now under the North Sea which once joined Britain to Europe

Earthworks: Literally a series of 'humps and bumps' on the surface that indicate the buried remains of buildings, boundaries and field systems

Ecofacts: Natural material that is of archaeological interest. It could include human remains, food waste or environmental material such as pollen or snails. In contrast to 'artefacts'.

Emporium: A settlement which has developed as a major trading centre or market

Entoptic: Internally produced. For example, entoptic images are generated by the brain itself rather than reflecting what has been seen.

Ethnicity: Identity of different groups based on their distinctive cultures

Ethnoarchaeology: Studying modern groups of people to understand the behaviour that leads to particular patterns of deposition

Ethnography: Observation-based study of modern social groups

Excarnation: Defleshing a corpse in some way as part of mortuary ritual or leaving a body exposed to the elements

Exchange: Not just trade, but any interaction where something passes between people. It could include information, gifts or money.

Extraction: Technologies used to acquire resources, particularly through mining

Fall-off analysis: Measuring the rate at which the number of particular artefacts declines as the distance from their source increases. It is used to diagnose particular modes of exchange.

Faunal dating: Relative dating based on the evolutionary sequence in which mammals have developed

Feature: Non-portable archaeological remains such as aspects of a site; for example, postholes or hearths

Field evaluation: Where desk-based assessment suggests a potential risk there would be a survey of the site, which usually includes trial trenching to establish the depth, nature and condition of remains

Fieldwalking: Systematically searching ploughed fields for the remains of artefacts and buildings to detect likely settlement areas

Flotation: Putting soil into a tank of water to separate ecofacts and tiny artefacts which are then recovered with a mesh

Foragers: Groups subsisting on wild foods. Plant foods are usually the most important.

Formation processes: How archaeological material came to be created, buried and transformed to create the archaeological record

Funerary rites: Events to mark the final rite of passage of a person. Overlaps with, but is not the same as, mortuary practice.

Geochemical survey: Using techniques derived from chemistry to detect traces of past activity from soil samples. See phosphate analysis.

Geophysical survey: Using techniques derived from physics to detect remains under the ground. See resistivity and magnetometry.

GIS: Geographic Information Systems – linked maps and databases

Glyphs: Reliefs of figures or signs carved on stone. Usually Mesoamerican.

GPS: Global Positioning System. A handheld device for locating positions of sites or features using satellites.

Haplogroups: Particular sets of genetic variations. Think of them as branches of the Homo sapiens family tree. Y DNA haplogroups are traced back to the first individual with that particular genetic mutation and are passed on by males, mtDNA can be traced back to the first female with that mutation and are passed down by females.

Harris Lines: Horizontal lines in bones where growth was reduced during a period of stress

HER: Historic Environment Record. The new name for SMRs. The local authority archive of records and database covering archaeology and the built environment.

Heterarchy: A society with many, roughly equal power centres rather than one hierarchy

Hoards: Deliberately buried groups of artefacts. May have been placed in earth or water for security, as offerings, etc.

Hominans: Modern and extinct humans

Hominids: The great apes. Includes gorillas as well as human and many extinct species.

Hominins: Subcategory of hominids including humans and chimpanzees

Horticulturalist: Groups subsisting largely on plant foods, some of which they may plant. May be mobile and not using permanent fields.

Horticulture: Encouraging particular plants to grow; for example, by weeding round them. Used to identify a stage in food production before agriculture.

Human: Either just modern humans (us) or the Homo genus generally. Australopithecines were extinct African hominids living from 5 mya to around 1 mya. The gracile (slender) variants were the ancestors of the Homo genus.

Hunter-gatherers: Groups subsisting on a mixture of wild animal and plant foods. May be mobile.

Iconography: Art that may have a religious meaning

Inclusions: Material added to clay to provide strength and improve the firing process. Also known as temper.

Inhumation: Burial of a body

In situ: In its original place

Intensification: Increasing production. Usually applied to food production but can apply to extraction or manufacture.

Intra-site analysis: Study of the use of space on an archaeological site

Isotopes: Variations in the molecules of particular elements which have different numbers of neutrons

Isotopic analysis: Identifying different ratios of isotopes in materials in order to pinpoint their source

Kin: Relatives through blood and marriage

Levallois technique: A lithic technology which involved preparing a core to produce a particular size and shape of flake. Identified from 200,000 BP and associated with Neanderthals.

Lidar (Light Detection and Ranging): Similar to RADAR but transmitting and measuring the return of a short pulse of light (a laser) rather than radio waves. In aerial reconnaissance it measures the distance from the plane to the ground and is linked to a GPS system to provide a detailed contour survey.

Liminal: A boundary. Can be used for a place or group of people on the edge of normal society or even a time such as the start and end of a year. May be seen as dangerous and likely to require ritual to deal with it.

Lineage: A group sharing the same ancestor

Linearbandkeramik (LBK): The first farmers in central Europe, named after their pottery which was decorated with bands running around the vessels

Lipids: Fats

Lithics: Stone tools

Magnetometry: Detecting buried remains through magnetic variations between them and the surrounding soil

Market exchange: A system of exchange where producers compete in terms of prices. It is often associated with money or bartering and particular exchange sites; for example, shops or markets.

Mastaba: Rectangular mudbrick structures that housed the entrance to underground tombs. These tombs were forerunners of the pyramids.

Material culture: The total physical remains of a former society including artefacts, buildings, etc.

Matrix: The type of soil or other material in which an artefact is found

Mesolithic: A label given to the period from the end of the last Ice Age until the development of farming. Sometimes used to refer to groups living by hunting and gathering. In Britain dates range from *c.* 8000 BC.

Metallography: Studying the composition and structure of metals

Metallurgy: Making artefacts from metal ores

Micro-contour survey: A detailed survey using accurate sensitive equipment to reveal subtle variations in the ground surface in order to reveal the plan of buried sites

Microliths: Tiny stone or flint blades 1–4cm long. Associated with the Mesolithic period.

Midden: A rubbish heap. In some periods may have had other functions including a source of fertiliser and a ritual site.

Mitigation strategy: Work undertaken to preserve or remove archaeological material threatened by destruction

Mixed farming: Arable and pastoral.

MNI: Minimum number of individuals. The smallest number of animals that could have produced the bones in an assemblage.

Moiety: Organisation of society based on the idea of two different subgroups

Monotheistic: Belief in one god

Mortuary practice: Ritual activity and preparation involving the disposal of a corpse

Mousterian: See Levallois. Neanderthal lithic industry from *c.* 150,000 BP.

Native American Graves Protection and Repatriation Act (NAGPRA): A 1990 US law protecting human and cultural remains and repatriating materials from existing collections

Natufian: The final Mesolithic culture of the Near East. Sedentary and with a range of tools for processing wild grains.

Neolithic: This label is used to describe the period of the first farmers, before the use of metal tools. Increasingly it is used to describe the process of domestication including changing ideas about the world. British dates range from *c.* 4500 BC.

Neolithic package: The assemblage associated with the spread of agriculture across Europe including querns and polished stone axes, domesticated animal bones and plant remains from emmer and einkorn wheat and barley

Neutron activation analysis (NAA): Highly sensitive analysis of trace elements undertaken within a reactor

NISP: Number of identified specimens. A count of all the bones of each species in an assemblage.

NMR: National Monuments Record

Numen: The spirit of a place (Roman). It could also reside in objects or be linked to particular deities.

Obsidian: Volcanic glass that can be worked to produce hard, sharp edges

Oldowan: The earliest lithic industry from around 2.6 mya. Associated with Homo habilis. Crude flaking of a stone to produce a cutting edge.

Optically Stimulated Luminescence (OSL) Dating: Similar to thermoluminescence. It calculates the length of time since sediments such as quartz were last exposed to light.

Organic residue analysis: Using chemicals to extract and identify traces of plant and animal materials from pottery

Ossuary: A place in which the bones of the dead are stored; for example, a charnel house

Palaeolithic: The first archaeological period. Before 8000 BC but subdivided into Lower, Middle and Upper on the basis of stone technology

Palimpsest: A collection of archaeological artefacts, ecofacts and material that may not be related. For example, they are together through accident or natural forces rather than human activity. Also used for a site with a mass of intercut features of different periods.

Palynology: Studying pollen for dating and environmental reconstruction

Pastoralists: People who subsist largely from the animals they herd. May be mobile.

Petrology: Studying the minerals in archaeological (lithics) material to identify their source of origin

Phosphate analysis: Analysing soil samples to detect high phosphate which can indicate human or animal habitation

Planum method: An approach to excavating deposits where stratigraphy is very hard to detect and the fill seems to be homogeneous such as graves. It is also used on large open sites with few if any features. It involves trowelling successive artificial layers. More widely used abroad than in the UK.

Pollen dating: Using local pollen sequences to provide a relative date for a site

Polytheistic: Belief in many gods

Preservation by record: Excavating and recording archaeological remains

Preservation in situ: Leaving archaeological remains where they are

Prestige goods chain: Where valuable items are exchanged between high-status individuals, often over a considerable area

Primary products: The material gained by killing an animal; for example, meat, skin

Probing: Using metal rods to detect walls and other buried features close to the surface

Propitiation: Offerings to gods; for example, offerings in pits or deposited in water

Radiocarbon dating (RC): Absolute dating technique based on the known rate of decay of Carbon 14

Reciprocity: Exchange between social equals. Balanced reciprocity implies things of equal value are exchanged.

Redistribution: A form of exchange where goods are collected by a central authority and then given to other people or places

Regression: Using clues from the earliest known maps and documents from an area and projecting them back in time to produce a picture of an earlier period

Relative dating: Determining where a site or artefact sits in a sequence in relation to other sites or artefacts

Remote sensing: Detecting archaeological remains from above the surface of the earth, usually from a satellite

Resistivity: Detecting buried remains through differences between them and the surrounding soil in their ability to carry an electrical current

Rites of intensification: Ritual to mark times of change or danger

Rites of passage: Ritual to mark events in the lives of individuals

Sampling: The careful selection of areas to investigate or materials to analyse. Usually based on mathematical probability to ensure that what is selected is representative of wider evidence.

Secondary products: Materials gained from animals without killing them; for example, milk, wool

Sedentary: Where a group is settled, that is, staying in one place. Semi-sedentary groups stay for considerable periods, perhaps moving between sites on a seasonal basis.

Segmentary society: Small, relatively self-contained social groups who may sometimes combine with similar groups to form wider alliances

SEM: Scanning electron microscope

Shadow sites: Sites that survive as low earthworks and are seen from the air in conditions of low sunlight

Shaman: Individual who can communicate with, and often interact with, spirits

Shovel pit testing: An alternative to fieldwalking for woods, pasture and gardens. Samples of soil from carefully selected test pits are sieved for artefacts.

Sidescan sonar: A series of sonar pulses are emitted from a ship or towed device in a wide beam and the returning signal is recorded. The results provide an image of the seabed in the direction travelled.

Signature: Traces in the archaeological record that can be linked to particular patterns of activity

Site: A place where human activity has taken place

Site catchment analysis: Reconstructing the available natural resources within easy reach of an archaeological site to help construct a model of its economy and the diet of its people

SMR: Sites and Monuments Record. Today more likely to be an HER.

Social complexity: When a society has a high degree of specialisation and different roles

Social storage: When an individual gives something of value to another individual, creating an obligation on the part of the second person to return something at a later date. What is exchanged can vary enormously from an exotic gift to a meal, from military service to a bride.

Soil marks: Variations in the tone or colour of ploughed soil due to the destruction of buried features

Sonar: Form of underwater detection based on sound waves

Specialisation: This term can be used in several ways. Economic specialisation can be used to describe a group who rely on one primary means of supporting themselves; for example, pastoralists. It can also mean a division of labour where different individuals perform particular tasks rather than working in similar ways; for example, miners, iron smelters and smiths in the production of iron tools.

State: Society with a territory, central authority and permanent institutions

Stelae: Carved stone pillars or statues

Stratification: A series of layers, strata or deposits laid down over time. **Stratigraphy** is the analysis of stratification or its use in relative dating.

Structured deposition: Material entering the archaeological record through specific (possibly ritual) activities or behaviour patterns (not random). For example, particular animal bones being placed in ditches.

Subsistence: The way in which a group acquires the food it needs; for example, fishing or herding. A subsistence economy is one which just produces enough to live on.

Superposition: The principle that in undisturbed stratification, the oldest layer in the sequence is at the bottom

Surface collection: American version of fieldwalking. It can usefully be applied to the systematic recovery of artefacts from places other than fields.

Surface survey: Examining the landscape for evidence of underlying archaeological remains

Surveying: Precisely measuring the dimensions, position and orientation of archaeological sites and features

Syncretism: Fusion of different systems of belief

Taphonomy: 'The law of burial'. The processes which transform organic archaeological material in the ground.

TAQ: Terminus ante quem. The latest possible date for a site or layer.

Tell: A large mound created by successive settlement layers on a site over thousands of years

Temper: Material added to clay to give it strength and prevent it cracking during firing

Thiessen polygons: Shapes created by joining the mid-point between economic centres to provide models for exploring territories

Thin sections: Samples of rock taken for petrological analysis

TL: Thermoluminescence dating

Totemism: A natural object is adopted by a group as their emblem and as an object of worship

TPQ: Terminus post quem. The earliest possible date for a site or layer.

Trace elements: Tiny amounts of rare elements within stone and metal. The balance of trace elements varies according to the geological source of the material.

Transect: Walking or taking a sample across a landscape

Transegalitarian: A society where there is some inequality but individual families do not amass sufficient wealth to make the differences permanent

Transformation (T) processes: The way in which archaeological material has been shaped by human and natural forces since its abandonment. Also known as formation processes.

Transhumance: A yearly cycle of movement between higher or cooler pastures during the early summer and more sheltered areas for the winter. Practised by herding societies.

Trend surface analysis: A way of illustrating the distribution of artefacts by using mathematical formulae to create a contour map

Tribe: A society that is larger than a band but still linked together by kinship ties. May number between several hundred and a few thousand people. Likely to be farmers or pastoralists. Unlikely to have wide variations in wealth and status.

Typology: Organising artefacts into types based on similar attributes and studying the development of such objects

Unit: An archaeological trust or commercial company that tenders (bids) to do survey and excavation work

Use wear analysis: Using high-powered microscopes to study marks on tools and bones in order to identify the activity that caused them

Valletta Convention (1992)**:** A Council of Europe agreement to document and preserve archaeological heritage. It has been ratified by the parliament.

Varves: Annual deposits of sediments in lakes which can be counted and used for dating.

Votives: Artefacts deposited as offerings to gods or spirits

Watching brief: Literally that. Typically an archaeologist observes the work of developers to see if archaeological remains are uncovered.

X-ray fluorescence (XRF): A non-destructive method of analysing the mineral composition of the surface of artefacts

Ziggurat: A Mesopotamian mudbrick temple. Stepped and shaped like a pyramid.

Bibliography

Abrams, E. (1994) *How the Maya Built Their World: Energetics and Ancient Architecture*. Austin: University of Texas Press.

Aitchison, K. (2009) What is the value of an archaeology degree? *Papers from the Institute of Archaeology* 17: 41–2.

Aldenderfer, M. (1996) *Anthropology, Space, and Geographic Information Systems*. Oxford: Oxford University Press.

All-Party Parliamentary Archaeology Group (2003) *The current state of Archaeology in the UK*. London: APPAG.

Alsford, S. (2009) History of Medieval Ipswich. Online: http://users.trytel.com/~tristan/towns/ipswich1.html.

Ammerman, A. and Cavalli-Sforza, L. L. (1984) *The Neolithic Transition and the Genetics of Populations in Europe*. Princeton: Princeton University Press.

Anderson, S. (1985) Tybrind Vig. *Journal of Danish Archaeology* 4. Odense: Odense University Press.

Anderson, S. (1995) Ringkloster: Ertebølle trappers and wild boar hunters in eastern Jutland – a survey. *Journal of Danish Archaeology* 12 (1): 13–64.

Anthony, D. (2007) *The Horse, the Wheel, and Language: How Bronze-Age Riders from the Eurasian Steppes Shaped the Modern World*. Princeton: Princeton University Press.

Armit, I. (2003) *Towers in the North*. Stroud: Tempus.

Arneborg, J. et al. (2012) Human diet and subsistence patterns in Norse Greenland AD c.980–AD c.1450: archaeological interpretations. *Journal of the North Atlantic* (Special Volume) 3: 94–133.

Arnold, B. (1990) The past as propaganda: totalitarian archaeology in Nazi Germany. *Antiquity* 64 (244): 464–78.

Arnold, E. and Greenfield, H. (2006) *The Origins of Transhumant Pastoralism in Temperate South Eastern Europe*. Oxford: BAR International Series 1538.

Artusson, M. (2009) The power structure of Bronze Age societies was based on social networks. *Science Daily*, 9 April.

Ashmore, W. and Sharer, R. (1999) *Discovering Our Past*. Mountain View, CA: Mayfield.

Aston, M. (1985) *Interpreting the Landscape*. London: Routledge.

Aston, M. and Gerrard, C. (2013) *Interpreting the English Village. Landscape and Community at Shapwick, Somerset*. Macclesfield: Windgather Press.

Auel, J. (1980) *The Clan of the Cave Bear*. London: Hodder and Stoughton.

Bahn, P. and Vertut, J. (1988) *Images of the Ice Age*. Leicester: Windward.

Bailey, D. W. (2000) *Balkan Prehistory: Exclusion, Incorporation and Identity*. London: Routledge.

Bailey, R. (1991) *The Behavioural Ecology of the Efe Pygmy Men in the Huri Forest, Zaire*. University of Michigan Museum.

Balaresque, P. et al. (2010) A predominantly Neolithic origin for European paternal lineages. *PLoS* 8 (1).

Balter, M. (2004) *The Goddess and the Bull: Çatalhöyük*. New York: Free Press.

Balter, M. (2006) First jewellery? Old shell beads suggest early use of symbols. *Science* 312: 1731.

Bang-Andersen, S. (2003) Encircling the living space of early postglacial reindeer hunters in the interior of southern Norway. In Larsson, L. et al. (eds) *Mesolithic on the Move*. Papers presented at the sixth International Conference on the Mesolithic in Europe, Stockholm 2000. London: Oxbow Books, pp. 193–204.

Bang-Andersen, S. (2009) Prehistoric reindeer trapping by stone-walled pitfalls: news and views. In Finlay, N. et al. (eds) *From Bann Flakes to Bushmills: Papers in Honour of Professor Peter Woodman*. Oxford: Oxbow Books, pp. 61–9.

Barclay, G. and Russell-White, C. (1993) Excavations in the ceremonial complex of the fourth to second millennium BC at Balfarg/Balbirnie, Glenrothes, Fife. *Proceedings of the Society of Antiquaries of Scotland* 123, pp. 43–211.

Barker, G., Gilbertson, D. and Mattingly, D. (2008) *Archaeology and Desertification*. Levant Supplementary Series 6. Oxford and Amman: Council for British Research in the Levant.

Barley, N. (1984) *Adventures in a Mud Hut: An Innocent Anthropologist Abroad*. New York: Vanguard Press.

Barnett, J. (1998) Monuments in the landscape: thoughts from the Peak. Lecture at conference on Prehistoric Ritual, Oxford.

Barrett, J. (1994) *Fragments from Antiquity*. Oxford: Blackwell.

Barrett, J. and Bradley, R. (eds) (1980) *Settlement and Society in the British Later Bronze Age*. Oxford: BAR 83.

Barrett, J. et al. (2004) The origins of intensive marine fishing in medieval Europe: the English evidence. *Proceedings: Biological Sciences* 271, 1556: 2417–21.

Barrett, J. et al. (2007) Interpreting the plant and animal remains from Viking-age Kaupang. In Skre, D. (ed.) *Kaupang in Skiringssal*. Aarhus: Aarhus University Press, pp. 283–319.

Barrett, J. et al. (2008) Detecting the medieval cod trade: a new method and first results. *Journal of Archaeological Science* 35 (4): 850–61.

Barth, F. (1999) Archaeological heritage of the Hallstatt region. From the Austrian application to the World Heritage Committee of UNESCO.

Barton, N. (1997) *Stone Age Britain*. London: Batsford.

Bartosiewicz, L. (2005) Plain talk: animals, environment and culture in the Neolithic of the Carpathian Basin and adjacent areas. In Bailey, D. et al. (eds) *Unsettling the Neolithic*. Oxford: Oxbow Books.

Bar-Yosef, O. (1998) The Natufian Culture in the Levant: threshold to the origins of agriculture. *Evolutionary Anthropology* 6 (5): 159–77.

Bateman, C. et al. (2003) Prehistoric and Anglo-Saxon Settlements to the rear of Sherborne House, Lechlade: excavations in 1997. *Transactions of the Bristol and Gloucestershire Archaeological Society* 121: 23–96.

Bayliss, A. (2009) Rolling out revolution: using radiocarbon dating in archaeology. *Radiocarbon* 51 (1): 123–47.

Bayliss-Smith, T. (1996) People–plant interaction in the New Guinea highlands. In Harris, D. (ed.) *The Origins and Spread of Agriculture and Pastoralism in Eurasia*. London: UCL.

Bay-Petersen, J. (1978) Animal exploitation in Mesolithic Denmark. In Mellars, P. (ed.) *The Early Postglacial Settlement of Northern Europe: An Ecological Perspective*. London: Duckworth, pp. 115–45.

Bednarik, R. G. (1992) Paleoart and archaeological myths. *Cambridge Archaeological Journal* 2: 27–57.

Bednarik, R. G. (1995) Towards a better understanding of the origins of body decoration. *Anthropologie* 33: 201–12.

Bednarik, R. G. (2000) Beads and the origins of symbolism. Online: www.semioticon.com/frontline/bednarik.htm.

Beja-Pereira, A. et al. (2006) The origin of European cattle: Evidence from modern and ancient DNA. *Proceedings of the National Academy of Sciences* 103 (2): 8113–18.

Benner Larsen, E. (1985) The Gundestrup Cauldron, identification of tool traces. *Iskos* 5: 561–74.

Bentley, R. et al. (2003) Human mobility at the early Neolithic settlement of Vaihingen, Germany: evidence from strontium isotope analysis. *Archaeometry* 45 (3): 4714–86.

Bentley, R. et al. (2008) Isotopic signatures and hereditary traits: snapshot of a Neolithic community in Germany. *Antiquity* 82 (316): 290–304.

Bentley, A. (2012) Community differentiation and kinship among Europe's first farmers. *PNAS* 109 (24): 9326–30.

Bickle, P. and Whittle, A. (2013) *The First Farmers of Central Europe*. Oxford: Oxbow Books.

Biel, J. (2006) Eberdingen-Hochdorf. *Brathair* 6 (1): 3–9.

Binford, L. (1978) *Nunamiut Ethnoarchaeology*. Orlando: Academic Press.

Binford, L. (1983) *In Pursuit of the Past*. New York: Thames and Hudson.

Binford, L. (1989) *Debating Archaeology*. San Diego: Academic Press.

Blinkhorn, P. (1997) Stranger in a strange land: Middle Saxon Ipswich Ware. Paper presented to the Pottery in the Making Conference at the British Museum.

Blinkhorn, P. (1999) Of cabbages and kings: production, trade, and consumption in middle-Saxon England. In Anderton, M. (ed.) *Anglo-Saxon Trading Centres: Beyond the Emporia*. Glasgow: Cruithne Press, pp. 42–3.

Blinkhorn, P. (2012) *The Ipswich Ware Project*. Medieval pottery reseach group occasional paper 7. Dorchester: Dorset Press.

Blom, R. et al. (1997) Space technology and the discovery of the lost city of Ubar. *IEEEE Aerospace Conference Proceedings* 1: 19–28.

Blumenschine, R. et al. (1987) Characteristics of an early hominid scavenging niche. *Current Anthropology* 28 (4): 383–407.

Bogaard, A. et al. (2013) Crop manuring and intensive land management by Europe's first farmers. *PNAS* 110 (31): 12589–94.

Bogucki, P. (2000) How agriculture came to north-central Europe. In Price, T. (ed.) *Europe's First Farmers*. Cambridge: Cambridge University Press, pp. 197–218.

Bogucki, P. (2004) The Neolithic mosaic on the North European Plain. Online: www.princeton.edu/~bogucki/mosaic.html.

Bogucki, P. (2011) How wealth happened in Neolithic Central Europe. *Journal of World Prehistory* 24 (2–3): 107–15.

Boismier, W. et al. (2012) *Neanderthals Among Mammoths. Excavations at Lynford Quarry, Norfolk*. English Heritage.

Bokelmann, K. (1991) Some new thoughts on old data on human and reindeer in the Ahrensburg tunnel valley in Schleswig-Holstein, Germany. In Barton, R. et al. (eds) *Late Glacial in North-west Europe: Human Adaptation and Environmental Change at the End of the Pleistocene*. Oxford: CBA, pp. 72–81.

Bollongino, R. et al. (2012) Modern Taurine cattle descended from small number of Near-Eastern founders. *Molecular Biology and Evolution* 29 (7): 2101–04.

Boulestin, B. et al. (2009) Mass cannibalism in the Linear Pottery Culture at Herxheim. *Antiquity* 83: 968–82.

Boyadzhiev, K. (2011) *Development and Distribution of Close Combat Weapons in Bulgarian Chalcolithic*. Studia Praehistorica 14. Bulgarian Academy of Sciences.

Bradley, R. (1984) *The Social Foundations of Prehistoric Britain*. London: Longman.

Bradley, R. (1997) *Rock Art and the Prehistory of Atlantic Europe: Signing the Land*. London: Routledge.

Bradley, R. (1998) *The Significance of Monuments*. London: Routledge.

Bradley, R. (2000a) *The Good Stones*. Edinburgh: The Society of Antiquaries of Scotland.

Bradley, R. (2000b) *An Archaeology of Natural Places*. London: Routledge.

Bradley, R. (2007) *The Prehistory of Britain and Ireland*. Cambridge: Cambridge University Press.

Bradley, R. and Edmonds, M. (2005) *Interpreting the Axe Trade: Production and Exchange in Neolithic Britain*. Cambridge: Cambridge University Press.

Branigan, K. (ed.) (2001) *Urbanism in the Aegean Bronze Age*. Sheffield: Sheffield University Press.

Bratlund, B. (1996) Hunting strategies in the late glacial of northern Europe: A survey of the faunal evidence. *Journal of World Prehistory* 10 (1): 1–48.

British Museum (2006) *The British Museum Policy on Human Remains*.

British Tourist Authority (2012) *Annual Report and Financial Statements for the Year Ended 31 March 2012*. Visit Britain.

Bronk-Ramsey, C. et al. (2004) Dating the volcanic eruption at Thera. *Radiocarbon* 46 (1): 325–44.

Brotherton, P., Haak, W. et al. (2013) Neolithic mitochondrial haplogroup H genomes and the genetic origins of Europeans. *Nature Communications* 4: 1764.

Brück, J. (1995) A place for the dead: the role of human remains in late Bronze Age Britain. *Oxford Journal of Archaeology* 61: 245–77.

Bruins, H. et al. (2009) The Minoan Santorini eruption and tsunami deposits in Palaikastro: dating by geology, archaeology, RC and Egyptian chronology. *Radiocarbon* 51 (2): 397–411.

Buckland, P. (1976) The use of insect remains in the interpretation of archaeological environments. In Davidson, D. and Shackley, M. (eds) *Geoarchaeology*. London: Duckworth.

Bunn, H. and Kroll, E. (1986) Systematic butchery by Plio-Pleistocene hominids at Olduvai Gorge, Tanzania. *Current Anthropology* 27: 431–52.

Bunson, M. (1995) *A Dictionary of Ancient Egypt*. Oxford: Oxford University Press.

Burenhult, G. (ed.) (2003) *People of the Past*. San Francisco: Fog City Press.

Burger, J. et al. (2005) Ancient DNA from the First European Farmers in 7500-year-old Neolithic sites. *Science* 310: 1016–18.

Burger, J. et al. (2009) The origins of lactase persistence in Europe. *PLoS Computational Biology* 5 (8): e1000491.

Burra Charter (1999) Online: http://australia.icomos.org/publications/charters/.

Callum, R. (2007) *The Unnatural History of the Sea*. Washington DC: Ocean Island Press/Shearwater Books.

Canaanite Amphorae Project (nd) www.amarnaproject.com/pages/recent_projects/material_culture/canaanite.shtm.

Cann, R., Stoneking, M. and Wilson, A. (1987) Mitochondrial DNA and human evolution. *Nature* 325: 31–6.

Carneiro, R. (1970) A theory of the origin of the state. *Science* 169 (3947): 733–8.

Caspari, R. and Lee, S. (2004) Older age becomes common late in human evolution. *Proceedings of the National Academy of Sciences* 101: 10895–900.

Çatal Höyük project (nd). Online: www.catalhoyuk.com/.

Champion, T. and Collis, J. (eds) (1996) *The Iron Age in Britain and Ireland: Recent Trends*. Sheffield: Sheffield Academic Press.

Champion, T. et al. (1984) *Prehistoric Europe*. San Diego: Academic Press.

Chapman, R., Kinnes, I. and Randsborg, K. (eds) (1981) *The Archaeology of Death*. Cambridge: Cambridge University Press.

Cherry, J. (1983) Evolution, revolution, and the origins of complex society in Minoan Crete. In Krzyszkowska, O. and Nixon, L. (eds) *Minoan Society*. Bristol Classical Press, pp. 33–45.

Cherry, J. (1986) Polities and palaces: some problems in Minoan state formation. In Renfrew, C. and Cherry, J. (eds) *Peer Polity Interaction and Socio-Political Change*. Cambridge: Cambridge University Press.

Childe, V. (1931) *Skara Brae, a Pictish Village in Orkney*. Monograph of the Royal Commission on the Ancient and Historical Monuments of Scotland.

Childe, V. (1936) *Man Makes Himself*. London: Watts.

Clark, R. (2000) *Mesolithic Hunters of the Trentino*. Oxford: BAR 832.

Clarke, D. (ed.) (1972) *Models in Archaeology*. London: Methuen.

Cohen, M. (1979) *The Food Crisis in Prehistory: Overpopulation and the Origins of Agriculture*. New Haven: Yale University Press.

Cohen, M. (1991) *Health and the Rise of Civilization*. New Haven: Yale University Press.

Colburn, C. (2008) Exotica and the Early Minoan elite: eastern imports into prepalatial Crete. *American Journal of Archaeology* 112: 203–24.

Coles, B. and Coles, J. (1976) *Sweet Track to Glastonbury*. London: Thames and Hudson.

Coles, J. (1979) *Experimental Archaeology*. London: Academic Press.

Coles, J. and Lawson, A. (eds) (1987) *European Wetlands in Prehistory*. Oxford: Clarendon Press.

Collis, J. (1984) *The European Iron Age*. London: Batsford.

Collis, J. (1996) *Hillforts, enclosures and boundaries*. In Champion, T. and Collis, J. (eds) *The Iron Age in Britain and Ireland: Recent Trends*. Sheffield: Sheffield Academic Press.

Collis, J. (2003) *The Celts: Origins, Myths and Inventions*. Stroud: Tempus.

Cook, B. et al. (2012) Deforestation as an amplifier of drought in Mesoamerica. *Geophysical Research Letters* 39 (16).

Cook, J. and Ward, C. (2008) *Conservation assessment of the Neanderthal human remains from Krapina, Croatia and its implications for the debate on the display and loan of human fossils*. BM technical research bulletin no 2.

Cooney, G. and Grogan, E. (1999) *Irish Prehistory: A Social Perspective*. Dublin: Wordwell.

Cooper, N. (2000) *The Archaeology of Rutland Water: Excavations at Empingham 1967–73 and 1990*. Leicester: Leicester University Press.Copley, M. et al. (2005) Dairying in antiquity I. Evidence from absorbed lipid residues dating to the British Iron Age. *Journal of Archaeological Science* 32(4): 485–503.

Cornwell, B. (1999) *Stonehenge*. London: HarperCollins.

Coulter, D. (2009) The fall of the Maya: 'They did it to themselves'. *Science@NASA Headline News*. 6 October.

Craddock, P. (1995) *Early Metal Mining and Production*. Edinburgh: Edinburgh University Press.

Craig, O. et al. (2011) Ancient lipids reveal continuity in culinary practices across the transition to agriculture in Northern Europe. *Proceedings of the National Academy of Sciences* 108 (44): 17910–15.

Craig, O. et al. (2013) Earliest evidence for the use of pottery. *Nature* 496 (7445): 351–4.

Crossley, D. (1994) *Post Medieval Archaeology in Britain*. Leicester: Leicester University Press.

Crow, J. (2004) *Housesteads*. London: Batsford.

Crumlin-Pedersen, O. (ed.) (2003) *Hjortspring*. Roskilde: The Viking Ship Museum.

Cunliffe, B. (1992) Pits, preconceptions and propitiation in the British Iron Age. *Oxford Journal of Archaeology* 11: 69–83.

Cunliffe, B. (1993) *Danebury*. London: English Heritage.

Cunliffe, B. (ed.) (1994) *The Oxford Illustrated Prehistory of Europe*. Oxford: Oxford University Press.

Cunliffe, B. (1995) *Iron Age Britain*. London: Batsford.

Cunliffe, B. and Koch, J. (2012) *Celtic from the West: Alternative Perspectives from Archaeology, Genetics, Language and Literature*. Oxford: Oxbow Books.

Cuno, J. and Martin, E. (2009) *Who Owns Antiquity? Museums and the Battle over our Ancient Heritage*. Princeton: Princeton University Press.

Dalén, L. et al. (2012) Partial genetic turnover in Neandertals: continuity in the east and population replacement in the west. *The Oxford Journal of Molecular Biology and Evolution* 29 (8): 1893–7.

Dark, K. and Dark, P. (1997) *The Landscape of Roman Britain*. Stroud: Sutton Publishing.

Darvill, T. and Fulton, A. (1998) *MARS: The Monuments at Risk Survey of England*. Bournemouth and London: Bournemouth University and English Heritage.

Darvill, T. and Thomas, J. (eds) (2000) *Neolithic Houses in North-west Europe and Beyond*. Oxford: Oxbow Books.

Davidson, D. and Shackley, M. (eds) (1976) *Geoarchaeology*. London: Duckworth.

Defleur, A. et al. (1999) Neanderthal cannibalism at Moula-Guercy, Ardèche, France. *Science* 286 (5437): 128–31.

De la Bédoyère, G. (1998) *Hadrian's Wall: History and Guide*. Stroud: Tempus.

Deloitte, with Oxford Economics (2010) *The Economic Contribution of the Visitor Economy: UK and the Nations*. Visit Britain.

Dennell, R. (1978) *Early Farming in South Bulgaria from the 6th to 3rd millennium B.C.* British Archaeological Reports International Series 47.

Department for Culture, Media and Sport (2005) *Guidance for the Care of Human Remains in Museums*. London: DCMS.

Derevenski, J. (1997) Age and gender at the site of Tiszapolgar-Basatanya, Hungary. *Antiquity* 71: 875–89.

Dery, C. (1997) Food and the Roman army: travel, transport and transmission. In Walker, H. (ed.) *Proceedings of the Oxford Symposium on Food and Cookery*. Chippenham: Prospect Books.

Diamond, J. (1998) *Guns, Germs and Steel: A Short History of Everybody for the Last 13,000 Years*. London: Vintage.

Diamond, J. (2005) *Collapse: How Societies Choose to Fail or Succeed*. New York: Penguin Books.

Dietler, M. (1994) Our ancestors the Gauls: archaeology, ethnic nationalism and the manipulation of Celtic identity in modern Europe. *American Anthropologist* 96 (3): 584–605.

Domi'nguez-Rodrigo, M. and Pickering, T. (2003) Early hominid hunting and scavenging: a zooarcheological review. *Evolutionary Anthropology* 12: 275–82.

Drewett, P. (1982) Later Bronze Age downland economy at Black Patch, East Sussex. *Proceedings of the Prehistoric Society* 48: 321–409.

Drewett, P. (1999) *Field Archaeology*. London: UCL Press.

Driessen, J. (2001) History and hierarchy. Preliminary observations on the settlement pattern in Minoan Crete. In Branigan, K. (ed.) *Urbanism in the Aegean Bronze Age*. Sheffield: Sheffield University Press.

Duarte, C. et al. (1999) The early Upper Paleolithic human skeleton from the Abrigo do Lagar Velho (Portugal) and modern human emergence in Iberia. *PNAS* 96 (13): 7604–9.

Dudd, S., Regert, M. and Evershed, R. (1998) Assessing microbial lipid contributions during laboratory degradations of fats and oils and pure triacylglycerols absorbed in ceramic potsherds. *Organic Geochemistry* 29 (5–7): 1345–54.

Durham, A. (1988) The Vučedol Culture. In *Vučedol: 3000 Years B.C.* Zagreb: Muzejski prostor.

Elliott, S. (nd) Pits, wells and associated slumps from the Roman town of Silchester. Conference poster, University of Reading. Online: www.reading.ac.uk/web/FILES/QUEST/Silchester_poster_-_Phytoliths_SE.pdf.

Ellison, A. (1980) Settlements and regional exchange: a case study. In Barrett, J. and Bradley, R. (eds) *Settlement and Society in the British Later Bronze Age*. Oxford: BAR 83.

English Heritage (2000) *The Power of Place*. EH.

English Heritage (2002) *With Alidade and Tape*. EH.

English Heritage (2006) *Understanding Historic Buildings: A Guide to Good Recording Practice*. EH.

English Heritage (2013) *Heritage at Risk*. EH.

Enloe, J. (1992) *Food Sharing in the Paleolithic: Carcass Refitting at Pincevent*. Oxford: BAR International Series.

Enloe, J. (1997) Seasonality and age structure in remains of Rangifer tarandus: Magdalenian hunting strategy at Verberie. *Anthropozoologica* 25–26: 95–102.

Enloe, J. (2006) Geological processes and site structure: assessing integrity at a late Palaeolithic open-air site in northern France. *Geoarchaeology: An International Journal* 21 (6): 523–40.

Evans-Pritchard, E. (1937) *Witchcraft, Oracles and Magic Among the Azande*. Oxford: Oxford University Press.

Evershed, R. (2002) Identification of animal fats via compound specific 13C values of individual fatty acids: assessments of results for reference fats and lipid extracts of archaeological pottery vessels. *Documenta Praehistorica* 29: 73–96.

Evershed, R. et al. (2003) Direct chemical evidence for widespread dairying in prehistoric Britain. *Proceedings of the National Academy of Sciences, USA* 100 (4): 1524–9.

Evershed, R. et al. (2005) Processing of milk products in pottery vessels through British prehistory. *Antiquity* 79: 895–908.

Fabech, C. and Ringtved, J. (eds) (1999) Settlement and Landscape. Proceedings of a conference in Aarhus, Denmark, 4–7 May. Jutland Archaeological Society, Aarhus University Press.

Faegre, T. (1979) *Tents: Architecture of the Nomads*. Garden City, New York: Anchor Press/Doubleday.

Fagan, B. (1995) *Time Detectives*. New York: Simon and Schuster.

Fagan, B. (2000) *In the Beginning*. New York: Prentice-Hall.

Fairclough, J. (2010) *Boudica to Raedwald: East Anglia's Relations with Rome*. Suffolk: Malthouse Press.

Fash, W. L. (1991) *Scribes, Warriors and Kings*. New York: Thames and Hudson.

Faulkner, N. (2000) Archaeology from below. *Public Archaeology* 1 (1): 21–33.

Festi, D. et al. (2011) The Late Neolithic settlement of Latsch, Vinschgau, northern Italy: subsistence of a settlement contemporary with the Alpine Iceman, and located in his valley of origin. *Vegetation History and Archaeobotany* 20: 367–79.

Fforde, C. et al. (eds) (2004) *The Dead and their Possessions: Repatriation in Principle, Policy and Practice*. Abingdon: Routledge.

Fifield, T. (1996) Human remains found in Alaska reported to be 9,730 years old. *Society for American Archaeology* 14 (5) bulletin.

Fischer, A. (ed.) (1995) *Man and Sea in the Mesolithic*. Oxford: Oxbow Books.

Flannery, K. (1969) Origins and ecological effects of early domestication in Iran and the Near East. In Ucko, P. J. and Dimbleby, G. W. (eds) *The Domestication and Exploitation of Plants and Animals*. Chicago: Aldine, pp. 73–100.

Fleming, A. (1988) *The Dartmoor Reaves*. London: Batsford.

Fleming, A. (1998) *Swaledale, Valley of the Wild River*. Edinburgh: Edinburgh University Press.

Forenbaher, S. (1994) The late Copper Age architecture at Vučedol, Croatia. *Journal of Field Archaeology* 21: 307–23.

Foster, S. (1989) Analysis of spatial patterns in buildings as an insight into social structure: examples from the Scottish Atlantic Iron Age. *Antiquity* 63 (238): 40–50.

Freter, A. (1993) Obsidian hydration dating: its past, present and future application in Mesoamerica. *Ancient Mesoamerica* 4 (4): 285–303.

Fried, M. (1978) The State, the chicken and the egg. In Cohen, N. and Service, E. (eds) *Origins of the State*. Philadelphia: ISHI.

Frost, P. (2006) European hair and eye color: a case of frequency-dependent sexual selection? *Evolution and Human Behavior* 27: 85–103.

Gaffney, V. and Stanic, Z. (1991) *GIS Approaches to Regional Analysis: A Case Study of the Island of Hvar*. University of Ljubljana.

Gaffney, V., Thomson, K. and Fitch, S. (2007) *Mapping Doggerland: The Mesolithic Landscapes of the Southern North Sea*. Oxford: Archaeopress.

Gamble, C. (1986) *The Palaeolithic Settlement of Europe*. Cambridge: Cambridge University Press.

Gamble, C. (1999) *Palaeolithic Societies of Europe*. Cambridge: Cambridge University Press.

Gamble, C. (2000) *Archaeology: The Basics*. London: Routledge.

Gaudzinski, S. (1999) Middle Palaeolithic bone tools from the open-air site Salzgitter-Lebenstedt. *Journal of Archaeological Science* 26 (2): 125–41.

Gaudzinski, S. (2000) Adults only: Reindeer hunting at the Middle Palaeolithic site Salzgitter-Lebenstedt, Northern Germany. *Journal of Human Evolution* 38: 497–521.

Gebhard, R. et al. (2004) Ceramics from the Celtic Oppidum of Manching and its influence in Central Europe. *Hyperfine Interactions* 154: 199–214.

Gibbons, A. (2000) Evolutionary genetics. Europeans trace ancestry to Palaeolithic people. *Science* 290 (5494): 1080–1.

Giddens, A. (1989) *Sociology*. London: Polity.

Gilchrist, R. (1995) *Contemplation and Action: The Other Monasticism*. London: Leicester University Press.

Gilman, A. (1981) The development of social stratification in Bronze Age Europe. *Current Anthropology* 22 (1): 1–23.

Gimbutas, M. (1991) *The Civilization of the Goddess*. New York: Harper Collins.

Gimbutas, M. and Dexter, M. (1999) *The Living Goddesses*. Berkeley: University of California Press.

Golitko, M. and Keeley, L. (2007) Beating ploughshares back into swords: warfare in the Linearbandkeramik. *Antiquity* 81: 332–42.

Grabner, M. et al. (2009) Wood supply of the Bronze Age salt mining site at Hallstatt, Austria. *Proceedings for the 1st Mining in European History-Conference 12–15 November, Universität Innsbruck*. Innsbruck University Press.

Graslund, B. (1994) Prehistoric soul beliefs in Northern Europe. *Proceedings of the Prehistoric Society* 60: 15–26.

Graves-Brown, P. et al. (1996) *Cultural Identity and Archaeology: The Construction of European Communities*. TAG. London: Routledge.

Grayson, D. and Delpech, F. (2001) Specialized Early Upper Palaeolithic hunters in Southwestern France? *Journal of Archaeological Science* 29: 1439–49.

Grayson, D. and Delpech, F. (2003) Ungulates and the Middle-to-Upper Palaeolithic transition at Grotte XVI. *Journal of Archaeological Science* 30 (12): 1439–49.

Green, M. (2000) *A Landscape Revealed*. Stroud: Tempus.

Greene, K. (2002) *Archaeology: An Introduction*. London: Routledge.

Grogan, E. (1999) Hilltop settlement in South West Ireland. Lecture at conference on Late Bronze Age Landscapes, Oxford.

Gross, P. and Levitt, N. (1997) *The Flight from Science and Reason*. Annals of the New York Academy of Sciences, Vol. 775. New York: Annals of the New York Academy of Sciences.

Haak, W. et al. (2008) Ancient DNA, Strontium isotopes, and osteological analyses shed light on social and kinship organization of the Later Stone Age. *Proceedings of the National Academy of Sciences* 105 (47): 18226–31.

Halstead, P. (1981a) Counting sheep in Neolithic and Bronze Age Greece. In Hodder, I. et al. (eds) *Pattern of the Past: Studies in Honour of David Clarke.* Cambridge: Cambridge University Press.

Halstead, P. (1981b) From determinism to uncertainty: social storage and the rise of the Minoan Palace. In Sheridan, A. and Bailey, G. (eds) *Economic Archaeology.* Oxford: British Archaeological Reports, pp. 187–213.

Hamilakis, Y. and Alouri, E. (1996) Antiquities as symbolic capital in modern Greek society. *Antiquity* 70: 117–29.

Hammond, C. and O'Connor, T. (2013) Pig diet in medieval York: carbon and nitrogen stable isotopes. *Archaeological and Anthropological Sciences* 5 (2): 123–7.

Hansen, I. and Wickham, C. (2000) *The Long Eighth Century.* Leiden: Brill.

Hårdh, B. and Larsson, L. (2002) *Central places in the migration and the merovingian periods.* Papers from the 52nd Sachsen symposium, Lund, August 2001. Stockholm: Almqvist and Wiksell International.

Hardy, B. and Moncel, M. (2011) Neanderthal use of fish, mammals, birds, starchy plants and wood 1252–50,000 years ago. *Public Library of Science* 6 (8): e23768.

Hardy, K. and Wickham-Jones, C. (2002) Scotland's first settlers: the Mesolithic seascape of the Inner Sound, Skye and its contribution to the early prehistory of Scotland. *Antiquity* 76: 825–33.

Hardy, K. and Wickham-Jones, C. R. (2009) Mesolithic and later sites around the Inner Sound, Scotland: the work of the Scotland's First Settlers project 1998–2004. *Scottish Archaeological Internet Reports* 31. Online: www.sair.org.uk.

Härke, H. (1979) Settlement types and settlement patterns in the West Hallstatt province: an evaluation of evidence from excavated sites. Oxford: British Archaeological Reports.

Härke, H. (1990) Warrior graves? The background of the Anglo-Saxon burial rite. *Past and Present* 126: 22–43.

Harris, D. (ed.) (1996) *The Origins and Spread of Agriculture and Pastoralism in Eurasia.* London: UCL.

Haselgrove, C. et al. (2012) *Development-led Archaeology in North-West Europe.* Oxford: Oxbow Books.

Haviland, W. (2000) *Anthropology.* New York: Harcourt Brace.

Hawkes, C. (1954) Archaeological theory and method: some suggestions for the Old World. *American Anthropologist* 56: 155–68.

Hayden, B. (1995) Pathways to power. Principles for creating socioeconomic inequalities. In Price, T. D. and Feinman, G. M. (eds) *Foundations of Social Inequality.* New York: Plenum Press, pp. 15–86.

Hayden, B. (2009) The proof is in the pudding: feasting and the origins of domestication. *Current Anthropology* 50 (5): 708–9.

Hayden, B. and Dietler, M. (2010) *Feasts: Archaeological and Ethnographic Pespectives on Food, Politics, and Power.* Tuscaloosa: University of Alabama Press.

Healy, J. (1978) *Mining and Metallurgy in the Greek and Roman World.* London: Thames and Hudson.

Hedeager, L. (2002) Scandinavian 'central places' in a cosmological setting. In Hårdh, B. and Larsson, L. (eds) *Central Places in the Migration and the Merovingian Periods.* Papers from the 52nd Sachsen symposium, Lund, August 2001. Stockholm: Almqvist and Wiksell International, pp. 3–18.

Hedges, J. (2000) *Tomb of the Eagles.* John and Erica Hedges.

Helmer, D. and Vigne, J. (2007) Was milk a 'secondary product' in the Old World Neolithisation process? Its role in the domestication of cattle, sheep and goats. *Anthropozoologica* 42 (2): 9–40.

Henson, D. (2005) *Television Archaeology: Education or Entertainment?* Institute of Historical Research.

Herschend, F. (2000) Ship grave hall passage – the Oseberg monument as compound meaning. 11th International Saga Conference, Sydney, 142–51.

Higgs, E. and Vita Finzi, C. (1970) Prehistoric economy in the Mount Carmel area of Palestine: site catchment analysis. *Proc. Prehist. Soc.* 36: 1–37.

Higham, T. et al. (2007) New perspectives on the Varna cemetery (Bulgaria) – AMS dates and social implications. *Antiquity* 81 (313): 640–54.

Highfield, R. (2006) The birth of bling. *Daily Telegraph Online*, 24 June.

Hill, J. D. (1996a) Hillforts and the Iron Age of Wessex. In Champion, T. and Collis, J. (eds) *The Iron Age in Britain and Ireland: Recent Trends.* Sheffield: Sheffield Academic Press.

Hill, J. D. (1996b) Weaving the strands of a new Iron Age. *British Archaeology* 17: 8–9.

Hiller, S. and Nikolov, V. (eds) (1997) *Karanovo I.* Salzburg: Verlag Ferdinand Berger & Sohne.

Hillman, G. et al. (2001) New evidence of Lateglacial cereal cultivation at Abu Hureyra on the Euphrates. *The Holocene* 11 (4): 383–93.

Hines, J. (2003) *The Anglo-Saxons from the Migration Period to the Eighth Century: An Ethnographic Perspective.* Woodbridge: Boydell Press.

Hirth, K. (2010) Housework: craft production and domestic economy in ancient Mesoamerica. *Archaeological Papers of the American Anthropological Association* 19, February.

Hobsbawm, E. and Ranger, T. (eds) (1983) *The Invention of Tradition.* Cambridge: Cambridge University Press.

Hodder, I. (2004) Women and men at Çatalhöyük. *Scientific American* 290 (1): 66–73.

Hodges, R. (1982) *Dark Age Economics: The Origins of Town and Trade.* London: Duckworth.

Hoffecker, J. (2005) Innovation and technological knowledge in the Upper Palaeolithic of northern Eurasia. *Evolutionary Anthropology* 14: 186–98.

Hoffmann, R. (1996) Economic development and aquatic ecosystems in medieval Europe. *American History Review* 101: 631–69.

Hughey, G. et al. (2013) A European population in Minoan Bronze Age Crete. *Nature Communications* 4: 1861.

Hunter, J. et al. (1995) *Studies in Crime: An Introduction to Forensic Archaeology.* London: Batsford.

Hunter, J. and Ralston, I. (eds) (1999) *The Archaeology of Britain.* London: Routledge.

Hurst, D. (2001) *Skull Wars: Kennewick Man, Archaeology and the Battle for Native American Identity.* New York: Basic Books.

Hutton, B. (1986) *Recording Standing Buildings.* Sheffield: Sheffield University Press and Rescue (The British Archaeological Trust).

IFA (2011) *The Southport Group Report: Realising the Benefits of Planning-led Investigation of the Historic Environment.* Institute for Archaeologists.

IFA (2013) *Prospect Archaeologists Branch and Diggers' Forum Joint Day Conference Saturday 2nd November 2013.* Institute for Archaeologists.

Ilkjaer, J. (2002) *Illerup Ådal: Archaeology as a Magic Mirror.* Aarhus: Aarhus University Press.

Isaac, G. (1978) The food-sharing behaviour of protohuman hominids. *Scientific American* 238 (4): 901–08.

Isern, N. and Fort, J. (2010) Anisotropic dispersion, space competition and the slowdown of the Neolithic transition. *New Journal of Physics* 12.

Ixer, R. and Bevins, R. (2010) The detailed petrography of six orthostats from the bluestone circle, Stonehenge. *Wiltshire Archaeological and Natural History Magazine* 104: 1–14.

Jackson, P. (1995) Footloose in archaeology. *Current Archaeology* 144: 466–70.

James, S. (1999) *The Atlantic Celts: Ancient People or Modern Invention?* London: British Museum Press.

James, S. (2000) Simon James Ancient Celts Page. Online: www.ares.u-net.com/celtindx.htm.

Jansma, E. and De Natris, M. (2009) Dendrochronological analysis of barrels from the Early Medieval trade centre Dorestad. Thesis, University of Utrecht.

Janusek, J. et al. (2004) Top-down or bottom-up: rural settlement and raised field agriculture in the Lake Titicaca Basin, Bolivia. *Journal of Anthropological Archaeology* 23 (4): 404–30.

Jenkins, T. (2010) *Contesting Human Remains in Museum Collections: The Crisis of Cultural Authority.* Abingdon: Routledge Research in Museum Studies.

Jochim, M. (1976) *Hunter Gatherer Subsistence and Settlement: A Predictive Model.* New York: Academic Press.

Jovanović, B. (2009) Beginning of the metal age in the central Balkans according to the results of archaeometallurgy. *Journal of Mining and Metallurgy* 45 (2): B 143–8.

Kauffman, N. (2004) *Cultural Heritage Needs Assessment: Phase I.* Washington, DC: National Park Service, Department of the Interior.

Keeler, D. (2007) Intrasite spatial analysis of a late Upper Palaeolithic French site using geographic information systems. *Journal of World Anthropology: Occasional Papers* III (1): 1–40.

Keeley, L. (1996) *War Before Civilization: The Myth of the Peaceful Savage.* Oxford: Oxford University Press.

Kemp, B. J. (1993) *Ancient Egypt.* New York: Routledge.

Kennett, D. et al. (2012) Development and disintegration of Maya Political Systems in response to climate change. *Science* 338 (6108): 7887–91.

Kent, S. (1989) *Farmers as Hunters.* Cambridge: Cambridge University Press.

Kern, A. et al. (2009) *Kingdom of Salt.* Vienna: Natural History Museum.

Knapp, A. et al. (2002) Excavations at Politiko Phorades: a Bronze Age copper smelting site on Cyprus. *Antiquity* 76 (292): 319.

Knecht, L. (1994) Late Ice Age hunting technology. *Scientific American*, July: 82–7.

Kosian, M. et al. (2013) The city and the river: a reconstruction of the strategic position of early 9th century Dorestad, The Netherlands. *Geophysical Research Abstracts* 15.

Kowarik, K. et al. (2009) Modeling a mine. Agentbased Modeling, System dynamics and Experimental Archaeology applied to the Bronze Age Saltmines of Hallstatt. *Proceedings for the 1st Mining in European History Conference 12–15 November*, Universität Innsbruck.

Krell, K. (1998) Gimbutas' Kurgans-PIE homeland hypothesis: a linguistic critique. In Blench, R. and Spriggs, M. (eds) *Archaeology and Language, II*. London: Routledge.

Kreuz, A. et al. (2005) A comparison of early Neolithic crop and weed assemblages from the Linearbandkeramik and the Bulgarian Neolithic cultures: differences and similarities. *Vegetation History and Archaeobotany* 14: 237–58.

Kristiansen, K. and Larsson, T. (2005) *The Rise of Bronze Age Society: Travels, Transmissions and Transformations*. Cambridge: Cambridge University Press.

Kubiak-Martens, L. (1996) Evidence for possible use of plant foods in Palaeolithic and Mesolithic diet from the site of Całowanie in the central part of the Polish Plain. *Vegetation History and Archaeobotany* 5 (1–2): 33–8.

Larsen, E. (2005) Technical investigations: work in progress. In Nielsen, S. et al. (eds) *The Gundestrup Cauldron: New Scientific and Technical Investigations*. Acta Archaeological 76. Denmark: Acta Archaeologica, pp. 9–20.

Lee, E. (2012) Emerging genetic patterns of the European Neolithic: perspectives from a late Neolithic bell Beaker burial in Germany. *American Journal of Physical Anthropology* 148 (4): 571–9.

Lee, R. and DeVore, I. (eds) (1968) *Man the Hunter*. New York: Aldine de Gruyter.

Leroi-Gourhan, A. and Brézillion, M. (1966) L'habitation Magdalénienne No. 1 de Pincevent près Monereau. *Gallia Préhistoire* 9 (2): 263–385.

Levitt, N. and Gross, P. (1997) *Prometheus Bedeviled: Science and the Contradictions of Contemporary Culture and co-author of Higher Superstition: The Academic Left and Its Quarrels with Science*. Baltimore, MD: Johns Hopkins University Press.

Lewis, C. (1996) Prehistoric mining at the Great Orme. M.Phil thesis, University of Wales, Bangor.

Lewis-Williams, J. D. and Dowson, T. A. (1988) The signs of all times: entoptic phenomena in Upper Palaeolithic Cave Art. *Current Anthropology* 29: 201–45.

Linderholm, A. et al. (2010) High frequency of lactose intolerance in a prehistoric hunter-gatherer population in northern Europe. *BMC Evolutionary Biology* 10: 89.

Lönnqvist, M. (2013) SYGIS – Jebel Bishri: The Finnish Project in Syria. Online: www.helsinki.fi/hum/arla/sygis/.

Lordkipanidze, D. et al. (2013) A complete skull from Dmanisi, Georgia, and the evolutionary biology of early homo. *Science* 342 (6156): 326–31.

Loveday, R. (1998) Mother Dunche's Buttocks: a focus for Neolithic interest. Lecture to Neolithics Studies Group, London.

Loveluck, C. and Tys, D. (2006) Coastal societies, exchange and identity along the Channel and southern North Sea shores of Europe, AD 600–1000. *Journal of Maritime Archaeology* 1 (2): 140–61.

Madella, S. et al. (2013) Phytoliths in pottery reveal the use of spice in European prehistoric cuisine. *Public Library of Science* 8 (8).

Mallory, J. (1991) *In Search of the Indo-Europeans: Language, Archaeology, and Myth*. London: Thames and Hudson.

Mania, D. (1991) The zonal division of the lower palaeolithic open-air site Bilzingsleben. *Anthropologie* 29 (Brno): 172–4.

Mannermaa, K. et al. (2008) Birds in late Mesolithic burials at Yuzhniy Oleniy Ostrov. *Fennoscandia archaeologica* XXV.

Marcus, J. and Flannery, K. (1994) *Zapotec Civilization*. London: Thames and Hudson.

Mattingly, T. et al. (2008) *Archaeology and Desertification: The Wadi Faynan Landscape Survey, Southern Jordan*. Oxford: Oxbow Books.

Mays, S. (1998) *The Archaeology of Human Bones*. London: Routledge.

McCormick, M. (2003) *Origins of the European Economy: Communications and Commerce AD 300–900*. Cambridge: Cambridge University Press.

McNeil, C. (2009) Evidence disputing deforestation as the cause for the collapse of the ancient Maya polity of Copan, Honduras. *Proceedings of the National Academy of Sciences of the USA*, 107 (3): 1017–22.

Medieval Origins of Commercial Sea Fishing Project. Online: www.mcdonald.cam.ac.uk/projects/Medieval_Fishing/.

Megaw, J. and Megaw, M. (1998) The mechanism of (Celtic) dreams?: A partial response to our critics. *Antiquity* 72 (276): 432.

Mellaart, J. (1967) *Çatal Hüyük: A Neolithic Town in Anatolia*. London: Thames and Hudson.

Mellars, P. (1987) *Excavations on Oronsay: Prehistoric Human Ecology on a Small Island*. Edinburgh: Edinburgh University Press.

Mellars, P. (ed.) (1990) *The Emergence of Modern Humans*. Edinburgh: Edinburgh University Press.

Mellars, P. (1996) *The Neanderthal Legacy*. Princeton: Princeton University Press.

Mellars, P. (2001) The Upper Palaeolithic Revolution. In Cuncliffe, B. (ed.) *The Oxford Illustrated Prehistory of Europe*. Oxford: Oxford University Press, pp. 42–78.

Mellars, P. and French, J. (2011) Tenfold population increase in Western Europe at the Neanderthal-to-Modern Human transition. *Science* 333 (6042): 623–7.

Mellars, P. and Stringer, C. (eds) (1989) *The Human Revolution: Behavioural and Biological Perspectives on the Origins of Modern Humans*. Edinburgh: Edinburgh Free Press.

Milisauskas, S. (2002) *European Prehistory: A Survey*. New York: Springer.

Millett, M. (1995) *Roman Britain*. London: English Heritage.

Milner, N. (2007) *Star Carr: Past, Present and Future*. Oxford: Lecture.

Mithen, S. (1989) New evidence for Mesolithic settlement on Colonsay. *Proceedings of the Society of Antiquaries of Scotland* 119: 33–41.

Mithen, S. (1990) *Thoughtful Foragers: A Study of Prehistoric Decision Making*. Cambridge: Cambridge University Press.

Mithen, S. (2006) *After the Ice: A Global Human History, 20.000–5.000 BC*. Cambridge, MA: Harvard University Press.

Molleson, T. (1994) The eloquent bones of Abu Hureyra. *Scientific American* 271 (2): 70–5.

Molleson, T. et al. (1993) *The Spitalfields Project, vol. 2, the Anthropology: The Middling Sort*. CBA Research Report 86, Council for British Archaeology.

Molleson, T. et al. (2003) Dietary change and the effects of food preparation on microwear patterns in the Late Neolithic of Abu Hureyra, northern Syria. *Journal of Human Evolution* 24 (6): 455–68.

Montgomery, J. et al. (2005) Continuity or colonisation in Anglo-Saxon England? Isotope evidence for mobility, subsistence practice, and status at West Heslerton. *American Journal of Physical Anthropology* 126 (2): 123–38.

Moore, A., Hillman, G. and Legge, A. (2000) *Village on the Euphrates*. Oxford: Oxford University Press.

Muir, R. (1981) *Reading the Landscape*. London: Michael Joseph.

Murdock, G. and Morrow, D. (1970) Subsistence economy and supportive practices: cross-cultural codes. *Ethnology* 9 (3): 302–30.

Museums and Galleries Commission (2000) *Restitution and Repatriation: Guidelines for Good Practice*. Museums and Galleries Commission.

Nadel, D. et al. (2012) New evidence for the processing of wild cereal grains at Ohalo II, a 23 000-year-old campsite on the shore of the Sea of Galilee, Israel. *Antiquity* 86 (334): 990–1003.

Nafplioti, A. (2008) Mycenaean political domination of Knossos following the Late Minoan IB destructions on Crete: negative evidence from strontium isotope ratio analysis. *Journal of Archaeological Science* 35 (8): 2307–17.

Nakassis, D. et al. (2011) Redistribution in Aegean Palatial Societies. Redistributive economies from a theoretical and cross-cultural perspective. *American Journal of Archaeology* 115 (2): 175–244.

Nilsson Stutz, L. (2003) Embodied rituals and ritualised bodies: tracing ritual practise in Late Mesolithic burials. *Acta Archaeologica Lundensia*, 46.

Nilsson Stutz, L. (2010) The way we bury our dead. Reflections on mortuary ritual, community and identity at the time of the Mesolithic–Neolithic transition. *Documenta Praehistorica* XXXVII.

Nowicki, K. (2002) The end of the Neolithic in Crete. *Aegean Archaeology* 6: 7–72.

O'Connor, T. (1991) *Bones from 46–54 Fishergate*. CBA Publications.

Oeggl, K. (2008) The Neolithic agricultural regime in the Inner Alps. Online project: www.uibk.ac.at/himat/sfb-himat/pps/pp11/transhumance/transhumance.html.en.

O'Flaherty, R. (2007) A weapon of choice: experiments with a replica EBA halberd. *Antiquity* 81: 423–34.

Oppenheimer, S. (2007) *The Origins of the British: A Genetic Detective Story*. London: Robinson Publishing.

Orme, B. (1981) *Anthropology for Archaeologists*. London: Duckworth.

Orschiedt, J. (1998) Linear pottery settlement burials in West Germany. Archaeological and anthropological findings. *Intern. Arch.* 43: 1–34.

Orschiedt, J. and Haidle, M. (2007) The LBK enclosure at Herxheim: theatre of war or ritual centre? *Journal of Conflict Archaeology* 2 (1): 153–67.

Orton, C. (2010) Stable isotopes and cod fishing: methodological considerations and preliminary evidence for human impact on marine ecosystems. Talk at Trinity College Dublin, November.

Orton, C. et al. (1993) *Pottery in Archaeology*. Cambridge: Cambridge University Press.

Orton, D. and Barrett, J. (2012) What fish bones can tell: Marine bioarchaeology as historical ecology. The Birds and the Fishes Conference, Macdonald Institute, 7 July.

Orwell, G. (2000) *1984*. London: Penguin Classics (first published 1949).

O'Shea, J. (1981) Social configurations and the archaeological study of mortuary practices: a case study. In Chapman, R., Kinnes, I. and Randsborg, K. (eds) *The Archaeology of Death*. Cambridge: Cambridge University Press.

Outram, A. et al. (2009) The earliest horse harnessing and milking. *Science* 323: 1332–5.

Ozkan, H. et al. (2002) AFLP analysis of a collection of tetraploid wheats indicates the origin of emmer and hard wheat domestication in southeast Turkey. *Molecular Biology and Evolution* 19: 1797–801.

Paine, R. and Freter, A. (1996) Environmental degradation and the Classic Maya Collapse at Copan, Honduras (A.D. 600–1250): evidence from studies of household survival. *Ancient Mesoamerica* 7 (01): 37–47.

Parezek, K. (2007) Aswan obelisk quarry more than meets the eye. *Science Daily*, 19 October.

Parker-Pearson, M. (1993) *Bronze Age Britain*. London: Batsford.

Parker-Pearson, M. (1999) *The Archaeology of Death and Burial*. Stroud: Sutton.

Parker-Pearson, M. (2011) The value of archaeological research. In Bate, J. (ed.) *The Public Value of the Humanities*. London: Bloomsbury Academic, pp. 30–43.

Parker-Pearson, M. (2012) *Stonehenge: Exploring the Greatest Stone Age Enigma*. London: Simon and Schuster.

Patterson, N. et al. (2012) Ancient admixture in human history. *Genetics* 192 (3): 1065.

Paver, M. (2005) *Wolf Brother: Chronicles of Ancient Darkness*. London: Orion Childrens.

Pearce, E. et al. (2013) New insights into differences in brain organization between Neanderthals and anatomically modern humans. *Proceedings of the Royal Society B: Biological Sciences*, 280 (1758).

Pedersen, L. et al. (eds) (1998) *The Danish Storebælt since the Ice Age*. Copenhagen: Storebaelt.

Pike-Tay, A. and Bricker, H. (1993) Hunting in the Gravettian: an examination of evidence from Southwestern France. *Archeological Papers of the American Anthropological Association* 4 (1): 127–43.

Pinhasi, R. (2011) Revised age of late Neanderthal occupation and the end of the Middle Paleolithic in the northern Caucasus. *Proceedings of the National Academy of Sciences of the USA*, 108: 8611–16.

Pinhasi, R. et al. (2012) The genetic history of Europeans. *Trends in Genetics* 28 (10): 496–505.

Pirenne, H. (1927/1969) *Medieval Cities: Their Origins and the Revival of Trade*. Reprint, Princeton: Princeton University Press.

Pitts, M. and Roberts, M. (1997) *Fairweather Eden*. London: Century.

Pohl, M. (2010) Quernstones and Tuff as indicators for Medieval European trade patterns. *Papers from the Institute of Archaeology* 20: 148–53.

Politiko Phorades project. Online: www.scsp.arts.gla.ac.uk/Phorades/.

Pollington, S. (2003) *Mead-Hall: The Feasting Tradition in Anglo-Saxon England*. Norfolk: Anglo-Saxon Books.

Potts, R. and Shipman, P. (1981) Cutmarks made by stone tools on bones from Olduvai Gorge, Tanzania. *Nature* 291: 577–80.

Powell, A. (2004) Harvard researchers push human cereal use back 10,000 years. *Harvard Gazette Archives*, 22 July.

Powlesland, D. J. (2000) *The Heslerton Parish Project: 20 Years of Archaeological Research in the Vale of Pickering*. Landscape Research Centre.

Price, N. (2001) *The Archaeology of Shamanism*. London: Routledge.

Price, T. (ed.) (2000) *Europe's First Farmers*. Cambridge: Cambridge University Press.

Price, T. et al. (2008) Late palaeolithic reindeer on the north European plain. In Sulgostowska, Z. and Tomaszewski, A. J. (eds) *Man – Millennia – Environment*. Warsaw: Institute of Archaeology and Ethnology, pp. 1231–32.

Prior, F. (1991) *Flag Fen*. London: Batsford.

Project Gutenberg (2005) *Beowulf: An Anglo-Saxon Epic Poem*. Translation by Leslie Hall. eBook: www.gutenberg.org/files/16328/16328-h/16328-h.htm.

Racimo, F. et al. (2014) The complete genome sequence of a Neanderthal from the Altai Mountains. *Nature* 505: 43–49.

Rackham, J. (1994) *Animal Bones*. Berkeley and London: University of California Press and British Museum.

Rackham, O. (1986) *The History of the Countryside*. London: Phoenix.

Ramsey, B. et al. (2004) Dating the volcanic eruption at Thera. *Radiocarbon* 46 (1): 325–44.

Rasmussen, M. et al. (2014) The genome of a Late Pleistocene human from a Clovis burial site in Western Montana. *Nature* 506: 225–29.

Rathje, W. and Murphy, C. (1991) *Rubbish! The Archaeology of Garbage*. New York: Harper Collins.

Reece, R. (1998) Research in progress on the potential of hedges for locating early medieval settlement. Unpublished research manuscript.

Renfrew, C. (1972) *The Emergence of Civilization*. London: Methuen.

Renfrew, C. (1973) *Before Civilization.* London: Jonathan Cape.

Renfrew, C. (1984) *Approaches to Social Archaeology.* Edinburgh: Edinburgh University Press.

Renfrew, C. (1987) *Archaeology and Language: The Puzzle of Indo-European Origins.* London: Pimlico.

Renfrew, C. and Bahn, P. (2004) *Archaeology: Theories, Methods and Practice,* 4th edn. London: Thames and Hudson.

Renfrew, C. and Cherry, J. (eds) (1986) *Peer Polity Interaction and Socio-Political Change.* Cambridge: Cambridge University Press.

Renfrew, C. and Shennan, S. (1982) *Ranking, Resource, and Exchange: Aspects of the Archaeology of Early European Society.* Cambridge: Cambridge University Press.

Reynolds, P. (1979) *Iron Age Farm: The Butser Experiment.* London: British Museum Publications.

Reynolds, P. (1989) Reconstruct or construct: the Pimperne House. *British Archaeology* 11: 34–7.

Richards, J. (1997) *Stonehenge: The Story so Far.* London: English Heritage.

Richards, M. and Mellars, P. (1998) Stable isotopes and the seasonality of the Oronsay midden. *Antiquity* 72 (275): 178–84.

Richards, M. and Schulting, R. (2006) Touch not the fish: the Mesolithic-Neolithic change of diet and its significance. *Antiquity* 80 (308): 4444–56.

Rigaud, J. et al. (1995) Mousterian FIRES from Grotte XVI. *Antiquity* 69: 266.

Roberts, C. (2009a) *Human Remains in Archaeology: A Handbook,* Practical handbooks in archaeology (19). York: Council for British Archaeology.

Roberts, C. (2009b) *The Unnatural History of the Sea.* Washington, DC: Island Press.

Roebroeks, W. and Kolfschoten, T. (eds) (1995) *The Earliest Occupation of Europe.* Leiden: University of Leiden.

Rousseau, J. (1754) *A Discourse on the Origins of Inequality.* Mineola, New York: Dover Press.

Rowley-Conwy, P. (1995) Meat, furs and skins: Mesolithic animal bones from Ringkloster, a seasonal hunting camp in Jutland. *Journal of Danish Archaeology* 12 (1): 87–98.

Rowley-Conwy, P. et al. (2002) Derivation and application of a Food Utility Index for European wild boar. *Environmental Archaeology* 7: 77–87.

Rue, D. (1989) Archaic Middle American agriculture and settlement: recent pollen dating from Honduras. *Journal of Field Archaeology* 10: 177–84.

Rundkvist, M. (2011) *Mead-halls of the Eastern Geats. Elite Settlements and Political Geography AD 375–1000 in Östergötland,* Sweden. Antikvariska series, 49. Stockholm: The Royal Swedish Academy of Letters, History and Antiquities.

Russo, D. (1998) *Town Origins and Development in Early England: c.4009–50 A.D.* Westport, CN: Greenwood Press.

Saul, H. et al. (2013) Phytoliths in pottery reveal the use of spice in European prehistoric cuisine. *PLoS ONE* 8(8): e70583.

Saunders, N. (2002) Excavating memories: archaeology and the Great War, 1914–2001. *Antiquity* 76 (291): 101–8.

Schele, L. and Matthews, P. (1983) *The Code of Kings.* New York: Thames and Hudson.

Schele, L. and Miller, M. (1986) *The Blood of Kings.* Austin: University of Texas Press.

Schick, K. and Toth, N. (1993) *Making Silent Stones Speak.* London: Weidenfeld and Nicolson.

Schmidt, R. (1938) *Die Burg Vučedol.* Zagreb: Kroatisches Archäologisches Staatsmuseum (1945).

Schreve, D. (2006) The taphonomy of a Middle Devensian vertebrate assemblage from Lynford, Norfolk, UK, and its implications for Middle Palaeolithic subsistence strategies. *Journal of Quaternary Science* 21 (5): 543–56.

Schulting, R. (2007) What the bones say: a bioarchaeological approach to Mesolithic burial remains. Oxford: Lecture.

Scull, C. (1998) Early medieval cemeteries at Boss Hall and Buttermarket, Ipswich. Spring lecture, *Saxon* – newsletter of the Sutton Hoo Society no. 29.

Scull, C. (2009) *Early medieval (late 5th–early 8th centuries AD) cemeteries at Boss Hall and Buttermarket.* Ipswich: Society for Medieval Archaeology Monograph 27.

Service, E. (1971) *Primitive Social Organisation: An Evolutionary Perspective.* New York: Random House.

Sharples, N. (1991) *Maiden Castle.* London: Batsford.

Shennan, S. (1975) The social organisation at Branc. *Antiquity* 49: 279–88.

Sherratt, A. (1981) Plough and pastoralism: aspects of the secondary products revolution. In Hodder, I. et al. (eds) *Patterns of the Past.* Cambridge: Cambridge University Press, pp. 261–305.

Sherratt, A. (1997) *Economy and Society in Prehistoric Europe.* Edinburgh: Edinburgh University Press.

Sindbæk, S. (2007a) Networks and Nodal Points. The Emergence of Towns in Early Viking Age Scandinavia, *Antiquity* 81, 1191–32.

Sindbæk, S. (2007b) Part 2: northern Europe. In Graham-Campbell, J. (ed.) *The Archaeology of Medieval Europe, Volume 1: Eighth to Twelfth Centuries AD*. Aarhus: Aarhus University Press.

Skoglund, P. et al. (2012) Origins and genetic legacy of Neolithic farmers and hunter-gatherers in Europe. *Science* 336 (6080): 466–9.

Skyre, D. (2013) From Dorestad to Kaupang: Frankish traders and settlers in a 9th century Scandinavian town. In Willemsen, A. and Kik, H. (eds) *Dorestad in an International Framework: New Research on Centres of Trade and Coinage in Carolingian Times*. Chicago: Brepols Publishers, pp. 137–41.

Smith, G. (2012) Middle Palaeolithic subsistence: the role of hominins at Lynford, Norfolk, UK. *Quaternary International* 252: 61–81.

Soffer, O. et al. (1997) Cultural stratigraphy at Mezhirich, an Upper Palaeolithic site in Ukraine with multiple occupations. *Antiquity* 71: 48–62.

Soffer, O. et al. (2009) *The Invisible Sex: Uncovering the True Roles of Women in Prehistory*. New York: Harper Collins.

Spratling, M. (1979) The debris from metal working. In Foster, J. (ed.) (1980) *The Iron Age Moulds from Gussage All Saints*. London: British Museum.

Stevens, R. et al. (2013a) One for the master and one for the dame: stable isotope investigations of Iron Age animal husbandry in the Danebury environs. *Archaeological and Anthropological Sciences* 5 (2): 95–109.

Stevens, R. et al. (2013b) Investigating dietary variation with burial ritual in Iron Age Hampshire: an isotopic comparison of Suddern Farm Cemetery and Danebury Hillfort pit burials. *Oxford Journal of Archaeology* 32 (93): 257–73.

Stone, E. and Zimansky, P. (2004) *The Anatomy of a Mesopotamian City*. Winona Lake: Eisenbrauns.

Stone Pages (nd) News bulletins on world archaeology. Online: www.stonepages.com/news/.

Stott, A. et al. (2003) Direct dating of archaeological pottery by compound-specific 14C analysis of preserved lipids. *Analytical Chemistry* 75 (19): 5037–45.

Stringer, C. (2005) *The Complete World of Human Evolution*. London: Thames and Hudson.

Stringer, C. and McKie, R. (1997) *African Exodus: The Origins of Modern Humanity*. London: Pimlico.

Strudwick, N. and Strudwick, H. (1989) *Thebes in Egypt*. London: BM Press.

Svoboda, J. and Klima, B. et al. (2000) The Gravettian in Moravia: climate, behaviour and technological complexity. In Mussi, M. et al. (eds) *Hunters of the Golden Age*. Leiden: University of Leiden, pp. 198–217.

Sykes, B. (2001) *The Seven Daughters of Eve: The Science that Reveals Our Genetic Ancestry*. New York: W. W. Norton.

Sykes, B. (2006) *Blood of the Isles: Exploring the Genetic Roots of Our Tribal History*. London: Bantam.

Szczepanski, S. (2009) Archaeology in the service of the Nazis: Himmler's propaganda and the excavations at the hillfort site in Stary Dzierzgoń. *Lietuvos Archeologija* 35: 83–94.

Taylor, T. (1997) *The Prehistory of Sex*. London: Fourth Estate.

Tegel, W. et al. (2012) Early Neolithic water wells reveal the world's oldest wood architecture. *PLoS* 7(12): e51374.

Thackray, D. and Payne, S. (2009) *Report on Consultation on the Request for Reburial of Prehistoric Human Remains from the Alexander Keiller Museum at Avebury*. English Heritage.

Thomas, D. (2001) *Skull Wars: Kennewick Man, Archaeology and the Battle for Native American Identity*. New York: Basic Books.

Thomas, J. (1991) *Understanding the Neolithic*. London: Routledge.

Tilley, C. (1994) *A Phenomenology of Landscape*. Oxford: Berg.

Tilley, C. (1996) *An Ethnography of the Neolithic*. Cambridge: Cambridge University Press.

Tomkins, P. and Schoep, I. (2010) The Early Bronze Age: Crete. In Cline, E. (ed.) *The Oxford Handbook of the Bronze Age Aegean*. Oxford: Oxford University Press, pp. 66–82.

Trbojević Vukičević, T. (2006) Archaeozoological and taphonomic investigation of enolithic cattle from Vucedol site. PhD thesis, University of Zagreb.

Trigger, B. (1989) *A History of Archaeological Thought*. Cambridge: Cambridge University Press.

Tringham, R. (2013) Destruction of places by fire: domicide or domithanasia. In Driessen, J. (ed.) *Destruction: Archaeological, Philological and Historical Perspectives*. Louvain: Louvain University Press, pp. 89–108.

Trinkaus, E. (2005a) Anatomical evidence for the antiquity of human footwear use. *Journal of Archaeological Science* 32: 1515–26.

Trinkaus, E. (2005b) The adiposity paradox in the Middle Danubian Gravettian. *Anthropologie* XLIII (2–3): 263–71.

Tubb, J. (1997) Interim report on the ninth season (1996) of excavations at Tell es-Sa'idiyeh, Jordan. *Palestine Exploration Quarterly* 129: 54–77.

UNWTO (2013) *Annual Report*. Madrid: United Nations World Tourist Organisation.

Ur, J. et al. (2007) Early urban development in the Near East. *Science* 317 (5842): 1188.

Van Andel, T. and Runnels, C. (1988) An essay on the 'emergence of civilization' in the Aegean world. *Antiquity* 62: 234–47.

Van Es, W. (1990) Dorestad. In Besteman, J. et al. (eds) *Medieval Archaeology in the Netherlands: Studies Presented to H.H. van Regteren.* Assen/Maastricht: Altena, pp. 151–82.

Van Es, W. and Verwers, W. (2010) Early medieval settlements along the Rhine: precursors and contemporaries of Dorestad. *Journal of Archaeology in the Low Countries* 2–1: 5–39.

Van Gennep, A. (1909) *Les rites de passage.* Paris: E. Nourry.

Vanhaeren, M. et al. (2004) Tracing the source of Upper Palaeolithic shell beads by strontium isotope dating. *Journal of Archaeological Science* 31 (10): 1481–8.

Vanhaeren, M. et al. (2006) Middle Palaeolithic shell beads in Israel and Algeria. *Sciences* 312: 1785.

Vanhaeren, M. et al. (2013) Thinking strings: additional evidence for personal ornament use in the Middle Stone Age at Blombos Cave, South Africa. *Journal of Human Evolution* 64 (6): 500–17.

Veldhuijzen, H. and Rehren, T. (2007) Slags and the city: early iron production at Tell Hammeh, Jordan and Tel Beth-Shemesh, Israel. In La Niece, S. et al. (eds) *Metals and Mines – Studies in Archaeometallurgy.* London: Archetype/British Museum, pp. 189–201.

Visit Britain (2012) *Annual Report and Accounts.* London: HMSO.

Vollbrecht, J. (2000) The antler finds at Bilzingsleben, excavations 1969–1993. *Internet Archaeology* 8.

Von Däniken, E. (1969) *Chariots of the Gods?* New York: Souvenir Press.

Waddell, J. (2000) *The Prehistoric Archaeology of Ireland.* Dublin: Wordwell.

Waddington, C. (1998) Cup and rings in context. *Cambridge Archaeological Journal* 8 (1): 29–54.

Waddington, C. (1999) *A Landscape Archaeological Study of the Mesolithic-Neolithic in the Milfield Basin, Northumberland.* British Archaeological Reports. Oxford: Archaeopress.

Wade, K. (2001) The evidence for early trading sites around the North Sea coast from the 7th to the 9th century. *Saxon* 34 (The Sutton Hoo Society).

Waelkens, M. and Herz, M. (1992) *Ancient Stones: Quarrying, Trade and Provenance: Interdisciplinary Studies.* Leuven: Leuven University Press.

Wainwright, G. (1979) *Gussage All Saints: An Iron Age Settlement in Dorset.* London: HMSO.

Walker, A. and Shipman, P. (1997) *The Wisdom of the Bones: In Search of Human Origins.* New York: Vintage Books.

Warmuth, V. et al. (2012) Reconstructing the origin and spread of horse domestication in the Eurasian steppe. *Proceedings of the National Academy of Sciences Early edition.*

Wass, S. (1999) *The Amateur Archaeologist,* 2nd edn. London: Batsford.

Watson, A. (1997) Hearing again the sound of the Neolithic. *British Archaeology* 23 (April).

Webster, D. (1989) *The House of the Bacabs, Copan, Honduras.* Pre-Columbian Art and Archaeology Studies Series 29. Washington DC: Dumbarton Oaks.

Webster, D. and Freter, A. (1990) Settlement history and the classic collapse at Copan: a redefined chronological perspective. *Latin American Antiquity* 1: 66–85.

Webster, D. et al. (1992) A simulation of Copán population history and its implications. *Ancient Mesoamerica* 3 (1): 189–201.

Webster, D., Freter, A. and Rue, D. (1993) The Obsidian Hydration Dating Project at Copán: a regional approach and why it works. *Latin American Antiquity* 4 (4): 303–24.

Weinstock, J. (2000) Osteometry as a source of refined demographic information: sex-ratios of reindeer hunting strategies and herd control at the Late Glacial site of Stellmoor. *Journal of Archaeological Science* 27: 1187–95.

Weiss, E. et al. (2004) The broad spectrum revisited: evidence from plant remains. *PNAS* 101 (26): 9551–5.

Welch, M. (1992) *Anglo-Saxon England.* London: Batsford.

Wenke, R. (1999) *Patterns in Prehistory.* Oxford: Oxford University Press.

West, S. (1985) *West Stow: The Anglo-Saxon Village.* East Anglian Archaeology 24. Suffolk County Department of Planning.

White, R. (2007) Systems of personal ornamentation in the Early Upper Palaeolithic: methodological challenges and new observations. In Mellars, P. et al. (eds) *Rethinking the Human Revolution: New Behavioural and Biological Perspectives on the Origin and Dispersal of Modern Humans.* Cambridge: McDonald Institute for Archaeological Research, pp. 287–302.

White, R. et al. (2012) Context and dating of newly discovered Aurignacian rock art from Abri Castanet (Dordogne, France). Paléo. English online version.

Whitelaw, T. (2001) From sites to communities: defining the human dimensions of Minoan urbanism. In Branigan, K. (ed.) *Urbanism in the Aegean Bronze Age.* Sheffield: Sheffield University Press.

Whitelaw, T. (2004) Alternative pathways to complexity in the southern Aegean. In Barrett, J. and Halstead, P. (eds) *The Emergence of Civilization Revisited.* Oxford: Oxbow Books, pp. 232–56.

Whitfield, S. et al. (2010) *IDP:* Mapping of archaeological sites uncovered in the early twentieth century along the Silk Road. ArchAtlas, Version 4.1. Online: www.archatlas.org/workshop09/works09-whitfield.php.

Whittle, A. (1996) *Europe in the Neolithic.* Cambridge: Cambridge University Press.

Whittle, A. (1998) *Sacred Mound, Holy Rings.* Oxford: Oxbow Books.

Wiessner, P. (1982) Risk, reciprocity and social influences on !Kung San economics. In Leacock, E. and Lee, R. (eds) *Politics and History in Band Societies.* Cambridge: Cambridge University Press, pp. 61–84.

Wild, J. (2003) Anatolia and the Levant in the Bronze Age. In Jenkins, D. (ed.) *The Cambridge History of Western Textiles.* Cambridge: Cambridge University Press.

Wilkinson, K. and Stevens, C. (2003) *Environmental Archaeology.* Stroud: Tempus.

Wilkinson, R. (2000) *The Temples of Ancient Egypt.* London: Thames and Hudson.

Willcox, G. (2012) Pre-domestic cultivation during the Late Pleistocene and Early Holocene in the Northern Levant. In Gepts, P. et al. (eds) *Biodiversity in Agriculture: Domestication, Evolution, and Sustainability.* Cambridge: Cambridge University Press.

Willey, P. and Emerson, T. (1993) The osteology and archaeology of the Crow Creek Massacre. *Plains Anthropologist* 38 (145): 227–69.

Wilson, D. (1976) *The Archaeology of Anglo-Saxon England.* London: Routledge.

Wittfogel, K. (1957) *Oriental Despotism: A Comparative Study of Total Power.* New York: Random House.

Wong, K. (2000) Palaeolithic pit stop. *Scientific American* 283: 18–20.

Wood, R. et al. (2013) Radiocarbon dating casts doubt on the late chronology of the Middle to Upper Palaeolithic transition in southern Iberia. *Proceedings of the National Academy of Sciences of the USA*, 110 (8): 2781–6.

Wordsworth, P. (2010) Traversing the Karakum: approaches to defining trade networks through the desert landscapes of Medieval Central Asia. ArchAtlas, Version 4.1. Online: www.archatlas.org/workshop09/works09-wordsworth.php.

Wordsworth, P. (2013) Exploring medieval routes. Online: www.ucl.ac.uk/merv/our_research/routes_medieval.

World Archaeological Congress (1989) The Vermillion Accord, archaeological ethics and the treatment of the dead. A statement of principles agreed by archaeologists and indigenous peoples at the World Archaeological Congress.

World Tourism Organization (2013) *2013 Tourism Highlights.* UNWTO.

Young, R. (ed.) (2000) *Mesolithic Lifeways.* Leicester: University of Leicester.

Zvelebil, M. et al. (eds) (1998) *Harvesting the Sea, Farming the Forest.* Sheffield: Sheffield Academic Press.

Index